INTERNATIONAL FINANCIAL
REPORTING AND ANALYSIS

FOURTH EDITION

INTERNATIONAL FINANCIAL REPORTING AND ANALYSIS

DAVID ALEXANDER, ANNE BRITTON AND ANN JORISSEN

CENGAGE
Learning™

Australia • Brazil • Japan • Korea • Mexico • Singapore • Spain • United Kingdom • United States

SOUTH-WESTERN
CENGAGE Learning

International Financial Reporting and Analysis, Fourth Edition
David Alexander, Anne Britton and Ann Jorissen

Publishing Director: Linden Harris

Publisher: Brendan George

Development Editor: Charlotte Loveridge

Content Project Editor: Jamina Ward

Head of Manufacturing: Jane Glendening

Production Controller: Tom Relf

Marketing Manager: Amanda Cheung

Typesetter: KnowledgeWorks Global Ltd.

Cover design: Adam Renvoize

Text design: Design Deluxe, Bath, UK

For product information and technology assistance, contact **emea.info@cengage.com**.
For permission to use material from this text or product, and for permission queries, email **clsuk.permissions@cengage.com**.

British Library Cataloguing-in-Publication Data
A catalogue record for this book is available from the British Library.

ISBN: 978-1-4080-1792-0

Cengage Learning EMEA
Cheriton House, North Way, Andover, Hampshire, SP10 5BE, United Kingdom

Cengage Learning products are represented in Canada by Nelson Education Ltd.

For your lifelong learning solutions, visit **www.cengage.co.uk**

Purchase your next print book, e-book or e-chapter at **www.CengageBrain.co.uk**

Printed by Zrinski D.D., Croatia
2 3 4 5 6 7 8 9 10 – 12 11 10

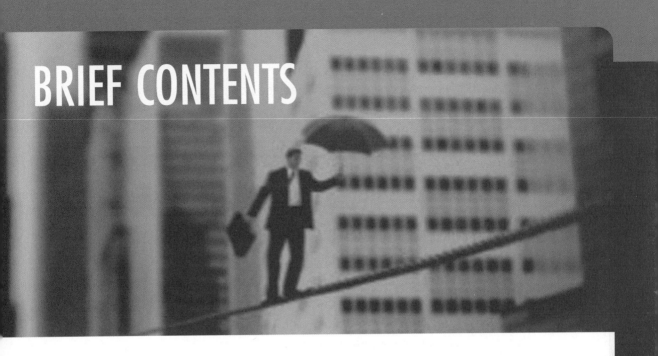

BRIEF CONTENTS

CONTENTS

PART TWO ANNUAL FINANCIAL STATEMENTS

PART THREE CONSOLIDATED ACCOUNTS
AND THE MULTINATIONAL

FOREWORD TO PREVIOUS EDITION

This book is overdue. With the decision taken by the European Union (EU) to require all listed EU companies to prepare their consolidated accounts in accordance with International Accounting Standards (IAS) from 2005 onwards, there is a pressing need to train people in the financial reporting language of the future. New is not so much that new standards are replacing old standards. New is that as a result of the political decision to use IAS in the future, accounting is no longer a national matter, which differs from country to country. The financial reporting language of the future is an international language. This requires an international approach in the teaching of that language.

The authors have opted for such an approach. They are right. Financial reporting is dealt with in this book as a subject in its own right without too much reliance on standards of one or more particular countries. The authors also put the emphasis on the whys and wherefores. More than ever, accountants and students of accountancy need to be trained to think about accounting. Although knowledge of the standards is important, those who favour IAS favour a principles-based approach to standard-setting. This requires those who apply the standards to carefully consider what the standard is trying to achieve rather than how a particular event or transaction can be brought into the scope of the standard so as to obtain the desired result.

Financial reporting is the only matter concerning listed EU companies which is now uniform throughout the EU. This is quite a radical change from the past. That change affects all member states, although some more than others. For continental Europe, IAS is very much an Anglo-Saxon inspired reporting model. Applying and understanding IAS in these countries requires a considerable effort in getting to know the new concepts and the approach of the standard-setters with the trilogy of recognition, measurement and disclosure. But, as the authors of the book point out, there is virtually no UK listed company yet that already applies IAS. There is too often an inclination in the UK to believe that with the knowledge of UK GAAP, one is perfectly ready for the IAS revolution. This is clearly untrue.

Although the requirement to apply IAS does not extend to small and medium-sized companies (at least not as an EU requirement), many member states of the EU will, as a result of the modernisation of the accounting Directives, amend their national accounting legislation in a manner which brings it closer to IAS. There can therefore be no doubt that it is difficult to conceive an accounting training in any member state of the EU which does not enter into a detailed examination of IAS and the conceptual framework that underpins IAS. Equally, given the adoption of IAS also in Australia and a number of other countries in the world and the rapidly increasing influence of International Accounting Standards worldwide, the book should meet an important need in regions outside Europe.

I hope that this book will find a good reception and I congratulate the authors on their initiative.

Karel VAN HULLE
Head of Unit, Insurance and Pensions, Financial Institutions
European Commission
(formerly Head of Financial Reporting and
Company Law, European Commission)

PREFACE

WHY THIS BOOK?

Financial reporting is changing. Accounting has always been a reactive service, changing and developing to meet the practical needs created by the environment in which it operates. This process of change can be illustrated by both time considerations and place considerations. In particular, in the days when most business operations were largely organised within national boundaries, accounting thought, practices and regulation grew up in significantly different ways in different countries, consistent with national environments and characteristics, a process discussed in more detail in Chapter 2.

Now, however, big business is international, and the process and its implications are moving at a very fast rate. Big business is global in its operations; the demand for finance is global and the supply of finance is global. The provision of information, the oil which lubricates any working market, is global in its reach and instantaneous in its transmission. Financial reporting must of necessity become global too. From slow beginnings, the International Accounting Standards Board is now poised to become the generally accepted regulator at this international level. From 2005, every listed EU company (and also in Australia) has been *required* to produce its group financial statements in accordance with International Accounting Standards and International Financial Reporting Standards. Other countries, as diverse as the USA and China, are seeking close convergence, at minimum, with IASB requirements. The USA is at last proposing to allow full acceptance of IFRS, without a reconciliation, for US stock exchange listing.

The effects on accounting and reporting for business entities operating at a national or local level, many of them of the small-medium entity (SME) size, are unclear, and are likely to differ in different places. Two points are very clear to us, however. First, national needs, characteristics and ways of thinking will remain significant at the SME level. Second, the application of agreed International Accounting Standards, a subjective process of necessity, will continue to be influenced by the context and environment in which the application takes place.

This new book is written to reflect this new situation and its implications. A knowledge of the requirements of the International Accounting Standards is now essential to anyone studying financial accounting and reporting, whether the aim is the preparer focus implied by a desire to enter the accounting professions or the user focus implied by finance, business or MBA-type programmes aimed at management or the educated public.

But, of course, knowledge is not enough. A critical understanding of issues and alternatives, of the whys and wherefores, is also required. The author team has been carefully constructed to contain significant academic, pedagogic and writing experience and to reflect the diversity of European and international thought and experience. Our approach is to expose the reader to the issues by a carefully developed sequence of exposition, student-centred activity and constructive feedback. This process provides a framework with which the reader can assimilate, understand and appraise the exposition of international requirements that follows. Only with such an overall understanding, enhancing both depth and breadth, will the reader be able to follow, and hopefully to take an active part in, the future development of financial accounting and reporting as the process of international change continues.

It is important to be clear that our emphasis is on the IASB requirements, and on a full understanding thereof. How those requirements will actually be applied in detailed practice in the many different countries and cultures involved has to be largely outside our scope. As already indicated, we certainly believe that there will continue to be material differences in the practical interpretation and application of international standards. We give a full justification and explanation of that belief, and provide a framework for analysing its implications. Nevertheless, it has to be up to the individual reader and/or teacher, situated in a 'local' context, to explore what the implications of that local context may be.

The fourth edition differs from the third edition on the following aspects. More attention is devoted to the regulatory framework of the IASB. A new chapter 'Basics of financial statement analysis' is included in order to introduce the students to the fundamentals of financial analysis. More coverage is given to the definition, recognition, measurement and disclosure of fixed assets. Part Three on consolidated accounts has been significantly restructured and resequenced, into four separate chapters for consolidation plus one for foreign currency translation, and we believe that this makes the exposition significantly easier to follow. Further the discussion of all standards is updated (summer 2008) and brought in line with the latest developments in the IFRS standard-setting programme of the IASB. This implies that at the time of writing, attention has been paid to current evolutions and possible changes in the standards taking place in the near future. Last, but not least, new exercises have been included at the end of each chapter and the number of downloadable PowerPoint slides has increased substantially.

STRUCTURE AND PEDAGOGY

The broad structure of the book is as follows: Part One provides the essential conceptual and contextual background. Parts Two and Three explore the detailed issues and problems of financial reporting both in general and through the specific regulatory requirements of the International Accounting Standards Board – for individual company issues in Part Two and for group and multinational issues in Part Three. Part Four provides a summation by an in-depth consideration of financial statement analysis within a dynamic international context.

Each chapter follows a similar pattern in terms of pedagogic structure. Learning objectives set out what the student should be aiming to achieve, with an introduction to put the chapter in context. There are frequent activities throughout the chapter, with immediate feedback so that students can work through practical examples and reflect on the points being made. The chapter closes with a summary and exercises. Answers to some of the exercises can be found on the students' area of the website, the remainder on the lecturers' password-protected area at www.cengage.co.uk/abj4e.

SUPPLEMENTARY MATERIALS

Companion website

A companion website to the book can be found at www.cengage.co.uk/abj4e. The site has an open access student area and a password-protected lecturer area, as follows:

Student area (OPEN ACCESS)

- Answers to students' exercises (at end of chapters)
- Sample chapter – Chapter 23 on Statements of Cash Flows
- Online chapters – on industry-specific IFRSs – mineral resources exploration and agriculture
- Accounting and Finance Definitions from the Pocket IEBM
- Related links

Lecturer area (PASSWORD-PROTECTED)

- Answers to students' exercises
- Answers to lecturers' exercises
- PowerPoint slides
- Online chapters – on industry-specific IFRSs – mineral resources exploration and agriculture

TARGET AUDIENCE

This is not a book for those with no prior exposure to accounting. A one-year introductory course in accounting and a basic understanding of the principles of double-entry, or some practical business exposure, are assumed. However, we recognise that such earlier work may have taken any of a wide variety of different forms, have approached the subject from any of several different directions, and indeed may well not have been studied in the English language. The book will be particularly suitable for the middle and advanced years of undergraduate 3- or 4-year degree programmes, for post-graduate programmes requiring an internationalisation of prior studies of a national system and for MBA-type programmes where a true understanding of the issues and the implication of accounting subjectivity and diversity is required. Readers requiring a training manual of 'how to do it', whether 'it' is preparation or unintelligent interpretation and analysis, may perhaps do better elsewhere.

LIST OF REVIEWERS

The publishers would like to thank the following academics for their insightful feedback and suggestions which helped shape the 4th edition:

Dr Danny Chow, Birkbeck College, University of London
Franz Josef Gellert, Hanze University of Applied Sciences, Groningen
Dr Agnieszka Herdan, University of Greenwich
Suzanne McCallum, University of Glasgow
Libby Scott, London South Bank University
Stefan Sundgren, Umeå School of Business, Sweden
Idlan Zakaria, University of Essex

ACKNOWLEDGEMENTS

We are grateful for constructive help and support from several quarters. First of all the authors are indebted to Christoph Müller (DHL) for the assistance given and the insight into the airline industry derived from discussion with him. Further, the authors want to thank Leo van der Tas (Erasmus University Rotterdam and Ernst & Young) for his comments on Chapter 2. We are especially grateful to Karel van Hulle for not only writing the Foreword, but also providing helpful comments to us. Pat, Charlotte, our Production Editor Jamina and many others have given every encouragement from Cengage Learning. Three spouses and ten offspring have coped with the conflicting demands on our time and thoughts. Now, perhaps, it is your turn to help us, or to help us to help you. Suggestions for further development and improvement would be gratefully received by authors or publisher.

Finally, to come back to where we started, we hope that you, the reader, will be interested and stimulated. The internationalisation of accounting is an unstoppable force, which will create new and demanding challenges. We believe that participation in this process will be a fascinating and rewarding experience. We hope that you will agree when you have finished studying this book.

David Alexander, University of Birmingham
Anne Britton, Leeds Metropolitan University
Ann Jorissen, University of Antwerp

WALK THROUGH TOUR

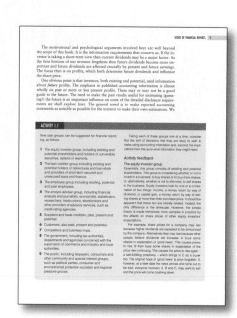

Learning Objectives These appear at the start of each chapter to help you monitor your understanding and progress through each chapter. Learning objectives are followed by an introduction which puts the chapter's content in context.

Activity (and Activity Feedback) With immediate feedback, these activities provide an opportunity to work through practical examples and reflect on the points being made.

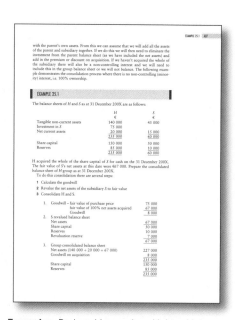

Chapter Summary Each chapter ends with a comprehensive summary that provides a thorough re-cap of the issues in each chapter, helping you to assess your understanding and revise key content.

Examples Real-world examples with broad international and sector spread demonstrate the principles set out in the book and link theory to practice.

Illustrations Providing an example of a detailed, practical application, the illustrations work through core concepts to aid understanding.

Exercises Appearing at the end of each chapter, these help reinforce and test your knowledge and understanding, and provide a basis for group discussions and activities. Answers to questions marked with $\sqrt{}$ are available in the students' area of the website and the remainder in the lecturers' area.

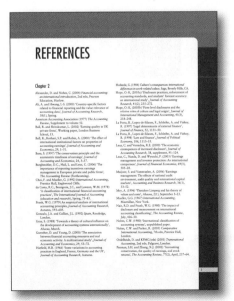

References Comprehensive references at the end of the book allow you to explore the subject further, and act as a starting point for projects and assignments.

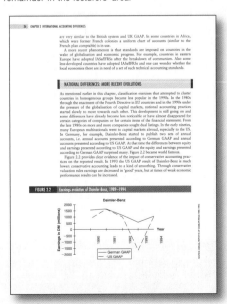

Figures Throughout the chapters, figures and tables help explain the subject by giving a visual representation of key concepts or data.

ABOUT THE WEBSITE

Visit the *International Financial Reporting and Analysis* companion website at:
www.cengage.co.uk/abj4e to find valuable teaching and learning material including:

FOR STUDENTS

- Answers to Student's Exercises (At end of chapters)
- Sample chapter – Chapter 23 on Cashflow Statements
- Online chapters – on industry-specific IFRS – mineral resources exploration and agriculture
- Accounting and Finance Definitions from the Pocket IEBM
- Related Links

FOR LECTURERS

- Answers to Student's Exercises
- Answers to Lecturer's Exercises
- PowerPoint Slides
- Online chapters – on industry-specific IFRS – mineral resources exploration and agriculture

PART ONE
FRAMEWORK, THEORY AND REGULATION

In this first part we look at what financial reporting is all about – what it is trying to achieve and how the accountant sets about achieving it. We explore the international context, reasons for national differences in accounting practice and tradition and the developing international regulatory system designed to achieve greater harmonisation.

BASICS OF FINANCIAL REPORTING

1

> **OBJECTIVES** After studying this chapter you should be able to:
>
> - explain and discuss the scope of accounting in general and of financial reporting in particular
>
> - describe the major types of user of published financial information and discuss the implications of their different needs
>
> - list and discuss the characteristics of accounting information that are likely to maximise its usefulness
>
> - describe and apply the traditional conventions applied in financial reporting
>
> - discuss and illustrate the internal coherence or inconsistency of these conventions.

INTRODUCTION

At its simplest level, accounting is about the provision of figures to people about their resources. It is to tell them such things as:

1 what they have got
2 what they used to have

3 the change in what they have got

4 what they may get in the future.

You may have done quite a lot of 'accounting' already. In many cases, this will have consisted largely of technical manipulation – writing up ledger accounts, preparing profit and loss accounts and balance sheets and so on. Much of the emphasis is likely to have been on 'doing things with numbers'. Given a figure to start with, you can probably record it in a proper double-entry manner and see its effect through onto a balance sheet that actually balances.

But this is only part of the story. Suppose you are not 'given a figure'. Suppose you are given, or have available, a whole variety of figures all related to a particular item or transaction. Which figure or figures should you actually put into the double-entry system? More fundamentally, *how* are you going to decide which ones to put in? In very general terms, we can answer this question by going back to our original simple definition of accounting. Namely, that it concerns the provision of figures to people about their resources. Presumably, therefore, the figures that we as accountants should provide to people are the figures that they need to know for their own particular purpose.

So the key question is: What do people want to know about their resources? What use do they wish to make of the figures we as accountants provide? Once we have answered this question, we can go on to say that the figure we should put into our double-entry system is the one likely to be *most useful to the user of our accounting reports*.

Accounting therefore needs:

- an effective and efficient data handling and recording system
- the ability to use that system to provide something useful to somebody.

This book is essentially concerned with the second of these needs. We have to consider three fundamental issues:

1 Who are the users of accounting statements?

2 What is the purpose for which each particular type of user requires the information?

3 How can we provide the user with the information best suited to their needs?

However, we have also to remember that the accountant and the user have themselves to operate within, and under the control of, the community at large. There is, therefore, an element of *regulation* that has to be taken into account.

USERS OF FINANCIAL REPORTS

As readers will be aware, accounting can be divided into management accounting and financial accounting. Very broadly, management accounting is designed for the management user, i.e. for internal decision-making, and financial accounting is designed for all other users. The theoretical distinction is that management, by definition, can obtain whatever information it needs from within the organisation. External users, however, have to rely on negotiation or regulation in order to obtain information. Financial reporting is only concerned with external users and so is this book.

ACTIVITY 1.1

Nine user groups can be suggested for financial reporting, as follows:

1 The equity investor group, including existing and potential shareholders and holders of convertible securities, options or warrants.

2 The loan creditor group including existing and potential holders of debentures and loan stock and providers of short-term secured and unsecured loans and finance.

3 The employee group including existing, potential and past employees.

4 The analyst-adviser group, including financial analysts and journalists, economists, statisticians, researchers, trade unions, stockbrokers and other providers of advisory services, such as credit-rating agencies.

5 Suppliers and trade creditors, past, present and potential.

6 Customers, also past, present and potential.

7 Competitors and business rivals.

8 The government, including tax authorities, departments and agencies concerned with the supervision of commerce and industry and local authorities.

9 The public, including taxpayers, consumers and other community and special interest groups, such as political parties, consumer and environmental protection societies and regional pressure groups.

Taking each of these groups one at a time, consider first the sort of decisions that they are likely to wish to make using accounting information and, second, the implications from this as to what information they might need.

Activity feedback

The equity investor group

Essentially, this group consists of existing and potential shareholders. This group is considering whether or not to invest in a business: to buy shares or to buy more shares; or, alternatively, whether or not to disinvest, to sell shares in the business. Equity investors look for one or a combination of two things: income, a money return by way of dividend, or capital gain, a money return by way of selling shares at more than their purchase price. It should be apparent that these two are closely related. Indeed, the only difference is the timescale. However, the simple theory is made immensely more complex in practice by the effects on share prices of other equity investors' expectations.

For example, share prices for a company may rise because higher dividends are expected to be announced by the company. Alternatively they may rise because other people *believe* dividends will increase. A buys some shares in expectation of 'good news'. This causes prices to rise. B then buys some shares in expectation of the price rise continuing. This causes the price to rise again – a self-fulfilling prophecy – which brings in C as a buyer too. The original hope of 'good news' is soon forgotten. If, however, at a later date the news arrives and turns out to be bad, everyone involved, A, B and C, may want to sell and the price will come crashing down.

The motivational and psychological arguments involved here are well beyond the scope of this book. It is the information requirements that concern us. If the investor is taking a short-term view then current dividends may be a major factor. As the time horizon of our investor lengthens then future dividends become more important and future dividends are affected crucially by present and future *earnings*. The focus then is on profits, which both determine future dividends and influence the share price.

One obvious point is that investors, both existing and potential, need information about *future* profits. The emphasis in published accounting information is almost wholly on past or more or less present profits. These may or may not be a good guide to the future. The need to make the past results useful for estimating (guessing) the future is an important influence on some of the detailed disclosure requirements we shall explore later. The general trend is to make reported accounting statements as suitable as possible for the investor to make their own estimations. We should note an alternative possibility, however. This is that the company itself – through either the management or possibly through the auditors – should make a forecast. After all, the management and the auditor have a much greater insight into possibilities and risks than the external shareholder.

The loan creditor group

This group consists of long-, medium- or short-term lenders of money. The crucial question an existing or potential loan creditor wishes to consider is obvious: Will he or she get their money back? A short-term loan creditor will primarily be interested, therefore, in the amount of cash a business has got or will very soon get. As a safeguard, they will also be interested in the net realisable value (NRV) of all the assets and the priority of the various

ACTIVITY 1.1   (Continued)

claims, other than their own, on the available resources. Longer-term lenders will clearly need a correspondingly longer-term view of the firm's future cash position. Their needs are thus similar to the needs of the equity investor group – they need to estimate the overall strength and position of the business some way into the future.

The employee group

Employees or their representatives need financial information about the business for two main reasons:

1 fair and open collective bargaining (i.e. wage negotiations)

2 assessment of present and future job security.

In these respects they also need to be able to assess the economic stability and vulnerability of the business into the future.

The employees, actual or potential, will also have additional requirements, however:

1 They will often need detailed information at 'local' level, i.e. about one particular part of the business or one particular factory.

2 They will need information in a clear and simple non-technical way.

3 They will need other information that is inherently non-financial. They will want to know, for instance, about management attitudes to staff involvement in decision-making, about 'conditions of service' generally, promotion prospects and so on. It can thus be seen that the employee group may require particular statements for its own use and that it may require information not traditionally regarded as 'financial' at all.

The analyst-adviser group

In one sense this is not a separate group. It is a collection of experts who advise other groups. Stockbrokers and investment analysts will advise shareholders, trade union advisers will advise employees, government statisticians will advise the government and so on. The needs of the analyst-adviser group are obviously essentially the needs of the particular group they are advising. However, being advisers and presumably experts they will need more detail and more sophistication in the information presented to them.

Suppliers and trade creditors need similar information to that required by short-term loan creditors. But they will also need to form a longer-term impression of the business's future. Regular suppliers are often dependent on the continuation of the relationship. They may wish to consider increasing capacity specifically for one particular purchaser. They will therefore need to appraise the future of their potential customers both in terms of financial viability and in terms of sales volume and market share.

Customers will wish to assess the reliability of the business both in the short-term sense (will I get my goods on time and in good condition?) and in the long-term sense (can I be sure of after-sales service and an effective guarantee?). Where long-term contracts are involved, the customer will need to be particularly on his or her guard to ensure that the business appears able to complete the contract successfully.

Competitors and business rivals will wish to increase their own effectiveness and efficiency by finding out as much as possible about the financial, technical and marketing structure of the business. The business itself will naturally not be keen for this information to become generally available within the industry and it is generally recognised that businesses have a reasonable right to keep the causes of their own competitive advantage secret. Competitors may also wish to consider a merger or an amalgamation or a straight takeover bid. For this purpose they need all this information, plus the information required by the equity investor group. They also need information about what they – the bidders – could do with the business. In other words, they need to be able to form an opinion on both:

● what the existing management is likely to achieve

● and what new management could achieve with different policies.

The government

Everybody is aware that governments require financial information for purposes of taxation. This may be the most obviously apparent use by governments, but it is not necessarily the most important. Governments also need information for decision-making purposes. Governments today take many decisions affecting particular firms or particular industries, both in a control sense and in government's capacity as purchaser or creditor. Also, governments need information on which to base their economic decisions as regards the economy as a whole. This information is likely to need to be very detailed and to go well beyond the normal historic information included in the usual published accounting reports. Again, there is an obvious need for future-oriented information.

The public

Economic entities, i.e. businesses in the broadest and most general sense, do not exist in isolation. They are

ACTIVITY 1.1 *(Continued)*

part of society at large and they react and interact with society at every level. At the local level, there will be concern at such things as employment, pollution and health and safety. At the wider level, there may be interest in, for example, pollution and 'green' issues, energy usage, effective use of subsidies, dealings with

foreign governments and contributions to charities in money or kind. Much of this information is non-financial. Indeed, some of it cannot be effectively measured at all. Whether it is accounting information is an open question. But it is certainly useful information about businesses.

Summary of user needs

Several general points emerge from the preceding discussion:

1 Many, although not all, of the information requirements are essentially forward looking.
2 Different users, with different purposes, may require *different* information about the *same* items.
3 Different users will require (and be able to understand) different degrees of complexity and depth.
4 Not all the information required is likely to be included in financial accounts.

CHARACTERISTICS OF USEFUL INFORMATION

ACTIVITY 1.2

Make a list of the desirable attributes or characteristics (such as relevance, for example) that financial information should have if it is likely to be useful.

Activity feedback
Seven general ideas occur to us, as follows.

Relevance
This sounds obvious, but on reflection is difficult to define and therefore to achieve. A report must give the user what he or she wants. As already indicated this presupposes that we, the accountants preparing the report, know:

1 who the user is
2 what their purpose is
3 what information he or she requires for this purpose.

Clearly these requirements may change as time goes by.

Understandability
Different users will obviously have different levels of ability as regards understanding accounting information. Understandability does not necessarily mean simplicity. It means that the reports must be geared to the abilities and knowledge of the users concerned. Complex economic activities being reported to an expert user may well require extremely complicated reports. Simple aspects being reported to users with little or no background knowledge will need to be very simple. The problems really arise when we have the task of reporting on complex activities but to the non-expert user.

Reliability
The user should be able to have a high degree of confidence in the information presented to him or her. This does not necessarily mean that the information has to be factually correct, but it should be as credible, as believable, as possible. Preferably, it should be independently verified, e.g. by an independent, qualified auditor.

ACTIVITY 1.2 *(Continued)*

However, unverified – or unverifiable – information may be better than no information at all.

Completeness

The user should be given a total picture of the reporting business as far as possible. This is a tall order. It implies large and complex collections of information. It may also imply problems of understandability.

Objectivity

The information presented should be objective or unbiased in that it should meet all proper user needs and be neutral in that the perception of the measurer should not be biased towards the interest of any one user group. Objectivity is a confused notion, with several different possible meanings. We shall consider the problems in more detail later. The present proposition is that reports should not be biased by the personal perception, the personal opinion, of the preparer of those reports. The stated need is not for reports with no personal opinion, but for reports with *unbiased* personal opinion.

Timeliness

Essentially, this means that information should be provided to the user in time for use to be made of it. Information presented should be as up to date as possible. Approximate information, made available in time to assist with some decision or action, is likely to be more useful than precise and accurate information presented after the decision has already been made.

Comparability

Information about any one business for any one period should be presented so that:

1 it can be easily compared with information about the same business for a different period

2 it can be easily compared with information about a different business for the same, or even a different, period.

Clearly, consistency of treatment is very important here – the application of generally accepted standards (and generally accepted regulatory standards).

NEED FOR COMMUNICATION

So we have some idea of the various characteristics of useful information. But, more fundamentally, what is information? Remember our earlier suggestion that 'accounting is about the provision of useful figures to people about their resources'. The accountant has to provide figures to the user. But 'provide' does not just mean 'send'. It is not enough to send, to deliver, sheets of paper with words and figures on. There has to be *communication*, there has to be *understanding* by the user. The point about communication, the point about information, is that the receiver is genuinely informed. He or she must become mentally and personally aware.

If effective communication is to take place the language used must be such that the signs employed evoke in others the same response as if those others were to see the object represented instead of the signs. This is, of course, an idealistic position. A television news film can never really put the viewer in the same position in every respect as if they were physically present at the actual event filmed. Even less successful is a verbal description by 'someone who was present'. In accounting, the means of communication is essentially a few numbers, usually prepared by someone who was not actually involved in the financial events supposedly being portrayed anyway. But it is a useful idea to bear in mind, however impossible to achieve.

Another problem is the likely ignorance of the intended receiver of the information. Accounting 'signs' are highly 'coded'. The accountant knows what he or she means, but does anybody else? And how is the user requiring the information to specify exactly what is wanted from the accountant if they cannot 'speak the language'? Clearly, when we think about it, the accountant has to communicate the main features of the reports in non-accounting terms.

Financial accounting conventions

We have looked at some of the possible things that financial accountants could do in order to provide useful figures to people about their resources. We have looked at who the users are and what sort of information they might want. In this and the following chapters we look at what accountants usually *do* do. Many different words are used in textbooks, articles and statements to describe these ideas – concepts, conventions, assumptions, postulates for example. Some of them are described as being more 'fundamental' than the others. In this chapter we shall simply refer to all of them as 'conventions'. Later we shall look at how international bodies define and divide them, but here we concentrate on the ideas themselves.

We shall consider 12 separate conventions, as follows: business entity, duality, monetary measurement, cost, accounting period, continuity (going concern), conservatism (prudence), consistency, materiality, objectivity, realisation of revenue and matching.

Business entity

This states that the business has an identity and existence distinct from its owners. To the accountant, whatever the legal position, the business and the owner(s) are considered completely separately. Thus the accountant can always speak of the business owing the owner money, borrowing money from the owner, owing profits to the owner and so on. Think of the basic business balance sheet:

Fixed assets	Capital
Current assets	Liabilities
Total	Total

As we know, a properly prepared balance sheet can always be relied on to balance. Why is this? The simple answer is because capital is the balancing figure. Capital is the amount of wealth invested in the business by the owner, the amount of money borrowed by the business from the owner or the amount the business owes the owner. None of these three statements could be made unless the accountant is treating the business as separate from, and distinct from, the owner. The accountant usually prepares the accounts of, i.e. the balance sheet of, the business. Transactions of the business are recorded as they affect the business, not as they affect the owner. In principle, another balance sheet always exists, namely for the owner as an individual. This will contain the owner's investment in the business, shown as one of his or her assets.

Duality

This may be regarded as a formalisation of the basis of double-entry. It states that in relation to any one economic event, two aspects are recorded in the accounts, namely:

1 the source of wealth

2 the form it takes (i.e. its application).

In the simplest of terms, 1 is 'where it comes from' and 2 is 'what we have done with it'. The source it came from will have a claim back on it. Thus, again in balance sheet terms, we can say that the balance sheet shows the array of resources at a point in time (assets) and the claims on those resources (liabilities); it shows the application of what was available (assets) and the source of what is available (liabilities or claims).

Monetary measurement

Accountants regard their job as dealing with *financial* information. This convention states that the accountant only records those facts that are expressed in money terms. Any facts, however relevant they may be to the user of the information, are ignored by the accountant if they cannot conveniently be expressed in money terms. It is often said that the greatest asset an effective and efficient business possesses is its workforce. So why does the workforce never appear on a business balance sheet? The short answer is that it would be extremely difficult to 'put a figure on' the workforce, i.e. to express this asset, this resource, in money terms. So the accountant does not even bother to try. Facts and outcomes that cannot be expressed in money terms are ignored. This convention and its limitations are sometimes queried.

Cost

This convention states simply that resources acquired by the business are recorded at their original purchase price. It follows on from the previous convention in that it tells us how that item is actually to be measured. This is the well-known historical cost (HC) convention. It does not always now receive the near universal support of earlier years.

Accounting period

This very simple convention recognises that profit occurs over time and we cannot usefully speak of the profit 'for a period' until we define the length of the period. The maximum length of period normally used is one year. This is supported by legislation normally requiring the preparation of full audited accounts annually. This does not, of course, preclude the preparation of accounts for shorter periods as well. But the formal 'published accounts' period is nearly always one year.

Continuity (going concern)

This important convention states that in the absence of evidence to the contrary it is assumed that the business will continue into the indefinite future. This convention has a major influence on the assumptions made when evaluating particular items in the balance sheet. For example, the convention allows us to assume that inventory will eventually be sold in the normal course of business, i.e. at normal selling prices. Perhaps even more obviously it allows for the principle of depreciation. If we depreciate an item of plant over ten years, then we are assuming that the plant will have a useful life to the business (not necessarily a useful total *physical* life) of ten years. This assumption can only be made if we are first assuming that the business will continue – or keep going – for at least ten years. Notice, incidentally, that the going concern assumption does not say that the business is going to keep being profitable into the indefinite future. It merely assumes that the business will manage not to collapse altogether.

Conservatism (prudence)

This convention refers to the accounting practice of recognising all possible losses, but not anticipating possible gains. This will tend to lead to an understatement of profits – to an understatement of asset values with no corresponding understatement of liability.

The accounts are in essence trying to give an indication of the current position (the balance sheet) and of the degree of success achieved through the accounting period (the profit and loss (P&L) account). This convention requires the accountant to attempt to ensure that the position or the degree of success is not overstated. Recognising that absolute accuracy is not possible, the accountants, according to this convention, should ensure the avoidance of overstatement by deliberately setting out to achieve a degree of understatement. This requires that similar items, some of which are positive and some of which are negative, should not be treated identically or symmetrically (see Activity 1.3).

Consistency

This is the practice of applying the same accounting rules, methods or procedures in each similar case. This convention should:

1 avoid short-term manipulation of reported results
2 facilitate comparisons within the firm over different accounting periods (intra-firm comparisons)
3 facilitate comparison between different entities (inter-firm comparisons).

Consistency can, of course, never overrule the requirements of proper and useful reporting. But the convention does certainly support the argument that where several alternative treatments or approaches are acceptable, the business should make a decision and then stick to it year by year for all similar items.

Materiality

This is a statistical concept that, in its application to accounting, implies that insignificant items should not be given the same emphasis as significant items. The insignificant items are, by definition, unlikely to influence decisions or provide useful information to decision makers, but they may well cause complication and confusion to the user of accounts. Their detailed treatment may also involve a great deal of time and effort – and therefore of money! – for no useful purpose. Many firms, for example, treat smallish items that fulfil all the theoretical requirements of the definition of

ACTIVITY 1.3

Give some examples of regular non-symmetrical treatment of positive and negative aspects of otherwise similar items.

Activity feedback
There are many examples to choose from. Two examples are:

1 the treatment of inventory, which is usually shown at cost or NRV if lower (but not at NRV if higher) – see Chapter 16

2 the whole approach to contingent items – see Chapter 19.

fixed assets, but cost below a defined minimum amount, as simple current expenses. This is not done because it is correct. It is done because it is easier and because it is 'good enough' for practical purposes and for users' informational needs.

Objectivity

This convention refers to an attribute or characteristic of accounting information generally regarded as desirable. This is that accounting measurements and information should permit qualified individuals working independently to develop similar measures or conclusions from the same evidence. In a nutshell, accounting information should be verifiable. Two schools of thought seem to have arisen in recent years over the full implications of this. One argues that the desire for objectivity implies as much factual content as possible. Facts, e.g. the actual cost figure specified in a contract, are easily verifiable. This idea surely corresponds with the everyday meaning of objectivity, i.e. the avoidance of subjectivity, the avoidance of personal opinion.

The second school of thought seems to argue that the degree of objectivity can be indicated not by the amount of formal (factual) verifiability, but by the degree of consensus achieved by several independent opinions. The question of whether a young woman is pretty or a young man is handsome clearly depends on the person giving the opinion ('beauty is in the eye of the beholder'). But this second school of thought would presumably argue that if, say, six people all say that they agree with such a statement, it becomes objective, becomes a fact ('the majority is always right'). You, the reader, must make your own mind up. But what is clear in any event is the convention that verifiability is a desirable element in accounting.

Realisation of revenue

We have just established the convention that an asset acquired by the business is usually recorded at the original purchase price. It is thus based on a market transaction. It is obvious that, at the latest, when the asset is disposed of by the business, we must record the actual disposal price. So if we buy inventory for €30, €30 has to be recorded as having gone and inventory (of €30, cost convention) has to be recorded as being present. If we then sell the inventory for €50, we must record €50 as being present and inventory has to be removed from the accounts. Thus an asset of €30 has been replaced by an asset of €50, giving a profit of €20. Once the €50 is physically in, there is no other possibility than to record an asset of €50. But is there no possibility of recognising an asset of €50 before, i.e. earlier than, the physical arrival of the money? Suppose we sell the inventory on 1 December and receive the money on 10 December. When did assets of €30 turn into assets of €50? Was it 10 December when we received the money? Or was it 1 December, when we acquired the expectation – indeed the right – to receive the money?

More importantly perhaps what criteria are we going to use to answer this question? On what *grounds* should we decide when the total asset figure increased, i.e. when the profit was made? This is a very complicated matter. We can first of all state the usual conventional answer: revenue is recognised as soon as, and is allocated to the period in which:

1 it is capable of objective measurement and

2 the asset value receivable in exchange is reasonably certain.

But this is really rather simplistic and we need to explore the area in more detail. (See Chapter 18.)

Before we do that, we should complete our overview by seeing how the revenue recognition question leads on to the calculation of profit. Since profit is revenue less expenses, we must explore the idea of matching expenses and revenues together.

Matching

Looking back over the conventions we have discussed so far, we have:

1 decided on the basic characteristics of the recording system (*business entity and duality*)
2 decided on how we are going to record items entering the business's control (monetary *measurement and cost*)
3 decided on how to record the proceeds from the disposal of such items (*revenue recognition*).

The essential item missing is clearly the mechanism for recording the actual loss of the item – its removal from the financial statements about the business. The earlier question was: When did assets of €30 turn into assets of €50? It is intuitively clear that whenever this did happen (and the revenue recognition convention tells us when), a profit of €20 was made. Thus, if the revenue, the benefit, is €50, then the expense, the amount used or lost, is €30. The matching convention covers this final stage in the process of profit calculation. It states that:

> Income (or profit) determination is a process of matching against revenue the expenses incurred in earning that revenue.

When an asset gets used, it becomes an expense. The question in effect is: At precisely what point does the accountant regard an asset as being 'used'? The answer is: At the point when the related revenue is recognised, so the process of profit calculation can be summarised as follows. First, we determine the point at which the revenue is to be recognised, the time when the proceeds are 'made'. Second, we match the expense against the revenue, i.e. we regard the expense as occurring at the same time as the revenue. So if the revenue from selling an item of inventory is recognised on 28 December as €50 then the expense of €30 is also recognised on 28 December. Accounts prepared on 31 December will include profit of €20 and an asset of €50 (debtors or cash). But if the revenue from selling an item of inventory is recognised on 2 January, then the expense will also be recognised on 2 January. Accounts prepared on 31 December will include an asset of €30 (inventory), no revenue and no expense, and therefore no profit or loss from this transaction.

The **matching convention** is often referred to as the **accruals convention**, although some writers distinguish between them. The accruals convention should be contrasted with the ideas of cash flow accounting (Chapter 23). The essence of the accruals convention is that the time when an item of benefit should be recognised and recorded by the accountant is determined by the reasonably ascertainable *generation* of the benefit – not by the date of the actual (cash) *receipt* of the benefit. Similarly, the time when an item of expense should be recognised and recorded as such by the accountant is determined by the usage of the item, not by the date of the acquisition of the item or of the *payment* for the item. The accruals convention is therefore another way of saying that the process of profit calculation consists of relating (matching) together the revenues with the expenses. It is not directly concerned with cash receipts and cash payments.

COHERENT FRAMEWORK

Thus far we have considered, separately, 12 conventions. How do they relate together? The idea of an all-embracing framework is discussed more fully in Chapter 8. What we can usefully do at this stage is to look at the 12 conventions to consider whether they are 'coherent' or consistent with each other.

One of the most problematic conventions is that of prudence or conservatism. At its most basic this derives from the obviously sensible belief that it is important not to encourage the users of accounts to spend money or to consume resources they do not have. Consideration of this convention, together with several of the other conventions, gives rise to certain difficulties.

ACTIVITY 1.4

Suggest pairs of conventions that we have already discussed, which are, or may be, contradictory or in opposition to each other, and illustrate the possible problems between them.

Activity feedback

Here are some possibilities we thought of:

1 **Prudence** and **going concern**. The going concern convention argues that the firm will 'keep going', e.g. that it will not be forced out of business by competition or bankruptcy. This may be a likely and rational assumption, but it is not necessarily prudent – in certain circumstances it could be decidedly risky.

2 **Prudence** and **matching**. The matching convention, building on the going concern convention, allows us to carry forward assets into future periods on the grounds that they will be used profitably later. This obviously makes major assumptions about the future that may not be at all prudent. The contradiction between these two conventions is one of the major problems of accounting practice. Should we, when in doubt, emphasise prudence or matching? Should we ensure that we never overstate the position or should we do our professional best to 'tell it like it is'? Should we report the worst possible position (prudence) or the most likely position (matching)?

3 **Prudence** and **objectivity**. Objectivity implies certainty and precision. It implies freedom from personal opinion, freedom from bias. Prudence, quite explicitly, implies that we should bias the information we choose to report in a certain direction. If accounting information could be genuinely objective, then prudence would be irrelevant by definition, because any bias would be impossible. In practice, of course, since accounting always has to make assumptions about future events, objectivity can never be completely achieved.

4 **Prudence** and the **cost concept**. This is a particularly interesting pairing of ideas. The cost concept is supported by objectivity (not on the grounds that it is objective, but on the grounds that it usually has a greater objective element than alternative valuation concepts) and is often regarded as being supported by prudence and, in some respects, it is.

Prudence suggests that in areas of valid choice, lower asset figures should be incorporated in accounts. In times of rising prices, use of replacement costs (RCs) could therefore be seen as imprudent, as compared with use of HCs. But consider the effect on reported profits of using an RC basis rather than HCs (Chapter 5). This splits up the HC profit into operating profit and holding gain, enabling the 'genuine', and therefore safely distributable, operating profit to be distinguished. Nothing could be more imprudent than to distribute resources needed to maintain the business and HC accounting can easily permit this to happen. Now try the following activity.

ACTIVITY 1.5

On 20 December 20X7 your client paid €10 000 for an advertising campaign. The advertisements will be heard on local radio stations between 1 January and 31 January 20X8. Your client believes that, as a result, sales will increase by 60% in 20X8 (over 20X7 levels) and by 40% in 20X9 (over 20X7 levels). There will be no further benefits.

Required

Write a memorandum to your client explaining your views on how this item should be treated in the accounts for the three years 20X7 to 20X9. Your answer should include explicit reference to at least three relevant traditional accounting conventions and to the requirements of two classes of user of published financial accounts.

Activity feedback

To : Client

From : Accountant

Treatment of advertising costs

There are a number of possible treatments:

- Write off the whole amount in 20X7. This could be justified on the grounds of *prudence* – any return being highly speculative.

- Write off the amount in strict proportion to the expected benefits. This would be supported by the *matching* convention, i.e. to allocate the expenses over the period of benefit in proportion to that benefit. This would imply expenses of €0 in 20X7 (as benefit does not commence in 20X7), €6000 in 20X8 and €4000 in 20X9.

- The conflict between prudence and matching is usually resolved through compromise, although in areas of real doubt and difficulty prudence should prevail and be given greater emphasis. A reasonable compromise in this case might well be to charge all the €10 000 as an expense in 20X8 – any returns in 20X9 being much more speculative than those expected in 20X8.

- The validity of this suggestion would depend on the particular circumstances, advice of advertising and industry experts, your earlier treatment of similar items (*consistency* is an important accounting convention) and also on the *materiality* of the amounts concerned. If the amounts concerned are small in relation to your results as a whole, then it is pointless to spend my time (and your money!) in a lengthy and detailed investigation.

- We should perhaps also consider the users of your accounting reports. For example, a *trade creditor* will be particularly interested in your assets and liability position. From this point of view, an asset that exists because of the speculative expectation of higher sales next year is not exactly a safe 'near-cash' security. Contrariwise, a *shareholder* will be concerned with the future trend of profits, and application of the matching convention is arguably an essential requirement for showing a fair indication of present profit and current and future trends.

The general conclusion from Activity 1.5 should be clear. A great deal of choice and subjectivity is involved in trying to produce useful financial information.

INTERNATIONAL DIMENSION

This introductory chapter has discussed basic and general ideas. We have not been at all concerned with what is likely to happen in any particular country or any particular jurisdiction. Historically, accounting and reporting grew up largely independently, and often very differently, in different countries. Practice, regulation and, indeed, the mode and volume of regulation, differed, often very greatly.

With the global economy, instant communication and a global finance market, this situation has changed sharply and this process of change is continuing.

The historical developments, and the reasons for them, are discussed in Chapter 2. The institutional and regulatory developments in the ongoing process of increasing harmonisation, involving the European Union (EU) and the International Accounting Standards Board (IASB) in particular are discussed in Chapter 3. The speed of this process has increased sharply in recent years; all listed (quoted) companies within the EU are using International Accounting Standards (IASs) for their consolidated financial statements for year-ends beginning on or after 1 January 2005; Australia switched to IASs from the same date, and an active process of 'convergence' between the IASB and the American regulatory body is ongoing.

A process of rapid change is under way. It is this process of change that necessitates the international approach taken by this book.

TERMINOLOGY AND THE ENGLISH LANGUAGE

Many readers of this book will be trying not only to master a subject new to them but also doing so in a language that is not their first. One added difficulty is that there are several forms of the English language, particularly for accounting terms. UK terms and US terms are extensively different. Some examples are shown in the first two columns of Table 1.1. At this stage, you are not expected to understand all these terms; they will be introduced later, as they are needed.

The IASB operates and publishes its standards in English, although there are approved translations in several languages. The IASB uses a mixture of UK and US terms, as shown in the third column of Table 1.1. On the whole, this book uses IASB terms, but UK terms tend to be used in the Fourth EU Directive. Familiarity with both is essential.

TABLE 1.1	Some examples of UK, US and IASB terms	
UK	**US**	**IASB**
Stock	Inventory	Inventory
Shares	Stock	Shares
Own shares	Treasury stock	Treasury shares
Debtors	Receivables	Receivables
Creditors	Payables	Payables
Finance lease	Capital lease	Finance lease
Turnover	Sales (or revenue)	Sales (or revenue)
Acquisition	Purchase	Acquisition
Merger	Pooling of interests	Uniting of interests
Fixed assets	Non-current assets	Non-current assets
Profit and loss account	Income statement	Income statement

SUMMARY

Financial reporting is concerned with the provision of information about business organisations to people outside the management function. We have thought about the various users of financial reporting, and the type and characteristics of information they might need. Finally we have explored the accountant's traditional approach to meeting these needs, i.e. the traditional underlying conventions of accounting. It can be demonstrated that they are often not mutually consistent. As we shall see in Chapter 2, different national traditions have sharply differing views on which conventions should be given priority.

EXERCISES

Suggested answers to exercises marked ✓ are to be found on the Student side of the companion website.

Suggested answers to the remaining exercises are to be found on the Instructor side of the companion website.

✓ **1** Look up as many definitions of accounting as you can find, noting the source, country, original language and date of publication. Note, and try to explain, their differences.

✓ **2** Consider the relative benefits to users of financial statements of:

- information about the past
- information about the present
- information about the future.

✓ **3** Do you think that a single set of financial statements can be prepared that will be reasonably adequate for all major external users and their needs?

4 Which of the suggested conventions do you regard as most important? Why?

5 Which of the suggested conventions do you regard as most useful? Why?

6 Explain the differences, if any, between your answers to questions 4 and 5.

✓ **7** How objective is the traditional HC balance sheet?

8 Completeness is not compatible with the monetary measurement convention. Discuss.

9   A firm spends €10 000 developing a new product and €5000 on an advertising campaign for it. Which conventions will help you in deciding on the appropriate accounting treatment and what do they imply?

10   Which conventions underlie the usual accounting treatment of inventory and work in progress?

11   HC accounts are neither objective nor useful. Discuss.

12   The normal accounting practice of revenue recognition proves that accountants are prudent. Discuss.

13   How do accountants decide when to recognise revenue?

14   When do accountants usually recognise revenue?

15   Do your answers to questions 13 and 14 satisfy the objectivity convention?

16   Explain the relationship between revenue recognition and asset valuation.

17   A local group collects subscriptions from its members, and also has to pay 60% of them to central funds. In the year to 31 December 20X8 the group receives:

for 20X7	€20
for 20X8	€60
for 20X9	€10

It pays to central funds in that year:

for 20X7	€12
for 20X8	€30
for 20X9	nil

Required:

(a) Produce a summary of the subscription position for the group for the year 20X8, on

   (i)   a receipts and payments basis
   (ii) a revenue and expenses basis.

(b) Outline the advantages and disadvantages of each basis with reference to appropriate accounting conventions. Give the group leader your recommended method, with reasons. Discuss also any difficult decisions you have to make in deciding your answer to (a) above.

(ACCA – adapted)

INTERNATIONAL ACCOUNTING DIFFERENCES

2

OBJECTIVES   After studying this chapter you should be able to:

- describe and explain how the following elements influenced the development of financial reporting and the existing accounting systems in a country:

  - provision of finance
  - the legal system
  - the system of taxation
  - cultural values

- explain and appraise the influence of cultural values on accounting values

- explain how different systems of accounting regulation could develop

- describe the purpose of country classification exercises

- appraise whether these country classification exercises are still relevant today.

INTRODUCTION

Chapter 1 introduced you to the subject of accounting and why accounting matters. It also touched on the importance of international harmonisation with respect to financial reporting. In this chapter we will focus on why accounting and financial reporting systems developed differently in different countries. At the end of this chapter we will pay attention to research approaches which try to explain with the help of these national characteristics the differences in the degree of accounting quality observed between various countries.

In Activity 2.1 we take another look at the main issues of Chapter 1. The limits mentioned in Activity 2.1 are set by standard setters in different countries or international standard setters such as the IASB, which promulgate the methods of recognition and measurement, consolidation presentation and disclosure that the company must comply with. Some standard setters allow many options with regard to those issues. Other standard setters are strict and prescribe, for example, one specific measurement method for a specific asset. Companies located in countries where standard setters allow many choices with regard to recognition and measurement issues etc. have much more accounting flexibility in the presentation and valuation of their assets, liabilities, earnings and financial position. As a result, users of financial statements of companies located in countries with accounting flexibility will face more problems comparing the performance of different companies with one another than users of annual accounts of companies located in countries with very little accounting flexibility. A discussion of the influence of accounting flexibility on financial analysis can be found in Chapter 30.

These differences in accounting systems are an obstacle towards the comparability of financial information published by companies using different sets of accounting standards. Companies operating in different countries and raising capital on different capital markets insist on more harmonisation of accounting standards in the first place. Harmonisation would increase the comparability of financial information and would create more transparency for the users of financial information. As a result, the information asymmetry between stakeholders and the companies would decrease. This will lead to a lower cost of capital for companies (see, for example, Leuz and Verrechia, 2000).

All over the world stakeholders use the information provided by financial statements in their decision-making process for the purposes enumerated earlier. Although the use of the information is more or less the same worldwide, the communication of that information can differ according to the location of the company (type of

ACTIVITY 2.1

Try to formulate in your own words the subject of accounting and especially financial reporting. Why does international harmonisation matter?

Activity feedback

A company draws up its financial statements to reflect the effects of transactions and events within and outside the company on its assets and liabilities, financial position and income. Whether and in what way, events and trans-

actions are reflected in the financial report depends on the accounting policies chosen by the company's management. For every kind of transaction and event, management must decide, either explicitly or implicitly, whether and how to reflect it in the financial statements. The methods of recognition and measurement, consolidation, and presentation must be chosen and decisions made as to what data to disclose in what degree of detail. Within limits, these choices are at the management's discretion.

ACTIVITY 2.2

Remember the contents of Chapter 1 and list again a number of users of financial information and for what purpose they will use the information.

Activity feedback

From Chapter 1 we know that different external stakeholders of financial statements exist and that they use the information of the annual accounts in their own decision-making process.

Shareholders: They use information from the financial statements in order to determine whether or not they are going to invest or disinvest in a company.

Creditors: On the basis of the financial statements creditors will assess the capability of a company to repay its debt in the long term. Based on the results of that analysis, credit will be granted or denied and the conditions will be negotiated.

Suppliers: They will assess the capability of the firm to repay their invoices in the short term before they decide to grant short-term credit.

Workforce: Employees will use financial statement data to get an idea about the financial health of their company.

Government: Governments use financial statements for several purposes, including for determining taxable income, controlling compliance with regulation or making decisions about government grants to certain industries.

accounting standards used) or other influencing factors (e.g. legal system, development of the capital market, culture and so on).

Information from the annual accounts becomes useful for decision-making if it can be compared to a certain benchmark. Very often data taken from the financial statements of other companies are used as a benchmark. As already mentioned in the feedback discussion of Activity 2.1, comparability will be hindered if the level of accounting flexibility differs among the companies. Accounting flexibility means that because of the freedom of choice the same kind of transactions and events can be reflected differently by different companies. This accounting flexibility is not only a problem related to comparability in those countries where accounting standards allow large freedom of accounting choices. It was, and still is to a certain extent, also a major problem when shareholders and other external stakeholders compare the financial statement information provided by companies located in different countries with each other.

The performance of another company is only a yardstick for evaluation if comparability is not jeopardised by accounting flexibility or other factors (see Part Four of this textbook). Comparing two financial reports that are based on different accounting policies is like comparing two lengths without knowing that one is in centimetres and the other in inches.

So if readers want to compare financial reports, which are the reflections of transactions and events as recorded under a particular accounting policy, it is important that the accounting policies do not differ to such an extent that the comparison of financial reports is meaningless. The accounting policies or accounting decisions of a company were, and still are to a large extent, influenced by the national environment and national accounting standards and practices.

As these national standards and practices differ from each other we will focus in this chapter on the differences between national accounting practices and standards and national accounting environments. In a period where international harmonisation or even standardisation seems to be almost realised, national differences still play a role. Empirical evidence exists (as we will see later in this chapter) that even the reporting behaviour of multinational companies listed on several international stock markets is still influenced by national accounting characteristics. That is the reason why we still pay attention to these national differences in the current volume.

ORIGIN OF NATIONAL DIFFERENCES

Financial reporting in general can be viewed as part of a communication process. The report is a medium through which information is transferred by a sender to a receiver.

The nature and functions of reporting with respect to organisations differ depending on the nature of the sender and the receiver as well as on the nature of the information transferred. The sender and the receiver form an integral part of their environment, which at the time that financial reporting developed in the past centuries was merely a national environment.

Financial reporting was, to start with, mainly internal reporting. Early financial reports can hardly be called external, they were a means by which the owners could get an insight into their income and capital. The company was a part of and managed by its owners. One could hardly distinguish between internal and external financial reports. From the early 1800s on, the increasing scale of companies resulted in finance problems and the need for a disconnection of management and capital supply. Private capital alone was insufficient to finance business activities, so capital was gathered from people outside the company.

This separation of ownership and management makes it possible to have the company managed by people specialising in management. The owners delegate control and the evaluation of the management to the board of directors. The board of directors also has the power to hire and fire top management and to approve any strategic decisions. The directors, by way of contrast, are accountable towards the owners for their deeds, decisions and policy. The external financial report provides a means of rendering account of this authority. Besides the functions of profit and capital determination, already mentioned, the financial report now also serves a stewardship role. An example of early external financial reporting are the accounts 'published' by the East India Company in the 18th century.

Financial reporting evolved from internal to external reporting, but for a long time external reporting meant providing information within the borders of a specific country. Because national environments have different characteristics, standard setters and accounting bodies have chosen different alternatives for recognition, measurement and presentation of assets, liabilities, equity, revenue and expenses. They have chosen those recognition, measurement, consolidation, presentation and disclosure policies that best fitted their national environments. In each country annual accounts provide information on the financial position of a company and its result. Although the general mission is similar in most countries many differences between countries occur. In each country there was and still is a different mix of influences on financial reporting. These differences result from different environmental, institutional and cultural influences in the individual countries. We will now focus on the most important environmental, institutional and cultural differences that shaped financial reporting in the individual countries.

The causes discussed thus far have been identified by several researchers who focused on this topic especially in the last 25 years of the 20th century when the need for accounting harmonisation started, as a result of increasing globalisation of the business world. Among the most important causes referred to in the literature are: provision of finance; the existing legal system; the link between accounting and taxation; and cultural differences between societies.

Provision of finance

According to Nobes and Parker (2003, p. 21): 'This difference in providers of finance (creditors/insiders) versus (equity/outsiders) is the key cause of international differences in financial reporting.' We saw earlier in this chapter that through the increasing scale of companies two centuries ago, firms had to find extra capital to finance growth. Companies in different countries responded differently to this increased need for funds. In countries such as Germany, France, Italy and Belgium, banks became the major supplier of extra funds. Companies in these countries relied more on debt to finance their activities than on equity. In contrast, in the UK and the USA the extra funds tend to be provided by shareholders, often by many shareholders for small amounts. Companies in those countries rely more on equity for the financing of their activities. In those countries an active stock exchange was and still is present.

Table 2.1 presents some examples of countries in which companies are more shareholder-oriented and countries in which companies are more credit/family/state-oriented. This divide represents the situation in the 20th century. To a large extent, it is still representative for today's situation, especially for non-listed groups and SMEs. (See Activity 2.3)

So in countries where companies are largely financed through equity, financial statements will have an investor or shareholder orientation. This means that financial statements must provide the kind of information that will enable a potential shareholder to make the best investment decision. Financial information that enables investors to make those investment decisions is called 'high-quality' accounting information. In the last decade empirical research on the measurement of 'accounting quality' and 'quality of accounting earnings' has indicated that in those countries with a strong capital market influence, the quality of accounting earnings is higher than in countries with a creditor orientation (see the discussion of today's role of national differences later in this chapter). In countries where companies rely more on debt financing, the financial statements have a creditor orientation. In those countries information provided through the annual accounts must be useful to judge whether a company is able to repay its debt. Creditor protection becomes important in this respect. These differences in financing are worth bearing in mind when companies from different countries are compared with each other for financial analysis purposes. (See further Chapters 30 and 31.)

TABLE 2.1	Shareholder-oriented versus credit-oriented countries
Shareholder-oriented	**Credit/family/state-oriented**
United States	Germany
United Kingdom	France
The Netherlands	Belgium
Sweden	Italy
Australia	Spain
Canada	Portugal

Source: Adapted from Alexander and Nobes (2004), Nobes and Parker (2003) and Ordelheide and KPMG (2001).

ACTIVITY 2.3

Could you argue why especially the difference between credit/insiders versus equity/outsiders has an impact on financial reporting?

Activity feedback

Insiders or parties that have a power relation towards a company are in a position to ask for internal data about the financial position of the firm towards which they exercise power. The power relation of outsiders is much weaker: they are not in a position to ask for extra information and have to rely on public information. Especially in countries where widespread shareholdership exists, the power of the individual shareholder to get financial information is limited. Although the power of the individual shareholder is weak, in those countries where companies rely on the capital market for extra funding there is a strong incentive towards high-quality external financial reporting. Through financial reports, companies communicate their financial situation to existing and potential shareholders.

ACTIVITY 2.4

If you were to compare the financial risk between companies on the basis of the debt/equity ratio calculated from the published annual accounts, in which countries would you come across firms with the highest ratio?

Activity feedback

If we exclude the impact of other influencing factors on the debt/equity ratio (e.g. type of industry, profit distribution versus reservation) and take into account only these national differences, then you would find, for example in Germany and France, companies with higher debt/equity ratios than in companies in the USA or in the UK. This difference is then due solely to national differences with regard to the way in which companies are financed.

Existing legal system

Over the years in the western world two types of legal system have developed: the so-called common law system and the code law system. Both legal systems were exported in the 20th century to different parts of the world. The common law system originated in England and is developed from case law. The legal system in most Commonwealth countries is the common law system. Common law is characterised as a legal system that is developed case by case and does not prescribe general rules that could be applied to several cases. In a common law situation accounting rules are not a part of the law. In common law countries accounting regulation is in the hands of professional organisations of the private sector. Company law in these countries is kept to a minimum. Detailed accounting regulation is produced by the private standard setter, as we will discuss later when we look at accounting regulation.

The code law system originated in Roman law and has developed in continental Europe. It is characterised by a wide set of rules that try to give guidance in all situations. In code law countries the company law is very detailed and accounting standards are often embodied in the company law. Accounting regulation in code law countries is in the hands of the government and financial reporting is in those circumstances often reduced to complying with a set of very detailed legal rules.

Table 2.2 gives some examples of code law and common law countries. (See also La Porta, Lopez-de-Silanes, Schleifer and Vishny, 1997 and 1998.)

TABLE 2.2	Common law versus code law countries	
Common law countries		**Code law countries**
England and Wales		Scotland
United States		France
Australia		Germany
Canada		Belgium
Ireland		The Netherlands
New Zealand		Portugal
Singapore		Spain
		Japan

Source: Adapted from Alexander and Nobes (2004), Nobes and Parker (2003) and Ordelheide and KPMG (2001).

Link between accounting and taxation

In some countries the fiscal authorities use information provided in the financial statements in order to determine taxable income. In a number of continental European countries expenses are tax deductible only if they are also recognised in the profit and loss account. As a result financial reporting becomes tax influenced or even tax biased. In this respect Germany is well known for its *Massgeblichkeitsprinzip*, which stands for the fact that the tax accounts (*Steuerbilanz*) should be identical to the accounts published for external stakeholders (*Handelsbilanz*). This link between financial reporting and taxation is often found in those countries that do not have an explicit investor approach in their financial reporting orientation.

In countries like the USA, the UK and the Netherlands the link between taxable income and accounting income is much weaker. Separate accounts are filed for tax purposes. The measurement and recognition rules and estimates used in the tax accounts can differ from the valuation rules used in the preparation of the financial statements published for all external stakeholders.

Table 2.3 shows the general relationship between accounting and taxation using some examples based on the situation in the 1990s.

TABLE 2.3	General relationship between accounting and taxation	
Independence		**Dependence**
Denmark		Germany
Ireland		France
United Kingdom		Belgium
The Netherlands		Italy
Czech Republic		Sweden
Poland		Norway

Source: Adapted from Alexander and Nobes (2004), Nobes and Parker (2003) and Ordelheide and KPMG (2001).

This relationship between accounting income and tax income can vary over time. For example, Spain was for a long time in the column of dependence; with the reform of 1989, however, the link between taxable income and accounting income became less strong and they are now moving towards independence. The introduction of International Accounting Standards will have an impact on the relation between accounting and taxation in those countries characterised by a dependence relationship, especially when SMEs will start to use IFRS for private entities in the near future.

Cultural differences

Research indicates that another cause of variation between national accounting systems is cultural differences. Cultural differences between nations are identified as an important influencing factor on reporting and disclosure behaviour with regard to financial statements. One of the prominent researchers on cultural differences is Hofstede (1984). He used four constructs to classify countries according to the cultural differences he observed in his empirical research. The constructs resulted from empirical survey-based research in one multinational (IBM; survey population 100 000 employees in 39 countries, 1984). Hofstede labelled his constructs as follows: individualism, power distance, uncertainty avoidance and masculinity. According to Hofstede these labels describe the following characteristics of a society.

Individualism versus collectivism Individualism stands for the preference for a loosely knit social framework in society wherein individuals are supposed to take care of themselves and their immediate families only. Collectivism describes the preference for a tightly knit social framework in which individuals expect their relatives, clan or other in-group to look after them in exchange for unquestioning loyalty. The fundamental issue addressed by this dimension is the degree of interdependence a society maintains among individuals. This difference relates to the people's self-concept: 'I' or 'we'.

Large versus small power distance Power distance is the extent to which the members of a society accept that power in institutions and organisations is distributed unequally. People in larger power distance societies accept a hierarchical order in which everybody has a place that needs no further justification. The fundamental issue addressed by this dimension is how a society handles inequalities among people when they occur.

Strong versus weak uncertainty avoidance Uncertainty avoidance is the degree to which the members of a society feel uncomfortable with uncertainty and ambiguity. This feeling leads them to beliefs promising certainty and to maintain institutions protecting conformity. Strong uncertainty avoidance societies maintain rigid codes of belief and behaviour and are intolerant of deviant people and ideas. Weak uncertainty avoidance societies maintain a more relaxed atmosphere in which practice counts more than principles and deviance is more easily tolerated.

Masculinity versus femininity Masculinity stands for the preference in society for achievement, heroism, assertiveness and material success. Its opposite, femininity, stands for the preference for relationships, modesty, caring for the weak and the quality of life.

Based on Hofstede's classification scheme Gray (1988) defined 'accounting values' that can be linked to the different cultural values as follows:

- professionalism versus statutory control
- uniformity versus flexibility
- conservatism versus optimism
- secrecy versus transparency.

Professionalism versus statutory control The accounting value professionalism links to individualism. Professionalism is consistent with a society where the emphasis is on 'I' rather than 'we'. Professionalism also goes together with a society with small power distance. Statutory control is observed in the opposite situation, namely in societies with large power distance. In relation to the accounting profession, professionalism implies self-regulation by the accounting profession itself. Statutory control implies control by the government. Statutory control could also be linked to strong uncertainty avoidance.

Uniformity versus flexibility First of all, uniformity can be linked to strong uncertainty avoidance. Uniformity leads to detailed regulations embedded in the law and adherence to consistency. Uniformity is therefore also associated with large power distance societies and societies in which the emphasis is on 'we' rather than 'I'. Flexibility, however, can be associated with weak uncertainty avoidance, small power distance and individualism.

Conservatism versus optimism Conservatism could be linked to uncertainty avoidance. In these societies one is more conservative with regard to profit recognition and asset measurement. Conservatism is an important value for accountants, especially in continental Europe where financial reporting is more creditor-oriented and where there is a strong link between accounting income and taxable income.

Secrecy versus transparency Secrecy implies a preference for confidentiality. Secrecy can be linked to uncertainty avoidance, but also to societies with large power distances. Information asymmetry will then reinforce inequalities and power relations between the different parties. Secrecy will have a direct impact on the level of information disclosure by companies.

The most important economic and cultural elements cited in the literature as causes for differences between national accounting systems have now been discussed. Other factors also listed in the literature as contributors to those differences are, for example, the level of economic development in a country, the degree of industrialisation, inflation levels, the adherence to accounting theory (e.g. in the Netherlands income determination and valuation is inspired by the theory of Limperg, financial reporting in Germany was inspired by the theory of Schmalenbach).

ACTIVITY 2.5

Consider again the cultural values described by Hofstede. How do they link with the accounting value dimensions defined by Gray? Is there a direct link or an indirect link?

Activity feedback
Between some variables there is a direct relationship; between other characteristics and values the relationship is rather indirect.

In the next part of the chapter we will analyse how these different economic and cultural factors shaped financial reporting practices and standards in each individual country. The causes for differentiation had their influence on the existing accounting system in a country.

DIFFERENCES IN ACCOUNTING SYSTEMS

Since accounting responds to its environment, different cultural, economic, legal and political environments produce different accounting systems, while similar environments produce similar accounting systems.

In this section we focus on these differences in accounting systems. In the next section, the emphasis lies on the different sets of domestic generally accepted accounting principles (GAAP). Under the heading of accounting systems we discuss two elements that characterise accounting systems, namely the organisation of accounting regulation and the organisation of the accounting profession.

Types of accounting regulation

When shareholders are the main providers of capital we expect them to have great interest in the way in which companies communicate their financial information. The shareholders will definitely want to have a hand in the communication process, including the financial reporting process. The shareholders are mainly trying to achieve this objective by hiring professional accountants who check on their behalf the communication process and its outcome within a company. In order to be able to fulfil their task properly the accountants started to play a major role in the standard-setting process of those countries.

We observe that in those countries with a code law system and a creditor orientation the government often makes use of financial reporting for their own purposes. First of all, in those countries the annual accounts are often used for tax purposes which serves the government. Second, the financial statements may be used for specific information needs of the government (e.g. in Belgium, the social balance sheet [a document containing employment statistics, e.g. number of employees, breakdown

ACTIVITY 2.6

Consider Tables 2.1 and 2.2, which provide information on the different sources of finance in each country and the existing legal system. What kind of accounting regulation would you expect in those countries?

Activity feedback

If we consider Tables 2.1 and 2.2 again, we observe to a certain extent a correlation between the provision of finance (debt versus equity) and the legal system in place (code law/common law). In most countries with active equity markets the legal system is the common law system. This is in favour of the private sector developing financial reporting rules or standards. In countries in which companies are financed to a large extent through debt, the code law system is present as the legal system. In those countries creditor protection is high on the agenda. Because large creditors such as banks are able to obtain inside information from the companies, they are less in need of financial information published by these companies. In these countries accounting regulation is in the hands of the government.

into different categories, change in the workforce, use of government incentives for the creation of employment] must be included in the financial statements by Royal Decree of 1996. It mainly serves the need of the government for information with regard to employment in order to evaluate the effectiveness of their governmental employment policies). Financial reporting in those countries essentially comes down to compliance with legal requirements and tax laws.

These observations show that there are two types of accounting regulation, each of which is embedded in a different economic and legal environment. First of all, there are countries in which accounting regulation is in the hands of the private sector: the UK, the USA, Australia and the Netherlands. In these countries private standard setting goes together with a shareholder orientation of the financial information published and, in most countries, a common law system. Second, there are countries in which the government plays a major part in accounting regulation. This system is observed in many continental European countries. In those countries detailed accounting rules are embodied in the law, normally the company law. Financial information has mainly a creditor orientation in those countries and they are further characterised by a code law system. These two types of accounting regulation still apply for the time being to non-listed groups and small and medium-size entities. With the compulsory introduction of the International Financial Reporting Standards a substantial number of countries with diverse backgrounds now operate in a similar setting with regard to accounting regulation.

Differences in the organisation of the accounting profession

When companies are financed by equity capital and if this equity capital is in the hands of a widespread group of small shareholders, these shareholders are in need of a well-organised control system with regard to the quality and reliability of the information provided by the financial statements. The strength and size of the accounting profession is directly influenced by the need for the external control mechanisms or audit of the published financial information. Table 2.4 illustrates that in those countries with active capital markets the profession developed earlier than in countries where companies are more financed by debt.

In countries with a well-organised accounting profession we observe that the influence of that profession on local accounting practices and on national GAAP is larger than in countries with smaller and later developed professional organisations.

CHARACTERISTICS AND DIFFERENCES IN NATIONAL GAAP

Economic and environmental differences lead to differences in accounting systems (e.g. regulation). These accounting systems produce different national or domestic accounting standards. The following points illustrate several differences in financial reporting characteristics. Although they are presented as separate items, they are linked together.

Shareholder orientation versus stakeholder orientation

In countries with widespread ownership there is a need for high-quality published financial information. As companies have to rely to a large extent on the capital market, information disclosure becomes extremely important because existing and potential shareholders do not have access to internal information in order to assess the financial situation of the company they might want to invest in or increase their investment in. In those countries the pressure for disclosure is much greater than in countries where providers of finance have the power to obtain internal information. Besides the need for more disclosure and more auditing, the debt versus equity orientation also has a direct influence on valuation issues.

In equity-oriented countries financial reporting is aimed at communicating the performance and efficiency of the business to existing and potential shareholders. Profit measurement is very important and reported data on earnings, financial position and cash flow will be used to make predictions about the future earnings, cash flow and financial position of the company. In countries where companies are financed through debt, financial statements serve the information needs of many different stakeholders, especially creditors, and also the government. Their information needs are concerned with the underlying assets of the company and the determination of taxable income. The debt/equity orientation lies at the origin of the different reporting and principles described next.

TABLE 2.4	Dates of establishment of professional accountancy bodies	
Country	Professional body	Founding date (founding date of predecessor)
Belgium	Instituut der Bedrijfsrevisoren/Institut des Reviseurs d'Entreprises	1953
England and Wales	Institute of Chartered Accountants in England and Wales	1880 (1870)
Denmark	Foreningen af Statsautoriserede Revisorer	1912
Finland	KHT-yhdistys	1925 (1911)
France	Ordre des Experts Comptables	1942
Germany	Institut der Wirtschaftsprüfer	1932
Ireland	Institute of Chartered Accountants of Ireland	1888
Italy	Consiglio Nazionale dei Dottori Commercialisti	1924
	Collegio dei Ragionieri e Periti Commerciali	1906
Japan	Japanese Institute of Certified Public Accountants	1948 (1927)
Norway	Den norske Revisorforening	1999 (1930)
Portugal	Sociedade Portuguesa de Contabilidade	1930
Scotland	Institute of Chartered Accountants of Scotland	1951 (1854)
Spain	Institut of Sworn Auditors of Accounts	1943
Sweden	Föreningen Auktoriserade Revisorer (FAR)	1923
	Svenska Revisorsamfundet (SRS)	1899
Netherlands	Nederlands Instituut voor Registeraccountants	1967 (1895)
New Zealand	New Zealand Society of Accountants	1909 (1894)
United States	American Institute of Certified Public Accountants	1887

Source: Alexander and Nobes (2004), Nobes and Parker (2003) and Ordelheide and KPMG (2001).

Fairness versus legality

In common law countries the aim of financial reporting is a fair representation of the financial situation of the company. In the UK this is translated into the 'true and fair view' concept. In code law countries financial reporting is focused on compliance with the legal requirements and tax laws. This often leads the 'legal form' to dominate 'the substance'. The most cited example in this respect is the accounting treatment of a lease contract. In countries with strong shareholder orientation and emphasis on fairness, lease contracts are accounted for on the balance sheet although the company is not the legal owner of the assets (e.g. the UK and USA). In countries where the legal form prevails, these assets used by the company are kept off balance sheet as the company is not the legal owner (e.g., until recently, France). This difference can have a major impact on the debt/equity ratio of companies (for example Euro Disney SCA, see Chapter 30).

Conservatism versus accruals

In countries in which financial reporting is more creditor-oriented and used for tax purposes, valuation rules will be more conservative or prudent than in countries with a shareholder orientation. Adherence to conservatism versus accruals will lead to a different choice in valuation rules and accounting practices. For example, with regard to depreciation, the declining balance method will be used more often than the straight line method, if conservatism is an important characteristic in financial reporting. Further, more use will be made of provisions in these countries, especially when provisions are tax deductible. Conservative accounting is often regarded as a system in which lower profits are reported than under a system driven by accrual accounting. However, with the use of extensive depreciation and creation of provisions, those companies are also able to increase results in periods with weak economic performance.

Much research is currently being undertaken with regard to the quality of earnings reported under conservative accounting. With quality of accounting information one refers to the use of accounting data for the prediction of future performance (value relevance of accounting information). The results of these studies reveal that information provided under conservative accounting practices is less value relevant (see, for example, Basu, 1997; Pope and Walker, 1999; Penman and Zhang, 2002).

Uniformity, accounting plans and formats

In code law countries we observe that the regulator attaches importance to uniformity. Compliance with prescribed accounting plans (France, Spain and Belgium) and detailed formats for the balance sheet and the profit and loss account are a result of this drive for uniformity. When regulation is in the hands of the government the layout of the balance sheet, profit and loss accounts and notes is much more detailed. The schemes for balance sheet and profit and loss account put forward by the Fourth and Seventh Directives of the EU are more detailed than the layout presented by the IASB (see Chapter 9). On the other hand the level of detail in the notes to the balance sheet and profit and loss account is much higher when accounts in compliance with IFRS are prepared.

Consolidated accounts

In countries where financial reporting has a strong shareholder orientation, the practice of preparing and publishing consolidated financial statements emerged much earlier. Preparing consolidated financial statements was already common practice at the beginning of the 20th century in the USA (in the 1920s). In the UK and the Netherlands consolidation became common practice in the 1930s. In typical creditor orientation countries, which are usually also code law countries, consolidation was introduced by law. This was done in the late second half of the 20th century (Germany, 1965, *Aktiengesetz* for public companies; France, 1985, a law which obliged listed companies to publish consolidated accounts; Belgium, the Royal Decree of March 1990; in Italy consolidation became compulsory in the early 1990s).

Deferred taxation

In countries with no direct link between tax income and accounting income the practice of recording deferred taxes on the balance sheet is well-established and common practice. For countries in which there is a strong link between accounting income and tax income the practice of recording and calculating deferred taxes is relatively new. Further, in the individual accounts of companies in those countries the amounts recorded under deferred taxes will be rather small.

COUNTRY CLASSIFICATION

Research into the possible causes to explain the observed differences in national accounting practices reveal several moderating or intervening variables (e.g. providers of finance, legal system, cultural differences and taxation). These variables shape the existing accounting systems in the different countries (accounting regulation and organisation of the profession), accounting values and financial reporting practices.

These different factors are used by researchers as cluster variables in order to classify different countries into separate more homogeneous groups according to their characteristics. These classification exercises were very popular in the 1970s and the 1980s. Examples can be found in the following publications: Hatfield (1966), Mueller (1967), Seidler (1967), American Accounting Association (1977), da Costa, Bourgeois and Lawson (1978), Frank (1979) and Nair and Frank (1980). The most cited classification pattern of countries is that of Nobes (1980).

To illustrate these country classification exercises, we now look at the classification system of Nobes. The popularity of classification attempts based purely on observed differences dropped in the 1990s, although Nobes' classification scheme still figures in many textbooks.

Nobes based his classification research on the financial reporting practices of public companies in the western world. The date of classification was 1980, that is, before the enactments in EU countries of the Fourth Directive on company law and before the emergence of IAS. Nobes selected the following nine discriminating variables:

1 type of user of the published accounts of listed companies
2 degree to which law or standards prescribe in detail and exclude judgement
3 importance of tax rules in measurement
4 conservatism/prudence
5 strictness of application of historical cost

6 susceptibility to replacement cost adjustments in main or supplementary accounts

7 consolidation practices

8 ability to be generous with provisions and to smooth income

9 uniformity between companies in application of rules.

Some of the discriminating factors relate to explanatory variables (for example factors one and two) while other variables relate more to valuation practices (for example, four and eight) (see Figure 2.1).

In the 1990s classification attempts were carried out, but they were becoming less popular. The classification exercises that were undertaken in the 1990s (e.g. d'Arcy, 2001), show us that clusters are moving towards each other and that more countries are now clustered into one group, especially when group accounting is considered. The clustering research of d'Arcy (2001) which is based on data from the second half of the 1990s, shows not only that national differences matter in explaining financial reporting, but also that firm characteristics play an important role in the quality and characteristics of financial reporting (e.g. single versus dual listing status, industry influence, firm dimension, geographical diversification and global player).

So far in this chapter we have explained how an existing accounting system in a specific country (financial reporting standards and practices, type of accounting regulator and strength of the accounting profession) is a result of national or local characteristics or influences. There are countries, however, in which the accounting systems in place do not result from national characteristics but are 'exported' to them or 'economically' or 'politically' imposed on them.

Western countries have exported their accounting systems to their colonies in the past. For example the accounting system in place in Singapore and the local GAAP

FIGURE 2.1   Suggested classification of accounting 'systems' in some developed countries

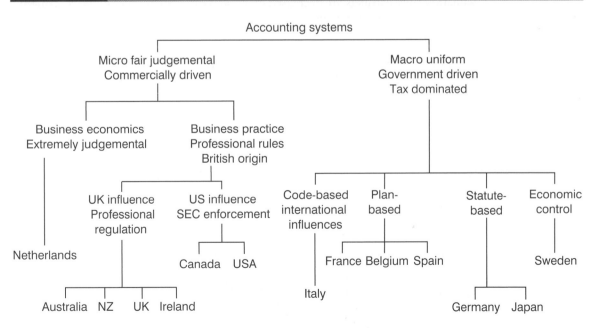

SOURCE: NOBES (1980)

are very similar to the British system and UK GAAP. In some countries in Africa, which were former French colonies, a uniform chart of accounts (similar to the French plan comptable) is in use.

A more recent phenomenon is that standards are imposed on countries in the wake of globalisation and economic progress. For example, countries in eastern Europe have adopted IASs/IFRSs after the breakdown of communism. Also some less-developed countries have adopted IASs/IFRSs and one can wonder whether the local economies there are in need of a set of such technical accounting standards.

NATIONAL DIFFERENCES: MORE RECENT EVOLUTIONS

As mentioned earlier in this chapter, classification exercises that attempted to cluster countries in homogeneous groups became less popular in the 1990s. In the 1980s through the enactment of the Fourth Directive in EU countries and in the 1990s under the pressure of the globalisation of capital markets, national accounting practices started slowly to move towards each other. This development is still going on and some differences have already become less noticeable or have almost disappeared for certain categories of companies or for certain financial statement items. From the late 1980s on more and more companies sought dual listings. In the early 1990s, many European multinationals went to capital markets abroad, especially to the US. In Germany, for example, Daimler-Benz started to publish two sets of annual accounts, i.e. annual accounts presented according to German GAAP and annual accounts presented according to US GAAP. At that time the differences between equity and earnings presented according to US GAAP and the equity and earnings presented according to German GAAP surprised many. Figure 2.2 became world famous.

Figure 2.2 provides clear evidence of the impact of conservative accounting practices on the reported result. In 1993 the US GAAP result of Daimler-Benz is much lower: conservative accounting leads to a kind of smoothing. Through conservative valuation rules earnings are decreased in 'good' years, but at times of weak economic performance results can be increased.

| FIGURE 2.2 | Earnings evolution of Daimler-Benz, 1989–1994 |

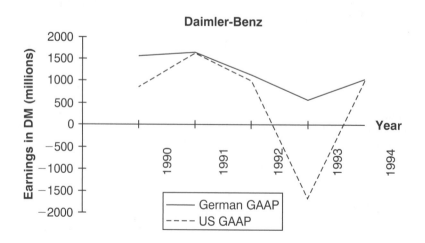

SOURCE: ANNUAL REPORTS OF DAIMLER-BENZ (1989–1994)

Many Swiss, German and Scandinavian multinationals switched to IAS in the second half of the 1990s. In France a number of listed companies prepared their consolidated accounts using US GAAP (e.g. Total Fina, Suez) or IAS (e.g. Eutelsat, Rémy Cointreau, Renault). Academics started to study the reaction of the capital market to these voluntary switches of companies from 'conservative or low-quality' accounting standards to a set of 'higher-quality' accounting standards (IAS or US GAAP). Empirical research results showed that capital markets reacted positively to the voluntary switch, since capital markets perceived the switch as a reduction in information asymmetry between firms and investors. As a result the cost of capital dropped for these companies (see, for example, Leuz and Verrechia, 2000).

This evolution resulted in the emergence of two groups of companies in most countries. The first group consists of companies that made an appeal to the international capital market for funds and subsequently started to apply accounting rules that would lead to an increase of comparability of their financial information worldwide. This group started to use 'high-quality' accounting standards such as IAS/IFRS, US GAAP and UK GAAP, whereby 'high-quality' standards are defined as follows: 'Financial reporting quality relates to the usefulness of financial statements for contracting, monitoring, valuation and other decision-making by investors, creditors, managers and all other parties contracting with the firm' (Ball and Shivakumar, 2002). The second group consists of non-listed domestic companies, predominantly small and medium-sized, who would continue to apply national GAAP.

At the turn of the century following up on this situation governments and regulatory authorities issued regulations that listed groups would have to comply with IFRS or US GAAP. In the first years of the 21st century, non-listed global players started to use IAS or US GAAP as well. Nowadays we observe that also medium-sized companies issue financial statements in compliance with IFRS.

Due to the drive towards global harmonisation of reporting practices, one might expect that national influences on reporting behaviour would soon vanish. Academic research however provides evidence that besides company characteristics, national influences still play an important role in the quality of financial reporting. The variables which influence national accounting characteristics and which were discussed in prior sections of this chapter, are still significant independent variables in regression models explaining differences in accounting quality between companies from different countries.

NATIONAL DIFFERENCES: DO THEY STILL PLAY A ROLE IN AN ERA OF GLOBALISED ACCOUNTING?

Even when all companies comply with US GAAP or IAS/IFRS, academic research provides evidence that national influences still affect the quality of financial reporting in the different countries. Current empirical research provides us with evidence of this influence, and this is another reason why we have paid so much attention to such national variables in this chapter.

The variables pointed out by researchers in the 1970s and 1980s as causes that might explain and have led to differences in national accounting systems and national GAAP are now used in empirical multi-country studies in which different aspects of the financial reporting practices of companies are researched. These studies focus, among other things, on the value relevance of accounting information, on earnings management practices and on characteristics of the audit market and audit process. A few examples of these empirical studies will be presented here together with their research results.

Ali and Hwang (2000) found that the value relevance of accounting information is lower for countries with bank-oriented (as opposed to market-oriented) financial systems. Value relevance was specified in terms of explanatory power of accounting variables (earnings and book value of equity) for security returns. Their results indicate further that value relevance of accounting income is lower for countries where private sector bodies are not involved in the standard-setting process. This finding is consistent with the premise that government standard setters use financial accounting rules to satisfy their own regulatory needs such as computing income taxes or demonstrating compliance with the national government policies and macroeconomic plans (Choi and Mueller, 1992). The research provides further evidence for the fact that value relevance is lower for continental model countries than for British-American model countries, plus that value relevance is lower when there is a strong link between accounting results and tax results and finally they find that value relevance is higher when more is spent on external auditing services.

Ball, Kothari and Robin (2000) investigated two properties of accounting income (conservatism and timeliness) and the influence of international institutional factors on accounting income. The property timeliness is defined as the extent to which current period accounting income incorporates current period economic income. Conservatism has been used in this study using the definition of Basu (1997), which regards conservatism as the extent to which current period income asymmetrically incorporates economic losses, relative to economic gains. Their central result is that accounting income in common law countries is significantly more timely than in code law countries, due entirely to quicker incorporation of economic losses which means more income conservatism.

Guenther and Young (2000) investigated how cross-country differences in legal systems, differences in legal protection for external shareholders, and differences in the degree of tax conformity affect the relation between financial accounting earnings and real economic value-relevant events that underlie those earnings. The results provide evidence that the association between financial accounting earnings and real economic activity in a country is related in predictable ways to the legal and economic systems that underlie financial accounting standard setting and the demand for financial accounting standards. The high association for the UK and the USA and the low association for France and Germany are consistent with expectations that accounting earnings in common law countries, countries with legal systems that protect external shareholder rights, countries with market-oriented (rather than bank-oriented) capital markets and countries where financial accounting rules are independent of tax rules better reflect underlying economic activity. Not only the traditional elements of differentiation (provision of capital, legal system, link with taxation) seem to be relevant, but also elements such as risk of litigation, investor protection and enforcement of accounting rules are important factors that explain differences in reporting behaviour.

Leuz, Nanda and Wysocki (2003) found that the quality of financial reports increased in countries where investor protection is stronger. Their findings suggest an important link between legal institutions and the quality of financial information provided. The legal rights accorded to outside investors, especially minority investors, and the quality of their enforcement are both associated with the properties of firms' accounting earnings. Their study indicated further that a switch to high-quality standards alone was not a guarantee for high-quality financial information. Other academics had also put forward this issue. For example,

Schipper (2000) stated that: 'Reporting quality is not only a function of the set of standards applied. High-quality standards implemented in a defective manner will not result in high-quality financial reports.' Without adequate enforcement, even the best accounting standards will be inconsequential. Hope (2003(a); 2003(b)) constructed an enforcement index which took into account judicial efficiency, rule of law, anti-director rights, audit firm type, audit spending, stock exchange listings and insider trading. Hope found evidence that the enforcement score varied widely among countries. Therefore accounting quality will still differ among countries even if they apply the same set of accounting standards.

Maijoor and Vanstraelen (2006) in their study put forward the idea that the international comparability of earnings reported depends not only on the set of accepted accounting standards, but also on the national quality of audits and the constraints imposed on earnings management by the national audit environment. In their research they studied earnings management in France, Germany, the Netherlands and the United Kingdom. Although companies in all four countries engage in earnings management, its magnitude is not uniform across the four. Prior research focused almost exclusively on differences in earnings quality among the national jurisdictions with regard to listed companies. Recent research paying attention to non-listed companies confirms to a large extent the results found in relation to listed companies (Burghstahler, Hail and Leuz, 2006).

The research results in the articles cited above are based on financial information published by companies that complied on a voluntary basis with IFRS. A stream of research is now under way to find out whether accounting quality differs among countries in which listed groups have to comply on a mandatory basis with IFRS. The first articles researching accounting quality among companies which now comply with IFRS on a mandatory basis still point at differences in accounting quality among IFRS accounts driven by national institutional differences. It is still too early to argue that the switch to IFRS for group accounts could not eliminate national differences in accounting quality. Further we have to be aware that companies applying IFRS for the first time since 2005 are going through a learning curve. This learning curve might have an impact on the quality of the information published.

SUMMARY

In this chapter we outlined the major influencing factors which led to differences in the development of national accounting environments and national reporting practices from the 18th century until the end of the 20th century and beyond. Empirical research conducted in the 1970s and the 1980s indicated the following variables as important determinants of those differences: provision of finance, the legal system, the link between accounting and taxation and cultural values.

From the 1970s on, a movement towards harmonisation of financial reporting started slowly to emerge. From the 1990s on, under pressure from multinational companies seeking dual listings to attract capital, the request for one set of GAAP to be applied worldwide emerged. Whether this goal will be obtained in the near future is the subject of part of Chapter 3. Meanwhile, as attempts for worldwide harmonisation and standardisation are undertaken, national institutional differences still influence, to some extent, the output of the financial reporting process.

EXERCISES

Suggested answers to exercises marked ✓ are to be found on the Student side of the companion website.

Suggested answers to the remaining exercises are to be found on the Instructor side of the companion website.

✓ **1** Discuss whether, in essence, accounting is law-based or economics-based.

✓ **2** If accounting is culture-based and national, indeed local, cultures are different, international harmonisation will obviously be impossible. Discuss.

3 In this chapter several causes are discussed which had some influence on existing accounting systems. Which of the causes listed played a significant role in your country? Discuss.

4 If you take Hofstede's (1984) framework for describing cultural differences, how would you describe your own country in relation to these constructs?

5 Do you notice in your country an evolution in the existing accounting system? What would you suggest are the driving forces? Explain.

6 If you consider Gray's (1988) adaptation of Hofstede's framework in relation to accounting values, could you describe which accounting values are prevalent in your country?

7 Is Gray's (1988) adaptation of the Hofstede (1984) framework of cultural differences able to explain the observed differences concerning voluntary disclosures made to the financial statements?

8 Discuss recent research articles which examine the accounting quality or the degree of earnings management after mandatory IFRS adoption.

THE PROCESS OF HARMONISATION

OBJECTIVES After studying this chapter you should be able to:

- outline the role of the EU in the development of accounting harmonisation

- describe in your own words the meaning of endorsement of IFRS in the EU

- outline the history and changing role of the International Accounting Standards Committee/Board in the development of accounting harmonisation

- describe in your own words the different steps in the due process of standard setting of the IASB

- understand current developments and their implications (developments are current when you read the chapter!).

INTRODUCTION

Chapter 2 gave some idea of the very real historical differences between accounting thinking and practice across the world. Since accounting is essentially a communication process, such differences are not helpful in the context of multinational and international business. Either reporting entities need to prepare multiple sets of financial statements under different bases or users have to familiarise themselves with, and understand, a variety of different accounting preparation systems. Both alternatives are time consuming and costly, and can easily lead to confusion and error.

Reduction in such differences, and ideally, the elimination of such differences, is desirable. This process is also difficult, because of the deep-seated causes discussed in Chapter 2. However for listed companies the harmonisation process on a global scale is well under way (at the time of writing – summer 2008). We provide in this chapter an overview of harmonisation processes undertaken in the past decades and recently. A number of attempts have been made on a regional basis, of which that of the EU is perhaps the most significant, to reduce country differences. The International Accounting Standards Board (IASB) and its predecessor the International Accounting Standards Committee (IASC) pursue harmonisation at the global level. In this chapter, we discuss first the EU efforts towards harmonisation and later we pay attention to the international harmonisation on a global level. In the early years, the EU had a much greater effect than the IASC, so we look at the EU first. Now, however, its influence relative to the IASB has declined.

A note on terminology, which can be very confusing, is necessary. 'Harmonisation' is a process of increasing the compatibility of accounting practices by setting bounds to their degree of variation. 'Standardisation' appears to imply the imposition of a more rigid and narrow set of rules. However, within accounting these two words have almost become technical terms and one cannot rely on the normal difference in their meanings. Harmonisation is a word that tends to be associated with the supranational legislation promulgated in the EU, while standardisation is a word often associated with the IAS Board (IASB) and its predecessor the International Accounting Standards Committee (IASC). In practice, the words are often used interchangeably.

It is possible to distinguish between de jure harmonisation (that of rules, standards, etc.) and de facto harmonisation (that of corporate financial reporting practices). For any particular topic or set of countries, it is possible to have one of these two forms of harmonisation without the other. For example, countries or companies may ignore the harmonised rules of standard setters or even lawmakers. By contrast, market forces persuade many companies in France or Switzerland to produce English-language financial reports that approximately follow Anglo-American practice.

EU DIRECTIVES

For many years the major method of engendering change across the EU has been by means of Directives. Once agreed (a process that can take and has taken over 20 years), a Directive is a binding agreement by all the member states of the EU that they will introduce national legislation. It is important to clarify precisely what this means and what it does not mean. It does mean that all member states are required to implement the Directives. It does not mean that citizens or institutions within a member state are required to follow the Directive, unless and until the contents of the Directive are enacted by legislation within the state. Another important point is that each Directive exists not merely in one language version, but in each of the official EU languages. It is the language version applicable to a particular member state that is to be enacted into the law of that country. There may not be perfect semantic equivalence between different language versions of the Directives. Furthermore, where the contents of the national legislation following from a Directive differs from that Directive (either by restricting allowed options or by going against the terms of the Directive itself), only European legal procedures can be used to enforce the Directive requirements.

The fundamental EU Directive relating to financial reporting is the Fourth Company Law Directive of 25 July 1978. This relates to the annual accounts of limited companies. It was followed by the Seventh Company Law Directive of 13 June 1983, which extended the principles of the Fourth Directive to the preparation of consolidated (group) accounts. The Fourth Directive seeks to provide a minimum of coordination of national provisions for the content and presentation of annual financial accounts and reports, of the valuation methods used within them and of the rules for publication. It applies to 'certain companies with limited liability' – broadly, all those above defined minimum size criteria – and aims to ensure that annual accounts disclose comparable and equivalent information.

It is important to place the Fourth Directive into its historical context. It was drafted and debated over a period of some ten years, beginning when the EU had six members and ending when it had ten. The pre-Directive national characteristics of the accounting practices of the member states were significantly different, both in degree of sophistication and in direction. When appraising the success (or otherwise) of this Directive we must measure its achievements against those, at times, startlingly diverse existing practices.

Crucial to the content of the Fourth Directive is the requirement that published accounts should show a 'true and fair view'. The implications and origin of the phrase are discussed in some detail in Chapter 8. Briefly, however, this is a classic example of the cultural divide between the common law tradition and the tradition of codified law. In the former, definitions of such concepts are typically provided by courts in relation to specific situations, rather than by legislative texts intended to apply to many different situations. In the latter, the converse is true; the courts have a role of interpretation and clarification of legislative texts, but not of providing situationally appropriate legal definitions. Thus, the tradition of economic liberalism of the English-speaking countries, the faith in markets and the suspicion of technocracy, go hand in hand with an essentially pragmatic common law tradition and a belief that the accounting profession can largely lay down its own rules in the form of 'generally accepted accounting principles'. By contrast, the countries of continental Europe have less historical attachment to economic liberalism, more faith in technocracy and a preference for explicit legal texts, which extends to the framing of accounting rules. Harmonisation of accounting within the EU has involved bringing these two traditions into some degree of harmony and it is in this respect that the inclusion of the 'true and fair' requirement in the Fourth Directive was both crucial and controversial.

The Fourth Directive contained many options with regard to recognition and measurement of a substantial number of balance sheet items and profit and loss items. Analysing the different national implementations of the Fourth Directive in the EU member states revealed that huge differences still existed with regard to the individual financial statements published in the different member states. The Seventh Directive, which was developed in the 1980s, contained less options than the Fourth Directive. The latter was due to the fact that consolidation practices were less developed in a number of EU member states (see Chapter 2), therefore less national practices and interests had to be defended during the development of the Seventh Directive.

By the early 1990s it had become clear, even to the European Commission, that Directives were too cumbersome and slow to achieve further useful harmonisation.

The Fourth Directive, agreed in 1978, did not cover several topics and it had been too complicated to amend it often. Furthermore, global harmonisation had become more relevant than regional harmonisation.

It had also become clear that, for large European companies, voluntary harmonisation might focus on US rules over which the European Commission and other Europeans have no influence. Consequently, from the middle of the 1990s, the European Commission began to support the increasingly important efforts of the IASC.

In 1995 the European Commission developed its new 'Accounting Strategy'. Within the frame of that new strategy the contact committee on Accounting Directives analysed the degree of conformity between the IASs and the content of the European Accounting Directives. With the results of this analysis the individual EU member states could decide whether or not they would allow national companies to comply with IAS instead of the domestic GAAP.

In May 1999 the European Commission agreed on the Financial Services Action Plan. One of the objectives of this Plan is to create a single large capital market within the EU. To facilitate this creation of a large single capital market the European Commission proposed in 2000 that all listed companies should use one set of accounting standards for financial reporting purposes. The International Accounting Standards (IAS) were chosen to be that set of accounting standards. In 2002, Regulation (EC) No. 1606/2002 on the application of International Accounting Standards was approved by the European Parliament.

Unlike an EU Directive, the Regulation has the force of law and no further action is required by member states before the Regulation comes into effect. The Regulation applies in all member states plus Iceland, Norway and Liechtenstein.

The Regulation requires all listed companies within the EU and the European Economic Area to publish IAS consolidated financial statements for accounting periods beginning on or after 1 January 2005. The term IAS encompasses all standards and interpretations issued or adopted by the IASB. Member states could allow a two-year extension for companies that have their securities publicly traded outside the EU and which, for that purpose, had already been using internationally accepted standards (in practice, US GAAP) since a financial year that started before the Regulation was published. Member states could also allow a two-year extension for companies that have only debt securities listed on a regulated market. These extension periods are now over and all groups listed in the EU (with equity or debt instruments) now have to comply with IFRSs.

Although the Regulation requires the publication of IAS/IFRS consolidated financial statements, this does not imply that when the IASB issues standards and interpretations, they become immediately applicable in the EU. The European Commission is required to decide on the applicability of individual IASs/IFRSs and Interpretations within the EU. The latter implies that it may adopt an IAS only if:

- it is not contrary to the principles of the EU Fourth and Seventh Directives
- it is conducive to the European public good
- it meets the criteria of understandability, relevance, reliability and comparability required of financial information needed for making economic decisions and assessing stewardship of management.

The EU decision on applicability of standards and interpretations issued by the IASB in the EU is called the enforcement process. The European Commission is assisted in its decision on the applicability of the IAS/IFRS and SIC/IFRICs in the EU by three different committees. First there is the Accounting Regulatory Committee (ARC). The ARC consists of representatives from member states and its function is to provide an opinion to the Commission on proposals to adopt (endorse) an IAS. The governments of member states try to influence this endorsement process through the ARC. Second, a group called the European Financial Reporting Advisory Group (EFRAG) advises the European Commission in this endorsement process. The EFRAG is a private institution, set up in 2001 by organisations active in the area of financial reporting. Its activities are:

- providing proactive advice to the IASB
- advising the European Commission on the acceptability of IFRSs for endorsement in Europe
- advising the European Commission on any resulting changes to be made to the Accounting Directives and related topics.

Within EFRAG a 12-member Technical Experts Group considers each standard and each interpretation for its acceptability for endorsement in the EU. Based on the advice of its Technical Expert Group, EFRAG will provide advice to the Commission. Since EFRAG is not defined in the EU Regulation on the adoption of IFRSs, the Commission has no regulatory obligation to listen to EFRAG.

In 2006 the European Commission added another player to this endorsement process. The Standards Advice Review Group was created. This group consists of seven independent experts. This group is expected to give advice to the Commission that is not influenced by governments (unlike ARC) or by audit firms or companies (unlike EFRAG).

Since the establishment of this endorsement process, the original text of all standards (IAS/IFRS) and interpretations (SIC/IFRIC) of the IASB have been endorsed in full except for IAS 39 and IFRICs. A few other standards and interpretations generated a lot of controversy but were finally endorsed in full. We first pay attention to the endorsement process of IAS 39.

Political interference and lobbying by European banks anxious to maintain secretive traditions have so far prevented endorsement of IAS 32 or 39, despite significant conciliatory amendments made by the IASB. Legalistically speaking, considerable difficulties could result if the EU authorities continue to allow or facilitate such interference (a practice they have learnt from the US Congress). In early 2005 the European Commission confirmed the adoption of IAS 39 in Europe, minus two (significant) sections. These two sections were called carve-outs and will be removed later. It is interesting to stress that EFRAG gave a positive opinion in relation to IAS 39, but that the ARC under political pressure opposed the endorsement of IAS 39.

In 2005 the EU refused to endorse IFRIC 3 on accounting for emission rights. The reason for the non-endorsement was not a political issue, but a technical issue. This time the IASB withdrew IFRIC 3 and a problem of non-endorsement was avoided. Next IFRS 8 on operating segments generated a lot of protest at the IASB level as well as at EU level. In the end the EU after commissioning a study on IFRS 8 and its implications fully endorsed the standard on segmental disclosure. Finally IFRIC 12 on service concession arrangements generated controversy from the member states as well. All other standards and interpretations were endorsed without major discussions.

ACTIVITY 3.1

Go the website of EFRAG and check the endorsement processes of standards and interpretations issued by the IASB recently (www.efrag.org–endorsement status).

Activity feedback

On EFRAG's website you will find a list of standards and interpretations for which the endorsement process is on its way. The comment letters EFRAG receives from European constituents with regard to the standards and interpretations to be endorsed can be found on EFRAG's website.

As soon as a standard or interpretation (SIC/IFRIC) is endorsed, it is translated in the official languages of the EU. When companies do prepare financial statements using IAS, they have to declare that their financial statements are in compliance with IAS/IFRS as endorsed by the EU. If a company uses carve-outs foreseen through the endorsement process of the EU, this company complies with IAS/IFRS as endorsed by the EU, however it does not comply with the IAS/IFRS as issued by the IASB. The latter element is important for the recognition of accounts in compliance with the international standards outside the EU (e.g. in the US as we will see later in this chapter).

Member states have the option of extending the application of the Regulation to unlisted companies and to legal entity, rather than consolidated, financial statements. In many member states of the EU non-listed groups and legal entities are allowed to prepare their accounts in compliance with IAS/IFRS. Only in a few EU countries are legal entities not allowed to prepare their individual accounts in compliance with IAS (e.g. Germany, Belgium, France).

The EU updated in 2003 the Fourth and Seventh Directives to make them more receptive to the international standards. Major amendments include to:

- empower member states to allow or require a cash flow statement
- bring the definition of parent and subsidiary fully into line with IAS 27 (see Chapter 26)
- require the consolidation of all subsidiaries, even those with dissimilar activities
- achieve consistency between the formal requirements for the financial statements and IAS requirements
- allow for likely IAS requirements on performance reporting
- allow the revaluation of intangible assets and any other class of assets
- extend the disclosures about environmental and social aspects of a business
- modify the format and content of the audit report to reflect current best practice and achieve harmonisation.

The EU has issued a regulation which ensures compulsory compliance with IFRS by listed groups on stock exchanges in Europe, however at the same time no uniform enforcement mechanism is foreseen. Enforcement is still a national matter. A step towards unified enforcement was the creation of the Commission of European Securities Regulators (CESR). CESR meets regularly and tries to improve consistent application of IFRS all over Europe.

ACTIVITY 3.2

Check CESR's website on pronouncements with regard to application of certain international standards and interpretations (www.cesr-eu.org).

ards and interpretations. After deliberations CESR formulates an opinion on application problems.

Activity feedback

On CESR's website you will find pronouncements with regard to problems of application of a number of standards

After the discussion of harmonisation efforts in the EU, we now focus on the worldwide harmonisation efforts of the IASB and its predecessor the IASC

INTERNATIONAL ACCOUNTING STANDARDS

The IASC and the start of international harmonisation

The IASC was created in 1973. Its creation was related to that of the International Federation of Accountants (IFAC), which is the worldwide umbrella organisation of accountancy bodies. It is independent of government or pseudo-government control. Its stated purpose is to develop and enhance a coordinated worldwide accountancy profession with harmonised standards. All members of the IFAC were, under the old IASC constitution, automatically members of the IASC.

IASC's description of itself as an 'independent private sector body' is accurate and revealing. It was, in essence, a private club, with no formal authority. This is in contrast to national regulatory or standard-setting bodies, which operate within a national jurisdiction and some form of legal and governmental framework that delineates, defines and provides a level of authority. The IASC, however, operated throughout its existence in the knowledge that in the last resort, it and its standards have no formal authority. It therefore always had to rely on persuasion and the quality of its analysis and argument. This can be seen to have had two major effects. First, the quality of logic and discussion in its publications was generally high and its conclusions were – if sometimes debatable – feasible and clearly articulated. Second, however, the conclusions and recommendations of many of the earlier published IAS documents often had to accommodate two or more alternative acceptable treatments, simply because both or all were already being practised in countries that were members of IASC and were too significant to be ignored.

The disadvantages of this state of affairs are obvious and were well-recognised by the IASC itself. Toward the end of the 1980s the IASC decided it would attempt a more proactive approach and early in 1989 it published an exposure draft (E32) on the comparability of financial statements. This proposed the elimination of certain treatments permitted by particular IASs and the expression of a clear preference for one particular treatment, even where two alternatives were still to be regarded as acceptable.

This 'comparability project' led to a large number of revised standards operative from the mid-1990s, which did indeed considerably narrow the degree of optionality compared with the earlier versions of the standards issued in the 1970s and 1980s.

The comparability project, therefore, can be said to have made the set of IAS more meaningful and significant. Of course, it did nothing to increase the formal authority of the IASC.

Towards acceptance of IAS by IOSCO

In 1995, as the next stage in its development, IASC entered into an agreement with the International Organisation of Securities Commissions (IOSCO) to complete a 'core set' of IAS by 1999. With regard to the agreement, the IOSCO's Technical Committee stated that completion of 'comprehensive core standards acceptable to the Technical Committee' would allow it to 'recommend endorsement' of those standards for 'crossborder capital raising in all global markets'. The significance of this agreement is great. It would mean that one set of financial statements, properly prepared in accordance with IAS GAAP, would automatically be acceptable for listing purposes without amendment and without any reconciliation to national (i.e. local) GAAP on each and all of the world's important stock exchanges. This would save huge resources at the international and multinational level, both for preparers and for users and analysts. The role of national standard setters, except arguably for small and medium-sized entities, would simply disappear, if enforcement were left to bodies other than the standard setter.

From the IAS viewpoint, successful implementation of this process would provide the de facto authority that it needs and craves. Any entity failing to accept the authority of IAS would know that its shares would be likely to be de-listed.

This, of course, raises the issue of effective enforcement, for which IASB is dependent on securities regulators and other bodies with the power to impose de-listing and other sanctions and on a mechanism for bringing breaches of IASs to the attention of such bodies.

In December 1998 the then IASC completed its 'core standards' programme with the approval of IAS 39, *Financial Instruments Recognition and Measurement*. Following the publication of the report of IASC's Strategic Working Party, *Recommendations on Shaping IASC for the Future*, in November 1999, the board of IASC approved proposals in December 1999 to make significant changes to IASC's structure, in order to prepare it for an enhanced role as a global accounting standard setter.

Following these preparations, the year 2000 was a momentous one for IASC. In May the proposed structural changes were approved by IASC's membership. (The results of these changes are outlined in the following section.) Also in May, the IOSCO formally accepted the IASC's 'core standards' as a basis for cross-border securities-listing purposes worldwide (although for certain countries, notably the United States, reconciliations of items such as earnings and stockholders' equity to national GAAP would still be required). In June, the European Commission issued a Communication proposing that all listed companies in the EU would be required to prepare their consolidated financial statements using IASs, a proposal that has since been adopted.

International Accounting Standards: From voluntary adoption to compulsory adoption

We have discussed in this chapter that EU-listed companies need to prepare their consolidated accounts in compliance with IAS/IFRS. But preparing annual accounts in compliance with IAS is no longer limited solely to listed firms in the EU. A number of member states in the EU have already extended this compulsory application of IAS to financial institutions, group accounts of unlisted companies and even individual accounts (e.g. Czech Republic, Estonia, Malta, Lithuania). In other member states companies are allowed to prepare their group accounts or individual accounts according to IAS/IFRS on a voluntary basis. These statements then replace the statements which would have been prepared according to national GAAP. Only a few member states still prohibit companies from preparing their individual accounts in compliance with IAS/IFRS (e.g. Austria, Belgium, France, Spain and Sweden).

Not only in Europe but also on a worldwide scope more and more companies are using IASs/IFRSs. Listed companies in Australia and in New Zealand now have to comply with IASs/IFRS as well. Further we are able to distinguish a number of countries in which the domestic GAAP are identical to the IAS/IFRS. These countries are South Africa, Singapore, the Philippines and Hong Kong. There is always a period of time which elapses between the issuance of a new international standard (IAS/IFRS) or interpretation (SIC/IFRIC) and the moment it is translated into these national GAAP rules. Auditors when certifying these accounts, state that the financial statements are in compliance with the national GAAP, although the national GAAP is similar to IAS.

Next we observe countries which stopped developing their own national GAAP and have substituted their national GAAP with IASs. We find this situation in Bahrain, the Emirates, Croatia, Dominican Republic, Kenya, Haiti, Nepal and Venezuela. These international accounting standards receive a national label.

Worldwide use of IASs/IFRSs will increase in the near future, since regulatory authorities in a number of countries have decided to move towards compulsory application of IFRS for listed groups. The following is a list of these decisions (current in summer 2008). We notice that IFRS adoption increases in Asia as well as in the Americas. Korea has decided that from 2009 any company can choose to apply IFRS, with the use of IFRS becoming mandatory for all listed companies from 2011 (IASB Insight, Q1/Q2, 2008, page 10). China announced that its central-level state-owned enterprises and large to mid-scale companies will adopt China's new accounting standards that comply with IFRSs by the end of 2009 (IASB Insight, Q3, 2007, page 17). In Brazil banks have to comply with IFRSs from 2009 onwards and listed companies from 2010 onwards (IASB Insight, Q1/Q2, 2008, page 5). Canada is working towards a deadline of 2011 to implement IFRS (IASB Insight, Q1/Q2 2008, page 11).

One global set of accounting standards or worldwide use of IASs/IFRSs will only be achieved if the American SEC accepts international accounting standards for listing purposes without reconciliations towards US GAAP. Recently historic changes have been announced and decided by the SEC. These decisions made by the SEC turn the first sentence from a wish to a possible reality in the near future. The Securities and Exchange Commission approved in November 2007 that for 'foreign private issuers' (a corporation or other organisation incorporated or organised under the laws of any foreign country) financial statements prepared in accordance 'with IFRS as issued by the IASB' would be accepted on American stock exchanges without reconciliation to US GAAP. This new regulation will apply to financial statements covering years ended after 15 November 2007. This is a very significant step towards global harmonisation of accounting. At the time of writing (summer 2008) it is highly likely that the SEC will also allow US issuers to prepare financial statements in accordance with IFRS in the near future without reconciliation to US GAAP. This implies also that American companies can prepare their accounting in compliance with IAS/IFRS and use these accounts for listing purposes in the US.

The process of acceptance of IAS/IFRS in the US

The change in attitude of the SEC dates back to the turn of the century. The collapse of Enron and subsequent further 'scandals' have shaken the complacency of American regulation to the core. Early accusations against Enron did not accuse the company of not following US GAAP, merely of following it in an inappropriate manner. This has led to the suggestion, which the IASB was very quick to take up, that the US desire for evermore detailed standards has been demonstrated to be unhelpful. Rather, standards based on general principles, as international (and also UK) standards generally are, would perhaps be more effective. The EU (and not merely the UK) is strongly behind the IASB on this issue. At almost the same time, a new chairman was appointed to the US Financial Accounting Standards Board (FASB), Robert Herz. Herz was one of the two half-time appointments to the new IASB and was an active supporter of convergence between the USA and IAS, and of a more principles-based, rather than detail-based, approach for US standards, which would obviously make such convergence easier.

The process of convergence between the IASB and the FASB started in September 2002 when after a joint meeting by the two bodies the 'Norwalk Agreement' was issued in which both parties acknowledged their commitment to the development of high quality, compatible accounting standards that could be used for both domestic and cross-border financial reporting. On 27 February 2006 a Memorandum of Understanding between the FASB and the IASB was issued. The title of the MOU was 'A Roadmap for Convergence between IFRSs and US GAAP – 2006–2008'. The FASB and the IASB agreed on the following guidelines regarding their approach to the convergence programme:

- convergence of accounting standards can best be achieved through the development of high-quality, common standards over time
- trying to eliminate differences between two standards that are in need of significant improvement is not the best use of the FASB's and the IASB's resources – instead, a new common standard should be developed that improves the financial information reported to investors
- serving the needs of investors means that the boards should seek convergence by replacing weaker standards with stronger standards.

The IASB and the FASB agreed on a convergence programme 2006–2008 after discussions with the representatives of the European Commission and the American Securities and Exchange Commission. The convergence process can in fact be divided into two distinct groups of projects. On the one hand there is the short-term convergence project whereby a limited list of topics is on the agenda of both organisations to remove the differences before 2008. If we consult the update of the IASB on the convergence project with the FASB, we learn that convergence has been reached on the following items. US GAAP was brought in line with IFRS through the introduction of a fair value option in a number of standards and the adoption of the IFRS approach with regard to acquired R&D in business combinations. Converging IFRSs with US GAAP was done through the new standards on borrowing costs and segment reporting. A number of short-term convergence projects are still outstanding (summer 2008): income taxes, valuation of investment properties and intangibles. On the other hand there are projects with a longer time frame where current practices will be studied in order to find out how the current standards can be improved.

ACTIVITY 3.3

Go to the website of the IASB (www.iasb.org) and check the status of the convergence project of the IASB with the FASB.

Activity feedback

On the website of the IASB under the heading current projects, you will find the information on the Memorandum of Understanding with the FASB and its current status. List the items they are still working on at the time when you consult the website. See if there is any progress compared to the situation of summer 2008.

In order to become a world leader in standard setting, it was necessary to change the structure of the IASC at the turn of the century. This happened in 2001. We discuss below the structure of the IASB and subsequently we pay attention to its due process of standard setting. At the time of writing the manuscript for this textbook, new changes in the structure of the IASB are on the agenda. These changes will be included in the last section of this chapter, 'The future?'

STRUCTURE OF THE IASB

Like the Financial Accounting Standards Board (FASB) in 1972 and the UK Accounting Standards Board in 1990, which replaced the APB and the ASC, respectively, the new IASB differs from its predecessor by having a two-tier structure, based on an organ of governance not involved in standard setting (the trustees) and a standard-setting board. According to Clause 3 of the Constitution (governance of the IASC Foundation):

> The governance of IASC shall rest with the Trustees and such other governing organs as may be appointed by the Trustees in accordance with the provisions of this Constitution. The Trustees shall use their best endeavours to ensure that the requirements of this Constitution are observed; however, they are empowered to make minor variations [in the Constitution] in the interest of feasibility of operation if such variations are agreed by 75% of all the Trustees.

The new structure is the one proposed in the Strategic Working Party's November 1999 report, *Recommendations on Shaping IASC for the Future*. This structure was articulated in the IASC Foundation Constitution on 24 May 2000. The Constitution has been adapted several times since 2000. The latest changes were approved on 31 October 2007. There are 22 Trustees, of whom six are from North America, six from Europe, six from the Asia/Oceania region and four from any area, subject to establishing 'overall geographical balance'.

Para 7 of the Constitution stipulates that Trustees shall comprise individuals that as a group provide an appropriate balance of professional backgrounds, including auditors, preparers, users, academics, and other officials serving the public interest. Two of the Trustees shall normally be senior partners of prominent international accounting firms. To achieve such a balance, Trustees should be selected after consultation with national and international organisations of auditors (including the International Federation of Accountants), preparers, users and academics. Trustees are appointed for a three-year term with a possibility for renewal once.

The task of standard setting lies with the IASB. The new Board differs significantly from its predecessor (the Committee) by having 12 full-time members as well as two part-time members. Moreover, its members are chosen for their technical expertise and background experience and (in contrast to the Trustees) not on the basis of geographical representation. However the Trustees shall ensure that the IASB is not dominated by any particular constituencies or geographical interest. The IASB will, in consultation with the Trustees, be expected to establish and maintain liaison with national standard setters and other official bodies concerned with standard setting in order to promote the convergence of national accounting standards and IAS/IFRS.

Before the latest change in the Constitution the Board had to comprise a minimum of five members with a background as practising auditors, at least three with a background as preparers of financial statements, at least three with a background as users of financial statements and at least one must have an academic background. In the revised Constitution there is no longer an explicit numerical mix of members from different backgrounds foreseen. In the revised Constitution the qualifications to become a Board member are stipulated in para 19 as follows:

> The main qualifications for membership of the IASB shall be professional competence and practical experience. The Trustees shall select members of the IASB so that it will comprise a group of people representing, within that group, the best available combination of technical expertise and diversity of international business and market experience in order to contribute to the development of high-quality, global accounting standards.

With regard to the composition of the Board the Constitution now stipulates (para 21) that the Trustees shall select IASB members so that the IASB as a group provides an appropriate mix of recent practical experience among auditors, preparers, users and academics.

Each member has one vote. On both technical and other matters, proxy voting shall not be permitted nor shall members of the IASB be entitled to appoint alternates to attend meetings. The publication of an exposure draft, final IAS, or final interpretation of the Standing Interpretations Committee requires approval by at least nine of the 14 members of the IASB. Other decisions of the IASB, including the publication of a discussion paper, shall require a simple majority of the members of the IASB present at a meeting that is attended by at least 60% of the members of the IASB, in person or by telecommunications.

Next to the Trustees and to the Board, the structure includes an Interpretations Committee named the International Financial Reporting Interpretations Committee (IFRIC and its predecessor SIC – similar to its predecessor in the previous structure) and a Standards Advisory Council. The members of both these two bodies are also appointed by the Trustees.

Since 2001, the name of the SIC has been changed to the International Financial Reporting Interpretations Committee (IFRIC) and for Standards issued by IASB the term 'International Financial Reporting Standard' (IFRS) is used. The International Financial Reporting Interpretations Committee (IFRIC) consists of 14 voting members appointed by the Trustees (par 33). The Trustees have the task to select members of the Committee so that it comprises a group of people representing, within that group, the best available combination of technical expertise and diversity of international business and market experience in the practical application of IFRSs and analysis of financial statements prepared in accordance with IFRSs. The task of this committee according to the Constitution is to interpret the application of IASs and IFRSs and provide timely guidance on financial reporting issues not specifically addressed in IASs and IFRSs, in the context of the IASB framework, and undertake other tasks at the request of the IASB. In carrying out this work IFRIC needs to work together with national standard setters to bring about convergence and to reach high-quality solutions.

The Standards Advisory Council, with 30 or more members, provides a forum for participation by organisations and individuals with an interest in international financial reporting and having diverse geographic and functional backgrounds, with the objective of giving advice to the Board on agenda decisions and priorities, informing the Board of the view of members of the Council on major standard-setting projects and giving other advice to the Board or the Trustees. The Chairman of the Council is appointed by the Trustees and shall not be a member of the IASB or its staff.

The objectives of the IASB

When the IASC was established in the 1970s its mission statement was:

- to formulate and publish in the public interest accounting standards to be observed in the presentation of financial statements and to promote their worldwide acceptance and observance; and
- to work generally for the improvement and harmonisation of regulations, accounting standards and procedures relating to the presentation of financial statements.

In this mission statement the emphasis lies on harmonisation of financial reporting and promoting worldwide acceptance of these standards. In order to gain this

FIGURE 3.1   The structure of the international accounting standard setter

worldwide acceptance, the IASC allowed many options in the standards it promulgated in the early years.

Together with the reorganisation of the IASC in 2001, its mission was reformulated. In the Constitution of the International Accounting Standards Committee Foundation (October 2007) the mission statement includes the following objectives (Constitution – Part A – Name and objectives):

The objectives of the IASC Foundation are:

(a) to develop, in the public interest, a single set of high quality, understandable and enforceable global standards that require high quality, transparent and comparable information in financial statements and other financial reporting to help participants in the world's capital markets and other users make economic decisions

(b) to promote the use and rigorous application of those standards

(c) in fulfilling the objectives associated with (a) and (b), to take account of, as appropriate, the special needs of small and medium-sized entities and emerging economies

(d) to bring about convergence of national accounting standards and IAS and IFRS to high quality solutions.

We do observe an evolution in the objectives of the IASC; the focus lies now on developing one single set of high-quality and enforceable standards. The role of the IASB has evolved towards the role of a global standard setter. This implies however that the IASB will issue standards that have to be applied in a variety of different legal and cultural contexts. This will require the use of IFRS by companies that vary considerably in size, ownership structure, capital structure, political jurisdiction, and financial reporting sophistication (Schipper, 2005). Financial reports must be comprehensible across countries, across jurisdictions, and across cultures. This universality of IAS application is increasingly being questioned, especially as the direction of US and EU influence is likely to push IASs further towards a large enterprise multinational focus. The relevance of this focus to small or medium-sized enterprises (SMEs) or to developing economies is debatable. The latter has come to the attention of the IASB which has issued an exposure draft on how IAS/IFRS can be used by private entities.

It is important to underline that the IASB has no authority with regard to the application of its standards in the different jurisdictions. The enforcement of the IAS or IFRS is still a national matter. A first step in the direction of single enforcement within the EU might be the establishment of the Commission of European Securities Regulators (CESR) which will supervise consistent application of the IASs by listed companies within the EU. There is a real need, again strongly expressed from the USA, for visible enforcement and adequately uniform application of international standards. The people applying those standards will come from many different countries with many different native languages. Their attitudes will inevitably be influenced by all the historical and cultural baggage inherent in our discussion in Chapter 2. The precise outcome is uncertain. But the future is going to be interesting!

The IASB's due process of standard setting

In order to achieve its objectives, it is necessary for the IASB to develop accounting standards along a transparent process in which the different constituent parties could have their voices heard. Therefore the standards promulgated by the IASB are developed through a formal system of due process and broad international consultation that involves accountants, financial analysts and other users of financial statements, the business community, stock exchanges, regulatory and legal authorities, academics and other interested individuals, and organisations from around the world. This group of parties interested in influencing the outcome of the standard-setting process are called the constituent parties. The IASB consults, in public meetings, the Standards Advisory Council (SAC) on major projects, agenda decisions and work priorities, and discusses technical matters in meetings that are open to public observation.

It is stipulated in the Constitution and in the IASB's due process handbook that the IASB has to cooperate with national standard setters in its standard-setting process. The IASB will meet the chairmen of its partner and other accounting standard setters regularly. With a number of standard setters convergence programmes have been agreed (the American standard setter, the Japanese standard setter and the Canadian standard setter). In addition, staff members of the IASB and partner standardsetters cooperate on a daily basis on projects, sharing resources whenever necessary and appropriate.

The IASB's due process of standard setting involves six stages (see due process handbook for the IASB – March 2006) which we will briefly enumerate here.

Stage 1: Setting the agenda The IASB will set the agenda for the future by taking into account the users' needs in relation to high-quality accounting standards. The IASB will evaluate the merits of adding a potential item to its agenda mainly by reference to the needs of investors. According to the IASB their needs will also meet most needs of other users like employees, lenders, suppliers and other trade creditors, customers, government and their agencies and the public. Whether the latter is true is an issue of debate, certainly in Europe.

When deciding whether a proposed agenda item will address users' needs the IASB considers:

(a) the relevance to users of the information and the reliability of information that could be provided

(b) existing guidance available

ACTIVITY 3.4

While you are reading the different stages of the standard-setting process it is interesting to look at the website of the IASB (http://www.iasb.org.uk) and consult its timetable of projects.

Activity feedback
You will find a timetable of the IASB's agenda for the future. This agenda lists the standards, the exposure drafts of standards, the discussion documents and the research projects the IASB is working on in the coming years. A projected timetable of the IASB workplan is posted on the website. A distinction is drawn in their active agenda between new standards, major projects, amendments to standards, the conceptual framework and research projects. Except for the text of a standard which is going to be approved, you will find the texts of all the other documents (exposure drafts, discussion papers, research reports) on the IASB website. Besides the texts of these documents you are able to consult the comment letters sent by the constituent parties in relation to exposure drafts and discussion documents. Looking at the website helps you better understand the process described below.

(c) the possibility of increasing convergence

(d) the quality of the standard to be developed

(e) resource constraints.

When the IASB considers potential agenda items, it may decide that some issues require additional research before it can take a decision on whether to add the item to its active agenda. Such issues may be addressed as research projects on the IASB's research agenda. A research project may be undertaken by the IASB or by another standard setter. The IASB discusses potential agenda items with the SAC, IFRIC, other standard setters and other interested parties.

Stage 2: Project planning When adding an item to its active agenda, the IASB also decides whether to conduct the project alone, or jointly with another standard setter. The due process of standard setting is similar under both approaches. After considering the nature of the issues and the level of interest among constituents, the IASB may establish a working group at this stage.

Stage 3: Development and publication of a discussion paper Although a discussion paper is not a mandatory step in its due process, the IASB normally publishes a discussion paper as its first publication on any major new topic as a vehicle to explain the issue and solicit early comment from constituents. If the IASB decides to omit this step, it will state its reasons.

Typically, a discussion paper includes a comprehensive overview of the issue, possible approaches in addressing the issue, the preliminary views of its authors or the IASB, and an invitation to comment. This approach may differ if another accounting standard setter develops the research paper. The IASB normally allows a period of 120 days for comment on a discussion paper, but may allow a longer period on major projects (which are those projects involving pervasive or difficult conceptual or practical issues).

Stage 4: Development and publication of an exposure draft Publication of an exposure draft is a mandatory step in due process. Irrespective of whether the IASB has published a discussion paper, an exposure draft is the IASB's main vehicle for consulting the public. Unlike a discussion paper, an exposure draft sets out a specific proposal in the form of a proposed standard (or amendment to an existing standard). The development of an exposure draft begins with the IASB considering issues on the basis of staff research and recommendations, as well as comments received on any discussion paper, and suggestions made by the SAC, working groups and accounting standard setters and arising from public education sessions.

An exposure draft contains an invitation to comment on a draft standard, or amendment to a standard, that proposes requirements on recognition, measurement and disclosures. The draft may also include mandatory application guidance and implementation guidance, and will be accompanied by a basis for conclusions on the proposals and the alternative views of dissenting IASB members (if any). The IASB normally allows a period of 120 days for comment on an exposure draft. However this period can be extended if the standard deals with a major issue or the period can be shortened to 30 days if there is already broad consensus on the topic.

Stage 5: Development and publication of an IFRS The development of an IFRS is carried out during IASB meetings, when the IASB considers the comments received on the exposure draft. Changes from the exposure draft are posted on the website. After resolving issues arising from the exposure draft, the IASB considers whether it should expose its revised proposals for public comment, for example by publishing a second exposure draft.

When the IASB is satisfied that it has reached a conclusion on the issues arising from the exposure draft, it instructs the staff to draft the IFRS. A pre-ballot draft is usually subject to external review, normally by the IFRIC. Shortly before the IASB ballots the standard, a near-final draft is posted on its limited access website for paying subscribers. Finally, after the due process is completed, all outstanding issues are resolved, and the IASB members have balloted in favour of publication, the IFRS is issued.

Stage 6: Procedures after an IFRS is issued After an IFRS is issued, the staff and the IASB members hold regular meetings with interested parties, including other standard-setting bodies, to help understand unanticipated issues related to the practical implementation and potential impact of its proposals.

The aim of this elaborated due process of standard setting is that all constituent parties from the different regions of the world do participate in this process. Whether or not this goal is achieved is not that easy to observe. Constituent parties often meet with members of the IASB or its staff to discuss items. No tracks are left of this kind of lobbying activities. Lobbying activities which are traceable are the comment letters sent by constituent parties in response to discussion documents and exposure drafts of standards.

Figure 3.2 presents a graphical overview of the IASB's due process of standard setting.

Table 3.1 provides an overview of the participation levels of the different constituents in sending comment letters on discussion documents and exposure drafts to the IASB. The data were collected by analysing the origin of the comment letters sent between 2002 and the summer of 2005 (Jorissen, Lybaert and Van de Poel, 2006).

We observe that preparers take a much more active role than users in influencing the standard-setting process. This is not surprising since the benefits of lobbying probably outweigh the costs of lobbying for the preparers of financial statements (see also Sutton, 1984; Watts and Zimmerman, 1978).

The data in the table indicate that the financial institutions have played an active role in the standard-setting process in the time period under study. This could be explained by the fact that IAS 39 and several amendments have been on the agenda of the IASB in that period.

We notice however that the constituent party for which all the financial information is prepared, namely the user of the financial statements, is remaining rather silent in this standard-setting process. There is so far one exception to this observation and this exception relates to Exposure Draft 8 in relation to segmental reporting. A number of non-governmental organisations have sent an identical comment letter complaining about the loss of information with the new standard on segment reporting.

If we consider global participation in this due process of standard setting, we observe that preparers originate mainly from the Western world; however in relation to the other constituent parties we do observe worldwide participation especially from national standard setters, stock exchanges and professional organisations of accountants and auditors (Jorissen, Lybaert and Van de Poel, 2006).

In the last part of this chapter we will pay attention to the future agenda of the IASB.

FIGURE 3.2   The IASB's due process of standard setting

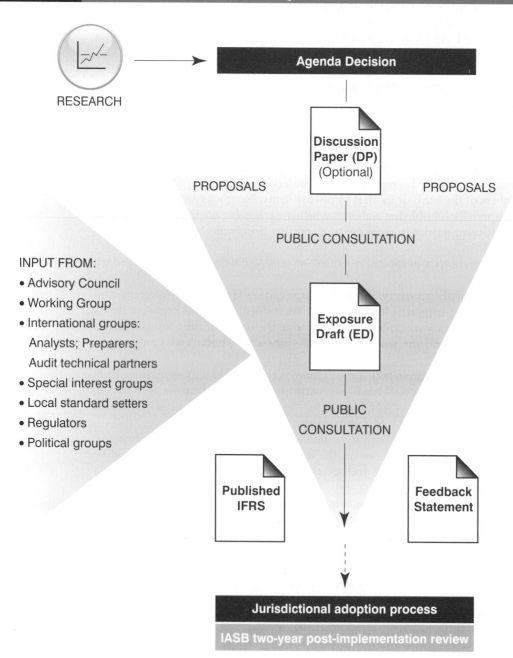

TABLE 3.1	Number of comment letters received from different constituent parties between 2002 and summer 2005		
Preparers		**1051**	**(47%)**
Individual companies		263	(12%)
Associations of companies		222	(10%)
Individual banks and the like		249	(11%)
Association of banks and the like		317	(14%)
The accounting profession		**587**	**(26%)**
Audit firms		134	(6%)
Associations of accountants and auditors		453	(20%)
Users		**30**	**(1%)**
National standard setters		**296**	**(13%)**
Stock exchanges		**35**	**(2%)**
Governments		**33**	**(1%)**
Individuals		**77**	**(3%)**
Academics		**36**	**(2%)**
Other interested parties		**100**	**(4%)**
Consultants		60	(3%)
Actuaries		40	(2%)
Total		**2245**	**(100%)**

THE FUTURE?

Of course there will be the ongoing effort to improve standards and issue new standards. We will pay attention to that in the second half of this section on the future of the IASB. First however we concentrate on changes in the structure of the IASB which are proposed at the time of writing this manuscript (summer 2008). On 21 July 2008 the IASCF communicated two important changes for the future in a document *Review of the Constitution: Public Accountability and the Composition of the IASB – Proposals for change*. Since comments on this document must be submitted by the end of September 2008, we will concentrate on the proposed changes in this textbook and not on the discussion which will take place during the autumn of 2008 and later on. It is up to the reader to follow up the discussion on these proposed changes and their implementation.

The IASCF proposed the following changes:

(a) establish a formal link between the organisation and a Monitoring Group comprising representatives of public authorities and international organisations that have requirements for accountability to public authorities

(b) expand the membership of the IASB to 16 members and add new guidelines regarding the geographical diversity of the members of the IASB.

The first point is aimed at enhancing the transparency and public accountability of the IASCF, while not impairing the independence of the standard-setting process. The Monitoring Group will consist of public authorities outside the IASC

Foundation's organisational framework. In the proposal of the IASCF initial membership would comprise the responsible member of the European Commission, the managing director of the International Monetary Fund, the chair of the IOSCO Emerging Markets Committee, the chair of the IOSCO Technical Committee, the commissioner of the Japan Financial Services Agency, the chairman of the US Securities and Exchange Commission and the president of the World Bank. The Monitoring Group would have the responsibility of approving the selection of Trustees. The Trustees would also report to the Monitoring Group regularly to enable it to address whether and how the Trustees are fulfilling their role set out in the Constitution.

The second item in their proposal for changes relates to the composition of the IASB. When we discussed the composition of the standard setting body, we stressed that no geographical equilibrium is prescribed for this body. With the second item of their proposals the IASCF would like to introduce a geographical component into this group, although the Trustees stress that 'professional competence and practical experience' remain paramount in order to be a member of this group. However the addition of a geographical component would strengthen the legitimacy of the IASB in the view of the countries choosing to adopt IFRS.

The Trustees expect to complete the first part of the Constitution Review, the addition of a Monitoring Group to the structure of the IASB, by 1 January 2009. The second point will come into effect later on.

With regard to the standard-setting issue, we can be certain that the future agenda of the IASB will be dominated to a large extent by a number of convergence projects. Besides the convergence project with the FASB, the IASB will also seek convergence in the near future with the Japanese standard setter, and other standard-setting authorities. Another major project is the issuance of a standard which deals with the use of IASs/IFRSs by private entities. With this standard for private entities the IASB hopes to influence financial reporting quality of medium-sized enterprises around the world. At the same time the IASB hopes that this standard for private entities will also solve the needs of businesses in the developing countries. Along with these large projects on convergence and private entities, the IASB also embarked on a review of its conceptual framework and a revision of existing standards on financial instruments. It is possible however that due to the financial crisis, the latter project will be speeded up, since fair value has come under serious discussion (summer 2008).

ACTIVITY 3.5

By means of the IASB website (http://www.iasb.org.uk), websites of regulatory and professional accounting organisations in your own country and any other convenient sources, update this chapter for yourself. This chapter was written in summer 2008.

Activity feedback
Up to you, of course. Think about the political dimension as well as about the pure accounting issues.

SUMMARY

This chapter has provided a background of history and understanding behind current international accounting developments, with an emphasis on the increasing importance of the IASB. Thirty years ago the EU started with the harmonisation of financial reporting. The EU changed its accounting strategy in the mid-1990s and started to back the efforts of the IASC and later on the IASB. The new accounting strategy of the EU, the acceptance by IOSCO of IASs for listing purposes and the change in the structure of the international standard setter in 2001 paved the way for the IASB to become a global standard setter. It seems that the final steps towards this status will be taken in the very near future.

EXERCISES

Suggested answers to exercises marked ✓ are to be found on the Student side of the companion website.

   Suggested answers to the remaining exercises are to be found on the Instructor side of the companion website.

✓ **1** The European Commission has handed over accounting regulation in Europe to the IASB. Discuss.

2 The European Commission, through its 2005 requirement, has given the IASB authority that it could never have achieved by itself. Discuss.

3 Global accounting ignores the needs of developing economies. Discuss.

4 Enumerate which of the steps of the due process of standard setting is necessary in issuing a standard.

ECONOMIC VALUATION CONCEPTS

4

OBJECTIVES After studying this chapter you should be able to:

- provide an overview and context of the asset valuation debate

- explain definitions and interrelationships of income, capital and value

- describe the variety of alternatives that need to be explored within the parameters of the valuation debate

- outline the concepts of income developed by Fisher (1930) and Hicks (1946)

- contrast *ex ante* and *ex post* economic income

- outline the scope of economic thinking in this area.

INTRODUCTION

This chapter is the first of a series that explores the whole area of asset valuation and income measurement. A number of separated research traditions have grown up, some over several centuries, often associated with particular individuals. There is a tendency in the English-speaking world to think that most of the important ideas involved were invented by Anglo-Saxons, but this is far from the truth.

Nevertheless, since, as we have shown in Chapter 2, IASB capital market-driven accounting has largely developed from Anglo-Saxon thinking (very broadly defined), it is suitable to present the analysis in something of what in the old nationalistic days would have been regarded as an Anglo-Saxon context. We briefly relate the ideas to a number of other research traditions at the end of Chapter 7. It is also important to realise that the principles underlying much of this theoretical debate are directly applicable to regulatory issues and debates considered in Parts Two and Three.

More pertinently, it is important to accept that we are here concerned with theoretical analysis, i.e. with what could be done, and what appear to be the advantages and disadvantages of doing it. Practical traditions are, again, outlined at the end of Chapter 7.

THE BASIC EQUATION

We have already established that a well-behaved balance sheet does not balance just because accountants are good at adding up. It balances because it is defined in such a way that it must balance. Following from the business entity convention, capital is the balancing figure. Capital is the liability of the business entity to the ownership entity. The business owns a collection of assets, and owes a collection of borrowings to lenders and unpaid suppliers of goods and services. Deducting these borrowings from the assets enables us to say that the business owns a collection of net assets. So the owners own the business and the business owns the net assets. Therefore the owners' investment in the business – i.e. the capital – must equal the net assets.

That much is couched in static terms. But we can easily modify the wording to allow for profit or income. To avoid possible confusion, we use profit and income as, in the accounting context, completely synonymous terms. Profit (income) means the positive difference between revenues and expenses for a given period. If a business makes a profit then money or money's worth received or to be received increases by more than money or money's worth consumed. This is a complicated way of saying that its net assets go up by the amount of the profit. But in logic and in bookkeeping profit represents an increase in capital. Profit is attributable to owners, is owned by owners and is therefore owed by the business to the owners.

So the amount of profit equals the amount of the increase in the net assets, which, in turn, equals the amount of the increase in the capital. In practice, drawings or dividends are likely to occur. These obviously represent a withdrawal of money or money's worth and therefore a reduction in net assets. They also mean that the business has paid the owners some of what is owed to them. There is therefore a reduction in what remains owing to them, i.e. a reduction in capital. If drawings in a period equal profits for the period then capital (and net assets) is maintained at its original level. If profit exceeds drawings in a period capital (and net assets) increase.

This can usefully be summarised schematically. Let W_1 be the opening wealth (net assets of the business) and W_2 be the closing net assets. Let P be the profit for the period and D be the (net) drawings. Then:

$$W_1 + P - D = W_2$$

Or in more purely accounting terms: Opening capital plus profit minus drawings equals closing capital

It is obvious that the $W_1 + P - D = W_2$ equation fits our traditional accounting model. But it is in no way restricted to that model. It is expressed in the most general of terms. It can be reduced to:

> What you had
> $+$ What you've added to it
> $-$ What you've removed from it
> $=$ What you've got

This is a truism, mere tautology. The unit of measurement could be absolutely anything. But in accounting we take a particular view. First, we measure the elements in money terms. Second, we traditionally measure the sums of money in a particular way, following the concepts we considered in Chapter 1. We record assets using the historic cost convention and we recognise revenue and net asset increases following the realisation and accrual conventions. We are so used to this procedure that we tend to do it automatically, without considering the alternatives. We tend to accept normal practice out of sheer habit. Such acceptance will not do.

INCOME AND CAPITAL

A useful starting point is the work of the economist Irving Fisher (1930). He defines capital thus: 'Capital is a stock of wealth at an instant in time.' In contrast to this, we can say that: Income is a flow of benefits or services arising through time. This is quite consistent with our earlier tautological equation. What you had (capital, stock) plus additions (income, flow) less withdrawals equals what you have got.

Capital is a stock of wealth that generates income. Income is the enjoyment from the use of capital. These seem like circular and therefore inadequate definitions. The way round this difficulty is to distinguish between *capital*, on the one hand, and *the value of capital*, on the other. *Capital* is a stock of assets capable of generating future services. *The value of capital* is dependent on the value of those future services. For example, a field is a stock of wealth, a field is capital. The value of the field, the value of the capital, is dependent on the (net) value of crops to be grown on the field, i.e. on the income.

All this makes income and the value of capital sound like forward-looking concepts. Perhaps they are!

ACTIVITY 4.1

Go to a library and look up the words 'income' (or 'profit') and 'capital' in (a) a number of accounting texts, (b) a number of economics texts, (c) general dictionaries and encyclopaedias. Record book titles under these three subheadings and summarise the definitions given. Record book titles that fail to include definitions of either concept (you may wish to avoid these in the future). Does a clear consensus and a clear understanding emerge?

Activity feedback

You may have more luck than we did, but likely conclusions are:

1   The terms have a wide variety of different meanings.

2   Clear definition is extremely difficult.

3   Many accounting texts evade the difficulties by talking in purely bookkeeping terms.

WEALTH AND VALUE

It should be clear by now that we can talk about evaluating the assets of an entity, we can talk about evaluating the wealth of an entity and we can talk about evaluating the capital of an entity. Each of these descriptions amounts to exactly the same thing. It amounts to an evaluation of what the entity 'has got'. Whichever way we look at this problem, whichever word we wish to use, the key point is the obvious need for evaluation. We noticed earlier that any measuring unit will do. But there must be a measuring unit – certainly a generally understandable one and preferably one generally accepted as a means of exchange (i.e. acceptable as 'money'). You are already familiar with the ways in which accountants usually evaluate different assets in a balance sheet. You are familiar, at least intuitively, with ideas of the 'A is better off than B' or 'this car is worth more than that one' variety. Try the next activity – it may be both more fun and more productive if you try it in a group, but if this is not possible think it over for half an hour while doing something else and then summarise your ideas.

ACTIVITY 4.2

A brief case study

We have an asset, for example a briefcase, and we wish to evaluate it, to attach a monetary value to it. List and describe all the possible ways of doing this you can think of. Illustrate each possible way by making up some simple figures. Which is the best method?

Activity feedback

One of the purposes of this activity is simply the realisation that there is a very large number of possible answers. Here are some possibilities:

1　We could take as our basic figure the amount of money we originally paid for the briefcase:

　(a)　We could simply use this base figure as being our 'value'.

　(b)　We could reduce it according to the life of the item. Thus, if the briefcase cost €10, is expected to last for ten years and is now eight years old, we could retain the figure of €10 as giving the 'value', but it arguably makes more sense to say that since the briefcase is eight-tenths 'used up', then eight-tenths of the €10 has been 'used up' and therefore the remaining 'value' is €2.

2　We could take as our basic figure the amount of money we would now have to pay to buy the briefcase. Again there are several specific possibilities arising from this basis:

　(a)　We could take the cost, today, of buying a new briefcase.

　(b)　We could take the cost, today, of buying a second-hand briefcase in this particular condition.

　(c)　We could take the cost, today, of buying a new briefcase and reduce it according to the life of our briefcase. Thus, if a new briefcase costs €20, the second-hand cost of an old one is €3 and other information is as before, the alternative figures under this basis would be (a) €20; (b) €3; (c) eight-tenths of €20, i.e. €4.

　　　A variant of this basis is not to consider the cost of replacing the asset, but rather to consider the cost of replacing its function. Thus, in our example, we would consider the cost of enabling me to carry my bits and pieces if my briefcase were lost, rather than the cost of replacing my briefcase. In situations of rapid technology change, this variant may be the only practical possibility, as the original assets are no longer available.

3　We could take as our basic figure the amount of money we would get if we sold the briefcase in its existing condition – say, €1. This should be the net figure after deducting any selling expenses.

4　We could take as our basic figure an evaluation of the future usefulness to us of the briefcase if

(Continued)

ACTIVITY 4.2   (*Continued*)

we keep it and use it. We might say that the value of the use we shall get from the briefcase in the two final years of its life is €3 and €2, respectively. This does not mean that our basic figure would be $3 + 2 = €5$. The question is not: what is the sum of the valuations of the usefulness in each year over the remaining life of the briefcase, but rather: what is the value today of the receipts of usefulness expected in the future. Thus, in our example, we need to find the value today of receiving a benefit of €3 in one year's time and a further €2 in two year's time. (Strictly, this assumes that the whole of a year's benefit or usefulness occurs on the last day of the year.)

The essence of this problem can be considered as follows. Suppose I owe you €80. If I say, 'Would you pre-fer €80 now or €90 in one year?', you would probably say you would take €80 now. If I were to say, 'Would you prefer €80 now or €150 in one year?', however, you would probably prefer the €150 in one year.

There will be some point between €90 and €150 at which you are completely indifferent as between the €80 and the higher figure in one year. If that point occurs at €100, i.e., you are completely indifferent between €80 now and €100 in one year, then the rate of discount is 25% ($25\% \times 80 = 20$; $100 - 20 = 80$). This enables us to say that €100 expense in one year is the equivalent of €80 expense today and, equally, that €100 benefit in one year is only 'worth' €80 benefit today.

Suppose a project involves expenses of €100 pa for three years and then benefits of €200 for a further two years. At a 25% discount rate the present 'value' of this project is found as follows:

End year				
$1 - 100 \times 80\% =$				-80
$2 - 100 \times 80\% =$	$80 \times 80\% =$			-64
$3 - 100 \times 80\% =$	$80 \times 80\% =$	$64 \times 80\% =$		-51
$4 + 200 \times 80\% =$	$160 \times 80\% =$	$128 \times 80\% =$		
		$102 \times 80\% =$		$+80$
$5 + 200 \times 80\% =$	$160 \times 80\% =$	$128 \times 80\% =$		
		$102 \times 80\% =$		
		$80 \times 80\% =$		$\underline{+64}$
				$\overline{€ -51}$

Therefore, the project, involving net cash inflow of €100 (2×200) – (3×100), has a net present 'value' (discounted value) of -51 and is not worth pursuing (unless all available alternatives give even greater negative present values).

The problem, of course, is finding the rate of discount, which is influenced by alternative uses of the resource (e.g. interest on money) and by future expectations, which are of necessity subjective. Even if a discount rate as of now can be found, the implied assumption used here, that the rate remains constant, is almost certainly false.

If we take the same 25% discount factor as in the example, then €3 in one year will be evaluated at 80% of €3 today, i.e. €2.40, and €2 in two years will be eval-uated at 80% of 80% of €2, i.e. €1.28. Thus, the value today of the future usefulness to us of the briefcase would, under these assumptions, be €2.40 + €1.28 = €3.68.

We can label these four evaluation approaches:

1 historic cost

2 replacement cost

3 net realisable value

4 net present value or economic value.

You may, of course, have thought of other ideas or other combinations. Our suggestions are restricted in at least two ways. First, we have thought purely in monetary terms. Second, we have assumed that money is a per-fectly acceptable measuring unit – that we know exactly what one euro means. Both these assumptions require critical consideration.

ACTIVITY 4.3

Analyse and summarise the thought process that made you decide this book was worth buying.

Activity feedback

These suggestions make the assumption, not necessarily valid, that you did actually buy it. Whatever the price you paid, we can logically deduce that you considered that having the book was worth more to you than having the money. But you do not want the book in order to have the book. You bought the book in order to read it, to learn from it, to enjoy and savour its every word. This cannot be precisely evaluated. Equally, if you had not bought the book it would not be because you wanted to have the money. It would be because you wanted to spend the money on something else even more advantageous than ownership of your own copy. This also would not mean that you had evaluated the benefits of this alternative with any precision. There is no need to evaluate the benefits of these alternative courses of action, merely to rank them. So in order to take this significant investment decision it is not obvious that we can necessarily restrict our thinking to the financially quantifiable. This idea is further explored in Chapter 10.

ACTIVITY 4.4

Obtain a pencil, a measuring rule and an elastic band. Now attempt to measure the length of the pencil (a) with the rule and (b) with the elastic band.

Activity feedback

Quite! Stupid, isn't it? A centimetre is a precisely defined concept. But the idea of measuring a length with an elastic band is nonsensical because, of course, we do not know how far we have stretched it – it is continually changing by unknown amounts.

But a euro is as elastic a concept as an elastic band! In relative terms, for example in relation to the US dollar, the euro keeps changing, as published exchange rates tell us. Even more importantly, the euro keeps changing in absolute terms – indeed, is undefinable in absolute terms – as published inflation rates confirm. The value of a euro is neither clearly defined nor constant. Yet accountants use it as if it were both. This is another idea requiring detailed analysis and we return to it in Chapter 7.

AN ARRAY OF VALUE CONCEPTS

A fuller explanation of some possible value concepts is given in a book that every accounting student should read (Edwards and Bell, 1961). We are asked to consider a semi-finished asset, i.e. part-way through the production process, to enumerate the various dimensions through which we can describe this asset and thus to calculate and define all possible permutations arising from this multidimensional consideration. Three dimensions are suggested:

1 the form (and place) of the thing being valued
2 the date of the price used in valuation
3 the market from which the price is obtained.

The form can be of three types. First, the asset could be described and valued in its present form, e.g. a frame for a chair. Second, it could be described and valued in terms of the list of inputs – wood, labour, etc., its initial form. Third, it could be described and valued as the expected output, less the additional inputs necessary to reach that stage – a chair less a padded seat, for example: its ultimate form.

The date of the price used in valuation, when applied to any of these three forms, gives rise to three possibilities – past, current and future. We can talk about past

TABLE 4.1	An array of value concepts		
	Form and place of asset		
Value date, market	***Initial inputs***	***Present form***	***Ultimate form***
Past, entry	*Historic costs*	Discarded alternatives	Irrelevant
Past, exit	Discarded alternatives	Discarded alternatives	Irrelevant
Current, entry	*Current costs*	*Present costs*	Irrelevant
Current, exit	Irrelevant	*Opportunity costs*	*Current values*
Future, entry	Possible replacement costs	Possible replacement costs	Irrelevant
Future, exit	Irrelevant	Possible selling values	*Expected values*

costs, current costs or future costs of the initial inputs. We can talk about past costs of the present form (i.e. what we could have bought it for in the past as bought-in work in progress), about current costs of the present form or about future costs of the present form. Finally, the prices assigned to the asset in its ultimate form (and to the inputs which must be deducted) could also bear past, current or future dates.

This now yields nine possible alternatives for our asset. But we have still to consider the third dimension – the market from which the price is obtained. Two basic types of market need to be distinguished, the market in which the firm could buy the asset in its specified form at the specified time, giving entry prices, and the market in which the firm could sell the asset in its specified form at the specified time, giving exit prices. Adding this third dimension with its two possibilities leads to a total of 18 possible alternatives for the asset. Edwards and Bell summarise this in Table 4.1.

ACTIVITY 4.5

Articulate and explain the meaning of each of the 18 alternatives shown in Table 4.1.

Activity feedback
Your words will undoubtedly be different from ours but your ideas should be somewhat on the following lines.

Initial inputs

Past, entry	original costs of raw inputs
Past, exit	past selling prices of those raw inputs in their raw form
Current, entry	cost of those raw inputs today
Current, exit	today's potential selling price of those raw inputs if still in their original form (which they are not)
Future, entry	expected future costs of those same raw inputs in their original form
Future, exit	the expected future selling price of those raw inputs if still in their original form (which they are not)

Present form

Past, entry	the past cost at which the product could have been purchased in its present partially completed form (it was not)
Past, exit	past selling prices at which the product could have been sold in its present partially completed form (but it was not)
Current, entry	the cost at the present time of buying the asset in its present partially completed form
Current, exit	today's selling price of the product in its present partially completed form
Future, entry	the expected future cost of buying the asset directly from a supplier in its present partially completed form

(Continued)

ACTIVITY 4.5   (*Continued*)

Future, exit — the expected future selling price of the product in its present partially completed form

Ultimate form

Past, entry — the past cost at which the product could have been purchased directly from a supplier in its final fully completed form (but it was not)

Past, exit — the past selling price at which the product could have been sold in its final fully completed form (if we had had the product in that form, which we did not)

Current, entry — the cost at the present time of buying the product in its final fully completed form (which we did not)

Current, exit — today's selling price of the product in its final fully completed form

Future, entry — the expected future cost of buying the product directly from a supplier in its final fully completed form

Future, exit — the expected future selling price of the product in its final fully completed form

ACTIVITY 4.6

You may have found Activity 4.5 rather mind-bending! It is a good example of the type of mental flexibility required if we are going to analyse from first principles without being influenced by prior experience. Now a rather easier task. Select the six alternatives from the total of 18 that you think are most likely to lead to the provision of useful information.

Activity feedback

The six as selected and defined by Edwards and Bell (1961) themselves are shown in Table 4.2. It is clear from the feedback to Activity 4.5 that not all the other tasks are totally irrelevant (although some of them obviously are). So you may have included one or two different ones. Satisfy yourself, however, that you at least agree that the six alternatives selected in Table 4.2 will indeed provide useful information for decision-making purposes. These six ideas, as developed by later thinking, are all explored in subsequent chapters.

TABLE 4.2   Edwards and Bell's useful valuation possibilities

Exit values

1 *Expected values* (ultimate, future, exit) – values expected to be received in the future for output sold according to the firm's planned course of action

2 *Current values* (ultimate, current, exit) – values actually realised during the current period for goods or services sold

3 *Opportunity costs* (present, current, exit) – values that could currently be realised if assets (whether finished goods, semi-finished goods or raw materials) were sold (without further processing) outside the firm at the best prices immediately obtainable

Entry values

1 *Present costs* (present, current, entry) – the cost currently of acquiring the asset being valued

2 *Current cost* (initial, current, entry) – the cost currently of acquiring the inputs which the firm used to produce the asset being valued

3 *Historic cost* (initial, past, entry) – the cost at time of acquisition of the inputs which the firm in fact used to produce the asset being valued

ECONOMIC VALUE

We have already met the idea of this in our brief case study (Activity 4.2). It is mentioned again here in order to point out that the Edwards and Bell exposition of the array of value concepts is clearly incomplete in that it excludes the economic value possibility. To extend their own illustration, one possible course of action with a partly completed chair is to complete it and hire it out for rental or use it oneself by sitting on it, in either case producing returns over a number of periods capable of being evaluated using the discounting process. Economic value, too, requires proper exploration in a later chapter.

CAPITAL MAINTENANCE

We established with our tautology that profit is an increase in capital. Turning the argument around, we can suggest that profit is the increase in the closing capital after having maintained the original capital. This provides a different but often useful way of looking at problems of income measurement. For each and every value concept that we can define, with its corresponding income concept, there is also a clearly definable capital maintenance concept. (See Activity 4.7.)

CRITERIA FOR APPRAISING ALTERNATIVE VALUATION CONCEPTS

We discussed the definition and role of accounting together with suggested characteristics of useful information. In essence, accounting communicates useful information for decision-making. We need to analyse each valuation concept to be considered so as to understand in detail the meaning and significance of the information it gives. Different users face different decisions. Users are asking a number of questions. An array of valuation bases are providing a number of answers. If we can match up question with answer then we are being useful. Many valuation bases may be useful, but for different purposes. The question is generally not 'which is the best valuation concept?', but 'which is the best valuation concept to answer this question or help this decision?'. Appraisal is a way of analysing and a way of thinking, never an absolute.

ACTIVITY 4.7

Under traditional accounting conventions, based on historical cost, what precisely is the definition of capital that has to be maintained before a profit is reported?

Activity feedback
Traditionally, profit is the numerical quantity of money units generated by the business for the owners over a period. If opening money capital is 100 and closing money capital 103, then (ignoring dividends and capital infusions) profit is 3. Profit is the excess after having maintained the original 100, so it is the original money capital, the number of euros originally invested, which has to be maintained under this traditional thinking. If the 100 were in 1898 and the 103 in 2008, this statement still applies!

We shall return to the idea of capital maintenance for each of the methods we consider in detail. It will help considerably in appraising the usefulness of the various alternatives. It is also an important element in the IASB conceptual framework discussed in Chapter 8.

ACTIVITY 4.8

What are the questions, what are the decisions, for which traditional historical cost accounting as outlined in Chapter 1 appears to provide the relevant information?

Activity feedback

One safe answer, following from our discussion on capital maintenance, is that it tells us our gain, our profit, after ensuring the retention of the number of euros we originally invested. It does not seem obvious, however, that this is very useful information. Investment and expansion decisions as regards future activity require projections into the future based on today's euros. Reports on past activity related to euros of the day the business started seem a pretty illogical substitute. But you may, of course, have other ideas!

FISHER AND PSYCHIC INCOME

The implication of Activity 4.3 was that people buy something, not because of the object itself, but because of what they can do with it. This idea leads us into Fisher's concept of psychic income. People do things because of the satisfaction they derive from so doing. Satisfaction is a mental occurrence, an event of the mind. It is a psychic rather than a physical happening. People act, and make decisions about actions, so as to maximise their personal, mental or psychic satisfaction. Fisher (1930) puts the argument as follows:

> For each individual only those events which come within the purview of his experience are of direct concern. It is these events – the psychic experiences of the individual mind – which constitute ultimate income for that individual. The outside events have significance for that individual only in so far as they are the means to these inner events of the mind. The human nervous system is, like a radio, a great receiving instrument. Our brains serve to transform into the stream of our psychic life those outside events which happen to us and stimulate our nervous system.
>
> Directors and managers providing income for thousands of people sometimes think of their corporation merely as a great money-making machine. In their eyes its one purpose is to earn money dividends for the stock-holders, money interest for the bond-holders, money wages and money salaries for the employees. What happens after these payments are made seems too private a matter to concern them. Yet that is the nub of the whole arrangement. It is only what we carry out of the market place into our homes and our private lives which really counts. Money is of no use to us until it is spent. The ultimate wages are not paid in terms of money but in the enjoyments it buys. The dividend cheque becomes income in the ultimate sense only when we eat the food, wear the clothes, or ride in the automobile which are bought with the cheque.

The essence of this proposition seems to us to be obviously correct. How do we decide whether to work overtime and earn an extra €20 or to go for a walk in the sunshine? We shall take the decision that, we believe (possibly wrongly, of course), will lead to the greater pleasure. Clearly the pleasure to be derived from spending the €20 is relevant in this equation. Equally obviously, such pleasure or satisfaction – enjoyment income as Fisher terms it – cannot be measured directly or objectively. He proposes a series of approximations. The first approximation he calls real income.

This involves physical events and material things. A litre of milk and a daily newspaper are both examples of real income. Real income consists of:

> those final physical events in the outer world which give us our inner enjoyments. This real income includes the shelter of a house, the music of a radio, the use of clothes, the eating of food.

In one sense real income is measurable – litre is an objective term (although 'milk' is less so!). But there is no additivity – no standard measuring unit or common denominator. To achieve this we need to move to a second approximation, which Fisher calls the cost of living. This consists of the money paid to obtain the real income – the cost of the litre of milk and the daily newspaper. Fisher's exposition of the argument has something of a period flavour:

> So, just as we went behind an individual's enjoyment income to his real income, we now go behind his real income, or his living, to his cost of living, the money measure of real income. You cannot measure in dollars either the inner event of your enjoyment while eating your dinner or the outer event of eating it, but you can find out definitely how much money that dinner cost you. In the same way, you cannot measure your enjoyment at the cinema, but you do know what your house shelter is really worth to you, you can tell how much you pay for your rent, or what is a fair equivalent for your rent if you happen to live in your own house. You cannot measure what it is worth to wear an evening suit, but you can find out what it costs to hire one, or a fair equivalent of its hire if, perchance, the suit belongs to you. Deducing such equivalents is an accountant's job.
> The total cost of living, in the sense of money payments, is a negative item, being outgo rather than income; but it is our best practical measure of the positive items of real income for which those payments are made.

The problem with this as Fisher himself recognises is that money paid out (outgo) does not seem to make much sense as a measure of income in money terms. We therefore move to a third approximation, that of money income:

> All money received and readily available and intended to be used for spending is money income.

We can illustrate Fisher's arguments by considering eating a meal. If we wish to eat, we have to go out and earn some money. This means that we have a money income – in this case, wages. This money income, of course, is the idea that corresponds to the everyday use of the words 'income' or 'earnings'. Having some money, we go out to a restaurant where we eat, and pay for, a meal. Here we have real income. We have the 'final physical event', namely the actual eating of the food. This is approximately measured by the 'cost of living', i.e. by the cost of the meal – the amount we pay the restaurant. This idea of taking a cost-based approach is clearly not a new one to an accountant.

But this is not the end of the story. Fisher argues further. We did not eat a meal for the sake of it, we ate a meal to receive the satisfaction, the pleasure of having eaten (or to avoid the unpleasantness, the pain, of feeling hungry). This satisfaction, this pleasure, is the 'enjoyment' or 'psychic' income. It may be unmeasurable, at least in a manner that can be recorded, but it is still, argues Fisher, the most important. After all, if it did not exist, we would have had no reason to buy the meal. And without a reason to buy the meal, we have no reason to earn the wages.

Fisher thus distinguishes three successive stages, or aspects, of a person's income:

1 *enjoyment* or psychic income, consisting of agreeable sensations and experiences
2 *real income* 'measured' by the cost of living
3 *money income*, consisting of the money received by someone for meeting their costs of living.

The last – money income – is most commonly called income; and the first – enjoyment income – is the most fundamental. But for accounting purposes real income, as measured by the cost of living, is the most practical.

This last statement may seem surprising, Fisher dismisses money income as being unimportant (enjoyment income is the most important, the cost of living is the most practical).

Notice again the definition he gives of money income, emphasis now added:

All money received and readily available and *intended* to be used for spending is money income.

So if we receive a salary of $10 000 (Fisher's figures, writing in 1930!), save $4000 and put $6000 as available for spending, the significant figure to Fisher is the $6000, not the $10 000. Real income as measured by the cost of living may be more or less than money income. Real income is a closer approximation to ultimate reality (i.e. psychic satisfaction) than money income, so real income is the preferable concept:

A definition of income which satisfies both theory and practice, in both economics and accountancy, must reckon as income in the most basic sense all those uses, services, or living for which the cost of living is expended even though such expenditure may exceed the money income.

What this all boils down to is that Fisher's definitions of income *do not involve a concept of capital maintenance*. It is this point that distinguishes Fisher's ideas from the mainstream of both accounting and economic thinking. Fisher's measure of income is really a measure of *consumption*.

HICKS AND CAPITAL MAINTENANCE

We have already seen (Activity 4.2) that in very general terms economic value is based on a current evaluation of future streams of (net) receipts. It is also obvious that in our earlier equation $W_1 + P - D = W_2$ capital maintenance requires that W_2 is at least equal to W_1. Another way of putting this is that D (= drawing or consumption) cannot exceed P (= profit or income). The classic analysis of the implications of this thinking is by Hicks (1946). The opening of the following quote makes it clear just how fundamental he feels capital maintenance to be:

The purpose of income calculations in practical affairs is to give people an indication of the amount which they can consume without impoverishing themselves. Following out this idea, it would seem that we ought to define a man's income as the maximum value which he can consume during a week, and still expect to be as well off at the end of the week as he was at the beginning. Thus, when a person saves, he plans to be better off in the future; when he lives beyond his income, he plans to be worse off. Remembering that the practical purpose of income is to serve as a guide for prudent conduct, I think it is fairly clear that this is what the central meaning must be.

However, business men and economists alike are usually content to employ one or other of a series of approximations to the central meaning. Let us consider some of these approximations in turn.

Hicks moves on to attempt to operationalise this 'central meaning'. Like Fisher, Hicks is obviously adopting a forward-looking approach to valuation and income measurement. We have seen in Activity 4.2 that we can operationalise such an approach (once we have invented the raw figures!) by calculating net present value figures for expected receipts. Putting these two ideas together, we can regard capital, wealth, 'well-offness' as being the net present value of expected receipts. If we put this notion into the original definition in place of the vague 'as well off', we arrive at a first approximation:

Income No. 1 is thus the maximum amount which can be spent during a period if there is to be an expectation of maintaining intact the capital value of prospective receipts (in money terms). This is probably the definition which most people do implicitly use in their private affairs; but it is far from being in all circumstances a good approximation to the central concept.

ACTIVITY 4.9

Suppose that at the beginning of the week our individual possesses property worth €10 010 and no other source of income. If the rate of interest were one-tenth per cent per week, income would be €10 for the week. For if €10 were spent, €10 000 would be left to be reinvested; and in one week this would have accumulated to €10 010 – the original sum. This is income No. 1. But suppose that the rate of interest per week for a loan of one week is one-tenth per cent, that the corresponding rate expected to rule in the second week from now is one-fifth per cent and that this higher rate is expected to continue indefinitely afterwards. What is the individual's income for: (a) week 1, (b) week 2?

Activity feedback
At the beginning of week 1 the individual is bound to spend no more than €10 in the current week, if he is to expect to have €10 010 again at his disposal at the end of the week; but if he desires to have the same sum available at the end of the second week, he will be able to spend nearly €20 in the second week, not €10 only. The same sum (€10 010) available at the beginning of the first week makes possible a stream of expenditures:

€10, €20, €20, €20, . . .

while if it is available at the beginning of the second week it makes possible a stream:

€20, €20, €20, €20, . . .

It is obvious that these two alternative possible expenditure streams do not give equal well-offness. One is worth more than the other. If we put the income as €10 for week 1 and €20 for week 2, then we are not 'maintaining intact the capital value of prospective receipts (in money terms)'. The amount the individual can spend each week while still maintaining well-offness intact **must**, under these conditions, be the same in week 1 and in week 2 (and subsequent weeks):

This leads us to the definition of Income No. 2. We now define income as the maximum amount the individual can spend this week, and still expect to be able to spend the same amount in each ensuing week. So long as the rate of interest is not expected to change, this definition comes to the same thing as the first; but when the rate of interest is expected to change, they cease to be identical. Income No. 2 is then a closer approximation to the central concept than Income No. 1 is.

There are several problems with this as an operational concept. First, interest rates may change. The second problem is that prices may be expected to change. In principle we can deal with this easily by a small addition to the wording:

(Continued)

ACTIVITY 4.9   *(Continued)*

Income No. 3 must be defined as the maximum amount of money which the individual can spend this week, and still expect to be able to spend the same amount in real terms in each ensuing week. If prices are expected to rise, then an individual who plans to spend €10 in the present and each ensuing week must expect to be less well off at the end of the week than he is at the beginning. At each date he can look forward to the opportunity of spending €10 in each future week; but at the first date one of the €10s will be spent in a week when prices are relatively low. An opportunity of spending on favourable terms is present in the first case, but absent in the second. Thus, if €10 is to be his income for this week, according to definition No. 3 he will have to expect to be able to spend in each future week not €10, but a sum greater or less than €10 by the extent to which prices have risen or fallen in that week above or below their level in the first week.

In practice, of course, the apparent simplicity of this change is false. We need expectations of price changes for every individual for every commodity of projected purchase for every need of each anticipated expenditure!

In addition to this practical difficulty Income No. 3 also has the problem of how to deal with long-term assets, i.e. fixed assets or 'durable consumption goods':

Strictly speaking, saving is not the difference between income and expenditure, it is the difference between income and consumption. Income is not the maximum amount the individual can spend while expecting to be as well off as before at the end of the week; it is the maximum amount he can consume. If some part of his expenditure goes on durable consumption goods, that will tend to make his expenditure exceed his consumption; if some part of his consumption is consumption of durable consumption goods, already bought in the past, that tends to make consumption exceed expenditure.

It should be noted that we have now come full circle back to an emphasis on consumption. But Hicks is concerned with consumption and capital maintenance, whereas Fisher is only concerned with consumption. We can summarise the basic difference between Fisher and Hicks by realising that while Fisher is concerned with consumption, Hicks is concerned with the capacity to consume. This is clearly a long-run concept. To take an obvious example, consider the farmer's seed corn. This is the basis of next year's crops. It is available now and it could be eaten (consumed). But if it is eaten now there will be no crop next year and therefore no possibility of consumption next year. Therefore, if we wish to maintain the capacity to consume next year, the seed corn must not be consumed now. In other words it must be saved. This is, to put it mildly, useful information.

CALCULATION OF ECONOMIC INCOME

One way of summarising what we have just looked at is to say that for Fisher:

$$\text{Income} = \text{Consumption}$$

But for Hicks:

$$\text{Income} = \text{Consumption and Saving}$$

which can be expressed as:

$$Y = C + S$$

Savings can be expressed as $(K_e - K_s)$ where:

$$K_e = \text{value of capital at the end of a period}$$
$$K_s = \text{value of capital at the start of a period}$$

Thus:

$$Y = C + (K_e - K_s)$$

For example, if income = €100, capital at the end of the period = €280 and capital at the beginning of the period was €300, then: €100 = 120 + (280 − 300).

This tells us that consumption has exceeded income by €20, because of dis-saving of €20. 'Well-offness' has not been maintained.

In the business world rather than the personal consumption world, C is redefined as the realised cash flows of the period. We will illustrate this as simply as possible.

ACTIVITY 4.10

An investment on 1 January year 1 has expected receipts on 31 December each year of €1000 for three years. The discount rate to reflect the time value of money is 10%. Calculate the capital as at 1 January for each of the years 1, 2 and 3.

Activity feedback
On 1 January year 1 the expected receipt on 31 December year 1 needs to be discounted back by one year, the expected receipt on 31 December year 2 needs to be discounted back by two years and the expected receipt on 31 December year 3 needs to be discounted back by three years.

Thus capital at 1 January year 1 is:

$$\frac{1000}{1.1} + \frac{1000}{(1.1)^2} + \frac{1000}{(1.1)^3}$$
$$= 909 + 826 + 751 = €2486$$

On 1 January year 2 the receipt on 31 December year 1 is now irrelevant. The expected receipt on 31 December year 2 now needs to be discounted back to 1 January year 2, i.e. by one year and the expected receipt on 31 December year 3 also needs to be discounted back to 1 January year 2, i.e. by two years. Similarly, on 1 January year 3 only the expected receipt on 31 December year 3 is of any relevance and this needs to be discounted back to 1 January year 3, i.e. by one year. Thus capital at 1 January year 2 is:

$$\frac{1000}{1.1} + \frac{1000}{(1.1)^2}$$
$$= 909 + 826 = €1735$$

and capital at 1 January 03 is:

$$\frac{1000}{1.1} = €909$$

ACTIVITY 4.11

Considering the investment in the previous activity, now suppose that the actual cost of the investment, on 1 January year 1, is €2486. According to the Hicksian way of thinking, what is the income for each year?

Activity feedback
Our formula was:

$$Y = C + (K_e - K_s)$$

So in year 1:

$$Y = 1000 + (1735 - 2486)$$
$$= 1000 - 751$$
$$= €249$$

In year 2:

$$Y = 1000 + (909 - 1735)$$
$$= 1000 - 826$$
$$= €174$$

In year 3:

$$Y = 1000 + (0 - 909)$$
$$= 1000 - 909$$
$$= €91$$

In year 1, the cash receipts are €1000, but the income is stated as €249. The difference (€751) needs to be reinvested (saved), in order to facilitate *future* spending. This reinvestment of €751 on 1 January year 2 will by itself earn 10% in the year 2, i.e. €75. So total income in year 2 is €174, from the original investment, plus €75 from the reinvestment, i.e. again €249.

In year 2, the cash receipts from the original investment are €1000, but the income is stated as €174. The difference (€826) again needs to be reinvested. This investment of €826 will itself earn €83 in year 3, giving total cash receipts in that year of €91 from the original investment, €75 from the first reinvestment and €83 from the second reinvestment, i.e. €249 once again. Similarly

(Continued)

ACTIVITY 4.11   *(Continued)*

TABLE 4.3   Hicks' economic income model

	1	2	3	4	5	6	7	8	9
Year	C	K_e	K_s	Y	Reinvestment	Cumulative reinvestment	Total reinvestment	Income from reinvestment	Total economic income
0	0	2 486	0	0	0	0	2 486	0	0
1	1 000	1 735	2 486	249	751	751	2 486	0	249
2	1 000	909	1 735	174	826	1 577	2 486	75	249
3	1 000	0	909	91	909	2 486	2 486	158	249
4	0	0	0	0	0	2 486	2 486	249	249

Notes: 4 = 1 + 2 − 3
5 = 1 − 4
7 = 2 + 6
9 = 4 + 8

in year 3, cash receipts will be €1000, but the income is stated as €91. The difference (€909) will be reinvested at 10%, earning itself €91 in each year. Total cash receipts in year 4, all from reinvestments, will therefore be 75 + 83 + 91 = €249 and similarly in year 5 onwards. This of course satisfies our original conditions. The income of year 1 is the amount 'that can be spent while still enabling the income of all future periods to be the same amount'. This

has been shown to be €249 under the given assumptions. These results are summarised in Table 4.3.

The present value of an annual income stream of €249, to infinity, at a 10% discount rate is €2490. This, allowing for rounding errors, gives us our original 'capital' figure of €2486, which of course is what it should do. So the answer may possibly have come as no surprise. But you should still make sure you understand all the logic involved.

INCOME *EX ANTE* AND INCOME *EX POST*

We have assumed that we are in a world of perfect knowledge and perfect foresight – an ideal world in fact. The economic income devised under these assumptions is known as ideal income. It is obviously an unreal oversimplification. We can, however, extend our analysis to allow for estimates of future events and this leads to two further models, income *ex ante* and income *ex post*. Income *ex ante* means income measured before the event; income *ex post* means income measured after the event.

Two possibilities for changes exist: in the timing and/or amount of forecast cash flow and in the appropriate discount rate. Formally, income *ex ante* can be expressed as:

$$Y = C_1 + (K_e^1 - K_s)$$

where C_1 is the expected realised cash flow for the period anticipated at the beginning of the period, K_e^1 is the closing capital as measured (estimated) at the beginning of the period, and K_s is the capital at the beginning of the period as measured (estimated) at the beginning of the period.

ACTIVITY 4.12

Assume the same original information as in the previous two activities. Now suppose that at the end of year 2, the expected return from the investment in the year 3 increases to €1100. Using an *ex ante* approach consider the effects on the calculations for each of the years.

Activity feedback

Using an *ex ante* approach the effects will be:

Year 1 – No change

Year 2 – Still no change. The calculations for the year 2 are based on expectations as at the beginning of the year 2 and they had not altered at that time

Year 3 – The opening capital K_s will no longer be the same as the closing capital K_e at the end of year 2. It will now be:

$$K_s = \frac{1100}{1.1} = €1000$$

This compares with the corresponding figure of €909 for K_s in year 3 under the ideal income calculations. There is therefore a windfall gain of €91 appearing under the *ex ante* way of thinking in year 3.

Income *ex post* can be expressed correspondingly, as:

$$Y = C + (K_e - K_s^1)$$

where C is the actual realised cash flow of the period, K_e^1 is the closing capital measured (estimated) at the end of the period and K_s^1 is the opening capital measured (estimated) at the end of the period.

ACTIVITY 4.13

Given all the information of the previous activity, reconsider the effects of the change in expectations which occurs at the end of year 2.

Activity feedback

Again there will be no change in year 1 but, using an *ex post* approach, there will be a change in the calculations for year 2, because at the end of year 2 our expectations had already altered. Capital at 1 January year 2, based on expectations as at the end of year 2, is:

$$\frac{1000}{1.1} + \frac{1100}{(1.1)^2}$$
$$K_s = 909 + 909 = €1818$$

This compares with the corresponding figure of €1735 for K_s in year 2 under the ideal income calculations, giving rise to a windfall gain of €83 appearing in year 2. For present purposes, it is not considered necessary to pursue the calculations any further as regards recalculation of reinvestment amounts and so on. However, several points should be noted:

1 Income *ex post* is measured after the event, but it is still based on expectations of the future, income *ex post* for year 2 is derived from the expectations held as at the end of year 2, but

these expectations relate to years 3, 4 and so on to infinity. Economic income *ex post* is therefore just as subjective as economic income *ex ante*.

2 Is the windfall gain realised? This is relatively straightforward. The gain becomes realised as the cash flow whose estimation gave rise to it is actually received.

3 Is the windfall gain income or capital, i.e. should it be saved (reinvested) or can it be spent? This is not so clear cut, as it depends on where we consider our starting point to be. Taking our original example, if our original, and permanent, intention is to maintain the capacity to consume €249 each year to infinity, then it is clear that we have already achieved that requirement without taking account of the windfall gain. The gain is, therefore, 'spare', it need not be reinvested and so it is available for immediate consumption. Notice carefully that the windfall gain is available for consumption as soon as it is recognised, *whether or not it has been realised*, i.e. in year 2 under the *ex post* method and in year 3 under the *ex ante* method. Thus the windfall gain could be regarded as a simple one-off increase in possible consumption (do not forget it could be a windfall loss, leading to a one-off decrease in possible consumption).

(Continued)

ACTIVITY 4.13   *(Continued)*

However, the change in expectations might cause us to amend the permanent annual consumption requirement in some way. We might, for example, wish to redo the complete calculations taking year 2 as a new starting point, giving 2 years of cash flow only. Here the windfall gain would not, or not necessarily, be spendable at all (even if it is already realised!).

It is, of course, possible, taking the original ideal income scenario as our starting point, to consider an almost infinite number of changes in expectations, variable as to timing of the change in expectations, changes in the expected timing of receipts, changes in the expected amounts of receipts and changes in discount rates. In every case, under both *ex ante* and *ex*

post thinking, we need to establish whether the effect of the change is on income or on capital before we can attempt to rework all the calculations and this depends entirely on the intentions of the decision maker concerned. If these intentions remain unaltered despite the change in expectations then the windfall will be income.

Refer back to Hicks' Income No. 3 definition: the maximum amount of money the individual can spend this week and still expect to be able to spend the same amount in real terms in each ensuing week. If 'this week' is and remains week 1, then the windfall is income. But if 'this week' means 'the current week', e.g. the week when expectations change, then the windfall affects capital and requires that a new permanently spendable weekly consumption be calculated.

SUMMARY

Income, capital and value are interrelated concepts. Value can be defined and enumerated in a variety of ways and detailed description, analysis and appraisal of the alternatives is required.

It is suggested that the economic ideas outlined in this chapter are:

1   theoretically sound and logically sensible

2   highly subjective in application as regards

   (a)   size of future cash flows

   (b)   timing of future cash flows

   (c)   discount rate to apply to future cash flows

3   problematic as regards windfall gains and losses

4   and therefore, as far as accounting is concerned, they probably represent an unattainable ideal.

EXERCISES

Suggested answers to exercises marked ✓ are to be found on the Student side of the companion website.

Suggested answers to the remaining exercises are to be found on the Instructor side of the companion website.

1   Obtain three sets of published accounts of quoted companies. Look carefully at the consolidated balance sheets and notes thereto and read the 'accounting policies'. Taking each

item in the balance sheet separately describe how the item is evaluated. Are these evaluations consistent? I.e. in mathematical terms, do we have genuine additivity?

✓ **2** Two retail businesses, *A* and *B*, run a similar trade from similar shops in similar areas. *A* bought its shop in 1950 for €5000 and *B* bought its shop in 1990 for €105 000. Both businesses consistently prepare their accounts on historic cost principles and they have identical operating profits. To what extent do the resulting accounts give a true (and fair) representation of the relative performance of the two businesses?

✓ **3** It is never possible to define capital or income, only to define capital and income. Do you agree?

4 (a) Outline Fisher's thinking on the concept of income.
   (b) Outline Hicks' thinking on this topic.
   (c) Relate and compare the two.

5 Explain the principles of economic income, carefully distinguishing income *ex ante* and income *ex post*.

6 'Economic income is an unattainable ideal.' Consider and discuss.

7 Spock purchased a space invader entertainment machine at the beginning of year 1 for €1000. He expects to receive at annual intervals the following receipts; at the end of year 1 €400; end of year 2 €500; end of year 3 €600. At the end of year 3 he expects to sell the machine for €400.
   Spock could receive a return of 10% on the next best investment. The present value of €1 receivable at the end of a period discounted at 10% is as follows:

End of year 1   0.909
End of year 2   0.826
End of year 3   0.751

Required:
Calculate the ideal economic income, ignoring taxation, and working to the nearest whole euro.
   Your answer should show that Spock's capital is maintained throughout the period and that his income is constant.

(ACCA – adapted)

CURRENT ENTRY VALUE

5

OBJECTIVES After studying this chapter you should be able to:

- explain the effects and implications of using current entry values to record the possession and usage of economic resources

- carry out the necessary technical manipulation

- explain the strengths, usefulness and weaknesses of the resulting information.

INTRODUCTION

The ideas of the previous chapter are of fundamental importance. But they are inherently highly subjective to apply. Of crucial importance from the point of view of accounting thinking, they are far removed from the marketplace. All 18 of the value concepts considered by Edwards and Bell (1961) (see Chapter 4) relate directly to actual or expected market values. One of these, past entry values, i.e. the historical cost (HC) of the initial inputs, is the traditional process which we summarised in Chapter 1.

Four of the remaining five are current values, two being current entry values and two current exit values. We look first at current entry values. Remember that entry values represent a market buying price, i.e. current entry values represent a cost-based process (but not a historical cost-based process).

BACK TO BASICS

ACTIVITY 5.1

On 1 January, Mr Jones starts off in business with 100 cents. His transactions are as follows:

2 January	Buys one bag of sugar for 40c
4 January	Sells one bag of sugar for 50c
5 January	Buys one bag of sugar for 44c

Prepare balance sheets on 2 January and on 6 January and a P&L account for the intervening period.

Activity feedback

This should not present major problems.

Balance sheet 2 January

Inventory	40	Capital	100
Cash	60		
	100c		100c

Balance sheet 6 January

Inventory	44	Capital	110
Cash	66		
	110c		110c

Profit and loss

Sales	50
Cost of sales	40
	10c

In terms of our very general equation, $W_1 + P - D = W_2$:

$$100 + 10 - 0 = 110$$

So Jones has made a profit of 10c. This, of course, is the usual accounting approach. But it is important to notice that there are really two stages in the progress from 2 January to 6 January. Between 2 January and the evening of 4 January, after the sale was made, Jones has turned 100c into 110c. On 4 January he actually has physically 110c and nothing else. Then between the evening of 4 January and 6 January he has changed 110c plus nothing into 66c plus a bag of sugar. Since the second bag of sugar cost 44c and we are recording all our resources at original, or historical cost, it necessarily follows that we show total resources of 110c on both 4 January and 6 January. The 4 January balance sheet was as follows:

Balance sheet 4 January

Cash	110	Capital	110
	110c		110c

Comparing this 4 January position with the 2 January and 6 January balance sheets confirms that:

1 A profit of 10c was made between 2 January and 4 January.

2 No profit or loss at all was made between 4 January and 6 January.

Jones, of course, is running a business. He also has to live. So he decides to withdraw the business profit for his own spending purposes.

If he takes 10c out then, by the accountant's definition, he has still left in all the money originally put in. This 10c must therefore be genuine gain, so it can obviously be withdrawn from the business without in any way reducing the resources of the business. So we can rewrite our 6 January sheet, after the withdrawal, as follows:

Balance sheet 6 January

Inventory	44	Capital	100
Cash	56		
	100c		100c

Our equation now becomes:

$$100 + 10 - 10 = 100$$

ACTIVITY 5.2

Compare the physical possessions of Jones' business on 2 January with those on 5 January, assuming still that Jones withdraws his 10c profit.

Activity feedback

In physical terms the business possesses:

On 2 January:

1 one bag of sugar

2 a pile of 60 shiny bright 1c pieces.

On 6 January:

1 one bag of sugar

2 a pile of 56 shiny bright 1c pieces.

Now, by simple subtraction, we can compare the physical position between 2 January and 6 January in terms both of sugar and of shiny bright 1c pieces. In terms of sugar, we are comparing one bag with one bag. There is no difference. In terms of bags of sugar, the business is exactly the same size as it was before. In terms of shiny bright 1c pieces, the business had 60 on 2 January and 56 on 6 January. There is therefore a reduction of four shiny bright 1c pieces. In terms of shiny bright 1c pieces the business has got smaller by four pieces.

Something must be wrong somewhere. The accountant has shown us that there is a 'genuine gain' of 10c over and above the original 100c capital put in. Jones has therefore withdrawn the 10c, and yet the result is *not* that the business is 'back where it started'. The result is that the business *has got smaller* to the tune of 4c.

Surely, either the physical comparison is wrong or the profit and loss statement prepared in Activity 5.1 is wrong. If the physical comparison is correct (try it yourself) then the 'genuine gain' of 10% mentioned is quite simply not genuine! Further thinking is needed. On 4 January we had, in physical terms, as we have already seen, a pile of 110 shiny bright 1c pieces. We have also already seen that the profit of 10c was made by 4 January. It therefore follows that the accountant's statement at 4 January is identical with the actual physical position at that date. The accountant says cash is 110c and profit is 10c. The physical position shows a pile of 110 shiny bright 1c pieces. It is obvious that since the physical

position and the accounting position were identical as at 4 January the divergence, the difference between the two, must have occurred after 4 January. But only one event has happened *after* 4 January. This was the purchase of the second bag of sugar on 5 January. So the problem *must* be something to do with the accounting treatment of the second bag.

Question: Why did Jones have to buy a second bag of sugar for 44c? The answer is because he has sold the first bag of sugar (for 50c). He would not have bought the second bag of sugar had he not sold the first one. It seems, therefore, that the selling of the first bag of sugar and the buying of the second bag of sugar are really two parts of one complete action. If he does not sell the first bag of sugar and does not buy the second bag of sugar, he obviously ends up with the same amount of cash on 6 January as he had on 2 January, i.e. 60c. If he does sell the first bag of sugar for 50c and does buy the second bag of sugar for 44c, he will end up with 6c more cash on 6 January than he had on 2 January. So the result of selling bag 1 and buying bag 2, as compared with doing neither, is a gain of 6c.

We can show this as follows:

Sales	50c
Costs incurred as a direct result of making sale	44c
Profit	6c

We are now suggesting a profit of 6c, as compared with the earlier suggestion of 10c. This will presumably reduce the maximum drawing payable by 10c − 6c = 4c. And remember, we argued earlier that the error, the difference between the original accountant's calculations and physical reality, the amount by which Jones' business had unintentionally 'got smaller' was 4c. We seem to have corrected the error exactly. We have produced an accounting calculation that agrees with actual physical events:

$$W_1 + P - D = W_2$$
$$100 + 6 - 6 = 100$$

THE BUSINESS ITSELF

It is essential to remember the purpose and nature of Jones' business. It is a sugar-selling business. The essence of our conclusion is a very simple one. It is that the cost of sales figure that we should relate to any particular sale should be calculated as equal to the *cost of the resulting replacement*, assuming that the replacement occurs immediately. The cost of sales figure should not be related to the cost of the item actually sold. This raises a difficulty. In order to be able to transfer this higher replacement figure out of the balance sheet and into the profit and loss calculation, the higher replacement figure must obviously first be recorded in the balance sheet. The complete picture is most easily seen by a series of balance sheets:

1 January

Cash	100	Capital	100
	100c		100c

2 January

Sugar	40	Capital	100
Cash	60		
	100c		100c

3 January

Sugar (1st bag)	44	Capital	100
Cash	60	Gain	4
	104c		104c

4 January

Cash	110	Capital	100
		Gain	4
		Profit	6
	110c		110c

5 January

Sugar (2nd bag)	44	Capital	100
		Gain	4
Cash	66	Profit	6
	110c		110c

Now, we must choose our words carefully. It is perfectly correct to say that Jones began his business on 1 January with 100c. But that is not the point. The point is that Jones began the business on 1 January with *60c plus the capacity to buy a bag of sugar*. Jones is setting up in business for the purpose of acquiring and selling bags of sugar. Therefore, we need to evaluate his position at any time in terms of his capacity, his ability, to carry out his purpose. In other words, his capacity to acquire and sell sugar.

So on 1 January Jones had the capacity to buy one bag of sugar (for 40c) plus also 60c. On 4 January Jones had 110c. More usefully, we can say that on 4 January Jones had the capacity to buy one bag of sugar (for 44c), plus also 66c. Comparing the 4 January position with the 1 January position clearly shows that Jones has:

1 maintained his capacity to buy one bag of sugar

2 and gained 6 shiny bright 1c pieces.

This calculation agrees with the real physical events. Jones has:

1 6 more shiny bright 1c pieces

2 and a statement from his accountant giving a figure for profit of 6c.

ACTIVITY 5.3

Open individual accounts to reflect Jones' balance sheet on 2 January (as before). Record in these and any other necessary accounts the increase in inventory figure leading to the 3 January balance sheet, then the full effect of the sales transaction on 4 January.

Inventory			Cash	
Bal b/f	40		Bal b/f 60	
Holding gain	4	44 Bal c/d		
	44	44		
Bal b/f	44			

Activity feedback

We have on 2 January, the inventory T account shows a debit of 40c and on 3 January, a total debit of 44c. In full we have on 2 January:

Capital		Holding gain	
	100 Bal b/f		4 Inventory

This enables us to show on 4 January:

Inventory	Cash	Capital
40	60	100

On 3 January we increase the inventory so as to bring the recorded figure up to the current level of replacement cost (RC). Thus there is a debit of 4c to inventory and a credit of 4c somewhere else. This credit cannot be to cash, neither can it be to capital, so it must be to a new T account. Now this 4c represents a gain that has arisen as a result of *holding* our inventory over a period of time. We did not sell it, but we held it over a period during which the replacement cost rose. We shall more formally refer to this gain as a holding gain. So on 3 January:

Inventory			Cash	
Bal b/f 44	44 to P&L		Bal b/f	60
			To P&L	50

Capital		Holding gain	
	100 Bal b/f		4 Bal b/f

P&L account			
Inventory sold	44	50 Cash sales	
Bal c/d	6		
	50	50	
		6 Bal b/f	

On the assumptions that Jones wishes to carry on selling and buying bags of sugar this is obviously the correct answer.

We have solved a major problem. We have shown the accountant how to produce a profit figure that actually makes physical sense and that Jones can actually believe. But we have created another difficulty. The statement from the accountant showed not only a *profit* of 6c, but also a separate, different *gain* of 4c. This gain of 4c occurred earlier than the profit. The gain was included in the balance sheet of 3 January and the profit did not appear until 4 January. We know that this 'gain' is not the same as profit – the whole point of all this is that the 'total' profit, i.e. the total increase in the capacity of the business to do things, is only 6c. So if the 'gain' is not profit, what on earth is it?

In the most simple of terms it is the double-entry for an increase in the recorded figure for an item of inventory.

CAPITAL MAINTENANCE

Given that we are considering a different profit concept from the traditional historic profit, we are necessarily implying also a different capital maintenance concept from that discussed in Activity 4.7.

ACTIVITY 5.4

Define clearly the capital maintenance concept implied by the T account calculations just examined.

Activity feedback

Profit could here be defined as the amount generated by the business over and above that necessary to replace the assets. The capital maintenance concept could therefore be said to be the maintenance of the capacity to replace the resources of the business.

A more rigorous analysis

If an item of inventory is bought for €10, held until its buying price increases to €12, and then sold for €15 then the HC profit is €15 − €10 = €5. But we know from the previous discussion that this can be split into two parts as follows.

During the time the inventory is held, the cost price rises from €10 to €12. There is therefore a holding gain of €2, giving a recorded inventory figure immediately before the sale of €12. When the inventory is sold, an asset of €12 (inventory) is transformed into an asset (cash) giving rise to a profit from operating of €3. Clearly we have split the HC profit into two elements, namely the operating profit (revenue minus current replacement cost) and the holding gain (current replacement cost minus original purchase cost). In these circumstances both elements would be regarded as 'realised' (see Chapter 1).

More normally, both realised and unrealised gains will be involved, as in the following example:

1 October 20X1	Buy 2 at €30
1 November 20X1	Sell 1 at €50, when RC is €35
31 December 20X1	RC is €38 .
31 January 20X2	Sell 1 at €60, when RC is €40

The HC profits are:

Year 1	50 − 30 = €20
Year 2	60 − 30 = €30

A fuller analysis gives the following:

1 Between 1 October and 1 November, there has been a holding gain of
   $2 \times (35 - 30) = €10$.

2 On 1 November one of the items is sold; therefore on 1 November:

(a) half of the holding gain becomes realised (i.e. $1 \times [35 - 30]$), as the item to which it relates has been sold.

(b) there is a (realised) operating profit of 50 − 35 = €15.

3 On 31 December there is an additional holding gain of 38 − 35 = €3. This will be unrealised as the item is still unsold. Between 31 December 20X1 and 31 January 20X2 there has been a holding gain of 40 − 38 = €2.

4 On 31 January the second item is sold and therefore:

(a) there is a (realised) operating gain of 60 − 40 = €20

(b) all the unrealised holding gain related to the second item becomes realised.

To summarise, for year 1 we have:

Operating profit	€15
Realised holding gain	€5
Unrealised holding gain	€8 (5 + 3 or 38 − 30)

For year 2 we have:

Operating profit	€20
Realised holding gain	€10
Unrealised holding gain	€0

Note carefully that the €10 holding gain realised in the year 2 includes the €8 holding gain that was *recognised* and *recorded* in year 1, but which had not become realised in year 1, as well as the €2 of holding gain recognised in year 2.

These figures demonstrate that the HC profit consists of two of the three elements involved:

HC profit = Operating profit + Realised holding gains

In year 1	€20 = 15 + 5
In year 2	€30 = 20 + 10

Notice that we include all the holding gains realised in the year, whether or not they have been recognised

(Continued)

ACTIVITY 5.4   (Continued)

and recorded (as unrealised) in earlier years. Edwards and Bell (1961) referred to the reported results under an RC system as business income, which they defined as follows:

$$\text{Business income} = \begin{cases} \text{Operating profit} + \text{Realised holding recognised in the} \\ \text{period} + \text{Unrealised holding gains recognised in the period} \end{cases}$$

Thus business income in year 1 is:

$$15 + 5 + 8 = €28$$

And in year 2 is:

$$20 + 2 + 0 = €22$$

Observe that the proportion of the realised holding gain in year 2 which had already been included in business income of year 1 (as an unrealised holding gain) is not included in year 2. To do so would, of course, involve double counting.

Examination will show that the differences between accounting (HC) income and business income are caused by different elements of the holding gains being included.

ACTIVITY 5.5

Derive the formal relationship between accounting income and business income and apply it to the preceding situation.

Activity feedback

Accounting income includes:

1 realised holding gains of the period recognised in the period

2 plus realised holding gains of the period recognised in previous periods.

Business income includes:

3 realised holding gains of the period recognised in the period

4 plus unrealised holding gains recognised in the period.

Since **1** and **3** are the same, it follows that:

Accounting income – 2 = Business income – 4

Or:

Accounting income = Business income – 4 + 2

(as defined earlier).

For the year 1   €20 = 28 – 8 + 0
For the year 2   €30 = 22 – 0 + 8

The important thing about all this analysis is that it enables us to discuss and decide which elements we wish to include in our own preferred definition of income. Edwards and Bell, arguing in favour of a current entry (RC) approach, include all the holding gains recognised in the period as being included in income. This has been criticised on two grounds. First, it is suggested that no unrealised gains should be included, as this would lack prudence. Second, and more importantly, it is suggested that all the holding gains, whether realised or unrealised, need to be retained in the business in order to enable it to replace resources as they are used. Using the terminology we developed earlier, the operating profit is the gain after having retained sufficient resources to enable us to do those things that we originally had the capacity to do. If we ask the question: 'How much profit can I remove without impairing the substance, the operating capability of the business?' then the answer is the operating profit. Only the operating profit should be regarded and reported as income. Holding gains, whether realised or not, should be excluded. This objection to the Edwards and Bell conclusion is generally regarded as a valid one and most authors argue that the central profit figure under a current entry value system should consist of the operating profit alone.

Remember the capital maintenance concept as we defined it in Activity 5.4, i.e. the maintenance of the

(Continued)

ACTIVITY 5.5   *(Continued)*

capacity to replace the resources of the business. The holding gains represent reserves – i.e. ownership claims on resources – corresponding to the resources which will have to be used in addition to replace existing assets if they are replaced at current prices. Income, within this capital maintenance requirement, therefore excludes all such holding gains.

In practice, the changes in cost levels are likely to be approximated to by the use of appropriate price indices. Activity 5.6 provides an example of the application of this mechanism to the principles already discussed. Study the activity carefully and try to at least rough out a solution before you work through the feedback which follows.

ACTIVITY 5.6

Chaplin Ltd's balance sheet on 31 December, year 1, after one year's trading was as follows:

	€			€	€
Capital – €1		Land and buildings at cost			110 000
Ordinary shares	200 000	Plant and equipment at cost	40 000		
Profit	26 000	*less* Depreciation	4 000		36 000
	226 000				146 000
Creditors	50 000	Inventory		90 000	
Loan	50 000	Debtors		90 000	
					180 000
	326 000				326 000

1 The capital and loan had been contributed in cash and the land and buildings, plant and equipment and opening inventory of €60 000 had been purchased on 1 January.

2 Transactions took place evenly during the year. The situation may therefore be treated as if all opening balances were held from 1 January until 30 June, as if all transactions took place on 30 June and as if all closing balances were held from 30 June until 31 December.

3 Price indices were as follows:

	General inflation	Plant	Inventory
1 January	100	100	100
30 June	110	105	115
31 December	120	110	130

4 The land and buildings were professionally valued at 31 December at €135 000.

Prepare a closing balance sheet on RC lines.

Activity feedback

Chaplin Ltd – RC solution
HC profit   26 000
less Adjustments:

Depreciation	$4\,000 \times \dfrac{(110 - 100)}{100}$	400	
Inventory	$60\,000 \times \dfrac{(115 - 100)}{100}$	9 000	9 400

Current operating profit   16 600
add Holding gains:

Inventory: realised as previously		9 000	
unrealised	$90\,000 \times \dfrac{(130 - 115)}{115}$	11 740	

(Continued)

ACTIVITY 5.6   (Continued)

Plant and equipment: realised as previously unrealised	$40\,000 \times \dfrac{110-100}{100} - 400$	400 3 600	
Land and buildings: unrealised	$135\,000 - 110\,000$	25 000	49 740
			€66 300

Business income

The general view today is that the holding gains should be shown separately as holding gains, rather than combining all gains of every sort as 'business income'. This leads to the following balance sheet:

		€
Share capital		200 000
Holding gain reserve		49 740
P&L account		16 600
		266 340
Loan		50 000
Creditors		50 000
		€366 340

Fixed assets

		€	€
Land and building			135 000
Plant and equipment	$40\,000 \times \dfrac{110}{100}$	44 000	
less Depreciation	$4\,000 \times \dfrac{110}{100}$	4 400	39 600
			174 600

Current assets

		€	€
Inventory	$90\,000 \times \dfrac{130}{115}$	101 740	
Debtors		90 000	191 740
			€366 340

In checking through Activity 5.6 note the treatment of the inventory gains; it is assumed that the opening inventory was all sold on 30 June, so the relevant holding gain is realised, the €90 000 closing inventory is treated as being purchased on 30 June and held ever since. Check that you understand the usage of all the index adjustments (and note the irrelevance of the general inflation index here). As regards the distinction between realised and unrealised holding gains, note that only the current operating profit can be distributed without impairing the ability to replace physical assets.

REPLACEMENT COST ACCOUNTING AND DEPRECIATION

ACTIVITY 5.7

There is one particular problem with replacement cost (RC) accounting and depreciation that is not revealed by the Chaplin illustration. Consider the following:

A fixed asset costs €100, has an expected useful life of four years, with zero scrap value and the RC of a new asset rises by €20 each year. Calculate the profit and loss (P&L) account charge and show the balance sheet position, for each of the first two years, under RC.

Activity feedback

The year 1 position is simple enough. We have:

Cost (RC)	€120
Depreciation (25%) (in P&L a/c)	30
Balance sheet	€ 90

But year 2 is problematic. From a P&L account viewpoint we have an RC figure of €140 and we have had

(Continued)

ACTIVITY 5.7 *(Continued)*

25% of the benefit, therefore we should have an expense to match of 25% of 140 = €35. This leaves total accumulated depreciation of €65 and a balance sheet figure of €75 (140 – 65). But taking a balance sheet view we have an asset with an RC of €140 that is exactly half used up. Therefore, again following the matching convention, we should have accumulated depreciation of exactly half of €140, leaving a balance sheet figure also of exactly half of €140 to carry forward for future matching. This implies an expense figure in year 2 of €40 (closing depreciation balance €70, opening balance €30, therefore necessary charge for this year €40).

We are obviously in trouble. In year 2 we need a €35 charge in the P&L account (25% 140) and at the same time a deduction of €40 (70 – 30) in the balance sheet. From a double-entry viewpoint this is somewhat disturbing. This problem is usually solved by the idea of backlog depreciation. The year 2 balance sheet deduction is regarded as consisting of two elements:

1 the proper annual charge (€35)

2 the extra figure necessary to bring the accumulated depreciation at the beginning of year 2 up to what it would have been if the current (end of year 2) RC had been prevailing earlier (€5).

Thus we have a credit of €40 to depreciation provision, a debit of €35 to P&L account and a debit of €5 to – well, where?

Since the €5 relates in effect to the correction of what we now know with hindsight to have been under-depreciation in earlier years, one possibility would seem to be to reduce the accumulated revenue reserves figure brought forward – like a prior year adjustment. By the same token, the earlier years' accounts were certainly correct at that time with the matching convention properly applied in the then current circumstances. It could be argued that the problem of this backlog adjustment is covered by the existence and recording of holdings gains. Therefore the €5 could be 'charged to' holding gain account. This last argument is usually followed. This would give year 2 balance sheet entries as follows in our example:

Fixed asset	RC		140
	Depreciation		70
	(Net book value) NBV		70
Holding gain reserve	b/f	20	
	add	20	
	less	5	35

CURRENT ENTRY VALUES: PRELIMINARY APPRAISAL

ACTIVITY 5.8

Prepare a list, in point form, of advantages and disadvantages which you think could reasonably be said to apply to current entry value accounting.

Activity feedback
Possible, but not necessarily exhaustive, suggestions are as follows:

Advantages

1 It provides more information in that it splits the total profit into holding gains and operating profit. This permits better appraisal of earlier actions and provides more useful data for decision-making purposes.

2 By permitting holding gains to be excluded from reported profit, it allows for a proper maintenance of operating capacity – the 'business substance'.

3 It provides a balance sheet based on current value, on figures relevant to the date of the balance sheet.

4 It is consistent with accounting concepts – if holding gains are excluded from reported profit it is more prudent than HC.

5 Holding gains are recognised and reported when they occur.

(Continued)

ACTIVITY 5.8 *(Continued)*

6 Comparisons over time, and performance analysis, are more valid and meaningful.

7 It is practicable, it has been shown to be feasible in practical application.

Disadvantages

1 It requires more subjectivity (or arbitrary choice between different available indices). It is therefore less 'auditable'.

2 It requires the use of replacement cost figures for assets that the firm does not intend, or perhaps could not possibly, replace.

3 It still fails to give an indication either of the current market value of most assets in their present state or of the business as a whole.

4 It fails to take account of general inflation, of changes in the purchasing power of money.

You may recall from the array of value concepts analysed by Edwards and Bell that they suggested that two different concepts of current entry value were worthy of more detailed consideration. They named and defined these as:

1 *Present cost* – the cost currently of acquiring the asset being valued.

2 *Current cost* – the cost currently of acquiring the inputs which the firm used to produce the asset being valued.

So far in this chapter we have ignored this distinction. We would suggest, broadly following the thinking of Edwards and Bell themselves, that the route to making a rational choice between them lies in remembering the underlying arguments for using current entry values in the first place. As we saw in Activity 5.4 we are seeking the maintenance of the capacity to replace the resources of the business. We are therefore seeking to ensure the continued long-run operation of the business. The approach we need to adopt, therefore, is that which accords with the expected operations of the firm in the ordinary course of its business. Given that the going concern convention applies and given that the firm is going to continue operations in the long run, it is clear that current cost rather than present cost (both as defined earlier) will better reflect the reality of transactions and economic events in most cases. To a firm in business to manufacture motorcars and aiming for long-run operations as a manufacturer of motorcars, it is the cost of the replacement inputs which it needs to manufacture motorcars which is the relevant datum to ensure the maintenance of operating capacity. The cost to a manufacturer of motorcars of buying in complete motorcars (at present cost) is not normally an operationally relevant figure.

So it is argued that current cost is normally the appropriate current entry value to use, on the grounds of its relevance to normal ongoing business operations. It follows, however, that where this justification ceases to be true, because, for example, the inputs are no longer available, then the conclusion may well no longer be correct. If the firm *would* as a matter of expected action (not merely *should* as a matter of efficient management) replace an asset in a more complete state than with the previous raw components, then the appropriate present cost should be used instead.

It could be suggested that in arguing for the relevance of current cost as a useful entry value measure leading to the practical maintenance of operational capability, we are failing to follow properly the logic of the arguments put forward. The essence of the whole thinking is that a firm should charge as an expense the costs of replacing the resources used or consumed. Past (historical) costs are useless for this purpose. But what is theoretically needed is obviously the amount that *will* have to be paid for the replacement items at the time when they are replaced. The *current* cost may or may not be identical to the actual cost when replacement eventually occurs. In many cases current cost will be the same as expected actual cost. But if it is not, should we make some adjustment?

Theoretically, at least from the viewpoint of the income statement and capital maintenance in the operating sense, the answer seems to be yes. But there are at least two arguments against this. The first is the essentially practical one that a considerably greater degree of subjectivity is introduced which may more than outweigh the theoretical advantages. The second argument is that there are perhaps implications for the matching principle and the balance sheet. A current entry value balance sheet can be argued as being consistent within itself, giving proper additivity in the mathematical sense. But a future entry value balance sheet, with the timing implications of the word future being different for different items, is of more suspect validity. And since today's asset figure affects next period's results there are possible implications for future periods too.

SUMMARY

In this chapter we have explored the logic of using current entry values for the preparation of accounting results, analysed the effects and usefulness of the additional information derived, related the approach to capital maintenance and prepared and interpreted current entry value information.

The main advantages of current entry value accounting lie in its effects on the profit and loss account information given. It can be argued as giving more effective application of the matching and accruals conventions (*current* costs against current revenues) and, through its long-run economically rational capital maintenance concept, of the going concern convention. It provides important information, at minimum, about those elements of historical cost profit which do not represent increases in economic wealth (given continuing operation). As regards the balance sheet it gives figures based on up-to-date market numbers. However, the approach is still clearly to determine profit and loss figures and then to 'stick what is left' in the balance sheet. The balance sheet is still essentially a statement of unexpired expenses, not a list of marketable assets at valuation.

EXERCISES

Suggested answers to exercises marked ✓ are to be found on the Student side of the companion website.

Suggested answers to the remaining exercises are to be found on the Instructor side of the companion website.

1   Explain and demonstrate how replacement cost accounting affects reported profit as compared with historical cost accounting.

✓ 2   Is replacement cost accounting more or less prudent than historical cost accounting?

3   Under a replacement cost accounting system, which holding gains should be reported as:

(a)   realised

(b)   part of profit

(c)   distributable?

Why?

4   In general, replacement cost accounting produces reported profit figures which are a better indication of long-run future performance than historical cost accounting does. Discuss.

5   A replacement cost balance sheet is just as useless as a historical cost balance sheet. Discuss.

✓ **6**   I.M. Confused, computer dealer.

From the following information compute

(a)   Profit and loss accounts and closing balance sheets for each of the years 20X1 and 20X2 under historical cost principles.

(b)   Profit and loss accounts and closing balance sheets for each of the years 20X1 and 20X2 under current replacement cost principles.

Comment briefly on the significance of the results.

Date	Event relating to trading in computers	'Wealth' Computers	€ cash
01/01/X1	Set up business with €10 000 in the bank		10 000
02/01/X1	Buy six computers for €1 000 each	6	4 000
01/05/X1	Sell two for €1 500 each (RC = €1 100)	4	7 000
01/09/X1	Buy two computers for €1 200 each	6	4 600
01/10/X1	Pay annual rent of €600	6	4 000
31/12/X1	Financial year-end. Pay tax of €200	6	3 800
03/03/X2	Sell two computers for €1 800 each (RC = €1 300)	4	7 400
01/10/X2	Pay annual rent €700	4	6 700
01/11/X2	Buy two computers for €1 400 each	6	3 900
31/12/X2	Financial year-end. Pay tax €450	6	3 450

7   Mallard Co. was formed on 1 January 20X1 with 10 000 issued €1 ordinary shares. The same day they obtained a 12% loan of €8 000 and bought fixed assets for €9 000. During 20X1 their purchases and sales of widgets were as follows:

	Purchases		Sales	
3 January	100 at €80	8 000		
1 February			60 at €120	7 200
1 April	110 at €75	8 250		
1 May			90 at €120	10 800
1 July	100 at €85	8 500		
1 August			130 at €120	15 600
1 October	120 at €90	10 800		
1 November			110 at €130	14 300

(a)   Purchases and sales were all paid for in cash.

(b)   The loan interest was paid early in the following year (20X2).

(c)   The buying price of widgets changed on 1 March, 1 June, 1 September and on 1 December (when it was €100).

(d)   The fixed assets are to be depreciated at 10% p.a. At 31 December 20X1 their buying price was €12 600.

(e)   General expenses during the year were €13 200.

(i)   Prepare a balance sheet as at 31 December, 20X1 together with a trading profit and loss account for the year to 31 December 20X1, on replacement cost lines.

(ii)   What are holding gains? In what circumstances are they distributable?

8   *L and H*

On 1 January, L and H each started a business by investing €100 in cash, and then immediately purchasing one widget.

L sold her widget on 3 March for €110, but on 1 April discovered that she needed to pay this to buy another, which she did.

On 30 June this was sold for €120, and a new one bought in July for €120.

On 29 September this was sold for €130, and a replacement purchased on 30 September for €130.

H had been less active and had merely kept his first widget and read the newspaper. Both have decided to adopt 30 September as their accounting date, and come to you for accounting services.

(a)   How would the above appear under

   (i)   historic cost

   (ii)   replacement cost.

(b)   Which results make more sense, and why?

CURRENT EXIT VALUE AND MIXED VALUES

6

OBJECTIVES After studying this chapter you should be able to:

- explain the effects and implications of using current exit values to record the possession and usage of economic resources

- outline the implications of using an ad hoc mixture of valuation methods

- define and explain the effects and implications of deprival values as the basis of recording the possession and usage of economic resources

- discuss the overall relevance of current values

- outline the concept of fair value.

INTRODUCTION

In this chapter we look first of all at remaining current values worthy of consideration, current output or exit values. We then explore the possibility of using a combination of different valuation methods in preparing financial reports and, in particular, the concept of deprival value. In each case, as in earlier chapters, we seek to investigate both the techniques and logic of calculation and the meaning and usefulness of the resulting information.

CURRENT EXIT VALUE ACCOUNTING

Edwards and Bell suggested two current exit value concepts as worthy of consideration (see p. 68). These were current values and opportunity costs.

Current values they defined as 'values actually realised during the current period for goods or services sold'. On reflection, however, it quickly becomes apparent that the idea of substituting current values so defined into our basic equation of $W_1 + P - D = W_2$ does not make a great deal of sense. Values actually realised for goods and services already sold cannot obviously be argued as relevant to resources still possessed at the date or dates under consideration. Rather, of course, these realised values are the basis of revenue flows.

It is the second concept, that of opportunity costs, which we need to develop. Edwards and Bell (1961) defined this as 'values that could currently be realised if assets were sold (without further processing) outside the firm at the best prices immediately obtainable'. This is certainly a concept relevant to the resources possessed at the date under consideration. It shows the amount of money we could derive immediately (currently) from the resources held, or to take the alternative viewpoint it shows the amount of money we choose not to derive immediately if we retain the resources for any reason. We can adapt the application of the definition slightly to allow for further unavoidable processing or expenses of disposal and consider the concept of net realisable value (NRV), i.e. the proceeds after deducting these additional unavoidable expenses of disposal. These ideas are explored further in this chapter.

We intend to base our valuation figure on the current market selling price, more precisely, on NRV. So if an asset could be sold for €250, but the sale would involve €10 of selling expenses, the NRV is €240. The income under this method is based on the difference between the NRV of all resources at the two chosen dates. Following Edwards and Bell, it is often referred to as realisable income. It can be defined as follows:

$$Y_r = D + (R_e - R_s)$$

where Y_r is the exit value income, D is the distributions (less new capital inputs), R_e is the NRV of the assets at the end of the period and R_s is the NRV of the assets at the start of the period.

In practice, several possibilities exist as to exactly what we mean by NRV.

ACTIVITY 6.1

Consider an item of work in progress that has an NRV today of €10 in its existing state. The finished product (which would require a further €4 of expenses) has an NRV today of €20, but by the time the actual item of current work in progress is finished and sold, it is expected to have an NRV of €22. On a forced sale (e.g. if all the assets have to be sold off at once by a liquidator), the item in its existing state would realise €6.

Suggest possible figures for the exit value and which one you would normally find most useful.

Activity feedback

Possible figures for the exit value would seem to include €6, €10, €(20 − 4) and €(22 − 4). It is generally agreed that exit values should refer to assets in their existing state, on the assumption that they are sold in an orderly manner, i.e. in the normal course of business. Thus in our example the exit value for the work in progress would be €10.

It is clear that the exit value capital (R) at any particular date shows the amount of money that the business

ACTIVITY 6.1   (Continued)

could obtain from its assets as on that date. Turning this round, exit value is seen as an opportunity cost concept – it shows the amount of cash that the business could obtain if it did not keep the asset. The opportunity cost of having an asset is the amount of cash the business sacrifices by retaining the asset instead. Advocates of exit value accounting argue that it is necessary to know the cash resources tied up in a business in order to measure efficiency. The amount of cash potentially available – the 'current cash equivalent' of the resources of a business – also provides a genuinely common measuring unit when comparing different businesses.

It is often argued – indeed often merely stated – that exit value accounting does not conform to the going concern convention. Its advocates argue that it is not intended to show what will happen, rather it is intended to show the results of what could happen, in order to assist decision-making and internal appraisal.

We can usefully divide the exit value income (Y_r) into four elements:

Y_r = realised operating gains
  + unrealised operating gains   i.e. on assets held for resale

  + realised non-operating gains
  + unrealised non-operating gains   i.e. on assets held for use

Before looking at an example, it is important to understand the effect of exit value accounting on the P&L account. Since the opening and closing balance sheets are now value based, and not cost based, it necessarily follows that the P&L account is also value based and not cost based. For example 'depreciation' is no longer a process of cost allocation under the matching convention. It simply becomes the loss in value of the asset in the period. This is such a fundamental change that it would be better to invent a different word, but unfortunately nobody has yet done so.

Now work through the following example. Remember particularly that an unrealised gain in year 1, reported as such, will become a realised gain in a later year and will need to be reported as a realised gain. Care is needed to ensure that gains are not reported twice, as both unrealised and realised. This of course would be double counting.

Example

A company commences business with capital in cash of €15 000. It buys a fixed asset for €10 000. The following information is available:

	Year 1		Year 2	
	€		€	
NRV of fixed asset	6 000		4 000	
Sales	20 000		25 000	
Cost of sales	11 000		12 000	
Closing inventory: cost	2 000		3 000	
NRV	2 500		3 800	
Exit value revenue statements				
Sales	20 000		25 000	
Cost of sales	11 000		12 000	
	9 000		13 000	
'Depreciation'	4 000	(1)	2 000	(2)
	5 000		11 000	
less Operating gain included in previous year	–		500	(3)
	5 000		10 500	
add Unrealised operating gain	500	(4)	800	(5)
Realisable income	5 500		11 300	

| | Year 1 | | Year 2 | |
	€		€	
Exit value balance sheets				
Fixed assets	6 000		4 000	
Inventory	2 500		3 800	
Cash	12 000	(6)	24 000	(7)
	20 500		31 800	
Capital	15 000		15 000	
Realisable income	5 500		16 800	
	20 500		31 800	

Notes

1 10 000 – 6 000

2 6 000 – 4 000

3 Included as realised in the 11 000, but already included, as unrealised, in the 5 500 for year 1

4 2 500 – 2 000

5 3 800 – 3 000

6 15 000 – 10 000 + 20 000 – (11 000 + 2 000)

7 12 000 + 25 000 – (12 000 + 1 000)

The unrealised gain on inventory is here calculated on an annual basis, inventory during the year being left at cost. It would be possible, although more complicated, to record such unrealised gains more frequently – even daily if desired. Care must be taken, however, to ensure that a previously recorded unrealised gain is not again added into 'realisable income' when it is realised.

Now try the following activity, making a proper attempt before looking at the feedback which follows.

ACTIVITY 6.2

Bonds plc commenced business on 1 January year 7. Let us assume all transactions are by cheque and no credit is given or taken and that Bonds plc deals only in one type of item of inventory.

1 January Year 7
Introduced capital of €25 000 and purchased a machine for €9 000.
Purchased 500 items of inventory for €15 each.

31 December Year 7
Sold 300 items of inventory for €30 each.
Paid rent for the year of €1 000.
Paid other expenses for the year of €1 000.

1 January Year 8
Purchased 400 items of inventory for €17 each.

31 December Year 8
Sold 500 items of inventory for €33 each.
Paid rent for the year of €1 100.
Paid expenses for the year of €1 200.

The following information relates to the machine:

| | 31.12.7 | 31.12.8 |
	€	€
Replacement cost	10 000	12 000
Realisable value	8 000	6 000
Cost of realisation	1 000	1 000

Required Produce a set of realisable value accounts for years 7 and 8.

ACTIVITY 6.2   (Continued)

Activity feedback
Bonds plc Trading and P&L account for the year ended 31 December

	31.12.7		31.12.8	
	€		€	
Sales		9 000		16 500
Less cost of				
sales		(4 500)		(8 100)
Gross profit		4 500		8 400
Rent	1 000		1 100	
Expenses	1 000		1 200	
Depreciation				
(note 2)	2 000		2 000	
		(4 000)		(4 300)
Gross profit		500		4 100
Holding gain				
(note 3)		3 000		(1 400)
		3 500		2 700

Balance sheet as at 31 December

	31.12.7		31.12.8	
	€		€	
Fixed assets				
Machine at NRV		7 000		5 000
Current assets				
Inventory at NRV				
(note 1)	6 000		3 300	
Bank	15 500		22 900	
		21 500		26 200
		28 500		31 200
Share capital		25 000		25 000
Profit		3 500		6 200
		28 500		31 200

2 *Depreciation.* The depreciation is the difference between the NRV of the asset at the end of each year less the NRV of the asset at the beginning of the year. Note that the NRV is after deducting the costs of realising the asset.

Year 1	€7 000	–	€9 000
Year 2	€5 000	–	€7 000

3 *Holding gain.* In year 7 the holding gain is the unrealised holding gain on the closing inventory:

200 units × €15 (i.e. €30 – €15) = €3 000

In year 8 the holding gain of year 7 has now been realised (and therefore included in the trading account for year 8) while there is an unrealised holding gain on the closing stock of:

100 units × €16 (i.e. €33 – €17) = €1 600

Therefore, in year 8 the holding gain (loss) is:

	€
Unrealised holding gain in year 8	1 600
less: unrealised holding gain from year 7 now realised in year 8	3 000
	(1 400)

In effect we have a holding loss.

Notes
1 The inventory is also brought into the balance sheet at the end of each year at its net realisable value.

31.12.7	200 units × €30 = €6 000
31.12.8	100 units × €33 = €3 300

CURRENT EXIT VALUES: PRELIMINARY APPRAISAL

ACTIVITY 6.3

Prepare a list, in point form, of advantages and disadvantages which you think could reasonably be said to apply to current exit value accounting.

Activity feedback

Advantages

1 It follows the economic 'opportunity cost' principle. It reveals the money sacrifice being made by keeping an asset. This permits rational decision-making on the alternative uses of resources.

2 Exit values facilitate comparisons. They provide a genuinely common measure for the value of assets – cash or current cash equivalent.

3 The concept of realisable value is easy for the non-accountant to understand.

4 Useful information about assets is provided to outsiders, e.g. creditors.

5 It is already widely used, e.g. debtors, inventory at lower of historical cost (HC) and NRV, revaluation of land and buildings.

Disadvantages

1 It is highly subjective. Arguably more so than replacement cost (RC) accounting.

2 It fails to follow the going concern assumption, fails to recognise that firms do not usually sell all their assets (the proponents of exit value accounting explicitly deny this charge, arguing that it makes no assumptions either way, it merely provides useful information).

3 It fails to concentrate attention on long-run operational effectiveness.

4 It fails to give realistic information about the internal usefulness of assets – particularly of highly specialised assets that could have a very low NRV on the general market.

You may, of course, have some slightly different views. One point we should certainly consider is the possible relevance of expected values, which Edwards and Bell (1961) suggested to be a concept worth further exploration. They defined expected values (see Table 4.2) as 'values expected to be received in the future for output sold according to the firm's planned course of action'. Expected values are therefore a future exit rather than a current exit way of thinking. Expected values defined in this way certainly give useful information. In fact they form the raw material for the preparation of both cash and revenue budget statements. However, our essential purpose here is to prepare statements of current position and similar arguments apply to those already considered in relation to future entry values. To use future exit values would introduce greater subjectivity, greater possible inconsistency of evaluation and could be argued as failing to reflect current reality. Current exit values are suggested as a more useful concept.

It is essential to remember that exit value NRV accounting tends to focus on the balance sheet to a considerably greater extent than current entry value RC accounting. Profit or gain is very much determined by a consideration of changes in output values of resources. The balance sheet under NRV can be regarded as a consistent statement, with all figures on the same basis and as at the same date. This balance sheet is not just a list of 'balances left over' in the sense that a current entry value balance sheet is (see Chapter 5). However, it follows from this that it is the profit and loss calculation which in a sense picks up and contains 'the figures lying around'. Current exit value is essentially a short-run concept. It provides valuable information about market values of business resources and therefore about short-term alternatives and possibilities. This is clearly seen in the capital maintenance concept associated with NRV. This could be expressed as: the maintenance of the NRV, the current cash equivalent, of the resources of the business. But exit value accounting information does not provide us with the information necessary for management to seek to ensure the long-run operational capability of the business.

MIXED VALUES – AD HOC METHODS

As we shall see in detail later on, companies following IAS, and also some national systems, may have a great deal of flexibility in practice as regards the valuation policy they wish to adopt. There is no requirement for any consistency of approach as between one asset and another. It is in fact extremely common for businesses that broadly follow historical cost accounting principles to revalue some of their fixed assets at intervals (not necessarily annually), sometimes then depreciating on the revalued figure, sometimes not depreciating at all. This may well lead to the provision of more useful information as regards particular resources. For example, a current or recent valuation of land or factory is surely more useful than a 50-year-old cost figure. But, of course, it further increases the inconsistencies within the accounting reports as a whole, making the balance sheet as a statement of resources and the sources thereof ever more difficult to understand, usually influencing the size of expense figures charged and certainly influencing any interpretational ratios relating return with the source base being employed.

MIXED VALUES – DEPRIVAL VALUE

A much more theoretically defensible approach to the idea of using different valuation bases for different assets, or more accurately for using different valuation bases for assets in different circumstances, is the concept of deprival value.

Assume that a business owns an asset. What is that asset 'worth' to the business? The deprival value (DV) approach says that the DV of an asset is the loss that the rational businessman or businesswoman would suffer if he or she were deprived of the asset. This loss will depend on what would rationally have been done with the asset if he or she had not lost (been deprived of) it.

ACTIVITY 6.4

Six people, A to F, are possessors and owners of six assets, U to Z, respectively. The various monetary evaluations (in €) of each asset by its owner are shown in the following table.

Person	Asset	HC	RC	NRV	EV
A	U	1	2	3	4
B	V	5	6	8	7
C	W	9	12	10	11
D	X	16	15	14	13
E	Y	17	19	20	18
F	Z	23	22	21	24

All six people signed a contract with an insurance agent, Miss Prue Dential, under which they shall be reimbursed, in the event of loss of their assets, by 'the amount of money a rationally acting person will actually have lost as a result of losing the asset'.

Put yourself in the position of the rationally acting person, decide what action you would take in each circumstance and then calculate the net effect on your monetary position.

Activity feedback

In each situation the first question to ask is: Would the rationally acting businessman or businesswoman replace the asset or not? He or she will replace it if the proceeds of *either* selling it (NRV) *or* using it (economic value, EV) are higher than the costs of replacing it. If it is going to be replaced, then the loss suffered is clearly the cost of replacement. Thus, in situations where the rationally acting businessman or businesswoman would replace the asset, DV is RC. If he or she would not replace it, the loss suffered is given by the value of the benefits that *would have derived from* the asset but which he or she will now never receive. Being rational, the intention must have been to act

(Continued)

ACTIVITY 6.4   (Continued)

so as to derive the highest possible return, i.e. the higher of NRV and economic value (EV). Therefore, in situations where the rationally acting businessman or business-woman would not replace the asset if deprived of it, DV is the higher of NRV and EV. This last element, the higher of NRV and EV, is known as the 'recoverable amount'.

So we can formally state that DV is the lower of RC and recoverable amount, where recoverable amount is the higher of NRV and EV (see Figure 6.1). Given three different concepts (RC, NRV and EV) there are in fact only six possible different rankings:

EV	>	NRV	>	RC
NRV	>	EV	>	RC
RC	>	EV	>	NRV
RC	>	NRV	>	EV
NRV	>	RC	>	EV
EV	>	RC	>	NRV

The example contains all six of these alternatives. The DV in each situation is as follows:

FIGURE 6.1   Relationship between DV, RC, NRV and EV

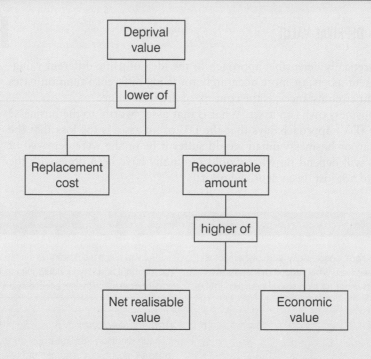

Person	DV	Reason
A	2	Cost of replacement
B	6	Cost of replacement
C	11	EV not received
D	14	Realisable value not received
E	19	Cost of replacement
F	22	Cost of replacement

Make sure that you understand why, in the context of the logic of the DV definition (and notice the irrelevance of the HC figures).

DEPRIVAL VALUE: APPRAISAL

Deprival value (DV) has a clearly definable concept of capital maintenance. Profit is here being regarded as the excess after maintaining the 'value to the business' of its assets. The value to the business is clearly seen to be related to actual operations (what the business would do). Following from this, we can say that DV seeks to maintain the business's capacity to do things, usually expressed as the *operating capacity* or *operating capability*. We saw earlier that in four of the six possible rankings, DV equals RC. In the practical business situation, the chances of replacement cost being higher than both NRV and EV will generally be relatively small, so the other two rankings will in practice not occur frequently. This means that in a practical business context, DV usually comes back to RC.

Theoretically, therefore, it can be suggested that deprival value provides an improvement and refinement on current replacement cost accounting. It reduces itself to replacement cost when the economically logical action is to replace and uses the more relevant benefit foregone figure in those situations where replacement would logically not occur. Notice, of course, that it is not strictly a completely current concept at all, as the EV possibility is a future orientation. Another way to look at the implications of the previous discussions would be to take the more practical line of arguing that deprival value shows that replacement cost is relevant most of the time. In other words, deprival value thinking positively explores the possibilities of refining replacement cost thinking and shows that in most situations the refinements introduce difficulty and subjectivity, for very little benefit in terms of extra relevance of information.

As a final thought, what about additivity? Is deprival value a separate concept, leading to a balance sheet consistently valued in deprival terms? Or is deprival value merely a formula for choosing which of the three (RC, NRV, EV) valuation bases to use in any particular situation? Under the latter way of thinking, deprival value obviously leads to a variety of bases in the balance sheet and therefore to a lack of additivity.

ACTIVITY 6.5

Prepare a list, in point form, of advantages and disadvantages which you think could reasonably be said to apply to deprival value accounting.

Activity feedback

Advantages

1 All the advantages of RC accounting can be claimed here also.

2 As a 'mixed value' system it is more realistic and relevant than either RC or NRV. It values resources at RC if it is profitable to replace them and at the expected proceeds if they would not be replaced.

Disadvantages

1 Disadvantages 1, 3 and 4 of RC accounting can be claimed here too.

2 It is more subjective than RC.

3 If the balance sheet is expressed in 'mixed values', what do the asset and capital employed totals mean? Can mixed values be validly added at all?

4 Firms are not in practice being continually deprived of their assets.

FAIR VALUES

The concept of fair value seems to have become popular in recent years. It is very important to be careful how you use the phrase and even more important to work out very carefully how another author has used it when you come across it. It seems sometimes to be used loosely and vaguely to mean 'current value' or 'market value'. It appears in US regulations from around the early 1980s, but apparently with a slightly different meaning from that discussed here.

We take fair value, here, as having the general IASB definition, used in a number of standards and in the IASB glossary of terms:

> Fair value is the amount for which an asset could be exchanged, or a liability settled, between knowledgeable willing parties in an arm's length transaction.

The concept of fair value in IAS regulations has emerged gradually over the last 20 years or so. Comparing IAS 41 (Agriculture, issued in 2001) with IAS 40 (Investment

---

ACTIVITY 6.6

S takes a product to market, incurring transport costs of €2 and exchanges it with B, in an arm's length (i.e. independent) transaction at an agreed exchange price of €30. B takes the product to his own entity, incurring transport costs of €3. Calculate each of the following within the limits of the given data:

(a) S's selling price

(b) S's net realisable value

(c) B's buying price

(d) B's historical cost

(e) B's current replacement cost

(f) Fair value to S before the sale

(g) Fair value to B after the sale

Activity feedback

Answers would seem to be as follows:

(a)	S's selling price	€30
(b)	S's net realisable value	€28
(c)	B's buying price	€30
(d)	B's historical cost	€33
(e)	B's current replacement cost	€33
(f)	Fair value to S before sale	€30
(g)	Fair value to B after purchase	€30

A number of points emerge: **(a)** and **(c)** are necessarily equal, **(f)** and **(g)** are necessarily equal at least instantaneously before and after the transaction. Further **(a)**, **(c)**, **(f)** and **(g)** are all necessarily equal. Third, **(b)** < **(c)** < **(e)**,

i.e. in the general case where disposal and acquisition costs are not nil:

$$NRV < Fair\ value < CRC$$

So, is fair value an entry value, an exit value, both or neither?

The short answer seems to be that nobody is quite sure. We suggest that two propositions can safely be made. First, from a theoretical perspective, taking the definition at face value and ignoring transaction costs, fair value is both entry and exit value at the same time. Since it is the agreed price between buyer and seller, there can be no other answer.

Second, from a practical point of view and allowing for the reality of transaction costs, it is arguably neither, being in between NRV (an operational exit value) and CRC (an operational entry value), as Activity 6.6 illustrates.

These two propositions taken together arguably suggest that the fair value concept as defined by IASB breaks down on rigorous examination and can neither be rationally analysed and positioned within the analysis of alternatives created in these chapters nor operationalised without the introduction of market costs, with which the definition is incompatible. When you come across this fair value concept in the context of particular applications and IASs, as you will a number of times in Part Two, try to relate the application to the general issues discussed here. The implications of the fair value concept, both theoretically and in practice, have not yet been fully explored. But the IASB's enthusiasm for fair value is still increasing.

Properties, issued in 2000) it is clear that the concept is still developing. It is also very important to note that IAS requirements based on the fair value concept do not necessarily require the actual recorded figure (carrying value) to be fair value as defined in the relevant standard. Details are discussed in the appropriate chapters in Part Two. Fair value is also closely related to the idea of asset impairment, discussed in several places in Part Two, especially Chapter 14. The general points to note are:

- Fair value may not necessarily be defined or operationalised identically in all situations.
- Carrying value may differ from fair value (and for different reasons) under particular standards.

Here we are concerned only to attempt an understanding and analysis of the central concept. This has its difficulties. IASB seems to be working backwards from the pronouncements in its standards and is now recognising the need to clarify fair value as a theoretical concept and we are forced to follow the same process. Creating the concept clearly, before applying it, would be a more valid scientific process. (See Activity 6.6)

The IASB and other regulators round the world have been giving much attention in recent years to the problem of how fair value can be obtained in practice. The general IASB view is illustrated by the example in IAS 40 (paras 45 and 46, see Chapter 12) that the best evidence of fair value is normally given by current prices on an active market for similar property in the same location and condition and subject to similar lease and other contracts.

In the absence of current prices on an active market, an entity considers information from a variety of sources, including:

- Current prices in an active market for properties of a different nature, condition or location (or subject to different lease or other contracts), adjusted to reflect those differences.
- Recent prices of similar properties on less active markets, with adjustments to reflect any changes in economic conditions since the date of the transaction that occurred at those prices.
- Discounted cash flows, supported by the terms of any existing lease and other contracts and by any external evidence such as current market rents for similar properties in the same location and condition, and using discount rates that reflect current market assessments of the uncertainty in the amount and timing of the cash flows.

An interesting slant on all this is given by the discussion paper, 'Measurement Bases for Financial Accounting – Measurement on Initial Recognition' (IASB, 2005). This document was written by staff of the Canadian Accounting Standards Board, and published for discussion by the IASB, and several other bodies. This proposes a four-level measurement hierarchy for assets and liabilities on initial recognition, as follows.

Level 1 – observable market prices; any adjustments are consistent with those that market participants can be expected to make.
Level 2 – accepted valuation models or techniques; all significant inputs are consistent with those which market participants can be expected to use.

Level 3 – current cost (i.e. reproduction cost and replacement cost); with the possibility of substituting historical cost, provided a reliable estimate can be made and the amount can be expected to be recoverable.

Level 4 – models and techniques that use entity-specific inputs only; when unavoidable and when not demonstrably inconsistent with those which market participants can be expected to use.

The discussion paper then makes two very significant further propositions.

1 Only Level 1 and 2 measurements should be described as 'fair value'. Level 3 and 4 measurement bases have sufficient relevance and reliability to be used as substitutes for fair value, but are not sufficiently based on market expectations to be described as 'fair value'.

2 If none of the above measurement alternatives is feasible, the item in question fails to meet the conditions for recognition as an asset or liability.

In essence, therefore, this discussion paper gives a significant push towards current values in general and towards fair value in particular, but also strongly insists that fair value, as such, must be genuinely based on *market* expectations, i.e. again, not entity-specific.

It remains to be seen how the debate progresses. However, the comment letter from EFRAG, circulated in July 2006, contains the following paragraph:

> We think that a number of important statements the paper makes are neither generally accepted nor justified in the paper. We are also not convinced by the reasoning underlying a number of important conclusions. For example – and probably most important of all – we are not convinced by the arguments advanced in the paper in support of the statements that (a) the market value measurement objective provides superior information to entity-specific measurement objectives, at least on initial recognition (paragraph 60) and (b) fair value is more relevant than measurement bases that depend on entity-specific expectations (paragraph 102). If the arguments in the paper are the only arguments in favour that exist and have been expressed in the paper in the best way possible, we do not understand how the paper could have reached the conclusions it has.

We tend to be supportive of current values, regard fair value as a valid contender for an appropriate current value, but, like EFRAG, are not at all convinced by the apparent determination to avoid entity-specific measurements. If a user of financial statements is making a detailed comparison of, say, Daimler-Benz and Peugeot-Citroen, surely figures related to Daimler-Benz and Peugeot-Citroen are likely to be more relevant than figures related to the world markets for steel, rubber, cars, etc. Let the debate continue!

Parallel to the theoretical uncertainty of what fair value actually implies in terms of real-life calculation, there is great political uncertainty regarding the future of, and desirability of, the use of fair values. As a general, and oversimplified, comment, we suggest that the greater the emphasis by users of published financial reports on the estimation of long-run cash flows, and therefore on long-run profitability, the greater the support for fair values in some form is likely to be. It follows from the discussions on user needs in Chapter 1 and on international differences in Chapter 2, that those countries and traditions tending to take a common law economic focus are likely to be more receptive to fair values than those taking a code law legislation focus. It further follows within any given tradition that, other things equal, companies whose shares are actually traded are likely to be relatively favourable towards fair values, whereas companies where the only users in practice are creditors/bankers and taxation authorities are likely to be critical.

The implications of these tensions and differences are nowhere near resolution amongst legal and regulatory authorities. A further complication is that the American regulators, the FASB, at the same time as professing a desire for convergence with the IASB have issued, in FAS 157 of 2006, a *different* definition of fair value, i.e. the price that would be received to sell an asset or paid to transfer a liability in an orderly transaction between market participants at the measurement date. This, unlike the IASB definition, is explicitly an exit concept. It is not obvious that other players will accept this unilateral move.

CURRENT VALUES: SOME OVERALL THOUGHTS

In Chapter 1 we revised and developed the traditional historical cost model. This is backwards looking and relatively objective (remember the relatively!). In Chapter 4 we considered the thinking of important economists in this area, the psychic theories of Fisher – unmeasurable in money terms by very definition but properly recognising that only human beings take decisions and that they are the ultimate consumers – and the more quantifiable work of Hicks with its important capital maintenance implications. These economic-based ideas are properly forward looking and logically relevant to the decision-making process, but they are highly subjective. Current values lie in the middle of this spectrum both in terms of their time relationship (in between past and future) and in terms of their degrees of objectivity/subjectivity. In this sense they are clearly worth exploring as a compromise between relevance and verifiability.

There are stronger claims that can be made, however. The usual financial reporting statements essentially claim to report on the position at a (current) date and on the results ending on that date. Current values can properly claim to provide information consistent with this approach. The question follows, of course, which current value? The discussions in this and the previous chapter suggest that each of the suggested bases has particular merits. All provide useful information. All give good and relevant answers to some questions. One obvious suggestion to follow from this is that the preferable method in any situation depends on the particular situation itself – in other words, the abstract question 'Which is the best method?' has no answer and indeed is simply a silly question. We should be prepared to use different valuation methods and different reporting methods for different purposes.

A second suggestion is an idea for you to take away and think about. The practice and application of double-entry channel us unthinkingly into the assumption that the balance sheet and the income statement are two elements in the same system and that they therefore have to be fully compatible with each other. But our basic purpose is to produce meaningful reports and there is no logical reason why they should be in any way constrained by data-recording systems. Perhaps we should consider producing smaller more ad hoc statements, using *combinations* of valuation bases depending on the purpose of each statement.

SUMMARY

In this chapter we have analysed the logic and implications of current exit value accounting and prepared accounting statements on a current exit (NRV) basis. We then explored the possibility of ad hoc mixtures within the framework of traditional accounting reports and analysed the logic and implications of deprival value accounting and of fair values. Finally, we asked ourselves to consider the usefulness of current values generally and individually.

EXERCISES

Suggested answers to exercises marked ✓ are to be found on the Student side of the companion website.

Suggested answers to the remaining exercises are to be found on the Instructor side of the companion website.

1   Explain the principles of exit value accounting, providing a simple made-up illustration.

2   Explain the principles of deprival value accounting, providing a simple made-up illustration.

✓ 3   Discuss the proposition that businesses should be required to publish their P&L statement on replacement cost lines and their balance sheet on net realisable value lines.

4   Deprival value removes significant disadvantages of replacement cost, while retaining its advantages. Discuss.

5   (a)   Provide a definition of the deprival value of an asset.

(b)   For a particular asset, suppose the three bases of valuation relevant to the calculation of its deprival value are (in thousands of euros): €12, €10 and €8. Construct a matrix of columns and rows showing all the possible alternative situations and, in each case, indicate the appropriate deprival value.

(c)   Justify the use of deprival value as a method of asset valuation, using the matrix in (b) to illustrate your answer.

✓ 6   Steward plc commences business on 1 January year 1. Let us assume all transactions are by cheque and no credit is given nor taken and that Steward deals only in one type of item of inventory.

1 January Year 1
Introduced capital of €30 000.
Purchased machine for €10 000.
Purchased 1000 items of inventory for €10 each.

31 December Year 1
Sold 800 items of inventory for €15 each.
Paid expenses for the year of €1000.
The NRV of the machine is €9000.

1 January Year 2
Purchased 800 items of inventory for €13 each.

31 December Year 2
Sold 500 items of inventory for €20 each.
Paid expenses for the year of €1200.
The NRV of the machine is €8000.

Produce profit and loss accounts and balance sheets relating to years 1 and 2 using NRV accounting.

7 On 1 January, Stan and Oliver each started a business by investing €100 in cash, and then immediately purchasing one widget, which at that date could have been resold for €120.

Stan sold his widget on 31 March for €130, but on 1 April discovered that he needed to pay €115 to buy another, which he did. On 30 June this was sold for €140, and a new one bought on 1 July for €125.

On 29 September this was sold for €150, and a replacement purchased on 30 September for €130, on which date the new one could have been sold for €160.

Oliver had been less active and had merely kept his first widget and read the newspaper.

Both have decided to adopt 30 September as their accounting date, and come to you for accounting services.

All widgets are identical.

Replacement costs changed on 31 March, 30 June, 29 September. How would the above appear under:

(a) historic cost

(b) replacement cost

(c) net realisable value

You may find it helpful to do this by using a table with each date on the left and columns for Cash, Inventory, Profit, Holding Gains, etc. across the top.

CURRENT PURCHASING POWER ACCOUNTING

7

OBJECTIVES After studying this chapter you should be able to:

- explain the concept of general inflation and its implications for accounting measurement

- explain the mechanisms for taking account of general inflation in financial reporting, especially, but not exclusively, in the context of historical cost accounting

- discuss theoretical arguments, and practical considerations, for and against current purchasing power accounting

- outline present attitudes to the whole changing prices and inflation debate.

INTRODUCTION

In our discussion so far we have considered various methods of 'putting a monetary figure on something'. There are many ways of deriving a figure with a € sign in front that we must consider and appraise. But we have not yet stopped to consider what we mean by the € sign. What is a euro? It is a unit of money – and money is of no use by itself. Money has no intrinsic value. Its value is related to what we can get with it, what we can do with it. When most prices are rising, then we can obtain gradually less and less with any given number of euros. This means that if, under any particular valuation basis, we have maintained our capital appropriately defined in terms of numbers of euros, we have not necessarily maintained our capital in terms of the purchasing power of those euros. *Current purchasing power* (CPP) accounting attempts to take account of this.

THE MEASURING UNIT PROBLEM

There are many examples of difficulties with measuring units. Litres and gallons or inches and centimetres are classic examples. But in these cases the use of different measuring units may be a nuisance, but the problems are capable of rapid and objective solution. An inch has a precise or standard specification. A centimetre has a precise or standard specification. It follows, of course, that the relationship between the two also has a precise or standard specification. We can very exactly convert one to the other and, even more significantly, the conversion factor is fixed and constant between different people, between different places and between different times.

None of this is true of money as a measuring unit. A unit of money is an artificial construct. It is related to spending power and spending patterns, and these are personal and individual. It follows that a unit of money is not fixed as between different people, is not fixed between different places and, crucially for accounting, it is not fixed between different times. We need a conversion factor between our altering measuring units. But since our units (euros) are not fixed in inherent valuation, it follows that the conversion factor cannot be fixed either. The solution (or evasion) which current purchasing power provides to this problem is to use averages as an approximate surrogate for the theoretically unique conversion factor required. The euro is converted, or adjusted, by means of general indices.

CURRENT PURCHASING POWER

It is vital to understand that current purchasing power (CPP) is a general purchasing power concept. We are concerned with general inflation, usually expressed as the average rise in the cost of living, i.e. with inflation in the politicians' sense. If inflation in the last year is 10%, then €100 last year has the same general (i.e. average) purchasing power as €110 this year. This means that in order to know what we are talking about we have to 'date' all our euros. Euros at different dates can no longer be regarded as the same, as a common measuring unit. In order to return to the position, essential for proper comparison, of having a common measuring unit, we have to convert euros of one date's purchasing power into euros of the other date's purchasing power. This needs illustrating!

Basic figures (all at 31 December) are:

20.1   €200
20.2   €250

The general inflation index stood at 300 in 20.1 and 330 in 20.2 (i.e. inflation in the year was 10%). Over the year $200_{20.1}$ euros have been changed into $250_{20.2}$ euros. How much better off are we?

The description 'basic figure' is deliberately vague. The idea of CPP adjustments can be superimposed on any valuation basis. The practical proposals made in recent

ACTIVITY 7.1

Well. How much better off are we?

$$200 \times \frac{330}{300} = €_{20.2}\ 220$$

Activity feedback

To answer this, we need to calculate the equivalent in $€_{20.2}$, of $€_{20.1}$ 200. In terms of general purchasing power this will be:

So in terms of a common measuring unit ($€_{20.2}$) we have an increase in well-offness of $250 - 220 = €_{20.2}\ 30$.

years for the introduction of CPP have generally assumed an HC basis and for the present we will discuss and illustrate the ideas under this assumption.

It is important to distinguish, when considering CPP accounting, between monetary and non-monetary items. Monetary items are items fixed by contract, custom or statute in terms of numbers of euros, regardless of changes in the general price level and the purchasing power of the euros. Examples are cash, debtors and creditors and longer term loans. Non-monetary items are all items not so fixed in terms of number of euros, for example land, buildings, plant, inventory, shares held as investments.

Suppose I held a monetary asset in 20.1 of €200 (i.e. $€_{20.1}$ 200). If I still hold this asset, untouched and unchanged, a year later, it will be worth €200. It might even be a pile of 200 physical € coins, although it could equally be a debtor or a loan. But in 20.2 what sort of euro is it worth 200 of? The answer is 20.2 euros. By definition the item is fixed in terms of number of euros. So I have turned $€_{20.1}$ 200 into $€_{20.2}$ 200. But we know that in terms of general purchasing power $€_{20.2}$ is worth less than $€_{20.1}$ was. Therefore, in maintaining my position in terms of the number of euros of my monetary asset, I have failed to maintain my position in terms of purchasing power.

Contrariwise, suppose we borrow €100 in 20.1 and repay the loan, €100, one year later. We have borrowed $€_{20.1}$ 100 and repaid $€_{20.2}$ 100. We have repaid the same number of euros that we borrowed, but each euro is of lower purchasing power. Therefore, in terms of (general) purchasing power we have repaid less than we borrowed, so we have gained. (We shall also have to pay interest of course, which may have attempted to take account of the effects of inflation.) These gains and losses on monetary items are an important part of the argument in favour of CPP accounting – it is suggested that such gains and losses should be calculated and reported.

With monetary items, then, when considering two sets of accounts at different dates, no *adjustment* to the € figure reported is needed, but care must be taken in interpretation. However, when *comparing* two sets of accounts of the same business at different dates it is necessary to adjust all the contents of one balance sheet into the measuring unit (dated euro) of that of the other. The question may be: what is the current (today) purchasing power of the €100 I held one year ago (and still hold)? The answer is 100 of today's euros. But the question might be: If I have €200 today and I had €100 one year ago, how much better off am I in terms of purchasing power? The answer, in terms of today's euros is:

$$200 - 100 \times \frac{\text{(RPI today)}}{\text{(RPI 1 year ago)}}$$

For example:

$$200 - 100 \times \frac{(330)}{(300)}$$
$$= 200 - 110$$
$$= € \text{ today } 90$$

This process leads to a good deal of confusion. Study the following example carefully.

Example

Given: All the information of Chaplin Ltd, as on pp. 88–89.
Prepare: A closing balance sheet under CPP principles.

Chaplin Ltd – CPP solution

		€	€
Capital	$200\ 000 \times \frac{120}{100}$		240 000
Operating profit			21 382
			261 382
Gain on net monetary liabilities			2 000
			263 382
Loan			50 000
Creditors			50 000
			363 382
Land and buildings	$110\ 000 \times \frac{120}{100}$		132 000
Plant and equipment: cost	$40\ 000 \times \frac{120}{100}$	48 000	
depreciation	$4\ 000 \times \frac{120}{100}$	4 800	43 200
			175 200
Inventory	$90\ 000 \times \frac{120}{110}$	98 182	
Debtors		90 000	
			188 182
			363 382

Notes

1 *Operating profit*. Balancing figure or provable as follows:

Per HC results		26 000
less Depreciation adj.	$4\ 000 \times \frac{110 - 100}{100}$	400
Inventory sold adj.	$60\ 000 \times \frac{110 - 100}{100}$	6 000
Adjusted profit as *30 June prices*		19 600
Adjusted profit at 31 December prices	$19\ 600 \times \frac{120}{110}$	€ 21 382

2 *Gain on net monetary liabilities.*

(a) In total this is easily provable as follows:
Net monetary liabilities 1 January €10 000 (loan 50 000 less cash 40 000).
Net monetary liabilities 31 December €10 000 (loan 50 000 plus creditors 50 000 less debtors 90 000).

Therefore gain is $10\ 000 \left(1 - \dfrac{120}{100}\right) = €2\ 000$ (at 31 December prices).

(b) More generally, however, the figures should be considered individually:

Debtors – arose on 30 June, remained until 31 December:

$$90\ 000 \left(1 - \frac{120}{110}\right) = \text{Loss} \qquad\qquad\qquad €\ 8\ 181$$

Creditors – arose on 30 June, remained until 31 December:

$$50\ 000 \left(1 - \frac{120}{110}\right) = \text{Gain} \qquad\qquad\qquad €\ 4\ 545$$

Loan – arose on 1 January, remained until 31 December:

$$50\ 000 \left(1 - \frac{120}{100}\right) = \text{Gain} \qquad\qquad\qquad €10\ 000$$

Cash – arose on 1 January, remained until 30 June:

$$40\ 000 \left(1 - \frac{110}{100}\right) = \text{Loss} \qquad\qquad\qquad €\ 4\ 000$$

But this loss on holding cash is expressed in 30 June euros.
This figure must be converted to 31 December euros i.e.:

$$4\ 000 \times \frac{120}{110} = \text{Loss} \qquad\qquad\qquad\qquad €\ 4\ 364$$

So in summary, we have:

Losses of 8 181 + 4 364	€12 545
Gains of 4 545 + 10 000	€14 545
Giving a net gain on net monetary liabilities of:	€ 2 000

Is this €2 000 gain distributable? Is it realised? In fact as the practical businessman or businesswoman might say, where is it?

3 *Indices used.* Study carefully which index number is used where and make sure you see why. Remember the simplifying assumption that all sales, purchases and associated payments occurred on 30 June and also that monetary items need no adjustment for balance sheet purposes. Note the irrelevance of the plant and inventory indices.

4 *Complexity.* This example is highly simplified yet the numbers and, more important, the logic, are not at all easy.

5 *Comparatives.* Next year this balance sheet will be used as a comparative for next year's results. For this purpose it will need, next year, to be multiplied by:

$$\frac{\text{(RPI at 31 December next year)}}{120}$$

This will need to be done to every figure, whether monetary or non-monetary. Thus, for example, the loan figure at the end of the year 2 will be 50 000 year 2 euros. If the RPI is then 150, then the comparative figure from year 1, as updated to year 2 euros will be:

$$50\ 000 \times \frac{150}{120} = €62\ 500$$

This cannot, of course, mean that the loan has been reduced in monetary amount by €12 500. What it does mean is that the loan has reduced in value in terms of year 2 euros (i.e. there has been another gain on monetary liabilities).

Now try the following activity. Our solution follows, but we strongly suggest that you make a serious attempt at your own solution first.

ACTIVITY 7.2

Mushroom Ltd was established on 1 January 20X4. Its opening balance sheet (on this date) was as follows:

	€
Land	6 000
Equipment	4 000
Inventory	2 000
Equity	12 000

During 20X4, the company made the following transactions:

(a) purchased extra inventory €10 000

(b) sold inventory for €11 000 cash, which had an historical cost value of €9 000

(c) closing inventory on 31 December 20X4 had an historical cost of €3 000 and was bought when the RPI index was 115 (average)

(d) the equipment has an expected life of four years and nil residual value. The straight line method of depreciation is used

(e) the general price index stood at:

100 on 1 January 20X4
110 on 30 June 20X4
120 on 31 December 20X4

You should assume that purchases and receipts occur evenly throughout the year. There are no debtors or creditors.

Required

Calculate the CPP profit for 20X4 and prepare the CPP balance sheet as at 31 December 20X4.

Activity feedback

		€CPP	€CPP
Sales	11 000 × 120/110		12 000
Opening			
inventory	2 000 × 120/100	2 400	
Add purchases	10 000 × 120/110	10 909	
		13 309	
less Closing			
inventory	(3 000 × 120/115)	3 130	
			10 179
			1 821
less			
Depreciation			1 200
			621
Loss on holding monetary assets (cash)*			91
CPP profit			530

* If cash accrues evenly over the year, the loss is

$$€(1000 \times 120/110) - €1\ 000 = €91$$

The historical cost profit (€11 000 − €9 000 − €1 000 for depreciation = €1 000) and the CPP profit can be reconciled as follows:

	€
Historical cost profit	1 000

Inventory
Additional charge based on restating the cost of inventory at the beginning and end of the year in euros of current purchasing power, thus taking the inflationary element out of the profit on the sale of inventory.

Opening inventory + 400 − closing inventory − 130	(270)

(Continued)

ACTIVITY 7.2 (Continued)

Depreciation
Additional depreciation based on cost, measured in euros of current purchasing power of fixed assets €1 200 − €1 000   (200)

Monetary items
Net loss in purchasing power resulting from the effects of inflation on the company's net monetary assets   (91)

Sales, purchases and all other costs*
These are increased by the change in the index between the average date at which they occurred and the end of the year. This adjustment increases profit as sales exceed the costs included in this heading   91

CPP profit   530

   * The historical cost profit is based on:

	€	€CPP	€
Sales	11 000	12 000	1 000
Purchases	10 000	10 909	(909)
Net difference			91

Calculation of balance sheet items, and reconciliation of profit figure with balance sheet:

1 Value of equity, 1 January 20X4	€12 000
Revalued in terms of €CPP at 31 December 20X4	
(€12 000 × 120/100)	€CPP14 400

2 Mushroom Ltd
CPP balance sheet as at 31 December 20X4

		€CPP	€CPP
Land	6 000 × 120/100		7 200
Equipment	4 000 × 120/100	4 800	
less Depreciation	1 000 × 120/100	1 200	
			3 600
			10 800
Inventory	3 000 × 120/115	3 130	
Cash	(11 000 − 10 000)	1 000	
			4 130
			14 930
Financed by equity and reserves			14 930
CPP profit − €CPP			
(14 930 − 14 400) =		€CPP	530

COMBINATION OF METHODS

As already stated, CPP thinking can be applied to any valuation basis, not just historical costs. It is often suggested that CPP adjustments could and indeed should be applied to replacement cost calculations. It is important to remember that:

1 RC accounting deals with specific price rises only

2 CPP accounting deals with general price rises only

3 both types of change are in fact occurring at the same time.

Thus to take the simplest of examples, if HC = 10 and a year later RC = 13, there is a holding gain of €3. But if the GI has increased by 10% then (10 × 110/100) = €1 of that holding gain of 3 (closing date) euros is not 'real' because it cannot be translated into increased purchasing power. The 'real' holding gain is arguably only 2 (3 − 1) (closing date) euros. This combined approach, known as *stabilised accounting*, is shown for Chaplin Ltd in the following example.

Example

Chaplin Ltd – stabilised (RC plus CPP) solution

	€
Capital (per CPP answer)	240 000
Operating profit	18 328
	258 328
Real holding gain	8 012
	266 340

Loan	50 000
Creditors	50 000
	366 340
Land and building (per RC answer)	135 000
Plant and equipment (per RC answer)	39 600
Inventory (per RC answer)	101 740
Debtors	90 000
	366 340

Notes

1 *Operating profit*

Per HC answer $\qquad 26\,000 \times \dfrac{120}{110} = 28\,364$

Depreciation RC 30 June $\qquad$ 4 200

Depreciation *less* HC $\qquad$ 4 000

$\qquad\qquad\qquad\qquad 200 \times \dfrac{120}{110} = \qquad (218)$

Cost of sales $\qquad\qquad\qquad 120$

(per RC answer) $\qquad 9\,000 \times \dfrac{120}{110} = (9\,818)$

$\qquad\qquad\qquad\qquad\qquad\qquad\qquad\qquad 18\,328$

2 *Real holding gain*

Gain on net monetary items (per CPP answer) $\qquad\qquad\qquad$ 2 000

Land and buildings $\qquad 110\,000 \times \left(\dfrac{135}{110} - \dfrac{120}{100}\right) = \qquad$ 3 000

Plant and equipment:

Cost $\qquad\qquad\qquad\qquad 40\,000 \times \left(\dfrac{110}{100} - \dfrac{120}{100}\right) = (4\,000)$

Depreciation $\qquad \left(400 \times \dfrac{105}{100}\right) \times \left(\dfrac{110}{105} - \dfrac{120}{100}\right) = \quad 182 \quad (3\,818)$

$\qquad\qquad\qquad\qquad\qquad\qquad\qquad\qquad\qquad\qquad\qquad\qquad 1\,181$

Cost of sales:

Opening inventory $\quad \left(60\,000 \times \left(\dfrac{115}{110} - \dfrac{110}{100}\right)\right) \times \dfrac{120}{110} = 3\,273$

Closing inventory $\qquad \left(90\,000 \times \left(\dfrac{130}{115} - \dfrac{120}{110}\right)\right) = 3\,557 \quad 6\,830$

$\qquad\qquad\qquad\qquad\qquad\qquad\qquad\qquad\qquad\qquad\qquad\qquad €8\,012$

CURRENT PURCHASING POWER – WHAT DOES IT REALLY MEAN?

It is most important when thinking about CPP accounting to be fully aware of exactly what it is doing and what it is not doing. The crucial point is that it is not producing a current valuation of the term concerned in any sense. What it is doing, in general terms, is to re-express in terms of current euros, the figures as originally calculated under the original measurement basis, whatever that was. It does not alter the basis of valuation. It alters the measuring unit which is being applied to the original basis of valuation.

ACTIVITY 7.3

Look at the figure of €132 000 for land and buildings shown in the Chaplin CPP example on p. 114 and think about it carefully. What does it mean?

Activity feedback

We would suggest it means something like: the number of current euros that would have to be spent today to buy the land and buildings if all economic circumstances were exactly unaltered from when the original purchase was made. Since all economic circumstances will most certainly not be unaltered from when the original purchase was made, it is not obvious that this is particularly useful information.

The other point that could be made concerns the assumption that a *general* adjustment to purchasing power is of relevance even when viewed in measuring unit terms to the *particular* user of the *particular* set of accounts of the *particular* business being considered. Can the spending or purchasing power of one euro be equated as between a retail shop and a chemical manufacturer? Can the spending or purchasing power of one euro be equated as between a non-smoking pensioner and a smoking teenager? Is general purchasing power so general that it is not really relevant to any particular user?

SOME INTERNATIONAL PRACTICES AND TRADITIONS

No attempt is made here to replicate a full coverage of either national research traditions or of national practices. Readers wishing to investigate the story as it applies in their own country should look elsewhere. We merely present a brief sketch and overview.

A significant starting point is the publication of a French *ordinance* (law) in 1673 and an authorised (by Royal Decree) commentary on it published in 1675 by Jacques Savary. Savary argued that an annual inventory – which we would now call balance sheet – had two functions. The first function is to give an indication of the position of the business as a performing (and continuing) operation. This function logically requires that assets are measured on a cost basis if not yet sold. The second function

ACTIVITY 7.4

Prepare a list, in point form, of advantages and disadvantages which you think could reasonably be said to apply to current purchasing power accounting.

Activity feedback
Advantages

1 All necessary figures are stated or restated in terms of a common measuring unit (CPP units). This facilitates proper comparison.

2 It distinguishes between gains or losses on monetary liabilities and assets, on the one hand, and 'real' gains or losses through trading activities, on the other.

3 It requires only a simple objective adjustment to HC accounts. Easily auditable.

Disadvantages

1 It is not clear what CPP units are. They are not the same as monetary units.

2 *General* purchasing power, by definition, has no direct relevance to any *particular* person or situation.

3 When CPP is applied to HC-based accounts, the resulting figures necessarily contain all the disadvantages of the original HC accounts.

4 It fails to give any sort of meaningful 'value' to balance sheet items, although it gives the impression to non-accountants that it has done precisely that.

5 It is extremely difficult to understand and interpret.

is an indication of debt coverage, i.e. to give an indication of the risk of bankruptcy. This function logically requires that assets are measured on a net realisable value basis.

These two functions, and the resulting balance sheets, later became known as dynamic and static respectively. These are the terms used in the German tradition, developed to considerable sophistication by theorists in the early years of the 20th century. Schmalenbach wrote *Dynamische Bilanz*, in several editions to 1926 (also available in English), which argues for a reporting system based on historical costs together with general indexation adjustment. This is in contrast with Schmidt, who supported the essentially static view (in the sense already described) that current values should be used, actually current entry (replacement cost) figures under his proposals.

The Dutch academic Theodor Limperg broadly followed and developed the Schmidt approach in the years to 1940, see for example Mey (1966). The essential argument is that replacement cost is the sacrificed value for production resources used. Distributable income is then logically defined as the difference between revenue and the value sacrificed in order to obtain that revenue, i.e. profit is revenue less replacement cost of consumption.

A connection into the English-speaking world was made through the publication by Sweeney of *Stabilised Accounting* (1936). Sweeney had access to the German literature and was strongly influenced by Schmidt. Sweeney went further, however, and demonstrates in detail the feasibility of a full-scale combination of replacement cost measurement in combination with general indication, i.e. RC + CPP at the same time.

The 'resources sacrificed' approach, essentially an opportunity cost philosophy, can be traced into *The Valuation of Property*, by Bonbright, published in the USA in 1937. It was this book that provided the foundations for the development of the concept of deprival value, already discussed.

Practice since the middle of the 20th century bears little resemblance to the earlier research developments. The general middle European practical approach, influenced by the factors discussed in Chapter 2, has been a strict adherence to historical costs. The same is true in the USA, although perhaps more for reasons of objectivity (and fear of the power of lawyers) than for reasons of prudence. The UK (and also the Netherlands) have adopted a more flexible approach, both in law and in practice. The large Dutch company, Phillips, used a broadly Limpergian reporting system for several decades.

In the 1970s the UK experimented with a compulsory supplementary *Current Purchasing Power System* (SSAP 7, 1974). Following the government-sponsored (and influenced) Sandilands Report (1975), an expanded (and excessively complicated) development of deprival value, known as *Current Cost Accounting* (SSAP 16, 1980) was required (without general indexation). Neither lasted very long. Moves along similar lines were made over this period in a number of other countries, including the USA, which briefly introduced additional note disclosures using both specific and general adjustments. But the timing of these events strongly influenced the content and wording of the Fourth European Directive on the accounts of limited companies, published in 1978 and still very much with us today. This Directive allows a very wide variety of different approaches.

In terms of the future, general inflation adjustments are regularly employed in hyperinflationary economies, such as some South American countries and supported by requirements in IAS 29, discussed in Chapter 22. Specific price change adjustments are not generally in fashion at present, but as trends of price rise tend to increase, then the debate is likely to return. Any such system in practice is not likely to be more complicated than the system briefly operated in the UK in the 1980s, which had four major elements. The last two of these, the monetary working capital adjustment and the gearing adjustment, raise important conceptual issues. Either of them could be dropped from a practical system without affecting the other. As an exposition of the issues involved, we discuss the requirements of this former Standard here. It is never likely to be reintroduced, in this form, in any jurisdiction, but the issues and arguments are permanent ones.

The profit calculation is divided into two stages. The first stage is to arrive at the current cost operating profit. This is calculated by starting from the historical cost profit and then making three adjustments. These are the depreciation and cost of sales adjustments and the monetary working capital adjustment. All three will usually, although not universally, be debits.

The second stage is to calculate the current cost profit attributable to shareholders. This is calculated by starting from the current cost operating profit and then making the gearing adjustment. This will normally be a credit.

The methodology of the depreciation adjustment and the cost of sales adjustment will be exactly the same as for replacement cost accounting as considered earlier (see Chapter 5). The only difference is that the calculations will be based on the 'value to the business', which is usually the replacement cost, rather than on the replacement cost, which, of course, is always the replacement cost. The other two adjustments require more detailed consideration.

Monetary working capital adjustment

If profit is revenue less expenses and the HC profit is correctly calculated to include all expenses, then adjustments for cost of sales and depreciation would seem to be all that is necessary to update the reported profit figure. Incidental expenses can reasonably be assumed to be 'current' already (e.g. administrative wages, the telephone bill and so on). An alternative argument, however, points out that rising costs will, other things being equal, have an effect on working capital needs as a whole, not just on inventory. Rising costs of inputs will lead to higher cash payments and these cash payments are not replaced in cash terms until the debtors resulting from the eventual sale actually pay. Therefore, the amount of cash the firm needs to finance from its own resources is increased because of the rise in the replacement cost of the inputs. Rising costs therefore lead to an increased burden because of rising debtors. Conversely, creditors will tend to protect the business to some extent because the business will lag behind current prices in its rate of payment.

For example, if inventory costing €100 is bought and not paid for and then inventory costing €110 is bought and not paid for, but the first inventory is now paid for, then the business has not, at this point, had to pay any extra money because of the rise in cost levels. The amount of extra finance needed to support the level of activity has arguably not increased. Therefore the unfavourable inventory (cost of sales) adjustment of €10 can be offset by a favourable monetary working capital adjustment (MWCA) of €10.

There are several problems arising from this idea:

1 How do we determine which monetary items are part of monetary *working* capital? It should include trade creditors, trade debtors, cash floats necessary

in operating the business, any items of inventory not included in the cost of sales adjustment (COSA) and any part of bank balances or overdrafts relating to fluctuations in inventory, debtors or creditors. It should not include loans, idle money or any 'non-operating' items. In practice, this obviously leads to difficult distinctions.

2 Which index should be used? It is usually argued that a specific cost index is often used as for the COSA. However, it could be argued that a selling price index should be used – if selling price goes up 15% and input costs go up 10% then the money tied up in debtors, the money the firm would have already had if debtors had paid immediately, has gone up by 15% not 10%. Alternatively, it could be suggested that a general index should be used on the grounds that money is by definition available for any purpose and anything other than a general index makes unjustified assumptions about intentions.

3 Why regard an 'amount of money' as an expense? The MWCA does not reduce profit by the cost of the extra finance. It reduces profit by the amount of the extra finance. It could therefore be suggested that it confuses expenses with increases in necessary investment. This, of course, brings us back to the capital maintenance concept of operating capability.

MWCA is a difficult concept and opinions differ as to its desirability. Both elements of this statement are even more true of the gearing adjustment.

Gearing adjustment

In essence, the argument for a gearing adjustment can be stated very simply. The depreciation and COSA and the MWCA if present, have, by definition, related to the business as a whole. The depreciation entries relate to all the fixed assets, and so on. This is obviously necessary, as the whole point of the operation is to maintain the operating capability (of the business as a whole). But for the gearing adjustment we take a different standpoint.

We consider how the total assets of the business (regarding net working capital as 'an asset' for this purpose) have been financed. The assets have generally been financed from two sources:

1 shareholders' equity – capital and reserves of all kinds
2 loans and borrowings from non-shareholders.

So, we have adjusted (generally reduced) profit by a series of adjustments that relate to all the assets. But we are reporting primarily to shareholders and, therefore, what we *should* be doing is adjusting profit by adjustments that relate to those assets financed by the shareholders. Therefore we have over-adjusted and we need to 'add a bit back again' – to adjust the adjustments, in fact!

To calculate the gearing adjustment the basic procedure is as follows:

1 add the adjustments made in arriving at current cost operating profit
2 calculate the gearing proportion. The gearing proportion is the relationship between the average net borrowing (L) and the average total capital employed figure (the ordinary shareholders' equity $S + L$), i.e.:

$$\text{Gearing proportion} = \frac{L}{L + S}$$

3 multiply the total arrived at in 1 by the proportion arrived at in 2.

This procedure arrives at the gearing adjustment, which then reduces the effect of the 'operating' adjustments. In the general case where the operating adjustments reduce profit (i.e. are debits) the gearing adjustment will be a credit. Using the terminology of SSAP 16, we have:

HC profit			X
less	Depreciation adjustment	X	
	COSA	X	
	MWCA	$\underline{X}$	
		X	
CC operating profit			X
plus	Gearing adjustment		$\underline{X}$
CC profit attributable to shareholders			$\underline{X}$

The double-entry for these adjustments goes into the revaluation reserve, now called *current cost reserve*, on the balance sheet.

The following example shows the replacement cost (RC) solution to Chaplin, reworked to include an MWCA and a gearing adjustment. Study it carefully.

Example

Chaplin – SSAP 16 accounts

		€	€
HC profit			26 000
less	Adjustments		
	Depreciation	400	
	Inventory	9 000	
	MWCA	$\underline{4\ 615}$	$\underline{14\ 015}$
CC operating profit			11 985
add	back gearing adjustment		
	(not applicable to shareholders)		
	18% × 14 015		$\underline{2\ 524}$
CC profit attributable to shareholders			$\underline{14\ 509}$

Balance sheet

	€		€
Share capital	200 000	Assets (per RC answer)	366 340
Profit	14 509		
Holding gains	$\underline{51\ 831}$		
	266 340		
Loan	50 000		
Creditors	$\underline{50\ 000}$		$\underline{}$
	$\underline{366\ 340}$		$\underline{366\ 340}$

		€
Holding gains	Per RC answer	49 740
	+ MWCA	4 615
	less Gearing	(2 524)
		51 831

Notes

1 *Calculation of MWCA*

	Actual		Mid-year €
Opening MWC	$0 \times \dfrac{115}{100}$	=	0
Closing MWC	$40\ 000 \times \dfrac{115}{130}$	=	35 385
Increase	40 000		35 385

This mid-year increase is the 'real' increase, therefore the 'price effect' increase must be 40 000 − 35 385 = €4 615.

2 *Calculation of gearing adjustment*
Closing capital, on a current cost basis, equals closing assets on a current cost basis less closing liabilities:

366 340	(as RC solution)
− 100 000	(50 000 + 50 000)
€266 340	

Opening capital = €200 000

$$\text{Average capital} = \frac{200\,000 + 266\,340}{2} = €233\,170$$

$$\text{Gearing proportion} = \frac{50\,000}{50\,000 + 233\,170} = 18\%$$

The idea of the gearing adjustment is difficult and controversial. If we look at the business as a whole, as an entity in itself, then a gearing adjustment seems unnecessary. This is known as the 'entity view'. In order to maintain the operating capability and assuming that the assumptions made in calculating value to the business adjustments are valid, all the appropriate operating adjustments must be made to HC profit. Gains on borrowing are not represented by cash inflows to the business and they are not available for distribution as dividends without reducing the business's 'well-offness'.

This means that the 'CC profit attributable to shareholders' does not generally show the amount that can be paid out as dividends without reducing the operating capacity of the business. This maximum amount of dividend that can be paid out without defeating the stated capital maintenance concept of operating capacity is given by the CC operating profit.

Alternatively, we can take what is known as the 'proprietary view'. This suggests that we should look at the company through the eyes of the shareholders; we should look at the business as it affects the shareholders and not as an entity in itself. This would seem to support the idea of a gearing adjustment. It is additionally argued by supporters of this viewpoint that the business, although admittedly unable to distribute the gearing adjustment from its own resources, can always borrow the additional cash necessary for this distribution without increasing (worsening) the gearing proportion. This argument is technically correct, but the relevance of a *financing* argument to a *profit* calculation is not universally accepted. A second major problem is that the gearing adjustment as illustrated here is closely related to the operating adjustments and the logic of this can be criticised. First, it can be criticised as being too conservative. Consider the treatment of the plant and equipment in the Chaplin CC accounts (pp. 88–89). The CC reserve has been increased by €4 000, the debit being to the balance sheet. Arising from this, €400 has been deducted from profit as depreciation adjustment, the credit being to the balance sheet. This €400 adjustment is usually regarded as realised. Our gearing adjustment has increased profit attributable to shareholders by the gearing proportion of the (realised) depreciation adjustment, i.e. by 18% of the €400. But the total gain is €4 000. Since 18% of this 4 000 can clearly be deemed to be financed by borrowing, why not increase profit attributable to shareholders by 18% of the whole €4 000? Certainly it cannot be argued as being realised, but remember that even 'realised' gains are not necessarily distributable anyway.

Additionally, remember that what the gearing adjustment does is to 'do something about monetary items'. We have argued earlier that gains or losses on monetary items are perhaps best measured in terms of purchasing power – the fall in the value of money. This implies the use of a general index and that any gearing adjustment must be calculated completely independently of the operating adjustments. If we are focusing our attention on the assets, which are financed by borrowing, perhaps a specific asset index is suggested. If we are focusing our attention on the borrowings of the business and on opportunity costs and future effects, perhaps a general index is indicated.

SUMMARY

In this chapter we have explored the concept of general inflation and current purchasing power adjustments and seen how the figures are calculated. Finally, we attempted to consider the meaning and usefulness of the resulting accounts and statements and to explore some national and practical developments.

EXERCISES

Suggested answers to exercises marked ✓ are to be found on the Student side of the companion website.

Suggested answers to the remaining exercises are to be found on the Instructor side of the companion website.

✓ **1** What do CPP adjustments do and how do they do it?

2 Are general indices more or less useful in financial reporting than specific price changes?

3 Look at the figure of €240 000 for capital shown in the Chaplin CPP example on p. 114 and think about it carefully. What does it mean?

4 To what extent do current purchasing power adjustments to historical cost figures lead to up-to-date valuations in a balance sheet?

5 Current purchasing power adjustments are simple to apply, but hard to explain and interpret. Discuss.

6 From the following historic cost accounts of Page plc, prepare a set of CPP accounts for the year-ended 31.12.8.

	31.12.7 €000		31.12.8 €000	
Fixed assets				
Cost (purchased 1.1.5)		500		500
less depreciation		300		400
		200		100
Current assets				
Inventory (purchased 31.10)	100		150	
Debtors	200		300	
Bank	150		350	
	450		800	
less Current liabilities	300		400	
		150		400
		350		500
Share capital		100		100
Reserves		250		400
		350		500

Profit and loss account for the year-ended 31 December year 8:

		€000
Sales		1 850
Cost of goods sold		
Opening inventory	100	
Purchases	1 350	
	1 450	
less closing inventory	150	
		1 300
Gross profit		550
Expenses	300	
Depreciation	100	
		400
Net profit		150

The movement on the retail price index has been as follows:

1 January year 5	180
1 January year 7	200
Average for year 7	210
31 October year 7	215
31 December year 7	220
Average for year 8	230
31 October year 8	235
31 December year 8	240

Assume all sales, purchases and expenses accrue evenly throughout the year.

✓ 7 From the following information produce a set of current cost accounts as per SSAP 16. Calgary plc had the following historic cost profit and loss account for the year-ended 30 June:

		Year 4 €000
Sales		7 000
Profit before interest and taxation		1 560
Interest	140	
Taxation	300	
		440
Profit attributable to shareholders		1 120
Dividends		300
Retained profit for the year		820
Balance brought forward		1 420
Balance carried forward		2 240

Balance sheet as at 30 June:

	Year 3 €000		Year 4 €000	
Fixed assets				
Land at cost		1 500		1 500
(purchased 1 July year 2)				
Plant and machinery at cost		1 200		1 200
(purchased 1 July year 2)				
less depreciation		(240)		(480)
		2 460		2 220
Current assets				
Inventory (purchased 30 April)	650		900	
Debtors	830		1 300	
Bank	10		620	
	1 490		2 820	
Less Current liabilities				
Creditors	790		1 060	
		700		1 760
		3 160		3 980
Share capital		1 040		1 040
Profit and loss		1 420		2 240
		2 460		3 280
Loan capital		700		700
		3 160		3 980

The following index numbers are applicable.

	RPI	Land	Inventory	Plant and machinery
1 July year 2	120	213	412	610
30 April year 3	125	232	423	639
30 June year 3	131	241	431	649
31 December year 3	139	263	442	661
30 April year 4	148	278	456	678
30 June year 4	158	289	462	691

8   You are the management accountant of a manufacturing company where production is capital-intensive using machinery that is estimated to have a five-year life. The present machinery is now approximately three years old. Whilst raw material stocks have a low turnover due to supply problems, finished goods are turned over rapidly and there is minimal work-in-progress at any one time. The technology incorporated in the means of production is thought to be stable.

In recent years, it has not been possible to increase the price of the company's outputs beyond the rate of general inflation without diminishing market share, due to keen competition in this sector. The company does not consider that it has cash-flow problems. The company is all equity financed. Although a bank overdraft is a permanent feature of the balance sheet this is primarily due to customers being given a 60-day credit period, whilst most suppliers are paid within 30 days. There is always a positive balance of short-term monetary assets.

In the previous financial year, net profit after taxation on a strict historic cost basis was considered very healthy, and the directors felt that they could prudently distribute a major portion of this by way of dividend. The directors are considering whether, and if so how, to reflect price-level changes in their financial statements. They are concerned that this would affect their profit figure and therefore the amount they could distribute as dividend.

The following price-level changes have been brought to the attention of the directors:

	Retail price index	Index for company's machinery	Raw materials stock index
3 years previously	100	100	100
2 years previously	104	116	102
1 year previously	107	125	108
Present	112	140	120

You are required to prepare a report for your directors setting out in general terms how to explain to the shareholders the likely impact on the historic cost profit of possible methods of accounting for price-level changes.

(CIMA – adapted)

ACCOUNTING THEORY AND CONCEPTUAL FRAMEWORKS

8

> **OBJECTIVES**   After studying this chapter you should be able to:
>
> - explain what accounting theory is
>
> - describe the main attempts at constructing an accounting theory
>
> - appraise current developments in the area
>
> - describe and discuss the contents of the IASB Framework
>
> - appraise the quality and usefulness of the IASB Framework in the context of its self-declared purposes
>
> - describe and discuss the parts of IAS 1 relating to accounting concepts and policies
>
> - appraise the overall effect of the Framework and comparable parts of IAS 1
>
> - describe and appraise the requirements of IAS 8 relating to accounting policies
>
> - outline the requirements of IFRS 1 relating to first-time adoption of IFRS.

INTRODUCTION

This chapter is about to deal with something that many people believe does not exist – a single generally accepted accounting theory. There is no generally accepted accounting theory at this time even though many attempts have been made to formulate one. According to Eldon S. Hendriksen in *Accounting Theory* (1977):

> Theory as it applies to accounting is the coherent set of hypothetical, conceptual and pragmatic principles forming the general frame of reference for a field of inquiry. Thus accounting theory may be defined as logical reasoning in the form of a set of broad principles that
>
> 1 Provide a general frame of reference by which accounting practices can be evaluated and
> 2 Guide the development of new practices and procedures.
>
> Accounting theory may also be used to explain existing practices to obtain a better understanding of them. But the most important goal of accounting theory should be to provide a coherent set of logical principles that form the general frame of reference for the evaluation and development of sound accounting practices.

Let us compare this with what many believe is the accounting framework, the IASB Framework for the Preparation and Presentation of Financial Statements. This Framework purports to:

1 assist the board of IASB in the development of standards and review of existing standards
2 provide a basis for reducing the number of permitted alternative accounting treatments
3 assist preparers in dealing with topics that have yet to form the subject of a standard.

This certainly sounds like an accounting theory. But if it is, then this theory would clearly determine how we should provide information to users and different practices would not prevail. The primary purpose of an accounting theory should be to provide a basis for the prediction and explanation of accounting behaviour and events.

IS AN ACCOUNTING THEORY POSSIBLE?

According to both Hendriksen (1977) and McDonald (1972) the development of an accounting theory should be possible. McDonald argues that a theory must have three elements:

1 encoding of phenomena to symbolic representation
2 manipulation or combination according to rules
3 translation back to real-world phenomena.

ACTIVITY 8.1

Do the three elements that McDonald states are necessary for a theory exist in accounting?

Activity feedback

The first obviously exists as we have the symbols of 'debits and credits' and we have also developed accounting terminology, e.g. depreciation, accruals, matching, current cost, revaluation, etc., which are all unique to accounting.

The second also exists as we have a wealth of rules and regulations for manipulating or combining these debits and credits. Translation is evidenced in how we present these debits and credits to users in the form of financial reports.

APPROACHES TO THE FORMULATION OF ACCOUNTING THEORY

If it *is* possible to develop an accounting theory (Hendriksen, 1977; McDonald, 1972), how do we approach its development? Research in this area has centred on traditional approaches, regulatory approaches and what have come to be regarded as new approaches. We will look briefly at each type.

Traditional approaches

Traditional approaches cover:

- non-theoretical
- theoretical.

Non-theoretical approaches to accounting theory are concerned with developing a theory or accounting techniques and principles that will be useful to users, particularly decision makers. This approach can be developed in a pragmatic or authoritarian way. In essence, this is the approach the accounting profession has used in the past to develop an accounting theory and it is fairly apparent it has not been able to resolve conflict in accounting practices or principles. Theoretical approaches to the development of an accounting theory are many but Belkaoui, in his text *Accounting Theory* (2000), categorises these as:

- deductive
- inductive
- ethical
- sociological
- economic
- eclectic.

Deductive approach This approach involves developing a theory from basic propositions, premises and assumptions that results in accounting principles that are logical conclusions about the subject. The theory is tested by determining whether its results are acceptable in practice. Edwards and Bell (1961) are deductive theorists (Chapter 4) and historical cost accounting was also derived from a deductive approach.

Inductive approach For this approach we start with observed phenomena and move towards generalised conclusions. The approach requires empirical testing, i.e. the theory must be supported by sufficient instances/observations that support the derived conclusions. Quite often the deductive and inductive approaches are mixed as researchers use their knowledge of accounting practices. As Belkaoui states: General propositions are formulated through an inductive process, but the principles and techniques are derived by a deductive approach. He also observes that when an inductive theorist, Littleton (1953), collaborates with a deductive theorist, Paton (1922), a hybrid results showing compromise between the two approaches.

Ethical approach

ACTIVITY 8.2

Identify concepts that could be at the core of the ethical approach to an accounting theory.

Activity feedback

Basically, this approach consists of the concepts of 'true and fair' or 'fair presentation'. These concepts have, of course, been taken on board by the EU in the Fourth Directive and by the IASB.

Writers/researchers in this area include D. R. Scott (1941) and Yu (1976).

Sociological approach This is actually an ethical approach that centres on social welfare. In other words, accounting principles and techniques are evaluated for acceptance after considering all effects on all groups in society. Thus within this approach we would need to be able to account for a business entity's effect on its social environment. We consider this type of reporting in Chapter 10.

Economic approach This approach focuses on general economic welfare. Thus accounting principles and techniques are evaluated for acceptance depending on their impact on the national economy. Sweden, in its national GAAP, uses an economic approach to its development. The IASB in developing its standards does tend to take an economic approach into account. For example, the current discussion on accounting for leases focuses on the effect that a standard requiring the capitalisation of all leases, whether finance or operating, might have on the economy or business in general. Traditionally, accounting standards have been set without considering economic consequences but lobby pressures from groups who perceive themselves as being affected can be strong.

Eclectic approach This is perhaps our current approach where we have a combination of all the approaches already identified appearing in our accounting theory. This approach has come about more by accident than as a deliberate attempt, due to the interference in the development of accounting theory by professionals, governmental bodies (including the EU) and individuals. This eclectic approach has also led to the development of new approaches to accounting theory.

Regulatory approaches

Many would regard this as the approach we currently have to accounting theory. They hold this view because to them it does not appear that standards, even those of the IASB, are based on broad, relevant theories but are developed as solutions to current conflicts that emerge in our attempts to provide useful information to users. Indeed, they might argue that new standards are only developed when a particular user complains about misinformation or non-information. But there are questions to consider if we do adopt this approach to the development of accounting theory. In the main these questions centre on whether we should adopt a free market approach to the regulation, a private sector regulatory approach or public sector regulatory approach.

This regulatory approach is also one that tends to identify solutions to difficulties that have occurred in our reporting rather than providing us with a theory that anticipates the issues.

New approaches

These attempt to use both conceptual and empirical reasoning to formulate and verify an accounting framework (Belkaoui, *Accounting Theory*, Chapter 10). The approaches are:

- events
- behavioural
- human information processing
- predictive
- positive.

Events approach The events approach was developed in 1969 by George Sorter and was defined as 'providing information about relevant economic events that might be useful in a variety of decision models'. The events approach leaves the user to aggregate and assign weights and values to the event. The accountant would only provide information on the economic event to the user, he would not assume a decision model. Thus, for example, the events approach income statement would not indicate financial performance in a period but would communicate events that occurred during the period without any attempt to determine a bottom line.

Behavioural approach The behavioural approach attempts to take into account human behaviour as it relates to decision-making in accounting. Devine (1960) stated the following:

> On balance it seems fair to conclude that accountants seem to have waded through their relationships to the intricate psychological network of human activity with a heavy handed crudity that is beyond belief. Some degree of crudity may be

ACTIVITY 8.3

Identify advantages and disadvantages of the events approach to the development of an accounting theory.

Activity feedback

1 Research has shown that structured/aggregate reports are preferable for high-analytic decision makers but not for low-analytic decision makers. Thus, the success of the events approach is dependent on the analytical skills of the user.

2 Users, in attempting to evaluate all information provided, may reach 'information overload'.

3 No criteria have yet been developed for the choice of events to be reported.

4 It will probably prove difficult to measure all characteristics of an event.

excused in a new discipline, but failure to recognise that much of what passes as accounting theory is hopelessly entwined with unsupported behaviour assumptions is unforgivable.

This to us seems a fair comment. Given that financial reporting is about communicating information to users to enable them to make decisions, a lack of consideration of how that information influences their behaviour is indeed unforgivable. Studies in this area have tended to concentrate on:

- the adequacy of disclosure
- usefulness of financial statement data
- attitudes about corporate reporting practices
- materiality judgements
- decision effects of alternative accounting practices.

In one of these areas, materiality, it was discovered that users' assessment of materiality was individualistic and that the provider of the information was not in the best position to determine materiality for a user. There is much work still to do within the behavioural approach.

Human information processing approach This is similar to a behavioural approach in that it focuses on how users interpret and use the information provided.

Predictive approach This approach attempts to formulate an accounting theory by focusing on the predictive nature/ability of a particular method of reporting an event that would be of use to the user. Such approaches are most prevalent in what could be regarded as management accounting. Efficient market hypothesis, Beta models, chaos theory are all examples of this approach.

Positive approach This can be best explained by quoting Jensen (1976), who called for the:

> development of a positive theory of accounting which will explain why accounting is what it is, why accountants do what they do, and what effects these phenomena have on people and resource utilisation.

The approach is based on the proposition that managers, shareholders and regulators are rational and that they attempt to maximise their utility. The theory became known as 'the Rochester school of accounting'. The positive approach is completely opposite to the normative approach and attempts to explain why accounting procedures and policies are as they are, whereas the normative approach attempts to prescribe the accounting procedures and policies to be implemented.

The future of theory

This section has been very brief and has mainly merely listed the approaches to the development of an accounting theory that exist in the current literature. For an in-depth study of this area we recommend *Accounting Theory* by Belkaoui.

This does, however, leave us with several questions:

- Can we develop an all-encompassing accounting theory?
- Would such a theory be useful to users?

- Should any theory be global in aspect and take into account behavioural aspects?
- Do researchers need to take into account their own underlying cultural beliefs and behaviour when developing an accounting theory?

As Glen Lehman states in *Accounting Forum* (2001) in his editorial:

Accounting might benefit by exploring its direction and future. Accounting must improve 'community usefulness' and not just simply expand into other fields such as information technology if it is to remain committed to the public interest. The technology of accounting might benefit through consideration of the relationships between regulation and construction of community virtues. Accountants have been criticised for assuming that if the 'figures' are constructed in line with current mandatory and legislative requirements, then the accounts are true and fair. Yet what is reported often bears little relation to a reasonable view of the true financial health of the entity. Future accounting research might work toward explaining the means through which corporations might be enabled to act in the interests of the communities they serve.

This statement is particularly pertinent given the Enron and WorldCom disasters in the USA.

THE IASB CONCEPTUAL FRAMEWORK

We have already outlined some of the fundamental general concepts of accounting in Chapter 1. We quickly noted that they are not always compatible between themselves and that they do not necessarily provide a prescriptive solution to a given problem. They do not, therefore, provide a rational coherent basis, which can be applied, in a scientific sense, to solve problems in ways which are likely to be themselves consistent and compatible. They are not true 'theories' in the sense discussed earlier.

A number of attempts have been made since the 1970s to create some form of more coherent conceptual framework. The IASB version, known as the Framework for the Preparation and Presentation of Financial Statements, was issued in 1989. It belongs to the family of conceptual frameworks for financial reporting that have been developed by accounting standard setters in a number of countries where accounting standard setting is carried out by a private sector body. On one level, such conceptual frameworks may be considered attempts to assemble a body of accounting theory (or interrelated concepts) as a guide to standard setting, so that standards are (as far as possible) formulated on a consistent basis and not in an ad hoc manner. On another, but complementary, level, they may be thought of as devices to confer legitimacy and authority on a private sector standard setter that lacks the legal authority of a public body. The IASB, as a private sector standard setter, shares these reasons for developing a conceptual framework.

Conceptual frameworks developed by accounting standard setters are essentially based on identification of 'good practice' from which principles are derived inductively. The criteria for identifying 'good practice' are related to the assumed objectives of financial reporting. At the same time, attention is paid to conceptual coherence, and the development process typically involves 'conceptual tidying up'.

Conceptual frameworks may be written in a prescriptive style or a descriptive style, or a mixture of the two. In any event, they are essentially normative, since they seek to provide a set of principles as a guide to setting and interpreting accounting standards. Such guidance, however, does not necessarily preclude a standard being issued that, for compelling pragmatic reasons, departs from a principle set out in the applicable conceptual framework.

The IASB's Framework is written in a descriptive style (in fact, it is IASB policy to use the word 'should' only in standards) and seeks to avoid being excessively prescriptive. One principal reason for this is that it needs to have broad international applicability. In the final paragraph of the Framework, the IASB states:

> This Framework is applicable to a range of accounting models and provides guidance on preparing and presenting the financial statements constructed under the chosen model. At the present time [1989], it is not the intention of the Board of IASB to prescribe a particular model other than in exceptional circumstances, such as . . . a hyperinflationary economy.

The Framework was intended to be separate from the IASs and to avoid binding the IASB to particular accounting treatments in IASs. It was approved and issued in April 1989 and has not been revised since that time, although the need to update it is now clearly recognised by the new Board.

However, the Framework has been quite influential in the recent development of IASs and in major revisions. For example, its definitions (and especially those of assets and liabilities) were highly influential in the preparation of IFRS 3, *Business Combinations*; IAS 37, *Provisions, Contingent Liabilities and Contingent Assets*; IAS 38, *Intangible Assets* and IAS 39, *Financial Instruments: Recognition and Measurement*.

The Framework is not an IAS and does not override any specific IAS; in case of conflict between it and an IAS, the requirements of the latter prevail. *One may, however, consider the Framework as embodying IAS GAAP in respect of issues that are not dealt with in any IAS.* This is apparent from the way in which the purpose and status of the Framework are described (see points 4 and 5 in the following list). For example, in the case of topics that have not yet been the subject of an IAS, the purpose of the Framework is to assist preparers in dealing with such topics. Moreover, the IASB will be guided by the Framework in the development of future IASs and in reviewing existing ones, so that the number of cases of conflict between the Framework and IASs are likely to diminish over time. The Framework itself will be subject to revision in the light of experience. The IASB and the (American) FASB are now attempting to create a new jointly agreed Framework. Progress appears difficult and slow. We outline the latest thinking as we go to press after our discussion of the original Framework contents.

The IASB Framework

As indicated earlier, the Framework does not have the status of an IAS, does not override any specific IAS and, in case of conflict between the Framework and an IAS, the latter prevails (paras 2–3). The purpose of the Framework is stated as follows (para. 1):

1 To assist the Board of IASB in the development of future IASs and in its review of existing IASs;

2 To assist the Board of IASB in promoting harmonisation of regulations, accounting standards and procedures relating to the presentation of financial statements by providing a basis for reducing the number of alternative accounting treatments permitted by IASs;

3 To assist national standard-setting bodies in developing national standards;

4 To assist preparers of financial statements in applying IASs and in dealing with topics that have yet to form the subject of an IAS;

5 To assist auditors in forming an opinion as to whether financial statements conform with IASs;

6 To assist users of financial statements in interpreting the information contained in financial statements prepared in conformity with IASs;

7 To provide those who are interested in the work of the IASB with information about its approach to the formulation of accounting standards.

The overall scope of the document covers:

1 objectives of financial statements

2 qualitative characteristics that determine the usefulness of financial statement information

3 definition, recognition and measurement of financial statement elements

4 concepts of capital and capital maintenance.

The Framework is concerned with 'general purpose financial statements', including consolidated financial statements. These are described as being prepared and presented at least annually and being directed toward the common information needs of a range of users. They do not include special purpose reports such as prospectuses and tax computations (para. 6). The Framework applies to the financial statements of all commercial, industrial and business reporting entities, whether in the private or public sectors (para. 8). The Framework first of all outlines the users of accounting information in a manner broadly similar to our discussion in Chapter 1:

- *Investors.* The providers of risk capital and their advisers are concerned with the risk inherent in and return provided by, their investments. They need information to help them determine whether they should buy, hold or sell. Shareholders are also interested in information which enables them to assess the ability of the entity to pay dividends.

- *Employees.* Employees and their representative groups are interested in information about the stability and profitability of their employers. They are also interested in information which enables them to assess the ability of the entity to provide remuneration, retirement benefits and employment opportunities.

- *Lenders.* Lenders are interested in information that enables them to determine whether their loans, and the interest attaching to them, will be paid when due.

- *Suppliers and other trade creditors.* Suppliers and other creditors are interested in information that enables them to determine whether amounts owing to them will be paid when due. Trade creditors are likely to be interested in an entity over a shorter period than lenders unless they are dependent on the continuation of the entity as a major customer.

- *Customers.* Customers have an interest in information about the continuance of an entity, especially when they have a long-term involvement with, or are dependent on, the entity.

- *Governments and their agencies.* Governments and their agencies are interested in the allocation of resources and, therefore, the activities of entities. They also require information in order to regulate the activities of entities, determine taxation policies and as the basis for national income and similar statistics.
- *Public.* Entities affect members of the public in a variety of ways. For example, entities may make a substantial contribution to the local economy in many ways including the number of people they employ and their patronage of local suppliers. Financial statements may assist the public by providing information about the trends and recent developments in the prosperity of the entity and the range of its activities.

Paragraph 10 states the following:

While all of the information needs of these users cannot be met by financial statements, there are needs which are common to all users. As investors are providers of risk capital to the entity, the provision of financial statements that meet their needs will also meet most of the needs of other users that financial statements can satisfy.

The Framework then goes on to summarise the overall objectives of financial statements. This is pretty standard stuff and can be briefly extracted here:

12 The objective of financial statements is to provide information about the financial position, performance and changes in financial position of an entity that is useful to a wide range of users in making economic decisions.
13 Financial statements prepared for this purpose meet the common needs of most users. However, financial statements do not provide all the information that users may need to make economic decisions since they largely portray the financial effects of past events and do not necessarily provide non-financial information.
15 The economic decisions that are taken by users of financial statements require an evaluation of the ability of an entity to generate cash and cash equivalents and of the timing and certainty of their generation. This ability ultimately determines, for example, the capacity of an entity to pay its employees and suppliers, meet interest payments, repay loans and make distributions to its owners. Users are better able to evaluate this ability to generate cash and cash equivalents if they are provided with information that focuses on the financial position, performance and changes in financial position of an entity.
19 Information about financial position is primarily provided in a balance sheet. Information about performance is primarily provided in an income statement. Information about changes in financial position is provided in the financial statements by means of a separate statement.

ACTIVITY 8.4

Does the last sentence of para. 10 follow logically?

Activity feedback

As a matter of logic, the answer is definitely not. The suggestion that because investors are providers of risk capital, information meeting the needs of investors will also meet most of the needs of, say, employees is clearly nonsense. Nevertheless, as an empirical pragmatic issue, the emphasis on investors, or at least an emphasis on providers of finance generally, may have some validity. Either way it is widely accepted in practice.

20 The component parts of the financial statements interrelate because they reflect different aspects of the same transactions or other events. Although each statement provides information that is different from the others, none is likely to serve only a single purpose or provide all the information necessary for particular needs of users. For example, an income statement provides an incomplete picture of performance unless it is used in conjunction with the balance sheet and the statement of changes in financial position.

Next the Framework discusses the various 'assumptions and characteristics' of accounting statements. These correspond closely to the conventions and characteristics of Chapter 1, but they are arranged in a series of subgroups with various headings and subheadings, which give interesting nuances of degrees of relative significance and importance. In order to give the full flavour of this the Framework is quoted here at some length.

Underlying assumptions

Accrual basis

22 In order to meet their objectives, financial statements are prepared on the accrual basis of accounting. Under this basis, the effects of transactions and other events are recognised when they occur (and not as cash or its equivalent is received or paid) and they are recorded in the accounting records and reported in the financial statements of the periods to which they relate. Financial statements prepared on the accrual basis inform users not only of past transactions involving the payment and receipt of cash but also of obligations to pay cash in the future and of resources that represent cash to be received in the future. Hence, they provide the type of information about past transactions and other events that is most useful to users in making economic decisions.

Going concern

23 The financial statements are normally prepared on the assumption that an entity is a going concern and will continue in operation for the foreseeable future. Hence it is assumed that the entity has neither the intention nor the need to liquidate or curtail materially the scale of its operations; if such an intention or need exists, the financial statement may have to be prepared on a different basis and, if so, the basis used is disclosed.

Qualitative characteristics of financial statements

24 Qualitative characteristics are the attributes that make the information provided in financial statements useful to users. The four principal qualitative characteristics are understandability, relevance, reliability and comparability.

Understandability

25 An essential quality of the information provided in financial statements is that it is readily understandable by users. For this purpose, users are assumed to have a reasonable knowledge of business and economic activities and accounting and a willingness to study the information with reasonable diligence. However, information about complex matters that should be included in the financial statements because of its relevance to the economic decision-making needs of users should not be excluded merely on the grounds that it may be too difficult for certain users to understand.

Relevance

26 To be useful, information must be relevant to the decision-making needs of users. Information has the quality of relevance when it influences the economic decisions of users by helping them to evaluate past, present or future events or confirming, or correcting, their past evaluations.

27 The predictive and confirmatory roles of information are interrelated. For example, information about the current level and structure of asset holdings has value to users when they endeavour to predict the ability of the entity to take advantage of opportunities and its ability to react to adverse situations. The same information plays a confirmatory role in respect of past predictions about, for example, the way in which the entity would be structured or the outcome of planned operations.

28 Information about financial position and past performance is frequently used as the basis for predicting future financial position and performance and other matters in which users are directly interested, such as dividend and wage payments, security price movements and the ability of the entity to meet its commitments as they fall due. To have predictive value, information need not be in the form of an explicit forecast. The ability to make predictions from financial statements is enhanced, however, by the manner in which information on past transactions and events is displayed. For example, the predictive value of the income statement is enhanced if unusual, abnormal and infrequent items of income or expense are separately disclosed.

Materiality

29 The relevance of information is affected by its nature and materiality. In some cases, the nature of information alone is sufficient to determine its relevance. For example, the reporting of a new segment may affect the assessment of the risks and opportunities facing the entity irrespective of the materiality of the results achieved by the new segment in the reporting period. In other cases, both the nature and materiality are important, for example, the amounts of inventories held in each of the main categories that are appropriate to the business.

30 Information is material if its omission or misstatement could influence the economic decisions of users taken on the basis of the financial statements. Materiality depends on the size of the item or error judged in the particular circumstances of its omission or misstatement. Thus, materiality provides a threshold or cut-off point rather than being a primary qualitative characteristic which information must have if it is to be useful.

Reliability

31 To be useful, information must also be reliable. Information has the quality of reliability when it is free from material error and bias and can be depended on by users to represent faithfully that which it either purports to represent or could reasonably be expected to represent.

32 Information may be relevant but so unreliable in nature or representation that its recognition may be potentially misleading. For example, if the validity and amount

of a claim for damages under a legal action are disputed, it may be inappropriate for the entity to recognise the full amount of the claim in the balance sheet, although it may be appropriate to disclose the amount and circumstances of the claim.

Faithful representation

33 To be reliable, information must represent faithfully the transactions and other events it either purports to represent or could reasonably be expected to represent. Thus, for example, a balance sheet should represent faithfully the transactions and other events that result in assets, liabilities and equity of the entity at the reporting date which meet the recognition criteria.

34 Most financial information is subject to some risk of being less than a faithful representation of that which it purports to portray. This is not due to bias, but rather to inherent difficulties either in identifying the transactions and other events to be measured or in devising and applying measurement and presentation techniques that can convey messages that correspond with those transactions and events. In certain cases, the measurement of the financial effects of items could be so uncertain that entities generally would not recognise them in the financial statements; for example, although most entities generate goodwill internally over time, it is usually difficult to identify or measure that goodwill reliably. In other cases, however, it may be relevant to recognise items and to disclose the risk of error surrounding their recognition and measurement.

Substance over form

35 If information is to represent faithfully transactions and other events that it purports to represent, it is necessary that they are accounted for and presented in accordance with their substance and economic reality and not merely their legal form. The substance of transactions or other events is not always consistent with that which is apparent from their legal or contrived form. For example, an entity may dispose of an asset to another party in such a way that the documentation purports to pass legal ownership to that party; nevertheless, agreements may exist that ensure that the entity continues to enjoy the future economic benefits embodied in the asset. In such circumstances, the reporting of a sale would not represent faithfully the transaction entered into (if indeed there was a transaction).

Neutrality

36 To be reliable, the information contained in financial statements must be neutral, that is, free from bias. Financial statements are not neutral if, by the selection or presentation of information, they influence the making of a decision or judgement in order to achieve a pre-determined result or outcome.

Prudence

37 The preparers of financial statements do, however, have to contend with the uncertainties that inevitably surround many events and circumstances, such as the collectability of doubtful receivables, the probable useful life of plant and equipment and the number of warranty claims that may occur. Such uncertainties are recognised by the disclosure of their nature and extent and by the exercise of prudence in the preparation of the financial statements. Prudence is the inclusion of a degree of caution in the exercise of the judgements needed in making the

estimates required under conditions of uncertainty, such that assets or income are not overstated and liabilities or expenses are not understated. However, the exercise of prudence does not allow, for example, the creation of hidden reserves or excessive provisions, the deliberate understatement of assets or income or the deliberate overstatement of liabilities or expenses, because the financial statements would not be neutral and, therefore, not have the quality of reliability.

Completeness

38 To be reliable, the information in financial statements must be complete within the bounds of materiality and cost. An omission can cause information to be false or misleading and thus unreliable and deficient in terms of its relevance.

Comparability

39 Users must be able to compare the financial statements of an entity through time in order to identify trends in its financial position and performance. Users must also be able to compare the financial statements of different entities in order to evaluate their relative financial position, performance and changes in financial position. Hence, the measurement and display of the financial effect of like transactions and other events must be carried out in a consistent way throughout an entity and over time for that entity and in a consistent way for different entities.

40 An important implication of the qualitative characteristic of comparability is that users be informed of the accounting policies employed in the preparation of the financial statements, any changes in those policies and the effects of such changes. Users need to be able to identify differences between the accounting policies for like transactions and other events used by the same entity from period to period and by different entities. Compliance with International Accounting Standards, including the disclosure of the accounting policies used by the entity, helps to achieve comparability.

41 The need for comparability should not be confused with mere uniformity and should not be allowed to become an impediment to the introduction of improved accounting standards. It is not appropriate for an entity to continue accounting in the same manner for a transaction or other event if the policy adopted is not in keeping with the qualitative characteristics of relevance and reliability. It is also inappropriate for an entity to leave its accounting policies unchanged when more relevant and reliable alternatives exist.

42 Because users wish to compare the financial position, performance and changes in financial position of an entity over time, it is important that the financial statements show corresponding information for the preceding periods.

Constraints on relevant and reliable information

Timeliness

43 If there is undue delay in the reporting of information it may lose its relevance. Management may need to balance the relative merits of timely reporting and the provision of reliable information. To provide information in a timely basis it may often be necessary to report before all aspects of a transaction or other event are known, thus impairing reliability. Conversely, if reporting is delayed until all aspects are known, the information may be highly reliable but of little use to users who have had to make decisions in the interim. In achieving a balance between relevance and reliability, the overriding consideration is how best to satisfy the economic decision-making needs of users.

Balance between benefit and cost

44 The balance between benefit and cost is a pervasive constraint rather than a qualitative characteristic. The benefits derived from information should exceed the cost of providing it. The evaluation of benefits and costs is, however, substantially a judgemental process. Furthermore, the costs do not necessarily fall on those users who enjoy the benefits. Benefits may also be enjoyed by users other than those for whom the information is prepared; for example, the provision of further information to lenders may reduce the borrowing costs of an entity. For these reasons, it is difficult to apply a cost benefit test in any particular case. Nevertheless, standard setters in particular, as well as the preparers and users of financial statements, should be aware of this constraint.

Balance between qualitative characteristics

45 In practice a balancing, or trade-off, between qualitative characteristics is often necessary. Generally the aim is to achieve an appropriate balance among the characteristics in order to meet the objective of financial statements. The relative importance of the characteristics in different cases is a matter of professional judgement.

True and fair view/fair presentation

46 Financial statements are frequently described as showing a true and fair view of, or as presenting fairly, the financial position, performance and changes in financial position of an entity. Although this framework does not deal directly with such concepts, the application of the principal qualitative characteristics and of appropriate accounting standards normally results in financial statements that convey what is generally understood as a true and fair view of or as presenting fairly such information.

This last paragraph concerning fair presentation has been rather overtaken by events, and is effectively superseded by IAS 1, discussed next.

It is worth emphasising the suggested interrelationships between these various notions. There are two, and only two, *underlying assumptions*, the accrual basis and the going concern assumption. There are four *principal qualitative characteristics*, some with related sub-characteristics, as shown in Table 8.1.

There are a number of peculiarities about these suggested relationships. Not every national tradition would accept them. Note that the importance of prudence is significantly downgraded, to the lowest level. Neither is it at all obvious how prudence (which is hardly 'neutral') is necessary for 'reliability', however important one may think prudence is in itself.

Elements of financial statements

The section of the Framework concerning the elements of financial statements (paras 47–80) consists essentially of definitions of the elements of financial statements as identified by the Framework. The definitions given in this section, and especially

TABLE 8.1	Assumptions and characteristics of accounting statements
Principal characteristic	*Sub-characteristic*
Understandability	
Relevance	
Reliability	Materiality
	Faithful representation
	Substance over form
	Neutrality
	Prudence
	Completeness
Comparability	

those of assets and liabilities, are the core of the Framework as a prescriptive basis for standard setting. The section on 'Recognition of Elements' (paras 82–98) acts to reinforce this core. In particular:

1 The Framework defines income and expenses in terms of increases and decreases in economic benefits that are equated with changes in assets and liabilities.

2 The latter are defined in terms of 'resources controlled' and 'present obligations' to exclude some of the types of items that have been recognised as assets or liabilities (accruals and deferrals) in the name of 'matching' expenses and revenues.

In other words, the definitions of assets and liability are the starting point for the entire edifice, putting the focus on balance sheet items, not on profit (revenue and expense) calculation.

The elements considered to be 'directly related to the measurement of financial position' are assets, liabilities and equity, which are defined as follows (para. 49):

1 An asset is a resource

   (a) controlled by the entity,

   (b) as a result of past events, and

   (c) from which future economic benefits are expected to flow to the entity.
   Recognition as an asset thus requires that all three components of the definition, (a), (b) and (c), be satisfied.

2 A liability is

   (a) a present obligation of the entity,

   (b) arising out of past events,

   (c) the settlement of which is expected to result in an outflow from the entity of resources embodying economic benefits.
   Recognition as a liability thus requires that all three components of the definition, (a), (b) and (c), be satisfied.

3 Equity is defined as the residual interest in the assets of the entity after deducting all its liabilities.

Merely satisfying these definitions does not entail recognition, since the recognition criteria in paras 82–98 must also be satisfied and also the principle of 'substance over form' must be respected. For example, this principle requires fixed assets held under finance leases to be recognised by the lessee as fixed assets (with corresponding leasing liabilities), while the lessor recognises a financial asset (paras 50–51).

Balance sheets drawn up in accordance with 'current' [in 1989] IASs may include items the treatment of which does not satisfy these definitions, but the definitions will underlie 'future' reviews of existing standards and the formulation of new ones (para. 52). As noted earlier, the IASB has acted accordingly and it would be unusual to find an item whose treatment according to a recently issued IAS would conflict with the definitions.

Assets The 'future economic benefit embodied in an asset' is defined as 'the potential to contribute, directly or indirectly, to the flow of cash and cash equivalents to the entity', including 'a capability to reduce cash outflows'. In case that definition should leave the status of cash itself as an asset unclear, it is stated that cash satisfies this definition, because it 'renders a service to the entity because of its command over other resources'. Assets embody future economic benefits that may flow to the entity by having one or more of the following capabilities:

- being exchanged for other assets
- being used to settle a liability
- being distributed to the entity's owners.

Cash conspicuously possesses these three capabilities; as well as that of being used singly or in combination with other assets in the production of goods and services to be sold by the entity (paras 53–55).

Neither having physical form nor being the object of a right of ownership is an essential attribute of an asset. Intangible items such as patents and copyrights may satisfy the definition of an asset, as may a fixed asset held under a finance lease (by virtue of which it is a resource controlled though not owned by the entity and from which future benefits are expected to flow). Moreover, knowledge obtained from development activity may meet the definition of an asset (capitalised development costs) even though neither physical form nor legal ownership is involved, provided there is de facto control such that, by keeping the knowledge secret, the entity controls the benefits that are expected to flow from it (paras 56–57).

Assets may result from various types of past transactions and other past events. Normally, these are purchase transactions and the events associated with production, but they may include donation (for example, by way of a government grant) or discovery (as in the case of mineral deposits). Expected future transactions or events do not give rise to assets; for example, a binding contract by an entity to purchase inventory does not cause the inventory in question to meet the definition of an asset of that entity until the purchase transaction that fulfils the contract has occurred. While expenditure is a common way to acquire or generate an asset, expenditure undertaken with a view to generating future economic benefits may fail to result in an asset, for example, if the intended economic benefits cannot be expected or are not controlled by the entity (paras 58–59).

ACTIVITY 8.5

Consider whether each of the following are assets, giving reasons for your answers.

1 A heap of rusty metal worth €10 as scrap but costing €20 to transport to the scrap dealer.

2 A municipal or trades union social or welfare centre outside the factory that substantially improves the overall working conditions of a firm's employees.

3 The benefits derived from next year's sales.

Activity feedback
None of these is an asset because it:

1 has no probable future benefit

2 is not possessed or controlled by the business

3 contains no earlier transaction or event.

Assets are always divided into *fixed assets* and *current assets*. The definition of fixed assets is often misunderstood. A fixed asset is not an asset with a long life. The essential criterion is the *intention* of the owner, the intended use of the asset. A fixed asset is an asset that the firm intends to use within the business, over an extended period, in order to assist its daily operating activities. A current asset, by way of contrast, is usually defined in terms of time. A current asset is an asset likely to change its form, i.e. likely to undergo some transaction, usually within 12 months. Consider two firms, A and B. Firm A is a motor trader. It possesses some motor vehicles that it is attempting to sell, and it also possesses some desks used by the sales staff, management and so on. Firm B is a furniture dealer. It possesses some desks that it is attempting to sell and it also possesses some motor vehicles used by the sales staff and for delivery purposes. In the accounts of A, the motor vehicles are current assets and the desks are fixed assets. In the accounts of B, the motor vehicles are fixed assets and the desks are current assets. Note incidentally that a fixed asset, which, after several years' use, is about to be sold for scrap, remains in the fixed asset part of the accounts even though it is about to change its form.

These two definitions, because they are based on different criteria (one on use and one on time), are not mutually exclusive. It is possible to think of assets that do not conveniently appear to be either fixed or current. Investments, for example, or goodwill.

Liabilities An essential characteristic of (or necessary condition for) a liability is that the entity should have a 'present obligation'. An obligation is 'a duty or responsibility to act or perform in a certain way'. The duty or responsibility may arise from the law, for example, the law of contract; or it may arise from normal business practice, which leads to legitimate expectations that the entity will act or perform in a certain way (that is, a constructive obligation). An example of the latter is a constructive obligation to extend the benefits of a warranty for some period beyond the contractual warranty period, because this is an established practice (para. 60).

A present obligation (in the relevant sense) is not the same as a future commitment. An entity may have a commitment to purchase an asset in the future at an agreed price; however, this does not entail a net outflow of resources. The commitment does not give rise to a liability, which arises only when the purchase has actually taken place and title in the asset has passed to the entity, leaving the latter with an obligation to pay for it. (In the case of a cash transaction, no liability would arise (para. 61).)

There are a number of ways in which a liability may be settled or discharged, which include replacement by another obligation, conversion into equity and the creditor waiving or forfeiting his rights. There are also various types of 'past transactions or past events' from which liabilities may result (paras 62–63). If a provision involves a present obligation and satisfies the rest of the definition of a liability given in the Framework, it is a liability even if the amount has to be estimated (para. 64). Paragraph 64 does not emphasise the equally important point that a provision that fails to satisfy the criterion of being an *obligation* arising from a past transaction or past event is not a liability. This point, however, was crucial in arriving at the requirements for recognition of provisions in IAS 22, *Business Combinations* (now IFRS 3) and IAS 37, *Provisions, Contingent Liabilities and Contingent Assets* (see Chapters 25 and 19).

Equity Paragraphs 65–68 are concerned with equity. The fact that equity is defined as a residual interest (assets minus liabilities) does not mean that it cannot be meaningfully divided into sub-classifications that are shown separately in the balance sheet. Examples are the difference among the following:

- paid-in capital (capital stock and paid-in surplus)
- reserves representing appropriations of retained earnings
- reserves representing the amounts required to be retained in order to maintain 'real' capital, that is, either real financial capital or (real) physical capital (para. 65).

There are various legal, tax and valuation considerations that affect equity, such as requirements for legal reserves and whether or not the entity is incorporated. It is emphasised that transfers to legal, statutory and tax reserves are appropriations of retained earnings and not expenses. (Likewise, releases from such reserves are credits to retained earnings and not income, but this is not spelled out.) The rather obvious point is made that the amount at which equity is shown in the balance sheet is not intended to be a measure of the market value of the entity, either as a going concern or in a piecemeal disposal. It is stated that the definition and treatment of equity in the Framework are appropriate for unincorporated entities, even if the legal considerations are different.

Performance

Paragraphs 69–81 contain the section of the Framework in which definitions of the financial statement elements relating to performance are given. 'Profit is frequently used as a measure of performance or as the basis for other measures, such as return on investment and earnings per share' (para. 69). However, this section of the Framework does not discuss the relationship between the elements of performance and the profit measure, except to say that 'the recognition and measurement of income and expenses, and hence profit, depends in part on the concepts of capital and capital maintenance used by the entity in preparing its financial statements'. The determination of profit and related issues are discussed in a later section of the Framework (paras 102–110).

The elements of income and expenses are defined as follows:

1 Income is increases in economic benefits during the accounting period in the form of inflows or enhancements of assets or decreases of liabilities that result in increases in equity, other than those relating to contributions from equity participants.

2 Expenses are decreases in economic benefits during the accounting period in the form of outflows or depletions of assets or incurrences of liabilities that result in decreases in equity, other than those relating to distributions to equity participants (para. 70).

These definitions identify the essential features of income and expenses but do not attempt to specify their recognition criteria (para. 71). The definition makes it clear that the Framework's approach treats the definitions of assets and liabilities as *logically prior* to those of income and expenses. This is sometimes characterised as a 'balance sheet approach' to the relationship between financial statements. This term is potentially misleading, however. The Framework's approach should certainly not be understood as implying the subordination of the income statements to the balance sheet from an *informational* perspective.

Income The Framework's definition of income encompasses both revenue and gains. Revenue is described as arising in the course of the ordinary activities of an entity and includes sales, fees, interest, royalties and rent. Gains may or may not arise in the course of ordinary activities. Gains may arise on the disposal of non-current assets and also include unrealised gains such as those arising on the revaluation of marketable securities and from increases in the carrying amount of long-term assets. Gains, when recognised in the income statements, are usually displayed separately because their economic significance tends to differ from that of revenue, and they are often reported net of related expenses (paras 74–77).

The counterpart entry corresponding to a credit for income may be to various asset accounts (not only cash or receivables) or to a liability account such as when a loan is discharged by the provision of goods or services (para. 77).

Expenses The Framework's definition of expenses encompasses losses as well as expenses that arise in the course of the ordinary activities of the entity. Examples given of expenses that arise in the course of ordinary activities are cost of sales, wages and depreciation. They usually take the form (that is, are the accounting counterpart) of an outflow or depletion of assets such as cash and cash equivalents, inventory, property or plant and equipment (para. 78).

Losses represent items that may or may not arise in the course of ordinary activities. They include those that result from such disasters as fire or flood, as well as those arising on the disposal of non-current assets and also encompass unrealised losses, such as those arising from the effects of adverse currency exchange rate movements on financial assets or liabilities. Losses, when recognised in the income statement, are usually displayed separately because their economic significance tends to differ from that of other expenses and they are often reported net of related income (paras 79–80).

Recognition of the elements of financial statements

Recognition issues are dealt with in paras 82–98. Recognition is described as 'the process of incorporating in the balance sheet or [the] income statement an item that meets the definition of an element and satisfies the criteria for recognition set out in paragraph 83'. (The statement of changes in financial position is not mentioned because its elements consist of those that are also elements of financial position or performance.) Failure to recognise *in the main financial statements* items that satisfy the relevant definition and recognition criteria is not rectified by disclosure of the accounting policies used or by use of notes or other explanatory material.

The recognition criteria set out in para. 83 are that an item that meets the definition of an element should be recognised if:

1 it is probable that any future economic benefit associated with the item will flow to or from the entity

2 the item has a cost or value that can be measured with reliability.

Recognition is subject to materiality. Accounting interrelationships are also significant, since recognition in the financial statements of an item that meets the definition and recognition criteria for a particular element, for example an asset, entails the recognition of another (counterpart) element, such as income or a liability (para. 84). (This refers, strictly speaking, to the initial recognition of an item. However, a similar point could be made about the implications of re-measurement or valuation adjustments.)

Probability of future economic benefit The concept of *probability* is used in the recognition criteria 'to refer to the degree of uncertainty [as to whether] the future economic benefits associated with the time will flow to or from the entity ... in keeping with the uncertainty that characterises the environment in which an entity operates'. Assessments of such uncertainty are made on the basis of the evidence available when the financial statements are prepared. In regard to receivables, for example, for a large population of accounts, some statistical evidence will usually be available regarding collectibility (para. 85).

Reliability of measurement Reliability, the second recognition criterion, was discussed earlier in the section on qualitative characteristics of financial statements. If an item does not possess a cost or value that can be measured with reliability (so that the information has that qualitative characteristic), then it is not appropriate to recognise it. However, in many cases, cost or (more particularly) value must be estimated; indeed, the use of reasonable estimates is an essential part of the financial reporting process and need not undermine reliability. In cases where an item satisfied the definition of an element but not the recognition criteria, it will not be recognised in the financial statements themselves, but its relevance is likely to require its disclosure in the notes to the financial statements or in other supplementary disclosures. This applies when the item meets the probability criterion of recognition but not the reliability criterion, but may also apply to an item that meets the definition of an element when neither recognition criterion is met. The key issue here is whether the item is considered to be relevant to the evaluation of financial position, performance or changes in financial position. An item that does not satisfy the recognition criteria for an asset or a liability at one time may do so later, if more information relevant to estimating its probability, cost or value becomes available (paras 86–88).

It is important to note that 'probable' and 'reliability' are both relative and subjective concepts. The Framework does not pretend otherwise. Professional judgement is required in the context of the particular situation in which the entity concerned operates.

Recognition of assets An asset is recognised in the balance sheet when it is probable that future economic benefits will flow to the entity (as a result of its control of the asset) and the asset's cost or value can be measured reliably. When expenditure has been incurred but it is not considered probable that economic benefits will flow to the entity beyond the current accounting period, this expenditure will be recognised as an expense, not as an asset. The intention of management in undertaking the expenditure is irrelevant (paras 89–90).

Recognition of liabilities A liability is recognised in the balance sheet when it is probable that an outflow of resources embodying economic benefits will result from the settlement of a present obligation and the amount of that settlement can be measured reliably. Obligations under executory contracts, that is, non-cancellable contracts that are equally proportionately unperformed (such as the amount that will be a liability when inventory ordered and awaiting delivery is received), are not generally recognised as liabilities in the balance sheet, neither are the related assets recognised in the balance sheet. In some cases, however, recognition may be required (para. 91).

Recognition of income Recognition of income occurs simultaneously with the recognition of increases in assets or decreases in liabilities (or a combination of the two). The normal recognition procedures used in practice are applications of the Framework's recognition criteria. An example is the requirement that revenue should be earned (that is, it should be associated with a simultaneous increase in assets or decrease in liabilities). These procedures are concerned with restricting the recognition of income to items that, in effect, meet the Framework's recognition criteria of probability (a sufficient degree of certainty that an economic benefit has flowed or will flow to the entity) and reliability of measurement (paras 92–93).

Recognition of expenses Recognition of expenses occurs simultaneously with the recognition of an increase in liabilities or a decrease in assets (or a combination of the two). Expenses are commonly recognised in the income statement on the basis of an association (matching) between the incurrence of costs and the earning of specific items of revenue, that result directly and jointly from the same transactions or other events. An example is the matching of the cost of goods sold with the associated sales revenue. However, the Framework does not permit the application of the matching procedure to result in the recognition of items in the balance sheet that do not meet the definition of assets or liabilities (paras 94–95).

Measurement of the elements of the financial statements

Paragraphs 99–101 deal with measurement issues, insofar as these are covered in the Framework. The treatment here is descriptive and avoids being prescriptive. Measurement is described as 'the process of determining the monetary amounts at which the elements of the financial statements are to be recognised and carried in the balance sheet and income statement'. It involves the selection of a particular basis of measurement.

Four different measurement bases are specifically mentioned and described (without any claim to exhaustiveness): historical cost, current cost (of replacement or settlement), realisable or (for liabilities) settlement value and present value. Historical cost is mentioned as the measurement basis most commonly adopted by entities in preparing their financial statements, usually in combination with other measurement bases. An example of the latter is the carrying of inventories at the lower of historical cost and net realisable value. Marketable securities may be carried at market value and pension liabilities are carried at their present value. Current cost may be used as a means of taking account of the effects of changing prices of non-monetary assets.

Concepts of capital and capital maintenance

Concepts of capital The Framework identifies two main concepts of capital: the financial concept and the physical concept. The financial concept of capital may take two forms: invested money (nominal financial) capital or invested purchasing power (real financial) capital. In either case, capital is identified with the equity of the entity (in either nominal or real financial terms) and with its net assets measured in those terms. The physical concept of capital is based on the notion of the productive capacity or operating capability of the entity, as embodied in its net assets. Most entities adopt a financial concept of capital, normally (in the absence of severe inflation) nominal financial capital (para. 102).

Capital maintenance and the determination of profit Choice of a concept of capital is related to the concept of capital maintenance that is most meaningful, given the implications of the choice for profit measurement and the needs of the users of the financial statements in that regard, as follows:

- *Maintenance of nominal financial capital.* Under this concept a profit is earned only if the money amount of the net assets at the end of the period exceeds the money amount of the net assets at the beginning of the period, after excluding any distributions to, and contributions from, equity owners during the period.

- *Maintenance of real financial capital.* Under this concept a profit is earned only if the money amount of the net assets at the end of the period exceeds the money amount of the net assets at the beginning of the period, restated in units of the same purchasing power, after excluding distributions to, and contributions from, owners. Normally, the units of purchasing power employed are those of the currency at the end of the period, into which the net assets at the beginning of the period are restated.

- *Maintenance of real physical capital.* Under this concept a profit is earned only if the operating capability embodied in the net assets at the end of the period exceeds the operating capability embodied in the net assets at the beginning of the period, after excluding distributions to, and contributions from, owners. Operating capability embodied in assets may, in principle, be measured by employing the current cost basis of measurement (paras 103–106).

The main difference among the three concepts of capital maintenance is the treatment of the effects of changes in the carrying amounts of the entity's assets and liabilities. Under nominal financial capital maintenance, increases in the money-carrying amounts of assets held over the period (to the extent that they are recognised as gains) are part of profit.

Under real financial capital maintenance, such increases are part of profit only if they are 'real' increases, that is, increases that remain after money-carrying amounts have been restated in units of the same purchasing power. The total amount of the restatement is known as a 'capital maintenance adjustment' and is transferred to a capital maintenance reserve, which is part of equity (but not of retained profits). Real financial capital maintenance may be used in conjunction with historical cost as a measurement basis but would more normally be used in conjunction with the current cost basis. (See Illustration.)

Developments towards a revised IASB Framework

The IASB and the FASB are in the process of developing a common conceptual framework to replace their two different existing sets of documents. This process has been divided into a number of different sections or sub-projects. These are moving at different speeds. Some have not yet been started and, at the time of writing (early in

---

ILLUSTRATION

Let us assume that a company begins with capital stock of €100 and cash of €100. At the beginning of the year, one item of inventory is bought for €100. The item of inventory is sold at the end of the year for €150, its replacement cost at that time is €120 and general inflation throughout the year is 10%. Profit measured using each of the capital maintenance concepts mentioned earlier would be as shown:

	Nominal financial capital maintenance	Real financial capital maintenance	Real physical capital maintenance
Sales	€150	€150	€150
less Cost of sales	(100)	(100)	(120)
Operating profit	50	50	30
less Inflation adjustment	–	(10)	–
Total gain	€50	€40	€30
Capital maintenance adjustment	€0	€10	€20

Column 1 shows the gain after ensuring the maintenance of the stockholders' opening capital measured as a sum of money. Column 2 shows the gain after ensuring the maintenance of the stockholders' opening capital measured as a block of purchasing power. Both of these are concerned, under different definitions, with the maintenance of financial capital – in terms either of its money amount or of its general purchasing power. Column 3 shows the gain after ensuring the maintenance of the company's initial operating capacity and is therefore of a completely different nature.

Under real physical capital maintenance, changes in the money prices at current costs of assets and liabilities held over the period are considered not to affect the amount of operating capability embodied in those items and therefore the total amount of those changes is treated as a capital maintenance adjustment and excluded from profit.

Different combinations of measurement bases and capital maintenance concepts provide different accounting models, between which management should choose, taking into account relevance and reliability. Readers should be very familiar with the concepts underlying these alternatives, which have been fully discussed in Chapters 4–7.

2009), none have been finalised, although one has reached the formal exposure draft stage. Experience shows that significant changes of thinking can and do take place at any stage in the long deliberative process. We outline the current situation here, but nothing below should be taken as definitive.

As of late 2008, the project was established in eight phases:

A Objectives and qualitative characteristics

B Definitions of elements, recognition and derecognition

C Measurement

D Reporting entity concept

E Boundaries of financial reporting, and presentation and disclosure

F Purpose and status of the framework

G Application of the framework to not-for-profit entities

H Remaining issues, if any

At that time, an exposure draft of A and a discussion paper for D had been issued. 'Initial consultative documents' for B and C are 'planned for publication' in 2009 and E to H are not 'currently active'. In summary, therefore, progress is slow.

The exposure draft for A may be reasonably close to an essential definitive version, and we summarise it here.

Chapter 1 The objective of financial reporting

The objective of general purpose financial reporting is to provide financial information about the reporting entity that is useful to present and potential equity investors, lenders and other creditors in making decisions in their capacity as capital providers. Capital providers are the primary users of financial reporting. To accomplish the objective, financial reports should communicate information about an entity's economic claims on those resources, and the transactions and other events and circumstances that change them. The degree to which that financial information is useful will depend on its qualitative characteristics.

Chapter 2 Qualitative characteristics and constraints of decision-useful financial reporting information

Qualitative characteristics are the attributes that make financial reporting information useful. The qualitative characteristics are complementary concepts that each contribute to the usefulness of financial reporting information. However, for analysis purposes it is helpful to distinguish the qualitative characteristics as either fundamental or enhancing, depending on how they affect the usefulness of information. Providing useful financial reporting information is limited by two pervasive constraints on financial reporting – materiality and cost.

Fundamental qualitative characteristics distinguish useful financial reporting information from information that is not useful or is misleading. For financial information to be useful, it must possess the two fundamental qualitative characteristics – relevance and faithful representation. Relevant information is capable of making a difference in decision making by virtue of its predictive or confirmatory value. Financial reporting information is a faithful representation if it depicts the substance of an economic phenomenon completely, neutrally and without material error.

Financial reporting information may have varying degrees of usefulness to different capital providers. Enhancing qualitative characteristics distinguish more useful information from less useful information. They enhance the decision-usefulness of financial reporting information that is relevant and faithfully represented. Enhancing qualitative characteristics (comparability, verifiability, timeliness and understandability) should be maximised to the extent possible. However, the enhancing qualitative characteristics, either individually or in concert with each other, cannot make information useful for decisions if that information is irrelevant or not faithfully represented.

Comparable information enables users to identify similarities in and differences between two sets of economic phenomena. Verifiable information lends credibility to the assertion that financial reporting information represents the economic phenomena that it purports to represent. Timeliness provides information to decision makers when it has the capacity to influence decisions. Understandability is the quality of information that enables users to comprehend its meaning.

Providing useful financial reporting information is limited by two pervasive constraints, *materiality* and *cost*. Information is material if its omission or misstatement could influence the decisions that users make on the basis of an entity's financial information. The benefits of providing financial reporting information should justify the costs of providing that information.

Phase D is in such an early stage that any detail would be dangerous. The concept of control is emphasised (as a matter of fact and not of legal structure) and an entity rather than proprietorial focus is preferred (e.g. focusing on a parent company/group, and not on the majority shareholders of the group).

Check out the IASB website for updates on this whole process.

IAS 1 *PRESENTATION OF FINANCIAL STATEMENTS*

It is most important to remember that the Framework has not been revised since 1989 and is now, as the IASB is well aware, in need of further development. However, to complicate the situation further, a revised version of IAS 1, *Presentation of Financial Statements*, was issued in 1997 and this covers some of the topics discussed in the Framework. As a full Standard, IAS 1 automatically takes priority over the Framework where there is any overlap or conflict. A further revision was finalised in 2004, effective from 1 January 2005, with earlier adoption being 'encouraged'. A further disclosure requirement was added in August 2005 and finally several significant further amendments were made in a revised version of IAS 1 that was issued in September 2007, required from 1 January 2009 at the latest. It is this last version that we discuss here.

Presentation of Financial Statements represents an attempt to cover several important aspects. The objective of the Standard is to prescribe the basis for presentation of general purpose financial statements, in order to ensure comparability both with the entity's own financial statements of previous periods and with the financial statements of other entities. To achieve this objective, the Standard sets out overall considerations for the presentation of financial statements, guidelines for their structure and minimum requirements for the content of financial statements.

In principle, therefore, IAS 1 applies to all aspects of all businesses. Many aspects of financial reporting are covered additionally by other more specific International

Accounting Standards, as detailed elsewhere in this volume. However, some other aspects are not further developed and IAS 1 therefore comprises the IAS GAAP in those respects. For example, disclosure of fixed assets is discussed in IAS 16, *Property Plant and Equipment* (see Chapter 12), but disclosure of current assets has no additional Standard, except for component parts such as inventories, covered by IAS 2, *Inventories* (see Chapter 16).

Broadly speaking, IAS 1 consists of two parts. Part 1 discusses a number of 'overall considerations' consisting of general principles, conventions and requirements. Much of Part 1 is a restatement of aspects of the Framework, as discussed already. Part 2 discusses in some detail the required contents of general purpose financial statements. It is worth noting that most national accounting standards operate, and are designed to operate, within the context of national legislation, especially for corporations. There is, of course, no single international company or corporation statute. To some extent, IAS 1 provides a minimal filling in of this lacuna.

Consistent with our chapter structure in this book, the first part of IAS 1 is discussed here. Part 2 is covered in Chapter 9.

SCOPE OF IAS 1

The scope and applicability of IAS 1 revised (hereafter IAS 1) is very wide. It should be applied in the presentation of all general purpose financial statements prepared and presented in accordance with International Accounting Standards.

General purpose financial statements are those intended to meet the needs of users who are not in a position to demand reports tailored to meet their specific information needs. They include statements presented separately or those within another public document such as an annual report or prospectus.

IAS 1 does not apply to condensed interim financial information, but it must be applied in full to all general purpose statements as already described which claim to be in accordance with International Accounting Standards. Not-for-profit organisations can also apply the Standard (and IAS GAAP generally) by amending item descriptions in the financial statements as appropriate.

IAS 1 repeats the objective of general purpose financial statements from the Framework, as being to provide information about the financial position, performance, and cash flows of an entity that is useful to a wide range of users in making economic decisions. Financial statements also show the results of management's stewardship of the resources entrusted to it. Financial statements provide information about an entity's (para. 9):

1 assets
2 liabilities
3 equity
4 income and expenses, including gains and losses
5 contributions by and distributions to owners in their capacity as owners, and
6 cash flows.

A complete set of financial statements, therefore, includes the following components (para. 10):

(a) a statement of financial position as at the end of the period

(b) a statement of comprehensive income for the period

(c) a statement of changes in equity for the period

(d) a statement of cash flows for the period

(e) notes, comprising a summary of significant accounting policies and other explanatory information; and

(f) a statement of financial position as at the beginning of the earliest comparative period when an entity applies an accounting policy retrospectively or makes a retrospective restatement of items in its financial statements, or when it reclassifies items in its financial statements.

An entity may use titles for the statements other than those used in this Standard.

An entity shall present with equal prominence all of the financial statements in a complete set of financial statements. The implications of this are discussed and illustrated in more detail in Chapter 9.

IAS 1 encourages, but does not require, the additional presentation, 'outside the financial statements', of a management report about the financial performance and financial position of the enterprise, and about its environment, risks and uncertainties. Brief suggestions as to coverage are made in paragraph 8, but none of the suggestions are mandatory. Further additional statements and reports, for example, on environmental matters, are also encouraged.

FAIR PRESENTATION AND COMPLIANCE WITH INTERNATIONAL ACCOUNTING STANDARDS

The first substantive part of IAS 1 concerns the vexed question of the override. The issue at stake is whether or not the detailed regulations, i.e. the Standards in this case, are always and automatically both necessary and sufficient conditions for the preparation of adequate financial statements or whether some more fundamental overriding criterion, such as the provision of a true and fair view, a requirement to present fairly or a requirement not to mislead users is, when a clash occurs, the determining requirement (hence 'overriding' the Standards). IAS 1 recognises that compliance with the International Standards may be insufficient or inadequate 'in extremely rare circumstances'.

Entities which comply with IAS should say so. This requires that they comply with all applicable aspects of all applicable Standards and with all applicable interpretations of the Standing Interpretations Committee. However, the overall requirement is that financial statements should present fairly the financial position, financial performance and cash flows of an entity. Fair presentation requires the faithful representation of the effects of transactions, other events and conditions in accordance with the definitions and recognition criteria for assets, liabilities, income and expenses set out in the Framework. The appropriate application of IAS, with additional disclosure when necessary, results, in 'virtually all circumstances', in financial statements that achieve a fair presentation.

In the extremely rare circumstances when management concludes that compliance with a requirement in a Standard would be misleading and therefore that departure from a requirement is necessary to achieve a fair presentation, an entity should (not may) depart from that requirement 'if the relevant regulatory framework requires, or otherwise does not prohibit, such a departure'.

When an entity departs from a requirement of a standard or an interpretation, it shall disclose (para. 20):

(a) that management has concluded that the financial statements present fairly the entity's financial position, financial performance and cash flows;

(b) that it has complied with applicable Standards and Interpretations, except that it has departed from a particular requirement to achieve a fair presentation;

(c) the title of the Standard or Interpretation from which the entity has departed, the nature of the departure, including the treatment that the Standard or Interpretation would require, the reason why that treatment would be so misleading in the circumstances that it would conflict with the objective of financial statements set out in the Framework, and the treatment adopted; and

(d) for each period presented, the financial impact of the departure on each item in the financial statements that would have been reported in complying with the requirement.

The question of terminology and national positions here is both important and potentially confusing. The US requirement to present fairly in accordance with (US) GAAP means to follow GAAP, at least as far as accounting standards are concerned, although the situation is slightly less clear as regards US auditing standards. The UK requirement to give a true and fair view equally clearly means to follow Standards where suitable, but to depart from them if a true and fair view requires it. The UK position in essence found its way into the EU Fourth Directive and hence, subject to varying degrees of bastardisation, into other European countries. IAS 1 follows the US wording but the UK/EU philosophy. Table 8.2 makes this clear.

This is not to imply that the override is likely to be used in similar ways or in similar volumes in the various jurisdictions where it exists. We predict that its usage under the IASB will indeed be rare. But an important issue of principle is at stake. Can the qualitative characteristics required of financial reporting be ensured by compliance with a set of (static) rules, or is some professional judgement involved which may, in principle, entail departure from one or more rules?

Although no attempt to define 'fair presentation' is provided (rightly in our view), the presumption 'in virtually all circumstances' is that a fair presentation is achieved by compliance in all material respects with applicable IAS. A fair presentation requires (para. 17):

TABLE 8.2	Terminology versus philosophy	
Jurisdiction	*Terminology*	*Overriding*
UK	True and fair view	Yes
EU	True and fair view	Yes
USA	Fair presentation	No
IASB	Fair presentation	Yes

1 selecting and applying accounting policies as described later

2 presenting information, including accounting policies, in a manner which provides relevant, reliable, comparable and understandable information

3 providing additional disclosures when the requirements in International Standards are insufficient to enable users to understand the impact of particular transactions or events on the entity's financial position and financial performance.

In extremely rare circumstances, application of a specific requirement in an International Accounting Standard might result in misleading financial statements. In such circumstances departure from the Standard is required. IASB is at pains to minimise the likelihood of this happening. The override can only be applied when following the Standard plus providing additional information would not give a fair presentation (i.e. presumably, would mislead). The existence of national regulations which conflict with IASB Standards is not an adequate reason for departing from an International Standard. IAS 1 requires in addition, as detailed earlier, if the override is employed, that full details of the departure are given in the financial statements, sufficient to enable users to make an informed judgement on whether the departure is necessary and to calculate the adjustments that would be required to comply with the Standard.

ACCOUNTING POLICIES

The actual process of selecting accounting policies by a particular entity was discussed in the 1997 version of IAS 1, but in 2004 was transferred to the new version of IAS 8. This is discussed below. However, IAS 1 proceeds to incorporate and discuss some, but not all, of the assumptions and qualitative characteristics of financial statements included in the Framework. The two 'underlying assumptions' are going concern and the accrual basis of accounting. The going concern assumption means that it is assumed that the entity will continue in operation for the foreseeable future. Financial statements should be prepared on a going concern basis unless management either intends to liquidate the entity or to cease trading or has no realistic alternative but to do so. When management is aware, in making its assessment, of material uncertainties related to events or conditions which may cast significant doubt on the entity's ability to continue as a going concern, those uncertainties should be disclosed. When the financial statements are not prepared on a going concern basis, that fact should be disclosed, together with the basis on which the financial statements are prepared and the reason why the entity is not considered to be a going concern. When the financial statements are prepared on the going concern basis it is not necessary to say so. Judgement, and in uncertain cases detailed investigation, may be required.

The accrual basis of accounting (except for cash flow statements) is also an automatic assumption that need not be explicitly stated. Under the accrual basis of accounting, transactions and events are recognised when they occur (and not as cash or its equivalent is received or paid) and they are recorded in the accounting records and reported in the financial statements of the periods to which they relate.

The actual wording indicates that the application of the matching concept in IAS GAAP does not allow the recognition of items in the balance sheet which do not meet the IAS definition of assets or liabilities.

The Framework states, however, that financial statements may include items not falling within these definitions if specific Standards require their recognition. Some other Standards do so require, e.g. with regard to the deferral of government grants (IAS 20, see Chapter 12) and the deferral of income and expenses relating to operating leases (IAS 17, Chapter 15). Although there seems to be conflict between the Framework and IAS 1 on this point, standards, explicitly, override the Framework.

IAS 1 also incorporates the principle of consistency from para. 39 of the Framework, but, oddly, only as regards presentation. A change in presentation and classification of items in financial statements between one period and another is permitted only when it results in a more appropriate presentation (which is expected to continue) or is required by a specific International Standard or interpretation. The Framework principle continues to relate, of course, to recognition and measurement.

The issue of materiality and aggregation raises some important considerations. Each material item should be presented separately in the financial statements. Immaterial amounts should be aggregated with amounts of a similar nature or function and need not be presented separately. In this context, information is material if its non-disclosure could influence the economic decisions of users taken on the basis of the financial statements. Materiality depends on the size and nature of the item judged in the particular circumstances of its omission. In deciding whether an item or an aggregate of items is material, the nature and the size of the item are evaluated together. Depending on the circumstances, either the nature or the size of the item could be the determining factor. For example, evidence of breaking the law causing a fine could be significant in principle, even if the amount is small. But similar items should be aggregated together however large they or the resulting total are in relation to the entity as a whole.

It is important that both assets and liabilities, and income and expenses, when material, are reported separately. Offsetting in either the income statement or the balance sheet, except when offsetting reflects the substance of the transaction or event, would detract from the ability of users to understand the transactions undertaken and to assess the future cash flows of the entity. Assets and liabilities, and income and expenses, should not be offset except when offsetting is required or permitted by another International Accounting Standard.

It is often not fully appreciated that the prevention of offsetting between assets and liabilities and between income and expenses is not at all the same thing as the prevention of netting out between debits and credits in a bookkeeping sense. Receipts and payments in relation to the purchase of one asset, for example, involve the netting out of debits and credits and are not examples of offsetting as discussed in IAS 1.

It should also be noted that there are several examples where other International Accounting Standards do 'require or permit' offsetting. One such example is IAS 11 (see Chapter 16), where contract costs plus recognised profits less losses are offset against progress billings to give a net figure of amount due from customers.

It is explicitly stated that the specific disclosure requirements of International Accounting Standards need not be met if the resulting information is not material. It thus follows that full compliance with IAS GAAP requires the following of complete IAS GAAP except for immaterial disclosure requirements, not the following of complete IAS GAAP period.

The 'presentation' section of IAS 1 concludes with requirements about comparative figures. Unless a Standard or Interpretation permits or requires otherwise, comparative information should be disclosed in respect of the previous period for all numerical information in the financial statements. Note that this now includes the need for an opening comparative statement of financial position (balance sheet). Comparative narrative and descriptive information should be included when it is relevant to an understanding of the current period's financial statements.

Comparative information should be restated if necessary if the presentation or classification of items in the current financial statements is altered, unless it is impractical to do so, in which case the reason for not reclassifying should be disclosed together with 'the nature of the adjustments that would have been made if the amounts had been reclassified'. Five- or ten-year summaries should logically be changed as well, although IAS 1 does not consider this point.

It should be noted that IAS 8, *Accounting Policies, Changes in Accounting Estimates and Errors*, applies if changes constitute a change in accounting policy as discussed in that Standard.

As already indicated, the remainder of IAS 1 relates to the structure and content of published financial statements, which is dealt with in the next chapter.

Accounting policies, changes in accounting estimates and errors – IAS 8

By now we have mentioned several times that financial statements serve as a means for communicating the economic health of a company to external parties. For a proper assessment of the performance and the financial status of a company external stakeholders need a benchmark with which to compare the financial accounting information. This will be discussed and illustrated extensively in Part Four of this textbook. Data taken from the financial statements of other companies are often used for benchmarking purposes. In this respect comparability of financial accounting information is extremely important. Comparability refers not only to inter-firm comparability but also to the comparability over time of company data of the same enterprise. Techniques for inter-firm comparisons and within firm comparisons over time are presented in Part Four of this textbook.

The objective of IAS 8 is to enhance comparability of financial statement data over time within the same firm and between firms. In order to improve comparability IAS 8 focuses on the criteria for selecting accounting policies, the accounting treatment and disclosure of changes in accounting policies, changes in accounting estimates and errors. The purpose of the standard is to ensure that entities prepare and present their financial statements on a consistent basis. IAS 8 shall be applied in selecting and applying accounting policies and accounting for changes in accounting policies, changes in accounting estimates and corrections of prior period errors. The tax effects of corrections of prior period errors and retrospective adjustments made to apply changes in accounting policies are accounted for and disclosed in accordance with IAS 12, *Income Taxes*.

The first part of IAS 8, which deals with accounting policies, determines first how to select and apply accounting policies (see paras 7–13). Accounting policies are defined as specific principles, bases, conventions, rules and practices adopted by an entity in preparing and presenting financial statements (para. 5). The selection process for an accounting policy starts with determining if there is a specific Standard that deals with the transaction or event that has to be reported.

IAS 8 states that when a Standard or an Interpretation specifically applies to a transaction, other event or condition, the accounting policy or policies applied to that item shall be determined by applying the Standard or Interpretation and considering any relevant Implementation Guidance issued by the IASB for the Standard or Interpretation (paras 7–9). It is interesting to note that the IASB stipulates that the Implementation Guidance for Standards does not form part of those Standards, and therefore does not contain requirements for financial statements (para. 9).

In the absence of a particular Standard or an Interpretation of a Standard that specifically applies to an item in the financial statements, management shall use its judgement in developing and applying an accounting policy that results in information that is (para. 10):

- relevant to the decision-making needs of users; and reliable in that the financial statements:
  - represent faithfully the results and financial position of the entity
  - reflect the economic substance of transactions and other events, and not merely the legal form
  - are neutral, i.e. free from bias
  - are prudent
  - are complete in all material respects.

In making the judgement described in para. 10, management shall consider the following sources in descending order:

- the requirements and guidance in Standards and Interpretations of Standards, dealing with similar and related issues
- the definitions, recognition criteria and measurement concepts for assets, liabilities, income and expenses set out in the Framework for the Preparation and Presentation of Financial Statements
- the most recent pronouncements of other standard-setting bodies that use a similar conceptual framework to develop accounting standards, other accounting literature and accepted industry practices, to the extent, but only to the extent, that these are consistent with the first two points of this paragraph.

IAS 8 states explicitly that accounting policies should be applied consistently for similar transactions, other events and conditions, unless a Standard or an Interpretation specifically requires or permits categorisation of items for which different policies may be appropriate. If a Standard or an Interpretation requires or permits such categorisation, an appropriate accounting policy shall be selected and applied consistently to each category (para. 13).

Accounting policy changes

Once an accounting policy is chosen it needs to be applied on a consistent basis over the years. Although consistency is the rule, changes in accounting policies are permitted if the change:

(a) is required by a Standard or an Interpretation

(b) or results in the financial statements providing reliable and more relevant information about the effects of transactions, other events or conditions on the entity's financial position, financial performance or cash flows (para. 14).

ACTIVITY 8.6

Can you think of events or elements which might induce a voluntary change in accounting policies?

Activity feedback

● Company A becomes a subsidiary of company B, subsequently the accounting policies within com- pany A should be harmonised with the accounting policies of company B.

● All changes between benchmark treatments and allowable treatments prescribed in the IAS/IFRS, e.g. a switch from capitalising borrowing costs to expensing them, due to changes in the finance policy of a company.

IAS 8 addresses changes of accounting policy arising from three sources:

1 initial application (including early application) of a Standard or Interpretation containing specific transitional provisions

2 initial application of a Standard or Interpretation which does not contain specific transitional provisions

3 voluntary changes in accounting policy.

Policy changes under 1 should be accounted for in accordance with the specific tran- sitional provisions of that Standard or Interpretation.

A change of accounting policy under 2 or 3 should be applied retrospectively, that is applied to transactions, other events and conditions as if it had always been applied (paras 5–19). The standard goes on to explain that retrospective application requires adjustment of the opening balance of each affected component of equity for the earliest prior period presented and the other comparative amounts disclosed for each prior pe- riod presented as if the new accounting policy had always been applied (para. 22). The Standard observes that the amount of the resulting adjustment relating to periods before those presented in the financial statements (which is made to the opening balance of each affected component of equity of the earliest prior period presented) will usually be made to retained earnings. However, it goes on to note that the adjustment may be made to another component of equity (for example, to comply with a Standard or an Interpretation). IAS 8 also makes clear that any other information about prior periods, such as historical summaries of financial data, should be also adjusted (para. 26).

It will frequently be straightforward to apply a change in accounting policy retro- spectively. However, the Standard accepts that sometimes it may be impractical to do so. Accordingly, retrospective application of a change in accounting policy is not required to the extent that it is impracticable to determine either the period-specific effects or the cumulative effect of the change (para. 23). The concept 'impracticable' occurs also in relation to the accounting treatment of prior period errors. As noted above, in the absence of a specifically applicable Standard or an Interpretation an entity may apply an accounting policy from the most recent pronouncements of another standard-setting body that uses a similar conceptual framework. The Stand- ard makes clear that a change in accounting policy reflecting a change in such a pro- nouncement is a voluntary change in accounting policy which should be accounted for and disclosed as such (para. 21).

We have noticed that the IASB introduced the concept of impracticability in rela- tion to the retrospective application of accounting policy changes. Since this concept can be used to circumvent the retrospective application of an accounting policy change, the Standard devotes a considerable amount of guidance to discussing what 'impracticable' means for these purposes.

The Standard states that applying a requirement is impracticable when an entity cannot apply it after making every reasonable effort to do so. It goes on to note that, for a particular prior period, it is impracticable to apply a change in an accounting policy retrospectively or to make a retrospective restatement to correct an error if:

1 the effects of the retrospective application or retrospective restatement are not determinable

2 the retrospective application or retrospective restatement requires assumptions about what management's intent would have been in that period

3 or the retrospective application or retrospective restatement requires significant estimates of amounts and it is impossible to distinguish objectively information about those estimates that:

   (i) provides evidence of circumstances that existed on the date(s) as at which those amounts are to be recognised, measured or disclosed

   (ii) would have been available when the financial statements for that prior period were authorised for issue, from other information.

IAS 8 observes that it is frequently necessary to make estimates in applying an accounting policy and that estimation is inherently subjective and that estimates may be developed after the balance sheet date. But developing estimates is potentially more difficult when retrospectively applying an accounting policy or making a retrospective restatement to correct a prior period error, because of the longer period of time that might have passed since the affected transaction, other event or condition occurred.

However, the objective of estimates related to prior periods remains the same as for estimates made in the current period, namely, for the estimate to reflect the circumstances that existed when the transaction, other event or condition occurred. Hindsight should not be used when applying a new accounting policy to, or correcting amounts for, a prior period, either in making assumptions about what management's intentions would have been in a prior period or estimating the amounts recognised, measured or disclosed in a prior period. For example, if an entity corrects a prior period error in measuring financial assets previously classified as held-to-maturity investments in accordance with IAS 39, it should not change their basis of measurement for that period if management decided later not to hold them to maturity.

Therefore, retrospectively applying a new accounting policy or correcting a prior period error requires distinguishing information that:

   (a) provides evidence of circumstances that existed on the date(s) as at which the transaction, other event or condition occurred

   (b) and would have been available when the financial statements for that prior period were authorised for issue from other information.

The Standard states that for some types of estimate (e.g. an estimate of fair value not based on an observable price or observable inputs), it is impracticable to distinguish these types of information. When retrospective application or retrospective restatement would require making a significant estimate for which it is impossible to distinguish these two types of information, it is impracticable to apply the new accounting policy or correct the prior period error retrospectively.

The concept of impracticability introduces limitations to the retrospective application of accounting policy changes. The future will tell us if this concept of impracticability will be used to avoid the retrospective application of accounting policy changes.

Although IAS 8 and similar standards of other GAAP systems require all these types of disclosure, we do observe in practice a difference in the quality of disclosure relating to changes in accounting policy or accounting methods. Less quality implies that external parties are hindered in comparing financial data from subsequent years or between firms. If accounting changes are used for example for earnings management purposes, then there is an incentive to drop the quality level of these disclosures. As disclosure requirements concerning these accounting method changes have become stricter over the years, accounting method changes are now less used for annual accounts' management purposes. The stricter disclosure requirements allow external parties to 'undo' the effect of the change and to detect the 'real' underlying economic performance.

The issue of accounting quality will be discussed further in Chapter 30.

First-time adoption of IFRS

When a company changes from its domestic GAAP to IAS/IFRS Standards, this change does not belong to the scope of IAS 8. IFRS 1, *First-time adoption of IFRS*, provides guidance for all companies, which change either compulsorily, or voluntarily to IAS/IFRS Standards.

An entity's first IFRS financial statements are the first annual financial statements in which the entity adopts IFRSs, by an explicit and unreserved statement in those financial statements of compliance with IFRSs. Financial statements under IFRSs are an entity's first financial statements if, for example, the entity:

(a) presented its most recent previous financial statements:

    (i) under national requirements that are not consistent with IFRSs in all respects;

    (ii) in conformity with IFRSs in all respects, except that the financial statements did not contain an explicit and unreserved statement that they complied with IFRSs;

    (iii) containing an explicit statement of compliance with some, but not all, IFRSs;

    (iv) under national requirements inconsistent with IFRSs, using some individual IFRSs to account for items which national requirements did not exist; or

    (v) under national requirements, with a reconciliation of some amounts to the amounts determined under IFRSs;

(b) prepared financial statements under IFRSs for internal use only, without making them available to the entity's owners or any other external users;

(c) prepared a reporting package under IFRSs for consolidation purposes without preparing a complete set of financial statements as defined in IAS 1, *Presentation of Financial Statements*; or

(d) did not present financial statements for previous periods.

If a company presents its financial figures for a particular financial year, these figures are usually accompanied by prior year figures. For the sake of comparability these figures should be prepared using the same GAAP. This implies that the prior year figures in an entity's first IFRS financial statements should also be prepared with the use of IAS/IFRS. If we apply this principle to the compulsory change to IAS/IFRS for listed companies in the EU we obtain the following situation.

The reporting date for entity A's first IFRS financial statements is 31 December 2005. If entity A decides to present comparative information in those financial statements for one year only, the date of transition to IFRSs is the beginning of business on 1 January 2004 (or, equivalently, close of business on 31 December 2003). Entity A will have presented financial statements under its previous GAAP annually to 31 December each year up to and including 31 December 2004. In this case entity A is required to apply the IFRSs effective for periods ending on 31 December 2005 in:

- preparing its opening IFRS balance sheet at 1 January 2004
- and preparing and presenting its balance sheet for 31 December 2005 (including comparative amounts for 2004), income statement, statement of changes in equity and cash flow statement for the year to 31 December 2005 (including comparative amounts for 2004) and disclosures (including comparative information for 2004).

If a new IFRS is not yet mandatory but permits early application, entity A is permitted, but not required, to apply that IFRS in its first IFRS financial statements. For many preparers which present their first IFRS financial statements the main question is: 'Which accounting policies need to be applied for the recognition and measurement of the items of the financial statements?' The main rule is that an entity shall use the same accounting policies in its opening IFRS balance sheet and throughout all periods presented in its first IFRS financial statements. Those accounting policies shall comply with each IFRS effective at the reporting date for its first IFRS financial statements. This general rule implies that an entity shall not apply different versions of IFRSs that were effective at earlier dates.

In its opening IFRS balance sheet an entity shall (para. 10):

(a) recognise all assets and liabilities whose recognition is required by IFRSs

(b) not recognise items as assets or liabilities if IFRSs do not permit such recognition

(c) reclassify items that it recognised under previous GAAP as one type of asset, liability or component of equity, but are a different type of asset, liability or component of equity under IFRSs and

(d) apply IFRSs in measuring all recognised assets and liabilities.

The accounting policies that an entity uses in its opening IFRS balance sheet may differ from those that it used for the same date using its previous GAAP. The resulting adjustments arise from events and transactions before the date of transition to IFRSs. Therefore, an entity shall recognise those adjustments directly in retained earnings (or, if appropriate, another category of equity) at the date of transition to IFRSs (para. 11).

In essence, companies have to use all IFRSs that are effective at reporting date for all the information included in the annual accounts. However, there are two categories of exception. First, IFRS 1 specifies a number of optional exemptions from retrospective application (paras 13–25). First-time adopters can elect to apply all, some or none of these optional exemptions. Second, IFRS 1 foresees mandatory exceptions from retrospective application. In Table 8.3 we list both the optional and mandatory exceptions, with the corresponding paragraph references.

TABLE 8.3	Optional and mandatory exceptions from retrospective application

An entity may elect to use one or more of the following exemptions:

(a) business combinations (paragraph 15);

(b) *fair value* or revaluation as *deemed cost* (paragraphs 16–19);

(c) employee benefits (paragraphs 20 and 20A);

(d) cumulative translation differences (paragraphs 21 and 22);

(e) compound financial instruments (paragraph 23);

(f) assets and liabilities of subsidiaries, associates and joint ventures (paragraphs 24 and 25);

(g) designation of previously recognised financial instruments (paragraph 25A);

(h) share-based payment transactions (paragraphs 25B and 25C);

(i) insurance contracts (paragraph 25D);

(j) decommissioning liabilities included in the cost of property, plant and equipment (paragraph 25E);

(k) leases (paragraph 25F);

(l) fair value measurement of financial assets or financial liabilities at initial recognition (paragraph 25G);

(m) a financial asset or an intangible asset accounted for in accordance with IFRIC 12 *Service Concession Arrangements* (paragraph 25H); and

(n) borrowing costs (paragraph 25I).

The IFRS prohibits retrospective application of some aspects of other IFRSs relating to:

(a) derecognition of financial assets and financial liabilities (paragraphs 27 and 27A);

(b) hedge accounting (paragraphs 28–30);

(c) estimates (paragraphs 31–34);

(d) assets classified as held for sale and discontinued operations (paragraphs 34A and 34B); and

(e) some aspects of accounting for non-controlling interests (paragraph 34C).

The switch from a previous GAAP system to IFRS will have an impact on the published figures of a company. IFRS 1 requires that in the notes to the accounts the impact of the transition from the previous GAAP to IAS/IFRS on the financial position, the financial performance and the cash flow should be explained.

Observing reporting practices of companies that switched to IAS/IFRS during 2005/2006, we notice that there is an enormous difference with regard to the level of detail that is presented to users of financial statements in relation to the impact of the switch on a form's financial position. Some companies provide several pages of explanation with regard to the impact on the company's equity, other companies just disclose a few lines.

A number of companies divided the impact of the IAS/IFRS transition over a number of years. Some companies started complying with IAS standards which have a favourable impact on equity in the financial years before the 'official' financial transition year. Compliance with IAS standards that have an unfavourable impact on equity takes place in the 'official' transition year.

Changes in accounting estimates

IAS 8 defines a change in accounting estimates as an adjustment of the carrying amount of an asset or a liability, or the amount of the periodic consumption of an

ACTIVITY 8.7

Think of some balance sheet or profit and loss account elements in which estimates are needed for valuation purposes.

Activity feedback

Estimates are required for example in the valuation of:

- allowances for bad debts
- inventory obsolescence
- determination of the fair value of assets
- determination of the useful life of an asset.

Indeed it is difficult to think of elements that do not include estimations.

asset, that results from the assessment of the present status of and expected future benefits and obligations associated with assets and liabilities. Changes in accounting estimates result from new information or new developments and, accordingly, are not corrections for errors.

Valuing balance sheet and profit and loss account items often involves making estimates. The use of reasonable estimates is an essential part of the preparation of financial statements. However, estimates may need to be revised over the years in light of new or changing information. The revision of an estimate does not affect the original classification of the transaction. As changes of accounting estimates imply in most circumstances elements of judgement, the IASB states explicitly in IAS 8 that the change of the estimate should not undermine the reliability of the financial statements.

IAS 8 requires that changes in estimate be accounted for prospectively; defined as recognising the effect of the change in the accounting estimate in the current and future periods affected by the change (IAS 8, paras 36–38). The Standard goes on to explain that this will mean (as appropriate):

- adjusting the carrying amount of an asset, liability or item of equity in the balance sheet in the period of change
- recognising the change by including it in profit and loss in:
  - the period of change, if it affects that period only (for example, a change in estimate of bad debts)
  - or the period of change and future periods, if it affects both (for example, a change in estimated useful life of a depreciable asset or the expected pattern of consumption of the economic benefits embodied in it).

Further, the Standard states explicitly that a change in an accounting estimate does not result from a change in the measurement basis or method applied, which is a change in an accounting policy. When it is difficult to distinguish between a change in an accounting policy and a change in an accounting estimate, the change is treated as a change in an accounting estimate, with appropriate disclosure.

Prospective recognition of the effect of a change in an accounting estimate means that the change is applied to transactions, other events and circumstances from the date of the change to estimate. A change in an accounting estimate may affect the current period only or both the current period and future periods.

So a change in an accounting estimate involves less administrative work and is somehow less visible than a change in accounting policy or method. The latter is applied retrospectively and therefore prior year comparative data need to be restated as well. All these changes will probably catch the eye of the user of the annual accounts sooner or later. Empirical evidence exists (this will be discussed in Chapter 30) that changes in accounting estimates are now more popular for earnings management purposes than accounting policy changes as they are less costly and less visible.

Errors

IAS 8 also deals with the treatment of prior period errors. Prior period errors are omissions from, and mis-statements in, the entity's financial statements for one or more prior periods arising from a failure to use, or misuse of, reliable information that:

- was available when financial statements for those periods were authorised for issue
- could reasonably be expected to have been obtained and taken into account in the preparation and presentation of those financial statements.

Such errors include the effects of mathematical mistakes, mistakes in applying accounting policies, oversights or misinterpretations of facts and fraud.

Paragraph 4 stipulates that the correction of the error has to be accounted for in a retrospective way, in the first set of financial statements authorised for issue after their discovery by:

- restating the comparative amounts for the prior period(s) in which the error occurred
- or, if the error occurred before the earliest prior period presented, restating the opening balances of assets, liabilities and equity for the earliest prior period presented.

In this way the financial statements are presented as if the error had never occurred.

Also in the case of prior period errors, comparative information presented for a particular prior period need not be restated if restating the information would be impracticable (paras 43–45).

ACTIVITY 8.8

Think of an example of a change in an accounting estimate which affects only the current period. Then think of an example which might affect the current period as well as subsequent periods.

Activity feedback

For example, a change in the estimate of the amount of bad debts affects only the current period and is therefore recognised in the current period. However, a change in the estimated useful life of or the expected pattern of consumption of the future economic benefits embodied in a depreciable asset affects depreciation expense for the remainder of the current period and for each future period during the asset's remaining useful life. In both cases, the effect of the change relating to the current period is recognised as income or expense in the current period. The effect, if any, on future periods is recognised in future periods.

An entity shall disclose the nature and amount of a change in an accounting estimate that has an effect in the current period or is expected to have an effect in future periods, except for the disclosure of the effect on future periods when it is impracticable to estimate that effect (para. 39).

If the amount of the effect in future periods is not disclosed because estimating it is impracticable, an entity shall disclose that fact (para. 40).

Special disclosure requirements apply in relation to such prior period errors (para. 49):

(a) the nature of the prior period error;

(b) for each prior period presented, to the extent practicable, the amount of the correction:

  (i) for each financial statement line item affected; and

  (ii) if IAS 33 applies to the entity, for basic and diluted earnings per share;

(c) the amount of the correction at the beginning of the earliest prior period presented; and

(d) if retrospective restatement is impracticable for a particular period, the circumstances that led to the existence of that condition and a description of how and from when the error has been corrected.

Financial statements of subsequent periods need not repeat these disclosures.

ACTIVITY 8.9

During 20X2, company A discovered that certain products that had been sold during 20X1 were incorrectly included in inventory at 31 December 20X1 at €3250.

Company A's accounting records for 20X2 show sales of €52 000, cost of goods sold of €43 250 (including €3250 for error in opening inventory) and income taxes of €2625.

In 20X1, company A reported:

Sales	36 750
Cost of goods sold	26 750
Profit from ordinary activities before	
Income taxes	10 000
Income taxes	(3 000)
Net profit	7 000

20X1 opening retained earnings were €10 000 and closing retained earnings were €17 000. Company A's income tax rate was 30% for 20X2 and 20X1.

Show the necessary disclosures in the financial statements for the year 20X2.

Activity feedback

Company A – an extract from the income statement

	20X2	20X1 (restated)
Sales	52 000	36 750
Cost of goods sold	40 000	30 000
Profit from ordinary activities before		
Income taxes	12 000	6 750

	20X2	20X1 (restated)
Income taxes	3 600	2 025
Net profit	8 400	4 725

Company A
Statement of retained earnings

	20X2	20X1 (restated)
Opening retained earnings as previously reported	17 000	10 000
Correction of fundamental error (Net of income taxes of €975) (Note 1)	2 275	–
Opening retained earnings as restated	14 725	10 000
Net profit	8 400	4 725
Closing retained earnings	23 152	14 725

Extracts from notes to the financial statements

1 Certain products that had been sold in 20X1 were incorrectly included in inventory at 31 December, 20X1 at €3250. The financial statement of 20X1 has been restated to correct this error.

Once again, we notice that the restatement is made on the judgement of the management whether or not the restatement is impracticable.

SUMMARY

This chapter began with an outline of 'theories about theories' in the accounting context. We then looked at the nearest that accounting seems to have got to a generally agreed theory, as illustrated by the IASB Framework and relevant parts of IAS 1. These documents, however, seem far removed from theory in a scientific sense. We also discussed changes in accounting policies (IAS 8) and the first-time adoption of IFRS (IFRS 1).

EXERCISES

Suggested answers to exercises marked ✓ are to be found on the Student side of the companion website.

Suggested answers to the remaining exercises are to be found on the Instructor side of the companion website.

✓ **1**   To what extent is financial reporting a suitable subject for theorising about?

✓ **2**   Positive research is a necessary starting point on the road to normative thinking, but can never be enough by itself. Discuss.

3   Is the IASB Framework useful in its present form? How could it be improved?

4   Accounting standards and regulations should aim to state how to deal with all situations. Discuss.

5   Rework question 9 from Chapter 1, specifically by applying the IASB Framework. Does it alter or improve your original answer? Does IAS 1 make any difference?

STRUCTURE OF PUBLISHED FINANCIAL STATEMENTS

9

OBJECTIVES After studying this chapter you should be able to:

- describe and apply the format requirements of the EU Fourth Directive

- describe and apply the format and disclosure requirements of IAS 1

- discuss the adequacy of the disclosure requirements of IAS 1 and the EU Fourth Directive and to suggest and appraise possible alterations thereto.

INTRODUCTION

There has been an increasing tendency over recent decades to regulate not only the contents of published financial statements, but also the precise layout and format in which those contents must be presented. Former country traditions in this respect varied considerably, as Chapter 2 should have made you expect. The central European countries usually had a much higher degree of precise specification than the UK- and US-influenced regions of the world.

There are two non-nationalistic influences of importance on the structure and contents of published financial statements. The first one chronologically, and in some ways the most detailed, is the Fourth Directive of the EU. This obviously only directly affects those countries that are members of the EU and also those trying to join. The more recent influence, and the more general one, but becoming the more pervasive, is the IASB, as represented by IAS 1, *Presentation of Financial Statements*, issued in its current form in 2007.

The requirements from these sources are presented in this chapter in logical rather than chronological order. Thus, the IAS 1 requirements, both more general and more wide-ranging in the countries they are likely to influence, are presented first in each section, followed by EU Directive considerations.

IAS 1 requires that financial statements that claim to follow IASs should be clearly distinguished from any other information that is included in the same published document. Figures, components and separate pages must be fully and clearly described. Financial statements should be presented at least annually, normally for a 12-month period, and any exceptions (such as a change in reporting date following an acquisition by another entity) should be clearly explained.

BALANCE SHEETS/STATEMENTS OF FINANCIAL POSITION

It is usual in Europe (and required by the Fourth Directive even though not at present by IAS 1) for a balance sheet to present current and non-current (fixed) assets and current and non-current liabilities, as separate classifications on the face of the balance sheet. When an entity chooses not to make this analysis, assets and liabilities should still be presented broadly in order of their liquidity, although this alternative is only allowed when it would lead to information that is 'reliable and more relevant'. In such circumstances, the IAS does not specify 'which way up' the liquidity analysis should go. For example, it is European practice for assets to end with cash (which is required by the Directive), whereas it is North American, Japanese and Australian practice to start with cash. Whichever method of presentation is adopted, an entity should disclose the amounts included in each item that are expected to be recovered or settled before and after 12 months.

Where, as is usually the case, the current/non-current classification is followed, then IAS GAAP specifies the distinctions as now described. IAS 1 deals with assets first, by defining a current asset.

An asset should be classified as a current asset when it (para. 66):

1 is expected to be realised in or is held for sale or consumption in the entity's normal operating cycle

2 is held primarily for trading purposes or expected to be realised within 12 months after the reporting period

3 is cash or a cash equivalent which is not restricted in its use.

All other assets should be classified as non-current assets.

This definition of a current asset requires careful consideration. Only one of the three conditions needs to be met for classification as a current asset to be required. Thus, an asset which meets condition 1 in a business which has a two-year operating cycle is a current asset even if it is not expected to be realised within 12 months.

Although the wording on the matter is perhaps not as clear as it might be, a non-current asset remains non-current throughout its useful life to the entity, as it is not held primarily for trading purposes. It does not eventually become 'current' merely because its expected disposal is within less than 12 months. The IASB definition also implies that the currently due portion of a long-term non-trading receivable is similarly not to be reclassified as current.

The classification of liabilities, when undertaken by the reporting entity, must follow a comparable distinction. A liability should be classified as current when it satisfies any of the following criteria:

1 it is expected to be settled in the entity's normal operating cycle

2 it is held primarily for the purpose of being traded

3 it is due to be settled within 12 months after the balance sheet date

4 the entity does not have an unconditional right to defer settlement of the liability for at least 12 months after the balance sheet date.

All other liabilities shall be classified as non-current.

Again, only one of these criteria needs to apply, so a long operating cycle could lead to the classification as current liabilities of items due to be settled in more than 12 months. The 'current' (i.e. due within 12 months) portion of long-term interest-bearing liabilities is to be classified as 'current' in most cases.

It is common for loan agreements to contain clauses such that, in the event of defined undertakings by the borrower not being satisfied (e.g. maintenance of an agreed maximum leverage ratio), the liability becomes payable on demand. If this happens, then the liability would in general immediately become 'current' under IAS GAAP. The liability would continue to be classified as non-current, however, if the lender has agreed, before the approval of the financial statements, not to demand payment within 12 months of the balance sheet date.

As a minimum, the face of the balance sheet (i.e. not the notes to the balance sheet) should include separate line items that present the following amounts (para. 54):

1 Property, plant and equipment

2 Investment property

3 Intangible assets

4 Financial assets (excluding amounts shown under 5, 8 and 9)

5 Investments accounted for using the equity method

6 Biological assets

7 Inventories

8 Trade and other receivables

9 Cash and cash equivalents

10 The total of assets classified as held for sale and assets included in disposal groups classified as held for sale in accordance with IFRS 5, *Non-Current Assets Held for Sale and Discontinued Operations*

11 Trade and other payables

12 Provisions

13 Financial liabilities (excluding amounts shown under 11 and 12)

14 Liabilities and assets for current tax, as defined in IAS 12, *Income Taxes*

15 Deferred tax liabilities and deferred tax assets, as defined in IAS 12

16 Liabilities included in disposal groups classified as held for sale in accordance with IFRS 5

17 Non-controlling interests, presented within equity

18 Issued capital and reserves attributable to owners of the parent.

Additional line items, headings and subtotals should be presented on the face of the balance sheet when their presentation is relevant to an understanding of the entity's financial position. When an entity presents current and non-current assets, and current and non-current liabilities, as separate classifications on the face of its balance sheet, it must not classify deferred tax assets (liabilities) as current assets (liabilities). Amounts included in line items in relation to IFRS 5 should not be also included elsewhere.

The necessity or otherwise of additional line items is obviously a subjective matter. Judgement on this should be based on assessment of the nature and liquidity of assets; the function of assets within the entity; and the amounts, nature and timing of liabilities.

It should be noted that IAS 1 does not prescribe any particular balance sheet format. The so-called horizontal and vertical formats are equally acceptable. The descriptions used and the ordering of items may be amended according to the nature of the enterprise and its transactions, to provide information that is necessary for an overall understanding of the enterprise's financial position. For example, a financial institution amends the above descriptions in order to apply the more specific relevant requirements of financial institutions. Other amendments not prescribed by promulgated IASB GAAP may be necessary in other industrial or commercial situations.

IAS 1 states that the use of different measurement bases for different classes of assets suggests that their nature or function differs and, therefore, that they should be presented as separate line items. It gives as an example the carrying of certain classes of property, plant and equipment at cost, and other classes at revalued amounts, under IAS 16, *Property, Plant and Equipment* (see Chapter 12).

It seems to us that the above proposition, or at least the example given, is not logical. The recording of different subsets of property, plant, and machinery under different valuation bases does not necessarily suggest any difference in nature or function. Further disclosure in the notes may well be desirable, as discussed below, but that is a separate matter. A more logical example might be the different treatments allowed for investment properties (see Chapter 12), where the function of the property may affect the accounting treatment.

A further category of required disclosure relating to the balance sheet can be presented either on the face of the balance sheet or in the notes. Further subclassifications of the line items should be presented, classified in a manner appropriate to the enterprise's operations.

The detail provided in subclassifications, either on the face of the balance sheet or in the notes, depends on the requirements of International Standards and the size, nature and function of the amounts involved. In some cases, other International Standards provide requirements (subject always to the materiality consideration). Tangible assets, for example, are classified by class as required by IAS 16, *Property, Plant and Equipment* (see Chapter 12), and inventories are subclassified in accordance with IAS 2, *Inventories* (see Chapter 16). Other applications will be more subjective. For example, the standard states that receivables are analysed between amounts receivable from trade customers, receivables from related parties, prepayments, and other amounts and that provisions are analysed showing separately provisions for employee benefit costs and any other items. Extensive detailed disclosure regarding owner's equity is required, either on the face of the balance sheet or in the notes, as follows (para. 79):

1 For each class of share capital:

   (a) The number of shares authorised

   (b) The number of shares issued and fully paid and issued but not fully paid

(c) Par value per share or that the shares have no par value

(d) A reconciliation of the number of shares outstanding at the beginning and at the end of the period

(e) The rights, preferences and restrictions attaching to that class, including restrictions on the distribution of dividends and the repayment of the capital

(f) Shares in the entity, held by the entity or by its subsidiaries or associates and

(g) Shares reserved for issue under options and sales contracts, including the terms and amounts.

2 A description of the nature and purpose of each reserve within equity.

Entities without share capital are required to present equivalent information showing details and movements of each category of equity interest.

The Fourth Directive sets out considerably more detail in its specifications regarding balance sheets. It requires that all member states should prescribe one or both of the layouts specified by its Articles 9 and 10. Article 9, reproduced in Table 9.1, gives a 'horizontal' format with the debits on one side and the credits on the other, following the general continental European tradition. Article 10, reproduced in Table 9.2, gives a 'vertical' format of the type more traditional in the UK. Companies are required to show the items in these tables in the order specified, except that the headings preceded by Arabic numbers may be combined or taken to the notes.

In the EU, companies that fall below a given size limit, which is updated as circumstances change, may be permitted by the laws of member states to produce abridged accounts. As far as the balance sheet is concerned these would consist of only those items preceded by letters and roman numerals in Table 9.1 and Table 9.2.

INCOME STATEMENTS/STATEMENTS OF COMPREHENSIVE INCOME

As outlined briefly in Chapter 8, the new version of IAS 1, mandatory from 1 January 2009, has made major changes regarding the reporting of performance over the period (and the corresponding comparatives). A 'statement of comprehensive income' is required, and its specifications are given with precision (paras 81–87).

An entity shall present all items of income and expense recognised in a period:

(a) in a single statement of comprehensive income, or

(b) in two statements: a statement displaying components of profit or loss (separate income statement) and a second statement beginning with profit or loss and displaying components of other comprehensive income (statement of comprehensive income).

Information to be presented in the statement of comprehensive income

As a minimum, the statement of comprehensive income shall include line items that present the following amounts for the period:

(a) revenue

(b) finance costs

TABLE 9.1	Fourth Directive: Horizontal balance sheet format

Assets

A Subscribed capital unpaid

B Formation expenses

C Fixed assets

   I *Intangible assets*
     1 Costs of research and development
     2 Concessions, patents, licences, trademarks and similar rights and assets
     3 Goodwill, to the extent that it was acquired for valuable consideration
     4 Payments on account

  II *Tangible assets*
     1 Land and buildings
     2 Plant and machinery
     3 Other fixtures and fittings, tools and equipment
     4 Payments on account and tangible assets in course of construction

 III *Financial assets*
     1 Shares in affiliated undertakings
     2 Loans in affiliated undertakings
     3 Participating interests
     4 Loans to undertakings with which the company is linked by virtue of participating interests
     5 Investments held as fixed assets
     6 Other loans
     7 Own shares

D Current assets

   I *Stocks*
     1 Raw materials and consumables
     2 Work in progress
     3 Finished goods and goods for resale
     4 Payments on account

  II *Debtors*
     (Amounts becoming due and payable after more than one year must be shown separately for each item.)
     1 Trade debtors
     2 Amounts owed by affiliated undertakings
     3 Amounts owed by undertakings with which the company is linked by virtue of participating interests
     4 Other debtors
     5 Subscribed capital called but not paid
     6 Prepayments and accrued income

 III *Investments*
     1 Shares in affiliated undertakings
     2 Own shares
     3 Other investments

 IV *Cash at bank and in hand*

E Prepayments and accrued income

F Loss for the financial year

TABLE 9.1	*(Continued)*

Liabilities

A Capital and reserves
  I   *Subscribed capital*
  II *Share premium account*
  III *Revaluation reserve*
  IV *Reserves*
      1 Legal reserve
      2 Reserve for own shares
      3 Reserves provided for by the articles of association
      4 Other reserves
  V   *Profit or loss brought forward*
  VI *Profit or loss for the financial year*

B Provisions for liabilities and charges
  1 Provisions for pensions and similar obligations
  2 Provisions for taxation
  3 Other provisions

C Creditors
  (Amounts becoming due and payable within one year and amounts becoming due and payable after more than one year must be shown separately for each item and for the aggregate of these items.)
  1 Debenture loans, showing convertible loans separately
  2 Amounts owed to credit institutions
  3 Payments received on account of orders insofar as they are now shown separately
     as deductions from stocks
  4 Trade creditors
  5 Bills of exchange payable
  6 Amounts owed to affiliated undertakings
  7 Amounts owed to undertakings with which the company is linked by virtue of participating interests
  8 Other creditors including tax and social security
  9 Accruals and deferred income

D Accruals and deferred income

E Profit for the financial year

(c) share of the profit or loss of associates and joint ventures accounted for using the equity method

(d) tax expense

(e) a single amount comprising the total of:

  (i) the post-tax profit or loss of discontinued operations and

  (ii) the post-tax gain or loss recognised on the measurement to fair value less costs to sell or on the disposal of the assets or disposal group(s) constituting the discontinued operation

(f) profit or loss

TABLE 9.2	Fourth Directive: Vertical balance sheet format

A Subscribed capital unpaid

B Formation expenses

C Fixed assets

 I *Intangible assets*
  1 Costs of research and development
  2 Concessions, patents, licences, trademarks and similar rights and assets
  3 Goodwill, to the extent that it was acquired for valuable consideration
  4 Payments on account

 II *Tangible assets*
  1 Land and buildings
  2 Plant and machinery
  3 Other fixtures and fittings, tools and equipment
  4 Payments on account and tangible assets in course of construction

 III *Financial assets*
  1 Shares in affiliated undertakings
  2 Loans to affiliated undertakings
  3 Participating interests
  4 Loans to undertakings with which the company is linked by virtue
     of participating interests
  5 Investments held as fixed assets
  6 Other loans
  7 Own shares

D Current assets

 I *Stocks*
  1 Raw materials and consumables
  2 Work in progress
  3 Finished goods and goods for resale
  4 Payments on account

 II *Debtors*
  (Amounts becoming due and payable after more than one year must be
  shown separately for each item.)
  1 Trade debtors
  2 Amounts owed by affiliated undertakings
  3 Amounts owed by undertakings with which the company is linked by virtue
     of participating interests
  4 Other debtors
  5 Subscribed capital called but not paid
  6 Prepayments and accrued income

 III *Investments*
  1 Shares in affiliated undertakings
  2 Own shares
  3 Other investments

 IV *Cash at bank and in hand*

E Prepayments and accrued income

TABLE 9.2   *(Continued)*

F Creditors: amounts becoming due and payable within one year
1 Debenture loans, showing convertible loans separately
2 Amounts owed to credit institutions
3 Payments received on account of orders insofar as they are not shown separately as deductions from stocks
4 Trade creditors
5 Bills of exchange payable
6 Amounts owed to affiliated undertakings
7 Amounts owed to undertakings with which the company is linked by virtue of participating interests
8 Other creditors including tax and social security
9 Accrual and deferred income

G Net current assets/liabilities

H Total assets less current liabilities

I Creditors: amounts becoming due and payable after more than one year
1 Debenture loans, showing convertible loans separately
2 Amounts owed to credit institutions
3 Payments received on account of orders in so far as they are not shown separately as deductions from stocks
4 Trade creditors
5 Bills of exchange payable
6 Amounts owed to affiliated undertakings
7 Amounts owed to undertakings with which the company is linked by virtue of participating interests
8 Other creditors including tax and social security
9 Accruals and deferred income

J Provisions for liabilities and charges
1 Provisions for pensions and similar obligations
2 Provisions for taxation
3 Other provisions

K Accruals and deferred income

L Capital and reserves
   I   *Subscribed capital*
   II   *Share premium account*
   III *Revaluation reserve*
   IV   *Reserves*
        1 Legal reserve
        2 Reserve for own shares
        3 Reserves provided for by the articles of association
        4 Other reserves
   V   *Profit or loss brought forward*
   VI   *Profit or loss for the financial year*

(g) each component of other comprehensive income classified by nature (excluding amounts in (h))

(h) share of the other comprehensive income of associates and joint ventures accounted for using the equity method; and

(i) total comprehensive income.

An entity shall disclose the following items in the statement of comprehensive income as allocations of profit or loss for the period:

(a) profit or loss for the period attributable to:

    (i) non-controlling interests, and

    (ii) owners of the parent

(b) total comprehensive income for the period attributable to:

    (i) non-controlling interests, and

    (ii) owners of the parent.

An entity shall present additional line items, headings and subtotals in the statement of comprehensive income and the separate income statement (if presented), when such presentation is relevant to an understanding of the entity's financial performance.

An entity shall not present any items of income or expense as extraordinary items, in the statement of comprehensive income or the separate income statement (if presented), or in the notes.

Profit or loss for the period

An entity shall recognise all items of income and expense in a period in profit or loss unless an IFRS requires or permits otherwise.

Other comprehensive income for the period

An entity shall disclose the amount of income tax relating to each component of other comprehensive income, including reclassification adjustments, either in the statement of comprehensive income or in the notes.

An entity shall disclose reclassification adjustments relating to components of other comprehensive income.

Other IFRSs specify whether and when amounts previously recognised in other comprehensive income are reclassified to profit or loss. Such reclassifications are referred to in this Standard as reclassification adjustments. A reclassification adjustment is included with the related component of other comprehensive income in the period that the adjustment is reclassified to profit or loss. For example, gains realised on the disposal of available-for-sale financial assets are included in profit or loss of the current period. These amounts may have been recognised in other comprehensive income as unrealised gains in the current or previous periods. Those unrealised gains must be deducted from other comprehensive income in the period in which the realised gains are reclassified to profit or loss to avoid including them in total comprehensive income twice.

Additional line items, headings and subtotals shall be presented on the face of the income statement when such presentation is relevant to an understanding of the entity's financial performance.

It is important to note that no line item for 'extraordinary items' is allowed, IAS 33, *Earnings per Share*, requires the disclosure of earnings per share data on the face of the income statement (see Chapter 24). IAS 1 explicitly accepts that considerations of materiality and the nature of an entity's operations may require addition to, deletions from, or amendments of descriptions within, the list. The ordering of items may be changed from that given 'when this is necessary to explain the elements of performance' (which seems likely to occur only very rarely).

The requirement for further disclosure is drawn widely and in general terms. An entity should present, either on the face of the income statement, which is encouraged but not obligatory or in the notes to the income statement, an analysis of expenses using a classification based on either the nature of expenses or their function within the entity. The implications of this distinction between classification by nature and classification by function are conveniently illustrated by turning to the Fourth Directive's specifications for the income statement. The Directive requires that member states allow one or more of the four layouts in its Articles 23 to 26.

These four layouts are necessary to accommodate the possibility of following either an analysis by nature or an analysis by function combined with either a horizontal-type presentation or a vertical-type presentation. Table 9.3 classifies the expense items by nature showing, for example, staff costs as a single separate figure. Table 9.4 classifies by function. Thus for example staff costs as a total are not shown, being split up between the various functional heads related to staff activity, such as distribution and administration.

The formats in Tables 9.3 and 9.4 are vertical in style, treating the revenues (credits) as pluses and the expenses (debits) as minuses. However, the Directive allows a horizontal double-entry style of income statement. Table 9.5 shows the horizontal version of the by nature format, i.e. a rearrangement of Table 9.3. Although the Directive also allows a horizontal by function format this is not used in practice and is not illustrated here.

ACTIVITY 9.1

Consider the relative advantages and usefulness of the four Directive formats for the income statement.

Activity feedback

As regards the financial reports of large listed entities there is no doubt that the vertical presentations are increasingly predominant. As between the by nature and by function classification, both methods have advantages. Showing expenses by nature requires less analysis and less judgement, but is arguably less informative. It shows the amount *incurred* on production for the period, but does not highlight the total *expenses* under the accruals convention. It fails to reveal the cost of sales, and therefore the gross profit and it has the logical disadvantage that it might seem to imply (see Tables 9.3 or 9.5) that changes in inventory are an expense or a revenue in their own right, which they are not. They are logically an adjustment to purchases.

However, because information on the nature of expenses is regarded as useful in predicting future cash flows, IAS 1 and the Directive require additional disclosure on the nature of expenses, including depreciation and amortisation expenses and staff costs, when the by function classification is used.

TABLE 9.3	Fourth Directive: Vertical profit and loss account by nature

Item	Description
1	Net turnover
2	Variation in stocks of finished goods and in work in progress
3	Work performed by the undertaking for its own purposes and capitalised
4	Other operating income
5	(a) Raw materials and consumables
	(b) Other external charges
6	*Staff costs*
	(a) wages and salaries
	(b) social security costs with a separate indication of those relating to pensions
7	(a) Value adjustments in respect of formation expenses and of tangible and intangible fixed assets
	(b) Value adjustments in respect of current assets, to the extent that they exceed the amount of value adjustments which are normal in the undertaking concerned
8	Other operating charges
9	Income from participating interests, with a separate indication of that derived from affiliated undertakings
10	Income from other investments and loans forming part of the fixed assets, with a separate indication of that derived from affiliated undertakings
11	Other interest receivable and similar income, with a separate indication of that derived from affiliated undertakings
12	Value adjustments in respect of financial assets and of investments held as current assets
13	Interest payable and similar charges, with a separate indication of those concerning affiliated undertakings
14	Tax on profit or loss on ordinary activities
15	Profit or loss on ordinary activities after taxation
16	Extraordinary income
17	Extraordinary charges
18	Extraordinary profit or loss
19	Tax on extraordinary profit or loss
20	Other taxes not shown under the above items
21	Profit or loss for the financial year

STATEMENT OF CHANGES IN EQUITY

The radical changes made by IAS 1 in 2007 regarding the statement of comprehensive income have necessitated changes also in the statement of changes in equity. The effect of all this, in simple terms, is that much of the data previously presented in the separate statement of changes in equity as required from 1 January 2005 until 1 January 2009, is now presented in the statement of comprehensive income, as discussed above.

The requirements for the statement of changes in equity are now as follows (paras 106–7).

TABLE 9.4	Fourth Directive: Vertical profit and loss account by function

Item	Description
1	Net turnover
2	Cost of sales (including value adjustments)
3	Gross profit or loss
4	Distribution costs (including value adjustments)
5	Administrative expenses (including value adjustments)
6	Other operating income
7	Income from participating interests, with a separate indication of that derived from affiliated undertakings
8	Income from other investments and loans forming part of the fixed assets, with a separate indication of that derived from affiliated undertakings
9	Other interest receivable and similar income, with a separate indication of that derived from affiliated undertakings
10	Value adjustments in respect of financial assets and of investments held as current assets
11	Interest payable and similar charges, with a separate indication of those concerning affiliated undertakings
12	Tax on profit or loss on ordinary activities
13	Profit or loss on ordinary activities after taxation
14	Extraordinary income
15	Extraordinary charges
16	Extraordinary profit or loss
17	Tax on extraordinary profit or loss
18	Other taxes not shown under the above items
19	Profit or loss for the financial year

An entity shall present a statement of changes in equity showing in the statement:

- total comprehensive income for the period, showing separately the total amounts attributable to owners of the parent and to non-controlling interests
- for each component of equity, the effects of retrospective application or retrospective restatement recognised in accordance with IAS 8 and
- for each component of equity, a reconciliation between the carrying amount at the beginning and the end of the period, separately disclosing changes resulting from:
  - **(i)** profit or loss
  - **(ii)** each item of other comprehensive income and
  - **(iii)** transactions with owners in their capacity as owners, showing separately contributions by and distributions to owners and changes in ownership interests in subsidiaries that do not result in a loss of control.

An entity shall present, either in the statement of changes in equity or in the notes, the amount of dividends recognised as distributions to owners during the period, and the related amount per share.

IAS 1 presents (non-mandatory) illustrations which are useful in showing the implications of these radical and complicated new requirements, and we reproduce extracts below. We omit the statement of financial position (balance sheet), which is relatively straightforward. We also omit all comparatives, which of course must be included in practice, and notes.

TABLE 9.5	Fourth Directive: Horizontal profit and loss account by nature

Item	Description

A   **Charges**

1 Reduction in stocks of finished goods and in work in progress
2 (a) Raw materials and consumables
   (b) Other external charges
3 *Staff costs*
   (a) wages and salaries
   (b) social security costs with a separate indication of those relating to pensions
4 (a) Value adjustments in respect of formation expenses and of tangible and intangible fixed assets
   (b) Value adjustments in respect of current assets, to the extent that they exceed the amount of value adjustments which are normal in the undertaking concerned
5 Other operating charges
6 Value adjustments in respect of financial assets and of investments held as current assets
7 Interest payable and similar charges, with a separate indication of those concerning affiliated undertakings
8 Tax on profit or loss on ordinary activities
9 Profit or loss on ordinary activities after taxation
10 Extraordinary charges
11 Tax on extraordinary profit or loss
12 Other taxes not shown under the above items
13 Profit or loss for the financial year

B   **Income**

1 Net turnover
2 Increase in stocks of finished goods and in work in progress
3 Work performed by the undertaking for its own purposes and capitalised
4 Other operating income
5 Income from participating interests, with a separate indication of that derived from affiliated undertakings
6 Income from other investments and loans forming part of the fixed assets, with a separate indication of that derived from affiliated undertakings
7 Other interest receivable and similar income, with a separate indication of that derived from affiliated undertakings
8 Profit or loss on ordinary activities after taxation
9 Extraordinary income
10 Profit or loss for the financial year

XYZ Group – Statement of comprehensive income for the year ended 31 December 20X7

(Illustrating the presentation of comprehensive income in one statement and the classification of expenses within profit by function)

	(in thousands of currency units) 20X7
Revenue	390 000
Cost of sales	(245 000)
Gross profit	145 000
Other income	20 667
Distribution costs	(9 000)
Administrative expenses	(20 000)
Other expenses	(2 100)
Finance costs	(8 000)
Share of profit of associates	35 100
Profit before tax	161 667
Income tax expense	(40 417)
Profit for the year from continuing operations	121 250
Loss for the year from discontinued operations	–
PROFIT FOR THE YEAR	121 250
Other comprehensive income:	
Exchange differences on translating foreign operations	5 334
Available-for-sale financial assets	(24 000)
Cash flow hedges	(667)
Gains on property revaluation	933
Actuarial gains (losses) on defined benefit pension plans	(667)
Share of other comprehensive income of associates	400
Income tax relating to components of other comprehensive income	4 667
Other comprehensive income for the year, net of tax	(14 000)
TOTAL COMPREHENSIVE INCOME FOR THE YEAR	107 250

XYZ Group – Statement of comprehensive income for the year ended 31 December 20X7

(Illustrating the presentation of comprehensive income in one statement and the classification of expenses within profit by function)

	(in thousands of currency units) 20X7
Profit attributable to:	
Owners of the parent	97 000
Non-controlling interests	24 250
	121 250
Total comprehensive income attributable to:	
Owners of the parent	85 800
Non-controlling interests	21 450
	107 250

	(in thousands of currency units) 20X7
Earning per share (in currency units):	
Basic and diluted	0.46

Alternatively, components of other comprehensive income could be presented in the statement of comprehensive income net of tax:

	20X7
Other comprehensive income for the year, after tax:	
Exchange differences on translating foreign operations	4 000
Available-for-sale financial assets	(18 000)
Cash flow hedges	(500)
Gains on property revaluation	600
Actuarial gains (losses) on defined benefit pension plans	(500)
Share of other comprehensive income of associates	400
Other comprehensive income for the year, net of tax	(14 000)

XYZ Group – Income statement for the year ended 31 December 20X7
(Illustrating the presentation of comprehensive income in two statements and classification of expenses within profit by nature)

	(in thousands of currency units) 20X7
Revenue	390 000
Other income	20 667
Changes in inventories of finished goods and work in progress	(115 100)
Work performed by the entity and capitalised	16 000
Raw material and consumables used	(96 000)
Employee benefits expense	(45 000)
Depreciation and amortisation expense	(19 000)
Impairment of property, plant and equipment	(4 000)
Other expenses	(6 000)
Finance costs	(15 000)
Share of profit of associates	35 100
Profit before tax	161 667
Income tax expense	(40 417)
Profit for the year from continuing operations	121 250
Loss for the year from discontinued operations	–
PROFIT FOR THE YEAR	121 250
Profit attributable to:	
Owners of the parent	97 000
Non-controlling interests	24 250
	121 250
Earnings per share (in current units):	
Basic and diluted	0.46

XYZ Group – Statement of comprehensive income for the year ended
31 December 20X7
(Illustrating the presentation of comprehensive income in two statements)

	(in thousands of currency units)
	20X7
Profit for the year	<u>121 250</u>
Other comprehensive income:	
Exchange differences on translating foreign operations	5 334
Available-for-sale financial assets	(24 000)
Cash flow hedges	(667)
Gains on property revalution	933
Actuarial gains (losses) on defined benefit pension plans	(667)
Share of other comprehensive income of associates	400
Income tax relating to components of other comprehensive income	<u>4 667</u>
Other comprehensive income for the year, net of tax	(14 000)
TOTAL COMPREHENSIVE INCOME FOR THE YEAR	<u>107 250</u>
Total comprehensive income attributable to:	
Owners of the parent	85 800
Non-controlling interests	<u>21 450</u>
	<u>107 250</u>

Alternatively, components of other comprehensive income could be presented, net of tax. Refer to the statement of comprehensive income illustrating the presentation of income and expenses in one statement.

XYZ Group – Disclosure of components of other comprehensive
income – Notes – Year ended 31 December 20X7

	(in thousands of currency units)	
		20X7
Other comprehensive income:		
Exchange differences on translating foreign operations		5 334
Available-for-sale financial assets:		
Gains arising during the year	1 333	
Less: Reclassification adjustments for gains included in profit or loss	<u>(25 333)</u>	(24 000)
Cash flow hedges:		
Gains (losses) arising during the year	(4 667)	
Less: Reclassification adjustments for gains (losses) included in profit or loss	3 333	
Less: Adjustments for amounts transferred to initial carrying amount of hedged items	667	(667)
Gains on property revaluation		933
Actuarial gains (losses) on defined benefit pension plans		(667)
Share of other comprehensive income of associates		<u>400</u>
Other comprehensive income		(18 667)
Income tax relating to components of other comprehensive income		<u>4 667</u>
Other comprehensive income for the year		<u>(14 000)</u>

XYZ Group – Disclosure of tax effects relating to each component of other comprehensive income – Notes – Year ended 31 December 20X7

	(in thousands of currency units) 20X7		
	Before-tax amount	Tax (expense) Benefit	Net-of-tax amount
Exchange differences on translating foreign operations	5 334	(1 334)	4 000
Available-for-sale financial assets	(24 000)	6 000	(18 000)
Cash flow hedges	(667)	167	(500)
Gains on property revaluation	933	(333)	600
Actuarial gains (losses) on defined benefit pension plans	(667)	167	(500)
Share of other comprehensive income of associates	400	–	400
Other comprehensive income	(18 667)	4 667	(14 000)

The whole issue of the appropriate format for presentation of these aspects of financial performance is in something of a state of flux. Much debate is under way within and between the world's major standard-setting bodies. There are two important questions. One concerns the question of what is known as recycling. Suppose an unrealised gain is recorded, outside the income statement, in year 1. In year 2 this gain becomes realised and now meets the criteria for inclusion in the income statement. How, *if at all*, should this be recorded in year 2? At the time of writing, to give two examples under IAS GAAP, IAS 16, *Property, Plant and Equipment*, requires in para. 41 that a transfer from revaluation surplus to retained earnings, on realisation, 'is not made through the income statement' (see Chapter 12). However IAS 21, *The Effects of Changes in Foreign Exchange Rates*, requires in para. 37 that, when a foreign entity is disposed of, related cumulative deferred exchange differences 'should be recognised as income or as expenses' in the period in which the gain or loss is recognised (see Chapter 29). The issue requires clarification as a matter of general principle.

The other major question, not entirely unrelated to the first, concerns the very idea of the separation of the two statements (i.e. of income and of gains/losses in equity). Because the second is an extension of the first or the first is merely a detailed breakdown of one element (net profit) of the second, why require separation at all? The idea of a single statement sounds quite simple in one sense, but it carries the fundamental implication, objectionable to some, that the sanctity of the realisation convention regarding the income statement would be downgraded or defiled. This debate is still ongoing and we expect to see yet further developments and changes to IAS 1 in the future.

CASH FLOW STATEMENTS

The widespread inclusion of cash flow statements in annual financial reporting packages is a relatively recent phenomenon in some countries. There was no mention at all in the EU Directives of the possibility or need to provide such statements. This formal regulatory position as regards the reporting of cash flows may seem rather surprising given the demonstrable importance of cash availability and cash flows in the management of an entity. This is presumably because at the time of the creation of the directives there was no general practice of any such thing in the major countries involved. The effect was that when national governments came to enact national legislation derived from the directives, there was usually still no mention of any such statement.

Nevertheless the rise of the cash flow statement as a necessary part of a comprehensive reporting package has been rapid. Something like it became a standard requirement in the UK in 1975, in IASs in 1977 and eventually in German law, for listed companies in 1998. There have been a number of developments in the format – and indeed, in the underlying principles – of such statements and there have been two different versions of an International Accounting Standard in the area, IAS 7. This is dealt with in full in Chapter 23.

NOTES TO THE FINANCIAL STATEMENTS

In one sense, the notes to the financial statements are 'where everything else goes'. IAS 1 summarises the functions of the notes as being to (para. 103):

1 Present information about the basis of preparation of the financial statements and the specific accounting policies selected and applied for significant transactions and events.

2 Disclose the information required by International Standards that is not presented elsewhere in the financial statements.

3 Provide additional information which is not presented on the face of the financial statements but that is relevant to an understanding of those statements.

Notes to the financial statements should be presented in a systematic manner. Each item on the face of the balance sheet, income statement and cash flow statement should be cross-referenced to any related information in the notes.

The Standard suggests that notes 'are normally' presented in the following order:

1 a statement of compliance with IFRSs

2 a summary of significant accounting policies applied

3 supporting information for items presented on the face of the balance sheet, income statement, statement of changes in equity and cash flow statement, in the order in which each statement and each line item is presented

4 other disclosures, including:

   (a) contingent liabilities (see IAS 37, Chapter 19) and unrecognised contractual commitments

   (b) non-financial disclosures, such as the entity's financial risk management objectives and policies (see IFRS 7, Chapter 17).

Being a recent revision and subject to the IASB's recent whim for detail and the laborious statement of common sense, IAS 1 goes to considerable length in discussing disclosure requirements in the notes. However, the central requirements are reasonably clear and reasonably succinct – an entity must disclose the following:

- *In the summary of significant accounting policies* – the measurement basis or bases used in preparing the financial statements and the other accounting policies used that are relevant to an understanding of the financial statements.

- *In the summary of significant accounting policies or other notes* – the judgements, apart from those involving estimations (see below), management has made in the process of applying the entity's accounting policies that have the most significant effect on the amounts recognised in the financial statements.

- *In the notes* – information about the key assumptions concerning the future, and other key sources of estimation uncertainty at the balance sheet date, that have a significant risk of causing a material adjustment to the carrying amounts of assets and liabilities within the next financial year. In respect of those assets and liabilities, the notes shall include details of their nature and their carrying amount as at the balance sheet date.

- *In the notes* – the amount of dividends proposed or declared before the financial statements were authorised for issue but not recognised as a distribution to equity holders during the period, and the related amount per share; and the amount of any cumulative preference dividends not recognised.

- *In information published with the financial statements (if not disclosed elsewhere)*:
  - the domicile and legal form of the entity, its country of incorporation, and the address of its registered office (or principal place of business, if different from the registered office)
  - a description of the nature of the entity's operations and its principal activities
  - the name of the parent and the ultimate parent of the group
  - if it is a limited life entity, information regarding the length of its life.

In August 2005 the Board added further disclosure requirements relating to capital. These disclosures were formally obligatory for annual periods beginning on or after 1 January 2007 (details can be found in paras 124A and B). The rationale for this addition is that such disclosures are necessary in order to assist users in appraising the risk profile of an entity.

An entity shall disclose information that enables users of its financial statements to evaluate the entity's objectives, policies and processes for managing capital. Therefore, to comply with para. 124A, the entity must disclose the following:

1 Qualitative information about its objectives, policies and processes for managing capital, including (but not limited to):

   (a) a description of what it manages as capital

   (b) when an entity is subject to externally imposed capital requirements, the nature of those requirements and how those requirements are incorporated into the management of capital

   (c) how it is meeting its objectives for managing capital.

2 Summary quantitative data about what it manages as capital. Some entities regard some financial liabilities (e.g. some forms of subordinated debt) as part of capital; other entities regard capital as excluding some components of equity (e.g. components arising from cash flow hedges).

3 Any changes in items 1 and 2 from the previous period.

4 Whether, during the period, it complied with any externally imposed capital requirements to which it is subject.

5 When the entity has not complied with such externally imposed capital requirements, the consequences of such non-compliance.

These disclosures shall be based on the information provided internally to the entity's key management personnel.

SUMMARY

This chapter has described and discussed the requirements of the EU Fourth Directive and IAS 1 in relation to the structure of published financial statements. The major revisions to performance reporting introduced from 1 January 2009 have as their fundamental purpose the prevention of information being 'hidden away' outside the essential statement of performance, now designated the statement of comprehensive income. The word comprehensive is precisely the point. All adjustments and events should be clearly reported in vision. The success of this policy remains to be seen.

EXERCISES

Suggested answers to exercises marked ✓ are to be found on the Student side of the companion website.

Suggested answers to the remaining exercises are to be found on the Instructor side of the companion website.

1 Are fixed formats for the key financial statements a good thing? If they are, why are several different ones allowed?

✓ 2 It is important that revenues as determined under the realisation convention are reported in a separate statement from any other gains and asset increases. Discuss.

3 The accountant is entitled to assume that readers of financial statements will read and understand all the notes to the accounts. Discuss.

4 The latest formats of reporting comprehensive income, required by the latest version of IAS 1 and described in this chapter, will be coming into regular use during 2009 and 2010. Obtain two sets of consolidated IAS accounts for groups based in different countries. Consider whether these recent requirements:

(a) increase comparability

(b) increase the information content of the reports.

CORPORATE GOVERNANCE AND PROVISION OF INFORMATION TO STAKEHOLDERS

10

OBJECTIVES After studying this chapter you should be able to:

- identify the need for additional statements to be included in a reporting package

- outline, and comment on the importance of, a variety of possible additional statements and reports which could be included in a reporting package including corporate responsibility reports and management commentary

- identify and comment on the issue of corporate governance in respect of financial reporting

- consider ethics and the accountant.

INTRODUCTION

Earlier chapters have considered a wide range of alternative ways of evaluating financial events. However, in terms of the basic statements that are to be used for presentation to the users of accounting information nothing fundamentally new has been discussed. It has been implicitly assumed throughout that two essential statements are to be created:

- some form of position statement (balance sheet)
- some form of income statement.

Several possible extensions or alternatives have been suggested in recent years and we will consider some of these here.

In addition this chapter will consider the issue of corporate governance, which, given the events in the financial markets of September 2008, is highly relevant. We will also look at ethics in accounting for the accountant.

But first we look at the variety of additional statements and reports that have been suggested as inclusions in a reporting package.

NEED FOR ADDITIONAL STATEMENTS

All the varied analysis of the last few chapters has been based on the concepts of income and value. We have been thinking about different ways of producing a statement of wealth and about different ways of producing a statement of income, i.e. a change in wealth over time. All of these methods and methodologies, even when reporting on past periods, contain significant assumptions and estimates, and it can be argued that this makes them all less than satisfactory.

Even the traditional accounting process is, as we have seen, an uncertain and complex process. Not only is profit determination complex, it is potentially misleading.

ACTIVITY 10.1

Make a list of further information additional to the income statement, balance sheet and some form of cash statement that might be significantly useful to one or more of the user groups involved in an entity.

Activity feedback

(a) A statement showing how the benefits of the efforts of an entity are shared between employees, providers of capital, the state and reinvestment. This statement will assist users to evaluate the economic performance of the entity. It is generally known as a 'value added statement'.

(b) Users will need to assess the performance of the entity in relation to employees. A report showing the size and composition of the workforce relying on the entity for its livelihood, the work contribution of employees and the benefits earned would be useful. This is often known as an employment report.

(c) Users may wish to assess the relationship between the entity and the state. Thus a statement of money exchanges with government will assist users to assess the economic function of the entity in relation to society.

(d) A statement of future prospects, showing likely future profit, employment and investment levels. This statement will assist users to evaluate the future prospects of the entity and assess managerial performance.

(e) A statement of corporate objectives showing management policy and medium-term strategic targets. This statement will assist users to evaluate managerial performance, efficiency and objectives.

(f) A statement of the social and environmental impact of the entity on the society surrounding it.

(g) A statement on the 'risks' inherent in the entity. Providing information on the potential risks associated with an entity's activities may enable users to assess the possible consequence of materialisation of that risk and whether suitable measures have been taken to mitigate it.

(h) Past trends in key financial figures and ratios, key financial highlights and stock trend data.

(i) Information in respect of innovations in the organisation that will develop tangible and intangible capital/assets in the future.

You may not have identified all of these but we hope you identified some of them. In the first part of this chapter we will discuss all of them.

In any accounting year, there will be a mixture of complete and incomplete transactions. Transactions are complete when they have led to a final cash settlement and these cause no profit measurement difficulties. However, considerable problems arise in dealing with incomplete transactions, where the profit or loss figure can only be determined by means of the accruals concept. Thus, the profit for the past year is dependent on the validity of many assumptions about the future. The greater the volume of incomplete transactions, the greater the degree of estimation and, accordingly, the greater the risk that investors could turn out to have been misled if actual outcomes deviate from estimates.

Thus, one possible extension to the accounting framework would be to provide information on cash inflows and outflows for an entity. This is considered further in Chapter 23. Another possible extension would be to provide information on individual segments within an entity. It is quite possible for one particular segment of an entity to earn all the profit and the others to provide none. The information provided on segments would allow us to assess the risks inherent in the entity. We will look at segmental reports in Chapter 24.

However, if users wish to make decisions on the stewardship of the entity's management and to make their own economic decisions on investing either their cash and/or employee skills in the entity, they arguably need further information.

POSSIBLE ADDITIONAL STATEMENTS

Value added statements

Value added is the wealth that an entity has been able to create by its own and its employees' efforts. It is defined as 'sales income less materials and services purchased'. In rough and ready terms then, it consists of the sales proceeds, reduced by resources given to other parties not connected with the entity. In this context, employees, providers of capital and the government are regarded as connected to the business. This thinking enables the second half of the statement to show how the total value added is shared between employees, providers of capital, the state, and finally the business itself for reinvestment. The statement will show how value added has been used to pay those contributing to its creation. An example of a value added statement is given in Table 10.1 taken from Bayer's Annual Report 2001.

ACTIVITY 10.2

Identify information in the value added statement in Table 10.1 that is not provided in the published financial statements.

Activity feedback
Rather difficult to do as a value added statement does not give any information that is not already in traditional published accounts. What it does do is to rearrange the information and present it from a different perspective.

The emphasis on shareholders inherent in the income statement is removed and instead attention is focused on the wealth created by the business as a whole and on how that created wealth has been split up for various subgroups of the community. It is therefore arguable that a much more rounded picture is presented both of the business as a whole and of the interrelationships between the various essential inputs that make the business operations possible.

TABLE 10.1	Value added by continuing operations					
Source				**Distribution**		
Million euros	**2001**	**Change in %**		**Million euros**	**2001**	**Share in %**
Net sales	28 938	+1.1		Stockholders	657	6.7
Other income	701	−22.5		Employees	7 576	77.1
Total operating				Governments	826	8.4
performance	29 639	+0.4				
Cost of materials	11 057	+10.1		Lenders	463	4.7
Depreciation	2 403	+20.8		Earnings retention	304	3.1
Other expenses	6 353	+0.5				
Value added	9 826	−10.1		Value added	9 826	100.0

Note that depreciation is not shown as providing for the maintenance of assets as retained profit does but is shown as a deduction from turnover. Thus the value added shown is an indicator of wealth created over and above that required for current maintenance.

There are no formal requirements from any source on the necessity to include a value added statement in the reporting package, but in spite of this many entities do publish a statement of this type.

Employment report

Employees are obviously closely involved in business. They have to make many important decisions for themselves that will be heavily influenced by the activities, actions and prospects of business organisations. It could be argued that they have much more to lose than many shareholders or lenders, particularly as they are unable to spread their risk. Employees almost always have to put their faith in one business, they cannot involve themselves with large numbers, as investors or lenders can.

Employees certainly need some indication of future profitability, as do other users, but they also need additional information. Some of this may be financial, e.g. relating to the profitability of their own particular plant, but much of it will not be best presented in financial terms at all. In spite of this, many accountants would regard the provision of information useful to employees as being a necessary component of the total reporting package.

Employment reports could contain the following information:

- numbers employed, average for the financial year and actual on the first and last day
- broad reasons for changes in the numbers employed
- age, distribution, sex and functions of employees
- geographical location of major employment centres
- major plant and site closures, disposals and acquisitions during the period
- hours scheduled and worked by employees giving as much detail as possible concerning the differences between groups of employees
- employment costs including fringe benefits

- costs and benefits associated with pension schemes and the ability of such schemes to meet future commitments
- cost and time involved in training
- names of unions recognised by the entity for the purpose of collective bargaining and membership figures where available or the fact that this information has not been made available by the unions concerned
- information concerning safety and health including the frequency and severity of accidents and occupational diseases
- selected ratios relating to employment.

Some of this information can be found in the current management reports that are provided by most entities in Europe. These management reports are additional to the financial statements but are generally consistent with them. In general auditors when reporting on the financial statements also report on the management report: 'In our opinion, the management report provides, on the whole, a fair understanding of the group's position and adequately presents the risks related to its future development' (extract from auditor's report Bayer Annual Report, 2001).

Statement of money exchanges with government

Part of the purpose of this idea is to emphasise the extent to which businesses provide governments with money and therefore to show the importance of business organisations to the community as a whole:

> The purpose of the statement is to present the direct flow of money between the entity and the government with the object of demonstrating the degree of interdependence between the entity and the state. It does not purport to reflect the full extent of the direct and indirect benefits derived by entities from social services and public facilities provided by government.
>
> (UK ASC Corporate Report 1975)

Statement of future prospects

Two points are absolutely clear. First, many users want to assess an entity's future prospects. Second, any such assessment of future prospects involves a high degree of uncertainty. Forecasts of future prospects do not predict the future but they do set out in a logical and systematic manner the future implications of past and present known facts adjusted by reference to estimates of likely future developments. These projections will have different degrees of probability attached to them that the user will need to judge. It is the certainty of uncertainty that makes entities unwilling to make public projections, although all those acquainted with such exercises are perfectly familiar with the limits on reliability that are inherent in them (see Activity 10.3).

However, such forecasts are certainly desired by users and competitors and, in general, management and accountants are likely to be able to make better and more rational projections that can then be reported than the external users can make for themselves. Forecast statements could include information covering:

- future profit levels
- future employment levels and prospects
- future investment levels.

ACTIVITY 10.3

Identify three objections to publishing such forecasts.

Activity feedback

- Forecasts are concerned with the future and are therefore inherently uncertain. Unless carefully presented, users may regard forecasts as presenting facts rather than best estimates.
- Management will be judged by how well it has met its forecasts and may be encouraged to lower its

targets by publishing only conservative forecasts it knows are wholly attainable and to accept results that meet those forecasts.

- The provision of forecasts by entities suffering from financial difficulties may result in the withdrawal of support and thus precipitate an otherwise avoidable collapse.

It should be remembered that these forecasts will be highly subjective and based on various management assumptions. The following 'Further prospects/forecast' is taken from the management report of Beiersdorf Annual Report, 2000:

> In the financial year 2001 Beiersdorf will implement the announced changes in the structure of the business. In April 2001, the Tesa business was hived-off as an independent corporation with retrospective effect from 1 January. This gives Tesa the organisational and legal structures appropriate to the requirements of the market and form the basis for further successful development in the future. The joint venture BSN medical GmbH & Co. HG has also commenced operations, beginning 1 April. This company brings together the professional businesses of Beiersdorf and Smith & Nephew in the field of conventional wound care. With annual sales of around 490 million euros, BS medical will occupy a leading position worldwide in its competence areas: professional wound care, casting, bandages and compression stockings.
>
> These two projects have high priority for Beiersdorf. We are confident that with these changes we have taken the right steps to ensure successful development of Medical's professional business and Tesa's business in the future.
>
> In our core business we will concentrate entirely on retail consumer sales of big brands. We expect 2001 to bring a worldwide continuation of the generally good economic situation. In Germany and Western Europe, however, the growth of our sales markets will be slow. We also expect a slackening of the pace of growth in North America. International competition and trend to concentration among our customers will continue to increase. We will counteract these developments by focusing on our strong brands. This will further increase our attractiveness as a strong partner for the distributive trade. In 2001 we plan to increase our sales by some 8 to 10% to around 4500 million euros. These figures include 50% of sales by BSN medical and also take account of the sale of the advanced wound care business to Smith & Nephew. We also expect that, after allowing for all remaining restructuring measures, we will achieve an EBIT operating result of around 450 million euros. The profit for the year will come to about 270 million euros. Thus Beiersdorf will probably achieve a net return on sales of 6% in 2001.

It is not until the last paragraph of this forecast that we see some quantitative information.

Statement of corporate objectives

It can be argued that the objectives being pursued by a business need to be publicised for two reasons. First, so that users can see the extent to which management objectives differ from their own and, second, so that management's ability to achieve the stated objectives can be assessed.

Again, of course, there is a distinct danger that management will declare objectives that it feels it can be almost certain of achieving.

Other information

Many entities provide information in their annual reports that they believe investors will find useful. Such information covers:

- Stock data where share prices, market capitalisations, number of shares traded in a period and dividends are tracked for a number of years.
- Balance sheet ratios where the traditional ratios of return on capital employed etc., are tracked. Bayer 2001 shows information as seen in Table 10.2.
- Financial highlights where the entity identifies key changes from one to the next in such items as sales, capital expenditure, personnel expenses, research and development expenses, etc.
- Ten-year summary information of sales, assets, financial obligations, etc.

TABLE 10.2 Balance sheet ratios tracking ROCE etc.	2001	2000
Non-current assets/total assets %	58.6	55.8
Depreciation/capital expenditure %	94.2	80.2
Net sales/inventories	5.2	5.1
Net sales/trade accounts receivable	5.6	5.0
Stockholders' equity-total assets %	45.7	44.3
Stockholders' equity/non-current assets %	78.0	79.3
Short-term liabilities/total liabilities %	51.9	53.8

- Risk management issues where entities report, as part of best practice within corporate governance, on the potential risks associated with their activities, the assessment of the possible consequences of their materialisation and measures available to mitigate them.

Social accounting

Social accounting has been defined as:

> The process of communicating the social and environmental effects of organisations' economic activities to particular interest groups within society at large. As such, it involves extending the accountability of organisations, beyond the traditional role of providing a financial account to the owners of capital, in particular, shareholders. Such an extension is predicated upon the assumption that companies do have wider responsibilities than simply to make money for their shareholders.
>
> (Gray, Owen and Adams, 1996)

As long ago as 1975 social accounting was suggested in the UK via the corporate report.

Through legislation, both country and EU based, society is imposing duties on entities to comply with anti-pollution, safety and health and other socially beneficial requirements. Legislation of this type will continue to increase in the future. Such legislation imposes costs on entities that were previously borne by the community at large and there is therefore good reason to require such expenditure, both compulsory and voluntary expenditure, to be reported. If entities do disclose information on their impact on social and environmental effects then we will, of course, need generally agreed measurement and recognition criteria for such impacts. Much work has been done, in the USA and Europe, to measure environmental costs. An attempt was made to measure pollution costs caused by employees driving to work. However, quite often in such studies, the costs and benefits of interest are not always quantifiable in money terms. This does not mean that such attempts at recognition and measurement should not be considered but does mean that we might have to design radically different measuring tools if we wish to provide useful information in this area to users. The attention of the community is increasingly focused on the 'quality of life' rather than money and if accountants do not attempt to produce useful information in this area then someone else will.

The last 15 years or so have seen an extensive growth in environmental reporting and legislation, which has forced entities to begin to assess their environmental liabilities and risks. Shell plc discovered the pressure that environmental groups can assert, as they were forced to abandon their attempts to dump the Brent Spar oil platform at sea. Users of Shell's financial statements may now demand a great deal more information in respect of Shell's environmental risks and liabilities.

Several research initiatives into social and environmental reporting have been established, in particular a centre has been established at the University of Dundee in the UK and the Canadian Institute of Accountants has produced a discussion paper.

Social and environmental reporting is gaining in importance politically, for example the EU has produced a regulation – Community Eco-management and Audit Schemes (EMAS) – where participating entities must establish environmental goals and report on their performance in meeting those goals. These reports will require external verification, surely a job for accountants as auditors. Environmental auditing was defined by the Canadian Institute as 'a systematic process of objectively obtaining and evaluating evidence regarding a verifiable assertion about activities and events to ascertain the degree of correspondence between the assertion and established criteria and then communicating the results to interested users'.

Most environmental reporting tends to be narrative and descriptive with entities using the document as a public relations exercise rather than as a true measure of the environmental risks and liabilities they carry. This is due to the inherent difficulties of measurement of environmental factors and of applying accounting concepts to these factors.

Environmental information is, however, becoming essential for many businesses and their users. Indeed some organisations, which see environmental issues as important, are becoming market leaders in this area. Businesses are becoming 'greener' and we must develop accounting systems to enable environmental performance reporting to take place.

ACTIVITY 10.6

Traditionally, accounting was based around the concepts of money measurement, going concern and accruals. Identify whether environmental issues are taken into account in the application of these concepts to a business and, if not, why not.

Activity feedback

Money measurement requires that only those facts that can be recorded in monetary terms with some objectivity are taken into account even if other facts are extremely relevant. Environmental factors are very difficult to measure in monetary terms. How, for example, do you place a monetary measure on the damage being done to the environment through car exhaust emissions of employees travelling to work?

The going concern convention requires that in the absence of evidence to the contrary it is assumed that the entity will continue into the future. This concept is principally concerned with solvency and financial performance, not with the impact of environmental factors. For example, in assessing going concern for Shell, little regard was given as to whether pressure groups could ever force them out of business.

Accruals requires a matching of expenses used up in generating revenues. However, entities make no assessment of the expense of environmental factors such as their contribution to global warming through the emission of carbon dioxide or to acid rain from the emission of sulphur and nitrogen oxides.

The international scene in respect of environmental reporting is developing. FEE, the Fédération des Experts Comptables Européens, established an environmental taskforce to review the current body of IASs and to recommend improvements in those standards. A report by the United Nations Conference on Trade and Development (UNCTAD) Secretariat, *Environmental Financial Accounting and Reporting at the Corporate Level*, was also issued on 19 November 1997. The report aimed to identify best practice for reporting and communicating environmental performance both in terms of reporting costs of environmental risks and in presenting non-financial information. The report was actually synthesised from two others:

- accounting and reporting for environmental liabilities and costs within the existing financial reporting framework (David Moore, Canadian Institute of Chartered Accountants, 1997)

- making environmental and financial performance: a survey of best practice techniques (Roger Adams, ACCA, 1997).

The findings of the report were that financial sector investors were placing increasing importance on environmental data in forming their decisions, although no obvious causal mechanism could be identified.

The EC has also urged greater corporate social responsibility (CSR) in Europe through a green paper promoting a European framework for CSR. The aim of the paper is to trigger debate on all aspects of CSR and views on it were requested by 31 December 2001. When the paper was launched two commissioners, Diamantopouilou and Liikanen stated: 'More and more firms are realising the link between profitability and best ethical and environmental practice. Conscientious firms not only attract and retain best workers, they can also get ahead in the technology game, vital for that all-important competitive edge.'

The debate on CSR is also influenced by the Commission's proposals for a European strategy on sustainable development endorsed at the Gothenburg Summit in June 2001. At this stage it might be useful to identify for you the meaning of several terms used in the environmental debate.

- CSR is about entities taking account of the social and environmental impact of their decisions when making business decisions. Entities who voluntarily do this will be seen as 'good corporate citizens'.

- Sustainable development is about ensuring that business decisions taken by entities now do not limit the range of economic, social and environmental options available to others in the future. In other words we must ensure that entities do not 'rape the planet'.

- Socially responsible investing (SRI) is a phenomenon that has grown in recent years. Many investors now take account of how entities impact on society as well as their financial performance when making investment decisions. There is currently a growth in 'ethical' investment funds.

- Triple bottom line (TBL) is a concept whereby companies voluntarily take on board social, environmental and economic issues and report on them. The EC endorses this triple bottom line approach in its green paper and suggests that all the elements, social, environmental and economic can, taken together, create more productive and profitable business. Under the TBL approach information is provided on:

ACTIVITY 10.7

Identify reasons why European entities should take CSR accounting seriously.

Activity feedback
The list is probably endless and we identify only a few here:

- The growth of SRI means entities will have to report on their social and environmental impact or risk losing investors.
- Environmental disasters caused by entities are now widely reported through the global media and entities are thus under greater scrutiny and pressure to disclose information.
- An entity's value in the market can be damaged if it does not take on board social and environmental risk factors. Its brand and reputation are likely to be damaged.
- An entity's reputation as a good 'corporate citizen' can have a positive effect on employee recruitment and retention.
- Good corporate citizenship can also generate customers and forge better links with suppliers.

- economic – covering financial and non-financial information as we currently have in annual reports
- environmental – effect of the products or services on the environment
- social – covering values, ethics and relationships with various stakeholders.

Shell in its Annual Report 2000 made the following statement:

Sustainable development underlies our strategy and is being integrated into everything Shell companies do – in oil and gas as much as renewables. We have to do business in the real world, with all its complexities. We look to governments to create conditions that foster social and economic development but some lack the means. We believe responsible business promotes development. We support Kofi Annan's Global Compact and the Global Sullivan Principles.

Since 2000 Shell have produced comprehensive sustainability reports providing an overview of their efforts to live up to their commitment to contribute to sustainability development. In their 2007 report they state, 'our commitment means helping meet the world's growing energy needs in economically, environmentally and socially responsible ways. This includes both running our operations responsibly today and helping build a responsible energy system for tomorrow.'

Produced below is an extract from Shell's Sustainability Review showing some performance data. The preamble to that data in respect of its limitations and comparison to financial data is quite interesting.

Reporting environmental and social data differs from financial data in a number of important ways. There are inherent limitations to the accuracy, precision and completeness of environmental and social data. These limitations stem from the nature of the data. Certain parameters rely on human behaviour and are affected by culture and personal perception. Other parameters rely on complex measurements that require constant tuning. Still others rely on estimation and modelling. We accept that our published environmental and social data will be affected by these inherent limitations. We continue to improve data integrity by strengthening internal controls. We have summarised our performance below, but more details can be found at www.shell.com/performancedata.

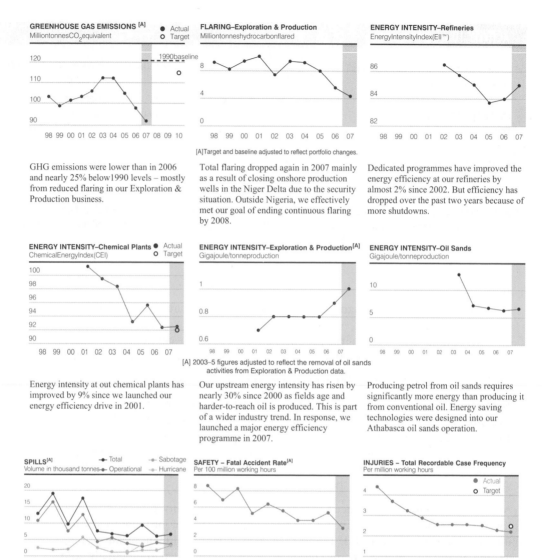

GHG emissions were lower than in 2006 and nearly 25% below 1990 levels – mostly from reduced flaring in our Exploration & Production business.

Total flaring dropped again in 2007 mainly as a result of closing onshore production wells in the Niger Delta due to the security situation. Outside Nigeria, we effectively met our goal of ending continuous flaring by 2008.

Dedicated programmes have improved the energy efficiency at our refineries by almost 2% since 2002. But efficiency has dropped over the past two years because of more shutdowns.

Energy intensity at out chemical plants has improved by 9% since we launched our energy efficiency drive in 2001.

Our upstream energy intensity has risen by nearly 30% since 2000 as fields age and harder-to-reach oil is produced. This is part of a wider industry trend. In response, we launched a major energy efficiency programme in 2007.

Producing petrol from oil sands requires significantly more energy than producing it from conventional oil. Energy saving technologies were designed into our Athabasca oil sands operation.

Our total spill volume rose in 2007, mainly because more spills, due to sabotage, occurred in Nigeria. Spills from corrosion or other operational problems fell again thanks to continued improvements in our downstream business.

Sadly, two employees and 28 contractors lost their lives in confirmed incidents while working for Shell in 2007. Our fatal accident rate has continued to improve since 1997.

Our injury rate – down by more than 50% since 1998 – was our lowest ever in 2007. This performance reflects the big push we are making to strengthen our safety culture.

Bayer's sustainability report for 2007 runs to 112 pages and for the first time includes a Performance Report. This Performance Report includes financial data as well as quantitative and qualitative data in the subject areas of economics, employees, human rights, social responsibility, and ecology and product steward-ship. This is very extensive information but will users read it and gain any benefit

ACTIVITY 10.8

Identify key criteria for CSR in order for it to be useful to users.

Activity feedback

- Continuity – in that the same methods and metrics are used year after year.
- Comparability – to allow for benchmarking and assessing progress.
- Credibility – to ensure that the information provides a 'true and fair' picture of the company's environmental performance.

---

from it? It has though been subject to an assurance process by Ernst and Young. Now look at Activity 10.8.

In Activity 10.8 you could, of course have listed understandability, comparability, relevance and reliability just as easily. The ACCA identify the following principles on which social accounting should be based:

- complete
- comparable – to aid comparison with previous years and others
- embedded – integration of CSR into everything that the company does
- externally verifiable
- continuous improvement – to work up to and beyond the minimum.

Several worldwide companies produce CR reports and make these freely available on their websites.

Nokia, in its CR report for 2005, makes the following statements:

At Nokia reporting is an integral part of our corporate responsibility work. We see clear and consistent communications on our progress as fundamental to building trust and reputation that goes far beyond the financial community. We produced our first CR report in 2002. Since then, we've worked steadily to increase the quality and scope of our reporting content as well as raise the level of awareness on ethical and environmental issues internally and with our stakeholders.

McDonald's publishes a *Europe Corporate Responsibility Report* within which it makes the following statement:

Corporate responsibility in McDonald's Europe is not an 'add-on' programme: it is an intrinsic part of our decision-making. One of the best ways to ensure that CR is fully embedded within our organisation is to present management at regular intervals with the expectations of stakeholders. Our three priority focus areas for CR are nutrition, food quality and safety, and employment practices.

McDonald's also provides a table outlining its responsibilities (Table 10.3).

TABLE 10.3	Extract from McDonald's Europe Corporate Responsibility Report (*How we view our responsibility at McDonald's*)	
	Plan to Win vision	**Our responsibility**
People	Our well-trained people will proudly provide a friendly, accurate and fast 'i'm lovin' it' service with a smile that delights our customers.	We have a responsibility to maintain a work environment where everyone feels valued and accepted, to provide training and other opportunities for personal and professional growth, and to promote job satisfaction.
Products	We will serve food and beverages people prefer to enjoy regularly.	We have a responsibility to provide a variety of quality product choices that our customers trust and to partner with suppliers that operate ethically and meet our social responsibility standards.
Place	Our restaurants and drive-thrus will be clean, relevant and inviting to the customers of today and tomorrow.	We have a responsibility to manage our business by integrating environmental considerations into daily operations and by constantly seeking ways to add value to the community.
Price	We will be the most efficient provider so that we can be the best value to the most people.	We have a responsibility to maintain our values and high standards as we provide food that is affordable to a wide range of customers.
Promotion	All of our marketing and communications will be relevant to our customers and consistent with our brand.	We have a responsibility to maintain and build trust with all our stakeholders by ensuring that our marketing and communications efforts are truthful and appropriate.

Source: McDonald's Worldwide Corporate Responsibility Report 2006.

McDonald's performance report for CSR includes some key performance indicators that are reproduced below.

McDONALD'S KEY PERFORMANCE INDICATORS[3]	2004	2005
BALANCED, ACTIVE LIFESTYLES		
OFFERING MENU CHOICE		
Average # of items, per market menu, that contain at least 1 serving of fruit or vegetables	n/a	6.4
Average # of items, per market menu, that contain at least 1/2 a serving of fruit or vegetables	n/a	9.8
PROVIDING NUTRITION INFORMATION		
% of markets providing nutrition information:		
In-restaurant (*i.e.* trayliners, nutrition brochures)	100%	100%
Out-of-restaurant (*i.e.* websites)	100%	100%

McDONALD'S KEY PERFORMANCE INDICATORS[3]	2004	2005
RESPONSIBLE SUPPLY SYSTEM		
SUPPLIER SOCIAL ACCOUNTABILITY (WORLDWIDE)		
% of food, packaging and tier-1 equipment suppliers that have affirmed our Code of Conduct	57.0%	89.0%
ENVIRONMENTAL IMPACTS OF CONSUMER PACKAGING[4] (NOT INCLUDING BRAZIL)		
Amount of packaging used, by weight, per transaction count	n/a	0.14 lbs.
% of packaging material that is made from recycled paper	n/a	31.5%
ANIMAL WELFARE (WORLDWIDE)		
# of supplier meat (beef, pork and poultry) processing plants audited	534	521
PEOPLE[5]		
OPPORTUNITY		
% of company-operated restaurant managers, started as crew members	n/a	63.6%
% of non-restaurant staff above administrative level, started as crew members	n/a	18.4%
% of operations staff at consultant level or above, started as crew members	n/a	31.5%
% of worldwide top management team who started as crew members	n/a	42.0%
EMPLOYEE TRAINING & DEVELOPMENT		
% of crew members satisfied that they receive the training needed to do a good job (NOT INCLUDING AUSTRALIA, CANADA, CHINA, JAPAN)	79.4%	80.6%
% of managers who feel the person they report to supports their professional development (NOT INCLUDING AUSTRALIA, CANADA, CHINA, JAPAN, U.K.)	80.3%	81.6%
EMPLOYEE SATISFACTION (NOT INCLUDING AUSTRALIA, CANADA, CHINA, JAPAN)		
% of crew who would recommend working at McDonald's to a friend	82.2%	83.2%
% of crew who feel valued as a McDonald's employee	76.5%	79.1%
% of managers who would recommend working at McDonald's to a friend	80.8%	81.6%
% of managers who feel proud to work for McDonald's	82.0%	83.5%
MANAGEMENT OPPORTUNITIES FOR WOMEN		
% of company-operated restaurant managers who are women	n/a	44.0%
% of mid-management office staff who are women	n/a	39.9%
% of mid-management operations staff who are women	n/a	31.5%
% of worldwide top management team who are women	n/a	15.3%

McDONALD'S KEY PERFORMANCE INDICATORS[3]	2004	2005
SOCIAL TAXES		
Total social taxes paid by McDonald's[6]	$345.3m	$382.3m
PLACE		
PHILANTHROPIC ACTIVITIES (WORLDWIDE)		
Total raised by the McDonald's System, including employees, owner/operators and suppliers, and with the help of customers, for RMHC & other charities[7]	n/a	$60.9m
Total corporate cash & in-kind contributions	$9.2m	$13.3m
LOCAL ECONOMIC IMPACTS (NOT INCLUDING JAPAN)		
Total capital expenditures (investments in new and existing restaurants)	$0.94 b	$1.14 b
RESTAURANT-LEVEL ELECTRICAL ENERGY USE (NOT INCLUDING CHINA, U.S.)		
Kilowatt hours used per transaction count (TC), resulting from electrical energy use in company-operated restaurants[8]	0.85 kwh/TC	0.85 kwh/TC
GREENHOUSE GAS EMISSIONS (NOT INCLUDING CHINA, U.S.)		
CO_2 emissions (in tons) resulting from electrical energy use in company-operated restaurants[9]	591 000	643 800

[3] Except as otherwise indicated, figures are for our nine major markets: Australia, Brazil, Canada, China, France, Germany, Japan, the U.K. and the U.S.

[4] Consumer packaging does not include pre-packaged items such as salad dressing packets.

[5] Data for restaurant employees are for company-operated stores.

[6] Social taxes support government programs that may benefit company employees (retirement, health, unemployment).

[7] Inclusive of a portion of the corporate contribution funds noted below.

[8] U.S. data are available only for 2005 and, if included, would skew 2004 and 2005 comparability. U.S. 2005 data for company-operated restaurants represent 1.20 kWh per transaction count.

[9] U.S. data are available only for 2005 and, if included, would skew 2004 and 2005 comparability. U.S. 2005 data for company-operated restaurants represent 173 168 tons of CO_2.

You might like to compare this with the performance data from Shell.

Nike only issued its second corporate responsibility report in 2005. The report follows closely the guidelines issued by GRI (global reporting initiative) and also outlines the company's three strategic corporate responsibility priorities going forward, which are:

- to effect positive, systemic changes in working conditions within the footwear, apparel and equipment industries
- to create innovative and sustainable products
- to use sport as a tool for positive social change and to campaign to turn sport and physical activity into a fundamental right for every young person.

A key driver of the European Alliance on CSR is CSR Europe's European Competitive and Sustainable Enterprise launched in March 2005; and another example of how seriously CR is taken in Europe was the European Conference on CSR and the Finance Sector in December 2005. The conference was designed to encourage a move beyond CSR to the wider goals of sustainable development. Some key findings from that conference were:

- CSR is gradually being mainstreamed
- CSR enables businesses to increase competitiveness, increases their ability to attract and retain quality staff, and taps into new opportunities in terms of clients and markets
- EU governments need effective policy, long-term leadership and commitment, regulations and consistency in policy to promote CSR
- CSR is not just about assessing companies but also about strengthening governments and the partnerships between private and public sectors.

The 2007 conference emphasised the need to move from process reporting to outcome reporting in CSR.

We will return to these issues again when we look in more detail at corporate governance (p. 215).

Table 10.4 provides an example of a CR action plan taken from AstraZeneca's CR Summary Report 2005.

You can find lots of examples of CSRs on company websites and in addition to those reports referenced previously we would also refer you to starbucks.com/csr to gain an insight into the type of information that entities are producing.

In conclusion to the discussion on CSR we return to Hicks and his theory of capital maintenance, which we dealt with in Chapter 4. Remember the quote: 'The purpose of income calculations in practical affairs is to give people an indication of the amount which they can consume without impoverishing themselves.'

This can be applied to the environment because if we continue to consume the environment we will impoverish perhaps not ourselves, but certainly future generations. Economic activity affects the environment as natural resources are depleted or polluted through for example usage, the effects of global warming and acid rain. There is a need to look forward, as the theory of capital maintenance does, to ensure natural wealth – the environment – is maintained and therefore a system of stewardship and maintenance of this natural wealth is a necessity. Reporting in respect of stewardship and maintenance of assets is the accountant's domain. If the objective of financial statements is to provide useful information to users in order for them to assess the stewardship of management and for making economic decisions then, in the view of many, financial statements will need to incorporate the issue, certainly, of environmental reporting and possibly CSR to meet this objective. This will not be an easy task as systems will be difficult to design, but, through their training, accountants are ideally placed to play a leading role in this area. As you may have noticed from the CSR examples we gave, many of these reports are assured by accountancy firms.

ELECTRONIC DISSEMINATION

Information, to be useful, requires the characteristic of timeliness. One means of ensuring timely information is to place financial statements and other information on the internet. Many countries now facilitate this further by permitting electronic

TABLE 10.4 Extract from AstraZeneca's CR Summary Report 2005

Issue	Objective	Action Plan
Integration of CR into all our activities	CR considerations are included in all relevant strategies and decisions.	Continued integration of CR into personal performance objectives. Continued internal communication of policies, framework, standards and guidelines. Continued local implementation. Continued integration of CR into learning and development programmes. Continued sampling of employee understanding and opinion.
Corporate governance and compliance	Application of highest ethical standards in all dealings with stakeholders. Global consistency of implementation of CR standards including all new governance laws and regulations.	Continued communication of revised Code of Conduct including the procedure of reporting concerns. Continued development of audit processes to include CR. Continued global auditing.
Patient safety	Patient safety continues to be a fundamental Company consideration for all our medicines, throughout their lifecycles.	Continued focus on drug safety throughout discovery, development, launch and marketing of each of our products. Continued communication to build understanding of the benefits and risks associated with all medicines.
Sales and marketing	High ethical standards of sales and marketing practice in all countries of operation.	Ongoing training of sales and marketing staff. Ongoing monitoring and review of compliance.
Access to medicines, including diseases of the developing world	Access to medicines considered when defining pricing and market access strategies for new brands. In the developing world, apply our skills and experience to helping to improve healthcare delivery in a sustainable way.	Continued communication of our framework for considering access. Continued monitoring of local alignment with global principles. Apply our skills in infection research to finding a new treatment for TB. Continued discussions with relevant external organisations regarding development and delivery.
Animal research	Use the minimum number of animals to achieve our scientific objectives. Maximise the use of non-animal methods in drug discovery. Enhance the welfare of those animals we have to use.	Annual site improvement plans covering animal welfare and the replacement, reduction and refinement (3Rs) of animal use at all AstraZeneca sites using animals. Formal programme of animal welfare inspection of sites where studies conducted by, or on behalf of, AstraZeneca.
Clinical trials	Our clinical trial programmes continue to be safe, well-designed and appropriate wherever they take place. Open communication of appropriate data.	Maintenance of consistent ethical standards worldwide, in line with our global policy requirements. Continued updating of AstraZeneca's public global clinical trials website with latest information.

TABLE 10.4 (*Continued*)

Human rights	We consistently live up to our core values and our commitment to the principles of the UN Declaration of Human Rights worldwide.	Establish a means of collecting human resources data on a consistent global basis. Establish KPI based on the planned areas of data collection.
Diversity and inclusion	Diversity and inclusion is appropriately supported in our global workforce and reflected in our leadership, and integrated into business and people strategies.	Build diversity and inclusion into business performance management. Focus on minimum standards including talent management, staffing, performance review and reward, and learning and development. Establish a means of collecting human resources data on a consistent global basis and monitor progress.
Driver safety	Promote the safety of all those that drive on Company business.	Continued implementation of driver safety programmes worldwide with a particular focus on areas of greatest driving activity.
Climate change	Minimise the impact of our business activities worldwide.	Further substantial efforts to be made to produce by 2010 an absolute reduction of 11% in global warming emissions for all sources other than pMDIs. Our target is to ensure that our emissions for all sources in 2010, including releases from the use of pMDI products, will be no greater than they were in 2000 and 40% less than they were in 1990.
Pharmaceuticals in the environment	Continue to refine our understanding of how products interact with the environment and pursue opportunities to reduce or eliminate potential adverse impacts.	Continue to work both independently and in collaboration with other organisations to advance research in this area, particularly with regard to environmental toxicity. Pursue site-specific opportunities to minimise the amount of product lost to waste water during manufacturing activities.
Suppliers	Encourage our suppliers to embrace CR standards similar to our own and work with them to share best practice and help them to improve, if appropriate.	Continue to include CR in our global purchasing category management processes. In addition to the US, the UK and Sweden, the CR in Purchasing Guideline to be implemented in other countries where we have major marketing, manufacturing or research activities. These will include Japan, China, India, Mexico, Canada and Puerto Rico as well as more countries in Europe.

Note: This year, we have included Patient Safety, Climate Change and Driver Safety in the plan and removed the broader Safety, Health and Environmental objectives, included in previous years. This does not reflect a diminishing effort in these areas, but for this Plan to be meaningful, we believe it should be used to communicate (both internally and externally) the highest priority issues for the year.

filing of statutory reports. Almost all large entities have their own website and provide not only the financial statements but also environmental statements and CSRs. However, not all financial information posted on the internet is verified by auditors, and users need to beware.

In addition, new digital languages are being developed to speed up and increase transparency of reporting to users. XBRL 'extensible business reporting language' is one example and many believe that it will revolutionise financial reporting. However, it will also bring its own problems of verification of information and we will need to ensure (otherwise we will undermine corporate governance) that XBRL information is relevant, reliable, understandable and comparable, and free from interference. XBRL could, if not closely governed, become the next 'creative accounting arena'.

OTHER EXTENSION FRAMEWORKS

Throughout the accounting world examples of different (better) reporting are being considered. In the UK in 2000 the Institute of Chartered Accountants produced an exemplar report for a fictitious company, Prototype plc. This suggested that future reporting would consist of a core document of summary information supported by additional reports of financial and economic information, people report, sustainability report and supply chain report.

Perhaps it is also worth considering the adoption of a 'balanced scorecard' (Kaplan and Norton, Harvard Business School Press, 1996) approach to company reporting.

From work in the field of human asset accounting the idea of intellectual capital accounts (ICAs) has developed. Edvinsson, who in 1991 was appointed Director of Intellectual Capital at Skandia Assurance and Financial Services stated that the difference between the market value of a firm and its financial or book value is represented by the firm's stock of intellectual capital. He defined intellectual capital as 'the process of knowledge, applied experience, organisational technology, customer relationships, and the professional skills that provide an entity with a competitive edge in the market'.

He makes a fundamental distinction between human capital and structural capital. Structural capital is composed of customer, image, innovation, process and IT capital. Carl Bro Group, a Danish company, provides their users with ICAs but they

ACTIVITY 10.9

Suggest possible performance indicators for human, customer, image, innovation, process and IT capital within the ICAs model.

Activity feedback

- Human – number of staff, age distribution, training costs, staff satisfaction surveys, etc.
- Customer – customer satisfaction index, turnover by customer, largest customer's share of turnover, etc.
- Image – among executives and students, surveys of entity as potential future employer.
- Innovation – number of development projects, number of first-time sales of new products, innovation rate per employer, etc.
- Process – gross sales, interdisciplinary projects, shared knowledge documents on the internet.
- IT – cost per employee, size of shared knowledge bases, employees with option of teleworking etc.

are not subject to audit. Carl Bro Group has also attempted to identify performance indicators in this area. Look at Activity 10.9.

There is much development work to do in the area of ICAs.

MANAGEMENT COMMENTARY

In 2005 the IASB issued a discussion paper entitled 'Management Commentary'. The IASB definition of a management commentary is:

> Information that accompanies financial statements as part of an entity's financial reporting. It explains the main trends and factors underlying the development, performance and position of the entity's business during the period covered by the financial statements. It also explains the main trends and factors that are likely to affect the entity's future development, performance and position.

The discussion paper suggests that the content of the commentary should be as follows:

- nature of the business
- objectives and strategies
- key resources, risks and relationships
- results and prospects
- performance measures and indicators.

In December 2007 the topic of management commentary was moved from the IASB's research agenda to its active agenda and an exposure draft is expected in the fourth quarter of 2008. Around 92% of the respondents to the 2005 discussion paper agreed that a Management Commentary is an integral part of a financial report.

CORPORATE GOVERNANCE

The issue

The issue of information through additional statements has also been brought to the fore by the corporate governance debate. Corporate governance is:

> the system by which business corporations are directed and controlled. The corporate governance structure specifies the distribution of rights and responsibilities among different participants in the corporation, such as, the board, managers, shareholders and other stakeholders, and spells out the rules and procedures for making decisions on corporate affairs. By doing this, it also provides the structure through which the company objectives are set, and the means of attaining those objectives and monitoring performance.
>
> (OECD, April 1999)

Corporate governance is therefore multi-faceted, covering processes, systems, culture, etc. from the viewpoint of many stakeholders. Corporate scandals such as Enron, WorldCom and Parmalat have focused attention on governance, accountability and disclosure and we, as accountants, must consider our role in it. Indeed the

2008 credit crunch and the turmoil within financial markets in September 2008 have placed even more emphasis on corporate governance.

Corporate governance is not static but evolutionary and practices and principles of it will need to change to enable corporations/businesses to remain competitive in a changing world. The Organisation for Economic Co-operation and Development (OECD) has a steering group to coordinate and guide its work on corporate governance, and in 2004 it issued its updated *Principles of Corporate Governance*.

The OECD sees corporate governance as one key element in improving economic efficiency and growth as well as enhancing investor confidence. Good corporate governance should provide proper incentives for the board and management to pursue objectives that are in the interests of the company and its shareholders and should facilitate effective monitoring. The presence of an effective corporate governance system, within an individual company and across an economy as a whole, helps to provide a degree of confidence that is necessary for the proper functioning of a market economy. As a result, the cost of capital is lower and firms are encouraged to use resources more efficiently, thereby underpinning growth.

The OECD sees financial reporting as one of the cornerstones in corporate governance, and within its principles statements it includes a section on disclosure and transparency covering:

1 Disclosure inclusions (but not limited to):

- the financial and operating results
- company objectives
- major share ownership and voting rights
- remuneration policy for members of the board and key executives
- related party transactions
- foreseeable risk factors
- issues regarding employees and other stakeholders
- governance structure and policies.

2 Information should be prepared and disclosed in accordance with high-quality standards of accounting and financial and non-financial disclosure.

3 An annual audit should be conducted by an independent, competent and qualified auditor.

4 External auditors should be accountable to the shareholders and owe a duty to the company to exercise due professional care.

5 Channels for disseminating information should provide for equal, timely and cost-efficient access to relevant information by users.

ACTIVITY 10.10

Identify the role of financial reporting within corporate governance.

Activity feedback

Financial reporting is about providing useful information to users to enable them to make informed decisions regarding stewardship and the future and therefore must be key to corporate governance.

6 The corporate governance framework should be complemented by an effective approach that addresses and promotes the provision of analysis or advice by analysts, brokers, rating agencies and others, which is relevant to decisions by investors, free from material conflicts of interest that might compromise the integrity of their advice or analysis.

Throughout this text we will reiterate time and again that users of company reports require access to regular, reliable and comparable information governed by a strong principles-based disclosure regime that is transparent. Weak and non-transparent regimes will lead to unethical behaviour, as we have seen in the recent corporate scandals, and a loss of market integrity. It is therefore important, as the OECD states, that transactions relating to an entire group of companies be disclosed in line with high-quality, internationally recognised standards and include information about contingent liabilities and off-balance sheet transactions, as well as special purpose entities. You, as a future accountant, will be required to abide by professional ethical guidelines and operate with honesty, integrity and reliability within this corporate governance regime.

History of corporate governance

The 1970s and 80s Corporate governance is not new – it has been around for as long as corporate entities, but the study of corporate governance is relatively new. Governance issues arise as soon as we separate ownership from management as we did with the invention of the limited liability company. Even Adam Smith (*The Wealth of Nations* 1776) understood the concept of governance; 'The directors of companies being managers of other people's money than their own, it cannot well be expected that they should watch over it with the same anxious vigilance with which the partners in a private copartnery frequently watch over their own.' Corporate governance has its beginnings in company law.

The 'Principal/Agency' problem concerns potential conflicts arising between the owners (principals) and boards of directors (agents) who have effective control over the company.

In the 1970s emphasis on independent outside directors, audit committees and the establishment of two-tier boards in companies drew attention to the governance issue. The EEC in its 5th draft directive 1972 advocated two-tier board governance as seen in Germany and Holland. Increasing litigation in the USA, where shareholders of failed companies sought recompense from directors, etc., again emphasised the need for appropriate governance.

The 1970s also saw a growth in the idea that public companies, in addition to their duty to shareholders (owners) also had responsibilities to other stakeholders such as employees, customers, suppliers, lenders, community and government. A list very similar to that we identified as the users of financial reports in Chapter 1, Activity 1.1.

In the UK the collapse of several companies in the 1970s, e.g. Pergamon Press, Rolls Royce, Lonhro, also enhanced the interest in corporate governance.

During the 1980s action on corporate governance was minimal and more company collapses and questionable practices were seen throughout the world attributed by many to the power of executive directors who had no checks or balances upon them. In particular the combination of the chief executive officer and chairman role was questioned, as was the lack of power of non-executive directors.

1990s The 1990s saw the growth in power of major institutional investors and they also began to focus on corporate governance.

In the UK the issue was brought to the fore by the Cadbury Report 1992 and the establishment of the Cadbury Code that focused on the financial aspects of corporate governance, corporate behaviour and ethics and led to improved boardroom practice. In 1995 the Greenbury Report added Principles on the Remuneration of Executive Directors in an attempt to curb CEO salaries. These two reports were brought together by the Hampel Report of 1998 and formed the first Combined Code. The Hampel Report had three main themes:

- Good corporate governance needs broad principles not prescriptive rules. This sounds like a familiar theme from financial reporting where the IASB wish to adopt a principles-based approach rather than a rule-based approach as was practised in the USA.
- A unitary board is acceptable, thus rejecting the proposal of two-tier boards.
- The board is accountable to shareholders thus downgrading the need for responsibility to other stakeholders.

1999 saw the publication of the Turnbull Report that concentrated on risk management and internal controls. All of these reports were as a result of shareholder disquiet as regards corporate performance and to avoid the threat of government legislation if such codes were not developed voluntarily by the business sector.

The Cadbury Report had great influence around the world and several other countries published their own corporate governance reports in the 1990s. All of these reports were concerned with the abuse of corporate power and recommended wider use of audit committees, outside non-executive directors, remuneration committees composed of independent outside directors to advise on director remuneration and separation of the chairman and CEO role. In 1998 the OECD proposed the development of global guidelines for corporate governance and emphasised the difference between the strong external investment culture of the USA and UK with the firm corporate governance practices in Japan, France and Germany where employees had more influence and investors seemed to take a longer-term view.

The 21st century The turn of the century saw the growth in global corporate structures with vast networks of subsidiaries, strategic alliances and related parties. Directors of major entities now wield extensive power. Another report on corporate governance was issued in the UK in 2003, the Higgs Report, which built on all the previous reports to produce a single combined code. The recommendations from Higgs were:

- To define 'independence' and the proportion of independent non-executive directors on the board and its committees.
- To expand the role of the senior independent director to provide an alternative channel for shareholders and to lead evaluations on the chairman's performance.
- To enhance the process of nominations to the board through a transparent and rigorous process and evaluation of the performance of the board, its committees and individual directors.

The FRC in the UK took this report forward together with the Smith Report on Audit Committees to publish its Combined Code of Corporate Governance in July 2003. This was further revised by the Turnbull Review Group and a revised code issued by the FRC in 2005. About this time the European Commission also issued its Corporate Governance and Company Law Action Plan covering disclosure requirements, exercise of voting rights, cross-border voting, disclosure by institutional investors and responsibilities of board members.

The events of 2008 have shown us that bankers, traders and financial institutions around the world wield extensive power and for all the reports, codes, action plans and publications on corporate governance it still remains an issue. James Wolfensohn, President of the World Bank stated in 2008: 'The governance of companies is more important for world economic growth than the government of countries.' The events of September 2008 certainly support this view and the consequent lack of investor confidence and public trust that will ensue from the collapse of major financial institutions will probably see an increased focus on corporate governance. The public at large will no doubt wish to see improved integrity and oversight of management, increased scrutiny of board composition and independence, more effective use of internal and external audit functions, greater levels of disclosure and transparency and more engagement with investors.

Combined Code on corporate governance

The FRC first published its corporate governance code in 2003 and its latest update was 2007. In the normal course of events the next review will take place in 2010. Given the abnormal recent events in the world financial markets this could be brought forward. The FRC states that:

> Good corporate governance should contribute to better company performance by helping a board discharge its duties in the best interests of shareholders; if it is ignored, the consequence may well be vulnerability or poor performance. Good governance should facilitate efficient, effective and entrepreneurial management that can deliver shareholder value over the long term. The Combined Code on Corporate Governance is published by the FRC to support these outcomes and promote confidence in corporate reporting and governance.

ACTIVITY 10.11

Identify three main principles that you believe should be included in the Combined Code in relation to the board of directors.

Activity feedback
The Code covers seven main principles as follows:

- Every company should be headed by an effective board, which is collectively responsible for the success of the company.

- There should be a clear division of responsibilities at the head of the company between the running of the board and the executive responsibility for the running of the company's business. No one individual should have unfettered powers of decision.

- The board should include a balance of executive and non-executive directors (and in particular independent non-executive directors) such that no

individual or small group of individuals can dominate the board's decision taking.

- There should be a formal, rigorous and transparent procedure for the appointment of new directors to the board.

- The board should be supplied in a timely manner with information in a form and of a quality appropriate to enable it to discharge its duties. All directors should receive induction on joining the board and should regularly update and refresh their skills and knowledge.

- The board should undertake a formal and rigorous annual evaluation of its own performance and that of its committees and individual directors.

- All directors should be submitted for re-election at regular intervals, subject to continued satisfactory performance. The board should ensure planned and progressive refreshing of the board.

The Code itself is not a rigid set of rules and does recognise that non-compliance may be justified in particular circumstances if good governance can be achieved by other means. The reasons for non-compliance should however be explained to shareholders. Thus the Code relies on a 'comply or explain approach.'

The Code provides best practice principles on directors, remuneration, accountability and audit, relations with shareholders, institutional shareholders and disclosures of corporate governance.

These seven main principles it identifies are each enhanced by supporting principles and code provisions. For example for principle one:

Supporting Principles

The board's role is to provide entrepreneurial leadership of the company within a framework of prudent and effective controls which enables risk to be assessed and managed. The board should set the company's strategic aims, ensure that the necessary financial and human resources are in place for the company to meet its objectives and review management performance. The board should set the company's values and standards and ensure that its obligations to its shareholders and others are understood and met.

All directors must take decisions objectively in the interests of the company.

As part of their role as members of a unitary board, non-executive directors should constructively challenge and help develop proposals on strategy. Non-executive directors should scrutinise the performance of management in meeting agreed goals and objectives and monitor the reporting of performance. They should satisfy themselves on the integrity of financial information and that financial controls and systems of risk management are robust and defensible. They are responsible for determining appropriate levels of remuneration of executive directors and have a prime role in appointing, and where necessary removing, executive directors, and in succession planning.

Code Provisions

A.1.1 The board should meet sufficiently regularly to discharge its duties effectively. There should be a formal schedule of matters specifically reserved for its decision. The annual report should include a statement of how the board operates, including a high level statement of which types of decisions are to be taken by the board and which are to be delegated to management.

A.1.2 The annual report should identify the chairman, the deputy chairman (where there is one), the chief executive, the senior independent director and the chairmen and members of the nomination, audit and remuneration committees. It should also set out the number of meetings of the board and those committees and individual attendance by directors.

A.1.3 The chairman should hold meetings with the non-executive directors without the executives present. Led by the senior independent director, the non-executive directors should meet without the chairman present at least annually to appraise the chairman's performance (as described in A.6.1) and on such other occasions as are deemed appropriate.

A.1.4 Where directors have concerns which cannot be resolved about the running of the company or a proposed action, they should ensure that their concerns are recorded in the board minutes. On resignation, a non-executive director should provide a written statement to the chairman, for circulation to the board, if they have any such concerns.

A.1.5 The company should arrange appropriate insurance cover in respect of legal action against its directors.

The Code in respect of accountability and audit is quite pertinent and we reproduce it below for you. You can access the whole of the code on the FRC website www.frc.org.

C.1 Financial Reporting

Main Principle The board should present a balanced and understandable assessment of the company's position and prospects.

Supporting Principle The board's responsibility to present a balanced and understandable assessment extends to interim and other price-sensitive public reports and reports to regulators as well as to information required to be presented by statutory requirements.

Code Provisions

C.1.1 The directors should explain in the annual report their responsibility for preparing the accounts and there should be a statement by the auditors about their reporting responsibilities.

C.1.2 The directors should report that the business is a going concern, with supporting assumptions or qualifications as necessary.

C.2 Internal Control

Main Principle The board should maintain a sound system of internal control to safeguard shareholders' investment and the company's assets.

Code Provision

C.2.1 The board should, at least annually, conduct a review of the effectiveness of the group's system of internal controls and should report to shareholders that they have done so. The review should cover all material controls, including financial, operational and compliance controls and risk management systems.

C.3 Audit Committee and Auditors

Main Principle The board should establish formal and transparent arrangements for considering how they should apply the financial reporting and internal control principles and for maintaining an appropriate relationship with the company's auditors.

Code provisions

C.3.1 The board should establish an audit committee of at least three, or in the case of smaller companies two, independent non-executive directors. In smaller companies the company chairman may be a member of, but not chair, the committee in addition to the independent non-executive directors, provided he or she was considered independent on appointment as chairman. The board should satisfy itself that at least one member of the audit committee has recent and relevant financial experience.

C.3.2   The main role and responsibilities of the audit committee should be set out in written terms of reference and should include:

- to monitor the integrity of the financial statements of the company, and any formal announcements relating to the company's financial performance, reviewing significant financial reporting judgements contained in them;

- to review the company's internal financial controls and, unless expressly addressed by a separate board risk committee composed of independent directors, or by the board itself, to review the company's internal control and risk management systems;

- to monitor and review the effectiveness of the company's internal audit function;

- to make recommendations to the board, for it to put to the shareholders for their approval in general meeting, in relation to the appointment, re-appointment and removal of the external auditor and to approve the remuneration and terms of engagement of the external auditor;

- to review and monitor the external auditor's independence and objectivity and the effectiveness of the audit process, taking into consideration relevant UK professional and regulatory requirements;

- to develop and implement policy on the engagement of the external auditor to supply non-audit services, taking into account relevant ethical guidance regarding the provision of non-audit services by the external audit firm; and to report to the board, identifying any matters in respect of which it considers that action or improvement is needed and making recommendations as to the steps to be taken.

C.3.3   The terms of reference of the audit committee, including its role and the authority delegated to it by the board, should be made available. A separate section of the annual report should describe the work of the committee in discharging those responsibilities.

C.3.4   The audit committee should review arrangements by which staff of the company may, in confidence, raise concerns about possible improprieties in matters of financial reporting or other matters. The audit committee's objective should be to ensure that arrangements are in place for the proportionate and independent investigation of such matters and for appropriate follow-up action.

C.3.5   The audit committee should monitor and review the effectiveness of the internal audit activities. Where there is no internal audit function, the audit committee should consider annually whether there is a need for an internal audit function and make a recommendation to the board, and the reasons for the absence of such a function should be explained in the relevant section of the annual report.

C.3.6 The audit committee should have primary responsibility for making a recommendation on the appointment, reappointment and removal of the external auditors. If the board does not accept the audit committee's recommendation, it should include in the annual report, and in any papers recommending appointment or re-appointment, a statement from the audit committee explaining the recommendation and should set out reasons why the board has taken a different position.

C.3.7 The annual report should explain to shareholders how, if the auditor provides non-audit services, auditor objectivity and independence is safeguarded.

OECD Principles of Corporate Governance

OECD originally issued their principles of corporate governance in 1999 and a revised version in 2004. In the preamble to the code they state:

The principles are intended to assist OECD and non-OECD governments in their efforts to evaluate and improve the legal, institutional and regulatory framework for corporate governance in their countries, and to provide guidance and suggestions for stock exchanges, investors, corporations, and other parties that have a role in the process of developing good corporate governance. The Principles focus on publicly traded companies both financial and non-financial. Increasingly, the OECD and its member governments have recognised the synergy between macroeconomic and structural policies in achieving fundamental policy goals. Corporate governance is one key element in improving economic efficiency and growth as well as enhancing investor confidence.

The events of September 2008 perhaps lead us to question whether there is an effective corporate governance system in operation in the USA and Europe.

The Principles focus on governance problems that result from the separation of ownership and control but also take a broader approach than this as they recognise that governance issues arise when controlling shareowners have power over minority shareholders and when employees have legal rights irrespective of their ownership rights.

Another pertinent paragraph from the OECD preamble is:

The degree to which corporations observe basic principles of good corporate governance is an increasingly important factor for investment decisions. Of particular relevance is the relation between corporate governance practices and the increasingly international character of investment. International flows of capital enable companies to access financing from a much larger pool of investors. If countries are to reap the full benefits of the global capital market, and if they are to attract long-term 'patient' capital, corporate governance arrangements must be credible, well understood across borders and adhere to internationally accepted principles.

The OECD principles are divided into six sections as follows:

- Ensuring the basis for an effective corporate governance framework
- The rights of shareholders and key ownership functions
- The equitable treatment of shareholders

- The role of stakeholders in corporate governance
- Disclosure and transparency
- The responsibilities of the board.

You can of course access the full Principles on the OECD website www.oecd.org.

The future for corporate governance

We would expect to see further emphasis on corporate governance in light of the events in the financial markets of September 2008. As the OECD state in their preamble, 'The Principles are evolutionary in nature and should be reviewed in light of significant changes in circumstances. Governments have an important responsibility for shaping an effective regulatory framework that provides for sufficient flexibility to allow markets to function effectively and to respond to expectations of shareholders and other stakeholders.' Indeed the OECD Secretary-general Angel Gurria called on 25 September 2008 for a new drive in corporate governance to raise standards and performance in this area stating that,

> Rebuilding investor confidence will be vital to helping the economy get back on track. Strengthening the rules, regulations and codes of corporate governance will be central to this. I call on member countries to work urgently with us to address major corporate governance failures. This will be a vital step to reinforcing market integrity.

A statement on the way forward is expected from the OECD in November 2008.

The future of corporate governance will also be affected by the outcome of the USA Federal Bureau of Investigation (FBI) into the events surrounding the demise of Freddie Mac, Freddie Mae, AIG, Lehman Brothers and other companies in September 2008. Much of the FBI investigation may well focus on creative accounting, especially the absence of billions of dollars of liabilities from the companies' balance sheets.

We expect much activity within the financial reporting standard setters of the world as well. They will need to focus on issues such as going concern, reporting of liabilities, financial instruments, cash accounting and perhaps more disclosure requirements. All of which is likely to lead to more complexity and perhaps less relevance in financial reporting. The UK's FRC in July 2008 identified complexity as a major project within their future work plan with the head of the project stating: 'We need to offer a vision of less complexity that stakeholders support so we can begin to move in the right direction.' Complexity in financial reporting is seen as one of the more serious threats to confidence.

ETHICS IN ACCOUNTING

Introduction

Users of financial reports expect the accountants who have prepared and audited them to have carried out their duties in a true and fair manner. Accountants within all their dealings must act with honesty, integrity, and reliability if they expect public trust to be placed in them. Unfortunately many corporate scandals such as Polly Peck, Maxwell, Enron, Guinness, Parmalat, WorldCom and the events of September 2008 have drawn that trust into question. The accounting profession and the associated professional bodies have established peer groups that oversee the discipline of members if their behaviour is not as expected. Penalties imposed by these professional bodies cover suspension of practising licences, fines, and termination of membership. In addition accountants are also of course subject to the law of the country in which they practice.

IFAC and ethics

The mission of IFAC is to:

> serve the public interest, continue to strengthen the accountancy profession worldwide, contribute to the development of strong international economies by establishing and promoting adherence to high quality professional standards, furthering the international convergence of such standards, and speaking out on public interest issues where the profession's expertise is most relevant.

In pursuing this mission IFAC has established the International Ethics Standards Board for Accountants that has developed a Code of Ethics for Professional Accountants for use around the world. The fundamental principles of the Code are:

- Integrity – a professional accountant should be straightforward and honest in performing professional services.
- Objectivity – a professional accountant should not allow bias, conflict of interest or undue influence of others to override professional or business judgements.
- Professional competence and due care – a professional accountant has a continuing duty to maintain professional knowledge and skill at the level required to ensure that a client or employer receives competent professional service based on current developments. A professional accountant should act diligently and in accordance with applicable technical and professional standards when providing professional services. From the above it is apparent that accountants will need to commit to continuing professional development.
- Confidentiality – a professional accountant should respect the confidentiality of information acquired as a result of professional and business relationships and should not disclose any such information to third parties without proper and specific authority unless there is a legal or professional right or duty to disclose. Confidential information acquired as a result of professional and business relationships should not be used for the personal advantage of the professional accountant or third parties.
- Professional behaviour – a professional accountant should comply with relevant laws and regulations and should avoid any action that discredits the profession.

Threats to adherence to the Code The Code, as much else in accounting, is principles-based not rules-based and therefore does not provide an extensive set of rules to follow. It considers how threats such as self-interest, intimidation, self review and familiarity create the conditions in which people might be tempted to act contrary to the principles and invites the application of safeguards in the form of institutional procedural frameworks and personal responses to overcome them. The Code is also divided into two sections, one dealing with accountants in public practice and the other with accountants in business.

ACTIVITY 10.12

The Code states that:

- Self-interest threats can occur as a result of the financial or other interests of an accountant or of an immediate or close family member.
- Intimidation can occur when a professional accountant may be deterred from acting objectively by threats, actual or perceived.

  Give examples of self-interest threats and intimidation threats for both accountants in public practice and in business.

Activity feedback

Self-interest threats could be:

- A financial interest in a client or jointly holding a financial interest with a client
- Undue dependence on total fees from a client
- Concern about the possibility of losing a client
- Having a close business relationship with a client
- Potential employment with a client
- Contingent fees relating to an assurance engagement
- Financial interest, loans or guarantees in the business

- Incentive compensation arrangements, e.g. bonuses
- Inappropriate personal use of corporate assets
- Concern over employment security
- Commercial pressure from outside the employing organisation.

  Intimidation threats could be:

- Threat of dismissal or replacement
- Threat of litigation
- Pressure to reduce inappropriately the extent of the work performed to reduce costs
- Threat of dismissal or replacement of the professional accountant in business or a close or immediate family member over a disagreement about the application of an accounting principle or the way in which financial information is to be reported
- A dominant personality attempting to influence the decision-making process, for example with regard to the awarding of contracts or the application of an accounting principle.

ACTIVITY 10.13

Identify safeguards to guard against the threats to professional accountants that could be employed in the workplace.

Activity feedback

The safeguard examples given by the Code are:

- The employing organisation's systems of corporate oversight or other oversight structures
- The employing organisation's ethics and conduct programmes
- Recruitment procedures in the employing organisation emphasising the importance of employing high calibre competent staff
- Strong internal controls
- Appropriate disciplinary processes

- Leadership that stresses the importance of ethical behaviour and the expectation that employees will act in an ethical manner
- Policies and procedures to implement and monitor the quality of employee performance
- Timely communication of the employing organisation's policies and procedures, including any changes to them, to all employees and appropriate training and education on such policies and procedures
- Policies and procedures to empower and encourage employees to communicate to senior levels within the employing organisation any ethical issues that concern them without fear of retribution

ACTIVITY 10.13   *(Continued)*

- Consultation with another appropriate professional accountant. (Several professional accountancy bodies provide networks to facilitate this.)

    The Code also includes what might be regarded as the final safeguard:

    In circumstances where a professional accountant in business believes that unethical behaviour or actions by others will continue to occur within the employing organisation, the

professional accountant in business should consider seeking legal advice. In those extreme situations where all available safeguards have been exhausted and it is not possible to reduce the threat to an acceptable level a professional accountant in business may conclude that it is appropriate to resign from the employing organisation.

Safeguards to such threats The Code advocates the employment of safeguards to eliminate or reduce the threats to the professional accountant. These safeguards can be created by the profession, legislation or regulation or can be created within the workplace.

Acting with sufficient expertise We outlined the fundamental principles of the Code in the introduction. One of these, acting with sufficient expertise, we would like to consider in a little more detail. This principle requires that the accountant only undertakes significant tasks for which he/she has, or can obtain, sufficient specific training or experience. Within the workplace there can be many potential threats to the maintenance of this principle by the accountant.

The full Code can be accessed on the IFAC website, www.ifac.org, as can the exposure draft issued by IFAC in July 2008 to clarify issues within the Code.

ACTIVITY 10.14

Identify circumstances that could exist within the workplace that would threaten the ability of the accountant to perform his duties within his given level of expertise. In addition identify safeguards that the accountant could employ to ensure he/she maintains this fundamental principle.

Activity feedback
The Code gives the following threats:

- Insufficient time for properly performing or completing the relevant duties
- Incomplete, restricted or otherwise inadequate information for performing the duties properly
- Insufficient experience, training and/or education
- Inadequate resources for the proper performance of the duties.

Safeguards that may be considered are:
- Obtaining additional advice or training
- Ensuring that there is adequate time available for performing the relevant duties
- Obtaining assistance from someone with the necessary expertise
- Consulting where appropriate, with superiors, independent experts, and a relevant professional body.

    The final safeguard is of course to refuse to perform the task/duties but remember to communicate to your superiors the reasons for the refusal.

ACTIVITY 10.15

Brief case study

You are a second-year trainee accountant about to go on study leave. Your manager asks you to complete some complicated reconciliation work before your study leave commences as your senior colleague who was due to do the work is on long-term sick leave. You feel the deadline given for the complicated task is unrealistic. You also do not feel sufficiently experienced to complete the work. You have asked your manager for additional supervision to complete the work but this has been refused. Your manager reiterates that he expects the work to be competed before you can take your study leave.

State which principles of the Ethical Code you think the above scenario brings into question, what threats exist and the action you would take to resolve the issue.

Activity feedback

The fundamental principles involved in this scenario are integrity, professional competence and due care and professional behaviour.

The threat is intimidation.

A suitable course of action would be to explain, politely, to your manager that you do not have sufficient time to complete the work before your study leave; that if you do undertake the work you will need suitable supervision; and that you will of course complete the work when you return from study leave. If this action does not resolve the issue you must obtain advice from a senior colleague or from your professional body.

(Adapted CIPFA ethics code case studies)

SUMMARY

There is a school of thought that more information is always, provided it is properly presented, a good thing. The list of possibilities is almost endless as we have hopefully indicated in this chapter. But there is a danger that the purpose of the whole operation becomes lost. We need to provide information that is useful to the typical user. What evidence there is tends to suggest that many users are not able to understand the information they are already getting. It could be argued that the priority for accountants should be to improve their ability to communicate understanding, rather than to increase the detail and complexity of their reports. Is the graph or the pie chart more useful than the beautifully balanced balance sheet? Is the 'chatty' chairman's statement of more use than the precisely detailed and carefully audited accounts and voluminous notes? Is the CSR report or TBL report of more use than the seg-

mental report even if they do lack a degree of reliability? And how can we audit this CSR and TBL report? How will we verify information on the internet and that provided through the use of new digital languages? These are all questions that the accounting profession will need to answer.

In this chapter we have outlined a wide variety of possible developments and extensions to the accounting framework and reporting practice. All involve additional effort and therefore additional cost. But if the advantages to some users or potential users outweigh those costs then we should perhaps produce them.

Whatever additional statements accountants become involved in preparing or verifying they will need to be trusted by all users and our ethical behaviour will become a powerful means of creating confidence in the business world. It is essential that you as a student of financial reporting understand and are guided by the fundamental principles of the IFAC Ethical Code so that the accountant retains a position of trust within society.

We have also considered the issue of corporate governance within this chapter and identified that the principles of corporate governance are evolutionary and will need to be reviewed in the light of significant changes in worldwide financial markets. As the OECD states in its Principles of Corporate Governance:

To remain competitive in a changing world, corporations must innovate and adapt their corporate governance practices so that they can meet new demands and grasp new opportunities. Similarly, governments have an important responsibility for shaping an effective regulatory framework that provides for sufficient flexibility to allow markets to function effectively and to respond to expectations of shareholders and other stakeholders.

EXERCISES

Suggested answers to exercises marked ✓ are to be found on the Student side of the companion website.

Suggested answers to the remaining exercises are to be found on the Instructor side of the companion website.

1   Using the annual report of any entity of your choice discuss whether the information provided therein is of use to users.

2   For the same entity identify what, if any, additional information you as a potential shareholder would have wished to be available and what use you would make of the information.

3   Using the information given in Activity 10.2 in respect of Bayer's value added statement identify possible conclusions that could be drawn in respect of Bayer's performance for the year and any caveats you would place on these conclusions.

4   Using the management report from any entity of your choice identify all information it contains relevant to employees and discuss the importance of this information to the employees of the entity.

5   Critically appraise the following statement: *All information provided by an entity in addition to that required by country law is potentially misleading to users.*

✓ **6**   Discuss the need for entities to provide additional information to users.

✓ **7**   Identify the potential drawbacks of entities providing additional information and suggest possible means of overcoming these drawbacks.

8   In the last analysis, financial reporting is about numbers. Discuss.

9   *When users are asked what they want from corporate environmental statements, there appears to be the usual mix of that which is deliverable, that which would be nice if only the accountants could find a way of delivering it and that which will never be deliverable – available or not – because of commercial sensitivity.* (Roger Adams, *Accountancy Age*, May 1994, p. 16.) Is this pessimistic or realistic today? Discuss and illustrate.

10   Corporate governance was established in response to shortcomings in business practices. Appraise the development of corporate governance in meeting the needs of business and its stakeholders in the 21st century.

11   Identify the recent developments in corporate social reporting and evaluate the effect such reporting has on alleviating social and environmental problems.

12   Identify the fundamental ethical principles that professional accountants must abide by and the threats they may be subject to in their working environment.

BASICS OF INTERPRETATION OF FINANCIAL STATEMENTS

11

OBJECTIVES After studying this chapter you should be able to:

- identify the needs of users wishing to make use of accounting information

- explain the technique of ratio analysis and calculate appropriate ratios

- explain what each of the ratios means, and discuss their limitations.

- identify additional information that users may require to aid their analysis

INTRODUCTION

We will be concerned in Parts Two and Three of this book with the provision of financial information to users which presents a true and fair view of the entity. Users will use this information to gain some insight as to the reporting entity's stability, performance, future prospects and/or whatever else may interest them.

In this chapter we will introduce the basic instruments of financial statement analysis. The presentation of these topics in this chapter will enable you to understand the discussion on financial statement analysis in Part Four of this book.

ACCOUNTING INFORMATION AND USERS

Financial statements provide valuable information for both the owners of the business, and any potential owners/investors, and for other stakeholders of the company. Within Chapter 1 we identified the users of accounting information and their differing needs (see Activity 11.1).

Financial statement data serve as an input to these economic decisions of the different stakeholders of the company. The financial statements provide information on the financial position, the changes in the financial position and the performance of the company. These financial data are more appropriate for certain economic decisions than for others. For example regulatory authorities will probably have to combine financial statement data with other data for their decision-making process. Regulatory authorities overseeing the competition in certain industries will also need to collect data on market shares or pricing policies of the different companies. So financial as well as non-financial data from other sources will be added to financial statement data in order to make decisions.

The analysis of the economic decisions carried out in Activity 11.1 indicates that it is possible to identify three general areas of interest in which users' needs and objectives may lie.

Although all the information needs of users cannot be met solely by financial statement data, there are needs that are common to all interested parties. The first two items below might interest a wide group of users. The third need relates to owners and potential owners.

- *Financial status* – can the business pay its way in the short term as well as in the long term, so is it in fact *liquid and solvent*?

ACTIVITY 11.1

In its preface to the conceptual framework, the IASB gives a list of examples of different economic decisions which are made by users on the basis of the financial statements of a company. Consider this list of examples of economic decisions and try to figure out which group of users will be especially interested in the answer to that question:

(a) decide when to buy, hold or sell an equity investment

(b) assess the stewardship or accountability of management

(c) assess the ability of the entity to pay and provide other benefits to its employees

(d) assess the security for amounts lent to the entity

(e) determine taxation policies

(f) determine distributable profits and dividends

(g) prepare and use national income statistics or

(h) regulate the activities of entities.

Activity feedback

The decisions listed in (a) and (b) will be taken by owners of the company and potential owners. Among the owners of the company, we can distinguish different groups of owners, such as shareholders with small amounts of shares or large institutional investors, such as pension funds.

The decision listed in (c) will be an issue of concern to owners, but also to the creditors of the company and the employees. In a number of countries like France, Germany and Belgium the law prescribes that financial information should be provided in specific formats to the workforce. To make sure that the information is reliable, auditors have to certify the economics and financial information provided to the employees by corporate management. Decision (d) will concern especially the suppliers of long-term credit to the company. Decision (e) is important for owners as well as for the government. Owners try to establish the most favourable tax regime for their operations. Decisions (f), (g) and (h) refer to governmental decisions or decisions of regulatory authorities. These governmental or regulatory bodies can be national or supranational.

- *Performance* – how successful is the business, is it making a reasonable profit, is it utilising its assets to the fullest, is it in fact *profitable* and *efficient*?
- *Investment* – is the business a suitable investment for shareholders or would returns be greater if they invested elsewhere, is it a good *investment*?

BENCHMARKING

These three general areas of interest require answers to questions which are subjective in nature, not objective. For instance, how do we judge whether a profit is reasonable? We could do so by comparing current profit to profit made in previous years or to profit made by other businesses. In other words we use benchmarks against which we compare current performance, financial status and investment potential. However, we need to take great care in carrying out this benchmarking so that we do not invalidate the results. Consider, for example, your opinion of the disco you attended last night. You may think it was the best disco you have ever attended; your friend may think it was the worst night out he or she ever had. This is because the experiences/benchmarks you each have are different and you are making a subjective judgement on how the current disco compares with those you previously attended. Thus, in setting benchmarks against which we can compare a company we must be aware of the limitations of this comparison.

First we need to identify benchmarks/indicators we can use, then consider their limitations. Four possible benchmarks are:

- past period achievements
- budgeted achievements
- other businesses' achievements
- averages of businesses' achievements in the same area.

ACTIVITY 11.2

Identify for each indicator above its uses and limitations.

Activity feedback

- Past periods
  Uses – to identify whether current activity is better or worse than previous periods.
  Limitations – external factors may have influenced activity levels, e.g. public awareness of environmental issues may have necessitated a change in manufacturing process leading to increased costs.

- Budgets
  Uses – has current activity matched planned activity?
  Limitations – the budget may not be a valid standard of performance, e.g. underlying assumptions may have been unrealistic or set at too high a level.

- Other businesses
  Uses – is our business performing as well?
  Limitations – businesses may not be truly comparable with regard to size and type, e.g. grocery sole trader compared to supermarket; manufacturer compared to retailer.
  External factors may affect one business, e.g. lengthy strike.
  Accounting policies and bases on which accounting information is prepared may be different, e.g. stock valuations, depreciation, historic cost or revalued amount, treatment of research and development, treatment of goodwill.

- Industry averages have uses and limitations very similar to those of other businesses.
  Additionally, an average is simply that – an average which takes account of the best and the worst.

Each of the four benchmarks identified are commonly used in assessing business status, performance and potential, but interpretation of accounts is highly subjective and requires skilled judgement, bearing in mind the limitations of these benchmarks.

In Part Four of this book we will discuss further the pitfalls in the interpretation of the information included in the annual accounts of a company. We will also study the techniques of industry analysis and horizontal and vertical analysis (= trend analysis and common size analysis). In this chapter we will concentrate on the techniques of analysis which can be applied to financial statements without elaborating further on the issues of the benchmarks.

TECHNIQUE OF RATIO ANALYSIS

Financial statements identify for us a multitude of figures, for example profit before tax, gross profit, total of fixed assets, net current assets. However, these figures do not mean very much unless we can compare them to something else. For example, looking at a set of financial statements for a high street retailer may tell us that profit before tax is £3 million, but will not tell us if this is a good profit. It will probably be more than the profit of a sole trader in the same industry but does it mean that the high street retailer is performing better? Now look at Activity 11.3.

What we did in Activity 11.3 was calculate a ratio. We will illustrate in the remainder of this chapter how different ratios can be calculated in order to help solve the three information needs mentioned above and facilitate the decision-making process of the different stakeholders of the company.

The next section identifies which figures in a set of financial statements it would be useful to compare to evaluate financial status, performance and investment potential of a business. The financial statements used are those of Serendipity plc which are reproduced below.

The layout and format of these financial statements is not the layout put forward in IAS 1. The format below is chosen for pedagogical reasons. The information provided in relation to the company Serendipity relates to the components which determine the profit or loss of the period. We will not include elements of other comprehensive income for the period in this example.

ACTIVITY 11.3

You have £1150 to invest and discover that type 1 investment will provide interest of £68 per annum and type 2 investment will provide a single interest payment of £341 after five years. Which investment would you choose, assuming no compound interest and no change in the value of the pound?

Activity feedback
Investment 1 provides a return of 68/1150 = 5.91% per annum. Investment 2 provides a return of 68.2/1150 = 5.93% per annum. Thus, investment 2 provides the highest return. In the above example we compared the return with the amount invested and expressed the figures in the same units – percentage per annum. We were then able to identify which investment provided the better return.

Serendipity P&L accounts

	Year-ended 31.12.X4		Year-ended 31.12.X5	
	£000	£000	£000	£000
Sales		584		972
Opening inventory	31		47	
Purchases	405		700	
	436		747	
Closing inventory	47		62	
Cost of goods sold		389		685
Gross Profit		195		287
Wages and salaries	78		101	
Depreciation	16		31	
Debenture interest	–		8	
Other expenses	54		62	
		148		202
Net profit before tax		47		85
Taxation		16		39
Net profit after tax		31		46
Proposed dividend		16		23
Retained profit for year		15		23

Serendipity balance sheet as at

	31.12.X4		31.12.X5	
	£000	£000	£000	£000
Assets				
Non-current assets		280		428
Current assets				
Inventories	47		62	
Debtors	70		156	
Bank	39		16	
Total current assets		156		234
Total assets		436		662
Equity		365		411
Share capital	272		295	
Retained earnings	93		116	
Non-current liabilities		–		80
10% debentures	–		80	
Current liabilities				
Creditors	39		109	
Taxation	16		39	
Proposed dividends	16		23	
Total current liabilities		71		171
Total equity and liabilities		436		662

Strictly speaking in IAS jargon, current and non-current refers to the fact whether or not an asset will be expected to be realised in, or is intended for sale or consumption in, the entity's normal operation cycle (IAS 1, para. 66(a)) and a liability is expected to be settled in the entity's normal operating cycle or due to be settled within 12 months (IAS 1, para. 69(a) and (c)). Net current assets are current assets minus current liabilities.

In the format of the previous balance sheet total assets and total equity and liabilities are presented separately.

With regard to the profit and loss account, the information on the changes in inventory levels and purchases will be provided in the notes to the accounts. On the face of an IAS profit and loss account itself you might only find the costs of goods sold, which is calculated by combining the changes in inventory levels together with the purchases.

The ratios which will be introduced to you in the following sections are calculated with information found either on the face of the balance sheet or on the face of the profit and loss account or in the notes to the accounts.

Before beginning any ratio analysis it is useful to look at the accounts and identify any changes from one year to the next (see Activity 11.4).

Having identified various points of interest in Activity 11.4 we are now ready to carry out the ratio analysis. We will start with those ratios that are helpful in deciding whether or not a business is successful and whether or not it is operated in an efficient way.

Performance

The first ratio to be considered in this respect is return on capital employed (ROCE):

$$ROCE = \frac{\text{Profit before taxation and long-term loan interest}}{\text{Net assets (Equity + Long-term debt)}}$$

This ratio identifies how much profit the business has made from the capital invested in it and answers the question: would the owners be better off selling the business and placing the proceeds in a bank deposit account?

In fact this ratio measures the return on investment. The question however is what amount do we need to consider as invested capital? In the ROCE ratio above, net assets or equity with long-term debt is used as denominator. One could also use the total assets instead of net assets as a denominator. In the latter ratio we assume that all assets contribute to the profit of the company. Further the ratio 'return on total assets' (ROA) is not influenced by the financial structure of the company, whereas the ROCE ratio is to a certain extent, namely the trade-off between short-term and long-term financing. In the literature and in practice both ratios are used (ROA and ROCE).

$$ROA = \frac{\text{Profit before taxation + Interest}}{\text{Total assets}}$$

ACTIVITY 11.4

Compare and contrast each item on the balance sheet and profit and loss account of Serendipity plc with the figure for the previous year. Note five points of interest from this comparison.

Activity feedback

You should have identified five from the following:

- sales have increased in X5
- cost of sales has increased
- expenses have increased
- profit after tax has increased by 50%
- fixed assets have increased substantially
- net current assets have reduced
- shares and debentures have been increased in X5.

ACTIVITY 11.5

Calculate the ROCE and ROA for Serendipity plc for X4 and X5.

This ratio has increased from X4 to X5 indicating an increase in profitability of the business.

Activity feedback

	X4	X5
ROCE	47/365 = 12.87%	93/491 = 18.9%
ROA	47/436 = 10.77%	93/662 = 14.04%

But where has this increased profitability come from? Is it because the business has increased sale prices or reduced expenses, that is, increased net profit margins, or is it because the business has increased the volume of trade compared to the capital employed?

In the following part we continue with the ROCE ratio; the sub-analysis of the ROA ratio proceeds in exactly the same way and the interpretations are similar. The only difference is that capital employed is substituted by total assets and in those circumstances where one needs to take into account the interest expense, interest expense on short-term liabilities should be added to the interest expense which relates to long-term liabilities.

These two questions can be expressed as ratios as follows:

$$\text{Net profit margin} = \frac{\text{Profit before tax and Long-term interest}}{\text{Sales}}$$

$$\text{Volume of trade} = \frac{\text{Sales}}{\text{Capital employed}}$$

Calculating these two ratios for Serendipity plc we have:

	X4	X5
Net profit margin	47/584 = 8%	93/972 = 9.6%

Net profit margin has increased, indicating benefit gained from control of expenses or increased sale prices. An answer to that question will be given later on, with the help of other ratios:

Volume of trade   584/365 = 1.6 times   972/491 = 1.98 times.

This indicates that Serendipity plc is earning more sales per pound of net assets or capital employed in X5 than X4.

The three ratios we have looked at so far have the following relationship:

$$\text{ROCE} = \text{Margin} \times \text{Volume}$$

$$\frac{\text{Profit}}{\text{Capital employed}} = \frac{\text{Profit}}{\text{Sales}} \times \frac{\text{Sales}}{\text{Capital employed}}$$

This relationship can be shown as a family tree:

ROCE

Profit before tax + Long-term interest/Sales   Sales/Capital employed

This family tree can be expanded and will provide a framework for the analysis of the performance and efficiency of the company. For example:

Net profit/Sales = Gross profit/Sales − Expenses/Sales

whereby Gross profit = Sales − Cost of goods sold

or, in brief:

$$\frac{GP}{S} - \frac{E}{S}$$

Sales/capital employed can be inverted to capital employed/sales, which is the value of assets held per pound of sales, and then expanded to:

Fixed assets/Sales + Net current assets/Sales or, in brief

$$\frac{FA}{S} + \frac{NCA}{S}$$

ACTIVITY 11.6

Calculate these four further ratios for Serendipity plc and interpret them.

Activity feedback

	X4	X5
Gross profit margin	195/584 = 33.3%	287/972 = 29.5%

This demonstrates a reduction in gross profit.

This could be due to several reasons. First of all we observe an increase in the relative cost of goods sold/sales. This percentage has increased from X4 to X5:

Cost of goods sold/ sales	X4	X5
	389/584 = 66%	685/972 = 70%

This could point at an inflation in the price of purchased goods or less efficient negotiations from the purchase department.

Another element could be that there is a decrease in sale prices which has generated more sales and a resulting increase in cost of goods sold:

Expenses/sales	X4	X5
	148/584 = 25.3%	194/972 = 20%

This has decreased from X4 to X5 indicating a better control of all other expenses:

FA/S	280/584 = 0.48	428/972 = 0.44

If we invert the above, then for X4 we have 2.08 and for X5 2.27, that is, fixed assets have generated 2.08 times their value in sales in X4 and 2.27 times their value in sales in X5.

Fixed assets are earning more sales or are operated in a much more efficient way:

NCA/S	85/584 = 0.15	63/972 = 0.06

Inverting gives X4 6.87 and X5 15.4.

Net current assets are also earning more sales in X5 than X4.

So all assets are used more efficiently in X5. Thus, we observe that the overall increase in profitability is positively influenced by the efficient use of the fixed assets and net current assets in X5, and the control of all expense except the cost of goods sold. The profitability was negatively influenced by the decrease in the gross profit margin.

The family tree of ratios, or pyramid, now looks like this:

The pyramid can be extended to level 4 by comparing individual expenses to sales and breaking down the fixed assets and net current assets into their constituent parts:

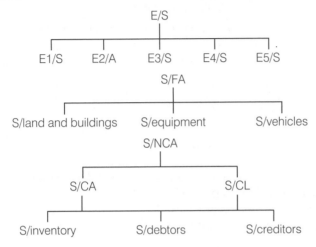

However, as inventory is recorded at cost not selling price then a more appropriate ratio than sale/inventory would be cost of goods sold/inventory, and as creditors relates to goods purchased on credit it would be better to look at credit purchases/creditors. Lastly sales/debtors would be more appropriate to credit sales/debtors.

Illustration 1 demonstrates the calculation and interpretation of these level 4 ratios.

ILLUSTRATION 1

The following information is provided for TAX Ltd as at 31 December 20X4:

	£000s
Cost of goods sold	220
Average inventory for the year	50
Trade creditors	86
Credit purchases	216
Trade debtors	96
Credit sales	284

Cost of goods sold/inventory = 220/50 = 4.4, that is, 4.4 times the average inventory level has been used in cost of goods sold for the year. This could be written much simpler as: inventory is turned over every 83 days, i.e. 365/4.4 = 83 days.

The ratio is therefore:

$$\frac{\text{Average inventory}}{\text{Cost of goods sold}} \times 365$$

The lower the ratio the more efficiently the company is operated. A low ratio means that investment is only tied up in non-income-generating investments for a short period. What is meant by a high ratio or a low ratio is dependent on the industry (see Part 4 of this book). These ratios, as many other ratios, have industry-specific outcomes. Inventory days will be much higher in the steel industry than in industries which sell perishable goods.

The debtors and creditors' ratios are written as:

$$\frac{\text{Trade debtors}}{\text{Credit sales}} \times 365$$

which will tell us on average how long it takes debtors to pay:

$$\frac{\text{Trade creditors}}{\text{Credit purchases}} \times 365$$

which will tell us how long on average it takes the business to pay its creditors.

The information provided above does not give a figure for credit sales or credit purchases; therefore we will have to use total sales and total purchases as an approximation:

$$\text{Debtors' period} = 96 \times 365/284 = 123 \text{ days}$$
$$\text{Creditors' period} = 86 \times 365/216 = 145 \text{ days}$$

Whether or not these level 4 ratios should be calculated when carrying out a ratio analysis will depend upon the information produced at previous levels. For example, when considering Serendipity plc we noted a marked improvement in the efficiency of net current assets; therefore, calculating the fourth level ratios may tell us where this improvement came from (see Activity 11.7).

Within the analysis of Serendipity plc at level 3 there was also a benefit gained from control of expenses. Therefore fourth level analysis here would also be beneficial, see Activity 11.8.

Other expenses have also been controlled as a percentage of sales. These three ratios, as we saw earlier, when combined gave an increase in profit margin – increased *profitability*. The pyramid also demonstrates that the ratios on the left-hand side show

---

ACTIVITY 11.7

Calculate inventory, debtor and creditor turnover periods for Serendipity plc and interpret them.

Activity feedback

	X4	X5
Inventory turnover	$(31 + 47)/2 \times 365/389$	$(47 + 62)/2 \times 365/685$
Number of inventory days	36.6 days	29 days

Thus, inventory is being turned over quicker in X5, demonstrating greater efficiency.

	X4	X5
Debtors' turnover period	$70/584 \times 365$	$156/972 \times 365$
	44 days	58 days

Thus, debtors have been allowed (or have taken) 14 more days on average in X5 than X4 in which to pay their debts to the business. This could possibly indicate that Serendipity plc is losing control of its debtor collection or that it has purposely allowed debtors more time to pay so as to encourage more sales.

	X4	X5
Creditors' turnover period	$39/405 \times 365$	$109/700 \times 365$
	35 days	57 days

(Note that cost of goods sold could be used as a substitute for purchases if the financial statements do not provide a figure for purchases.) This indicates that Serendipity plc is taking longer to pay its suppliers – 22 days longer. This may damage relations with suppliers if Serendipity does not take care, but also demonstrates how Serendipity is using creditors to finance its business operations. A balance has to be struck within this dichotomy.

profitability and those on the right show efficiency in the use of assets. Before moving on to consider financial status within ratio analysis we need to take another look at the first ratio on the pyramid – ROCE. Capital employed consists of shareholder funds, that is share capital and reserves, and long-term debt, for example debentures. In the example of Serendipity plc ROCE was:

X4	12.87%
X5	18.9%

However, the debentures in X5 only required a return to be paid to the holders of 10% even though the capital invested, £10 000, earned 18.9%. The earnings over and above the 10% will then accrue to the shareholders and their return will be increased beyond the 18.9% that the total capital earned. This phenomenon can be demonstrated by calculating the ratio of return on equity:

$$ROE = \frac{\text{Profit before tax, but after interest}}{\text{Shareholders' equity (or owners' equity)}}$$

X4	X5
47/365 = 12.88%	85/411 = 20.68%

The shareholders have increased their earnings in the business partly due to the benefit gained by borrowing at a lower rate of return than the business is earning. However, the converse can also occur! Note that ROCE and ROE were both the same in X4 as there was no long-term debt.

Whereas ROCE or ROA provides an answer to the question whether the business is worthwhile to invest in, the ROE ratio takes the perspective of the shareholder and tries to answer the question whether the investment in the share capital of the company is beneficial for the owners of the shares.

This is the opposite of the Serendipity case. Attracting external funds on which interest needs to be paid irrespective of the result of the company might be beneficial for the shareholders if ROA is higher than the interest rate paid by the firm on its debt. It is detrimental for the shareholders if ROA is lower than the interest rate paid by the firm on its debt. We need to compare ROCE with the interest paid on long-term debt.

After the discussion of the ratios which could help in determining whether or not a company is successful and operated in an efficient way, we turn our attention to the information needs in relation to the financial status of the company. The following questions will be asked by the interested parties:

1 Can the business pay its way? Is it liquid?

2 Has the company the ability to repay its debt? What is the security for the amounts lent to the company?

FINANCIAL STATUS

It is essential for a business to be able to pay its debts as and when they fall due, otherwise its chances of remaining in operation become remote. Thus there is a need to analyse the assets available to meet liabilities. This can be done in the short, medium and long term, since some debt will have to be repaid on short notice and other amounts will only fall due in the distant future.

Within the group of ratios which analyse the financial structure of the company, we distinguish on the one hand the liquidity ratios which are used to assess the company's ability to meet its short-term obligations. On the other hand we have the group of solvency ratios which concentrate on the question whether or not a company will repay its debt in the long term.

Liquidity ratios

Liquidity refers to the capacity of a company to generate liquidity from its current operations to repay its current debt. Therefore ratios concentrating on the liquidity question will focus on the current assets or short-term assets and the current or short-term liabilities of the firm. The first liquidity ratio is the current ratio:

$$\frac{\text{Current assets}}{\text{Current liabilities}}$$

In most industries this ratio needs to be higher than one in order to indicate that no liquidity problem will arise. However within the current assets there are items which might not be realisable in the very short term, e.g. inventory items which are damaged. Therefore there is a second liquidity ratio, the quick ratio or the acid test ratio:

$$\frac{\text{Current assets} - \text{Inventory}}{\text{Current liabilities}}$$

The acid test is often called the short-term liquidity test and the current ratio the medium-term liquidity test.

Solvency

Solvency ratios try to measure the risk involved in the repayment of debt and the ability of a company to meet its debt in the long run. A key element in this respect is the capital structure of the firm. Companies have two main resources of funds, namely debt and equity. Each has different well-known characteristics (e.g. fixed versus variable rewards, fixed repayment schedules versus repayment when the company liquidates). The financial risk or financial strength of a company is measured by ratios which relate debt to equity. The most commonly used ratio worldwide in this respect is the debt/equity ratio. A high debt/equity ratio implies higher financial risk, since a higher ratio points at higher interest charges and a wider exposure to possible interest changes. Further debt needs to be repaid often at a fixed date irrespective of whether or not the company has sufficient funds available. Several alterations can be made to the numerator and the denominator of this ratio in relation to the focus of the analysis, for example:

$$\frac{\text{Debt}}{\text{Equity}} \qquad or \qquad \frac{\text{Long-term debt}}{\text{Equity}}$$

The ratios mentioned above are often called gearing ratios.

$$\frac{\text{Debt}}{\text{Equity} + \text{Debt}} \qquad or \qquad \frac{\text{Equity}}{\text{Equity} + \text{Debt}}$$

The interest cover ratio is a ratio which indicates the safety margin between profits generated and interest charges and is calculated as follows:

$$\frac{\text{Net profit before interest and taxes}}{\text{Total interest charges}}$$

Whether or not a company is able to repay its debt in the long term depends on the ability of the company to generate cash flow from operations, from the disposal of assets or from external funding. The future cash flow generating capacity of a company can be estimated on the basis of the current cash flow. Whether or not a company will dispose of its assets depends on its strategy and the role of these assets in implementing the strategy. The possibility to attract external funds will depend on the appreciation of the company by the capital markets and the suppliers of the long-term and short-term credit. These items will be explained further in Part Four of this book.

The last grouping of ratios we will discuss in this chapter relate specifically to the information needs of current and potential shareholders. This group is especially interested in finding out whether or not the investment they make or intend to make in a company is a profitable investment compared to other investment possibilities they have (e.g. buying shares in other companies subscribing to debentures or putting their money into a savings account).

ACTIVITY 11.10

Calculate the two liquidity ratios, the gearing ratio, the interest cover ratio, the debt/equity ratio and the debt/(equity + debt) ratio for Serendipity plc and interpret them.

Activity feedback

$$\begin{array}{ccc} & X4 & X5 \\ \text{Acid test} & \dfrac{156 - 47}{71} = \dfrac{109}{71} & \dfrac{234 - 62}{171} = \dfrac{172}{171} \end{array}$$

expressed as   1.5:1   1:1

The ratio has decreased from X4 to X5 quite considerably but there are still plenty of liquid assets. The ratio will need careful monitoring to control this downward trend.

Current ratio $156/71 = 2.2{:}1$ $234/171 = 1.4{:}1$

Again this ratio has been substantially reduced but still appears adequate. Monitoring of this downward trend is again required.

Gearing ratio   not relevant $80/411 = 19.5\%$

This is low and we would consider this company low geared. If a company is high geared then it may have difficulty meeting the required interest payments. However this needs to be interpreted not only within the specific industry context, but also within the national environment (more on these items in Part Four of the book).

Debt/Equity	$71/365 = 19.45\%$	$251/411 = 61.07\%$
Debt/Equity + Debt	$71/436 = 16.28\%$	$251/662 = 37.91\%$

We notice a deterioration of the financial structure.

Interest cover   not relevant $(85 + 8)/8 = 12$

In X5 the profit covered the required interest payment 12 times indicating no immediate problem for Serendipity plc. Notice how consideration of all four ratios helped to build up a picture of the financial status of Serendipity plc.

Investment potential

Before looking in detail at investment ratios it is useful to carry out some practical research (see Activity 11.11).

Book value per share

This is the ordinary shareholders' equity/number of shares. This book value is the value each share would have if the company's assets and liabilities were sold at

ACTIVITY 11.11

Obtain a fairly recent copy of a financial newspaper (for example, *The Wall Street Journal* or *The Financial Times*), or the equivalent in your own country. Look up the share information service and make a note of the data provided for each company. Also read the 'company news section' either in a financial newspaper or any other quality newspaper and note down any ratios or indicators used to evaluate the companies.

Activity feedback

Your list possibly included the following:

● book value per share compared with market value per share

● net dividend
● dividend cover
● earnings per share
● gross dividend yield
● price earnings ratio.

We will look at each of these ratios in turn.

their balance sheet (book) value. The market value is the price a potential shareholder is willing to pay to acquire a share in the company. Comparing these two values identifies whether the market values the company at more or less than its book value.

Net dividend

This is the amount of dividend declared in any one year per share which equals paid and proposed dividends divided by the number of shares. People invest in shares for one of two reasons: either to earn dividends or to earn capital growth in the value of the share, or both. The level of dividend and its comparison with previous years is generally regarded as an important indicator of future expectations. However, one danger with this comparison is that dividends are not necessarily just paid out of the current year's earnings but can be paid out of retained earnings. It is therefore important to look at dividend cover in any one year.

Dividend cover

$$\frac{\text{Net profit available to ordinary shareholders}}{\text{Total ordinary dividend}}$$

ACTIVITY 11.12

The following information is available in respect of Kit plc:

	X4 £	X5 £
Ordinary shares issued £1	1 875 000	1 875 000
8% preference shares £1	660 000	660 000
Dividend ordinary shares	225 000	187 500
Net profit after tax	257 500	231 900

Calculate dividend per share in pence for both preference and ordinary shares, and dividend cover.

Activity feedback

	X4	X5
Dividend per preference share	8p	8p
Dividend per ordinary share	12p	10p

Dividend cover   257 500/277 800   231 900/240 300
0.93   0.97

Thus the dividend per share has reduced from X4 to X5, but the dividend cover has improved. However, this dividend cover is less than one, which indicates that the company is not earning enough in either year to pay the dividend and is therefore using past earnings retained to fund the dividend payment. This may be a danger sign for potential investors.

Earnings per share

This is another indicator used widely by the investment community. It represents the amount of profit available to ordinary shareholders, the company has earned during the year for each ordinary share.

For the example of Kit plc (see Activity 11.12) the earnings per share in X4 is 204 700/1 875 000 = 10.9p and in X5 is 179 100/1 875 000 = 9.6p. We will provide more information on this ratio in Chapter 24 and Part Four of this book.

Gross dividend yield

This is calculated from the formula:

$$\frac{\text{Gross dividend}}{\text{Market price of ordinary share}}$$

Shareholders may be willing to accept a low gross dividend yield if there is a greater than average capital growth in share value expected or if the company is a safe investment. Gross dividend is calculated by grossing up the dividend declared in the accounts for basic rate taxation as dividends are always declared and paid net of basic income tax.

For example, in the case of Kit plc if the basic rate of tax is 20% then the gross dividend is:

	X4	X5
	225 000/80%	187 500/80%
	281 250	234 375
or per share	15p	12.5p

If the market value per share for Kit was £1.75 in X4 and £1.82 in X5, then the gross dividend yield is

15/175	12.5/182
8.6%	6.9%

Price/earnings (PE) ratio

The formula for this is:

$$\frac{\text{Market price per share}}{\text{Earnings per share}}$$

For Kit this is:

175/10.9	182/9.6
16.1	19

Like the dividend yield the PE ratio will change as the market price per share changes. It represents the market's view of the growth potential of the company, its dividend policy and the degree of risk involved in the investment. In general a high PE indicates that the market has a high/good opinion of these factors, a low PE a low/poor opinion. Another way of looking at the PE is that it represents the number of years' earnings it is necessary to have at the current rate to recover the price paid for the share. For Kit this was 19 years at the X5 rate of earnings.

In the discussion of investment ratios, we have covered the three principal areas in which users need information to make economic decisions. Although financial statement data represent an important source of information, they have to be interpreted with caution and must be combined with additional information to make sound business decisions. The pitfalls in ratio analysis will be discussed further in Part Four of this book, as well as an analysis of the additional information needed. To provide an idea on this additional information, see Activity 11.13.

ACTIVITY 11.13

Identify additional information that you would like when undertaking a ratio analysis of a company.

Activity feedback

- Inflation effects on the company.
- Does the balance sheet represent the position of the business throughout the year or just at the year-end?
- Cash flow throughout the year.

- Forecast business plans in the form of budgets and cash flows.
- Information in respect of the quality of goods and services and other factors affecting the assessment of goodwill in the business.
- Industrial averages of ratios.
- Differences in accounting policies between businesses.

ADDITIONAL INFORMATION

Ratio analysis is a tool that aids the user in building up an overall picture of the condition/state of a business entity. Other information can help to fill in more of this picture (see Activity 11.13).

Much of the information in Activity 11.13 will not be available to all users. For example, it would be very difficult, probably impossible, for a potential investor to obtain detailed information in respect of future plans of the business apart from that disclosed in the directors' report in the financial statements.

SUMMARY

Within this chapter we considered the users of the financial statements and their needs. We identified a tool – ratio analysis – in an attempt to meet these needs. We have illustrated how individual components of the balance sheet, the profit and loss account and the notes can be used in ratio analysis in order to provide useful data for economic decision-making. In this chapter the illustrations of performance, liquidity, solvency and investment ratios only allowed us to judge whether or not the position of Serendipity had improved from year X4 to year X5. To make sound business decisions we need however to compare the outcomes of the ratios not only over a longer time span than just two years, but we also need to compare with the outcomes of other companies. This will be elaborated further in Part Four of this book. We will now continue in Part Two and Part Three of this book with the analysis of the definition, recognition and measurement of the individual components of the balance sheet and profit and loss account. We will also pay attention to the disclosures in the notes. The choices made in these domains of definition, recognition and measurement will without doubt influence the outcome of the ratios and subsequently influence the appreciation of the stakeholders of the company with regard to the company's efficiency, success and financial position.

EXERCISES

Suggested answers to exercises marked ✓ are to be found on the Student side of the companion website.

Suggested answers to the remaining exercises are to be found on the Instructor side of the companion website.

✓ **1** The following are extracts from an industrial performance analysis for two groups, Alpha Group plc and Omega Group plc.

The two groups operate in different industrial sectors and have accordingly adopted different operating and financial strategies.

Alpha Group plc	20X3 £000	20X2 £000	20X1 £000
Profit and loss data			
turnover	20 915	19 036	16 929
operating profit	1 386	1 189	943
depreciation	299	264	214
income from investments	23	20	14
interest payable	95	66	60
Balance sheet data			
intangible fixed assets	636	660	484
tangible fixed assets	7 213	5 605	4 654
investments	234	201	148
	8 083	6 466	5 286
Stocks	1 405	1 312	1 217
Trade debtors	65	54	57
Cash	97	62	43
Other current assets	1 000	550	700
Total current assets	2 567	1 978	2 017
Trade creditors	1 651	1 521	1 381
Overdraft	150	–	160
Short-term loans	300	151	200
Other current liabilities	1 371	1 271	1 008
Total current liabilities	3 472	2 943	2 749
Total assets less current liabilities	7 178	5 501	4 554
Creditors: amounts falling due after more than 1 year	904	604	239
Provisions for liabilities and charges	180	159	158
Minority interests	150	132	130
	5 944	4 606	4 027
Ordinary shares	3 000	3 000	3 000
Preference shares, redeemable 20X6	2 000	–	–
Reserves	944	1 606	1 027
	5 944	4 606	4 027

Omega Group plc	*20X3*	*20X2*	*20X1*
	£000	*£000*	*£000*
Profit and loss data:			
turnover	19 540	15 260	16 320
operating profit	620	340	220
depreciation	240	220	220
income from investments	20	20	20
interest payable	720	660	720
Balance sheet data:			
intangible fixed assets	–	–	–
tangible fixed assets	1 620	1 360	1 360
investments	220	280	240
	1 840	1 640	1 600
Stocks	3 870	2 540	2 040
Trade debtors	2 660	1 920	2 040
Cash	800	480	400
Other current assets	4 000	4 000	3 580
Total current assets	11 330	8 940	8 060
Trade creditors	2 700	1 620	1 020
Overdraft	60	180	–
Short-term loans	1 800	1 200	1 820
Other current liabilities	1 140	840	740
Total current liabilities	5 700	3 840	3 580
Total assets less current liabilities	7 380	6 740	6 080
Creditors: amounts falling due after			
more than 1 year	5 400	5 100	4 660
Provisions for liabilities and charges	260	300	360
Minority interests	200	180	200
	1 520	1 160	860
Ordinary shares	600	600	600
Preference shares, redeemable 20X6	200	200	200
Reserves	720	360	60
	1 520	1 160	860

Required:

(a) A set of five key ratios of use in monitoring the operational performance of the two groups over three years. Show clearly your workings and justify the definitions of the inputs to your ratio calculations.

(b) A set of three key ratios of use in monitoring the financial structure of the two groups over three years. Show clearly your workings and justify the definitions of the inputs to your ratio calculations.

(c) Identify the contrasting operating and financing strategies of the two groups as revealed by your ratio analysis.

(d) For each group suggest an industrial sector for which such a strategy would give a best fit. Give reasons for your suggestions.

(e) List five ways in which financial statements could be improved in order to make them more useful as the basis for input to ratio analysis. Identify the constraints on implementation of these improvements.

(ACCA)

2 Obtain a set of accounts for a supermarket and a manufacturer. You can do this by accessing the website of the company and searching for the annual report, probably under the information headings 'investor relations'. Compare and contrast the nature of the current assets and liabilities of your two companies.

3 You are given the following information in relation to Olivet Ltd.

P&L accounts	20X4 £	20X5 £
Sales	100 000	100 000
Cost of sales	50 000	60 000
	50 000	40 000
Expenses	30 000	30 000
	20 000	10 000
Dividends	10 000	10 000
	10 000	–
Balance b/d	2 500	12 500
	12 500	12 500

Balance sheets as at	20X4 £	20X5 £
Land	21 500	31 500
Buildings	20 000	39 500
Equipment	3 000	3 000
	44 500	74 000
Investments at cost	25 000	40 000
Stock	27 500	32 500
Debtors	20 000	25 000
Bank	1 500	–
	118 500	171 500
Ordinary £1 shares	20 000	25 000
Share premium	6 000	7 000
Revaluation reserve	–	10 000
Profit and loss	12 500	12 500
Debentures 10%	50 000	75 000
Creditors	20 000	30 000
Proposed dividend	10 000	10 000
Bank	–	2 000
	118 500	171 500

Required:
You are required to comment on the financial position of Olivet Ltd as at 20X5. Calculate any ratios you feel necessary.

4 You are given the attached information about Fred plc, comprising summarised P&L accounts, summarised balance sheets, and some suggested ratio calculations. You should note that there may be alternative ways of calculating some of these ratios. The holder of a small number of the ordinary shares in the business has come to you for help and advice. There are a number of things he does not properly understand, and a friend of his who is an accountancy student has suggested to him that some of the ratios show a distinctly unsatisfactory position, and that he should sell his shares as quickly as possible.

Required:

Write a report to the shareholder commenting on the apparent position and prospects of Fred plc, as far as the information permits. Your report should include reference to liquidity and profitability aspects, and should advise whether, in your view, the shares should indeed be sold as soon as possible.

Fred plc
Some possible ratio calculations (which can be taken as arithmetically correct).

	20X2	20X1
Current ratio	54/147 = 36.7%	56/172 = 32.6%
Acid test ratio	12/147 = 8.2%	15/172 = 8.7%
ROCE	57/249 = 22.9%	41/161 = 25.5%
eps	31/190 = 16.3p	22/190 = 11.6p
Trade debtors' turnover	4/910 × 365 = 2 days	4/775 × 365 = 2 days
Trade creditors' turnover	60/730 × 365 = 30 days	60/633 × 365 = 35 days
Gross profit %	180/910 = 19.8%	142/775 = 18.3%
Operating profit %	57/910 = 6.3 p	41/775 = 5.3%
Stock turnover	42/730 × 365 = 21 days	41/633 × 365 = 24 days
Gearing	61/188 = 32.4%	1/160 = 0.6%

Fred plc
Summarised balance sheets at year-end (£m)

	20X2		20X1	
Fixed assets				
tangible – not yet in use		49		41
– in use		295		237
		344		278
investments		1		1
loan redemption fund		1		1
			346		280
Current assets				
stocks		42		41
debtors – trade	4		4	
– other	4		4	
		8		8
bank		2		5
cash		2		2
		54		56

Creditors – due within 1 year

– trade	60		60	
– other	87		112	
		147		172

Net current liabilities	93	116
Total assets less current liabilities	253	164
Creditors – due between one and five years	61	1
Provision for liabilities and charges	4	3
Net assets	188	160

Capital and reserves

ordinary shares of 10p each	19	19
preference shares of £1 each	46	46
share premium	1	1
profit and loss account	122	94
	188	160

Fred plc
Summarised P&L accounts for the year (£m)

			20X2		20X1
Sales			910		775
Raw materials and consumables			730		633
			180		142
Staff costs	77			64	
Depreciation of tangible fixed assets	12			10	
Other operating charges	38			30	
			127		104
			53		38
Other operating income			4		3
			57		41
Net interest payable			5		4
			52		37
Profit sharing – employees			2		1
			50		36
Taxation			17		12
			33		24
Preference dividends			2		2
			31		22
Ordinary dividends			3		2
			28		20

Note
Net interest payable:

interest payable	12	9
interest receivable	(1)	(1)
interest capitalised	(6)	(4)
	5	4

5 You are given summarised results of an electrical engineering business, as follows. All figures are in £000.

Profit and loss account

	year-ended	
	31.12.20X1	*31.12.20X0*
Turnover	60 000	50 000
Cost of sales	42 000	34 000
Gross profit	18 000	16 000
Operating expenses	15 500	13 000
	2 500	3 000
Interest payable	2 200	1 300
Profit before taxation	300	1 700
Taxation	350	600
(Loss) profit after taxation	(50)	1 100
Dividends	600	600
Transfer (from) to reserves	(650)	500

Balance sheet

Fixed assets		
intangible	500	–
tangible	12 000	11 000
	12 500	11 000
Current assets		
stock	14 000	13 000
debtors	16 000	15 000
bank and cash	500	500
	30 500	28 500
Creditors due within 1 year	24 000	20 000
Net current assets	6 500	8 500
Total assets less current liabilities	19 000	19 500
Creditors due after 1 year	6 000	5 500
	13 000	14 000
Capital and reserves		
share capital	1 300	1 300
share premium	3 300	3 300
revaluation reserve	2 000	2 000
profit and loss	6 400	7 400
	13 000	14 000

Required:

(a) Prepare a table of the following 12 ratios, calculated for both years, clearly showing the figures used in the calculations:

current ratio
quick assets ratio

stock turnover in days
debtors' turnover in days
creditors' turnover in days
gross profit %
net profit % (before taxation)
interest cover
dividend cover
ROCE
gearing

(b) Making full use of the information given in the question, your table of ratios, and your common sense, comment on the apparent position of the business and on the actions of the management.

PART TWO
ANNUAL FINANCIAL STATEMENTS

In this part we look in detail at the international rules that accountants have created for themselves to govern financial reporting. In each case, we explore the underlying issues involved, applying the principles developed in Part One, and consider the International Standards requirements. Do these Standards achieve what they are setting out to do when considered individually? Do they make sense, when looked at as a whole? As with Part One, you are invited to form your own opinion on 'the story so far'.

FIXED (NON-CURRENT) TANGIBLE ASSETS

12

OBJECTIVES After studying this chapter you should be able to:

- discuss and apply the principles, concepts and major methods of providing for depreciation

- explain what depreciation does and does not do

- explain the issues involved in determining appropriate treatments for government grants

- describe, apply and appraise the requirements of IAS 20, relating to government grants

- explain the issues involved in determining appropriate treatments for borrowing costs

- describe, apply and appraise the requirements of IAS 23 relating to borrowing costs

- describe, apply and appraise the requirements of IAS 16, *Property, Plant and Equipment*

- discuss alternative treatments for investment properties

- describe, apply and appraise the requirements of IAS 40 related to investment properties.

INTRODUCTION

Assets have been defined (in Chapter 8) as follows (Framework, para. 49a):

An asset is a resource controlled by the entity as a result of past events and from which future economic benefits are expected to flow.

Assets are divided into fixed assets and current assets. The IAS terms are non-current assets and current assets respectively. The distinction is formally defined in IAS 1 (para. 66), as discussed in more detail in Chapter 9.

An asset should be classified as a current asset when it is:

1 expected to be realised in, or is intended for sale or consumption in, the normal course of the entity's operating cycle

2 held primarily for the purpose of being traded

3 expected to be realised within 12 months after the balance sheet date reporting period

4 cash or cash equivalent (as defined by IAS 7, see Chapter 23), unless it is restricted from being exchanged or used to settle a liability for at least 12 months after the reporting period.

All other assets should be classified as non-current assets.

The definition of non-current assets is often misunderstood. A non-current asset is not an asset with a long life. The essential criterion is the *intention* of the owner, the intended use of the asset. A non-current asset is an asset that the firm intends to use within the business, over an extended period, in order to assist its daily operating activities. A current asset, by way of contrast, is usually defined in terms of time. A current asset is an asset likely to change its form, i.e. likely to undergo some transaction, within 12 months.

PRINCIPLES OF ACCOUNTING FOR DEPRECIATION

The first major problem with depreciation, perhaps surprisingly, is to agree on what it is and what it is for. The generally agreed view nowadays is that it is in essence a straightforward application of the matching, or accruals, convention. With a non-current asset the benefit from the asset is spread over several years. The matching convention requires that the corresponding expense be matched with the benefit in each accounting period. This does not simply mean that the total expense for the

ACTIVITY 12.1

Consider two firms, *A* and *B*. Firm *A* is a motor trader. It possesses some motor vehicles that it is attempting to sell and it also possesses some desks used by the sales staff, management and so on. Firm *B* is a furniture dealer. It possesses some desks that it is attempting to sell and it also possesses some motor vehicles used by the sales staff and for delivery purposes. How are these items treated in each case?

Activity feedback

In the accounts of *A*, the motor vehicles are current assets and the desks are non-current assets. In the accounts of *B*, the motor vehicles are non-current assets and the desks are current assets. Note incidentally that a fixed asset which, after several years' use, is about to be sold for scrap, remains in the fixed asset part of the accounts even though it is about to change its form.

asset's life is spread over the total beneficial life. It means, more specifically, that the total expense for the asset's life is spread over the total beneficial life *in proportion to the pattern of benefit*. Thus, to take a simple example, if a non-current asset gives half of its benefit, or usefulness, in year 1, one-third in year 2 and one-sixth in year 3 and the total expenses arising are €1 200, then the matching convention requires the charging of €600 in year 1, €400 in year 2, and €200 in year 3, in the annual profit calculation. This charge is known as the *depreciation charge*.

In order to calculate a figure for this charge it is necessary to answer four basic questions:

1 What is the cost of the asset?

2 What is the estimated useful life of the asset to the business? (This may be equal to, or may be considerably less than, its technical or physical useful life.)

3 What is the estimated residual selling value ('scrap value') of the asset at the end of the useful life as estimated?

4 What is the pattern of benefit or usefulness derived from the asset likely to be (not the amount of the benefit)?

It is perfectly obvious that the second, third and fourth of these involve a good deal of uncertainty and subjectivity. The 'appropriate' figures are all dependent on future plans and future actions. It is important to realise that even if the first figure, the cost of the fixed asset, is known precisely and objectively, the basis of the depreciation calculation as a whole is always uncertain, estimated and subjective.

The estimates should, as usual, be reasonable, fair and prudent (whatever precisely this implies!). But the first figure is often not at all precise and objective, for several reasons.

ACTIVITY 12.2

Suggest reasons why the cost of a particular fixed asset may be difficult to determine with precision.

Activity feedback
Possible reasons include the following:

1 Incidental expenses associated with making the asset workable should be included, e.g. installation costs carried out by the business's own staff, probably including some overhead costs.

2 The non-current asset may be constructed within the business by its own workforce, giving rise to all the usual costing problems of overhead definition and overhead allocation.

3 Depending on the accounting policies used by the firm generally, the 'basic' figure for the fixed asset may be revalued periodically. Additionally, if land is not depreciated but the building on the land is, then this requires a split of the total cost (or value) figure for the land and buildings together into two possibly somewhat arbitrary parts.

4 Major alterations/improvements may be made to the asset part way through its life. If these appear to increase the benefit from the asset over the remaining useful life and perhaps also to increase the number of years of the remaining useful life, and are material, then the costs of these improvements should also be capitalised (i.e. treated as part of the non-current asset from then on). However, maintenance costs, including a major overhaul that does not occur frequently, are 'running' expenses and should be charged to the income statement as incurred. In practice, this distinction can be difficult to make.

5 Accounting policies in relation to government grants receivable and to capitalisation of borrowing costs may influence the figures. These two issues are the subjects of separate International Standards. They are considered later in the chapter.

The total figure to be depreciated, known as the *depreciable amount*, will consist of the cost of the asset less the scrap value. This depreciable amount needs to be spread over the useful life in proportion to the pattern of benefit. Once the depreciable amount has been found, with revision if necessary to take account of material improvements, several recognised methods exist for spreading, or allocating, this amount to the various years concerned. The more important possibilities are outlined next. It is essential to understand the implicit assumption that each method makes about the pattern of benefit arising and therefore about the appropriate pattern of expense allocation.

Methods of calculating depreciation

Straight line method The depreciable amount is allocated on a straight line basis, i.e. an equal amount is allocated to each year of the useful life. If an asset is revalued or materially improved then the new depreciable amount will be allocated equally over the remaining, possibly extended, useful life. (See Activity 12.3.)

Reducing balance method Under this method, depreciation each year is calculated by applying a constant percentage to the net book value (NBV) brought forward from the previous year. (Note that this percentage is based on the cost less depreciation to date.) Given the cost (or valuation) starting figure and the useful life and 'scrap' value figures, the appropriate percentage needed to make the NBV at the end of the useful life exactly equal to the scrap value can be found from a formula:

$$d = 1 - \sqrt[n]{S/C}$$

where d is the depreciation percentage, n is the life in years, S is the scrap value and C is the cost (or basic value).

This formula is rarely used. In practice, when this method is used a standard 'round' figure is usually taken, shown by experience to be vaguely satisfactory for the particular type of asset under consideration. Notice, incidentally, that the formula fails to work when the scrap value is zero and produces an extreme and possibly distorted allocation of expense when the scrap value is very small.

A particular variant found in practice in some countries is known as the double-declining balance method. This involves calculating the appropriate 'straight line' depreciation percentage, then doubling it and applying the resulting percentage on the reducing balance basis.

ACTIVITY 12.3

Using the straight line method calculate the annual depreciation charge from the following data:

Cost ('basic' value figure)	€12 000
Useful life	4 years
Scrap value	€2 000

Activity feedback

$$\text{Annual charge} = \frac{€12\,000 - €2\,000}{4}$$
$$= €2\,500$$

This is by far the most common method. It is the easiest to apply and also the preparation of periodic, e.g. monthly, accounts for internal purposes is facilitated. This method assumes, within the limits of materiality, that the asset is equally useful, or beneficial, each year. Whether this assumption is as frequently justified as the common usage of the method suggests, is an open question.

ACTIVITY 12.4

Using the data from the previous activity and assuming a depreciation percentage of 40%, calculate the depreciation charge for each of the four years using the reducing balance method.

Activity feedback

Year 1	Cost	€12 000
	Depreciation 40%	4 800
Year 2	NBV	7 200
	Depreciation 40%	2 880

Year 3	NBV	4 320
	Depreciation 40%	1 728
Year 4	NBV	2 592
	Depreciation 40%	1 037
	NBV	€ 1 555

If the estimated scrap value turns out to be correct, then a 'profit' on disposal of 445 would be recorded also in year 4. This is an example of a reducing charge method or of an accelerated depreciation method. The charge is highest in the first year and gradually reduces over the asset's life.

ACTIVITY 12.5

Suggest, and critically appraise, arguments in favour of using the reducing balance method rather than the straight line method.

Activity feedback

1 It better reflects the typical benefit pattern, at least of some assets.

2 It could be argued that, where the pattern of benefit is assumed to be effectively constant, the appropriate 'expense', which needs to be correspondingly evenly matched, is not the pure depreciation element, but the sum of:

(a) the pure depreciation element

(b) and the maintenance and repair costs.

Because (b) will tend to increase as the asset gets older, it is necessary for (a) to be reduced as the asset gets older, in the hope that the total of the two will remain more or less constant. This may be a valid argument in the most general of terms, but of course there is no reason why an arbitrary percentage applied in one direction should even approximately compensate for flexible and 'chancy' repair costs in the other.

3 It better reflects the probable fact that the value (i.e. the market or resale value) of the asset falls more sharply in the earlier years. This argument, often advanced, is questionable in principle. Depreciation is concerned with appropriate allocation of expense, applying the matching convention. It is not concerned with an annual revaluation of the fixed assets, so whether or not a particular method is good or bad from this viewpoint is, or should be, irrelevant. So long as the original estimate of future benefit is still valid, the fact that current market value is small, at an intermediate time, is not of concern.

4 Since it frontloads the depreciation expense charge in the earlier years of the useful life, it is consistent with the prudence principle. It is indeed true that prudence can be said to support the reducing balance method rather than the straight line method. What is not clear is whether this is a valid *advantage*. This is a particular example of the general debate concerning the relative importance of the prudence principle as discussed in Chapter 1.

Sum of the digits method This is another example of a reducing charge method. It is based on a convenient 'rule of thumb' and produces a pattern of depreciation charge somewhat similar to the reducing balance method.

Using the same figures as before, we give the four years' weights of 4, 3, 2 and 1, respectively and sum the total weights. In general terms we give the n years weights of $n, n - 1, \ldots, 1$ respectively, and sum the total weights, the sum being $n(n + 1)/2$. The depreciable amount is then allocated over the years in the proportion that each year's weighting bears to the total.

ACTIVITY 12.6

Use the sum of the digits method to calculate annual depreciation charges for the data in the previous activities.

Activity feedback

1 $4 + 3 + 2 + 1 = 10$ (the 'sum' of the 'digits')

2 Depreciable amount = €12 000 – €2 000
 = €10 000

Depreciation charges are:

Year 1	$4/10 \times 10\,000 = €4\,000$
Year 2	$3/10 \times 10\,000 = €3\,000$
Year 3	$2/10 \times 10\,000 = €2\,000$
Year 4	$1/10 \times 10\,000 = €1\,000$

This gives NBV figures in the balance sheet of €8 000, €5 000, €3 000 and €2 000 for year ends 1–4, respectively.

Output or usage method This is particularly suitable for assets where the rate of usage or rate of output can be easily measured. For example, a motor vehicle might be regarded as having a life of 100 000 miles, rather than a life of four years. The depreciable amount can then be allocated to each year in proportion to the recorded mileage, e.g. if 30 000 miles are covered in year 1, then 3/10 of the depreciable amount will be charged in year 1. The life of a machine could be defined in terms of machine hours. The annual charge would then be:

$$\text{Depreciable amount} \times \frac{\text{Machine hours used in the year}}{\text{Total estimated life in machine hours}}$$

Revaluation or arbitrary valuation This approach is occasionally used with minor items such as loose tools. An estimated or perhaps purely arbitrary figure for the value of the items (in total) is chosen at the end of each year. Depreciation is then the difference between this figure and the figure from the previous year. Strictly, of course, this is not a method of depreciation at all, but a lazy alternative to it.

All these methods can be criticised on the grounds that they ignore the fact that the resources 'tied up' in the fixed asset concerned have an actual cost to the business in terms of interest paid or an implied (opportunity) cost in terms of interest foregone. This could well be regarded as an essential expense that should be matched appropriately against the benefit from the asset. The 'actuarial' methods that attempt to take account of interest expense are complicated to apply and in financial accounting are hardly ever used.

Some misconceptions underlined

The process of depreciation calculation is not designed to produce balance sheet numbers that are either particularly meaningful or particularly useful, as measurements of value; in fact, they are measurements of unexpired costs.

It must be remembered that depreciation is a process of matching expenses in proportion to benefits. Given that the depreciable amount has been agreed, the annual charge is based on actual or implied assumptions as to the pattern of benefit being derived and nothing else. In simple bookkeeping terms, all that is happening is that a transfer is being made from the non-current assets section in the balance sheet to the expenses section in the income statement. And it is the expense that is being positively calculated, not the reduction in the asset figure. It follows from this that:

1 The asset figure for an intermediate year has no very obvious or useful meaning. It can only be defined in a roundabout way. For example, under historical cost (HC) accounting, it is the amount of the original cost not yet

deemed to have been used, or not yet allocated. This intermediate figure is often called 'net book value' but it is not a value at all within the proper meaning of the word.

2 Depreciation has nothing to do with ensuring that the business can 'afford' to buy another asset when the first one becomes useless. This is true even if we

---

ACTIVITY 12.7

In the year to 31 December, Hans bought a new fixed asset and made the following payments in relation to it:

	€	€
Cost as per supplier's list	12 000	
less Agreed discount	1 000	11 000
Delivery charge		100
Erection charge		200
Maintenance charge		300
Additional component to increase capacity		400
Replacement parts		250

Required

1 State and justify the cost figure which should be used as the basis for depreciation.

2 What does depreciation do and why is it necessary?

3 Briefly explain, without numerical illustration, how the straight line and reducing balance methods of depreciation work. What different assumptions does each method make?

4 Explain the term, 'objectivity' as used by accountants. To what extent is depreciation objective?

5 It is common practice in published accounts of individual entities in Germany to use the reducing balance method for a fixed asset in the early years of its life, and then to change to the straight line method as soon as this would give a higher annual charge. What do you think of this practice? Refer to relevant accounting conventions in your answer.

Activity feedback

1 This figure should be the total cost of making the fixed asset usable, excluding all costs of actually using it. Therefore:

$$11\,000 + 100 + 200 + 400 = €11\,700$$

The additional component is the cost of machine as it enhances the revenue earning capacity of the asset but the replacement parts are cost of using machine – hence the difference in treatment between the two. Maintenance is obviously a cost of usage.

2 Depreciation spreads the cost (or value) of an item over its useful life, in appropriate proportion to the benefit (usefulness). It is necessary in accordance with the matching convention – allocating expense against corresponding benefit, as part of the profit calculation.

3 The straight line method charges a constant percentage of the cost (or value) each year. The reducing balance method charges a constant percentage of the net book value (cost less accumulated depreciation brought forward). Thus the straight line method has a constant charge but the reducing balance method has a charge reducing each year of the asset life. The two methods therefore make different assumptions about the usefulness, the trend or pattern of benefit, of the fixed asset concerned.

4 Objectivity implies lack of bias. It removes the need for and the possibility of subjectivity, of personal opinion. For an accounting figure to be objective, it must be expected that all accountants would arrive at the same figure. Clearly, the figure stated on an invoice has a high degree of objectivity. However, the calculation of depreciation is based on estimates of future life and future usefulness and is therefore highly subjective.

5 This practice can claim the advantage of greater prudence, as the expense is always the higher of the two possibilities. However, it seems to lack consistency. Perhaps more importantly, it obviously fails to attempt to follow the matching convention. It makes no attempt to make the trend of expenses consistent with the trend of benefit or usefulness.

ignore the likelihood of rising price levels. Depreciation does not increase the amount of any particular asset, cash or otherwise.

3 However, depreciation, like any other expense figure, does have the effect of retaining *resources* (or total assets) in the business. By reducing profit we reduce the maximum dividend payable (which would reduce resources) and therefore increase the 'minimum resources remaining' figure. This is, in fact, a particular illustration of the idea of capital maintenance discussed in Chapter 4.

DETERMINING THE COST OF A FIXED ASSET

In the following sections we look at two particular problem areas regarding cost determination, i.e. government grants and interest capitalisation. Before that, as a check on your understanding of general principles, try Activity 12.7.

GOVERNMENT GRANTS

Entities which receive a material amount of assistance from government or state sources are clearly in a different economic position from otherwise comparable entities which receive no such assistance. In order to allow proper appraisal of the results of the entity activities and to facilitate comparisons, disclosure of this government assistance in as much detail as practicable is necessary.

More specifically, government grants are usually easily quantifiable and the general principle of transparency requires that they are both properly accounted for and clearly disclosed. Government grants typically represent a reduction in net cash outflows and, therefore, at least ultimately, an increase in entity earnings.

Suppose a government grant is paid to an entity because, and under the condition that, the entity purchases a depreciable non-current asset. The figures concerned are as follows:

Purchase price of asset	€12 000
Expected useful life	4 years
Expected residual value	Nil
Government grant	€2 000
Annual profits before depreciation, and grants relating to the asset	€20 000

It is possible to suggest at least four possible different ways of treating the grant:

1 to credit the total amount of the grant immediately to the income statement

2 to credit the amount of the grant to a non-distributable reserve

3 to credit the amount of the grant to revenue over the useful life of the asset by:

(a) reducing the cost of the acquisition of the non-current asset by the amount of the grant or

(b) treating the amount of the grant as a deferred credit, a portion of which is transferred to revenue annually.

ACTIVITY 12.8

Which of these methods do you prefer? Give reasons.

Activity feedback

The first two methods may be rejected on the grounds that they provide no correlation between the accounting treatment of the grant and the accounting treatment of the expenditure to which the grant relates. The first method would increase the profits in the first year by the entire amount of the grant, failing to associate the grant with the useful life of the asset. It thus ignores both the prudence convention and the matching convention. The second method means that the grant will *never* affect the profit figure. It also therefore ignores the matching convention and, additionally, leaves the 'non-distributable reserve' in the balance sheet, presumably for ever, i.e. it is treated as paid-in surplus.

The third and fourth methods both follow and apply the matching convention. They both have exactly the same effect on reported annual profits, the differences only being concerned with balance sheet presentation.

Illustration of different accounting treatments

Using the data just given, the two 'acceptable' methods give the following results.

Method 3(a)	€	€	€	€
Profit before depreciation etc.	20 000	20 000	20 000	20 000
Depreciation	(2 500)	(2 500)	(2 500)	(2 500)
Profit	17 500	17 500	17 500	17 500
Balance sheet extract at year end				
Non-current asset at (net) cost	10 000	10 000	10 000	10 000
Depreciation	2 500	5 000	7 500	10 000
Carrying amount	7 500	5 000	2 500	0

Method 3(b)				
Profit before depreciation etc.	20 000	20 000	20 000	20 000
Depreciation	(3 000)	(3 000)	(3 000)	(3 000)
Grant released	500	500	500	500
Profit	17 500	17 500	17 500	17 500
Balance sheet extract at year end				
Non-current asset at cost	12 000	12 000	12 000	12 000
Depreciation	3 000	6 000	9 000	12 000
Carrying amount	9 000	6 000	3 000	0
Deferred credit				
Government grant	1 500	1 000	500	0

Thus method (a) shows assets of 7500, 5000, 2500 and 0 over the four years and method (b) shows assets of 9000, 6000, 3000 and 0 together with 'liabilities' of 1500, 1000, 500 and 0.

From a pragmatic point of view, method (a) has the obvious advantage of simplicity. No entries and no thought are required in the second and subsequent years. However, method (b) has the advantage that assets acquired at different times and locations are recorded on a uniform basis regardless of changes in governmental policy. But what is the cost of the asset? Is it 12 000 or is it 10 000? IAS 16, *Property, Plant and Equipment* (see later) states that cost is the amount of cash or cash equivalents paid, net of any trade discounts and rebates. This statement does not seem to categorically resolve the question. The government grant is not a trade discount. It is not a trade rebate, but it is a rebate. This would seem to imply that the cost in the sense of IAS 16 is 10 000. This is surely the net outflow arising because of the purchase. Yet IAS 20, as discussed in detail on shortly, allows both methods.

A difficult conceptual problem arises with the deferred credit under method (b), e.g. the 1500 at the end of year 1. We described it earlier as a 'liability'. As discussed in Chapter 8, IASB defines a liability as a present obligation of the entity arising from past events, the settlement of which is expected to result in an outflow of resources embodying economic benefits. On the assumption that the grant cannot be reclaimed by the governmental body concerned (the usual situation), the 1500 is clearly not a liability as no outflow of resources is foreseeable. It is more logically either a reserve (not yet realised) or a contra-asset. It could be suggested that this leads to a different possible treatment, i.e. regular inclusion in the balance sheet as a visible contra-asset, i.e. included as a negative balance among the 'assets' instead of as a positive balance among the liabilities. This would raise its own problems – not least the lack of user friendliness involved in the concept of a negative asset. Such conceptual difficulties do not appear to worry either IASB or other national regulators.

The IASB requirements relating to government grants are contained in IAS 20, effective since 1984. The full title of IAS 20 is *Accounting for Government Grants and Disclosure of Government Assistance*. Its coverage therefore extends beyond the area of fixed assets, but for completeness we deal with all aspects of IAS 20 here. Where IAS 41, *Agriculture*, applies, government grants are to be treated under IAS 41 (see appendix), not under IAS 20. Key concepts introduced in IAS 20 are as follows.

Government assistance is action by government designed to provide an economic benefit specific to an entity or range of entities qualifying under certain criteria. Government assistance for the purpose of this Standard does not include benefits provided only indirectly through action affecting general trading conditions, such as the provision of infrastructure in development areas or the imposition of trading constraints on competitors.

A specific subset of government assistance is government grants. *Government grants* are assistance by government in the form of transfers of resources to an entity in return for past or future compliance with certain conditions relating to the operating activities of the entity. They exclude those forms of government assistance that cannot reasonably have a value placed on them and transactions with government that cannot be distinguished from the normal trading transactions of the entity.

The notion of government is to be interpreted broadly. *Government* refers to government, government agencies and similar bodies whether local, national or international.

Government grants may be related to revenue/expense items, such as repayment of 10% of the wages bill, or to capital/asset items, such as repayment of 10% of the cost of a machine. These two types are formally distinguished by IAS 20:

- *Grants related to assets* are government grants whose primary condition is that an entity qualifying for them should purchase, construct or otherwise acquire long-term assets. Subsidiary conditions may also be attached restricting the type or location of the assets or the periods during which they are to be acquired or held.

- *Grants related to income* are government grants other than those related to assets.

The Standard gives two other definitions, including the familiar fair value.

- *Forgivable loans* are loans that the lender undertakes to waive repayment of under certain prescribed conditions.

- *Fair value* is the amount for which an asset could be exchanged between a knowledgeable, willing buyer and a knowledgeable, willing seller in an arm's-length transaction.

Government assistance

Despite the inclusion of government assistance in the title of IAS 20, the statements about it are brief and rather obscure. The definitions given suggest, in effect, that government grants are government assistance that is distinguishable and quantifiable. Turning this round, references to government assistance in the Standard are to government activities that cannot be quantified or clearly distinguished. It follows, of course, that government assistance in this sense cannot be included numerically in the financial statements.

Examples of assistance that cannot reasonably have a value placed on it are free technical or marketing advice and the provision of guarantees. An example of assistance that cannot be distinguished from the normal trading transactions of the entity is a government procurement policy that is responsible for a portion of the entity's sales. The existence of the benefit might be unquestioned but any attempt to segregate the trading activities from government assistance could well be arbitrary.

The significance of the benefit in the examples just presented may be such that disclosure of the nature, extent and duration of the assistance is necessary in order that the financial statements may not be misleading (para. 36). The Standard explicitly stated (para. 37) that while loans at nil or low interest rates are a form of government assistance, the 'benefit is not quantified by the imputation of interest'. This has now been reversed with effect from 1 January 2009 (see below).

The disclosure requirement implied in this seems rather weakly stated. Non-quantified government support, which explicitly included loans at low or zero interest, need not be disclosed at all unless its omission would be so serious as to be 'misleading'.

Treatment of government grants

The major portion of IAS 20 is concerned with the treatment of government grants. The first issue to deal with is the timing of recognition. The IAS requirement (para. 7) is that government grants, including non-monetary grants at fair value, should not be recognised until there is reasonable assurance that the entity will comply with the conditions attaching to them and that the grants will be received. Receipt of a grant does not of itself provide conclusive evidence that the conditions attaching to the grant have been or will be fulfilled.

'Reasonable assurance' is not, of course, definable or defined, but it is clearly less rigorous or demanding than, for example, 'virtual certainty' or 'beyond all reasonable doubt'. The Standard confirms (para. 10) that a forgivable loan (as defined above) is treated as a government grant when there is reasonable assurance that the entity will meet the terms for forgiveness of the loan. Once a government grant is recognised, any related contingency would be treated in accordance with IAS 37, *Provisions, Contingent Liabilities and Contingent Assets* (see Chapter 19).

The benefit of a government loan at a below-market rate of interest is treated as a government grant. The loan shall be recognised and measured in accordance with IAS 39, *Financial Instruments: Recognition and Measurement*. The benefit of the below-market rate of interest shall be measured as the difference between the initial carrying value of the loan determined in accordance with IAS 39 and the proceeds received. The benefit is accounted for in accordance with the Standard. The entry shall consider the conditions and obligations that have been, or must be, met when identifying the costs for which the benefit of the loan is intended to compensate (para. 10A, inserted in 2008).

The key requirement of the Standard (para. 12) is that government grants should be recognised as income over the periods necessary to match them with the related costs they are intended to compensate, on a systematic basis, i.e. following method 3(a) or (b) as discussed at the beginning of this chapter. They should not be credited directly to shareholders' interests. SIC 10, *Government Assistance – No Specific Relation to Operating Activities*, effective from 1 August 1998, has confirmed that government assistance to entities is a grant under IAS 20, even if granted generally to all entities within certain regions or industry sectors.

The matching principle will usually be simple to apply, as illustrated earlier in this chapter. Grants related to non-depreciable assets may also require the fulfilment of certain obligations and would then be recognised as income over the periods that bear the cost of meeting the obligations. As an example, a grant of land may be conditional on the erection of a building on the site and it may be appropriate to recognise it as income over the life of the building. A government grant that becomes receivable as compensation for expenses or losses already incurred or for the purpose of giving immediate financial support to the entity with no future related costs should be recognised as income of the period in which it becomes receivable. Separate disclosure and explanation may be required.

Usually, a careful reading of the contract with the governmental body will determine the appropriate accounting treatment, although an intelligent appraisal of the in-substance thrust of the contract may be required. For example, a grant towards building a factory, stipulating that the factory must remain operating and employing at least 30 people for at least three years, is clearly in essence a grant towards building a factory, not a revenue grant towards reducing net wage costs. However, where a grant clearly relates in material terms to both specific capital and specific revenue items, the Standard is silent on appropriate treatment. Accounting common sense obviously requires an apportionment in such cases.

The Standard is surprisingly vague about non-monetary government grants, such as land donated by a government. IAS 20 merely notes (para. 23) that:

> It is usual to assess the fair value of the non-monetary asset and to account for both grant and asset at that fair value. An alternative course that is sometimes followed is to record both asset and grant at a nominal amount.

This is worded as a description, not as a requirement, although the preference is clear enough. Our view is that merely to record the event at nominal amount lacks transparency to an unacceptable degree. Also it is not consistent with the substance over form principle and would lead to an inconsistent treatment of assets affecting both inter-entity and intra-entity comparisons.

Presentation of government grants

Regarding the presentation of grants related to assets, IAS 20 allows both methods (a) and (b) as discussed and illustrated earlier. Thus, government grants related to assets, including non-monetary grants at fair value, should (paras 24–28) be presented in the balance sheet either by setting up the grant as deferred income or by deducting the grant in arriving at the carrying amount of the asset. The Standard spells out that separate disclosure of the gross cash flows in the cash flow statement is likely to be necessary, whatever treatment is followed in the balance sheet. IAS 7,

Cash Flow Statements (see Chapter 23), is more explicit in making this grossing up of cash flows a requirement.

Regarding the presentation of grants related to income, the Standard again accepts either of two alternatives (paras 29–31). It states, with approval, that grants related to income are sometimes presented as a credit in the income statement, either separately or under a general heading such as 'Other income'; alternatively, they are deducted in reporting the related expense.

A proper understanding of the financial statements may require separate disclosure of the grant and of its effects on particular items of income or expense.

Repayment of government grants

A grant to which conditions were attached may have been properly recognised under the 'reasonable assurance' criterion discussed earlier. However, it may still become repayable in whole or in part if, in fact, the conditions are not met. IAS 20 requires (para. 32) that such a grant, as soon as the repayment becomes foreseeable (which might be significantly earlier than when the repayment actually occurs) should be accounted for as a revision to an accounting estimate, under IAS 8, *Accounting Policies, Changes in Accounting Estimates and Errors* (see Chapter 8). This essentially requires that the entries be made in the financial statements of the year concerned. Repayment of a grant related to income should be applied first against any unamortised deferred credit set up in respect of the grant. To the extent that the repayment exceeds any such deferred credit, or where no deferred credit exists, the repayment should be recognised immediately as an expense. Repayment of a grant related to an asset should be recorded by increasing the carrying amount of the asset or reducing the deferred balance by the amount repayable. The cumulative additional depreciation that would have been recognised to date as an expense in the absence of the grant should be recognised immediately as an expense. Circumstances giving rise to repayment of a grant related to an asset may require consideration to be given to the possible impairment of the new carrying amount of the asset (see IAS 36, *Impairment of Assets*, discussed in Chapter 14).

Disclosure

Key disclosure requirements are as follows:

- the accounting policy adopted for government grants, including the methods of presentation adopted in the financial statements
- the nature and extent of government grants recognised in the financial statements and an indication of other forms of government assistance from which the entity has directly benefited
- unfulfilled conditions and other contingencies attaching to government assistance that has been recognised.

National requirements

US GAAP, or at least promulgated US GAAP, appears to be silent on this whole area. FAS 116, *Accounting for Contributions Received and Contributions Made*, applies to not-for-profit organisations and explicitly excludes transfer of assets from governments to businesses. The US promulgated GAAP for the treatment of investment tax credits, perhaps analogous, permits either deferral and gradual release of the benefit to income or instant release to income.

UK GAAP in SSAP 4 does not permit the netting out of capital grants in the balance sheet and allows only the treatment retaining a separate deferred income balance. This is under the stated, but mistaken, belief that UK law, following European Directive wording, prohibits such setting off. UK (and European) legal requirements forbid the netting out of assets and liabilities, but of course deferred income is not a liability, as already discussed, so therefore netting would be perfectly legal!

The IASB, as part of its convergence project with US GAAP, has been considering possible revisions to IAS 20. Such considerations have been postponed until the possible revisions to IAS 37 have been resolved, which, at the time of writing, does not seem likely to be soon (see Chapter 19).

BORROWING COSTS

The second particular problem area related to the cost of fixed assets is that of interest costs. In the general case, interest cost is a straightforward periodic expense, it should be charged against revenues in proportion to the benefit received, i.e. on a time basis. This is a normal application of the matching principle. The benefit is the existence of the loan and the expense is the interest cost, allocated proportionate to the size of the borrowing.

However, there are circumstances in which accounting theory seems to rationalise an alternative argument. We pointed out in our feedback to Activity 12.2 that 'cost of an asset' includes any item which is necessary to obtain the asset and make it workable. Suppose a loan is necessary in order to obtain the funds without which the asset cannot be obtained. Can it be argued that the cost of the loan (i.e. the interest) is part of the 'cost of the asset'? Clearly, once the asset is workable, i.e. able to function and generate revenues, then there can be no question of this argument justifying non-expensing of interest. But can interest be capitalised as part of the cost of an asset during the period of its creation or construction (see Activity 12.9)?

ACTIVITY 12.9

From your knowledge of accounting principles, what do you think the answer to this question should be?

Activity feedback

As far as it goes, the logic of the 'cost' argument seems inescapable. With a typical self-constructed asset, all direct costs and, in some circumstances, some allocable indirect costs are properly regarded as part of the total historical cost. It follows that any borrowing costs that can be directly linked to the financing of the asset concerned are also logically part of the total historical cost, as an application of the matching principle.

However, it is not difficult to find arguments which point in a different direction. It is clearly not very prudent to avoid the immediate expensing of interest payments that undeniably relate to periodic costs of the accounting period in question. Further, is not the economic argument, i.e. that the cost of necessary finance is part of the cost of production, true *whether or not* a separate source of finance related to the particular asset can be distinguished? If it is true, as we would certainly suggest that it is, then an imputed interest charge should be included even if not supported by any payments or external documentation. This arguably departs much too far from the traditional function of accounting as the recording of transactions. A problem of consistency in asset cost calculations thus arises if some interest costs are capitalised (relatable to specific loans) and others are not.

IAS 23, *Borrowing Costs*

IASB GAAP on the treatment of borrowing costs are set out in IAS 23, *Borrowing Costs*. The original 1984 version of the Standard permitted a free choice between systematically expensing costs and capitalising them when certain conditions were met. In its comparability project in the early 1990s, the IASC proposed in E32 that a 'benchmark' treatment should be for borrowing costs to be expensed, with capital-isation as an alternative treatment when certain conditions were met. The responses to E32 were divided on this issue; however, the IASC then issued E39, according to which capitalisation would be required if certain conditions were met, and expensing would be required otherwise. This position is similar to that in US GAAP (FAS 34). Again, responses to E39 were mixed. In particular, there is the argument that capital structure would lead to different carrying values of 'qualifying assets.' Hence, IAS 23 *Capitalisation of Borrowing Costs,* issued in 1994, restored the choice between expensing and capitalisation subject to certain conditions being met, but expensing became the 'benchmark treatment' and capitalisation the 'alternative treatment.'

In March 2007, as part of the programme of convergence between IASB GAAP and US GAAP, a revised IAS 23, *Borrowing Costs,* was issued, which reverted to the posi-tion proposed in ED 39. In fact, IASB GAAP on 'Borrowing Costs' now align in this respect with US GAAP (see FAS 34, FAS 42, and FAS 58), with the result that capitalisa-tion is required if certain conditions are met and expensing is required otherwise.

The 'core principle' of the revised IAS 23 is that borrowing costs that are directly attributable to the acquisition, construction, or production of a qualifying asset form part of the cost of that asset (i.e. are capitalised). Other borrowing costs are recog-nised as an expense (IAS 23, para. 1).

IAS 23 is to be applied in accounting for borrowing costs. It does not deal with the actual or imputed cost of equity, including that of preferred capital not classified as a liability. Borrowing costs are not required to be capitalised in the case of qualify-ing assets that are (1) measured at fair value (e.g., biological assets) or (2) inventories manufactured or otherwise produced in large quantities on a repetitive basis (IAS 23, paras 2–4). The exclusion of (1) qualifying assets measured at fair value, such as biological assets, from the scope of IAS 23, is logical in that, as such assets are not measured on the basis of cost, the cost of borrowings is irrelevant to their measure-ment. The exclusion of (2) inventories manufactured or otherwise produced in large quantities on a repetitive basis is based on pragmatic reasons.

Qualifying assets are assets that necessarily take a substantial period of time to pre-pare for their intended use or sale, and depending on the circumstances may include:

- certain inventories (e.g. construction work-in-process).
- manufacturing plants
- power generation facilities
- intangible assets (e.g. patents)
- investment properties.

Qualifying assets do not include:

- financial assets
- inventories that are manufactured or otherwise produced over a short period of time
- assets that are ready for their intended use or sale when they are acquired.

(IAS 23, paras 5–7)

Borrowing costs that are directly attributable to the acquisition, construction, or production of a qualifying asset are those borrowing costs that would have been avoided if the expenditure on the qualifying asset had not been made.

When funds are borrowed specifically for the purpose of obtaining a particular qualifying asset, it is clear that these funds are easily identified as directly attributable borrowing costs. If such borrowings are temporarily invested before being expended for the purpose of obtaining the asset, it is likewise clear that any investment income earned is to be deducted from the cost of the borrowings.

In other circumstances, identifying a direct relationship between particular borrowings and a qualifying asset, and determining the borrowings that would otherwise have been avoided, may be difficult, and judgement may have to be exercised. To the extent that funds that have been borrowed for general purposes are used for obtaining a qualifying asset, the amount of borrowing costs that are eligible for capitalisation should be determined by applying a capitalisation rate to the expenditures on that asset. This capitalisation rate is calculated as the weighted average of the borrowing costs applicable to the borrowings that are outstanding during the period excluding any borrowings made specifically for the purpose of obtaining the particular qualifying asset or any other qualifying asset. The amount of borrowing costs capitalised by an entity during a period must not exceed the total amount of borrowing costs that it incurred during that period.

The commencement date for capitalisation is that date on which the entity first meets all of the following three conditions:

1 Expenditures on the qualifying assets are being incurred.

2 Borrowing costs are being incurred.

3 Activities that are necessary to prepare the asset for its intended use or sale are in progress.

Expenditures on the qualifying asset should include only those that have resulted in payments of cash, transfers of other assets, or the assumption of interest-bearing liabilities. They are reduced by any progress payments received (for work-in-process) and grants received in connection with the asset. For the application of the capitalisation rate, a reasonable approximation of the balance of expenditures to which it should be applied for a period is given by the average carrying amount of the asset during that period including all borrowing costs capitalised in prior periods.

Activities necessary to prepare the asset for its intended use or sale include technical and administrative work prior to the start of physical construction. However, the mere holding of the asset in the absence of such work does not count as an activity, and borrowing costs incurred during such a period of inactivity (e.g. when land acquired for building purposes is held without any associated development activity) do not qualify for capitalisation (IAS 23, paras 17–19).

Moreover, capitalisation of borrowing costs is suspended during extended periods in which active development of a qualifying asset is discontinued and no substantial technical or administrative work is carried out, except in the case of a temporary delay that is a necessary part of the process of preparing the asset for its intended use or sale (e.g. suspension of the building of a bridge during an extended period of high water levels) (IAS 23, paras 20–21).

Capitalisation of borrowing costs should cease when substantially all of the activities necessary to prepare the qualifying asset for its intended use or sale are complete. When a qualifying asset is completed in parts, and each part is capable of being sold or used while work continues on the others (e.g., in the case of a business park comprising several buildings), the capitalisation of borrowing costs on a substantially completed part should cease.

An asset is normally considered as 'ready for its intended use or sale' when its physical construction is complete, even though (1) some routine administrative work may still continue, or (2) minor modifications, such as the decoration of the property to the purchaser's or user's specification, may still be outstanding (IAS 23, paras 22–25).

An entity should disclose in the notes to its financial statements:

- The amount of borrowings capitalised during the period.
- The capitalisation rate used to determine the amount of borrowing costs eligible for capitalisation (IAS 23, para. 26).

PROPERTY, PLANT AND EQUIPMENT

We are now, at last, in a position to look at the central requirements of IAS GAAP in relation to accounting for fixed assets. Even now, four different aspects and four different IASs need to be considered, i.e. property, plant and equipment; investment properties; intangibles; and finally the whole question of impairment of fixed assets. Although there are relationships and interlinking between all of these, it will aid understanding to explore them separately. We begin with property, plant and equipment, IAS 16, which is the general Standard regarding the treatment of fixed (non-current) assets. We deal only with the latest version of IAS 16, as revised in 2004, applicable from 1 January 2005, with further minor amendments effective from 2009.

The Standard notes that the general definition and recognition criteria for an asset given in the Framework for the Preparation and Presentation of Financial Statements (discussed in Chapter 8) must be satisfied before IAS 16 applies. Subject to that, IAS 16 applies to accounting for all property, plant and equipment except when another IAS requires or permits a different accounting treatment (para. 2).

There are, in fact, a number of exclusions. It is explicitly stated (para. 2) that IAS 16 does not apply to biological assets related to agricultural activity (to which IAS 41 applies: see Appendix), and the recognition and measurement of exploration and evaluation assets (to which IFRS 6 applies: see appendix). However, it does apply to property, plant and equipment used to develop or maintain these activities or assets but separable from those activities or assets. IAS 16 also does not apply to property, plant and equipment classified as held for sale in accordance with IFRS 5, *Non-current Assets Held for Sale and Discontinued Operations* (see Chapter 14).

An entity applies IAS 40, *Investment Property*, rather than IAS 16, to its investment property (see below). With effect from 1 January 2009, IAS 40 applies to property being constructed or developed for future use as an investment property. IAS 40 also applies to existing investment property being redeveloped for future continued use as investment property.

If any other IAS permits a particular approach to the initial recognition of the carrying amount of property, plant and equipment, then that Standard will prevail as regards this initial carrying value, but IAS 16 would then apply to all other aspects, including depreciation. An example of this would be IFRS 3, *Business Combinations*, which requires property, plant and equipment acquired in a business combination to be measured initially at fair value (see Chapter 26).

The Standard then gives a number of key definitions as follows:

- *Property, plant and equipment* are tangible items that:
  - **(a)** are held for use in the production or supply of goods or services, for rental to others, or for administrative purposes, and
  - **(b)** are expected to be used during more than one period.
- *Depreciation* is the systematic allocation of the depreciable amount of an asset over its useful life.
- *Depreciable* amount is the cost of an asset, or other amount substituted for cost, less its residual value.
- *Useful life* is:
  - **(a)** the period of time over which an asset is expected to be used by an entity
  - **(b)** or the number of production or similar units expected to be obtained from the asset by an entity.
- *Cost* is the amount of cash or cash equivalents paid or the fair value of the other consideration given to acquire an asset at the time of its acquisition or construction or, where applicable, the amount attributed to that asset when initially recognised in accordance with the specific requirements of other IFRSs, e.g. IFRS 2, *Share-based Payment*.
- *The residual value* of an asset is the estimated amount that an entity would currently obtain from disposal of the asset, after deducting the estimated costs of disposal, if the asset were already of the age and in the condition expected at the end of its useful life.
- *Entity-specific value* is the present value of the cash flows an entity expects to arise from the continuing use of an asset and from its disposal at the end of its useful life, or expects to incur when settling liability.
- *Recoverable amount* is the higher of an asset's fair value less costs to sell and its value in use.
- *Fair value* is the amount for which an asset could be exchanged between knowledgeable, willing parties in an arm's length transaction.
- An *impairment* loss is the amount by which the carrying amount of an asset exceeds its recoverable amount.
- *Carrying amount* is the amount at which an asset is recognised after deducting any accumulated depreciation and accumulated impairment losses.

These definitions contain no real surprises and confirm the general earnings calculation focus of the depreciation process. The first issue to deal with is the issue of when an item of PPE should be recorded, i.e. *recognised*, in the financial statements.

An item of property, plant and equipment should be recognised (para. 7) as an asset if, and only if:

1. it is probable that future economic benefits associated with the item will flow to the entity and
2. the cost of the item to the entity can be measured reliably.

In determining whether an item satisfies the first criterion for recognition, an entity needs to assess the degree of certainty attaching to the flow of future economic benefits on the basis of the available evidence at the time of initial recognition. Existence of sufficient certainty that the future economic benefits will flow to the entity necessitates an assurance that the entity will receive the rewards attaching to the asset and will undertake the associated risks. The second criterion for recognition is usually readily satisfied because the exchange transaction evidencing the purchase of the asset identifies its cost.

IAS 16 allows for the aggregation of items which may individually be insignificant (para. 9), giving 'moulds, tools and dyes' as an example. The aggregation is then treated as '*an asset*' if the recognition criteria are met. Conversely, when it is clear that, although an asset may initially be acquired as a whole, significant components of it will have significantly different useful lives, then the expenditure on the asset should be allocated to the component parts and each part should be accounted for as a separate item. An aircraft and its engines are given as a likely example. This separate treatment allows depreciation figures to properly reflect the different consumption patterns of the various components.

Subsequent costs

The first and obvious point is that costs of day-to-day servicing of an item of property, plant and equipment, often described as 'repairs and maintenance', are expenses, not additions to costs. However, major parts of some items of property, plant and equipment may require replacement at regular intervals. For example, a furnace may require relining after a specified number of hours of use; aircraft interiors such as seats and galleys may require replacement several times during the life of the airframe. Items of property, plant and equipment may also be acquired to make a less frequently recurring replacement, such as replacing the interior walls of a building or to make a non-recurring replacement. Under the recognition principle in para. 7, an entity recognises in the carrying amount of an item of property, plant and equipment the cost of replacing such a part of an item when that cost is incurred if the recognition criteria are met. The carrying amount of those parts that are replaced is derecognised in accordance with the derecognition provisions of the Standard.

Note that in order to facilitate this, the component parts of the original item need to have been accounted for separately in the first place.

A major inspection or refit, even if it does not 'improve' the original item, may logically be treated the same way. Thus para. 14 notes that a condition of continuing to operate an item of property, plant and equipment (for example, an aircraft) may be performing regular major inspections for faults regardless of whether parts of the item are replaced. When each major inspection is performed, its cost is recognised in the carrying amount of the item of property, plant and equipment as a replacement if the recognition criteria are satisfied. Any remaining carrying amount of the cost of the previous inspection (as distinct from physical parts) is derecognised. This occurs regardless of whether the cost of the previous inspection was identified in the transaction in which the item was acquired or constructed. If necessary, the estimated cost of a future similar inspection may be used as an indication of what the cost of the existing inspection component was when the item was acquired or constructed.

Once the criteria for recognition have been met, the issue of measurement arises. This is considered in two stages: initial measurement and subsequent remeasurement.

Initial measurement

The essential requirement is straightforward and can be simply stated (para. 15). An item of property, plant and equipment that qualifies for recognition as an asset should initially be measured at its cost. The cost of an item of property, plant and equipment comprises its purchase price, including import duties and non-refundable purchase taxes and any directly attributable costs of bringing the asset to working condition for its intended use; any trade discounts and rebates are deducted in arriving at the purchase price. Examples of directly attributable costs are:

- cost of site preparation
- initial delivery and handling costs
- installation costs
- professional fees such as for architects and engineers
- the estimated cost of dismantling and removing the asset and restoring the site, to the extent that it is recognised as a provision under IAS 37, *Provisions, Contingent Liabilities and Contingent Assets* (see Chapter 19).

In practice, however, a number of complications are likely to arise. The Standard goes into some detail about several aspects (paras 18–28). It notes that in cases where payment is deferred beyond normal credit terms, defined or imputed interest must be removed from the total of the payments, thus reducing the cost to the cash purchase price equivalent. General and administration overheads are not likely to be 'directly attributable costs' as the term was used earlier, but, for example, pension costs of direct labour could be.

The question of what is an essential cost of 'bringing the asset to working condition' is likely to be difficult and subjective.

The basic principle is that recognition of costs in the carrying amount of an item of property, plant and equipment ceases when the item is in the location and condition necessary for it to be capable of operating in the manner intended by management. For example, the following costs are not included in the carrying amount of an item of property, plant and equipment:

- costs incurred while an item capable of operating in the manner intended by management has yet to be brought into use or is operated at less than full capacity
- initial operating losses, such as those incurred while demand for the item's output builds up
- costs of relocating or reorganising part or all of an entity's operations
- costs of opening a new facility
- costs of introducing a new product or service (including costs of advertising and promotional activities)
- costs of conducting business in a new location or with a new class of customer (including costs of staff training)
- administration and other general overhead costs.

Measurement subsequent to initial recognition

The IASB has always operated on the basis that a strict adherence to historical cost is not required and, indeed, has recognised the possibility of rejecting historical cost accounting as the normal basis (see Chapter 8). Consistent with this approach, two alternative approaches to subsequent measurement are allowed under IAS 16 (paras 30 and 31). The first is described as the cost model and is simply stated:

> After recognition as an asset, an item of property, plant and equipment shall be carried at its cost less any accumulated depreciation and any accumulated impairment losses.

The second is the revaluation model.

> After recognition as an asset, an item of property, plant and equipment whose fair value can be measured reliably shall be carried at a revalued amount, being its fair value at the date of revaluation less any subsequent accumulated depreciation and subsequent accumulated impairment losses. Revaluations shall be made with sufficient regularity to ensure that the carrying amount does not differ materially from that which would be determined using fair value at the balance sheet date.

In the previous version of IAS 16, these were presented as the benchmark treatment and the alternative treatment, respectively. However, they are now presented simply as two alternatives.

The fair value of land and buildings will usually be its market value as determined by professional qualified valuers. It is the fair value on the open market which should be used, and note again that fair value is likely to be higher than net realisable value. When there is no evidence of market value because of the specialised nature of the plant and equipment and because these items are rarely sold, except as part of a continuing business, they are valued at their depreciated replacement cost. Appropriate specific price indices may if necessary be used to determine replacement cost.

IAS 16, para. 35 discusses the treatment of accumulated depreciation. The wording is obscure and we quote the paragraph in full:

> When an item of property, plant and equipment is revalued, any accumulated depreciation at the date of the revaluation is treated in one of the following ways:
>
> (a) restated proportionately with the change in the gross carrying amount of the asset so that the carrying amount of the asset after revaluation equals its revalued amount. This method is often used when an asset is revalued by means of an index to its depreciated replacement cost; or
>
> (b) eliminated against the gross carrying amount of the asset and the net amount restated to the revalued amount of the asset. This method is often used for buildings.
>
> The amount of the adjustment arising on the restatement or elimination of accumulated depreciation forms part of the increase or decrease in carrying amount that is accounted for in accordance with paragraphs 39 and 40.

As already indicated, the treatment of increases and decreases arising on revaluation is dealt with in IAS 16, paras 39 and 40.

If an asset's carrying amount is increased as a result of a revaluation, the increase shall be recognised in other comprehensive income and accumulated in equity under the heading of revaluation surplus. However, the increase shall be recognised in profit or loss to the extent that it reverses a revaluation decrease of the same asset previously recognised in profit or loss.

ACTIVITY 12.10

Suppose we have an asset to which IAS 16 applies, cost 10 000, useful life 5 years, estimated residual value nil, now 3 years old. The asset is then revalued to a new gross figure of 15 000, that is the new 'cost' is 15 000, for the purpose of treatment (a). Alternatively the asset is now revalued to a current fair value *in its existing state* of 6000, for the purpose of treatment (b). Show the implications of each of these two treatments.

Activity feedback

(a) Suggests the following:

Cost	Depreciation	Carrying amount
10 000	6 000	4 000

The asset is now revalued, by index or otherwise, to a new gross figure of 15 000, i.e. the new 'cost' is 15 000. The depreciation is now 'restated proportionately', i.e. it is also increased by 50%. We thus end up with:

Gross revaluation	Depreciation	Carrying amount
15 000	9 000	6 000

This increase in carrying amount of 2000 is then dealt with as discussed later.

(b) Suggests a different sequence. Suppose the asset is again recorded before revaluation:

Cost	Depreciation	Carrying amount
10 000	6 000	4 000

The new carrying value is to be 6000. Other balances will need to be altered or eliminated as shown.

Asset revaluation Account

Transfer of cost	10 000		6 000	Transfer of depreciation
Surplus				New carrying value
(calculated)	2 000		6 000	(given)
	12 000		12 000	

If an asset's carrying amount is decreased as a result of a revaluation, the decrease shall be recognised in profit or loss. However, the decrease shall be recognised in other comprehensive income to the extent of any credit balance existing in the revaluation surplus in respect of that asset. The decrease recognised in other comprehensive income reduces the amount accumulated in equity under the heading of revaluation surplus.

Such a revaluation surplus reserve is not 'realised', and is therefore not 'earned' and not available for dividend. However it is likely to become realised over time. Such revaluation surplus included in equity may be transferred directly to retained earnings when the surplus is realised. The whole surplus may be realised on the retirement or disposal of the asset. However, some of the surplus may be realised as the asset is used by the entity; in such a case, the amount of the surplus realised is the difference between depreciation based on the revalued carrying amount of the asset and depreciation based on the asset's original cost.

It is noteworthy that the word 'may' is used three times in the last three sentences. The increase in carrying amount may be transferred to retained earnings eventually when the asset is disposed of or gradually over the remaining useful life – thus, in effect, offsetting in the retained earnings balance the effect of 'extra' depreciation. Note that in neither case is there any effect on the income statement for any year; this will be charged in full with the new depreciation expense. Alternatively, it appears that the increase could be left in revaluation surplus forever. Under a historical cost accounting philosophy this last possibility seems illogical, though under a current cost philosophy it would be logically correct (see Chapter 7).

The Interpretations Committee issued IFRIC 1 in May 2004, effective for annual periods beginning on or after 1 September 2004, earlier application being encouraged. IFRIC 1, *Changes in Existing Decommissioning, Restoration and Similar Liabilities*, provides guidance on how to account for the effect of changes in the measurement of existing such liabilities. The details of IFRIC 1 are complicated, pedantic and common sense.

Depreciation

The formal requirement of IAS 16 for the calculation of depreciation should by now have a familiar ring (para. 50). The depreciable amount of an item of property, plant and equipment should be allocated on a systematic basis over its useful life. The depreciation method used should reflect the pattern in which the asset's economic benefits are consumed by the entity. The depreciation charge for each period should be recognised as an expense unless it is included in the carrying amount of another asset (e.g. as part of the manufacturing cost of inventories).

The Standard goes into detail about a number of aspects. The residual value and the useful life of an asset shall be reviewed at least at each financial year-end and, if expectations differ from previous estimates, the change(s) shall be accounted for as a change in an accounting estimate in accordance with IAS 8, *Accounting Policies, Changes in Accounting Estimates and Errors*.

Depreciation is recognised even if the fair value of the asset exceeds its carrying amount, as long as the asset's residual value does not exceed its carrying amount. Repair and maintenance of an asset do not negate the need to depreciate it. The depreciable amount of an asset is determined after deducting its residual value. In practice, the residual value of an asset is often insignificant and therefore immaterial in the calculation of the depreciable amount. The residual value of an asset may increase to an amount equal to or greater than the asset's carrying amount. If it does, the asset's depreciation charge is zero unless and until its residual value subsequently decreases to an amount below the asset's carrying amount. This last point is rather significant. It recognises and confirms that, while a depreciation charge is *required* for all items of property, plant and machinery, the correctly calculated charge may well be zero.

Land and buildings are separable assets with different accounting characteristics and should be considered separately, even if acquired as a single purchase.

The Standard mentions three depreciation methods by name: straight line, reducing (or diminishing) balance and the units of production (usage) method (para. 62). This list is neither exhaustive nor in order of preference. The method used for an asset is selected based on the expected pattern of economic benefits and is consistently applied from period to period unless there is a change in the expected pattern of economic benefits from that asset. This implies that for any particular asset, with its own particular expected pattern of economic benefits, there is one particular appropriate method. Once the method has been chosen, consistency is required. Now look at Activity 12.11 on the next page.

Derecognition

The carrying amount of an item of property, plant and equipment shall be derecognised:

- on disposal
- or when no future economic benefits are expected from its use or disposal.

The gain or loss arising from the derecognition of an item of property, plant and equipment shall be determined as the difference between the net disposal proceeds, if any, and the carrying amount of the item. The gain or loss is to be included in profit or loss when the item is derecognised (unless IAS 17 requires otherwise on a sale and leaseback). Gains shall not be classified as revenue.

This confirms that any element of revaluation reserve relating to the item will not pass through the income statement.

However, an entity that, in the course of its ordinary activities, routinely sells items of property, plant and equipment that it has held for rental to others shall transfer such assets to inventories at their carrying amount when they cease to be rented and become held for sale. The proceeds from the sale of such assets shall be recognised as revenue in accordance with IAS 18, *Revenue*. IFRS 5 does not apply when assets that are held for sale in the ordinary course of business are transferred to inventories (para. 68A inserted in 2008).

The disposal of an item of property, plant and equipment may occur in a variety of ways (e.g. by sale, by entering into a finance lease or by donations). In determining the date of disposal of an item, an entity applies the criteria in IAS 18, *Revenue*, for recognising revenue from the sale of goods. IAS 17 applies to disposal by a sale and leaseback.

Disclosure

The disclosure requirements under IAS 16 are lengthy and incapable of effective summarisation. In general, full details and reconciliations of movements concerning additions, disposals, impairments and revaluations are required.

ACTIVITY 12.11

It is sometimes argued, for example in the case of hotels, that depreciation of the building is not necessary, on the grounds that its fair value is being maintained by the incurrence of expensive maintenance costs which are being charged as expenses. To charge depreciation as well could appear to be 'double-counting'. What do you think of this argument?

Activity feedback

Standard setters generally are at pains to counter this argument. It is not valid to argue that maintenance increases residual value at the end of economic life, so in principle the proposition is invalid, although maintenance is certainly a factor in determining the *length* of the economic life. However, the useful life could, it must be remembered, be significantly shorter than the economic life. It certainly seems theoretically valid for a hotel owner to argue that expected residual value at the end of the expected useful life (to him) is equal to or greater than the initial carrying value. This would suggest that, while depreciation needs to be provided, the 'correct' figure will be nil! Auditors may be suspicious of this argument although, as discussed earlier, IAS 16 now recognises its possible legitimacy.

The depreciation method applied to an asset shall be reviewed at least at each financial year-end and, if there has been a significant change in the expected pattern of consumption of the future economic benefits embodied in the asset, the method shall be changed to reflect the changed pattern. Such a change shall be accounted for as a change in an accounting estimate in accordance with IAS 8.

It is necessary to determine whether or not an item of property, plant and equipment has become impaired. This area is covered by IAS 36, *Impairment of Assets* (see Chapter 14). Impairments or losses of items of property, plant and equipment, related claims for or payments of compensation from third parties and any subsequent purchase or construction of replacement assets are separate economic events and are accounted for separately as follows:

- impairments of items of property, plant and equipment are recognised in accordance with IAS 36

- derecognition of items of property, plant and equipment retired or disposed of is determined in accordance with IAS 16

- compensation from third parties for items of property, plant and equipment that were impaired, lost or given up is included in determining profit or loss when it becomes receivable

- the cost of items of property, plant and equipment restored, purchased or constructed as replacements is determined in accordance with IAS 16.

ACCOUNTING FOR INVESTMENT PROPERTIES

Principles and definitions

The classic perception of a non-current asset is that of a long-term resource that is necessary to support the day-to-day operational activities of a business. It is used in production or administration, but is not itself sold. It generally wears out, as its use value, or service potential, is consumed, in recognition of which depreciation is charged in the annual profit calculation. The classic perception of an investment is that of an asset held so that the asset itself will earn positive returns, either through regular inflows such as interest, dividend, or rent or through capital appreciation. With an investment, the key issue is impairment or capital appreciation, rather than consumption of use value or service potential.

The specific problem with properties is that they can be held for either purpose or for both purposes at different times. Because of a general tendency, over the long term, for property prices to rise significantly in nominal terms, the distinction in practice is often particularly significant.

Until at least the 1970s, property held as an investment was generally treated for accounting purposes like any other property, with or without the possibility of revaluation and with or without the possibility of non-depreciation, depending on the jurisdiction. This approach began to be challenged, notably in the United Kingdom. It was argued that if a property is held as an investment then:

1 the matching convention is arguably not relevant, as no service potential is being used up

2 the current values of such investments and any change therein are of prime importance and relevance.

ACTIVITY 12.12

We have seen that, under IAS, a non-current asset is any asset other than a current asset, where a current asset is an asset which (IAS 1, para. 66) is:

1 expected to be realised in, or is intended for sale or consumption in, the entity's normal operating cycle

2 held primarily for the purpose of being traded

3 expected to be realigned within 12 months after the balance sheet date

4 cash or cash equivalent (as defined by IAS 7, see Chapter 23), unless it is restricted from being exchanged or used to settle a liability for at least 12 months after the balance sheet date.

If an entity owns a property which it intends to hire out in the short-to-medium term and eventually sell or possibly to sell in the short-to-medium term, consider:

(i) whether it is a non-current or current asset

(ii) whether the economic substance of the situation implies a need for annual depreciation.

Activity feedback

The answer to (i) seems to depend on the particular situation. If the entity is actually trading in properties as an operating activity, then the property does seem to be a current asset. In this case, the question of depreciation does not arise, either logically under the matching principle, or in legal or regulatory terms under EC Directives or IAS GAAP.

If the entity is intending to hold the property for a number of accounting periods, for rental and/or capital gain, then the current/non-current distinction is less clear, although perhaps non-current better reflects the substance. However, the property is still not being consumed in supporting the operating activities of the entity. Further, the key information of relevance to stakeholders should accord with the expected future outcomes, i.e. some kind of rental income and an eventual profitable disposal, not the wearing out of the asset. Arguably, therefore, depreciation is neither logical nor relevant, although this can raise legal and regulatory issues. This whole area needs separate discussion.

IAS 25, *Accounting for Investments*, effective from 1 January 1987 until 31 December 2000, was constructed to allow, but not to require, the treatment of an investment property as a long-term investment under IAS 25, rather than as property under IAS 16, *Property, Plant and Equipment*. Even under IAS 25, such a property could be carried at either cost or revalued amount. Thus there was a great deal of choice involved.

The IASB issued an exposure draft on investment properties, E64, in July 1999. This proposed a mandatory fair value model for investment properties. However, in the resulting debate, IAS was forced to backtrack and the Standard, IAS 40, gives a choice.

Investment property, as defined later, can be treated in either of two ways. Entities can choose between a fair value model and a cost model. The fair value model is the model proposed in E64: investment property should be measured at fair value and changes in fair value should be recognised in the income statement.

The cost model is as defined in IAS 16, *Property, Plant and Equipment*: investment property should be measured at depreciated cost (less any accumulated impairment losses). An entity that chooses the cost model should additionally disclose the fair value of its investment property in the notes to the financial statements.

IAS 40 gives the following key definitions:

- *Investment property* is property (land or a building or part of a building – or both) held (by the owner or by the lessee under a finance lease) to earn rentals or for capital appreciation or both, rather than for:
  - use in the production or supply of goods or services or for administrative purposes, or
  - sale in the ordinary course of business.
- *Owner-occupied property* is property held (by the owner or by the lessee under a finance lease) for use in the production or supply of goods or services or for administrative purposes.

It follows from the definition of investment property that an investment property will generate cash flows 'largely independently' of other assets held by an entity. It is this which distinguishes investment property from owner-occupied property, as owner-occupied property only generates cash flows in conjunction with other operating assets necessary for the production or supply process.

An investment property within the definition should be recognised as an asset when, and only when:

1 it is probable that the future economic benefits that are associated with the investment property will flow to the entity

2 the cost of the investment property can be measured reliably.

Figure 12.1 summarises the various alternatives for treating a property under IAS GAAP (based on a figure in the appendix to the 2000 version of IAS 40).

Note that in marginal cases, judgement will be needed in distinguishing investment properties from owner-occupied properties. For example, an owner-managed hotel is essentially concerned with the provision of services to guests, so it is not an investment property. However, the owner of a building which is managed as a hotel by a third party is in the position of holding an investment, with 'largely independent' cash flows arising, hence creating an investment property. In complex intermediate situations, the substance of the situation and the balance of emphasis should be followed. Disclosure of the criteria used is required when classification is difficult.

FIGURE 12.1   Decision tree for treatment of most property under IAS GAAP

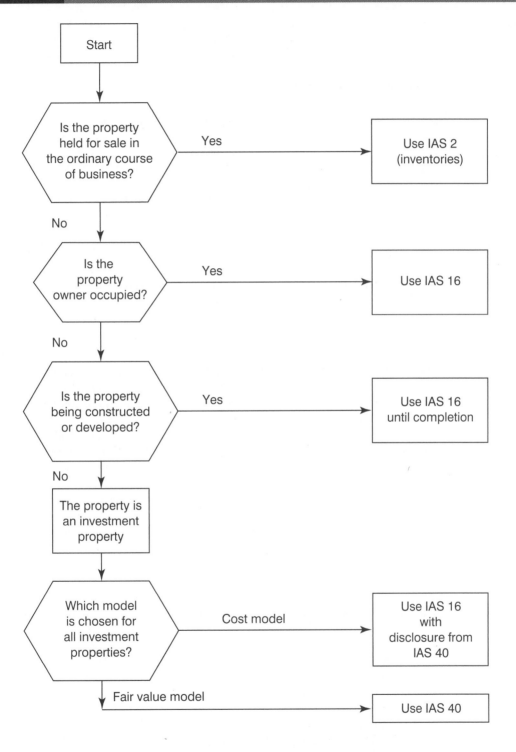

ACTIVITY 12.13

Consider each of the assets described in (a) to (i) and indicate whether they are or are not investment properties as defined in IAS 40:

(a) Land held for long-term capital appreciation rather than for short-term sale in the ordinary course of business.

(b) Land held for a currently undetermined future use.

(c) Property that is being constructed or developed for future use as investment property.

(d) A building owned by the entity (or held by the entity under a finance lease) and leased out under one or more operating leases.

(e) A building that is vacant but is held to be leased out under one or more operating leases.

(f) Property intended for sale in the ordinary course of business, for example, property held for trading by property traders or for development and resale by property developers.

(g) Property being constructed for third parties.

(h) Owner-occupied property.

(i) Property that is leased to another entity under a finance lease.

Activity feedback

(a), (d), and (e) are clearly held for investment purposes and are investment properties. (b) cannot really be regarded as other than a speculative purchase at the time it was acquired and so is an investment property unless and until, presumably, it eventually becomes part of an owner-occupied property. (c), however, does not at present meet the definition; it is property under construction, and IAS 16 would apply. None of the final four is an investment property and IAS 40 would not apply to them. (f) would be dealt with as inventory under IAS 2 (see Chapter 16), (g) as a construction contract under IAS 11 (see Chapter 16), (h) and (i) as property, plant and equipment under IAS 16.

A new introduction in the 2004 version of IAS 40 concerns property interests under operating leases. It was widely suggested that, in substance, given the long life of most property, these should be treatable similarly to finance leases. Accordingly (para. 6), a property interest that is held by a lessee under an operating lease may be classified and accounted for as investment property if, and only if, the property would otherwise meet the definition of an investment property and the lessee uses the fair value model for the asset recognised. This classification alternative is available on a property-by-property basis. However, once this classification alternative is selected for one such property interest held under an operating lease, all property classified as investment property shall be accounted for using the fair value model. When this classification alternative is selected, any interest so classified is included in the disclosures required. Note that this is an option, not a requirement.

Measurement

The initial measurement of a newly acquired investment property under IAS 40 is reasonably simple, but the issue of subsequent measurement is much more complicated. An investment property should be measured initially at its cost, which is the fair value of the consideration given for it. Transaction costs are included in the initial measurement. The cost of a purchased investment property comprises its purchase price and any directly attributable expenditure. Directly attributable expenditure includes, for example, professional fees for legal services and property transfer taxes.

When an investment property has already been recognised, subsequent expenditure on that investment property should be recognised as an expense when it is incurred unless it is probable that this expenditure will enable the asset to generate future economic benefits in excess of its originally assessed standard of performance and the expenditure can be measured and attributed to the asset reliably.

The initial cost of a property interest held under a lease and classified as an investment property shall be as prescribed for a finance lease by para. 20 of IAS 17, i.e. the asset shall be recognised at the lower of the fair value of the property and the present value of the minimum lease payments. An equivalent amount shall be recognised as a liability in accordance with that same paragraph. Note that this applies both to finance leases and to property interests under operating leases treated as investment properties under the option introduced in para. 6.

As suggested, the question of measurement subsequent to the initial measurement is more complicated. As already outlined, two models are available: the fair value model and the cost model. An entity has a choice between these two models under IAS and should apply the chosen model to all of its investment property. Although the choice given in IAS 40 between these two models is a free one, and there is no stated 'benchmark' treatment, it is very clear that the preference indicated in E64 for a fair value model remains. Fair value has to be determined in *all* cases – for measurement in the financial statements if the fair value model is used and for disclosure in the notes if the cost model is used. The Standard notes that IAS 8 (see Chapter 8) states that a voluntary change in accounting policy should be made only if the change will result in a more appropriate presentation of events or transactions in the financial statements of the entity. IAS 40 explicitly states that it is highly unlikely that a change from the fair value model to the cost model will result in a more appropriate presentation.

Some insurers and other entities operate an internal property fund that issues notional units, with some units held by investors in linked contracts and others held by the entity. A newly introduced para. (32A) states that an entity may:

(a) choose either the fair value model or the cost model for all investment property backing liabilities that pay a return linked directly to the fair value of, or returns from, specified assets including that investment property; and

(b) choose either the fair value model or the cost model for all other investment property, regardless of the choice made in (a).

After initial recognition, an entity that chooses the cost model should measure all its investment property using the cost-based treatment in IAS 16, that is, at cost less any accumulated depreciation and any accumulated impairment losses. In other words, if choosing the cost model, an entity proceeds, in measurement (but not disclosure) terms to follow IAS 16 as if IAS 40 did not exist.

However, investment properties that meet the criteria to be classified as held for sale (or are included in a disposal group that is classified as held for sale) shall be measured in accordance with IFRS 5 (see Chapter 14).

There is a rebuttable presumption that an entity will be able to determine the fair value of an investment property reliably on a continuing basis. After initial recognition, an entity that chooses the fair value model should measure all its investment property at its fair value, unless this presumption is not valid.

A gain or loss arising from a change in the fair value of investment property should be included in net profit or loss for the period in which it arises. The Standard makes it absolutely explicit that changes in fair value are to be taken directly to earnings and not taken to or from reserves.

We have discussed the concept of fair value elsewhere (see Chapter 7). Fair value is the amount for which an asset could be exchanged between knowledgeable, willing parties in an arm's length transaction. Note that the fair value figure used in a balance sheet should reflect the actual market state and circumstances as of the balance sheet date, not as of either a past or a future date. It follows, for example, that the cost of any anticipated future capital expenditure that will enhance the property and any related expected increase in benefits are both omitted from the estimation of fair value at the current date.

The best evidence of fair value is normally given by current prices on an active market for similar property in the same location and condition and subject to similar lease and other contracts. In the absence of current prices on an active market, an entity considers information from a variety of surrogate sources, including different properties, less active markets adjusted as appropriated and net present value calculations.

In the rare situations in which fair value measurement proves impossible for a particular property, the entity should measure that investment property using the cost model treatment in IAS 16. The residual value of the investment property should be assumed to be zero. The entity should continue to apply IAS 16 until the disposal of the investment property. In such circumstances, the entity measures all its other investment properties at fair value. IAS 40 requires that once an entity has begun measuring an investment property at fair value, it should continue to do so, even if the measurements subsequently become less reliable.

Transfers and disposals

Under IAS 40, transfers to or from investment property should be made only when there is a clearly evidenced change of use. When the cost model is being used for investment properties, transfers between investment property, owner-occupied property and inventories do not change the carrying amount of the property transferred and they do not change the cost of that property for measurement or disclosure purposes. The Standard does not remind us, but we should note, that the fair value of investment properties measured under the cost model has to be disclosed in the notes, a requirement that does not extend to owner-occupied property or to inventory.

A transfer to or from investment properties which are being carried at fair value obviously has potentially very significant effects on the measurement process and the carrying amount of an asset. If an investment property carried at fair value becomes an owner-occupied property or is transferred to inventory, then the property's cost for subsequent accounting purposes is its fair value as at the date of the change in use.

If an owner-occupied property becomes an investment property carried at fair value, then IAS 16 should be applied up to the date of the change of use, i.e. the entity continues to depreciate the property and to recognise any impairment losses. A difference between the carrying amount of the asset under IAS 16 at the date of the change of use and the fair value at that date is dealt with in the same way as a revaluation under IAS 16.

If a property classed as inventory is transferred to become an investment property carried at fair value, then the treatment is consistent with that of a sale of inventory under IAS 2. A difference between the fair value of the property at that date and its previous carrying amount is therefore part of net profit or loss for the period. Similarly, a self-constructed investment property that will be carried at fair value will give rise, on completion, to an effect on reported net profit or loss for the period equal to the difference between the fair value on the completion date and its previous (cost-based) carrying amount.

ACTIVITY 12.14

Read the immediately preceding paragraph again. Does it meet the requirement in IAS 1 and the underlying concept in the IAS Framework to be prudent?

Activity feedback

There is, certainly in comparison with what many would regard as normal, an apparent lack of prudence, and of strict adherence to the realisation principle, inherent in the previous paragraph. However, this is the whole point of the fair value concept. There is, by definition, reliable evidence to determine fair value, which is a market-based concept and therefore it follows logically and consistently with a true sale, that a gain relating to operating processes has been 'made'. Anybody who regards only a completed transaction as providing adequate evidence for fair value should reject the whole notion of fair value accounting.

An investment property should be eliminated from the balance sheet (derecognised) on disposal. The disposal of an investment property may occur by sale or by enter-

ing into a finance lease. In determining the date of disposal for investment property, an entity applies the criteria in IAS 18, for recognising revenue from the sale of goods (see Chapter 17). IAS 17 applies on a disposal by entering into a finance lease or by a sale and leaseback (see Chapter 14). An investment property must also be derecognised when it is permanently withdrawn from use and no further economic benefits are expected from its disposal. Gains and losses arising on derecognition, i.e. the difference between the net disposal proceeds and the carrying amount, are recognised as income or expense in the income statement, unless IAS 17 requires otherwise in the case of a sale and leaseback. This is, of course, consistent with the treatment of annual changes in fair value of a retained investment property, which are likewise taken directly to the income statement.

IAS 40 gives extensive and detailed disclosure requirements. The crucial point to remember is that if the cost model is used, then disclosure of fair values, by way of note, is still required.

Some national considerations

Broadly speaking, the treatment of investment properties in important accounting jurisdictions mirrors the general characteristics of those jurisdictions, as discussed in Chapter 2. It may be suggested that the attitude to investment properties often illustrates these characteristics quite strongly. It is generally argued that the Fourth EU Directive, as agreed in 1978, does not allow non-depreciation of property, although of course the true and fair override in Article 2 can be used to justify departure from this, at least in those countries that believe in the override anyway. National practice in 'continental' European countries would be, at least up to the present, to use the cost model.

The so-called Anglo-Saxons are clearly split on the matter. At the time of writing, UK Standards *require* investment properties to be evaluated on a broadly fair value basis, in SSAP 19. US GAAP, as currently constituted (ARB 43, APB 6), require that investment properties be treated the same way as any other properties and are, therefore, squarely inconsistent with the original E64 proposals and with the UK requirements.

It is important to note, however, that although at first sight IAS 40 seems to be a compromise in that it allows both the UK to use fair values and the US to forbid them, this is oversimplistic. There is in fact a major difference between the UK and IAS. SSAP 19 in the UK, at para. 13, requires that changes in the market value of investment properties should not be taken to the income statements but should be taken to the statement of total recognised gains and losses (being a movement on an investment revaluation reserve), unless a deficit (or its reversal) on an individual property is expected to be permanent, in which case it should be charged (or credited) in the profit and loss account of the period.

This is in sharp contrast to the IAS 40 requirements, which, as discussed earlier, generally require such changes in market value to be taken directly to annual reported earnings. As regards the important concept of reported earnings, therefore, current UK GAAP is significantly more prudent than the requirements of the fair value alternative in IAS GAAP.

It should also be noted that IAS 40 has gone out of its way to give the impression that it is a stepping stone towards an eventual compulsory fair value model for investment properties. Time will tell.

ACTIVITY 12.15

An extract from the financial statements of the British Land Company PLC for the year to 31 March 2008 is shown in Table 12.1.

Briefly explain how the group measures its properties, and what has happened during the year in relation to them.

At 31 March 2008, the Group book value of properties of £10 469m (2007: £14 047m) comprises freeholds of £9357m (2007: £13 118m); virtual freeholds of £303m (2007: £106m); long leaseholds of £802m (2007: £820m) and short leaseholds of £7m (2007: £3m). The historical cost of properties was £7315m (2007: £8897m).

At 31 March 2008, the book value of owner-occupied property is £53m (2007: £50m) after charging £nil (2007: £nil) depreciation to the income statement for the year.

The property valuation does not include any investment properties held under operating leases (2007: nil).

The property valued at £7162m (2007: £9194m) were subject to a security interest and other properties

of non-recourse companies amounted to £2m (2007: £128m).

Cumulative interest capitalised in investment and development properties amounts to £33m and £84m (2007: £28m and £46m) respectively.

Activity feedback

Most of the group properties are held as investments, with a significant minority under development. They are generally held at fair value. During the year there has been little acquisition of properties, and significant disposals. In addition, a sizeable downward revaluation has been recorded, taken directly to reported earnings. The absolute historical cost of the properties has therefore fallen, as also has the excess of valuation over historical cost for those remaining. Note also that most of the properties are pledged as security against group borrowings. The quality of disclosure and transparency seems quite high.

TABLE 12.1   Extract from financial statements of British Land plc for the year ended 31 March 2008

	Investment £m	Development £m	Owner occupied £m	Total £m
Carrying value at 1 April 2007	12 891	1 106	50	14 047
Additions – property purchases	115			115
Other capital expenditure	253	292		545
Disposals	(2 694)	(24)		(2 718)
Reclassifications	360	(360)		
Revaluations: in income statement	(1 569)	(19)		(1 588)
in statement of recognised income and expense		57	3	60
Increase in tenant incentives and guaranteed rent uplift balances	33	10		43
Carrying value at 31 March 2008	9 389	1 062	53	10 504
Head lease liabilities				(35)
Total Group property portfolio valuation 31 March 2008				10 469

SUMMARY

In this long chapter we have explored a number of aspects of IAS thinking in relation to the accounting treatment of fixed (non-current) assets. We looked at problems of cost determination, in particular IAS 20 on government grants and IAS 23 on borrowing costs and on the recognition and measurement of property, plant and equipment (IAS 16), including alternative methods of depreciation calculation. We also exposed alternative views on the treatment of investment properties, and the IAS requirements on this in IAS 40.

EXERCISES

Suggested answers to exercises marked ✓ are to be found on the Student side of the companion website.

Suggested answers to the remaining exercises are to be found on the Instructor side of the companion website.

1 What are fixed (non-current) assets?

2 Outline four different depreciation methods and appraise them in the context of the definition and objectives of depreciation.

3 Are government grants related to the purchase of fixed assets by an entity a reduction in cost of acquisition?

4 Can the receipt of a government grant create a liability?

5 In what circumstances, if at all, should borrowing costs be capitalised, in your opinion?

✓ 6 Should land be allowed to be, or required to be, revalued?

✓ 7 Should buildings be allowed to be, or required to be, revalued?

8 In what circumstances, if any, do you think that regulation should allow the non-depreciation of owned buildings?

9   IAS 40 gives a choice of accounting policy in relation to investment properties. Is a choice acceptable? If not, how should IAS 40 be altered?

(i)   Discuss the arguments in favour of, and those against, the capitalisation of borrowing costs as part of the cost of an asset.

On 1 April 20X2, Webster commenced the construction of a large development consisting of several separate retail premises. It had a policy of capitalising borrowing costs under IAS 23. At 31 March 20X3 the amount of expenditure on the development totalled $12 million. These expenditures can be taken to have been incurred evenly throughout the year. The development is being financed from funds generally borrowed for the construction of similar development projects. Webster's cost of capital on these funds can be calculated from the following:

> $2 million overdraft at 15% per annum
> $3 million 5 year secured 8% loan note
> $5 million 5 year unsecured 10% loan note

Construction of the development was halted twice during the accounting period to 31 March 20X3. The first occasion, for a two-week period, was due to the discovery of ancient artefacts unearthed during excavation work. The second, an extended period of two months, was due to an industrial relations dispute.

(ii)   Calculate the amount of finance costs that Webster should capitalise for the period to 31 March 20X3.

(ACCA June 2003 adapted)

✓ **10**   The following is an extract of Errsea's balances of property, plant and equipment and related government grants at 1 April 2006.

	Cost $'000	Accumulated depreciation $'000	Carrying amount $'000
Property, plant and equipment	240	180	60
Non-current liabilities			
Government grants			30
Current liabilities			
Government grants			10

Details including purchases and disposals of plant and related government grants during the year are:

(i)   Included in the above figures is an item of plant that was disposed of on 1 April 2006 for $12 000 which had cost $90 000 on 1 April 2003. The plant was being depreciated on a straight-line basis over four years assuming a residual value of $10 000. A government grant was received on its purchase and was being recognised in the income statement in equal amounts over four years. In accordance with the terms of the grant, Errsea repaid $3000 of the grant on the disposal of the related plant.

(ii) An item of plant was acquired on 1 July 2006 with the following costs:

	$
Base cost	192 000
Modifications specified by Errsea	12 000
Transport and installation	6 000

The plant qualified for a government grant of 25% of the base cost of the plant, but it had not been received by 31 March 2007. The plant is to be depreciated on a straightline basis over three years with a nil estimated residual value.

(iii) All other plant is depreciated by 15% per annum on cost.

(iv) $11 000 of the $30 000 non-current liability for government grants at 1 April 2006 should be reclassified as a current liability as at 31 March 2007.

(v) Depreciation is calculated on a time apportioned basis.

Required:

Prepare extracts of Errsea's income statement and balance sheet in respect of the property, plant and equipment and government grants for the year ended 31 March 2007.

Note: Disclosure notes are not required.

(ACCA June 2007)

✓ **11** Omega is an entity that owns three properties. All three properties were purchased on 1 October 2004. Details of the purchase price and market values of the properties are as follows:

	Property 1 $'000	Property 2 $'000	Property 3 $'000
Purchase price	15 000	10 000	12 000
Market value 30 September 2005	16 000	11 000	13 500
Market value 30 September 2006	17 000	9 000	14 500

Properties 1 and 2 are used by Omega as factories whilst property 3 is let to a non-related third party at a commercial rent. Omega does not depreciate any of the properties on the basis that they are valued at market values that are generally expected to increase over time.

Required:

(a) Assess whether Omega's policy of non-depreciation of properties 1–3 is in accordance with international financial reporting standards.

(b) Show how the movements in the carrying amount of each property will be reflected in the financial statements of Omega for the years ended 30 September 2005 and 2006. You can assume that any relevant depreciation is immaterial.

Where necessary you should justify your treatment with reference to appropriate international financial reporting standards. Where more than one treatment is permitted under international financial reporting standards you should show the impact of both treatments.

(ACCA December 2006)

✓ **12** Omega prepares financial statements under International Financial Reporting Standards. In the year ended 31 March 2007 the following transactions occurred:

Transaction 1

On 1 April 2006 Omega began the construction of a new production line. Costs relating to the line are as follows:

Details	Amount $'000
Costs of the basic materials (list price $12·5 million less a 20% trade discount)	10 000
Recoverable sales taxes incurred not included in the purchase cost	1 000
Employment costs of the construction staff for the three months to 30 June 2006 (Note 1)	1 200
Other overheads directly related to the construction (Note 2)	900
Payments to external advisers relating to the construction	500
Expected dismantling and restoration costs (Note 3)	2 000

Note 1

The production line took two months to make ready for use and was brought into use on 31 May 2006.

Note 2

The other overheads were incurred in the two months ended 31 May 2006. They included an abnormal cost of $300 000 caused by a major electrical fault.

Note 3

The production line is expected to have a useful economic life of eight years. At the end of that time Omega is legally required to dismantle the plant in a specified manner and restore its location to an acceptable standard. The figure of $2 million included in the cost estimates is the amount that is expected to be incurred at the end of the useful life of the production plant. The appropriate rate to use in any discounting calculations is 5%. The present value of $1 payable in eight years at a discount rate of 5% is approximately $0.68.

Note 4

Four years after being brought into use, the production line will require a major overhaul to ensure that it generates economic benefits for the second half of its useful life. The estimated cost of the overhaul, at current prices, is $3 million.

Note 5

Omega computes its depreciation charge on a monthly basis.

Note 6

No impairment of the plant had occurred by 31 March 2007.

Transaction 2

On 31 December 2006 the directors decided to dispose of a property that was surplus to requirements. They instructed selling agents to find a suitable purchaser and advertised the property at a commercially realistic price.

The property was being measured under the revaluation model and had been revalued at $15 million on 31 March 2006. The depreciable element of the property was estimated as $8 million at 31 March 2006 and the useful economic life of the depreciable element was estimated as 25 years from that date.

On 31 December 2006 the directors estimated that the market value of the property was $16 million, and that the costs incurred in selling the property would be $500 000. The property was sold on 30 April 2007 for $16.1 million. Omega incurred selling costs of $550 000. The actual selling price and costs to sell were consistent with estimated amounts as at 31 March 2007.

The financial statements for the year ended 31 March 2007 were authorised for issue on 15 May 2007.

Required:

Show the impact of the above transactions on the income statement of Omega for the year ended 31 March 2007, and on its balance sheet as at 31 March 2007. You should state where in the income statement and the balance sheet relevant balances will be shown.

(ACCA June 2007)

INTANGIBLE ASSETS

13

OBJECTIVES After studying this chapter you should be able to:

- define and distinguish intangible assets, and goodwill

- describe, apply and appraise the requirements of IAS 38 relating to intangible assets

- discuss alternative possible treatments for purchased goodwill

- describe, apply and appraise the requirements of IFRS 3 relating to purchased goodwill.

INTRODUCTION

The accounting treatment of goodwill and intangible assets has caused great difficulty and confusion over the years. Part of the trouble was a failure to distinguish clearly between the two. Much of the confusion has been removed by recent international developments, but the future treatment of goodwill is under active consideration and discussion, as regulators move further towards an acceptance of the use of fair values.

In the 'bad old days' goodwill was often very loosely regarded as a conglomerate figure for all unrecorded net asset values. In other words, if a business were bought for €1 million and the recorded net assets had 'book values' of €600 000, then the difference of €400 000 was considered to be goodwill. This adherence to book values, which are by definition largely meaningless in market terms, is now generally unacceptable. IASB now defines goodwill (IFRS 3, Appendix A) as follows:

> Future economic benefits arising from assets that are not capable of being individually identified and separately recognised.

In principle, goodwill is in existence all the time. Its value is difficult to define, and is constantly changing. Its value can, of course, be negative. But goodwill is always there, it is inherent in the business. This is often referred to as *inherent goodwill*, *non-purchased goodwill* or *internally generated goodwill*. It is contrasted with purchased goodwill. This contrast is not for reasons of principle, but purely for the practical reason that purchased goodwill has a convenient cost figure. There has been a transaction, the cost convention can be applied, we have a figure capable of being audited. If we buy a business for €100 000 and the net separable assets have fair value of €60 000 then we can certainly say that goodwill is, or at least at that instant was, worth €40 000.

The accounting treatment for purchased goodwill is regarded as an aspect of accounting for business combinations. IASB covers this in IFRS 3 and we discuss purchased goodwill separately in the next section. We first consider in detail the problems of accounting for intangibles other than purchased goodwill; this is covered by IAS 38, *Intangible Assets*.

INTANGIBLE ASSETS

In IAS GAAP, an intangible asset is defined as an '*identifiable* non-monetary asset without physical substance'. This excludes goodwill, which is by definition non-identifiable.

Identifiability in IAS GAAP does not equal separability, since an asset of an entity is defined as '*a resource* [that is] (a) *controlled* by the entity as a result of past events; and (b) from which future economic benefits are expected to flow to the entity'. For an intangible asset to be recognised, the future economic benefits must be 'probable', and it must be possible to measure the cost of the asset reliably. 'Control' encompasses both the right to obtain the benefits and the ability to restrict access to them by others. It is not necessarily considered to imply the ability to sell the item separately from other assets of the entity. These criteria thus permit the recognition as assets, in appropriate circumstances, of non-separable items such as development costs that have not been converted into (separable) patents. They do not permit the recognition of internally generated goodwill.

IAS 38 is a relatively recent standard. At its original creation in 1998 the IASB decided to include the requirements on research and development (R&D) costs, originally separately stated in IAS 9, with those on other intangibles because R&D costs are intangible in nature, any value attributable to them being due to the know-how embodied in them rather than to physical items such as prototypes. The IASB was concerned to achieve, as far as possible, uniformity of treatment for all long-term non-financial assets, whether tangible or intangible, and for intangibles whether internally generated or acquired. This concern is manifested in IAS 38 in the following ways:

- many of the paragraphs of IAS 38 are similar in wording and in places virtually identical, to paragraphs of IAS 16, *Property, Plant and Equipment*

- the recognition as assets of internally generated intangibles is allowed, subject to stringent and cumbersome criteria.

Although the principle is that any intangibles that meet the asset recognition criteria should be recognised (except in the case of the 'alternative treatment' discussed later), it remains to be seen whether the effect of these criteria acts as a deterrent to a reporting entity from so doing, in the absence of a powerful reason.

The treatment of R&D costs has been the subject of particular controversy internationally. While there is general (but not universal, e.g. Norwegian law explicitly states the opposite) agreement that research does not give rise to intangible values that can be recognised as assets, there is disagreement as to whether development may do so, subject to certain criteria. In its 1993 revision of IAS 9, *Research and Development Costs*, the IASB changed its preferred (benchmark) treatment from that proposed in its Exposure Drafts E32 and E47, namely, the immediate expensing of all development costs, to capitalisation (i.e. recognition as an asset), provided certain criteria were met. It was thought that this was more consistent with the concept of an asset as set out in the IASB's Framework. In IAS 38, capitalisation is maintained, but the criteria for recognition have been tightened up; immediate expensing is not allowed as an alternative treatment if these criteria are met.

Another area of controversy has been the treatment of brands. Here, however, the IASB has felt able to take a firm line: internally generated brands are not to be recognised as assets. Brands acquired in a business combination are not considered to be separately identifiable assets and are thus part of goodwill.

The new version of IAS 38, applicable from 1 January 2005, makes various amendments and clarifications and, in a major development, requires the non-depreciation of intangible assets with indefinite lines, as defined, requiring regular impairment tests instead.

Scope of IAS 38

The scope of IAS 38 is clarified in paras 2 and 3 by stating which categories of item are not included, namely:

(a) intangible assets that are within the scope of another Standard

(b) financial assets, as defined in IAS 39, *Financial Instruments: Recognition and Measurement*

(c) the recognition and measurement of exploration and evaluation assets (covered by IFRS 6) and

(d) expenditure on the development and estimation of minerals, oil, natural gas and similar non-regenerative resources.

If another Standard prescribes the accounting for a specific type of intangible asset, an entity applies that Standard instead of IAS 38. For example:

(a) intangible assets held by an entity for sale in the ordinary course of business (see IAS 2, *Inventories*, and IAS 11 *Construction Contracts*)

(b) deferred tax assets (see IAS 12, *Income Taxes*)

(c) leases that are within the scope of IAS 17, *Leases*

(d) assets arising from employee benefits (see IAS 19, *Employee Benefits*)

(e) financial assets as defined in IAS 39; recognition and measurement of some financial assets are covered by IAS 27, *Consolidated and Separate Financial Statements*, IAS 28, *Investments in Associates*, and IAS 31, *Interests in Joint Ventures*

(f) goodwill acquired in a business combination (see IFRS 3, *Business Combinations*)

(g) deferred acquisition costs, and intangible assets, arising from an insurer's contractual rights under insurance contracts within the scope of IFRS 4, *Insurance Contracts*

(h) non-current intangible assets classified as held for sale (or included in a disposal group that is classified as held for sale) in accordance with IFRS 5, *Non-current Assets Held for Sale and Discontinued Operations*.

The term *intangible assets* raises the major issue of which intangible items should be recognised as assets and which should not. Hence, IAS 38 mentions numerous items of expenditure on what may be termed *intangible resources*, many of which do not meet its asset recognition criteria. Such intangible resources include expenditure on advertising, training, start-up, research and development activities, and computer software, patents, copyrights, motion picture films. A good number of these do not qualify for recognition as assets in terms of the criteria set out in the IASB's Framework and one of the main purposes of IAS 38 is to distinguish between those that do and those that do not. Examples of expenditure that do not meet these criteria are start-ups, research, training, advertising and/or promotion and relocation or reorganisation. Paragraph 63 adds internally generated brands, mastheads, publishing titles, customer lists and items similar in substance as items not qualifying for recognition as assets.

According to IAS 38, para. 6, an intangible asset held by a lessee under a finance lease is considered, after initial recognition, to be an asset falling within the scope of IAS 38.

Recognition under IAS 38

Three criteria need to be satisfied before an item should be recognised as an intangible asset under IAS 38. These are identifiability, control and reliable measurability.

Identifiability (IAS 38, paras 11–12) is necessary in order to distinguish an intangible asset from goodwill. Separability is a sufficient condition for identifiability, but in IAS GAAP not a necessary one. An asset is separable if the entity could rent, sell, exchange or distribute the specific future economic benefits attributable to the asset without also disposing of other assets or future economic benefits that flow from them. (Future economic benefits include both revenues and cost savings.)

An entity, however, may be able to identify an intangible asset in some other way. If an intangible asset is acquired together with a set of other assets, it may be separately identifiable by virtue of separate legal rights attaching to it. An internally generated intangible asset may also result from an internal project that gives rise to legal rights for the entity. Nevertheless, usually legal rights are transferable, so that such assets are separable (an exception is rights resulting from a legal duty on employees to maintain confidentiality). But identifiability in IAS GAAP can be achieved even if an asset generates future economic benefits only in combination with other assets, that is, it is not separable, provided the entity can identify the future economic benefits that will flow from the asset. In that case, however, the second criterion, control, is particularly crucial.

Control (IAS 38, paras 13–16) is exercised by an entity over an asset if the entity:

- has the power to obtain the future economic benefits flowing from the underlying resource
- can also restrict the access of others to such benefits.

The resource itself is not recognisable as an asset unless the criterion of control (as well as that of identifiability) is met. Control will generally result from legal rights enforceable in law and such rights provide a sufficient condition for control. IAS GAAP do not exclude the possibility that control over the future economic benefits could be exercised in some other way, but give no examples of this.

In the case of such intangible resources as benefits arising from a team of skilled staff and from training, even if the identifiability criterion can be satisfied, the criterion of controllability will most likely not be met in the absence of protection by legal rights. The same is true for customer lists or market shares. Such intangible resources therefore do not usually qualify for recognition as intangible assets.

Reliable measurability is also a necessary precondition for the recognition of intangible assets.

IAS 38, paras 21 and 24, state that an intangible asset (that has met the other recognition criteria) should be recognised only if its cost can be measured reliably and that it should be measured initially at that cost.

For the purpose of determining cost, four different modes of acquisition are considered (paras 25–47): separate acquisition; acquisition as part of a business combination; acquisition by way of a government grant; and acquisition by exchange of assets. Little needs to be said in explanation of this.

In the case of separate acquisition, the rules for determining cost are the same as those for assets generally, discussed in Chapter 12. The rules for determining cost in the case of acquisition as part of a business combination are given in IFRS 3 (see Chapter 26). In the case of acquisition by way of a government grant, the rules in IAS 20 are applicable (see Chapter 12).

In general, exchanges of assets are accounted for at fair value, the fair value of the asset given being treated as the cost of the asset acquired, subject to any necessary adjustments for any other partial consideration such as cash. In the case of an intangible asset that is exchanged for an equity interest in a similar asset (such as a share in a research and development joint venture), the cost of the new asset is the carrying amount of the asset given up, with no gain or loss being recognised on the transaction, unless the fair value of the asset received is less than the carrying amount of the asset given up.

Internally generated intangible assets

Note that internally generated goodwill cannot be an intangible asset within the terms of IAS 38 and so cannot be capitalised. In order to assess whether an internally generated intangible resource meets the criteria for recognition as an asset, IAS 38 sets out the following methodology (paras 51–64).

The entity, first, classifies the internal project resulting in the generation of the resource into two phases: a research phase and a development phase. If this distinction cannot be made for the internal project, then the entire project should be considered as a research phase.

Research is defined as original and planned investigation undertaken with the prospect of gaining new scientific or technical knowledge and understanding. Development is the application of research findings or other knowledge to a plan or design for the production of new or substantially improved materials, devices, products, processes, systems or services before the start of commercial production or use (IAS 38, para. 8).

It is worth pausing at this point to remind ourselves about the general principles involved here. It is obvious that the management of an entity will authorise the expenditure of money and resources on either research or development only if there is in some sense or other an expectation of benefit to the entity. It can be argued that an expectation of future benefit from a past event automatically creates the expectation of an asset now. However, the IAS definition of an asset needs to be remembered in full, i.e. an asset is a resource:

- controlled by an entity as a result of past events
- and from which future economic benefits are expected to flow.

ACTIVITY 13.1

From your knowledge of the IASB Framework and general accounting concepts, suggest briefly, with justification, how expenditure in the research and development phases should be treated.

Activity feedback

In essence, the matching convention argues in favour of capitalisation now, in order to permit expensing later against resulting benefit. The asset figure will need to be charged to the P&L account over the period of benefits, in approximate proportion to the benefit pattern. In effect, we would have a fixed asset that would require depreciating. And since there is likely to be a gap, perhaps of several years, between expenditure and eventual benefit in terms of production and sales, it follows that the expense or depreciation may be zero for one or more accounting periods. If the benefit has not begun to appear yet, then under the matching convention we should not yet begin to write off the asset as an expense.

It can be suggested that this treatment is inconsistent with the prudence convention. Research and development expenditure is by definition speculative and, particularly with more basic investigation, the outcome is highly uncertain. It is perhaps difficult to argue that the existence of future benefit, of greater amount than the expenditure, can be established with 'reasonable certainty'. It is even harder to argue that the *relationship* to the revenue or benefit in any particular future period can be established with 'reasonable certainty'. It must also be remembered that a successful profitable outcome is crucially dependent on the validity of the going concern convention.

There is clearly a tension regarding research and development expenditure between matching and prudence. Whatever detailed views an individual holds, it is obvious that research is significantly more speculative than development and that development expenditure becomes less speculative and more reasonably predictable in its outcome, as actual production and sale of the product comes nearer. The IASB solution is to forbid the capitalisation of all research and development expenditure, except for development phase items which meet specified conditions, in which case they are required (not just permitted) to be capitalised.

Thus under IAS 38, no intangible asset should be recognised as resulting from research or from the research phase of an internal project. Expenditure on research should be recognised as an expense when incurred.

An intangible resource arising from development (or from the development phase of an internal project) should be recognised as an intangible asset if, and only if, an entity can demonstrate all the following:

- the technical feasibility of completing the intangible asset so that it will be available for use or sale
- its intention to complete the intangible asset and use or sell it
- its ability to use or sell it
- how the intangible asset will generate probable future economic benefits. Among other things, the following should be demonstrated: the existence of a market for the intangible asset or its output or, if it is to be used internally, its usefulness to the entity
- the availability of adequate technical, financial and other resources to complete the development and

ACTIVITY 13.1   (Continued)

to use or sell the intangible asset, which may be demonstrated by an appropriate business plan

- the entity's ability to measure reliably the expenditure attributable to the intangible asset during its development, for example, by means of the entity's costing system.

To demonstrate how an intangible asset will generate probable future economic benefits, the principles set out in IAS 36, *Impairment of Assets*, especially paras 30–57 on value in use should be applied. If the asset will generate economic benefits only in combination with other assets, the principles for 'cash-generating units' set out in IAS 36 should be followed (IAS 36 is discussed in Chapter 14).

As discussed above, under the heading 'Scope of IAS 38', IAS 38 names a number of items that do not meet these criteria.

The cost of an internally generated asset is the sum of the expenditure incurred from the date when the intangible asset first meets the recognition criteria set out earlier. Cost includes all expenditure that is either directly attributable to generating the asset or has been allocated on a reasonable and consistent basis to the activity of generating it. Allocations of overheads should follow the principles set out in IAS 2, *Inventories* (see Chapter 16). With regard to the recognition of interest as a cost, IAS 23, *Borrowing Costs* (see Chapter 12) sets out the applicable principles.

Expenditure that is not part of the cost of the intangible asset includes that on selling, administration and training staff to operate the asset. Expenditure on an intangible resource that was initially recognised as an expense in previous financial statements or reports (for example, expenditure during the 'research phase' of an internal project) should not be recognised as part of the cost of an intangible asset at a later date (IAS 38, para. 71).

Any expenditure that is not part of the cost of an intangible asset properly recognisable as defined and discussed earlier is, naturally, to be recognised as an expense when incurred (unless the expenditure is part of the cost of a business acquisition, when IFRS 3 applies as already stated).

Subsequent expenditure

The view taken in IAS 38 is that only rarely will expenditure incurred after the initial recognition of a purchased intangible asset or after the completion of an internally generated intangible asset result in an addition to the amount of its capitalised cost. This is because it is generally difficult:

- to attribute such expenditure to a particular intangible asset rather than to the business as a whole
- and even when that difficulty does not arise, to determine whether such expenditure will enhance, rather than merely maintain, the probable economic benefits that will flow from the asset.

Consequently, subsequent expenditure should be recognised as an expense, except in the rare cases where:

- probable enhancement of the economic benefits that will flow from the asset can be demonstrated
- and the expenditure can be measured and attributed to the asset reliably (IAS 38, paras 18–20).

Measurement subsequent to initial recognition

Two treatments are available, the cost model and the revaluation model. In the 1998 version of IAS 38 these were characterised as 'benchmark' and 'alternative' treatments, respectively. These terms have been removed and the new IAS 38 gives the two alternatives ostensibly equal weighting.

The cost model is that an intangible asset should be carried at cost less any accumulated depreciation and (if any) accumulated impairment losses (IAS 38, para. 74).

The revaluation model is to carry the intangible asset at a revalued amount. The revalued amount should be the fair value of the asset at the date of revaluation less any subsequent accumulated depreciation and (if any) subsequent accumulated impairment losses (IAS 38, para. 75). This alternative treatment can only be applied after initial recognition, i.e. all the conditions and requirements stated earlier must previously have been fully satisfied.

If an intangible asset is revalued, revaluation of all the other assets in its class should also be carried out (i.e. those of similar nature and use within the entity's operations), except those for which there is no active market, which should be carried at cost less accumulated amortisation and impairment losses.

Fair value should be determined by reference to an active market and revaluations should be made with sufficient regularity so that the carrying amount does not diverge materially from the fair value at the balance sheet date. An active market is defined as one in which all the following conditions exist:

- the items traded within it are homogeneous
- willing buyers and sellers can normally be found at any time (within reason)
- prices are public information (IAS 38, para. 8).

It is considered unlikely that such an active market would exist for an intangible asset (IAS 38, para. 78), although there may be exceptions to this generalisation; for example, there may be active markets in freely transferable taxi licences, fishing licences, production quotas or airport takeoff and landing 'slots'. If an active market is not available, the revaluation model cannot be used.

The revaluation model cannot apply to initial recognition, which should be at cost, or to intangible resources that were not previously recognised as assets. However, if only part of the cost of an intangible resource was recognised as an asset because it did not meet the criteria for recognition until part of the way through an internal project, the revaluation treatment may be applied to the whole of the asset and not just to that proportion of it that would be represented by the amount recognised as its cost. The revaluation treatment may also be applied to an intangible asset received by way of a government grant and initially recognised at a nominal amount (IAS 38, para. 77).

An active market that has existed for an intangible asset may cease to exist. In that case, if the asset has been accounted for by using the alternative treatment, then its carrying amount should be its revalued amount at the date of the last revaluation by reference to the formerly active market less any accumulated depreciation and impairment losses. The cessation of the active market may be an indication of possible impairment of the asset's value and this should be tested in accordance with IAS 36, *Impairment of Assets* (see Chapter 14). If, at a subsequent measurement date, an active market is available again so that the fair value of the asset can be determined, the asset should be revalued at its fair value as of that date.

Recognition of revaluation gains and losses

The usual prudence and realisation conventions prevail. Increases in an intangible asset's carrying amount (gains) should be credited directly to equity under the heading of revaluation surplus, except to the extent that the increase is a reversal of a previous revaluation decrease (loss) recognised as an expense in respect of the same asset, in which case the amount of the reversal is recognised as income.

Revaluation decreases (losses) are recognised as expenses except to the extent that the decrease is a reversal of a revaluation increase (gain) that was previously credited to revaluation surplus in respect of the same asset, in which case the amount of the reversal should be charged against the revaluation surplus (IAS 38, paras 85–86).

According to IAS 38, para. 87, the cumulative revaluation surplus 'may' be transferred directly to retained earnings when the surplus is realised. Realisation of the surplus may occur through retirement or disposal of the asset or through the process of using up the asset, insofar as the amortisation based on the revalued carrying amount exceeds that which would have been calculated on the basis of the asset's historical cost. The transfer from revaluation surplus to retained earnings is not made through the income statement, but directly in the balance sheet, i.e. it does not affect reported earnings in the year the transfer is made.

Amortisation and depreciation

IAS 38 uses the terms *amortisation* and *depreciation* interchangeably with reference to intangible assets to refer to the process of systematic allocation of an asset's cost or revalued amount, less any residual value, over its useful life. The residual value should be assumed to be zero, unless:

- either there is a commitment by a third party to purchase the asset at the end of its estimated useful life to the entity (i.e. the period of time over which it is being depreciated)
- or there is an active market for the asset, such that the asset's residual value can be determined by reference to that market and it is probable that the market will exist at the end of asset's estimated useful life to the entity.

An estimate of an asset's residual value is based on the amount recoverable from disposal using prices prevailing at the date of the estimate for the sale of a similar asset that has reached the end of its useful life and has operated under conditions similar to those in which the asset will be used. The residual value is reviewed at least at each financial year end. A change in the asset's residual value is accounted for as a change in an accounting estimate in accordance with IAS 8, *Accounting Policies, Changes in Accounting Estimates and Errors*.

Useful life

The previous (1998) version of IAS 38 contained a 'rebuttable assumption' that the useful life for an intangible asset could not exceed 20 years, and, in all cases, required amortisation. The new version makes very significant changes. IAS 38 now requires (paras 88–89) that an entity shall assess whether the useful life of an intangible asset is finite or indefinite and, if finite, the length of, or number of production or similar units constituting, that useful life. An intangible asset shall be regarded by the entity as having an indefinite useful life when, based on an analysis of all the relevant factors, there is no foreseeable limit to the period over which the asset is expected to generate net cash inflows for the entity.

The accounting for an intangible asset is based on its useful life. An intangible asset with a finite useful life is amortised and an intangible asset with an indefinite useful life is not.

Factors that need to be considered in estimating an intangible asset's useful life include the following (IAS 38, paras 90 and 94):

1 The expected usage of the asset by the entity and whether the asset could be efficiently managed by another management team.

2 Typical product life cycles for the asset and public information on estimates of useful lives for similar assets that are used in a similar way.

3 Technical, technological, commercial or other types of obsolescence.

4 The stability of the industry in which the asset operates and changes in the market demand for the outputs of the asset.

5 Expected actions by competitors or potential competitors.

6 The level of maintenance expenditure required to obtain the expected future economic benefits from the asset and the entity's intent and ability to spend such amounts.

7 The entity's period of control over the asset and legal and similar limits on control or use, such as the expiration dates of related leases. If control over the future economic benefits from the asset is achieved though legal rights that have been granted for a finite period, the useful life of the asset should not exceed the duration of the legal rights unless they are renewable and renewal is virtually certain.

8 Whether the asset's useful life is dependent on that of other assets of the entity.

The term 'indefinite' does not mean 'infinite'. The useful life of an intangible asset reflects only that level of future maintenance expenditure required to maintain the asset at its standard of performance assessed at the time of estimating the asset's useful life and the entity's ability and intention to reach such a level. A conclusion that the useful life of an intangible asset is indefinite should not depend on planned future expenditure in excess of that required to maintain the asset at that standard of performance.

Intangible assets with finite useful lives The depreciable amount of an intangible asset with a finite useful life shall be allocated on a systematic basis over its useful life. Amortisation shall begin when the asset is available for use, i.e. when it is in the location and condition necessary for it to be capable of operating in the manner intended by management. Amortisation shall cease at the earliest date that the asset is classified as held for sale (or included in a disposal group that is classified as held for sale) in accordance with IFRS 5, *Non-current Assets Held for Sale and Discontinued Operations* (see Chapter 14), and the date that the asset is derecognised. The amortisation method used shall reflect the pattern in which the asset's future economic benefits are expected to be consumed by the entity. If the pattern cannot be reliably determined, the straight line method shall be used. The amortisation charge for each period shall be recognised in profit or loss unless IAS 38 or another Standard permits or requires it to be included in the carrying amount of another asset.

IAS 38 envisages a variety of amortisation methods that may be used to allocate systematically the depreciable amount of an intangible asset over the periods making up its useful life. The standard mentions the straight line, diminishing balance and units of production methods. The straight line method should be used unless the time pattern of consumption of the asset's economic benefits can be determined reliably and clearly indicates that one of the other methods is more suitable. There will rarely, if ever, be persuasive evidence to support a method for intangible assets that is less conservative (that is, results in a lower amount of accumulated depreciation) than the straight line method (IAS 38, paras 97–99).

The amortisation period and method should be reviewed at least at each financial year-end and the amortisation period should be changed if the expected useful life of the asset is significantly different from previous estimates (IAS 38, para. 104). If the expected time pattern of economic benefits has changed, the amortisation method should be changed accordingly. Such changes should be accounted for as changes in accounting estimates under IAS 8 (see Chapter 8).

In addition to all of the above, the requirements of IAS 36, *Impairment of Assets* (discussed in Chapter 14), will apply.

Intangible assets with indefinite useful lives The essential treatment is very simple. Such assets are not depreciated (i.e. shall not be, not need not be). IAS 36 is applied and an impairment test is carried out annually and whenever there is an indication that the intangible asset may be impaired. This will lead to reductions in carrying value to the recoverable amount at the date of the impairment test.

Retirements and disposals

An intangible asset shall be derecognised:

- on disposal
- or when no future economic benefits are expected from its use or disposal.

The gain or loss arising from the derecognition of an intangible asset shall be determined as the difference between the net disposal proceeds, if any, and the carrying amount of the asset. It shall be recognised in profit or loss when the asset is derecognised (unless IAS 17, *Leases*, requires otherwise on a sale and leaseback). Gains shall not be classified as revenue.

Amortisation of an intangible asset with a finite useful life does not cease when the intangible asset is no longer used, unless the asset has been fully depreciated or is classified as held for sale (or included in a disposal group that is classified as held for sale) in accordance with IFRS 5.

Disclosure

The disclosure requirements are, as usual, long and detailed. Full details of balances, movements over the year and any revaluations or impairment losses are specified.

INTERNATIONAL DIFFERENCES

The main differences between IAS GAAP and US GAAP regarding intangibles are the following:

1 With the exception of certain software development costs, which are required to be capitalised in accordance with FAS 86, *Accounting for the Costs of*

Computer Software to be Sold, Leased or Otherwise Marketed, US GAAP (FAS 2) require all R&D costs to be immediately expensed. Under IAS GAAP, the required treatment of development costs is that they should be capitalised if certain recognition criteria are met.

2 IAS GAAP permit the restatement of intangible assets to their fair values, provided fair value can be determined by reference to an active market for that type of asset. This is not permitted by US GAAP.

3 US GAAP permit useful lives of identified intangibles to have a duration of up to 40 years, like goodwill acquired in a business combination.

UK GAAP is difficult to map onto the IASB requirements. FRS 10 goes out of its way to treat both intangible assets and purchased goodwill in the same Standard and as consistently as possible. However, research and development expenditure is regulated separately, in SSAP 13 issued long ago. SSAP 13 is notable for specifying the same six criteria as IAS 38 related to the capitalisation of development expenditure, but saying that if they are all met then the expenditure 'may' be capitalised. Such a weak politically inspired compromise will undoubtedly be removed.

European practices in this area are historically variable. The general emphasis on prudence would suggest reluctance to capitalise, for example, development expenditure. Paradoxically, however, formation expenses, which require immediate write off under IAS, are commonly capitalised and written off over five years as explicitly allowed by the Fourth European Directive.

ACCOUNTING FOR PURCHASED GOODWILL

As we discussed earlier, purchased goodwill is regulated under IAS by IFRS 3 on business combinations, not by IAS 38 on intangible assets. Nevertheless the basic issues involved in its treatment are asset/expense questions, not principles of consolidations, and it is appropriate to deal with its treatment here. As already noted, goodwill is defined (IFRS 3, Appendix A) as follows:

> Future economic benefits arising from assets that are not capable of being individually identified and separately recognised.

It could be suggested that this rather strange wording (future economic benefits *arising from* assets …) implies that goodwill is not, itself, an asset (see Activities 13.2 and 13.3).

We are now in a position to explore the formal requirements of IFRS 3 in relation to goodwill on acquisition. First, look at Activities 13.2 and 13.3.

Goodwill and IFRS 3

Goodwill in IAS GAAP is the difference between the fair value of the purchase consideration given and the aggregate fair values of the identifiable assets and liabilities of the acquiree that are recognised on acquisition, as discussed earlier. What is recognised as goodwill on acquisition is therefore a function of the recognition criteria and valuation rules applied to the identifiable assets and liabilities (and notably those in IASs 36, 37, 38 and 39). As such, it is therefore not itself an identifiable asset or liability but a residual amount. Nevertheless, IAS GAAP require it to be shown as an asset.

ACTIVITY 13.2

Does goodwill on acquisition meet the IASB's own definition of an asset?

Activity feedback

An asset (Framework, para. 49a) is a resource controlled by the entity as a result of past events and from which future economic benefits are expected to flow. There is certainly a past event and there must logically be an expectation of future economic benefits in the eyes of the management of the acquirer. But is there a 'resource controlled' by the entity? Remember that, by definition, no 'identifiable asset' is involved. The issue is a complicated theoretical one and general opinion seems to be that goodwill on acquisition is certainly not a normal asset, but is at least sufficiently asset-like to be treated as if it was one.

A variety of ways can be suggested for how goodwill on acquisition might be treated after recognition. Here are seven possible ways:

1 carry it as an asset and amortise it over its estimated useful life through the profit and loss account

2 carry it as an asset and amortise it over its estimated useful life by writing off against reserves

3 eliminate it against reserves immediately on acquisition

4 retain it in the accounts indefinitely, unless a permanent reduction in its value becomes evident, when impairment is recognised

5 charge it as an expense against profits in the period when it is acquired

6 show it as a deduction from shareholders' equity (and either amortise it or carry it indefinitely)

7 revalue it annually to incorporate later non-purchased goodwill.

ACTIVITY 13.3

Comment on each of these seven possible treatments, in relation to rational justification and usefulness.

Activity feedback

Here are some thoughts, which you may or may not completely agree with:

1 is a straightforward application of matching the acquisition 'cost' in proportion to the benefit

2 seems illogical; amortisation represents an expense and therefore should appear in the profit and loss account

3 this solves the problem as if the item had never existed. It implies that no asset exists, and that equity must face the 'loss' immediately

4 this is rational if it is accepted that purchased goodwill can be maintained, as a building can. Arguably, however, the reality is that purchased goodwill is gradually being replaced by non-purchased goodwill. It can also be suggested that the costs of maintaining the goodwill are being expensed as they occur and that to charge amortisation as well would usually be simple double counting

5 seems illogical and excessively prudent

6 also seems illogical, and potentially confusing, being essentially a misrepresentation of either 1 or 4

7 would be consistent with the trend towards fair value generally, but highly subjective (and inconsistent with legal restrictions in many countries).

Goodwill on acquisition is calculated through the following process (paras 36–37).

The acquirer shall, at the acquisition date, allocate the cost of a business combination by recognising the acquiree's identifiable assets, liabilities and contingent liabilities that satisfy the recognition criteria in paragraph 37 at their fair values at that date, except for non-current assets (or disposal groups) that are classified as held for sale in accordance with IFRS 5, *Non-current Assets Held for Sales and Discontinued Operations*, which shall be recognised at fair value less costs to sell. Any difference between the cost of the business combination and the acquirer's interest in the net fair value of the identifiable assets, liabilities and contingent liabilities so recognised shall be accounted for as goodwill.

The acquirer shall recognise separately the acquiree's identifiable assets, liabilities and contingent liabilities at the acquisition date only if they satisfy the following criteria at that date:

- in the case of an asset other than an intangible asset, it is probable that any associated future economic benefits will flow to the acquirer and its fair value can be measured reliably
- in the case of a liability other than a contingent liability, it is probable that an outflow of resources embodying economic benefits will be required to settle the obligation and its fair value can be measured reliably
- in the case of an intangible asset or a contingent liability, its fair value can be measured reliably.

The excess of cost over the net fair value of the identifiable assets is the goodwill on acquisition figure. The acquirer is required to treat such goodwill as follows (paras 51–52):

The acquirer shall, at the acquisition date:

(a) recognise goodwill acquired in a business combination as an asset; and

(b) initially measure that goodwill at its cost, being the excess of the cost of the business combination over the acquirer's interest in the net fair value of the identifiable assets, liabilities and contingent liabilities recognised in accordance with para. 36.

Goodwill acquired in a business combination represents a payment made by the acquirer in anticipation of future economic benefits from assets that are not capable of being individually identified and separately recognised. Goodwill acquired in a business combination shall not be amortised. Instead, the acquirer shall test it for impairment annually, or more frequently if events or changes in circumstances indicate that it might be impaired, in accordance with IAS 36, *Impairment of Assets*.

Note that this treatment is exactly consistent with the requirements for identifiable intangible assets with indefinite lives, as discussed earlier in relation to IAS 38.

It is, of course, possible for the calculated goodwill figure to be negative. IFRS 3 studiously avoids calling this negative goodwill, stating that if the acquirer's interest in the net fair value of the identifiable assets, liabilities and contingent liabilities recognised in accordance with para. 36, exceeds the cost of the business combination, the acquirer shall:

- reassess the identification and measurement of the acquiree's identifiable assets, liabilities and contingent liabilities and the measurement of the cost of the combination
- recognise immediately in profit or loss any excess remaining after that reassessment.

It follows that, in future, negative goodwill, under that or any other label, will not appear in IAS group balance sheets. This is a major change. Any negative goodwill brought forward under previous IASB standards is to be derecognised and transferred to retained earnings.

International developments

Many different methods have been used over the years. The previous IAS requirement was essentially our suggested method 1, with compulsory impairment reviews added on in the case of a useful life over 20 years. The current IAS requirement is essentially our method 4. US GAAP allowed a useful life of up to 40 years until recently. Method 3 was common for many years in the UK and may still be found in a number of European national systems. UK GAAP now allows, in effect, a choice between methods 1 and 4. There is a presumption that useful life will not normally exceed 20 years (requiring method 1); impairment reviews at intervals are specified. A longer useful life or an unlimited life with no annual amortisation both require annual impairment reviews. US GAAP has now moved to annual impairment reviews, with amortisation prohibited. Harmonisation is getting closer, but has not yet been reached.

SUMMARY

This chapter, following the exploration of the treatment of tangible long-term assets in Chapter 12, has looked at the treatment of similar intangible assets. We considered in detail the requirements of IAS 38, dealing with separable intangible assets, and of IFRS 3 as regards the treatment of goodwill.

EXERCISES

Suggested answers to exercises marked ✓ are to be found on the Student side of the companion website.

Suggested answers to the remaining exercises are to be found on the Instructor side of the companion website.

✓ **1** Is goodwill an asset?

2 Identifiable intangible assets should be treated, for all accounting purposes, identically with tangible assets. Discuss.

3 Outline five different ways of treating goodwill in financial statements, discussing arguments for and against each one.

4   If depreciation is done properly, impairment adjustments will not arise. Discuss.

5   CD is a manufacturing entity that runs a number of operations including a bottling plant that bottles carbonated soft drinks. CD has been developing a new bottling process that will allow the bottles to be filled and sealed more efficiently.

   The new process took a year to develop. At the start of development, CD estimated that the new process would increase output by 15% with no additional cost (other than the extra bottles and their contents). Development work commenced on 1 May 2005 and was completed on 20 April 2006. Testing at the end of the development confirmed CD's original estimates.

   CD incurred expenditure of €180 000 on the above development in 2005/06.

   CD plans to install the new process in its bottling plant and start operating the new process from 1 May 2006.

   CD's balance sheet date is 30 April.

Required:

(i)   Explain the requirements of IAS 38, *Intangible Assets* for the treatment of development costs.

(ii) Explain how CD should treat its development costs in its financial statements for the year ended 30 April 2006.

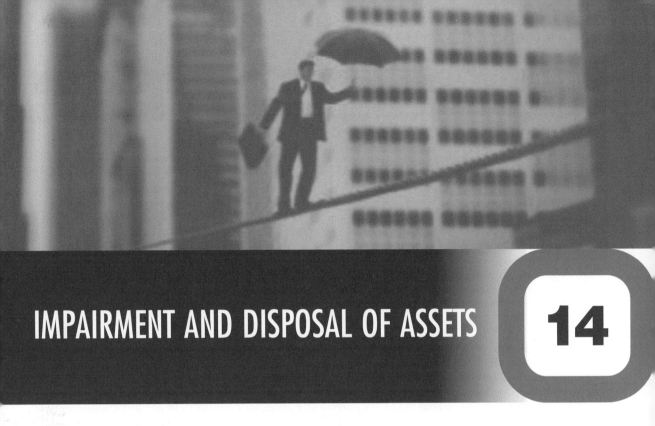

IMPAIRMENT AND DISPOSAL OF ASSETS   14

OBJECTIVES   After studying this chapter you should be able to:

- describe, apply and appraise the requirements of IAS 36 relating to impairment of assets

- explain what is meant by non-current assets held for sale

- describe how non-current assets held for sale should be recognised and measured in accordance with IFRS

- explain the purpose of issuing information on discontinuing operations, and how such information should be disclosed.

IMPAIRMENT OF ASSETS

The problem

Reference to impairment of assets has been made at a number of points in previous chapters. In very simple terms, the principle of deferring charges to future periods under the matching principle means, of course, that such deferred charges appear in an intermediate balance sheet as assets.

ACTIVITY 14.1

If there is a reasonable expectation of future revenues associated with the past expenditure being greater than the deferred expenses, does any other circumstance, such as a low current market value for the asset, lead to a need for immediate write off down to this lower figure?

Activity feedback

Prudence and the informational needs of lenders with a short-term focus might both suggest an argument for such an immediate expense charge and reduction in the balance sheet carrying value of the asset (i.e. the deferred expense). However, matching and the informational needs of investors suggest the opposite. Long-term assets should be appraised in a long-term context, it can be argued. The IASB generally takes this second argument.

Very broadly speaking, purchase transactions are recorded in accounting terms first by including the purchased item as an asset at its cost price, then by expensing the item over one or a number of accounting periods according to its usage or consumption pattern. The going concern convention supports this treatment as it explicitly assumes that there will be future operational accounting periods in which present assets can be transferred to expenses.

Strictly, this means that there is no need, at an intermediate stage in this process, to compare the temporary balance sheet number with any form of value – using the word value in its proper sense of monetary benefit to be derived. This would not be in accordance with the prudence convention, however, and would arguably be dangerously misleading to creditors and lenders. Over the years accounting has dealt with the inherent tension and conflict here in a variety of ways, all more or less ad hoc, depending on the accounting issue involved (and often depending also on the country involved).

The IASB has quite properly attempted to provide a general Standard, IAS 36, *Impairment of Assets*, to provide consistency and coherence to this whole matter.

The principle of the Standard is clear and simple. First, the carrying amount of an asset is determined in accordance with accounting principles and other relevant International Standards. Second, the 'recoverable amount' of the asset is determined as of that date, being the higher of fair value less costs to sell and the asset's value in use (to the existing entity). If the recoverable amount is lower than the carrying value as recorded, then an impairment loss must be recognised immediately, that is, the carrying value is lowered to the recoverable amount. Otherwise, no impairment loss is required. It is important to emphasise that recoverable amount is a very different concept from fair value and, for non-current assets, will often be significantly higher than fair value. IAS 36 does not require assets within its scope to be recorded at the lower of cost and market or fair value.

The question of which assets IAS 36 does apply to is rather complicated and the following section on scope should be read carefully. Unfortunately, although the principle of IAS 36 is simply stated, the IASB, perhaps influenced by American tradition, found it necessary to specify considerable operational detail in relation to its application. We examine these details later, to the extent that we consider it necessary. However, we are writing a textbook, not a manual for practitioners, and IAS 36 is very much a technical 'how to do it' Standard. It would be unhelpful to attempt to cover all this technical specification here.

A revised version of IAS 36 was effective from 31 March 2004 (not 1 April 2004). The only major changes of principle relate to impairment tests for goodwill and are linked with contemporaneous changes introduced by IFRS 3, *Business Combinations* (see Chapter 13).

However, the opportunity has been taken to amend and clarify (and make more complex) much of the detailed specification. A further more fundamental reconsideration of the whole impairment area is ongoing; any resulting changes are not likely to appear in the short term.

Scope and coverage

The essential objective of IAS 36 is to ensure that assets are not carried at a figure greater than their recoverable amount. The Standard itself says nothing about possible or normal methods of arriving at carrying value. The Standard applies whatever the underlying basis of valuation of the asset is.

The Standard begins by saying that it applies to all assets except ... and then gives a significant number of exceptions (para. 2). These are generally items that are covered in detail by other International Accounting Standards. Thus IAS 36 does not apply to:

1 inventories (see IAS 2, *Inventories*, discussed in Chapter 16)

2 assets arising from construction contracts (see IAS 11, *Construction Contracts*, discussed in Chapter 16)

3 deferred tax assets (see IAS 12, *Income Taxes*, discussed in Chapter 20)

4 assets arising from employee benefits (see IAS 19, *Employee Benefits*, discussed in Chapter 21)

5 financial assets that are included in the scope of IAS 39, *Financial Instruments: Recognition and Measurement* (see Chapter 17)

6 investment property that is measured at fair value (see IAS 40, *Investment Property*, discussed in Chapter 12)

7 biological assets related to agricultural activity that are measured at fair value less estimated point-of-sale costs (see IAS 40, *Agriculture*, website appendix)

8 deferred acquisition costs, and intangible assets, arising from an insurer's contractual rights under insurance contracts within the scope of IFRS 4, *Insurance Contracts* (see Chapter 17)

9 non-current assets (or disposal groups) classified as held for sale in accordance with IFRS 5, *Non-current Assets Held for Sale and Discontinued Operations* (see below).

In relation to point 5, it must be noted that financial assets excluded from IAS 39 are automatically excluded from the exclusion! Thus, investments in:

1 subsidiaries, as defined in IAS 27, *Consolidated Financial Statements and Accounting for Investments in Subsidiaries*

2 associates, as defined in IAS 28, *Accounting for Investments in Associates*

3 and joint ventures, as defined in IAS 31, *Financial Reporting of Interests in Joint Ventures*

are financial assets but are excluded from the scope of IAS 39. Therefore, IAS 36 applies to such investments. Note carefully that the Standard very deliberately describes itself as dealing with impairment of assets, not with impairment of non-current assets. However, it then excludes inventories and construction contracts (IAS 2 and IAS 11) and accounts receivable and cash (both covered by IAS 39). In many, if not most businesses, this will mean that all current assets are excluded from consideration under IAS 36. However, the IAS definition of current assets (discussed in Chapter 9) is more generally expressed and IAS 36 could be applicable to certain current assets in special cases.

Terminology

IAS 36 gives a number of definitions of key terms. Many of these definitions are interrelated, one term being used in the definition of another (para. 6).

An impairment loss is the amount by which the carrying amount of an asset or a cash-generating unit exceeds its recoverable amount.

Carrying amount is the amount at which an asset is recognised after deducting any accumulated depreciation (amortisation) and accumulated impairment losses thereon.

Depreciation (amortisation) is the systematic allocation of the depreciable amount of an asset over its useful life.

Depreciable amount is the cost of an asset or other amount substituted for cost in the financial statements, less its residual value.

Useful life is:

- either the period of time over which an asset is expected to be used by the entity

- or the number of production or similar units expected to be obtained from the asset by the entity.

Fair value less costs to sell is the amount obtainable from the sale of an asset or cash-generating unit in an arm's-length transaction between knowledgeable, willing parties, less the costs of disposal.

Costs of disposal are incremental costs directly attributable to the disposal of an asset or cash-generating unit, excluding finance costs and income tax expense.

Value in use is the present value of the future cash flows expected to be derived from an asset or cash-generating unit.

The *agreement date* for a business combination is the date that a substantive agreement between the combining parties is reached and, in the case of publicly listed entities, announced to the public. In the case of a hostile takeover, the earliest date that a substantive agreement between the combining parties is reached is the date that a sufficient number of the acquiree's owners have accepted the acquirer's offer for the acquirer to obtain control of the acquiree.

An *active market* is a market in which all the following conditions exist:

- the items traded within the market are homogeneous

- willing buyers and sellers can normally be found at any time

- prices are available to the public.

Most of these terms should be fairly easy to understand, but they can be difficult to calculate. Two further definitions are given, as follows:

A *cash-generating unit* is the smallest identifiable group of assets that generates cash inflows that are largely independent of the cash inflows from other assets or groups of assets.

Corporate assets are assets other than goodwill that contribute to the future cash flows of both the cash-generating unit under review and other cash-generating units.

When several assets are interrelated in their usage in a way which makes it impossible meaningfully to attribute cash inflows to each individual asset, they are to be considered together as a single cash-generating unit as just defined. In effect, therefore, a cash-generating unit is 'an asset' for the purposes of IAS 36. Corporate assets do not generate their own cash flows, but, as described earlier, are necessary for the generation of cash flows by other units. Special considerations, discussed below, apply to such assets.

Identifying an asset that may be impaired

It is important to be clear that IAS 36 does not require that the recoverable amount of all assets must be determined annually in order to test for impairment. Rather, it postulates a two-stage process. The first stage is to assess, at each balance sheet date, whether there is any indication that an asset may be impaired. If any such indication exists, the entity should estimate the recoverable amount of the asset.

These are two different formal requirements. The first relates to all assets (para. 9). This is that an entity should assess at each reporting date whether there is any indication that an asset may be impaired. If such an indication exists, the entity should estimate the recoverable amount of the asset. The second is more stringent, but relates only to certain intangible assets. This is that (para. 10), irrespective of whether there is any indication of impairment, an entity shall also:

- test an intangible asset with an indefinite useful life or an intangible asset not yet available for use for impairment annually by comparing its carrying amount with its recoverable amount; this impairment test may be performed at any time during an annual period, provided it is performed at the same time every year; different intangible assets may be tested for impairment at different times, however, if such an intangible asset was initially recognised during the current annual period, that intangible asset shall be tested for impairment before the end of the current annual period
- test goodwill acquired in a business combination for impairment annually in accordance with paras 80–99, as described later.

The concept of materiality applies to the general requirement in para. 9, but not to the specific requirement of para. 10, which, in its defined circumstances, is absolute.

Only if an indication of likely impairment exists (see Activity 14.2) do we need, in the general case, to move on to the second stage and actually measure the recoverable amount.

ACTIVITY 14.2

Suggest situations that may indicate that an asset has been impaired.

Activity feedback
IAS 36 suggests that, when assessing whether there is any indication that an asset may be impaired, an entity should consider, *as a minimum*, the following indications (para. 12):

External sources of information:

1 During the period, an asset's market value has declined significantly more than would be expected as a result of the passage of time or normal use.

2 Significant changes with an adverse effect on the entity have taken place during the period or will take place in the near future in the technological, market, economic or legal environment in which the entity operates or in the market to which an asset is dedicated.

3 Market interest rates or other market rates of return on investments have increased during the period and those increases are likely to affect the discount rate used in calculating an asset's value

in use and decrease the asset's recoverable amount materially.

4 The carrying amount of the net assets of the reporting entity is more than its market capitalisation.

Internal sources of information:

1 Evidence is available of obsolescence or physical damage of an asset.

2 Significant changes with an adverse effect on the entity have taken place during the period or are expected to take place in the near future in the extent to which, or manner in which, an asset is used or is expected to be used. These changes include the asset becoming idle, plans to discontinue or restructure the operation to which an asset belongs, plans to dispose of an asset before the previously expected date and reassessing the useful life of an asset as finite rather than indefinite.

3 Evidence is available from internal reporting that indicates that the economic performance of an asset is, or will be, worse than expected.

Several of these considerations require some comment. Items 1 and 2 (under external sources of information) are fairly obviously indicators of a possible fall in recoverable amount, relating directly to net selling price and value in use, respectively. In neither case, however, does a low or lower recoverable amount *necessarily* follow, as recoverable amount is the *higher* of fair value less costs to sell and value in use. The relevance of item 3 is that value in use, as defined earlier, is the *present value* of future cash flows. Discounting is thus central to the calculation or recoverable amount and an increase in discount rate may significantly reduce the value in use of an asset, as defined, if the new discount rate is regarded as relevant in the long term. Item 4, again, is a fairly obvious indicator that something is widely perceived as being wrong somewhere, although not, of course, that every, or any one particular, asset is impaired.

Measurement of recoverable amount

IAS 36 devotes no fewer than 39 paragraphs to the measurement of recoverable amount, not including another 42 paragraphs on cash-generating units, and sets out detailed computations. Nevertheless, a number of simplifications may be justified. If either fair value less costs to sell or value in use exceeds the asset's carrying amount, then the other figure need not be determined at all. If fair value less costs to sell is unobtainable even by reliable estimate, because of the absence of an active market, then the recoverable amount can be taken as equal to value in use. Conversely, the recoverable amount may be taken or given by fair value less costs to sell if the nature of the asset or the nature of its usage by entity is such that value in use is unlikely to differ materially from fair value less costs to sell, which will usually be the case with active and competitive factor markers (i.e. in developed economies).

Fair value less costs to sell This will often be straightforward to determine, being fair value less any incremental costs that would be directly attributable to the disposal of the asset. Fair value may need to be estimated by reference to comparable transactions. Costs of disposal, other than those that have already been recognised as liabilities, are deducted in determining net selling price. Examples of such costs are legal costs, stamp duty and similar transaction taxes, costs of removing the asset and direct incremental costs to bring an asset into condition for its sale. However, termination benefits (as defined in IAS 19, *Employee Benefits*; see Chapter 21) and costs associated with reducing or reorganising a business after the disposal of an asset are not direct incremental costs to dispose of the asset (see IAS 37, *Provisions, Contingent Liabilities and Contingent Assets*, discussed in Chapter 19).

Value in use Estimating the value in use in a realistic way is often likely to be rather more difficult. It involves the following steps (para. 31):

1 estimating the future cash inflows and outflows to be derived from continuing use of the asset and from its ultimate disposal

2 applying the appropriate discount rate to these future cash flows.

Estimates of future cash flows should include:

1 projections of cash inflows from the continuing use of the asset, net of projections of cash outflows that are necessarily incurred to generate the cash inflows (including cash outflows to prepare the asset for use) and that can be

directly attributed, or allocated on a reasonable and consistent basis, to the asset

2 net cash flows, if any, to be received (or paid) for the disposal of the asset at the end of its useful life.

Future cash flows should be estimated for the asset in its current condition. It follows that estimates of future cash flows should not include estimated future cash inflows or outflows that are expected to arise from:

1 a future restructuring to which an entity is not yet committed

2 or future (uncommitted) capital expenditure that will improve or enhance the asset in excess of its originally assessed standard of performance.

The issue of when an entity is 'committed to a future restructuring' is discussed in IAS 37, *Provisions, Contingent Liabilities and Contingent Assets* (see Chapter 19). If it is so committed, then obviously the related cash inflows and outflows **are** to be included.

The estimate of net cash flows to be received (or paid) for the disposal of an asset at the end of its useful life is determined in a similar way to an asset's fair value less costs to sell, except that, in estimating those net cash flows:

1 an entity uses prices prevailing at the date of the estimate for similar assets that have reached the end of their useful life and that have operated under conditions similar to those in which the asset will be used

2 those prices are adjusted for the effect of both future price increases due to general inflation and specific future price increases (decreases). However, if estimates of future cash flows from the asset's continuing use and the discount rate exclude the effect of general inflation, this effect is also excluded from the estimate of net cash flows on disposal.

Discount rate The key points can be very briefly stated. The discount rate (or rates) should be a pre-tax rate (or rates) that reflect(s) current market assessments of the time value of money and risks specific to the asset (para. 55). The discount rate(s) should not reflect risks for which future cash flow estimates have been adjusted, as this would involve double counting. The standard rightly makes no attempt to argue that this process is other than subjective. It does try to suggest a suitable thought process (Appendix A).

As a starting point, the entity may take into account the following rates:

1 the entity's weighted average cost of capital determined using techniques such as the capital asset pricing model

2 the entity's incremental borrowing rate

3 other market borrowing rates.

These rates are adjusted:

1 to reflect the way that the market would assess the specific risks associated with the projected cash flows

2 to exclude risks that are not relevant to the projected cash flows.

Consideration is given to such risks as country risk, currency risk, price risk and cash flow risk. This makes it clear, for example, that the appropriate discount rate may be different for different types of asset or different circumstances, within the same entity. What is crucial, above all else except basic rationality and common sense, is that the chosen method should be applied consistently.

Recognition and measurement of impairment losses

After all the subjectivity, complexity, and detail of earlier sections of IAS 36 it is easy to lose sight of the importance of those paragraphs dealing with recognition and measurement of impairment losses. This is the point and purpose of the entire Standard. The Standard requires that if, and only if, the recoverable amount of an asset is less than its carrying amount, the carrying amount of the asset should be reduced to its recoverable amount. That reduction is an impairment loss (para. 59).

An impairment loss should be recognised immediately as an expense in the income statement, unless the asset is carried at revalued amount under another Standard (for example, under IAS 16, *Property, Plant and Equipment* (see Chapter 12)). Any impairment loss of a revalued asset should be treated as a revaluation decrease under the other Standard.

In the general case, if the estimated impairment loss is greater than the carrying value of the relevant asset, the asset is simply reduced to nil, with a corresponding expense. Only if so required by another Standard should a liability be recognised.

Common sense indicates, but the Standard feels it necessary to state, that after the impairment loss has been recognised, the depreciation charge for the asset should be adjusted to allocate the revised carrying amount, net of any expected residual value, on a systematic basis over its remaining useful life.

This is all very well when 'an asset' means 'an asset'. But when 'an asset' means 'a cash-generating unit', as discussed earlier, the treatment is not so easy in practice – as the Standard's need for over 40 paragraphs on the topic would suggest. If it is not possible to estimate the recoverable amount of an individual asset, an entity should determine the recoverable amount of the cash-generating unit to which the asset belongs (the asset's cash-generating unit) (para. 66). Identification of an asset's cash-generating unit involves judgement. If the recoverable amount cannot be determined for an individual asset, an entity identifies the lowest aggregation of assets that generate largely independent cash inflows from continuing use.

In other words, an asset's cash-generating unit is the smallest group of assets that includes the asset and that generates cash inflows from continuing use that are largely independent of the cash inflows from other assets or groups of assets.

Perhaps inevitably, the standard resorts to a series of examples in order to try and indicate more precisely how the analysis of any particular situation should proceed. Common sense and economic substance are perhaps the key watchwords. Thus if an active market exists for the output produced by an asset or a group of assets, this asset or group of assets should be identified as a cash-generating unit, even if some or all of the output is used internally. If this is the case, management's best estimate of future market prices for the output should be used (para. 70):

1 in determining the value in use of this cash-generating unit, when estimating the future cash inflows that relate to the internal use of the output

2 in determining the value in use of other cash-generating units of the reporting entity, when estimating the future cash outflows that relate to the internal use of the output.

As an indicative illustration, the example given by IAS 36 in relation to this specification follows.

ILLUSTRATION

A significant raw material used for plant Y's final production is an intermediate product bought from plant X of the same entity. X's products are sold to Y at a transfer price that passes all margins to X. 80 per cent of Y's final production is sold to customers outside the reporting entity. 60% of X's final production is sold to Y and the remaining 40% is sold to customers outside the reporting entity.

For each of the following cases, what are the cash-generating units for X and Y?

Case 1: X could sell the products it sells to Y in an active market. Internal transfer prices are higher than market prices.

Case 2: There is no active market for the products X sells to Y.

Case 1

X could sell its products on an active market and so generate cash inflows that would be largely independent of the cash inflows from Y. Therefore, it is likely that X is a separate cash-generating unit, although part of its production is used by Y.

It is likely that Y is also a separate cash-generating unit. Y sells 80% of its products to customers outside the reporting entity. Therefore, its cash inflows can be considered to be largely independent.

Internal transfer prices do not reflect market prices for X's output. Therefore, in determining value in use of both X and Y, the entity adjusts financial budgets/forecasts to reflect management's best estimate of future arm's length market prices for those of X's products that are used internally (see para. 70 of IAS 36).

Case 2

It is likely that the recoverable amount of each plant cannot be assessed independently from the recoverable amount of the other plant because:

1 The majority of X's production is used internally and could not be sold in an active market. So, cash inflows of X depend on demand for Y's products. Therefore, X cannot be considered to generate cash inflows that are largely independent from those of Y.

2 The two plants are managed together.

As a consequence, it is likely that X and Y together is the smallest group of assets that generates cash inflows from continuing use that are largely independent.

Once the cash-generating unit has been defined, the next step is to determine and compare the recoverable amount and carrying amount of that unit. It should go without saying, but the Standard reminds us, that the carrying amount of a cash-generating unit should be determined consistently with the way the recoverable amount of the cash-generating unit is determined.

This means, for example, that the carrying amount of a cash-generating unit includes the carrying amount of only those assets that can be attributed directly or allocated on a reasonable and consistent basis to the cash-generating unit and that will generate the future cash inflows estimated in determining the cash-generating unit's value in use and does not include the carrying amount of any recognised liability, unless the recoverable amount of the cash-generating unit cannot be determined without consideration of this liability. However, the Standard notes that in practice the recoverable amount of a cash-generating unit may be considered either including or excluding assets or liabilities that are not part of the cash-generating unit – for example a net selling price of a business segment might be determined on the assumption that either the vendor or the purchaser accepts certain obligations. Consistency requires that if the obligation is included in the evaluation of recoverable amount, it is the net carrying value with which this recoverable amount must be compared in determining whether an impairment loss exists.

There are two problems that need special consideration, namely goodwill and corporate assets (as already defined). In essence these two problems are related.

Goodwill, by definition, does not generate cash flows independently from other assets or groups of assets and, therefore, the recoverable amount of goodwill as an individual asset cannot be determined. As a consequence, if there is an indication that goodwill may be impaired, the recoverable amount is determined for the cash-generating unit to which the goodwill belongs. This amount is then compared to the carrying amount of this cash-generating unit and any impairment loss is recognised, attributed first to the goodwill as discussed later.

It is particularly in relation to the treatment of possible impairment of goodwill that the new version of IAS 36 has been made much more detailed (and therefore, at least apparently, more complex). The previous version of IAS 36 required goodwill acquired in a business combination to be tested for impairment as part of impairment testing of the cash-generating unit(s) to which it related. It employed a 'bottom-up/top-down' approach under which the goodwill was, in effect, tested for impairment by allocating its carrying amount to each cash-generating unit or smallest group of cash-generating units to which a portion of that carrying amount could be allocated on a reasonable and consistent basis. The Standard now similarly requires goodwill acquired in a business combination to be tested for impairment as part of impairment testing the cash-generating unit(s) to which it relates. However, IAS 36 now clarifies that:

1 The goodwill should, from the acquisition date, be allocated to each of the acquirer's cash-generating units, or groups of cash-generating units, that are expected to benefit from the synergies of the business combination, irrespective of whether other assets or liabilities of the acquiree are assigned to those units or groups of units.

2 Each unit or group of units to which the goodwill is allocated should:

   (i) represent the lowest level within the entity at which the goodwill is monitored for internal management purposes

   (ii) not be larger than a segment based on either the entity's primary or the entity's secondary reporting format determined in accordance with IAS 14, *Segment Reporting*.

3 If the initial allocation of goodwill acquired in a business combination cannot be completed before the end of the annual period in which the business combination occurs, that initial allocation should be completed before the end of the annual period beginning after the acquisition date.

4 When an entity disposes of an operation within a cash-generating unit (group of units) to which goodwill has been allocated, the goodwill associated with that operation should be:

   (i) included in the carrying amount of the operation when determining the gain or loss on disposal

   (ii) measured on the basis of the relative values of the operation disposed of and the portion of the cash-generating unit (group of units) retained, unless the entity can demonstrate that some other method better reflects the goodwill associated with the operation disposed of.

5 When an entity reorganises its reporting structure in a manner that changes the composition of cash-generating units (groups of units) to which goodwill has been allocated, the goodwill should be reallocated to the units (groups of units) affected. This reallocation should be performed using a relative value approach similar to that used when an entity disposes of an operation within a cash-generating unit (group of units), unless the entity can demonstrate that some other method better reflects the goodwill associated with the reorganised units (groups of units).

By way of example, to illustrate point 4, suppose that an entity sells for €100 an operation that was part of a cash-generating unit to which goodwill has been allocated. The goodwill allocated to the unit cannot be identified or associated with an asset group at a level lower than that unit, except arbitrarily. The recoverable amount of the portion of the cash-generating unit retained is €300. Because the goodwill allocated to the cash-generating unit cannot be non-arbitrarily identified or associated with an asset group at a level lower than that unit, the goodwill associated with the operation disposed of is measured on the basis of the relative values of the operation disposed of and the portion of the unit retained. Therefore 25% of the goodwill allocated to the cash-generating unit is included in the carrying amount of the operation that is sold and 75% is left in the retained portion.

The Standard permits (not requires) the annual impairment test for a cash-generating unit (group of units) to which the goodwill has been allocated to be performed at any time during an annual reporting period, provided that the test is performed at the same time every year and different cash-generating units (groups of units) are tested for impairment at different times. However, if some of the goodwill allocated to a cash-generating unit (group of units) was acquired in a business combination during the current annual period, the Standard requires that unit (group of units) to be tested for impairment before the end of the current period.

The Standard also permits the most recent detailed calculation made in a preceding period of the recoverable amount of a cash-generating unit (group of units) to which goodwill has been allocated to be used in the impairment test for that unit (group of units) in the current period, provided specified criteria are met, as follows:

- the assets and liabilities making up the unit have not changed significantly since the most recent recoverable amount calculation

- the most recent recoverable amount calculation resulted in an amount that exceeded the carrying amount of the unit by a substantial margin

- based on an analysis of events that have occurred and circumstances that have changed since the most recent recoverable amount calculation, the likelihood that a current recoverable amount determination would be less than the current carrying amount of the unit is remote.

Similarly, corporate assets, also by definition, do not generate independent cash flows and, again, recoverable amount is determined by reference to the cash-generating unit to which the corporate asset belongs. In testing a cash-generating unit for impairment, an entity shall identify all the corporate assets that relate to the cash-generating unit under review. If a portion of the carrying amount of a corporate asset can be allocated on a reasonable and consistent basis to that unit, the entity shall compare the carrying amount of the unit, including the portion of the carrying amount of the corporate asset allocated to the unit, with its recoverable amount. Any impairment loss shall be recognised in accordance with para. 104, discussed later. If a portion cannot be allocated on a reasonable and consistent basis to that unit, the entity shall:

1 compare the carrying amount of the unit, excluding the corporate asset, with its recoverable amount and recognise any impairment loss in accordance with para. 104

2 identify the smallest group of cash-generating units that includes the cash-generating unit under review and to which a portion of the carrying amount of the corporate asset can be allocated in a reasonable and consistent basis

3 compare the carrying amount of that group of cash-generating units, including the portion of the carrying amount of the corporate asset allocated to that group of units, with the recoverable amount of the group of units. Any impairment loss shall be recognised in accordance with para. 104.

An amazingly lengthy illustrative example (No. 8) is given in an accompaniment to the Standard.

Once the impairment loss for a cash-generating unit has been determined, it has to be deducted from the carrying amounts of specific assets that are part of that unit, in some systematic manner. IAS 36 specifies its requirements with precision (paras 104 and 105).

An impairment loss should be recognised for a cash-generating unit if, and only if, its recoverable amount is less than its carrying amount. The impairment loss should be allocated to reduce the carrying amount of the assets of the unit in the following order:

1 first, to goodwill allocated to the cash-generating unit (if any)

2 then, to the other assets of the unit on a pro rata basis based on the carrying amount of each asset in the unit.

In allocating an impairment loss the carrying amount of an asset should not be reduced below the *highest* of:

1 its fair value less costs to sell (if determinable)

2 its value in use (if determinable)

3 zero.

The amount of the impairment loss that would otherwise have been allocated to the asset should be allocated to the other assets of the unit on a pro rata basis. A liability should be recognised for any remaining amount of an impairment loss for a cash-generating unit, if, and only if, that is required by other International Accounting Standards.

The effect of this is, first, to eliminate goodwill, but then to ensure that the carrying amount of any individual asset is not reduced so far as to produce a figure not economically relevant to that asset.

Reversal of an impairment loss The whole point, in a sense, of impairment losses is that they represent unusual or 'extra' reductions in asset numbers (carrying values) as used in financial statements. If regular depreciation is a downward slope, then an impairment loss is a step downward. The basic cause of this downward step is something unusual and/or extraneous to the asset and its regular accounting treatment. It follows that this cause, this unusual or extraneous factor, may be removed over time. In such a situation, as explained and defined in IAS 36, the original impairment loss must be reversed; *except* for goodwill.

As with impairment losses, we again have a two-stage process. An entity first checks to see whether there is any *indication* that an impairment loss recognised in earlier years may have decreased significantly. IAS 36 spells out a series of likely indicators (para. 111) that mirror those discussed earlier under 'identifying an asset that may be impaired'.

The formal requirement for reversing impairment losses for an asset other than goodwill (para. 114) is that an impairment loss recognised for an asset in prior years must be reversed if, and only if, there has been a change in the estimates used to determine the asset's recoverable amount since the last impairment loss was recognised. If this is the case, the carrying amount of the asset should be increased to its recoverable amount. That increase is a reversal of an impairment loss. It is important to note that an asset's value in use may become greater than the asset's carrying amount simply because the present value of future cash inflows increases as they become closer. However, the service potential of the asset has not increased. Therefore, such an impairment loss is not reversed, even if the recoverable amount of the asset becomes higher than its carrying amount.

The reversal of an impairment loss should in no circumstances increase the carrying value of an asset above what it would have been at this balance sheet date if no impairment loss had been recognised in prior years. This means, in particular, that the carrying value of assets subject to depreciation cannot be increased above the figure which the pre-impairment depreciation policy applied to the pre-impairment recoverable amount would have given at this balance sheet date, that is, the amount of the reversal will be less than the amount of the original impairment. The new carrying value forms the basis for a systematic depreciation policy to allocate the carrying value, less estimated residual value if any, over the remaining useful life.

A reversal of an impairment loss for an asset as above should be recognised as income immediately in the income statement, unless the asset is carried at revalued amount under another International Accounting Standard (for example, under the allowed alternative treatment in IAS 16, *Property, Plant and Equipment* (see Chapter 12)). Any reversal of an impairment loss on a revalued asset should be treated as a revaluation increase under that other Standard.

A reversal of an impairment loss for a cash-generating unit should be allocated to increase the carrying amount of the assets of the unit on a pro rata basis based on the carrying amount of each asset in the unit and then to goodwill allocated to the cash-generating unit.

In allocating a reversal of an impairment loss for a cash-generating unit, the carrying amount of an asset should not be increased above the lower of:

1 the recoverable amount (if determinable)

2 the carrying amount that would have been determined (net of amortisation or depreciation) had no impairment loss been recognised for the asset in prior years.

The amount of the reversal of the impairment loss that would otherwise have been allocated to the asset should be allocated to the other assets of the unit, except for goodwill, on a pro rata basis.

The treatment of a reversal of an impairment loss for goodwill has changed significantly in the new version of IAS 36 (i.e. with effect from 31 March 2004) as compared with the earlier version. The previous version of IAS 36 required an impairment loss recognised for goodwill in a previous period to be reversed when the impairment loss was caused by a specific external event of an exceptional nature that was not expected to recur and subsequent external events have occurred that reverse the effect of that event. The Standard now completely prohibits the recognition of reversals of impairment losses for goodwill.

The rationale for prohibiting the reversal of impairment losses for goodwill is presented by the IASB as follows. The key point is that IAS 38, *Intangible Assets* (see Chapter 13) prohibits the recognition of internally generated goodwill. This prohibition is theoretically debatable, but is undoubtedly widely supported, and is consistent with national laws in many countries including the whole of the EU, following the Fourth Directive.

Given this prohibition, there is still no *theoretical* problem in arguing, supported by analogy with other assets, that *previously purchased* goodwill that has been subsequently impaired because of a circumstance now reversed should have the impairment loss reversed. However, there is a *practical* problem in distinguishing, numerically as well as conceptually, between a reversal of a previous impairment to previously purchased goodwill, on the one hand, and the appearance of new internally generated goodwill, which cannot be recognised, on the other. It is because of this practical impossibility, and the resulting 'danger' of effectively capitalising internally generated goodwill that the change to an outright prohibition of the recognition of a reversal of an impairment loss for goodwill has been introduced.

The IASB notes that internally generated goodwill may in fact be involved at an earlier stage in the whole impairment process, in that purchased goodwill may not be impaired in the first place because its recoverable amount is kept up through the creation of new goodwill to replace the old, but also notes that, again on purely practical grounds, such a position cannot be numerically demonstrated and therefore cannot be prevented.

Disclosure

The disclosure requirements of IAS 36, like much else in the Standard, are extensive. They are also quite straightforward, requiring detailed numerical, explanatory and background information.

NON-CURRENT ASSETS HELD FOR SALE AND DISCONTINUED OPERATIONS

The structure or dimension of most companies changes over the years. On the one hand, companies can grow through acquisitions or/and organic growth. On the other hand, companies might also discontinue activities and as a result may decrease in size. If a relatively large component of the entity is discontinued then substantial financial disclosure about these activities which are discontinued is required.

It is intuitively likely that assets associated with discontinued operations, or with operations that are approaching a discontinued status, are likely to suffer impairment, and it seems logical to bring such assets, and the IAS 36 impairment Standard, into proximity. Nevertheless, they are technically separate issues, and need to be carefully distinguished when considering the detail.

These requirements are part of IFRS 5, *Non-current Assets Held for Sale and Discontinued Operations*. IFRS 5, which was issued in spring 2004, is one of the first Standards that is a result of the IASB's convergence project. IFRS 5 is meant to close the gap between, on the one hand, FASB Statement No. 144, *Accounting for the Impairment or Disposal of Long-lived Assets* (SFAS 144), which was issued in 2001 and, on the other hand, the recognition and valuation rules for those assets under IAS/IFRS. SFAS 144 addresses three areas:

1 impairment of long-lived assets to be held and used

2 classification, measurement and presentation of assets held for sale

3 classification and presentation of discontinued operations.

IFRS 5 only deals with the issues mentioned in (2) and (3). With regard to the impairment of long-lived assets to be held and used, the existing differences between the FASB and the IASB were not solved. The difference between US GAAP and IAS/IFRS is often called a difference between rules-based versus principles-based accounting standards. If one considers IFRS 5, which is a product of the convergence project, one will notice that the criteria for a non-current asset to be defined as 'held for sale' are rather detailed. It is highly likely that the convergence project might move the IAS/IFRS standards away from a purely principles-based accounting system and drive it towards a more rules-based system. Although a substantial convergence is reached for these recognition and measurement items (namely non-current assets held for sale and discontinued operations) differences with SFAS 144 still exist. First, we will present the treatment of non-current assets held for sale under IFRS 5 and, second, we will focus on the information to be reported in relation to discontinuing operations.

Non-current assets held for sale

Definition IFRS 5 presents the definition, the recognition and measurement of non-current assets held for sale. Non-current assets are defined as assets that do not meet the criteria of a current asset. The definition of a current asset is found in IAS 1, para. 66 and is as follows:

An asset shall be classified as current when it satisfies any of the following criteria:

(a) it is expected to be realised in, or is intended for sale or consumption in, the entity's normal operating cycle;

(b) it is held primarily for the purpose of being traded;

(c) it is expected to be realised within twelve months after the balance sheet date; or

(d) it is cash or the cash equivalent (as defined in IAS 7, *Cash Flow Statements*) unless it is restricted from being exchanged or used to settle a liability for at least 12 months after the balance sheet date.

All other assets are classified as non-current assets. So non-current assets include tangible, intangible and financial assets of a long-term nature. IFRS 5 not only considers individual non-current assets, but it also prescribes the definition, the recognition and the valuation rules for disposal groups. In these circumstances, a common example would be the disposal of a subsidiary. The standard observes that an entity will dispose of a group of assets, possibly with some directly associated liabilities, together in a single transaction (para. 4). The disposal group might include goodwill acquired in a business combination if the group is a cash-generating unit to which goodwill has been allocated or if it is an operation within a cash-generating unit as defined in Appendix A of IFRS 5. In this respect a disposal group can be a group of cash-generating units, a single cash-generating unit or part of a cash-generating unit.

IFRS 5 states explicitly that the rules of measurement and recognition stipulated in IFRS 5 do not apply to the following assets since they are covered by other Standards: deferred tax assets, assets arising from employee benefits, financial assets within the scope of IAS 39, non-current assets that are accounted for in accordance with the fair value model in IAS 40, *Investment Property*, non-current assets that are measured at fair value less estimated point-of-sale costs in accordance with IAS 41,

Agriculture, and contractual rights under insurance contracts as defined in IFRS 4, *Insurance Contracts*.

Essential to the definition of non-current assets held for sale is that the carrying amount of the assets will be recovered principally through sale rather than continuing use in the business (para. 6). Besides these general definitions on the concept of non-current assets held for sale IFRS 5 goes further into detail by providing more characteristics that need to be fulfilled before a non-current asset can be classified as held for sale. These characteristics are laid down (in paras 7–14) and have a more rules-based character.

With regard to the interpretation of 'held for sale' we summarise the main items of paras 7–14 here.

For an asset (or disposal group) to be classified as held for sale:

- it must be available for immediate sale in its present condition, subject only to terms that are usual and customary for sales of such assets (or disposal groups)

- its sale must be highly probable, the appropriate level of management must be committed to a plan to sell the asset (or disposal group), and an active programme to locate a buyer and complete the plan must have been initiated

- the sale should be expected to qualify for recognition as a completed sale within one year from the date of classification (exception is permitted if the delay is caused by events or circumstances beyond the entity's control and there is sufficient evidence that the entity remains committed to its plan to sell the asset (or disposal group)

- it must genuinely be sold, not abandoned. The sale transactions, referred to (in paras 7–14) include exchanges of non-current assets for other non-current assets when the exchange has commercial substance in accordance with IAS 16.

Measurement of non-current assets and disposal groups held for sale

Measurement on initial classification as held for sale IFRS 5 requires that immediately before the initial classification of an asset (or disposal group) as held for sale, the carrying amount of the asset (or all the assets and liabilities in the group) should be measured in accordance with applicable IFRSs. In other words, an entity should apply its usual accounting policies up until the criteria for classification as held for sale are met.

Thereafter a non-current asset (or disposal group) classified as held for sale should be measured at the lower of its carrying amount and fair value less costs to sell. According to IFRS 5 the fair value is defined as 'the amount for which an asset could be exchanged, or a liability settled, between knowledgeable, willing parties in an arm's-length transaction'. Costs to sell are defined as 'the incremental costs directly attributable to the disposal of an asset (or disposal group), excluding finance costs and income tax expense'. When the sale is expected to occur beyond one year, the costs to sell should be measured at their present value. Any increase in the present value of the costs to sell that arises from the passage of time should be presented in profit or loss as a financing cost. There is no similar requirement to present that element of an increase in fair value that also relates to just the passage of time as finance income.

For the disposal groups, the standard adopts a portfolio approach. It requires that if a non-current asset within the scope of its measurement requirements is part of a disposal group, the measurement requirements should apply to the group as a whole, so that the group is measured at the lower of its carrying amount and fair value less costs to sell. It will still be necessary to apportion any write down to the underlying assets of the disposal group, but no element is apportioned to items outside the scope of the Standard's measurement provisions.

If a newly acquired asset (or disposal group) meets the criteria to be classified as held for sale (which are subtly different for assets acquired exclusively with a view to subsequent disposal), applying the above requirements will result in the asset (or disposal group) being measured on initial recognition at the lower of its carrying amount had it not been so classified (for example, cost) and fair value less costs to sell. This means that, if the asset (or disposal group) is acquired as part of a business combination, it will be measured at fair value less costs to sell.

While a non-current asset is classified as held for sale or while it is part of a disposal group classified as held for sale it should not be depreciated or amortised. Interest and other expenses attributable to the liabilities of a disposal group classified as held for sale should continue to be recognised.

On subsequent remeasurement of a disposal group, the standard requires that the carrying amounts of any assets and liabilities that are not within the scope of its measurement requirements, be remeasured in accordance with applicable IFRSs before the fair value less costs to sell of the disposal group is remeasured.

Recognition of impairment losses and reversals The requirement to measure a non-current asset or disposal group held for sale at the lower of carrying amount less costs to sell may give rise to a write down in value (impairment loss) and possibly its subsequent reversal. As noted earlier, the first step is to account for any items within the scope of the Standard in the normal way. After that, any excess of carrying value over fair value less costs to sell should be recognised as an impairment.

Any subsequent increase in fair value less costs to sell of an asset up to the cumulative impairment loss previously recognised either in accordance with IFRS 5 or in accordance with IAS 36, *Impairment of Assets*, should be recognised as a gain. In the case of a disposal group, any subsequent increase in fair value less costs to sell should be recognised:

- to the extent that it has not been recognised under another Standard in relation to those assets outside the scope of IFRS 5's measurement requirements
- but not in excess of the cumulative amount of losses previously recognised under IFRS 5 or before that under IAS 36 in respect of the non-current assets in the group that are within the scope of the measurement rule of IFRS 5.

Any impairment loss (or any subsequent gain) recognised for a disposal group should be allocated to the non-current assets in the group that are within the scope of the measurement requirements of IFRS 5. The order allocation should be:

- first, to reduce the carrying amount of any goodwill in the group
- then, to the other assets of the group pro rata on the basis of the carrying amount of each asset in the group.

When assets meet the criteria to be classified as held for sale they have to be presented separately on the balance sheet. In the notes disclosures have to be made in relation to the facts and circumstances of the sale and the gains or losses recognised after the classification of the non-current assets as 'held for sale'. If assets are no longer used in the operational activities of the firm, they will no longer generate revenues, expenditures and cash. Information on the impact of the disappearance of these items should be presented as information on discontinued operations.

Discontinued operations

IFRS 5 deals also with the presentation of information on discontinued operations. This type of information disclosure had been regulated already, namely under the superseded IAS 35. IFRS 5 requires the presentation of a single amount on the face of the income statement relating to discontinued operations, with further analysis either on the face of the income statement or in the notes. (See Activity 14.3.)

ACTIVITY 14.3

Why do you think financial information about discontinuing operations should be provided to the external user of the financial statements?

Activity feedback

A discontinuing operation is a relatively large component of an entity that is either being disposed of completely or substantially or is being terminated through abandonment or piecemeal sale. The effects of such discontinuation are likely to be significant both in their own right and in changing the future results of the remaining components of the entity.

Distinguishing between the financial impact of the discontinuing and the continuing operations on the financial situation of an entity will improve the ability of investors,

creditors and other users of financial statements to make projections of the entity's cash flows, earnings generating capacity and financial position.

In order to be useful for decision purposes, the results of an entity need to be presented in a manner that will satisfy the two following objectives. First, the activities and results of the year under review must be reported fully and clearly. Second, readers of the financial statements should be able to understand the implications of the current period results for future periods. This relates to the relevance of accounting information. So the objective of IFRS 5 is to establish a basis for segregating information about a major operation that an entity is discontinuing from information about its continuing operations and to specify minimum disclosures about a discontinuing operation.

Definition of a discontinued operation IFRS 5 defines a discontinued operation as 'a component of an entity that either has been disposed of, or is classified as held for sale, and:

(a) represents a separate major line of business or geographical area of operations

(b) is part of a single co-ordinated plan to dispose of a separate major line of business or geographical area of operations, or

(c) is a subsidiary acquired exclusively with a view to resale.'

For the purposes of this definition, a 'component of an entity' is also defined by the Standard as comprising 'operations and cash flows that can be clearly distinguished, operationally and for financial reporting purposes, from the rest of the entity'. In other words, a component of an entity will have been a cash-generating unit or a group of cash-generating units while being held for use.

Business entities frequently close facilities, abandon products or even product lines and change the size of their workforce in response to market forces. Those kinds of termination do not qualify as discontinuing operations but they can occur in connection with a discontinuing operation. A list of such activities which do not qualify as discontinuing operations is presented below:

- gradual or evolutionary phasing out of a product line or class of service
- discontinuing, even if relatively abruptly, several products within an ongoing line of business
- shifting of some production or marketing activities for a particular line of business from one location to another
- closing of a facility to achieve productivity improvements or other cost savings
- selling a subsidiary whose activities are similar to those of the parent or other subsidiaries.

These examples could bring along the recording of impairments or restructuring provisions.

With regard to the presentation of information on those discontinued operations IFRS 5 stipulates (from para. 33) that an entity shall disclose:

(a) a single amount on the face of the income statement comprising the total of:

    (i) the post-tax profit or loss of discontinued operations and

    (ii) the post-tax gain or loss recognised on the measurement to fair value less costs to sell or on the disposal of the assets or disposal group(s) constituting the discontinued operation.

(b) an analysis of the single amount of (a) into:

    (i) the revenue, expense and pre-tax profit or loss of discontinued operations and related income tax expense;

    (ii) the gain or loss recognised on the measurement to fair value less costs to sell or on the disposal of the assets or disposal group(s) constituting the discontinued operation and related income tax expense.

The analysis may be presented in the notes or on the face of the income statement. If it is presented on the face of the income statement it shall be presented in a section identified as relating to discontinued operations, i.e. separately from continuing operations. The analysis is not required for disposal groups that are newly acquired subsidiaries that meet the criteria to be classified as held for sale on acquisition.

(c) the net cash flow attributable to the operating, investing and financing activities of discontinued operations.

The Standard also makes clear that any gain or loss on the remeasurement of a non-current asset (or disposal group) classified as held for sale that does not meet the definition of a discontinued operation should not be included within these amounts for discontinued operations, but be included in profit or loss from continuing operations.

Further, IFRS 5 requires that these disclosures be re-presented for prior periods presented in the financial statements so that the disclosures relate to all operations that have been discontinued by the balance sheet date for the latest period presented. Accordingly, adjustments to the comparative information as originally reported will be necessary for those disposal groups categorised as discontinued operations.

ACTIVITY 14.4

Alpha has three segments: pharmaceuticals, chemicals and soft drinks. In 20X3 after an assessment of the corporate strategy for the future, the company decides to concentrate on chemicals and pharmaceuticals.

On 30 September 20X3 the board of directors voted in favour of a disposal plan which would either try to sell off the *soft drinks* segment as a whole or, if not successful by the end of 20X3, dispose of the assets of the segment in a piecemeal fashion. An announcement of the plan was made the same day. A month later the company enters into a legally binding sales agreement with one of the major producers of soft drinks in the world. The parties expect the sale to be completed in February 20X4.

The following information for the soft drink segment is available for the financial year 20X3 (figures and transactions are simplified):

	Book value at 30 September	Recoverable amount at 30 September	Book value/ result at 31 December
Assets	450	400	400
Liabilities	200	200	200
Revenue	–	–	300
Operating expenses	–	–	125

An amount of 25 is representing non-cash expenses.

As you are aware, information relating to a discontinuing operation should be presented separately from continuing operations. You should now prepare the information that needs to be disclosed in the financial statements on 31 December 2003. Assume a corporate income tax rate of 30% on the accounting profit for the segment.

Also comment on what other information must be given regarding the discontinuing operation.

Activity feedback

- As a single amount on the income statement, para. 33 (a): profit for the period from discontinued operations

(i) the post-tax result on discontinued operations	122.5
(ii) the post-tax gain or loss on the measurement of the assets held for sale	35
Total	157.5

- An analysis of the single amount, para. 33(b)

revenue from discontinued operations	300
expenses from discontinued operations	125
(i) pre-tax result	175
(ii) related income tax expense	52.5
(iii) the loss on non-current assets held for sale	50
(iv) related income tax result	15

- On the asset side of the balance sheet we should present as a single line item: non-current assets classified as held for sale   400

- Among the liabilities we should disclose as a single line item: liabilities directly associated with non-current assets held for sale   200

- Net cash flow attributable to discontinued operations: 200

Note that comparative figures for 20X2 should be restated as well (para. 34). Disclosure requirements (refer to IFRS 5, para. 41):

- a description of the segment soft drinks (also comment on the reason for the disposal)

- segments in which the discontinuing operation is reported (is a segment in this case)

- the date on which the company announced the plan to discontinue the soft drink segment (also comment on the date when it entered into the binding sales agreement)

- the date when the discontinuance is expected to be completed.

SUMMARY

This chapter has completed the coverage, begun in Chapter 12, of the accounting treatment of fixed (non-current) assets. We looked in some detail at the issue of impairment of assets in general and of fixed assets in particular and at the contents of IAS 36. Finally we explored the requirements of IFRS 5 relating to non-current assets held for sale, and to the reporting of discontinued operations.

EXERCISES

Suggested answers to exercises marked ✓ are to be found on the Student side of the companion website.

Suggested answers to the remaining exercises are to be found on the Instructor side of the companion website.

1   If depreciation is done properly, impairment adjustments will not arise. Discuss.

2   What is 'recoverable amount' as the phrase is used in IAS 36? How does it relate to the alternative valuation bases discussed at length in Part One of this book?

✓ **3**   A cash-generating unit was reviewed for impairment at 31 May 20X3 as required by IAS 36, *Impairment of Assets*. The impairment review revealed that the cash-generating unit has a value in use of $25 million and a net realisable value of $23 million.

The carrying values of the net assets of the cash-generating unit immediately prior to the impairment review were as follows:

	$000
Goodwill	5 000
Property, plant and equipment	18 000
Net current assets	4 000
	27 000

The review indicated that an item of plant (included in the above figure of $18 million) with a carrying value of $1 million had been severely damaged and was virtually worthless.

There was no other evidence of obvious impairment to specific assets.

What is the carrying value of the goodwill relating to the unit immediately after the results of the impairment review have been reflected in accordance with IAS 36?

A	$1 million
B	$2 million
C	$3 million
D	$4 million

(CIMA November 2003)

4   On 31 December 20X1, U purchased 100% of the equity share capital of V and V became a subsidiary of U on that date. U paid $110 million for the shares, and the fair value of the net assets of V at 31 December 20X1 was $100 million. Goodwill on consolidation is written off over 10 years, starting in 20X2. At 31 December 20X2, the balance sheet of V showed the following balances:

	$ million
Property, plant and equipment:	
Land and buildings	50
Plant and machinery	30
Net current assets	15
	95

On 31 December 20X2, the directors of U carried out an impairment review in which V was treated as a single cash-generating unit. The recoverable amount of the cash-generating unit at 31 December 20X2 was computed as $96 million. No assets within the cash-generating unit had suffered obvious impairment.

What is the reduction in the consolidated reserves of U as a result of the impairment review of V (not including the normal annual write-off of goodwill)?

A	$1 million
B	$5 million
C	$8 million
D	$9 million

(CIMA May 2003)

5   (a)   IAS 36, *Impairment of Assets* was published in June 1998. Its primary objective is to ensure that an asset is not carried on the balance sheet at a value that is greater than its recoverable amount. The Standard does not apply to inventories (including construction contracts). It replaces guidance given in several other International Financial Reporting Standards.

Required:

   (i)   Describe the circumstances where an impairment loss is deemed to have occurred and explain when companies should perform an impairment review of tangible and intangible assets.

   (ii)   Describe the matters to be considered in assessing whether an asset may be impaired.

(b)   Avendus is preparing its financial statements to 30 September 20X3. It has identified the following issues:

   (i)   Avendus owns and operates an item of plant that had a carrying value of $400 000 and an estimated remaining life of 5 years. It has just been damaged due to incorrect operation by an employee. It is not economic to repair the plant but it still operates in a limited capacity although it is now no longer expected to last for 5 years. As the plant is damaged it could only be sold for $50 000. The cost of replacing the plant is $1 million. The plant does not generate cash flows independently and is part of a group of assets that have a carrying value of $5 million and an estimated recoverable amount of $7 million.

Required:
Explain how the above item of plant should be treated in the financial statements of Avendus for the year to 30 September 20X3. Your answer should consider the situations where the plant continues to be used and where it would be replaced.

(ii) Avendus owns an investment property which has a remaining useful economic life of five years. The property has a carrying value of $200 000 on 30 September 20X3. It is currently let to Marchant at an annual rental of $50 000 per annum. A surveyor has estimated that Avendus could expect net proceeds of $165 000 from sale of the property. The lease and the rental are due for renegotiation on 1 October 20X3. There is currently a surplus of rental properties and this has affected rental incomes and selling prices considerably. Aware of this, Marchant has offered to rent the property for a further five years, but for an annual rental, payable in advance, of only $40 000. The rental would be payable in full on 1 October each year. The current cost of capital of Avendus is 10% per annum, but current market assessments of a widely expected increase in interest rates means this will soon rise to 12% per annum. Avendus uses the cost method in IAS 40, *Investment Property*. The following information can be taken as correct:

	10%	12%
Interest rate		
Present value of 4 year annuity	3.2	3.0
Present value of 5 year annuity	3.8	3.6

Required:
Explain how the above investment property should be treated in the financial statements of Avendus for the year to 30 September 20X3.
Your answer should be supported with numerical calculations.

(iii) Avendus recently acquired a company called Fishright, a small fishing and fish processing company for $2 million. Avendus allocated the purchase consideration as follows:

	$000
Goodwill	240
Fishing quotas	400
Fishing boats (2 of equal value)	1 000
Other fishing equipment	100
Fish processing plant	200
Net current assets	60
	2 000

Shortly after the acquisition, one of the fishing boats sank in a storm and this has halved the fishing capacity. Due to this reduction in capacity, the value in use of the fishing business as a going concern is estimated at only $1.2 million. The fishing quotas now represent a greater volume than one boat can fish and it is not possible to replace the lost boat as it was rather old and no equivalent boats are available. However, the fishing quotas are much in demand and could be sold for $600 000. Avendus has been offered $250 000 for the fish processing plant. The net current assets consist of accounts receivable and payable.

Required:
Calculate the amounts that would appear in the consolidated financial statements of Avendus in respect of Fishright's assets after accounting for the impairment loss.

(ACCA December 2003)

6   Outline the requirements of IFRS 5, *Non-current Assets Held for Sale and Discontinued Operations.*

7   (a)   IAS 36, *Impairment of Assets*, was issued in June 1998 and subsequently amended in March 2004. Its main objective is to prescribe the procedures that should ensure that an entity's assets are included in its balance sheet at no more than their recoverable amounts. Where an asset is carried at an amount in excess of its recoverable amount, it is said to be impaired and IAS 36 requires an impairment loss to be recognised.

Required:

(i)   Define an impairment loss explaining the relevance of fair value less costs to sell and value in use; and state how frequently assets should be tested for impairment;
    Note: your answer should NOT describe the possible indicators of an impairment.

(ii)   Explain how an impairment loss is accounted for after it has been calculated.

(b)   The assistant financial controller of the Wilderness group, a public listed company, has identified the matters below which she believes may indicate an impairment to one or more assets:

(i)   Wilderness owns and operates an item of plant that cost $640 000 and had accumulated depreciation of $400 000 at 1 October 2004. It is being depreciated at 12½% on cost. On 1 April 2005 (exactly halfway through the year) the plant was damaged when a factory vehicle collided into it. Due to the unavailability of replacement parts, it is not possible to repair the plant, but it still operates, albeit at a reduced capacity. Also it is expected that as a result of the damage the remaining life of the plant from the date of the damage will be only two years. Based on its reduced capacity, the estimated present value of the plant in use is $150 000. The plant has a current disposal value of $20 000 (which will be nil in two years' time), but Wilderness has been offered a trade-in value of $180 000 against a replacement machine which has a cost of $1 million (there would be no disposal costs for the replaced plant). Wilderness is reluctant to replace the plant as it is worried about the long-term demand for the product produced by the plant. The trade-in value is only available if the plant is replaced.

Required:
Prepare extracts from the balance sheet and income statement of Wilderness in respect of the plant for the year ended 30 September 2005. Your answer should explain how you arrived at your figures.

(ii) On 1 April 2004 Wilderness acquired 100% of the share capital of Mossel, whose only activity is the extraction and sale of spa water. Mossel had been profitable since its acquisition, but bad publicity resulting from several consumers becoming ill due to a contamination of the spa water supply in April 2005 has led to unexpected losses in the last six months. The carrying amounts of Mossel's assets at 30 September 2005 are:

	$'000
Brand (Quencher – see below)	7 000
Land containing spa	12 000
Purifying and bottling plant	8 000
Inventories	5 000
	32 000

The source of the contamination was found and it has now ceased.

The company originally sold the bottled water under the brand name of 'Quencher', but because of the contamination it has rebranded its bottled water as 'Phoenix'. After a large advertising campaign, sales are now starting to recover and are approaching previous levels. The value of the brand in the balance sheet is the depreciated amount of the original brand name of 'Quencher'.

The directors have acknowledged that $1.5 million will have to be spent in the first three months of the next accounting period to upgrade the purifying and bottling plant.

Inventories contain some old 'Quencher' bottled water at a cost of $2 million; the remaining inventories are labelled with the new brand 'Phoenix'. Samples of all the bottled water have been tested by the health authority and have been passed as fit to sell. The old bottled water will have to be relabelled at a cost of $250 000, but is then expected to be sold at the normal selling price of (normal) cost plus 50%.

Based on the estimated future cash flows, the directors have estimated that the value in use of Mossel at 30 September 2005, calculated according to the guidance in IAS 36, is $20 million. There is no reliable estimate of the fair value less cost to sell of Mossel.

Required:

Calculate the amounts at which the assets of Mossel should appear in the consolidated balance sheet of Wilderness at 30 September 2005. Your answer should explain how you arrive at your figures.

(ACCA December 2005)

LEASES

OBJECTIVES After studying this chapter you should be able to:

- explain the issues underlying the accounting treatment of leases

- discuss alternative accounting treatments for leases of various types

- describe, apply and appraise the requirements of IAS 17 in relation to leased assets for lessor and lessee

- understand, and contribute to, ongoing debates concerning the treatment of leases in financial statements.

INTRODUCTION

A lease is an agreement that conveys to one party (the lessee) the right to use property, but does not convey legal ownership of that property. It follows that if an asset is defined as something which is legally owned (i.e. that has been acquired in an exchange transaction), then leases will not give rise to an asset in the financial statements of the lessee. It also follows that if nothing has been 'acquired', then nothing is unpaid for, that is, the lease agreement will also not give rise to a liability in the financial statements of the lessee.

If, however, the lease agreement allows the lessee to use the property for all or most of its useful life, requires the lessee to pay total amounts close to and possibly greater than the normal buying price of the item and requires or assumes that the lessee will look after the item as if the item belonged to it (e.g. insurance, repairs and maintenance), then it is clear that in substance the lessee would be in the same position, both economically and in terms of production and operating capacity, *as if* the lessee actually owned the asset. Furthermore, a contractual requirement to make future payments greater than the net cost of a straightforward purchase of the item means that the lessee is in the same position *as if* it had taken out a loan under agreed regular repayment terms and at an agreed rate of interest. Thus, in such circumstances, the economic substance of the situation is that the lessee has an asset and a liability, although the legal form of the agreement makes it quite clear that the legal ownership of the item remains with the other party (the lessor). (See Activity 15.1)

Under this method of accounting only one asset would be shown under fixed assets and only the liability to pay for one asset would be shown. The fact that the company has the use of another fixed asset and that they have the liability outstanding for lease payments is not shown and this could be considered misleading to shareholders and to other potential lenders.

If the two assets are obtained in these different ways by two different companies then the difference will be even more obvious. If the assets are being used equally profitably, then one company will appear to be using significantly fewer resources and significantly less finance than the other one, to achieve comparable operating activities. This apparent economic (and managerial) efficiency of the company which leases the asset is not logically justified and, in addition, unavoidable obligations are not being recorded as liabilities.

The general principle of substance over form discussed in Chapter 8 requires that, in such circumstances, the lessee *does* record an asset and a liability in its balance sheet and also that the lessor records a sale and a debtor in its financial statements.

In broad terms, the whole issue of accounting for leases can be summarised very simply. If a lease agreement essentially gives the parties rights and obligations similar to those arising from a legal purchase, then the accounting proceeds as if it *were* a legal purchase. This gives rise to a fixed asset and an obligation. If, by way of contrast, a lease agreement is, in the context of the particular characteristics of the object in question, essentially a short-term rental, then the accounting treats it as such, giving rise in the books of the lessee to a simple expense, normally allocated on a time basis.

Unfortunately, this simple division masks a considerable amount of practical difficulty. There are problems involved in creating a clear demarcation line between the two situations and a number of particular issues and problems have arisen over the years which IASB and various national Standards have tried to tackle.

As an introduction to the accounting principles involved, consider Activity 15.2.

ACTIVITY 15.1

A company obtains the use of two identical assets costing €100 000 by obtaining one asset on a credit sale agreement and the other on a lease. Assuming fixed assets are only recorded on a company's balance sheet when it has legal ownership, show the adjustments that would be necessary to the company's accounts and identify the problems, if any, with this method of accounting.

Activity feedback

	€
Fixed assets	100 000
Creditors	100 000

ACTIVITY 15.2

A company signs a lease agreement under which it will pay €2000 at the end of each of years 1–6 inclusive. The purchase cost of the asset concerned is €10 000 and the asset is expected to be worthless after six years. Discuss what the accounting entries in year 1 should be.

Activity feedback

In substance, this transaction is clearly a purchase on deferred credit terms. There should be an immediate recording of an asset of €10 000 on day 1, with an equal liability. At the end of year 1, a payment of €2000 is recorded, i.e. a credit. The double-entry for this payment will need to be split two ways. There is a total interest cost of €2000 over the six-year period ((2000 × 6) − 10 000) and some of the €2000 payment at the end of year 1 will be the payment of the interest relating to year 1, say X^i. This will be an expense of year 1 and the remainder of this payment, i.e. $(2000 - X^i)$ will be a partial settlement of the liability. There will also be a depreciation charge made at the end of year 1, of €1667 if the straight line basis is used. This gives entries as follows:

Leasehold asset			
1/1/1 cost	10 000	1 667 depreciation	31/12/1

Lease liability		
	10 000	1/1/1
	$(2\ 000 - X^i)$	31/12/1

Profit and loss	
31/12/1 interest	X^i
31/12/1 depreciation 1 667	

In year 2 the payment, interest and depreciation entries will be repeated, but the interest expense of X^{ii} should be less than X^i, because the liability during year 2 was lower than that during year 1. This follows the basic matching principle by allocating the total interest charge of €2000 over the six years pro rata to the benefit, thus the annual interest charge reduces as the amount borrowed reduces.

We first of all explore the considerable number of definitions given by IAS 17, the key standard on this issue, and consider the whole issue of the classification of leases into two distinct types, i.e. those that are, in substance, creating fixed assets and long-term debt and those that are not. We then look separately at accounting requirements for lessees, and lessors. Finally, we look at an actual case study and consider possible future developments. IAS 17 was originally issued in 1982, as *Accounting for Leases*, but was replaced by a new standard, *Leases*, issued in 1997 but standard from 1 January 1999. A further revision appeared in March 2004, effective for annual periods beginning on or after 1 January 2005, with earlier application encouraged. The main (but limited) objective of this revision was to clarify the classification of a lease of land and buildings and to eliminate accounting alternatives for initial direct costs in the financial statements of lessors.

DEFINITIONS OF IAS 17

- A *lease* is an agreement whereby the lessor conveys to the lessee in return for a payment or series of payments the right to use an asset for an agreed period of time.
- A *finance lease* is a lease that transfers substantially all the risks and rewards incidental to ownership of an asset. Title may or may not eventually be transferred.
- An *operating lease* is a lease other than a finance lease.

The risks of ownership relating to a finance lease are those of breakdown, damage, wear and tear, theft, obsolescence and so on. The rewards of ownership are extracted by using the asset for substantially all its productive usefulness, that is, its economic life, and by receiving its residual value at the time of its disposal.

- *Economic life* is either:
  - the period over which an asset is expected to be economically usable by one or more users
  - or the number of production or similar units expected to be obtained from the asset by one or more users.
- *Useful life* is the estimated remaining period, from the commencement of the lease term, without limitation by the lease term, over which the economic benefits embodied in the asset are expected to be consumed by the entity.

Note that the useful life relates to the expected situation for the lessee. The economic life relates to the asset, whether or not the current lessee is the only presumed user. Thus, although the useful life can exceed the lease term, the useful life cannot exceed the economic life.

- The *lease term* is the non-cancellable period for which the lessee has contracted to lease the asset together with any further terms for which the lessee has the option to continue to lease the asset, with or without further payment, when, at the inception of the lease, it is reasonably certain that the lessee will exercise the option.
- A *non-cancellable lease* is a lease that is cancellable only in one of the following four circumstances:
  - on the occurrence of some remote contingency
  - with the permission of the lessor
  - if the lessee enters into a new lease for the same or an equivalent asset with the same lessor
  - on payment by the lessee of an additional amount such that, at inception, continuation of the lease is reasonably certain.
- The *inception of the lease* is the earlier of the date of the lease agreement and the date of commitment by the parties to the principal provisions of the lease. As at this date:
  - a lease is classified as either an operating or a finance lease
  - and, in the case of a finance lease, the amounts to be recognised at the commencement of the lease term are determined.
- The *commencement of the lease term* is the date from which the lessee is entitled to exercise its right to use the leased asset. It is the date of initial recognition of the lease (i.e. the recognition of the assets, liabilities, income or expenses resulting from the lease, as appropriate).

One of the major criteria for deciding whether or not a finance lease exists is the total amount or more accurately the total minimum amount payable under the lease contract. This leads to a set of related terms, as follows:

- *Minimum lease payments* are the payments over the lease term that the lessee is, or can be, required to make excluding contingent rent, costs for services and taxes to be paid by and reimbursed to the lessor, together with:

- in the case of the lessee, any amounts guaranteed by the lessee or by a party related to the lessee
- or in the case of the lessor, any residual value guaranteed to the lessor by either: ·

  1 the lessee

  2 a party related to the lessee

  3 or a third party unrelated to the lessor that is financially capable of discharging the obligations under the guarantee.

However, if the lessee has an option to purchase the asset at a price that is expected to be sufficiently lower than the fair value at the date when the option becomes exercisable so that, at the inception of the lease, it is reasonably certain to be exercised, that is, a 'bargain purchase option' exists, then the minimum lease payments comprise the minimum payments payable over the lease term and the payment required to exercise this purchase option.

- *Fair value* is the amount for which an asset could be exchanged or a liability settled, between knowledgeable, willing parties in an arm's-length transaction.
- From the viewpoint of the lessee, the *guaranteed residual value* is that part of the residual value which is guaranteed by the lessee or by a party related to the lessee (the amount of the guarantee being the maximum amount that could, in any event, become payable).
- From the viewpoint of the lessor, the *guaranteed residual value* is that part of the residual value which is guaranteed by the lessee or by a third party unrelated to the lessor who is financially capable of discharging the obligations under the guarantee.
- *Unguaranteed residual value* is that portion of the residual value of the leased asset, the realisation of which by the lessor is not assured or is guaranteed solely by a party related to the lessor.
- The lessor's *gross investment in the lease* is the aggregate of the minimum lease payments receivable by the lessor under a finance lease and any unguaranteed residual value accruing to the lessor.
- *Net investment in the lease* is the gross investment in the lease discounted at the interest rate implicit in the lease.
- *Unearned finance income* is the difference between:
  - the gross investment in the lease
  - and the net investment in the lease.

Some of the greatest technical difficulties are caused by the need, at least theoretically, to calculate backwards the interest rates implicitly included in arriving at the total payments under the lease.

- The *interest rate implicit in the lease* is the discount rate that, at the inception of the lease, causes the aggregate present value of (a) the minimum lease payments and (b) the unguaranteed residual value to be equal to the sum of fair value of the leased asset and any initial direct costs of the lessor.
- The *lessee's incremental borrowing rate of interest* is the rate of interest the lessee would have to pay on a similar lease or, if that is not determinable, the

rate that, at the inception of the lease, the lessee would incur to borrow over a similar term, and with a similar security, the funds necessary to purchase the asset.

- *Contingent rent* is that portion of the lease payments that is not fixed in amount but is based on the future amount of a factor that changes other than with the passage of time (e.g. percentage of sales, amount of usage, future price indices, future market rates of interest).

LEASE CLASSIFICATION

As already indicated, the form of words which determines the classification of a lease as either a finance lease or an operating lease is very simple. A lease is classified as a finance lease if it transfers substantially all the risks and rewards incidental to ownership. A lease is classified as an operating lease if it does not transfer substantially all the risks and rewards incidental to ownership. Because the transaction between a lessor and a lessee is based on a lease agreement common to both parties, it is appropriate to use consistent definitions. The application of these definitions to the differing circumstances of the two parties, however, may sometimes result in the same lease being classified differently by lessor and lessee.

The Standard makes no attempt to define 'substantially all'. Some national GAAPs take a much more numerical approach to this question, for example requiring

ACTIVITY 15.3

A lessee leases an asset on a non-cancellable lease contract with a primary term of five years from 1 January 20X1. The rental is €650 per quarter payable in advance. The lessee has the right to continue to lease the asset after the end of the primary period for as long as they wish at a nominal rent. In addition, the lessee is required to pay all maintenance and insurance costs, as they arise. The leased asset could have been purchased for cash at the start of the lease for €10 000 and has a useful life of eight years.

Calculate the interest rate implicit in the lease.

Activity feedback

From the definition of 'interest rate implicit in the lease' we can state that:

1 €10 000 (fair value) = the present value at implicit interest rate of 20 quarterly rentals payable in advance of €650

2 the present value of the first rental payable is €650 as it is paid now

3 thus €9350 = the present value at implicit interest rate of 19 rentals of €650

4 therefore 9350/650 = 14.385 = present value at implicit interest rate of 19 rentals of €1

5 using discount tables we can determine the interest rate as 2.95%.

In principle, IAS 17 and the definitions just given apply to all leases when IAS GAAP is to be followed. However, a number of exceptions are given. IAS 17 does not apply to:

- lease agreements to explore for or use minerals, oils, natural gas and similar non-regenerative resources

- or licensing agreements for items such as motion pictures, video recordings, plays, manuscripts, patents and copyrights.

Additionally, IAS 17 should not be applied to the measurement by:

- lessees of investment property held under finance leases (see IAS 40, *Investment Property*, Chapter 12)

- lessors of investment property leased out under operating leases (see IAS 40)

- lessees of biological assets held under finance leases (see IAS 41, *Agriculture*, Appendix)

- lessors of biological assets leased out under operating leases (see IAS 41).

the present value of the minimum lease payments to be 90% or more of the fair value of the asset at the inception of the lease (e.g. USA, Germany). Others, such as the UK, suggest that 90% gives a 'presumption' of a finance lease, but make it clear that the determining factor is 'substantially all', not 90%.

What IAS 17 does do is to give a number of examples of situations that 'would normally' (paras 1–5) or that 'could' (paras 6–8) point to a lease being properly classified as a finance lease. These are as follows (paras 10 and 11):

1 The lease transfers ownership of the asset to the lessee by the end of the lease term.

2 The lessee has the option to purchase the asset at a price that is expected to be sufficiently lower than the fair value at the date the option becomes exercisable such that, at the inception of the lease, it is reasonably certain that the option will be exercised (i.e. a bargain purchase option exists).

3 The lease term is for the major part of the economic life of the asset even if title is not transferred.

4 At the inception of the lease the present value of the minimum lease payments amounts to at least substantially all of the fair value of the leased asset.

5 The leased assets are of a specialised nature such that only the lessee can use them without major modifications being made.

6 If the lessee cancels the lease, the lessor's losses associated with the cancellation are borne by the lessee.

7 Gains or losses from the fluctuation in the fair value of the residual accrue to the lessee (for example in the form of a rent rebate equalling most of the residual sales proceeds at the end of the lease).

8 The lessee has the ability to continue the lease for a secondary period at a rent which is substantially lower than market rent (i.e. a bargain rental option).

ACTIVITY 15.4

Explain briefly in your own words why each of these situations points towards a finance lease.

Activity feedback

Our suggested wording is as follows. Because, under situations 1 and 2 the lessee ends up with legal ownership, the validity of a finance lease classification is obvious. Situation 3 assumes, reasonably enough, that a major part of the economic life (measured in years) must imply transfer of substantially all the risks and rewards of ownership (measured in money). Situation 4 argues that payment of substantially all the purchase price, after discounting to present value, must again imply that the substance of the transaction is a purchase on credit terms and situation 5 indicates by definition that only the lessee can derive 'rewards' from possession of the particular items. The remaining three situations, 6, 7, and 8, while perhaps less definitive, all clearly point to the likelihood of the lessee being in the in-substance ownership position of deriving the benefits and 'paying the price'.

The US prescriptive approach is continued in other respects. For example, the US version of situation 3 specifies that for a finance lease the lease term is 75% or more of the economic life of the asset. The UK leasing Standard contains no similar consideration at all, relying on the 'substantially all the risks and rewards' criterion.

Note that the lease classification is to be made at the inception of the lease.

ACTIVITY 15.5

Costa uses three identical pieces of machinery in its factory. These were all acquired for use on the same date by the following means:

1 Machine 1 rented from Brava at a cost of €250 per month payable in advance and terminable at any time by either party.

2 Machine 2 rented from Blanca at a cost of eight half-yearly payments in advance of €1500.

3 Machine 3 rented from Sol at a cost of six half-yearly payments in advance of €1200.

The cash price of this type of machine is €8000 and its estimated life is four years. Are the three machines rented by operating or finance leases?

Activity feedback

Machine 1 is held on an operating lease as there is no transfer of the risks or rewards of ownership. Machine 2 involves a total payment of €12 000. In present value terms this will almost certainly be more than the €8000 fair value of the asset and therefore clearly more than 'substantially all of the fair value of the leased asset' (see our earlier situation 4). Machine 2 is therefore held on a finance lease. Machine 3 involves a total payment of €7200, the present value of which will be significantly less than €8000, so that situation 4 will not apply. The question is whether or not situation 3 applies, that is, whether or not three years is a 'major part of the economic life' of the machine (which is four years). Under US GAAP, which specifies an arbitrary 75% ratio here, this would be a finance lease under situation 3 (in which circumstance the lease agreement would probably have been changed before signing in order to be a week or two shorter). Under UK GAAP, which focuses more exclusively on situation 4, machine 3 would, on the available information, be an operating lease. Our interpretation of IAS 17 would be that situation 3 does not apply to machine 3, i.e. that this would be treated as an operating lease under IAS GAAP. This example well illustrates the practical difficulties which may arise in lease classification.

The latest (2004) revision added a number of detailed requirements relating to leases of land and buildings (paras 14–19). The essential point is that the land and buildings elements of a lease of land and buildings are considered separately for the purposes of lease classification. If title to both elements is expected to pass to the lessee by the end of the lease term, both elements are classified as a finance lease, whether analysed as one lease or as two leases, unless it is clear from other features that the lease does not transfer substantially all risks and rewards incidental to ownership of one or both elements. When the land has an indefinite economic life, the land element is normally classified as an operating lease unless title is expected to pass to the lessee by the end of the lease term. The buildings element is classified as a finance or operating lease in accordance with the above specifications.

Separate measurement of the land and buildings elements is not required when the lessee's interest in both land and buildings is classified as an investment property in accordance with IAS 40 and the fair value model is adopted. Detailed calculations are

ACTIVITY 15.6

Do you think the use of numerical specifications in the finance/operating lease distinction is beneficial?

Activity feedback

The desirability of creating a precise numerical distinction is very much open to question. It has the obvious surface advantage of apparent objectivity and precision. However, the chosen figure is purely arbitrary. More importantly, the creation of a definitive numerical distinction allows, and arguably encourages, business entities to structure lease contracts so that they fall just marginally below the chosen criterion, even though the whole purpose may, quite visibly, be, in substance, to finance the 'purchase' of major resources by borrowing. The use of a fixed numerical boundary may substantially reduce subjectivity for the accountant and the auditor, but it may at the same time substantially increase creative accounting and the likelihood of misleading or unfair financial statements.

required for this assessment only if the classification of one or both elements is otherwise uncertain. In accordance with IAS 40, it is possible for a lessee to classify a property interest held under an operating lease as an investment property. If it does, the property interest is accounted for as if it were a finance lease and, in addition, the fair value model is used for the asset recognised. The lessee should continue to account for the lease as a finance lease, even if a subsequent event changes the nature of the lessee's property interest so that it is no longer classified as investment property.

Yet another attempt to tighten up the requirements for lease capitalisation was made by the issue in December 2004 of IFRIC 4, *Determining Whether an Arrangement Contains a Lease*. The interpretation notes that in recent years arrangements have developed that do not take the legal form of a lease but convey rights to use assets in return for a payment or series of payments, such as outsourcing arrangements, telecommunication contracts that provide rights to capacity, and take-or-pay and similar contracts, in which purchasers must make specified payments, regardless of whether they take delivery of the contracted products or services.

The interpretation specifies that an arrangement that meets both the following criteria is, or contains, a lease that should be accounted for in accordance with IAS 17:

> Fulfilment of the arrangement depends upon a specific asset. The asset need not be explicitly identified by the contractual provisions of the arrangement. Rather, it may be implicitly specified because it is not economically feasible or practical for the supplier to fulfil the arrangement by providing use of alternative assets. The arrangement conveys a right to control the use of the underlying asset.

ACCOUNTING AND REPORTING BY LESSEES – FINANCE LEASES

In the case of finance leases, the substance and financial reality are that the lessee acquires the economic benefits of the use of the leased asset for the major part of its economic life in return for entering into an obligation to pay for that right an amount approximating to the fair value of the asset and the related finance charge.

Lessees should recognise finance leases as assets and liabilities in their balance sheets at amounts equal at the inception of the lease to the fair value of the leased property or, if lower, at the present value of the minimum lease payments (para. 20). In calculating the present value of the minimum lease payments, the discount factor is the interest rate implicit in the lease, if this is practicable to determine; if not, the lessee's incremental borrowing rate should be used. At the inception of the lease, the asset and the liability for the future lease payments are recognised in the balance sheet at the same amounts.

During the lease term, each lease payment should be allocated between a reduction of the obligation and the finance charge so as to produce a constant periodic rate of interest on the remaining balance of the obligation over the amortisation period, in the manner illustrated earlier. The asset initially recorded is depreciated in a manner consistent with that used by the lessee for owned assets.

If the circumstances described in situations 1 or 2 earlier are present, that is a transfer of ownership is clearly foreseeable, then depreciation is usually based on the economic life of the leased asset; otherwise, it is based on the shorter of economic life and lease term. Contingent rentals are generally not included in the minimum lease payments and are not accounted for as part of the capitalised lease. They should be charged to expense in the period to which they relate.

ACTIVITY 15.7

Using the information given in Activity 15.3, assuming the asset has a nil residual value and assuming the asset is leased for a further two years after the primary period, show the accounting entries over the life of the lease required in the lessee's books by IAS 17.

Activity feedback

The lease falls within the definition of a finance lease, therefore the 'rights in the lease' will be capitalised at fair value of €10 000 and the obligation under the lease of €10 000 will be shown as a liability:

		€	€
1.1.XI	Fixed asset	10 000	
	Creditors (lessor)		10 000

The minimum lease payments amount to 20 × €650 = €13 000, the cash price was €10 000, hence the total finance charge will be €3000.

Remembering that this total finance charge should be allocated to accounting periods during the lease so as to produce a constant periodic rate of charge on the remaining balance of the obligation for each accounting period, then an appropriate method of allocation would be the actuarial method as follows:

Period	Capital sum at start of period	Rental paid	Capital sum during period	Finance charge (2.95% per quarter)*	Capital sum at end of period
	€	€	€	€	€
1/X1	10 000	650	9 350	276	9 626
2/X1	9 626	650	8 976	265	9 241
3/X1	9 241	650	8 591	254	8 845
4/X1	8 845	650	8 195	242	8 437
				1 037	
1/X2	8 437	650	7 787	230	8 017
2/X2	8 017	650	7 367	217	7 584
3/X2	7 584	650	6 934	205	7 139
4/X2	7 139	650	6 489	191	6 680
				843	
1/X3	6 680	650	6 030	178	6 208
2/X3	6 208	650	5 558	164	5 722
3/X3	5 722	650	5 072	150	5 222
4/X3	5 222	650	4 572	135	4 707
				627	
1/X4	4 707	650	4 057	120	4 177
2/X4	4 177	650	3 527	104	3 631
3/X4	3 631	650	2 981	88	3 069
4/X4	3 069	650	2 419	71	2 490
				383	
1/X5	2 490	650	1 840	54	1 894
2/X5	1 894	650	1 244	37	1 281
3/X5	1 281	650	631	19	650
4/X5	650	650	–		–
				110	
		13 000		3 000	

We can now apportion the annual rental of €2600 (i.e. 4 × €650) between a finance charge and a capital repayment as follows:

ACTIVITY 15.7   (Continued)

	Total rental €	Finance charge €	Capital repayments €
X1	2 600	1 037*	1 563
X2	2 600	843	1 757
X3	2 600	627	1 973
X4	2 600	383	2 217
X5	2 600	110	2 490
	13 000	3 000	10 000
	(a)	(b)	(a) – (b)

*as calculated using actuarial method

We also need to calculate a depreciation charge. The period for depreciation will be seven years as this is the lesser of economic life (eight years) and lease period (seven years). The annual depreciation charge on a straight line basis is therefore:

$$€10\,000 \div 7 = €1429$$

The accounting entries in the lessee's books will be as follows assuming year end as 31 December.
Profit and loss account charges

	Depreciation	Finance charge	Total
X1	1 429	1 037	2 466
X2	1 429	843	2 272
X3	1 429	627	2 056

	Depreciation	Finance charge	Total
X4	1 429	383	1 812
X5	1 428	110	1 538
X6	1 428	–	1 428
X7	1 428	–	1 428
	10 000	3 000	13 000

Balance sheet entries
Assets held under finance leases

	Cost €		Accumulated depreciation €		Net book value of assets held under finance leases €
31.12.X1	10 000	–	1 429	=	8 571
31.12.X2	10 000	–	2 858	=	7 142
31.12.X3	10 000	–	4 287	=	5 713
31.12.X4	10 000	–	5 716	=	4 284
31.12.X5	10 000	–	7 145	=	2 855
31.12.X6	10 000	–	8 574	=	1 426
31.12.X7	10 000	–	10 000	=	–

Obligations under finance leases (i.e. the capital element of future rentals payable)

ACTIVITY 15.7   (Continued)

	Obligations under finance leases outstanding at start of year €		Capital repayment €		Obligations under finance leases outstanding at year-end €
31.12.X1	10 000	–	1 563	=	8 437
31.12.X2	8 437	–	1 757	=	6 680
31.12.X3	6 680	–	1 973	=	4 707
31.12.X4	4 707	–	2 217	=	2 490
31.12.X5	2 490	–	2 490	=	–
31.12.X6					–
31.12.X7					–

ACCOUNTING AND REPORTING BY LESSEES – OPERATING LEASES

Lease payments under an operating lease should be recognised as an expense in the income statement on a straight line basis over the lease term unless another systematic basis is more representative of the time pattern of the user's benefit (para. 33). Note that the pattern of payment is not relevant. Remember that contingent rent, as defined earlier, is not included in the original calculations. It therefore follows that the rental expense for any year will consist of:

1 the minimum rent under the lease divided equally over the number of years

2 plus any contingent rent relating to that year.

Now look at Activity 15.8.

ACCOUNTING AND REPORTING BY LESSORS – FINANCE LEASES

As is the case with the financial statements of lessees, the approach is to follow and record the substance of the situation. From the viewpoint of the lessor, the substance

ACTIVITY 15.8

If the lease in Activity 15.6 were to be treated as an operating lease, show the entries in the lessee's books.

Activity feedback
The only entries in the lessee's books would be the following annual entry:

Rental expense	(4 × 650)	2 600	
Creditors	(4 × 650)		2 600

During the negotiation of a new operating lease or the renewal of an existing one, the lessee may receive incentives to sign the agreement from the lessor. Incentives take many forms, including rent-free periods, reduced rents for a period of time, leasehold improvements on the lessor's account or a cash signing fee. IAS 17 is silent on this matter, but the Standing Interpretations Committee has clarified the position in SIC 15, *Incentives in an Operating Lease*. This requires that the benefit of such incentives be recognised at the inception of the lease and treated as a reduction of rental expense over the term of the lease. The benefit is recognised on a straight line basis, unless another systematic basis is more representative of the time pattern in which benefit is derived from the leased asset.

is that the lessor has an amount receivable, much of it usually non-current, due from the lessee. In direct relation to the lease contract, the lessor has no other assets or liabilities. The amounts received from the lessee will embrace two elements, i.e. a repayment of 'loan' and an interest revenue.

Lessors should recognise assets held under a finance lease in their balance sheets and present them as a receivable at an amount equal to the net investment in the lease (paras 36–41). A lessor aims to allocate finance income over the lease term on a systematic and rational basis. This income allocation is based on a pattern reflecting a constant periodic return on the lessor's net investment outstanding in respect of the finance lease. Lease payments relating to the accounting period, excluding costs for services, are applied against the gross investment in the lease to reduce both the principal and the unearned finance income.

Estimated unguaranteed residual values used in computing the lessor's gross investment in a lease are reviewed regularly. If there has been a reduction in the estimated unguaranteed residual value, the income allocation over the lease term is reviewed and any reduction in respect of amounts already accrued is recognised immediately.

Initial direct costs are often incurred by lessors and include amounts such as commissions, legal fees and internal costs that are incremental and directly attributable to negotiating and arranging a lease. They exclude general overheads such as those incurred by a sales and marketing team. For finance leases other than those involving manufacturer or dealer lessors, initial direct costs are included in the initial measurement of the finance lease receivable and reduce the amount of income recognised over the lease term. The interest rate implicit in the lease is defined in such a way that the initial direct costs are included automatically in the finance lease receivable; there is no need to add them separately. Costs incurred by manufacturer or dealer lessors in connection with negotiating and arranging a lease are excluded from the definition of initial direct costs. As a result, they are excluded from the net investment in the lease and are recognised as an expense when the selling profit is recognised, which for a finance lease is normally at the commencement of the lease term.

An asset under a finance lease that is classified as held for sale (or included in a disposal group that is classified as held for sale) in accordance with IFRS 5, *Non-current Assets Held for Sale and Discontinued Operations*, shall be accounted for in accordance with that IFRS (see Chapter 14).

Finance leasing by manufacturers or dealers

The manufacturer or dealer may be the person who actually provides the asset, as well as the finance. A finance lease of an asset by a manufacturer or dealer lessor gives rise to two types of income:

1 the profit or loss equivalent to the profit or loss resulting from an outright sale of the asset being leased, at normal selling prices, reflecting any applicable volume or trade discounts

2 the finance income over the lease term.

The sales revenue recorded at the commencement of a finance lease term by a manufacturer or dealer lessor is the fair value of the asset or, if lower, the present value of the minimum lease payments accruing to the lessor, computed at a commercial rate of interest (para. 44). The cost of sale recognised at the commencement of the lease term is the cost, or carrying amount if different, of the leased property less the present value of the unguaranteed residual value. The difference between the sales revenue and the cost of sale is the selling profit, which is recognised in accordance with the policy followed by the entity for sales which will be consistent with IAS 18 (see Chapter 18).

Manufacturer or dealer lessors sometimes quote artificially low rates of interest in order to attract customers. The use of such a rate would result in an excessive portion of the total income from the transaction being recognised at the time of sale. If artificially low rates of interest are quoted, selling profit must be restricted to that which would apply if a commercial rate of interest were charged. Initial direct costs should be charged as expenses at the inception of the lease.

ACTIVITY 15.9

A lessor leases out an asset on terms which constitute a finance lease. The primary period is five years commencing 1 July 20X0, and the rental payable is €3000 per annum (in arrears). The lessee has the right to continue the lease after the five-year period referred to for an indefinite period at a nominal rent. The cash price of the asset in question at 1 July 20X0 was €11 372, and the rate of interest implicit in the lease can be calculated to be 10%.

Show the entries in the lessor's books.

Activity feedback

The finance charge is simply the difference between the fair value of the asset (in this case being the cash price of the new asset) and the rental payments over the lease period, i.e. of €15 000 less €11 372 or €3628.

Using the actuarial method with an interest rate of 10%, the allocation of the finance charge will be as follows:

Year ended 30 June	Balance b/f		Finance charge (10%)		Rental		Balance c/f (in year-end balance sheet)
	€		€		€		€
20X1	11 372	+	1 137	−	(3 000)	=	9 509
20X2	9 509	+	951	−	(3 000)	=	7 460
20X3	7 460	+	746	−	(3 000)	=	5 206
20X4	5 206	+	521	−	(3 000)	=	2 727
20X5	2 727	+	273	−	(3 000)	=	0
			€3 628		€15 000		

The relevant extracts from the income statements of the years in question will thus appear as follows:

	20X1	20X2	20X3	20X4	20X5	Total
Rentals	3 000	3 000	3 000	3 000	3 000	15 000
less Capital repayments	1 863	2 049	2 254	2 479	2 727	11 372
Finance charges	1 137	951	746	521	273	3 628
Interest payable	(x)	(x)	(x)	(x)	(x)	
Overheads	(x)	(x)	(x)	(x)	(x)	

The relevant balance sheets will appear as follows:

	Year ended June 30			
	20X1	20X2	20X3	20X4
Net investment in finance lease				
Current	2 049	2 254	2 479	2 727
Non-current	7 460	5 206	2 727	–
	9 509	7 460	5 296	2 727

ACCOUNTING AND REPORTING BY LESSORS – OPERATING LEASES

As IAS 17 (para. 49) unsurprisingly says, lessors should present assets subject to operating leases according to the nature of the asset. The asset subject to the operating lease is, in substance as well as in form, a non-current asset of the lessor. Such an asset should be depreciated on a basis consistent with the lessor's policy for similar assets. IAS 16, *Property, Plant and Equipment*, or IAS 38, *Intangible Assets*, will apply (see Chapters 12 and 13). In addition IAS 36, *Impairment of Assets*, will need to be considered (see Chapter 14).

Costs, including depreciation, incurred in earning the lease income are recognised as an expense. Lease income (excluding receipts for services provided such as insurance and maintenance) is recognised in income on a straight line basis over the lease term even if the receipts are not on such a basis, unless another systematic basis is more representative of the time pattern in which use benefit derived from the leased asset is diminished. By definition, no element of selling profit can arise.

Initial direct costs incurred specifically to earn revenues from an operating lease are added to the carrying amount of the leased asset and recognised as an expense over the lease term on the same basis as the lease income.

Disclosure

The disclosure requirements are extensive for both lessors and lessees. Leases are a form of financial instrument and disclosure requirements relating to financial instruments generally will apply to leases. IAS 17 specifies detailed additional requirements. These include details designed to give a clear indication of the timing of future cash movements and of future expected expense and revenue outcomes.

SALE AND LEASEBACK TRANSACTIONS

A sale and leaseback transaction involves the sale of an asset by the vendor and the leasing of the same asset back to the vendor. The lease payment and the sale price are usually interdependent as they are negotiated as a package. The accounting treatment of a sale and leaseback transaction depends on the type of lease involved. Again, the principle of substance over form is fundamental.

If the leaseback is an operating lease and the lease payments and the sale price are established at fair value, there has in effect been a normal sale transaction and any profit or loss is recognised immediately. If the sale price is below fair value, any profit or loss should be recognised immediately except that, if the loss is compensated by future lease payments at below market price, it should be deferred and amortised in proportion to the lease payments over the period for which the asset is expected to be used. If the sale price is above fair value, the excess over fair value should be deferred and amortised over the period for which the asset is expected to be used. Also, for operating leases, if the fair value at the time of a sale and leaseback transaction is less than the carrying amount of the asset, a loss equal to the amount of the difference between the carrying amount and fair value should be recognised immediately.

If the leaseback is a finance lease, the transaction is a means whereby the lessor provides finance to the lessee, with the asset as security. For this reason it is not appropriate to regard an excess of sales proceeds over the carrying amount as income because there has, in substance, been no sale. Such excess is deferred and amortised over the lease term. For finance leases, if the fair value at the time of the sale and leaseback transaction is less than the carrying amount of the asset, then no recognition of the difference between the two is necessary (again, because there has in substance not been a sale). However, such a difference might indicate an impairment in accordance with IAS 36, *Impairment of Assets*, which Standard would then be applied (see Chapter 14).

SIC 27 extends the principles of the sale and leaseback discussion earlier to situations of linked multiple transactions in general. The principle of following the substance of the overall situation remains crucial.

Case study

The published consolidated financial statements of Euro Disney SCA for the year to 30 September 2000 provided a sharp illustration of how significant the leasing question can be. Broadly speaking, this is a consolidation of the French part of the worldwide Disney organisation. It is published in English, but is explicitly stated to follow 'French accounting principles' in the audit report and 'French GAAP' elsewhere. Most of the land and property utilised by Euro Disney is owned, through complicated relationships, by financing companies. Under French GAAP at the time, the leases involved were operating leases and the financing companies are not consolidated. The effect is that major obligations are not revealed. However, a detailed reconciliation is given to US GAAP which, in broad terms, has the same effect as using IAS GAAP as regards the relevant leases.

Four reconciliations are now given.

Reconciliation of net income (loss)

	30 September	
(€ *in millions*)	*2000*	*1999*
Net income, as reported under French GAAP	38.7	23.6
Lease and interest adjustments	(106.0)	(74.5)
Other	1.1	1.0
Net loss under US GAAP	(66.2)	(49.9)

Reconciliation of shareholders' equity

	30 September	
(€ *in millions*)	*2000*	*1999*
Shareholders' equity, as reported under French GAAP	1 247.5	1 140.8
Cumulative lease and interest adjustments	(1 172.9)	(1 067.0)
Effect of revaluing the ORAs and sale/leaseback transactions	178.1	26.7
Other	(14.6)	(15.6)
Shareholders' equity under US GAAP	**238.1**	**84.9**

Reconciliation of borrowings

(€ in millions)	30 September 2000	1999
Total borrowings, as reported under French GAAP*	873.8	941.4
Unconsolidated Phase 1 SNCs debt	1 245.4	1 249.6
Lease financing arrangements with TWDC	236.9	236.9

	30 September 2000	1999
Borrowings including unconsolidated Financing Companies	2 356.1	2 427.9
US GAAP adjustments to revalue lease financing arrangements and ORAs	(6.3)	(8.5)
Total US GAAP borrowings*		

*(excluding accrued interest)

Balance sheet under US GAAP

(€ in millions)	30 September 2000	1999
Cash and short-term investments	452.9	347.6
Receivables	203.2	184.6
Fixed assets	2 493.3	2 455.5
Other assets	169.4	161.4
Total assets	**3 318.8**	**3 149.1**
Accounts payable and other liabilities	730.9	644.8
Borrowings*	2 349.8	2 419.4
Shareholders' equity	238.1	84.9
Total liabilities and equity	**3 318.8**	**3 149.1**

*(excluding accrued interest)

Total assets under French GAAP were 2 793.8 for 2000 and 2 518.8 for 1999.

Possible future developments

In December 1999 the IASC published a discussion paper on the subject of leases entitled *Leases: Implementation of a New Approach*. The paper had been developed by the G4 + 1 group. This group consisted of representatives of accounting standard setters from Australia, Canada, New Zealand, UK and USA working with the IASC.

The essential, and apparently very radical, proposal is that the arbitrary distinction between operating and finance leases is unsatisfactory and should be abolished, to be replaced by an approach that applies the same regulations for all leases. The IASC noted in the paper that many analysts recast financial statements by applying the same approach to operating and finance leases. G4 + 1 believed that recognition in a lessee's balance sheet of material assets and liabilities arising from operating leases should take place:

> The general effect of the approach proposed is that the amounts recognised as an asset and a liability by a lessee in respect of a lease of a given item would vary in amount depending on the nature of the lease.

ACTIVITY 15.10

Calculate the following ratios, within the limits of the given information in the Euro Disney case study, under (a) French GAAP and under (b) US GAAP and comment.

$$\frac{\text{net income}}{\text{shareholders' equity}}$$

$$\frac{\text{borrowings}}{\text{equity} + \text{borrowings}}$$

$$\frac{\text{net income}}{\text{total assets}}$$

$$\frac{\text{net income}}{\text{total assets}} \quad \frac{38.7}{2\,793.8} = 1\% \quad \frac{23.6}{2\,518.8} = 1\%$$

(b) *US GAAP*

$$\frac{\text{net income}}{\text{shareholders' equity}} \quad \frac{(66.2)}{238.1} = -28\% \quad \frac{(49.9)}{84.9} = -58\%$$

$$\frac{\text{borrowings}}{\text{equity} + \text{borrowings}} \quad \frac{2\,349.8}{2\,349.8 + 231.8} = 91\% \quad \frac{2\,419.4}{2\,419.4 + 8.94} = 97\%$$

$$\frac{\text{net income}}{\text{total assets}} \quad \frac{(66.2)}{3\,318.8} = -2\% \quad \frac{(49.9)}{3\,149.1} = -2\%$$

Activity feedback
(a) *French GAAP*

	2000		1999	
$\dfrac{\text{net income}}{\text{shareholders' equity}}$	$\dfrac{38.7}{1\,247.5}$	= 3%	$\dfrac{23.6}{1\,140}$	= 2%
$\dfrac{\text{borrowings}}{\text{equity} + \text{borrowings}}$	$\dfrac{873.8}{873.8 + 1\,247.5}$	= 41%	$\dfrac{941.4}{941.4 + 1\,140.8}$	= 45%

To state the obvious, a very different picture is given. When the substance of the situation is recorded and the contracted (legally as well as economically) liabilities related to the operations are involved, the whole entity is shown to be very highly geared (leveraged), as well as unprofitable. Can both sets of figures be validly regarded as equally fairly presenting the position to readers of the financial statements?

TABLE 15.1   Lessee's liabilities and items excluded

Items included in initial assets and liabilities	*Items excluded from initial assets and liabilities*
Minimum payments required by lease	
Amounts payable in respect of obtaining renewal options	Rentals relating to optional renewal periods
Contingent rentals that represent consideration for the fair value of rights conveyed to lessee	Contingent rentals relating to optional additional usage
Fair value of residual value guarantees	Residual values guaranteed where transfer of economic benefits in settlement is not probable

The financial statements would thus reflect the extent to which differing lease arrangements result in financial obligations and provide financial flexibility.

Table 15.1 provides an overview of the items that would be included in the liabilities of a lessee and reported at the beginning of the lease with an asset and those that would not according to the discussion paper (p. 13).

The discussion paper debates the issue of recognition and measurement in relation to those leases to be included on the balance sheet.

For a lease contract the recognition point could be:

- signing a contract to lease
- purchase or manufacture by the lessor of the specific item of property that is the subject of the lease
- delivery of the property to the lessee
- rental payments falling due during the lease term.

ACTIVITY 15.11

A lessee agrees to hire a piece of equipment for three years at an annual rental of €10 000. The lessee returns the equipment to the lessor at the end of the three-year period. Rights and obligations of the lessee are thus:

● right to use for three years

● obligation to pay €10 000 per annum for three years

● obligation to return the equipment to lessor after three years.

At which point should the lessee recognise an asset and at what value in accordance with the discussion paper?

Activity feedback

When the equipment is delivered to the lessee he should recognise an asset equivalent to the present value of three annual payments of €10 000 and a corresponding liability. The asset would subsequently require depreciation and impairment.

The discussion paper works through even more complicated examples involving lessee interest in residual values and various optional features, e.g. lease payments that vary with price changes and considers the measurement problems involved. It then moves on to the issue of discount rates. Recording fair value of rights and obligations in a lease requires the discounting of future payments, thus there is a need to settle on a discount rate. The rate suggested by the discussion paper is the rate at which the lessee could borrow money for the term of the lease and with similar security to that of the lease.

The paper also proposes significant changes to lessor accounting practices. Lessors would report financial assets (representing amounts receivable from the lessee) and residual interests as separate assets. In the group's view, this would be a marked improvement in lessor accounting because a lessor's investment in a leased asset has two distinct elements, receivables and residual interest, which are subject to quite different risks.

The IASB has been too busy dealing with a multitude of urgent matters relevant to the 1 January 2005 deadline for implementation of many new Standards to devote much attention to these radical proposals. But they have not been removed from the longer-term agenda.

The discussion paper suggests that recognition take place at delivery of the property to the lessee.

For measurement of a lease we have to remember the principle that assuming an arm's-length transaction the cost of an acquired asset is normally measured by fair value of the consideration given. Thus the objective is to record at the beginning of the lease term the fair value of the rights and obligations that are conveyed by the lease.

SUMMARY

This chapter has explored the accounting measurement and disclosure problems relating to leases in the financial statements of both lessors and lessees. The requirements of IAS 17 have been explored and illustrated. Finally, suggestions that the distinction between finance and operating leases should be abolished have been considered.

EXERCISES

Suggested answers to exercises marked ✓ are to be found on the Student side of the companion website.

Suggested answers to the remaining exercises are to be found on the Instructor side of the companion website.

✓ **1**   Explain the theoretical distinction between finance leases and operating leases.

2   IAS 17 fails to give a clear definitional distinction between finance and operating leases. Discuss.

3   IAS 17 states that a particular lease which is a finance lease for the lessee need not automatically be a finance lease as regards the lessor. Can this make sense?

4   The need to account for lease transactions in a useful way proves that the principle of substance over form is essential. Discuss.

5   All unavoidable obligations relating to all lease contracts should be shown in the balance sheet of published financial statements. Discuss.

6   The following figures have been extracted from the accounting records of Lavalamp on 30 September 20X3:

	$000	$000
Sales revenue		112 500
Cost of sales (note (i))	78 300	
Operating expenses	11 400	
Lease rentals (note (iii))	2 000	
Loan interest paid	1 000	
Dividends paid	1 200	
Leasehold (20 years) factory at cost (note (ii))	25 000	
Plant and equipment at cost	34 800	
Depreciation 1 October 20X2 – leasehold		6 250
– plant and equipment		12 400
Accounts receivable	25 550	
Inventory – 30 September 20X3	21 800	
Cash and bank		4 000
Accounts payable		7 300
Ordinary shares of $1 each		20 000
Share premium		10 000
8% Loan note (issued in 20X0)		25 000
Accumulated profits – 1 October 20X2		3 600
	201 050	201 050

(i) Lavalamp has spent $6 million (included in the cost of sales) during the year developing and marketing a new brand of soft drink called Lavaflow. Of this amount $1 million is for advertising and the remainder is the development costs. A firm of consultants has been reviewing the sales of the new product and based on this, it has valued the brand name of Lavaflow at $10 million and expects the life of the brand to be 10 years. Lavalamp wishes to capitalise the maximum amount of intangible assets permitted under International Financial Reporting Standards.

(ii) Due to a sharp increase in the values of properties, Lavalamp had its leasehold property revalued on 1 October 20X2 with the intention of restating its carrying value. A firm of surveyors contracted to value the property found that it had suffered some damage which will cost $1.5 million to rectify. They gave a valuation of $24 million for the property on the assumption that the repairs are carried out. Lavalamp has informed Capitalrent, the owner of the property, of the repairs needed. Capitalrent has since sent their own surveyors to inspect the property and have informed Lavalamp that they believe the damage is due to the type of machinery being used in the building and accordingly have requested that Lavalamp pay for the repairs. Lavalamp has taken professional advice on this matter which concluded that the property was not in good condition when it was originally leased, but the use of the plant is making the damage worse. Lavalamp has offered to share the cost of the repairs with Capitalrent, but it has not yet had a reply.

(iii) Included in the income statement charge of $2 million for lease rentals is a payment of $600 000 in respect of a five-year lease of an item of plant (requiring ten payments in total). The payment was made on 1 April 20X3. The fair value of this plant at the date it was leased (1 April 20X3) was $5 million. Information obtained from the finance department confirms that this is a finance lease with an implicit interest rate of 10% per annum. The company depreciates plant used under finance leases on a straight line basis (with time apportionment) over the life of the lease. Other plant is depreciated at 20% per annum on cost. The remaining payments were confirmed as being for operating leases of office equipment.

(iv) A provision for income tax for the year to 30 September 20X3 of $3 470 000 is required.

(v) Lavalamp made and accounted for a rights issue on 1 October 2002 of 1 new share for every 4 held at a price of $1.60 per share. The issue was fully subscribed.

Required:

Prepare the financial statements for the year to 30 September 20X3 for Lavalamp in accordance with International Financial Reporting Standards as far as the information permits. They should include:

(a) an income statement;

(b) a statement of changes in equity, and

(c) a balance sheet.

Other than for item (ii) above, notes to the financial statements are NOT required, nor is a calculation of earnings per share. Ignore deferred tax.

(ACCA Dec 2003)

✓ **7**   (i)   Different accounting practices for leases are an area that, without a robust accounting standard, can be used to manipulate a company's financial statements. IAS 17 *Leases* was revised in 1999 and has as its objective to prescribe the appropriate accounting policies and disclosures for financial and operating leases.

Required:

Summarise the effect on the financial statements of a lessee treating a lease as an operating lease as opposed to a finance lease; and describe the factors that normally indicate a lease is a finance lease.

(ii)   Gemini leased an item of plant on 1 April 20X1 for a five-year period. Annual rentals in advance were $60 000. The cash price (fair value) of the asset on 1 April 20X1 was $260 000. The company's depreciation policy for this type of plant is 25% per annum on the reducing balance.

Required:

Assuming the lease is a finance lease and the interest rate implicit in the lease is 8%, prepare extracts of the financial statements of Gemini for the year to 31 March 20X3.

(ACCA December 2003)

INVENTORIES AND CONSTRUCTION CONTRACTS

16

OBJECTIVES After studying this chapter you should be able to:

- explain the composition of inventories

- describe five inventory cost assumptions, i.e. unit cost, first in first out (FIFO), last in first out (LIFO), weighted average and base inventory

- show the effect on annual profit and profit trends of using different inventory cost assumptions

- discuss IAS 2 requirements relating to inventories

- define construction contracts, attributable profit and foreseeable losses

- appraise IAS 11 requirements relating to construction contracts

- calculate amounts to be disclosed in financial statements relating to construction contracts

- identify the disclosure requirements of IAS 2 and 11.

INTRODUCTION

Inventories, including work in progress, present several problems to the accountant. First, we have to determine the value of the inventories, taking into account that the number of items in inventory changes constantly over time. Second, when inventory items are sold, we need to determine the cost of goods sold and recognise the related revenue. For this purpose we need to determine the revenue recognition (sale) point. The latter issue is solved in the international reporting standards by IAS 18, *Revenue*. So the valuation of inventories requires care as it is a key determinant of cost of goods sold and therefore in determining net income. Commercial companies purchase goods with the purpose of reselling them to third party customers. Inventories of commercial companies mainly consist of goods purchased for resale. Industrial companies on the other hand produce the products which they sell to their customers. Within industrial companies inventories consist of raw materials, work in progress and finished goods. Most industrial companies first produce goods and in a second step they face the commercial risk of finding a customer for those products. In a number of cases however a contract with the customer in which the revenue is determined has already been negotiated and signed before the start of the production of the goods according to the specifications agreed with the customer. In these cases companies do not bear a commercial risk after signing the contract with their customers, their main concern is to keep production costs under control. The latter types of contracts are called construction contracts and are treated in a separate standard, namely IAS 11, *Construction Contracts*. All other types of inventories are dealt with in IAS 2. In this chapter we consider first all types of inventories other than construction contracts. We start with a discussion of all methods available for inventory valuation purposes, and thereafter we focus on those methods which are permitted according to IAS 2. Next we discuss the valuation of construction contracts.

INVENTORIES

Inventories include:

1 goods or other assets purchased for resale
2 consumable stores
3 raw materials and components purchased for incorporation into products for sale
4 products and services in intermediate stages of completion
5 finished goods.

The 'cost' of each item at each of these stages is the key to determining the costs of goods sold and the value of inventory still left in the business, the closing inventory. Commercial companies will include in the valuation of the inventory mainly goods purchased for resale. Industrial companies in determining the cost of their inventory need to consider not only the cost of the raw materials but also the cost of converting raw materials into products and services for sale. Thus, we need to include in our valuation of inventory the following items: costs of purchase and costs of conversion including both direct and indirect overhead costs.

A moment's reflection will make it obvious that there are practical problems here. 'Direct' items should present no difficulties as figures can be related 'directly' by definition. But overhead allocation necessarily introduces assumptions and approximations – what is the normal level of activity taking one year with another? – can overheads be clearly classified according to function? – which other (non-production) overheads are 'attributable' to the present position and location of an item of inventory? So for any item of inventory that is not still in its original purchased state, it is a problem to determine the cost of a unit or even of a batch. Methods in common use include job, process, batch and standard costing. All include more or less arbitrary overhead allocations. We will elaborate on this issue when we discuss the IASB's definition of costs of conversion included in IAS 2.

Once we have found a figure for the unit cost per product 'in its present location and position', the next difficulty will arise when we have to select an appropriate method for calculating the related cost where several identical items have been purchased or made at different times and therefore at different unit costs.

Consider the following transactions for company Tradex:

Purchases:	January	10 units at €25 each
	February	15 units at €30 each
	April	20 units at €35 each
Sales:	March	15 units at €50 each
	May	18 units at €60 each

How do we calculate inventory, cost of sales and gross profit? There are several ways of doing this, based on different assumptions as to which unit has been sold or which unit is deemed to have been sold.

Inventory cost assumptions

Five possibilities are now discussed.

Unit cost Here we assume that we know the actual physical units that have moved in or out. Each unit must be individually distinguishable, e.g. by serial numbers. In these circumstances, we simply add up the recorded costs of those units sold to give cost of sales and of those units left to give stock. This needs no detailed illustration.

First in, first out (FIFO) Here it is assumed that the units moving out are the ones that have been in the longest (i.e. came in first). The units remaining will therefore be regarded as representing the latest units purchased (see Activity 16.1).

Last in, first out (LIFO) Here we reverse the assumption. We act as if the units moving out are the ones which came in most recently. The units remaining will therefore be regarded as representing the earliest units purchased (see Activity 16.2).

Weighted average Here we apply the average cost, weighted according to the different proportions at the different cost levels, to the items in inventory. Activity 16.3 shows the fully worked out method, involving continuous calculations. In practice, an average cost of purchases figure is often used rather than an average cost of inventory figure. This approximation reduces the need for calculation to a periodic, maybe even annual, requirement.

ACTIVITY 16.1

Calculate the cost of sales and gross profit based on FIFO inventory cost assumption from the data for company Tradex.

Activity feedback

				€	Cost of sales €
January	10	at €25	=	250	
February	15	at €30	=	450	
February total	25			700	
March	−10	at €25 (Jan.)	=	250	
	− 5	at €30 (Feb.)	=	150	400
March total	10			300	
April	+ 20	at €35	=	700	
April total	30			1 000	
May	−10	at €30 (Feb.)	=	300	
	− 8	at €35 (Apr.)	=	280	580
May total	12	at €35		420	
					980

Sales are 750 + 1080 = €1830
Purchases are 250 + 450 + 700 = €1400

This gives:		€	Cost of sales €
	Sales		1 830
	Purchases	1 400	
	Closing inventory	420	
	Cost of sales		980
	Gross profit		850

ACTIVITY 16.2

Calculate the cost of sales and gross profit based on LIFO inventory cost assumption using the data on p. 361.

Activity feedback

				€	Cost of sales €
January		10 at €25	=	250	
February		15 at €30	=	450	
February total		25	=	700	
March		−15 at €30 (Feb.)	=	450	450
March total		10	=	250	
April		+20 at €35	=	700	
April total		30	=	950	
May		−18 at €35 (Apr.)	=	630	630
May total		2 at €35 & 10 at €25	=	320	
					1 080
This gives:	Sales		1 830	
	Purchases	1 400		
	Closing inventory	320		
	Cost of sales		1 080	
	Gross profit		750	

Base inventory This approach is based on the argument that a certain minimum level of inventory is necessary in order to remain in business at all. Thus, it can be argued that some of the inventory viewed in the aggregate, is not really available for sale and should therefore be regarded as a fixed asset. This minimum level defined by management, remains at its original cost and the remainder of the inventory above this level is treated, as inventory, by one of the other methods. In our example, the minimum level might be ten units (see Activity 16.4).

So which approach or approaches are preferable or acceptable?

In selecting a method management presumably must exercise judgement to ensure that the methods chosen provide the fairest practicable approximation to cost. If standard costs are used to value inventory they will need to be reviewed frequently

---

ACTIVITY 16.3

Calculate the cost of sales and gross profit based on weighted average inventory cost assumption.

Activity feedback

Working: $\dfrac{(10 \times 25) + (15 \times 30)}{(10 + 15)} = 28^*$

$\dfrac{(10 \times 28) + (20 \times 35)}{(10 + 20)} = 32^{2/3**}$

			Cost of sales	
			€	€
January	10 at €25	=	250	
February	15 at €30	=	450	
February total	25 at €28*	=	700	
March	−15 at €28	=	420	420
March total	10 at €28	=	280	
April	+20 at €35	=	700	
April total	30 at €32²/₃**	=	980	
May	−18 at €32²/₃	=	588	588
May total	12 at €32²/₃	=	392	
				1 008

This gives:		Cost of sales	
		€	€
	Sales		1 830
	Purchases	1 400	
	Closing inventory	392	
	Cost of sales		1 008
	Gross profit		822

ACTIVITY 16.4

Calculate the cost of sales and gross profit based on a minimum inventory level of ten units and using FIFO.

Activity feedback

January purchase of base stock: 10 at €25 = €250

			Cost of sales	
			€	€
February	15 at €30	=	450	
March	−15 at €30	=	450	450
March total	0		0	
April	+20 at €35	=	700	
April total	20		700	
May	−18 at €35	=	630	630

May total	2 at €35	=	Cost of sales	
			€	€
May total	2 at €35	=	70	
				1 080

This gives:			
	Sales		1 830
	Purchases	1 150	
	Closing inventory	70	
	Cost of sales		1 080
	Gross profit		750

In this particular case, the gross profit is the same with this method (base inventory + FIFO) as with LIFO. Can you work out why? This will not generally be the case.

to ensure that they bear a reasonable relationship to actual costs incurred during the period. Methods such as base stock and LIFO often result in inventories being stated in the balance sheet at amounts that bear little relationship to recent cost levels. When this happens, not only can the presentation of current assets be misleading, but there is potential distortion of subsequent results if inventory levels reduce and out of date costs are drawn into the income statement. However, the method of arriving at cost by applying the FIFO method could be as unacceptable in principle because it is not necessarily the same as actual cost and, in times of rising prices, will result in the taking of a profit which has not been realised. To amplify, consider the cost of sales figure for the May sales in the earlier FIFO and LIFO calculations. Is it preferable to match an April cost level against an April revenue (LIFO) or, partially at least, to match a February cost level against an April revenue level (FIFO)? From a balance sheet viewpoint, however, the criticism of LIFO perhaps makes more sense. The balance sheet total under both LIFO and base stock is likely to be badly out of date. Applying the latest purchase price level to all units, sometimes called next in first out (NIFO), could also be rejected in principle for the same reason as LIFO.

Before we consider IAS 2 and how it attempts to answer this puzzle there is another problem to consider. In the activities so far we have virtually been able to match an inventory item with its sale but this is not the general case.

INVENTORY SYSTEMS

Periodic systems

Within this system inventory is determined by a physical count at a specific date. As long as the count is made frequently enough for reporting purposes, it is not necessary to maintain extensive inventory records. The inventory shown in the balance sheet is determined by the physical count and is priced in accordance with the inventory method used. The net charge between the beginning and ending inventories enters into the computation of costs of goods sold.

Perpetual system

In a perpetual system, inventory records are maintained and updated continuously as items are purchased and sold. The system has the advantage of providing inventory information on a timely basis but requires the maintenance of a full set of inventory records. Audit practice will certainly require that a physical check of perpetual inventory records be made periodically.

IAS REQUIREMENTS FOR INVENTORY

It is now quite clear that the calculation of the appropriate inventory at 'cost' figure is by no means clear cut. Assumptions in two respects have to be made. First the determination of the cost of the unit and second the matching of these costs with the items sold. With regard to the first item, IAS 2 states that 'Inventories shall be measured at the lower of cost and net realisable value' (NRV) (para. 9, IAS 2). With regard to the second item, namely the matching issue, IAS 2 allows three of the five methods discussed earlier, namely the unit cost, FIFO and weighted average. In certain circumstances the retail method is allowed. We concentrate in the sections below first on the determination of the unit cost of an item in inventory and afterwards we pay attention to inventory valuation methods allowed by IAS 2. We start the discussion with a review of the scope of IAS 2 and the definitions provided in the Standard for a number of concepts.

Definitions

In para. 6 of IAS 2 inventories are defined as assets:

(a) held for sale in the ordinary course of the business;

(b) in the process of production for such sale; or

(c) in the form of materials or supplies to be consumed in the production process or in the rendering of services.

Excluded from the scope of IAS 2 are construction contracts, financial instruments and biological assets related to agricultural activity and agricultural produce at the point of harvest (dealt with under IAS 41, *Agriculture*: for a discussion of IAS 41, see the accompanying website to this book). With regard to the scope of IAS 2, the text of the Standard (para. 3) mentions further that the Standard does not apply to producers of agricultural and forest products, agricultural produce after harvest, and minerals and mineral products, to the extent that they are measured at net realisable value in accordance with well-established practices in those industries. Neither does the Standard apply to commodity broker-traders who measure their inventories at fair value less cost to sell. In both cases changes in fair values are recognised in profit or loss in the period of change.

IAS 2 (para. 6) defines the concepts of net realisable value and fair value. *Net realisable value* is defined as the estimated selling price in the ordinary course of business less the estimated costs of completion and the estimated costs necessary to make the sale. *Fair value* is defined as the amount for which an asset could be exchanged, or a liability settled, between knowledgeable, willing parties in an arm's-length transaction.

Paragraph 8 of IAS 2 provides a number of examples of items which will be recorded under inventories. For example, merchandise purchased by a retailer and held for resale or land and other property held for resale. They also encompass finished goods produced or work in progress being produced by the entity and include materials and supplies awaiting use in the production process being produced by the entity and include materials and supplies awaiting use in the production

ACTIVITY 16.5

An entity has three products in its inventory with values as follows:

Product	Cost	NRV
A	10	12
B	11	15
C	12	9
Total	33	36

At what value should the inventory be stated in the balance sheet in accordance with IAS 2?

Activity feedback

If the inventory is not separated into each type then we would value at the lower of cost of 33 and NRV of 36. The answer is 33. However, IAS 2 requires us to value each type of inventory separately and therefore the lower in each case is A 10, B 11 and C 9 giving us an inventory valuation of 30.

process. In the case of a service provider, inventories include the costs of the service for which the entity has not yet recognised the related revenue.

After a discussion on the scope of IAS 2, we return to the heart of the matter, namely the valuation of the inventories. IAS 2 states that inventories must be measured at the lower of cost and net realisable value (NRV). IAS 2 defines (para. 10) the concept of cost of inventories as follows: 'The cost of inventories shall comprise all costs of purchase, costs of conversion and other costs incurred in bringing the inventories to their present location and condition.' The definition of net realisable value is provided above (see the discussion on the scope of IAS 2). It is obvious that for each separate item of inventory we need to determine both the cost, and the NRV.

The separate item point is significant and this is shown in Activity 16.5.

In the next section we concentrate on the concept 'cost of inventory' for industrial companies. In industrial companies the calculation of the unit cost involves a lot more decisions in order to arrive at the unit cost which can be used for financial reporting purposes.

Cost of inventory

IAS 2 gives guidance on the costs of the different elements included in the definition of the cost of inventories as follows (see para. 10: 11–18). The cost of inventories should include: all costs of purchase, costs of conversion and other costs incurred in bringing the inventories to their present location and condition. Further amplification of cost is given in para. 11 as follows.

The costs of purchase of inventories comprise the purchase price, import duties and other taxes (other than those subsequently recoverable by the entity from the taxing authority) and transport, handling and other costs directly attributable to the acquisition of finished goods, materials and services. Trade discounts, rebates and other similar items are deducted in determining the costs of purchase.

It must be noted here that IAS 2 does *not* permit exchange differences arising directly on the recent acquisition of inventories invoiced in a foreign currency to be included in the costs of purchase of inventories. This change is because the improved IAS 21 has eliminated the allowed alternative treatment of capitalising certain exchange differences. The cost of purchase applies to the inventories in commercial companies as well as to all materials used in the production process of industrial companies and materials awaiting use in the production process.

The item costs of conversion is explained in paragraphs, 12, 13 and 14 of IAS 2, indicating the associated problems. Costs of conversion include direct labour, the systematic allocation of fixed production overheads, e.g. depreciation, maintenance charges and the allocation of variable production overheads, e.g. indirect materials and labour. (Remember here that fixed overheads are those indirect costs of production that remain relatively constant regardless of volume of production whereas variable overheads are those that vary directly or nearly with volume of production.) IAS 2 prescribes a different allocation procedure for fixed and variable overheads. Variable overheads are allocated to the units produced based on the actual use of production facilities.

The allocation of fixed overheads is based on the normal capacity of production facilities, taking into account the loss of capacity resulting from planned maintenance. However IAS 2 also proposes two other treatments for the allocation of fixed overhead costs. First the actual level of production may be used if it approximates normal capacity. Second, in periods of abnormally high production, the amount of fixed overhead allocated to each unit of production is decreased so that of variable overheads on the actual use of production facilities, inventories are not measured above cost. Where joint products are concerned a rational basis for allocation of costs of conversion between them needs to be found.

The Standard suggests the use of relative sale value or gross contribution margin as rational and consistent bases. This can be seen as somewhat arbitrary and subjective but nevertheless is at least a consistent, if not entirely logical, method for dealing with a difficult issue.

We now focus on the definition of the third element included in the cost of conversion namely other costs included in the concept 'cost of inventories'. According to para. 15 other costs are included in the inventory only to the extent that they are incurred in bringing the inventories to their present location and condition. Para. 16 lists a number of items which are excluded from the cost of inventories and as a result they should be recognised as expenses in the period in which they are incurred:

(a) abnormal amounts of wasted materials, labour and other production costs;

(b) storage costs, unless those costs are necessary in the production process before a further production stage;

(c) administrative overheads that do not contribute to bringing inventories to their present location and condition; and

(d) selling costs.

A good example of storage costs that can be included in the cost of inventory is those involved in the ageing of whisky. As ageing is essential to the production of whisky, whatever storage costs are incurred can be capitalised to the cost of inventory.

Techniques for the measurement of the cost of inventories

For companies producing products and services, IAS 2 permits the use of the standard cost method where normal levels of materials, supplies, labour, efficiency and capacity utilisation will be used to calculate a standard cost. These standard costs have to be reviewed regularly if this method is used.

ACTIVITY 16.6

Determine the valuation of inventory items A and B from the following data:

	A	B
Direct labour charge per item	2	4

Fixed production overheads total €50 000 and normal capacity of production is 5200 for product A and 10 200 for product B but this is reduced by 200 for A and 200 B for planned maintenance. The target of production was 6000 for A and 12 000 B. Variable production overheads are calculated as €10 000 in total and are to be allocated on a machine hour basis. Each A item takes two hours of machine time and each B one hour.

Activity feedback

Fixed production overheads will be charged over 5000 A and 10 000 B as normal capacity is after planned maintenance allowance. The target of production is irrelevant in the calculation unless this high production level is actually achieved in which case the fixed overheads to each unit will be decreased so as not to measure the item above cost.

	A	B
Direct labour	2	4
Fixed overheads (allocated in ratio of 1:2 and on number of items)	2	4
Variable overheads (0.5 per hour)	1	0.5
	5	8.5

ACTIVITY 16.7

Calculate the cost of inventories in accordance with IAS 2 using the following data relating to Unipoly Company for the year ended 31 May 20X7.

	€
Direct materials cost of can opener per unit	1
Direct labour cost of can opener unit	1
Other direct costs of can opener unit	1
Production overheads per year	600 000
Administration overheads per year	200 000
Selling overheads per year	300 000
Interest payments per year	100 000

There were 250 000 units in finished goods at the year-end. You may assume that there were no finished goods at the start of the year and that there was no work in progress. The normal annual level of production is 750 000 can openers, but in the year ended 31 May 20X7 only 450 000 were produced because of a labour dispute.

Activity feedback

The direct costs of the inventory are straightforward to calculate as follows:

	€
250 000 units at €1 direct material cost	250 000
250 000 units at €1 direct labour cost	250 000
250 000 units at direct €1 cost	250 000
	750 000

IAS 2 only permits the inclusion of production overheads in the valuation of inventories and therefore the administration, selling and interest costs (if interest costs meet the requirements identified in IAS 23, *Borrowing Costs*, see Chapter 12) are not relevant here.

To allocate production overhead the normal production capacity will be used as an allocation basis (600 000/750 000) = 0.8 € per unit. In order to calculate the overhead which will be assigned to the inventory we multiply the overhead cost per unit by the number of units in inventory (0.8 x 250 000 = 200 000). The abnormal costs associated with the labour dispute will be charged as an expense in the period they are incurred. So we arrive at a cost of finished inventory of:

Cost of finished inventory = €950 000

ACTIVITY 16.8

Which of the following costs, listed below can be included in the cost of inventory in accordance with IAS 2? Reference to paras 9–20 of IAS 2 will help in completing this activity.

Discounts on purchase price
Travel expenses of buyers
Import duties
Transport insurance
Commission and brokerage costs
Storage costs after receiving materials that are
   necessary in the production process
Salaries of sales department
Warranty cost
Research for new products
Audit and tax consultation fees

Activity feedback

Discounts on purchase price	yes
Travel expenses of buyers	no
Import duties	yes
Transport insurance	yes
Commission and brokerage costs	yes
Storage costs after receiving materials that are necessary in the production process	yes
Salaries of sales department	no
Warranty cost	no
Research for new products	no
Audit and tax consultation fees	no

IAS 2 also permits the use of the retail method. The retail method is generally used in the retail industry where there are large numbers of rapidly changing items that have similar margins. The cost of the inventory is determined by reducing the sales value of the inventory by the appropriate gross profit margin. Problems occur with this method when a retailer deals in products of widely differing profit margins or discounts slow moving items.

Once the cost of inventories is determined, the next cost formulae are available to determine the value of the costs of goods sold. In the introduction to this chapter, we explained that five methods or cost formulas are available in order to determine the value of the inventory and the costs of goods sold.

Cost formulas for the determination of the value of the inventory and the costs of goods sold

IAS 2 distinguishes between interchangeable goods and non-interchangeable goods. Items that are not ordinarily interchangeable and goods or services produced and segregated for specific projects should be assigned by using specific identification of their individual costs (para. 23). This approach equates to the unit cost method described in the introductory section.

For all other types of inventories, IAS 2 advocates the use of FIFO or the weighted average cost formula. We note that IAS 2 does not permit the use of LIFO.

Remember the use of LIFO in a period of rising costs will reduce profits and value inventory on the balance sheet at older costs whereas FIFO shows inventory on the balance sheet at newer costs and what many would regard as a more relevant cost.

The elimination of LIFO, however, does not rule out specific cost methods that reflect inventory flows that are similar to LIFO. For example, when stock bins of coal, cement, etc. are replenished by 'topping up', then LIFO may reflect the actual physical flow of inventories.

When inventories are sold, the carrying amount of those inventories shall be recognised as an expense in the period in which the related revenue is recognised. The closing inventory will appear on the balance sheet at the lower of cost or net realisable value.

Net realisable value

In order to determine the net realisable value, the company deducts from the selling price in the ordinary course of the business the estimated costs of completion and the estimated costs necessary to make the sale (= marketing, selling and distribution costs). When the cost of the inventory will not be recoverable due to damage, the cost of the inventory will be written down to net realisable value. The amount of any write-down of inventories to net realisable value and all losses of inventories shall be recognised as an expense in the period the write-down or loss occurs. The amount of any reversal of any write-down of inventories, arising from an increase in the net realisable value, shall be recognised in the period in which the reversal occurs.

Comparison with other GAAPs

US GAAP – inventory is carried at lower of cost or market with market generally meaning replacement cost. Under US GAAP reversals on write-downs of inventory cannot be recognised.

Otherwise, in general, the UK and US GAAPs are comparable to IAS.

Disclosure requirements

According to IAS 2, financial statements have to disclose:

- the accounting policies adopted in measuring inventories, including the cost formulas used
- the total carrying amount of inventories and the carrying amount in classifications appropriate to the entity

- the carrying amount of inventories carried at fair value less costs to sell
- the amount of any write-down of inventories recognised as an expense in the period in accordance with para. 34
- the carrying amount of inventories pledged as security for liabilities
- the cost of inventories recognised as an expense during the period
- the amount of any reversal of any write-down that is recognised as a reduction in the amount of inventories recognised as an expense in the period in accordance with para. 34
- the circumstances or events that led to the reversal of a write-down of inventories in accordance with para. 34.

In the 2005 annual report of IBM the reader is provided with 'critical accounting estimates'. These are estimates requiring degrees of judgement on the application of GAAP. They have this to say on inventories:

> The company reviews the market value and demand for its inventory on a quarterly basis to ensure recorded inventory is stated at the lower of cost or market. Inventories at higher risk for writedowns or writeoffs are those in the industries that have lower relative gross margins and that are subject to a higher likelihood of changes in industry cycles. The semiconductor business is one such industry.
>
> Factors that could impact estimated demand and selling prices are the timing and success of future technological innovations, competitor actions, supplier prices and economic trends. To the extent that total inventory losses differ from management estimates by 5 percent, the company's consolidated net income in 2005 would have improved/declined by an estimated $22 million using 2005 results, depending upon whether the actual results were better/worse, respectively, than expected.

This quite clearly demonstrates that valuation of inventory is not an exact science.

CONSTRUCTION CONTRACTS

Introduction

Construction contracts generally last over a long period of time, certainly longer than one accounting period. Another feature is that the purchase contract for these items is already agreed before production starts. A sales price is determined in the contract. Such contracts involve all the difficulties discussed earlier in the context of inventories, with one major addition. This is the question of profit allocation over the various accounting periods. If a contract extends over, say, three years, should the contribution to profits be 0%, 0% and 100%, respectively, for the three years? Can we make profits on something before we have finished it? The realisation convention might seem to argue against doing so and the old idea of prudence would certainly argue against it too. But would this give a 'fair presentation' of the results for each period? And would it be of any use? All the various users want regular information on business progress. Remember the desirability of timeliness of information. Can we not argue that we can be 'reasonably certain' during the contract, of at least some profit? This discussion has led to two basic methods of dealing with construction contracts: 'completed-contract method' and 'the percentage-of-completion method'. This latter method requires allocation over accounting periods of the total profit on the contract while the former delays profit recognition until completion (see Activity 16.9).

In Activity 16.9 the percentage of completion was determined on the basis of the proportion of costs already incurred. Having decided on the use of percentage-of-completion method our next problem is to determine how this profit and indeed any sale and therefore resulting contract work in progress should be shown in the accounts. If the contract work in progress is shown as a current asset with its attributable profit, as implied by the percentage-of-completion method then this is in direct conflict with the requirement to show inventories at cost or NRV, whichever is the lower included in IAS 2. Therefore construction contracts are dealt with in a separate Standard, namely IAS 11.

IAS 11

Construction contracts are defined (para. 3) as contracts specifically negotiated for the construction of an asset or a combination of assets that are closely interrelated or interdependent in terms of their design, technology and function of their ultimate purpose or use. IAS 11 distinguishes between two types of construction contracts, namely 'a fixed price contract' and 'a cost plus contract'. The essential difference between the two types of contracts is the way in which the revenue of the transaction is determined:

- A *fixed price contract* is a construction contract in which the contractor agrees to a fixed contract price or a fixed rate per unit of output, which in some cases is subject to cost escalation clauses.

- A *cost plus contract* is a construction contract in which the contractor is reimbursed for allowable or otherwise defined costs, plus a percentage of these costs or a fixed fee.

However, in practice, the type of contract is not always so clear cut and many have characteristics of both types. It is also worth noting that there is no definition given for 'contractor' which appears to be used in a general sense in the Standard.

ACTIVITY 16.9

Zen entity is contracted to Alpha for $2m to construct a building. The following data are available in relation to the contract:

	20X5	20X6	20X7
Costs incurred during year	500 000	700 000	300 000
Year-end estimate costs to complete	1 000 000	300 000	
Bills raised during year	400 000	700 000	900 000
Cash received during year	200 000	500 000	1 200 000

Show the profit to be included in the accounts under both the percentage-of-completion method and completed-contract method assuming that degree of completion is based on costs incurred.

Activity feedback

Under the completed-contract method the profit of 500 000 will not be recognised until 20X7 whereas under the percentage-of-completion method it will be allocated to each accounting year as follows:

$$20X5 \; \frac{500\,000}{1\,500\,000} \times 500\,000$$

$$- \text{previously recognised}(0) \qquad 166\,667$$

$$20X6 \; \frac{1\,200\,000}{1\,500\,000} \times 500\,000 - 166\,667 \qquad 233\,333$$

$$20X7 \; \frac{1\,500\,000}{1\,500\,000} \times 500\,000$$

$$- \; 233\,333 - 166\,667 \qquad \underline{100\,000}$$

$$\underline{\underline{500\,000}}$$

The Standard also discusses the separability issue. Many contracts can cover the construction of a number of assets and in these cases each asset must be treated as a separate contract if:

- separate proposals have been submitted for each asset
- each asset has been subject to separate negotiations and the contractor and customer have been able to accept or reject that part of the contract relating to each asset
- the costs and revenues of each asset can be identified.

Conversely, a group of contracts may in substance be a single construction contract and is required to be treated as such when:

- the group of contracts is negotiated as a single package
- the contracts are so clearly interrelated that they are in effect part of a single project with an overall profit margin
- the contracts are performed concurrently or in a continuous sequence.

After these definitions and explanations the Standard finally arrives at the heart of the problem, namely the recognition of the revenues and costs involved in the contract. Contract revenue should comprise (para. 11):

(a) the initial amount of revenue agreed in the contract; and

(b) variations in contract work claims and incentive payments:

    (i) to the extent that it is probable that they will result in revenue; and

    (ii) they are capable of being reliably measured.

Contract costs consist of (para. 16):

- costs that relate directly to the specific contract
- costs that are attributable to contract activity in general and can be allocated to the contract
- such other costs as are specifically chargeable to the customer under the terms of the contract.

Thus, in determining appropriate figures for construction contracts, first we calculate the total costs attaching to the contract to date, including appropriate production overheads, which could include borrowing costs. Second, we calculate revenue attributable to the contract to date and therefore attributable profit.

The Standard provides lists of costs that may and may not be charged to a specific contract (see Activity 16.10).

So far we have discussed all items, which need to be taken into account in the valuation process of construction contracts. Next we focus on the amounts which need to be recorded in the balance sheet and the profit and loss account during the construction period. IAS 11 requires the percentage-of-completion method to be used for the valuation of these contracts. When the outcome of a construction contract can be estimated reliably, contract revenue and contract costs associated with the construction contract shall be recognised as revenue and expenses respectively by reference to the stage of completion of the contract activity at the end of the reporting period (para. 22).

The stage of completion of a contract is determined by the method that measures reliably the work performed and this could be:

- proportion that costs incurred for work performed to date bear to total
- estimated costs;

ACTIVITY 16.10

Identify four costs that could be charged to a specific contract and four that may not.

Activity feedback

Paragraph 17 of the Standard gives a number of items, as follows:

Costs that may be charged are:

- site labour costs
- materials used in construction
- depreciation of assets used on construction
- costs of moving assets to and from the site
- hire charges
- design and technical assistance that is directly related

- estimated costs of rectification and guarantee work, including warranty costs
- claims from third parties
- insurance
- construction overheads.

Costs that may not be charged are:

- general administration costs not specified in the contract
- selling costs
- research and development costs not specified
- depreciation of idle assets not used on a specific contract.

- surveys of work performed; or
- completion of a physical proportion of the contract work.

IAS 11 pays a lot of attention to the recognition of the revenues of the construction contracts. In para. 22 and para. 23 the standard spells out in detail when revenue can be recognised for a fixed price contract and for a cost plus contract.

In the case of a fixed price contract, the outcome of a construction contract can be estimated reliably when all the following conditions are satisfied (para. 23):

(a) total contract revenue can be measured reliably;

(b) it is probable that the economic benefits associated with the contract will flow to the entity;

(c) both the contract costs to complete the contract and the stage of contract completion at the end of the reporting period can be measured reliably; and

(d) the contract costs attributable to the contract can be clearly identified and measured reliably so that actual contract costs incurred can be compensated.

In relation to cost plus contracts, the outcome of a construction contract can be estimated reliably when all the following conditions are satisfied:

(a) it is probable that the economic benefits associated with the contract will flow to the entity; and

(b) the contract costs attributable to the contract, whether or not specifically reimbursable, can be clearly identified and measured reliably.

When it is probable that total contract costs will exceed total contract revenue, the expected loss shall be recognised as an expense immediately (para. 36).

In Activities 16.11–16.17 we will illustrate the principles laid down in IAS 11 with regard to the recognition and valuation of construction contracts.

IAS 11 requires that, 'an expected loss should be recognised as an expense immediately'. It also requires that the gross amount due from customers for contract work

ACTIVITY 16.11

The following data are available in respect of a construction contract:

Costs to date	$2m
Total contract revenue expected	$2m
Further costs to completion	$0.5m

How should this contract be treated in the accounts?

Activity feedback

The problem here is that the contract is forecast to make a loss of $0.5m and we need to determine how much of this loss should be recognised at the current stage of completion. The percentage-of-completion method might imply we should recognise $2/2.5 \times 0.5 = 0.4$ but prudence would suggest we should recognise all the foreseeable loss immediately it becomes apparent.

should be shown as an asset and gross amount due to customers for contract work as a liability. The gross amount due from customers is defined as the net amount of:

costs incurred + recognised profits

— the sum of recognised losses and progress billings

for all contracts in progress for which costs incurred plus recognised profits (less recognised losses) exceeds progress billings.

The gross amount due to customers is defined as the net amount of:

costs incurred + recognised profits

— the sum of recognised losses and progress billings

for all contracts in progress for which progress billings exceed costs incurred plus recognised profits (less recognised losses).

Activity 16.12 should demonstrate these requirements.

ACTIVITY 16.12

The following data are available in respect of five contracts in progress at the end of year 1 by Gamma Entity. Identify how each contract should be shown in the accounts in accordance with IAS 11.

		Contracts				
	A	B	C	D	E	Total
Contract revenue recognised	145	520	380	200	55	1 300
Contract expenses recognised	110	450	350	250	55	1 215
Expected losses				40	30	70
Contract costs incurred in period	110	510	450	250	100	1 420
Contract costs recognised as contract expenses	110	450	350	250	55	1 215
Contract costs relating to future activity		60	100		45	205
Progress billings	100	520	380	180	55	1 235
Payments in advance of billings		80	20		25	125

Activity feedback

We will explain the treatment of each contract separately.

Contract A
Income statement

Shown as contract revenue	145
Shown as contract expenses	110
Gross profit	35

Balance sheet
The amount to be included in current assets under amounts due from customers calculated as follows:

Cumulative revenue	145
less Cumulative billings	100
Amounts due from customers	45

This can also be calculated as:

Costs incurred, 110 plus recognised profits, 35 less progress billings, 100 = 45. In this case all the costs incurred to date relate to the contract activity recorded as revenue and are transferred to income statement as contract expenses leaving a zero balance.

Contract B
Income statement

Shown as contract revenue	520
Shown as contract expenses	450
Gross profit	70

Balance sheet
As cumulative billings are greater than revenue there is a credit balance, calculated as follows:

Cumulative revenue	520
Billing plus advances	600
Advances received (shown under current liabilities)	80

Contract costs incurred to date	510
Contract expenses	450
Amounts due from customers, current assets	60

(also calculated as 510 + 70 – 520)

Contract C

Contract revenue	380
Contract expenses	350
Gross profit	30

Balance sheet
As with contract B cumulative billings and payments in advance are greater than contract revenue and there is a credit balance calculated as follows:

Contract revenue	380
Billings plus advances	400
Advances received – current liabilities	20

The amount to be included in current assets is calculated as follows:

Contract costs incurred to date	450
Contract expenses	350
Amounts due from customers – current asset	100

(also calculated as 450 + 30 – 380)

Contract D
Income statement

Contract revenue	200
Contract expenses (costs 250 + loss 40)	290
Gross loss	90

Balance sheet
The amount to be included in current assets is calculated as follows:

Cumulative revenue	200
Billings	180
Balance	20

However, there is also a foreseeable loss credit balance sitting in the accounts and this 40 is transferred to the balance creating a liability of 20 – amounts due to customers. This can also be calculated via costs incurred 250, less foreseeable losses 90, less billings, 180 = (20).

Contract E
Income statement

Contract revenue	55
Contract expenses (costs incurred 55 + loss 30)	85
Gross loss	30

Balance sheet
As cumulative billings are greater than contract revenue there is a credit balance calculated as follows:

Contract revenue	55
Billings plus advances	80
Advance payment – current liabilities	25
Contract costs incurred	100
Contract expenses	85
Due from customers – current asset	15

(also calculated as 100 – 30 – 55)

Thus, in total for contracts A to E, we have:

Contract revenue		1 300
Contract expenses	1 215	
Expected losses	70	1285
Profit		15
Payments in advance shown as creditor (0 + 80 + 20 + 0 + 25)		125
Payments due from customers shown as current asset (45 + 60 + 100 + 0 + 15)		220
Payments due to customers shown as liability (contract D)		20

To test your understanding of Activity 16.12 we include Activity 16.13 which is slightly easier.

ACTIVITY 16.13

Show how the following information for two construction contracts should be recorded in the financial statements.

	Contract X	Contract Y
Contract revenue	500	350
Contract expenses	450	400
Billings	500	200
Payments in advance of billings	25	–
Contract costs incurred	600	400
Foreseeable additional losses	–	60

Activity feedback

Contract X

Contract revenue	
P&L 500(2)	Debtors 500(1)

Contract costs incurred			
Costs incur.	600	P&L	450(3)
		Bal.c/d	150
	600		600
Bal.b/d	150		

Bal.b/d 150 is shown as due from customers under current assets on BS (also calculated as 600 + 50 – 500)

Income statement					Debtors			
Contract expenses	450(3)	Contract revenue	500(2)		Revenue	500	Billing	500
Profit	50							

Billings			
Debtor	500	Payments	525
Bal. pays in advance	25		

Contract Y

Contract revenue			Contract costs incurred			
P&L 350(2)	Debtors 350(1)		Costs incur.	400	P&L	400(3)

Income statement					Debtors			
Contract costs	400(3)	Contract rev	350(2)		Contract rev	350	Billing	200
Prov. for losses	60(4)	Loss	110				Bal.c/d	150
						350		350
					Bal.b/d	150	Prov.loss	60(5)
							Bal.c/d	90
Prov. for loss account						150		150
Debtors	60(5)	P&L	60(4)		Bal.b/d	90		

Bal. b/d 90 shown as due from customers under current assets (400 – 110 – 200)

(1) raise the contract revenue

(2) transfer contract revenue to income statement

(3) transfer proportion of contract costs incurred to date to income statement or contract expenses

(4) raise provision for foreseeable losses

(5) transfer provision to debtors.

In total, the contracts will be shown as follows:

Income statement		
Contract revenue	(500 + 350)	850
Contract expenses	(450 + 460)	910
Loss		60
Balance sheet		
Current assets		
Due from customers construction contracts	(90 + 150)	240
Current liabilities		
Payments in advance construction contracts		25

Estimating the stage of completion of a contract relies on estimates of total costs and these may well change throughout the life of the contract. Paragraph 38 of IAS 11 requires us to treat the changes as a change in accounting estimate in accordance with IAS 8, *Accounting Policies*.

ACTIVITY 16.14

A construction contract with revenue of £15m is initially estimated to have total costs of £9m and is expected to take four years to complete. In year 2 the costs are re-estimated at £10m the increased cost being attributed as follows, £0.6m to year 3 and £0.4m to year 4. If we assume the initial costs were attributed as follows, £2m year 1, £2.5m year 2, £3m year 4 and £1.5m year 4 we can calculate the stage of completion of the contract both before and after the re-estimate.

	Year 1 £m	Year 2 £m	Year 3 £m	Year 4 £m
Initial estimate				
Revenue	15	15	15	15
Contract costs to date	2	4.5	7.5	9
Contract costs to complete	7	4.5	1.5	-
	9	9	9	9
Profit estimate	6	6	6	6

% complete	22.2%	50%	83.3%	100%
Profit recognised in year	1.33	1.67	2	1
Re-estimate				
Revenue	15	15	15	15
Contract costs to date	2	4.5	8.1	10
Contract costs to complete	7	5.5	1.9	-
	9	10	10	10
Profit estimate	6	5	5	5
% complete	22.2%	45%	81%	100%
Profit recognised in year	1.33	0.92	1.8	0.95

Year 2 profit is reduced from £1.67m to £0.92m to take account of the adjustment to the year 1 profit subsequent to the re-estimate. Note that no change is made to the year 1 profit figure in accordance with IAS 8.

So far we have dealt with construction contracts where the outcome can be reliably estimated. For those contracts that cannot be reliably estimated the Standard requires that revenue should be recognised only to the extent of contract costs incurred that it is probable will be recoverable and contract costs should be recognised as an expense immediately.

ACTIVITY 16.15

An entity is involved in two construction contracts the outcome of which cannot be assessed with reliability for which the following data are available:

Contract A   contract costs incurred 30 000 all probably recoverable

Contract B   contract costs incurred 100 000, similar contracts have shown a loss of 15% on contract sale price due to pending legislation affecting the construction. Contract sale price 1m.

Identify how these two contracts should be treated in the accounts of the entity.

Activity feedback

Contract A	Contract revenue	30 000
	Contract costs	30 000
Contract B	Contract revenue	0
	Contract costs recognised as expense	150 000

ACTIVITY 16.16

Using the data from the feedback to Activity 16.13 show, as far as possible, the disclosure requirements for contracts X and Y in accordance with IAS 11.

Activity feedback

Contract revenue recognised as revenue in period	850

Contract costs incurred and recognised profits less losses	
600 + 400 + 50 − 110	940
Advances received	25
Amounts due from customers (150 + 90)	240

Disclosure requirements

These are detailed at paras 39–45 of the Standard and cover such items as:

- amount recognised as revenue in the period
- method used to determine revenue and stage of completion
- aggregate amounts relating to costs and profits recognised, advances received and retentions.

In addition, amounts due to and from customers must be presented as a current asset and liability respectively.

Another activity for you to try.

ACTIVITY 16.17

The following data is available in respect of two contracts:

	£000s Contract A	£000s Contract B
Contract revenue recognised	1 000	400
Contract expenses recognised	600	400
Foreseeable additional losses		200
Progress billings	700	100
Payments made by customer	500	80

Show how the above should be recorded in the financial statements.

Activity feedback

Income statement	£000s Total	£000s Contract A	£000s Contract B
Contract revenue	1 400	1 000	400
Contract expenses	1200	600	600
			(400 + 200 loss)
Gross profit	200	400	(200)
Balance sheet			
Gross amount due from customers	400	300 (1000 − 700)	100 (400 − 100 − 200 loss)
Trade receivables	220	200 (700 − 500)	20 (100 − 80)

Note the billings not paid by customers are shown as trade receivables.

The following extract from the annual report of Vitec Group plc for the year ended 31 December 2005 shows a typical accounting policy under IFRSs:

Long term contracts (IAS 11 'Construction contracts'):
Contract revenue and expenses are recognised in the income statement in proportion to the stage of completion of the contract. The stage of completion is assessed by reference to surveys of work performed. An expected loss on a contract is recognised immediately in the income statement.

Contract work in progress is stated at costs incurred, less those transferred to the income statement, after deducting foreseeable losses and payments on account not matched with turnover.

Amounts recoverable on contracts are included in debtors and represent turnover recognised in excess of payments on account.

In the financial statements of EADS for the year 2007 (a company active in the air, space and defence transport sectors) we find information on write-downs on their A-380 programme.

Inventories at 31st December 2007 and 2006 consist of the following:

(in €m)	31st December 2007	31st December 2006
Raw materials and manufacturing supplies	1 596	1 283
Work in progress	12 253	11 260
Finished goods and parts accounted for at lower of cost and net realisable value	1 217	1 224
Advance payments to suppliers	3 840	3 125
Total	**18 906**	**16 892**

The increase in work in progress of €993 million was mainly driven by the Airbus A380 programme, the A400M programme and the ramp-up at Eurocopter partly compensated by the MBDA quotation change from 50% to 37.5% in the amount of €(318) million. The increase of advance payments provided to suppliers mainly reflects activities in Airbus for supplier funding and in Defence of Eurofighter Series Production Equipment.

The finished goods and parts for resale before write-down to net relisable value amunt to €1,565 million in 2007 (2006: €1,559 million) and work in progress before write-down to net realisable value amunts to €13,632 million (2006: €12,186 million). Write-downs for finished goods and services are recorded when it becomes probable that total estimated contract costs will exceed total contract revenues. The impairment charges in 2007 and 2006 for work in progress mainly relate to the A380 programme.

Comparison with different GAAPs

UK GAAP in SSAP 9, *Stocks and Long-term Contracts*, is similar to IAS 11 except for some differences in the offset of final balances on the contracts.

US GAAP – if an entity cannot determine contract revenue or costs, estimated costs to completion or the stage of completion then the completed-contract method is required. IAS 11 prohibits the use of the completed-contract method.

SUMMARY

This chapter has defined inventories and construction contracts and identified the accounting requirements for them in accordance with IAS 2 and 11. Valuation of inventories using the unit cost, FIFO, LIFO, weighted average and base inventory are all possible but all lead to a different profit figure and asset figure. Remember the improved IAS 2 has now eliminated the use of LIFO.

It should be clear to you that valuation of inventories is by no means a straightforward task and it requires management to make several judgements.

EXERCISES

Suggested answers to exercises marked ✓ are to be found on the Student side of the companion website.

Suggested answers to the remaining exercises are to be found on the Instructor side of the companion website.

1　P Forte commences business on 1 January buying and selling pianos. He sells two standard types, upright and grand, and his transactions for the year are given in the table below.

	Upright		Grand	
	Buy	*Sell*	*Buy*	*Sell*
1 January	2 at €400		2 at €600	
31 March		1 at €600		
30 April	1 at €350		1 at €700	
30 June		1 at €600		1 at €1 000
31 July	2 at €300		1 at €800	
30 September		3 at €500		2 at €1 100
30 November	1 at €250		1 at €900	

You observe that the cost to P Forte of the pianos is changed on 1 April, 1 July and 1 October and will not change again until 1 January following.

Required:

(a)　Prepare a statement showing gross profit and closing inventory valuation, separately for each type of piano, under each of the following assumptions:

　　(i)　FIFO

　　(ii)　LIFO

(iii) weighted average

(iv) RC.

(b) At a time of rising prices (i.e. using the grand pianos as an example) comment on the usefulness of each of the methods.

2 Using any information you wish from exercise 1 illustrate and discuss the effects on the income statement and balance sheet from using the different cost assumptions available to value closing inventory.

3 Critically appraise the different cost assumptions underlying the valuation of closing inventory.

4 Discuss the solution offered by IAS 2 to the valuation of inventories.

5 IAS 11 uses the percentage-of-completion method for the valuation of construction contracts. Discuss the advantages and disadvantages of this method and appraise whether it results in useful information for users.

✓ **6** Explain the rationale behind the prohibition of the completed-contract method for valuing construction contracts by IAS 11 given that US GAAP permits this option under certain circumstances.

7 The inventory of Base at 30 September 200X was valued at cost €28.5 million. This included €4.5 million of slow-moving stock that Base had been trying to sell to another retailer. The best price Base has been offered for this slow moving stock is €2 million. Identify how Base should record its inventory in its year-end accounts at 30 September 200X.

8 Gear Software, a public limited company, develops and sells computer games software. The revenue of Gear Software for the year ended 31 May 2003 is $5 million, the balance sheet total is $4 million and it has 40 employees. There are several elements in the financial statements for the year ended 31 May 2003 on which the directors of Gear require advice.

(i) Gear has two cost centres relating to the development and sale of the computer games. The indirect overhead costs attributable to the two cost centres were allocated in the year to 31 May 2002 in the ratio 60:40 respectively. Also in that financial year, the direct labour costs and attributable overhead costs incurred on the development of original games software were carried forward as work-in-progress and included with the balance sheet total for inventory of computer games. Inventory of computer games includes directly attributable overheads. In the year to 31 May 2003, Gear has allocated indirect overhead costs in the ratio 50:50 to the two cost centres and has written the direct labour and overhead costs incurred on the development of the games off to the income statement. Gear has stated that it cannot quantify the effect of this write-off on the current year's income statement. Further, it proposes to show the overhead costs relating to the sale of computer games within distribution costs. In prior years these costs were shown in cost of sales.

(ii) In prior years, Gear has charged interest incurred on the construction of computer hardware as part of cost of sales. It now proposes to capitalise such interest and to change the method of depreciation from the straight line method over four years to the reducing balance method at 30% per year. Depreciation will now be charged as cost of sales rather than administrative expenses as in previous years. Gear currently recognises revenue on contracts in proportion to the progression and activity on the contract. The normal accounting practice within the industrial sector is to recognise revenue when the product is shipped to customers. The effect of any change in accounting policy to bring the company in line with accounting practice in the industrial sector would be to increase revenue for the year by $500 000.

The directors have requested advice on the changes in accounting practice for inventories and tangible non-current assets that they have proposed.

(ACCA June 2003)

9 At 30 September 2003 Bowtock had included in its draft balance sheet inventory $250 000 valued at cost. Up to 5 November 2003, Bowtock had sold $100 000 of this inventory for $150 000. On this date new government legislation (enacted after the year-end) came into force which meant that the unsold inventory could no longer be marketed and was worthless.

Bowtock is part way through the construction of a housing development. It has prepared its financial statements to 30 September 2003 in accordance with IAS 11 *Construction Contracts* and included a proportionate amount of the total estimated profit on this contract. The same legislation referred to above (in force from 5 November 2003) now requires modifications to the way the houses within this development have to be built. The cost of these modifications will be $500 000 and will reduce the estimated total profit on the contract by that amount, although the contract is still expected to be profitable.

Required:
Assuming the amounts are material, state how the information above should be reflected in the financial statements of Bowtock for the year ended 30 September 2003.

(ACCA Dec 2003)

10 (i) Linnet is a large public listed company involved in the construction industry. Accounting standards normally require construction contracts to be accounted for using the percentage-(stage)-of-completion basis. However under certain circumstances they should be accounted for using the completed-contracts basis.

Required:
Discuss the principles that underlie each of the two methods and describe the circumstances in which their use is appropriate.

(ii) Linnet is part way through a contract to build a new football stadium at a contracted price of $300 million. Details of the progress of this contract at 1 April 2003 are shown below:

	$ million
Cumulative sales revenue invoiced	150
Cumulative cost of sales to date	112
Profit to date	38

The following information has been extracted from the accounting records at 31 March 2004:

	$ million
Total progress payment received for work certified at 29 February 2004	180
Total costs incurred to date (excluding rectification costs below)	195
Rectification costs	17

Linnet has received progress payments of 90% of the work certified at 29 February 2004. Linnet's surveyor has estimated the sales value of the further work completed during March 2004 was $20 million.

At 31 March 2004 the estimated remaining costs to complete the contract were $45 million. The rectification costs are the costs incurred in widening access roads to the stadium. This was the result of an error by Linnet's architect when he made his initial drawings. Linnet calculates the percentage of completion of its contracts as the proportion of sales value earned to date compared to the contract price. All estimates can be taken as being reliable.

Required:

Prepare extracts of the financial statements for Linnet for the above contract for the year to 31 March 2004.

(ACCA June 2004)

ACCOUNTING FOR FINANCIAL INSTRUMENTS

17

OBJECTIVES After studying this chapter you should be able to:

- describe a financial instrument

- identify the need to account for them

- outline the history of accounting for financial instruments

- define the scope of IASs regarding financial instruments

- identify and explain the requirements of the IASB for financial instruments

- critically appraise these current requirements

- identify and appraise current international accounting requirements for insurance contracts – IFRS 4.

INTRODUCTION

Financial instruments, which include such things as interest rate swaps, Treasury bond options, credit swaps, equity swaps, bonds, receivables, loans, shares, etc., have become more complex over the past 20 years. This complexity has led to difficulties in recognising, measuring, presenting and disclosure of such instruments in the financial statements of an entity. The international work on accounting for financial instruments began in 1988 but it was in 1995 that a Standard was issued on presentation and disclosure and 1998 for a Standard on recognition and measurement.

The complexity of the whole issue had led to the decision by the IASC to split the project on financial instruments into two parts, first, presentation and disclosure and, second, recognition and measurement. The real stumbling block in the entire debate on financial instruments is around the issue of whether the financial assets and liabilities involved should be valued at fair value.

IAS 39, *Financial Instruments: Recognition and Measurement* first issued 1998 and revised 2000, was seen as an interim solution to accounting for financial instruments. Its publication was driven by the need for the IASB to have a set of core standards available for approval by IOSCO by early 1999. The Standard was further revised as part of the improvement project and it is this extant version of 2004 that we consider here, together with its various amendments up to May 2008.

The complexity of the whole area was further demonstrated by the fact that the IASB decided there was a need to issue guidance on IAS 39 in the form of questions and answers. This guidance was included in a publication from the IASB entitled *Accounting for Financial Instruments – Standards, Interpretations and Implementation Guidance*. Several SICs have also been issued: SIC 5, *Classification of Financial Instruments – Contingent Settlement Provisions*; SIC 16, *Share Capital – Reacquired Own Equity Instruments*; SIC 17, *Equity – Costs of an Equity Transaction*; and IFRIC 9, *Reassessment of Embedded Derivatives*. The new Standard 2004 supersedes the previous interpretations and implementation guidance as these are now included in the Standard as Implementation Guidance. SIC 5 is also now withdrawn and superseded by the revised IAS 32, as are SIC 16 and 17. IFRIC 2, *Members' Shares in Co-operative Entities and Similar Instruments* should also be referenced.

IAS 32, *Financial Instruments: Disclosure and Presentation*, was, as IAS 39, revised in December 2003 but IAS 32 has now been split into two Standards:

- IAS 32, *Financial Instruments: Presentation*
- IFRS 7, *Financial Instruments: Disclosures*.

The latter was published in August 2005 and IAS 32 was amended in February 2008. In addition to these changes there is also a very complex situation as regards the adoption of IAS 39 by the EU. In November 2004 the European Commission adopted what became known as a 'carve-out' version of IAS 39. This 'carve-out' version prohibited the use of the fair value option for financial liabilities. The amendment to IAS 39 in June 2005 has dealt with the fair value option but there still remain some differences between the full IAS 39 and the 'carve-out' version endorsed by the EU. The IASB still continues with its working group on financial instruments which it set up in September 2004 with the aim of taking a fresh look at IAS 39. At that time the Board stated that:

> The review will focus on improving, simplifying and ultimately replacing IAS 39 and will examine broader questions of the application and extent of fair value accounting – a topic on which the IASB has not reached any conclusion. Although any major revision of IAS 39 may take several years to complete, the IASB is willing to revise the standard in the short term if any immediate solutions emerge from the working group's discussions. (Note that the June 2005 amendment was such a revision.)

Currently the IASB jointly with the FASB is seeking input from users of financial statements in respect of the kinds of information on fair values of financial instruments, and changes in those fair values, that are useful to users. We are unlikely to see any definitive new versions of IAS 39 before 2008 and certainly not until the IASB reaches its conclusions on fair value measurement. However in March 2008 the IASB published a discussion paper, *Reducing Complexity in Reporting Financial Instruments*. This paper runs to 92 pages!

The complexity is caused by the many ways of measuring financial instruments. The discussion paper proposes that a long-term solution to the complexity is to measure all financial instruments at fair value but acknowledges that there are issues and concerns to be addressed before the IASB can require general fair value measurement.

The two main concerns are:

- volatility of earnings arising from changes in fair value
- presentation of unrealised gains and losses in earnings.

Further the IASB will need to address the following four issues:

- Presentation: how should the effects of changes in fair values be presented in earnings?
- Disclosure: what information about financial instruments should be disclosed?
- Measurement: what is the definition of fair value and how should fair value be measured?
- Scope: what is the appropriate definition of a financial instrument and which financial instruments, if any, should be outside the scope of a standard for financial instruments?

This chapter, as you can imagine from the outline, is highly complex and, on many issues, controversial. We advise you to work through the chapter methodically, completing all the activities as you go.

HISTORY OF ACCOUNTING FOR FINANCIAL INSTRUMENTS

The IASC's work on financial instruments began in 1988 following an OECD symposium on the issue. Even at this early stage the most difficult issue to deal with concerned the valuation of the instruments and whether this should be at fair value or not. The first Draft Statement of Principle (DSOP) was issued in March 1990 and this advocated fair value measurement for financial assets and liabilities held for trading but not for others. The DSOP was approved by the IASC in November 1990.

In June 1991 E40 was issued. It advocated a benchmark treatment consisting of fair value for trading items and cost for others and an allowed alternative of fair value for all items; a compromise solution.

An agreement had also been made between the IASC and the Canadian Institute of Chartered Accountants (CICA) to cooperate on the development of the IASC Standard on financial instruments. However, in 1991 the CICA issued an exposure draft which did not allow fair value accounting for other than trading items. The two drafts were also at odds over the criteria for designation of a hedge. Both IASC and CICA published revised exposure drafts in 1994 and after consultation with standard-setting bodies in 20 countries the IASC decided to split its work on financial instruments into two stages. The first stage was to deal with presentation and disclosure and the second with recognition and measurement. The time scales set for these two stages were optimistic but IAS 32 was published in March 1995 on time. For recognition and measurement the IASC had to establish a further steering group which issued a discussion paper jointly with CICA in March 1997. Even at this stage, however, consensus could not be reached on whether to use fair values and where the resulting unrealised recognised gains and losses should be reported. Events then speeded up, as the IASC had to produce a core set of Standards by early 1999 to meet the IOSCO agreement. One of these core Standards had to deal with financial instruments. IAS 39 was issued in March 1999 and it took a cautious approach to fair value accounting. This cautious approach gave rise to complex requirements for hedging. The standard was so complex that guidance notes in the form of questions and answers were issued during 2000.

However, the Standards produced in 2000 were not universally accepted. A working group of standard setters and professional organisations from several countries produced draft revisions to the Standard on financial instruments, in December 2000, which proposed radical changes. One of their proposals was that virtually all financial instruments should be measured at fair value. The improvement project to IAS 32 and IAS 39 took this proposal up and fair value is now an option under IAS 39. However, such has been the controversy surrounding the new Standard, with uncertainty surrounding its adoption by several countries as well as Europe, that the IASB has issued further exposure drafts. It also set up (in September 2004) a further working party to analyse accounting issues relating to financial instruments. In the meantime, partial (as opposed to full) adoption of IAS 39 by Europe could cause long-term damage to the credibility and quality of financial reporting in Europe.

PROBLEMS IDENTIFIED

Information available

The growth in the variety of financial instruments available over the past 20 years had given rise to a lack of understanding by users of financial statements of the significance of such instruments on an entity's financial performance, position and cash flows. Many of the instruments were carried off balance sheet and the user was unable to access the effect of these unless there was adequate presentation and disclosure. In addition, an entity, by the use of financial instruments, can significantly change its financial risk profile resulting in excessive gains or losses depending on whether prices of such instruments move in favour of or against the entity.

Measurement practice

Measuring financial instruments at historical cost does not always provide the most relevant or consistent information for users. Throughout the programme of work on financial instruments the view grew that using fair values for such assets and liabilities could provide more relevant information.

However, the use of fair values then raises the question of where the unrealised gain or loss should be reported, in the income statement or as a change in equity. Historically the principal driver in the recognition of gains was 'realisation' but this may have less relevance in a situation where entities are trading underlying risks. Careful consideration would need to be given to information derived by measuring financial instruments at fair value and recognising that gain or loss in the income statement as compared with valuation at historical cost.

ILLUSTRATION

Entity *A* enters into an interest swap with *B*. The notional amount of the swap is €1m but this amount is not exchanged. *A* pays interest to *B* at three-month intervals at 7% and *B* pays interest to *A* at London Interbank Offered Rate (LIBOR). If LIBOR moves above 7% then *A* gains on the deal, otherwise he loses. On a historical cost basis no asset or liability would be recorded by either party and interest payments would be shown through the income statement. It could be the case that at a year-end, if LIBOR has moved to 10%, the fair value of this interest swap is €50 000. If fair value accounting is used then the interest rate swap would be recorded at €50 000 and presumably this gain would be shown in the income statement. In six months' time the fair value of this swap could have dropped to €10 000. Which method of accounting for the swap would provide relevant and reliable information to the user? We leave this question for you to debate.

WHAT IS A FINANCIAL INSTRUMENT?

IAS 32 and 39 define a financial instrument as 'any contract that gives rise to a financial asset of one entity and a financial liability or equity instrument of another entity'.

A financial asset is any asset that is:

(a) cash

(b) an equity instrument of another entity

(c) a contractual right:

- to receive cash or another financial asset from another entity
- to exchange financial instruments or financial liabilities with another entity under conditions that are potentially favourable to the entity

(d) a contract that will or may be settled in the entity's own equity instruments and is:

- a non-derivative for which the entity is or may be obliged to receive a variable number of the entity's own equity instruments; or
- a derivative that will or may be settled other than by the exchange of a fixed amount of cash or another financial asset for a fixed number of the entity's own equity instruments. For this purpose the entity's own equity instruments do not include instruments that are themselves contracts for the future receipt or delivery of the equity's own equity instruments.

A financial liability is any liability that is:

(a) a contractual obligation:

- **(i)** to deliver cash or another financial asset to another enterprise entity; or
- **(ii)** to exchange financial instruments assets or financial liabilities with another enterprise entity under conditions that are potentially unfavourable to the entity; or

(b) a contract that will or may be settled in the entity's own equity instruments and is:

- **(i)** a non-derivative for which the entity is or may be obliged to deliver a variable number of the entity's own equity instruments: or

(ii) a derivative that will or may be settled other than by the exchange of a fixed amount of cash or another financial asset for a fixed number of the entity's own equity instruments. For this purpose the entity's own equity instruments do not include puttable financial instruments that are classified as equity instruments in accordance with paragraphs 16A and 16B, instruments that impose on the entity an obligation to deliver to another party a pro rata share of the net assets of the entity only on liquidation and are classified as equity instruments in accordance with paragraphs 16C and 16D, or instruments that are themselves contracts for the future receipt or delivery of the entity's own equity instruments.

A puttable instrument is a financial instrument that gives the holder the right to put the instrument back to the issuer for cash or another financial asset or is automatically put back to the issuer on the occurrence of an uncertain future event or the death or retirement of the instrument holder. An example of a puttable instrument is a redeemable, at the option of the holder, share.

From these definitions we can assert that a financial instrument is the contract, not the asset or liability, and thus we must be clear what is meant by contract, contractual right and obligation. Neither Standard defines these terms but IAS 32 does state that 'contract' and 'contractual' refer to an agreement between two or more parties that has clear economic consequences that the parties have little, if any, chance of avoiding, because generally the agreement is enforceable in law. Contracts need not, however, be in writing.

ACTIVITY 17.1

Identify which of the following are financial instruments:

- cash
- gold bullion
- debtors
- creditors
- loans
- bank deposits
- debentures
- a promissory note payable in government bonds
- ordinary shares
- preference shares
- plant and equipment previously bought and paid for by the entity
- pre-payments for goods or services.

Activity feedback

Clearly, the last two are not financial instruments as there is no contract to settle anything in cash or another financial instrument.

Cash is clearly not a financial instrument but it *is* a financial asset. Gold bullion, contrariwise, is a commodity or physical asset as there is no contractual right to receive cash or other financial asset.

Debtors are financial assets but *not* financial instruments as they cannot be described as a contract although they quite possibly arose from a contract. Creditors are likewise a financial liability. Loans, bank deposits and debentures are financial assets of one entity and liabilities of another but it is debatable whether they are actually a financial instrument as this requires a contract. Presumably there is a contract behind these assets and liabilities and it should be this that is the financial instrument. The Standard tends to confuse the terms financial assets, financial instruments and financial liabilities.

A promissory note payable in government bonds is a financial instrument as the note is the contract that gives the holder the contractual right to receive and the issuer the contractual obligation to deliver government bonds. The bonds themselves are financial assets of one entity and liabilities of another. Ordinary and preference shares can also be regarded as financial instruments if we regard them as a contract that will ultimately result in the entity paying cash to the holder. The Standard defines an equity instrument as any contract that evidences a residual interest in the assets of an entity after deducting all of its liabilities.

ACTIVITY 17.1   (Continued)

This activity is somewhat tortuous given that the Standard uses the terms financial instrument, financial asset and financial liability rather loosely.

Other examples of financial instruments given in the Standards are derivatives such as financial options, futures and forwards, interest rate swaps and currency swaps. The Standard gives further examples of contracts that do not give rise to financial instruments as they do not involve the transfer of a financial asset. For example, an operating lease for the use of a physical asset can be settled only by the receipt and delivery of services and is therefore not a financial instrument.

Finance leases are, however, financial instruments as they are contracts which result in a financial asset of one entity and a financial liability of another. (Finance leases are outside the scope of IAS 32 and 39 as they are subject to IAS 17, *Leases*.)

A derivative is defined in the Standards as: a financial instrument:

(a) whose value changes in response to the change in a specified interest rate, security price, commodity price, foreign exchange rate, index of prices or rates, a credit rating or credit index or similar variable (underlying)

(b) that requires no initial net investment or little initial net investment relative to other types of contracts that have a similar response to changes in market conditions, and

(c) that is settled at a future date.

ACTIVITY 17.2

Are the following contracts financial instruments?

1 Entity A enters into both derivatives and an interest rate swap with another, B, that requires A to pay a fixed rate of 7% and receive a variable amount based on three-month LIBOR. The notional amount of the swap is €1 million but this amount is not exchanged. A pays or receives a net cash amount each quarter based on the difference between 7% and LIBOR.

2 A also enters into a pay fixed, receive variable interest swap with C. The notional amount is for €100 million and fixed rate 10%. The variable rate is based on three-month LIBOR. A prepays its fixed interest rate obligation as 100m × 10% × 5 years discounted at market interest rates at inception of the swap.

3 A enters into a contract to pay 10 million if X shares increase by 5% or more during a six-month period and to receive 10 million if the share price decreases by 5% or more in the same period. No payment is made if the price swing is less than 5% up or down.

Activity feedback

1 There is no initial net investment, settlement occurs at a future date and its value changes based on changes in LIBOR, the underlying variable, therefore this is a financial instrument as it meets the definition of a derivative.

2 This is also a derivative and therefore a financial instrument even though there is an initial net investment. The payment of the fixed interest at inception will be regarded as 'little' compared with other similar contracts such as a variable rate bond where the notional amount of €100m would be paid over.

3 There is no initial net investment, settlement occurs at a future date and the underlying variable is the share price. This is a derivative and therefore a financial instrument.

CATEGORIES OF FINANCIAL LIABILITY OR EQUITY

Distinction between equity and liability

At this stage we need to differentiate between a financial liability and equity. IAS 32 tells us that to determine whether a financial instrument is an equity instrument rather than a financial liability certain conditions must be met. These conditions are:

(a) The instrument includes no contractual obligation to deliver cash or another financial asset/liability to another entity or to exchange financial assets or financial liabilities with another entity under conditions that are potentially unfavourable to the issuer.

(b) If the instrument will or may be settled in the issuer's own equity instruments, it is:

- A non-derivative that includes no contractual obligation for the issuer to deliver a variable number of its own equity instruments; or
- A derivative that will be settled only by the issuer exchanging a fixed amount of cash or another financial asset for a fixed number of its own equity instruments. For this purpose the issuer's own equity instruments do not include instruments that have all the features of puttable instruments or instruments that are contracts for the future receipt or delivery of the issuer's own equity instruments.

The Standard does provide us with an exception to the definition of a financial liability. If an instrument meets the definition of a financial liability but meets certain conditions then it is classified an equity instrument. For example a puttable financial instrument sounds like a financial liability but if it has all the following features it will be classed as equity:

- it entitles the holder to a pro-rata share of the entity's net assets in the event of liquidation
- it is subordinate to all other classes of instruments, i.e. it has no priority under liquidation before others and it does not need to be converted into another instrument before it is subordinate
- in the subordinate class all instruments have identical features
- it does not include an obligation to deliver cash or another financial asset except for the redemption
- its cash flows are based substantially on profit or loss attained.

ACTIVITY 17.3

Ram has two classes of shares; founder shares and investor shares. The fund has issued 1000 founder shares with a par value of £1 which are held for regulatory purposes. The founder shares are not redeemable, carry voting rights but are not entitled to dividends. The investor shares issued are 900 000 with a par value of 1p each, they are redeemable at fair value at the option of the holder, carry no voting rights, but are entitled to dividends. In the case of liquidation the founder shares rank equally with the investor shares with each entitled to an amount equal to its par value. The investor shares are entitled to any surplus after payment of par values.

Which, if any, of the shares is equity?

Activity feedback
The investor shares are not equity as they do not form part of the subordinate class of instruments. The founder shares are the most subordinate as they do not gain any of the surplus, nor do the investor shares have the same features as the founder shares. If however the founder shares were repurchased by Ram then the investor shares would be reclassified as equity.

The founder shares are equity as they are not puttable, they are subordinate and there is no obligation on the entity to deliver cash or other financial assets to the holder.

It is worth noting at this point that in general redeemable preference shares will be liability not equity

Compound financial instruments

Some financial instruments can contain both an equity element and a liability element. For example a bond convertible by the holder into a fixed number of shares of the entity is a compound financial instrument. This is because the instrument comprises a liability to deliver cash or another financial asset on redemption and a call option granting the holder the right to convert it into a fixed number of shares. IAS 32 requires us to account for the substance of this transaction, both a liability and an equity element, not the legal form. The substance is basically that of issuing a debt instrument with an early settlement provision and warrants to purchase ordinary shares.

IAS 39 tells us how to measure the component parts and we will deal with this in the measurement section.

CATEGORIES OF FINANCIAL ASSET/LIABILITY

IFRS 7, *Financial Instruments: Disclosures*, categorises financial assets/liabilities as:

- held for trading
- held-to-maturity investments
- loans and receivables
- available for sale.

Held for trading asset is one, regardless of why it was acquired, which is part of a portfolio for which there is evidence of short-term profit taking or was initially acquired for purposes of generating a profit through short-term fluctuations in price or dealer's margins.

Held-to-maturity investments are financial assets with fixed or determinable payments and fixed maturity that an entity has the positive intent and ability to hold to maturity. The Standard subsequently defines what it means by 'positive intent' and 'ability to hold to maturity' in an appendix at paras AG 16–AG 25.

Loans and receivables originated by the entity are financial assets created by the entity by providing money, goods, or services directly to a debtor.

Available for sale are those that are not loans and receivables originated by the entity, held to maturity or held for trading.

These definitions are very important as the Standard requires available for sale and held for trading to be measured at fair value and the loans and receivables and held to maturity to be measured at amortised cost using the effective interest method. In

ACTIVITY 17.4

Which categories of financial asset/liability do the following fit into:

1 a non-derivative financial asset acquired with the intent to hold for a long period irrespective of short-term fluctuations in price

2 a bond purchased at original issuance where funds are transferred directly to the issuer?

Activity feedback

1 held for maturity

2 originated loan.

addition, any financial asset that does not have a quoted market price in an active market and whose fair value cannot be reliably measured is measured at amortised cost.

MEASUREMENT OF FINANCIAL INSTRUMENTS

From the preceding paragraph it becomes apparent that we need a definition of amortised cost and effective interest method. IAS 39, *Financial Instruments: Recognition and Measurement* defines these as follows:

Amortised cost is the amount at which the financial asset or liability is measured at initial recognition minus principal repayments, plus or minus the cumulative amortisation of any difference between the initial amount and the maturity amount, and minus any write-down for impairment or uncollectability.

Effective interest method is a method of calculating amortisation using the effective rate of a financial asset or liability. The effective interest rate is the rate that exactly discounts the expected stream of future cash payments through maturity or the next market-based repricing date to the current net carrying amount of the financial asset or liability. That computation should include all fees and points paid or received between parties to the contract. The effective interest rate is sometimes termed the level yield to maturity or to next repricing date and is the internal rate of return of the financial asset or liability for that period.

ILLUSTRATION

On 1 January 2000, an entity acquires €100 000 par value 9% bonds of Paper Co. priced to yield 10% with a maturity date of 31.12.2004. The value of the bonds on acquisition is

Market value	96 209
Discount from par value therefore is	3 791
Par value	100 000
Thus the bonds are initially recognised at	€ 96 209

	€
Present value of interest payments	
9% of €100 000 for five years discounted	
at 10% = 9 000 × 3.79079 (annuity	
factor at 10% for 5 years)	34 117
Present value of maturity value =	
100 000 × 0.62092	
(annuity factor at 10% in 5 years)	62 092

Subsequent recognition of the bonds each year requires amortisation using the effective interest rate method. Thus, we need to amortise the discount from par value over the five years recognising this together with interest received as interest income.

Table 17.1 shows the carrying amount (amortised cost) (column E) of the instrument each year and the interest income (column A).

TABLE 17.1   Amortisation of bonds

Year	Interest income CA × 10%	Cash received	Discount amortised	Discount remaining	Carrying amount
	A	B	C	D	E
1.1.00				3 791	96 209
31.12.00	9 621	9 000	621	3 170	96 830
31.12.01	9 683	9 000	683	2 487	97 513
31.12.02	9 751	9 000	751	1 736	98 264
31.12.03	9 826	9 000	826	910	99 090
31.12.04	9 910	9 000	910		100 000

Any financial asset or financial liability can be designated as at fair value through the profit and loss account. This option overrides the other measurement requirements of IAS 39 such that any financial asset or liability so designated will be revalued to fair value at each accounting period date. As this facility is an option any financial asset or financial liability not designated as at fair value through the profit and loss account will be initially recognised and subsequently measured in accordance with IAS 39 (see summary at end of chapter). Fair value of the consideration is generally estimated as the sum of all future cash payments or receipts discounted using prevailing market rate of interest for a similar instrument of an issuer with a similar credit rating. Transaction costs are also included in the initial measurement of all financial assets and liabilities. Transaction costs include fees and commissions and costs of issuing debt.

Fair value is defined by the Standard as the amount for which an asset could be exchanged or a liability settled, between knowledgeable, willing parties in an arm's-length transaction. If the fair value of the instrument cannot be reliably measured then the instrument is carried at amortised cost if it has a fixed maturity and at cost if no fixed maturity. Look at Activities 17.5 and 17.6.

Gains and losses on remeasurement to fair value

The Standard requires that a gain or loss from a change in fair value of a financial instrument (FI) held for trading should be included in net profit or loss for the period but a similar gain or loss on an FI available for sale is recognised directly in equity except for impairment losses and foreign exchange gains and losses, which are both recognised in profit or loss. Note here that this is one of the changes made by the

---

ACTIVITY 17.5

Identify three situations in which the fair value of a financial instrument (FI) could be reliably measured and one in which it might not.

Activity feedback
Reliable measurement:

- a financial instrument for which there is a published price quoted in an active public securities market for the instrument

- a debt instrument that has been rated by an independent rating agency and whose cash flows can be reasonably estimated

- a financial instrument for which there is an appropriate valuation model and for which the data inputs to that model can be measured reliably because the data come from active markets.

Unreliable measurement of fair value:

- no quoted market price available in an active market and for which other methods of reasonable estimation of fair value are unworkable.

ACTIVITY 17.6

Company A holds 15% of the share capital of B which is publicly traded in an active market. Quoted price is €100 and the daily trading volume is 0.1% of outstanding shares. Company A believes that if it sold its shares in B in one lot it would obtain greater than the quoted market price. Several independent estimates have confirmed this and suggested a price about €105. At what value should A record its holding?

Activity feedback
The holding needs to be measured at fair value as it is an instrument held for trading. Fair value is the current quoted price €100; €105 will not be regarded as the fair value unless company A has entered into a contract to sell at that price.

improvement to IAS 39 as previously entities had a choice of where they recognised the gain or loss – profit or loss or equity. This choice had a marked effect on profits!

Once the available for sale FI is derecognised the cumulative gain or loss is moved from equity to profit or loss.

All financial instruments have to be reviewed for impairment at each balance sheet date. For loans and receivables and held-to-maturity investments carried at amortised cost the impairment loss is measured as the difference between the asset's carrying amount and the present value of future estimated future cash flows.

Initial recognition

According to the Standard an entity should only recognise a financial asset or liability on its balance sheet when it becomes a party to the contractual provisions of the instrument. Put simply this means that even where a firm commitment to buy or sell goods exists this would not be recognised until the goods have been shipped, delivered or services rendered and that planned future transactions, no matter how likely, are not recognised. However, a forward contract which is a commitment to purchase or sell a specified FI or commodity on a future date at a specified price is recognised on the commitment date rather than the closing date.

The Standard (and this is rather confusing so take your time reading this) then deals with something called 'regular way contracts'.

Regular way contracts are those for the purchase or sale of financial assets that require delivery of the assets within the timeframe generally established by regulation or convention in the market concerned. For these contracts recognition is permitted at either trade date or settlement date but the policy chosen must be applied consistently.

Settlement date accounting, when applied, does, however, require the entity to recognise any change in the fair value of the asset that occurs between the trade and settlement date. This is a somewhat strange requirement given that the financial asset itself is not yet recognised. Regular way contracts actually meet the definition of a derivative as they are forward contracts but are not recognised as derivatives because of the short duration of the commitment.

An example of a regular way contract is where a bank makes a loan commitment at a specified rate of interest and then takes a commitment period to enable it to complete its underwriting and to provide time for the borrower to execute the transaction that is the subject of the loan. This commitment period would have to be of a normal duration for such an agreement. The loan, once recognised at either trade date or settlement date, would be carried at amortised cost.

ACTIVITY 17.7

On 29 December 20X1 an entity commits to buy a financial asset for €1000 which is its fair value on commitment date (trade date). On 31.12.X1 and 4.1.X2, the settlement date, the fair value of the asset is €1002 and €1003 respectively.

Show the amounts to be recorded for the asset at 29.12.X1, 31.12.X1 and 4.1.X2 using both settlement and trade date accounting and identify where any change in value will be recognised. Note you do not know whether this asset is held to maturity or available for sale.

Activity feedback

There is a lot to sort out in this question.

If the asset is held to maturity then it will be carried at amortised cost but if available for sale it will need to be remeasured to fair value. On remeasurement to fair value the change is taken to equity. We also have to choose between initial recognition at trade (Table 17.2) or settlement date (Table 17.3).

ACTIVITY 17.7 *(Continued)*

TABLE 17.2 Trade date accounting

Date of balance	Held to maturity	Available for sale
29.12.X1		
Financial asset	1 000	1 000
Liability	(1 000)	(1 000) Note 1
31.12.X1		
Financial asset	1 000	1 002
Liability	(1 000)	(1 000)
P&L	Note 2	
Equity		(2)
		Note 4
4.01.X2		
Financial asset	1 000	1 003
Liability	Note 3	
P&L		
Equity		(1) in addition to the previous 2

Note 1: At this stage in the recognition we have both a financial asset that we have purchased and the liability outstanding to pay for this asset.

Note 2: We still haven't settled this transaction so the liability still remains and as it is held for maturity we carry at amortised cost.

Note 3: Settlement date is now reached so the liability is removed but note that other assets, perhaps cash, would be reduced.

Note 4: Only the value of the financial asset changes to fair value, not that of the liability.

TABLE 17.3 Settlement date accounting

Date of balance	Held to maturity	Available for sale
29.12.X1	–	–
31.12.X1		
Financial asset	–	2 Note 5
Liability	–	
P&L	–	
Equity	–	(2)
4.1.X2		
Financial asset	1 000	3
Liability		
P&L		
Equity		(1) in addition to the previous 2

Note 5: In both cases here we need to recognise the change in fair value that has occurred between trade and settlement date even though the full financial asset is not yet recognised.

Compound financial instrument measurement

We previously identified a redeemable bond with an option to convert to a fixed number of ordinary shares as a compound financial instrument. We now need to deal with the measurement of its separate parts.

The standard tells us to first determine the carrying amount of the liability component by measuring the fair value of a similar liability. The carrying amount of the equity element is then determined by deducting the fair value of the financial liability from the fair value of the compound instrument as a whole (see Activity 17.8).

ACTIVITY 17.8

On 1 April 20X6 Beta entity issued at par an 8% convertible loan note with a nominal value of £600 000. It is redeemable at par on 31 March 20Y0 or it may be converted into equity shares of Beta on the basis of 100 new shares for each £200 of loan note. An equivalent loan note without the conversion option would have carried an interest rate of 10%. Within the financial statements for the year ended 31 March 20X7 interest of £48 000 has been charged as a finance cost and the loan note is shown under non-current liabilities at £600 000. The present value of £1 receivable at the end of each year, based on discount rates of 8% and 10%, are:

End of year	8%	10%
1	0.9259	0.9091
2	0.8573	0.8264
3	0.7938	0.7513
4	0.7350	0.6830

Show how the loan note should be presented in the financial statements ended 31 March 20X7 in accordance with IASs.

Activity feedback

IAS 32 (paras 28–32) requires a convertible loan note to be separated into its equity and liability component. The liability component is equal to the fair value of a similar liability that does not have an equity component. In this example we therefore need to determine the present value at a discount rate of 10% (the comparator) of the future cash flows.

End of year	Future cash flows	Discount rate 10%	FV
1	48 000 (interest at 8%)	0.9091	43 637
2	48 000	0.8264	39 667
3	48 000	0.7513	36 062
4	648 000 (capital + interest)	0.6830	442 584
Liability element			561 950
Equity element			38 050
			600 000

Financial statements 31 March 20X7

Balance sheet

Equity – equity option	38 050
Non-current liabilities – 8% convertible loan note	
Loan note 561 950 + 8 000 (note a)	569 950

Income statement

Finance costs convertible 8% loan – 8% 600 000 + 8 000 (note a)	56 000

note a - the interest on the loan is increased to the equivalent rate of 10% and the accrual of £8 000 added to the liability

Derecognition

The Standard states the following:

17 An entity shall derecognise a financial asset when and only when:

   (a) The contractual rights to the cash flows from the financial assets expires; or

   (b) It transfers the financial asset as set out in paragraphs 18 and 19 and the transfer qualifies for derecognition in accordance with paragraph 20.

18 An entity transfers a financial asset if, and only if, it either:

   (a) Transfers the contractual rights to receive the cash flows of the financial asset; or

   (b) Retains the contractual rights to receive the cash flows of the financial asset, but assumes a contractual obligation to pay the cash flows to one or more recipients in an arrangement that meets the conditions in paragraph 19.

19 When an entity retains the contractual rights to receive the cash flows of a financial asset (the 'original asset'), but assumes a contractual obligation to pay those cash flows to one or more entities (the 'eventual recipient'), the entity treats the transaction as a transfer of financial asset if, and only if, all of the following three conditions are met:

   (a) The entity has no obligation to pay amounts to the eventual recipient unless it collects equivalent amounts for the original asset. Short-term advances by the entity with the right of full recovery of the amount lent plus accrued interest at market rates do not violate this condition.

   (b) The entity is prohibited by the terms of the transfer contract from selling or pledging the original asset other than as security to the eventual recipients for the obligation to pay them cash flows.

   (c) The entity has an obligation to remit any cash flows it collects on behalf of the eventual recipients without material delay. In addition, the entity is not entitled to reinvest such cash flows, except for investment in cash or cash equivalents (as defined in IAS 7, *Cash Flow Statements*) during the short settlement period from the collection date to the date of required remittance to the eventual recipients, and interest earned on such investments is passed to the eventual recipients.

20 When an entity transfers a financial asset (see paragraph 18) it shall evaluate the extent to which it retains the risks and rewards of ownership of the financial asset. In this case:

   (a) If the entity transfers substantially all the risks and rewards of ownership of the financial asset, the entity shall derecognise the financial asset and recognise separately as assets or liabilities any rights and obligations created or retained in the transfer;

   (b) If the entity retains substantially all the risks and rewards of ownership of the financial asset, the entity shall continue to recognise the financial asset;

(c) If the entity neither transfers nor retains substantially all the risks and rewards of ownership of the financial asset, the entity shall determine whether it has retained control of the financial asset. In this case:

(i) If the entity has not retained control, it shall derecognise the financial asset and recognise separately as assets or liabilities any rights and obligations created or retained in the transfer,

(ii) If the entity has retained control, it shall continue to recognise the financial asset to the extent of its continuing involvement in the financial asset (see paragraph 30).

Derecognition is used by the IASB as a term meaning 'to remove from the balance sheet'. This area is again complex, given that derecognition of a portion of the asset is permitted and there is the possibility of repurchase options or other derivatives being involved. From, the paragraphs above it is apparent that the issue of derecognition involves determination of whether an entity has lost control of the financial asset; has the transferor given the rights to obtain benefits from the financial asset to the transferee?

Derecognition accounting treatment The accounting treatment on derecognition requires the entity to recognise in the net profit or loss for the period the difference between the carrying amount of the asset, or portion, transferred to another party

---

ACTIVITY 17.9

In each of the following cases state, with reasons, whether the financial asset should be derecognised in the books of entity A.

1 A transfers a loan it holds to a bank but stipulates that the bank cannot sell or pledge the loan (this is to protect the customer to whom the loan was originally made).

2 A transfers a financial asset to B on terms that stipulate that A can repurchase the asset before the expiry of a specific period and that repurchase is at the value at transfer date plus interest at a market rate on that value.

3 A transfers a financial asset to B on terms that stipulate that A must repurchase the asset before the expiry of a specific period at market value at the date of repurchase.

4 A sells receivables to B and provides a guarantee with that sale to pay for any credit losses that may be incurred on the receivables as a result of the failure of the debtor to pay when due. All other substantive risks and rewards of the receivables are transferred to B.

Activity feedback

1 Even though the transferee, the bank, cannot sell or pledge the loan it does receive all other benefits from holding the loan and therefore A would derecognise this financial asset. However, A would also need to show the separate forward commitment to repurchase the loan.

2 This is in effect similar to B making a loan to A secured on the financial asset. A does not lose control of any risks or rewards in the financial asset and therefore the asset remains recognised throughout the period in A's books. No derecognition.

3 This might seem similar to example 2 but it isn't. In this case, the risks and rewards associated with the asset have been transferred to B as he will bear the loss if the market value falls and the gain if it increases. The asset will be derecognised by A and recognised when it is repurchased.

4 A derecognises these receivables. A has lost control of the financial asset and his risk is limited to a credit risk in the case of default. This credit risk would need to be recognised by A as a financial liability, a separate financial instrument.

ILLUSTRATION

(Adapted from IAS 39 implementation guide.)

A purchases €100 of bonds in the marketplace with an effective yield of 11%. An 80% portion of the principal amounts of these bonds is sold on to investors. The investors purchase 80% of the bonds at par at interest of 6%. The 80% of the bonds transferred need to be derecognised and to do so we need to allocate the carrying amount of the bonds based on their fair values at date of sale. At the date of sale A estimates that the present value of the cash flows from the 20% it retains is equal to 25% of the principal amount of the bonds, i.e. €25. The fair value of the portion sold is €80 as that was what the investors paid. The carrying amount of the asset, €100, needs allocating to the portion retained and portion sold based on fair values at date of sale.

Carrying amount is €100

Fair value of portion sold €80

Fair value of 100% of bonds is €105 (80 + 25)

Carrying amount allocated to sold portion is $100 \times 80/105 = 76.19$

Profit on sale is therefore €3.81

and the sum of the proceeds received or receivable and any prior adjustment to reflect the fair value of that asset that had been reported in equity.

Partial derecognition Derecognition of part of a financial asset is again complex. Paragraph 27 of IAS 39 requires that if an entity transfers a part of a financial asset to others and retains the other part, then the part transferred/sold must be derecognised. To do this the carrying amount of the financial asset must be allocated between the part sold and the part retained based on their relative fair values at the date of sale. The gain or loss recognised is based on the proceeds for the part sold. (See the 'Illustration' above.)

Occasionally, it could be the case that an entity is unable to estimate reliably the fair value of the portion of the asset retained. In this case para. 47 of the Standard requires us to allocate zero value to the portion retained and to allocate the entire carrying amount to the portion sold/derecognised. (See Activity 17.10.)

Derecognition coupled with new asset or liability Quite often asset derecognition is coupled with the recognition of a new financial asset or liability. When this occurs IAS 39 requires recognition of the new financial asset or liability at fair value and the recognition of a gain or loss on the transaction based on the difference between:

- the proceeds
- the carrying amount of the financial asset sold plus the fair value of any new financial liability assumed, minus the fair value of any new financial asset acquired and plus or minus any adjustment that had been previously reported in equity to reflect the fair value of that asset.

ACTIVITY 17.10

Entity A with receivables in its books at a carrying amount of €100 sells them for €90. The entity continues to service the receivables even after they have been sold for a fee, which is expected to exceed the cost of servicing. The fair value of this fee cannot be reliably estimated. How should this transaction be shown in the books of A?

Activity feedback

The receivables are derecognised from A's books and a loss of €10 shown in the net profit and loss account. The servicing asset would be recorded at zero. A more complicated example is given in Activity 17.11.

ACTIVITY 17.11

A holds originated loans of €1000 yielding 10% interest p.a. for their nine-year life. The loans are sold to B entity at €1000 with an interest rate of 8% pa. A continues to service the loans at a fee equivalent to half of the interest not sold. The other half of the interest not sold is to be regarded as an interest-only strip receivable. The fair value of the loan plus servicing at date of transfer is €1100 including fair value of servicing and interest-only strip as €40 and €60 respectively. Identify the treatment of this transaction in A's books.

Activity feedback

The loans will be derecognised and a servicing asset and an interest-only strip receivable will be recognised in the balance sheet. The €1000 carrying amount of the loan is allocated as follows:

	Fair value	%	Carrying amount
Loans sold	1 000	91	910
Servicing asset	40	3.6	36
Interest-only strip receivable	60	5.4	54
	1 100	100.0	1 000

Thus a gain of €90 (1000 – 910) will be shown in the net profit and loss account on the sale of the loan, the servicing asset will be recorded at €36 in the balance sheet and interest-only strip receivable at €54.

Derecognition of a financial liability Derecognition of a financial liability is also relatively straightforward. We remove the financial liability from the balance sheet when the obligation specified in the contract is discharged, cancelled or expires. Occasionally, one financial liability will be exchanged for a similar one with the same lender, if the terms of the new agreement are substantially different from the old then the old is derecognised and the new recognised. The problem with this requirement from the Standard, para. 61, is that we need to set boundaries to 'substantially'. The Application Guidance to the Standard at para. 62 states the following:

> The terms are substantially different if the discounted present value of the cash flows, under the new terms, including any fees paid net of any fees received, is at least 10% different from the discounted present value of the remaining cash flows of the original debt instrument.

Reclassifications

Paragraph 50 of IAS 39 informs us that an entity cannot reclassify a financial instrument into or out of the fair value through profit or loss category while it is held or issued. Paragraph 51 also informs us that an investment held to maturity, if circumstances surrounding it change, can be reclassified as available for sale and remeasured at fair value.

HEDGING

The Standard takes 30 paragraphs to deal with this issue and we recommend you read the Standard in detail if you want complete information on this issue. Hedging is about offsetting the loss or potential loss on one item against the gain or potential gain on another. The loss or gain on the hedging arises from changes in fair values or cash flows. The rules in relation to hedging are complex because IAS 39 does not require all financial instruments to be carried at fair value. Remember loans and receivables originated by the entity and held to maturity as investments are carried at amortised cost. Only financial assets and liabilities held for trading and available for sale, and derivatives are carried at fair value. Thus, the Standard permits the use of hedging where derivatives are designated as the hedge instrument but only permits non-derivatives to hedge a foreign currency risk. The hedging relationship only qualifies for the special accounting arrangements in IAS 39 if:

- formal documentation of the detail of the hedge relationship exists
- the hedge is expected to be highly effective or highly probable
- the effectiveness of the hedge can be reliably measured.

These requirements need full expansion in the Standard to ensure consistency and comparability in the application of the hedging allowance. This expansion covers numerous detailed paragraphs.

Hedged relationships are of three types:

1 fair value hedge where the change in fair value of the asset or liability is hedged

2 cash flow hedge where the variability to cash flows in the hedged item is hedged

3 foreign currency hedge, which we consider in Chapter 29.

Fair value hedges

For fair value hedges the gain or loss from remeasuring the hedging instrument at fair value is recognised immediately in net profit or loss and the gain or loss on the hedged item is recognised immediately in net profit or loss (see Activity 17.12).

ACTIVITY 17.12

On 1 January 20X0 a fixed interest debt security is purchased by an entity for $100. Its current fair value at 31 December 20X0 is $110. The investment is regarded as an available for sale financial asset and the entity adopts the policy of equity accounting on remeasurement. The entity acquires a derivative asset on 31 December 20X0. By 31 December 20X1 the fair value of the derivative has increased by $4 but the security has reduced to $105.

Show the accounting entries if:

1 no hedging is designated

2 the derivative is designated as a hedge as from 1 January 20X1.

Activity feedback

1 The investment would be shown at fair value at 31.12.X0 and 31.12.X1 as $110 and $105

respectively. The first-year gain of $10 and second-year loss of $5 would both be taken to equity. The increase in the fair value of the derivative would be taken to income. Thus at 31.12.X1 the balance sheet will show an investment at $105, a derivative at $4 and over the two years a change in equity year 1 of $10 and year 2 of ($5).

2 For the first year the increase in fair value of the investment will be taken to equity as before and the balance sheet will record a fair value of $110. For the second year the loss on the investment of $5 will be taken to net profit and loss and hedged by the increase from the derivative of $4. At 31.12.X1 the balance sheet will show an investment at $105, a derivative at $4, and a −$1 effect on the net profit or loss.

The hedging accounting rules force the gains or losses on the FIs through the profit or loss account but these are offset by the loss or gain on the hedge.

Cash flow hedges

For cash flow hedges that portion of the gain or loss on the hedging instrument which is determined to be an effective hedge should be recognised directly in equity, as follows: the component of equity associated with the hedged item should be adjusted to the lower of (a) the fair value of the cumulative change in expected future cash flows of the hedged item from the inception of the hedge and (b) the cumulative gain or loss on the hedging instrument needed to offset the cumulative change in expected cash flows of the hedged item from the inception of the hedge. Any remaining gain or loss on the hedging instrument constitutes the ineffective portion and should be reported (a) if the hedging instrument is a derivative, immediately in net profit or loss, and (b) if the hedging instrument is not a derivative, in accordance with the requirement for reporting fair value remeasurement gains and losses for the type of instrument involved. The following should help to illustrate the difference in treatment between a fair value hedge and a cash flow hedge.

ILLUSTRATION

An export sale is made at a price denominated in foreign currency for which an account receivable is raised payable in 90 days. In addition a 90-day foreign exchange contract to hedge the foreign currency exposure is taken out. The hedge can be designated as either a fair value or a cash flow hedge.

Under normal foreign currency transaction rules the sale will be recorded at the spot rate at the day of sale and the receivable will be restated during the 90-day period with any difference being taken to net profit or loss.

However, if the foreign exchange contract is designated as a fair value hedge, then the gain or loss from remeasuring the forward exchange contract at fair value is also recognised in the net profit or loss thereby offsetting the gain or loss on the receivable.

If the foreign exchange contract is designated as a cash flow hedge then the portion of the gain or loss that is determined to be an effective hedge is recognised directly in equity and the ineffective portion in net profit and loss. When the receivable remeasurement gain or loss is recognised in net profit and loss then the effective portion of the hedge is transferred from equity to profit.

ACTIVITY 17.13

1 An entity plans to issue a fixed rate debt in six months. The forecasted issue is hedged by a eurodollar future derivative. At the end of the six months the derivative has losses of $2m and the forecasted debt issuance has accumulated $1.8m of positive expected future cash flows at fair value (i.e. after discounting).

2 On 4.1.X0 the entity has a forecasted sale of 500 tonnes of wheat, cost £1m, which is expected to occur on 31.12.X0. On 4.1.X0 a hedge is designated against the cash flows of the forecasted sale. The hedge is a future contract (derivative) to sell 500 tonnes at £1.1m on 31.12.X0. On 31.12.X0 the derivative has a fair value of £25 000 and is closed. The inventory is sold by the entity at £1 075 000 on 31.12.X0.

Show how both these cash flow hedges should be accounted for.

Activity feedback

1 The ineffective part of the hedge, $200 000, will be recognised as a loss immediately. The remainder of the hedged loss of $1.8m is recognised in equity. When the debt is issued and the hedge cleared the $1.8m is transferred out of equity and recorded as a reduction to the debt. Thus the debt is recorded as issued at a discount.

2 The wheat future is entered in the books at £25 000 as an asset with the gain of £25 000 taken to equity. This gain remains in equity until the forecasted sale takes place. When the inventory sale occurs on 31.12.X0, £75 000 profit will be shown in the net profit and loss. At the same time £25 000 will be transferred from equity to profit making a total profit of £100 000. The total cash flow will be £1.1m, £1 075 000 from the sale and £25 000 from the hedge as cash is received from the hedge on 31.12.X0.

All of this is quite complicated and requires judgement as to the effectiveness of the hedge at the outset. This 'effectiveness' also needs to be kept under review throughout the life of the hedge and the accounting changed if it is no longer effective. A hedge is normally regarded as effective if expected changes in the hedged item are almost fully offset by changes in the hedging instrument. The actual results need to be in the range of 80% to 125%.

Foreign entity investment hedges

Hedges of a net investment in a foreign entity are accounted for in a similar fashion to cash flow hedges. Thus the gain or loss on the hedging instrument is recognised immediately in equity. On recognition of the foreign currency translation gain or loss the hedging gain or loss will be recognised in the same manner.

PRESENTATION AND DISCLOSURE

The presentation and disclosure requirements in relation to financial instruments were detailed in IAS 32, which was revised in 1998 and further revised under the Board's improvement project, and are added to in relation to hedging by those of IAS 39. As mentioned in the introduction to this chapter, IAS 32 now only covers presentation and IFRS 7 has been issued detailing *Financial Instruments: Disclosures*. IFRS 7 incorporates many of IAS 32 original disclosures as well as additional and qualitative and quantitative disclosures on risks arising from financial instruments. The requirements for presentation and disclosure cover:

- classification of the FI as a liability or equity using substance over form
- separate classification of component parts of the FI in equity and liabilities
- reporting of interest, dividends, losses and gains from a FI
- offsetting of a financial asset and a financial liability that can only occur if there is a legally enforceable right to offset or if the entity intends to settle on a net basis or to realise the asset and settle the liability simultaneously
- disclosure such that understanding of the significance of on-balance sheet and off-balance sheet FIs on an entity's financial position, performance and cash flows is given to users
- disclosure of risk management policies of an entity including its policy for hedging
- disclosure of terms, conditions and accounting policies in relation to all financial assets, financial liabilities and equity
- exposure to interest rate risk and credit risk in all financial assets and financial liabilities
- information on fair values, for example method used to determine fair value
- description of hedging instruments.

ACTIVITY 17.14

Identify whether the following financial instruments should be classified by the issuer as a liability (debt) or equity in accordance with IASs.

- *A* has issued a perpetual preference share redeemable only at *A*'s option. Interest of 8% is paid annually provided there are sufficient distributable profits.

- *B* has issued a perpetual convertible bond. Interest of 10% on the bond is paid if a dividend is paid on the ordinary shares of *B*.

- *C* issues a perpetual preference share carrying a fixed dividend rate of 5%. If the dividend is deferred then the dividend is accumulated for future payout together with additional interest at 30%.

- *D* issues specific preference shares to its fund managers. They carry the right to an annual payment based on 25% of realised gains on the fund recorded in the period by *D*.

- *E* has issued perpetual preference share that carry a non-cumulative fixed rate dividend. This dividend is payable only if the parent company of *E* declares a dividend on its ordinary shares.

Activity feedback

- *A*. This is a *liability* as management does not have discretion over payment of interest. The critical feature of a liability remember is the existence of an obligation to pay cash or to exchange another instrument under conditions that are potentially unfavourable to the issuer.

- *B*. This should be included in *equity* as cash is paid over only if a dividend is paid to ordinary shareholders and thus the interest decision is discretionary.

- *C*. Given the interest obligation on the non-payment of dividend this must be treated as a *liability*.

- *D*. Again this is a *liability* as management have no discretion over the calculation of timing of the amount to be paid.

- *E*. This appears to be similar to *B* and therefore equity but the management of *E* does not have discretion over payment; the parent company does, and therefore this must be classified as a *liability*.

(adapted from *Accountancy* April 2003, p. 89)

REVISIONS TO IAS 39

IAS 39 before revision in June 2005 permitted users the option of designating all financial assets and liabilities at fair value with gains and losses recognised in the profit or loss. The IASB changed this option as it was possible that it might be used inappropriately.

Now an entity on initial recognition can only designate a financial asset/liability at fair value through profit and loss if by doing so more relevant information is provided to users:

A designation of a financial instrument as at fair value through profit and loss will result in more relevant information when either:

- it eliminates or significantly reduces a measurement or recognition inconsistency; or

- a group of financial assets, financial liabilities or both is managed and its performance evaluated on a fair value basis, in accordance with a documented risk management strategy and information about the group of financial instruments is provided internally on that basis to the entity's key management personnel. (IAS 39, para. 9)

However, an equity instrument that cannot be reliably measured is prohibited from being recognised as at fair value through profit and loss as this would not lead to more relevant information being provided to users.

One issue you might like to debate in relation to FIs is that of realisation. Historically, the principal driver of recognition of gains has been the realisation concept, but perhaps this is unrealistic in a marketplace involving complex financial instruments that trade on the basis of their underlying risks.

IFRS 4 *INSURANCE CONTRACTS*

Introduction

Before the issue of IFRS 4, *Insurance Contracts*, in March 2004 there was no International Accounting Standard to deal with the diverse practices of insurance contract accounting. The IASC had established a steering committee in 1997 to investigate the issues surrounding insurance contracts but the IASB did not really discuss the matter until 2001. As with many other controversial issues, the IASB has split the project for insurance contracts into two:

Phase I **(a)** to make limited improvements to accounting practices for insurance contracts without requiring major changes that may need to be reversed in phase II **(b)** to require disclosure that (i) identifies and explains the amounts in an insurer's financial statements arising from insurance contracts and (ii) helps users of those financial statements understand the amount, timing and uncertainty of future cash flows from insurance contracts. Phase I resulted in IFRS 4, which is basically a presentation and disclosure Standard.

Phase II will be concerned with the recognition and measurement of an insurance contract.

The basic issue with an insurance contract is determining the risks and rewards in the contract and who in substance owns them and in addition how to treat payments received and made within the contract.

Insurance contract

As defined by IFRS 4, this is a contract under which one party (the insurer) accepts significant insurance risk from another party (the policyholder) by agreeing to compensate the policyholder if a specified uncertain future event (the insured event) adversely affects the policyholder.

Several terms used in the above definition are also defined in IFRS 4:

Insurance risk: risk, other than financial risk, transferred from the holder of a contract to the issuer
Insured event: an uncertain future event that is covered by an insurance contract and creates insurance risk.

Risk is the essence of an insurance contract and as such at least one of the following will be uncertain at the inception of the contract:

1 whether an insured event will occur

2 when it will occur

3 and how much the insurer will need to pay if it occurs.

For example, insurance against theft or damage to property is an insurance contract as 1 and 2 above are uncertain and the contract will compensate the policyholder for the loss or damage, albeit generally to a limited amount. Life insurance is also deemed an insurance contract under IFRS 4, as, although death is certain, the timing is uncertain.

ACTIVITY 17.15

Identify which of the following are insurance contracts:

(a) compensation in cash or kind to contract holders for losses suffered while travelling

(b) financial guarantee contract that requires payment even if the holder has not insured a loss on the failure of the debtor to make payments when due

(c) deferred annuity contract where the holder will receive or can elect to receive a life contingent annuity at rates prevailing when the annuity begins

(d) a contract that requires specified payments to reimburse the holder for a loss it incurs because a specified debtor fails to make payment when due

(e) a catastrophe bond in which principal, interest payments or both are reduced significantly if a specified triggering event occurs and the triggering event includes a condition that the issuer of the bond suffered a loss

(f) loan contract containing a prepayment fee that is waived if prepayment results from the borrower's death.

Activity feedback
(a), **(d)** and **(e)** are insurance contracts.

In **(b)** there is no specified uncertain future event, the payment is required whatever happens to the debt. In **(c)** the insurer can reprice the mortality risk. It will become an insurance contract only when the annuity rate is fixed. Before the contract in **(f)**, the borrower faced no risk corresponding to the prepayment fee thus no risk has been transferred.

Scope

An entity applies IFRS 4 to:

- Insurance contracts that it issues and reinsurance contracts that it holds. A reinsurance contract is defined as an insurance contract issued by one insurer (the reinsurer) to compensate another insurer (the cedant) for losses on one or more contracts issues by the cedant.
- Financial instruments that it issues with a discretionary participation feature.

(IFRS 4, para. 2)

Excluded from the requirements of IFRS 4 are:

- product warranties issued directly by a manufacturer, dealer or retailer
- employers' assets and liabilities under employee benefit plans
- contractual rights or contractual obligations that are contingent on the future use of, or right to use, a non-financial item (for example, some licence fees, royalties, contingent lease payments and similar items), as well as lessee's residual value guarantee embedded in a finance lease
- financial guarantees into which an entity enters or retains on transferring to another party financial assets or financial liabilities within the scope of IAS 39, regardless of whether the financial guarantees are described as financial guarantees, letters of credit or insurance contracts
- contingent consideration payable or receivable in a business combination
- direct insurance contracts that the entity holds (i.e. direct insurance contracts in which the entity is the policyholder). However a cedant shall apply this IFRS to reinsurance contracts that it holds.

(IFRS 4, para. 4)

A sells computer hardware and offers to its customers an extended warranty for a fixed period covering servicing, repairs and maintenance for an annual fixed fee. Is this an insurance contract requiring disclosure under IFRS 4?

Activity feedback

A is accepting significant insurance risks under this contract as neither the number of services that *A* will be required to perform nor their nature is predetermined so this does meet the definition of an insurance contract. However, IFRS 4 specifically excludes product warranties issued by a retailer so this falls outside the scope of IFRS 4. If the extended warranty had been provided by a third party, i.e. a specialist repair firm or even a competing manufacturer or retailer, then the exclusion would not apply and IFRS 4 would need to be applied.

Disclosure

IFRS 4 requires disclosure of:

1 information that identifies and explains the amounts in its financial statements arising from insurance contracts

2 information that helps users to understand the amount, timing and uncertainty of future cash flows from insurance contracts.

Under **1** accounting policies, recognised assets, liabilities, income and expense will be disclosed as well as processes used to determine assumptions within these amounts and the effects of changes in these assumptions. Under **2** terms and conditions of the insurance contract that have a material effect on the cash flows of the insurer, and actual claims compared with previous estimates, will be disclosed.

ILLUSTRATION

A policyholder pays premiums of €100 every year for 5 years. The policy provider establishes an experience account equal to 90% of the cumulative premiums (including additional payments as below) less 90% of cumulative claims. If the experience account is negative (claims exceed premiums) the policyholder has to pay an additional payment equal to the experience account balance divided by the number of years left to run on the contract. At the end of the contract if the experience account is positive (premiums exceed claims) it is refunded to the policyholder; if the balance is negative that amount is paid to the insurer. Other terms of the contract are that it cannot be cancelled before maturity and maximum loss of the insurer in any one period is €2000.

This contract is obviously an insurance contract as significant risk is transferred to the insurer and there is uncertainty in respect of the experience account as the claims are uncertain. Let us assume that in the above case there are no claims by the policyholder during the five-year period, then at the end of the five years the policyholder will receive €450 (90% of cumulative premiums of €500). In substance, the policyholder has made a loan to the insurer, which is repaid in one instalment in year five, thus we need to unbundle the loan and the insurance contract. We therefore need to measure the loan advance each year at fair value in accordance with IAS 39. Assuming a discount rate of 10%, and that the insurance premium is equal in each year, then each payment of €100 is made up of a loan advance of €67 (see data that follow) and premium of €33.

Year	Opening balance	10% interest	Advance	Closing balance
0	0	0	67	67
1	67	6.7	67	140.7
2	140.7	14.1	67	221.8
3	221.8	22.2	67	311
4	311	31.1	67	409.1
5	409.1	40.9	(450)	–
Total		**115**	**(115)**	

Unbundling of deposit components

Some insurance contracts contain both an insurance component and a deposit component (see the 'Illustration' on p. 409). A deposit component is defined by IFRS 4 as:

> A contractual component that is not accounted for as a derivative under IAS 39 and would be within the scope of IAS 39 if it were a separate instrument. This requirement ensures that assets and liabilities are not omitted from the balance sheet.

Other main features

Other main features of IFRS 4 are:

1 The Standard exempts an insurer temporarily (until Phase II of the project is complete) from some requirements of other IFRSs.

2 Permits an insurer to change its accounting policies but only if the resulting financial statements would be more relevant but no less reliable or vice versa.

3 Permits insurers to introduce an accounting policy that would see the insurance liabilities in each period reflected at market interest rates.

4 Does not require the insurer to change its accounting policies even if they are excessively prudent.

When an insurer changes its accounting policies for insurance liabilities, it may reclassify some or all financial assets as 'at fair value through profit or loss', i.e. at the date of change the financial asset is measured at fair value with any gain or loss from the carrying amount reflected in profit or loss.

Financial guarantee contracts

IAS 30 defines a financial guarantee contract as a contract that requires the issuer to make specified payments to reimburse the holder for a loss it incurs because a specified debtor fails to make payment when due in accordance with the original or modified terms of a debt instrument.

ILLUSTRATION

Entity Alpha provides a financial guarantee to a third party entity Beta on 1 January 200X. Under the guarantee if entity Beta defaults on a specific loan of £10 000 that it has with a bank Alpha will become liable to repay the loan to the bank excluding interest. The guarantee lasts for five years.

On the date of the guarantee being provided Beta paid Alpha £500 which it considered to be the fair value of granting the guarantee. In 200Y the credit market has deteriorated to such a degree that it has become probable that Beta will default on its loan to the bank. How should Alpha account for the guarantee in its accounts in accordance with IAS 39?

On initial recognition the guarantee must be recognised at fair value, that is £500, thus Alpha will show a financial guarantee liability of £500. Subsequently it will be amortised over its life of five years. Thus Alpha will credit income with £100 and reduce the liability by £100 for the year ended 31 December 200X.

During 200Y when the possibility arises that Beta will default on the loan then Alpha will have to apply IAS 37 to account for the financial guarantee liability. This means Alpha needs to determine the best estimate of the expenditure it would incur if it had to settle the loan. If we assume the best estimate of the liability at 31 December 200Y is £9650 then Alpha will need to charge £9250 as an expense in the income statement and credit the financial guarantee liability account with £9250. The balance on the financial guarantee liability will now be £9650 the amount required to settle the loan.

These could also be regarded as insurance contracts. However IAS 39 states that these financial guarantee contracts are within its scope but permits an issuer to elect to apply either IAS 39 or IFRS 4 on those contracts where it has previously asserted explicitly that it regards such contracts as insurance contracts.

IAS 39 requires that such contracts are initially measured at fair value and subsequently amortised and recorded as income over the period the guarantees applies unless the liability measured in terms of IAS 37 exceeds the carrying amount.

The illustration on page 410 should help you understand this.

Insurance contract – Phase II

Currently IFRS 4 permits the use of existing accounting policies for insurance contracts. Phase II of the insurance contract project will introduce a comprehensive set of principles and requirements for the recognition and measurement of these contracts. A Standard on the matter is not expected until 2011. Measurement methods for insurance contracts currently under discussion are:

- current entry value
- current exit value.

The main difference between the two values occurs when evaluating risk to be measured in the contract. Under the current entry value method risk will be evaluated by reference to the price charged to the policyholder at the inception of the contract. This risk may well vary over the life of the contract. Under the current exit value method risk will be evaluated by reference to the amount that the insurer would have to pay to another entity to transfer all remaining contractual rights and obligations. The decisions made under Phase II will need to be consistent with the IASB's revenue recognition and fair value measurement projects.

SUMMARY

A complicated chapter and one where we advise you to read carefully the actual Standards. Table 17.4 on page 412, summarising the current major requirements of IAS 39 (excluding hedged items), might be useful for you. The table clearly shows that full fair value accounting for financial assets and liabilities is still not a requirement of IAS 39 on initial recognition. In addition, IAS 39 has introduced an option whereby entities can designate a financial asset or liability as 'at fair value through profit or loss account' and measure it at fair value for the whole period of its recognition.

Derivatives are always assumed to be held for trading, unless specifically designated as effective hedges. The information required to be kept and disclosed in respect of hedging instruments is substantial. Hedging instruments, if they are not effective hedges, will increase the volatility of earnings as the ineffective hedge will be recorded immediately in earnings. Remember that hedge accounting has the effect that an asset or liability that would otherwise be measured on a cost basis is measured on a fair value basis and the gain or loss is taken to profit and loss either immediately or via recycling at a later date.

(continued)

SUMMARY *(Continued)*

TABLE 17.4 Summary of current major requirements of IAS 39

	Loans and receivables originated by the entity	Held-to-maturity investments	Financial assets held for trading	Available for sale financial assets	Financial liabilities held for trading	Financial asset or financial liability at fair value through profit or loss account (option)
Recognition	When becomes a party to the transaction					
Derecognition	When loses control of contractual rights				When obligation discharged, cancelled or expired	When loses control of contractual rights
Gain or loss on derecognition	To net profit for period					
Initial measurement	Cost equals fair value of consideration given or received					
Subsequent measurement	At cost less amortisation	At cost less amortisation	At fair value subject to rebuttable assumption re reliable estimation	At fair value subject to rebuttable assumption re reliable estimation	At fair value with minor exceptions	At fair value subject to rebuttable assumption re relative estimation
Gain or loss on remeasurement	N/A	N/A	To income	To equity	To income	To income

Accountants, analysts and many others are struggling with the detail of IAS 39, and its impact cannot yet be fully measured. It is however a Standard that moves accounting beyond the traditional methods and attempts to capture the rights and obligations of complicated financial instruments which in the long term should provide more useful information to users if it is made understandable to them.

As at September 2008 the IASB has three current projects on financial instruments:

1 Revision to IAS 32 to improve and simplify the financial reporting requirements for FIs with characteristics of equity. Within the discussion paper issued on this matter the IASB proposes the use of a 'basic ownership' approach to determine which instruments should be classified as equity. A basic ownership instrument has the following characteristics according to the IASB:

 (a) the holder has a claim to a share of the assets of the entity that is subordinate to all other claims if the issuer were to liquidate on the date the classification decision is being made, and

 (b) the holder is entitled to a percentage of the assets of the entity that remain after all higher priority claims have been satisfied.

 This approach would classify even fewer instruments as equity than IAS 32 does.

2 Revision to IAS 39 in respect of derecognition of financial assets. A discussion paper has not yet been issued at the time of writing.

3 The complexity project which we identified for you at p. 387.

IFRS 4 fills a gap in international accounting standards but it is a stopgap until Phase II of the project on insurance contracts is complete. This is not expected until 2011 at the very earliest. IFRS 4 has not eliminated the diverse practices in accounting for insurance contracts, but it has ensured there will be more disclosure to improve comparability and provide risk information. However, IFRS 4 has defined an insurance contract, this definition it is intended will continue into Phase II of the project, which will provide more consistency. The biggest challenge for Phase II of the project is the decision whether or not to apply fair value measurement to insurance liabilities. Given the problems this fair value measurement has presented in IAS 39, the IASB will need to tread carefully and consult widely to ensure the result provides useful information to users that has the characteristics of relevance, reliability, comparability and understandability.

EXERCISES

Suggested answers to exercises marked ✓ *are to be found on the Student side of the companion website.*

Suggested answers to the remaining exercises are to be found on the Instructor side of the companion website.

✓ **1** Discuss the problems faced by users of financial reports if financial instruments are kept off balance sheet.

2 What is a financial instrument?

3 How does the IASB determine differentiation between financial instruments and other assets and liabilities?

4 What is a derivative?

5 Discuss the IASB's methodology for the recognition of gains and losses on remeasurement of financial instruments to fair value and illustrate the effects on the income statement.

6 Appraise the effect of using settlement date accounting as opposed to trade date accounting for regular way contracts.

7 Discuss the proposal by the IASB to move to full fair value accounting for financial instruments and identify the effects this move would have on an entity's income statement and balance sheet.

✓ **8** It is unrealistic to apply the realisation concept to complex financial instruments. Discuss.

9 Ambush, a public limited company, is assessing the impact of implementing the revised IAS 39 *Financial Instruments: Recognition and Measurement*. The directors realise that significant changes may occur in their accounting treatment of financial instruments and they understand that on initial recognition any financial asset or liability can be designated as one to be measured at fair value through profit or loss (the fair value option). However, there are certain issues that they wish to have explained and these are set out below.

Required

(a) Outline in a report to the directors of Ambush the following information:

   (i)   How financial assets and liabilities are measured and classified, briefly setting out the accounting method used for each category. (Hedging relationships can be ignored.)

   (ii) Why the 'fair value option' was initially introduced and why it has caused such concern.

(b) Ambush loaned $200 000 to Bromwich on 1 December 2003. The effective and stated interest rate for this loan was 8%. Interest is payable by Bromwich at the end of each year and the loan is repayable on 30 November 2007. At 30 November 2005, the directors of Ambush have heard that Bromwich is in financial difficulties and is undergoing a financial reorganisation. The directors feel that it is likely that they will only receive $100 000 on 30 November 2007 and no future interest payment. Interest for the year ended 30 November 2005 had been received. The financial year-end of Ambush is 30 November 2005.

Required:

   (i)   Outline the requirements of IAS 39 as regards the impairment of financial assets.

   (ii) Explain the accounting treatment under IAS 39 of the loan to Bromwich in the financial statements of Ambush for the year ended 30 November 2005.

(ACCA 3.5 int, December 2005)

10 The directors of QRS, a listed entity, have met to discuss the business's medium to long-term financing requirements. Several possibilities were discussed. including the issue of more shares using a rights issue. In many respects this would be the most desirable option because the entity is already quite highly geared. However, the directors are aware of several recent cases where rights issue have not been successful because share prices are currently quite low and many investors are averse to any kind of investment in shares.

Therefore, the directors have turned their attention to other options. The finance director is on sick leave, and so you, her assistant, have been given the task of responding to the following note from the Chief Executive:

Now that we've had a chance to discuss possible financing arrangements, the directors are in agreement that we should structure our issue of financial instruments in order to be able to classify them as equity rather than debt. Any increase in the gearing ratio would be unacceptable. Therefore, we have provisionally decided to make two issue of financial instruments as follows:

1   An issue of non-redeemable preferred shares to raise $4 million. These shares will carry a fixed interest rate of 6%, and because they are shares they can be classified as equity.

2   An issue of 6% convertible bonds, issued at par value, to raise $6 million. These bonds will carry a fixed date for conversion in four years' time. Each $100 of debt will be convertible at the holder's option into 120 $1 shares. In our opinion, these bonds can actually be classified as equity immediately, because they are convertible within five years on terms that are favourable to the holder.

Please confirm that these instruments will not increase our gearing ratio should they be issued.

Note: You determine that the market rate available for similar non-convertible bonds is currently 8%.

Required:

Explain to the directors the accounting treatment, in respect of debt/equity classification, required by IAS 32, *Financial Instruments: Disclosure and Presentation* for each of the proposed issues, advising them on the acceptability of classifying the instruments as equity.

Your explanation should be accompanied by calculations where appropriate.

(CIMA P8 PILOT PAPER)

REVENUE

OBJECTIVES After studying this chapter you should be able to:

- define revenue and what type of transactions it arises from

- determine when it should be recognised by an entity

- explain how it should be measured

- critically appraise IAS 18 in relation to revenue recognition and measurement

- identify the disclosure requirements in respect of revenue in accordance with IAS 18

- compare IAS GAAP with other GAAPs.

INTRODUCTION

The income statement reports the profit of an entity by matching expenses to revenues, but before we can carry out this matching we need to define revenues and expenses and identify at what point we should recognise them. Many Standards that we have already considered are about the expense side of these issues but as yet we have given very little consideration to the revenue.

Chapter 8 dealt with the general principles in respect of revenue but this chapter will consider them in more detail and also IAS 18, *Revenue*. IAS 18 was originally issued in 1982 and revised in 1993 and is effective for financial statements covering periods beginning on or after 1 January 1995. It is worth noting at this point that neither the US nor the UK has a specific Standard on 'revenue'.

WHAT IS REVENUE?

The Framework for the Preparation and Presentation of Financial Statements defines income as increases in economic benefits during the accounting period in the form of inflows or enhancements of assets or decreases of liabilities that result in increases in equity, other than those relating to contributions from equity participants. It further states that income encompasses both revenues and gains. Revenues are further described as arising in the course of the ordinary activities of an entity. So what is this revenue and how do we distinguish it from other gains?

Revenue is regarded by many as simply the cash that you are paid for selling things and this simple idea also implies exchange – cash for things. We have also carried this idea of exchange through to the balance sheet. Consider the simple exchange of selling an item of inventory for cash, the accounting entries would be to derecognise the item of inventory in the balance sheet and recognise the asset of cash. The asset of cash would qualify as revenue and against this we would match relevant expenses to determine profit. Traditionally, we have not regarded the item of inventory as revenue until it is sold or at least until we have exchanged it for another asset, perhaps a debtor. This approach seems to equate revenue with economic activity involving exchange with a customer and ignores other items such as gains on assets that are revalued or carried at current value.

IAS 18 (para. 7) defines revenue as:

The gross inflow of economic benefits during the period arising in the course of the ordinary activities of an entity when those inflows result in increases in equity, other than increases relating to contributions from equity participants.

There are several important notions in this definition.

1 Revenue is the *gross inflow*, i.e. before the deduction of any expenses. We must also presume that this gross inflow is to the entity although it isn't specifically stated in the definition.

2 Revenue results from ordinary activities. This notion distinguishes revenue from other gains. Gains are defined in the Framework as 'other items that

ACTIVITY 18.1

An entity receives €100 for the sale of an item of inventory. This amount includes a sales tax at 25% on cost which is payable to the tax authorities. The entity also sells another item of inventory on behalf of an agent for which it only retains a 10% commission charge on sale price. Identify the revenue to the entity in both cases in accordance with the IAS 18 definition.

Activity feedback

The first item of inventory only results in an increase in equity of €80, the other €20 is paid directly to the tax authorities and is effectively collected by us on their behalf.

The second item of inventory has only generated revenue and subsequent increase in equity to the entity of €10. The other €90 is collected on behalf of the agent.

ACTIVITY 18.2

Two entities both sell an item of real estate (cost €1m) for €2m. One entity operates in the chemical industry; the other is a property development company. Identify the revenue for both entities.

Activity feedback

For the chemical entity the income of €2m will be regarded as a gain as the sale of real estate is not regarded as part of the ordinary activities. For the property development company the income of €2m would be regarded as revenue.

ACTIVITY 18.3

The following transactions occur in an accounting period for A entity:

- 1m €1 shares are issued at a premium on nominal value of €2
- property is sold for €2m
- the entity deals in the retail of widgets and makes sales of €150 000, 50% of which are on credit.

Identify the revenue for the entity in accordance with IAS 18 for the period.

Activity feedback

All these transactions give rise to an increase in equity but only the last is regarded as revenue. The share issue is income received from equity participants and the second is not part of the ordinary activities of the entity.

meet the definition of income and may, or may not, arise in the ordinary activities of an entity'.

3 Revenue gives rise to an increase in equity.

FROM WHAT DOES REVENUE ARISE?

So far we have defined revenue as arising from exchange transactions that give rise to gross inflows from ordinary activities. However, exchange transactions, as we have already seen, can take many forms and we need to consider whether all of them or only some give rise to revenue.

Exchange transactions can be viewed as contracts between a seller and a buyer but would we regard interest received and royalties as part of such an exchange contract and therefore revenue?

Interest received results from the use by another of entity cash or cash equivalent and thus we have an exchange contract that gives rise to an increase in equity, and therefore the interest can be regarded as revenue. Note that when the principal element of the loan is repaid this will not be regarded as revenue as it will not result in an increase in equity, only an asset of cash replacing the debt. Royalties are similar, as they are charges for the use of long-term assets of the entity such as copyrights, patents, trademarks, etc. IAS 18 states that revenue arises from three types of transaction and event:

- the sale of goods
- the rendering of service
- the use by others of entity assets yielding interest, royalties and dividends.

There is some revenue that the Standard does not deal with and this is generally that which is dealt with by another Standard, e.g. construction contracts, leases, dividends from associated companies, changes in the fair value of financial assets and liabilities or their disposal (dealt with under financial instruments). Changes in other non-current assets, extraction of mineral ores, insurance contracts of insurance entities and natural increases in herds, agricultural and forestry products are also outside the scope of IAS 18.

In determining whether or not a sale has been made or a service has been rendered the Standard requires us to determine whether certain conditions have been met before we recognise revenue (see Activity 18.4).

ACTIVITY 18.4

An entity transfers assets to a customer as follows:

- €2000 of bottles of wine in exchange for €2000 cash with the option for the customer to return as many of the bottles, unopened, within seven days and claim a refund of the cash paid for each.

- €200 of glasses in exchange for €50 cash where the customer is required to return all glasses within seven days or pay the full price for them.

Identify in each case whether a sale has occurred and therefore whether revenue should be recognised.

Activity feedback

The answer here involves us looking at the substance of the transactions and deciding whether the customer, on receipt of the asset, has acquired the associated risks and rewards of the asset.

In the case of the wine it would seem that the customer has received the risks and rewards associated with it, but do we recognise all the €2000 or do we only recognise 90% of it, assuming it is normal that 10% is returned. Alternatively, we could delay the recognition of the revenue until the return time has expired.

In the case of the glasses the customer is not acquiring all the risks and rewards associated with them, only a very limited proportion of them. Indeed, the entity retains effective control over them.

Sale of goods

IAS 18 identifies several criteria that must be met before revenue can be recognised on sale of goods as follows:

- the entity has transferred to the buyer the significant risks and rewards of ownership of the goods
- the entity retains neither continuing managerial involvement to the degree usually associated with ownership nor effective control over the goods sold
- the amount of revenue can be measured reliably
- it is probable that the economic benefits associated with the transaction will flow to the entity
- the costs incurred or to be incurred in respect of the transaction can be measured reliably.

ACTIVITY 18.5

Identify, for the following transactions, if and when the risks and rewards associated with the transaction have passed between the parties concerned:

1. A publisher sells books to a retailer on sale or return. If the books are not sold the retailer returns them to the publisher for a refund. It is impossible to estimate reliably how many books will remain unsold.

2. A retailer offers a 12-month guarantee on all its products whereby a customer can return the product for whatever reason and have a full refund. In the normal course of business it has been found that 1% per annum of sales is subject to such refunds.

3. A software house develops a customised finance system for a customer. Title to the software passes to the customer on a given date but included in the agreement is a three-month warranty period beyond this date to cover the need for any amendments or debugging of the system. It is impossible to estimate the potential for these costs.

4. A piece of machinery is sold by Alpha entity to Beta for €100 000. In addition Beta is required to pay €75 000 to Alpha for the installation of the machinery. The machinery is inoperable without installation.

5. Alpha sells another machine to Gamma but under an agreement that allows Gamma to return the machine if a contract Gamma is seeking, and for which it needs the machine, is not won. No information is available on the likelihood of Gamma winning the contract.

Activity feedback

1. In this example, the receipt of revenue to the publisher is dependent on the derivation of revenue by the retailer from the sale of the goods and thus the risks and rewards do not pass until the retailer has sold the books. This would not be regarded as a sale and revenue would only be recognised when the books are sold by the retailer.

2. In this case the retailer retains very little risk associated with the products and therefore revenue should be recognised when the sale is made and an accrual made for the expected returns.

3. Legal title has passed to the customer but the risks and rewards still remain with the developer until the end of the three-month period. Revenue will not be recognised until the end of the three-month period.

4. This sale will not be completed until the installation, which is a material part of the cost, is complete. Revenue will be recognised on completion of installation.

5. Revenue cannot be recognised by Alpha until and if Gamma wins the contract.

ACTIVITY 18.6

An advertising entity Choice contracts to produce an advert about TV1 for it to show on air. The contract entitles Choice to a fee of £100 000 on the first showing of the advert and a repeat fee of £10 000 for each subsequent showing. How should Choice account for the revenue from the contract?

Activity feedback

IAS 18 requires that revenue should be recognised on a service contract when the revenue flow to the entity is probable and the revenue, the stage of completion of the transaction and the costs to complete can be reliably measured. The revenue of £100 000 should be recognised by Choice when the advertisement is handed over to TV1. The repeat fees should be recognised as repeats occur as this is the only time when the revenue can be measured reliably. This contract could also be regarded as comprising of two separate elements (see Activity 18.11) which would give the same answer.

RECOGNITION

The Standard provides other examples of when to recognise revenue on sale of goods in an appendix. This covers such things as 'bill and hold' sale – where the buyer accepts the billing for the product but the products are left with the seller until the buyer requests delivery – goods shipped subject to conditions, lay away sales, orders when payment is received in advance, sale and repurchase agreements, sales to intermediate parties, subscription sales, instalment sales and real estate sales. It is worth noting at this stage that the recognition of revenue on sale of goods involves management in a subjective decision, i.e. revenue is recognised when significant risks and rewards have been transferred to the buyer.

Rendering of services   Criteria for recognition are also required for rendering of services. Consider Activity 18.7 and the two illustrations below.

Stage of completion recognition of revenue is often referred to as percentage-of-completion method (see Chapter 16). The percentage of completion can be estimated by one of several methods but management must choose the most reliable. The methods available are:

ACTIVITY 18.7

Suggest criteria for the recognition of revenue from services rendered.

Activity feedback

The criteria are quite similar to those for sale of goods:

- The amount of revenue can be measured reliably.

- It is probable that the economic benefits associated with the transaction will flow to the entity.

- The stage of completion of the transaction at the balance sheet date can be measured reliably.

- The costs incurred for the transaction and the costs to complete the transaction can be measured reliably.

   The stage of completion criterion is most important here.

ILLUSTRATION

Alpha has a contract with Beta to provide daily security services for a period of three years. The contract involves payment by Beta of €10 000 per annum and commences at Alpha's opening balance sheet date.

   At each balance sheet date Alpha will recognise revenue of €10 000 for the period of three years as this is in line with the performance of the service.

ILLUSTRATION

A recruitment agency has a contract with Gamma to seek and appoint a new chief executive. The contract is for a period of 18 months. On the appointment of the CE the agency will receive a payment of €25 000.

   This revenue will not be recognised by the agency until the service is actually rendered, that is, the CE is appointed. The specific act of finding the CE is the significant factor that results in revenue and therefore this service would not be recognised on a straight line basis over the period of the contract.

- surveys of work performed
- services performed to date as a percentage of total services to be performed
- the proportion that costs incurred to date bear to the estimated total costs of the transaction.

If the revenue cannot be measured reliably for a service then revenue should only be recognised to the extent that costs incurred can be recovered. If the costs cannot be recovered then these are recognised as an expense.

An interestingly problematic issue arises with customer loyalty programmes, popular with, for example, airlines. A 'sale' now involves immediate inflows, but also creates an expected future outflow (of uncertain amount, timing, and rate of take-up). Common practice is to recognise the full revenue immediately, and also to recognise an expense (and provision) for the expected costs of supplying the loyalty award.

IFRIC 13, *Customer Loyalty Programmes*, requires an entity that grants loyalty award credits (such as points or travel miles) to customers who buy other goods or services to allocate some of the proceeds of the initial sale to the award credits and recognise these proceeds as revenue only when they have fulfilled their obligations. The amount allocated to the award credits should be measured by reference to their fair value; that is, the amount for which the award credits could be sold separately (which will logically be less than the cost of actually supplying the loyalty award, to allow for expected non-take-up).

If the entity supplies the awards itself, it recognises the amounts allocated to the award credits as revenue when the credits are redeemed and the entity fulfils its obligation to supply the awards. If a third party supplies the awards, the entity needs to assess first whether it is collecting the amount allocated to the award credits on its own behalf or as an agent for a third party. Note also that a correction to the unrecognised revenue may be needed from time to time to take account of expired unused loyalty rights.

Interest, royalties and dividends The criteria for recognition of these are:

- It is probable that the economic benefits associated with the transaction will flow to the entity.
- The amount of revenue can be measured reliably.

IAS 18 also specifies the period over which these amounts are recognised: 'Interest should be recognised on a time proportion basis that takes into account the effective yield on the asset.' The effective yield is the rate of interest required to discount the stream of future cash receipts expected over the life of the asset to the initial carrying amount of the asset. An example of this is given in Activity 18.8.

'Royalties should be recognised on an accrual basis in accordance with the substance of the relevant agreement.' Generally, royalty payments are based on time or sales. If it is time based then the revenue should be recognised on the same time base. If sales based then revenue is recognised, say, on the budgeted sales with an adjustment to reflect actual sales at the year-end.

'Dividends should be recognised when the shareholder's right to receive payment is established.' This means that the revenue in this case is recognised in accordance with legal form rather than substance.

ACTIVITY 18.8

An entity sells a product to another under an agreement that allows for payment to be made by a series of annual instalments of €4000 for four years. The product generally sells for cash €16 000. The buyer would, under normal circumstances, be able to obtain finance at a cost of 10% per annum. (Note the buyer is acquiring the product under a 0% financing agreement.) Identify the revenue to be recognised at the outset by the seller and any other accounting entries to be made over the five-year period.

Activity feedback

The revenue must be recognised at fair value which equates to discounting the cash payments made at 10%. The buyer has received the product at a discounted price from normal sale value of €16 000. A corresponding debtor would be raised at the date of sale. As the instalments are received these will be split between the principal amount which reduces the debt and an amount of interest which will be recognised as revenue.

HOW SHOULD IT BE MEASURED?

'Revenue is measured at the fair value of the consideration received or receivable' (IAS 18, para. 9). This sounds simple enough and as fair value is the amount for which an asset could be exchanged or a liability settled between knowledgeable, willing partners in an arm's-length transaction then we would measure the revenue after trade discounts, early payment discounts or volume rebates.

A problem does arise, however, in the case where revenue is not received by the seller for a period of time. In this case, the consideration eventually received, due to the time value of money, will be less than that originally agreed. It is therefore necessary for the nominal amount of revenue to be discounted where there would be a material difference in the amount received due to the time value of money. The question then needing an answer is 'what discount rate should be used?' The Standard answers as follows.

The imputed rate of interest is the more clearly determinable of either:

- the prevailing rate for a similar instrument of an issuer with a similar credit rating, or
- a rate of interest that discounts the nominal amount of the instrument to the current cash sales price of the goods or services.

It is often the case that goods or services are swapped, not for cash, but for other goods and/or services. These swaps, barter transactions, can occur of both like and dissimilar products. We need to determine whether or not these barter transactions should be treated as revenue and, if they are, how that revenue should be measured.

Where the products are alike, which generally occurs for commodities such as milk, gas or oil where suppliers exchange inventories in different locations to fulfil demand, then the exchange is not regarded as one which generates revenue by IAS 18. Where products are dissimilar then, according to IAS 18, revenue is generated and should be measured at the fair value of the goods or services received or, if this cannot be reliably measured, then at the fair value of the goods or services given up. (See Activity 18.9.)

In relation to barter transactions involving advertising a specific SIC, SIC 31, *Barter Transactions Involving Advertising Services*, has been issued. The SIC is concerned with the fair value of the revenue and states that:

ACTIVITY 18.9

Explain the basis of the logic used by IAS 18 in accounting for barter transactions.

Activity feedback

IAS 18 defines revenue as a gross inflow of economic benefits that should be recognised when an entity has transferred to the buyer the significant risks and rewards of ownership of the goods.

In a barter transaction involving the exchange of oil in Saudi Arabia for oil in Russia, barter of similar products, then the entities involved are not in a substantially different position to that before the exchange assuming that the barter was a fair exchange. Each will still have the same risks associated with the oil and neither party will actually have been rewarded. There is no revenue, because, in substance there is no sale.

In the situation involving different products then the barter will result in each entity placing itself in a different position in its operating cycle. Each entity has reached the end of the operating cycle in relation to its product and dispensed with the risks and rewards associated with that product. In exchange they have started on the operating cycle in relation to the new product and are now subject to the new risks and rewards associated with it. So revenue does exist and will be measured by each entity at the fair value of the goods it has received.

The revenue in these transactions can only be reliably measured by reference to non-barter transactions that:

- involve advertising similar to the advertising in the barter transaction;
- occur frequently;
- represent a predominant number of transactions and amount when compared to non-barter transactions to provide advertising that is similar to the advertising in barter transactions;
- involve cash and/or another form of consideration (e.g. marketable securities) that has a reliably measurable fair value; and
- do not involve the same counterparty as in the barter transaction.

Transactions made up of parts

Transactions can often be made up of several components and to identify their substance we will need to unbundle them and recognise the revenue on the separate parts and perhaps at different times.

Activity 18.11 involves transactions made up of parts.

In some business sectors multiple element arrangements are increasingly complex. For example consider your mobile phone package which probably includes a handset sale, pre-paid minutes for calls and texts, message services, discounts and many

ACTIVITY 18.10

An entity sells a product plus a servicing agreement for three years for €15 000. The product without the servicing could be sold at fair value of €9000. At what point should any revenue be recognised?

Activity feedback

At the initial point of sale €9000 will be recognised as revenue, always assuming all other criteria have been met for recognition. The servicing revenue will be deferred and only be recognised when that service is rendered.

ACTIVITY 18.11

Silver is a supplier of silver candlesticks. It currently supplies to several retailers but it has recently contracted to supply only to Sable over the next two years. This contract requires a payment, which is non-refundable, from Sable to Silver of £200 000 on signing and an agreement that Sable will pay Silver £30 for each candlestick. The fair value of the candlesticks to retailers is £30. Although Silver cannot sell candlesticks to anyone but Sable, Sable can buy from other suppliers. How should the revenue, i.e. the lump sum of £200 000, and each sale be recognised in Silver's accounts?

Activity feedback

There are two separately identifiable elements in this contract:

- the £200 000 which is a payment to Silver for not selling candlesticks to another retailer for two years. However this cannot be recognised as revenue in full on signing the contract but must be spread over the two-year period
- the sale of each candlestick which will be recognised as each sale is made in accordance with IAS 18.

other special offers and incentives. How do we separate all these things and account for the separate transactions as revenue, as IAS 18 requires?

Activity 18.13 should test your understanding of this chapter.

Disclosure requirements

The disclosure requirements of IAS 18 are quite straightforward and what we would expect. They cover accounting policy adopted to recognise revenue, method of determining stage of completion of services, the amount of significant revenue from sale of goods, rendering of services, interest, royalties and dividends and the amount of revenue recognised from exchanges of goods or services.

The following is an example of an accounting policy for revenue taken from Vitec group plc financial statements for the year ended 31 December 2005.

Revenue

Turnover, which excludes value added tax and sales between group companies, represents the value of products and services sold. Other than for long-term contracts, the treatment of which is set out separately below, revenue arising from product sales is recognised when the significant risks and rewards of ownership have been transferred to the buyer, which occurs normally when title passes to the customer.

Revenue arising from asset rental is recognised over the duration of the rental contract as the gross amount billed to the customer, where we act as the principal in the rental transaction. No revenue is recognised if there are significant uncertainties regarding the recovery of the consideration due, associated costs or the possible return of goods and continuing management involvement with the goods.

ACTIVITY 18.12

In Activity 18.11 if the contract specified that silver would sell candlesticks to Sable at £20, i.e. £10 less than the fair value sale to retailers, would the recognition of the revenue change?

Activity feedback

The answer is yes as cross-subsidisation now exists between the two elements in the contract. The lump sum of £200 000 now incorporates an element for the discount on fair value. An estimate of the total discount must be made and subtracted from the lump sum; the remainder of the lump sum will then be spread over the two-year period. The discount element will be recognised as each sale is made.

ACTIVITY 18.13

Identify when the revenue, if indeed there is such, in the following transactions should be recognised:

1 commitment fees received by an entity to originate or purchase a loan

2 advertising media commissions carried out for a client where inflows will be received when the advert is exposed in the media

3 tuition fees paid to a training entity

4 servicing fees included in the price of a product sold by an entity

5 an entity sells all its inventory of wine to the bank with the option to repurchase the wine at any time it wishes and at a price that increases by 5% per annum on the original sale price.

Activity feedback

1 If it is unlikely that a specific loan agreement will be entered into then the commitment fee will be recognised on a time basis over the commitment period. Otherwise, the commitment fee will be recognised when both parties legally agree to the loan.

2 These will be recognised when the advertisement is seen by the public.

3 Revenue will need to be recognised over the period of tuition.

4 The servicing amount included in the price of the product is separated out and deferred and recognised as revenue over the period of service generally on a straight line basis.

5 In this case it seems apparent that the seller has not transferred the risks and rewards associated with the wine to the bank. In fact, the substance of the transaction is that of a loan guaranteed on the value of the wine. No revenue will be recognised in this case, as it is a financing arrangement.

The following extract is taken from a summary of Rolls-Royce's new group accounting policies under IFRS.

Revenues

Revenues comprise sales to outside customers after discounts and excluding value added tax. Sales are recognised when the significant risk and rewards of ownership of the goods are transferred to the customer, the sales price agreed and the receipt of payment can be assured. Where the impact of discounting to present value is significant, revenues are recognised at present value.

Sales of services and long-term contracts are recognised when the outcome of the transaction can be assessed reliably. Revenue is recognised by reference to the stage of completion of the contract. The assessment of the stage of completion is dependent on the nature of the contract, but will generally be based on costs incurred to the extent relating to services performed up to the reporting date or achievement of contractual milestones where appropriate or flying hours for long-term aftermarket arrangements.

Linked sales of products and services are treated as a single long-term contract where they have been negotiated as a single package and are so closely interrelated that they effectively form a single product with an overall profit margin. Revenue is recognised on the same basis as for other long-term contracts described above.

GAAP comparisons

IAS is the only GAAP to have a specific Standard for revenue recognition. The IAS Framework defines income as including revenues and gains. The Standard defines revenues as the gross inflows of economic benefits during the period arising from the ordinary activities of an entity when the inflows result in an increase in equity, other than increases relating to contributions from equity participants.

All three frameworks, i.e. IASB, FASB and UK ASB, require measurement of revenues at fair value of consideration received or receivable and both IAS and UK permit discounting to present value where inflows are deferred. US GAAP does not permit this discounting.

UK GAAP does not define revenue but the Statement of Principles requires that a gain must be recognised if there is sufficient evidence that an asset has been created and the asset can be measured with sufficient reliability. Recognition occurs when a critical event in the operating cycle is reached, e.g. delivery of goods or services. It also states that in some cases it might be appropriate to recognise revenue earlier. In July 2001 the UK ASB issued a discussion paper entitled *Revenue Recognition* with the intention of provoking discussion, and with the longer-term aim of establishing a framework within which to consistently address revenue issues that arise in different contexts.

US GAAP focuses on realisation of revenue. Realisation occurs when the transaction is converted into cash or cash equivalents or the likelihood of its receipt is reasonably certain.

SUMMARY

We have seen throughout this chapter that the recognition of revenue, which is key in the determination of profit of an entity, is dependent on several factors. These factors also require judgements to be made by management, many of which will require subjectivity. Management has to take decisions on:

- what constitutes the ordinary activities of the entity
- whether or not significant risks and rewards of ownership have been transferred to a buyer
- whether the amount of revenue involved can be measured reliably, i.e. can its fair value be determined
- whether it is probable that economic benefits associated with the transaction (sale) will flow to the entity
- whether the costs in respect of the transaction can be measured reliably
- what stage a particular service has reached in its delivery.

We have also seen that revenue is distinguished from income, which incorporates gains as well as revenue. Gains are generally seen as being those items that result from activities outside the ordinary activities of the entity, e.g. gains from the sale of non-current assets or upward revaluations of non-current assets.

All of this ensures that the revenue that is recognised in financial statements is reliable and prudent but it may not be very relevant in a business world where most production is sold. Currently, we do not recognise gains on stocks of goods for sale but it is arguable that this information would be relevant to users. All we provide them with is information on the cost of the product (or NRV, whichever is the lower) not information on what the asset of stock could be sold for assuming a reasonable marketplace.

IAS 18 is 'principles-based' with few detailed rules. This leaves substantial scope for judgement and interpretation and could lead to a lack of consistency. However, in the US, where a 'rules-based' approach is adopted which leads to a plethora of rules on revenue recognition, the problems of revenue recognition are still rife. The IASB is currently working with the FASB to replace IAS 18. This process has been continuing for several years, and the discussions have clearly got into severe difficulties. A discussion paper (not an exposure draft), is scheduled for late 2008, but the original schedule has slipped badly. Follow developments when they eventually occur, but do not assume that emerging proposals will remain unchanged.

EXERCISES

Suggested answers to exercises marked ✓ are to be found on the Student side of the companion website.

Suggested answers to the remaining exercises are to be found on the Instructor side of the companion website.

✓ **1**   What is revenue? Distinguish it from other gains.

2   Useful information is provided to users by restricting the definition of revenue to that arising from ordinary activities only. Discuss.

3   IAS 18 is based on substance over form. Discuss.

4   Financial reports prepared under IAS 18 are irrelevant and unreliable. Discuss.

5   The IAS 18 method of revenue recognition proves that accountants are prudent. Discuss.

6   Explain the relationship between revenue recognition and asset valuation.

7   Analyse the need to discount deferred inflows to an entity as permitted by IAS 18.

✓ **8**   Recognition of revenue in accordance with IAS 18 is objective. Discuss.

9   (a)   Revenue recognition is the process by which companies decide when and how much income should be included in the income statement. It is a topical area of great debate in the accounting profession. The IASB looks at revenue recognition from conceptual and substance points of view. There are occasions where a more traditional approach to revenue recognition does not entirely conform to the IASB guidance; indeed neither do some International Accounting Standards.

Required:
Explain the implications that the IASB's Framework for the Preparation and Presentation of Financial Statements (Framework) and the application of substance over form have on the recognition of income. Give examples of how this may conflict with traditional practice and some accounting standards.

(b)   Derringdo sells good supplied by Gungho. The goods are classed as A grade (perfect quality) or B grade, having slight faults. Derringdo sells the A grade goods acting as an agent for Gungho at a fixed price calculated to yield a gross profit margin of 50%. Derringdo receives a commission of 12.5% of the sales it achieves for these goods. The arrangement for B grade goods is that they are sold by Gungho to Derringdo and Derringdo sells them at a gross profit margin of 25%. The following information has been obtained from Derringdo's financial records:

		$000
Inventory held on premises 1 April 2002	– A grade	2 400
	– B grade	1 000
Goods from Gungho year to 31 March 2003	– A grade	18 000
	– B grade	8 800
Inventory held on premises 31 March 2003	– A grade	2 000
	– B grade	1 250

Required:

Prepare the income statement extracts for Derringdo for the year to 31 March 2003 reflecting the above information.

(ACCA June 03)

✓ **10** Identify when the revenue, if indeed there is any, in the following transactions should be recognised in accordance with IAS 18, *Revenue Recognition*:

(a)   Land has been sold by *A* entity to Connect Housing Association entity for £1m unconditionally and irrevocably with contracts exchanged. £0.6m of the consideration is payable after six months and £0.4m 12 months after *A*'s year-end. Connect is expecting to build apartments on the land and the project is likely to receive lottery funding although this is not guaranteed. The uncertainty over the funding is the reason Connect has agreed delayed payment.

(b)   *B* entity rents cars to 'not own fault' accident victims. The rental for such cars is billed to the insurance company of the fault driver. Negotiations then take place between *B* and the insurance company as to how much of the charge for the rental car will be paid.

(c)   *Z* entity, a broadband network provider, supplies equipment and a maintenance service to its customers at a charge of £216 per annum. The price of the maintenance service is £160 per annum and the cost of the equipment £80 if purchased separately.

(d)   *Y* entity sells motorboats for £50 000 each. The company also provides moorings at £5000 per annum to customers. If a customer buys the boat and mooring package together he is given a 5% discount on the cost of the total package. The normal profit on the boat is 25% and the moorings 50% to *Y*.

(e)   *A* law firm provides services to defendants on a no-win/no-fee basis. Lawyers' fees are normally charged on a time basis and fees are billed monthly.

(f)   *A* entity sells materials for making doors to two manufacturers *X* and *Y* who assemble the frames and put glass in the doors. *A* receives the doors back from *X* and *Y* and sells them to a builder for installation in homes. The precise details of the sale of materials to *X* and *Y* are as follows:

- *X* buys the materials at £10 per door from *A* without any guarantee that *A* will purchase the assembled doors; *X* buys materials for assembly from other manufacturers; no price for the purchase of the doors by *A* is agreed on the sale of materials to *X*.

- Y buys the materials from *A*, which cost *A* £5, at £10 per door; *A* agrees to buy the finished doors back from *Y* at £50.

(g) Keepfit plc operates gyms that charge a joining fee of £250. This fee entitles members to life membership. In addition, members pay £6 per session. Non-members can use the gym at £8 per session. Historical records indicate that members use the gym about 50 times per year and that they hold membership for two years.

(h) Lowds plc manufactures and sells caravans. When a customer orders a caravan an advance payment of 10% of the sale price is required. In most cases orders are taken for caravans that are not yet completed.

(i) A university collects fees from its students at the beginning of the academic year in which the student enrols for the whole of their course. The course may last from one to three years.

11 Delta's accounting year-end is 30 September. The trial balance of Delta as at 30 September 2006 showed the following balances:

	$'000	$'000
Revenue (Note 1)		240 000
Purchases	90 000	
Employment costs (Note 2)	60 000	
Operating overheads (Note 2)	45 000	
Inventories as at 1 October 2005 (Note 3)	35 000	
Property, plant and equipment (Notes 4 and 5):		
– At cost 30 September 2006	100 000	
– Accumulated depreciation at 1 October 2005		26 500
Construction contract (Note 6)	7 000	
Financial asset (Note 7)	12 500	
Investment income (Note 7)		500
Long-term loan (fixed rate of interest 10% per annum)		30 000
Interest paid on long-term loan	3 000	
Trade receivables	50 000	
Cash and bank balances	43 300	
Trade and other payables		30 000
Current tax payable (Note 8)	200	
Deferred tax at 1 October 2005 (Note 9)		4 000
Equity share capital (ordinary shares of $1)		50 000
Share premium account		40 000
Dividend paid on ordinary shares	5 000	
Retained earnings at 1 October 2005		30 000
	451 000	451 000

Notes to the trial balance

Note 1 – Revenue

On 29 September 2006 Delta sold a consignment of products for $30 million and credited the entire amount to revenue, the debit entry being to trade receivables. The terms of sale of the products were that Delta would provide an after-sales service which required Delta to correct any defects that became apparent in the products for a one-year period from the date of sale. The directors of Delta estimated that the cost of correcting defects in the consignment over the relevant period would be $1 million. A reasonable gross profit margin for corrective work of this nature would be 20%.

Note 2 – Apportionment of costs

Employment costs and operating overheads (including depreciation and impairment of property, plant and equipment) should be apportioned between cost of sales, distribution costs and administrative expenses in the ratio 7:1:2.

Note 3 – Inventories

The carrying value of closing inventories at 30 September 2006 was $40 million.

Note 4 – Property, plant and equipment

	Cost at 30/09/06 $'000	Accumulated depreciation at 01/10/05 $'000
Properties	40 000	3 800
Plant and equipment	60 000	22 700
Total	100 000	26 500

Property, plant and equipment is depreciated on a straight line basis (with a full year's charge in the year of purchase and no charge in the year of sale) at the following rates:

– 2% per annum for properties.

– 25% per annum for plant and equipment (other than that used on the construction contract – see note 6 below)

Note 5 – Revaluation of properties

On 30 September 2006 the properties were revalued to their market values as indicated below:

	Cost at 30/9/06 $'000	Accumulated depreciation at 01/10/05 $'000	Market value at 30/09/06 $'000
Property A	15 000	1 500	20 000
Property B	15 000	300	18 000
Property C	10 000	2 000	6 000
	40 000	3 800	44 000

This revaluation is not reflected in the trial balance of Delta but the directors wish to reflect it in the financial statements.

Note 6 – Construction contract

On 1 January 2006 Delta commenced a construction contract that was estimated to last for a period of 24 months. Costs incurred on the contract to date (and debited to the contract account) and estimated future costs are as follows:

	Costs to date $'000	Estimated future costs $'000
Materials	5 000	3 000
Plant and equipment	6 000	–
Overheads	4 000	6 000

The purchased plant and equipment is not expected to have any residual value at the end of the contract.

The contract price was fixed at $32 million. On 20 September 2006 an independent expert certified that 25% of the contract work had been completed satisfactorily. The customer immediately made a progress payment of $8 million, which Delta received on 27 March 2006 and credited to the contract account.

Note 7 – Financial asset

On 1 October 2005 Delta purchased a loan investment that had a nominal value of $10 million at a cost of $12·5 million. The investment entitled the holder to a fixed rate of interest of 5% on the nominal value of the loan. Delta designated the investment as fair value through profit and loss. The investment had a fair value of $13 million at 30 September 2006.

Note 8 – Current tax payable

The current tax payable figure at 1 October 2005 comprised $5 million in respect of the estimated income tax liability of Delta for the year ended 30 September 2005. This liability was finally agreed at $5·2 million in early 2006 and this amount was duly paid and debited to current tax payable. The estimated income tax liability for the year ended 30 September 2006 is $6 million. The rate of income tax that is relevant for Delta is 20%.

Note 9 – Deferred tax

A transfer of $500 000 needs to be made to the deferred tax account at 30 September 2006. This transfer does not include any potential deferred tax implications of the properties revaluation (see note 5 above).

Required:

(a) Prepare the income statement for Delta for the year ended 30 September 2006.

(b) Prepare the statement of changes in equity for Delta for the year ended 30 September 2006.

(c) Prepare the balance sheet for Delta as at 30 September 2006.

Notes to the income statement and balance sheet are not required. However your workings should justify your treatment of items referred to in the trial balance and the notes with appropriate references to international financial reporting standards.

(ACCA 2.5 (INT) 7 December 2006)

12 LMN trades in motor vehicles, which are manufactured and supplied by their manufacturer, IJK. Trading between the two entities is subject to a contractual agreement, the principal terms of which are as follows:

● LMN is entitled to hold on its premises at any one time up to 80 vehicles supplied by IJK. LMN is free to specify the ranges and models of vehicle supplied to it. IJK retains legal title to the vehicles until such time as they are sold to a third party by LMN.

● While the vehicles remain on its premises, LMN is required to insure them against loss or damage.

● The price at which vehicles are supplied is determined at the time of delivery; it is not subject to any subsequent alteration.

- When LMN sells a vehicle to a third party, it is required to inform IJK within three working days. IJK submits an invoice to LMN at the originally agreed price; the invoice is payable by LMN within 30 days.

- LMN is entitled to use any of the vehicles supplied to it for demonstration purposes and road testing. However, if more than a specified number of kilometres are driven in a vehicle, LMN is required to pay IJK a rental charge.

- LMN has the right to return any vehicle to IJK at any time without incurring a penalty, except for any rental charge incurred in respect of excess kilometres driven.

Required:

Discuss the economic substance of the contractual arrangement between the two entities in respect of the recognition of inventory and of sales. Refer, where appropriate, to IAS 18 *Revenue*.

(CIMA P8 Financial Analysis 23 May 2006)

13 EJ publishes trade magazines and sells them to retailers. EJ has just concluded negotiations with a large supermarket chain for the supply of a large quantity of several of its trade magazines on a regular basis.

EJ has agreed a substantial discount on the following terms:

- the same quantity of each trade magazine will be supplied each month

- quantities can only be changed at the end of each six-month period

- payment must be made six monthly in advance.

The supermarket paid $150 000 on 1 September 2007 for six months supply of trade magazines to 29 February 2008. At 31 October 2007, EJ had supplied two months of trade magazines. EJ estimates that the cost of supplying the supermarket each month is $20 000.

Required:

(i)   State the criteria in IAS 18 *Revenue Recognition* for income recognition.

(ii) Explain, with reasons, how EJ should treat the above in its financial statements for the year ended 31 October 2007.

(CIMA P7 Financial Accounting & Tax Principles: 22 November 2007)

PROVISIONS, CONTINGENT LIABILITIES AND CONTINGENT ASSETS

19

OBJECTIVES   After studying this chapter you should be able to:

- describe the issues IAS 37 attempts to address

- define provisions and contingencies

- account for provisions and contingencies in accordance with IAS 37

- appraise the recognition and measurement criteria of IAS 37

- describe the presentation requirements in relation to provisions and contingencies

- identify the likely changes to IAS 37.

INTRODUCTION

Financial statements of all entities are prepared at an arbitrary date – the balance sheet date – which is a convenient cut-off point. However, no matter how sophisticated the information systems, judgements still have to be made concerning conditions existing at the balance sheet date with uncertain outcomes. In essence, IAS 37 deals with situations where obligations from an entity or to an entity are uncertain in either existence of event and/or amount of that event. The accounting or not for such conditions can have a marked effect on both the balance sheet and income statement of an entity.

PROBLEMS IDENTIFIED

ACTIVITY 19.1

PPR entity, a retailer of washing machines, has a year-end of 31 December. During December a washing machine was sold to a customer who carried out the plumbing himself. On 24 December the washing machine failed to operate correctly, resulting in the customer's house suffering severe damage due to flooding. The customer, together with several relatives, had to spend the festive season in an hotel as his home was uninhabitable. The customer is planning to sue PPR for a considerable amount of damages. Would you as an accountant for PPR accrue a loss for the damages pending or not?

Activity feedback

The first question to answer is, is there a liability? A liability is 'a present obligation of the entity arising from past events, the settlement of which is expected to result in an outflow from the entity of resources embodying economic benefits' (IASB Framework; para. 49(b)). The problem here is that the outcome will presumably only be confirmed when the claim for damages is settled. What view should we take of the outcome of this claim? Will we have to pay out damages? If so, how much? Should we assume the claim will be found against the entity and estimate how much that claim will be and accrue in the income statement or not? The decision as to whether we do or not is likely to have a profound effect on profits if the claim is substantial.

The area of provisions and contingencies has led to substantial creative accounting within accounts and has given rise to the term 'big bath accounting' which is discussed in more detail in Part Four. The following activity illustrates this term.

ACTIVITY 19.2

An entity with annual expected future profits of €2.5m decides to recognise a provision (on the grounds of prudence) for reorganisation costs for future years of €2m in the current year when its expected profits are €4.5m. The reorganisation involves decentralisation of all activities relating to purchases and sales to the entity's outlying units from the centre.

In the event the charges for the reorganisation are €0.5m next year, €0.5m the following year and thereafter no further costs arise.

Show the effect of the proposed accounting treatment for the reorganisation costs on the profits for the company for the current and future years. Comment on this treatment.

Activity feedback

	Year 1	Year 2	Year 3	Year 4
Provision b/f	0	2.0	1.5	0
Expense	0	(0.5)	(0.5)	0
Income statement charge	2.0	0	(1.0)	0
Provision c/f	2.0	1.5	0	0
Profits	4.5	2.5	2.5	2.5
Provision charged to income statement	(2.0)	0	1.0	0
Profit after provision	2.5	2.5	3.5	2.5

The entity has been able to charge the provision for the reorganisation against the profits in the first year which were higher than generally expected. In future years the entity has been able to charge €0.5m to the provision instead of the income statement, thus profits in these year have not been reduced. In addition, as all the provision has not been required, the excess provision has been released back to the income statement in year 3 increasing profits to €3.5m. In effect, the entity has taken a 'big bath' in year 1 when it had substantial profits and has protected future years' profits.

Activities 19.1 and 19.2 show the potential for creativity in the provisions area and therefore the need for a Standard on the issue. If recognition of a provision is further based on the intention to incur expenditure rather than an obligation to do so then this could create even more creativity in accounting. We could have the situation arising where a provision is provided, as for the reorganisation costs just given, and then if this reorganisation is not carried out the whole provision might be released to next year's profits. The recognition of such a provision does not reflect a change in economic position of the entity, since only an external commitment can affect the financial position at the balance sheet date. Without a complete framework for accounting for and disclosure of provisions users are not presented with a true and fair view of the state of affairs.

PROVISIONS, CONTINGENT LIABILITIES AND CONTINGENT ASSETS

IAS 37, issued by the IASB in 1998, and operative for annual financial statements beginning on or after 1 July 1999, updated those parts of IAS 10, *Contingencies and Events Occurring after the Balance Sheet Date* (1974) relating to contingencies but issued guidance also on provisions which were not covered by IAS 10.

IAS 37 effectively bans:

- big bath accounting
- creation of provisions where no obligation to a liability exists
- the use of provisions to smooth profits

and requires greater disclosure in relation to provisions to aid the user's understanding and present a true and fair view.

Scope

IAS 37 is to be applied to all entities when accounting for provisions, contingent liabilities and contingent assets except for those items resulting from executory contracts except where the contract is onerous, and those covered by another IAS. Examples of items covered by another IAS are IAS 11, *Construction Contracts*, and IAS 19, *Retirement Benefits*. Executory contracts also need some explanation. These are contracts where neither party has performed any of its obligations or both parties have partially performed obligations to an equal amount. The standard does not apply to financial instruments that are within the scope of IAS 39, *Financial Instruments: Recognition and Measurement*.

ACTIVITY 19.3

Identify an executory contract within entities.

Activity feedback
Such contracts generally cover delivery of future services, e.g.:

- gas, electricity, local taxes
- purchase orders
- employee contributions in respect of continued employment.

It is also worth clarifying at this point certain 'provisions' that IAS 37 does not cover. This arises because IAS 37 uses the word provisions to mean a liability of uncertain timing or amount but in the general language of accounting it is common for the word provision to be applied to:

- provision for depreciation
- provision for doubtful debts
- provision for impairment.

In these cases the 'provision' is adjusting the carrying amount of the asset; it is not a liability of uncertain timing or amount.

Objectives

The objectives of IAS 37 are fairly clear and laudable:

To ensure that appropriate recognition criteria and measurement bases are applied to provisions, contingent liabilities and contingent assets and that sufficient information is disclosed in the notes to the financial statements to enable users to understand their nature, timing and amount.

Definitions

We have already identified two of these for you:

A provision is a liability of uncertain timing or amount.

A liability is a present obligation of the entity arising from past events, the settlement of which is expected to result in the outflow from the entity of resources embodying economic benefits.

(IAS 37, para. 10)

One of the key words in the definition of a liability is 'obligation'. So what is an obligation? An obligation can be either legal or constructive:

A legal obligation is an obligation that derives from:

(a) a contract (through its explicit or implicit terms);

(b) legislation; or

(c) other operation of law.

A contract can become onerous and this occurs when 'the unavoidable costs of meeting the obligations under the contract exceed the economic benefits expected to be received under it'.

(IAS 37, para. 10)

A constructive obligation is an obligation that derives from an entity's actions where:

(a) by an established pattern of past practice, published policies or a sufficiently specific current statement, the entity has indicated to other parties that it will accept certain responsibilities; and

(b) as a result the entity has created a valid expectation on the part of those other parties that it will discharge those responsibilities.

(IAS 37, para. 10)

ACTIVITY 19.4

Identify which of the following is a constructive obligation of the entity:

1   *A*, a leisure entity causes severe damage to the habitat of wildlife in a country where there is no legal protection for the wildlife. The company has a high profile in the support of wildlife as it makes large contributions to the World Wildlife Fund and campaigns vigorously on its behalf. To rectify the damage to the habitat a charge of €1m is likely.

2   An entity in the oil industry causes severe pollution when one of its tankers grounds off a Pacific island. The entity has avoided costs of cleaning up such contamination in the past and pays little regard to environmental issues.

Activity feedback

1   This is a constructive obligation as there is a valid expectation that the entity will clean up the habitat.

2   This is not a constructive obligation as no valid expectation has been created by the entity that it will repair the damage to the ocean.

ACTIVITY 19.5

Identify, in your own words, the key differences between a provision and a contingent liability.

Activity feedback

Provisions require:

- a present obligation from past event
- a probable outflow of economic benefits
- an evaluation of timing and amount.

Contingent liabilities occur when one or more of the conditions for a provision are not met, i.e. either:

- a possible obligation from past event exists
- and/or an outflow of economic benefits is not probable
- and/or a reliable estimate of outflow cannot be made.

A contingent liability is:

- a possible obligation that arises from past events and whose existence will be confirmed only by the occurrence or non-occurrence of one or more uncertain future events not wholly within the control of the entity
- or a present obligation that arises from past events but is not recognised because:
    - it is not probable that an outflow of resources embodying economic benefits will be required to settle the obligation
    - or the amount of the obligation cannot be measured with sufficient reliability.

In essence, a contingent liability is a provision where one or more of the three requirements is not met. IAS 37 provides in an appendix a useful decision tree to determine whether a provision or contingent liability exists in a given set of circumstances and we reproduce this for you (Figure 19.1).

This is all rather confusing as a provision is, in fact, a liability which is contingent as its timing or amount is uncertain; but it is called a provision not a contingent liability. A contingent liability as defined by IAS 37 is by its name a liability but is not recognised as such as it is not charged in the accounts; it is only disclosed.

IAS 37 also defines a contingent asset for us as:

A possible asset that arises from past events and whose existence will be confirmed only by the occurrence or non-occurrence of one or more uncertain future events not wholly within the control of the entity.

(IAS 37, para. 10)

FIGURE 19.1   Decision tree to determine existence of provision or contingent liability

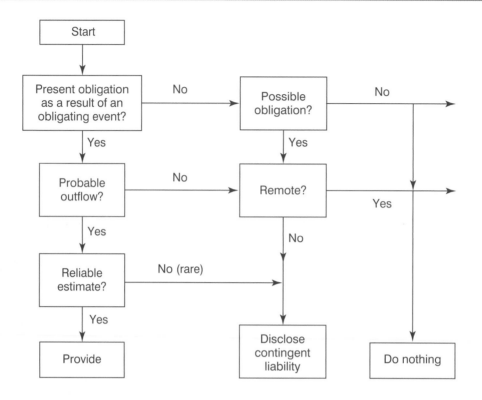

ACCOUNTING FOR PROVISIONS, CONTINGENT LIABILITIES AND CONTINGENT ASSETS

If the conditions for a provision are met and a reliable estimate can be made of the amount then this amount will be recognised in the income statement for the year and shown as a provision on the balance sheet. A contingent liability is not recognised in the financial statements but it is disclosed as follows:

- a brief description of the nature
- an estimate of its financial effect
- an indication of the uncertainties relating to the amount or timing of outflow
- the possibility of any reimbursement.

A contingent asset is not recognised in the accounts but it is disclosed if the inflow of economic benefits is probable.

You should have noted by now that how we treat future inflow or outflow of economic benefits in the accounts is dependent on how we/management/experts define the words: probable, possible, remote. IAS 37 gives us no definitions of these three words. A standard English dictionary provides us with the following definitions:

probable – likely to be or to happen but not necessarily so

possible – feasible but less than probable

remote – distant, slight, faint.

ACTIVITY 19.6

Identify how the following items should be treated in the accounts of the entity at year-end 31 December 20X1. All information is at year-end 31 December 20X1 unless stated otherwise.

1 An airline entity is required by law to overhaul its aircraft once every three years. The aircraft were purchased a year ago.

2 An entity has guaranteed a loan taken out by one of its subsidiary entities. In March 20X1 the subsidiary placed itself in liquidation and there would appear to be insufficient funds to repay the loan.

3 An entity catered for a wedding reception in September 20X1. Subsequent to the wedding several people have died of food poisoning. The entity is disputing liability for the case brought against it by the relatives of the dead and its lawyers advise that it is probable that they will not be found liable.

4 An entity leases a factory under an operating lease. During the year it moves production of its products to a new factory but the old factory lease cannot be cancelled and it cannot be relet.

5 The government of the country in which an entity operates makes substantial changes to the health and safety legislation under which it must operate. The entity will have to retrain a large proportion of its staff to ensure compliance with the new legislation. No retraining has yet taken place.

6 An entity at the year end had discounted €600 000 bills of exchange without recourse. At 15 March 20X2 €150 000 were still outstanding and are due to mature in one month's time.

7 No bill has been received for electricity supplied in the last quarter of the year.

Activity feedback

1 At the current balance sheet date no obligation to overhaul the aircraft exists independent of the entity's future action. The entity could sell the aircraft to avoid the overhaul cost. This is not a provision, neither is it a contingent liability.

2 The entity has an obligation to fulfil the guarantee given and it appears that an outflow of funds is probable. A provision should be recognised in the accounts.

3 There is no obligation and therefore no provision should be made. It is a contingent liability and a note should be made to the accounts unless the lawyers advise that the probability of any transfer of funds is extremely remote.

4 This is in fact an example of an onerous contract. There is a present legal obligation and a provision is required of the unavoidable lease payments in total. Prior to the contract becoming onerous it would have been treated in accordance with IAS 17, *Leases*.

5 There is no obligating event as no staff training has yet taken place and therefore no provision is recognised, neither is there a contingent liability. The entity might need to consider whether there is a possibility it is placing itself in a situation where it will be fined for non-compliance with the new regulations and if this is the case, that is the legislation is already in force, then a provision may need to be made for the fines, if any, that could be imposed.

6 The bills of exchange are without recourse and therefore no liability falls on the entity.

7 This is an accrual as there is very little uncertainty in respect of the timing or the amount due.

There is an example in the Standard of an application to an offshore oilfield. In this example, an entity operating an oilrig has a legal obligation to remove the rig and clean up the site at the end of the oil extraction. The Standard concludes that this cost should be charged as a provision at the outset of the operation. This appears to us to be in direct contrast to the example of the aircraft maintenance at point 1 in Activity 19.6. The oilrig could be sold as easily as the aircraft.

It is a requirement of IAS 37 that provisions be reviewed at each balance sheet date and adjusted where required and that the expenditure set against a provision is only that in relation to the intent of the provision. Therefore, a provision which we discover is no longer required cannot be used for the offset of other expenditure.

It is often the case that an entity can be reimbursed by another party for some of the expenditure in relation to a provision, e.g. insurance contracts, suppliers' warranties. In these cases the reimbursement must be treated as a separate asset and indeed only accounted for in the income statement, when the reimbursement is virtually certain.

Measurement of provisions

So far we have been concerned with the recognition of a provision or a contingent liability but we must also determine an amount. Remember a provision can only be recognised in the financial statements if a reliable estimate can be made of the amount. If no reliable estimate can be made of the amount then a contingent liability is disclosed (this will rarely occur).

IAS 37 requires that when determining a reliable estimate this should be 'the best estimate of the expenditure required to settle the present obligation at the balance sheet date' (para. 36). The best estimate is determined by the judgement of management supplemented by experience of similar transactions and/or reports from independent experts. The emphasis on present obligation in the measurement rule is deliberate and this means that the effect of future events in this measurement must be carefully evaluated. It is only where such future events are expected with some certainty and objectivity to occur that they will be taken account of. (See Activity 19.7.)

In practice the decision may not be as clear cut as we have just indicated. One future event that is not taken account of in measuring a provision is the gain on the expected disposal of a related asset. The Standard states that these gains must be dealt with in accordance with the standards dealing with the assets concerned. This is presumably because until there is a binding contract to sell the asset the management can change the decision in respect of the sale. We will deal with this issue again when we look at restructuring and provisions later in this chapter.

The best estimate of a provision can require the use of statistical methods of estimation. This can occur when a provision consists of a large population of items where possible outcomes have various probabilities attached. The method of estimation used in this case is known as 'expected value'.

If the provision relates to a single item or event or a small number of events then the expected value technique cannot be used. In this case the most 'likely outcome' is used.

ACTIVITY 19.7

An entity has a present obligation due to a past event to pay €2m to clean up a waste site. It is currently expected that technological developments that are near completion will decrease this cost to €1.5m. It has also been brought to management's attention that some research is under way, but in its infancy, that might reduce these costs further. At what value would the provision for the clean-up costs be shown in the accounts?

Activity feedback

The technological developments appear to have certainty and objectivity to them but the other research is much less objective and therefore the provision should be shown at €1.5m.

ILLUSTRATION

An entity sells goods under warranty. Past experience indicates that 80% of goods sold will have no defects, 15% will have minor defects and 5% major defects. If minor defects occurred in all goods sold the cost of rectification would be €5m and for major defects €15m. What is the expected value of the provision to be recorded in the financial statements of the entity at the balance sheet date?

The expected value is:

$$80\% \times 0 + 15\% \times 5 + 5\% \times 15 = 1.5m$$

ACTIVITY 19.8

An entity is facing a substantial legal claim for €5m. The lawyers estimate that there is a 40% chance of successfully defending the claim. At what value should this provision be shown in the accounts?

Activity feedback

Care needs to be exercised here as the answer is not 40% × €5m. We have to use the most likely outcome technique here. The most likely outcome, 60% chance, is of an unsuccessful defence against the claim and therefore the best estimate of the provision required is €5m.

ACTIVITY 19.9

An entity is under warranty to replace a major component in a computer hardware system. The major component costs €0.5m to replace and five of these components are used in the system. Experience shows that there is a 45% chance of only one component failing a 30% chance of two failing and 25% of three failures. It has never been known for more than three to fail. What is the value of the provision that should be shown in the accounts of the entity?

Activity feedback

At first glance the answer to the best estimate would appear to be the costs of one failure, €0.5m, as this is the most likely outcome at 45% occurrence. However, there is a 55% probability that more than one failure would occur and therefore the best estimate is €1m, that is of two failures. If the probabilities had been 25% one failure, 35% two and 40% three then the best estimate would again be €1m, two failures, as there is only a 40% chance of three failure and a 60% chance of fewer than three.

Provisions are measured before the effect of any tax consequences. The tax effect will be shown in accordance with IAS 12, *Income Taxes* (see Chapter 20).

Measurement at present value

'Where the effect of the time value of money is material, the amount of a provision should be the present value of the expenditure expected to be required to

ACTIVITY 19.10

The information in an earlier illustration enabled us to calculate the expected value for the provision for warranties. This provision was not discounted, even though it is expected that the time value of money will have a material effect on the provision. What type of discount rate should be applied, risk free or risk adjusted?

Activity feedback

Risk free, as the specific risk has already been accounted for in the information gathered about the number of warranties taken up.

ACTIVITY 19.11

An entity identifies a provision for €250 000 at the year-end 31 December 20X1. The outflow of this amount is expected at year-end 20X3. Specific risk associated with this provision has already been taken account of when calculating the best estimate for the provision. A suitable risk-free discount rate to use is identified as 5%.

Show the provision charged in the accounts for the year-ends 20X1, 20X2 and 20X3 assuming no change takes place in the best estimate and any other related entries required.

Activity feedback

As at 20X1 the provision of €250 000 is due for payment in two years' time and therefore will need to be discounted at 5% for a period of two years:

$$250\,000 \times 0.91 = 227\,500$$

As at 20X2 the provision is now due for payment in one year's time and therefore will be charged at:

$$250\,000 \times 0.95 = 237\,500$$

As at 20X3 the provision should have been paid at €250 000 and therefore will not be required at the year-end.

settle the obligation' (IAS 37, para. 45). This requirement of the Standard means that we must discount the expenditures required and the IAS specifies the discount rate as a pre-tax rate that reflects current market assessments of the time value of money and the risks specific to the liability. If future cash flows are adjusted to take account of risk then the discount rate used must be risk free and vice versa. This is to ensure that the risk involved in future cash flows is not allowed for twice. The best estimate measurement of the provision is becoming somewhat subjective! (See Activities 19.10 and 19.11.)

The problem inherent in the discounting of provisions is that the carrying amount of the provision increases as the discount unwinds. Where do we account for this unwinding? The IASB view this unwinding as a charge to interest. There is no doubt that this unwinding is a financial item but whether it should be regarded as an interest charge is debatable.

In Activity 19.11 in year ended 20X2 €10 000 would be charged to interest in the income statement and at year end 20X3 €12 500.

SPECIFIC APPLICATION OF RECOGNITION AND MEASUREMENT RULES

IAS 37 identifies three specific applications of recognition and measurement of provisions:

1 *Future operating losses*. These do not meet the definition of a liability as there is no present obligation and thus no liability. The loss will be recognised as it occurs. However, the possibility of future losses should lead management to test assets for impairment.

2 *Onerous contracts*. We discussed these at Activity 19.6. IAS 37 requires us to recognise the present obligation under an onerous contract as a provision.

3 *Restructuring*.

Other applications

In Activity 19.13 there are a further two circumstances outlined for the application of the recognition and measurement rules of IAS 37.

Disclosure

The disclosure requirements are fairly extensive but are those you would expect in terms of providing relevant information to users. The following disclosure in respect

---

ACTIVITY 19.12

The management board of Alex takes a decision on 24 March to close down one of its divisions. The board also agrees the detailed plan for closure put forward on 24 March. No further action is taken on the closure and the year-end for Alex is 31 March. What should Alex provide in the accounts in respect of the closure?

Activity feedback

First question to ask is: is there a present obligation (legal or constructive) as a result of a past event (see Figure 19.1).

The answer is no. The board of Alex can change their mind in regard to the closure. A constructive obligation will only exist when the closure is communicated in detail to employees and customers. A problem does exist here, however, as the point of recognition of the constructive obligation is dependent on a subjective judgement – at what point will the company make a sufficiently specific statement as to the closure? No provision will be made in the accounts as at 31 March.

IAS 37 tells us that a constructive obligation to restructure arises only when an entity:

● has a detailed formal plan for the restructuring identifying at least:

  – the business or part of a business concerned
  – the principal locations affected

  – the location, function and approximate number of employees who will be compensated for termination of their services
  – the expenditures that will be undertaken
  – when the plan will be implemented

● and restructures by starting to implement that plan or announcing its main features to those affected by it (para. 72).

This still leaves us with a subjective judgement to make.

In addition, we have to be careful about the expenditure included in a restructuring provision as we cannot include those costs associated with ongoing activities of the entity. Thus, we cannot include retraining or relocation costs of continuing staff, marketing or investment in new systems and distribution networks. We can only include the direct expenditures. Also remember that gains from expected disposal of assets should not be taken account of when measuring the provision for restructuring.

ACTIVITY 19.13

1 An entity has for many years made a provision for repair and maintenance of its assets. Should the entity continue to do so now IAS 37 is effective?

2 An entity that operates a chain of retail outlets decides not to insure itself in respect of the risk of minor accidents to its customers but to self-insure. Based on past experience it expects to pay €100 000 a year in respect of these accidents. Should provision be made for the amount expected to arise in a normal year?

Activity feedback

1 The entity has no constructive or legal obligation for repairs and maintenance as a result of a past event. No provision. Charge the amount of repairs and maintenance to the income statement as actually expensed.

2 There is no present obligation as a result of a past event as no event has occurred. No provision. However, as the minor accidents occur the expenditure associated with them will be charged to the income statement.

of provisions, contingent liabilities and contingent assets comes from Bayer's financial report 2000:

> Other provisions
> Other provisions are valued in accordance with IAS 37 using the best estimate of the extent of the obligation. Interest-bearing provisions are discounted to fair value.

There follows an example of an accounting policy for provisions and contingencies under the current requirements of IAS 37 taken from Vitec group accounts year ended 31 December 2005.

> Provisions
> Provisions are recognised in the balance sheet when the group has a present legal or constructive obligation as a result of a past event and it is probable that an outflow of economic benefits will be required to settle the obligation.
> Provisions for warranties, based on historical warranty data, are recognised when the underlying products or services are sold. Provisions for restructuring are recognised when the group has approved a detailed and formal restructuring plan and restructuring has either commenced or been announced. Provisions for onerous contracts are recognised when the expected benefits from a contract are lower than the unavoidable costs of meeting the contract's obligations.

GAAP comparison

UK GAAP (FRS 12) is very similar to IAS in this area. Indeed the examples and decision trees used in both Standards are identical.

US GAAP is again similar but with some minor differences as follows:

- *Measurement:*
  - discount rate is pre-tax reflecting current market assessment of time value of money (thus no account of risk is taken)
  - where a range of estimates of the outflow are available and all are equally likely then the lowest is taken (not mid-point as per IAS).

- *Restructuring:*
  - management approval and commitment is sufficient to recognise the restructuring. Thus, under US GAAP restructuring provisions are likely to occur at an earlier point than under IAS.
- *Contingent asset:*
  - under US GAAP insurance recoveries will be recognised when probable (IAS requires virtual certainty). Thus US GAAP will recognise the contingent asset at an earlier stage than IAS.

FOURTH DIRECTIVE AND IAS 37

There was some discrepancy between the Fourth Directive and IAS 37. The Directive required member states to ensure that accounts are drawn up in such a way as to take account of all foreseeable and potential losses arising in the financial year (Article 31(1)(c)(bb)). IAS 37 quite obviously does not do this. Article 31(1)(d) required that charges relating to the financial year irrespective of date of payment must be taken into account and Article 20 required the creation of a provision to cover charges that are likely to be incurred (or certain) but where amount or timing is uncertain.

Clearly, the Fourth Directive was written at a time when prudence was a key element, even a bias, of financial reporting and since then the underlying concepts of accounting have changed. This inconsistency between the Directive and IAS 37 has now been eliminated by changes in the Directive.

ACTIVITY 19.14

Felix, a commercial port operator, is uncertain how do deal with the following issues in its year-end accounts:

1 Significant one-off refurbishments of operational port assets that are required in the future.

2 A decision has been taken to alter employee conditions by reducing overtime payments from twice the normal rate to 1.5 times at one port. A one-off payment will be made to all employees who accept this change of condition. Employees and unions are aware of the proposed change and have also been informed that if agreement is not given to the proposal other ways will be found to avoid the overtime.

3 Felix has a contract to purchase items at €1 per unit. Current market price of these items is 50c. The items are used in a part of the business that is profitable. The management believes the contract is onerous.

4 Felix purchased four small ports for €100m during the year; however, the Monopolies and Mergers Commission has directed Felix to sell them. No sale has been made by the year-end but the best estimate of their sale value is €50m.

Activity feedback

1 There is no present obligation, either legal or obligatory, so no provision or contingent liability is shown.

2 The one-off payment is associated with future work not current and therefore no provision should be made.

3 The contract is not onerous as no loss is being made by Felix on these items as they form part of a profitable item.

4 A provision of €50m should be made in the accounts as this is a present obligation due to a past event and a reasonable estimate of the loss can be made.

FUTURE DEVELOPMENTS

In June 2005 the IASB published an exposure draft (ED) to amend IAS 37 as a result of the convergence work with the FASB and also as a result of the second phase of the business combinations project. As at autumn 2008 no amended standard has been issued.

The ED proposed to eliminate some familiar terms:

- provisions
- contingent liabilities
- contingent assets.

But more than this the ED proposed some very radical changes that would see many more liabilities appearing on the balance sheet and as a result charged against profits.

The ED 37 proposed definitions are as follows:

- A non-financial liability is a liability other than a financial liability as defined in IAS 32, *Financial Instruments* (see Chapter 17). This is the replacement for the term 'provision' but is much wider in its scope.
- A constructive obligation is a present obligation that arises from an entity's past actions when:
  - **(a)** by an established pattern of past practice, published policies or a sufficiently specific current statement, the entity has indicated to other parties that it will accept particular responsibilities, and
  - **(b)** as a result, the entity has created a valid expectation in those parties that they can reasonably rely on it to discharge those responsibilities.
- A legal obligation is a present obligation that arises from the following:
  - **(a)** a contract (through its explicit or implicit terms)
  - **(b)** legislation, or
  - **(c)** other operation of law.
- An onerous contract is one where the unavoidable costs of meeting its obligations exceed its expected benefits.

The ED requires that an entity should recognise a non-financial liability when:

(a) the definition of a liability has been satisfied, and

(b) the non-financial liability can be measured reliably.

To remind you, the definition of a liability is a present obligation of the entity arising from past events, the settlement of which is expected to result in an outflow from the entity of resources embodying economic benefits.

The idea of a contingent asset or liability as contained in IAS 37 disappears under the ED and the term 'contingency' will in future refer to uncertainty about the amount that will be required to settle a liability, rather than uncertainty about whether a liability exists. The ED further specifies that a liability for which the settlement amount is contingent on one or more uncertain future events is recognised independently of the probability that the uncertain future event will occur (or fail to occur).

The ED states that in many cases the amount of a non-financial liability must be estimated. This is certainly true, but then the ED states 'that except in extremely rare cases, an entity will be able to determine a reliable measure of a liability'. This will require subjective judgements and will raise questions about the reliability of the judgements made. It does however remove the necessity to classify obligations as present, probable or remote which was always difficult under IAS 37.

The ED has this to say on reliable measurement:

> In the extremely rare case in which an entity cannot measure a non-financial liability reliably, the liability does not qualify for recognition in accordance with this standard. In such cases, the entity discloses information about the non-financial liability in accordance with para. 69. The non-financial liability is recognised initially in the period in which it can be measured reliably. (para. 28)

> An entity shall measure a non-financial liability at the amount that it would rationally pay to settle the present obligation or to transfer it to a third party on the balance sheet date. (para. 29)

Let's look at some examples to show the changes proposed by the ED to IAS 37. The following are all adapted from the examples given by the IASB in the ED.

Example 19.1

Take the scenario as in Activity 19.6, item 3. Under IAS 37 we concluded that there was no obligation and therefore no provision required. A contingent liability did exist and a note of its effect was required to the financial statements unless it was judged that transfer of funds was remote.

Under the new ED it would be concluded that the entity *did* have a present obligation as the start of the legal proceedings requires the entity to stand ready to perform as the court directs. Thus a non-financial liability is recognised and we would need to place an estimated amount on it. This would be the amount that the entity would rationally pay to settle or transfer the obligation on the balance sheet date and would require consideration of:

- the possible outcomes of the lawsuit
- the cash flows associated with those outcomes
- the timing of the cash flows
- the probabilities of those outcomes
- the risks and uncertainties associated with the obligation – risk adjustment.

Let's suppose the entity is being sued for £20m in this case and that the entity estimates it has a 10% chance of losing the case. The entity will recognise £2m as a non-financial liability (and debit this to the income statement). This in no way reflects the likely outcome which is either win and pay nothing or lose and pay £20m.

Example 19.2

A patient dies in a hospital as a result of a mistake made during an operation. The hospital is aware that a mistake occurred. In these circumstances the hospital's past experience and lawyer's advice indicate that it is highly likely that the patient's relatives will start legal proceedings and, if the matter comes to court, that the hospital will be found guilty of negligence.

Under IAS 37 no obligation would be recognised and therefore no provision made. Under the ED a present obligation would be recognised as negligence occurred and a non-financial liability would be recognised. Measurement of the liability would be the problem.

Example 19.3

On 31 December 20X0 entity *A* gives a guarantee of specified borrowings of entity *B*, whose financial condition at that time is sound. During 20X1 the financial condition of *B* deteriorates and at 30 June 20X1 *B* files for protection from its creditors. Under IAS 37 a provision would only be recognised as at 30 June 20X1 but under the ED a liability would be recognised as soon as the guarantee was provided as *A* is required to stand ready to repay the borrowing of *B* from that date.

Example 19.4

Take the scenario as in Activity 19.6, item 5.

Under IAS 37 we concluded that there was no provision required for the retraining as no obligating event had taken place. The conclusion under the ED will be exactly the same; no obligation because no past event had taken place and therefore no liability exists.

The proposals in this 2005 exposure draft were heavily criticised, and the project has been delayed. No early progress seems likely.

TABLE 19.1	IAS 37: Summary of provisions and contingent liabilities	
Obligation	**Accounting result**	**Disclosure**
Present obligation that probably requires outflow	Provision recognised	Amounts, nature, uncertainties, assumptions, reimbursements
Possible obligation or present obligation that may require outflow	No provision recognised Contingent liability disclosed	Nature, estimate of financial effect, uncertainties, reimbursement
Possible obligation or present obligation where outflow remote	No provision recognised No contingent liability disclosed	Nil

TABLE 19.2	IAS 37: Summary of contingent assets	
Economic benefits	**Accounting result**	**Disclosure**
Inflow virtually certain	Asset rules apply	
Inflow probable	No asset recognised Contingent asset disclosed	Nature, financial effect
Inflow not probable	No asset recognised No contingent asset disclosed	Nil

SUMMARY

You should now realise that the area of provisions, contingent liabilities and contingent assets is controversial and requires a great deal of subjective judgement. Many people would argue that IAS 37 lacks prudence in that it does not require the recognition of and accounting for all future expenses. We would not argue this, as we view prudence as a state of being free from bias, not being overly pessimistic. The issues involved in this chapter have been quite difficult and Tables 19.1 and 19.2 summarise the position of IAS 37.

EXERCISES

Suggested answers to exercises marked ✓ are to be found on the Student side of the companion website.

Suggested answers to the remaining exercises are to be found on the Instructor side of the companion website.

1 Outline the recommended treatment of provisions, contingent liabilities and contingent assets in accordance with IAS 37, clearly defining and illustrating the meaning of each term.

2 Identify any other methods of accounting for provisions, contingent liabilities and contingent assets and discuss why IAS 37 rejects these methods in favour of its recommended treatment.

3 Discuss the statement that financial reports prepared under IAS 37 provide a 'true and fair view' to users.

4 Explain the terms:
  – big bath accounting
  – profit smoothing.

  Give an illustration of each.

5 IAS 37 ensures 'consistency between entities in the recognition and measurement of provisions and contingencies and that sufficient information is disclosed about them to users so that they can understand their effect on current and future results'. Discuss.

✓ **6** The distinction between a provision and a contingent liability is irrelevant. Discuss.

7 Describe the accounting arrangements in accordance with IAS 37 for provisions and contingent liabilities. Comment on whether these arrangements provide useful information to users.

8 Appraise the requirement in IAS 37 to measure a provision at the 'best estimate'.

✓ **9** Debate the contention that IAS 37 lacks prudence.

10 i) In relation to a failed acquisition, a firm of accountants has invoiced Gear for the sum of $300 000. Gear has paid $20 000 in full settlement of the debt and states that this was a reasonable sum for the advice given and is not prepared to pay any further sum. The accountants are pressing for payment of the full amount but on the advice of its solicitors, Gear is not going to settle the balance outstanding. Additionally Gear is involved in a court case concerning the plagiarism of software. Another games company has accused Gear of copying their games software and currently legal opinion seems to indicate that Gear will lose the case. Management estimates that the most likely outcome will be a payment of costs and royalties to the third party of $1 million in two years' time (approximately). The best case scenario is deemed to be a payment of $500 000 in one year's time and the worst case scenario that of a payment of $2 million in three years' time. These scenarios are based on the amount of the royalty payment and the potential duration and costs of the court case. Management has estimated that the relative likelihood of the above payments are best case – 30% chance, most likely outcome – 60% chance, and worst case – 10% chance of occurrence. The directors are unsure as to whether any provision for the above amounts should be made in the financial statements.

ii) In the event of the worst case scenario occurring, the directors of Gear are worried about the viability of their business as the likelihood would be that current liabilities would exceed current assets and it is unlikely that in the interim period there will be sufficient funds generated from operational cash flows.

　　The discount rate for any present value calculations is 5%.

Required:
Write a report to the directors of Gear Software explaining the implications of the above information contained in paragraphs (i) and (ii) for the financial statements.

(ACCA June 2003)

11 IAS 37, *Provisions, Contingent Liabilities and Contingent Assets* was issued in 1998. The Standard sets out the principles of accounting for these items and clarifies when provisions should and should not be made. Prior to its issue, the inappropriate use of provisions had been an area where companies had been accused of manipulating the financial statements and of creative accounting.

Required:

(a) Describe the nature of provisions and the accounting requirements for them contained in IAS 37.

(b) Explain why there is a need for an accounting standard in this area. Illustrate your answer with three practical examples of how the Standard addresses controversial issues.

(c) Bodyline sells sports goods and clothing through a chain of retail outlets. It offers customers a full refund facility for any goods returned within 28 days of their purchase provided they are unused and in their original packaging. In addition, all goods carry a warranty against manufacturing defects for 12 months from their date of purchase. For most goods the manufacturer underwrites this warranty such that Bodyline is credited with the cost of the goods that are returned as faulty. Goods purchased from one manufacturer, Header, are sold to Bodyline at a negotiated discount which is designed to compensate Bodyline for manufacturing defects. No refunds are given by Header, thus Bodyline has to bear the cost of any manufacturing faults of these goods.

Bodyline makes a uniform mark-up on cost of 25% on all goods it sells, except for those supplied from Header on which it makes a mark-up on cost of 40%. Sales of goods manufactured by Header consistently account for 20% of all Bodyline's sales.

Sales in the last 28 days of the trading year to 30 September 2003 were $1 750 000. Past trends reliably indicate that 10% of all goods are returned under the 28-day return facility. These are not faulty goods. Of these 70% are later resold at the normal selling price and the remaining 30% are sold as 'sale' items at half the normal retail price.

In addition to the above expected returns, an estimated $160 000 (at selling price) of the goods sold during the year will have manufacturing defects and have yet to be returned by customers. Goods returned as faulty have no resale value.

Required:
Describe the nature of the above warranty/return facilities and calculate the provision Bodyline is required to make at 30 September 2003:

i) for goods subject to the 28-day returns policy; and

ii) for goods that are likely to be faulty.

(d) Rockbuster has recently purchased an item of earth moving plant at a total cost of $24 million. The plant has an estimated life of 10 years with no residual value, however its engine will need replacing after every 5000 hours of use at an estimated cost of $7.5 million. The directors of Rockbuster intend to depreciate the plant at $2.4 million ($24 million/10 years) per annum and make a provision of $1500 ($7.5 million/5000 hours) per hour of use for the replacement of the engine.

Required:

Explain how the plant should be treated in accordance with International Accounting Standards and comment on the directors' proposed treatment.

(ACCA Dec 2003)

12 Nette, a public limited company, manufactures mining equipment and extracts natural gas. The directors are uncertain about the role of the IASB's 'Framework for the Preparation and Presentation of Financial Statements' (the Framework) in corporate reporting. Their view is that accounting is based on the transactions carried out by the company and these transactions are allocated to the company's accounting period by using the matching and prudence concepts. The argument put forward by the directors is that the Framework does not take into account the business and legal constraints within which companies operate. Further they have given a situation which has arisen in the current financial statements where they feel that the current accounting practice is inconsistent with the Framework.

Situation
Nette has recently constructed a natural gas extraction facility and commenced production one year ago (1 June 2003). There is an operating licence given to the company by the government which requires the removal of the facility at the end of its life which is estimated at

20 years. Depreciation is charged on the straight line basis. The cost of the construction of the facility was $200 million and the net present value at 1 June 2003 of the future costs to be incurred in order to return the extraction site to its original condition is estimated at $50 million (using a discount rate of 5% per annum). 80% of these costs relate to the removal of the facility and 20% relate to the rectification of the damage caused through the extraction of the natural gas. The auditors have told the company that a provision for decommissioning has to be set up.

Required:

(a) Explain the importance of the 'Framework' to the reporting of corporate performance and whether it takes into account the business and legal constraints placed upon companies.

(b) i) Explain with reasons and suitable extracts/computations the accounting treatment of the above situation in the financial statements for the year ended 31 May 2004.

ii) Discuss whether the treatment of the items appears consistent with the 'Framework'.

(ACCA June 2004)

13 NDL drilled a new oil well, which started production on 1 March 2003. The licence granting permission to drill the new oil well included a clause that requires NDL to 'return the land to the state it was in before drilling commenced'.

NDL estimates that the oil well will have a 20-year production life. At the end of that time, the well will be de-commissioned and work carried out to reinstate the land. The cost of this de-commissioning work is estimated to be $20 million.

Required:

As the trainee management accountant, draft a memo to the production manager explaining how NDL must treat the de-commissioning costs in its financial statements for the year to 31 March 2003. Your memo should refer to appropriate International Accounting Standards.

(CIMA pilot paper Fin. Acc. Tax Principles)

14 *U* manufactures refrigerators and freezers and sells them with a one-year warranty. It applies the requirements of IAS 37 *Provisions, Contingent Liabilities and Contingent Assets* to its financial accounts. *U* has made a provision for future warranty claims each year.

U did not keep accurate records of previous warranty claims, so when IAS 37 became effective, it estimated future warranty claims based on an estimated 10% of sales turnover. It also started keeping accurate records of warranty claims.

U has decided to change its method of calculating the provision for warranty claims to the weighted average of the last three years' actual claims paid.

A warranty claim provision of $900 000, calculated on the old basis, has already been entered in the accounts for the year ended 30 September 2004.

Year to 30 September	2002	2003	2004
	$000	*$000*	*$000*
Revenue	7 500	8 000	9 000
Actual warranty claims paid	375	400	325

Prepare the accounting entries required in *U*'s year-end accounts to reflect the above change.

(CIMA paper 6b November 2004)

INCOME TAXES

OBJECTIVES

OBJECTIVES After studying this chapter you should be able to:

- explain the concept of deferred taxes
- describe the arguments for and against providing for deferred tax
- identify several possible methods of accounting for deferred tax
- identify the requirements of IAS 12, *Income Taxes*
- critically appraise the IAS approach
- identify the possible amendments to IAS 12.

INTRODUCTION

The amount of tax charged against the profit in any period is an important determinant of the amount attributable to the owners of a company. This amount is determined by the earnings per share. It also obviously has an effect on all other ratios which are calculated after tax. However, the tax charge, calculated according to a country's tax legislation, is not necessarily the same as applying the tax rate to the accounting profits. This difference arises because of the different recognition and measurement rules in tax legislation compared to accounting GAAP. The implications arising from these differences have led to a long, complicated and sometimes badly argued debate over the last three decades or more, both in individual countries and internationally.

THE EXPENSE QUESTION

The first question to answer is 'Is tax a business expense?' At first glance your answer might be an unequivocal yes, but it needs further consideration. An expense is an outflow or other using up of assets or incurrences of liabilities during a period from delivering or producing goods, services, etc. Expenses are also discretionary in a sense, i.e. the business could avoid them if it wished. Tax is not a charge for the exchange of goods or services and cannot be avoided by the business. Many see tax not as an expense but as a distribution of income like distributions to shareholders. This view regards the tax authorities as a stakeholder in the business. If this distribution view of tax was adopted the rest of this chapter would be irrelevant. Tax is internationally treated as an expense but the argument for doing so is not very well founded.

THE DEFERRED TAX PROBLEM

In many countries the amount of tax payable by a business for a particular period often bears little relationship to the profit as reported by the accountants in the income statement. It is often the case that the tax authorities take the accountant's reported profit figure as their starting point but they make all sorts of adjustments to it in order to determine the amount of taxable income. One of these adjustments can be in respect of depreciation. As we have already seen in Chapter 12, the 'appropriate' charge for depreciation can be a highly uncertain, subjective amount which to many taxation authorities is unacceptable. Additionally, several national governments have felt that by specifying tax allowances (not equivalent to an accountant's depreciation figure) for capital assets against profits, which they can vary from year to year, they can provide incentives to businesses to invest more or to invest in some particular way. The first thing that such tax authorities do to the accountant's profit figure, as calculated and published in the income statement, is to remove all the depreciation entries put in by the accountant. In other words, the depreciation figure, which will have been deducted in arriving at the accountant's profit figure, is simply added back again (a profit on disposal that will have been added by the accountant will of course need to be removed by deduction). From the resulting figure the tax authority now deducts whatever the tax allowance for the capital asset is and tax is levied on this taxable profit.

Consider Activity 20.1, which illustrates the difference between accounting profits and tax authority profits or taxable income.

If the firm uses the taxes payable as tax expense on its income, the profit after tax figures would indicate that in year 2 the performance of the company decreased and continued to do so for the next three years. But have the firm and management been less successful? Arguably not! Over the five-year period the company has made the same accounting profit with the same resources each year (excluding the problems of historical cost here). Thus, the profit after accounting tax figures provides a better guide to performance of the company.

If we look carefully at the activity feedback we note that the total tax charge is €165 over the five-year period using either method. Thus, the use of tax allowances does not alter the total tax due, only the timing of those tax payments. The difference between the depreciation charge in any year and the tax allowance for that

ACTIVITY 20.1

An asset attracting 25% tax allowances per annum costs Deftax Ltd €100 (note that tax allowances apply to the reducing balance of the asset). The asset has an expected life of five years at the end of which it is estimated it can be sold for €25. In the books of Deftax the asset is depreciated each year with an amount of €15. Taxation is payable at the rate of 33%. Calculate the accounting profit as well as taxable income in the knowledge that the accounting profit below is presented after a depreciation charge of €100 each year.

Activity feedback

In order to determine both values, we first need to distinguish between the depreciation amounts according to accounting GAAP and the depreciation allowances according to the fiscal rules. The depreciation of the asset according to accounting GAAP is €15 per year (€75/5). The fiscal depreciation is a declining amount calculated each year as 25% of the remaining tax base of the asset, whereby the tax base is the amount attributed to that asset for tax purposes. In order to determine the taxable profit we start from the accounting profit and add back the depreciation amount according to accounting GAAP. Subsequently we deduct the tax allowances (depreciation amounts accepted for tax purposes). The outcome is the taxable profit. In the next step the taxes payable are calculated.

	Year				
	1	2	3	4	5
	€	€	€	€	€
Accounting profit (after depreciation charge)	100	100	100	100	100
Depreciation	15	15	15	15	15
Tax allowance	−25	−18	−14	−11	−8
Taxable profit	90	97	101	104	107
Taxes payable	30	32	33	34	36

	Year				
	1	2	3	4	5
	€	€	€	€	€
Profit before tax	100	100	100	100	100
Taxation 33% taxable profit	30	32	33	34	36
Profit after tax	70	68	67	66	64
Profit before tax	100	100	100	100	100
Taxation charge if calculated on accounting profit	33	33	33	33	33
Profit after accounting tax	67	67	67	67	67

year is referred to as the 'timing difference'. The tax allowance has the effect of deferring tax payments in year 1, €3 and year 2, €1, and then collecting these in years 4 (€1) and 5 (€3).

So in future years (4 and 5) we have an eventual payment that relates to year 1 and 2 and arises as a result of the transactions and results of years 1 and 2 and it is therefore arguable that there is a liability created at year 1 (of €3) and increased at year 2 (with €1). We are in effect suggesting that:

1 The tax charge reported on the income statement for years 1 and 2 should really be €33, as this is the amount that must eventually be paid as a result of years 1 and 2 activities.

2 There is a liability of €3 at the end of year 1, in respect of tax related to year 1 but payable in later years (4 and 5) which increases to €4 by the end of year 2.

We can easily allow for both these considerations by creating a liability account, known as a deferred tax account. This is shown below. The amount to be transferred to the credit of the deferred tax account can be formally calculated as follows. Amount equals:

Tax rate × (tax allowances given − depreciation disallowed)

Thus for year 1:

$$33\% \times (25 - 15) = 3$$
$$33\% \times (18 - 15) = 1$$

	Year					
	1	2	3	4	5	Total
	€	€	€	€	€	€
Profit before tax	100	100	100	100	100	500
Taxation: payable for year	30	32	33	34	36	165
Additional charge (credit) to deferred tax account	3	1	0	(1)	(3)	0
Total tax charge	33	33	33	33	33	165
Profit after tax	67	67	67	67	67	335

The tax expense is the aggregate amount included in the determination of the profit and loss account for the period in respect of current tax and deferred tax. As an illustration we present the journal entries which will be made in years 1 and 4 with regard to income taxes.

Year1
Tax expense	33	
Taxation payable for the year		30
Deferred tax liability		3

Year4
Tax expense	33	
Deferred tax liability		1
Taxation payable for the year		34

The deferred tax account will be credited in years 1 and 2 and debited in years 4 and 5.

Deferred tax account

	€		€
Balance c/d 31.12.01	3	Appropriation account 31.12.01	3
	3		3
		Balance b/d 1.1.02	3
Balance c/d 31.12.02	4	Approp. acc 31.12.02	1
	4		4
Balance c/d 31.12.03	4	Balance b/d 1.1.03	4
	4		4
Approp. acc. 31.12.04	1	Balance b/d 1.1.04	4
Balance c/d 31.12.04	3		4
	4		4
Approp. acc 31.12.05	3	Balance b/d 1.1.05	3

For year 4
$$33\% \times (11 - 15) = -1$$

And year 5
$$33\% \times (8 - 15) = -3$$

Arguments for deferred tax

From this discussion we can note that:

1   The tax charge by including deferred tax is €33 for years 1–5, which provides a profit after-tax figure of €67 which reflects the performance of the company.

2   There is a liability balance remaining at the end of each year in respect of tax related to the current or earlier years but not yet paid or due for payment. This, we also suggested, was a desirable outcome.

3   The total position viewed over the five years as a whole remains unaltered. This is to be expected as nothing we are doing and also nothing that the tax authorities are doing, through tax allowances, alters the total tax eventually payable as a result of a year's profits.

All this appears totally logical and in accord with accounting principles. So what is the problem?

Arguments against deferred tax

A problem occurs with the previous logic if a company buys assets regularly, which is a realistic assumption. Let us demonstrate the problem – see Activity 20.2.

Comparing the tables from Activities 20.1 and 20.2 we see that the total position over the five years is no longer the same. The total tax charge is increased by €8 (165–157). This is not surprising, as it equals the liability provided for at the end of year 5 on the deferred tax account. The transfer to the deferred tax account can be seen to be the result of an amalgam of positive originating timing differences relating to depreciation. The resultant figure of profit after tax, €67 per annum, reflects the underlying profitability of the company. It does not give an impression of improved profitability because of the effect of tax allowances related to asset acquisitions. Everything appears fine so where is the problem? The problem is the €8 remaining on the deferred tax account. Does this liability actually exist?

In the long term we can suggest that:

1   If the entity reaches the state where it has a constant volume of fixed assets, merely replacing its existing assets as they wear out and also the price it has to pay for replacement fixed assets does not rise over time, then the balance of liability on the deferred tax account will remain a more or less constant figure.

2   If the entity finds that it is effectively in the position of paying gradually more and more money for fixed assets each year, then the balance of liability on the deferred tax account will gradually rise, apparently without limit.

3   Only if the monetary amount of reinvestment in fixed assets actually falls will the balance of liability on the deferred tax account start to fall.

How likely is each of these three outcomes? In general 2 will tend to be the most frequent for three reasons:

1   Entities have a tendency to expand.

2   Entities have a tendency to become more capital intensive.

3   Inflationary pressures tend to cause the amount of money paid for assets to increase over time.

ACTIVITY 20.2

In addition to the information given in Activity 20.1 Deftax Ltd buys an asset in year 2 for €100, one in year 3 for €120 and one in year 4 for €220 and two in year 5 for €250 and €300, respectively. All these assets also have an expected life of five years, but unlike the first asset, all these later ones have an expected scrap value of zero. Complete the table in Activity 20.1 using the new information and show the deferred tax account over the five-year period. Comment on the results.

Activity feedback

To help you with the activity we provide the workings for years 2 and 3 for the calculation of depreciation and capital allowances. Years 4 and 5 follow the same pattern.

Workings

Year 2:

Asset 1 depreciation 75/5 = 15
Asset 2 depreciation 100/5 = 20
$$\underline{35}$$

Asset 1 tax allowance 25% × 75 = 18
Asset 2 tax allowance 25% × 100 = 25
$$\underline{43}$$

Year 3:

Asset 1 depreciation   = 15
Asset 2 depreciation   = 20
Asset 3 depreciation 120/5 = 24
$$\underline{59}$$

Asset 1 tax allowance 25% × (75 − 18) = 14
Asset 2 tax allowance 25% × (100 − 25) = 18
Asset 3 tax allowance 25% × 120   = 30
$$\underline{62}$$

	Year 1 €	Year 2 €	Year 3 €	Year 4 €	Year 5 €
Accounting profit (after deprec. charged)	100	100	100	100	100
Depreciation	15	35	59	103	213
Tax allowance	25	43	62	103	215
Taxable profit	90	92	97	100	98
Tax charge	30	30	32	33	32
Deferred tax charge	3	3	1	0	1
Total tax	33	33	33	33	33
Profit after tax	67	67	67	67	67

Deferred tax account

Balance c/d 31.12.01	3	3	Appropriation a/c	31.12.01
	3	3		
		3	Bal. b/d 1.1.02	
Balance c/d 31.12.02	6	3	Appropriation a/c	31.12.02
	6	6		
		6	Bal. b/d 1.1.03	
Bal. c/d 31.12.03	7	1	Appropriation a/c	31.12.03
	7	7		
		7	Bal. b/d 1.1.04	
Bal. c/d 31.12.04	7	0	Appropriation a/c	31.12.04
	7	7		
		7	Bal. b/d 1.1.05	
Bal. c/d 31.12.05	8	1	Appropriation a/c	31.12.05
	8	8		
		8	Bal. b/d 1.1.06	

So the most likely outcome, if full provision is to be made for deferred tax in this way, is of a liability figure on the balance sheet that is apparently ever increasing. But what is a liability? Informally, we can say that it is an amount to be paid out in the future. We have an account representing a liability to the tax authorities. The balance on this account is gradually getting bigger and bigger and, as far as can reasonably be foreseen, this process is going to continue. Therefore, the liability balance does not seem to be getting paid, neither in the foreseeable future is it likely to be paid. Therefore, it appears that it is not a liability at all within the meaning of the word liability! If the liability account seems all set to keep on growing, is there a probable future sacrifice?

It should be observed that one way of summarising the two arguments as regards the liability aspect is that we can consider the position for each individual asset or we can consider the position for all assets in the aggregate. In the former case the tax deferred will all have become payable by the end of the asset's life, so deferred tax provision would seem to be necessary. In the latter case the aggregate liability is likely to go on increasing so deferred tax provision would seem to be unnecessary.

Accountants' response

Formally, three approaches have been distinguished:

1 The *flow through approach*, which accounts only for that tax payable in respect of the period in question, i.e. timing differences are ignored.

2 *Full deferral*, which accounts for the full tax effects of timing differences, i.e. tax is shown in the published accounts based on the full accounting profit and the element not immediately payable is recorded as a liability until reversal.

3 *Partial deferral*, which accounts only for those timing differences where reversal is likely to occur in aggregate terms (because, for example, replacement of assets and expansion is expected to exceed depreciation).

These alternatives are discussed and explained in the following activities.

ACTIVITY 20.3

Should the flow through approach be identified as the method to be used for accounting for tax? Think of the discussion and illustrations in the activities above.

Activity feedback
Arguments in favour:

- Tax is assessed on taxable profits not accounting profits. The only liability for tax for the period therefore is that accordingly assessed.

- Future years' tax depends on future events and is therefore not a present liability (see definition of liability, Chapter 19).

- Even if current events were giving rise to future tax liabilities then, as the tax charge will be based on a complex set of future transactions, it cannot be measured with reliability and therefore should not be recognised.

Arguments against:

- As tax charges can be traced to individual transactions and events then any future tax consequences arising from these should be provided for at the outset.

- Flow through method can understate an entity's liability to tax.

ACTIVITY 20.4

Should the full deferral method be adopted as the method to be used for accounting for tax? Think of the discussion and illustrations in the activities above.

Activity feedback

The view can be taken that the amount of tax saving should not appear as a benefit of the year for which it was granted, but should be carried forward and recred-ited to the profit and loss account (by way of reduction of the tax charged therein) in the year or years in which there are reversing time differences.

In effect, therefore, the full unreversed element is shown as a liability. Applying this to the circumstances of Deftax Ltd, we arrive at the position in Activity 20.2. Thus, we could well be showing a liability that will never crystallise.

ACTIVITY 20.5

Should partial deferral be the method adopted for accounting for tax?

Activity feedback

As we have seen, the one major problem with full deferral is that the balance on the deferred tax account is likely to increase continuously where there is expansion and replacement at increased prices. If, however, timing differences are regarded in aggregate terms rather than as relating to individual assets, then this could be taken as evidence that the differences were not reversing. In short, is a liability that is never likely to become payable a liabil-ity at all? In many businesses, timing differences arising from accelerated capital allowances are of a recurring nature and reversing differences are themselves offset, wholly or partially, or are exceeded, by new originating differences thereby giving rise to continuing tax reduc-tions or the indefinite postponement of any liability attrib-utable to the tax benefits received. It is, therefore, appropriate that in the case of accelerated capital allow-ances, provisions be made for deferred taxation except insofar as the tax benefit can be expected with reasona-ble probability to be retained in the future in conse-quence of recurring timing differences of the same type.

ACTIVITY 20.6

On the assumption that the directors of Deftax Ltd fore-see no reversal of timing differences for some consider-able time and using the information from Activity 20.2, show the impact on tax charges and income figures of the firm using the partial deferral method.

Activity feedback

	Year				
	1	2	3	4	5
	€	€	€	€	€
Profit before tax	100	100	100	100	100
Taxation	30	30	32	33	32
Deferred tax charge	0	0	0	0	0
	70	70	68	67	68

Deferred tax calculation

Year	Originating (O) timing difference	Reversing (R) timing difference	Net timing difference
1	10 (25 capital allowance −15 depreciation)	–	10 (O)
2	18 (43 − 35)	–	8 (O)
3	6 (30 − 24)	3	3 (O)
4	11 (55 − 44)	11	(O)
5	28 (138 − 110)	26	2 (O)
6 onwards no net reversals			

The liability for tax will never crystallise, therefore no provision for deferred tax is required. No net reversal appears ever to be expected.

Deferral versus liability method

The deferred tax amount is dependent on the tax rate used. When calculating the amount we could either use:

- the tax rate applying when the timing difference originated – deferral method
- or the tax rate (or the best estimate of it) ruling when the tax will become payable – liability method.

A simple example is used to illustrate the difference.

ILLUSTRATION

An entity purchases a non-current asset for €5 000 000 on 1.1.X0. It is depreciated on a straight line basis over five years. It attracts tax allowances of €200 000 in X0 and €150 00 in X1. The tax rate in X2 is 30% and X1 is 25%.

	X0	X1
Depreciation charge	100 000	100 000
Tax allowance	200 000	150 000
Timing difference	100 000	50 000

Deferred tax provided

	Deferral method		Liability method	
	X0	X1	X0	X1
	30%	25%	30%	25%
Deferred tax charge	30 000	12 500	30 000	12 500

Deferred tax balance	30 000	42 500	(5 000)
		30 000	37 500

The (5000) in X1 under the liability method adjusts the carry forward of 30 000 to 25 000 which is the timing difference of 100 000 at 25% tax rate. The 37 500 is now the best estimate of the tax payable if the timing differences reversed, whereas the 42 500 does not represent the best estimate of the likely liability.

Income statement or balance sheet view of deferred tax

When the income statement view of deferred tax is taken, there is a focus on the difference between the accounting profit and taxable profit. This was the view of deferred tax taken internationally and in the UK and US until the 1990s. The balance sheet view focuses on the difference between carrying amount of assets and liabilities and their amount in tax terms and forms the basis for current IAS and US GAAP.

UK GAAP still focuses on the income statements. In some situations, it makes no difference whether we take an IS or BS view but in many it does, as the following illustration shows.

The argument for providing deferred tax on this temporary difference (note there is no timing difference) is that it is presumed that the revalued carrying amount of the asset will be recovered through use and will generate taxable income that will be taxable in the future and therefore there is a deferred tax liability. There is a problem with this logic, though, given the definition of a liability as 'a present obligation arising out of a past event'. The future taxable income referred to here is not a past event.

ILLUSTRATION

An entity buys an asset for €100 depreciated over five years on a straight line basis. Annual depreciation according to accounting GAAP is €20 per year. Tax allowances on capital assets are 50% in the first year and tax rate is 30%. Under the income statement view, known as limiting difference, the deferred tax provided for at the end of the first year is:

Tax allowance	50
Depreciation	20
Timing differences	30
Deferred tax	9

The balance sheet view, temporary difference, is:

Net book value of asset end year 1	80
Tax base (tax written down value)	50
	30
Deferred tax	9

In this example there is no difference between the two methods.

If the asset had been revalued to €200 at the end of year 1 then only the balance sheet calculation would change:

NBV	200
Tax base	50
Temporary differences	150
Deferred tax	45

IAS 12 AND TAX

Introduction

Revised IAS 12 was issued in 1996 and some slight changes were made in 2000. In addition there are two SICs, SIC 21, *Income Taxes – Recovery of Revalued Non-depreciable Assets* and SIC 25, *Income Taxes – Changes in the Tax Status of an Entity or its Shareholders*. The Standard deals with both current tax and deferred tax issues.

The current version of IAS 12 has major changes from the one first issued in 1979. This original Standard basically allowed deferred tax to be calculated based on any method available, deferral or liability method, full or partial provision, and was based on an income statement approach.

The current IAS 12 is based on a balance sheet approach and therefore a liability measurement of deferred tax together with a full provision method for all temporary differences.

Definitions

The definitions given in IAS 12 (para. 5) are now reproduced:

- Accounting profit is net profit or loss for a period before deducting tax expense.
- Taxable profit (tax loss) is the profit (loss) for a period, determined in accordance with the rules established by the taxation authorities, upon which income taxes are payable (recoverable).

- Tax expense (tax income) is the aggregate amount included in the determination of net profit or loss for the period in respect of current tax and deferred tax.
- Current tax is the amount of income taxes payable (recoverable) in respect of taxable profit (tax loss) for a period.
- Deferred tax liabilities are the amounts of income taxes payable in future periods in respect of taxable temporary differences.
- Deferred tax assets are the amounts of income taxes recoverable in future periods in respect of:

  (a) deductible temporary differences

  (b) the carryforward of unused tax losses, and

  (c) the carryforward of unused tax credits.
- Temporary differences are differences between the carrying amount of an asset or liability in the balance sheet and its tax base. Temporary differences may be either:

  (a) taxable temporary differences, which are temporary differences that will result in taxable amounts in determining taxable profit (tax loss) of future periods when the carrying amount of the asset or liability is recovered or settled; or

  (b) deductible temporary differences, which are temporary differences that will result in amounts that are deductible in determining taxable profit (tax loss) of future periods when the carrying amount of the asset or liability is recovered or settled. These lead to deferred tax assets.
- The tax base of an asset or liability is the amount attributed to that asset or liability for tax purposes.

Tax base

In many cases the tax base of an asset or liability is fairly obvious.

ACTIVITY 20.7

An entity buys an asset for €500 000, which it intends to depreciate equally over five years. Under tax legislation the asset attracts a 50% first-year allowance and then an equal allowance each year over the next four to write the asset down to zero.

What is the tax base of the asset (at the end of each year) and its carrying amount in the balance sheet.

Activity feedback

End year		Tax base	Carrying amount
	1	250 000	400 000
	2	187 500	300 000
	3	125 000	200 000
	4	62 500	100 000
	5	0	0

The tax base of an asset is the amount that will be deductible for tax purposes against any taxable economic benefits that will flow to an entity when it recovers the carrying amount of the asset. If those economic benefits will not be taxable then the tax base of the asset is equal to its carrying amount.

ACTIVITY 20.8

An entity has interest receivable of €200 and dividends receivable of €300 in its balance sheet (these amounts are thus the carrying amount of the assets). As far as tax legislation that the entity is subject to is concerned the interest will be taxed in full on a cash basis but the dividends are not taxable. Identify the tax base for the interest receivable and the dividends receivable.

Activity feedback

As the interest is taxed in full there is no deduction from the economic benefit and therefore the tax base is nil.

The benefit of the dividends is not subject to tax and therefore the whole €300 must have been deducted from the economic benefit and thus the tax base of €300. In the activity note the following:

	Tax base	Carrying amount	Temp. difference
Interest receivable	0	200	200
Dividends receivable	300	300	–

Thus, deferred tax liability would need to be recognised on the interest but not the dividend receivable.

A similar situation occurs in the case of liabilities where the tax base of a liability is its carrying amount less any amount that will be deductible for tax purposes in respect of that liability in future periods. For example, suppose an entity makes a provision in its accounts for €100 on which tax relief in full will be given when the liability is paid, then:

	Tax base	Carrying amount	Temp. difference
Provision	0	100	100

and a deferred tax asset will be required.

ACTIVITY 20.9

An entity has a loan of €500 repayable in five years' time. The principal repayment is not deductible for tax purposes. Identify the tax base and therefore the timing difference.

Activity feedback

	Tax base	Carrying amount	Temp. difference
Loan	500	500	0

There are several more examples of tax base calculations in the Standard.

Current tax liabilities and assets

The requirements of IAS 12 here are quite straightforward (para. 12–13). Unpaid current tax in relation to current or earlier periods is shown as a liability and if the amount paid exceeds the amount due then the excess is recognised as an asset. In addition where the benefit from a tax loss can be carried back to recover current tax of a previous period this should also be recognised as an asset.

Recognition of deferred tax liabilities

A deferred tax liability shall be recognised for all taxable temporary differences except to the extent that the deferred tax liability arises from:

1 the initial recognition of goodwill; or

2 the initial recognition of an asset or liability in a transaction which is not a business combination and at the time of the transaction affects neither accounting profit nor taxable profit.

We try to explain the reasoning for these two exceptions to the provision of deferred tax using the information you acquired so far in this chapter.

First goodwill is an asset and if we assume a carrying amount of €1000 then its tax base will be nil which implies a temporary difference of €1000, but if deferred tax is provided on this then the goodwill which is a function of all the net assets of the acquired business will change which will consequently change the deferred tax. This will keep occurring as we try to calculate the deferred tax and thus an exemption is made as the calculation becomes circuitous.

The second exemption can best be understood by an example.

Suppose a company buys a current asset for €100 which is not deductible for tax purposes when the asset is sold. Then:

	Tax base	Carrying amount	Temp. difference
Asset	nil	100	100

would imply a deferred tax liability should be recognised on the asset. However, the purchase of the asset had created no taxable or accounting income and therefore no timing difference and thus no need for deferred tax.

Temporary differences are differences between the carrying amount of an asset or a liability in the balance sheet or in the statement of financial position and its tax base. Temporary differences often occur due to timing differences, i.e. when income or expense is recognised in an accounting profit in a different period to when it is included in taxable profit. Remember the example of depreciation here. There are, however, temporary differences that are not timing differences.

Temporary differences that are not timing differences

IAS 12 discusses five circumstances where temporary differences arise that are not timing differences. We have already discussed two of these, goodwill and initial recognition of an asset or liability, and as we saw this temporary difference does not give rise to deferred tax as IAS 12 exempts them. The other three cases do give rise to deferred tax as we now describe.

Business combinations When a combination occurs under the acquisition method then the acquired assets and liabilities are revalued to fair value. However, the tax base of the asset or liability remains at its original figure within the subsidiary. (NB a group is not a taxable entity.) A temporary difference therefore arises on which a deferred tax liability is recognised.

Revaluation of assets Where assets are revalued to fair value there may be a temporary difference. This temporary difference will arise in tax jurisdictions where the tax base of the asset is not adjusted for the revaluation. IAS 12 requires deferred tax to be recognised on this temporary difference. This does seem somewhat illogical. If the tax base of the asset is not adjusted as there is no tax effect from the revaluation then how can a liability arise? The IASB justifies the recognition of the liability on the grounds that the asset will generate future taxable income but this is again debatable as it is difficult to see how future taxable income can equal a past event!

Investment in subsidiaries, branches, associates and joint ventures In the case of an entity with these types of investment the tax base of the investment is generally cost. The carrying amount of the investment, however, changes over time as undistributed profits are built up in the subsidiary, associate, etc. or due to foreign currency translation or when the investment is reduced to its recoverable amount. These changes will give rise to temporary differences and IAS 12 requires deferred tax to be recognised except where:

- the parent, investor or venturer is able to control the timing of the reversal of the difference
- and it is probable that the difference will not reverse in the foreseeable future.

One circumstance where a parent can control the difference is the declaration of dividends from the subsidiary but the parent could not control the difference in relation to foreign currency translation.

Recognition of a deferred tax asset

IAS 12 requires that a deferred tax asset is recognised for all deductible temporary differences to the extent that it is probable that taxable profit will be available against which the deductible temporary difference can be utilised. The meaning of 'probable' is to some extent subjective, as it is under IAS 37, *Provisions, Contingent Liabilities and Contingent Assets*. There are circumstances when a deferred tax asset should not be recognised and these are when it arises from the initial recognition of an asset or liability in a transaction that:

- is not a business combination
- at the time of the transaction affects neither accounting profit nor taxable profit (loss).

These mirror the exemptions under deferred tax liability.

Measurement of deferred tax

IAS 12 requires that deferred tax is measured by reference to tax rates and laws, as enacted or substantively enacted by the balance sheet date, that are expected to apply in the periods in which the assets and liabilities to which the deferred tax relates are realised or settled. This is the liability method discussed at p. 463.

Amount recognised in income statement

So far we have concentrated on the measurement of the deferred tax asset or deferred tax liability in the balance sheet as this is the approach adopted by IAS 12.

ACTIVITY 20.10

An entity has calculated deferred tax assets of €1m which will result in deductions in tax computations for the next three years. Deferred tax liabilities of €0.5m have also been calculated in accordance with IAS 12. Taxable profits, including reversal of deferred tax liabilities, are expected to be €0.2m per annum over the next three years. How much of the deferred tax asset should be recognised?

Activity feedback
As only €0.6m of the deferred tax asset can be reversed against future taxable profits then this is the only amount that should be recognised.

The amount recognised in the income statement of a period under this approach is the movement in deferred tax from the opening to closing balance sheet. This difference is recognised in arriving at the net profit and loss for the period except for tax arising from:

- a transaction or event which is recognised in any accounting period directly in equity, in which case the movement in deferred tax should be accounted for directly in equity
- or a business combination that is accounted for as an acquisition, in which case the movement in deferred tax is included in the resulting goodwill figure.

See Activities 20.11 and 20.12.

ACTIVITY 20.11

An entity purchases an asset, cost €50 000, on 1.1.X1. Depreciation is on a straight line basis over its useful life of five years. The taxable allowance for the asset is straight line over four years. On 31.12.X3 the asset is revalued to €45 000 but its useful life and method of depreciation remains unchanged. The revaluation of the asset is irrelevant for tax legislation. Show the charge to the income statement for deferred tax over the life of the asset given tax rate at 30% for all years and compare it with the situation where there is no revaluation.

Activity feedback
Revaluation:

Date	Carrying amount €	Tax base	Temp. difference
31.12.X1	40 000	37 500	2 500
31.12.X2	30 000	25 000	5 000
31.12.X3	45 000	12 500	32 500
31.12.X4	22 500	0	22 500
31.12.X5	0		

When the asset was revalued €25 000 would have been transferred to revaluation reserve. The charge against this amount (€25 000) for deferred tax is at 30% = €7 500. Therefore the net amount credited to revaluation reserve is €17 500 (€25 000 – €7 500).

Deferred tax liability at 30%	Movement in year	IS charge	Equity charge
750	750	750	0
1 500	750	750	0
9 750	8 250	750	7 500
6 750	(3 000)	(3 000)	(3 750)
0	(6 750)	(6 750)	(3 750)

Transfers from the equity revaluation reserve to retained earnings will be required for the excess depreciation charged over and above historical cost basis net of deferred tax in each of the final two years as follows:

Historical cost depreciation charge	10 000
Revaluation depreciation charge	22 500
Excess	12 500
Deferred tax 30%	3 750
	8 750

and therefore the €3750 will need to be credited to the revaluation reserve in the last two years. No revaluation:

Date	Carrying amount	Tax base	Temp. diff	DT liability	Movement in year	Income statement charge
31.12.X1	40 000	37 500	2 500	750	750	750
31.12.X2	30 000	25 000	5 000	1 500	750	750
31.12.X3	20 000	12 500	7 500	2 250	750	750
31.12.X4	10 000	0	10 000	3 000	750	750
31.12.X5	0	–	0	0	(3 000)	(3 000)

ACTIVITY 20.12

An entity purchases shares in another entity, leading to a parent/subsidiary relationship. The fair value of the net assets purchased included a deferred tax liability of €50 000 being temporary differences of €125 000 at 40%. In the accounting year after the purchase it is announced that the tax rate applicable for the following year is to change to 42%. By the end of the accounting year after the year of the purchase €40 000 of the temporary difference had reversed. Show the deferred tax liability at the end of the accounting year after the year of purchase and state where any changes would be charged.

Year	Tax rate	Temp. difference	DT liability
Of purchase	40%	125 000	50 000
After purchase	40%	85 000	34 000
Next year	42%		35 700

If the tax rate change had not been enacted or substantively enacted the deferred tax liability account would have remained at €34 000, but as the change is known about at the year-end the deferred tax under the liability method must be accounted for at €35 700 and thus €1700 will be charged to the income statement for the year after the purchase. The charge cannot be debited to any goodwill on the acquisition as it results from a post-acquisition event.

Activity feedback

In this activity the years are confusing and it is therefore easier to see the effects using a table.

Presentation and disclosure requirement

IAS 12 is quite prescriptive in the presentation of tax assets and liabilities in the accounts as follows:

- Tax assets and liabilities must be separated from other assets and liabilities in the balance sheet.
- Deferred tax should be distinguished from current tax.
- Deferred tax should be shown under non-current.
- Current tax assets and liabilities can be offset only where the entity has a legally enforceable right to do so and it intends to settle on a net basis or to realise the asset and settle the liabilities simultaneously.
- Deferred tax assets and liabilities can only be offset where the entity has a legally enforceable right to do so for current taxes and they relate to tax levies by the same taxation authority.

The disclosure requirements are extensive and we suggest you read the Standard in detail for these. In the main, disclosure is required of the:

- separate major components of the tax charge or credit in the income statement, e.g. current tax, deferred tax, changes in either due to tax rates
- charges in respect of tax charged to equity
- tax relating to extraordinary items
- reconciliation between tax charge and that calculated by applying the tax rate to accounting profit
- detail of temporary differences of deferred tax.

Discounting

IAS 12 does not permit the discounting of deferred tax balances with one exception, unlike UK GAAP, which does permit it. IAS 12 allows discounting of deferred tax where it relates to a pre-tax amount that is itself discounted. This exception is obvious as the application of a tax rate to the discounted item will automatically

ILLUSTRATION

Jor entity acquires an intangible asset for $200 000 with an expected life of five years. No tax deductions on amortisation or eventual sale are permitted on the asset in the country in which Jor operates, where the current tax rate is 20%.

Here, even though there is a temporary difference of $200 000 which implies a deferred tax liability of $40 000, IAS 12 currently requires no provision for this deferred tax. Under the proposed amendment this deferred tax would need to be provided.

result in a deferred tax charge that is discounted. Deferred tax is defined as a liability and as payment is some time in the future it is obvious that under the current regime of IAS 12 the amount shown as a liability does not reflect this deferment to the future. Discounting the deferred tax could be seen as an attempt to reflect the fair value but could also be seen as a method to reflect the time value of money. UK GAAP uses discounting to reflect the 'time value of money' effect on deferred tax but the whole issue is controversial. The IASB is reflecting on discounting but for the moment it does not permit discounting on deferred tax because:

- reliable calculation is complex and dependent on several factors not least of which is choice of discount rate and therefore if discounting was required 'reliability' would be questionable
- if discounting is permitted some entities would discount and others wouldn't leading to a lack of comparability.

Amendments to IAS 12

As stated at p. 462, IAS 12 is based on the balance sheet liability approach of calculating deferred tax. The IASB is considering amendments to IAS 12 through its convergence project with the FASB but the underlying approach is not to be altered. The project is intended to eliminate exceptions to this basic approach. For example the IASB suggests that the exception as regards the 'initial recognition of an asset or liability in a transaction which is not a business combination and at the time of the transaction affects neither accounting profit nor taxable profit' should be eliminated. The change if this proposal is approved is shown in the example above.

Another proposed amendment to IAS 12 is to clarify that 'substantially enacted' means that any anticipated change in the tax rate is 'virtually certain'.

The IASB also suggests an amendment to clarify the term 'probable' in the recognition of a deferred tax asset. Probable is to be clarified as 'more likely than not.' How useful this clarification will be remains to be seen.

Comparison between GAAPs

US GAAP IAS and US GAAP are fairly similar on the issue of current and deferred taxes as both require full provisioning for deferred tax based on temporary differences. There are, however, some differences in the types of temporary differences for which no deferred tax need be provided. For example, as we have seen, IAS does not require deferred tax on temporary differences arising from the initial recognition of assets or liabilities but US GAAP does.

UK GAAP UK GAAP is based on a full provisioning for incremental timing differences (income statement approach) and IAS is based on full provisioning on a temporary difference approach (balance sheet liability method). One of the major differences ensuing from the use of these two methods is that IAS GAAP will provide for deferred tax on revalued assets whereas UK GAAP will not. IAS 12 encompasses all timing differences from UK GAAP (FRS 19), but also includes many permanent differences. However, IAS 12 requires that deferred tax should not be recognised for certain temporary differences that would be permanent differences under UK GAAP.

UK GAAP, under FRS 19, permits the use of discounting.

Examples of disclosure from IAS accounts

The following disclosure is taken from the accounts of BMW, the car manufacturer for the year ended 31.12.2007. The disclosure with regard to taxes is quite extensive:

Income taxes

Taxes on income comprise the following:

in euro million	2007	2006
Current tax expense	1 002	993
Deferred tax expense	−263	257
	739	**1 250**

The deferred tax expense was euro 520 million lower than in the previous year, primarily reflecting the impact of the Business Tax Reform Act 2008, adopted by the German Bundesrat (Federal Council) on 6 July 2007.

Deferred taxes are recognised on temporary differences between the carrying amount of assets and liabilities for IFRS purposes and their tax bases. Deferred taxes are computed using enacted or planned tax rates which are expected to apply in the relevant national jurisdictions when the amounts are recovered. A corporation tax rate of 15.0 % applies in Germany with effect from 1 January 2008 onwards. After taking account of the average multiplier rate (Hebesatz) of 410 % for municipal trade tax and the solidarity charge of 5.5 %, the overall income tax rate for companies in Germany is 30.2 % (2006: 38.9 %). This reduced rate has been applied in 2007 to measure deferred tax assets and liabilities. As in the previous year, the tax rates for companies outside Germany remain in a range of between 12.5 % and 40.7 %. A valuation allowance is recognised on deferred tax assets when recoverability is uncertain. In determining the level of the valuation allowance, all positive and negative factors concerning the likely existence of sufficient taxable profit in the future are taken into account. These estimates can change depending on the actual course of events.

An analysis of deferred tax assets and liabilities by position at 31 December is shown below:

in euro million	Deferred tax assets		Deferred tax liabilities	
	2007	2006	2007	2006
Intangible assets	1	–	1 528	1 859
Property, plant and equipment	43	48	428	510
Leased products	558	572	3 205	3 368
Investments	2	2	1	–

in euro million	Deferred tax assets		Deferred tax liabilities	
	2007	2006	2007	2006
Other current assets	1 110	1 058	3 767	3 696
Tax loss carryforwards	1 072	849	–	–
Provisions	1 145	1 540	51	134
Liabilities	3 084	3 653	690	827
Consolidations	1 661	1 600	329	403
	8 676	**9 322**	**9 999**	**10 797**
Valuation allowance	−671	−528	–	–
Netting	−7 285	−8 039	−7 285	−8 039
	720	**755**	**2 714**	**2 758**

Compared to the previous reporting period, the main changes to deferred tax assets and liabilities were as follows:

Application of the income tax rate of 30.2 % (2006: 38.9 %), which is valid in Germany from 1 January 2008 onwards, significantly affected the measurement of deferred tax assets and liabilities relating to intangible assets, property, plant and equipment, leased products, provisions and liabilities.

The changes in deferred tax assets and liabilities relating to leased products and other current assets are attributable primarily to the financial services business.

Deferred tax assets on tax losses available for carryforward and on capital losses increased marginally on a net basis. Tax losses available for carryforward, which for the most part can be carried forward without restriction, totalled euro 1.8 billion at the year-end (2006: euro 1.7 billion). A valuation allowance of euro 43 million (2006: euro 65 million) was recognised in 2007 on deferred tax assets relating to tax losses. Capital losses in the United Kingdom increased to euro 2.2 billion at the end of 2007 (2006: euro 1.5 billion). In this context, a definitive agreement was reached with the UK tax authorities in 2007. As in previous years, these tax losses amounting to euro 628 million at the end of the year (2006: euro 463 million) were fully written down since they can only be utilised against future capital gains. Capital losses are not connected to ongoing business operations.

Deferred taxes recognised directly in equity amounted to euro 116 million (2006: euro 512 million). The decrease was due mainly to actuarial gains and losses (net) arising in conjunction with pension obligations and recognised directly in equity. The level of actuarial gains and losses in 2007 was affected in particular by the increase in the discount factors applied.

Deferred taxes are not recognised on retained profits of euro 13 925 million (2006: euro 13 866 million) of foreign subsidiaries, as it is intended to invest these profits to maintain and expand the business volume of the relevant companies. A computation was not made of the potential impact of income taxes on the grounds of disproportionate expense.

The tax returns of BMW Group entities are checked regularly by German and foreign tax authorities. Taking account of a variety of factors – including existing interpretations, commentaries and legal decisions taken relating to the various tax jurisdictions and the BMW Group's past experience – adequate provision has, as far as identifiable, been made for potential future tax obligations.

The actual tax expense for the financial year 2007 of euro 739 million (2006: euro 1 250 million) is euro 767 million (2006: euro 354 million) lower than the expected tax expense of euro 1 506 million (2006: euro 1 604 million) which would theoretically arise if the tax rate of 38.9 % (unchanged from the previous year), applicable for German companies, was applied across the Group. The difference between the expected and actual tax expense is attributable to the following:

in euro million	2007	2006
Expected tax expense	**1 506**	**1 604**
Variances due to different tax rates	−731	−213
Tax reductions (−)/tax increases (+) as a result of non-taxable income and non-deductible expenses	4	−68
Tax expense (+)/benefits (−) for prior periods	−4	−94
Other variances	−36	21
Actual tax expense	**739**	**1 250**

The sharp decrease in the effective tax rate was mainly caused by the significant increase in variances due to different tax rates. This includes the one-off impact of the remeasurement of deferred tax assets and liabilities at 31 December 2007. The total positive impact for the BMW Group was euro 491 million, most of which was due to the application of the tax rate of 30.2 % (valid from 1 January 2008) for German entities.

ACTIVITY 20.13

In all the following cases identify the amount of deferred tax that should be recognised and by whom.

1 Entity A, which bought a 35% interest in B, sold goods to B costing £20 000 for £30 000. B still holds these goods at the year-end in inventory. A recognises an adjustment in its consolidated accounts to eliminate its share of the unrealised profit on the goods. A pays tax at 30% and B at 40%.

2 Entity C recognises a liability at its year-end of £50 000 for accrued warranty costs. For tax purposes the product warranty costs are not deductible until claimed. Tax rate is 30%.

3 Entity D holds an asset with a carrying amount of £100 and a tax base of £60. A tax rate of 20% would apply if the asset were sold and a tax rate of 30% would apply to other income.

Activity feedback

1 There is a temporary timing difference in respect of A's share of the unrealised profit, i.e. 35% × £10 000 = £3500. This timing difference will reverse in the next 12 months if we assume that B sells all the goods and therefore a deferred tax asset of £3500 × 30% = £1050 is required. Note that A's tax rate is used here, not B's.

2 The temporary difference in respect of the warranties is £50 000 on which a deferred tax asset of £15 000 should be recognised.

3 If D expects to sell the asset without further use then a deferred tax liability of 8 (40 × 20%) would be recognised. If it intends to use the asset a deferred tax liability of 12 (40 × 30%) would be recognised.

SUMMARY

Within this chapter we have considered the principles of debate on accounting for tax and identified the regulations of IAS 12. We have seen that accounting standard-setting bodies, which all believe that they are issuing standards within a conceptual framework, can view the principles of deferred tax quite differently. Our debate in this chapter has considered deferred tax from a:

- balance sheet or income statement approach
- flow through, partial or full provision method
- deferral or liability method.

We also considered the possibility of discounting deferred tax. We leave you with the question: 'Does the required accounting treatment of taxation in published IAS accounts lead to a true and fair view as required by the Fourth Directive?'

EXERCISES

Suggested answers to exercises marked ✓ are to be found on the Student side of the companion website.

Suggested answers to the remaining exercises are to be found on the Instructor side of the companion website.

1   Outline the major arguments in favour of always providing for deferred tax where the amounts are material.

2   Outline the major arguments in favour of only providing for deferred tax when it is probable that a liability will crystallise.

3   Deferred tax should be ignored when preparing financial statements. Discuss.

✓ **4**   Explain and distinguish between:

- the flow through approach
- full deferral
- partial deferral.

5   Explain and distinguish between:

- the deferral method
- the liability method.

6   Comparability requires that either all entities provide in full for deferred tax or that it is always ignored. Discuss.

✓ **7** Explain to a non-accountant the difference between the income statement view and the balance sheet view of deferred tax.

8 Discounting deferred tax balances would provide useful information to users. Discuss.

9 Critically appraise the following statement: *The required accounting treatment of taxation in published IAS accounts does not lead to a true and fair view as required by the Fourth Directive.*

10 (i) IAS 12, *Income Tax* was issued in 1996 and revised in 2000. It details the requirements relating to the accounting treatment of deferred tax.

Required:
Explain why it is considered necessary to provide for deferred tax and briefly outline the principles of accounting for deferred tax contained in IAS 12, *Income Tax*.

(ii) Bowtock purchased an item of plant for $2 000 000 on 1 October 2000. It had an estimated life of eight years and an estimated residual value of $400 000. The plant is depreciated on straight line basis. The tax authorities do not allow depreciation as a deductible expense. Instead a tax expense of 40% of the cost of this type of asset can be claimed against income tax in the year of purchase and 20% per annum (on a reducing balance basis) of its tax base thereafter. The rate of income tax can be taken as 25%.

Required:
In respect of the above item of plant, calculate the deferred tax charge/credit in Bowtock's income statement for the year to 30 September 2003 and the deferred tax balance in the balance sheet at that date.
   Note: work to the nearest $000.

(ACCA Dec 2003)

11 Nette, a public limited company, manufactures mining equipment and extracts natural gas. The directors are uncertain about the role of the IASB's 'Framework for the Preparation and Presentation of Financial Statements' (the Framework) in corporate reporting. Their view is that accounting is based on the transactions carried out by the company and these transactions are allocated to the company's accounting period by using the matching and prudence concepts. The argument put forward by the directors is that the Framework does not take into account the business and legal constraints within which companies operate. Further they have given a situation which has arisen in the current financial statements where they feel that the current accounting practice is inconsistent with the Framework.

Situation
Nette purchased a building on 1 June 2003 for $10 million. The building qualified for a grant of $2 million which has been treated as a deferred credit in the financial statements. The tax allowances are reduced by the amount of the grant. There are additional temporary differences of $40 million in respect of deferred tax liabilities at the year-end. Also the company has sold extraction equipment which carries a five-year warranty. The directors have made a provision for the warranty of $4 million at 31 May 2004 which is deductible for tax when costs are incurred under the warranty. In addition to the warranty provision the company has unused tax losses of $70 million. The directors of the company are unsure as to whether a provision for deferred taxation is required.

(Assume that the depreciation of the building is straight line over ten years, and tax allowances of 25% on the reducing balance basis can be claimed on the building. Tax is payable at 30%.)

Required:

(a) Explain the importance of the 'Framework' to the reporting of corporate performance and whether it takes into account the business and legal constraints placed upon companies.

(b) (i) Explain with reasons and suitable extracts/computations the accounting treatment of the above situation in the financial statements for the year ended 31 May 2004.

  (ii) Discuss whether the treatment of the items appears consistent with the 'Framework'.

(ACCA June 2004)

12 On 1 January 2003, SPJ had an opening balance of $5000 on its tax account, which represented the balance on the account after settling its tax liability for the previous year. This balance arose from an overestimate of the tax due charged to the previous year's income statement. SPJ has a credit balance on its deferred tax account of $1.6 million at the same date.

SPJ has been advised that it should expect to pay $1 million tax on its trading profits for the year ended 31 December 2003 and increase its deferred tax account balance by $150 000.

Required:
Prepare extracts from the income statement for the year ended 31 December 2003, balance sheet at that date and notes to the accounts showing the tax entries required.

(CIMA pilot paper, Fin. Acc. & Tax principles)

13 *D* purchased all its tangible non-current assets new three years ago on 1 October 2001. The tangible non-current assets cost $720 000 and all qualified for tax depreciation at 25% per annum on the reducing balance method. *D's* depreciation policy is to depreciate tangible non-current assets at 20% per annum using the straight line method and assuming no residual value. *D* pays income tax at 30%.

Required:

(i) Calculate *D's* deferred tax balance at the end of each of the years ended 30 September 2002, 2003 and 2004.

(ii) Using the IASB's *Framework for the Preparation and Presentation of Financial Statements* definitions of assets and liabilities, justify the deferred tax balances at 30 September 2002, 2003 and 2004.

(CIMA paper 6(b), November 2004)

14 The directors of Panel, a public limited company, are reviewing the procedures for the calculation of the deferred tax provision for their company. They are quite surprised at the impact on the provision caused by changes in accounting standards such as IFRS 1, *First Time Adoption of International Financial Reporting Standards*, and IFRS 2, *Share-based Payment*. Panel is adopting International Financial Reporting Standards for the first time as at 31 October 2005 and the directors are unsure how the deferred tax provision will be calculated in its financial statements ended on that date including the opening provision at 1 November 2003.

Required:

(a) (i) Explain how changes in accounting standards are likely to have an impact on the provision for deferred taxation under IAS12, *Income Taxes.*

    (ii) Describe the basis for the calculation of the provision for deferred taxation on first-time adoption of IFRS including the provision in the opening IFRS balance sheet.

Additionally the directors wish to know how the provision for deferred taxation would be calculated in the following situations under IAS12, *Income Taxes*:

(i) On 1 November 2003, the company had granted 10m share options worth $40m subject to a two-year vesting period. Local tax law allows a tax deduction at the exercise date of the intrinsic value of the options. The intrinsic value of the 10m share options at 31 October 2004 was $16m and at 31 October 2005 was $46m; the increase in the share price in the year to 31 October 2005. The directors are unsure how to account for deferred taxation on this transaction for the years ended 31 October 2004 and 31 October 2005.

(ii) Panel is leasing plant under a finance lease over a five-year period. The asset was recorded at the present value of the minimum lease payments of $12m at the inception of the lease which was 1 November 2004. The asset is depreciated on a straight line basis over the five years and has no residual value. The annual lease payments are $3m payable in arrears on 31 October and the effective interest rate is 8% per annum. The directors have not leased an asset under a finance lease before and are unsure as to its treatment for deferred taxation. The company can claim a tax deduction for the annual rental payment as the finance lease does not qualify for tax relief.

(iii) A wholly owned overseas subsidiary, Pins, a limited liability company, sold goods costing $7m to Panel on 1 September 2005, and these goods had not been sold by Panel before the year-end. Panel had paid $9m for these goods. The directors do not understand how this transaction should be dealt with in the financial statements of the subsidiary and the group for taxation purposes. Pins pays tax locally at 30%.

(iv) Nails, a limited liability company, is a wholly owned subsidiary of Panel, and is a cash-generating unit in its own right. The value of the property, plant and equipment of Nails at 31 October 2005 was $6m and purchased goodwill was $1m before any impairment loss. The company had no other assets or liabilities. An impairment loss of $1.8m had occurred at 31 October 2005. The tax base of the property, plant and equipment of Nails was $4m as at 31 October 2005. The directors wish to know how the impairment loss will affect the deferred tax provision for the year. Impairment losses are not an allowable expense for taxation purposes.

Assume a tax rate of 30%.

Required:

(b) Discuss, with suitable computations, how the situations (i) to (iv) above will impact on the accounting for deferred tax under IAS12, *Income Taxes* in the group financial statements of Panel.

(ACCA 3.5 Int December 2005)

15 On 31 March 2006, CH had a credit balance brought forward on its deferred tax account of $642 000. There was also a credit balance on its corporate income tax account of $31 000, representing an overestimate of the tax charge for the year ended 31 March 2005.

CH's taxable profit for the year ended 31 March 2006 was $946 000. CH's directors estimated the deferred tax provision required at 31 March 2006 to be $759 000 and the applicable income tax rate for the year to 31 March 2006 as 22%. Calculate the income tax expense that CH will charge in its income statement for the year ended 31 March 2006, as required by IAS 12 *Income Taxes*.

(CIMA paper P7, May 2006)

EMPLOYEE BENEFITS

21

OBJECTIVES After studying this chapter you should be able to:

- explain how short-term employee benefits have to be accounted for

- explain the difference between defined contribution pension plans and defined benefit pension plans

- explain the purpose and function of actuarial cost or funding methods

- list several actuarial assumptions and discuss their impact on the pension cost and pension benefit obligation

- define the concept of total pension cost according to IAS 19

- define the concept of a defined benefit liability according to IAS 19

- describe what is meant by pension plan assets

- explain what is meant by the 'corridor' approach

- explain how equity-settled share-based payment transactions have to be accounted for

- explain how cash-settled share-based payment transactions have to be accounted for

- describe the contents of a pension plan report according to IAS 26.

INTRODUCTION

In every organisation, people are a very important resource. Without a competent and loyal staff of personnel, an entity will usually be unsuccessful. To keep the workforce motivated and loyal most, if not all, employers provide employees with certain benefits in addition to the wages paid. Employee benefits are usually furnished by the employer in full, but some types of benefits are paid for jointly by the employer and the employee. A benefit package may include: retirement plans; insurance plans such as hospital, dental, life and disability insurance; stock options; profit-sharing plans; recreational programmes; vacations and so on.

A number of these employee benefits have a long-term perspective, which implies that elements of uncertainty are involved. As a consequence, accounting for a number of these long-term employee benefits is not that straightforward and of a rather high technical level.

Most of the employee benefits are dealt with in IAS 19, *Employee Benefits*. One particular type of employee benefit, namely equity compensation or share-based benefits, is dealt with in IFRS 2, *Share-based Payment*. IFRS 2 describes the recognition and valuation rules when an entity undertakes a share-based payment transaction.

As you will notice, the scope of IFRS 2 encompasses all share-based payment transactions made by an entity, not just share-based transactions with employees and top management.

We will first present the definitions, recognition and measurement rules for those employee benefits that fall within the scope of IAS 19. Subsequently, we will discuss the accounting treatment of share-based compensation, which is dealt with in IFRS 2.

IAS 19 qualifies as short-term benefits wages, salaries and social security contributions, paid annual leave and paid sick leave, profit sharing and bonuses (if payable within 12 months of the end of the period) and non-monetary benefits (such as medical care, housing, cars and free or subsidised goods or services) for current employees.

Profit-sharing plans and bonus plans can be long term or short term, according to when they are payable (within 12 months or longer). Examples of long-term benefits are qualified post-employment benefits such as pensions, other retirement benefits, post-employment life insurance and post-employment medical care. Long-term employee benefits include long-service leave or sabbatical leave, jubilee or other long-service benefits and long-term disability benefits.

IAS 19 deals with further termination benefits.

If we discuss the issue of how these benefits should be accounted for then it is important to determine when a company is obliged or required to fulfil these employee benefits. The accounting treatment which IAS 19 prescribes for employee benefits is applicable if they result from:

- formal plans or other formal agreements between an entity and individual employees, groups of employees or their representatives
- legislative requirements, or from industry arrangements, whereby entities are required to contribute to national, state, industry or other multi-employer plans
- or informal practices that give rise to a constructive obligation. Informal practices give rise to a constructive obligation where the entity has no realistic alternative but to pay employee benefits. An example of a constructive obligation is where a change in the entity's informal practices would cause unacceptable damage to its relationship with employees.

Accounting for short-term employee benefits is straightforward as these elements do not include many uncertainties. We will look first at those short-term employee benefits. Then we will focus on the long-term employee benefits and, more specifically, on pension benefits.

ACCOUNTING FOR SHORT-TERM EMPLOYEE BENEFITS

Short-term benefits are salaries, paid leave, bonus plans payable within 12 months and other benefits payable. With regard to these benefits the basic valuation rule is as follows: When an employee has rendered service to an entity during an accounting period, the entity should recognise the undiscounted amount of short-term employee benefits expected to be paid in exchange for that service. The benefit will be reported as an expense, unless another International Accounting Standard requires or permits the inclusion of the benefits in the cost of an asset (see, for example, IAS 2, *Inventories*, and IAS 16, *Property, Plant and Equipment*) and as a liability (accrued expense), after deducting any amount already paid. If the amount already paid exceeds the undiscounted amount of the benefits, an entity should recognise that excess as an asset (prepaid expense) to the extent that the prepayment will lead to, for example, a reduction in future payments or a cash refund.

Compensated absences are short-term employee benefits. IAS 19 pays explicit attention to them. Concerning these short-term compensated absences IAS 19 makes a distinction between accumulating and non-accumulating compensated absences. The difference between the two will result in a different accounting treatment.

ACTIVITY 21.2

Can you think of some examples of paid absence? Can you distinguish between whether they arise from service rendered in the past (= accumulated absences) or whether they are not related to service rendered at work (= non-accumulated absences)?

Activity feedback
A typical example of an accumulated compensated absence is absence for vacation (holiday). According to the number of days worked an employee is entitled to a number of days of paid absence. Examples of non-accumulated

absences are sickness leave, maternity and paternity leave, military service.

In the case of accumulating compensated absences the expected cost of the short-term benefit has to be recognised when the employees render the service that increases their entitlement to future compensated absences.

In the case of non-accumulating compensated absence, the benefit should be recognised when the absence occurs, as in the latter case the absence is not linked to the service rendered by the employees in a period.

ACCOUNTING FOR PROFIT-SHARING AND BONUS PLANS

The compensation package of many executives, but also of higher and middle management these days often includes profit-sharing plans or bonus plans. When profit-sharing or bonus plans exist executives and employees receive a variable amount as compensation on top of their salary. These bonuses can be linked to financial indicators (for example accounting numbers such as earnings before interest and taxes (EBIT), return on assets (ROA), return on equity (ROE) or non-financial indicators (for example customer satisfaction) or a combination of both).

The obligation to pay an amount to the employees under a profit-sharing or bonus plan results from employee service and not from a transaction with the entity's owners. Therefore, an entity has to recognise the cost of profit-sharing and bonus plans as an expense and not as a distribution of net profit (para. 21). The bonus as such qualifies as an obligation. The amount linked to it is dependent on the realised performance in relation to the indicator specified in the profit-sharing or bonus plan.

As a result the expected cost of profit-sharing and bonus payments should be recognised as an expense and as a liability when, and only when (paras 10 and 17): the entity has a present legal or constructive obligation to make such payments as a result of past events and a reliable estimate of the obligation can be made. A present obligation exists when, and only when, the entity has no realistic alternative but to make the payments.

IAS 19 in itself, unfortunately, does not require specific disclosures about short-term benefits; other International Accounting Standards, however, may require disclosures concerning these short-term benefits. For example, where required by IAS 24, *Related Party Disclosures*, an entity has to disclose information about employee benefits for key management personnel or IAS 1, *Presentation of Financial Statements*, requires that an entity should disclose staff costs.

IAS 19 does not oblige a company to provide information about the formal terms of a bonus or profit-sharing plan to external stakeholders of the company. This information disclosure is left to the voluntary disclosure policy of the firm. Since empirical research related to earnings management found evidence that these bonus plans and profit-sharing plans can create incentives to manage the reported results of a firm, it would be interesting to know the amounts paid out in respect of these plans but even more interesting to know the indicator (financial or non-financial) which drives the bonus.

This would be useful information for financial analysis purposes (for a further discussion of this item see Chapter 30). Information on the formal terms of the plan (e.g. the indicators to which the bonus is linked) can give the external user of the financial statements an idea concerning the direction in which the results possibly could have been influenced. We might hope that in the wake of the 'accounting scandals of the year 2002', these practices become less common.

ACCOUNTING FOR EQUITY COMPENSATION BENEFITS

Bonus plans and profit-sharing plans have for a long time been the only widely used instrument to increase compensation of executives and employees. From the beginning of the 1990s stock-based compensation or share-based payment became very popular. Stock based compensation can take the form of stock options or gifts of shares for free or at lower than market values. Empirical research on incentives for earnings management also reveals that the existence of stock options might induce management to smooth reported income and to increase income upward in order to boost the share price. These elements are illustrated further in Chapter 30.

The instruments that qualify as equity-based compensation are:

(a) shares, share options and other equity instruments, issued to directors, senior executives and other employees; and

(b) cash payments, the amount of which will depend on the future market price of the reporting entity's shares or other equity instruments, again as part of a remuneration plan.

These instruments, without doubt, have an impact on the result, the financial position and the cash flow of an entity. If a company uses existing shares for the equity-based compensation plans, then the company has to buy the shares from existing shareholders. This implies a cost for the company. If a company chooses to issue extra shares (in that case employees can subscribe for new shares), there is a dilutive effect when the options are exercised (see Chapter 24).

Important elements concerning equity-based compensation are the grant date, the exercise date, the exercise price (strike price), the vesting date and vesting requirements. The difference between the exercise price and the market price is the key value driver of warrants/options. Simple methods (intrinsic value) only use this difference for valuation purposes. More sophisticated methods are using valuation methods (for instance the Black and Scholes model) which incorporate additional parameters (e.g. volatility).

Relevant accounting valuation issues concerning these benefits are: How to measure the cost of compensation offered by the company to the employees? When to recognise this cost in the profit and loss account? How to account for the financial impact of stock options (e.g. if existing shares are bought, how will they be financed by the company)?

Equity-based compensation is a hot topic in accounting regulation. Previous attempts of the United States Financial Accounting Standards Board to prescribe valuation and recognition rules whereby the cost of the share-based compensation had to be charged to the profit and loss account had to be withdrawn under the pressure of the business community. So SFAS 123, *Accounting for Stock-based Compensation*, is one of the exceptional standards where preparers can make a choice whether or not to include an item on the balance sheet or account for it off balance sheet. However, since Enron the attitude of the business world is changing. In July 2002 Coca-Cola was the first company to announce that it would recognise the cost of stock-based compensation in its profit and loss account from 2002 on; other companies followed the example of Coca-Cola.

ACTIVITY 21.3

Look at websites of several companies from different parts of Europe and worldwide and try to find information on stock-based compensation or other elements of compensation. What do you observe?

Activity feedback

Disclosure on equity-based compensation and about compensation at large differs among different countries. In the Anglo-Saxon world information on compensation has for some time found its way onto the financial statements. Compensation levels of individuals are disclosed in those financial statements. In continental Europe the presence of the value 'secrecy' (discussed in Chapter 2) probably has an impact on the amount and the way in which information is disclosed. Further a diversity of share-based compensation plans is found in the notes to the accounts of companies.

The disclosure of compensation benefits to the external stakeholders of the company is not only determined by accounting regulation. Codes of corporate governance in many countries include disclosure requirements with regard to top management compensation.

The choice left by SFAS 123 with regard to the recognition and measurement of equity-based remuneration instruments is unsatisfactory for the users of financial information. Studies by Bear Stearns and Credit Suisse First Boston, carried out at the start of the 21st century, show that if companies belonging to the Standard & Poor's 500 had accounted for their equity-based remuneration investments on the balance sheet with the use of the fair value, the earnings of those companies would have been significantly lower.

One of the first issues the Board, in its new composition, wanted to solve is the recognition and valuation of these equity benefit compensation schemes. In the beginning of 2004 IFRS 2, *Share-based Payment*, was issued. With IFRS 2, the Board has insisted on recognition and measurement of those equity-based remuneration instruments on balance sheet. A disclosure of these benefits in the notes only and no recognition on the balance sheet was no longer accepted.

The scope of IFRS 2 includes all share-based payment transactions. So IFRS 2 is applicable to more transactions than just equity-based compensation benefits. IFRS 2 defines share-based transactions as those transactions where an entity's equity instruments are transferred by its shareholder to parties that have supplied goods or services to the entity, unless the transfer is clearly for a purpose other than payment for goods or services supplied to the entity. IFRS 2 also applies to transfers of equity instruments of the entity's parent, or equity instruments of another entity in the same group as the entity, to parties that have supplied goods or services to the entity. However, an entity shall not apply this IFRS to transactions in which the entity acquires goods as part of the net assets acquired in a business combination to which IFRS 3, *Business Combinations*, applies (para. 5). A transaction with an employee (or other party) in his/her capacity as a holder of equity instruments of the entity is not considered to be a share-based payment transaction and does not fall under the scope of IFRS 2.

IFRS 2 distinguishes with regard to the nature of the share-based payment transactions between three different types of share-based transactions (para. 2):

(a) *equity-settled share-based payment transactions*, in which the entity receives goods or services as consideration for equity instruments of the entity (including shares or share options)

(b) *cash-settled share-based payment transactions*, in which the entity acquires goods or services by incurring liabilities to the supplier of those goods or services for amounts that are based on the price (or value) of the entity's shares or other equity instruments of the entity, and

(c) *share-based payment transactions with cash alternatives*, these are transactions in which the entity receives or acquires goods or services and the term of the arrangement provide either the entity or the supplier of those goods or services with a choice of whether the entity settles the transaction in cash (or other assets) or by issuing equity instruments.

Although the accounting treatment of these three types of share-based payment transaction will be different, the main objective will be that an entity should reflect in its results and in its financial position the effects of share-based payment transactions when the goods are obtained and services are received. We will now present and illustrate the definition, recognition and measurement rules of the three types of share-based payment transactions.

Equity-settled share-based payment transactions

In equity-settled share-based payment transactions an entity receives goods or services in exchange for equity instruments. For example, an entity acquires equipment from a manufacturer and uses shares as consideration. Another example is a top executive in a company who receives as part of their remuneration shares, share options or other equity instruments.

IFRS 2 (para. 10) states that for these equity-settled share-based payment transactions, the entity shall measure the goods or services received and the corresponding increase in equity, directly, at the fair value of the goods or services received, unless that fair value cannot be estimated reliably. If the entity cannot estimate reliably the fair value of the goods or services received, the entity shall measure their value, and the corresponding increase in equity, indirectly, by reference to the fair value of the equity instruments granted (see Activity 21.4).

So IFRS 2 distinguishes with regard to the valuation of these equity-settled share-based transactions between two possibilities, namely when the fair value of the goods received and the services rendered can be measured reliably and when it is not possible to determine this value in a reliable way. In the latter situation the fair value of the equity instrument will be used for reporting purposes (see IFRIC 8). For example if an entity grants shares to a charity organisation in order to enhance its image, the transaction shall be accounted for according to IFRS 2 and the value of the transaction is the fair value of the equity instruments.

Before focusing further on the recognition and measurement issues of these equity-settled share-based payment transactions, we will explain a number of concepts that play a role in the accounting treatment of these share-based transactions. First, there is the grant date of the share-based payment transaction. This is the date at

---

ACTIVITY 21.4

Consider the two examples just given (the acquisition of the equipment and the compensation of the top executive) and determine which amount will be used under IFRS 2 for the valuation of the transaction in the books of the entity.

Activity feedback
In the case of the equipment, the market value of the equipment will be used to measure, on the one hand, the increase in the fixed assets and, on the other hand, the increase in equity. In the situation where equity instruments are used as remuneration for services rendered by employees, directors or other senior executives, it is usually not possible to measure directly the services received for particular components of the employee's remuneration package. It might also not be possible to measure the fair value of the total remuneration package

independently, without measuring directly the fair value of the equity instruments granted. Furthermore, shares or share options are sometimes granted as part of a bonus arrangement, rather than as a part of the basic remuneration. By granting shares or share options, in addition to other remuneration, the entity is paying additional remuneration to obtain additional benefits. Estimating the fair value of those additional benefits is likely to be difficult. Because of the difficulty of measuring directly the fair value of the services received, the entity shall measure the fair value of the employee services received by reference to the fair value of the equity instruments granted. So the share-based remuneration will be recorded in the books of the company in the following manner. The amount of the fair value of the equity instrument will be debited on an expense remuneration account and credited on an equity account.

which the entity and another party (including an employee) agree to a share-based payment arrangement, being when the entity and the other contracting party have a shared understanding of the terms and conditions of the arrangement. At grant date the entity confers on the other contracting party the right to cash, other assets, or equity instruments of the entity, provided the specified vesting conditions, if any, are met. If that agreement is subject to an approval process (for example, by shareholders), grant date is the date when that approval is obtained.

In the definition of the grant date, we discover the concept of 'vesting conditions'. These are the conditions that must be satisfied for the counterparty to become entitled to receive cash, other assets or equity instruments of the entity, under a share-based payment arrangement. Vesting conditions include service conditions, which require the other party to complete a specified period of service, and performance conditions, which require specified performance targets to be met (such as a specified increase in the entity's profit over a specified period of time). Only these two conditions, namely service rendered and performance conditions, need to be considered to determine the vesting conditions. The latter was determined explicitly by the Board in 2006.

The fair value of the equity instruments granted should be determined at the measurement date. IFRS 2 defines the measurement date as the date at which the fair value of the equity instruments are granted. For transactions with employees and others providing similar services, the measurement date is the grant date. For transactions with parties other than employees (and those providing similar services), the measurement date is the date the entity obtains the goods or the counterparty renders service.

If market prices are available they should be used as fair value of the equity instruments. If market prices are not available, valuation techniques can be used to estimate the fair value of those equity instruments on the measurement date in an at-arm's-length transaction between knowledgeable willing parties. In relation to share options the Black-Scholes-Merton formula might be used. When the fair value of the equity instruments cannot be measured reliably, IFRS 2 stipulates that the intrinsic value of the instrument will be used for valuation purposes. The intrinsic value of the equity instrument is defined in the appendix to IFRS 2 as the difference between the fair value of the shares the counterparty has the right to and the price (if any) the counterparty is required to pay for those shares. In many cases, transactions will have an intrinsic value of nil at the date of the grant. Therefore, IFRS 2 requires that all share-based payments measured at intrinsic value be remeasured through profit or loss at each reporting date until the transaction is settled (e.g. the exercise of options granted).

If vesting requirements exist then the grant of the equity instruments is conditional on satisfying specified vesting conditions. For example, a grant of shares or share

ILLUSTRATION

A company, Amax, grants 50 share options to each of its 200 employees. If there is no vesting requirement the employees are entitled to receive these granted options immediately. The fair value of the share option at the grant date is €30. When the equity instruments granted vest immediately, implying that the counterparty is not required to complete a specific period of service before becoming unconditionally entitled to those equity instruments, the entity shall recognise on grant date the serv-ices received in full, with a corresponding increase in equity.

In this situation the expense related to these granted share options is:

$$10\ 000 \text{ options} \times €30 = €300\ 000$$

This amount will be debited on an expense account and credited in an equity account.

ILLUSTRATION

When company Amax wants to enter its share-based transaction in its books, it needs information on the probability that the employees will remain in service. On the basis of past experience, company Amax estimates that 10% of employees will leave during the three-year period and therefore forfeit their rights to the share options. If we take the example of the share option plan that is only dependent on the vesting condition that the employee remains in service for three years we will have the following amounts to be entered in the books of company Amax. For this illustration we assume that after three years the estimates used match exactly with the reality and that the fair value of the option at grant date is €30.

Year	Calculation	Amount debited on the expense account	Amount credited on an equity account
1	10 000 options × 90% × €30 × 1/3	€90 000	€90 000
2	(10 000 options × 90% × €30 × 2/3) − 90 000	€90 000	€90 000
3	(10 000 options × 90% × €30 × 3/3) − 180 000	€90 000	€90 000

Over the vesting period an amount of €270 000 has been reported on the profit and loss account as a remuneration expense and over the same period that amount has been credited to an equity account.

options to an employee is typically conditional on the employee remaining in the entity's employ for a specified period of time.

Suppose that company Amax still grants 50 share options to each of its 200 employees, but that each grant is conditional on the employee remaining in service over the next three years.

Vesting conditions might also take the form of performance conditions that must be satisfied, such as the entity achieving a specified growth in profit or a specified increase in the entity's share price. Suppose that company Amax grants 50 share options to each of its 200 employees, conditional on the employees remaining in the company for a period of two years. However, the shares will only vest if at the end of year 2 the return on equity of the company has increased by 4% over the vesting period. Company Amax combines a performance condition with a service condition to arrive at the vesting condition.

The entity shall recognise an amount for the goods or services received during the vesting period based on the best available estimate of the number of equity instruments expected to vest and shall revise that estimate, if necessary, if subsequent information indicates that the number of equity instruments expected to vest differs from previous estimates. On the vesting date, the entity shall revise the estimate to equal the number of equity instruments that ultimately vested. When vesting conditions exist the amount of the services received, measured by the fair value of the equity instruments, is allocated over the vesting period.

After the vesting period, the entity shall not make any subsequent adjustments to its equity. IFRS 2 describes further the recognition and measurement rules on how to deal with modifications to the terms and conditions on which equity instruments were granted, including cancellations and settlements. Discussing these elements in detail would go beyond the purpose of this book.

Cash-settled share-based payment transactions

For cash-settled share-based payment transactions, the entity shall measure the goods or services acquired and the liability incurred at the fair value of the liability.

ILLUSTRATION

Suppose Amax grants 50 share options to each of its 200 employees, on the condition that the employees remain in service for the next three years. The employees may choose to exercise their options at the end of year 3, year 4 or year 5. The payment will however be in cash. The amount of cash to be received will be determined by the value of the option at exercise date. During the first year eight employees leave the company, the entity estimates that 12 employees will leave the company in the next two years. During year 2 a total of eight employees leave the company and the company estimates that six employees will leave Amax in year 3. In the third year ten employees leave the company. At the end of year three the share options held by the remaining employees vest.

In the third year 30 employees exercise their options, in the fourth year another 40 employees exercise their options and in the fifth year the remaining 104 employees exercise their options.

Amax uses the following estimates for the valuation of this cash-settled share-based transaction in its books.

Year	Fair value	Intrinsic value
1	€10	
2	€11	
3	€14	€1 250
4	€17	€1 500
5		€2 000

This cash-settled share-based transaction will lead to the following amounts:

Year	Calculations	Expense	Liability
1	$(200 - 20) \times 50 \times €10 \times$ $1/3 = 30\,000$	30 000	30 000
2	$((200 - 22) \times 50 \times €11 \times 2/3)$ $- 30\,000 = 35\,266$	35 266	65 266
3	$((200 - 26 - 30) \times 50 \times €14)$ $- 65\,266 = 35\,534 + 30 \times$ $50 \times €12.5 = 18\,750$	54 284	100 800
4	$((144 - 40) \times 50 \times €17) -$ $100\,800 = -12\,400 + 40 \times$ $50 \times €15 = 30\,000$	17 600	88 400
5	$0 \times 88\,400 = -88\,400 + 104$ $\times 50 \times €20 = 104\,000$	15 600	0

The amount in the column 'Expense' represents the remuneration expense for the period and the amount in the column 'Liability' represents the amount on the liability account. In the example of the cash-settled share-based payment transaction presented above, we need to remeasure the liability at its fair value after the vesting date because not all options have been exercised. If all options are exercised at vesting date, no subsequent remeasurements are necessary.

Until the liability is settled, the entity shall remeasure the fair value of the liability at each reporting date and at the date of settlement, with any changes in fair value recognised in profit or loss for the period.

Share-based payment transactions with cash alternatives

In relation to this third group of share-based payment transactions a distinction is made between, on the one hand, share-based payment transaction in which the terms of the arrangement provide the counterparty with a choice of settlement and, on the other, share-based payment transactions in which the terms of the arrangement provide the entity with a choice of settlement.

In the first situation where an entity has granted the counterparty the right to choose whether a share-based payment transaction is settled in cash or by issuing equity instruments, the entity has granted a compound financial instrument, which includes a debt component (i.e. the counterparty's right to demand payment in cash) and an equity component (i.e. the counterparty's right to demand settlement in equity instruments rather than in cash). For transactions with parties other than employees, in which the fair value of the goods or services received is measured directly, the entity shall measure the equity component of the compound financial instrument as the difference between the fair value of the goods or services received and the fair value of the debt component, at the date when the goods or services are received.

For other transactions, including transactions with employees, the entity shall measure the fair value of the compound financial instrument at the measurement date, taking into account the terms and conditions on which the rights to cash or equity instruments were granted.

For a share-based payment transaction in which the terms of the arrangement provide an entity with the choice of whether to settle in cash or by issuing equity instruments, the entity shall determine whether it has a present obligation to settle in cash and account for the share-based payment transaction accordingly. The entity has a present obligation to settle in cash if the choice of settlement in equity instruments has no commercial substance (e.g. because the entity is legally prohibited from issuing shares), or the entity has a past practice or a stated policy of settling in cash, or generally settles in cash whenever the counterparty asks for cash settlement.

If the entity has a present obligation to settle in cash, it shall account for the transaction in accordance with the requirements applying to cash-settled share-based payment transactions.

If no such obligation exists, the entity shall account for the transaction in accordance with the requirements applying to equity-settled share-based payment transactions, in paras 10–29. On settlement:

(a) If the entity elects to settle in cash, the cash payment shall be accounted for as the repurchase of an equity interest, i.e. as a deduction from equity, except as noted in (c) below.

(b) If the entity elects to settle by issuing equity instruments, no further accounting is required (other than a transfer from one component of equity to another, if necessary), except as noted in (c) below.

(c) If the entity elects the settlement alternative with the higher fair value, as at the date of settlement, the entity shall recognise an additional expense for the excess value given, i.e. the difference between the cash paid and the fair value of the equity instruments that would otherwise have been issued, or the difference between the fair value of the equity instruments issued and the amount of cash that would otherwise have been paid, whichever is applicable.

In business combinations employees of subsidiary A might be entitled to share-based compensation whereby they receive shares of the parent entity B. In this situation subsidiary A accounts for this transaction in its own entity's books according to the principles set out in IFRS 2, as well as in IFRIC 11, which deals with group and treasury share transactions. For example, in case of an equity-settled share-based payment transaction, the account expenses in relation to employee services are debited and the equity account is credited. This credit can be regarded as a capital contribution from the parent, namely entity B in this particular case.

In the parent B's separate financial statements, the parent entity recognises on the one hand the grant of an equity instrument and on the other the capital contribution made to its subsidiary. This event will be recorded in the books of the parent entity by debiting the account investment in subsidiary A and by crediting the equity account.

When the consolidated group accounts are prepared, the increase in equity in A's financial statements and the increase in the investment asset in B's separate financial statements are both eliminated upon consolidation (see Activity 21.5).

Disclosures

Extensive information disclosures about these share-based transactions in the notes to the accounts are required by IFRS 2. In relation to these transactions an entity shall disclose information that enables users of the financial statement to:

ACTIVITY 21.5

A parent entity grants 200 employees of its subsidiary the right to receive 200 shares of the parent entity each, conditional upon the completion of two years' service with the subsidiary entity. The fair value of the shares on grant date is €40 per share. The subsidiary estimates that 90 per cent of the employees will complete the two-year vesting period. This estimate remains the same during the whole vesting period. At the end of the vesting period 92% of the employees complete the required two years of service.

Account for this transaction in the books of the subsidiary and in the books of the parent entity.

Activity feedback

The subsidiary will recognise this share-based payment transaction by debiting an expense account in relation to employee services and crediting an equity account, representing a capital contribution from the parent. The amounts which will be recorded in year 1 and year 2 are presented below:

Year 1: 200 employees × 200 shares × 90% estimated
vesting × $\frac{1}{2}$ years × €40 = €720 000

Year 2: 200 employees × 200 shares × 92% vesting ×
1 year × €40 − €720 000 = € 1 472 000 −
€720 000 = €752 000

The parent entity will increase its investment in its subsidiary by debiting this investment account for €720 000 in year 1 and €752 000 in year 2. The equity account will be credited for €720 000 in year 1 and €752 000 in year 2.

(a) understand the nature and the extent of share-based payment arrangements that existed during the period

(b) understand how the fair value of the goods or services received, or the fair value of the equity instruments granted, during the period was determined

(c) understand the effect of share-based payment transactions on the entity's profit or loss for the period and on its financial position.

These information requirements imply that a detailed description of all share-based payment arrangements have to be disclosed (e.g. the different types of share-based arrangements and their nature and conditions, the number and weighted average exercise price of share options for the outstanding options at the beginning of the period, the ones granted, forfeited, exercised and expired during the period and the ones outstanding at the end of the period and the ones exercisable at the end of the period) a description of how the fair value is determined, details on the expenses recognised and the liabilities recorded.

To illustrate all the information which needs to be disclosed in relation to these share-based payment transactions, an extract from the Annual Report 2005 of Adidas is included for illustration. Note that the vesting requirements are a combination of a service period and performance objectives.

32. Equity Compensation Benefits
Management Share Option Plan (MSOP) of adidas-Salomon AG
Under the share option plan adopted by the shareholders of adidas-Salomon AG on May 20, 1999, and amended by resolution of the Annual General Meeting on May 8, 2002, and on May 13, 2004, the Executive Board was authorised to issue non-transferable stock options for up to 1,373,350 no-par-value bearer shares to members of the Executive Board of adidas-Salomon AG as well as to managing directors/senior vice presidents of its related companies and to other executives of adidas-Salomon AG and its related companies until August 27, 2004. The granting of stock options was able to take place in tranches not exceeding 25% of the total volume for each fiscal year.

There is a two-year vesting period for the stock options and a term of approximately five years upon their respective issue.

The expense recognised for 2005 arising from share-based payment transactions amount to € 0.5 million and is recorded within the operating expenses.

Management Share Option Plan (MSOP)

	Tranche I (1999)		Tranche II (2000)		Tranche III (2001)		Tranche IV (2002)		Tranche V (2003)	
	No.	Exercise Price in €	No.	Exercise Price in €	No.	Exercise Price in €	No.	Exercise Price in €	No.	Exercise Price in €
Originally issued	**266 550**		**335 100**		**342 850**		**340 850**		**88 000**	
Outstanding as at Dec. 31, 2003	**175 550**		**172 700**		**312 000**		**327 150**		**87 500**	
Forfeited during the period	12 050		3 600		18 650		25 350		5 000	
Exercised during the period										
Jan. 2004	0		41 750	81.84	41 550	86.44	0			
Jul. 2004	0		56 450	64.87	94 900	72.97	0			
Oct. 2004	0		46 400	42.43	76 200	54.93	48 000	99.33		
Outstanding as at Dec. 31, 2004	**163 450**		**24 250**		**80 700**		**253 800**		**82 500**	
Exercisable as at Dec. 31, 2004	163 450		24 250		80 700		253 800			
Outstanding as at Dec. 31, 2004	**163 450**		**24 250**		**80 700**		**253 800**		**82 500**	
Forfeited during the period	4 450				1 900		3 200		2 500	
Exercised during the period										
Jan. 2005	0		6 800	21.75	25 000	37.95	49 250	90.85		
Jun. 2005	0		3 950	2.56	23 400	2.56	56 255	72.67		
Oct. 2005	82 950	116.26	800	2.56	9 500	2.56	71 700	2.56	41 900	2.56
Outstanding as at Dec. 31, 2005	**76 050**		**12 700**		**20 900**		**73 395**		**38 100**	
Exercisable as at Dec. 31, 2005	76 050		12 700		20 900		73 395		38 100	

No further stock options were issued during the year under review. The stock options may only be exercised subject to the attainment of at least one of the following performance objectives:

(1) **Absolute Performance:** During the period between the issuance and exercise of the stock options, the stock market price for the adidas-Salomon AG share – calculated upon the basis of the total shareholder return approach – has increased by an annual average of at least 8%.

(2) **Relative Performance:** During the same period, the stock market price for the adidas-Salomon AG share must have developed by an annual average of 1% more favorably than the stock market prices of a basket of competitors of the adidas Group globally and in absolute terms may not have fallen.

The stock options may only be exercised against payment of the exercise price. The exercise price corresponds to the arithmetical mean of the closing prices of the adidas-Salomon AG share over the last 20 trading days of the respective exercise period, less a discount, which is composed of the absolute and relative performance components. In any case, the exercise price shall be at least the lowest issue price as stated in § 9 section 1 of the German Stock Corporation Act (AktG), currently € 2.56.

The option terms and conditions stipulate that the stock options may be used for existing common shares in lieu of new shares from the contingent capital, or in the place of common shares the discount is paid in cash.

The new shares participate in profits from the beginning of the year in which they are issued.

(Adidas Annual Report 2005)

ACCOUNTING FOR LONG-TERM EMPLOYEE BENEFITS: PENSION BENEFITS

The most important long-term employee benefits are pension benefits. Other long-term employee benefits, including long-service leave or sabbatical leave, jubilee or other long-service benefits, long-term disability benefits or medical benefits, are accounted for in a similar manner as pension benefits. Therefore, we will only discuss the recognition and valuation issues related to pension benefits extensively. We will start the discussion by defining the concept of a pension benefit and by an analysis of the impact of a company pension plan on the financial situation of the company.

Existence of different pension systems

The purpose of a pension is to grant people some money when they are retired. Worldwide three different types of 'pension systems' can be distinguished, namely state pensions, pensions received from the employer resulting from an employment contract and individual pension savings plans. So an individual can be entitled to a state pension, on top of that a retirement benefit resulting from his employment contract (if retirement benefits were included) and finally a payment from an individual pension scheme if the individual has taken the initiative to contribute to an individual savings account. The importance and presence of each type of pension system in a single country is determined by characteristics of the local or national environment.

In some countries state pensions are the major source of income for retired people. In other countries initiatives such as company pension plans and individual pension schemes are stimulated by the government and are common practice, because of the lower levels of state pensions.

State pensions do not usually create any accounting problems for entities. The companies are collecting the premium from the employees (a deduction from the gross salary) and these amounts together with employer's contributions (if any) are paid to the government. If the premium due for an accounting period, which will be recorded as an expense is not equal to the amount transferred to the government, prepaid expenses or accrued expenses can be reported on the balance sheet. According to IAS 19 state pensions should be accounted for as multi-employer plans and these will often have the character of a defined contribution plan (this concept will be defined later on p. 519). The treatment stipulated in IAS 19 concerning state pensions is usually in line with what we have already mentioned.

Individual pension schemes are totally separate from employment contracts, so IAS 19 does not focus on them. IAS 19 deals especially with company pension plans as they have an impact on the financial situation of a company.

Company pension plans

A company pension plan can be defined as an agreement between an employer and its employees, whereby the former agrees to pay benefits to the latter after their retirement. The terms of the pension plan stipulate the retirement benefit to which an employee is entitled. There are two major categories of pension schemes or pension plans, namely defined benefit plans and defined contribution plans.

Definition of a pension benefit In a defined contribution plan the employer agrees to contribute a specific amount to the pension plan with or without a contribution from the employee. The benefits to be received by the employee at retirement are determined by the contributions transferred to the plan plus the investment return obtained on those contributions. This implies that an employee will only know the amount which he will receive as pension benefit on retirement. The contributions are usually paid into a separate entity (fund or insurance company). Further, the employee bears the risk under this type of pension plan as the amount is, in the end, dependent on the obtained investment return on the amounts contributed and invested.

A defined benefit plan is defined by IAS 19 as all plans other than defined contribution plans. If we want to describe defined benefit plans in somewhat more detail we would characterise them as those plans where the benefits promised are defined in advance, whereby the amount of pension benefit to be paid depends on the plan's benefit formula. Plans for which the pension benefit formula is based on compensation levels are called pay-related plans. The three most important types of pay-related plans are:

- the final pay plan in which the benefits are calculated as a percentage of the final salary before retirement
- the final average pay plan, where the benefits are calculated as a percentage of the average salary of the last three to five years before retirement
- the career average pay plan in which the benefits are related to the average salary someone has earned during his career.

In some defined benefit plans the state pensions are included in the benefit formula. This implies, however, that if the level of state pensions drops, the employer faces a higher cost. Plans for which the benefit formula is not based on compensation levels are called non-pay-related plans or flat benefit plans. For example, a pension plan whereby the pension benefit is defined as a benefit consisting of contributions plus a guarantee of fixed return is categorised as a defined benefit pension plan and shall be accounted for as such.

Organisation and financing of a company pension plan Providing retirement benefits to the employees involves many decisions. In addition to a decision about the type of pension benefit promised (defined contribution or defined benefit) decisions regarding the organisation and the financing or funding patterns of these benefits have to be made as well. The choices made by companies will not only be influenced by company characteristics but also by characteristics of the national environment. The latter will be illustrated on p. 497 and in Chapter 31.

When an employer provides his employees with a defined contribution plan, the finance pattern consists of the contributions, stipulated in the pension plan made to a pension account. The finance pattern and the responsibility of the employer can be determined in a very straightforward way. The pension account in which the funds are accumulated can be administered by the company or by a bank.

A defined benefit plan can be financed through the so-called pay as you go system or through a funding system. Under the pay as you go system the pensions are paid directly from the resources of the company as they fall due. The purpose of a funding system on the contrary is to make contributions through the whole employment period of the employee in order to accumulate enough funds to guarantee the pension payments. Usually actuarial cost methods (also called actuarial funding methods) are used to determine the amounts to be financed each period in order to have enough funds to pay the pension benefits when the employees retire.

If pension benefits are financed by means of a funding system two main types of organisational set-ups are possible: internal funding or external funding. In case of internal funding, resources are allocated in advance for the provision of benefits, but no separation of these amounts from the other assets of the employer is made. Benefit payments when due are made directly by the employer. In some countries employers are allowed to use those funds accumulated within the entity for financing the operational activities of the entity. In other countries those funds may be kept in the entity but they have to be invested in certain assets. Very often these plans, financed through internal funding, are called unfunded pension plans in the Anglo-Saxon world. This term might be misleading as it may sound as if no financing arrangements have been made yet, as in the case of the pay as you go system. In fact, internally funded plans is a better way to describe this financing system.

If an employer uses external funding the resources are accumulated in a separate legal entity (i.e. there is a separate fund). In the Anglo-Saxon world these plans, which are funded externally, are called funded pension plans. This separate fund may be a unique creation for only one employer or for many employers or it may be operated by a specialist insurance company running many such schemes. The contract with the insurance company has to stipulate what type of risks and responsibilities are transferred to the insurance company. The terms of this contract are extremely important for accounting purposes as they determine whether insured benefits will be considered a defined contribution type or a defined benefit type.

Paragraph 39 states in this respect:

An entity may pay insurance premiums to fund a post-employment benefit plan. The entity should treat such a plan as a defined contribution plan unless the entity will have (either directly, or indirectly through the plan) a legal or constructive obligation to either:

- pay the employee benefits directly when they fall due
- or pay further contributions if the insurer does not pay all future employee benefits relating to employee service in the current and prior periods.

If the entity retains such a legal or constructive obligation, the entity should treat the plan as a defined benefit plan for accounting purposes.

Whether an insured plan qualifies as a defined contribution plan or a defined benefit plan is an extremely important matter, since the way these plans have to be accounted for is totally different. Companies will have a tendency to try to qualify their insured plans as much as possible as defined contribution plans.

Although employers can choose between different types of pension benefit and different ways to organise and finance them, country-specific influences are often encountered. First of all the importance of the pension benefits granted by the employer versus state pensions differs among countries. In countries like the UK, the USA and the Netherlands the benefits of company pension plans are a major source of income for retired people. In countries in the south of Europe and also in Belgium and Scandinavian countries state pensions make up an important part of the income of people after retirement. A wide variety of differences in pension systems is also found on a global basis.

Further, companies may choose between internal funding or external funding. Very often the national environment, however, determines the choice. For example in the Netherlands and the UK companies usually fund their pension promises externally. German companies often use internal funding. This practice is responsible for large provisions on the balance sheets of German companies (see, for example, Chapter 31). Very often national legal requirements are the drivers for the observed differences. For example there might be laws which prohibit internal funding. The possibility of withdrawing funds from an external pension fund in times when surpluses are present will also be dependent on the existing laws of a particular country. In fact, IAS 19 has to take into account all these different possibilities existing worldwide. The IASB has to develop accounting regulations concerning these benefits which can be applied worldwide. IAS 19 is elaborately detailed in order to take into account all of these differences.

Another element which relates to organisational issues is whether an employer joins a multi-employer plan for the organisational and financial aspects in relation to pension benefits or whether he decides to set up the organisation and financing as a single-employer plan. In some countries such as the Netherlands employers often join multi-employer plans. In relation to multi-employer plans IAS 19 stipulates that multi-employer plans are defined contribution plans (other than state plans) or defined benefit plans (other than state plans) that:

- pool the assets contributed by various entities that are not under common control
- use those assets to provide benefits to employees of more than one entity, on the basis that contribution and benefit levels are determined without regard to the identity of the entity that employs the employees concerned.

Whether these multi-employer plans are of a defined benefit or a defined contribution type will depend on the terms of the plan.

ACTIVITY 21.6

How do you think these different types of pension plan affect the financial situation of the sponsoring company, namely the employer?

Activity feedback

- Pensions represent a cash outflow for the company. The timing of the cash flow will be different according to the funding system which is used by the company: pay as you go system, internal or external funding system and the finance pattern determined by the actuarial funding methods.
- The amount of pension benefits represents a cost for the company. This cost can be reduced through advanced funding if positive investment returns are obtained.
- When an employee renders service, his pension rights accrue. Depending on the terms of the pension plan or the existing company practice the employer has a legal or constructive obligation. At the time of retirement the employer owes the employee a certain amount of money. This amount of money is determined in advance in the case of a defined benefit plan or will be dependent on the realised investment return on the amounts contributed to a plan under a defined contribution plan.

Impact of company pension plans on the sponsoring company In this respect the concept of vested benefits is important as vested employee benefits are those benefits that are not conditional on future employment. The terms of a pension plan stipulate when pension benefits become vested. Usually an employee has to be in service for a minimum period (e.g. five years) before his pension rights become vested. If the benefits are vested, this means that the employee has earned his/her pension rights independent of whether the employee will stay further with the firm.

From the feedback of Activity 21.6, we have learned that pension benefits do have an impact on the result, cash flow and financial position of a company. Further we know that pensions and other retirement benefits are a major cost for many entities across many jurisdictions. For example, the overall deficit in defined benefit plans for the Standard & Poor's was $464 billion at 31 December 2005 (*The Analyst's Accounting Observer*, June 2006). The overall deficit for European companies in the Dow Jones Stoxx 50 was €116 billion at 31 December 2004 and in the UK FTSE 100 was £37 billion at July 2005 (Lane, Clark and Peacock, 'Accounting for Pensions Survey', 2005).

As a result these elements have to be accounted for in the financial statements of the employer. The way these benefits are accounted for will depend largely on the type of pension promise which has been made to the employee, namely a defined contribution into a plan or a promise for a defined benefit at the moment of retirement. Defined contribution plans are much simpler to account for. With regard to the recognition and valuation of pension benefits granted under a defined benefit plan, many technical issues have to be agreed on first.

Accounting for defined contribution plans

Under a defined contribution plan, the finance pattern and the responsibility of the employer can be determined in a very straightforward way. The amounts to be contributed, according to the terms of the pension plan, should be treated as pension costs for that particular period. If the employer has transferred all the contributions stipulated in the pension plan to a pension scheme, then the employer has fulfilled his pension commitments and no provision has to be shown on the balance sheet.

Paragraphs 44–46 of IAS 19 stipulate reporting and disclosure requirements in relation to a defined contribution plan as follows: When an employee has rendered service to an entity during a period, the entity should recognise the contribution payable to a defined contribution plan in exchange for that service as a liability (accrued expense), after deducting any contribution already paid. If the contribution already paid exceeds the contribution due for service before the balance sheet date, an entity should recognise that excess as an asset (prepaid expense) to the extent that the prepayment will lead to, for example, a reduction in future payments or a cash refund. The contribution payable to a defined contribution plan should also be recorded as an expense, unless another International Accounting Standard requires or permits the inclusion of the contribution in the cost of an asset (see, for example, IAS 2, *Inventories*, and IAS 16, *Property, Plant and Equipment*).

A company should always disclose in the notes the amount recognised as an expense in relation to the defined contribution plans of the company. When a pension plan consists of contributions which guarantee a fixed return, it is considered a defined benefit plan.

Accounting for defined benefit plans

As mentioned earlier, the pension benefit under this type of plan is determined by the pension plan formula and as such is defined in advance. The formula can be a function of the salary of the beneficiary or another variable.

Until recently most defined benefit plans determined the benefit to be received as a function of the salary of the employee. In the USA and (gradually) in Europe cash balance plans are becoming more popular. Cash balance plans are pension plans in which the pension benefit is determined by reference to amounts credited to an employee's account. Those amounts typically comprise in each year a principal amount based on current salary and a specified interest credit. The plan may or may not be funded. If the plan is funded, it may be invested in assets that differ from those which determine the interest credit. On retirement or leaving service (when vesting conditions are met) the employee is entitled to a lump sum equal to the total amount credited to this account.

According to IAS 19 cash balance plans are defined benefit plans. However they entail specific accounting problems which are not dealt with yet by IAS 19. As a result the Board will pay attention to these types of plans in the near future.

Under a defined benefit scheme the exact total amount of the benefit is known only at the moment of retirement (in case of a lump sum payment) or when the pensioner dies (in case of annual payments). Only at that moment are all uncertainties gone. The main problem, however, is how to charge this total cost over the subsequent service years of the employee. In many countries actuarial funding methods are used for this accounting allocation problem and IAS 19 has also opted for this approach by choosing one particular actuarial funding method, namely the projected unit credit method for accounting purposes. Because of the important role of actuarial funding methods in the recognition of pension costs and pension liabilities for accounting purposes we will pay attention in this section to the function and the mechanisms of those actuarial funding methods (often called by actuaries actuarial cost methods).

Mechanisms of actuarial funding methods We will illustrate the purpose and the mechanisms of actuarial funding methods with a numerical example relating to one person, Mr Dupont. This example is highly simplified for pedagogic reasons.

ACTIVITY 21.7

Assume Mr Dupont enters a pension scheme with a pension formula based on his final salary. The pension benefit he is entitled to receive is defined as follows:

$$Br = k(r - y)Sr$$

whereby:

  Br = pension benefit to be received at retirement
  k = % of salary
  r = retirement age
  y = age at which the employee is entitled to receive benefits
  Sr = last salary before retirement

The pension benefit for Mr Dupont is a lump sum payment at retirement. We will further assume the $k = 10\%$ and that Mr Dupont enters the company in year 1. His pension benefits are vested from the first moment of employment. The salary levels over the five years of his employment are:

Year 1: 100 000
Year 2: 110 000
Year 3: 120 000
Year 4: 140 000
Year 5: 160 000

Calculate the amount of earned pension benefit Mr Dupont is entitled to receive at the end of each year of service rendered.

Activity feedback

The pension benefit Mr Dupont is entitled to increases over the years in the following way.

Year 1: $B1 = 0.1 \times 1 \times (100\,000) = 10\,000$
Year 2: $B2 = 0.1 \times 2 \times (110\,000) = 22\,000$
Year 3: $B3 = 0.1 \times 3 \times (120\,000) = 36\,000$
Year 4: $B4 = 0.1 \times 4 \times (140\,000) = 56\,000$
Year 5: $B5 = 0.1 \times 5 \times (160\,000) = 80\,000$

Several actuarial cost or funding methods exist to determine the financing or funding pattern for the pension benefits. These different methods will all lead to different funding patterns for the same pension benefit to attain in the end, in the case of Mr Dupont at the end of year 5. The group of actuarial cost or actuarial funding methods which are most commonly used can be divided in two subgroups, namely accrued valuation methods and projected valuation methods. The first group, the accrued valuation methods, takes into account only the service rendered to date and the current salary level for the calculation of the amounts to be funded. The amount to be funded in a particular year under this method is equal to the present value of the benefit accrual in that particular year. Only the accrued or earned pension rights are financed under this method. Under the accrued valuation method expected future salary levels can be taken into account as well as in combination with service already rendered. The accrued benefit valuation method whereby future salary levels are taken into account is called the projected unit credit method. This method is chosen by IAS 19 for cost recognition and pension liability valuation purposes.

The second group of actuarial cost methods used by actuaries is called the projected benefit cost methods or projected valuation methods. These actuarial funding methods calculate the total pension benefit an employee will receive on retirement by taking into account the expected service to be rendered over the total service period and the expected salary level at retirement. They allocate that final amount, over the working life of the employee, as a yearly fixed amount or as a fixed percentage of salary.

The main difference in the funding patterns between the two families of actuarial funding methods (accrued valuation methods versus projected valuation methods) is that under the accrued methods the amounts to be funded at the start of a career of a person are lower than if one would finance the promised benefit under a projected valuation method, which takes into account from the start the whole expected service period.

Accrued benefit valuation methods use the pension plan formula in order to determine the accrual of pension rights over the years. The amount of accrued benefits at a particular moment can be defined as follows:

$$AB_x = B_x(_{r-x}P_xT)V_{r-x}\ddot{a}_r$$

whereby:

AB_x = actuarial value of accrued benefits at age x

B_x = accrued pension benefits at age x

$_{r-x}P_xT$ = the probability that the employee stays with the firm from age x till retirement with $P_xT = (1 - q_{mx})(1 - q_{wx})(1 - q_{dx})(1 - q_{rx})$

q_m = probability of mortality

q_w = probability of withdrawal from the plan

q_d = probability of disability

q_r = probability of early retirement

v_{r-x} = discount factor from retirement age to age x

$\ddot{a}_r$ = present value at retirement age of a long life annuity of a single currency unit at the start of each year (needed if the pension benefit will be paid out as an annual payment)

P_xT as such is often called the plan turnover assumption.

The function of actuarial assumptions It is clear from the formula just examined that in order to calculate the accrued benefits and the finance patterns related to it, the actuary must make assumptions about a number of variables, e.g. life expectancy, employee turnover, future salary levels, investment return and so on. These elements are called actuarial assumptions. Some of them are of a demographic nature (e.g. mortality, number of men and women in the plan) others are of an economic nature (e.g. inflation rate, investment return). When these actuarial funding methods are used to determine the finance pattern of the benefits a company is free to choose the value of these assumptions. When the outcome of the actuarial funding method is used for accounting purposes IAS 19 stipulates that (para. 72) the actuarial assumptions used should be unbiased and mutually compatible. By the latter IAS 19 means that (para. 75) actuarial assumptions are mutually compatible if they reflect the economic relationships between factors such as inflation, rates of salary increase, the return on plan assets and discount rates. For example all assumptions which depend on a particular inflation level (such as assumptions about interest rates and salary and benefit increases) in any given future period assume the same inflation level in that period.

Further, IAS states that financial assumptions should be based on market expectations at the balance sheet date, for the period over which the obligations are to be settled. The choice of the actuarial assumptions is not immaterial. Minor changes in the assumptions might have substantial impacts on the amounts reported, the assumption with the most material effect is the discount rate (see also the example in Activity 21.12). That is the reason why IAS 19 has paid special attention to the choice of the discount rate (para. 78). The rate used to discount post-employment benefit obligations (both funded and unfunded) should be determined by reference to market yields at the balance sheet date on high-quality corporate bonds. In countries where there is no deep market in such bonds, the market yields (at the balance sheet date) on government bonds should be used. The currency and term of the corporate bonds or government bonds should be consistent with the currency and estimated term of the post-employment benefit obligations.

It is important to state here that the discount rate reflects the time value of money and *not* the actuarial or investment risk.

ACTIVITY 21.8

Calculate the actuarial value of accrued benefits for Mr Dupont in each of the five years he is in service, based on the service rendered to that date and the current salary level at that time. Assume that the plan turnover assumption is equal to zero and the discount rate is 4%. The pension benefit is paid out as a lump sum at the moment of retirement. The actuarial calculations are made at the end of the year.

Activity feedback

$AB1 = [0.1 \times (1 \times 100\ 000)]/(1.04)^4 = 8\ 548$

$AB2 = [0.1 \times (2 \times 110\ 000)]/(1.04)^3 = 19\ 558$

$AB3 = [0.1 \times (3 \times 120\ 000)]/(1.04)^2 = 33\ 284$

$AB4 = [0.1 \times (4 \times 140\ 000)]/(1.04)^1 = 53\ 846$

$AB5 = [0.1 \times (5 \times 160\ 000)]/(1.04)^0 = 80\ 000$

These actuarial calculations can also be made at the start of each year: the interest factor will then be different. The present value of these accrued benefit obligations increases each year due to the year of extra service rendered by the employee and the interest accrual.

We will now analyse the impact on the amount of accrued benefits in Activity 21.9 when future salary levels are included in the calculations. IAS 19 requires the use of the projected unit credit method for the determination of the pension liability as well as for the determination of a part of the total pension cost. The projected unit credit method takes into account future salary increases.

Present value of the defined benefit obligation The present value of the defined benefit obligation, as calculated in Activity 21.9 plays an important role in the valuation of a possible pension liability under IAS 19. The PBO is the starting point for the recognition of a defined benefit liability or a pension asset in the financial statements of the employer (para. 54).

Paragraph 83 of IAS stipulates further that post-employment benefit obligations should be measured on a basis that reflects:

- estimated future salary increases
- the benefits set out in the terms of the plan (or resulting from any constructive obligation that goes beyond those terms) at the balance sheet date
- estimated future changes in the level of any state benefits that affect the benefits payable under a defined benefit plan, if, and only if, either:
  - those changes were enacted before the balance sheet date
  - or past history, or other reliable evidence, indicates that those state benefits will change in some predictable manner, for example in line with future changes in general price levels or general salary levels.

ACTIVITY 21.9

Take into account the expected future salary levels and calculate the projected benefit obligation (PBO) of Mr Dupont at the end of each year that he is in service. Since we take into account expected future salary levels, we can no longer talk about accrued benefits or earned benefits.

Activity feedback

$PBO1 = [0.1 \times (1 \times 160\ 000)]/(1.04)^4 = 13\ 677$

$PBO2 = [0.1 \times (2 \times 160\ 000)]/(1.04)^3 = 28\ 448$

$PBO3 = [0.1 \times (3 \times 160\ 000)]/(1.04)^2 = 44\ 379$

$PBO4 = [0.1 \times (4 \times 160\ 000)]/(1.04)^1 = 61\ 538$

$PBO5 = [0.1 \times (5 \times 160\ 000)]/(1.04)^0 = 80\ 000$

As a result of point 3 of para. 83 we notice in practice that when pension plan formulas are renegotiated or new pension plans are set up, the benefits resulting from state pensions are no longer included as a part of the company pension plan benefit formula. Employers clearly want to avoid elements which increase risk and uncertainty.

Now that you are familiar with the workings of actuarial cost methods, we are able to introduce the solution for the determination of the total pension cost and the valuation of pension liabilities and assets, which the IASB has opted for. Accounting for pensions is on the agenda of the IASB for revision in the frame of the convergence project with the FASB (see Chapter 3). In March 2008 a discussion paper, *Preliminary Views on Amendments to IAS 19 Employee Benefits*, was issued by the IASB. Responses to the issues raised in this discussion paper had to be submitted by 26 September 2008 (the date of delivery of the manuscript of this textbook to the publisher). The discussion paper raised a number of issues with regard to the recognition of the pension liability, the treatment of actuarial gains and losses, the treatment of the investment return and a number of other issues. It will probably take some time before discussion paper ideas will be finally crystallised in a new amended IAS 19, *Employee Benefits*. This implies that many elements explained in this chapter will remain in place for the next two or more years.

Below is the determination of the total pension cost. Subsequently, we will pay attention to the impact of the pension benefits on the balance sheet of the employer. However, first we will enumerate a number of decisions the Board has taken in relation to pension accounting:

1 Pension accounting will be based primarily on the plan's terms and benefit formula.
2 For accounting purposes, the projected unit credit method will be used.
3 A net pension obligation will be presented on the balance sheet, rather than a consolidation of pension assets and pension liabilities in the financial statements of the employer or the sponsor.
4 Future salary increases will be incorporated in the measurement of the pension liability.
5 The pension plan assets will be measured at fair value.
6 Preparers may choose to reduce the volatility of the total pension cost by opting for a 'corridor approach'.

Determination of the total pension cost The total pension cost in a particular year is defined by IAS 19 as follows:

(a) current service cost (see paras 63–91)
(b) interest cost (see para. 82)
(c) the expected return on any plan assets (see paras 105–107) and on any reimbursement rights (see para. 104A)
(d) actuarial gains and losses, as required in accordance with the entity's accounting policy (see paras 92–93D)
(e) past service cost (see para. 96)
(f) the effect of any curtailments or settlements (see paras 109–110)
(g) the effect of the limit in para. 58(B), unless it is recognised outside profit and loss in accordance with para. 93C.

We will explain below the different items which make up the total pension cost in a particular year.

Current service cost As illustrated in Activity 21.9, the current service cost should be calculated with the use of the projected unit credit method. The projected unit credit method attributes the amount to be funded each year on the basis of the plan's benefit formula. These amounts to be funded each year, which result from the projected unit credit method, represent the current service cost. However, if an employee's service in later years will lead to a materially higher level of benefit than in earlier years, an entity should attribute the benefit on a straight line basis from:

- the date when service by the employee first leads to benefits under the plan (whether or not the benefits are conditional on further service)
- until the date when further service by the employee will lead to no material amount of further benefits under the plan, other than from further salary increases.

In those cases the pension plan formula will no longer determine the cost allocation pattern. In fact IAS 19 allows in this case an allocation pattern which is more similar to the funding patterns used by the projected valuation methods (see earlier in this chapter).

The PBO in Activity 21.9 increases each year due to the service rendered in each year and the interest accrual on the amount of the PBO at the start of the year. Under IAS 19, the increase due to service rendered is called the current service cost.

Interest cost The current service cost calculated with the use of the projected unit credit method and the interest accrual are two components of the total pension cost which should be charged to the profit and loss account. Based on the data we have available so far the total pension cost in the subsequent years would be as shown in Table 21.1.

ACTIVITY 21.10

Calculate the current service cost and the interest accrual for Mr Dupont with the use of the projected unit credit method which takes into account the service rendered to date and the future salary levels. The calculations are made at the end of the year in this example.

Activity feedback

	Current service cost	Interest accrual	Projected benefit obligation (PBO)
Year 1	13 677	0	13 677
Year 2	14 224	547	28 448
Year 3	14 793	1 138	44 379
Year 4	15 384	1 775	61 538
Year 5	16 000	2 462	80 000

The current service cost is determined each year by the increase in earned pension rights according to the pension benefit formula:

$CSC\ 1 = [0.1 \times (1 \times 160\ 000)]/(1.04)^4 = 13\ 677$

$CSC\ 2 = [0.1 \times (1 \times 160\ 000)]/(1.04)^3 = 14\ 224$

$CSC\ 3 = [0.1 \times (1 \times 160\ 000)]/(1.04)^2 = 14\ 791$

$CSC\ 4 = [0.1 \times (1 \times 160\ 000)]/(1.04)^1 = 15\ 384$

$CSC\ 5 = [0.1 \times (1 \times 160\ 000)]/(1.04)^0 = 16\ 000$

The interest cost component is determined as follows:

$IC1 = 0.04\ (0) = 0$

$IC2 = 0.04\ (13\ 677) = 547$

$IC3 = 0.04\ (28\ 448) = 1\ 138$

$IC4 = 0.04\ (44\ 379) = 1\ 775$

$IC5 = 0.04\ (61\ 538) = 2\ 462$

TABLE 21.1	Total cost of pensions		
	Current service cost	**Interest accrual**	**Total pension cost**
Year 1	13 677	0	13 677
Year 2	14 224	547	14 771
Year 3	14 793	1 138	15 931
Year 4	15 384	1 775	17 159
Year 5	16 000	2 462	18 642

The interest cost component in Activity 21.10 is determined with the use of the discount rate of 4%. The discount rate reflects the time value of money. Paragraph 82 stipulates that the interest cost is computed by multiplying the discount rate as determined at the start of the period by the present value of the defined benefit obligation throughout that period, taking account of any material changes in the obligation. Since the amounts calculated in the activity are calculated at the end of the year there is no interest cost in the first year. (As we said earlier this example is simplified for pedagogic reasons.)

Expected return on plan assets If the amounts to be funded are invested an investment return can be realised. When investments are successful, meaning when the realised investment return is higher than expected return, the total pension cost can be decreased. Concerning this return on plan assets, we have to distinguish between the expected return on assets (again an actuarial assumption) and the realised return on assets. Note that the expected return on plan assets is not the same as the discount factor used in the actuarial calculation. At the start of a period an assumption must be made about the investment return to be realised in that period. Remember that the interest component reflects the time value of money. We will now add investment data to our example (see Activity 21.11).

If a company is virtually certain that another party will reimburse some or all the expenditures required to settle a defined benefit obligation, it shall recognise its right to reimbursement as a separate asset. The amount recognised for reimbursement in the period shall be deducted from the total pension cost and presented together with the expected return on plan assets.

ACTIVITY 21.11

Assume that in year 3 the expected return on assets will be 5% and in year 4 the expected return on assets is estimated to be 3%. What will be the impact on the pension cost so far? Determine the total pension cost with the elements you know at this stage.

Activity feedback

In year three when the expected return on plan assets is higher than the discount rate used this has so far a decreasing impact on the total pension cost to be reported, with the opposite situation arising the year afterwards.

	Year 3	Year 4
Current service cost	14 793	15 384
Interest cost	1 138	1 775
Expected return on plan assets	−1 422 = 0.05 (28 448)	−1 331 = 0.03 (44 379)

Actuarial gains and losses Intuitively, we feel that something is missing at the moment, namely information on the realised investment return. The difference between the expected return on plan assets and the realised return on plan assets is presented as an actuarial gain if the realised return is higher than the expected return, or as an actuarial loss if the realised return is lower than the expected return.

Actuarial gains and losses arise from two sources. If actuarial assumptions are different from reality a difference will occur. This difference can be positive or negative as in Activity 21.12. These differences are called experience adjustments. If this difference between the actuarial assumption and the reality continues to exist then it could be that the actuarial assumptions used in the actuarial calculations have to be changed. This is a second source of actuarial gains and losses. So actuarial gains and losses can also result from changes in the actuarial assumptions themselves. A change in the actuarial assumptions used has as a consequence that the future amounts to be funded will be higher or lower. Further, the PBO calculated with the new actuarial assumptions can also be higher or lower than the PBO calculated with the old actuarial assumptions. In the view of an actuary, actuarial gains and losses mean the following. If the PBO (new assumptions) is higher than the PBO (old assumptions) then an actuarial loss arises, since the difference is not yet funded and needs to be. In the opposite situation, where PBO (new assumptions) is smaller than the PBO (old assumptions), an actuarial gain arises, since there is now more funded than the present PBO (new assumptions) (see Activity 21.13).

ACTIVITY 21.12

Assume that at the end of year 3 the realised return on assets was €1300 and at the end of year 4 the realised return was €1500, present the total pension cost based on the information you now possess and under the assumption that the actuarial gains and losses are fully recognised immediately (= charged to the income statement for the total amount).

Activity feedback

	Year 3	Year 4
Current service cost	14 793	15 384
Interest cost	1 138	1 775
Expected return on plan assets	−1 422	−1 331
Actuarial gains or losses	+122	−169
Total	14 631	16 659

ACTIVITY 21.13

Assume that at the start of year 4 the discount rate used in the calculations in relation to the pension benefit of Mr Dupont will be changed from 4% to 5%. What will be the impact on the projected benefit obligation (PBO) at the start of year 4?

Activity feedback

The PBO at the start of year 4 using a discount rate of 5% is equal to:

PBO at the start of year 4 (new assumptions)

$$= [0.1 \times (3 \times 160\,000)]/(1.05)^2 = 43\,537$$

Remember that the PBO at the start of year 4 using the discount rate of 4% was PBO4 (old assumptions) 44 379.

In this situation we have an actuarial gain as the projected benefit obligation calculated with the new assumptions (in this case a new discount rate) is lower than the projected benefit obligation calculated with the old assumptions. The actuarial gain is 842 (we talk about a gain because the new PBO (43 537) is lower than the old PBO (44 379)).

A major question subsequently arises. How should we account for this actuarial result?

It is obvious that differences between reality and the actuarial assumptions used will occur frequently (e.g. realised salary increases or higher or lower than estimated salary increases). These differences are almost inherent to this process. Further, minor changes in the actuarial assumptions used might entail an impact on the amounts of the projected benefit obligation calculated. Immediate recognition of these elements has the consequence that the total pension cost will become a highly volatile element on the income statement. This is something that the business world absolutely does not like (for a further discussion of this aspect, see Chapter 30).

In order to reduce this volatility the IASB had initially chosen a so-called corridor approach whereby actuarial gains and losses, which fall within a corridor, need not be recognised. The amount of actuarial gains and losses falling outside the corridor had to be recognised over a certain period of time. This recognition procedure which is included in IAS 19 concerning these actuarial gains and losses is probably more inspired by concerns from the business world than by elements of the conceptual framework of the IASB. The corridor approach allows that actuarial gains and losses do not always have to be recognised. An element in support of this corridor approach might be that in the long term actuarial gains and losses may be offset against each other. Being aware of the fact that this 'corridor' approach is not in line with the conceptual framework, the IASB recently introduced the possibility for an entity to recognise the actuarial gains and losses in the period in which they occur and to report them in a statement of changes in equity titled 'statement of recognised income and expense' (see IAS, para. 96). This treatment allows preparers of financial statements to keep the influence of actuarial gains and losses outside the profit and loss account (IAS 19, para. 93). We will first illustrate the functioning of the 'corridor' approach. This is stipulated in paras 92 and 93 of IAS 19 in the following way.

An entity should recognise a portion of its actuarial gains and losses as income or expense if the net cumulative unrecognised actuarial gains and losses at the end of the previous reporting period exceeded the greater of (para. 92):

- 10% of the present value of the defined benefit obligation at that date (before deducting plan assets)
- 10% of the fair value of any plan assets at that date.

These limits should be calculated and applied separately for each defined benefit plan.

Paragraph 93 further states that the portion of actuarial gains and losses to be recognised for each defined benefit plan is the excess determined under para. 92, divided by the expected average remaining working lives of the employees participating in that plan. However, an entity may adopt any systematic method that results in faster recognition of actuarial gains and losses, provided that the same basis is applied to both gains and losses and the basis is applied consistently from period to period. An entity may apply such systematic methods to actuarial gains and losses even if they fall within the limits specified in para. 92.

If we apply these paras (92 and 93) to the example of Dupont, we notice that we indeed exceed the corridor of 10% namely 842 > 443 (= 0.10 (44 379)). The amount above 10% is equal to 399 (= 837 − 443). If we recognise the amount above 10% or outside the corridor by dividing it by the expected average remaining working life of Mr Dupont, then we will add an amount of 199.5 (= 399/2) to the total pension cost of year 4 and 199.5 will be taken into account as unrecognised actuarial gain for the determination of the defined benefit liability. In year 5 the remaining 199.5 will be charged to the income statement under the heading recognised actuarial gain.

IAS 19, however, also allows other systematic allocation methods on condition that they recognise the actuarial results faster. IAS 19 also allows companies to recognise actuarial results which lie within the corridor of 10%. As a result, companies have many options; however, if their aim is to reduce volatility of the pension cost, they will opt to recognise only actuarial results outside the 10% corridor. For external users of the annual accounts this results in less transparency about the current and future impact of the pension plan on a company's situation, especially if the quality of disclosure of the firm is low.

The possibility of recognising actuarial gains and losses in the year they occur and presenting them outside the profit and loss account on a 'statement of recognised income and expense' is inspired by the UK pension rules. The IASB felt that transparency around these actuarial gains and losses could be improved by allowing this treatment.

If we apply this method to the example of Dupont, this would imply that no actuarial gains and losses are included in the amount of the total pension cost, but that the total amount of 842 has a direct impact on the company's equity and that it is presented in a statement of recognised income and expenses.

With this treatment of actuarial gains and losses, it is not necessary to take into account unrecognised actuarial gains and losses in the coming years with regard to this particular loss or gain.

IAS 19, para. 93 permits this treatment only if it is used for all the defined benefit plans of the sponsoring company and for all its actuarial gains and losses. Although the immediate recognition of actuarial gains and losses in a statement of recognised income and expenses is taken by the IASB from the UK-GAAP situation, not all British companies adopt this approach. For example, British Airways opted for the corridor approach.

(vii) Employee benefit obligations

Under UK GAAP the measurement and recognition requirements of SSAP 24 were applied to accounting for pensions and post-retirement benefits in the financial statements, whilst disclosures were provided under FRS 17. IAS 19 takes a balance sheet approach to accounting for defined benefit schemes, similar to FRS 17. Therefore, on transition, the deficit, similar to that previously disclosed under FRS 17, has been recognised in the balance sheet. From April 1, 2004 the Group has elected to apply the 'corridor' treatment under IAS 19. The impact will be that actuarial gains and losses are only recognised to the extent that they exceed 10 per cent of the greater of the scheme assets or liabilities, and in that case are spread over the remaining average service lives of employees. Therefore, the net actuarial losses on the pension schemes for 2004/05 of £0.4 billion have not been recognised.

(British Airways Annual Report)

Vodafone, on the other hand, immediately recognises these actuarial gains and losses outside the profit and loss account.

b. Employee Benefits – actuarial gains and losses (IAS 19, 'Employee Benefits')

The Group has elected to recognise all cumulative actuarial gains and losses in relation to employee benefit schemes at the date of transition. The Group has recognised actuarial gains and losses in full in the period in which they occur in a statement of income and expense in accordance with the amendment to IAS 19, issued on 16 December 2004.

(Vodafone Annual Report 2005)

Past service cost The last major component of the total pension cost are the past service costs. Past service costs arise when an employer grants pension rights for the service rendered prior to the establishment of the pension plan or when an employer grants an increase in pension benefits also for service rendered in past periods. As a result the projected benefit obligation will increase. This increase in the amount of the projected benefit obligation resulting from those past service benefits should, on the one hand, be funded or financed and, on the other, be recognised for accounting purposes. The amounts recognised in relation to those past service benefits in a particular year on the income statement are called past service costs. The amount not yet recognised will be called a past service liability; alternatively, this may sometimes be referred to as 'past service cost'. (See Activity 21.14.)

ACTIVITY 21.14

Assume that from year 4 on Mr Dupont is entitled to a pension benefit of 0.15% of his final salary for each year he has been with the firm instead of 0.10% of his final salary.

The formula of the pension plan of Mr Dupont then becomes:

$$Br = 0.15 \ (r - y)Sr$$

The employer also grants this increase in pension benefits for the first three years of the career of Mr Dupont. We have to remember that the pension rights of Mr. Dupont are vested from the start of his employment.

Calculate the new PBO at the start of year 4 which takes into account this increase in pension benefits granted for past periods.

Activity feedback

PBO start year 4 = $0.15 \ [3 \times (160\ 000)]/(1.04)^2 = 66\ 568$

Remember that the PBO at the start of year 4 under the old pension benefit formula was 44 379. This is an increase of the projected benefit obligation of 22 189 = (66 568 − 44 379).

How should this increase be accounted for? IAS 19 makes a distinction between vested past service costs and non-vested past service costs. Remember vested pension benefits are pension benefits which are not conditional on further future employment. So the employee is entitled to them, even if he leaves the firm. When past service costs *are* vested, IAS 19 stipulates (para. 96) that these past service cost should be recognised immediately as cost. If past service costs are non-vested they should be recognised as an expense on a straight line basis over the average period until the benefits become vested.

In the example of Mr Dupont where these past service benefits are vested, the amount of 22 189 should be recognised immediately as part of the total pension cost in year 4. Because the amount of the past service benefits has been fully recognised on the income statement of year 4, it should not be taken into account for the determination of the amount recognised as a defined pension liability.

ACTIVITY 21.15

Assume that the pension rights of Mr Dupont would only become vested at the end of year 5. How would you then account for these past service benefits in accordance with IAS 19?

Activity feedback

The amount of 22 189 should then be allocated over years 4 and year 5. Half of it will be reported as part of

the pension cost in year 4 and the other half will be taken into account in the determination of the pension liability at the end of year 4. In year 5 the remaining half would then be charged to the income statement.

Curtailments or settlements The total pension cost will be affected by the effects of a curtailment or settlement. A curtailment arises when (para. 111) an entity either:

- is demonstrably committed to make a material reduction in the number of employees covered by a plan, or
- amends the terms of a defined benefit plan such that a material element of future service by current employees will no longer qualify for benefits or will qualify only for reduced benefits.

A curtailment may arise from an isolated event, such as the closing of a plant, discontinuance of an operation or termination or suspension of a plan. An event is material enough to qualify as a curtailment if the recognition of a curtailment gain or loss would have a material effect on the financial statements. Curtailments are often linked with a restructuring. Therefore, an entity accounts for a curtailment at the same time as for a related restructuring. We notice that it is up to the management to judge whether the effect is material.

A settlement occurs (para. 112) when an entity enters into a transaction that eliminates all further legal or constructive obligation for part or all of the benefits provided under a defined benefit plan, for example, when a lump-sum cash payment is made to, or on behalf of, plan participants in exchange for their rights to receive specified post-employment benefits.

What kind of treatment does IAS 19 prescribe for the results of those settlements and curtailments?

An entity should recognise gains or losses on the curtailment or settlement of a defined benefit plan when the curtailment or settlement occurs. The gain or loss on a curtailment or settlement should comprise:

- any resulting change in the present value of the defined benefit obligation
- any resulting change in the fair value of the plan assets
- any related actuarial gains and losses and past service cost that, under paras 92 and 96, had not previously been recognised.

Before determining the effect of a curtailment or settlement, an entity should remeasure the obligation (and the related plan assets, if any) using current actuarial assumptions (including current market interest rates and other current market prices) (para. 110).

All items making up the total pension cost (para. 61) have now been discussed except for one item, namely the effect of the limit in relation to the recognition of a net pension asset explained in para. 58(b), unless it is recognised outside profit and loss in accordance with para. 93C. This item will be illustrated below when we discuss the recognition and valuation of the net pension liability or the net pension asset.

Defined benefit liability

Following the analysis of the total pension cost, we now focus on the possible impact of company pension plans on the balance sheet of the employer. Paragraph 54 stipulates in this respect that the amount to be recognised as a defined benefit liability should be the net total of the following amounts:

- the present value of the defined benefit obligation at the balance sheet date (see para. 64)
- plus any actuarial gains (less any actuarial losses) not recognised because of the treatment set out in paras 92–93 and
- minus any past service cost not yet recognised (see para. 96)
- minus the fair value at the balance sheet date of plan assets (if any) out of which the obligations are to be settled directly (see paras 102–104).

We observe that a 'net' amount will appear on the balance sheet and not the total amount of pension liabilities and pension assets.

The first three components have been illustrated when the determination of the total pension cost was discussed. These three components make up the pension liability.

The present value of the defined benefit obligation calculated with the use of the projected unit credit method was illustrated in Activity 21.9 without a past service cost and Activity 21.14 when a past service cost was present. The treatment of the actuarial gains and losses was illustrated in Activity 21.13. The amounts outside the corridor of 10% and not yet recognised should be included in the determination of the amount of the defined benefit liability. However, we know that companies might also use other recognition procedures or recognise also the amount within the corridor. Actuarial gains and losses immediately recognised and included in the statement of recognised income and expenses must not be taken into account for the determination of the pension liability. So some flexibility exists with regard to this component. Also the treatment of past service costs was explained in Activity 21.14.

We will illustrate the determination of the first three components of the defined benefit liability using the data of Activity 21.13 and subsequently Activity 21.14. We determine the first three components of the calculation of the defined benefit liability at the end of year 4. In the case of Activity 21.13 an actuarial gain of 842 has arisen due to the change in discount factor from 4% to 5%. The first component will be determined as follows: the present value of the defined benefit obligation at balance sheet date:

$$PBO4 = 0.1(4 \times 160\ 000)/(1.05) = 60\ 952$$

The second component will arise only when the company has actuarial gains and losses which are not recognised yet. So only in the situation where the company has used the corridor approach in Activity 21.13 will an actuarial gain not recognised be added to the first component. In this situation the total of the first two components will be $60\ 952 + 199.5 = 61\ 151.\ 5$.

If the company opts for an immediate recognition of the actuarial gain the amount of the first two components will be only $60\ 952$.

In the case of Activity 21.13 there is no third component, since there are no past service costs in that example. The above amounts will be compared with the fair value of the plan assets. Assume that the fair value of the total plan assets is 60 000; then a net pension liability of 1151.5 will arise in the situation the company has chosen for the corridor approach. When the company has chosen for immediate recognition of the actuarial gain a net pension liability of 952 will arise.

We will now include the information of Activity 21.14 in this example. In Activity 21.14 a past service liability is created due to the benefit increase which was granted retrospectively. The first component of the pension liability will be:

$$PBO4 = 0.15(4 \times 160\ 000)/(1.04) = 92\ 307$$

Only when the total amount of past service costs is not recognised immediately, will this first component be decreased with a third component, namely the amount of the unrecognised past service cost. If this total amount of 22 189 of past service liabilities is allocated over two subsequent years 4 and 5, then an amount of 11 094.5 is deducted from the present value of the defined benefit obligation in order to arrive at the defined pension liability. The amount of the defined pension liability in this situation will be 81 212.5. If the total fair value of pension assets would be 90 000, a net pension asset or a negative net pension liability would arise in this case.

Following these numerical illustrations of the determination of the first three components of the defined benefit liability, we turn our attention to the determination of the fair value of the pension plan assets.

Plan assets

Plan assets include (according to the definitions of IAS 19) assets held by a long-term employee benefit fund and qualifying insurance policies. Reading the paragraphs on pension plan assets it becomes clear that the market value is regarded as the fair value. It is stipulated in para. 102 that when no market price is available, the fair value of plan assets is estimated; for example, by discounting expected future cash flows using a discount rate that reflects both the risk associated with the plan assets and the maturity or expected disposal date of those assets (or, if they have no maturity, the expected period until the settlement of the related obligation). Further, unpaid contributions due from the reporting entity to the fund, as well as any non-transferable financial instrument issued by the entity and held by the fund may not be included in the pension plan assets. Plan assets should be reduced further by any liabilities of the fund that do not relate to employee benefits. Where plan assets include qualifying insurance policies that exactly match the amount and the timing of some or all benefits payable under the plan, the fair value of those insurance policies is deemed to be the present value of the related obligations.

There might be occasions where the amount determined under para. 54 may be negative (an asset). If we suppose (taking into account the data presented above) that the fair value of pension plan assets was 65 000, then a negative amount of an asset would be the result of the determination of the existence of a 'defined benefit liability'. This situation arises when, for example, the investment policy of the fund has been highly successful and a surplus exists. An entity should then measure the resulting asset at the lower of:

- the amount determined under para. 54
- and the net total of:
  - any unrecognised actuarial losses and past service cost (see paras 92, 93 and 96)
  - the present value of any economic benefits available in the form of refunds from the plan or reductions in future contributions to the plan. The present value of these economic benefits should be determined using a discount rate which is calculated by reference to market yields at balance sheet date on high quality bonds (see para. 78).

We will illustrate this with the following activity.

ACTIVITY 21.16

The following data are available in relation to a defined benefit plan:

- the present value of the defined benefit obligation 5 000
- unrecognised actuarial losses 200
- unrecognised past service cost 400
- pension plan assets 6 000
- present value of available future refunds ... 50

Calculate the amount resulting from the determination of the defined benefit liability (para. 54) and compare this amount with the limit put forward in para. 58(b).

Activity feedback
Applying para. 54 to the data above results in a negative amount:

- the present value of the defined benefit obligation 5 000

- unrecognised actuarial losses .... –200
- unrecognised past service cost .... –400
- pension plan assets .... –6 000
- negative amount .... –1 600

We arrive at a negative amount of –1 600 (4 400 – 6 000).

The limit under para. 58(b) will be determined as follows:

- unrecognised actuarial losses 200
- unrecognised past service cost 400
- present value of available future refunds ... 50
- total amount 650

The limit of 650 is less than 1 600 (amount determined under para. 54), so the entity will recognise an asset of 650 on its balance sheet.

IAS 19 states further that an entity should determine the present value of defined benefit obligations and the fair value of any plan assets with sufficient regularity that the amounts recognised in the financial statements do not differ materially from the amounts that would be determined at the balance sheet date. IFRIC 14, titled *General Requirements Concerning the Limit on a Defined Benefit Asset*, states that economic benefits, in the form of refunds or reduced future contributions, are available if they can be realised at some point during the life of the plan or when the plan liabilities are settled.

Disclosure in the notes in relation to pension benefits

On the face of the balance sheet of the employer a liability or an asset will be presented. The underlying elements taken into account to determine this pension liability or asset have to be disclosed in the notes of the financial statements (para. 120). Some extensive disclosures are the result.

An entity should disclose the following information about defined benefit plans:

- the entity's accounting policy for recognising actuarial gains and losses
- a general description of the type of plan

- a reconciliation of the assets and liabilities recognised in the balance sheet, showing at least:
  - the present value at the balance sheet date of defined benefit obligations that are wholly unfunded
  - the present value (before deducting the fair value of plan assets) at the balance sheet date of defined benefit obligations that are wholly or partly funded
  - the fair value of any plan assets at the balance sheet date
  - the net actuarial gains or losses not recognised in the balance sheet (see para. 92), if the company uses the corridor approach
  - the past service cost not yet recognised in the balance sheet (see para. 96)
  - any amount not recognised as an asset, because of the limit in para. 58(b)
  - the total amount recognised in the statement of recognised income and expense for each of the following actuarial gains and losses and the effect of the limit in para. 58(b)
- the amounts included in the fair value of plan assets for:
  - each category of the reporting entity's own financial instruments
  - any property occupied by, or other assets used by, the reporting entity
- reconciliation showing the movements during the period in the net liability (or asset) recognised in the balance sheet.

The same remark holds for the total pension cost reported. On the profit and loss account of the employer a single amount will be recorded. The external stakeholder to the firm will gain insight in the individual sub-components of the total pension cost by a disclosure of these elements in the notes together with the actuarial assumptions used (para. 120):

- the total expense recognised in the income statement for each of the following and the line item(s) of the income statement in which they are included:
  - current service cost
  - interest cost
  - expected return on reimbursement right recognised as an asset in accordance with para. 104A
  - actuarial gains and losses
  - past service cost
  - the effect of any curtailment or settlement
- the actual return on plan assets
- the principal actuarial assumptions used as at the balance sheet date, including, where applicable:
  - the discount rates
  - the expected rates of return on any plan assets for the periods presented in the financial statements
  - the expected rates of salary increases (and of changes in an index or other variable specified in the formal or constructive terms of a plan as the basis for future benefit increases)
  - medical cost trend rates
  - any other material actuarial assumptions used.

An entity should disclose each actuarial assumption in absolute terms (for example, as an absolute percentage) and not just as a margin between different percentages or other variables.

To illustrate the level of detail which needs to be provided in relation to the pension plan of a company, the information disclosure of Inbev, the world's largest brewer, in their annual accounts of 2007 in relation to their pension plan is shown here as an example:

Note 24: Employee benefits

InBev maintains in several countries post-employment benefit plans such as pensions and medical care plans as well as other long-term employee benefit plans. In accordance with IAS 19 *Employee Benefits* post-employment benefit plans are classified as either defined contribution plans or defined benefit plans.

Defined contribution plans For defined contribution plans, InBev pays contributions to publicly or privately administered pension funds or insurance contracts. Once the contributions have been paid, the group has no further payment obligation. The regular contribution expenses constitute an expense for the year in which they are due. For 2007, the defined contribution expenses for the company amounted to 5m euro compared to 6m euro for 2006.

Defined benefit plans The company makes contributions to 52 defined benefit plans of which 40 are retirement plans and 12 are medical cost plans. Most plans provide benefits related to pay and years of service. The German, French, Luxemburg and part of the Belgian, Brazilian, Canadian, UK and US plans are unfunded. The assets of the other plans are held in legally separate funds set up in accordance with applicable legal requirements and common practice in each country. The medical cost plans in Canada, US, Belgium and Brazil provide medical benefits to employees and their families during the service period and after retirement in some cases.

The present value of funded obligations includes a 140m euro liability related to two medical plans, for which the benefits are provided through the Fundação Antonio Helena Zerrenner ('FAHZ'). The FAHZ is a legally distinct entity which provides medical, dental, educational and social assistance to current and retired employees of AmBev. On 31 December 2007, the actuarial liabilities related to the benefits provided by the FAHZ are fully offset by an equivalent amount of assets existing in the fund. The net liability recognised in the balance sheet is nil.

The net decrease in outstanding employee benefits by 130m euro as compared to 31 December 2006 is primarily the effect of contributions paid to pension plans (128m euro) and actuarial gains (55m euro), partly offset by 2007 expenses (62m euro) and exchange losses (5m euro).

The company's net liability for post-employment and long-term employee benefit plans comprises the following at 31 December:

Million euro	2007	2006
Present value of funded obligations	(2 241)	(2 289)
Fair value of plan assets	2 256	2 219
Present value of net obligations for funded plans	**15**	**(160)**
Present value of unfunded obligations	(400)	(412)
Present value of net obligations	**(385)**	**(572)**

Million euro	2007	2006
Unrecognised past service cost	3	7
Unrecognised asset	(217)	(154)
Net liability	**(599)**	**(719)**
Other long term employee benefits	(18)	(28)
Total employee benefits	**(617)**	**(747)**
Employee benefits amounts in the balance sheet:		
Liabilities	(624)	(753)
Assets	7	6
Net liability	**(617)**	**(747)**

The other long-term employee benefits balance of 18m euro at 31 December 2007 relates for an amount of 14m euro to long service leave and jubilee benefits while 4m euro represents the Quinsa profit sharing that is payable two years after the close of the related year in which profit was made.

The changes in the present value of the defined benefit obligations are as follows:

Million euro	2007	2006
Defined benefit obligation at 1 January	**(2 701)**	**(2 829)**
Service cost	(69)	(69)
New unvested past service cost		−10
Interest cost	(150)	(153)
Actuarial gains and (losses)	134	(17)
Gains on curtailments	1	1
Reclassifications from provisions	4	−
Reclassifications to assets held for sale	−	19
Exchange differences	(17)	121
Benefits paid	157	216
Defined benefit obligation at 31 December	**(2 641)**	**(2 701)**

The changes in the fair value of plan assets are as follows:

Million euro	2007	2006
Fair value of plan assets at 1 January	**2 129**	**2 005**
Expected return	177	169
Actuarial gains and (losses)	(57)	69
Contributions by InBev	128	177
Contributions by plan participants	11	11
Exchange differences	25	(86)
Assets distributed on settlement	−	(56)
Benefits paid	(157)	(160)
Fair value of plan assets at 31 December	**2 256**	**2 129**

The actual return on plan assets in 2007 and 2006 was 120m euro and 238m euro respectively.

The decrease in contributions by InBev (128m euro in 2007 versus 177m euro in 2006) is primarily explained by higher contributions in Canada in 2006 resulting from the wind-up of certain plans there following restructurings.

The expense recognised in the income statement with regard to defined benefit plans can be detailed as follows:

Million euro	2007	2006
Current service costs	(50)	(59)
Interest cost	(150)	(153)
Expected return on plan assets	177	169
Amortised past service cost	(6)	(1)
New vested past service cost	(7)	1
Gains on settlements or curtailments	1	–
Asset limitation	(27)	(23)
	(62)	**(66)**

The employee benefit expense is included in the following line items of the income statement:

Million euro	2007	2006
Cost of sales	(15)	(17)
Distribution expenses	(13)	(13)
Sales and marketing expenses	(8)	(13)
Administrative expenses	(21)	(20)
Non-recurring items	(5)	(3)
	(62)	**(66)**

Weighted average assumptions used in computing the benefit obligations at the balance sheet date are as follows[1]:

	2007	2006
Discount rate	4.9 %	4.3 %
Future salary increases	3.1 %	2.4 %
Future pension increases	1.8 %	1.1 %
Medical cost trend rate	6.5 % p.a. reducing to 3.8 %	6.5 % p.a. reducing to 3.1 %
Dental claims trend rate	4.1 %	3.9 %
Life expectation for a 40 year old male	81	81
Life expectation for a 40 year old female	85	85

Weighted average assumptions used in computing the net periodic pension cost for the year are as follows:

	2007	2006
Discount rate	4.3 %	4.1 %
Expected return on plan assets	6.6%	6.3 %
Future salary increases	2.4 %	2.3 %
Future pension increases	1.1 %	0.8 %
Medical cost trend rate	6.5 % p.a. reducing to 3.1 %	5.0 % p.a. reducing to 2.1 %
Dental claims trend rate	3.9 %	3.6 %

---

[1]Since the assumptions are nominal rates in different currencies we have converted the foreign rates into euro equivalents based on the 5 year forward currency exchange rates. The weighted average assumptions are calculated based on these euro equivalents.

Assumed medical cost trend rates have a significant effect on the amounts recognised in profit or loss. A one percentage point change in the assumed medical cost trend rates would have the following effects (note that a positive amount refers to a decrease in the obligations or cost while a negative amount refers to an increase in the obligations or cost):

Million euro	2007		2006	
	100 basis points increase	100 basis points decrease	100 basis points increase	100 basis points decrease
Medical cost trend rate				
Effect on the aggregate of the service cost and interest cost of medical plans	(4)	3	(3)	3
Effect on the defined benefit obligation for medical cost	(38)	33	(33)	28

To meet the IAS 1 *Presentation of Financial Statements* disclosure requirements on key sources of estimation uncertainty we have included the results of our sensitivity analysis with regard to the discount rate, the future salary increase and the longevity assumptions.

Million euro	2007		2006	
	50 basis points increase	50 basis points decrease	50 basis points increase	50 basis points decrease
Discount rate				
Effect on the aggregate of the service cost and interest cost of defined benefit plans	3	(3)	4	(4)
Effect on the defined benefit obligation	176	(192)	188	(203)

Million euro	2007		2006	
	50 basis points increase	50 basis points decrease	50 basis points increase	50 basis points decrease
Future salary increase				
Effect on the aggregate of the service cost and interest cost of defined benefit plans	(3)	3	(5)	5
Effect on the defined benefit obligation	(23)	21	(39)	37

Million euro	2007		2006	
	One year increase	One year decrease	One year increase	One year decrease
Longevity				
Effect on the aggregate of the service cost and interest cost of defined benefit plans	(5)	5	(5)	5
Effect on the defined benefit obligation	(71)	70	(72)	71

The above are purely hypothetical changes in individual assumptions holding all other assumptions constant: economic conditions and changes therein will often affect multiple assumptions at the same time and the effects of changes in key assumptions are not linear. Therefore, the above information is not necessarily a reasonable representation of future results.

The fair value of plan assets at 31 December consists of the following:

	2007	2006
Government bonds	35 %	30 %
Corporate bonds	11 %	12 %
Equity instruments	51 %	54 %
Property	1 %	1 %
Cash	1 %	1 %
Insurance contracts	1 %	2 %
	100 %	100 %

The plan assets include indirect investments in ordinary shares issued by the company for a total fair value of 1m euro. The expected rates of return on individual categories of plan assets are determined by reference to relevant indices based on advice of external valuation experts. The overall expected rate of return is calculated by weighting the individual rates in accordance with the anticipated share in the total investment portfolio.

The five year history of the present value of the defined benefit obligations, the fair value of the plan assets and the deficit in the plans is as follows:

Million euro	2007	2006	2005	2004	2003
Present value of the defined benefit obligations	(2 641)	(2 701)	(2 829)	(2 167)	(1 739)
Fair value of plan assets	2 256	2 129	2 005	1 514	1 094
Deficit	(385)	(572)	(824)	(653)	(645)
Experience adjustments : (increase)/ decrease plan liabilities	22	(6)	(33)	–	–
Experience adjustments : increase/ (decrease) plan assets	(57)	69	133	108	–

InBev expects to contribute approximately 92m euro to its defined benefit plans in 2008.

Multi-employer plans

In the introductory discussion on pension benefits, the concept of multi-employer plans was introduced. Paragraphs 29 and 30 of IAS define how a multi-employer should be accounted for. The terms of the plan will determine whether a multi-employer plan will be classified as a defined benefit plan or a defined contribution plan. Where a multi-employer plan is a defined benefit plan, the company shall account for its proportionate share of the defined benefit obligation, plan assets and costs with the plan in the same way as for any other defined benefit plans. When sufficient information is not available to use defined benefit accounting for a multi-employer plan that is classified as a defined benefit plan, the company might account for the plan as if it were a defined contribution plan. In this situation, the employer has to disclose in the notes to its accounts that the pension plan is, in fact, a defined benefit plan together with the reason why there is insufficient information to account for the plan as a defined benefit plan. If there is a surplus or a deficit in the plan that may affect the amount of future contributions, information about the surplus or the deficit (basis for the calculation and the implications) should be provided as well.

In the context of a multi-employer plan a contingent liability (IAS 37) might arise from, for example:

(a) actuarial losses relating to other participating entities because each entity that participates in a multi-employer plan shares in the actuarial risks of every other participating entity, or

(b) any responsibility under the terms of a plan to finance any shortfall in the plan if other entities cease to participate.

Defined benefit plans that share risks between various entities under common control

IAS 19 prescribes the accounting treatment of defined benefit plans that share risks between various entities under common control. How these individual entities under common control have to account for promised pension benefit in their separate annual accounts depends on whether or not a contractual agreement or stated policy exists for charging the net defined benefit cost for the plan as a whole to the individual group entities measured in accordance with IAS 19. If such a contract or policy exists the total pension cost determined according to IAS 19 for the group as a whole will be split over the individual accounts of the separate entities under common control. If no such policy or contracts exists, then the total pension cost determined in line with IAS 19 will be recognised in the individual statement of the group entity which is the legally sponsoring employer for the plan. The other group entities account only for their contribution to the plan in their individual accounts. Participation in such a plan is a related party transaction for each individual group entity and the necessary disclosures on related party transactions have to be made.

TERMINATION BENEFITS

An entity should recognise termination benefits as a liability and an expense when, and only when, the entity is demonstrably committed to either:

- terminate the employment of an employee or group of employees before the normal retirement date
- or provide termination benefits as a result of an offer made in order to encourage voluntary redundancy.

An entity is demonstrably committed to a termination when, and only when, the entity has a detailed formal plan for the termination and is without realistic possibility of withdrawal. The detailed plan should include, as a minimum:

- the location, function, and approximate number of employees whose services are to be terminated
- the termination benefits for each job classification or function

- the time at which the plan will be implemented. Implementation should begin as soon as possible and the period of time to complete implementation should be such that material changes to the plan are not likely.

Where termination benefits fall due more than 12 months after the balance sheet date, they should be discounted using the discount rate specified in para. 78.

In the case of an offer made to encourage voluntary redundancy, the measurement of termination benefits should be based on the number of employees expected to accept the offer (para. 140).

ACCOUNTING BY THE PENSION FUND

When pension benefits are externally funded the entity to which the amounts are transferred must also prepare financial statements. When the amounts are transferred to an insurance company, the financial statements of the insurance company will give a picture of the financial position of the insurance company.

Financial reporting by pension funds is regulated by IAS 26 *Accounting and Reporting by Retirement Benefit Plans*. The last revision of IAS 26 dates from 1994, which is important to stress, since IAS 19, which focuses on the financial statements of the employer, has been revised twice since then. The financial situation of a pension fund will not be presented in the 'classical' format of financial statements, namely consisting of a balance sheet and an income statement. IAS 26 defines the contents of a pension fund 'report' which should be prepared. Also in relation to this report the type of pension benefit (defined contribution or defined benefit) promised plays a role.

When amounts resulting from a defined contribution plan are transferred to a pension fund, the report (para. 13) contains a statement of net assets available for benefits and a description of the funding policy.

When amounts resulting from a defined benefit plan are transferred to a pension fund, the report of the fund should contain either (para. 17):

- a statement that shows:
  - the net assets available for benefits
  - the actuarial present value of promised retirement benefits, distinguishing between vested benefits and non-vested benefits
  - the resulting excess or deficit
- or a statement of net assets available for benefits including either:
  - a note disclosing the actuarial present value of promised retirement benefits, distinguishing between vested benefits and non-vested benefits – or a reference to this information in an accompanying actuarial report.

If an actuarial valuation has not been prepared at the date of the report, the most recent valuation should be used as a base and the date of the valuation disclosed.

We notice immediately that the concept of defined benefit obligation is not introduced here, IAS 26 only mentions actuarial present value of promised retirement benefits. In order to improve the information value of the annual reports of pension funds a revision of IAS 26 in line with the vision of IAS 19 would be welcome. It is not certain, however, whether the business world would also welcome a revision in the near future.

SUMMARY

IAS 19 is considered to be one of the more technical Standards.

The same remark applies to IFRS 2, *Share-based Payment*. Pension plans represent assets, liabilities and costs for the sponsoring company. The related amounts are not always easy to determine and the impact on a company may be overlooked. In the acquisition deal of KLM by Air France, the French made a surprising post-acquisition discovery. When the deal was closed and the acquisition price determined, the company management discovered pension surpluses in the pension plan of KLM. This surplus net pension asset could be regarded as an asset of the Air France–KLM group. This meant that Air France had acquired KLM with negative goodwill. The net pension asset was the difference between pension liabilities of €7627 million and pension assets of €8912 million, implying a surplus of €1285 million. To make sure that they accounted for this surplus, which occurred under IAS (KLM had used Dutch GAAP before the acquisition by Air France), Air France–KLM consulted the IASB on its interpretation of IAS 19.

This illustrates that pension valuation and pension accounting is not easy. The level of technicality however depends on the type of pension promise made.

Accounting for defined contribution plans is less technical than accounting for defined benefit plans. It has been noticed that in recent years defined contribution plans have become more popular. Could the stricter accounting requirements which make the uncertainties and the risks involved in a defined benefit plan more visible have something to do with this?

EXERCISES

Suggested answers to exercises marked ✓ are to be found on the Student side of the companion website.

Suggested answers to the remaining exercises are to be found on the Instructor side of the companion website.

✓ **1** Company Rebo has five directors, who all participate in the following share-based remuneration plan with cash alternatives. The directors have the right to choose between 600 shares or the value of 500 shares paid in cash at vesting date. If the directors opt for the shares they may not sell them for three years. The only vesting requirement is that the directors should remain three years with the company.

At the grant date the entity's share price is €30. At the end of years 1, 2 and 3 the share prices are €33, €36 and €40. The fair value of the share alternative is €28 per share. Calculate the remuneration expense for the equity-based remuneration system of Rebo. Indicate also which accounts are credited. Consider further both situations, namely the directors choose the cash alternative and the directors choose the equity alternative.

✓ **2** IAS 19, *Employee Benefits* was issued in February 1998. Amongst other things the Standard deals with the treatment of post-employment benefits such as pensions and other retirement benefits.

Post-employment benefits are classified as either defined contribution or defined benefit plans.

Klondike

	at 31 March 2001 $000	at 31 March 2002 $000
Present value obligation	1 500	1 750
Fair value of plan assets	1 500	1 650
Current service cost – year to 31 March 2002		160
Contributions paid – year to 31 March 2002		85
Benefits paid to employees – year to 31 March 2002		125
Net cumulative unrecognised gains at 1 April 2001	200	
Expected return on plan assets at 1 April 2001 is	12%	
Discount rate for plan liabilities at 1 April 2001	10%	

Required:

(a) Describe the relevant features and required accounting treatment of defined contribution and defined benefit plans under IAS 19.

(b) Klondike operates a defined benefit post-retirement plan for its employees. The plan is reviewed annually. Klondike's actuaries have provided the information in the table above.

The average remaining working lives of Klondike's employees at 31 March 2001 is ten years.

Required:

Prepare extracts of Klondike's financial statements for the year to 31 March 2002 in compliance with IAS 19, *Employee Benefits* insofar as the information permits.

(ACCA June 2002)

✓ **3** Company Crux grants share options to its employees at 1.1.X1. Each employee will receive ten options if he/she stays with the company for the next three years. At grant date the turnover percentage of employees is estimated at 20%. The fair value of the option at grant date is €20. The company grants these options to the 100 employees in service at grant date. During the first year four employees leave and the company revises its estimate on employee turnover from 20% to 15% (= 15 employees leaving). During year 2 another four employees leave, the entity revises the estimate to 12%. At the end of the third year six employees leave the company. The share options of the remaining employees vest at the end of year 3.

Calculate the remuneration expense for years 1, 2 and 3 following from this share option plan. What is the credit side when this expense is recorded in the books of the company?

✓ **4** At the beginning of year 1, an entity grants to 20 senior executives 1000 share options, each based on two conditions. First, the executive has to remain with the entity until the end of year 3. Second the share options may not be exercised unless the share price has increased from €100 at the beginning of year 1 to above €130 at the end of year 3. If the share price is above €130 at year 3, the share options may be exercised at any time during the next five years.

The entity applies a binomial option-pricing model, which takes into account the possibility that the share price will exceed €130 at the end of year 3 (in this case the share options become exercisable) and the possibility that the share price will not exceed €130 at the end of year 3 (and then the options will be forfeited). It estimates the fair value of the share options with this market condition to be €48 per option.

At the end of year 1, the company estimates the turnover of senior executives at 2%. In the second year one executive leaves the company, but the turnover estimate remains the same. During the third year two executives leave the company. Calculate the remuneration expense for each year in which an expense needs to be recorded. Which account will be credited when the remuneration expense is recorded.

5   An entity grants 100 share appreciation rights to its 200 employees on the condition that they remain with the firm for two years. At the end of these two years, the benefits vest and the employees may exercise the options in the two consecutive years. The benefits will be paid out in cash and the cash amount will be determined by the intrinsic value at the date of exercise. The fair value of the appreciation rights and the intrinsic value of the rights are presented below.

Year	Fair value	Intrinsic value
1	31	
2	36	30
3		40

At the end of the first year ten employees leave the company and the company estimates that in the next year 15 more employees will leave. In year 2, 16 employees leave and 74 employees exercise their share appreciation rights immediately when their benefits vest and the remaining 100 exercise their rights in year 3.

Calculate the remuneration expenses and the amount of the liability to be recognised as a result of these share-based payment transactions.

6   Discuss the 'corridor' approach for the recognition of actuarial gains and losses. Take into account in the discussion the framework for the preparation and presentation of financial statements. Do you agree with the 'corridor' approach or are you in favour of another recognition approach? Give arguments to support your decision.

7   For the determination and recognition of the current service cost and the defined pension liability one particular actuarial cost method has been chosen, namely the projected unit credit method. This method takes into account expected future salary increases. Comment on this decision. What is your opinion on taking into account these expected salary increases? What arguments could be used in favour of including future salary increases? Are there any arguments against the inclusion of future salary increases?

8   The actuarial assumptions 'discount factor' and 'expected market return' are different elements in the opinion of the IASB and as a result the impact of both assumptions is included separately in the total pension cost. Would the data be less reliable or value relevant if the same value were used for the discount factor and the expected market return? Comment on your opinion.

9   Consider the assumptions 'discount factor' and 'expected market return' again. Take into account the different funding or financing systems (internal and external funding) which companies can use. Does the separate disclosure of the interest cost component and the

return on assets increase the information value of the pension data communicated to external users of the financial statements? Discuss.

10 State pension plans are defined in IAS 19 as multi-employer plans. Multi-employer plans can be either of a defined benefit type or of a defined contribution type. Had you been in the position of the standard setter, would you have included the treatment of the state pension plans in the treatment of the multi-employer plans? Present arguments in favour of your answer.

11 The recognition of equity benefits on the balance sheet and income statement is currently under discussion. If you were in the standard setter's position, how would you recognise and measure equity benefits? Take into account the conceptual framework and try to be consistent with it.

12 The following statements relate to accounting for retirement benefits under the provisions of IAS 19, *Employee Benefits*. [The 'net pension asset' is the fair value of plan assets less the present value of plan liabilities.]

 (i) Other things being equal, the net pension asset increases when interest rates increase.

 (ii) Other things being equal, the net pension asset decreases when share prices fall.

 (iii) Where the terms of retirement benefits are altered so as to provide immediate additional benefits to retired members, then the cost of the additional benefits should be recognised in the income statement over a period equal to the average life expectancy of the retired members.

Which of the statements are true?

A (i) and (ii) only

B (i) and (iii) only

C (ii) and (iii) only

D All of them

(CIMA Nov 2003)

13 E pays contributions into a post-employment defined benefit plan on behalf of its employees. The balance sheet of the entity at 30 April 2003 showed a net pension liability of $60 million. During the year to 30 April 2004:

- The entity closed down a division and the curtailment of retirement benefits for employees made redundant resulted in a gain of $4 million.

- The estimated current service cost was $8 million.

- The expected return on assets was $6 million.

- The unwinding of the discount on the pension liability was $4 million.

- There was no recognition of actuarial gains or losses in the income statement.

The net pension liability at 30 April 2004 was $65 million [before incorporating the actuarial gain or loss for the year].
 What is the actuarial gain or loss for the year ended 30 April 2004?

A A loss of $1 million

B A gain of $1 million

C   A loss of $3 million

D   A gain of $3 million

(CIMA May 2004)

14   At 31 March 2007, the present value of AZB's pension obligation is $1 634 000. The fair value of the pension plan assets is $1 337 000. Unrecognised actuarial losses are $224 000.

What is the amount of the liability in respect of the pension scheme that should be recognised in the balance sheet?

A $73 000

B $297 000

C $521 000

D $1 634 000

(CIMA May 2007)

15   The following information relates to the defined benefits pension scheme of BGA, a listed entity.

The present value of the scheme obligations at 1 November 2006 was $18 360 000, while the fair value of the scheme assets at that date was $17 770 000. During the financial year ended 31 October 2007, a total of $997 000 was paid into the scheme in contributions. Current service cost for the year was calculated at $1 655 000, and actual benefits paid were $1 860 300. The applicable interest cost for the year was 6.5% and the expected return on plan assets was 9.4%.

The present value of the scheme obligations at 31 October 2007 was calculated as $18 655 500, and the fair value of scheme assets at that date was $18 417 180.

BGA adopts the '10% corridor' criterion in IAS 19 *Employee Benefits* for determining the extent of recognition of actuarial gains and losses. The average remaining service life of the employees was 10 years. Net unrecognised actuarial losses on 1 November 2006 were $802 000.

Required:

(a)   Calculate the actuarial gain or loss on BGA's pension scheme assets and liabilities for the year ended 31 October 2007.

(b)   Calculate the extent to which, if at all, actuarial gains or losses should be recognised in BGA's income statement for the year ended 31 October 2007, using the '10% corridor' criterion.

(CIMA NOV 2007)

16   Kappa is an entity that operates in a sector where the recruitment and retention of high-quality employees is particularly important in order to achieve corporate goals. You are the financial controller of Kappa and you have recently received a memorandum from a member of the board of directors. The memorandum includes the following key issues:

(i)   The board is eager to reward employees appropriately but is aware that large salary payments have an immediate impact on the liquidity and earnings per share of Kappa.

(ii)   A more appropriate method of remuneration is to grant key employees share options that will vest at a future date if the employees comply with specified conditions (such as continued employment) or achieve specific performance targets (such as completing an assignment to a specified standard or achieving a specified growth in the share price). This would allow employees to exercise the options at an appropriate time for them and would prevent an immediate impact on the liquidity or earnings per share of Kappa at the grant date.

Required:
Draft a reply that responds to the observations made by the board. Your reply should focus on the impact on the balance sheet and income statement of Kappa rather than the personal tax positions of the employees. Your reply should contain a summary of the appropriate provisions of IFRS 2, *Share-based Payment*.

(ACCA June 2007)

CHANGING PRICES AND HYPERINFLATIONARY ECONOMIES

22

OBJECTIVES After studying this chapter you should be able to:

- outline regulatory requirements in relation to the issues of accounting for inflation and changing prices discussed in Chapters 4–7

- describe, apply and appraise the requirements of IAS 29 concerning hyperinflationary economies

- explain the implications of adjusting, or not adjusting, for changes in general purchasing power in economies with material inflation.

INTRODUCTION

We spent considerable time on the alternative theoretical and practical possibilities regarding measurement alternatives in Part One, Chapters 4–7. We also briefly looked at some of the national attitudes and national regulations of earlier years. It is not necessary to repeat this material or to revisit the thinking behind it. This chapter limits itself to coverage of international regulation on the matter.

EU FOURTH DIRECTIVE

The majority of the Directive is couched in historical terms, but it does, in Article 33, permit member states to allow and to require a wide variety of alternative methods, provided only that, if such methods are used, information is given in the notes to the accounts sufficient for the reader to work out what the balance sheet figures would have been under the historical cost approach. National reactions to this in subsequent national legislation by European countries were broadly what we would expect from our discussion in Chapter 2, i.e. UK, Ireland and the Netherlands, for example, do allow such variations and most mainland European countries do not.

IAS GAAP

As we pointed out in Part One, inflation and price increases in the 1970s were much higher in the main developed economies than is the case now.

In 1977 the IASC issued IAS 6, *Accounting Responses to Changing Prices*, which required the disclosure of the effect of any procedures applied to reflect the impact of specific or general price changes. Subsequently the IASC replaced IAS 6 with IAS 15, which required the use of restatement on the basis of either the general price level or current costs when the reporting currency was subject to a significant (but unspecified) degree of inflation. In 1989 the IASC followed an approach similar to that of the FASB, by making IAS 15 optional. In the same year the IASC issued IAS 29, which requires general price level restatement when the reporting currency is subject to hyperinflation. It is worth noting, however, that IAS GAAP are applied in a number of countries with less developed economies, where significant inflation (but not necessarily hyperinflation) may be prevalent. Yet IAS 15 appears to have been little used in practice. It has now been completely withdrawn, with effect from 1 January 2005.

IAS 29, *Financial Reporting in Hyperinflationary Economies*, is another matter. IAS 29 requires that if the functional currency used by an entity is the currency of a hyperinflationary economy, then the entity's financial statements should be restated in units of the same purchasing power, using the measuring unit current at the balance sheet dates (units of current purchasing power). According to IAS 29, para. 37, this restatement should be made using 'a general price index that reflects changes in general purchasing power' and it is preferable that the same index be used by all entities that report in the currency of the same economy.

The restated financial statements should be presented as the primary financial statements and separate presentation of the unrestated financial statements is discouraged. The corresponding figures for the previous period required by IAS 1, *Presentation of Financial Statements* (see Chapter 8), and any information in respect of earlier periods should also be restated in terms of units of current purchasing power at the balance sheet date (IAS 29, paras 7–8). The gain or loss on net monetary position (see later) should be separately disclosed as part of net income (IAS 29, para. 9).

The determination of the functional currency in any particular case, previously discussed in SIC 19, is now covered in the newly revised IAS 21 (see Chapter 29). It is defined as the currency of the primary economic environment in which the group operates. As a result of these changes, an entity can no longer avoid restatement under IAS 29 by adopting a stable currency, such as the functional currency of its parent, as its functional currency, a dodge not prevented in the original IAS 21 and 29 taken together. The possible implications are well illustrated in the case study on Aeroflot, which follows on p. 533.

IAS 29, para. 3, sets out five characteristics of the economic environment as indicators of hyperinflation, of which the fifth is the most frequently cited:

1 The general population prefers to keep its wealth in non-monetary assets or in a relatively stable foreign currency.

2 The general population regards monetary amounts not in terms of the local currency but in terms of a relatively stable foreign currency.

3 Sales and purchases on credit take place at prices that compensate for the expected loss of purchasing power during the credit period even when it is short.

4 Interest rates, wages and prices are linked to a price index.

5 The cumulative inflation rate over three years is approaching or exceeds 100% (i.e. the average annual inflation rate over three years is approaching or exceeds $33^1/_3\%$).

The general principles of IAS 29, when applicable, are essentially the CPP approach discussed in Chapter 7. Monetary items are not restated because they are already expressed in terms of the monetary units current at the balance sheet date (current purchasing power unit). In the case of monetary items that are linked by agreement to changes in prices, such as index-linked bonds and loans, their carrying amounts adjusted in accordance with the agreement are used in the restated balance sheet. Other balance sheet amounts are restated to amounts in units of current purchasing power by applying a general price index, unless they are already carried at amounts in units of current purchasing power, such as current market value or net realisable value (IAS 29, paras 11–14).

For items carried at cost or cost less depreciation, the restated cost or cost less depreciation is determined by applying to the historical costs and accumulated depreciation (if any) the change in a selected general price index from the date of acquisition to the balance sheet date. For items carried at revalued amounts, the revalued amount and accumulated depreciation (if any) are restated by applying the change in the price index from the date of the latest revaluation to the balance sheet date.

If records of the acquisition of property, plant, and equipment do not permit the ascertainment or estimation of the acquisition dates, it may be necessary, when the Standard is first applied, to use an independent professional valuation of the items concerned as a basis for their restatement. If no general price index is available to cover the period between acquisition and the balance sheet date, an estimate of the changes in general purchasing power of the reporting currency over that period may be made by using the changes in the exchange rate between the reporting currency and a relatively stable foreign currency (IAS 29, paras 11–18).

The restated amount of a non-monetary item is reduced (in accordance with the appropriate IAS) when it exceeds the amount recoverable from the item's future use, sale or disposal (IAS 29, para. 19). It is not appropriate both to restate capital expenditure (fixed assets) financed by borrowing and to capitalise that part of the borrowing costs that compensates for inflation.

At the beginning of the first period of application of IAS 29, the components of owners' equity are restated by applying a general price index from the dates on which the components were contributed or otherwise arose, except for retained earnings and any revaluation surplus. Any revaluation surplus from prior periods is eliminated and restated retained earnings is the residual amount (balancing figure) in the restated balance sheet. Subsequently, all components of owners' equity are restated by applying a general price index from the beginning of the period (or the date of contribution, if later). The movements for the period in owners' equity should be disclosed in accordance with IAS 1, *Presentation of Financial Statements* (see Chapter 9) (IAS 29, paras 24–25).

All items in the income statement should be expressed in terms of end of year current purchasing power units. Hence, all income statement amounts need to be restated by applying the change in general price index between the dates at which the amounts were recorded and the balance sheet date. In practice, average index values for sub-periods, such as months, would normally be used, as in the case of average exchange rates used for the translation of foreign currency amounts under IAS 21 (see Chapter 29).

According to IAS 29, para. 27, the gain or loss on the entity's net monetary position may be estimated by applying the change in the general price index to the weighted average for the period of the difference between monetary assets and monetary liabilities.

The gain or loss on the net monetary position should be included in net income. Any adjustment to index-linked assets or liabilities (as mentioned earlier) is offset against the gain or loss on net monetary position. It is suggested that the gain or loss in net monetary position should be presented in the income statement together with interest income and expense and foreign exchange differences related to invested or borrowed funds (IAS 29, paras 27–28).

If an investee accounted for under the equity method reports in the currency of a hyperinflationary country, the financial statements of the investee are restated in accordance with IAS 29 in order to calculate the investor's share of its net assets and results of operations (IAS 29, para. 20).

All items in the cash flow statement should be restated in terms of current purchasing power units at the balance sheet date (IAS 29, para. 33). Comparative figures from the previous reporting period and other comparative information that is disclosed in respect of prior periods should be restated in terms of units of current purchasing power at the balance sheet date (IAS 29, para. 34).

These requirements assume an original historical cost set of financial statements. However, IAS 29 also allows for the possibility of 'current cost' financial statements as the basis. Items stated at current cost are already expressed in units of current purchasing power and so are not restated. Other items are restated as described for historical cost balance sheets earlier (IAS 29, para. 29).

The current cost income statement reports items in terms of the purchasing power of the monetary unit at the times when the underlying transactions or events occurred. For example, cost of goods sold and depreciation are recorded at their current costs at the time of consumption. Therefore, all amounts need to be restated into current purchasing power units at the balance sheet date (IAS 29, para. 30). Gain or loss on net monetary position should be calculated and accounted for as already described (IAS 29, para. 31).

A parent that reports in the currency of a hyperinflationary economy may have subsidiaries that also report in currencies of hyperinflationary economies. The financial statements of such subsidiaries should be restated in accordance with IAS 29 as described earlier, before being included in the process of consolidation. In the case of foreign subsidiaries, financial statements (restated as described earlier if they are in the currency of a hyperinflationary economy) should be translated into the reporting currency at closing rates as required by IAS 21.

If financial statements with different reporting dates are consolidated, all items, whether monetary or non-monetary, should be restated into units of current purchasing power at the date of the consolidated financial statements (IAS 29, paras 35–36).

When an entity discontinues the preparation and presentation of financial statements in accordance with IAS 29 because the economy of its reporting currency is no longer hyperinflationary, the amounts that are expressed in current purchasing power units as at the end of the previous reporting period should be treated as the basis for the carrying amounts in its subsequent financial statements (IAS 29, para. 38). In other words, these increased numbers are retained as the new 'cost' figure, which in a sense, they are not.

The following disclosures should be made:

1 The fact that the financial statements and the comparative figures have been restated for changes in the general purchasing power of the reporting currency and are stated in terms of the unit of purchasing power current at the balance sheet date.

2 Whether the underlying financial statements are based on historical costs or current costs.

3 The identity and level of the general price index used at the balance sheet date and the movement in this index during the current and previous reporting periods (IAS, para. 39).

Case study

If you have any doubts about technicalities involved in this discussion, you should reread Chapter 7 at this point. There is no doubt that the Russian airline, Aeroflot, was operating in a hyperinflationary economy according to IAS 29 in the year ended 31 December 1999. The Aeroflot financials quote annual inflation rates for the relevant three years as follows.

For year ended 31 December	Annual inflation
1999	36.70%
1998	84.40%
1997	11.00%

However, Aeroflot, among its 'principal accounting policies', reported as follows:

The statutory (i.e. Russian statutory) amounts of non-monetary assets and liabilities have been adjusted to their historical cost denominated in US dollars, the functional currency of the Group (except for certain older assets independently valued in US dollars) so as to present the financial statements in accordance with IAS. The US dollar has been determined as the reporting currency of the Group on the basis that the majority of revenues are denominated in US dollars and settled in US dollars or other foreign currency, the majority of assets and liabilities are denominated in foreign currency, as is a significant portion of operating expenses. Accordingly, these financial statements are presented in US dollars.... Since US dollars are not the currency of a hyperinflationary economy, the provisions of IAS 29 have not been applied.

The consolidated statement of operations of Aeroflot for 1999 is shown in Table 22.1. A very significant reduction in the scale of operations is indicated. Revenue in 1999 is 17% down on 1998 and operating costs are 18% down. However the exchange rates for the rouble to the dollar are given in the notes as follows:

At 31 December	Exchange rate
1997	$1 = 5.96 r
1998	$1 = 20.65 r
1999	$1 = 27.00 r

Making a rough and simplistic calculation, the average rate of exchange for 1999 can be taken as the mid-point of the beginning and end rates and similarly for 1998. This simplistic calculation gives an average rate for 1999 of 23.82 and for 1998 of 13.31.

TABLE 22.1	Aeroflot and subsidiaries' consolidated statements of operations, 1999

	Year ended 31 December 1999	Year ended 31 December 1998
	$ million	$ million
Traffic revenue	865.4	1 000.0
Other revenue	300.8	403.1
Revenue	**1 166.2**	**1 403.1**
Operating costs	(908.9)	(1 103.9)
Staff costs	(118.0)	(170.3)
Depreciation and amortisation expense	(132.0)	(135.1)
Operating costs	**(1 158.9)**	**(1 409.3)**
Operating income (loss)	7.3	(6.2)
Interest expense	(52.2)	(32.2)
Interest income	0.9	2.0
Share of income in associated undertakings	4.6	4.4
Foreign exchange and translation loss, net	(6.8)	(18.4)
Non-operating income (expenses), net	40.1	(25.1)
Loss before taxation and minority interest	(6.1)	(75.5)
Taxation	(52.2)	(134.2)
Loss after taxation	(58.3)	(209.7)
Minority interest	(1.3)	(1.2)
Loss	(59.6)	(210.9)
Loss per share	($0.05)	($0.19)

ACTIVITY 22.1

Recalculate the figure for revenues and operating costs from Table 22.1 into historical roubles using the multiplicands given in the illustration and comment on the results.

Activity feedback

The figures are as shown in Table 22.2.

Without claiming accuracy for the figures used, it is clear that the trend of activity indicated in nominal roubles is the exact opposite of that suggested in the published financials. A significant increase in the scale of operations is now indicated. Also, the result for 1999 in nominal roubles is a profit under these assumptions (albeit small), not a loss. A further refinement of the figures in Table 22.2 is possible. The 1998 figures are expressed (as calculated) in 1998 roubles. Arguably, these should be re-expressed into 1999 roubles for comparison with the reported 1999 figures, i.e. the entire 1998 column in Table 22.2 could be multiplied by 136.7%. This would suggest that in real terms that 1998 and 1999 revenues and expenses were not significantly different. Who said that accounting is an exact discipline?!

The other question that arises in relation to the Aeroflot example is whether or not the bold claim in the quoted accounting policy that the treatment used, in avoiding IAS 29 adjustments, was in accordance with IAS, is actually correct. The answer is, possibly but, from 1 January 2005, this treatment would definitely not be permitted.

TABLE 22.2	Aeroflot operating results (recalculated in roubles from Table 22.1)	
	Year ended 31 December 1999	*Year ended 31 December 1998*
	000 million roubles	000 million roubles
Traffic revenue	20.614	13.310
Other revenue	7.165	5.365
Revenue	27.779	18.675
Operating costs	21.650	14.693
Staff costs	2.811	2.267
Depreciation and amortisation	3.144	1.798
Operating costs	27.605	18.758
Operating income (loss)	0.174	(0.083)

SUMMARY

In this chapter we explored the IAS regulations relating to accounting for inflation, as contained in IAS 29 and related these regulations to the theoretical issues discussed in Part One.

EXERCISES

Suggested answers to exercises marked ✓ are to be found on the Student side of the companion website.

Suggested answers to the remaining exercises are to be found on the Instructor side of the companion website.

✓ **1** Which phenomena is IAS 29 adjusting for when it is applied in the preparation of financial statements?

2 The idea that a regular annual inflation rate of 35% requires CPP adjustments, but that a regular annual inflation rate of 25% does not, is quite absurd. Discuss.

3 Rework a numerical exercise from Chapter 7.

STATEMENTS OF CASH FLOWS

23

OBJECTIVES After studying this chapter you should be able to:

- identify the need for a statement of cash flows

- describe the difference between funds flow and cash flow

- explain why the IASB found it necessary to require cash flow rather than funds flow statements

- describe the requirements of IAS 7, *Statements of Cash Flow*

- prepare a statement of cash flows

- identify any problems in relation to a statement of cash flows

- compare different GAAPs for statements of cash flow.

INTRODUCTION

A statement of cash flows, as we will see later, provides additional useful information to users, additional, that is, to the income statement and balance sheet of an entity. The cash flow statement emphasises cash and liquidity rather than revenue, expenses and profit. IAS 7, which was first issued in 1977, originally required a funds flow statement not a statement of cash flows. IAS 7 was revised in 1992 and now requires a statement of cash flows. Also note that IAS 7's title before it was changed in 2007, as a result of changes in terminology introduced by IAS 1, was *Cash Flow Statements*. We will also discuss the difference between funds flow and cash flow within this chapter.

PROFIT VERSUS CASH

The traditional accounting process is an uncertain and complex process. Not only is profit determination complex, it is potentially misleading. In any accounting year there will be a mixture of complete and incomplete transactions. Transactions are complete when they have led to a final cash settlement and these cause no profit measurement difficulties. Considerable problems arise, however, in dealing with incomplete transactions, where the profit or loss figure can only be estimated by means of the accruals concept, whereby revenue and costs are:

> matched with one another so far as their relationship can be established or justifiably assumed and dealt with in the profit and loss account of the period to which they relate.

Thus, the profit for the past year is dependent on the validity of many assumptions about the future, e.g. the future life of assets is estimated in order to calculate the depreciation charge for the past year.

ACTIVITY 23.1

Two short statements about the same business in the same year follow. Summarise in words what each statement is telling us and suggest reasons for the differences between them.

A		€000s
Sales		410
less Cost of sales		329
		81
less Other expenses		36
		45
less Depreciation		13
		32
less Taxation provided		13
		19
less Dividend provided		8
Retained		11
B		€000s
Sales received		387
less Payments for goods for sale		333
		54
less Other expenses paid		32
		22
less Capital expenditure		20

		2
less Taxation paid		14
		(12)
less Dividend paid		7
Increase in borrowing		(19)

Activity feedback

Clearly, statement A is an income statement. It shows the revenues and expenses, calculated on the traditional bases, the taxation charges relating to the year and the dividends which it has been decided should be paid out to shareholders in relation to that year. It shows a profit and implies (although we do not know the size of the business) a successful year.

Statement B is a statement of cash movement in the year – a summary of the cash book but analysed into the various reasons the cash has moved. The individual differences between the two statements will be due to changes in accruals, prepayments and the like. Overall, statement B shows a reduction in the cash resources of the business before the payment of the dividend and obviously shows an even bigger contraction in the cash resources of the business after the dividend payout in the year. Statement B surely implies an unsuccessful year.

The greater the volume of incomplete transactions, the greater the degree of estimation and, accordingly, the greater the risk that investors could turn out to have been misled if actual outcomes deviated from estimates.

To explore the differences between cash flow and profit reporting, consider Activity 23.1 on the previous page.

CASH FLOW REPORTING

People often talk about 'cash flows' or claim to be in favour of 'cash flow statements' or 'cash flow reporting' without being too precise about what they mean. In fact, different people are likely to mean significantly different things and it is very important that we are able to separate out the various situations and arguments one from the other.

At one level, it can be suggested that cash flow reporting, actual and budgeted, should completely replace both the income statement (on whatever basis) and balance sheet. The argument for this (ignoring barter situations) is that only cash represents and demonstrates an increase or decrease in the business resources and that this suggests both that only cash should be reported and that only cash need be reported. This argument is surely untenable. Users need information about changes in the command of a business organisation over resources, over goods and services or the power to obtain goods and services.

At a second level, it can be suggested that some form of cash flow statement on the lines of statement B in Activity 23.1, since it obviously gives information which is potentially useful and which is additional to and different from the information in the income statement should be required as an additional statement in the final reporting package. This is surely logical. Indeed, it is arguably precisely because an income statement for the year is not a good indicator of the cash flow position for the year and because a cash flow statement for the year is not a good indicator of the profit and loss position for the year that the argument for including both is so powerful.

However a weakness of a statement of cash flows, like that in Activity 23.1, is that it is an historical statement, as is a balance sheet and income statement. It gives no indication of future cash flows and whether an entity will be able to meet its debts in the future. A forecast statement of cash flows would be required for this.

FUNDS FLOW OR CASH FLOW?

The funds flow statement as traditionally prepared for many years was, conceptually speaking, an extremely odd animal. It tried to adjust away some, but not all, of the accrual adjustments used in the creation of the income statement to start with. Historically, the reason for much of this obscurity was that the funds flow statement, being an additional statement not required by the law, was deliberately designed not to give additional information, merely to rearrange already available information in a different form. Basically the funds flow statement concentrated on changes in net current assets rather than cash.

So what is funds flow? Activity 23.2 should illustrate this for you.

ACTIVITY 23.2

An extract from the balance sheet of A entity as at 31 December 20X2:

	€000s 31.12.X9	€000s 31.12.X8
Inventory	4 300	4 600
Accounts receivable	2 600	1 300
Cash and bank	1 200	2 500
	8 100	8 400
Accounts payable	6 500	7 900
Working capital	1 600	500

Identify the change in funds.

Activity feedback

If we look solely at cash we could state that A had experienced a decrease in cash of €1 300 000 over the year. Contrariwise, looking at working capital/net current assets provides a much better position, an increase of €1 100 000 over the year. But which figure should users of accounts have regard to when taking decisions?

Advantages of cash flow over funds flow

These can be summarised as follows:

- Funds flow data based on movements in working capital can obscure movements relevant to the liquidity and viability of an entity. For example, a significant decrease in cash available may be masked by an increase in inventory or accounts receivable. Entities may, therefore, run out of cash while reporting increases in working capital. Similarly, a decrease in working capital does not necessarily indicate a cash shortage and a danger of failure.

- As cash flow monitoring is a normal feature of business life and not a specialised accounting technique, cash flow is a concept which is more widely understood than are changes in working capital.

- Cash flows can be a direct input into a business valuation model and, therefore, historical cash flows may be relevant in a way not possible for funds flow data.

ACTIVITY 23.3

State whether you believe, given your knowledge so far, that cash flow is understandable, relevant, reliable and complete.

Activity feedback

1 *Understandable.* Certainly, cash is a concept that most people understand, whereas accrual accounting takes us a few years to learn and even more years to understand the need for!

2 *Relevant.* Cash certainly is relevant as without it a business cannot operate. Entities may be able to show a healthy profit but have a very poor cash position as they are relying on borrowed funds.

3 *Reliable.* Cash is the end product of a transaction. It is realised! Whereas funds based on profit require us to estimate a point of realisation of revenue prior to receipt of cash and the ultimate realisation of cash can be in doubt. Cash is certainly free from bias.

4 *Complete.* Is anything that is historical information providing a complete picture? A statement of cash flows shows information about the reporting entity's cash flows in the reporting period, but this provides incomplete information for assessing future cash flows. Some cash flows result from transactions that took place in an earlier period and some cash flows are expected to result in further cash flows in a future period.

- A funds flow statement is based largely on the difference between two balance sheets. It reorganises such data, but does not provide new data. The statement of cash flows may include data not disclosed in a funds flow statement.

So does a statement of cash flows have the relevant characteristics of useful information? Let us see if you can answer the question (see Activity 23.3).

Looking back to Activity 23.2 where we noted that a healthy funds flow (working capital) of €1.1m masked a decrease in cash flow of €1.3m we can see that the selection of funds or cash flow can have a major impact on a user's interpretation of an entity's financial position. It is also worth noting that cash is the 'life blood' of an entity and without it they cannot operate. Cash is also rather a difficult figure to manipulate.

REQUIREMENTS OF IAS 7

Scope

The IASB viewed cash flow reporting as so important that there are no exemptions for any entities. No matter what an entity's principal revenue-producing activities might be they need cash to conduct their operation, to pay their obligations and to provide returns to their investors; their users need this information as they are interested in how the entity uses and generates cash.

Generation of cash flows and definitions

Cash flows within an entity can broadly be generated by three activities:

1 Operating or principal revenue-producing activities defined by IAS 7 as those activities that are not investing or financing.
2 Investing activities; the acquisition and disposal of long-term assets and investments not included in cash equivalents.
3 Financing activities; activities that result in changes in the size and composition of the equity capital and borrowings of the entity.

Some other definitions from IAS 7 for completeness are:

- *Cash*. Comprises cash on hand and demand deposits.
- *Cash equivalents*. Short-term, highly liquid investments that are readily convertible to known amounts of cash and which are subject to an insignificant risk of changes in value.

The amount of cash flows from operating activities is highly important for users to assess whether enough cash has been generated from this source for the entity to repay loans, make investments in assets and pay dividends. Cash flows under the heading of operating activities are primarily derived from the principal revenue producing activities of the entity.

Separating out the cash flows from investing activities is also seen as important as this provides users with information on investment made in resources that will potentially generate future income and cash flows. Users require information on cash

ACTIVITY 23.4

Provide examples of cash flows, both inflow and outflow, from operating, investing and financing activities. To help we provide an example for each category in Table 23.1. Now extend the table.

TABLE 23.1   Examples of cash flows

Operating activities	Investing activities	Financing activities
Cash receipts from sale of goods and rendering of services	Cash payments to acquire fixed assets	Cash proceeds from issue of shares and other equity instruments

Activity feedback

You may not have identified all the following but the definitive list as given by IAS 7 is shown in Table 23.2.

TABLE 23.2   Definitive list of cash flows as given by IAS 7

Operating activities	Investing activities	Financing activities
Cash receipts from sale goods and rendering services	Cash payments to acquire fixed assets	Cash proceeds from issue of shares and other equity instruments
Cash receipts from royalties, fees, commissions and other revenue	Cash receipts from sale of fixed assets	Cash payments to owners to acquire or redeem the entity's shares
Cash payments to suppliers for goods and services	Cash payments to acquire equity or debt instruments of other entities and interests in joint ventures	Cash proceeds from issuing debentures, loans, notes, bonds, mortgages and other short- or long-term borrowings
Cash payments to and on behalf of employees	Cash advances and loans made to other parties	Cash repayments of amounts borrowed
Cash payments or refunds of income taxes unless they can be specifically identified with financing or investing activities	Cash receipts from the repayment of advances and loans made to other parties	Cash payments by a lessee for the reduction of the outstanding liability relating to a finance lease
Cash receipts and payments from contracts held for dealing or trading purposes	Cash payments for futures, forward contracts, options and swaps except when the contracts are held for dealing or trading purposes or the payments are classified as financing activities	Cash receipts and cash payments of an insurance entity for premiums and claims, annuities and other policy benefits

ACTIVITY 23.5

Identify in which category the following cash flows would be included:

1 An entity purchases a motor vehicle that it intends to sell on to a customer.

2 An entity purchases a motor vehicle that it intends to use as part of its delivery fleet.

3 An entity purchases a motor vehicle using a finance lease.

4 An entity gains the use of a motor vehicle under an operating lease.

5 An entity holds securities for dealing/trading purposes.

6 Interest paid and received and dividends received by an entity.

7 Dividends paid by an entity.

8 An entity purchases a building which it intends to rent to others.

Activity feedback

1 This is purchase of an inventory item and therefore shown under operating activities.

2 This is purchase of a fixed asset for the entity and therefore part of investing activities.

3 The entity has acquired the use of a fixed asset but the cash flow of principal payments will be shown under financing activities. There will be no cash flow under investing activities.

4 This time the payments under the operating lease will be treated as cash flows under operating activities as they are viewed as a normal expense payment of the entity. Note that the motor vehicle, depending on the revenue-producing activities of the entity and how the financing of the motor vehicle is arranged, can be regarded as a cash flow of any of the three categories.

5 These are inventory to the dealing house and therefore part of operating activities as they relate to the principal revenue-producing activities.

6 These are usually classified as operating cash flows for a financial institution but may also be regarded as operating for other entities as they form part of the net profit calculation – IAS 7, para. 33. This paragraph also allows them to be treated as financing – interest paid, or investing – interest and dividends received. The later alternative seems more sensible to us.

7 Dividends paid are obviously financing as they are a cost of obtaining finance. However, IAS 7 allows an alternative categorisation under operating activities. This is to enable users to judge the ability of the entity to pay dividends out of operating cash flows. We find this lack of consistency over the treatment of interest and dividends received and paid confusing and it will certainly impair comparability of cash flows between entities where different alternatives have been used.

8 This is the purchase of an asset that results in rental income and therefore must be regarded as a cash outflow under operating activities not investing activities. The rental received will be cash inflow under operating activities.

flows within financing activities so that they can predict claims on future cash flows from providers of capital to the entity. (See Activity 23.5.)

Cash and cash equivalents

The definitions of these are important as cash flows are defined as inflows and outflows of cash and cash equivalents. It should be apparent to you that an investment, dependent on our view of short-term or highly liquid could be viewed as a cash and cash equivalent, cash flow item or an investing activity. Bank borrowings are generally viewed, according to IAS 7, as financing activities but in certain circumstances bank overdrafts can be viewed as part of cash and cash equivalents. These circumstances are where the overdraft forms an integral part of the entity's cash management.

ACTIVITY 23.6

Determine whether the following items are cash, cash equivalents, investing activities or financing:

1 An account held with a bank where withdrawals require 90 days' notice.

2 An account held with a bank where withdrawals require 95 days' notice.

3 An overdraft with the bank which is seen as short term and part of everyday cash flows of the entity.

4 A loan from the bank for 60 days for a specific purpose.

5 An investment with a bank which has 60 days to maturity, but its final value is subject to significant risk as it is based on the index achievable at that time from a highly fluctuating stock market.

Activity feedback

1 If you view 90 days as short term then this is cash equivalent.

2 If you view 95 days as long term then this would be investing.

3 Cash as part of cash management.

4 Financing as a loan for a specific purpose cannot be viewed as everyday cash management.

5 This investment has a significant risk attached to it in terms of its final value and therefore must be regarded as investing activities.

The decision as regards 1 and 2 in Activity 23.6 is clarified by IAS 7 (para. 7) as follows:

> An investment normally qualifies as a cash equivalent only when it has a short maturity of, say, three months or less from date of acquisition. It must be readily convertible to a known amount of cash and be subject to an insignificant risk of changes in value.

> The decisions required here are quite subjective and it is feasible for one entity to determine an investment as a cash equivalent and another as an investing item.

FORMAT OF CASH FLOW STATEMENT

IAS 7 requires entities to report cash flows during a period in a statement identifying cash flows classified by operating, investing and financing activities. This implies a simple statement as follows:

Cash flow statement	
Cash flows from operating activities	A
Cash flows from investing activities	B
Cash flows from financing activities	C
Net change in cash and cash equivalents	X

However, the Standard, in order to provide relevant information to users, requires each of these cash flows to be separated into their constituent parts, i.e.:

1 Gross cash receipts and gross cash payments arising from investing and financing activities. Note here that if a single transaction has cash flows involving financing, investing and operating activities then the transaction will need to be split into its constituent parts. An example of such a transaction is a finance lease payment where the principal repayment will be disclosed as a cash flow under financing and the interest payment can be disclosed under operating or financing.

2 Gross cash receipts and payments from operating activities or net profit adjusted for effects of a non-cash nature.

3 Cash flows under any of the three sections can be reported net where the cash flows reflect the activities of the customer rather than the entity or where items are large, maturities short and turnover quick.

4 Cash flows relating to extraordinary items should be identified separately under each category.

5 Cash flows relating to taxes, interest and dividends received and paid, acquisitions and disposals of subsidiaries and other business units.

In addition, the components of cash and cash equivalents are required, together with a reconciliation of the amounts in the cash flow statement with the equivalent items reported in the balance sheets.

Direct or indirect method of determining cash flows

Item 2 in the list indicates that there are two methods for determining cash flows from operating activities, from cash receipts and payments known as the direct method or from adjusting net profit for non-cash receipts and payments known as the indirect method. The Standard prefers the direct method as it 'provides information which may be useful in estimating future cash flows which is not available under the indirect method'. Strangely, the UK ASB requires the indirect method as it does not believe that the benefits to the users of the direct method outweigh the costs of preparing it.

ACTIVITY 23.7

1 What information would the direct method provide that the indirect method would not provide to users?

2 Why might the direct method be more costly to prepare than the indirect?

3 How should a non-cash transaction be dealt with in a cash flow statement?

Activity feedback

1 The direct method would identify cash receipts from customers and cash payments to suppliers and employees whereas the indirect method would only show net profit with its adjustments for depreciation, profit on disposal and changes in working capital, etc. The actual disclosure of cash receipts and payments enables users to evaluate future cash flows more easily.

2 Entities operate an accounting system that is geared towards accrual accounting. The direct method would require a company to use either an accounting system which directly records and analyses the cash flow in relation to each transaction, thus operating two accounting systems or to adjust sales, costs of sales and other items in the income statement for non-cash items, changes in working capital and other items which relate to investing or financing activities – a time-consuming and costly business. If we take the view that information should be provided that is useful to users, the view of the Framework, then we must support the direct method for the disclosure of operating cash flows.

3 Quite obviously it shouldn't be dealt with as it does not involve a cash flow!

Examples of non-cash transactions given in the Standard are:

● acquisition of assets either by assuming directly related liabilities or by means of a finance lease

● acquisition of an entity by means of an equity issue

● conversion of debt to equity.

All these involve the exchange of a non-cash asset for a non-cash liability or conversion from one asset or liability to another. These types of transaction will be reported elsewhere in the financial statements.

ACTIVITY 23.8

From the following information relating to Zen entity calculate the cash flows from operating activities using both the direct and indirect method.

Consolidated income statement for the period ended 31 December 20X2

	€000s
Sales	30 650
Cost of sales	26 000
Gross profit	4 650
Depreciation	(450)
Administration and selling expenses	(910)
Interest expense	(400)
Investment income	500
Foreign exchange loss	(40)
Net profit before taxation and extraordinary item	3 350
Extraordinary item – insurance proceeds from earthquake disaster	180
Net profit after extraordinary item	3 530
Taxes on income	(300)
Net profit	3 230

Consolidated balance sheet as at 31 December 20X2

	20X2		20X1	
	€000s	€000s	€000s	€000s
Assets				
Cash and cash equivalents		410		160
Account receivable		1 900		1 200
Inventory		1 000		1 950
Portfolio investments		2 500		2 500
Property, plant and equipment at cost	3 730		1 910	
Accumulated depreciation	1 450	2 280	1 060	850
Total assets		8 090		6 660
Liabilities				
Trade payables		250		1 890
Interest payable		230		100
Income taxes payable		400		1 000
Long-term debt		2 300		1 040
Total liabilities		3 180		4 030
Shareholders' equity		1 500		1 250
Retained earnings		3 410		1 380
Total shareholders' equity		4 910		2 630
Total liabilities and shareholders' equity		8 090		6 660

Other information is available as follows:

(a) All the shares of a subsidiary were acquired for €590 000. The fair values of assets acquired and liabilities assumed were as follows:

	€000s
Inventories	100
Accounts receivable	100
Cash	40
Property, plant and equipment	650
Trade payables	100
Long-term debt	200

(b) €250 000 was raised from the issue of shares and €250 000 from long-term borrowings.

(c) Interest expense was €400 000 of which €170 000 was paid during the period. €100 000 relating to interest expense of the prior period was also paid during the period.

(d) Dividends paid were €1 200 000.

(e) The liability for tax at the beginning and end of the period was €1 000 000 and €400 000 respectively. During the period a further €200 000 tax was provided for. Withholding tax on dividends received during the period of €200 000 amounted to €100 000.

(f) During the period, the group acquired property, plant and equipment with an aggregate cost of €1 250 000 of which €900 000 was acquired by means of finance leases. Cash payments of €350 000 were made to purchase property, plant and equipment.

(g) Plant with original cost of €80 000 and accumulated depreciation of €60 000 was sold for €20 000.

(h) Accounts receivable as at end 31 December 20X2 include €100 000 of interest receivable.
[adapted from example in Appendix A to IAS 7]

Activity feedback

Direct method
Cash flow from operations:

Cash receipts from customers (working 1)	30 150
Cash paid to suppliers and employees (working 2)	(27 600)
Cash generated from operations	2 550
Interest paid (170 + 100 note c)	(270)
Income taxes paid (1000 + 200 + 100 − 400)	(900)

ACTIVITY 23.8 (Continued)

Cash flow before extraordinary item		1 380	
Proceeds from earthquake disaster settlement*		180	
		1 560	

* (assume disaster gave rise to loss of operating activities)

Working 1

Sales – income statement	30 650	
add Opening accounts receivable	1 200	
less Closing accounts receivable	(1 800)	(1 900 – 100 note h)
add Subsidiary debtors	100	
	30 150	

Working 2

Cost of sales – income statement	26 000	
less Opening stock	(1 950)	
add Closing stock	1 000	
Purchases	25 050	
less Closing trade payables	(250)	
add Opening trade payables	1 890	
	26 690	
Admin and selling expenses	910	
	27 600	
Subsidiary trade payables note a	100	
less Subsidiary inventories note a	(100)	
	27 600	

(Note interest and income taxes paid are treated as part of operating activities, dividends paid are not.)

Indirect method

Net profit before tax and dividends	3 350	
add Back interest	(100)	
Foreign exchange loss	40	
Depreciation	450	
	3 740	
Increase in trade and other receivables	(500)	(700 – 100 subsidiary – 100 interest receivable)
Decrease in inventories	1 050	(950 + 100 subsidiary)
Decrease in trade payables	(1 740)	(1 640 + 100 subsidiary)
Cash generated from operations	2 550	
Interest paid	(270)	
Income taxes paid	(900)	
Cash flow before extraordinary item	1 380	
Proceeds from earthquake disaster settlement	180	
Net cash flow from operating activities	1 560	

Cash flows from investing activities

ACTIVITY 23.9

Now calculate the cash flow from investing activities from the data given in Activity 23.8.

Activity feedback

Investing activities cover cash flows in respect of fixed assets, investments in equity or debt, advances and loans to other parties. The balance sheet changes identify any increases/decreases in portfolio investments and property, plant and equipment and we were also informed about an acquisition of a subsidiary.

Therefore:

Cash flow from investing activities		
Acquisition of subsidiary less cash acquired	(550)	(590 – 40)
Purchase of property, plant and equipment	(350)	(note f) or (working 1)
Proceeds from sale of equipment	20	(note g)
Dividends received	200	(note c)
Interest received (investment income – dividends)	200	
Net cash used in investing activities	(480)	

Working 1

Opening balance sheet of property etc. at cost	1 910
add Subsidiary bought	650
less Sale	(80)
	2 480
Closing balance sheet at cost	3 730
	1 250
Leased assets so no cash flow	(900)
Therefore assets bought for cash	350

Cash flows from financing activities

ACTIVITY 23.10

Now identify the cash flows from financing activities from the data given in Activity 23.8.

Activity feedback

Cash flow from financing activities covers proceeds from the issue of shares, loans, etc. and repayments of amounts borrowed.

Cash flow from financing activities		
Proceeds from issuing shares	250	(note b)
Proceeds from long-term borrowings	250	(note b)
Payments of finance lease (working 1)	(90)	
Dividends paid	(1 200)	(note d)
	(790)	

Working 1	
Opening balance sheet long-term debt	1 040
add Finance lease principal	900
	1 940
add Subsidiary long-term loan	200
	2 140
New loans	250
	2 390
Closing balance sheet long term debt	2 300
Therefore lease principal repaid	90

Statement of cash flows

If you put the answers of Activities 23.8, 9, and 10 together and add on cash and cash equivalent changes you have a full cash flow statement for the data in Activity 23.8 as follows.

Direct Method Cash Flow Statement

Cash flow from operating activities		
Cash receipts from customers (working 1)	30 150	
Cash paid to suppliers and employees (working 2)	(27 600)	
Cash generated from operations	2 550	
Interest paid (170 + 100 note c)	(270)	
Income taxes paid (1 000 + 200 + 100 − 400)	(900)	
Cash flow before extraordinary item	1 380	
Proceeds from earthquake disaster settlement*	180	
Net cash flow from operating activities		1 560
Cash flow from investing activities		
Acquisition of subsidiary less cash acquired	(550)	(590 − 40)
Purchase of property, plant and equipment	(350)	(note f) or (working 1)
Proceeds from sale of equipment	20	(note g)
Dividends received	200	(note c)
Interest received (investment income − dividends)	200	
Net cash used in investing activities		(480)

Cash flow from financing activities
Proceeds from issuing shares   250   (note b)
Proceeds from long-term borrowings   250   (note b)
Payments of finance lease (working 1)   (90)
Dividends paid   (1 200) (note d)

Net cash used in financing activities   (790)
Net increase in cash and cash equivalents   290
Cash and cash equivalents at beginning of period
   (160 – 40 f.e.l.)   120
Cash and cash equivalents at end of period   410

Notes to statement of cash flows
Notes to this cash flow are required in respect of:

- the fair value of assets and liabilities of the subsidiary acquired
- the amount of property, plant and equipment acquired by finance lease
- detailed analysis of the cash equivalents
- segmental cash flows.

IAS 7, Appendix A illustrates these notes.

PREPARATION OF STATEMENT OF CASH FLOWS

The next activity requires you to prepare a rather more complicated cash flow than Activity 23.11.

ACTIVITY 23.11

The balance sheet of Axbrit entity for the year ended 31 March 20X2 is as follows:

Assets	20X2	20X1
Cash and cash equivalents	27	21
Accounts receivable	15	18
Inventory	25	20
Property, plant and equipment at cost	230	160
Accumulated depreciation	(60)	(44)
Total assets	237	175
Liabilities		
Trade payables	47	39
Income taxes payable	16	12
Long-term debt	32	30
Total liabilities	95	81

Shareholders' equity		
Share capital	33	27
Capital reserves	30	24
Retained earnings	79	43
Total shareholders' equity	142	94
Total liabilities and shareholders' equity	237	175

Prepare the statement of cash flows for the year ended 31 March 20X2 given that no property, plant and equipment was sold during the period and that the increase in long-term debt took place on 1 April 20X2 and carried a 10% rate of interest and that dividends paid during the year were €18.

(Continued)

ACTIVITY 23.11 *(Continued)*

Activity feedback

As we are not given the income statement or any other information to enable us to derive net cash flow from operating activities using the direct method we have to use the indirect method in this example.

Indirect method net cash flow from operating activities		
Net profit (change in retained earnings + dividends)		54
Add interest on long-term loans	3.2	
Add taxation charge (assume liability at end is charge for period)	16	
		19.2
Net profit before taxation		73.2
add Depreciation	16	
Increase in inventories	(5)	
Decrease in accounts receivable	3	
Increase in trade payables	8	22
Cash generated from operations		95.2

Interest paid		(3.2)
Income taxes paid		(12)
Net cash flow from operating activities		80
Cash flow from investing activities		
Purchase of property, plant and equipment	70	
Net cash used in investing activities		(70)
Cash flows from financing activities		
Proceeds from issues of shares	12	
Proceeds from long-term borrowings	2	
Dividends paid	(18)	
Net cash used in financing activities		(4)
Net increase in cash and cash equivalents		6
Cash and cash equivalents at beginning of period		21
Cash and cash equivalents at end of period		27

ACTIVITY 23.12

From the income statement and balance sheets of Thomas Manufacturing entity prepare the statement of cash flows for the year ended 31 December 20X5.

Thomas manufacturing income statement for the year ended 31.12.X5

	€000s	€000s
Sales		5 000
Change in inventories		500
Own work capitalised		150
Other operating income		50
Raw materials and consumables	(2 000)	
Other external charges	(750)	(2 750)
Employee costs		(1 500)
Depreciation and amortisation		(400)
Other operating charges		(100)
		950

	€000s	€000s
Income from investments – dividends		20
Other interest receivable		5
		975
Interest payable		(160)
Income before income taxes		815
Income taxes		(325)
Income after taxes		490
Extraordinary income	70	
Extraordinary charges	(90)	
Extraordinary loss	(20)	
Tax on loss	8	(12)
Income for period		478
Dividends paid for the period were €250 000		

ACTIVITY 23.12   (Continued)

	Balance Sheet as at 31.12.X4			31.12.X5	
	Cost €000s	Net €000s	Cost €000s	Deprec. €000s	Net €000s
Non-current assets					
Intangible	200	100	350	200	150
Property, plant and equip.	1 500	800	2 500	775	1 725
Investments	100	100	200		200
	1 800	1 000	3 050	975	2 075
Current assets					
Inventories		1 000		1 600	
Accounts receivable		1 000		1 200	
Investments		50			
Cash shareholders' equity		250		30	2 830
		2 300			4 905
		3 300			
Ordinary shares		1 000			1 500
Capital reserves		200			800
Retained earnings		177			405
		1 377			2 705
Liabilities					
Long term					
Loans		980			790
Short term					
Accounts payable	600		750		
Loans			257		
Taxation	243		274		
		843			1 281
Deferred taxes		100			129
		1 923			1 200
		3 300			4 905

Further information is available as follows:

- As at 1 January X5, freehold land was revalued from €500 000 to €1 000 000.

- During the year ended 31 December X5 plant and equipment costing €300 000, written down to €50 000 at 31 December X4, was sold for €75 000. These book gains and losses were adjusted into the depreciation charge in the income statement.

- Own work capitalised refers to development work carried forward as an intangible asset.

- Loans with a nominal value of €190 000 were redeemed at par during the year.

- Shares were issued for cash during the year; there were no purchases of the company's own shares.

- The investments shown as current assets at 31 December X4 and not regarded as cash equivalent were sold during the year for €50 000.

Activity feedback

Indirect statement of cash flows for Thomas Manufacturing

	€000s	€000s
Cash flow from operating activities		
Net profit before tax and extraordinary items		815
Adjustments for:		
Depreciation (400 + 25 gain adj. on sale into dep.)		425

(Continued)

ACTIVITY 23.12 (Continued)

	€000s	€000s		€000s	€000s
Profit on sale of plant and equipment	(25)		Dividends paid	(250)	
Investment income	(25)		Net cash from financing activities		417
Interest expense	160	535			
Operating profit before working capital changes		1 350	**Net decrease in cash and cash equivalents**		(220)
Increase in trade and other receivables	(200)		Cash and cash equivalents at beginning of period		250
Increase in inventories	(600)				
Increase in trade payables	150	(650)	Cash and cash equivalents at end of period		30
Cash generated from operations		700			
Interest paid		(160)			
Income taxes paid (see note 1)		(257)	Note 1		
Cash flow before extraordinary items		283	Opening balance of taxes (243 + 100)	343	
Proceeds from extraordinary items		(20)	Add income statement charge		
Net cash from operating activities		263	(325 − 8)	317	
				660	
Cash flow from investing activities			Closing balance of taxes (274 + 129)	403	
Purchase of intangible fixed assets	(150)		Therefore taxes paid during the year	257	
Purchase of property, plant and equipment (note 2)	(800)				
Purchase of investments	(100)		Note 2		
Proceeds from sale of investments	50		Opening balance of assets at cost	1 500	
Proceeds from sale of equipment	75		add Revaluation during the year	500	
Interest received	5		less Sale at cost	(300)	
Dividends received	20			1 700	
Net cash used in investing activities		(900)	Closing balance at cost	2 500	
			Therefore purchase of assets	800	
Cash flow from financing activities					
Proceeds from issues of shares	600				
Proceeds from long-term borrowings	257				
Redemption of loans	(190)				

Disclosure

As an example of disclosure required in respect of cash flow statements by IAS 7 we present that relating to the Bayer Group for the year ended 31 December 2007.

Bayer Group Statement of Cash Flows

	Note	2006	2007
€ million			
Income from continuing operations after taxes		1,526	2,306
Income taxes		454	(72)
Non-operating result		782	920
Income taxes paid		(763)	(915)
Depreciation and amortization		1,913	2,712
Change in pension provisions		(295)	(369)
(Gains) losses on retirements of noncurrent assets		(133)	(13)

€ *million*	Note	2006	2007
Non-cash effects of the remeasurement of acquired assets (inventory work-down)		429	215
Gross cash flow		**3,913**	**4,784**
Decrease (increase) in inventories		(155)	(347)
Decrease (increase) in trade accounts receivable		(201)	(183)
(Decrease) increase in trade accounts payable		130	189
Changes in other working capital, other non-cash items		241	(162)
Net cash provided by (used in) operating activities (net cash flow), continuing operations	[33]	**3,928**	**4,281**
Net cash provided by (used in) operating activities (net cash flow), discontinued operations	[6.3]	275	2
Net cash provided by (used in) operating activities (net cash flow) (total)		**4,203**	**4,283**
Cash outflows for additions to property, plant, equipment and intangible assets		(1,876)	(1,860)
Cash inflows from sales of property, plant, equipment and other assets		185	165
Cash inflows from divestitures		489	4,648
Cash inflows from noncurrent financial assets		850	70
Cash outflows for acquisitions less acquired cash		(15,351)	(491)
Interest and dividends received		686	636
Cash inflows (outflows) from current financial assets		287	18
Net cash provided by (used in) investing activities (total)	[34]	**(14,730)**	**3,186**
Capital contributions		1,174	0
Bayer AG dividend, dividend payments to minority stockholders, reimbursements of advance capital gains tax payments		(535)	(773)
Issuances of debt		13,931	2,155
Retirements of debt		(3,216)	(7,768)
Interest paid		(1,155)	(1,344)
Net cash provided by (used in) financing activities (total)	[35]	**10,199**	**(7,730)**
Change in cash and cash equivalents due to business activities (total)		**(328)**	**(261)**
Cash and cash equivalents at beginning of year		**3,290**	**(2,915)**
Change in cash and cash equivalents due to changes in scope of consolidation		(2)	(4)
Change in cash and cash equivalents due to exchange rate movements		(45)	(119)
Cash and cash equivalents at end of year	[36]	**2,915**	**2,531**

DISCLOSURE REQUIREMENTS OF IAS 7

As an example of disclosure required in respect of statements of cash flows by IAS 7 we present that relating to the Bayer Group for the year ended 31 December 2007.

Notes to the Statements of Cash Flows

The cash flow statement shows how the liquidity of the Bayer Group was affected by the inflow and outflow of cash and cash equivalents during the year. The effects of changes in the scope of consolidation are eliminated. Cash flows are classified by operating, investing and financing activities in accordance with IAS 7 (Cash Flow Statements). The cash and cash equivalents shown in the balance sheet comprise cash, checks, balances with banks and securities with original maturities of up to three months.

The amounts reported by consolidated companies outside the euro zone are translated at average exchange rates for the year, with the exception of cash and cash equivalents, which are translated at closing rates as in the balance sheet. The effect of changes in exchange rates on cash and cash equivalents is shown separately.

Cash and cash equivalents contain both the proceeds from divestitures of discontinued operations and the cash inflows from these operations prior to the divestitures. In principle, therefore, the statement of cash flows must account for all cash inflows and outflows from continuing and discontinued operations. However, IFRS 5 (Non-current Assets Held for Sale and Discontinued Operations) specifies that cash flows from operating, investing and financing activities be classified by continuing and discontinued operations. The discontinued operations' shares of the cash flows from operating, investing and financing activities are stated separately in Note [6.3].

In both the balance sheet and the income statement, however, the amounts corresponding to the components of the net operating cash flow are shown for continuing operations only. This is the case, for example, with the amounts of inventories, receivables and payables recognised in the balance sheet that determine the changes in working capital shown in the cash flow statement. The income from continuing operations after taxes that is recognised in the income statement forms the starting point for the cash flow statement. To ensure that the operating activities are consistently presented in the cash now statement, income statement and balance sheet, the net operating cash flow from continuing operations is stated first on the face of the cash flow statement. The total net operating cash flow from discontinued operations is shown in the next line, by analogy with the presentation of the income statement. The cash flows from continuing and discontinued operations are added together to give the net operating cash flow (total) for the entire business.

33. Net cash provided by (used in) operating activities

The gross cash flow for 2007 of €4 784 million (2006: €3 913 million) is the cash surplus from operating activities before any changes in working capital. The cash flows by segment are shown in the table in Note [1].

The net operating cash flow from continuing operations of €4 281 million (2006: €3 928 million) takes into account the changes in working capital and other non cash-relevant transaction, The €2 million (2006: €275 million) net cash flow from the discontinued operations comprises operating income from the H.C. Starck and Wolff Walsrode business units and the diagnostics business. The total net cash flow for 2007 is €4 283 million (2006: €4 203 million).

The line 'Non-cash effects of the remeasurement of acquired assets (inventory work-down)' has been inserted in the cash flow statement in order to eliminate the effects of the Schering purchase price allocation from gross cash flow. Thus, the non-cash effect of the work-down of the step-up from the remeasurement of Schering inventories to fair value as of June 23, 2006, the date of acquisition, on the gross cash flow is reversed. In 2007 €215 million (2006: €429 million) was transferred to this line from 'Decrease/ Increase in inventories.' These non-cash effects do not impact net cash flow.

34. Net cash provided by (used in) investing activities

In 2007, there was a net cash inflow of €3 186 million (2006: net cash out flow of €14 730 million), consisting principally of the proceeds from the divestitures of the Diagnostics Division, H.C. Starck and Wolff Walsrode. The principal acquisitions were those of the U.S. cotton seed producer Stoneville Pedigreed Seed Company, the Ure-Tech group of Taiwan, and a biologics manufacturing facility from Novartis. Further details of acquisitions and divestitures are given in Notes [6.2/6.3].

Cash outflows fur additions to property, plant and equipment and intangible assets in 2007 came to €1 860 million (2006: €1 876 million). Disbursements for property, plant and equipment and intangible assets included those for the acquisition of Zymo Genetics and the expansion of the production site for polymer products in Caojing, near Shanghai, China.

Inflows from sales of property, plant and equipment and other assets amounted to €165 million (2006: €185 million). An initial payment of €395 million on the divestiture of the diagnostics business, which was completed at the start of 2007, was received at the end of 2006.

Cash inflows from noncurrent financial assets amounted to €70 million (2006: €850 million).

35. Net cash provided by (used in) financing activities

In fiscal 2007 there was a net cash outflow of €7 730 million (2006: net cash in flow of €10 199 million) from financing activities. These disbursements served primarily to reduce debt by €5 613 million (2006: net borrowing of €10.7 billion to finance the acquisition of Schering).

Cash outflows for dividend payments amounted to €773 million (2006: €535 million – including the €176 million refund of advance capital gains tax payments made on intragroup dividends in 2004). Interest expense increased to €1 344 million (2006: €1 155 million).

36. Cash and cash equivalents

Cash and cash equivalents comprise cash, checks and balances with banks. In accordance with IAS 7 (Cash Flow Statements) this item also includes securities with original maturities of up to three months, reflecting their high liquidity. Cash and cash equivalents amounted to €2 531 million as of December 31, 2007 (2006: €2 915 million). Cash of €755 million (2006: €799 million) has been deposited in escrow accounts. This amount comprises €695 million (2006: €710 million) transferred to a guarantee account in light of the resolved squeeze-out of the remaining minority stockholders of Schering, and €60 million (2006: €89 million) to be used exclusively for payments relating to antitrust fines and civil law settlements.

GAAP COMPARISONS

UK versus IAS

The UK standard FRS 1 (revised 1996), *Cash Flow Statements*, defines cash flow as increases or decreases in cash. Thus those items that would be regarded as cash equivalents under IAS 7 are presented in accordance with FRS 1 under a heading of 'management of liquid resources'. FRS 1 also has many more headings than the IAS as can be seen in Table 23.3.

A note of the reconciliation of the movement in net debt is required by FRS 1 but not by IAS 7. There is also a difference in the treatment of cash flows from a foreign subsidiary. IAS 7 requires translation using exchange rates prevailing on dates of cash flows whereas FRS 1 requires the same rate as that used in the income statement, which will be the average or closing rate.

US versus IAS

US cash flow statements (SFAS 95 as amended by 102, 104 and 117) use the three headings of IAS 7 but there are some minor differences arising from permitted alternatives within the IAS.

THE FUTURE

The cash flow statement is set to be reviewed under the joint project of the IASB/FASB on presentation of financial information in individual statements.

Initial discussions are focusing on:

- The need to specify the direct method of calculating cash flows from operations as a requirement.
- The need to specify a reconciliation schedule of statements of cash flows to the statement of comprehensive income.

TABLE 23.3 FRS 1 and IAS 7 compared

FRS 1	IAS 7
Operating	Operating
Dividends from joint ventures and associates	Operating or investing
Returns on investments and servicing of finance	Operating or financing for interest paid, investing for interest and dividends received
Taxation	Operating
Capital expenditure and financial investment	Investing
Acquisition and disposals	Investing
Equity dividends paid	Financing or operating
Management of liquid resources	Investing or cash equivalent
Financing	Financing

Direct method

As we stated earlier the IASB prefer the use of the direct method but did not require it in IAS 7 due to the concerns about the cost of preparing a direct method statement of cash flows. It now emerges that there are two approaches to preparing the direct method of cash flows:

- The 'bottom-up' or 'cash ledger' approach (referred to as the 'direct-direct method'). Under this approach, cash receipts and payments are determined by aggregating cash flow amounts from cash ledgers. This is a costly approach.
- The 'top-down' or 'financial statement' approach (referred to as the 'indirect-direct method'). Under this approach, cash receipts and payments are determined by adjusting revenues, expenses, and gains and losses for the change in the related accrual over the period. This approach, it is thought, would be cheaper than the direct-direct method.

Reconciliation schedule

This would form a new schedule in the financial statements and would be columnar as follows:

Cash flows	Cash flows not affecting income	Valuation adjustments	All other changes	Comprehensive income
A	B	C	D	A − B + C + D

with a line for each item on the cash flow and comprehensive income statement.

Whether such a complicated reconciliation statement will be of use to users remains to be seen.

SUMMARY

Within this chapter we have attempted to show you how to draw up a statement of cash flows using both the direct and indirect method and we have highlighted some of the problems associated with it. These problems are:

- the arbitrary three-month cut off for cash equivalents
- the choice of category for interest and dividends
- the difficulty of producing direct cash flows
- the lack of user information in indirect cash flows.
- the historical nature of the statement of cash flows.

On the whole, however, the statement of cash flows under IAS 7 is certainly an improvement on the previous funds flow statement and the production of cash flow information provides important information to users. We will deal with the analysis of cash flow statements in Chapter 31.

EXERCISES

Suggested answers to exercises marked ✓ are to be found on the Student side of the companion website.

Suggested answers to the remaining exercises are to be found on the Instructor side of the companion website.

1 Comment on the usefulness of both funds flow statements and cash flow statements to users.

2 *Cash is a very difficult figure to fiddle* (David Tweedie). Discuss.

3 Compare and contrast the direct and indirect method of preparing a statement of cash flows and identify and comment on the reasons why the IASB prefers the direct method. (Note: This preference is not universal by accounting standards' boards.)

4 Using the statement of cash flows provided in respect of the Bayer Group analyse, as far as the information permits, the performance of the group.

✓ 5 Discuss the proposition that a cash flow statement is more useful to users than an income statement.

6 Differentiate, using illustrative examples where necessary, between cash and cash equivalents.

7 Cash flows should be defined as increases or decreases in cash. Discuss.

8 The following information is available in respect of Barn entity.
Income statement for the year ended 30 September 2007

	£m	£m	£m
Gross profit			280
Depreciation		60	
Interest receivable	(10)		
Interest payable	16	6	
Profit on sale of assets		(16)	
Impairment of intangibles		40	90
Net profit before tax			190
Tax			80
Net profit after tax			110
Dividends paid and proposed			80
Retained earnings			30

Balance sheets as at:

	30.9.06 £m	30.9.07 £m
Assets		
Non-current assets		
Intangibles	240	280
Property, plant and equipment	640	778
	880	1 058

	30.9.06 £m	30.9.07 £m
Current assets		
Inventory	60	68
Trade receivables	48	44
Cash and bank	128	144
	236	256
Total assets	1 116	1 314
Equity and liabilities		
Equity		
Ordinary share capital	500	600
Share premium	40	60
Retained earnings	192	222
	732	882
Non-current liabilities	200	240
Current liabilities		
Trade payables	64	72
Dividends	30	40
Tax	90	80
	184	192
Total equity and liabilities	1 116	1 314

The sale proceeds from the sale of non-current assets was £72m. All interest due has been received and the interest payable has been paid.

Required

(a) Prepare the statement of cash flows for Barn entity for the year ended 30 September 2007 in accordance with IAS 7, *Cash Flow Statements*. (Notes to the cash flow statement are not required.)

(b) Identify two limitations of a cash flow statement.

9   The following information is available in respect of Theta entity.
         Income statement for the year ended 31 December 2007

	£m	£m	£m
Gross profit			420
Depreciation		90	
Interest receivable	(15)		
Interest payable	24	9	
Profit on sale of assets		(24)	
Impairment of intangibles		60	135
Net profit before tax			285
Tax			120
Net profit after tax			165
Dividends paid and proposed			120
Retained earnings			45

Balance sheets as at:

	31.12.06	31.12.07
Assets	£m	£m
Non-current assets		
Intangibles	360	420
Property, plant and equipment	960	1 167
	1 320	1 587
	€m	€m
Current assets		
Inventory	90	102
Trade receivables	72	66
Cash and bank	192	216
	354	384
Total assets	1 674	1 971
Equity and liabilities		
Equity		
Ordinary share capital	750	900
Share premium	60	90
Retained earnings	288	333
	1 098	1 323
Non-current liabilities	300	360
Current liabilities		
Trade payables	96	108
Dividends	45	60
Tax	135	120
	276	288
Total equity and liabilities	1 674	1 971

The sale proceeds from the sale of non-current assets was £108m. All interest due has been received and the interest payable has been paid.

Required

(a) Prepare the statement of cash flows for Theta entity for the year ended 31 December 2007 in accordance with IAS 7, *Cash Flow Statements*. (Notes to the cash flow statement are not required.)

(b) Identify information that is provided by a cash flow statement to users that is not provided by an income statement and balance sheet.

✓ **10** Rytetrend is a retailer of electrical goods. Extracts from the company's financial statements are set out below:

	2003		2002	
Income statement for the year ended 31 March:	$000	$000	$000	$000
Sales revenue		31 800		23 500
Cost of sales		(22 500)		(16 000)
Gross profit		9 300		7 500
Other operating expenses		(5 440)		(4 600)
Operating profit		3 860		2 900

Income statement for the year ended 31 March:	2003 $000	2003 $000	2002 $000	2002 $000
Interest payable – loan notes	(260)		(500)	
– overdraft	(200)	(460)	nil	(500)
Profit before taxation		3 400		2 400
Taxation		(1 000)		(800)
Profit after taxation		2 400		1 600
Dividends		(600)		(400)
Net profit for the period		1 800		1 200
Accumulated profit – brought forward		5 880		4 680
Accumulated profit – carried forward		7 680		5 880

Balance Sheets as at 31 March	2003 $000	2003 $000	2002 $000	2002 $000
Non-current assets (note (i))		24 500		17 300
Current assets				
Inventory	2 650		3 270	
Receivables	1 100		1 950	
Bank	nil	3 750	400	5 620
Total assets		28 250		22 920
Equity and liabilities				
Ordinary capital ($1 shares)		11 500		10 000
Share premium		1 500		nil
Accumulated profits		7 680		5 880
		20 680		15 880
Non-current liabilities				
10% loan notes		nil		4 000
6% loan notes		2 000		nil
Current liabilities				
Bank overdraft	1 050		nil	
Trade payables	2 850		1 980	
Proposed dividends (declared before the year-end)	450		280	
Taxation	720		630	
Warranty provision (note (ii))	500	5 570	150	3 040
Total equity and liabilities		28 250		22 920

Notes

(i) The details of the non-current assets are:

	Cost $000	Accumulated depreciation $000	Net book value $000
At 31 March 2002	27 500	10 200	17 300
At 31 March 2003	37 250	12 750	24 500

During the year there was a major refurbishment of display equipment. Old equipment that had cost $6 million in September 1998 was replaced with new equipment at a gross cost of $8 million. The equipment manufacturer had allowed Rytetrend a trade-in allowance of $500 000 on the old display equipment. In addition to this Rytetrend used its own staff to install the new equipment. The value of staff time spent on the installation has been costed at $300 000, but this has not been included in the cost of the asset. All staff costs have been included in operating expenses. All display equipment held at the end of the financial year is depreciated at 20% on its cost. No equipment is more than five years old.

(ii)   Operating expenses contain a charge of $580 000 for the cost of warranties on the goods sold by Rytetrend. The company makes a warranty provision when it sells its products and cash payments for warranty claims are deducted from the provision as they are settled.

Required:

(a)   Prepare a statement of cash flows for Rytetrend for the year ended 31 March 2003.

(b)   Write a report briefly analysing the operating performance and financial position of Rytetrend for the years ended 31 March 2002 and 2003.

Your report should be supported by appropriate ratios.

(ACCA June 2003)

11   The following information relates to Planter, a small private company. It consists of an opening balance sheet as at 1 April 2003 and a listing of the company's ledger accounts at 31 March 2004 after the draft operating profit before interest and taxation (of $17 900) had been calculated.

Planter – Balance sheet as at	1 April 2003	
	$	$
Non-current assets		
Land and buildings (at valuation $49 200 less		
accumulated depreciation of $5 000)		44 200
Plant (at cost of $70 000 less accumulated		
depreciation of $22 500)		47 500
Investments at costs		16 900
		108 600
Current assets		
Inventory	57 400	
Trade receivables	28 600	
Bank	1 200	87 200
Total assets		195 800
Equity and liabilities		
Capital and Reserves:		
Ordinary shares of $1 each		25 000
Reserves:		
Share premium	5 000	
Revaluation reserve	12 000	
Accumulated profits	70 300	87 300
		112 300

Non-current liabilities

8% Loan notes		43 200
Current liabilities		
Trade payables	31 400	
Taxation	8 900	40 300
		195 800

Ledger account listings at 31 March 2004	**Dr**	**Cr**
	$	$
Ordinary shares of $1 each		50 000
Share premium		8 000
Accumulated profits – 1 April 2003		70 300
Profit before interest and tax – year to 31 March 2004		17 900
Revaluation reserve		18 000
8% Loan notes		39 800
Trade payables		26 700
Accrued loan interest		300
Taxation	1 100	
Land and buildings at valuation	62 300	
Plant at cost	84 600	
Buildings – accumulated depreciation 31 March 2004		6 800
Plant – accumulated depreciation 31 March 2004		37 600
Investments at cost	8 200	
Trade receivables	50 400	
Inventory – 31 March 2004	43 300	
Bank		1 900
Investment income		400
Loan interest	1 700	
Ordinary dividend	26 100	
	277 700	277 700

Notes

(i) There were no disposals of land and buildings during the year. The increase in the revaluation reserve was entirely due to the revaluation of the company's land.

(ii) Plant with a net book value of $12 000 (cost $23 500) was sold during the year for $7800. The loss on sale has been included in the profit before interest and tax.

(iii) Investments with a cost of $8700 were sold during the year for $11 000. The profit has been included in the profit before interest and tax. There were no further purchases of investments.

(iv) On 10 October 2003 a bonus issue of 1 for 10 ordinary shares was made utilising the share premium account. The remainder of the increase in ordinary shares was due to an issue for cash on 30 October 2003.

(v) The balance on the taxation account is after settlement of the provision made for the year to 31 March 2003. A provision for the current year has not yet been made.

Required:
From the above information, prepare a statement of cash flows using the indirect method for Planter in accordance with IAS 7, *Cash Flow Statements* for the year to 31 March 2004.

(ACCA June 2004)

12   The following information has been extracted from the draft financial statements of TEX, a manufacturing entity:

TEX – Income statement for the year ended 30 September 2003

	$000
Revenue	15 000
Cost of sales	(9 000)
Gross profit	6 000
Other operating expenses	(2 300)
	3 700
Finance cost	(124)
Profit before tax	3 576
Income tax expense	(1 040)
Dividends	(1 100)
	(1 436)

TEX – Balance sheets at 30 September

	2003 $000	2003 $000	2002 $000	2002 $000
Assets				
Non-current assets:		18 160		14 500
Current assets:				
Inventories	1 600		1 100	
Trade receivables	1 500		800	
Bank	150		1 200	
		3 250		3 100
Total assets		21 410		17 600
Equity and liabilities:				
Capital and reserves:				
Issued capital		10 834		7 815
Accumulated profits		5 836		4 400
		16 670		12 215
Non-current liabilities:				
Interest-bearing borrowings	1 700		2 900	
Deferred tax	600		400	
		2 300		3 300
Current liabilities				
Trade payables	700		800	
Proposed dividend	700		600	
Tax	1 040		685	
		2 440		2 085
		21 410		17 600

Non-current assets:

	Property $000	Plant $000	Total $000
At 30 September 2002			
Cost	8 400	10 800	19 200
Depreciation	1 300	3 400	4 700
Net book value	7 100	7 400	14 500
At 30 September 2003			
Cost	11 200	13 400	24 600
Depreciation	1 540	4 900	6 440
Net book value	9 660	8 500	18 160

(i) Plant disposed of during the year had an original cost of $2 600 000 and accumulated depreciation of $900 000; cash received on disposal was $730 000.

(ii) All additions to non-current assets were purchased for cash.

(iii) Dividends were declared before the balance sheet dates.

Required:
Prepare TEX's statement of cash flows and associated notes for the year ended 30 September 2003, in accordance with IAS 7, *Statements of Cash Flows*.

(CIMA paper, *Financial Accounting and Tax Principles* May 2005)

13 The financial statements of AG are given below:

Balance sheets as at	31 March 2005 $000	31 March 2005 $000	31 March 2004 $000	31 March 2004 $000
Non-current assets:				
Plant, property and equipment	4 500		4 800	
Development expenditure	370	4 870	400	5 200
Current assets:				
Inventories	685		575	
Trade receivables	515		420	
Cash and cash equivalents	552	1 752	232	1 227
Total assets		6 622		6 427
Equity and liabilities Equity:				
Share capital	2 600		1 900	
Share premium account	750		400	
Revaluation reserve	425		300	
Retained earnings	1 430		1 415	
Total equity		5 205		4 015

Balance sheets as at	31 March 2005		31 March 2004	
	$000	$000	$000	$000
Non-current liabilities:				
10% loan notes	0		1 000	
5% loan notes	500		500	
Deferred tax	250		200	
Total non-current liabilities:		750		1 700
Current liabilities:				
Trade payables	480		350	
Income tax	80		190	
Accrued expenses	107		172	
Total current liabilities:		667		712
Total equity and liabilities		6 622		6 427

Income statement for the year ended 31 March 2005

	$000	$000
Revenue		7 500
Cost of sales		4 000
Gross profit		3 500
Distribution costs	900	
Administrative expenses	2 300	3 200
Profit from operations		300
Finance costs		45
Profit before tax		255
Income tax expense		140
Profit for the period		115

Additional information:

(i)   On 1 April 2004, AG issued 1 400 000 $0.50 ordinary shares at a premium of 50%.

(ii) On 1 May 2004, AG purchased and cancelled all its 10% loan notes at par.

(iii) Non-current tangible assets include properties which were revalued upwards by $125 000 during the year.

(iv) Non-current tangible assets disposed of in the year had a net book value of $75 000; cash received on disposal was $98 000. Any gain or loss on disposal has been included under cost of sales.

(v)   Cost of sales includes $80 000 for development expenditure amortised during the year.

(vi) Depreciation charged for the year was $720 000.

(vii) The accrued expenses balance includes interest payable of $87 000 at 31 March 2004 and $12 000 at 31 March 2005.

(viii)   The income tax expenses for the year to 31 March 2005 is made up as follows:

	$000
Corporate income tax	90
Deferred tax	50
	140

(ix)   Dividends paid during the year $100 000.

Required:
Prepare a statement of cash flows, using the indirect method, for AG for the year ended 31 March 2005, in accordance with IAS 7, *Statements of Cash Flows.*

(CIMA paper, *Financial Accounting and Tax Principles* May 2005)

14   The financial statements of CJ for the year to 31 March 2006 were as follows:

Balance sheets at	31 March 2006		31 March 2005	
	$000	$000	$000	$000
Non-current tangible assets:				
Property	19 160		18 000	
Plant and equipment	8 500		10 000	
Available for sale investments	1 500		2 100	
		29 160		30 100
Current assets:				
Inventory	2 714		2 500	
Trade receivables	2 106		1 800	
Cash at bank	6 553		0	
Cash in hand	409		320	
		11 782		4 620
Total assets		40 942		34 720
Equity and liabilities				
Equity:				
Ordinary share $0.50 each	12 000			7 000
Share premium	10 000			5 000
Revaluation reserve	4 200			2 700
Retained profit	3 009			1 510
		29 209		16 210
Non-current liabilities:				
Interest bearing borrowings	7 000		13 000	
Provision for deferred tax	999	7 999	800	13 800
Current liabilities:				
Bank overdraft	0		1 200	
Trade and other payables	1 820		1 700	
Corporate income tax payable	1 914		1 810	
		3 734		4 710
		40 942		34 720

Income statement for the year to 31 March 2006

	$000
Revenue	31 000
Cost of sales	(19 000)
Gross profit	12 000
Other income	200
Administrative expenses	(3 900)
Distribution costs	(2 600)
	5 700
Finance cost	(1 302)
Profit before tax	4 398
Income tax expense	(2 099)
Profit for the period	2 299

Additional information:

(i)   On 1 April 2005, CJ issued 10 000 000 $0.50 ordinary shares at a premium of 100%.

(ii) No additional available for sale investments were acquired during the year.

(iii) On 1 July 2005, CJ repaid $6 000 000 of its interest bearing borrowings.

(iv) Properties were revalued by $1 500 000 during the year.

(v)   Plant disposed of in the year had a net book value of $95 000; cash received on disposal was $118 000.

(vi) Depreciation charged for the year was properties $2 070 000 and plant and equipment $1 985 000.

(vii) The trade and other payables balance includes interest payable of $650 000 at 31 March 2005 and $350 000 at 31 March 2006.

(viii) Dividends paid during the year, $800 000 comprised last year's final dividend plus the current year's interim dividend. CJ's accounting policy is not to accrue proposed dividends.

(ix) Other income comprises

	$
Dividends received	180 000
Gain on disposal of available for sales investments	20 000
	200 000

Dividends receivable are not accrued.

(x)   Income tax expense comprises:

	$
Corporate income tax	1 900 000
Deferred tax	199 000
	2 099 000

Required:

Prepare CJ's statement of cash flow for the year ended 31 March 2006, in accordance with IAS 7, *Statements of Cash Flows*.

(CIMA paper, *Financial Accounting and Tax Principles* May 2006)

15 (a) Casino is a publicly listed company. Details of its balance sheets as at 31 March 2005 and 2004 are shown below together with other relevant information:

Balance Sheet as at	31 March 2005		31 March 2004	
Non-current assets (note (i)):	$m	$m	$m	$m
Property, plant and equipment		880		760
Intangible assets		400		510
		1 280		1 270
Current assets:				
Inventory	350		420	
Trade receivables	808		372	
Interest receivable	5		3	
Short-term deposits	32		120	
Bank	15	1 210	75	990
Total assets		2 490		2 260
Share capital and reserves:				
Ordinary Shares of $1 each		300		200
Reserves				
Share premium	60		nil	
Revaluation reserve	112		45	
Retained earnings	1 098	1 270	1 165	1 210
		1 570		1 410
Non-current liabilities:				
12% loan note	nil		150	
8% variable rate loan note	160		nil	
Deferred tax	90	250	75	225
Current liabilities:				
Trade payables	530		515	
Bank overdraft	125		nil	
Taxation	15		110	
		670		625
Total equity and liabilities		2 490		2 260

The following supporting information is available:

(i) Details relating to the non-current assets are:
Property, plant and equipment at:

| | 31 March 2005 | | | 31 March 2004 | | |
	Cost/ Valuation $m	Depreciation $m	Value Carrying $m	Cost/ Valuation $m	Depreciation $m	Carrying value $m
Land and buildings	600	12	588	500	80	420
Plant	440	148	292	445	105	340
			880			760

Casino revalued the carrying value of its land and buildings by an increase of $70 million on 1 April 2004. On 31 March 2005 Casino transferred $3 million from the revaluation reserve to retained earnings representing the realisation of the revaluation reserve due to the depreciation of buildings.

During the year Casino acquired new plant at a cost of $60 million and sold some old plant for $15 million at a loss of $12 million.

There were no acquisitions or disposals of intangible assets.

(ii) The following extract is from the draft income statement for the year to 31 March 2005:

	$m	$m
Operating loss		(32)
Interest receivable		12
Finance costs		(24)
Loss before tax		(44)
Income tax repayment claim	14	
Deferred tax charge	(15)	(1)
Loss for the period		(45)
The finance costs are made up of:		
Interest expenses		(16)
Penalty cost for early redemption of fixed rate loan		(6)
Issue costs of variable rate loan		(2)
		(24)

(iii) The short-term deposits meet the definition of cash equivalents.

(iv) Dividends of $25 million were paid during the year.

Required:

As far as the information permits, prepare a statement of cash flows for Casino for the year to 31 March 2005 in accordance with IAS 7, *Statements of Cash Flows*.

(b) In recent years many analysts have commented on a growing disillusionment with the usefulness and reliability of the information contained in some companies' income statements.

Required:

Discuss the extent to which a company's statement of cash flows may be more useful and reliable than its income statement.

(CIMA paper, *Financial Accounting and Tax Principles* June 2005)

DISCLOSURE ISSUES

24

OBJECTIVES After studying this chapter, you should be able to:

- explain the purpose of segmental reporting or disclosure of segment information

- describe what is meant by an operating segment

- explain the criteria for the determination of a reportable segment

- describe what is meant by a post-balance sheet event or by an event after the reporting period

- explain the difference between an adjusting event and a non-adjusting event

- define basic earnings per share

- define diluted earnings per share

- describe the contents and appraise the statement IAS 33 on earnings per share

- describe the main issues of interim financial reporting under IAS 34.

INTRODUCTION

Most of the Standards that we are going to discuss in this chapter have in common, that they regulate supplemental information disclosure on top of the data reported in the balance sheet and income statement. The aim of the Standards discussed in this chapter is the improvement of the information disclosed in the financial statements for decision usefulness. Stakeholders will make economic decisions based on the reported information. The issues to be discussed are segmental reporting (IFRS 8), communication of information on post-balance sheet events (IAS 10), the determination of the earnings per share (IAS 33) and interim financial reporting (IAS 34).

DISCLOSURE OF SEGMENT INFORMATION

The first Standard that we will discuss in this chapter is IFRS 8 on the disclosure of segment information.

In the autumn of 2006, the IASB issued a new Standard on segmental reporting: IFRS 8, *Operating Segments*. IFRS 8 replaces the old IAS 14, *Segmental Reporting*. IFRS 8 is part of the convergence programme with the FASB and its purpose is to achieve convergence in the area of segment reporting with segmental reporting rules under US GAAP. In practice this specific convergence project (see also Chapter 3) implies that IAS 14 is substituted by SFAS 131, *Disclosures About Segments of an Entity and Related Information*, a financial accounting standard of the FASB. This time, like any other time when Standards on segmental reporting are on the agenda of a standard setter, these Standards generate a lot of discussions and controversy. According to preparers of financial information the Standard requires too much information to be disclosed whereas users complain about the lack of comparable information.

Why is disclosure of segment information such a topic of debate?

Purpose of the disclosure of segment reporting

In order to answer that question, we will first define what segmental reporting means and its purpose. On the balance sheet and profit and loss account of a company aggregated data on sales, expenses, assets and liabilities of a company as a whole are communicated to external parties. For companies active in a single industry, e.g. Pizza Hut, the risk and the volatility of the results disclosed by the company in the profit and loss account are tied to the characteristics of risk and volatility of that specific industry. In this case external stakeholders are able to make predictions about the future performance of the company based on an assessment of its prior year and current performance and on an assessment of the future evolution of the industry in which the company is active.

Very often, however, companies sell multiple products and are competing in different industries and on different regional markets, e.g. companies such as Nike and Adidas are active in the sport equipment industry and clothing industry and they are selling their products worldwide in markets with different levels of purchasing power. A company like the Scandinavian SAS group is active in the airline industry as well as in the hotel business. The corporate risk and the future performance of these companies or groups is influenced, first, by the individual risks and performance patterns of the different product groups and, second, by the individual risks of the different markets in which they are competing. The risks and volatility of the results of these individual products – or services groups or different markets – can be positively or negatively correlated to each other. If there is a positive correlation between the risks and returns of the individual segments then the risk of the company as a whole is increased and the corporate result will then be highly volatile. If the correlation is negative the corporate risk is reduced. So in order to make predictions about the future performance of multi-business and multinational companies, information on the performance of the individual groups of products or services and the different regional markets is essential.

Providing that financial information about these different product groups and separate markets is called segmental reporting or disclosure of segment information.

Think of some multinationals or other companies you are familiar with and try to determine whether they are single business or multi-business entities and if they are competing in different markets. What kind of information would you like about them?

Segmental reporting or disclosure of segment information is dealt with in IFRS 8, *Operating Segments*. As mentioned in the introductory paragraph the key objective of this Standard is to assist the user of financial statements in making judgements about the opportunities and risks facing an entity by the disclosure of more disaggregated information than that provided in the primary financial statements (meaning the balance sheet and profit and loss account of the group).

Information on the result obtained in each segment should be disclosed together with the capital employed in each segment. As the segmental information to be disclosed is more disaggregated, it enables the reader of the financial statements to analyse the financial performance of the entity in the various areas or segments in which it operates. In this respect segmental information increases the value relevance of the accounting information disclosed in the financial statements.

Companies, however, are not very eager to disclose segmental information as these segmental data are of strategic importance. The profitability of individual markets or business lines are revealed by it. Segmental data not only increase the value relevance of the accounts for investors, but also competitors will make use of those segmental data in their own decision process. As disclosing segmental data are experienced by companies as communicating proprietary information, firms have often tried in the past to provide segmental information of little value relevance. Analysts have consistently criticised the quality and inadequacy of the segment disclosures. Firms often argued that the benefits of informing the capital markets about firm value are smaller than the costs of aiding competitors with the information. The degree of flexibility permitted in segment disclosures was an issue for regulators in the 1980s and the 1990s (Fields, Lys and Vincent, 2001). In the mid-1990s the American FASB issued a new standard on segment reporting requiring disclosures on segment reporting that are consistent with the firm's internal reporting organisation. The IASB now takes a similar approach with IFRS 8, which does not differ from the American standard on segmental reporting.

Before we start with the discussion of the contents of IFRS 8, it is important to stress that IFRS 8 should be applied by those entities whose equity or debt securities are publicly traded and by entities that are in the process of issuing equity or debt securities in public securities markets (IFRS 8; para. 2). Companies that issue voluntarily segmental information in their IAS accounts should also fully comply with IFRS 8 (para. 2). According to IFRS 8 an entity shall disclose information to enable users of its financial statements to evaluate the nature and financial effects of the business activites in which it engages and the economic environments in which it operates.

Definition of segments

In order to provide guidance on the disclosure of segment information IFRS 8 starts with a discussion of the concept of an operating segment. The first step towards the disclosure of segmental information is the definition of the different operating segments present in the company. The principle underlying the approach in IFRS 8 is that the process of identifying segments for external reporting purposes begins with the information used by the board of directors and the chief executive officer to evaluate past performance and to make decisions about future allocations of resources. The former IAS 14 had as underlying principles that similar risks and returns were the basis to define the business and the geographical segments of a company, which would be the basis for segmental reporting.

Under IFRS 8 segments for which financial information has to be disclosed in the notes are identified on the basis of internal reports that are regularly reviewed by the entity's chief operating decision maker to allocate resources and to evaluate the performance of those segments. Through this management approach of segmental reporting, the user of the financial statements will receive segmental information in the same format and according to the same valuation rules as the management of the company. According to this approach no segments have to be created for external purposes. This certainly facilitates the task of preparers of financial statements. For users of the annual accounts, however, there is a danger that this 'look through the eyes of management' will create an obstacle to the comparability of segment information between different companies. This approach has generated a lot of comment letters from users of financial statements at the stage when Exposure Draft 8 on operating segments was issued.

IFRS 8 (para. 5) provides the following definition for the concept 'operating segment':

An operating segment is a component of an entity:

(a) that engages in business activities from which it may earn revenues and incur expenses (including revenues and expenses relating to transactions with other components of the same entity),

(b) whose operating results are regularly reviewed by the entity's chief operating decision maker to make decisions about resources to be allocated to the segment and assess its performance, and

(c) for which discrete financial information is available.

The above definition implies that internal segments which do not earn revenue, such as corporate headquarters, will not qualify as an operating segment. The term 'chief operating decision maker' identifies a function, not necessarily a manager with a specific title.

Generally, an operating segment has a segment manager who is directly accountable to and maintains regular contact with the chief operating decision maker to discuss operating activities, financial results, forecasts, or plans for the segment. An operating segment can be a business segment or a geographical segment or a combination of both.

We include the segmental reporting of Adidas in its annual report of 2007. The segmental information is disclosed based on the management approach, which is in compliance with IFRS 8 (see also page 576).

Notes – Additional Information 29 SEGMENTAL INFORMATION The Group operates predominately in one industry segment – the design, wholesale and marketing of athletic and sports lifestyle products. The Group is currently managed by brands.

Certain Group functions are centralised and an allocation of these functions to specific segments is not considered to be meaningful. This includes functions such as central treasury, worldwide sourcing as well as other headquarter departments. Assets, liabilities, income and expenses relating to these corporate functions are presented in the HQ/Consolidation column together with other non-allocable items and intersegment eliminations.

The Reebok segment includes the brands Reebok, Reebok-CCM Hockey and Rockport. The Greg Norman license, which was acquired with the Reebok business and subsequently sold in November 2006, was allocated to the TaylorMade-adidas Golf segment. In 2007, the remaining retail activities were allocated to the Reebok segment. Both the NBA and Liverpool licensed businesses were transferred to brand adidas in the first half of 2006.

Information about the Group's segments in accordance with the management approach is presented on the following page.

There are no intersegment sales between the brands. Net sales to third parties are shown in the geographic market in which the revenues are realised. The global sourcing function is included in the HQ/Consolidation column. Transactions between the segments are based on the dealing-at-arm's-length principle.

Segment assets include all operating assets and comprise mainly accounts receivable, inventory as well as property, plant and equipment and intangible assets. Segment liabilities comprise operating liabilities and consist principally of trade and other payables as well as accrued liabilities and provisions. Non-allocable items including financial assets or assets and liabilities relating to income taxes and borrowings, are included in the HQ/Consolidation column.

Capital expenditure, amortisation and depreciation relate to segment assets; the acquisition of goodwill and the inception of finance leases do not affect capital expenditure.

The second step in the disclosure of segmental information relates to the determination of the reportable segments on the basis of the operating segments present in a company according to IFRS 8 (para. 5). So in the next section we describe how operating segments will qualify to be reportable segments.

ADIDAS – PRIMARY SEGMENTAL INFORMATION BY BRAND

€ in millions

	adidas		Reebok		TaylorMade-adidas Golf		HQ/Consolidation		adidas Group	
	2007	2006	2007	2006	2007	2006	2007	2006	2007	2006
Net sales to third parties	7,113	6,626	2,333	2,473	804	856	49	129	10,299	10,084
Gross profit	3,370	3,059	902	865	360	376	250	195	4,882	4,495
in % of net sales	47.4%	46.2%	38.7%	35.0%	44.7%	43.9%	–	–	47.4%	44.6%
Operating profit	920	788	109	86	65	73	(145)	(66)	949	881
in % of net sales	12.9%	11.9%	4.7%	3.5%	8.1%	8.5%	–	–	9.2%	8.7%
Assets	3,329	3,211	2,913	3,217	629	656	1,454	1,295	8,325	8,379
Liabilities	900	752	421	477	106	106	3,865	4,208	5,292	5,543
Capital expenditure	150	135	57	72	12	13	70	57	289	277
Amortisation and depreciation	104	91	60	53	12	13	25	25	201	182
Impairment	2	11	1	–	–	–	–	–	3	11

SECONDARY SEGMENTAL INFORMATION BY REGION

€ in millions

	Europe		North America		Asia	
	2007	2006	2007	2006	2007	2006
Net sales to third parties	4,369	4,162	2,929	3,234	2,254	2,020
Assets	1,819	1,808	1,489	1,564	772	719
Capital Expenditure	105	84	34	49	49	74

	Latin America		HQ/Consolidation		adidas Group	
	2007	2006	2007	2006	2008	2006
Net sales to third parties	657	499	89	169	10,299	10,084
Assets	285	217	3,960	4,071	8,325	8,379
Capital Expenditure	10	7	91	63	289	277

Region Europe also includes Middle East and Africa, Region Asia also includes the Pacific region.

Reportable segments

A reportable segment is an operating segment for which segment information is required to be disclosed by the Standard. Only for reportable segments do segment data have to be disclosed in the notes to the balance sheet and the profit and loss account.

According to IFRS 8 (para. 11) an entity shall report separately information about each operating segment that has been identified or that results from aggregating two or more of those operating segments according to para. 12 of IFRS 8 if each operating segment or the aggregation of operating segments exceeds the quantitative thresholds (para. 13 of IFRS 8). So once a company knows which segments qualify under the definition of operating segments, a company will focus on the aggregation criteria and figure out whether or not operating segments can be combined for reporting purposes. Second, only information on an operating segment or aggregated segments needs to be disclosed if the segment or aggregated segments exceed a number of quantitative thresholds. So, to sum up, operating segments which comply with the aggregation criteria and meet the quantitative thresholds are externally reportable segments.

When operating segments have similar economic characteristics and subsequently similar long-term financial performance, they might be aggregated. The aggregation criteria are defined as follows (para. 12): Two or more operating segments may be aggregated into a single operating segment if the segments have similar economic characteristics and if they are similar in the following respects:

(a) the nature of the products and services

(b) the nature of the production processes

(c) the type or class of customer for their product and services

(d) the methods used to distribute their products or provide their services

(e) if applicable, the nature of the regulatory environment, for example banking, insurance or public utilities.

Second, only information on operating segments or aggregated operating segments need to be disclosed if the segment or aggregated segments exceed a number of quantitative thresholds specified in IFRS 8 (para. 13).

An entity shall report separately information about an operating segment that meets any of the following quantitative thresholds:

(a) its reported revenue, including both sales to external customers and intersegment sales or transfers, is 10% or more of the combined revenue, internal and external of all operating segments

(b) the absolute amount of its reported profit or loss is 10% or more of the greater, in absolute amount, of (i) the combined reported profit of all operating segments that did not report a loss, and (ii) the combined reported loss of all operating segments that reported a loss

(c) its assets are 10% or more of the combined assets of all operating segments.

Operating segments that do not meet any of the quantitative thresholds may be considered reportable, and separately disclosed, if management believes that information about the segment would be useful to users of the financial statements.

IFRS 8 specifies further that (para. 15) if the total external revenue reported by operating segments constitutes less than 75% of the entity's revenue, additional operating segments shall be identified as reportable segments (even if they do not

The management of a major multinational has identified the following reportable segments:

	Total segment revenues	Inter-segment revenues	Segment result	Identifiable segment assets
Segment A	750		300	800
Segment B	400	40	−50	450
Segment C	950		250	600
Segment D	500	50	200	900
Segment E	350	35	50	500
Segment F	500		150	700
Segment G	550		−100	750
Segment H	650		100	400
Total segments	4 650	125	900	5 100
Inter-company eliminations	125		50	150
Consolidated total	4 525		850	4 950

1 Assume segments A–H are business segments. Determine which of these business segments would classify as reportable segments.

2 Based on your answer on question 1, determine whether sufficient operations are represented by the reportable segments (75% threshold test).

Activity feedback

1 Reportable segments

	Segment revenue[1] >465 10% of 4 650	Segment result >105 10% of 1 050[2]	Identifiable segment assets >510 10% of 5 100	Reportable segment
Segment A	Yes	Yes	Yes	Yes
Segment B	No	No	No	No
Segment C	Yes	Yes	Yes	Yes
Segment D	Yes	Yes	Yes	Yes
Segment E	No	No	No	No
Segment F	Yes	Yes	Yes	Yes
Segment G	Yes	No	Yes	Yes
Segment H	Yes	No	No	Yes

[1] The majority of the segment revenue is from external sales in all segments.

[2] Combined result of segments in profit 1 050
Combined result of segments in loss 150
Chose the greater in absolute amounts, i.e. 1 050

2 Number of reportable segments

In order to determine the number of reportable segments the threshold of 75% of the external revenue reported by the segments applies. This implies that if the total external revenue reported by the segments constitutes less than 75 of the entity's revenue, additional segments must be identified as reportable segments until at least 75% of the entity's revenue is included in reportable segments.

So 75% (4525) = 3394 is the threshold. We will check whether we meet the threshold with individual segments which have passed the size criteria for being an individual reportable segment.

External revenue segment A	= 750
External revenue segment C	= 950
External revenue segment D	= 450
External revenue segment F	= 500
External revenue segment G	= 550
External revenue segment H	= 650
Total	3850

Even without segment D, the threshold of 75% is met.

meet the quantitative thresholds defined in para. 13) until at least 75% of the entity's revenue is included in reportable segments.

Activity 24.1 illustrates the application of the size criteria or quantitative thresholds in order to determine whether or not an individual segment qualifies to be a reportable segment and whether or not sufficient reportable segments have been distinguished for disclosure in the notes to the accounts.

Disclosure of segmental data

Once the reportable segments are determined, information on these segments must be disclosed in the notes in order to enable users of financial statements to evaluate the nature and financial effects of the business activities in which it engages and the economic environments in which it operates.

First of all some general information has to be provided with regard to the reportable segments (para. 22).

(a) factors used to identify the entity's reportable segments, including the basis of organisation (for example, whether management has chosen to organise the entity around differences in products and services, geographical areas, regulatory environments, or a combination of factors and whether operating segments have been aggregated), and

(b) types of products and services from which each reportable segment derives its revenues.

Afterwards specific information needs to be disclosed. IFRS 8 states explicitly which information needs to be included in the notes with regard to profit and loss items of the reporting segment. Remember that the internal information communicated and reviewed by the chief operating decision maker is the basis for segmental disclosure. However with regard to the items of the profit and loss and the total assets, IFRS 8 states explicitly that these items should be disclosed even if they are not included in the communication to the chief operating decision maker. With regard to segment liabilities IFRS 8 states that an entity shall report a measure of liability for each reportable segment only if such an amount is regularly provided to the chief operating decision maker. The old IAS 14 required the disclosure of segment liabilities. The following items need to be disclosed for each reportable segment.

(a) revenues from external customers

(b) revenues from transactions with other operating segments of the same entity

(c) interest revenue

(d) interest expense

(e) depreciation and amortisation

(f) material items of income and expense disclosed in accordance with paragraph 86 of IAS 1, *Presentation of Financial Statements*

(g) the entity's interest in profit or loss of associates and joint ventures accounted for by the equity method

(h) income tax expense or income, and

(i) material non-cash items other than depreciation and amortisation.

An entity shall report interest revenue separately from interest expense for each reportable segment unless a majority of the segment's revenues are from interest and the chief operating decision maker relies primarily on the net interest revenue to assess the performance of the segment and to make decisions about resources to be allocated to the segment. In that situation, an entity may report that segment's interest revenue net of its interest expense and inform the user of the financial statements about this decision. Further an entity shall disclose the following about each reportable segment whether or not this information is included in the information provided to the chief operating decision maker:

(a) the amount of investment in associates and joint ventures accounted for by the equity method, and

(b) total expenditures for additions to non-current assets other than financial instruments, deferred tax assets, post-employment benefit assets (see the discussion on employee benefits, Chapter 21) and rights arising under insurance contracts.

The measurement of the segment data under IFRS 8 is fundamentally different from the measurement under IAS 14. In contrast with segment data reportable under IAS 14 segment data separated under IFRS 8 do not need to be in compliance with IAS regulations. The amount of each segment item reported shall be the measure reported to the chief operating decision maker for the purposes of making decisions about allocating resources to the segment and assessing its performance. Adjustments and eliminations made in preparing an entity's financial statements and allocations of revenues, expenses, and gains or losses shall be included in determining reported segment profit or loss only if they are included in the measure of the segment's profit or loss that is used by the chief operating decision maker. Similarly, only those assets that are included in the measure of the segment's assets that is used by the chief operating decision maker shall be reported for that segment. If amounts are allocated to reported segment profit or loss or assets, those amounts shall be allocated on a reasonable basis. So in a nutshell segment revenue, segment expenses and segment assets can be valued according to other rules or principles other than IAS/IFRS.

Again we notice an element that might impede comparability of segment data between different companies as the valuation basis of the segment data can be different. Since there is no obligation for the disclosed segment data to comply with International Accounting Standards the reported totals over all segments might deviate from the figures which appear in the group financial statements which comply with IAS. In order to link the disclosed segment data with the data published in the balance sheet and the profit and loss account of the entity, the following reconciliations have to be provided.

(a) the total of reportable segments' revenues to the entity's revenue

(b) the total of the reportable segments' measures of profit or loss to the entity's profit or loss before income tax expense or income and discontinued operations. However, if an entity allocates to reportable segments items such as income tax expense or income, the entity may reconcile the total of the segments' measures of profit or loss to the entity's profit or loss after those items

(c) the total of the reportable segments' assets to the entity's assets

(d) the total of the reportable segments' amounts for every other material item of information disclosed to the corresponding amount for the entity. For example, an entity may choose to disclose liabilities for its reportable segments, in which case the entity would reconcile the total of reportable segments' liabilities to the entity's liabilities if the segment liabilities are material.

Besides this requirement to disclose segmental data, IFRS 8 also prescribes the disclosure of entity-wide data. These requirements for entity-wide disclosures also apply to entities that have only one single reportable segment. The IASB are well aware of the fact that some entities' business activities are not organised on the basis of differences in related products and services or differences in geographical areas of operations. In this case such an entity's reportable segments may report revenues from a broad range of essentially different products and services, or more than one of its reportable segments may provide essentially the same products and services. Similarly, an entity's reportable segments may hold assets in different geographical areas and report revenues from customers in different geographical areas, or more than one of its reportable segments may operate in the same geographical area.

In order to ensure that users of financial statements receive at least some information, which they can use for inter-firm comparison and which is understandable in a straightforward way, IFRS 8 states that entities must disclose the following in addition to their segmental data.

1 Information about products and services (revenues from external customers for each product and service or each group of similar products or services).

2 Information about geographical areas:

   (a) revenues from external customers:

   (i) attributed to the entity's country of domicile and

   (ii) attributed to all foreign countries in total from which the entity derives revenues. If revenues from external customers attributed to an individual foreign country are material, those revenues shall be disclosed separately. An entity shall disclose the basis for attributing revenues from external customers to individual countries

   (b) non-current assets other than financial instruments, deferred tax assets, post-employment benefit assets, and rights arising under insurance contracts:

   (i) located in the entity's country of domicile and

   (ii) located in all foreign countries in total in which the entity holds assets. If assets in an individual foreign country are material, those assets shall be disclosed separately.

The amounts reported in relation to 1 and 2 shall be based on the financial information that is used to produce the entity's financial statements. This implies that this information shall be prepared according to IFRS. If the information is not available in accordance with IFRS and if the cost of producing this information would be excessive, the information can be omitted.

3 Information about major customers. If revenues from transactions with a single external customer amount to 10% or more of an entity's revenues, the

entity shall disclose that fact, the total amount of revenues from each such customer, and the identity of the segment or segments reporting the revenues. The entity need not disclose the identity of a major customer or the amount of revenues that each segment reports from that customer. For the purpose of this IFRS, a group of entities known to a reporting entity to be under common control shall be considered a single customer, and a national government, a local government, or a foreign government shall each be considered a single customer.

These entity-wide disclosures must probably compensate for the loss of comparable information on business and geographical segments which was required by IAS 14 but abolished with the introduction of IFRS 8.

The primary reporting segment format chosen by Nestlé for its Annual Report in 2007 is probably already an indication of the kind of segmental information that forthcoming IFRS 8 will provide us with. We find a mixture of geographical and business segments.

InBev, now the world's largest brewer after the acquisition of Anheuser Busch, discloses that IFRS 8 will not alter its segment reporting. The notes to its 2007 accounts (see pages 584–5) reads as follows.

EVENTS AFTER BALANCE SHEET DATE OR AFTER THE REPORTING PERIOD

Financial statements are used for mainly two purposes. First of all, external stakeholders will use financial statement information as input in their own decision-making process and, second, financial statements can serve as a basis for control on stewardship. The latter means that management and directors could be held accountable for their policy decisions and actions on the basis of the financial statements.

With regard to the first aim of financial reporting, namely providing useful and reliable information, it is important that external stakeholders get a clear idea about which transactions and their related financial impact are included in the annual accounts and which transactions or events and their related financial impact have not been taken into account in the financial statements. Between the balance sheet date and the publication of the financial statements to the public time passes. Accounts, no matter how sophisticated the information technology, are never prepared, audited and approved by directors in a few days. Generally there is a time lag of a number of months between the balance sheet date and the 'signing off' of the accounts by directors. During this period numerous events can occur that may or may not have an influence on the information which is provided, by the final accounts, for users (see Activity 24.2).

The events listed in Activity 24.2 will have an impact on the financial situation of the company and it might well be that external stakeholders will change their decisions in relation to the company if they take into account the financial impact of the information becoming available after balance sheet date. IAS 10 deals with the communication of the impact of those post-balance sheet events on the financial situation of the company.

Definition of events after balance sheet date or after the reporting period

Paragraph 3 of IAS 10 defines events occurring after the balance sheet date as those events, both favourable and unfavourable, that occur between the balance sheet date

1. Segmental information
Nestlé Group – By management responsibility and geographic area

In millions of CHF

2007	Zone Europe	Zone Americas	Zone Asia, Oceania and Africa	Nestlé Waters	Nestlé Nutrition	Other Food and Beverages	Unallocated items	Inter-segment eliminations	Total Food and Beverages	Pharma	Total
Segment revenues and results											
Sales	28 464	32 917	16 556	10 404	8 434	3 458			100 233	7 319	107 552
EBIT Earnings Before Interest, Taxes, restructuring and impairments	3 412	5 359	2 697	851	1 447	548	(1725)		12 589	2 435	15 024
Segment assets and liabilities											
Segment assets	15 794	19 503	9 153	9 298	13 990	1 792	13 140	(1 565)	81 105	7 120	88 225
Non segment assets											26 434
Total assets											114 659
of which goodwill and intangible assets	3 457	7 702	2 113	2 859	10 070	237	10 667		37 105	3 535	40 640
Segment liabilities	6 096	4 067	2 595	2 220	1 385	768	796	(1 565)	16 362	1 090	17 452
Non segment liabilities											42 973
Total liabilities											60 425
Other segment information											
Capital additions	1 118	1 667	811	1 382	9 768	272	135		15 153	1 483	16 636
of which Capital expenditure	932	1 371	675	1 043	271	269	134		4 695	276	4 971
Depreciation of segment assets	878	753	458	527	155	31	146		2 948	263	3 211
Impairment of segment assets	85	66	13	243	–	4	–		411	71	482
Restructuring costs	89	15	60	237	46	7	–		454	27	481

InBev – Segment reporting
Primary segments
Million euro. except
volume (million hl)
and full time equivalents
(FTE in units)

	North America 2007	North America 2006	Latin America North 2007	Latin America North 2006	Latin America South 2007	Latin America South 2006	Western Europe 2007	Western Europe 2006	Central and Eastern Europe 2007	Central and Eastern Europe 2006	Asia Pacific 2007	Asia Pacific 2006	Global export and holding companies 2007	Global export and holding companies 2006	Consolidated 2007	Consolidated 2006
Volume	**13**	**14**	**101**	**94**	**31**	**23**	**36**	**39**	**49**	**43**	**36**	**31**	**5**	**2**	**271**	**247**
Revenue	**1 564**	**1 831**	**4 904**	**4 268**	**1 003**	**733**	**3 455**	**3 646**	**2 198**	**1 820**	**994**	**912**	**312**	**99**	**14 430**	**13 308**
Cost of goods sold	(491)	(680)	(1 664)	(1 491)	(425)	(313)	(1 616)	(1 619)	(1 013)	(840)	(495)	(467)	(233)	(67)	(5 936)	(5 477)
Distribution expenses	(275)	(270)	(551)	(500)	(82)	(56)	(403)	(416)	(292)	(242)	(68)	(66)	(41)	(1)	(1 713)	(1 551)
Sales and marketing expenses	(206)	(311)	(491)	(440)	(118)	(89)	(668)	(720)	(392)	(312)	(207)	(174)	(52)	(68)	(2 134)	(2 115)
Administrative expenses	(83)	(104)	(256)	(273)	(44)	(51)	(235)	(263)	(131)	(140)	(61)	(54)	(179)	(191)	(990)	(1 075)
Other operating income/(expenses)	3	(6)	121	61	(11)	(9)	(70)	(108)	(69)	(80)	-	(1)	289	276	263	133
Normalised profit from operations (EBIT)	**512**	**459**	**2 062**	**1 625**	**323**	**215**	**462**	**520**	**302**	**206**	**163**	**150**	**96**	**49**	**3 920**	**3 223**
Non-recurring items	14	(4)	14	60	(2)	4	347	(139)	(15)	(2)	3	(7)	12	(7)	374	(94)
Profit from operations (EBIT)	**526**	**455**	**2 076**	**1 684**	**320**	**219**	**809**	**381**	**287**	**204**	**167**	**143**	**108**	**42**	**4 294**	**3 129**
Net finance cost	(48)	(56)	(370)	(276)	(19)	(22)	(287)	(209)	(44)	(37)	(4)	(13)	173	140	(598)	(473)
Share of result of associates	-	1	-	-	1	-	(1)	-	-	-	-	-	-	-	1	1
Profit before tax	**479**	**400**	**1 706**	**1 407**	**303**	**197**	**521**	**173**	**244**	**168**	**163**	**130**	**282**	**182**	**3 697**	**2 657**
Income tax expense	(126)	(145)	(195)	(142)	(91)	(60)	(86)	(74)	(62)	(40)	(38)	(33)	(51)	(38)	(649)	(531)
Profit	**353**	**255**	**1 510**	**1 265**	**212**	**137**	**436**	**99**	**182**	**128**	**124**	**97**	**231**	**144**	**3 048**	**2 126**
Normalised profit	343	258	1 504	1 227	212	133	109	218	195	129	125	105	187	151	2 675	2 220
Normalised EBITDA	597	551	2 318	1 872	405	280	771	834	520	398	263	241	118	63	4 992	4 239
EBITDA margin (normalised) in %	38.2	30.1	47.3	43.9	40.3	38.2	22.3	22.9	23.6	21.8	26.5	26.4	-	-	34.6	31.9
Segment assets	2 271	2 333	10 059	8 321	2 388	2 405	4 602	4 908	3 058	2 910	2 664	2 825	1 497	962	26 540	24 664
Intersegment elimination															(668)	(151)
Non-segmented assets															2 827	2 097
Total assets															**28 699**	**26 246**

(Continued)

InBev – Segment reporting
Primary segments
Million euro. except volume (million hl) and full time equivalents (FTE in units)

	North America 2007	North America 2006	Latin America North 2007	Latin America North 2006	Latin America South 2007	Latin America South 2006	Western Europe 2007	Western Europe 2006	Central and Eastern Europe 2007	Central and Eastern Europe 2006	Asia Pacific 2007	Asia Pacific 2006	Global export and holding companies 2007	Global export and holding companies 2006	Consolidated 2007	Consolidated 2006
Segment liabilities	739	736	2 138	1 461	379	281	1 884	2 081	529	502	519	389	571	585	6 759	6 035
Intersegment elimination															(668)	(515)
Non-segmented liabilities															22 608	20 726
Total liabilities															**28 699**	**26 246**
Gross capex	74	76	367	332	132	117	367	332	415	377	158	84	58	63	1 571	1 380
Impairment losses/ (reversals)	(12)	22	3	(1)	–	–	(27)	61	4	(3)	1	1	–	–	(31)	81
Depreciation & amortisation	86	93	253	244	82	67	307	314	211	191	100	89	22	15	1 061	1 012
Additions to/ (reversals) of provisions	1	48	30	(30)	12	1	23	89	14	5	10	(1)	14	26	105	139
FTE	5 662	6 337	25 999	24 872	7 290	5 306	11 481	12 122	13 509	13 356	24 056	22 925	694	699	88 690	85 617

Secondary segments

Million euro, except volume (million hl)

	Beer 2007	Beer 2006	Non-beer 2007	Non-beer 2006	Consolidated 2007	Consolidated 2006
Volume	230	212	41	35	271	247
Revenue	13 237	12 313	1 193	995	14 430	13 308
Total assets	19 662	23 535	9 037	2 711	28 699	26 246
Gross capex	1 343	1 284	228	96	1 571	1 380

ACTIVITY 24.2

Can you think of activities after balance sheet date which might alter the financial picture presented by the financial statements closed at the balance sheet date?

Activity feedback

- The bankruptcy of an important customer.
- The levy of import tariffs in an important export market of the company.

- The acquisition of a large part of the shares of a company.
- A settlement of a court case in which the company is involved.

and the date when the financial statements are authorised for issue. Two types of event can be identified:

- those that provide evidence of conditions that existed at the balance sheet date (adjusting events after the balance sheet date)
- those that are indicative of conditions that arose subsequent to the balance sheet date (non-adjusting events after the balance sheet date).

Date of authorisation for issue

In order to judge the relevance of the information provided through the financial statements it is of extreme importance for the external stakeholders to know when the financial statements have been authorised for issue, as the financial statements do not reflect events after this date. Therefore para. 17 of IAS 10 states explicitly that an entity should disclose the date on which the financial statements were authorised for issue and who gave that authorisation. If the entity's owner or others have the power to amend the financial statements after issuance, the entity should disclose that fact (see Activity 24.3).

The process involved in authorising the financial statements for issue will vary depending on the management structure, statutory requirements and procedures followed in preparing and finalising the financial statements (para. 4). In some cases, an entity is required to submit its financial statements to its shareholders for approval after the financial statements have already been issued. In such cases, the financial statements are authorised for issue on the date of original issuance, not on the date when shareholders approve the financial statements (para. 5). In other cases,

ACTIVITY 24.3

Check the financial statements on several websites of listed companies. Is information disclosure clear on this issue (= date of authorisation for issue and who gave the authorisation)?

Activity feedback

As a user of the annual report and the financial statements you will have found out that it is not easily

retrievable and it is not obvious where to find that information, especially with regard to the item 'who gave the authorisation'.

An example of such disclosure is found in the financial statements of Anglo Gold United (Annual Report 2000, p. 42) (see Table 24.1).

TABLE 24.1	Annual accounts of Anglo Gold United

Directors' approval

The annual financial statements and group annual financial statements for the year ended 31 December 2000 were approved by the board of directors on 20 February 2001 and are signed on its behalf by:

Directors:

R M Godsell
Chairman and chief
executive officer

R P Edey
Deputy chairman

J G Best
Finance director

C B Brayshaw
Chairman, Audit
Committee

Managing secretary: **Ms Y Z Simelane**

---

the management of an entity is required to issue its financial statements to a supervisory board (made up solely of non-executives) for approval. In such cases, the financial statements are authorised for issue when the management authorises them for issue to the supervisory board. Care may need to be taken in determining the date of 'authorisation' for this purpose. The Standard has to allow for a variety of different national systems of corporate governance and of management structure.

IAS 10 makes a distinction between adjusting events after balance sheet date and non-adjusting events after balance sheet date. For both type of events the financial impact of the events has to be disclosed to the readers of the financial statements, however, the disclosure method differs.

Adjusting events

With regard to adjusting events an entity should adjust the amounts recognised in its financial statements to reflect adjusting events after the balance sheet date (para. 8). IAS 10 does not give an explicit definition as guidance for what might be an adjusting event. A list of examples of what the IASB considers to be adjusting events is presented. The following examples should serve as a point of reference for preparers of financial statements (para. 9):

- The settlement after the balance sheet date of a court case that confirms that an entity had a present obligation at the balance sheet date. The entity adjusts any provision previously recognised related to this court case in accordance with IAS 37, *Provisions, Contingent Liabilities and Contingent Assets* or recognises a new provision instead of merely disclosing a contingent liability because the settlement provides additional evidence that would be considered in accordance with para. 16 of IAS 37.

- The receipt of information after the balance sheet date indicating that an asset was impaired at the balance sheet date or that the amount of a previously recognised impairment loss for that asset needs to be adjusted. For example:
  - the bankruptcy of a customer which occurs after the balance sheet date usually confirms that a loss already existed at the balance sheet date on a

trade receivable account and that the entity needs to adjust the carrying amount of the trade receivable account

– the sale of inventories after the balance sheet date may give evidence about their net realisable value at the balance sheet date.

- The determination after the balance sheet date of the cost of assets purchased or the proceeds from assets sold before the balance sheet date.

- The determination after the balance sheet date of the amount of profit-sharing or bonus payments, if the entity had a present legal or constructive obligation at the balance sheet date to make such payments as a result of events before that date (see IAS 19).

- The discovery of fraud or errors that show that the financial statements were incorrect.

Non-adjusting events

The name already reveals that the amounts related to this type of post-balance sheet events should not be recognised in the financial statements themselves, but disclosed in the notes to the accounts. If non-adjusting events after the balance sheet date are material, non-disclosure could influence the economic decisions of users taken on the basis of the financial statements (para. 21). Accordingly, an entity shall disclose the following for each material category of non-adjusting event after the balance sheet date in the notes to the accounts:

- the nature of the event

- an estimate of its financial effect, or a statement that such an estimate cannot be made.

Again, examples of non-adjusting events are presented as guidance in IAS 10 (para. 22).

The following are examples of non-adjusting events after the balance sheet date that would generally result in disclosure:

- a major business combination after the balance sheet date (IFRS 3, *Business Combinations*, requires specific disclosures in such cases) or disposing of a major subsidiary

- announcing a plan to discontinue an operation

- major purchases of assets, classification of assets as held for sale in accordance with IFRS 5, *Non-current Assets Held for Sale and Discontinued Operations*, other disposals of assets or expropriation of major assets by government

- destruction of a major production plant by a fire after the balance sheet date

- announcing or commencing the implementation of a major restructuring (see IAS 37, *Provisions, Contingent Liabilities and Contingent Assets*)

- major ordinary share transactions and potential ordinary share transactions after the balance sheet date (IAS 33, *Earnings Per Share*, requires an entity to disclose a description of such transactions, other than when such transactions involve capitalisation or bonus issues, share splits or reverse share splits all of which are required to be adjusted under IAS 33)

- abnormally large changes after the balance sheet date in asset prices or foreign exchange rates

- changes in tax rates or tax laws enacted or announced after the balance sheet date that have a significant effect on current and deferred tax assets and liabilities (see IAS 12, *Income Taxes*)

- entering into significant commitments or contingent liabilities, for example, by issuing significant guarantees

- commencing major litigation arising solely out of events that occurred after the balance sheet date.

Since information on adjusting but also on non-adjusting events is extremely important for external parties, the disclosure rules on non-adjusting events became stricter over the past years. If an entity receives information after the balance sheet date about conditions that existed at the balance sheet date, they are now obliged to adjust disclosures that relate to these conditions, in the light of the new information.

If we study the list of examples of non-adjusting events described in para. 22 of IAS 10, we notice that some events lie within the decision power of the management (e.g. acquisitions, discontinuing operations) and other events are beyond the influence of the management (e.g. fire, change in tax laws). It is interesting to observe that many acquisitions or major investments seem to take place between the balance sheet date and the 'signing off' of the accounts. By signing the contract after balance sheet date, the acquisition becomes a non-adjusting event. If, through the acquisition, control was obtained over another entity, full consolidation of the entity in the group accounts could be avoided and the influence of the liabilities of that entity and goodwill paid on acquisition could be postponed for one year on the group's financial statements.

To illustrate this observation we include the information on past balance sheet events published by Adidas in its Annual Report 2005, p. 153.

> 36 Events after the Balance Sheet Date Group-Specific Subsequent Events
>
> The acquisition of Reebok International Ltd., Canton, Massachusetts (USA), with all its direct and indirect subsidiaries, announced on August 3, 2005, was completed on January 31, 2006. As a result, the Reebok business will be consolidated as a separate brand segment within the adidas Group from February 1, 2006, which will have an impact on the Group's balance sheet and cash flow statement.
>
> The total purchase price for 100% of the shares of Reebok International Ltd. was US$ 3.85 billion (€ 3.2 billion), fully paid in cash. Further disclosures according to IFRS 3 would be impracticable because of the not yet finalised year-end audit of the Reebok Group for 2005 as well as the ongoing purchase price allocation process on the basis of the opening balance sheet as at January 31, 2006.
>
> Date of Authorisation for Issue
>
> The Executive Board of adidas-Salomon AG approved the consolidated financial statements for submission to the Supervisory Board on February 17, 2006. It is the Supervisory Board's task to examine the consolidated financial statements and give their approval and authorisation for issue.
>
> Herzogenaurach, February 17, 2006. The Executive Board of adidas-Salomon AG
> (Adidas, Annual Report 2005)

For more information on these items see also Part Three of this book on group accounts. Further, the subjectivity inherent in the item of possible disclosure of non-adjusting events is not removed by the inclusion in IAS 10 of a list of examples. Words such as 'major' or 'significant' appear in nearly all the examples given, so the expert subjective judgement of the accountants responsible for the preparation of the financial statement package remains crucial.

In the following disclosure on events after balance sheet date of EADS, active in the air, space and defence industry, communicates in the notes to the financial statements information about contracts signed after the reporting date. EADS also mentions the date when the statements were authorised for issue.

Events after the Balance Sheet Date

On 29th February 2008, the U.S. Air Force awarded Northrop Grumman Corp., U.S.A. a contract for the development and procurement of up to 179 tanker aircraft for approximately $40 billion. This dollar amount includes both priced options for 80 aircraft and unpriced options for another 99 as well as estimated support costs (currently unpriced). The initial contract for the newly named KC-45A, is for the system design and development of four test aircraft for $1.5 billion. The Air Force will be funding this initial tranche over the next three years. EADS North America Inc., U.S.A. is the partner to Northrop Grumman Corp., U.S.A. on the new tanker contract, with responsibility for assembling airframes and providing completed flight-qualified aircraft and refueling sub-systems. The Military Transport Aircraft Division (MTAD) is responsible within the EADS Group for all military derivative programmes based on Airbus platforms, including tankers. Starting in 2011, production of KC-45A airframes will be performed at Airbus' new Mobile, Alabama aerospace centre which will house the Airbus KC-45A final assembly facility.

In addition, EADS Group and Airbus intend to transfer the final assembly of Airbus A330 civilian freighters there. Unsuccessful competitor Boeing announced its imminent intention to file a protest with the General Accounting Office, whose decision would have to be issued within 100 days of the filing as required by law.

With regard to the plan to sell the Airbus sites in Méaulte, St. Nazaire Ville, Nordenham, Varel, Laupheim and Filton and the EADS site in Augsburg negotiations with selected preferred bidders (Latécoère in France, GKN in the U.K. and MT Aerospace in Germany) are ongoing. So far, binding agreements have not been reached. Furthermore, the potential divestment of the sites is still subject to EADS' Board of Directors decision.

These Consolidated Financial Statements have been authorised for issuance by the Board of Directors on 10th March 2008.

Dividends

In the latest revision of IAS 10 the treatment of dividends was dealt with more explicitly. Paragraph 12 states that if dividends to holders of equity instruments (as defined in IAS 32, *Financial Instruments: Disclosure and Presentation*) are declared after the balance sheet date, an entity shall not recognise those dividends as a liability at the balance sheet date. In many countries dividends under these circumstances are disclosed as a liability in the national GAAP accounts, the IAS treatment is different.

The issue of going concern

There is, however, one item which applies to the definition of a non-adjusting event, but which entails an adjustment of the financial statements. We refer to para. 14 of IAS which stipulates that if management determines after the balance sheet date either that it intends to liquidate the entity or to cease trading or that it has no realistic alternative but to do so, the financial statements should no longer be prepared on a going concern basis.

This implies that the accounts have to be completely redrawn on a non-going concern basis. The latter has a tremendous impact on the data which will subsequently be presented in the financial statements.

EARNINGS PER SHARE

Most people or companies buy shares of other companies for investment purposes. Probably only fans of listed football clubs such as Manchester United, Barcelona or Ajax buy shares for purely emotional reasons. An indicator frequently used in the context of evaluating the investment performance of a company is earnings per share (see Chapter 11 and Part Four of this book). Earnings per share (EPS) is found by dividing profit attributable to the ordinary shareholders by the number of ordinary shares in issue. As an absolute, however, it has no meaning or relevance. Earnings per share becomes relevant in the context of the price/earnings ratio or when the growth rate of the EPS of a company is considered. This will be explained with the following example. If we are told that company A has an EPS of 6c whereas company B has an EPS of 25c, we are unable to compare the performance of the two because we know nothing about their relative size or, more specifically, about the number or value of shares in issue. For the same reasons, the quoted share price of the two companies provides no basis for comparison of the stockmarket's perceptions of either.

Thus analysts and investors require a basis of comparison and an indicator of confidence in particular companies. Such an indicator is the price/earnings (PE) ratio, which is simply calculated by dividing the share price by the EPS, thereby relating company performance to external perception.

The calculation and use of the PE ratio is illustrated in Activity 24.4, where the PE ratio for company X is calculated to be 7.5 and for company Y, 12.

ACTIVITY 24.4

In which company would you invest?

Company	X	Y
Price per share (a)	150c	96c
Earnings per share (b)	20c	8c
PE ratio (a/b)	7.5	12

Activity feedback

Company X has a higher share price and greater EPS, but company Y is expected to perform better in the future. Why? The normal action of supply and demand has bid up the share price of Y relative to current earnings and the market is therefore saying something about its confidence in Y relative to X. Market participants are willing to pay 12 times the EPS to acquire a share in company Y, whereas investors are only willing to pay seven-and-a-half times the EPS to invest in company X. This difference results from a different view on the future earnings generating power and prospects of both companies (e.g. markets of company Y represent more growth potential, company Y has more products in the early stage of the life cycle of company X). Clearly, a very high PE would indicate such extravagant expectations that there may be some element of risk, but generally a high PE is a good indicator of market support. People are willing to pay more for something they think more highly of.

If the PE ratio is used in this way, being quoted in the financial press and elsewhere, it matters greatly that its derivation is consistent and comparable. There are no problems with the price of the share, but what about the earnings per share?

In this section we will discuss the calculation of the EPS and in Part Four of the book we further illustrate the use of EPS in the context of the price/earnings ratio. In order to calculate earnings per share, first of all, the earnings number has to be defined and, second, the determination of the number of shares to be used in the denominator has to be specified as well. To enhance the comparability of the EPS measure between companies the IASB has issued IAS 33 which deals with the determination of EPS. The IASB is well aware of the fact that IAS 33 mainly improves consistency in the determination of the denominator of the EPS ratio. Companies can still influence their results by using different accounting valuation methods and accounting estimates, as we discuss in Chapter 30.

IAS 33 shall be applied by entities whose ordinary shares or potential ordinary shares are publicly traded and by entities that are in the process of issuing ordinary shares or potential ordinary shares in public securities markets (IAS 33, para. 2). An entity that discloses earnings per share shall calculate and disclose earnings per share in accordance with IAS 33, if they state that their annual accounts comply with IAS/IFRS, even those companies that disclose voluntarily EPS data in their IAS financial statements.

Two types of EPS ratio can be calculated: basic earnings per share (BEPS) and diluted earnings per share (DEPS). The main difference between the two EPS figures is the number of shares they take into account in the denominator. In the calculation of basic earnings per share (BEPS) the outstanding equity share capital during the financial year is taken into consideration. The diluted earnings per share (DEPS) takes into account, besides the outstanding shares, the existence of securities with no current claim on equity earnings, but which will give rise to such a claim in the future. This information gives potential investors an idea about future changes in the EPS.

As the main objective of IAS 33 is achieving consistency in the determination of the denominator of the EPS ratio, the elements to be included in the denominator should be defined first. Paragraphs 5 and 6 of IAS 33 provide the following definitions:

An *ordinary share* is an equity instrument that is subordinate to all other classes of equity instruments. Ordinary shares participate in net profit for the period only after other types of shares such as preference shares.

A *potential ordinary share* is a financial instrument or other contract that may entitle its holder to ordinary shares.

Warrants, options and their equivalents are financial instruments that give the holder the right to purchase ordinary shares.

Contingently issuable ordinary shares are ordinary shares issuable for little or no cash or other consideration upon the satisfaction of certain conditions pursuant to a contingent share agreement, whereby a contingent share agreement is an agreement to issue shares that is dependent on the satisfaction of specified conditions.

Put options on ordinary shares are contracts that give the holder the right to sell ordinary shares at a specified price for a given period.

Dilution is a reduction in earnings per share or an increase in loss per share resulting from the assumption that convertible securities were converted, that

ACTIVITY 24.5

The summarised income statement for EPS SA for the year ended 20X6 is as follows:

	€	€
Profit before taxation		1 000 000
Taxation (including deferred adjustment)		400 000
		600 000
Preference dividend	50 000	
Ordinary dividend	100 000	
		150 000
		450 000

The number of ordinary shares in issue is 200 000.

Calculate the basic EPS.

Activity feedback

From the definition of earnings per share:

$$\text{Basic EPS} = \frac{\text{Profit after tax} - \text{Preference dividend}}{\text{Number of ordinary shares}}$$

$$= \frac{600\,000 - 50\,000}{200\,000}$$

$$= €2.75 \text{ per share}$$

options or warrants were exercised or that ordinary shares were issued upon the satisfaction of certain conditions. As a result of these events the number of outstanding shares will increase.

Anti-dilution is an increase in earnings per share or a reduction in loss per share resulting from the assumption that convertible instruments are converted, that options and warrants are exercised, or that ordinary shares are issued upon the satisfaction of specified conditions. As a result of these events the number of outstanding shares will decrease.

Listed companies have to disclose the basic earnings per share and diluted earnings per share. We concentrate, first of all, on the basic earnings per share figure and all the issues which might arise in the calculation of the BEPS. Later on we discuss the diluted earnings per share.

Basic earnings per share

The basic earnings per share (BEPS) figure represents the amount attributable to the ordinary shareholders by dividing the earnings figure by the weighted average number of ordinary shares outstanding (the denominator) during the period. The calculation of the earnings figure is determined in para. 12. The earnings are equal to the profit and loss attributable to the parent entity. If there are discontinuing operations in a company then the BEPS should also be calculated on the basis of the profit or loss for the period from the continuing operations attributable to the parent entity. If there are no discontinuing operations there is just one basic earnings per share figure. Again, this is to improve the relevance of the information communicated.

The calculation of the earnings included in the numerator shall be the profit or loss adjusted for the after-tax amounts of preference dividends, differences arising on the settlement of preference shares and other similar effects of preference shares classified as equity. The reason is that ordinary shares are not entitled to those elements. The weighted average number of ordinary shares outstanding during the period will figure in the denominator.

Changes in equity share capital during the year In Activity 24.5 the number of shares in issue is given and remains constant over the financial period. However, in reality, there can be changes in the equity share capital during the financial year under consideration. For the purpose of calculating basic earnings per share, the number of ordinary shares should be the weighted average number of ordinary shares outstanding during the period. This is the number of ordinary shares outstanding at the beginning of the period, adjusted by the number of ordinary shares bought back or issued during the period multiplied by a time-weighting factor. The time-weighting factor is the number of days that the shares are outstanding as a proportion of the total number of days in the period; a reasonable approximation of the weighted average is adequate in many circumstances (see Activity 24.6).

In reality, shares can be issued at a price different from the market price or shares can be issued without a corresponding change in the resources of the company. Related to this, para. 26 of IAS 33 states that the weighted number of ordinary shares outstanding during the period and for all periods presented shall be adjusted for events, other than the conversion of potential ordinary shares, that have changed the number of ordinary shares outstanding without a corresponding change in resources. Ordinary shares may be issued or the number of ordinary shares outstanding may be reduced, without a corresponding change in resources. Examples include:

- a capitalisation or bonus issue (sometimes referred to as a stock dividend)
- a bonus element in any other issue, for example a bonus element in a rights issue to existing shareholders
- a share split
- a reverse share split (consolidation of shares).

In these circumstances the calculation of the EPS in Activity 24.6 needs to be modified. In all those circumstances where these 1 million ordinary shares have been issued at less than market price or for no consideration, the calculations in Activity 24.6 need to take into account this new element. This is illustrated below. A difference will be made between a change in the number of outstanding shares without a change in the resource of the company (e.g. bonus issue and share split) and a change in the number

ACTIVITY 24.6

Fullmar plc had issued share capital on 31 December X5 as follows:

500 000 preference shares (value €1 each) a preference dividend of 7% is attached 4 000 000 ordinary shares (value €0.25 each)

Profit after tax for the year ended 31 December X5 was €435 000. On 1 October X5 Fullmar had issued 1 million ordinary shares at full market price (= €0.25 each).

Calculate the EPS for Fullmar plc for the year ended 31 December X5.

Activity feedback

The number of ordinary shares in issue on 1 January X5 was 3 million and 1 million were issued on 1 October X5.

Thus the time weighted average number of ordinary shares in issue for the year was

$$(3\,000\,000 \times 9/12) + (4\,000\,000 \times 3/12) = 3\,250\,000$$
$$\text{or}$$
$$(3\,000\,000 \times 12/12) + (1\,000\,000 \times 3/12) = 3\,250\,000$$

The earnings for the year attributable to the ordinary shareholders is €435 000 − €35 000 preference dividend − €400 000. Therefore:

$$\text{EPS} = \frac{400\,000}{3\,250\,000} \text{ per share}$$
$$= \text{€}0.1230 \text{ per share}$$

Note that the 1 million ordinary shares are issued at full market price in this example.

of outstanding shares with a change in the resources of the company, but whereby the shares were not issued at market price. We will first illustrate a change in the number of outstanding shares without a change in the resources of the company.

A bonus issue In a capitalisation or bonus issue or a share split, ordinary shares are issued to existing shareholders for no additional consideration. Therefore, the number of ordinary shares outstanding is increased without an increase in resources. The number of ordinary shares outstanding before the event is adjusted for the proportionate change in the number of ordinary shares outstanding as if the event had occurred at the beginning of the earliest period presented. For example, on a two-for-one bonus issue, the number of ordinary shares that are outstanding before the issue is multiplied by three to obtain the new total number of ordinary shares or by two to obtain the number of additional ordinary shares.

In all these examples more shares have been issued at no 'cost'. The earnings of the business during the year can only be regarded as relating to the shares at the end of the year, i.e. to all the shares including the new ones. No distortion arises, as no resources were passed into the business when the new shares were created (see Activity 24.7).

We need to think about the implications of such changes for meaningful comparison with the prior year's figures. Adjusted earnings per share should be calculated in order to provide meaningful prior year comparative figures. Thus, the EPS figure which relates to year X4 needs to be restarted. This ratio then consists of the earnings of the year (X4) before divided by the new amount of outstanding shares of the current year, namely 4 000 000.

A consolidation of ordinary shares generally reduces the number of ordinary shares outstanding without a corresponding reduction in resources. However, where a share consolidation is combined with a special dividend and the overall effect is a share repurchase at fair value, the reduction in the number of ordinary shares outstanding is the result of a corresponding reduction in resources. The weighted average number of ordinary shares outstanding for the period in which the combined transaction takes place is adjusted for the reduction in the number of ordinary shares from the date the special dividend is recognised.

We will now illustrate the calculation of the EPS when the total number of outstanding shares changes, together with a change in the resources of the company.

ACTIVITY 24.7

Using the same data as in Activity 24.6 but assuming that the shares issued on October X5 were a capitalisation issue, calculate the EPS for the year. This means that we now have a bonus issue for no additional consideration, whereby for each three existing shares a new share is issued.

Activity feedback

We now have a capitalisation or bonus issue, not a full market price issue of shares, and therefore we assume 4 million shares in issue for the whole of the year. (Note this assumption would be the same no matter at what point during the year the capitalisation was made.) Thus: $= 3\,000\,000 + 1\,000\,000 = 4\,000\,000$.

The number of shares in issue can also be calculated from the following:

$$3\,000\,000 \times \frac{9}{12} \times \frac{4}{3} + 4\,000\,000 \times \frac{3}{12}$$

(bonus factor)

$$EPS = \frac{400\,000}{4\,00\,000} = €0.100 \text{ per share}$$

Rights issue at less than full market price In a rights issue, the exercise price is often less than the fair value of the shares, for example if Fullmar (see Activity 24.6) had issued the 1 million ordinary shares at a price less than market price. Therefore, such a rights issue includes a bonus element as indicated earlier. The number of ordinary shares to be used in calculating basic earnings per share for all periods before the rights issue is the number of ordinary shares outstanding before the issue, multiplied by the following factor:

$$\frac{\text{Fair value per share immediately before the exercise of rights}}{\text{Theoretical ex-rights value per share}}$$

The theoretical ex-rights value per share is calculated by adding the aggregate fair value of the shares immediately before the exercise of the rights to the proceeds from the exercise of the rights and dividing by the number of shares outstanding after the exercise of the rights or a theoretical ex-rights value per share =

$$\frac{\begin{array}{c}\text{Fair value of all outstanding shares before the exercise of rights}\\ +\ \text{total amount received from exercise of rights}\end{array}}{\begin{array}{c}\text{Number of shares outstanding before exercise}\\ +\ \text{number of shares issued in the exercise}\end{array}}$$

Where the rights themselves are to be publicly traded separately from the shares before the exercise date, fair value for the purposes of this calculation is established at the close of the last day on which the shares are traded together with the rights.

This is complicated! A rights issue combines the characteristics of a capitalisation issue and a full market price issue. New resources are passing into the business so a higher earnings figure, related to these new resources, should be expected. But at the same time there is a bonus element in the new shares, which should be treated like a capitalisation issue. To the extent that the rights issue provides new resources, i.e. equates to an issue at full market price, we need to calculate the average number of shares weighted on a time basis. To the extent that the rights issue includes a discount or bonus element we need to increase the number of shares deemed to have been in issue for the whole period. The theoretical ex-rights value per share can be calculated as follows:

1 Calculate the total market value of the equity before the rights issue (actual cumulative rights price × number of shares).
2 Calculate the total proceeds expected from the right issue (issue price × number of shares).
3 Add these two amounts and divide by the total number of shares involved altogether (i.e. by the total number after the rights issue).

We introduce two Activities 24.8 and 24.9 on the following page to illustrate the calculations.

Diluted earnings per share

Besides the basic earnings per share, a company must also disclose its diluted earnings per share. Where there are securities existing at the year end that will have a claim on equity earnings from some time in the future, then it is clear that at this future time the claim of each currently existing share will, other things being equal,

ACTIVITY 24.8

Company TEX wants to raise capital and decides to issue one share for each five outstanding shares. The new shares will be issued at a price of €10. The market value of the shares is €25. The one to five issue takes place on 1 March 20X5 and all shares issued are subscribed. The number of outstanding ordinary shares before the issue was 500. The profit for the year 20X4 is 1 €1600 and the profit for the year 20X5 is €2000. Calculate the EPS for 20X4 and 20X5.

Activity feedback

The increase in resources of company TEX takes place during the year, namely on 1 March 20X5. The shares are issued at less than market price so this includes a bonus element.

We will first determine the theoretical ex-rights value per share. Using that number we are able to calculate the factor by which we have to multiply the number of outstanding shares before the issue in order to take into account the bonus element included in this issue.

Theoretical ex-rights value per share:

$$((€25 \times 500 \text{ shares}) + (€10 \times 100 \text{ shares}))/(500 + 100)$$
$$= €22.5 \text{ per share}$$

Second, we calculate the multiplying factor = fair value per share immediately before the exercise of the rights/theoretical ex-rights value per share:

$$€25/€22.5 = 1.11$$

We calculate the EPS for 20X5 and take into account when the issue took place:

$$\text{EPS 20X5} = €2\,000/((500 \times 1.11 \times 2/12)$$
$$+ (600 + 10/12)) = €3.37$$

We need to recalculate the EPS for 20X4 = €1 600/(500 × 1.11) = €2.88

ACTIVITY 24.9

Trig plc as at 30 June X5 has €600 000 ordinary shares in issue with a current market value of €2 per share. On 1 July X5 Trig plc makes a four for six rights issue at €1.75 and all rights are taken up. Earnings for the year after tax and preference dividends are €81 579 and the previous year's EPS was declared as 9c. Calculate the EPS figure that should be shown in the financial statements for the year ended 31 December X5.

Activity feedback

We first need to calculate the theoretical ex-rights price of the shares:

Market value of equity		
before rights	= 600 000 × € 2	= 1 200 000
Proceeds from rights		
issue	= 400 000 × € 1.75 =	700 000
	1 000 000	1 900 000

Theoretical ex-rights value per share $= \dfrac{1\,900\,000}{1\,900\,000}$
$$= €1.90$$

Second, we calculate the weighted average number of shares:

$$\underset{\text{(time weighting)}}{600\,000 \times \frac{1}{2} \times \frac{2}{1.9}} + \underset{\text{(time weighting)}}{1\,000\,000 \times \frac{1}{2}} = 815\,789$$

Therefore EPS for year ending 31 December X5 =
$\dfrac{8\,157\,900}{8\,15\,789} = 10\text{c per share}$

Third, we need to recalculate the previous year's EPS:

$$9 \times 1.9/2 = 8.55\text{c per share}$$

A reduction has occurred in the previous year's EPS as we have inserted the bonus element of the rights, and we assume that this element has happened for the earlier period reported.

be reduced (or diluted). It is likely to be useful information to current shareholders and others to give them a picture of what the EPS would be if this dilution takes place. This is done by recalculating the current year's EPS as if the dilution had already occurred.

For the calculation of the numerator of the diluted EPS, the starting amount will be the earnings amount of the BEPS adjusted for the after-tax effect of:

1 any dividends or other items related to dilutive potential ordinary shares deducted in arriving at profit or loss attributable to ordinary equity holders of the parent entity as calculated in accordance with the calculation done for the BEPS

2 any interest recognised in the period related to dilutive potential ordinary shares

3 any other changes in income or expense that would result from the conversion of the dilutive potential ordinary shares.

In the denominator of the DEPS the number of ordinary shares shall be the weighted average number of ordinary shares calculated in accordance with paras 19 and 26 (which relate to the denominator of the BEPS), plus the weighted average number of ordinary shares that would be issued on the conversion of all the dilutive potential ordinary shares into ordinary shares. Dilutive potential ordinary shares shall be deemed to have been converted into ordinary shares at the beginning of the period or, if later, the date of issue of the potential ordinary shares.

Further it is interesting to note that potential ordinary shares shall be treated as dilutive when, and only when, their conversion to ordinary shares would decrease earnings per share or increase loss per share from continuing operations (para. 41). This implies that the impact of potential ordinary shares with anti-dilutive effect on EPS is not taken into account when calculating the DEPS. Potential ordinary shares are anti-dilutive when their conversion to ordinary shares would increase earnings per share or decrease loss per share from continuing operations. As a result an investor will only be informed numerically about the negative impact of potential ordinary shares on the future EPS figure. A positive impact will not be calculated.

We will illustrate the calculation of the DEPS in Activity 24.10.

In determining whether potential ordinary shares are dilutive or anti-dilutive, each issue or series of potential ordinary shares is considered separately rather than in aggregate. The sequence in which potential ordinary shares are considered may affect whether they are dilutive. Therefore to maximise the dilution of basic earnings per share, each issue or series of potential ordinary shares is considered in sequence from the most dilutive to the least dilutive, i.e. dilutive potential ordinary shares with the lowest 'earning per incremental share' are included in the diluted earnings per share calculation before those with a higher earning per incremental share. Options and warrants are generally included first because they do not affect the numerator of the calculation.

IAS 33 considers a number of financial instruments as potentially dilutive and describes their effect on the DEPS figure in the following order:

- options, warrants and equivalent instruments (paras 45–48)
- convertible instruments (paras 42–51)
- contingently issuable shares (paras 52–61)
- purchase options (para. 62)
- written put options (para. 63).

We will illustrate the impact of options on the DEPS figures in Activity 24.11. The impact of convertible instruments on DEPS figures has been illustrated in Activity 24.10.

The latest version of IAS 33 also pays attention to retrospective adjustments. IAS 33 (para. 64) states in this respect that if the number of ordinary or potential ordinary shares outstanding increases as a result of capitalisation, bonus issue or share

ACTIVITY 24.10

The summarised income statement for EPS plc for the year ended 20X1 is as follows:

	€	€
Profit before taxation		1 000 000
Taxation (including deferred adjustment)		400 000
		600 000
Preference dividend	50 000	
Ordinary dividend	100 000	
		150 000
		450 000

The number of ordinary shares in issue is 2 million.

In addition to the 2 million ordinary shares already in issue, however, there exists convertible loan stock of €500 000 bearing interest at 10%. This may be converted into ordinary shares between 20X3 and 20X6 at a rate of one ordinary share for every €2 of loan stock. Corporation tax is taken for convenience as 50%. Calculate the fully diluted EPS.

Activity feedback
The fully diluted EPS is found as follows. If the conversion is fully completed then there will be two effects:

1 The share capital will increase by 250 000 shares (1 share for every €2 of the €500 000 loan).

2 The profit after tax will increase by the interest on the loan no longer payable less the extra tax on this increase. The interest at 10% on €500 000 is €50 000, but the extra tax on this profit increase would be 50% of €50 000, i.e. €25 000.

So profit after tax, and therefore 'earnings', will increase by 50 000 – 25 000 = €25 000. Fully diluted EPS will therefore be:

$$\frac{600\,000 + 25\,000 - 50\,000}{2\,000\,000 + 250\,000}$$
$$= \frac{575\,000}{2\,250\,000}$$
$$= 25.6c \text{ per share}$$

Remember that the fully diluted EPS is a hypothetical calculation. It assumes total conversion into equity participation. The extent to which this assumption is likely in any particular circumstance is irrelevant.

ACTIVITY 24.11

Company Capsi realised a profit of 600 000 in the financial year 20X6 which is attributable to the ordinary shareholders. In the year 20X6 300 000 shares are outstanding. The BEPS for company Capsi is €2 (= 600 000/300 000). During the year 20X6 100 000 share options are outstanding of which the exercise price is €10 per share. The market price of the shares of company Capsi was €15 in 20X6. Calculate the DEPS for 20X6.

Activity feedback
We will assume that from the number of potentially outstanding shares a part will be issued at market price and

a part will be issued without consideration. The number of shares considered to be issued at market price will not influence the calculation of the DEPS. The number of shares considered to be issued with no increase in the resources of the company will be assumed to be present from the earliest period which is reported and will have a dilutive effect. So in fact the prior year DEPS should also be adjusted.

	Profit for ordinary shareholders	Number of shares	Earnings per share
Profit 20X6	600 000		
Weighted average number of shares outstanding in 2006		300 000	
Basic EPS			2
Weighted average number of shares under option		100 000	
Weighted average number of shares that would have been issued at average market price (100 000 × €10):€15		(66 666)	
Diluted EPS	600 000	344 444	1.74

split, or decreases as a result of a reverse share split, the calculation of basic and diluted earnings per share for all periods presented shall be adjusted retrospectively. If these changes occur after the balance sheet date but before the financial statements are authorised for issue, the per share calculations for those and any prior period financial statements presented shall be based on the new number of shares. The fact that per share calculations reflect such changes in the number of shares shall be disclosed. In addition, basic and diluted earnings per share of all periods presented shall be adjusted for the effects of errors and adjustments resulting from changes in accounting policies accounted for retrospectively.

The IASB attaches importance to the EPS figure as it requires in IAS 33 that the basic EPS as well as the diluted EPS should be disclosed on the face of the income statement for the current year as well as for all other years for which information is presented. EPS should be presented for each class of ordinary shares that has a different right to share in net profit for the period. We know that if there are discontinuing operations, two EPS figures have to be disclosed. An entity that reports a discontinuing operation shall disclose the basic and diluted amounts per share for this line item either on the face of the income statement or in the notes to the financial statements. Even if the EPS figure is negative the amounts should be presented.

On the face of the income statement EPS is presented as a single figure. In the notes to the accounts the user of the financial statements can obtain information on the composition of the numerator and the denominator of the basic EPS and the diluted EPS.

It is perhaps useful at this point to look at an example of a calculation of EPS involving more than one type of share issue. The following example (Activity 24.12) appears complicated but only requires a clear thought process and a knowledge of IAS requirements.

ACTIVITY 24.12

Part of a listed company's consolidated profit and loss account is as follows:

Chasewater Public Limited Company
Consolidated P&L account (extract) for the year ended
30 June 20X5

	€	€
Group net profit before taxation		500 000
Taxation		270 000
Group net profit after taxation		230 000
Minority interests in subsidiaries		20 000
Attributable to shareholders in Chasewater Plc		210 000
Extraordinary items (after taxation)		11 000
Net profit for year		221 000
Dividends (net)		
Preference	25 000	
Ordinary	100 000	
		125 000
Retained earnings for year		96 000

Notes

1 Issued share capital (fully paid), 1 July 20X4: 250 000 10% cumulative preference shares of €1 each and 4 million ordinary shares of 25c each.

2 Loan capital, 1 July 20X4: €500 000 7% convertible debentures (convertible into 200 ordinary shares per €100 debenture, with proportionate increases for subsequent bonus issues and for the bonus element in subsequent rights issues).

3 Changes during the year ended 30 June 20X5:
1 October 20X4 Rights issues of ordinary shares (ranking for dividend 20X4–5): 1 for 4 at €0.90 per share: market price before issue, €1.00: 1 January 20X5 Conversion of €100 000 of 7% convertible debentures: 1 March 20X5 Bonus issue of ordinary shares, 1 for 3

4 Basic earnings per share for the year ended 30 June 20X4 was 4c.

5 Corporation tax, 52%; income tax basic rate, 30%.

ACTIVITY 24.12   (Continued)

Required:

(a) compute the company's basic earnings per share for the current year and its comparative BEPS for the previous year; and

(b) compute the company's fully diluted earnings per share for the current year only.

Activity feedback

On reading the question you should have noted the following:

1 a rights issue on 1 October 20X4 of 1 million shares

2 a conversion of debentures on 1 January 20X5 to 200 000 shares plus the bonus of ordinary shares at 1 for 3 issue.

A quantity of convertible debentures still remain in issue. First, we calculate the earnings for the EPS calculation. This is straightforward:

Profit after tax after extraordinary items	221 000
Preference dividend	25 000
Earnings for basic EPS calculation	196 000

Second, as a rights issue has taken place we need to calculate the adjusting factor, i.e.:

$$\frac{\text{Actual cumulative rights}}{\text{Theoretical } ex\text{-rights}} =$$

Market value of equity

before rights =	$4\,000\,000 \times €1$	$= 4\,000\,000$	
Proceeds of rights issue =	$1\,000\,000 \times 90c$ =	$\underline{900\,000}$	
	$5\,000\,000$	$4\,900\,000$	

Theoretical ex-rights value

$$\text{per share} = \frac{4\,900\,000}{5\,000\,000} = 98c$$

Adjusting factor = 100/98 (this represents the bonus element of the rights issue).

Third, we need to calculate the time weighted *average number* of shares and remember to include the bonus issue for the whole of the year and multiply the proportion of capital in issue before rights by a factor of 100/98. Note the conversion of debentures on 1 January 20X5 will be to 200 000 × 100/98 shares = 204 082 shares and that the bonus issue will be calculated as follows:

Number of shares in issue *before bonus* =

4 000 000 + 1 000 000 rights + 204 082 conversion
= 5 204 082

$$\text{Bonus issue at 1 for 3} = \frac{5\,204\,082}{7} = 743\,440$$

Number of shares in issue after bonus = 6 938 776

Time weighted number of shares =

$$\left[4\,000 \times \frac{3}{12} \times \frac{100}{98} + 5\,000\,000 \times \frac{3}{12} \times 5\,204\,082 \times \frac{2}{12}\right]$$

$$\frac{4}{3}(\text{bonus factor}) + 6\,938\,776 \times \frac{4}{12}$$

$$= (1\,020\,408.1 + 1\,250\,000 + 867\,347)\frac{4}{3} + 2\,312\,925.3$$

$$= 3\,137\,755.1 \times \frac{4}{3} + 2\,312\,925.3 = 6\,496\,598.6$$

The fourth, fifth and sixth steps are as follows:

$$\text{Basic EPS 20X5} = \frac{19\,600\,000}{6\,496\,598.6} = 3.02c$$

$$\text{Revised EPS 20X4} = 4c \times \frac{3}{4}(\text{bonus factor})$$

$$\times \frac{98}{100}(\text{rights factor}) = 2.94c$$

Fully diluted EPS also needs to be calculated to see if there is a 5% dilution:

	£
Basic earnings	196 000
Add back debenture interest assuming full conversion took place at 1 July 20X4	
$\frac{6}{12} \times 7\% \times 500\,000 + 6\frac{6}{12} \times 7\% \times 4\,000\,000 =$	31 500
Corporate tax adjustment for non-payment of debenture interests	(16 380)
Diluted earnings	211 120

The weighted number of shares will need recalculating assuming all convertible debentures converted on 1 July 20X4, i.e. 1 million shares issued. Note the bonus issue will now be 2 083 333 shares on 1 March 20X5, and the rights issue 1 250 000 shares on 1 October 20X4.

Time weighted number of shares.

$$\left[5\,000\,000 \times \frac{3}{12} \times \frac{100}{98} + 6\,250\,000 \times \frac{5}{12}\right]\frac{4}{3} + 8\,333\,333$$

$$\times \frac{4}{12} = 7\,950\,680$$

$$\text{Diluted EPS} = \frac{21\,112\,000c}{7\,950\,680} = 2.66c$$

The following is an extract from the Annual Accounts of Adidas 2007, which illustrates the disclosure on EPS, this important financial figure.

28 Earnings Per Share

Basic earnings per share are calcuLated by dividing the net income attributable to shareholders by the weighted average number of shares outstanding during the year.

Dilutive potential shares arose under the Management Share Option Plan (MSOP) of adidas AG, which was implemented in 1999. As the required performance criteria for the exercise of the stock options of all tranches of the share option plan have been fulfilled, dilutive potential shares impact the diluted earnings per share calculation.

It is also necessary to include dilutive potential shares arising from the convertible bond issuance in October 2003 in the calculation of diluted earnings per share as at December 31, 2007 and 2006, respectively, as the required conversion criteria were fulfilled at the balance sheet date. As a result, the convertible bond is assumed to have been converted into ordinary shares and the net income is adjusted to eliminate the interest expense less the tax effect.

EARNINGS PER SHARE

	2007	Year ending Dec 31 2006
Net income attributable to shareholders (€ in millions)	551	483
Weighted average number of shares	203,594,975	203,386,104
Basic earnings per share (in €)	2.71	2.37
Net income attributable to shareholders (€ in millions)	551	483
Interest expense on convertible bond, net of taxes (€ in millions)	12	12
Net income used to determine diluted earnings per share (€ in millions)	563	495
Weighted average number of shares	203,594,975	203,386,104
Weighted share options	187,887	328,308
Weighted assumed conversion convertible bond	15,684,315	15,685,110
Weighted average number of shares for diluted earnings per share	219,467,177	219,399,522
Diluted earnings per share (in €)	2.57	2.25

INTERIM FINANCIAL REPORTING

All the Standards discussed in this chapter relate to the disclosure of information with the purpose of enhancing the decision usefulness of the data communicated through the financial statements. Investors, creditors, suppliers, the government and the workforce all make use of data taken from the financial statements. The financial statements are prepared on a yearly basis only. The investors' community, however, appreciates the provision of financial information on a more frequent basis.

Many stock exchanges require half-year interim reports. The US SEC even asks for quarterly interim reports. In Europe, the normal frequency of reporting is

ACTIVITY 24.13

Look at websites of listed companies and find out how they present their interim financial reports. Do they present other types of financial short-term information?

Activity feedback

Interim financial reports usually consist of a consolidated statement in a kind of abbreviated format and explanatory notes accompanied by a management report. Besides interim financial statements companies also often disclose on their website operating data on a half-year, quarterly or even monthly basis. If you look at the websites of some major airlines you will even find traffic statistics updated on a monthly basis.

biannual. Relatively few European companies follow the North American practice of reporting every quarter. The EU's Council of Economics and Finance Ministers (ECOFIN) approved and issued the Directive of the European Parliament and of the Council on the harmonisation of transparency requirements with regard to information about issuers whose securities are admitted to trading on a regulated market and amending Directive 2001/34/EC in its final form in the autumn of 2004. Article 5.3 of that Directive will require in respect of half-yearly financial reports that 'where the issuer is required to prepare consolidated accounts, the condensed set of financial statements shall be prepared in accordance with the international accounting standard applicable to the interim financial reporting as adopted pursuant to the procedure provided for under Article 6 of Regulation (EC) No. 1606/2002'. This means that half-yearly reports are expected to comply with IAS 34 once the draft Transparency Directive has been approved. However, quarterly reports will be exempt from this requirement. A company can publish interim financial reports as a result of a requirement by a stock exchange or another regulatory body. The practice of publishing an interim report can also result from a voluntary disclosure decision.

Before we present the contents of IAS 34, we want to underline that IAS does not require companies to publish interim financial reports. Only if an entity reporting under IAS does choose (or is required by other authorities) to issue such interim reports, then IAS prescribes the minimum content of an interim financial report and the principles for recognition and measurement in complete or condensed financial statements for an interim period.

According to accounting theory there are two different theoretical approaches towards interim reporting, namely the 'integral' approach and the 'discrete' approach. The 'integral' approach considers the interim report as part of the yearly financial report. This approach means that in order to prepare the interim reports, preparers will first determine the year totals and subsequently allocate these over the different interim periods.

The discrete approach considers an interim report as being independent from the 12-month financial accounts and will recognise assets, liabilities, expenses and revenue in the period in which they occur.

In principle the IASB has opted for the discrete approach; however, for a number of items we notice the influence of the integral approach.

Format of interim reports

Concerning the format of the interim report, IAS 34 leaves two options from which management has to choose. As an interim financial report a company can publish either a complete set of financial statements or a set of condensed financial statements for an interim period. The interim period is defined as a financial reporting period shorter than a full financial year. If an entity publishes a complete set of financial statements in its interim financial report, the form and content of those statements should conform to the requirements of IAS 1 for a complete set of financial statements.

If, however, the company chooses for a set of condensed financial statements then the minimum components of the interim financial report are presented in para. 8 of IAS 34, as follows:

- condensed balance sheet
- condensed income statement
- condensed statement showing either (i) all changes in equity or (ii) changes in equity other than those arising from capital transactions with owners and distributions to owners
- condensed cash flow statement
- selected explanatory notes.

What is meant by 'condensed' is explained further in the Standard: 'Those condensed statements should include, at a minimum, each of the headings and subtotals that were included in its most recent annual financial statements.' Additional line items or notes should be included if their omission would make the condensed interim financial statements misleading. Further basic and diluted earnings per share should be presented on the face of an income statement, complete or condensed, for an interim period.

It is important to stress that IAS 34 starts from the assumption that anyone who reads an entity's interim report will also have access to its most recent annual report. As a result, virtually none of the notes to the annual financial statements is repeated or updated in the interim report. Instead, the interim notes include primarily an explanation of the events and changes that are significant to an understanding of the changes in financial position and performance of the entity since the last annual reporting date. IAS 34 pays explicit attention to the notes accompanying the interim report.

Notes to the interim reports

Concerning these selected explanatory notes, which are typical for interim reports, para. 16 states which information as a minimum should be included if material and if not disclosed elsewhere in the interim financial report. The information should normally be reported on a financial year-to-date basis. However, the entity should also disclose any events or transactions that are material to an understanding of the current interim period:

- a statement that the same accounting policies and methods of computation are followed in the interim financial statements as compared with the most recent annual financial statements or, if those policies or methods have been changed, a description of the nature and effect of the change
- explanatory comments about the seasonality or cyclicality of interim operations
- the nature and amount of items affecting assets, liabilities, equity, net income or cash flows that are unusual because of their nature, size or incidence

- the nature and amount of changes in estimates of amounts reported in prior interim periods of the current financial year or changes in estimates of amounts reported in prior financial years, if those changes have a material effect in the current interim period
- issuances, repurchases and repayments of debt and equity securities
- dividends paid (aggregate or per share) separately for ordinary shares and other shares
- segment revenue and segment result for business segments or geographical segments, whichever is the entity's primary basis of segment reporting (disclosure of segment data is required in an entity's interim financial report only if IAS 14, *Segment Reporting*, requires that entity to disclose segment data in its annual financial statements)
- material events subsequent to the end of the interim period that have not been reflected in the financial statements for the interim period
- the effect of changes in the composition of the entity during the interim period, including business combinations, acquisition or disposal of subsidiaries and long-term investments, restructurings and discontinued operations. In the case of business combinations, the entity shall disclose the information required to be disclosed under paras 66–73 of IFRS 3, *Business Combinations*
- changes in contingent liabilities or contingent assets since the last annual balance sheet date.

IAS 34 gives the following examples of disclosures required in interim financial reports (para. 17):

- the write-down of inventories to net realisable value and the reversal of such a write-down
- recognition of a loss from the impairment of property, plant and equipment, intangible assets, or other assets, and the reversal of such an impairment loss
- the reversal of any provisions for the costs of restructuring
- acquisitions and disposals of items of property, plant and equipment
- commitments for the purchase of property, plant and equipment
- litigation settlements
- corrections of prior period errors
- any loan default or breach of a loan agreement that has not been remedied on or before the balance sheet date and
- related party transactions.

Furthermore, individual Standards and interpretations also provide guidance regarding disclosures for many of these items.

Valuation rules for interim reports

IAS 34 stipulates that an entity should apply the same accounting policies in its interim financial report as are applied in its annual financial statements, except for accounting policy changes made after the date of the most recent annual financial statements that are to be reflected in the next annual financial statements.

In many firms revenues and costs have a seasonal pattern. Think, for example, of firms in the tourism industry or in the ice cream industry. But in industries where one would not think about seasonal patterns, they may indeed exist, e.g. sale of cars.

With regard to revenue and expense recognition explicit guidance is given on revenues and costs which occur unevenly during the year. Revenues that are received seasonally, cyclically or occasionally within a financial year should not be anticipated or deferred as of an interim date if anticipation or deferral would not be appropriate at the end of the entity's financial year. Costs that are incurred unevenly during an entity's financial year should be anticipated or deferred for interim reporting purposes if, and only if, it is also appropriate to anticipate or defer that type of cost at the end of the financial year.

But, what shall we do with costs and revenues resulting from discretionary decisions by the management? The costs can be allocated evenly over the quarters or they can be changed to a specific quarter only according if they have occurred in that specific quarter. Consider again the valuation rules of IAS 34 mentioned earlier. They don't give that much guidance. To overcome this issue the IASB has presented in Appendix B to IAS 34 a list of examples of how to apply the general recognition and measurement principles in relation to interim reports. The examples relate to maintenance, provisions, pensions, intangible assets, year-end bonuses, tax credits and inventories, among other things.

Explicit attention is paid in IAS 34 to the use of accounting estimates. Paragraph 41 stipulates that the measurement procedures to be followed in an interim financial report should be designed to ensure that the resulting information is reliable and that all material financial information that is relevant to an understanding of the financial position or performance of the entity is appropriately disclosed. While measurements in both annual and interim financial reports are often based on reasonable estimates, the preparation of interim financial reports generally will require a greater use of estimation methods than annual financial reports. Again an appendix is used to give more guidance. Appendix C presents *Examples of the use of estimates* (for example, contingencies, pensions, income taxes, provisions, inventories, etc.).

Recently IFRIC No. 10, *Interim Financial Reporting and Impairment*, was issued to resolve a potential conflict between IAS 34 and the requirements of IAS 36 and IAS 39 not to reverse in the subsequent reporting periods impairments on goodwill, on investments in an equity investment classified as available for sale and financial assets covered at cost. In addition, when impairments are recorded in the interim statements, the requirements of IAS 36 and IAS 39 have to be complied with and reversals cannot be recorded in the subsequent (interim) periods.

The frequency of an entity's reporting – annual, half-yearly, or quarterly – should not affect the measurement of its annual results. To achieve that objective, measurements for interim reporting purposes are made on a year-to-date basis.

What does this mean?

The requirement to present information on a financial year-to-date basis and to ensure an understanding of the current interim period should be noted carefully. It logically has no effect in the context of half-yearly interim statements, but if interim statements are issued quarterly, then its implications could be significant. The financial report must satisfy the requirements of providing an understanding of the latest quarter (and its comparatives) and also an understanding of the year-to-date (and its comparatives). For example, a first-quarter report (e.g. 1.1.20X2-31.3.20X2) has to show the data for the three months and comparable figures for the first three months of the previous year (1.1.20X1–

31.3.20X1). For example a third-quarter report has to show the data for the first nine months of the current year (e.g. 1.1.20X2–30.9.20X2) and comparative data for the first nine months of the previous year (1.1.20X1–30.9.20X1) and data of the last three months as well (1.7.20X2–30.9.20X2) and the same period in the previous year (1.7.20X1-30.9.20X1).

In order to help the preparers of interim financial reports an extensive appendix can be found accompanying IAS 34 in which a large number of examples is given in relation to applying the recognition and measurement principles of IAS to interim financial reports.

With regard to interim reporting the IASB takes a framework-based approach in IAS 34 itself. As such, it seems that the IASB merely sees interim reporting as a frequent version of annual reporting, whereas the business community often uses the interim reports as a signalling device towards the total result of the financial period.

SUMMARY

In this chapter a set of individual Standards has been discussed and illustrated. They all had in common that their purpose is to increase the usefulness of the reported information so that external users of the annual accounts can make better decisions. We remember, however, that although the Standards have become stricter over the years, room for judgement is still left and this might threaten the value relevance of the accounting information. However, we must admit that judgement is always inherent to the process of financial reporting.

EXERCISES

Suggested answers to exercises marked ✓ are to be found on the Student side of the companion website.

Suggested answers to the remaining exercises are to be found on the Instructor side of the companion website.

✓ **1**   Calculate from the following information:

   (a)   the basic EPS

   (b)   the fully diluted EPS.

   The capital of the company is as follows:

   - £500 000 in 7% preference shares of £1 each
   - £1 000 000 in ordinary shares of 25p each

- £1 250 000 in 8% convertible unsecured loan stock carrying conversion rights into ordinary shares as follows: on 31 December 120 shares for each £100 nominal of loan stock.

The P&L account for the year ended 31 December showed:

(a) profit after all expenses, but before extraordinary items, loan interest and corporation tax £1 200 000. Extraordinary items £100 000 (expense)

(b) corporation tax is to be taken as 35% of the profits shown in the accounts after all expenses and after loan interest.

✓ **2** Extracts from the consolidated financial statements of Worldwide for the year ended 31 March 2004

INCOME STATMENT – YEAR ENDED 31 March 2004

	$'000
Revenue	665 000
Cost of sales	(312 000)
Gross profit	353 000
Distribution costs	(99 000)
Administrative expenses	(118 000)
Profit from operations	136 000
Income from investments	6 000
Finance cost	(25 000)
Profit before tax	117 000
Income tax expense	(28 000)
Profit after tax	89 000
Minority interests	(8 000)
Net profit for the period	81 000

BALANCE SHEET AS AT 31 March 2004

	$'000	$'000
ASSETS		
Non-current assets:		
Property, plant and equipment	340 000	
Financial assets	50 000	
		390 000
Current assets:		
Inventories	75 000	
Trade receivables	104 000	
Bank balances	24 000	
		203 000
		593 000
EQUITY AND LIABILITIES		
Capital and reserves:		
Issued capital	150 000	
Accumulated profits	180 000	
		330 000

	$'000	$'000
Non-current liabilities:		
Interest bearing borrowings	140 000	
Deferred tax	36 000	
		176 000
Current liabilities:		
Trade and other payables	70 000	
Short-term borrowings	17 000	
		87 000
		593 000

Requirement:

Prepare a segment report for Worldwide for the year ended 31 March 2004 that complies with IAS14. You need not address disclosures required by IAS14 that cannot be given from the information available.

(ACCA June 2004)

✓ **3** As the recently qualified accountant of Aveler plc, a food retailer with balance sheet date 31 December 20X1, you notice the following items occurring before the accounts are approved by the directors:

(a) the sale, during the period from 31 December 20X1 to the date the accounts are approved by the directors, of 1000 tins of baked beans

(b) the purchase, during the period from 31 December 20X1 to the date the accounts are approved by the directors, of 750 tins of baked beans

(c) the incurrence of other expenses, during the period from 31 December 20X1 to the date the accounts are approved by the directors, amounting to €125

(d) notification that a customer who owes the company €10 000 as at 31 December 20X1 has gone into liquidation on 17 January 20X2

(e) a fire on 4 January 20X2 destroys all the stock in one warehouse

(f) the receipt of a letter from the company's insurers stating that it is unclear whether Aveler was actually insured for loss of stock by fire.

Which of these items are relevant to the accounts for the period ending 31 December 20X1?

4 Outline the circumstances in which post-balance sheet events affect the contents of financial statements. In what different ways are those contents affected? Give examples to illustrate your points.

5 Outline the main difficulties with the disclosure of segmental information and outline possible arguments against the disclosure of segmental information.

6 In preparing the financial statements for the year ended 31 December 20X5 Alpha plc discovers the following, all of which are material in the context of the company's results:

• development expenditure that met the required criteria of IAS 38 was previously capitalised and amortised. Alpha now believes that writing off all expenditure on development work would give a fairer presentation of the results

• a debt that was previously considered to be collectable as at 31 December 20X4 now requires writing off

- the estimate of costs payable in respect of litigation was €250 000 as at 31 December 20X4. This has now materialised at €280 000
- the directors of Alpha are of the view that depreciating vehicles by the reducing balance method rather than the straight line method as previously used will present a fairer view of the financial performance of the company.

How would you treat the information above in preparing the financial statements at the end of 31 December 20X5? The treatment should be in line with IAS/IFRS.

7 Discuss the advantages and disadvantages of earnings per share as a measure of corporate performance.

8 Consider the information given in Table 24.2 and explain to the holders of equity in Interbrew the usefulness of information like basic earnings per share and diluted earnings per share.

TABLE 24.2	Interbrew shareholder information: Information to our shareholders					
Earnings, dividends, share and share price	**2001 IAS**	**2000 IAS**	**2000**	**1999**	**1998**	**1997**
Adjusted net profit per share {1} {2} (euro)	1.44	1.04	1.21	0.92	0.69	0.51
Dividend per share {1} (euro)	0.29	0.21	0.21	0.18	0.15	0.12
Average number of shares (in millions)	429	335	333	323	322	322
Fully dilated number of shares (in millions)	434	343	436	332	336	338
Share price high (euro)	37.5	38.1	38.1	N/A	N/A	N/A
Share price low (euro)	25.5	34.0	34.0	N/A	N/A	N/A
Year-end share price (euro)	30.75	37.12	37.12	N/A	N/A	N/A

{1} Adjusted for stack splits
{2} Net profit (share of the group) (before extraordinary xxxx goodwill impairment) plus amortisation of goodwill, divided by the number of shares outstanding

Source: Annual report, 2001, p. 118

9 Consolidated financial statements effectively aggregate the results of members of the group. Whilst this achieves the objective of showing the results of the group as if it were a single entity, it does have the disadvantage of hiding the relative performance of the different components of the entity. The International Accounting Standards Board's solution to this problem is to require disclosures relating to the different segments of the entity.

Required:

(a) (i) Discuss the objectives and usefulness of reporting segment information.

(ii) Define a reportable segment under IAS 14, *Segment Reporting*

(iii) Identify the main problems of providing segment information.

(b) Portico has identified the following distinguishable business segments, together with their relative sizes:

Engineering	23%
Textiles	22%
Chemicals	20%
Travel agency	8%
House building	7%
Four others of 5% each	20%

None of the smaller segments are similar enough to be combined with other segments. The sizes above can be taken to relate to segment revenues, profits and assets. The following additional information has been obtained:

(i) For cost control purposes, Portico's holding company is invoiced centrally and pays the utility costs (electricity and water) of each of its three reportable segments.

(ii) In its management accounts, central head office expenditure on research and development expenditure is allocated to reportable segments in relation to the relative turnover of each segment.

(iii) Certain assets, liabilities and expenses for the segments have been identified:

	Engineering $000	Textiles $000	Chemicals $000
Leased assets at cost	12 000	25 000	18 000
Annual depreciation based on life of lease	1 200	1 250	1 500
Outstanding lease liability (at year-end)	7 000	15 000	8 000
Lease interest for current year	800	1 300	600

Required:
Identify the reportable segments for Portico and state how you would recommend the items in (i) to (iii) above should be treated in Portico's segment report. (ACCA June 2002)

10 The IASB issued IAS 33, *Earnings Per Share* in 1997 with the objective of determining the principles for the calculation and presentation of earnings per share in order to improve performance comparison. Its main focus is on the denominator of the calculation.

Required:

(a) Explain the usefulness of disclosing:

(i) a company's basic earnings per share;

(ii) a company's diluted earnings per share.

(b) Below are extracts from the financial statements of Bovine for the year to 31 March 2003:
Income statement:

	Continuing operations $000	Discontinuing operations $000	Total $000
Profit (loss) before tax	1 580	(200)	1 380
Tax (charge) relief	(280)	50	(230)
Profit from the ordinary activities	1 300	(150)	1 150
Extraordinary item as part of			
continuing operations			(120)
(net of tax relief of $60)			1 030

Balance sheet:	
Ordinary shares of 25 cents each	1 800
6% Non-redeemable preference shares	500
10% Convertible preference shares $1 each	1 000
Non-current liabilities	
8% Convertible loan stock	1 500

Notes: all shares and loan stocks were in issue prior to the beginning of the current accounting year. The 10% convertible preference shares are convertible to ordinary shares on the basis of three ordinary shares for every five preference shares on 31 March 2005 at the option of the preference shareholders. The 8% convertible loan stock is redeemable on 31 March 2005 or can be converted to ordinary shares on the basis of 120 ordinary shares for each $100 of loan stock at the holder's option.

There are also in issue directors' share options for four million ordinary shares. These were issued on 31 March 2002 and are exercisable on 31 March 2005 at a price of $1.40 per share. The market price of Bovine's shares can be taken as $2.00 each.

Preference dividends are paid out of taxed profits. Interest on loan stock is an allowable tax reduction. The rate of income tax is 25%.

Required:
Calculate Bovine's basic and diluted earnings per share for the year ended 31 March 2003.

(ACCA June 2003)

11   Earnit plc is a listed company. The issued share capital of the company at 1 April 1999 was as follows:

- 500 million equity shares of 50p each.
- 100 million £1 non-equity shares, redeemable at a premium on 31 March 2004. The effective finance cost of these shares for Earnit plc is 10% per annum. The carrying value of the non-equity shares in the financial statements at 31 March 1999 was £110 million.

Extracts from the consolidated profit and loss account of Earnit plc for the year ended 31 March 2000 showed:

	£ million
Turnover	250
Cost of sales	(130)
Gross profit	120
Other operating expenses	(40)
Operating profit	80
Exceptional gain	10
Interest payable	(25)
Profit before taxation	65
Taxation	(20)
Profit after taxation	45
Appropriations of profit (see note)	(26)
Retained profit	19

Note appropriations of profit:
- to non-equity shareholders 11
- to equity shareholder 15

  26

The company has a share option scheme in operation. The terms of the option are that optionholders are permitted to purchase one equity share for every option held at a price of £1.50 per share. At 1 April 1999, 100 million share options were in issue. On 1 October 1999, the holders of 50 million options exercised their option to purchase, and 70 million new options were issued on the same terms as the existing options. During the year ended 31 March 2000, the average market price of an equity share in Earnit plc was £2.00.

There were no changes to the number of shares or share options outstanding during the year ended 31 March 2000 other than as noted in the previous paragraph.

Requirements:

(a) Compute the basic and diluted earnings per share of Earnit plc for the year ended 31 March 2000. Comparative figures are not required.

(b) Explain to a holder of equity shares in Earnit plc the usefulness of both of the figures you have calculated in part (a).

(CIMA May 2000)

12 IAS 10 (revised) was issued in May 1999. It deals with the accounting treatment of events occurring after the balance sheet date.

Required:

(a) In assessing the results of a company for the current year, explain why events occurring after the balance sheet date may be of importance; and describe the circumstances where the financial statements should and should not be adjusted.

(b) During a review of Penchant's draft financial statements (for the year ended 30 September 2003) in October 2003, the following matters came to light:

— The company's internal auditors discovered a fraud on one of the company's contracts. A senior employee had accepted an inducement of $200 000 for awarding the construction of roadways on one of the company's contracts to a particular sub-contractor. Investigations showed that the price of the subcontracting was $1 million higher than another comparable tender offer. At 30 September 2003 the contract was approximately 50% complete.

- An earthquake occurred on 10 October 2003. It caused damage to an in progress contract that it is estimated will cost $500 000 to rectify.
- At 30 September 2003 the company's head office premises were included in the draft financial statements at a value of $12 million. A building surveyor's report showed that they had fallen in value by $2 million. This was due partly to the discovery of ground subsidence and partly to a general fall of 10% in property prices caused by a sharp unexpected rise in interest rates announced in October 2003.
- In October 2003 there was a sharp fall in the value of a foreign currency. Penchant was owed a substantial amount for the final instalment of a completed contract whose price was fixed in that currency. The estimated loss due to the fall in the exchange rate has been translated at $250 000.

Note: you may assume the above figures are material.

Required:

For each of the items above, explain how Penchant should treat them under International Financial Reporting Standards.

(ACCA Dec 2003)

13   Classify the events below as adjusting events or non-adjusting events according to IAS 10:

(a)   shortly after the balance sheet date a survey of an item of property, plant and equipment revealed significant structural problems with the asset

(b)   a lawsuit alleging damages suffered from an accident that occurred after the balance sheet date

(c)   a bankruptcy of a customer that occurs after the balance sheet date

(d)   at year-end, management has the intention to decide upon the implementation of a restructuring plan. After the balance sheet date but prior to the issuance date of the company's financial statements, management approves and announces the plan.

14   Hamlet, a publicly listed company, is preparing its financial statements to 30 September 2003. In previous years it has chosen to write off all of its development expenditure even where management have been confident that the related projects would be profitable. The company is aware that development expenditure meeting the definition of an intangible asset in IAS 38, *Intangible Assets* should be capitalised. In the near future Hamlet intends to prepare its financial statements under International Financial Reporting Standards and as a step towards this, the management of Hamlet are to change their accounting policy for development expenditure for the current year to comply with IAS 38. Reproduced below are details of Hamlet's development expenditure for the relevant years. For the purpose of implementing the new policy management consider four years to be an appropriate amortisation period for all development expenditure. Amortisation should commence in the year following initial capitalisation.

		$million
Amounts written off in year to 30 September:	1999	500
	2000	400
	2001	900
	2002	640
	2003	720

No development expenditure occurred in any year prior to 30 September 1999. The accumulated profit of Hamlet at 1 October 2001 was $2500 million. You may assume that the above development expenditure meets the definition of a recognisable intangible asset in IAS 38.

Required:

(a) Describe the circumstances in which companies are permitted to change their accounting policies under International Financial Reporting Standards and discuss what constitutes a change of accounting policy.

(b) Prepare extracts of Hamlet's income statement and balance sheet for the year to 30 September 2003 together with comparative figures to reflect the change in accounting policy in respect of development expenditure; and calculate the restated accumulated profits at 1 October 2001.

Hamlet uses the benchmark treatment in IAS 8, *Net Profit or Loss for the Period, Fundamental Errors and Changes in Accounting Policies*. Ignore deferred tax.

(ACCA Dec 2003)

15 BJS, a listed entity, had a weighted average of 27 million ordinary shares in issue during its financial year ended 31 August 2006. It was also financed throughout the year by an issue of 12% convertible bonds with a par value of $50 million. The bonds are convertible at the option of the holders at the rate of 12 new ordinary shares for every $100 of bonds at par value. The tax rate applicable to BJS was 30% during the financial year. The profit attributable to ordinary shareholders for the year ended 31 August 2006 was $100 million. Calculate earnings per share, and diluted earnings per share, for BJS for the year ended 31 August 2006.

(CIMA Nov 2006)

PART THREE
CONSOLIDATED ACCOUNTS AND THE MULTINATIONAL

In this part we look in some detail at the preparation of financial statements for several entities that could be regarded as a group. Such statements are known as consolidated accounts and the techniques for preparing them are complicated and require detailed regulations. The preparation of consolidated accounts is covered in four chapters. The first, Chapter 25, provides an introduction to consolidated financial statements and deals with the basic techniques. The second, Chapter 26, details the IFRSs in relation to consolidated financial statements. The third, Chapter 27, is a chapter that we would encourage you to study, but is not essential if all you wish to gain from this text is 'How to prepare consolidated financial statements.' The fourth chapter deals with other relationships between entities and how we should display those relationships within financial statements.

Many groups of entities operate in different countries and, therefore, different currencies, so we need rules and regulations for conversion from one currency to another before we can prepare the consolidated financial statements. We also need to consider the accounting for the relatively simple operation of receiving or making payments in a foreign currency. The accounting for this may not be as easy as it first appears.

At the end of this part we invite you to form your own opinion as to whether the information provided by consolidated accounts and in respect of foreign entities and different currency transactions is helpful to users.

INTRODUCTION TO CONSOLIDATED FINANCIAL STATEMENTS

OBJECTIVES   After studying this chapter you should be able to:

- outline the need for consolidated financial statements

- explain a business combination

- consider the mechanics of preparing consolidated financial statements

- prepare consolidated income statements for combinations of more than one subsidiary

- prepare consolidated balance sheets for more than one subsidiary.

INTRODUCTION

Most people are vaguely familiar from their daily newspapers with such words as 'takeover', 'merger', etc., but few have need to understand how such business combinations are actually structured. There are two basic possibilities:

1   A new entity may be formed in order to absorb one or more existing entities. The essential feature here is that the new entity would physically take over the assets and liabilities of the entities absorbed and the latter would then cease to exist.

ACTIVITY 25.1

Entity A, an engineering firm, owns buildings and plant and machinery with NBV of $500 000. Entity B buys these assets on 1 January 200X from A at a cost of $650 000 and leases them back to A on an operating lease.

Entity C, on 1 January 200X purchases 55% of the ordinary voting shares of entity A on the open market.

Which entity, B or C, has control of A?

the use of that entity's resources. We are seeking to identify who controls the decision making in the entity.

B owns the assets A is using but in no way does B control the decisions of A's directors. Presumably, A could gain the use of assets from another company if necessary. C owns A's shares and therefore has controlling voting power over who is appointed to the board of directors and thus controls A.

Activity feedback

What do we mean by control? In relation to entities we are seeking to identify who controls, commands, regulates

---

2 An entity may be taken over by another entity, but in this case the entity being taken over would continue to exist (and would still, of course, keep its own assets and liabilities).

It is important here to recognise that in case 2 the acquiring entity obtains control over the action of the entity taken over, as opposed to simply acquiring the assets of that entity (case 1). In effect, with case 2 the purchasing entity is acquiring an investment rather than a collection of sundry assets and the cost of this investment would itself appear in the purchasing entity's balance sheet as an asset (in much the same way as individuals purchase investments (shares) in entities).

The twin elements in this transaction are an acquiring (or holding) entity and an entity (or entities) being acquired (subsidiaries) and these form the basis for an examination of the structure of groups of entities.

CONTROL IN GROUPS

We will deal with the IASB definition of control in Chapter 26 but, for now, we can generally define control as the power to govern the financial and operating policies of an entity or business so as to obtain benefits from its activities. A parent is an entity that has one or more subsidiaries. A subsidiary is an entity controlled by another entity. Note in these definitions that the word 'entity' is used, not 'company', so a subsidiary could be a partnership or unincorporated body as well as a company as long as the entity is controlled by another. Control is presumed to be obtained when one of the combining entities acquires more than one half of the voting rights of the other combining entity unless it can be demonstrated that such ownership does not constitute control. Even when ownership is not 50% or more of the voting shares, control could still be exercised by the holding (parent) entity.

ACTIVITY 25.2

Identify in each of the following circumstances whether B is a subsidiary of A, i.e. A exercises control over B.

1 A owns 40% of the voting rights of B and has an agreement with a shareholder who holds a further 15% of the voting rights that enables him to vote for these shares as well.

2 A owns 42% of the voting rights of B but also has an agreement to govern the financial and operating policies of B.

3 A owns 48% of the voting rights of B.

4 A owns 35% of the voting rights of B and also has the power to appoint or remove five of the nine members of the board of directors.

5 A owns 33% of the voting rights of B and 100% of the voting rights of C which in turn holds 20% of the voting rights of C.

Activity feedback

In cases 1, 2 and 4 A clearly controls the decisions of B and therefore B is a subsidiary of A.

Case 3 is not an example of a parent–subsidiary relationship.

Case 5 is an example of a subsidiary relationship and Figure 25.1 should show this more clearly. A controls C and therefore also 20% of B which together with its own 33% holding gives it control over 53% of B. This is an example of a mixed group.

FIGURE 25.1   A subsidiary relationship

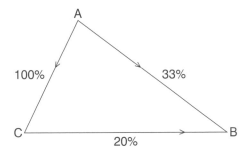

Further mixed groups

ACTIVITY 25.3

In the examples given identify the parent–subsidiary relationships:

1 H owns 75% of the voting shares of S which in turn owns 40% of the voting shares of S1. H also owns directly 15% of the voting shares of S1.

2 H owns 100% of the voting shares of S, which in turn owns 30% of S1. H also owns 75% of S2 which in turn owns 25% of S1.

3 H owns 60% of the voting shares of S which in turn owns 20% of the voting shares of S1. H also owns directly 20% of the voting shares of S1.

Activity feedback

1

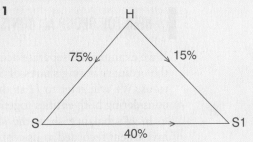

ACTIVITY 25.3 *(Continued)*

- S is a subsidiary of H (75% ownership), S1 is not a subsidiary of S (assuming no information in respect of dominant influence).
- H directly owns 75% × 40% of S1 + 15% of S1: = 30% + 15% = 45% which would imply no subsidiary relationship.
- However, H controls S thus controls 40% of S1 plus 15%.
- Therefore, S1 is a subsidiary of H and will be consolidated with a minority interest of 55%.

- However, H controls 30% + 25% + 55%.
- Thus, S1 is a subsidiary of H and will be consolidated with a minority interest of 51.25%.

3

- S is a subsidiary of H.
- H owns 60% × 20% + 20% of S1 = 32% of S1.
- H controls 20% + 20% of S1 = 40%.
- Thus, S1 is not a subsidiary of H (assuming no indication of dominant influence) and will not be consolidated.

2

- S and S2 are subsidiaries of H.
- H directly owns 100% × 30% + 75% × 25% of S1 = 305 + 18.75% = 48.75% only.

Minority interest (non-controlling interest)

We introduced the phrase minority interest at diagram 2 in the feedback to Activity 25.3. Put simply, minority interest is that part of the subsidiary that the holding (parent) entity does not own. This minority interest is usually less than 50% but can, as in item 2 Activity 25.3, be more than 50% if ownership does not define the control. Nowadays the phrase 'non-controlling interest' is more often used than minority interest.

NEED FOR GROUP ACCOUNTS

If we examine the separate accounts of two entities, *H* and *S*, where *H* holds 55% of the ordinary voting shares of *S* then we will find the following information available to us. We will refer to *H* as the 'holding' enterprise, *S* as the 'subsidiary' and when considering both entities together we will regard them as a 'group'.

In *H*'s balance sheet the shareholding (interest) in *S* will simply appear as an investment recorded at its cost of acquisition, historical cost. However, as with other assets in a balance sheet, the use of historical cost as the basis of valuation would not normally give the shareholders of *H* any indication of the value of the subsidiary or the underlying assets.

In relation to the holding entity's income statement the only reference to the subsidiary would be 'dividends received from S' (assuming there were any) and, of course, this would give no indication of the subsidiary's profitability.

As far as the group is concerned, the holding entity's accounts give no meaningful information about the group's activities, hence it would be useful to find a way to prepare information about the related activities of H and S in a consolidated (combined) format.

This is where the need for group accounts arises; to provide useful information to shareholders and other users of the holding entity's financial statements about the group as a whole.

GOODWILL IN GROUP ACCOUNTS

Premium on acquisition (goodwill)

From previous chapters you should by now be aware of the inadequacies of historic cost as a measure of asset value. It will be realised that the net book value (NBV) of an asset (or collection of assets) in the balance sheet of an entity will not necessarily bear any relationship to the market value of these assets or of that entity.

Obviously, when one entity acquires shares in another entity, then the price it is willing to pay for these shares will be computed by reference to the underlying value of the assets of the entity to be acquired and not of their book value as shown in the balance sheet. One would normally expect the assets of the entity being acquired to be revalued on the basis of the fair value of those assets for consolidation purposes. Further, since one entity is acquiring control of another entity (i.e. as opposed to simply buying a small (minority) shareholding), then the price to be paid for that controlling interest is very often a price in excess of the total of the fair value of the net assets of the subsidiary. Fair value is the price at which an asset would be purchased in an arm's-length transaction.

For accounting purposes this excess is termed goodwill or premium on acquisition. Obviously this 'difference' referred to earlier needs to be accounted for (if only to ensure that double entry is maintained) and it is usual for the total of such premium (goodwill) on acquisition of all group subsidiaries to be shown as an asset in the group balance sheet.

Discount on acquisition (negative goodwill)

Discount on acquisition can also occur. This relates to the possibility of one entity acquiring control of another at a discounted price (i.e. as opposed to at a premium).

In practice, this is not so far fetched as it might at first sight appear, in that an acquiring entity may for various reasons (e.g. empire building) be quite willing to purchase an entity with a recent history of trading losses, together with a forecast future of losses. This discount on the purchase price (i.e. the surplus of the fair value of tangible assets acquired over purchase consideration) at the date of acquisition may be thus thought of as compensation for anticipated future losses to the acquiring group. (One might also reasonably assume that in the medium-term future the group would hope to turn this subsidiary into profitability.) Alternatively, this discount may arise because the asset values agreed on acquisition may not be deemed to be fair values by the acquiring entity and may be revalued downwards on consolidation.

ACTIVITY 25.4

Identify the value of goodwill in each of the following acquisitions:

1 *H* acquired 100% of the net assets of *S* at a fair value of €1m. The net book value of *H*'s net assets was €750 000 and fair value €800 000.

2 *H* acquired 80% of the net assets of *S* at a fair value of €650 000. The fair value of the net assets of *S* at the date of acquisition was €700 000.

3 *H* acquired 75% of the net assets of *S* at a fair value of €400 000. The fair value of the net assets of *S* at the date of acquisition was €600 000.

Activity feedback

		€
1.	Fair value of the purchase price	1 000 000
	Fair value of the net assets acquired	800 000
	Goodwill on acquisition	200 000

2.	Fair value of the purchase price	650 000
	Fair value of the net assets acquired (80% × 700 000)	560 000
	Goodwill on acquisition	90 000
3.	Fair value of the purchase price	400 000
	Fair value of the net assets acquired (75% × 600 000)	450 000
	Discount on acquisition /negative goodwill	(50 000)

Note that in the answers above we always used the fair value of the purchase price and the fair value of the proportion of net assets acquired.

It must be emphasised at this stage that the calculation of the goodwill or discount on acquisition should be made after a fair valuation has been made of the net assets acquired. In practice, in many cases no revaluation occurs and it is then assumed that the book value reflects the fair value, as is the case with some of the illustrations used later in this chapter. Note also that for purposes of computation of goodwill or discount on acquisition we usually take the fair value of net assets as being equal to the proportion of the subsidiary's share capital plus reserves as at date of acquisition. The discount on acquisition is generally referred to as negative goodwill.

We will deal further with the treatment of this goodwill in accordance with international standards in the next chapter.

Treatment of consolidated goodwill

Once we have entered the consolidated goodwill in the consolidated balance sheet we will need to consider how we should treat it year on year. In Chapter 14 (p. 315) we identified the requirement from IAS 36 that goodwill on acquisition should be tested for impairment annually and the impairment charged to the consolidated income statement.

PREPARATION OF SIMPLE CONSOLIDATED BALANCE SHEETS

Balance sheet at date of acquisition

So far we have identified a need for group accounts to show useful information to users. But what would be useful information to these users? We can presume that they will need to know the total assets of the subsidiary that they control together with the parent's own assets. From this we can assume that we will add all the assets of the parent and subsidiary together. If we do this we will then need to eliminate the investment from the parent balance sheet (as we have included the net assets) and add in the premium or discount on acquisition. If we haven't acquired the whole of the subsidiary there will also be a non-controlling interest and we will need to include this in the group balance sheet or we will not balance. The following example demonstrates the consolidation process where there is no non-controlling (minority) interest, i.e. 100% ownership.

Example 25.1

The balance sheets of H and S as at 31 December 200X are as follows:

	H	S
	€	€
Tangible non-current assets	140 000	45 000
Investment in S	75 000	
Net current assets	20 000	15 000
	235 000	60 000
Share capital	150 000	50 000
Reserves	85 000	10 000
	235 000	60 000

H acquired the whole of the share capital of S for cash on 31 December 200X. The fair value of S's net assets at this date were €67 000. Prepare the consolidated balance sheet of H group as at 31 December 200X.

To do this consolidation there are several steps:

1 Calculate the goodwill
2 Revalue the net assets of the subsidiary S to fair value
3 Consolidate H and S.

1.	Goodwill – fair value of purchase price	75 000
	fair value of 100% net assets acquired	67 000
	Goodwill	8 000
2.	S revalued balance sheet	
	Net assets	67 000
	Share capital	50 000
	Reserves	10 000
	Revaluation reserve	7 000
		67 000
3.	Group consolidated balance sheet	
	Net assets (140 000 + 20 000 + 67 000)	227 000
	Goodwill on acquisition	8 000
		235 000
	Share capital	150 000
	Reserves	85 000
		235 000

Note that the share capital of S and the reserves from S at the date of acquisition, including the revaluation reserve, do not appear in the consolidated balance sheet. This is because they have been replaced with the net assets acquired and the goodwill value. In fact we have taken these items, the share capital and reserves of S to a cost of control account as follows and eliminated them:

Cost of control:

Fair value of purchase price	75 000
100% of share capital S	50 000
Pre-acquisition reserves	10 000
Revaluation acquisition	7 000
	67 000
Goodwill on acquisition	8 000

The following example shows the preparation of the group consolidated balance sheet when there is less than 100% ownership.

Example 25.2

The balance sheets of A and B as at 31 December 200X are as follows:

	A €	B €
Net assets	403 000	87 000
Investment in B	72 000	–
	475 000	87 000
Share capital	350 000	60 000
Reserves	125 000	27 000
	475 000	87 000

A bought 75% of S as at 31 December 200X and the fair value of the net assets bought equalled fair value.

Cost of control			Non-controlled interest	
Fair value of purchase price	72 000			
Purchased 75% of shares 60 000	45 000	25% × 60 000	15 000	
Plus 75% reserves at acquisition 27 000	20 250	25% × 27 000	6 750	
	65 250		21 750	
Goodwill	6 750			

Consolidated balance sheet for A group as at 31 December 200X

Net assets	490 000
Goodwill	6 750
	496 750
Share capital (only A even though ownership not 100%)	350 000
Reserves (only A)	125 000
	475 000
Non-controlling interest 25% × 87 000	21 750
	496 750

Note here that the reserves in the consolidated balance sheet are only those of *A* as *B*'s are either pre-acquisition or allocated to the non-controlling interest. We have also shown you two ways of calculating the non-controlling interest.

Now try Activity 25.5.

Consolidated balance sheet later than date of acquisition

We obviously have to prepare consolidated accounts subsequent to the date of acquisition and as long as we know the fair value of the assets acquired and the cost of that acquisition this is quite easy. What we must remember is that all reserves prior to acquisition belonging to the subsidiary are taken to the cost of control or belong to the non-controlling interest. Thus we can only include the parent share of the reserves post acquisition in the consolidation (see Activity 25.6).

Subsequent adjustments to purchase price

Acquisition agreements often provide for adjustment to the cost of an acquisition dependent on future events. These future events can be:

- the results of acquiree's operations exceeding or falling short of an agreed level
- the market price of securities issued as part of the purchase consideration being made (see Activities 25.7 and 25.8).

ACTIVITY 25.5

The balance sheets of *H* and *S* at the date *H* acquired 1 million 10p shares of *S* at a fair value of £120 000 for cash (the transaction has not yet been entered in *H*'s accounts) are as follows:

	H £000s	S £000s
Land and buildings	650	105
Plant and equipment	110	21
Net current assets	163	11
	923	137
Share capital £1 shares	800	
Share capital 10p shares		125
Reserves	123	12
	923	137

The fair value of *S*'s net assets at the date of acquisition were £142 000 (£108 000 land and buildings, £22 000 plant and equipment, £12 000 net current assets).

Prepare the consolidated balance sheet of *H* group as at 31 December 200X after the acquisition.

Activity feedback

Remember first to amend *H*'s balance sheet for the purchase of the shares in *S*. This will require an entry 'investment in *S* £120 000' and net current assets will be reduced to £43 000 for the cash payment.

H acquired 1 million 10p shares from a total of 1.25million, i.e. 80% ownership.

Cost of control		Non-controlled interest	
Purchase price FV	120		
80% shares	100	20% shares	25
80% reserves	9.6	20% reserves	2.4
80% revaluation	4	20% revaluation	1
	113.6		28.4
Goodwill	6.4		

Consolidated balance sheet of *H* group as at 31 December 200X

	£000s
Land and buildings (650 + 108)	758
Plant and equipment (110 + 22)	132
Goodwill	6.4
Net current assets (163 − 120 + 12)	55
	951.4
Share capital £1 shares (only *H*)	800
Reserves (only *H*, *S* either cost of control or non-controlled interest)	123
	923
Non-controlled interest	28.4
	951.4

20

ACTIVITY 25.6

H entity purchased 80% of the equity share capital of S Ltd for cash at 31 December year 1 at a price of €1.50 per share, when the balance on S entity's reserves stood at €2000.

The consolidation is required to be made at 31 December year 2, at which point the individual balance sheets of the two entities are as follows:

	€ H	€ S
Sundry current assets	35 000	6 000
Investment in S entity	9 600	–
Plant and machinery	60 000	5 000
	104 600	11 000
Represented by shares of €1	40 000	8 000
Reserves	64 600	3 000
	104 600	11 000

Activity feedback
The consolidated balance sheet as at 31 December year 2 would then be as follows:

	€
Sundry current assets	41 000
Plant and machinery	65 000
Goodwill on acquisition (note 1)	1 600
	107 600
Represented by shares of €1	40 000
Group reserves (note 2)	65 400
	105 400
Non-controlling interest (note 3)	2 200
	107 600

Notes

1 Cost of investment in S entity 9 600
Acquired ordinary shares at
31 December year 1
(80% × 8 000) 6 400
Acquired reserves at
31 December 1 600
(being 80% of balance of £2 000
on reserves of S entity at 31
December year 1) 8000
Goodwill on acquisition 1 600

2 Reserves of H entity at 31 December
year 2 64 600
Reserves of S entity accruing to group
since date of acquisition to 31
December year 2 = (3 000 − 2 000)
× 80% 800
65 400

3 Share capital as 31 December year 2 of
S entity accruing to non-controlling
interests (20% × 8 000) 1 600
Reserves at 31 December year 2 of S entity
accruing to non-controlling interests
(20% × 3 000) 600
2 200

ACTIVITY 25.7

Should subsequent adjustments to the cost of an acquisition be ignored or should a reasonable estimate of the probable effect be made?

Activity feedback
Accounting judgements concerned with probability and reliable estimates elsewhere should have led you to the conclusion that we should make a reasonable estimate of the purchase consideration including these future events based on the adjustment being probable and measurement reliable.

ACTIVITY 25.8

Entity *A* acquires all the issued share capital of entity *B* when the fair value of *B*'s net assets was €1m. The cost of the acquisition was €1.5m but included a proviso that unless earnings of *B* remained at 10% above the previous year the consideration would be reduced by €0.1m for each percentage point below that required. *A* expects *B* to meet this target. In addition, *A* guaranteed the market price of the securities issued to *B*'s shareholders on the acquisition for six months. The acquisition date was 1 October 200X and consolidated financial statements were drawn up as at 31 December 200X.

In the year ended 31 December 200Y it was noted that *B*'s earnings were 8% in excess of the previous year and that the market price of the securities had fallen by €0.2m.

Identify the goodwill on acquisition and adjustments necessary in the consolidated financial statements 31 December 200Y.

Activity feedback

	€
Purchase consideration	1.5
Fair value of net assets	1.0
Goodwill initially	0.5

Subsequent events change the purchase consideration to €1.3m and thus goodwill to €0.3m. Cost of acquisition will be shown in *A*'s individual books as €1.3m and the goodwill in the consolidated financial statements at 31.12.0Y as €0.3m.

The fall in the market price of the securities will be dealt with by a further issue of securities by *A* to *B*. The increase in securities will reduce the premium or increase the discount on the initial issue; it will not affect the purchase consideration.

Inter-company trading and the elimination of unrealised profits

When one member of a group, *S*, buys from an external supplier at a price (say) of €100, and sells those goods to a fellow group entity, *S1*, at a price of €140, then *S* can legitimately show a profit of €40 in its own income statement. However, on consolidation of the accounts of *S* and *S1* it should be recognised that this sale from *S* to *S1* couldn't give rise to a profit as far as the group income statement is concerned, as the sale is in effect an internal group transfer. In order for the group to realise a profit on sale, the sale must be made to a customer outside the group. This is shown diagrammatically in Figure 25.2 (the arrows represent sales either within or outside the group as indicated: R = realised group sales; UR = unrealised group sales).

Note, again, that although internal group sales reflect unrealised profit as far as the group is concerned, there is nonetheless a realised profit to be had from such transactions as far as the income statement of individual entities within the group is concerned.

Referring to the previous example if the individual accounts of *S* and *S1* are combined for consolidation purposes without further adjustment, then the group profit will show €40 and group stock will stand at €140. In other words, group profit will be overstated by €40 and also the stock of the group will be stated at €40 in excess of cost to the group (as opposed to *S*). (See Activity 25.9 on p. 631)

Reconciliation of inter-company balances

It is commonplace for entities within a group to shuffle liquidity and stocks between themselves as and when required and indeed this is one of the advantages of a group structure. Obviously with reference to such transactions, the indebtedness to/from

FIGURE 25.2	Inter-company trading an elimination of unrealised profits

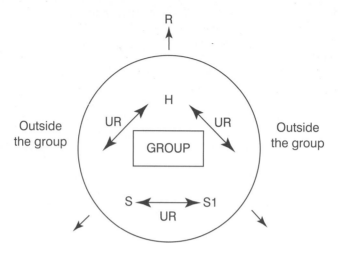

member entities will need to be recorded in the individual entities' books of account as appropriate. Hence, each entity will carry balances within the group. In relation to the group's position as regards the outside world, these balances are internal balances and will, therefore, not require to be shown in the group balance sheet. They are, in fact, cancelled on consolidation across the individual balance sheets of group members. Occasionally, however, it is not possible to cancel out such inter-entity balances, and this may often be due to transfer of goods or cash between group entities straddling the financial year-end. A consolidation adjustment is required at the year-end to adjust for goods or cash in transit between two entities before we can carry out the consolidation of accounts. The adjustment assumes that we account for the transit item as though it had reached its destination. It is important to note that these adjustments we are making here only affect the consolidated accounts; we make no adjustment for these inter-entity balances to the individual accounts of each entity (see Activity 25.10) on the next page.

Consistency of reporting dates and accounting policies within the group

Generally, the financial statement of a parent and its subsidiaries will be drawn up to the same date to enable easy preparation of consolidated financial statements. However, sometimes it is impracticable to do this and consolidation can take place using the accounts prepared to different dates provided the difference is no greater than a specified number of months. In the next chapter we will see how international standards explain this process. It would also make sense to ensure that the consolidation exercise employs the same accounting policies for the acquiree (subsidiary) and the acquirer (parent/holding entity). This means that the acquiree's (subsidiary's) financial statements will need to be adjusted before consolidation.

Activity 25.11 will test your understanding of the preparation of consolidated balance sheets for a parent and its subsidiary where there are several adjustments to make before consolidation can take place.

ACTIVITY 25.9

A entity owns 75% of the shares in B entity bought when the reserves of B were €200 000. The individual balance sheets of A and B as at 30 June 200X are given below. During the year B has sold goods to A at a profit margin of 25% on cost. €50 000 of these goods lie in A's closing stock as at 30 June 200X. Also B owes C an outside supplier €2000 and C owes A €5000 as at 30 June 200X.

	A	B
Assets	€000s	€000s
Land and plant	1 000	200
Stock	600	400
Debtors	200	40
Investment in B	275	–
	2 075	640
Liabilities		
Creditors	30	16
	2 045	624
Represented by		
Shares of €1	1 000	100
Reserves	1 045	524
	2 045	624

Prepare the consolidated balance sheet as at 30 June 200X.

Activity feedback

Consolidated balance sheet as at 30 June 200X:

Assets	€000s
Goodwill (note 1)	50
Land and plant	1 200
Stock (1 000 – 10)	990
Debtors (240 – 2)	238
	2 478
Liabilities	
Creditors (46 – 2)	44
	2 434
Represented by:	
Shares of €1	1 000
Reserves (Note 2)	1 280.5
	2 280.5
Non-controlling interests (note 3)	153.5
	2 434

Note 1

Cost of investment in B		275
Less ordinary shares acquired	75	
Reserves acquired 75% × 200	150	225
		50

Note 2

Reserves A		1 045
Reserves post-acquired B 75%		
(524 – 10 – 200)		235.5
		1 280.5

Note 3

Minority interest	
25% ordinary shares	25
25% reserves = 25% × 514	128.5
	153.5

ACTIVITY 25.10

The financial year-end of two entities A and B within the same group is 31 December. On 29 December A despatched goods to B to the invoice value of €40 000 and charges B's ledger account accordingly. B does not receive either goods or invoice until 4 January. Prepare the consolidation adjustment on B's books and note any other adjustment that may be required on consolidation.

Activity feedback

The adjustment will bring the goods into B's books as at 31 December.

B ledger books	Dr	Cr
Goods in transit	€40 000	
A current account		€40 000

On consolidation the respective inter-company balances in the current accounts which are now in agreement will cancel out.

However, we must remember that this stock of €40 000 in transit will contain an element of unrealised profit and this will need eliminating on consolidation.

ACTIVITY 25.11

On 1 October 2005 *H* entity acquired 2 million *of S* entity's ordinary shares paying £4.50 per share. At the date of acquisition the retained earnings of *S* were £4 200 000. The draft balance sheets of the two entities as at 30 September 2007 were as follows:

	H	S
Assets	£000	£000
Non-current assets		
Property	11 000	6 000
Plant and equipment	10 225	5 110
Investment in *S*	9 000	
	30 225	11 110
Current assets		
Inventory	4 925	3 295
Trade receivables	5 710	1 915
Cash	495	
	11 130	5 210
Total assets	41 355	16 320
Equity and liabilities		
Equity		
Ordinary shares £1	5 000	2 500
Retained earnings	25 920	8 290
	30 920	10 790
Non-current liabilities		
10% loans	6 000	2 000
Current liabilities		
Trade payables	3 200	2 255
Bank overdraft		285
Tax	1 235	990
	4 435	3 530
Total equity and liabilities	41 355	16 320

Extracts from the income statement of *S* entity before inter-group adjustments for the year ended 30 September 2007 are:

	£000s
Profit before tax	2 700
Taxation	800
Profit after tax	1 900

The following information is also relevant:

1 During the year *S* sold goods to *H* for £0.9 million. *S* adds a 20% mark-up on cost to all its sales. Goods with a transfer price of £240 000 were included in *H*'s inventory as at 30 September 2007.

2 The fair value of *S*'s land and plant and equipment at the date of acquisition was £1 million and £2 million respectively in excess of the carrying values. *S*'s balance sheet has not taken account of these fair values. Group depreciation policy is land not depreciated, plant and equipment depreciated 10% per annum on fair value.

3 An impairment review has been carried out on the consolidated goodwill as at 30 September 2007 and it has been found that the goodwill has been impaired by £400 000 during the year.

Required

Prepare the consolidated balance sheet of *H* group as at 30 September 2007

Activity feedback

Consolidated balance sheet for *H* group as at 30 September 2007

	£000s
Assets	
Non-current assets	
Land and property (11 000 + 6 000 + 1 000)	18 000
Plant and equipment (10 225 + 5 110 + 2 000 − 400 depreciation)	16 935
Intangible assets (1 240 goodwill − 400 impairment)	840
	35 775
Current assets	
Inventory (4 925 + 3 295 − 40 unrealised profit)	8 180
Trade receivables (5 710 + 1 915)	7 625
Cash	495
	16 300
Total assets	52 075
Equity and liabilities	
Equity	
Ordinary share capital	5 000
Retained earnings (25 920 + (8 290 − 4200 preacq − 400 dep − 40urp)80% − 400 impairment)	28 440
	33 440
Non-controlling interest (20%(10 790 − 400 − 40 + 3 000 revaluation)	2 670
Non-current liabilities	
10% loans (6000 + 2000)	8 000
Current liabilities	
Trade payables (3 200 + 2 255)	5 455
Bank overdraft	285
Tax (1 235 + 990)	2 225
	7 965
Total equity and liabilities	52 075

ACTIVITY 25.11 (Continued)

Cost of control			80% retained earnings at date of acquisition	
Paid 2m × £4.50		9 000	£4.2m	3 360
Bought				7 760
2m £1 shares		2 000	Goodwill	1 240
80% revaluation of assets £3m		2 400		

PREPARATION OF MORE COMPLEX CONSOLIDATED BALANCE SHEETS

Acquisition by stages

Sometimes one entity will acquire shareholdings in another in stages. For example, *A* may acquire 25% of the voting shares of *B* at 1.4.X1, a further 20% six months later and a further 30% 12 months later. In this example, it is only at the third stage that a subsidiary/parent relationship exists. The difficulty with staged acquisitions is in determining the date when a subsidiary relationship exists, what the cost was and what the fair value of the assets and liabilities acquired was.

The date of an acquisition by stages is fairly straightforward. This remains at the date when control is transferred. In our example, this is the third stage and therefore consolidation would take place as from that date. Prior to this date the investment would be recorded as a trade investment, associate (see p. 672 and IAS 28) or joint venture (see p. 696 and IAS 31). It had become general practice that when an acquisition involved more than one exchange transaction the cost of the acquisition was the aggregate cost of the individual transactions. When an acquisition was achieved in stages, the distinction between the date of acquisition and the date of the exchange transaction was important. While accounting for the acquisition commenced as from the date of acquisition, it used cost and fair value information determined as at the date of each exchange transaction.

You might like to consider whether perhaps changing the cost and the fair values of net assets at each exchange date to that of the acquisition date would provide a view that was true and fair as you will find that this is now the method required by the IASB for stage acquisitions, not the method describe above. This has been a recent change by the IASB.

Activity 25.12 should help to clarify general practice in relation to staged acquisitions.

We have shown you the old and new method of accounting for acquisitions in stages in the activity as this is a very recent change by the IASB. We will deal with this again in Chapter 26.

Reverse acquisitions

Normally in an acquisition the acquirer, who issues shares to the acquiree shareholders to gain control, still retains control of the combined enterprises.

ACTIVITY 25.12

H acquired an interest in S as follows:

- 10% of the voting shares for $150 000 on 1.4.01
- 30% of the shares for $460 000 on 1.4.02
- 40% of the voting shares for $800 000 on 1.4.03.

The fair values of the recognised assets and liabilities of S at these dates were $1m, $1.5m, and $1.75m respectively. Accounts are drawn up as at 31 March. Identify at what date S becomes a subsidiary of H and the goodwill to be shown in the consolidated financial statements after the final acquisition both under the previous method of the IASB and the new method.

Activity feedback

S becomes a subsidiary of H at the third purchase, 1.4.03, when 80% is then controlled. Goodwill will be recognised at the third stage but calculated by reference to each exchange transaction under the old method

	$
FV at first stage	1 000 000
Acquired 10%	100 000
Cost	150 000
Goodwill stage 1	50 000
FV at second stage	1 500 000
Acquired 30%	450 000
Cost	460 000
Goodwill stage 2	10 000

	$
FV at third stage	1 750 000
Acquired 40%	700 000
Cost	800 000
Goodwill stage 3	100 000
Total goodwill after third purchase	160 000

Under the **new method** required by the IASB for stage acquisitions we would need to identify the fair value of the whole of S by reference to the last purchase.

Fair value 800 000 × 100/40	= 2 000 000
Previous total holding was 40% which at fair value	800 000
However this would be recorded in H's books at 150 000 + 460 000 =	610 000
Recognise gain in profit and loss at 1.4.03 of	190 000
Ownership is now 80% at cost of 800 000 + 800 000	= 1 600 000
Fair value of net assets bought is 80% × 1 750 000 =	1 400 000
Goodwill	200 000

The goodwill on acquisition to be shown in the consolidated financial statements as at 1.4.03 under the new requirements of IASB will be £200 000.

Example 25.3

Entity A with a share capital of €100 shares issues a further 50 shares to acquire the complete shareholding of entity B consisting of 200 €1 shares, a one A share for four B shares exchange. In this case A now owns all of B's shares, 200, and A's shareholders hold 100 A shares. B shareholders hold 50 A shares. Thus A shareholders retain control of A. If, however, A had issued 200 A shares to acquire the 200 B shares then B shareholders would now hold two-thirds of the shareholding of A and in 'substance' the acquiree, B, becomes the acquirer.

When an entity obtains ownership of the shares of another entity but as part of the exchange transaction issues enough voting shares as consideration such that control of the combined entities passes to the owners of the entity whose shares have been acquired then we have what has become known as a reverse acquisition. Although legally the entity issuing the shares may be regarded as the parent or continuing entity, the entity whose shareholders now control the combined entity is in substance the acquirer. Using substance over form the entity issuing the shares can be deemed to have been acquired by the other entity; the latter entity is deemed to be the acquirer and would need to consolidate the assets and liabilities of the entity issuing the shares.

Adjustments to identifiable assets or liabilities

These can occur because:

- the acquirer was unaware of certain assets or liabilities of the acquiree
- the assets or liabilities did not satisfy recognition criteria
- or further information comes to light which enables more accurate estimation of fair values.

How these adjustments are dealt with depends on whether they occur before or after the first complete annual accounting period subsequent to acquisition:

- Before and the adjustment can easily be reflected in goodwill providing the amount will be recovered from expected future economic benefits, otherwise it would be recognised as an expense.
- After and the adjustment is reflected in income or expense not goodwill.

Disposal of part interest

When a group disposes of part of an interest in a subsidiary undertaking a profit or loss on disposal will obviously arise but how do we calculate this? We could record any profit or loss arising calculated as the difference between the carrying amount of the net assets of that subsidiary undertaking attributable to the group's interest before the reduction and the carrying amount attributable to the group's interest after the reduction together with any proceeds received (see Activity 25.13 and 25.14).

ACTIVITY 25.13

The value of a subsidiary's net assets at 31 March 200X is €400 000. At this date the parent, which held a 100% share in the subsidiary, disposes of 40% for €200 000. On the original acquisition of the subsidiary, goodwill of €80 000 arose. This goodwill has not subsequently been impaired and is in addition to the net assets of €400 000. Calculate the profit or loss on disposal.

Activity feedback

	€
Group share of net assets before disposal including goodwill (100% × (400 000 + 80 000))	480 000
Group share of net assets after disposal including goodwill (60% × (400 000 + 80 000))	288 000
Disposal proceeds	200 000
	488 000
Profit on disposal	8 000

If, for example the goodwill had been impaired to €60 000, then the impairment loss would have been recognised in previous profit and loss accounts. The profit on disposal, assuming no change in the proceeds, would then have been calculated as follows:

Group share of net assets before disposal including value of goodwill remaining (100% × 460 000)	460 000
Group share of net assets after disposal including goodwill (60% × 460 000)	276 000
Disposal proceeds	200 000
	476 000
Profit on disposal	16 000

The profit increases in this case by the €8 000 (40% of €20 000) which has previously been debited to the income statement.

We can usefully refresh our memory of group accounts and work through a full example at this point (Activity 25.14) using rules we have identified so far.

ACTIVITY 25.14

The balance sheets of Alexander and Britton on 30 June 20X1 were as follows:

	Alexander		Britton	
	€000s	€000s	€000s	€000s
Fixed assets				
Land and buildings	108		64	
less Depreciation	20	88	32	32
Plant and machinery	65		43	
less Depreciation	25	40	29	14
		128		46
Investments				
Shares in Britton		35		
Current assets				
Stock	25		27	
Debtors	48		21	
Bank	22		6	
	95		54	
Creditors <1 year				
Creditors	112	(17)	34	20
		146		66
Represented by				
Ordinary €1 share		100		50
Capital reserves		10		
Revenue reserves		36		16
		146		66

1 Alexander acquired 37 500 shares in Britton several years ago when there had been a debit balance on the revenue reserve of €3000.

2 During the year ended 30 June 20X1 Alexander purchased a machine from Britton for €5000 which had yielded a profit on selling price of 30% to that company. Depreciation on the machine had been charged in the accounts at 20% on cost.

3 Britton purchases goods from Alexander providing Alexander with a gross profit on invoice price of 33 1/3%. On 30 June 20X1 the stock of Britton included an amount of €8000 being goods purchased from Alexander for €9000.

Prepare the consolidated balance sheet of Alexander and its subsidiary as at 30 June 20X1.

Activity feedback

	€000	€000
Cost of control		35
Shares of net assets 75% (50 − 3)		35.25
Negative goodwill		0.25
Inter-group transfer of machine – unrealised profit		1 500
Excess depreciation charged 20% × 1 500		300
Britton's accounts unrealised profit		1 200
Inter-group stock transfer – unrealised profit 33 1/3 % × €9 000		3 000
		1 000
Reduction in value		2 000

Consolidated balance sheet as at 30 June 20X1

Fixed assets	
Land and buildings	120
Plant and machinery	52.8
	172.8
Current assets	
Stock	50
Debtors	69
Bank	28
	147
Creditors <1 year	
Creditors	146	1
	173.8
Represented by	
Ordinary €1 shares	100
Capital reserves	10
Revenue reserves	47.6
	157.6
Minority interest (25% (66 − 1.2))	16.2
	173.8

Note 1

Reserves of Alexander	36
Unrealised profit on stock	(2)
Post-acquisition profits of Britton: 75% (16 (30.6.X1) + 3 (debit balance at acq. date) − 1.2 (unrealised profit on sale of machine))	13.35
Negative goodwill	0.25
	47.6

Preparation of consolidated accounts involving more than one subsidiary

These are relatively straightforward if you remember the rules already explained. We include an activity here (Activity 25.15) of a consolidation involving several companies to test your understanding and application of the techniques of consolidation.

ACTIVITY 25.15

A plc acquired 5m €1 shares of *B* Ltd five years ago when the reserves of *B* stood at £6m. *B* Ltd acquired 2.25m €1 shares in *C* Ltd four years ago when the accumulated reserves of *C* were €0.5m. *A* plc also acquired 3m €1 share of *D* Ltd two years ago when *D*'s reserves were €0.3m. At the date of acquisition the net book value of all assets equated to fair value. There has been no issue of shares in any of these companies throughout the five-year period. The balance sheets relate to the group companies as at 31.12.200X.

	A €m	B €m	C €m	D €m
Fixed assets	45	5	1.5	2
Investment in *B*	16	–	–	–
Investment in *C*	–	4.5	–	–
Investment in *D*	4	–	–	–
Net current assets	32	18	2.5	1
	97	27.5	4	3
Share capital	18	7.5	3	4.
Reserves	79	20	1	(1)
	97	27.5	4	3

Prepare the consolidated balance sheet of *A* group as at 31.12.200X.

Activity feedback

B and *D* are subsidiaries of *A* with controlling interests of 66.6% and 75% respectively. *C* is a subsidiary of *B* at an ownership of 75% but as *B* is a subsidiary of *A* then *C* is also a subsidiary of *A* at a controlling interest of 50%. Figure 25.3 aids understanding here.

The goodwill calculations at acquisition are:

	B €m	C €m	D €m	Total €m
Cost of control	16	4.5	4	
Shares bought	5	2.25	3	
Reserves bought	4	0.375	0.225	
	9	2.625	3.225	
Goodwill	7	1.875	0.775	
Group share	7	1.25	0.775	9.025
Minority calculations:				
Total net assets	23	4	3	
MI% share	33.3	50	25	
MI	7.67	2	0.75	10.42

	€m
Goodwill	9.025
Fixed assets	53.5
Net current assets	53.5
	116.025
Share capital	18
Reserves	
[79 + (20 − 6)2/3 + (1 − 0.5)1/2	
+ (−1−0.3)3/4]	87.605
Minority interest	10.42
	116.025

FIGURE 25.3   Subsidiaries and controlling interest

PREPARATION OF CONSOLIDATED INCOME STATEMENT

The principles of preparation of a consolidated income statement are the same as those for the balance sheet. Thus we will add together each individual line from the income statements deducting inter-entity transactions as we go. At some point we will need to deduct the profit attributable to the non-controlling interest. A simple example demonstrates the preparation of a consolidated income statement.

Example 25.4

The individual income statements of High and Low as at 31 December 200X are as follows:

	High €	Low €
Turnover	100 000	50 000
Cost of sales	75 000	30 000
Gross profit	25 000	20 000
Distribution expenses	4 000	3 000
Administration expenses	7 000	8 000
	14 000	9 000
Investment income:		
Dividends received	2 250	
	16 250	
Taxation	7 000	3 000
Earnings	9 250	6 000
Retained earnings	22 000	4 000
	31 250	10 000

The share capital of Low consists of 100 000 €1 shares of which High bought 75 000 on 1 January 200X for €90 000. The fair value of Low's assets at date of acquisition equated to net book values and the only reserves existing when High bought in were retained profits. During the year High sold goods to Low for €12 000 which included a profit of €2000. As at 31.12.0X half of these goods still remain in Low's stocks. The dividends paid and proposed by Low are all paid out of current profits.

First, we need to identify the goodwill on acquisition:

	€	€
Cost of High's control of Low		90 000
Bought 75% of Low's shares	75 000	
Bought 75% of Low's retained profits	3 000	78 000
Goodwill		12 000
Next, we need to sort inter-company trading:		
Reduce High's sales by		12 000

	€	€
Reduce High's profits by		1 000
Reduce Low's stock by		1 000
Consolidated income statement for the year ended 31.12.0X		
Turnover (150 000 − 12 000)		138 000
Cost of sales (105 000 − 12 000 + 1 000)		94 000
		44 000
Distribution expenses	7 000	
Administration expenses	15 000	22 000
		22 000
Taxation		10 000
Consolidated earnings on ordinary activities after tax		12 000
Less attributable to non-controlling interest (25% × 6 000 − Low's profit after tax)		1 500
Consolidated earnings for the financial year		10 500
Retained earnings		22 000
		32 500

Note that all allocation of profits to the non-controlling interest for the year takes place after calculating consolidated earnings after tax and that the inter-entity transactions in relation to Low's dividends paid to high is eliminated.

Note that the total of income and expenditure for the parent and the subsidiary is included in the consolidated income statement. This is in accordance with the inclusion of the total of assets and liabilities in the consolidated balance sheet. However we perhaps need to show the division of this profit between the group and the non-controlling interest. In the example above the non-controlling interest allocation of profit is 1500 (25% × 6000). We could have prepared the consolidated income statement by only including the group share at each line of the income statement. However this would not have shown the income and expenses that the group controls. Including the full income and expenses and using a one line deduction from the non-controlling interest provided more useful information to users of what the group controls.

Acquisition part-way through a year

When the acquisition of a subsidiary occurs part-way through the year then a proportion of that year's profits of the subsidiary will be regarded as pre-acquisition. When preparing the consolidated income statement for the year of acquisition we could bring in only the post-acquisition amount at each line of consolidation (i.e. turnover, cost of sales, etc.) on a time basis or we could bring in the entire amount at each line and then make a deduction at the end of the income statement for pre-acquisition profits. In the next chapter we will identify the answer to this provided by international standards currently but you might like to consider which method would give a true and fair view.

Activity 25.16 requires you to prepare a consolidated balance sheet and a consolidated income statement.

ACTIVITY 25.16

The summarised statements for the year ended 30 June 2007 for A, B and C entities are as follows:

Income statement (Profit and loss account) for the year ended 30 June 2007

	A	B	C
	£000s	£000s	£000s
Revenue (Turnover)	15 000	8 000	6 000
Cost of sales	(7 200)	(4 300)	(4 100)
	7 800	3 700	1 900
Expenses	(3 300)	(2 100)	(1 100)
Profit before tax	4 500	1 600	800
Tax	(1 400)	(650)	(260)
Profit for the year	3 100	950	540

Balance sheet as at 30 June 2007

	A	B	C
ASSETS			
NON-CURRENT ASSETS			
(fixed assets)			
Property, plant and equipment	2 652	1 810	1 300
Investment in B	1 302		
Investment in C	1 256		
	5 210	1 810	1 300
CURRENT ASSETS			
Inventory (stock)	630	460	320
Trade receivables (debtors)	560	370	280
Cash	160	–	90
	1 350	830	690
TOTAL ASSETS	6 560	2 640	1 990
EQUITY AND LIABILITIES			
EQUITY			
Ordinary shares	1 600	850	900
Share premium	100	50	300
Retained earnings	3 850	1 210	360
	5 550	2 110	1 560
NON-CURRENT LIABILITIES (creditors due after one year)			
Loans	450	170	110
CURRENT LIABILITIES (creditors due within one year)			
Trade payables (creditors)	470	280	300
Bank overdraft	–	70	–

	A	B	C
Tax	90	10	20
	560	360	320
TOTAL EQUITIY AND LIABILITIES	6 560	2 640	1 990

The following information is also available:

(i)   A acquired a 70% share in B and an 80% share in C on 1 July 2006. The fair values of B's assets at that date equalled those shown on the balance sheet. As at 1 July 2007 the fair value of C's property was £500 000 in excess of the balance sheet value. A, B and C all depreciate their property, plant and equipment on the same basis. Property is depreciated on a straight line basis over 50 years.

(ii) As at 30 June 2007 the fair value of the consolidated goodwill was reviewed and found to have a value 5% less than its carrying value at the consolidation date. This impairment is to be accounted for in the consolidated accounts.

(iii) Inter-group sales (A to B) in the period from 1 July 2006 to 30 June 2007 are £3 100 000 on which A made a profit of 15% on selling price. Of these goods £500 000 (at selling price from A to B) are still in B's closing inventory (stock) amount.

Prepare the consolidated income statement (profit and loss account) for the year ended 30 June 2007 and the consolidated balance sheet as at that date for the group.

Activity feedback

	£000
Cost of control A in B	
Cost of 70% control	1 302
Ordinary shares 70% × 850	595
Share premium 70% × 50	35
Retained earnings at acquisition date (1 210 − 950 post acq.) × 70%	182
	812
Goodwill on consolidation	490
Impairment on review 5%	(24.5)
	465.5
Non-controlling interest	
Ordinary shares 30% × 850	255
Share premium 30% × 50	15
Attributable to NCI from retained earnings 30% × 1 210	363
	633

ACTIVITY 25.16   (Continued)

Cost of control A in C		£000
Cost of 80% control		1 256
Ordinary shares 80% × 900		720
Share premium 80% × 300		240
Fair value adjustment 500 × 80%		400
Retained earnings at acquisition date		
(360 − 540 post acq.) × 80%		(144)
		1 216
Goodwill on consolidation		40
Impairment on review 5%		(2)
		38
Non-controlling interest		
Ordinary shares 20% × 900		180
Share premium 20% × 300		60
Attributable to MI from retained earnings 20%		
× 360		72
20% fair value adjustment of 500		100
Depreciation charge on fair value 10 × 20%		(2)
		410
Total goodwill before impairment		530
Total impairment at 5%		26.5
Total goodwill after impairment		503.5
Total non-controlling interest (633 + 410)		1 043

Depreciation required on fair value of property 500/50 = 100

Inter-group sales reduce A's revenue by 3100, reduce B's cost of sales by 3100

Unrealised profit 15% × 500 = 75

Consolidated income statement for the year ended 30 June 2007

		£000s
Revenue	15 000 + 8 000 + 6 000	
	− 3 100	25 900
Cost of sales	7 200 + 4 300 + 4 100 −	
	3 100 + unrealised	
	profit 75	(12 575)
		13 325
Expenses	3 300 + 2 100 + 1 100 +	
	dep 10	(6 510)
	Goodwill Impairment 26.5	(26.5)

		£000s
		6 788.5
Taxation	1 400 + 650 + 260	(2 310)
		4 478.5
Attributable to	30% × 950 + 20% × 540	
N.C.I.		(393)
Retained profits		
for the year		4 085.5

Consolidated balance sheet as at 30 June 2007

		£000
Non-current assets		
Property, plant and	2 652 + 1 810 + 1 300	6 252
equipment	+ 500 − 10	
Goodwill		503.5
		6 755.5
Current assets		
Inventory	630 + 460 + 320 − 75	1 335
Trade receivables	560 + 370 + 280	1 210
Cash	160 + 90	250
		2 795
Total assets		9 550.5
Equity and liabilities		
Equity		
Ordinary shares		1 600
Share premium		100
Retained earnings	3 850 − 3 100 +	4 835.5
	4 085.5	
		6 535.5
Non-controlling interest		1 043
Non current liabilities		
Loans	450 + 170 + 110	730
Current liabilities		
Trade payables	470 + 280 + 300	1 050
Bank overdraft	70	70
Taxation	90 + 10 + 20	120
		1 240
Total equity and liabilities		9 550.5

SUMMARY

In this chapter we have dealt with the preparation of consolidated balance sheets and consolidated income statements. So far we have made little reference to accounting standards. This was deliberate as once you have mastered the techniques of consolidation you will be better placed to understand the issues that international accounting standards have to address in relation to business combinations. A brief list of these issues are:

- how to define a business combination
- how best to portray that combination to users to provide them with useful information
- how to deal with consolidated goodwill
- where to show the non-controlling interest on the consolidated balance and consolidated income statement
- how to deal with inter-group transactions and balances
- how to deal with stage acquisitions and disposals
- determining fair value of purchase price and net assets
- which entity is the acquirer (parent) and which the acquiree (subsidiary)
- how to deal with subsequent measurement of net assets.

We deal with the international accounting standards in relation to groups in the next chapter.

The exercises at the end of this current chapter will provide you with plenty of practice in preparing consolidated group financial statements.

EXERCISES

Suggested answers to exercises marked ✓ are to be found on the Student side of the companion website.

Suggested answers to the remaining exercises are to be found on the Instructor side of the companion website.

1 Construct (using appropriate assumptions) a mixed group structure bringing together a holding entity, a subsidiary and a sub-subsidiary.

✓ 2 Explain why the fair value of an entity's assets is used in the preparation of consolidated financial statements.

3 The preparation of consolidated financial statements provides useful information to users. Discuss.

4 Appraise the need for group accounts.

5 On 1 April 20X5 Hardy entity acquired 4 million of Sibling entity's common shares. paying €4.50 each. At the same time it also purchased at nominal value €500 000 of its 10% redeemable preference shares. At the date of acquisition the retained profit reserves of Sibling entity were €8 400 000. The draft balance sheets of the two entities at 31 March 20X8 were as follows:

	Hardy €000	Hardy €000	Sibling €000	Sibling €000
Non-current assets				
Land and buildings		22 000		12 000
Plant and equipment		20 450		10 220
Investment in Sibling: common shares		18 000		
Preference shares		500		
		60 950		22 220
Current assets				
Inventory	9 850		6 590	
Accounts receivable	11 420		3 830	
Cash	490		0	
	21 760		10 420	
Current liabilities				
Accounts payable	6 400		4 510	
Bank overdraft	0		570	
Provision for taxation	2 470		1 980	
	(8 870)		(7 060)	
Net current assets		12 890		3 360
Long-term liabilities				
10% loans		(12 000)		(4 000)
Net assets		61 840		21 580
Common shares of €1		10 000		5 000
10% preference shares				2 000
Retained profit reserves		51 840		14 580
		61 840		21 580

Extracts from the income statement of Sibling entity before intra-group adjustments, for the year to 31 March 20X8 are:

	€000
Profit before tax	5 400
Taxation	(1 600)
	3 800

The following information is relevant:

1 Included in the land and buildings of Sibling is a large area of developed land at its cost of €5 million. Its fair value at the date Sibling was acquired was €7 million and by 31 March 20X8 this had risen to €8.5 million. The group valuation policy for development land is that it should be carried at fair value and not depreciated.

2 Also at the date of Sibling's acquisition the plant and equipment included plant that had a fair value of €4 million in excess of its carrying value. This plant had a remaining life of five years. The group calculates depreciation on a straight line basis. The fair value of Sibling's other net assets approximated to their carrying values.

3   During the year Sibling sold goods to Hardy for €1.8 million. Sibling adds a 20% mark-up on cost to all its sales. Goods with a transfer price of €450 000 were included in Hardy's stock at 31 March 20X8. The balance on the current accounts of the parent and subsidiary was €240 000 on 31 March 20X8.

Prepare the consolidated balance sheet of Hardy as at 31 March 20X8.

6   The summarised statements for the year ended 31 December 2007 for Mat, Rug and Pet entities are as follows:

Income statement (Profit and loss account) for the year ended 31 December 2007

	Mat £000s	Rug £000s	Pet £000s
Revenue (Turnover)	23 500	11 700	8 900
Cost of sales	(15 400)	(8 700)	(6 800)
	8 100	3 000	2 100
Expenses	(4 600)	(1 800)	(900)
Profit before tax	3 500	1 200	1 200
Tax	(1 800)	(470)	(640)
Profit for the year	1 700	730	560

Balance sheet as at 31 December 2007

	Mat £000s	Rug £000s	Pet £000s
ASSETS			
NON-CURRENT ASSETS (fixed assets)			
Property, plant and equipment	7 030	2 130	1 760
Investment in Rug	2 680		
Investment in Pet	860		
	1 0570	2 130	1 760
CURRENT ASSETS			
Inventory	1 230	570	490
Trade receivables	1 100	190	560
Cash	430	–	110
	2 760	760	1 160
TOTAL ASSETS	13 330	2 890	2 920
EQUITY AND LIABILITIES			
EQUITY			
Ordinary shares	2 900	1 300	1 450
Share premium	700	700	110
Retained earnings	6 780	130	340
	10 380	2 130	1 900

	Mat £000s	Rug £000s	Pet £000s
NON-CURRENT LIABILITIES (creditors due after one year)			
Loans	760	340	90
CURRENT LIABILITIES (creditors due within one year)			
Trade payables	990	120	430
Bank overdraft	–	70	–
Tax	1200	230	500
	2 190	420	930
TOTAL EQUITIY AND LIABILITIES	13 330	2 890	2 920

The following information is also available:

(i) Dividends paid out of earnings for the year 31 December 2007 were as follows: Mat £600 000, Rug £550 000, Pet £440 000. The appropriate shareholders have received all these dividends. Mat has included its share in 'Revenue' on the income statement.

(ii) Mat acquired an 80% share in Rug and a 60% share in Pet on 1 January 2007. The fair values of Rug's assets at that date equalled those shown on the balance sheet. As at 1 January 2007 the fair value of Pet's property was £750 000 in excess of the balance sheet value. Mat, Rug and Pet all depreciate their property, plant and equipment on the same basis. Property is depreciated on a straight line basis over 50 years.

(iii) As at 31 December 2007 the fair value of the consolidated goodwill in Rug was reviewed and found to have a value 10% less than its carrying value at the consolidation date. This impairment is to be accounted for in the consolidated accounts. Any negative goodwill is to be taken to the income statement.

(iv) Intergroup sales (Mat to Rug) in the period from 1 January 2007 to 31 December 2007 are £6 200 000 on which Mat made a profit of 15% on selling price. Of these goods £1 000 000 (at selling price from Mat to Rug) are still in Rug's closing inventory amount.

Required:
Prepare the consolidated income statement for the year ended 31 December 2007 and the consolidated balance sheet as at that date for the group.

(ifa June 2008 q.1)

7   D has owned 80% of the equity shares of E since 1 January 1996. E has owned 60% of the equity shares of F since 1 January 1994. The accumulated profits of F at the latest balance sheet date, 31 December 2003, stood at $30m. The accumulated profits of F stood at $12m on 1 January 1994 and $14m on 1 January 1996.

Ignoring goodwill, what will be included in the consolidated accumulated profits of D at 31 December 2003 in respect of F?

8   At 1 April 20X3 S held 80 000 of the 100 000 issued ordinary shares of T. The acquisition of T took place on 1 April 20X2 and goodwill on acquisition was recorded at $120 000. The

directors of S have agreed that the goodwill on acquisition has been impaired by $36 000 as at 1 October 20X3. On 1 October 20X3, S disposes of $20 000 shares in T for $125 000. At that date T's total net assets are $400 000.

Calculate the consolidated profit and loss before tax on disposal of the shares.

9 As well as its investment in T (see question 8) S also held 75% of the shares of U. U sells goods to S. During the year ending 31 March 20X4, U sells goods to S for $100 000. The cost of the goods to U is $80 000. At the year end S's inventories include $16 000 of goods purchased from U.

Calculate the adjustment required in respect of unrealised profit, and describe the accounting treatment of the adjustment in the consolidated income statement and the consolidated balance sheet.

10 Base, a public limited company, acquired two subsidiaries, Zero and Black, both public limited companies, on 1 June 20X1. The details of the acquisitions at that date are as follows:

Subsidiary	Ordinary share capital of $1	Reserves	Fair value of net assets at acquisition	Cost of investment	Ordinary share capital acquired
	$m	$m	$m	$m	$m
Zero	350	250	770	600	250
Black	200	150	400	270	120

The draft income statements for the year ended 31 May 2003 are:

	Base	Zero	Black
	$m	$m	$m
Revenue	3 000	2 300	600
Cost of Sales	(2 000)	(1 600)	(300)
Gross profit	1 000	700	300
Distribution costs	(240)	(230)	(120)
Administrative expenses	(200)	(220)	(80)
Profit from operations	560	250	100
Finance cost – interest expense	(20)	(10)	(12)
Investment income receivable (including inter company dividends paid May 20X3)	100	–	–
Profit before tax	640	240	88
Income tax expense	(130)	(80)	(36)
Net profit from ordinary activities	510	160	52
Accumulated profit 1 June 20X2	1 400	400	190

The following information is relevant to the preparation of the group financial statements:

(i) On 1 December 20X2, Base sold 50 million $1 ordinary shares in zero for $155 million. The only accounting entry made by Base was to record the receipt of the cash consideration in the cash account and in a suspense account.

(ii) On 1 March 20X3, Black issued 100 million ordinary shares of $1 at a price of $2.65 per share. It was fully subscribed and paid up on that day. Base decided not to subscribe for the shares but the directors of Base had significant influence over the decision to issue the shares. The directors of Black had prepared financial information as at 28 February 20X3 for the purpose of the new issues of shares showing the carrying values of the net assets of Black to be $480 million.

(iii) Black had sold $150 million of goods to Base on 30 April 20X3. There was no opening inventory of inter-company goods but the closing inventory of the goods in Base's financial statements was $90 million. The profit on these goods was 30% on selling price.

(iv) Base has implemented in full IAS19, *Employee Benefits* in its financial statements. The directors have included the following amounts in the figure for cost of sales:

	$m
Current service cost	5
Actuarial deficit on obligation	4
Interest cost	3
Actuarial gainonassets	(2)
Charged to cost of sales	10

They are unsure as to the treatment of these amounts given their stated objective of maximising current year profit. The fair value of the plan assets at 31 May 20X2 was $48 million and the present value of the defined benefit obligation was $54 million at that date. The net cumulative unrecognised actuarial loss at 31 May 2002 was $3 million and the expected remaining working lives of the employees was ten years.

(v) Base invested on 1 June 20X2 in a convertible debt instrument at a cost of $20 million. The debt is repayable in four years at $16 million but the conversion terms are extremely favourable. Base has included the convertible debt in its balance sheet at $20 million.

(vi) Base had carried out work for a group of companies (Drum Group) during the financial year to 31 May 20X2. Base had accepted one million share options of the Drum Group in full settlement of the debt owed to them. At 1 June 2002 these share options were valued at $3 million which was the value of the outstanding debt. The following table gives the prices of these shares and the fair value of the option.

	Share price	Fair value of option
31 May 20X2	$13	$3
31 May 20X3	$10	$1

The options had not been exercised during the year and remained at $3 million in the balance sheet of Base. The options can be exercised at any time after 31 May 20X5 for $8.50 per share.

(vii) Base had paid a dividend of $50 million in the year and Zero had paid a dividend of $70 million in May 20X3.

(viii) The fair value adjustments have been incorporated into the subsidiaries' records.

(ix) Ignore the tax implications of any capital gains made by the Group and assume profits accrue evenly throughout the year.

Required:

Prepare a consolidated income statement for the Base Group for the year ended 31 May 20X3

(ACCA June 2003)

11   Highmoor, a public listed company, acquired 80% of Slowmoor's ordinary shares on 1 October 20X2. Highmoor paid an immediate $2 per share in cash and agreed to pay a further $1.20 per share if Slowmoor made a profit within two years of its acquisition. Highmoor has not recorded the contingent consideration.

The balance sheets of the two companies at 30 September 20X3 are shown in the table below.

| | Highmoor | | Slowmoor | |
	$ million	$ million	$ million	$ million
Tangible non-current assets		585		172
Investments (note (ii))		225		13
Software (note (iii))		nil		40
		810		225
Current assets				
Inventory	85		42	
Accounts receivable	95		36	
Tax asset	nil		80	
Bank	20	200	nil	158
Total assets		1 010		383
Equity and liabilities				
Capital and reserves:				
Ordinary shares of $1 each		400		100
Accumulated profits – 1 October 20X2	230		150	
profit/loss for year	100	330	(35)	115
		730		215
Non-current liabilities				
12% loan note	nil		35	
8% Inter-company loan (note (ii))	nil	nil	45	80
Current liabilities				
Accounts payable	210		71	
Taxation	70		nil	
Overdraft	nil	280	17	88
Total equity and liabilities		1 010		383

The following information is relevant:

(i)   At the date of acquisition the fair values of Slowmoor's net assets were approximately equal to their book values.

(ii)   Included in Highmoor's investments is a loan of $50 million made to Slowmoor. On 28 September 20X3, Slowmoor paid $9 million to Highmoor. This represented interest of $4 million for the year and the balance was a capital repayment. Highmoor had not received nor accounted for the payment, but it had accrued for the loan interest receivable as part of its accounts receivable figure. There are no other intra-group balances.

(iii)   The software was developed by Highmoor during 20X2 at a total cost of $30 million. It was sold to Slowmoor for $50 million immediately after its acquisition. The software had an estimated life of five years and is being amortised by Slowmoor on a straight line basis.

(iv) Due to the losses of Slowmoor since its acquisition, the directors of Highmoor are not confident it will return to profitability in the short term.

(v) For the purposes of realising any negative goodwill, in its acquisition plan, Highmoor had estimated at the date of acquisition that Slowmoor would make losses of $15 million (of which $12 million would be attributable to Highmoor) before returning to profitability. The remaining weighted average useful life at the date of acquisition of the acquired depreciable non-monetary assets can be taken as four years (straight line basis).

Required:

(a) Prepare the consolidated balance sheet of Highmoor as at 30 September 20X3, explaining your treatment of the contingent consideration.

(b) Describe the circumstances in which negative goodwill may arise. Your answer should refer to the particular issues of the above acquisition.

(ACCA December 2003)

12 In recent years Hillusion has acquired a reputation for buying modestly performing businesses and selling them at a substantial profit within a period of two to three years of their acquisition. On 1 July 20X2 Hillusion acquired 80% of the ordinary share capital of Skeptik at a cost of $10 280 000. On the same date it also acquired 50% of Skeptik's 10% loan notes at par. The summarised draft financial statements of both companies are:

Income statements: Year to 31 March 20X3

	Hillusion $000	Skeptik $000
Sales revenue	60 000	24 000
Cost of sales	(42 000)	(20 000)
Gross profit	18 000	4 000
Operating expenses	(6 000)	(200)
Loan interest received (paid)	75	(200)
Operating profit	12 075	3 600
Taxation	(3 000)	(600)
Profit after tax for the year	9 075	3 000
Accumulated profit brought forward	16 525	5 400
Accumulated profit per balance sheet	25 600	8 400

	Hillusion $000	Skeptik $000
Balance sheets: as at 31 March 20X3		
Tangible non-current assets	19 320	8 000
Investments	11 280	nil
	30 600	8 000
Current assets	15 000	8 000
Total assets	45 600	16 000
Equity and liabilities		
Ordinary shares of $1 each	10 000	2 000
Accumulated profits	25 600	8 400
	35 600	10 400

	Hillusion $000	Skeptik $000
Balance sheets: as at		
31 March 20X3		
Non-current liabilities		
10% Loan notes	nil	2 000
Current liabilities	10 000	3 600
Total equity and liabilities	45 600	16 000

The following information is relevant:

(i)   The fair values of Skeptik's assets were equal to their book values with the exception of its plant, which had a fair value of $3.2 million in excess of its book value at the date of acquisition. The remaining life of all of Skeptik's plant at the date of its acquisition was four years and this period has not changed as a result of the acquisition. Depreciation of plant is on a straight line basis and charged to cost of sales. Skeptik has not adjusted the value of its plant as a result of the fair value exercise.

(ii) In the post-acquisition period Hillusion sold goods to Skeptik at a price of $12 million. These goods had cost Hillusion $9 million. During the year Skeptik had sold $10 million (at cost to Skeptik) of these goods for $15 million.

(iii) Hillusion bears almost all of the administration costs incurred on behalf of the group (invoicing, credit control, etc.). It does not charge Skeptik for his service as to do so would not have a material effect on the group profit.

(iv) Revenues and profits should be deemed to accrue evenly throughout the year.

(v)   The current accounts of the two companies were reconciled at the year-end with Skeptik owing Hillusion $750 000.

(vi) Time apportionment should be used in the year of acquisition.

Required:

(a)   Prepare a consolidated income statement and balance sheet for Hillusion for the year to 31 March 20X3.

(b)   Explain why it is necessary to eliminate unrealised profits when preparing group financial statements; and how reliance on the entity financial statements of Skeptik may mislead a potential purchaser of the company.

NOTE: Your answer should refer to the circumstances described in the question.

(ACCA June 2003)

13   Alpha holds investments in two other entities, Beta and Gamma. All three entities prepare financial statements to 31 March and the balance sheets of the three entities at 31 March 2007 were as follows:

	Alpha $'000	Beta $'000	Gamma $'000
Assets			
Non-current assets:			
Property, plant and equipment	125 000	85 000	75 000
Investments (Note 2)	32 000	–	–
	157 000	85 000	75 000

	Alpha $'000	Beta $'000	Gamma $'000
Current assets:			
Inventories (Note 3)	33 000	30 000	28 000
Trade receivables (Note 4)	43 000	30 000	31 000
Cash and cash equivalents	11 000	10 000	9 000
	87 000	70 000	68 000
Total assets	**244 000**	**155 000**	**143 000**
Equity and liabilities			
Equity			
Share capital ($1 shares)	70 000	50 000	50 000
Retained earnings	55 000	44 000	28 000
Total equity	125 000	94 000	78 000
Non-current liabilities			
Long-term borrowings	50 000	25 000	22 000
Deferred tax	35 000	12 000	17 000
Total non-current liabilities	85 000	37 000	39 000
Current liabilities			
Trade and other payables (Note 4)	25 000	17 000	20 000
Current tax payable	9 000	7 000	6 000
Total current liabilities	34 000	24 000	26 000
Total equity and liabilities	**244 000**	**155 000**	**143 000**

Note 1 – purchase of shares in Beta

On 1 April 2006 Alpha purchased 40 million shares in Beta by issuing one share in Alpha for every two shares purchased in Beta. This share issue has not been recorded in the books of Alpha.

The quoted price of an Alpha share at 1 April 2006 was $6 and the quoted price of a Beta share at the same date was $2.40. Alpha incurred incremental legal and professional costs of $2 million in connection with the acquisition, of which $800 000 related to the cost of issuing its shares. These acquisition costs have been charged as an expense in the income statement of Alpha for the year ended 31 March 2007.

The retained earnings of Beta as shown in its balance sheet at 31 March 2006 were $35 million. The directors of Alpha carried out a fair value exercise on the net assets of Beta at that date. The following matters arose out of the exercise:

(i) Property, plant and equipment comprised non-depreciable land with a carrying amount of $50 million and a market value of $60 million, plus plant and equipment with a carrying amount of $30 million and a market value of $38 million. The estimated future economic life of the plant and equipment at 1 April 2006 was four years (straight line depreciation). None of the property, plant and equipment held by Beta at 1 April 2006 had been disposed of by 31 March 2007.

(ii) At 1 April 2006 Beta was engaged in legal action against a supplier in respect of damages caused by the supply of faulty products, Beta was claiming damages of $5 million. In the middle of March 2006 the customer had offered an out of court settlement of $3 million and Beta's lawyers advised that this was a fair offer given the likelihood of success in court. However Beta refused the offer, took the case to court, and subsequently won the case. The directors of Beta had not recognised any receivable in respect of the case in the balance sheet at 31 March 2006 because the claim was a contingent asset. The directors of Alpha considered that the fair value of the contingent asset at 1 April 2006 was $3 million.

(iii) At 1 April 2006 Beta had a long-standing portfolio of loyal customers that regularly ordered goods and services from Beta. In addition, the workforce of Beta was highly trained and the expertise of the workforce was seen by the directors as conferring significant competitive advantage to Beta. The customer relationships and the expertise of the workforce were not included in the balance sheet of Beta at 31 March 2006 because the directors did not consider that they met the recognition criteria in IAS 38 – *Intangible Assets* – for internally developed intangible assets. The directors of Alpha considered that the customer relationships had a market value of $20 million at 1 April 2006 and that based on the life cycle of the existing products, the existing customers would continue to order goods and services from Beta for at least five years from that date. They estimated that the fair value of the competitive advantage conferred by the workforce was $15 million at 1 April 2006 and that the average period to retirement for a typical employee was 20 years.

(iv) The financial director of Alpha has stated that the fair value adjustments will create temporary differences for deferred tax purposes.

Note 2 – purchase of shares in Gamma
On 1 April 2005 Alpha purchased 20 million shares in Gamma for a cash payment of $1.60 per share. The retained earnings of Gamma were $15 million at 1 April 2005. This shareholding has resulted in the directors of Alpha being able to exercise a significant influence over the operating and financial policies of Gamma. The fair value of the net assets of Gamma at 1 April 2005 was equal to their carrying amounts in Gamma's balance sheet.

Note 3 – inventories
The inventories of Beta and Gamma at 31 March 2007 included components purchased from Alpha during the year at a cost of $20 million to Beta and $16 million to Gamma. Alpha supplied these components at cost plus a mark-up of 25%.

Note 4 – trade receivables and payables
The trade receivables of Alpha included $5 million receivable from Beta and $4 million receivable from Gamma in respect of the purchase of components (see Note 3). The trade payables of Beta and Gamma include an equivalent amount payable to Alpha.

Note 5 – other information
(i) Neither the goodwill arising on acquisition of Beta nor the investment in Gamma has suffered any impairment since the dates of investment by Alpha in these entities.

(ii) The rate of tax to apply to temporary differences is 25%.

Required:
(a) Prepare the consolidated balance sheet of Alpha at 31 March 2007.

(b) Explain the effect on your answer to (a) if the acquisition agreement with the former shareholders of Beta provided for an additional cash payment of 50 cents per share acquired. The additional amount, payable on 31 March 2008, is contingent on the profits of Beta exceeding a given level in the two years ending 31 March 2008.

Note: You do NOT need to prepare the consolidated balance sheet under this revised assumption or perform any detailed numerical calculations.

(ACCA DIFR June 2007)

14 The income statements and summarised statements of changes in equity of Alpha, Beta and Gamma for the year ended 30 September 2006 are given below:

Income statements

	Alpha $'000	Beta $'000	Gamma $'000
Revenue	125 000	100 000	90 000
Cost of sales	(70 000)	(60 000)	(51 000)
Gross profit	55 000	40 000	39 000
Other operating expenses	(20 000)	(15 000)	(15 000)
Income from investments	9 000	5 000	4 500
Finance costs	(11 000)	(8 000)	(7 500)
Profit before tax	33 000	22 000	21 000
Income tax expense	(9 000)	(6 000)	(5 400)
Profit for the year	24 000	16 000	15 600

Summarised statements of change in equity

	Alpha	Beta	Gamma
Balance at 1 October 2005	110 000	60 000	56 000
Profit for the year	24 000	16 000	15 600
Dividends paid	(14 000)	(5 000)	nil
Balance at 30 September 2006	120 000	71 000	71 600

Notes to the financial statements

Note 1

(i)   On 1 October 2002 Alpha purchased an 80% equity shareholding in Beta. The equity of Beta as shown in its own financial statements at that date was $35 million. At the date of acquisition Beta owned some land with a book value of $25 million and a market value of $35 million, and some plant with a book value of $12 million and a market value of $16 million. The plant is depreciated on a straight line basis and the remaining useful economic life of the plant at 1 October 2002 was estimated at four years.

(ii) On 1 February 2006 Alpha purchased a 75% shareholding in Gamma. At the date of acquisition Gamma had registered a brand name that had a fair value of $27 million. Gamma had not recognised this amount in its own individual financial statements. The directors of Alpha estimated that this brand would provide Gamma with significant competitive advantage for a 15-year period from 1 February 2006.

(iii) Other than mentioned in notes (i) and (ii) above there were no fair value adjustments necessary on acquisition of Beta or Gamma.

(iv) Alpha presents depreciation and amortisation charges as part of cost of sales.

(v)   No impairment of goodwill on acquisition of either company has been identified up to and including 30 September 2006.

(vi) In addition to the equity investments made by Alpha in Beta and Gamma, on 1 February 2006 Alpha lent $20 million to Beta at an effective annual interest rate of 8%.

Note 2

Alpha supplies products used by Beta and Gamma. Sales of the products to Beta and Gamma during the year ended 30 September 2006 were as follows (all sales were made at a mark-up of 25% on cost):

- Sales to Beta $10 million.
- Sales to Gamma (all in the post-acquisition period) $3 million.

At 30 September 2006 and 30 September 2005 the inventories of Beta and Gamma included the following amounts in respect of goods purchased from Alpha.

	Amount in inventory at:	
	30/9/2006	*30/9/2005*
	$'000	*$'000*
Beta	2 000	1 200
Gamma	1 000	Nil

Required:

Prepare the consolidated income statement and summarised consolidated statement of changes in equity for Alpha for the year ended 30 September 2006. Ignore deferred tax.

(ACCA DIFR Dec 2006)

15 Parentis, a public listed company, acquired 600 million equity shares in Offspring on 1 April 2006. The purchase consideration was made up of:

- a share exchange of one share in Parentis for two shares in Offspring
- the issue of $100 10% loan note for every 500 shares acquired; and
- a deferred cash payment of 11 cents per share acquired payable on 1 April 2007.

Parentis has only recorded the issue of the loan notes. The value of each Parentis share at the date of acquisition was 75 cents and Parentis has a cost of capital of 10% per annum.

The balance sheets of the two companies at 31 March 2007 are shown below:

	Parentis		Offspring	
	$ million	*$ million*	*$ million*	*$ million*
Assets				
Property, plant and equipment (note (i))		640		340
Investments		120		nil
Intellectual property (note (ii))		nil		30
		760		370
Current assets				
Inventory (note (iii))	76		22	
Trade receivables (note (iii))	84		44	
Bank	nil	160	4	70
Total assets		920		440

	Parentis		Offspring	
	$ million	$ million	$ million	$ million
Equity and liabilities				
Equity shares of 25 cents each		300		200
Retained earnings – 1 April 2006	210		120	
– year ended 31 March 2007	90	300	20	140
		600		340
Non-current liabilities				
10% loan notes		120		20
Current liabilities				
Trade payables (note (iii))	130		57	
Current tax payable	45		23	
Overdraft	25	200	nil	80
Total equity and liabilities		920		440

The following information is relevant:

(i) At the date of acquisition the fair values of Offspring's net assets were approximately equal to their carrying amounts with the exception of its properties. These properties had a fair value of $40 million in excess of their carrying amounts which would create additional depreciation of $2 million in the post-acquisition period to 31 March 2007. The fair values have not been reflected in Offspring's balance sheet.

(ii) The intellectual property is a system of encryption designed for internet use. Offspring has been advised that government legislation (passed since acquisition) has now made this type of encryption illegal. Offspring will receive $10 million in compensation from the government.

(iii) Offspring sold Parentis goods for $15 million in the post-acquisition period. $5 million of these goods are included in the inventory of Parentis at 31 March 2007. The profit made by Offspring on these sales was $6 million. Offspring's trade payable account (in the records of Parentis) of $7 million does not agree with Parentis's trade receivable account (in the records of Offspring) due to cash in transit of $4 million paid by Parentis.

(iv) Due to the impact of the above legislation, Parentis has concluded that the consolidated goodwill has been impaired by $27 million.

Required:
Prepare the consolidated balance sheet of Parentis as at 31 March 2007.

(ACCA 2 SINT June 2007)

IFRSs AND PREPARATION OF CONSOLIDATED FINANCIAL STATEMENTS

26

OBJECTIVES After studying this chapter you should be able to:

- outline how the IASB requires the issues identified at the end of Chapter 25 to be dealt with

- describe the requirements of IAS 27, *Consolidated and Separate Financial Statements*

- describe the requirements of IFRS 3, *Business Combinations*

- prepare consolidated financial statements in accordance with IASs

- appraise the current position of regulation on the preparation of consolidated financial statements.

INTRODUCTION

In this chapter we will deal with the IASB regulation in respect of the preparation of consolidated financial statements. The following Standards issued by the IASB are relevant:

IAS 27, *Consolidated and Separate Financial Statements*
IFRS 3, *Business Combinations*

The IASB issued amended versions of these Standards in January 2008 as a result of its business combinations project commenced in 2001. The project began by reviewing IAS 22, *Business Combinations* (now replaced by IFRS 3) with the objective of improving the quality of and seeking international harmonisation on accounting for business combinations. The completion of Phase 1 of the project saw the issue of IFRS 3 and revised versions of IAS 36, *Impairment of Assets* and IAS 38, *Intangible* Assets to deal with the issue of goodwill generated in accounting for business combinations.

Phase 11 dealt with the method of accounting for combinations and proposed some radical changes, for example extending the use of fair value to the non-controlling interest and proposing that liabilities within a business combination should also be measured at fair value–settlement or exit values. Phase 11 also proposed that transactions with minority interest holders now to be referred to as non-controlling interests should be treated as if they are transactions with owners. This chapter deals with the current extant regulations but we will return to the Phase 11 debate at the end of this chapter as the IASB intend to issue a further exposure draft towards the end of 2008.

IAS 27 REGULATIONS

Scope

IAS 27 deals with the content of the consolidated financial statements not with the methods of accounting for business combinations nor the issue of goodwill on consolidation. These latter issues are dealt with in IFRS 3.

IAS 27 requires a parent to prepare consolidated financial statements except in the following circumstances:

- when the parent is a wholly-owned or partly-owned subsidiary of another enterprise
- the parent's debt or equity instruments are not traded in a public market or the parent is not in the process of issuing any class of instruments in a public market
- the ultimate or any intermediate parent produces consolidated statements available for public use that comply with IFRS.

Control

IAS 27 defines a subsidiary, as we did in Chapter 25, as an entity, including an unincorporated entity, that we control. Control under IAS 27 is again defined as we did in Chapter 25. IAS 27 emphasises that control is presumed to exist if a parent holds more than half of the entity's voting power unless it can be clearly demonstrated that such ownership does not constitute control; this is regarded as exceptional.

IAS 27 gives further guidance on control as follows:

- the existence and effect of potential voting rights that are currently exercisable or convertible should be taken into account when assessing whether control exists

- control also exists when the parent owns half or less of the voting powers of an entity when there is
  - power over more than half of the voting rights by virtue of an agreement with other investors
  - power to govern the financial and operating policies of the entity under a statute or an agreement
  - power to appoint or remove the majority of the members of the board of directors or equivalent governing body and control of the entity is by that board or body
  - power to cast the majority of votes at meetings of the board of directors or equivalent governing body and control of the entity is by that board or body.

Consolidation procedures

Under this section of the IAS we are told to:

- eliminate the carrying amount of the parent's investment and the parent's share of equity in each subsidiary
- allocate the profit or loss for the period on the face of the income statement between the parent and the non-controlling interest
- identify the non-controlling interest in consolidated subsidiaries' net assets and present them within equity on the balance sheet but separately from parent equity
- eliminate intra-group balances and transactions in full
- prepare the consolidated accounts using uniform accounting policies
- include the subsidiary's income and expenses only from the date of acquisition to the date when control ceases

---

ACTIVITY 26.1

1 H currently holds 48% of the shares of S. H does not have the power to govern the policies of S, nor the power to remove members of the board, nor the power to cast the majority of votes at meetings. The holders of the remaining 52% of S's shares do not have the ability to organise themselves so that they can cooperate on any voting issues at board meetings. Is S a subsidiary of H?

2 Entities A and B currently own 55% and 45% respectively of the ordinary voting right shares of entity C. Entity B also holds debt instruments that are convertible into ordinary shares of entity C at any time. If the debt were converted entity B would hold 70% of the voting shares and entity A's holding would become 30%. The conversion would require entity B to borrow additional funds to make the conversion payment. Is C a subsidiary of A, B or neither?

Activity feedback

1 Given that the 52% holding do not seem able to organise themselves in such a way as to vote against H it would appear that H does have a substantial amount of control over S. Given this it would seem that the true and fair view of the relationship may be given by consolidating S. However this is not the current requirement of IAS 27. Currently S would not be regarded as a subsidiary of H. It will be interesting to see if future amendments to IAS 27 deal with this issue.

2 The conversion rights owned by B give B the power to set the operating and financial policies of C. Therefore C is a subsidiary of B not of A.

- base income and expenses of the subsidiary on the values of the assets and liabilities recognised in the consolidated financial statements at the acquisition date
- make adjustments where reporting dates between parent and subsidiary are longer than three months.

The consolidation procedures identified by IAS 27 above are those we used in the examples in Chapter 25. To refresh your memory of these try the Activity 26.2.

Note that in the activity feedback we calculated the goodwill on consolidation but left it on the consolidated balance sheet. We need to look at IFRS 3, *Business Combinations* for further guidance on the treatment of the goodwill.

ACTIVITY 26.2

The balance sheets of Ric., Hel., Vic., and Mar. as at 30 June 2006 are as follows:

	Ric. £000	Hel. £000	Vic. £000	Mar. £000
Fixed assets				
Buildings nbv	110	27	46	11
Plant and machinery nbv	33	12	22	23
Investments:				
Shares in Hel.	86			
Shares in Vic.	45			
Shares in Mar.	74			
Loans to Hel.	14			
Loans to Vic.	14			
Net current assets	17	10	8	7
Loans from Ric.		(12)	(14)	
	393	37	62	41
Ordinary share capital	200	40	50	20
Revenue reserves	193	(3)	12	21
	393	37	62	41

(i) Ric. acquired 40 000 £1 shares in Hel. on 1 July 2002 when the balance on Hel.'s revenue reserve was £46 600.

(ii) Ric. acquired 40 000 £1 ordinary shares in Vic. on 1 July 2003 when the balance on Vic.'s revenue reserve was £7250

(iii) Ric. acquired 30 000 50p shares in Mar. (Mar. only has 50p shares in issue) when Mar.'s revenue reserves were £10 000

(iv) Hel. has repaid £2000 of the loan from Ric. but Ric. did not receive this amount by its year-end.

(v) Vic. purchased goods from Ric. providing Ric. with a gross profit on invoice price of 33⅓%. On 30 June 2006 the stock of Vic. included an amount of £9000 being goods purchased from Ric.

(vi) Both Hel. and Vic. depreciate their plant and machinery over 15 years straight line whereas Ric. uses 10 years straight line. The uniform policy chosen for consolidation is 10 years straight line. Further information is available as follows:

	Hel.	Vic.
All plant and machinery bought	1 July 2001	1 July 2002
Estimated residual value	£0	£0

Prepare the consolidated balance sheet for the Ric. group in accordance with international accounting standards for the year ended 30 June 2006.

Activity feedback

Adjustments and workings:

1 Stock – unrealised profit in stock £3000 debit Ric.'s reserves credit Vic.'s stock

2 Depreciation policy

	Hel.	Vic.
Plant and machinery dep. for	5 years	4 years
NBV after depreciation	£12 000	£22 000
Depreciation policy	15 years S.L.	15 years S.L.
Thus original cost	£18 000	£30 000
New dep. policy	10 year S.L.	10 year S.L.
Thus dep. to date	£9 000	£12 000
Thus new NBV	£9 000	£18 000
Adjustment required to reserves and nbv	(£3 000)	(£4 000)
Allocated pre-acquisition	(£600)	(£1 000)
Allocated post-acquisition	(£2 400)	(£3 000)

ACTIVITY 26.2   (*Continued*)

3 Loan – increase net current assets Ric. by £2000 for cash in transit and eliminate loans between Ric., Hel. and Vic.

4 Cost of control

	Ric in Hel.	Ric in Vic	Ric in Mar
Ownership	100%	80%	75%
Paid for investment	86 000	45 000	74 000
Bought:			
Ordinary shares	40 000	40 000	15 000
Revenue reserves	46 000 (46 600 – 600)	5 000 (7 250 – 1 000) × .8	7 500 (10 000 × .75)
	86 000	45 000	22 500
Goodwill	0	0	51 500

5 Post acq. reserves

52 000 ((3) – 46.6 – 2.4)   1 450 (12 – 7.25 – 3) × .8   8 250 (21 – 10) × .75

6 Non-controlling interest:

Shares	0	10 000	5 000
Reserves pre acq.	0	1 250	2 500
Reserves post acq.	0	350	2 750
	0	11 600	10 250

Consolidated balance sheet for Ric group as at 30 June 2006

	Calculations	£000
Fixed assets:		
Buildings net book value	110 + 27 + 46 + 11	194
Plant and machinery nbv	33 + 12 + 22 + 23 – 7	83
Goodwill	See above	51.5
Net current assets	17 + 10 + 8 + 7 + 2 – 3	41
Loans		0
		369.5
Ordinary shares		200
Revenue reserves	193 – 3 stock – 52 Hel. +1.4 Vic. + 8.25 Mar.	147.65
Non-controlling interests	See above 11.6 + 10.25	21.85
		369.5

Loss of control

A parent can lose control of a subsidiary by

- selling part of its ownership such that it is left with less than 50%
- the subsidiary becoming subject to control of a government, court administrator or regulator

● the subsidiary becoming subject to some other contractual agreement that results in the non-controlling interest gaining control.

If a parent loses control of a subsidiary then it must:

● derecognise the assets including any goodwill and liabilities of the subsidiary at their carrying amounts at the date when control is lost and the carrying amount of any non-controlling interest

● recognise the fair value of the consideration received in respect of the loss of control

● recognise any investment retained in the former subsidiary at its fair value.

We will deal with the accounting for loss of control under IFRS 3.

IFRS 3 REGULATIONS

Goodwill

IFRS 3 requires us to recognise goodwill as of the acquisition date measured as the excess of the aggregate of the fair value of the consideration given plus the amount of any non-controlling interest in the subsidiary over the net of the acquisition date amounts of the identifiable assets and liabilities of the subsidiary measured at fair value. This is basically what we did in Chapter 25. (See Activity 26.3.)

We have calculated the non-controlling interest in Activity 26.3 as a percentage of the fair value of the net assets at the acquisition date. If we had calculated the non-controlling interest, at what could be regarded as a more appropriate fair value, i.e. 20% of the fair value of the business as a whole (using the consideration given as an estimate of 80% of the fair value of the business as a whole), then the non-controlling interest would have been valued at $(650\,000 \times 100/80) \times 20\% = 162\,500$ and the goodwill £112 500. We might ask which method gives the more useful information to users.

Given, on consolidation, all assets and liabilities of the subsidiary are shown at fair value (but not necessarily those of the parent entity), then to show the non-controlling interest at fair value is logical. However, determining the fair value of the

---

ACTIVITY 26.3

H bought 80% of the net assets of S at a fair value of £650 000. The fair value of the net assets of S at the acquisition date were £700 000 (data as per activity 25.4(2)). Calculate the goodwill on consolidation in accordance with IFRS 3.

Activity feedback

Fair value of consideration given	650 000
Non-controlling interest 20% × 700 000 =	140 000
	790 000
Net assets at fair value	700 000
Goodwill	90 000

This is the same answer as activity 25.4 (2)

non-controlling interest can be difficult if there isn't a ready market in the shares. It is also true to say that the consolidated balance sheet may not all be at fair value especially if we have not revalued the net assets of the holding entity.

In the example above we assumed fair value by comparison with the purchase consideration but this is naive as the purchase price could include a premium on purchase. IFRS 3 permits a choice to the preparer for valuing the non-controlling interest as we will see later.

IAS GAAP, under IFRS 3, *Business Combinations*, requires that after initial recognition the business combination goodwill should be measured at cost less any accumulated impairment losses. Thus this goodwill is not amortised but tested for impairment. This impairment test is carried out in accordance with IAS 36, *Impairment of Assets*. Previously IAS GAAP did permit amortisation of business combination goodwill. Whether this change will result in a more robust view of goodwill on the balance sheet will depend on the robustness of the impairment reviews. The IASB states that goodwill arising from an acquisition represents a payment made by the acquirer in anticipation of future economic benefits which may result from synergy between the identifiable assets acquired or from assets which, individually, do not qualify, for recognition in the financial statements but for which the acquirer is prepared to make a payment in the acquisition.

The rationale for carrying goodwill on the balance sheet of the combined business at its impaired cost as opposed to amortising that goodwill through the profit or loss account is outlined in the IASB's Basis for Conclusions to IFRS3. The Board initially considered three possible treatments for goodwill arising on a business combination:

(a) straight line amortisation but with an impairment test whenever there was an indication that the goodwill might be impaired

(b) non-amortisation but with an impairment test annually or more frequently if events or changes in circumstances indicated that the goodwill was impaired

(c) permitting entities a choice between (a) and (b).

Point (c) was soon discounted in the deliberations as permitting such choices impairs the usefulness to users, as both comparability and reliability are diminished. However, many respondents to E3 supported method (a) as the acquired goodwill can be considered to be consumed over time and replaced with internal goodwill. The respondents felt that straight line amortisation over an arbitrary period, given that the pattern of use and useful life of goodwill is difficult to predict, with impairment tests was a reasonable balance between conceptual soundness and operational issues. In other words, (a) was the pragmatic solution. However, the Board was not impressed with pragmatism, being doubtful of the benefits of amortising acquired goodwill but not recognising internal goodwill. They felt that the amortisation was unhelpful, as unlike a tangible fixed asset, goodwill does not have a finite physical utility life. Thus the Board decided that (b) was the way forward; as long as a rigorous and operational impairment test could be devised (see IAS 36, Chapter 13) then more useful information would be provided to users by the use of (b). The proof of this decision will be tested in the future. Whatever method we use to account for acquired or inherent goodwill in the financial statements has a very large impact on the net assets and profit or loss recorded for the year. If users are not aware of this fact the decisions they make from using the information given could be flawed.

Discount on acquisition can also occur. This relates to the possibility of one company acquiring control of another at a discounted price (i.e. as opposed to at a premium). The Standard refers to this as a 'bargain purchase'.

In practice, this is not so far fetched as it might at first sight appear, in that an acquiring company may for various reasons (e.g. empire building) be quite willing to purchase a company with a recent history of trading losses, together with a forecast future of losses. This discount on the purchase price (i.e. the surplus of the fair value of tangible assets acquired over purchase consideration) at the date of acquisition may be thus thought of as compensation for anticipated future losses to the acquiring group. (One might also reasonably assume that in the medium-term future the group would hope to turn this subsidiary into profitability.) Alternatively, this discount may arise because the asset values agreed on acquisition may not be deemed to be fair values by the acquiring company and may be revalued downwards on consolidation.

It must be emphasised at this stage that the calculation of the goodwill or discount on acquisition should be made after a fair valuation has been made of the net assets acquired. In practice, in many cases no revaluation occurs and it is then assumed that the book value reflects the fair value. Note also that for purposes of computation of goodwill or discount on acquisition we usually take the fair value of net assets as being equal to the proportion of the subsidiary's share capital plus reserves as at date of acquisition. The discount on acquisition is generally referred to as negative goodwill.

If negative goodwill is identified then IFRS 3 requires the acquirer to reassess the calculation and to then recognise the negative goodwill that still exists in profit or loss.

(See Chapter 13 for goodwill in more detail.)

Business combination definitions

IFRS 3 defines a business combination as a 'transaction or other event in which an acquirer obtains control of one or more businesses'. It further defines a business as an 'integrated set of activities and assets that is capable of being conducted and managed for the purpose of providing a return in the form of dividends, lower costs or other economic benefits directly to investors or other owners, members or participants'.

The result of nearly all business combinations is that one entity, the acquirer, obtains control of one or more other businesses, the acquiree [para. 4].

Control is the power to govern the financial and operating policies of an entity or business so as to obtain benefits from its activities. A parent is an entity that has one or more subsidiaries.

A subsidiary is an entity controlled by another entity.

Note in these definitions that the word 'entity' is used, not 'company', so a subsidiary could be a partnership or unincorporated body as well as a company as long as the entity is controlled by another. Control was identified for us in IAS 27.

When preparing consolidated financial statements we need to identify the acquirer and acquiree. This acquirer is not always easy to identify but the standard tells us that we have to identify one and that usually there are indications available to us. For example:

- if the combination is effected by primarily transferring cash or other assets or by incurring liabilities, the acquirer is usually the entity that transfers the cash or other assets or incurs liabilities

- the acquirer is usually the entity whose owners as a group retain or receive the largest portion of the voting rights to the combined entity
- if the business combination results in the management of one of the combining entities being able to dominate the selection of the management team of the resulting combined entity, the entity whose management is able to so dominate is usually the acquirer
- the acquirer is usually the entity whose owners have the ability to elect or appoint or remove a majority of the members of the governing body of the combined entity.

Note the use of the word 'usually' in the examples.

Method of consolidation

IFRS 3 requires an entity to account for each business combination by applying the acquisition method. Applying the acquisition method requires:

- identifying the acquirer
- determining the acquisition date
- recognising and measuring the identifiable assets acquired, the liabilities assumed and any non-controlling interest in the acquiree
- recognising and measuring goodwill or a gain from a bargain purchase (negative goodwill).

The date of acquisition is defined as the date on which the acquirer obtains control of the acquiree.

Recognising and measuring the identifiable assets acquired, the liabilities assumed and any non-controlling interest in the acquiree

IFRS 3 requires us to allocate the cost of the combination by recognising the assets, liabilities and contingent liabilities at their fair values. The difference between the cost of the acquisition and the fair value of the net assets is recognised as goodwill, which is subsequently, measured at cost less any accumulated impairment losses. It is also important to note that the acquirer can only recognise intangible assets of the acquiree if these meet the definitions in IAS 38 at the acquisition date.

Non-controlling interests in the acquiree are required to be measured at either

1 fair value, or
2 at the non-controlling interest's proportionate share of the acquiree's identifiable net assets at fair value.

We discussed these two alternatives under goodwill. Method 2 was the only accepted method in the previous version of IFRS 3. On reviewing IFRS 3 the IASB wished to make method 1 – fair value – the required method for valuing the non-controlling interest. However they could not gain consensus on this and they therefore permitted the alternatives. Thus depending upon which method is chosen to value the non-controlling interest will result in different figures in the consolidated financial statements in respect of the non-controlling interest and goodwill. Note that all our examples in Chapter 25 used method 2 for valuing the non-controlling interest.

ACTIVITY 26.4

Identify four forms of consideration that could be given in a business combination.

Activity feedback
The consideration given can include:

- cash
- other assets
- a business or subsidiary of the acquirer
- ordinary or preference equity instruments of the acquirer
- options
- warrants
- contingent consideration.

Determining fair value of purchase price and net assets acquired

We have already noted that the purchase price/consideration given in a business combination must be measured at fair value (see Activity 26.4).

Business combination achieved in stages

An acquirer sometimes obtains control of an acquiree in which it already holds some of the equity shares. For example immediately prior to the parent obtaining control of the subsidiary it may have held a 35% non-controlling interest. If the parent then acquires another 30% which gives it control then we have a business combination achieved in stages. IFRS 3 requires us to remeasure the previously held equity interest at its acquisition date fair value recognising the resulting gain or loss in profit or loss.

ACTIVITY 26.5

H entity holds 30% of the voting shares of S entity which it purchased several years ago at a cost of €250k. As at 31 December 200X, H purchased a further 40% of S for a consideration of €450k. The fair value of S's net assets at 31 December 200X is €1m. It is estimated that H paid a premium of 10% on the purchase of the new 40% holding. Identify the goodwill to be included in the consolidated financial statements of H as at 1 January 200Y and the non-controlling interest.

Activity feedback
First we need to value the original holding at fair value. On the information we have available we must assume that the fair value of the original holding can be calculated by reference to the consideration paid for the new 40% holding after disregarding the premium on purchase.

Premium on purchase 450 – 450 × 100/110	41k
Consideration for 40% without premium	409k
Fair value of whole of S using consideration	
409 × 100/40	1 022.5

Fair value of 30% original holding	
30% × 1 022.5	306.75
Original cost of 30% holding	250
Gain on holding 306.75 – 250 transferred to	
profit and loss	56.75
Method 2 to value non-controlling interest:	
Consideration for 70% holding 306.75 + 450	756.75
70% of fair value of net assets of S 70% × 1m	700
Goodwill on consolidation using method 2	56.75
Non-controlling interest 30% × 1m	300
Method 1 to value non-controlling interest	
Fair value of non-controlling interest	
30% × 1 022.5	306.75
Consideration at fair value for 70% holding	756.75
	1 063.5
Fair value of net assets of S at acquisition	
date	1 000
Goodwill using method 1	63.5

The purchase consideration is now the aggregate of the fair value of the non-controlling interest previously held plus the consideration given for the new purchase to obtain control. The goodwill will be calculated by comparing this total consideration to the fair value of the controlling interest in net assets. This is how we dealt with a stage acquisition in Chapter 25. Try Activity 26.5 to refresh your memory.

Subsequent remeasurement of amounts in a business combination

Given that assets, liabilities, non-controlling interest and the consideration paid in a business combination all have to be measured at fair value there may be a need to include provisional amounts in the consolidation process. IFRS 3 identifies a measurement period within which adjustments can be made to these provisional amounts to ensure compliance with IFRS 3 requirements. The measurement period cannot exceed one year from the date of acquisition and ends when the acquirer receives the information it was seeking about facts and circumstances that existed as of the acquisition date that would change the provisional figures or the acquirer learns that the information is not obtainable.

When adjusting the provisional figures the acquirer needs to ensure that only adjustments pertinent to the circumstances at acquisition are included.

ACTIVITY 26.6

H entity acquired the whole of the voting shares of S entity on 31 December 200X. When preparing the consolidated financial statements on 31 December 200X H included provisional figures for the fair value of some of S's non-current assets and liabilities. As at 31 March 200Y the following information was available on these non-current assets and liabilities:

Non-current asset/(liability)	Provisional fair value 31 December 200X €	Fair value 31 March 200Y or sale proceeds €
Building 1	500 000	650 000
Building 2	350 000	750 000
Plant and equipment	90 000	85 500
(Liability to pay damages on accident)	250 000	300 000

Building 1 was sold on 10 January 200Y. Building 2 was sold on 31 March 200Y. The cost of buildings similar to building 2 had substantially increased during the two months from 1 February 200Y.

Plant and equipment is depreciated on a straight line basis and has an expected remaining life of five years and no residual value.

The damages are finally agreed with the third party involved as at 31 March 200Y. Identify the assets/liabilities that would require remeasurement in the consolidated financial statements as at the acquisition date.

Activity feedback

Building 1 will be adjusted in the consolidated statements at acquisition date from €500 000 to €650 000 as the sale value on 10 January is likely to reflect the fair value as at 31 December 200X.

Building 2 will not be adjusted as the increase in value is probably due to cost increase between February and end-March 200Y.

Plant and equipment will not be adjusted as the fall in value reflects to some extent the depreciation charged for that three-month period.

The damages will be adjusted to €300 000 as the final settlement figure provides evidence of the liability at acquisition date.

The two remeasurements will reduce goodwill on consolidation by €100 000.

Disclosure requirements of IFRS 3

IFRS 3 requires such disclosures that 'enable users of financial statements to evaluate the nature and financial effect of business combinations' (para. 59). Disclosure is required as follows:

- names and descriptions of combining entities
- acquisition date
- percentage of voting equity instruments acquired
- primary reason for the business combination and a description of how the acquirer obtained control of the acquiree
- cost of the combination and the components of the cost
- details of operations disposed of due to the combination
- details of fair values and carrying values of assets, liabilities and contingent liabilities acquired
- amount of any negative goodwill in a bargain purchase and a description of reasons why the transaction resulted in a gain
- amount of acquiree's profit or loss since the acquisition date included in the acquirer's profit or loss
- a reconciliation of the carrying amount of goodwill at the beginning and end of the reporting period.

You can read the full disclosure requirements at Appendix B of IFRS 3.

An example of such disclosure is taken from the accounts for the year ended 31 December 2000 of Charles Vogele Group (p. 51).

Composition of goodwill	Depreciation Period	Cost	Depreciation 2000	Accumulated depreciation	Book values
Acquisition of store locations in Switzerland 1995	5 years	9 500	(1 900)	(9 000)	500
Initial consolidation in connection with LBO 1997	20 years	76 632	(3 832)	(11 495)	65 137
Purchase of the minority interest in Charles Vogele (Austria) AG in 1998	20 years	33 012	(1 650)	(3 301)	29 711
Acquisition of store locations in the Netherlands 1999	20 years	4 663	(239)	(425)	4 238
Acquisition MacFash Group 2000	20 years	24 575	(5 029)	(4 915)	19 660
Balance 31.12.2000		148 382	(12 650)	(29 136)	119 246

Comments on acquisition of the MacFash Beteiligungsgesellschaft mbH as at 1 January 2000:

Purchase price	27 763
Cash	(3 045)
Other receivables	(15 409)
Inventories	(477)
Deferred tax assets	(1 915)
Bank overdraft	1 729
Trade payables	5 574
Accruals	1 395
Current tax liabilities	17
Provisions	9 512
Goodwill at the time of acquisition	25 144
Effect of exchange rates	(569)
Goodwill as at December 2000	24 575

The value of the goodwill represents the takeover of a profitable location already introduced in the market. In 2000, these 40 acquired stores contributed net sales of CHF 83.5 million. The goodwill was determined in local currency (DEM) at the time of acquisition and reported at 31 December 2000 in CHF using the year-end exchange rate. The purchase price was deposited in a fiduciary account in 1999 until the final conclusion of the transaction. Through the acquisition, the group at 1 January 2000 received cash and cash equivalents amounting to net CHF 1.3 million.

BUSINESS COMBINATIONS AND THE FUTURE

The IASB are expected to issue an exposure draft towards the end of 2008 to revise IAS 27. The ED is expected to specifically address the definition of control in respect of *all* legal entities. It is also expected to require enhanced disclosure requirements in respect of both consolidated and non-consolidated entities. The aim of the revision will be to improve comparability of financial statements and improve the information on legal entities not consolidated. The IASB, in its working paper issued in July 2008, are proposing to define a legal entity and change the definition of control. A legal entity may be defined as an entity that can assert legal ownership or title to assets and incur liabilities in their own names. It is expected that this will lead to the consolidation of more entities.

The new definition of control proposed is

as the current power sufficient to use or manage the assets and liabilities of that entity so as to benefit from them as if they are its own.

This will remove the requirement for controlling the strategic operations and financial policies and focus very clearly on who controls the assets and liabilities.

If this definition is adopted then example 1 in Activity 26.1 would be a subsidiary relationship.

The IASB is to keep the new version of IFRS 3 under review and has still to reach a conclusion on its wider fair value debate which will impact IFRS 3. Currently IFRS 3 uses exchange value as a definition of fair value but this could, in the future, be changed to an exit value definition. One of the changes to the original IFRS 3 that the IASB wanted to make on its revision in 2008 was to require the recognition of the full goodwill of a subsidiary. Current practice, as we have illustrated in Chapter 25 and this chapter, is that only the acquirer's proportion of goodwill is recognised. Recognising the full goodwill would mean valuing the subsidiary at fair value as a whole and this can be difficult and the value obtained unreliable. The proposal did however ensure consistency with other assets where we have always consolidated 100% of the fair value of the assets even where a non-controlling interest existed. Because the IASB could not gain consensus on the use of the full goodwill method the proposal was dropped when amending IFRS 3 in 2008. There are several other methods of consolidating parent and subsidiary entities besides the IFRS 3 and full goodwill method and we will discuss these in Chapter 27. It will be interesting to see the outcome of the post–implementation review on IFRS 3 and IAS 27 that will occur around 2011.

SUMMARY

There is much debate in the accounting world on the subject of business combinations and no doubt there will be further amendments to IAS 27 and IFRS 3 in the future. Changes may also occur if and when the IASB develops a complete conceptual framework. You might wish to debate whether the current extant regulation on business combinations provides useful information to users and particularly whether consolidated statements are understandable to them.

This chapter has dealt with the detailed regulation of IAS 27 and IFRS 3 and addressed the issues that we posed at the conclusion of Chapter 25. The exercises at the end of this chapter will provide further practice for you on preparing consolidated financial statements in accordance with IASs.

EXERCISES

Suggested answers to exercises marked ✓ are to be found on the Student side of the companion website.

Suggested answers to the remaining exercises are to be found on the Instructor side of the companion website.

1   What is 'control' as used in relation to consolidated financial statements?

2   On 30 June 2004, C purchased 75% of the equity shares of D for $16 million. The balance sheet of D showed net assets of $14 million. This was before taking account of the following items:

- The market value of D's properties at 30 June 2004 (included in the balance sheet of D at a carrying value of $8 million) was $10 million.

- On 30 June 2004, D was in the process of negotiating an insurance claim in respect of inventory that was damaged before that date. The claim was for $1 million and, although nothing has yet been received, the directors of D are confident that the claim will be successful.

What is the goodwill on consolidation that will appear in the consolidated balance sheet of C at 30 June 2004?

(CIMA paper November 2004)

3   Barking, an unlisted company, operates in the house building and commercial property investment development sector. The sector has seen an upturn in activity during recent years and the directors have been considering future plans with a view to determining their impact on the financial statements for the financial year to 30 November 20X4.

(a)   Barking wishes to obtain a stock exchange listing in the year to 30 November 20X4. It is to be acquired by Ash, a significantly smaller listed company in a share for share exchange whereby Barking will receive sufficient voting shares of Ash to control the new group. Due to the relative values of the companies, Barking will become the majority shareholder with 80% of the enlarged capital of Ash. The executive management of the new group will be that of Barking.

As part of the purchase consideration, Ash will issue zero dividend preference shares of $1 to the shareholders of Barking on 30 June 20X4. These will be redeemed on 1 January 20X5 at $1.10 per share. Additionally Ash will issue convertible interest free loan notes. The loan notes are unlikely to be repaid on 30 November 20X5 (the redemption date) as the conversion terms are very favourable. The management of Ash have excluded the redemption of the loan notes from their cash flow projections. The loan notes are to be included in long-term liabilities in the balance sheet of Ash. As part of the business combination Ash will change its name to Barking Inc.

(b)   The acquisition will also have other planned effects on the company. Barking operates a defined benefit pension scheme. On acquisition the scheme will be frozen and replaced by a group defined contribution scheme, and as a result no additional benefits in the old scheme will accrue to the employees. Ash's employees are also in a defined benefit scheme which has been classified as a multi-employer plan but it is currently impossible to identify its share of the underlying assets and liabilities in the scheme. After acquisition, Ash's employees will be transferred to the group's defined contribution scheme, with the previous scheme being frozen.

(c)   As a result of the acquisition the company will change the way in which it recognises sales of residential properties. It used to treat such properties as sold when the building work was substantially complete, defined as being when the roof and internal walls had been completed. The new policy will be to recognise a sale when a refundable deposit for the sale of the property has been received and the building work is physically complete. Legal costs incurred on the sale of the property are currently capitalised and shown as current assets until the sale of the property has occurred. Further, it has been decided by the directors that as at 30 November 20X4, the financial year-end, some properties held as trading properties of both companies would be moved from the trading portfolio to the investment portfolio of the holding company, and carried at fair value.

(d)   The directors intend to carry out an impairment review as at 30 November 20X4 in order to ascertain whether the carrying amount of goodwill and other non-current assets can be supported by their value in use. The plan is to produce cash flow projections up to 20X4 with an average discount rate of 15% being used in the calculations. The ten-year period is to be used as it reflects fairly the long-term nature of the assets being assessed. Any subsequent impairment loss is to be charged against the income statement.

Required:

Draft a report to the directors of Barking, setting out the financial reporting implications of the above plans for the financial statements for the year to 30 November 20X4.

(ACCA December 2003)

4   The balance sheets of George and its subsidiary entities Zippy and Bungle at 30 June 20X3 (the accounting date for all three entities) are given:

	George		Zippy		Bungle	
	$000	$000	$000	$000	$000	$000
ASSETS						
Non-current assets:						
Property, plant and						
equipment (Note 3)	45 000		25 000		20 000	
Financial assets						
(Notes 1 and 2)	20 000	65 000	Nil	25 000	Nil	20 000
Current assets:						
Inventories (Notes 3 and 4)	18 000		12 000		11 000	
Trade and other receivable						
(Notes 3 and 4)	15 000	33 000	10 000	22 000	9 000	20 000
Total assets		98 000		47 000		40 000

	George		Zippy		Bungle	
	$000	$000	$000	$000	$000	$000
EQUITY AND LIABILITIES						
Capital and reserves:						
Issued ordinary share						
capital ($1 shares)	25 000		15 000		10 000	
10% $1 preferred shares	Nil		10 000		Nil	
Share premium account	10 000		Nil		4 000	
Accumulated profits	24 000	59 000	8 000	33 000	9 300	23 300
Non-current liabilities						
Interest bearing borrowing						
(Note 3)	20 000		Nil		4 000	
Deferred tax (Note 3)	2 000	22 000	1 000	1 000	1 500	5 500
Current liabilities						
Trade payables (Note 4)	10 000		6 500		6 000	
Tax payable	2 000		1 500		1 000	
Proposed dividend (Note 5)	Nil		1 000		Nil	
Bank overdraft	5 000		4 000		3 000	
Provisions (Note 3)	Nil	17 000	Nil	13 000	1 200	11 200
Total equity and liabilities		98 000		47 000		40 000

Notes to the balance sheets

1   On 1 July 19W0, the date of incorporation of Zippy, George subscribed for all the ordinary shares of Zippy at par. Then, on 1 July 19X5, when its balance of accumulated profits was $3 million, Zippy issued 10 million $1 preferred shares at par. George subscribed for 50% of these shares.

2   On 30 June 20X3, George purchased 8 million $1 shares in Bungle. The terms of the purchase consideration were as follows:

    2.1 On 30 June 20X3, George issued 3 $1 ordinary shares for every 4 shares purchased in Bungle. The market value of the ordinary shares at 30 June 20X3 was $4 per share.

    2.2 On 30 June 20X5, George will pay the former shareholders of Bungle $1 in cash for every share in Bungle they have purchased. This payment is contingent on the cumulative profits after tax of Bungle for the two years ending 30 June 20X5 being at least $3 million. At the date of carrying out the fair value exercise (*see Note 3 below*), the directors of George considered it probable that this cash payment would be made.

    2.3 No entries in respect of the purchase of shares in Bungle have been made in the balance sheet of George.

3   Following the acquisition of Bungle, the directors of George carried out a fair value exercise. The following matters are relevant and all potential fair value adjustments are material:

    3.1 Property, plant and equipment comprise land and buildings and plant and machinery. At 30 June 20X3, the land and buildings had a carrying value of $12 million and a market value of $18 million.

        The plant and machinery had a carrying value of $8 million. All the plant and machinery was purchased on 30 June 20X0 and was being depreciated on a straight line basis over eight years. No reliable estimate was available of the current market value of the plant and machinery, but at 30 June 20X3, the plant would have cost $22 million to replace with new plant.

    3.2 The inventory at 30 June 20X3 comprised:

      • Finished goods which could be sold for $14.5 million. A reasonable profit allowance for the selling effort of the group would be $3 million.

      • Finished goods that had been damaged and could only be sold for $100 000, representing a significant loss on sale.

    3.3 Trade receivables includes an amount of $400 000 that the directors of George consider doubtful.

    3.4 The interest-bearing borrowing of Bungle is repayable at par on 30 June 20X6. Interest at 10% per annum is payable annually in arrears and the payment due on 30 June 20X3 has already been made. The relevant discount rate is 7%.

    3.5 The other provisions of Bungle comprise:

      • $400 000 in respect of the closure of various retail outlets to which the directors of Bungle became committed prior to entering into acquisition negotiations with the directors of George.

      • $800 000 in respect of the estimated cost of integrating Bungle into the George group. No detailed integration plans had been formulated by 30 June 20X3.

3.6 The additional deferred tax that needs to be provided on the adjustments that are necessary as a result of the fair value exercise is a liability of $3 million.

4   George supplies a component to Zippy at cost plus a mark-up of 20%. At 30 June 20X3, the inventories of Zippy included $1.5 million in respect of this component. At 30 June 20X3, the receivables of George showed an amount receivable from Zippy of $1.2 million, while the grade payables of Zippy showed an amount payable to George of $600 000. On 29 June 20X3, George sent a consignment of components to Zippy at an invoiced price of $600 000. The consignment was received and recorded by Zippy on 2 July 20X3.

5   On 15 July 2003, Zippy paid its preferred share dividend for the year ended 30 June 20X3. George made no entries in its financial statements in respect of this dividend unit it was received in cash.

Required:

(a)   Compute the goodwill on consolidation of Bungle that will be shown in the consolidated balance sheet of George at 30 June 20X3. Provide justification for your figures where you consider this is needed.

(b)   Prepare the consolidated balance sheet of George at 30 June 2003.

(IFRI November 2003)

5   The income statements and statements of changes in equity of Hansen and its subsidiary entities Williams and Charvis for the year ended 30 September 2004 are given below:

Income statement – year ended 30 September 2004	Hansen	Williams	Charvis
	$000	$000	$000
Revenue	60 000	45 000	35 000
Cost of sales	(30 000)	(25 000)	(19 000)
Gross profit	30 000	20 000	16 000
Other operating expenses	(15 000)	(10 000)	(8 000)
Profit from operations	15 000	10 000	8 000
Investment income	2 800		
Finance cost	(5 000)	(4 000)	(3 000)
Profit before income tax	12 800	6 000	5 000
Income tax expense	(3 500)	(2 000)	(1 800)
Net profit for the period	9 300	4 000	3 200

Statement of changes in equity – year ended 30 September 2004	Hansen	Williams	Charvis
	$000	$000	$000
Balance at 1 October 2003	30 000	17 000	16 000
Net profit for the year	9 300	4 000	3 200
Dividends paid 31 January 2004	(4 500)	(2 000)	(1 600)
Balance at 30 September 2004	34 800	19 000	17 600

Note 1 – Investments by Hansen

- On 1 October 1996, when the accumulated profits of Williams showed a credit balance of $6 million, Hansen purchased 4 million of Williams' 5 million $1 issued equity shares. Hansen paid $10.8 million for these shares.
- On 1 October 1997, when the accumulated profits of Charvis showed a credit balance of $4 million, Hansen purchased 4.5 million of Charvis' 6 million $1 issued equity shares. Hansen paid $8.7 million for these shares.
- All shares in Williams and Charvis have equal voting rights. Neither entity has any other reserves apart from its accumulated profits.
- No fair value adjustments were necessary in respect of either entity when it was first consolidated by Hansen.
- Goodwill on both acquisitions is written off on a straight line basis over 240 months [20 years]. Hansen presents the amortisation of goodwill on acquisition of subsidiaries in other operating expenses.

Note 2 – Sale of shares in Charvis

On 1 April 2004, Hansen sold a total of 3 million shares in Charvis for $3.50 per share. The sale was made to help finance organic growth and Hansen retained a significant influence over the operating and financial policies of Charvis following the sale. Under local tax legislation no tax is payable on the disposal.

Note 3 – Intra-group trading

Hansen levies a management charge [included in its revenue] of $1 million per annum on each of its subsidiaries. The subsidiaries presented this charge under other operating expenses. In the case of Charvis this charge ceased with effect from 1 April 2004. However, Charvis was obliged to incur equivalent costs from 1 April 2004 in order to replace the service formerly supplied by Hansen.

Note 4 – Profits of Charvis

All the profits of Charvis accrued evenly over the year ended 30 September 2004.

Required:

(a) Explain how the disposal of shares in Charvis will affect the method of consolidation of its profits by Hansen. You should make reference to appropriate International Financial Reporting Standards, but are NOT required to describe the consolidation method(s) in detail.

(b) Prepare the consolidated income statement of Hansen for the year ended 30 September 2004.

(CIMA paper November 2004)

6 Ejoy, a public limited company, has acquired two subsidiaries. The details of the acquisitions are as follows:

Company	Date of acquisition	Ordinary share capital of $1 $m	Reserves at acquisition $m	Fair value of net assets at acquisition $m	Cost of investment $m	Ordinary share capital of $1 acquired $m
Zbay	1 June 2004	200	170	600	520	160
Tbay	1 December 2005	120	80	310	216	72

The draft income statements for the year ended 31 May 2006 are:

	Ejoy $m	Zbay $m	Tbay $m
Revenue	2 500	1 500	800
Cost of sales	(1 800)	(1 200)	(600)
Gross profit	700	300	200
Other income	70	10	–
Distribution costs	(130)	(120)	(70)
Administrative expenses	(100)	(90)	(60)
Finance costs	(50)	(40)	(20)
Profit before tax	490	60	50
Income tax expense	(200)	(26)	(20)
Profit for the period	290	34	30
Profit for year 31 May 2005	190	20	15

The following information is relevant to the preparation of the group financial statements:

(i)   Tbay was acquired exclusively with a view to sale and at 31 May 2006 meets the criteria of being a disposal group. The fair value of Tbay at 31 May 2006 is $300 million and the estimated selling costs of the shareholding in Tbay are $5 million.

(ii) Ejoy entered into a joint venture with another company on 31 May 2006. The joint venture is a limited company and Ejoy has contributed assets at fair value of $20 million (carrying value $14 million). Each party will hold five million ordinary shares of $1 in the joint venture. The gain on the disposal of the assets ($6 million) to the joint venture has been included in 'other income'.

(iii) On acquisition, the financial statements of Tbay incluaded a large cash balance. Immediately after acquisition Tbay paid a dividend of $40 million. The receipt of the dividend is included in other income in the income statement of Ejoy. Since the acquisition of Zbay and Tbay, there have been no further dividend payments by these companies.

(iv) Zbay has a loan asset which is being carried at $60 million in the draft financial statements for the year ended 31 May 2006. The loan's effective interest rate is 6 per cent. On 1 June 2005 the company felt that because of the borrower's financial problems, it would receive

$20 million in approximately two years time, on 31 May 2007. At 31 May 2006, the company still expects to receive the same amount on the same date. The loan asset is classified as 'loans and receivables'.

(v)   On 1 June 2005, Ejoy purchased a five-year bond with a principal amount of $50 million and a fixed interest rate of 5% which was the current market rate. The bond is classified as an 'available for sale' financial asset. Because of the size of the investment, Ejoy has entered into a floating interest rate swap. Ejoy has designated the swap as a fair value hedge of the bond. At 31 May 2006, market interest rates were 6%. As a result, the fair value of the bond has decreased to $48.3 million. Ejoy has received $0.5 million in net interest payments on the swap at 31 May 2006 and the fair value hedge has been 100% effective in the period. No entries have been made in the income statement to account for the bond or the hedge.

(vi)   No impairment of the goodwill arising on the acquisition of Zbay had occurred at 1 June 2005. The recoverable amount of Zbay was $630 million and that of Tbay was $290 million at 31 May 2006. Impairment losses on goodwill are charged to cost of sales.

(vii)   Assume that profits accrue evenly throughout the year and ignore any taxation effects.

Required:
Prepare a consolidated income statement for the Ejoy Group for the year ended 31 May 2006 in accordance with International Financial Reporting Standards.

(ACCA 3.5int June 2006)

ALTERNATIVE METHODS OF PREPARING CONSOLIDATED FINANCIAL STATEMENTS

27

OBJECTIVES After studying this chapter you should be able to:

- explain the entity concept in consolidation processes

- explain the proprietary/parent concept in consolidation processes

- explain the uniting of interests concept in consolidation processes

- explain equity accounting

- consider the mechanics of preparing consolidated financial statements using different concepts.

INTRODUCTION

Within Chapters 25 and 26 we used a specific concept when preparing consolidated financial statements that was the parent concept. This is by no means the only concept/method that could be employed when preparing consolidated financial statements. Within this chapter we explore various other methods some of which have been used in the past, some in other countries in the world and some that, perhaps, may be used in the future.

THE PARENT APPROACH/PROPRIETARY CONCEPT

With this method of accounting the assumption is made that the consolidated financial statements are being prepared to be primarily of use by the shareholders of the controlling parent entity and the non-controlling interests are credited with their share of the net tangible assets of the subsidiary. This non-controlling shareholding can then be reflected either as a quasi-liability – the parent approach – or by omitting it entirely from the consolidated financial statements – the proprietary approach (see proportional consolidation method, p. 683).

A simple example is given here to demonstrate the parent company/proprietary concept approach.

Big entity acquired the whole of the outstanding common shares of Little entity at a price of €1.5 per share for cash as at 30 June, at which time their respective balance sheets were as follows:

	Big €	*Little* €
Investment in Little	75 000	
Land and buildings	100 000	25 000
Plant	40 000	20 000
Sundry other assets	20 000	15 000
	235 000	60 000
Share capital	150 000	50 000
Reserves	85 000	10 000
	235 000	60 000

As at this date, the estimated fair values of Little's assets were:

Land and buildings	30 000
Plant	22 000
Sundry other assets	15 000
Total	67 000

In Big's balance sheet, the investment in Little is shown at €1.50 × 50 000 shares, i.e. €75 000. In the group's balance sheet the subsidiary's assets would be best brought in at fair value amounting to €67 000, as this can be regarded as more useful than historic cost. We would need to account for the difference between this figure and the cost of the investment in Little of €75 000 and, as you know from Chapter 25, we refer to this difference as goodwill on consolidation (€8000). The consolidated balance sheet would look like this:

Land and buildings	130 000
Plant	62 000
Goodwill on consolidation	8 000
Sundry other assets	35 000
	235 000
Share capital	150 000
Reserves	85 000
	235 000

Parent concept consolidation with minority interest

Let's suppose Big only acquires 75% of the shares of Little at a price of €1.6 per share for cash. The fair value of Little's assets is:

Land and buildings	30 000
Plant	22 000
Sundry other assets	15 000
	67 000

and the balance sheets of the respective enterprises are:

	Big €	Little €
Investment in Little	60 000	
Land and buildings	100 000	25 000
Plant	40 000	20 000
Sundry other assets	20 000	15 000
	220 000	60 000
Share capital	150 000	50 000
Reserves	70 000	10 000
	220 000	60 000

The goodwill calculation is:

Paid for investment	60 000
Acquired 75% of fair value of net assets (67 000)	50 250
	9 750

On consolidation we need to remember to bring in 75% of the assets of Little at fair value, i.e. the group share, but to only incorporate the non-controlling interest share, 25%, at net book value. This is because the parent concept is only concerned with the fair value in relation to the holding (parent) entity share not that of the non-controlling interest.

The consolidated balance sheet is then:

	Calculation €	
Goodwill	See previous calculations	9 750
Land and buildings	100 000 + 25% × 25 000 + 75% × 30 000	128 750
Plant	40 000 + 25% × 20 000 + 75% × 22 000	61 500
Sundry assets	20 000 + 15 000 (NBV + FV)	35 000
		235 000
Share capital	Big only	150 000
Reserves	Big only	70 000
Non-controlling interest	25% × 60 000	15 000
		235 000

Note that in the above consolidated balance sheet the non-controlling interest is shown as their share of net assets of Little before fair value revaluation. This consolidated balance sheet does not include all net assets that Big controls at fair value as only those of Little have been revalued at the acquisition date.

ACTIVITY 27.1

Show the consolidated financial statement for A group using the parent extension method given that:

A buys 80% of B for cash $2200 when net assets of B have a fair value of $2000 and net book value was $1500. A's balance sheet at the date of acquisition was:

	$
Net assets (including investment in B)	5 000
Share capital	4 000
Reserves	1 000
	5 000

Consolidated balance sheet

Net assets [2 800 (5 000 – 2 200 inves. in B) + 2 000]	4 800
Goodwill	600
	5 400
Share capital	4 000
Reserves	1 000
Non-controlling interest 400 (20% of net assets FV 2000)	400
	5 400

Activity feedback

Goodwill calculation

Paid for investment in B	2 200
Bought 80% net assets at fair value 2000	1 600
	600

Parent concept extension method

This method adopts a fair value method to value the full net assets and the non-controlling interest of the subsidiary but does not include the full valuation of goodwill, only the parent share (see Activity 27.1).

Note here that the non-controlling interest is calculated by reference to the fair value of net assets but that the total fair value of goodwill is not included, i.e. no goodwill is allocated to the non-controlling interest. Note also that this is the method we used in Chapter 25 and is a permitted method of valuing the non-controlling interest under IFRS 3 (method 2) although not the preferred method of the IASB.

ILLUSTRATION

Use the data from Activity 27.1. Goodwill will need to be calculated for B as a whole not just 80% of it. Thus we need to assume that the consideration paid for 80% is indicative of the value of B as a whole. Thus we will assume for our illustration purposes that there is no premium on acquisition within the consideration.

Calculation of goodwill

Purchase consideration	2 200	for 80%
Total value of B 2200 × 100/80	2 750	
Fair value of net assets	2 000	
Goodwill	750	of which 20% attributable to non-controlling interest = 150

Consolidated financial statements using entity concept

Net assets	4 800
Goodwill	750
	5 550
Share capital	4000
Reserves	1 000
Non-controlling interest 20% × 2750	550
	5 550

ACTIVITY 27.2

Comment on the assets figure of $4 800 shown under the parent extension method and the entity method and identify how this figure would change if the parent method was used.

Activity feedback

Both the parent extension method and entity method include 100% of the net assets of B at fair value. Under the parent method only the parent share would be shown at fair value i.e. 1 600 (80% × 2 000) and the non-controlling interest would be included at book value 20% × 1 500 = 300, giving a total net assets of 4 700. The parent extension method is almost a halfway house between the parent and entity methods.

THE ENTITY CONCEPT

This concept views the group as a unit and makes no distinction between shareholders. The difference between the parent and entity concept only occurs where there is less than 100% purchase of the shares of an entity (see Illustration and Activity 27.2).

PROPORTIONAL CONSOLIDATION

This method is a variation of the parent method. It completely excludes the non-controlling interest from the consolidated financial statement which is in accord with the parent concept of providing information primarily for the majority shareholders (see Activity 27.3).

ACTIVITY 27.3

Show the consolidated financial statements for A group using proportional consolidation.

Activity feedback

Net assets [2 800 A + 80% of B's at FV]	4400
Goodwill	600
	5 000
Share capital	4 000
Reserves	1 000
	5 000

Proportional consolidation also has another disadvantage. When one entity acquires control of another entity (even though as in this case it does not acquire the whole of B's equity share capital), then A can determine the future action of B and can dictate the way in which B should utilise all (i.e. 100%) of its assets. This is the reality of the relationship between A and B (i.e. control) and it is quite different from the impression given in our balance sheet above, which implies that the group controls only 80% of B's various assets. Neither, of course, does this method give any indication of the existence of an external (non-controlling) interest in B.

COMPARISON OF ALL FOUR METHODS OF CONSOLIDATION

ACTIVITY 27.4

Compare and contrast the information provided in the consolidated balance sheet of A group using all four methods of consolidation – parent, entity, parent extension and proportional.

Activity feedback

This can best be seen by drawing up Table 27.1, containing information from the previous activities and the illustration of the entity concept.

Table 27.1 shows that the consistent figures throughout the four methods are only those of share capital and reserves of the holding company. The net assets change depending on how much of the fair value of the net assets each method considers attributable to the group. The proportional method excludes all reference to the portion of assets owned by the non-controlling interest whereas the entity and extension method assume that the group might not own all of the subsidiary's assets but it certainly controls them. The parent method only incorporates the net book value of the portion of assets owned by the non-controlling interest, it disregards the fair value of this portion. The goodwill only changes under the entity method where we include what could be regarded as the non-controlling interest goodwill. The non-controlling interest is shown at either 25% of NBV of net assets excluding goodwill (parent) or 25% of all net assets at fair value including goodwill (entity) or 25% of fair value of net assets excluding goodwill (extension). The proportional method of course makes no reference to a non-controlling interest.

TABLE 27.1 Information on balance sheets

	Proprietary	Entity	Proprietary extension	Proportional
Net assets	4 700	4 800	4 800	4 400
Goodwill	600	750	600	600
	5 300	5 550	5 400	5 000
Share capital	4 000	4 000	4 000	4 000
Reserves	1 000	1 000	1 000	1 000
Minority interest	300	550	400	N/A
	5 300	5 550	5 400	5 000

This plethora of methods requires us to decide which method we should use to reflect the consolidation of subsidiaries. As we saw in Chapter 26, the IASB have opted for the parent extension method plus a preferred option to include the non-controlling interest at its share of fair value of the subsidiary as a whole. It is worth noting here that the original ED for the amended IFRS 3 proposed the use of the entity concept where the full value of goodwill is included, not just the parent share.

PARENT EXTENSION METHOD REVISITED

The parent extension approach to consolidation was extensively used in the UK and became known as acquisition accounting and Activity 27.5 allows you to practise this method again as it is the method identified in IFRS 3 (using method 2 for valuing

ACTIVITY 27.5

Large Company acquired 75% of the share capital of Small Company at a price of €115 500 for cash as at 30 September, at which date their respective balance sheets were:

	Large Co €	Small Co €
Land and buildings	210 000	43 000
Investment in Small	115 500	–
Plant and equipment	75 000	22 000
Net current assets	63 500	18 000
	464 000	83 000
€2 shares	246 000	66 000
Reserves	218 000	17 000
	464 000	83 000

The estimated fair values at 30 September of Small assets were:

Land and buildings	49 000
Plant and equipment	19 000
Net current assets	18 000
	86 000

Prepare the consolidated balance sheet of Large as at 30 September using the parent company extension method.

Activity feedback

Goodwill calculation

	€
Purchase consideration	115 500
Purchased 75% of fair value	64 500
	51 000

Consolidation balance sheet for Large Group

	€
Land and buildings [210 000 + 49 000]	259 000
Plant and equipment [75 000 + 19 000]	94 000
Goodwill	51 000
Net current assets [63 500 + 18 000]	81 500
	485 500
Share capital	246 000
Reserves	218 000
	464 000
Non-controlling interest [25% × 86 000]	21 500
	485 500

Note again that under this treatment all the assets except goodwill are consolidated at 100% of fair value; goodwill included is only that in relation to the majority shareholding; the non-controlling interest is only valued at its share of fair value of net assets excluding goodwill.

the non-controlling interest). The parent company approach has also been termed the purchase method.

UNITING OF INTERESTS

Prior to the issue of IFRS 3, which requires that in any business combination an acquirer is identified, IAS 22 identified a 'uniting of interests' business combination. IAS 22 defined this as follows:

> A uniting of interests is a business combination in which the shareholders of the combining enterprises combine control over the whole, or effectively the whole, of their assets and operations to achieve a continuing mutual sharing in the risks and benefits attaching to the combined entity such that neither party can be identified as an acquirer.

Many respondents to the IASB on the issue of business combinations believe such uniting of interests still occur, even if only rarely, and that it will be impossible in such cases to identify an acquirer as required by IFRS 3. It was also previously the case that such uniting of interests was accounted for using the pooling of interests/merger method of accounting. IFRS 3 has now eliminated the use of merger accounting because:

- it has virtually eliminated the idea of uniting of interests
- in no circumstances, according to the Board, does the pooling of interests method provide superior information to that provided by the acquisition method.

The Basis for Conclusions to IFRS 3 does conclude that if true mergers exist, which it doubts, then a better accounting method to use for them could be the 'fresh start method'. This method requires both entities in the business combination to value all assets at fair value. However the IASB also disregarded the fresh start method and have no plans to debate it.

Differences between acquisition accounting and merger accounting

The main differences between the two methods can be examined under the headings of:

1 goodwill
2 share premium (paid-in surplus)
3 pre-acquisition profits.

Goodwill With a merger, there is no change in ownership and we merely have a pooling of resources, a consolidated balance sheet produced for a merger situation will simply combine the existing balance sheets and the assets will therefore remain at the book values at which they appear in the original balance sheets of the separate entities, that is to say no goodwill is recognised in the new balance sheet (since none is in fact acquired).

However, with acquisition accounting the net assets of the entity acquired will usually be revalued as at the date of acquisition and, of course, the difference between the purchase consideration and this asset revaluation will give rise to goodwill (premium) on acquisition.

Share premium With an acquisition where an entity issues shares to acquire another entity the cost of the investment is recorded in the acquirer's balance sheet and, of course, any shares issued in consideration are recorded at market value, i.e. nominal value plus share premium created. However, with a merger situation, shares issued in the share-for-share exchange involved are recorded at nominal value, i.e. no share premium is created.

Pre-acquisition profits For acquisition accounting purposes and in accordance with the concept of capital maintenance, the distributable profits of any acquired enterprise are frozen, i.e. are not legally regarded as available for distribution by the group.

By the same token, with merger accounting and in keeping with the spirit of a pooling of resources, the reserves of each participant entity are merely pooled, i.e. those that were distributable before the merger remain distributable after the merger.

It is obvious when one considers these differences why merger accounting was popular. Following from this, it can be seen that with merger accounting the balance sheet of the new entity does not carry a goodwill figure that might have to be impaired against income. Neither is there a non-distributable share premium account arising in the merged balance sheet and also the distributable reserves of the group are enlarged as opposed to the situation which would have prevailed under the acquisition accounting method.

It is appropriate here to consider an example of the application of merger accounting and also to contrast it with acquisition accounting (see Activity 27.6).

ACTIVITY 27.6

Two companies, A and M have the following respective balance sheets as at 30 June 200X:

	A $	M $
Common shares ($1)	9 000	6 000
Earned surplus	2 000	3 000
	11 000	9 000
Represented by		
Net current assets	5 000	2 000
Plant and machinery	6 000	7 000
	11 000	9 000

A acquired the whole of the share capital of M on the basis of a one-for-one share exchange as at the given date, at which point the market values of their respective shares were:

A	$4
M	$4

The fair values of M's tangible assets as at 30 June 200X were:

	$
Plant and machinery	8 000
Net current assets	2 500

Prepare the consolidated balance sheet for A using both acquisition/purchase (as per Chapter 25) and pooling methods.

Activity feedback

Consolidated balance sheet as at 30 June 200X

	Purchase		Pooling
Common shares ($1)	15 000	(note 1)	15 000
Share premium			
(paid-in surplus)	18 000	(note 2)	–
Earned surplus	2 000	(note 3)	5 000
	35 000		20 000

	Purchase		Pooling
Represented by:			
Net current assets	7 500	(note 4)	7 000
Plant and machinery	14 000	(note 4)	13 000
Goodwill on acquisition	13 500	(note 4)	–
	35 000		20 000

Notes

1 Based on a one-for-one exchange, A will need to issue a further 6 000 $1 shares (i.e. 9 000 + 6 000 = 15 000).

2 Issued at a price of $4 per share the share premium on the issue of A shares for acquisition accounting purposes will be $3 per share (i.e. 6 000 × €3 = €18 000).

3 For acquisition accounting purposes (but not for merger accounting) the reserves of M of €3 000 as at the date of acquisition will be frozen.

4 Cost of investment

(i.e. 6 000 shares at $4 each)	24 000
less Fair value of net assets	
acquired (i.e. $8 000 + 2 500)	(10 500)
	13 500

Despite the simplicity of this example the differences are amply illustrated:

1 Under acquisition accounting a non-distributable share premium account arises.

2 Under merger accounting the reserves of M at the date of acquisition are regarded as distributable by the group.

3 For acquisition accounting the assets of M are recorded at fair values, whereas for merger accounting purposes book values prevail.

EQUITY ACCOUNTING

We provide below an illustration of the equity method of accounting for you.

This particular method is only appropriate when there is no 'control' as it provides very little information to the user on the net assets of B that are controlled. Thus equity accounting is not a method to be used where we have a parent/subsidiary situation, but could be used where one entity has a significant interest in another, and in this connection the word 'associate' rather than 'subsidiary' is appropriate. A fuller discussion of the equity accounting method and its use for dealing with associated entities is given in the next chapter (Chapter 28), together with a consideration of IAS 28 and 31.

ILLUSTRATION

On 31 December 200X *A* entity acquired 1200 common shares in *B* entity (4000 common shares) at a cost of €3 per share. *B*'s net assets at 31.12.20X1 had a book value of €5600 and no *B* shares have been issued for several years.

The balance sheets of *A* and *B* as at 31.12.20X2 are as follows:

	A	*B*
	€	€
Net current assets	2 000	3 600
Property, plant and equipment	30 000	6 400
Investment in *B*	3 600	–
	35 600	10 000
Common shares €1	16 000	4 000
Reserves	19 600	6 000
	35 600	10 000

A is required to issue consolidated financial statements and decides to apply equity accounting to its investment in *B*.

First, we need to identify the goodwill, if any, in the investment as we did for acquisition accounting.

Consolidated balance sheet of *A* entity 31.12.02 using equity accounting for *B*

	€
Net current assets	2 000
Property, plant and equipment	30 000
Investment in *B* 3600 + 30% × earnings since purchase 4400	4 920
	36 920
Common shares €1	16 000
Reserves (19 600 + 1 320 share of *B* since purchase)	20 920
	36 920

	€
Cost of investment	3 600
Purchased 30% of *B*'s net assets	1 680 (or 30% of shares 4 000 = 1 200)
Goodwill	1 920 + 30% of reserves 1 600 = 480
	note reserves are €6000 so earnings since purchase are €4400

SUMMARY

The following is a useful summary of the methods that are available for accounting for a business combination:

- parent approach
- parent extension approach
- entity method
- proportional consolidation
- merger/uniting of interests
- equity accounting.

Remember also that we could have made the decision not to use any of these methods and just to leave the investment in the other entity as an investment on the balance sheet of the parent entity. However this would not have provided much useful information to users. Again remember that the method required in IFRS 3 to account for a subsidiary is the parent extension method plus the preferred option of showing the non-controlling interest as its share of the fair value of the entity as a whole.

EXERCISES

Suggested answers to exercises marked ✓ are to be found on the Student side of the companion website.

Suggested answers to the remaining exercises are to be found on the Instructor side of the companion website.

1 Appraise the effects on a group's financial statements of the use of merger accounting as opposed to acquisition accounting in order to account for business combinations.

✓ 2 Identify the essence of proportional consolidation and equity accounting and explain when each can be used in the preparation of consolidated financial statements in accordance with IAS GAAP.

ACCOUNTING FOR ASSOCIATES, JOINT VENTURES, SPECIAL PURPOSE ENTITIES AND RELATED PARTY TRANSACTIONS

28

OBJECTIVES After studying this chapter you should be able to:

- identify an associate and a joint venture

- identify a special purpose entity

- identify the need to disclose related party transactions

- consider the mechanics of accounting for an associate and a joint venture

- explain the requirements of IAS 24, *Related Party Disclosures*

- explain the requirements of IAS 28, *Investments in Associates*

- explain the requirements of IAS 31, *Interests in Joint Ventures*.

INTRODUCTION

So far within this section we have dealt primarily with the provision of information to users in respect of a holding in a subsidiary entity. However one entity may have a holding in another that does not give it control but does mean it has significant influence over the net assets of that entity. This chapter considers the appropriate methods to account for holdings/relationships where control is not achieved such that useful information is provided to users.

ACTIVITY 28.1

Using the illustration on p. 688 in Chapter 27 identify the main differences in the preparation of a consolidated balance sheet using equity accounting as opposed to acquisition accounting.

Activity feedback

The illustration shows us that equity accounting consolidates entity B as a one-line addition not by including the fair value of the net assets of B at each individual line of the balance sheet. This one line consolidation however does show us more than the original cost of the investment in B as it includes the goodwill and A's share of the earnings of B since it made the investment.

EQUITY ACCOUNTING AND ASSOCIATES

We gave you an example of equity accounting in Chapter 27. It will be useful (via Activity 28.1) for you to look back at the illustration we provided.

INVESTMENTS IN ASSOCIATES IAS 28

IAS 28 was originally issued in 1989 and amended in 1994, 1998, 1999 and 2000. Since then it has been further amended by changes made in other Standards, particularly IFRS 3. IAS 28's main objective was to reduce alternatives in the application of the equity method not to consider the fundamental approach of using the equity method to account for associates.

IAS 28 definitions

From Activity 28.1 we could define *equity method* of accounting as a method whereby the investment is initially recognised at cost and adjusted thereafter for the post-acquisition change in the investor's share of the net assets of the investee. The profit or loss of the investor includes the investor's share of the profit or loss of the investee. This is in fact how IAS 28 defines it.

The equity method in consolidated financial statements provides the user of the statements with much more information than recording the investment at cost and accounting for any distributions from the investee. The user is able to see his share of the results of the investment and calculate more useful ratios.

An associate is defined by IAS 28 as an entity, including an unincorporated entity such as a partnership, over which the investor has significant influence and that is neither a subsidiary nor an interest in a joint venture (para. 2).

Significant influence is defined as the power to participate in the financial and operating policy decisions of the investee but is not control or joint control over those policies.

Significant influence is amplified in IAS 28 as a situation where the investor holds, directly or indirectly through subsidiaries, 20% or more of the voting power of the

ACTIVITY 28.2

Identify whether an associate relationship exists in the following examples in accordance with IAS 28.

1 Entity A owns 20% of entity B and appoints one out of the seven directors. The remaining shares are held equally by two entities that both appoint three of the seven directors. A board meeting is quorate if four directors attend. In the event of tied decisions the Chair of the board who is appointed by one of the other entities has a casting vote.

2 Entity A owns 15% of B and appoints two of six directors to the board. Each director has one vote at meetings and the Chair who is from entity A has a casting vote. The other four directors do not represent a shareholding of more than 5%.

3 Entity A manufactures gadgets for retailer B. B designs the gadgets and normally 90% of A's sales are made to B. B owns 12% of the shares of A.

4 Entity A has a 16% holding in B. B retails software packages developed by A who holds the licence to the software. B retails no other software packages.

Activity feedback

1 Entity A has very little influence in entity B, as at any board meeting he will be outvoted. B is not an associate of A.

2 In this case although entity A holds less than 20% A has significant influence given his voting rights on the board, 33.3%, and his chair casting vote.

3 Although B only holds 12% of the shares B exerts significant influence as A is reliant on B for the continuation of the business. A is an associate of B.

4 B is dependent on A for technical information and therefore B is an associate of A.

investee and that if such a situation exists significant influence will be presumed unless it can be clearly evidenced otherwise and vice versa.

Significant influence is usually evidenced by:

- representation on the board of directors or equivalent governing body of the investee
- participation in policy making processes
- material transactions between the investor and the investee
- interchange of managerial personnel
- provision of essential technical information.

Goodwill in equity accounting

In the illustration in Chapter 27, p. 688 we identified goodwill but then appeared to do nothing with it. In accordance with IAS 28 this goodwill, if positive, is included in the carrying amount of the investment. (Under the previous version of IAS 28 the goodwill was amortised but remember amortisation of goodwill is no longer permitted under IASs.) The goodwill, unlike that in the case of a subsidiary, is not identified separately or subject to a separate impairment test. The investment in its entirety is tested for impairment. To do this test, in accordance with IAS 36, the recoverable amount of the investment, which is the higher of value in use and fair value less costs to sell, is compared with its carrying amount whenever there is an indication of impairment as prescribed by IAS 39. If the goodwill on the purchase of the associate is negative then this is excluded from the carrying amount of the investment and is included as income in the determination of the investor's share of the associate's profit or loss in the period in which the investment is acquired.

ILLUSTRATION

If the cost of the investment in the illustration in Chapter 27 p. 688 is €1500 and the reserves of the parent €17 500 then the identified goodwill would be as follows:

	€
Cost of investment	1 500
Purchased 30% of net assets	1 680
Negative goodwill	(180)

The balance sheet would be as follows:

	€	€
Net current assets		2 000
Property, plant and equipment		30 000
Investment in B – cost	1 500	
– share of earnings since purchase	1 320	
– exclusion of goodwill	180	3 000
		35 000
Capital shares		16 000
Reserves	17 500	
Reserves since purchase	1 320	
Negative goodwill	180	19 000
		35 000

Exemptions from the use of equity method

An investment in an associate shall be accounted for using the equity method except when:

(a) the investment is classified as held for sale in accordance with IFRS 5 *Non-current Assets held for Sale and Discontinued Operations*;

(b) the exception in paragraph 10 of IAS 27, allowing a parent that also has an investment in an associate not to present consolidated financial statements, applies; or

(c) all of the following apply:

- the investor is a wholly-owned subsidiary, or is a partially-owned subsidiary of another entity and its other owners, including those not otherwise entitled to vote, have been informed about, and do not object to, the investor not applying the equity method;

- the investor's debt or equity instruments are not traded in a public market (a domestic or foreign stock exchange or an over-the-counter market, including local and regional markets);

- the investor did not file, nor is it in the process of filing, its financial statements with a securities commission or other regulatory organisation, for the purpose of issuing any class of instruments in a public market; and

- the ultimate or an intermediate parent of the investor produces consolidated financial statements available for public use that comply with International Financial Reporting Standards. (IAS 28, para. 13)

Associate entities and losses

In the previous illustration if the reserves of B at 31.12.20X2 had stood at €14 000 debit then careful consideration would need to be given to how the loss was shown in the consolidated financial statements. If equity accounting was strictly applied the consolidated balance sheet would be:

	€
Net current assets	2 000
Property, plant and equipment	30 000
Investment in B	
3 600 + 30% (15 600)	(1 080)
	30 920
Common shares €1	16 000
Reserves (19 6007 – 4 680)	14 920
	30 920

This would imply that A has an obligation to transfer economic benefits of €1080 to the associate but this may not be the case. IAS 28, para. 29 states:

> If an investor's share of losses of an associate equals or exceeds its interest in the associate, the investor discontinues recognising its share of further losses. The interest in an associate is the carrying amount of the investment in the associate under the equity method together with any long-term interests that, in substance, form part of the investor's net investment in the associate.

For example, an item for which settlement is neither planned nor likely to occur in the foreseeable future is, in substance, an extension of the equity's investment in that associate. Such items may include preference shares and long-term receivables or loans but do not include trade receivables, trade payables or any long-term receivables for which adequate collateral exists, such as secured loans. Losses recognised under the equity method in excess of the investor's investment in ordinary shares are applied to the other components of the investor's interest in an associate in the reverse order of their seniority (i.e. prior to liquidation).

Thus, the consolidated balance sheet of A should be shown as follows if there is no obligation:

	€
Net current assets	2 000
Property, plant and equipment	30 000
Investments in B	–
	32 000
Common shares €1	16 000
Reserves (19 600 – 3 600)	16 000
	32 000

Alternatively, if there is an indication that the value of an investment may be impaired then IAS 36, *Impairment of Assets*, must be applied. The issue of impairment is dealt with in paras 33 and 34 of IAS 28. The associate must then be recorded at its value in use determined by estimating the enterprise's share of the present value of the estimated future cash flows expected to be generated by the investee as a whole, including the cash flows from the operations of the investee and the proceeds on the ultimate disposal of investment or the present value of the estimated future cash flows expected to arise from dividends to be received from the investment and from its ultimate disposal.

Both methods generally give the same result.

Disclosure requirements for associates

These are identified in paras 37–40 of IAS 28.

IAS 31 INTERESTS IN JOINT VENTURES

Introduction

So far we have defined investment in another entity as either a subsidiary relationship, a uniting of interests, an associate relationship or a simple trade investment.

There is one other type of investment we need to consider and that is a joint venture. The IASB issued a Standard on joint ventures in 1990 and has continued to update it since then. Currently, at the time of writing, there is an exposure draft in issue on joint ventures from which a new Standard is expected in the second quarter of 2009. We will deal with the issues of the exposure draft later.

Definitions

> '*A joint venture* is a contractual arrangement whereby two or more parties undertake an economic activity which is subject to joint control' (IAS 31, para. 3).
> '*Joint control* is the contractual agreed sharing of control over an economic activity' and exists only when the strategic financial and operating decisions relating to the activity require the unanimous consent of the parties sharing control (the venturers) (IAS 31, para. 3).

A joint venture is dependent on a contractual arrangement, usually in writing. This contract will cover several issues such as duration of the activity, reporting obligations, appointment of the governing body of the venture, capital contributions by each party (venturer) and the sharing of income, expenses or results. The contract will establish joint control by all ventures involved and will ensure that no one venturer can control the activity. Quite often though one venturer may be appointed as the operator or manager of the venture but he will still have to act within the financial and operating policies agreed by all the venturers. If this is not the case and one venturer can act unilaterally then the venture is not a 'joint venture' but probably a subsidiary of one venturer. (See Activity 28.3.)

Forms of joint venture

A joint venture can take many different forms both legally and in substance but IAS 31 categorises them into three areas:

- jointly controlled operations
- jointly controlled assets
- jointly controlled entities.

Jointly controlled operations are ventures where the assets and resources of the individual ventures are used. If a joint venture was established by three venturers to construct a spacecraft with one manufacturing the shell and furbishing the interior, the second the engines and the third the computer hardware and software, and each carried out the work alongside its normal activities using its own employees and incurring its own expenses and liabilities then this would be regarded as a jointly controlled operation. This presumes, of course, that the venture met the requirements to be defined a joint venture.

Jointly controlled assets occur when venturers jointly own and control specific assets for the purpose of a joint venture. For example, if two venturers acquired a refurbished castle and rented out rooms in the castle, each venturer receiving rents

ACTIVITY 28.3

Serp Company, a building firm, is involved in the following arrangements with other building entities:

- An interest in a project Castle Residential with Locking entity and Crawford entity. The project involves the renovation of the castle building to provide resident accommodation. The participants have equal shares in the project and are to share profits equally. Invoices are sent to Cork entity, which has contracted with the venturers for the work by each of the participants for their work done.

- A 30% interest in Alpha entity to the board of which Serp appoints two directors.

- A 70% interest in Beta entity.

- An equal interest with X entity in Gamma. The consent of Serp and X is required to all decisions on financial and operating policies of Gamma essential to activities, economic performance and financial position.

- A 15% interest in Wimp entity.

- A 22% interest in Alpine entity which is seen as a short-term investment.

- An interest in Delta entity. Serp, Delta and Condo are to share equally in the income, expenses and

results of Delta and they have each contributed the same capital. Condo has the power to vary the financial and operating policies of Delta as it sees fit.

Identify what type of relationship each of these arrangements is, as far as SERP is concerned, based on our discussions so far.

Activity feedback

Castle Residential is a joint venture as the venturers have joint control.

Alpha is an associate as we can presume significant influence from two directors.

Beta is a subsidiary if we assume 70% interest implies 70% voting rights.

Gamma is a joint venture as it is jointly controlled by Serp and X.

Delta is actually a subsidiary of Condo, not of Serp, and thus Serp will only account for the results of Condo as a trade investment.

Wimp and Alpine are trade investments as the former investment does not demonstrate any significant influence and the latter is for a short term.

and bearing expenses, then this would be regarded as a joint venture with jointly controlled assets. Many examples of this type of joint venture occur in oil, gas and mineral extraction industries. For example, three venturers could purchase a mine where each extracts a distinct mineral; each bearing their own costs of extraction and receiving sale revenues for their particular mineral.

Jointly controlled entities are examples of joint ventures where a distinct entity is formed in which each venturer has an interest. IAS 31 gives the following example:

(para. 26) A common example of a jointly controlled entity is when two enterprises combine their activities in a particular line of business by transferring the relevant assets and liabilities into a jointly controlled entity. Another example arises when an enterprise commences a business in a foreign country in conjunction with the government or other agency in that country, by establishing a separate entity, which is jointly controlled by the enterprise and the government or agency (para. 27).

Many jointly controlled entities are similar in substance to those joint ventures referred to as jointly controlled operations or jointly controlled assets. For example, the venturers may transfer a jointly controlled asset, such as an oil pipeline, into a jointly controlled entity, for tax or other reasons. Similarly, the venturers may contribute into jointly controlled entity assets, which will be operated jointly. Some jointly controlled operations also involve the establishment of a jointly controlled entity to deal with particular aspects of the activity, for example, the design, the marketing, distribution or after-sales service of the product.

ACTIVITY 28.4

Identify what form of joint venture Castle Residential and Gamma is (Activity 28.3, p. 697) in accordance with IAS 31.

Activity feedback

Castle Residential is a jointly controlled operation. Gamma is a jointly controlled entity.

Accounting for joint ventures

Jointly controlled operations will be accounted for in the venturer's own financial statements already as in this operation the venturer is using its own assets and liabilities and incurring its own income and expenses. There may need to be some adjustments to the venturer's statements for inter-venture transactions.

Separate financial statements for the joint venture are not required by law (as it is not a legal entity) but generally they are prepared for management purposes.

Jointly controlled assets are again already recorded in the venturer's financial statements so no further entries are required in the consolidated financial statements except to eliminate inter-venture transactions.

The accounting for a *jointly controlled entity* is by necessity different to the other two forms of joint venture as legally the entity must maintain its own accounting records and prepare financial statements. The venturer will have made contributions to the joint venture in terms of cash or other assets and these will be recorded in the venturer's individual statements as their investment in the jointly controlled entity.

However, this record of investment does not show the substance and economic reality of the joint venture to the user of the consolidated financial statements. In essence, without some different accounting method being used, the consolidated financial statements will not reflect the venturer's share of future economic benefits.

IAS 31 requires either proportional consolidation (the benchmark treatment/preferred method) or the equity method (allowed alternative treatment) to be used for jointly controlled entities. Both of these methods have been discussed already in Chapter 27.

Under the proportional consolidation method it is permitted either to combine the venturer's share of assets, liabilities, income and expenses in the joint venture with its own or to show the share of joint venture items as individual items at each line on the balance sheet and income statement. The latter method is preferred by some, as it does not sum whole and part items.

The equity method is as used for associates and is supported by those who believe that joint control is similar to significant influence. The IAS did not when issuing IAS 31 support this view but did, however, permit the alternative treatment. The Board did not recommend equity method because it believed 'proportionate consolidation better reflects the substance and economic reality of a venturer's interest in a jointly controlled entity, that is to say, control over the venturer's share of the future economic benefits' (para. 40). Note that if an enterprise had two investments, one in an associate and the other in a joint venture defined as a jointly controlled entity then in the consolidated financial statements of the venturer there would be no difference in the accounting for either investment if the alternative treatment was used for the joint entity.

Exposure draft joint ventures

ED9 issued September 2007 was titled *Joint Arrangements* and represents the first major review to IAS 31 since it was issued. The ED focuses on two aspects:

- Currently IAS 31 focuses on the legal form in which joint arrangements take place. In other areas the IASB focuses on substance over form. The ED therefore proposes to shift the focus to the contractual rights and obligations agreed to by the parties involved rather than the legal form.

● Currently the existing Standard permits a choice when accounting for interests in jointly controlled entities – proportional consolidation or equity accounting. The ED proposes to remove the option to use proportional consolidation. Parties to joint arrangements will be required to recognise both the individual assets to which they have rights and the liabilities for which they are responsible. If the parties only have a right to a share of the outcome of the activities their net interest in the arrangement will be recognised using the equity method.

The ED provides us with a flow chart to aid recognition of arrangements in joint arrangements which we produce below for you. It will be interesting to see if the ED proposed changes to IAS 31 are carried out.

The following flow chart illustrates how a party to a joint arrangement recognises its interests in the arrangement.

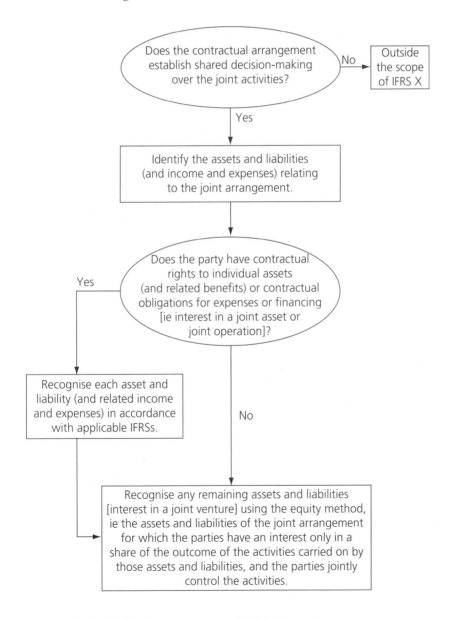

ACTIVITY 28.5

X entity acquired 600 $1 common shares in Y entity at a price of $1.50 per share on 31 December 20X1 at which point the income statement of Y had a credit balance of $800. The respective balance sheets of X and Y as at 31 December 20X2 are summarised here:

	X	Y
	$	$
Net current assets	1 000	1 800
Property plant and equipment	15 000	3 200
Investment in Y	900	–
	16 900	5 000
Common shares $1	8 000	2 000
Reserves	8 900	3 000
	16 900	5 000

X is required to prepare consolidated financial statements as it has several subsidiaries for the year ended 31 December 20X2. You are required to draft the initial consolidated balance sheet of the group as at December 20X2 before the inclusion of the subsidiaries but after the inclusion of Y assuming, first, that the investment in Y is an associate and, second, a jointly controlled entity.

Activity feedback

Y as an associate or as a jointly controlled entity using the alternative accounting treatment as permitted by IAS 31:

	€	€
Net current assets	1 000	
Property, plant and equipment	15 000	
Investment in Y (see note 1)	1 560	
	17 560	
Common shares € 1	8 000	
Reserves (see note 2)	9 560	
	17 560	

	€		€
Note 1: Goodwill calculation		**Note 2: Reserve calculation**	
Cost of investment	900	X reserves	8 900
Assets acquired 30% × 2800	840	30% of Y post-quisition (2200)	660
Goodwill	60		9 560

Share of net assets 30% × 5000 + goodwill 60 = 1 560

Y as a joint controlled entity using proportional consolidation as preferred by IAS 31 (summed method).

	€
Net current assets [1000 + 30% × 1800]	1 540
Property plant and equipment [15 000 + 30% × 3200]	15 960
Goodwill in joint venture [60]	60
	17 560
Common shares €1	8 000
Reserves (see note 2)	9 560
	17 560

Y as a jointly controlled entity using proportional consolidation as preferred by IAS 31 (individual line method).

	€	€
Net current assets	1 000	
Net current assets joint venture	540	
Property, plant and equipment	15 000	1 540
Joint venture	960	15 960
Goodwill of consolidation of JV		60
		17 500

Transactions between a venturer and a joint venture

When a venturer contributes or sells assets to a joint venture, recognition of any proportion of a gain or loss from the transaction should reflect the substance of the transaction. While the assets are retained by the joint venture and provided the venturer has transferred the significant risks and rewards of ownership, the venturer should recognise only that portion of the gain or loss, which is attributable to the interests of the other venturers. The venturer should recognise the full amount of any loss when the contribution or sale provides evidence of a reduction in the net realisable value of current assets or impairment loss. (IAS 31, para. 48.)

ACTIVITY 28.6

A joint venture, Gamma entity, is set up between A, B, and C entities. All venturers share equally in the joint venture. After establishment of the joint venture A sells to Gamma for cash some items of equipment, carrying value in A's books €1m, for €1.6 m.

Show the adjustments to be made in A's consolidated financial statements in respect of the above transaction.

Activity feedback

In A's individual statements the transaction will have been recorded as a sale of equipment thus:

Dr Cash	1.6m
Cr Equipment	1m
Cr Income statements – gain on sale	0.6m

The gain on sale of 0.6m, in accordance with IAS 31, should only be recognised in the consolidated financial statements as that part which is attributable to the other venturers. Thus only 2/3 × 0.6m = €0.4 m should be recognised.

In the consolidated financial statements using proportional consolidation the following adjustments to A's individual accounts will be required.

Cr Cash	0.533
Dr Equipment	0.333
Dr Income statement gain on sale	0.2

Thus the consolidated statements will still show one-third of the equipment and the gain on sale will have been reduced to €0.4m. It will be as though only two-thirds of the equipment has been sold.

Under the equity method the following adjustments will be required.

Cr Investments in JV	0.2
Dr Income statement	0.2

When a venturer purchases assets from a joint venture, the venturer should not recognise its share of the profits of the joint venture from the transaction until it resells the assets to an independent party. A venturer should recognise its share of the losses resulting from these transactions in the same way as profits except that losses should be recognised immediately when they represent a reduction in the net realisable value of current assets or impairment loss. (IAS 31, para. 49.)

Disclosure in respect of joint ventures

These are as expected:

- listing and description of interest in significant joint ventures
- proportion of ownership interest held
- aggregate amounts of each of current assets, long-term assets, current liabilities, long-term liabilities, income and expenses related to interest in joint ventures
- aggregate amount of certain contingencies incurred in relation to joint venture
- share of capital commitments of joint venture
- method it uses to recognise its interest in jointly controlled entities.

An example of a disclosure note in respect of consolidation methods is shown from Bayer Group's financial report 2002.

Consolidation methods: Capital consolidation is performed according to IAS 22 (Business Combinations) by offsetting investment in subsidiaries against the underlying equities at the dates of acquisition. The identifiable assets of subsidiaries and joint ventures are included at their fair values in proportion to Bayer's interest. Remaining differences are recognised as goodwill.

ACTIVITY 28.7

Determine from Bayer's disclosure whether accounting methods used are in accordance with current IASs.

Activity feedback

Bayer has obviously used the benchmark treatment under the previous version of IAS 22, as fair values have only been included in proportion to Bayer's interest. Thus, the value of assets and liabilities displayed in the group accounts will include the subsidiaries' assets partly at fair value (that part owned by Bayer), and partly (the minority interest), at some other value which equates to balance sheet carrying value of the subsidiary before taking account of fair value on consolidation. Thus the assets and liabilities displayed by Bayer in the consolidation are a mix of values. The allowed alternative treatment would have avoided this mix of values being incorporated from subsidiaries, as 100% of these would have to be incorporated at fair value (including the minority interest share).

> Where the statements of individual consolidated companies reflect write-downs or write-backs of investments in other consolidated companies, these are reversed for the Group statements.
>
> Intragroup sales, profits, losses, income, expenses, receivables and payables are eliminated. Deferred taxes are recognised for temporary differences related to consolidation entries. Joint ventures are included by proportionate consolidation according to the same principles. Intercompany profits and losses on transactions with companies included at equity were immaterial in 2002.

See Activity 28.7. Would Bayer's accounts have been more understandable and/or 'truer and fairer' if the alternative treatment had been used?

RELATED PARTY TRANSACTIONS

So far in this chapter we have dealt with accounting for business combinations, subsidiaries, associates and joint ventures. However, what we have not considered is that the parties in these business combinations often enter into transactions with each other that unrelated parties would not undertake. For example:

- Assets and liabilities may be transferred between parties at values above or below market value.
- One party may make a loan to another at a beneficial interest rate or without taking into account the full risk involved.
- Services carried out by one party for another may be charged for at a reduced rate.

When working through the accounting techniques for business combinations we learnt that such transactions required eliminating in the group consolidated accounts.

However, one of our basic assumptions within accounting is that transactions are carried out at arm's length between independent parties. If they are not, then users of financial statements will be misled if they are not provided with information in respect of these related party transactions. However, if we wish to give such information to users we need to have uniformity of information provided by enterprises and to clearly define when parties are related. This issue is dealt with by IASB in IAS 24 first issued in July 1984 and updated as part of the Board's improvement project.

ACTIVITY 28.8

Identify a related party situation where:

- A transaction occurs that affects the financial position and operating results of the reporting enterprise.

- A situation where no transaction occurs but an effect is still felt on the financial position and operating results of the reporting enterprise.

Activity feedback

- There are several situations you could have identified here and three of them we identified for you

above. Others are agency arrangements, leasing arrangements, licence agreements, guarantees and collaterals, management contracts and transfer of research and development.

- Such a situation could be where a subsidiary may terminate relations with a trading partner on acquisition by the parent of a fellow subsidiary engaged in the same trade as the former partner. Another such situation would be where a subsidiary, once acquired, is instructed by its parent not to engage in certain activities, e.g. research and development.

Related party issue

IAS 24 in its consideration of the related party issue maintains that related party relationships could have an effect on the financial position and operating results of the reporting enterprise and that this effect can occur even if no transactions have taken place (see Activity 28.8).

IAS 24 definitions

Related party A party is related to an entity if:

(a) Directly, or indirectly through one or more intermediaries, the party:

   (i) controls, is controlled by, or is under common control with, the entity (this includes parents, subsidiaries and fellow subsidiaries)

   (ii) has an interest in the entity that gives it significant influence over the entity

   (iii) or has joint control over the entity.

(b) The party is an associate (as defined in IAS 28, *Investments in Associates*) of the entity.

(c) The party is a joint venture in which the entity is a venturer (see IAS 31, *Interest in Joint Ventures*).

(d) The party is a member of the key management personnel of the entity or its parent.

(e) The parent is a close member of the family of any individual referred to in (a) or (d).

(f) The party is an entity that is controlled, jointly controlled or significantly influenced by or for which significant voting power in such entity resides with, directly or indirectly, any individual referred to in (d) or (c).

(g) The party is a post-employment benefit plan for the benefit of employees of the entity, or of an entity that is a related party of the entity.

Close members of the family of an individual are defined as those family members who may be expected to influence, or be influenced by, that individual in their dealings with the entity. They may include:

- the individual's domestic partner and children
- children of the individual's domestic partner
- dependants of the individual or the individual's domestic partner.

Compensation includes all employee benefits (as defined in IAS 19, *Employee Benefits*) including employee benefits to which IFRS 2, *Share-based Payment*, applies. Employee benefits are all forms of consideration paid, in exchange for services rendered to the entity. It also includes such consideration paid on behalf of a parent of the entity in respect of the entity.

Compensation includes:

(a) short-term employee benefits, such as wages, salaries, and social security contributions, paid annual leave and paid sick leave, profit sharing and bonuses (if payable within 12 months of the end of the period) and non-monetary benefits (such as medical care, housing, cars and free or subsidised goods or services) for current employees;

(b) post-employment benefits such as pensions, other retirement benefits, post-employment life insurance and post-employment medical care;

(c) other long-term employee benefits, including long-service leave or sabbatical leave, jubilee or other long-service benefits, long-term disability benefits and, if they are not payable wholly within 12 months after the end of the period, profit-sharing, bonuses and deferred compensation;

(d) termination benefits; and

(e) share-based payments (IAS 24, para. 9).

Related party transaction – a transfer of resources, services or obligations between related parties, regardless of whether a price is charged.

Control – the power to govern the financial and operating policies of an entity so as to obtain benefits from its activities.

Significant influence (for the purpose of this standard) – participation in the financial and operating policy decisions of an enterprise, but not control of these policies. Significant influence may be gained by share ownership, statute or agreement (IAS 28, para. 9).

Disclosure requirements of IAS 24

This breaks down into two areas:

1 Where no transactions have occurred between the parties but control exists. In this case the relationship must be disclosed so that the user can form a view about the effect of the relationship on the reporting enterprise.

2 Where transactions have occurred between related parties. In this case the nature of the relationship, the types of transactions and elements of the transactions necessary for an understanding of the financial statements must be disclosed.

ACTIVITY 28.9

Identify those elements of a related party transaction that you believe should be disclosed so as to provide an understanding of the financial statements.

Activity feedback
You probably identified:

- name of related party
- volumes and amounts involved in the transactions
- amounts and volumes outstanding at the balance sheet date
- amounts written off in respect of debts due from the related party
- pricing policies
- transfer of a major asset at a reduced price
- those where a free service was given.

IAS 24 requires disclosure of four elements:

- amount of the transactions
- amount of outstanding balances
- provision for doubtful debts
- expense recognised during the period in respect of bad or doubtful debts together with the name of the entity's parent and key management personnel compensation in total and for each of:

  – short-term employee benefits

  – post-employment benefits

  – other long-term benefits

  – termination benefits

  – share-based payment.

SPECIAL PURPOSE ENTITIES

Introduction

These are entities that have been created to accomplish a narrow and well-defined objective. For example, such a special purpose enterprise (SPE) could be set up to carry out a specific research project. The SPEs are generally set up under tight legal arrangements and the sponsor may transfer assets and liabilities to it. Within such arrangements we need to determine whether the sponsor has control over the SPE, as if he has, then it must be consolidated as it is in essence no different to a subsidiary.

Currently there is only a Standing Interpretations Committee – SIC 12 to regulate SPEs but any revision to IAS 27 is likely to incorporate regulation on SPEs such that the IASB develops consistent control criteria for subsidiaries and SPEs. SPEs are sometimes known as quasi-subsidiaries.

Accounting

SIC 12 states that an SPE shall be consolidated when the substance of the relationship between an entity and the SPE indicates that the SPE is controlled by that entity. For an SPE control by another entity might exist even in cases where an entity owns little or none of the SPE's equity. SIC 12 provides us with further guidance on identifying control of a SPE in addition to paragraph 13 of IAS27. This guidance is:

- in substance the activities of the SPE are being conducted on behalf of the entity according to its specific business needs so that the entity obtains benefits from the SPE's operations

- in substance the entity has the decision-making powers to obtain the majority of the benefits of the activities of the SPE or, by setting up an 'autopilot' mechanism, the entity has delegated these decision-making powers
- in substance the entity has rights to obtain the majority of the benefits of the SPE and therefore may be exposed to risks incident to the activities of the SPE
- in substance the entity retains the majority of the residual or ownership risks related to the SPE or its assets in order to obtain benefits from its activities.

'Autopilot' just means that the SPE has been set up in a way such that all its activities etc. have been predetermined.

SUMMARY OF ACCOUNTING METHODS FOR BUSINESS COMBINATIONS

The following might be a useful summary of methods available to account for different types of business relationships that we have covered in Chapters 25–28. We also provide a list of those different relationships.

Methods available:

- proprietary/parent entity
- parent entity extension
- entity concept
- proportional consolidation
- merger/uniting of interests
- equity accounting
- record as a trade investment.

Relationships:

- subsidiary
- merger
- associate
- special purpose entity
- joint venture
- jointly controlled operations
- jointly controlled assets
- jointly controlled entities
- trade investment.

To refresh your memory of the different methods of accounting for business combinations available we provide Activity 28.10.

ACTIVITY 28.10

The following information is available in respect of Serp company and the other entities for the year ended 31 March 20X8 (see Activity 28.3).

Income statement for the year ended 31.3.X8

	Serp €000	Gamma €000	Alpha €000	Beta €000
Turnover	9 000	6 000	15 000	10 000
Cost of sales	3 900	2 200	8 000	5 000
Gross profit	5 100	3 800	7 000	5 000
Administration and distribution	900	1 200	2 100	1 100
Operating profit	4 200	2 600	4 900	3 900
Dividends received	50			
Interest payable	150	170		1 100
Profit before tax	4 100	2 430		2 800
Taxation	1 750	1 100	4 900	1 100
Profit after tax	2 350	1 330	2 100	1 700

1 Serp has not received any dividends from any of its investments except for those from Wimp and Alpine.

2 Net assets of Alpha at acquisition, 1 April 20X3 were €18 000 000 and of Beta purchased 1 April 20X4 €15 000 000.

3 Serp bought its share in Gamma at 1 April 20X7.

4 Information in respect of Castle Residential project is as follows:

Memorandum income statement as at 31.3.X8

	Serp €000	Locking €000	Crawford €000
Turnover	2 000	700	1 500
Cost of sales	950	400	600
Gross profit	1 050	300	900
Administration and distribution	300	20	100
Operating profit	750	280	800
Interest payable	50	—	100
Profit before tax	700	280	700
Taxation	170	—	100
Profit after tax	530	280	600

These figures in respect of Serp are included in Serp's profit and loss account but no adjustment has been made in respect of the turnover and costs reported by Locking and Crawford on the project.

Balance sheet as at 31.3.X8 for Serp and other entities

	Serp €000	Gamma €000	Alpha €000	Beta €000
Non-current assets	16 500	10 130	30 000	27 500
Investments in:				
Beta	12 000			
Gamma	2 500			
Alpha	5 700			
Wimp, Alpine	5 000			
Current assets	3 200	1 000	4 000	2 500
Current liabilities	(2 900)	(800)	(2 700)	(900)
	42 000	10 330	31 300	29 100
Long-term liabilities	(2 200)	(4 000)	(7 500)	(9 000)
	39 800	6 330	23 800	20 100
Share capital	10 000	5 000	4 000	8 000
Reserves	29 800	1 330	19 800	12 100
	39 800	6 330	23 800	20 100

Required:
Prepare the consolidated accounts for the Serp group for the year ended 31.3.X8 using equity accounting for Gamma and Alpha, parent entity extension method for Beta and account for Castle Residential in accordance with the terms of the agreement.

Activity feedback

1 The jointly controlled operation, Castle Residential, has to be accounted for in Serp's accounts in accordance with the terms of that arrangement, i.e. equal shares:

	Project €000	Equalisation €000	Equal shares €000
Turnover	4 200	(600)	1 400
Cost of sales	1 950	(300)	650
Gross profit	2 250	(300)	750
Administration and distribution	420	(160)	140
Operating profit	1 830	(140)	610
Interest payable	150	0	50
Profit before tax	1 680	(140)	560
Taxation	270	(80)	90
Profit after tax	1 410	(60)	470

ACTIVITY 28.10 (Continued)

2 Goodwill calculations:

		€000
Joint venture Gamma	Purchase price	2 500
	50% × 5000	2 500
	Goodwill	0
Subsidiary Beta	Purchase price	12 000
	70% × 15m	10 500
	Goodwill	1 500
Associate Alpha	Purchase price	5 700
	30% × 18m	5 400
	Goodwill	300

3 Consolidated income statement for Serp group for the year ended 31.3.X8

	€000	€000
Group turnover (9000 − 600 equal + 10 000 subsid)		18 400
Cost of sales (3900 − 300 equal + 5000 sub)		8 600
Gross profit		9 800
Administration and distribution costs (900 − 160 + 1100)		1 840
Group operating profit		7 960
Share of operating profit in:		
Joint venture	1 300	
Associate	1 470	2 770
		10 730
Dividends received trade investments		50
		10 780
Interests payable		
Group (150 + 1100)	1 250	
Associate		
Joint venture	85	1 335
Profit on ordinary activities before tax		9 445
Tax:		
Group (1750 + 1100 − 80)	2 770	
Joint venture (50% × 1100)	550	
Associate (30% × 2100)	630	3 950

	€000	€000
Profit on ordinary activities after tax		5 495
Minority interest (30% × 1700)		510
Retained profit for group and its share of associate and joint ventures		4 985

Consolidated balance sheet for Serp group as at 31.3.X8

	€000	€000
Non-current assets		
Goodwill (1500)		1 500
Property, plant and equipment (16 500 + 27 500)		44 000
Investments		
Investments joint ventures		3 165
Investments in associates:		
Share of net assets (30% × 23 800)	7 140	
Goodwill	300	7 440
Trade investments		5 000
		61 105
Current assets (3200 + 2500)	5 700	
Current liabilities	3 860	1 840
		62 945
Long-term liabilities (2200 +9000)		11 200
		51 745
Equity minority interest (30% × 20 100)		6 030
		45 715
Share capital		10 000
Reserves		35 715
		45 715
Reserves		
Serp	29 800	
less Equalisation	60	29 740
Alpha (5800 × 30%) Gamma		1 740
		665
Beta (5 100 × 70%)		3 570
		35 715

SUMMARY

There is much debate in the accounting world on the subject of business combinations. Currently we are awaiting the issue of discussion papers on consolidation, expected at the end of 2008, a new Standard on *Joint Ventures* expected at the beginning of 2009, and a new Standard on *Related Party Disclosures* expected at the end of 2008.

To date the IASB have not debated the 'fresh-start method' and whether it should be applied to circumstances where an acquirer cannot be identified in a combination.

To recap, under current extant international standards we have the following:

Relationship	*Accounting method in consolidated statements*
Subsidiary	acquisition accounting parent company approach (choice of method permitted for valuing the non-controlling interest)
Associated entity	equity accounting
Jointly controlled entities	proportional consolidation or equity accounting (the new Standard is likely to opt for one method only – equity).

Note that the merger accounting (pooling of interests) method is not permitted.

Is this a suitable point to question whether it is possible to reach definitive solutions for business combinations without a complete conceptual framework being developed by the IASB? It is also debateable whether users will actually understand the consolidated statements produced whatever methods of preparation are finally chosen and whether they will be presented with useful information.

EXERCISES

Suggested answers to exercises marked ✓ are to be found on the Student side of the companion website.

Suggested answers to the remaining exercises are to be found on the Instructor side of the companion website.

1 Define a subsidiary, associate and related party entity.

2 Identify how a subsidiary, associate and related party will be dealt with in the financial statements of a group.

3 Using any information you can find in respect of 'Enron' discuss the following statement: *If Enron had prepared its financial statements using IAS GAAP instead of US GAAP it would have had to account for special purpose entities differently.*

✓ **4** The following draft balance sheets relate to Largo, a public limited company, Fusion, a public limited company and Spine, a public limited company, as at 30 November 20X3.

	Largo $m	Fusion $m	Spine $m
Non-current assets			
Tangible non-current assets	329	185	64
Investment in Fusion	150		
Investment in Spine	30	50	
Investment in Micro	11		
	520	235	64
Current assets	120	58	40
	640	293	104
Capital and reserves			
Called up ordinary share capital of $1	460	110	50
Share premium account	30	20	10
Accumulated reserves	120	138	35
	610	268	95
Non-current liabilities – deferred tax	20	20	5
Current liabilities	10	5	4
	640	293	104

The following information is relevant to the preparation of the group financial statements:

(i)   Largo acquired 90% of the ordinary share capital of Fusion and 26% of the ordinary share capital of Spine on 1 December 20X2 in a share for share exchange when the accumulated reserves were Fusion $136 million and Spine $30 million. The fair value of the net assets at 1 December 20X2 was Largo $650 million, Fusion $330 million and Spine $128 million. Any increase in the consolidated fair value of the net assets over the carrying value is deemed to be attributable to property held by the companies. There had been no new issue of shares since 1 December 20X2.

(ii) In arriving at the fair value of net assets acquired at 1 December 20X2, Largo has not accounted for the deferred tax arising on the increase in the value of the property of both Fusion and Spine. The deferred tax arising on the fair valuation of the property was Fusion $15 million and Spine $9 million.

(iii) Fusion had acquired a 60% holding in Spine on 1 December 19W9 for a consideration of $50 million when the accumulated reserve of Spine was $10 million. The fair value of the net assets at that date was $80 million with the increase in fair value attributable to property held by the companies. Property is depreciated within the group at 5% per annum.

(iv) The directors of Largo wish to account for the business combination as a uniting of interests. On 1 December 20X2, before the share exchange, the market capitalisation of the companies was $644 million: Largo; $310 million: Fusion; and $310 million: Spine. The number of employees of Largo was 50% more than the combined total of the employees of both Fusion and Spine. The new Board of Directors will comprise ten directors, seven of whom will be nominated by Largo. As a result of the directors' wish to use the pooling accounting method, the cost of the investment in Fusion and Spine, shown in the financial statements of Largo, is simply the nominal value of the share capital issued. The directors feel that pooling accounting is appropriate as former institutional shareholders of Fusion own a substantial amount of equity in the new business combination with the result that

Largo cannot dominate the new business combination because of their influence over the management of the new entity.

(v) Largo purchased a 40% interest in Micro, a limited liability investment company on 1 December 20X2. The only asset of the company is a portfolio of investments which is held for trading purposes. The stake in Micro was purchased for cash for $11 million. The carrying value of the net assets of Micro on 1 December 20X2 was $18 million and their fair value was $20 million. On 30 November 20X3, the fair value of the net assets was $24 million. Largo exercises significant influence over Micro. Micro values the portfolio on a 'mark to market' basis.

(vi) Fusion has included a brand name in its tangible non-current assets at the cost of $9 million. The brand earnings can be separately identified and could be sold separately from the rest of the business. The fair value of the brand at 30 November 20X3 was $7 million. The fair value of the brand at the time of Fusion's acquisition by Largo was $9 million.

Required:

Prepare the consolidated balance sheet of the Largo Group at the year ended 30 November 20X3 in accordance with International Financial Reporting Standards, explaining the reasons why pooling of interests accounting would not be used for the business combination.

(ACCA December 2003)

5   The following statements refer to a situation where an investing entity K seeks to exert control or influence over another entity L. Assume that K is required to prepare consolidated accounts because of other investments.

(a) If K owns more than 20%, but less than 50% of the equity shares in L, then L is bound to be an associate of K.

(b) If K controls the operating and financial policies of L, then L cannot be an associate of K.

(c) If L is an associate of K, then any amounts payable by L to K are not eliminated when preparing the consolidated balance sheet of K.

Which of the statements are true?

(i)   (a) and (b) only
(ii) (b) only
(iii) (b) and (c) only
(iv) (a) and (c) only.

6   Disclosure of related party transactions in financial statements provides no useful information to users. Discuss.

7   Explain what a special purpose entity is and identify how the IASB requires these to be accounted for.

8   Hosterling purchased the following equity investments:
    On 1 October 2005: 80% of the issued share capital of Sunlee. The acquisition was through a share exchange of three shares in Hosterling for every five shares in Sunlee. The market price of Hosterling's shares at 1 October 2005 was $5 per share.

On 1 July 2006: 6 million shares in Amber paying $3 per share in cash and issuing to Amber's shareholders 6% (actual and effective rate) loan notes on the basis of $100 loan note for every 100 shares acquired.

The summarised income statements for the three companies for the year ended 30 September 2006 are:

	Hosterling $'000	Sunlee $'000	Amber $'000
Revenue	105 000	62 000	50 000
Cost of sales	(68 000)	(36 500)	(61 000)
Gross profit/(loss)	37 000	25 500	(11 000)
Other income (note (i))	400	nil	nil
Distribution costs	(4 000)	(2 000)	(4 500)
Administrative expenses	(7 500)	(7 000)	(8 500)
Finance costs	(1 200)	(900)	nil
Profit/(loss) before tax	24 700	15 600	(24 000)
Income tax (expense)/credit	(8 700)	(2 600)	4 000
Profit/(loss) for the period	16 000	13 000	(20 000)

The following information is relevant:

(i)   The other income is a dividend received from Sunlee on 31 March 2006.

(ii) The details of Sunlee's and Amber's share capital and reserves at 1 October 2005 were:

	Sunlee $'000	Amber $'000
Equity shares of $1 each	20 000	15 000
Retained earnings	18 000	35 000

(iii) A fair value exercise was carried out at the date of acquisition of Sunlee with the following results:

	Carrying amount $'000	Fair value $'000	Remaining life (straight line)
Intellectual property	18 000	22 000	still in development
Land	17 000	20 000	not applicable
Plant	30 000	35 000	five years

The fair values have not been reflected in Sunlee's financial statements.
Plant depreciation is included in cost of sales.
No fair value adjustments were required on the acquisition of Amber.

(iv) In the year ended 30 September 2006 Hosterling sold goods to Sunlee at a selling price of $18 million. Hosterling made a profit of cost plus 25% on these sales. $7.5 million (at cost to Sunlee) of these goods were still in the inventories of Sunlee at 30 September 2006.

(v)   Impairment tests for both Sunlee and Amber were conducted on 30 September 2006. They concluded that the goodwill of Sunlee should be written down by $1.6 million and, due to its losses since acquisition, the investment in Amber was worth $21.5 million.

(vi) All trading profits and losses are deemed to accrue evenly throughout the year.

Required:

(a) Calculate the goodwill arising on the acquisition of Sunlee at 1 October 2005.

(b) Calculate the carrying amount of the investment in Amber at 30 September 2006 under the equity method prior to the impairment test.

(c) Prepare the consolidated income statement for the Hosterling Group for the year ended 30 September 2006.

(ACCA 2.5 INT Dec 2006)

9 The consolidated financial statements of Dietronic, a public limited company, for the year ended 30 November 20X3 are:

Income Statement		Balance Sheet	
	$000		$000
Group operating profit	13 000	Tangible non current assets	18 500
Interest income	940	Goodwill	1 500
Profit on sale of subsidiary	100	Current assets	8 000
Profit before tax	14 040		28 000
Taxation	(5 000)	Share capital $1 ordinary Shares	5 000
Minority interests	(3 000)	Reserves	10 000
Profit after tax	6 040	Minority interest	6 000
			21 000
		Current liabilities	4 000
		Long-term debt	3 000
			28 000

There have been a number of changes in the composition of the group during the year. The changes in the group and the accounting practices used are set out below:

(i) Dietronic had created on 1 July 20X3 a new management company in which it holds 80% of the ordinary share capital with the remainder being held by an employee share ownership trust. Dietronic had invested $160 000 in the company at the balance sheet date, and had incurred $400 000 in administrative set-up costs. These costs have been treated as goodwill on consolidation as the setting up of the new company constitutes a 'notional' acquisition with the set-up costs being included in the cost of acquisition. The shares held by the employee share ownership trust were issued at a price of $2 per share and are included in the consolidated balance sheet of Dietronic at this amount within current assets. The share capital of the management company is 100 000 ordinary shares of $1.

(ii) Dietronic acquired 70% of the ordinary share capital of Dairy, a public limited company, on 31 October 20X2. On acquisition of Dairy, the financial assets of the company were reduced from the book value of $1.2 million to $600 000. This reduction came about as a result of the directors' assessment of the fair value of the investments after taking into account the 'marketability' of the portfolio. On 31 December 20X2, all the investments were sold for $1 million net of costs and the profit on disposal reported in 'interest income' in the consolidated income statement. The financial assets sold were wholly unquoted investments.

(iii) Dietronic had a 100% owned German subsidiary which was set up in 20X0 by Dietronic. The subsidiary was sold on 1 December 20X2 for €600 000 ($400 000). The subsidiary is included in the holding company's accounts at a cost of $300 000 at 30 November 20X2 and the net assets at the same date included in the consolidated financial statements were €540 000 ($360 000). All exchange differences arising on the translation of the subsidiary's financial statements have been taken to a separate exchange reserve and the cumulative total on this reserve is $40 000 debit as at 1 December 20X2 before the receipt of the dividend. Dietronic has calculated the gain on the sale of the subsidiary as follows:

	$000
Sale proceeds	400
Cost of investment	(300)
Gain on sale	100

The closing rate/net investment method was used to consolidate the financial statements of the subsidiary. During the year to 30 November 20X2, the German subsidiary had declared and accounted for a proposed dividend of €48 000. This had been included in the holding company's financial statements at the exchange rate ruling when the dividend was declared ($1 = €1.6). This dividend was received on 1 December 20X2 by Dietronic and recorded in the cash book and dividends receivable account. The shareholders of the subsidiary approved the dividend on 1 October 20X2 and the exchange rate at 1 December 20X2 was ($1 = €1.5).

(iv) On 1 June 20X3 Dietronic acquired a 25% share in a newly formed company, Diet, a public limited company. Diet has been classified as an associated company in the financial statements but no details have been shown on the face of the balance sheet or income statement as Dietronic feels that the results and net assets of the associate are immaterial. The only amount included in the financial statements as regards the associate is the purchase consideration of $2.1 million which has been added to tangible non-current assets. The fair value of the net assets of Diet at the date of acquisition was $6.8 million. The directors are confident that Diet will be successful in future years with profits in the next financial year and dividends of 10c per share forecast for five years. If the investment in Diet were to be sold at 30 November 20X3, it is anticipated that it would realise $1.8 million.

The directors are seeking advice as to the acceptability of the accounting practices used for the above changes in the composition of the group. A discount rate of 5% should be used in any calculations.

Summarised Balance Sheet at 30 November 20X3

	Diet $000	$000
Tangible non-current assets		5 000
Net current assets		2 000
		7 000
Ordinary share capital of $1		7 600
Reserves at 30 November 2002	80	
Loss for year to 30 November 2003	(680)	(600)
		7 000

Required:

(a) Discuss the nature of any amendments required to the consolidated financial statements of Dietronic in order to bring the accounting practices used for the changes in the composition of the group into line with International Financial Reporting Standards.

(b) Redraft the consolidated financial statements of Dietronic in accordance with these amendments.

(ACCA December 2003)

✓ **10** (a) **Hapsburg, a public listed company, acquired the following investments:**

- On 1 April 2003, 24 million shares in Sundial. This was by way of an immediate share exchange of two shares in Hapsburg for every three shares in Sundial plus a cash payment of $1 per Sundial share payable on 1 April 2006. The market price of Hapsburg's shares on 1 April 2003 was $2 each.

- On 1 October 2003, 6 million shares in Aspen paying an immediate $2.50 in cash for each share.

Based on Hapsburg's cost of capital (taken as 10% per annum), $1 receivable in three years' time can be taken to have a present value of $0.75.

Hapsburg has not yet recorded the acquisition of Sundial but it has recorded the investment in Aspen.

The summarised balance sheets at 31 March 2004 are:

	Hapsburg $000	Hapsburg $000	Sundial $000	Sundial $000	Aspen $000	Aspen $000
Non-current assets						
Property, plant and equipment		41 000		34 800		37 700
Investments		15 000		3 000		nil
		56 000		37 800		37 700
Current assets						
Inventory	9 900		4 800		7 900	
Trade and other receivables	13 600		8 600		14 400	
Cash	1 200	24 700	3 800	17 200	nil	22 300
Total assets		80 700		55 000		60 000
Equity and liabilities						
Capital and reserves						
Ordinary shares $1 each		20 000		30 000		20 000
Reserves:						
Share premium	8 000		2 000		nil	
Accumulated profits	10 600	18 600	8 500	10 500	8 000	8 000
		38 600		40 500		28 000
Non-current liabilities						
10% loan note		16 000		4 200		12 000
Current liabilities						
Trade and other payables	16 500		6 900		13 600	
Bank overdraft	nil		nil		4 500	
Taxation	9 600	26 100	3 400	10 300	1 900	20 000
Total equity and liabilities		80 700		55 000		60 000

The following information is relevant:

(i) Below is a summary of the results of a fair value exercise Sundial carried out at the date of acquisition:

Asset	Carrying value at acquisition $000	Fair value at acquisition $000	Notes
Plant	10 000	15 000	remaining life at acquisition four years
Investments	3 000	4 500	no change in value since acquisition

The book values of the net assets of Aspen at the date of acquisition were considered to be a reasonable approximation to their fair values.

(ii) The profits of Sundial and Aspen for the year to 31 March 20X4, as reported in their entity financial statements, were $4.5 million and $6 million respectively. No dividends have been paid by any of the companies during the year. All profits are deemed to accrue evenly throughout the year.

(iii) In January 20X4 Aspen sold goods to Hapsburg at a selling price of $4 million. These goods had cost Aspen $2.4 million.
Hapsburg had $2.5 million (at cost to Hapsburg) of these goods still in inventory at 31 March 20X4.

(iv) All depreciation is charged on a straight line basis.

Required:
Prepare the consolidated balance sheet of Hapsburg as at 31 March 20X4 in accordance with current IASs.

(b) Some commentators have criticised the use of equity accounting on the basis that it can be used as a form of off-balance sheet financing.

Required:
Explain the reasoning behind the use of equity accounting and discuss the above comment.

(ACCA June 2004)

11 Jay, a public limited company, has acquired the following shareholdings in Gee and Hem, both public limited companies.

Date of acquisition	Holding acquired	Fair value of net assets $m	Purchase consideration $m
Gee			
1 June 2003	30%	40	15
1 June 2004	50%	50	30
Hem			
1 June 2004	25%	32	12

The following balance sheets relate to Jay, Gee and Hem at 31 May 2005:

	Jay $m	Gee $m	Hem $m
Tangible non-current assets	300	40	30
Investment in Gee	48		
Investment in Hem	22		
Current assets	100	20	15
Total assets	470	60	45
Share capital of $1	100	10	6
Share premium account	50	20	14
Revaluation reserve	15		
Retained earnings	135	16	10
Total equity	300	46	30
Non-current liabilities	60	4	3
Current liabilities	110	10	12
Total equity and liabilities	470	60	45

The following information is relevant to the preparation of the group financial statements of the Jay Group:

(a) Gee and Hem have not issued any new share capital since the acquisition of the shareholdings by Jay. The excess of the fair value of the net assets of Gee and Hem over their carrying amounts at the dates of acquisition is due to an increase in the value of Gee's non-depreciable land of $10 million at 1 June 2003 and a further increase of $4 million at 1 June 2004, and Hem's non-depreciable land of $6 million at 1 June 2004. There has been no change in the value of non-depreciable land since 1 June 2004. Before obtaining control of Gee, Jay did not have significant influence over Gee but has significant influence over Hem. Jay has accounted for the investment in Gee at market value with changes in value being recorded in profit or loss. The market price of the shares of Gee at 31 May 2005 had risen to $6 per share as there was speculation regarding a takeover bid.

(b) On 1 June 2004, Jay sold goods costing $13 million to Gee for $19 million. Gee has used the goods in constructing a machine which began service on 1 December 2004. Additionally, on 31 May 2005, Jay purchased a portfolio of investments from Hem at a cost of $10 million on which Hem had made a profit of $2 million. These investments have been incorrectly included in Jay's balance sheet under the heading 'Investment in Hem'.

(c) Jay sold some machinery with a carrying value of $5 million on 28 February 2005 for $8 million. The terms of the contract, which was legally binding from 28 February 2005, was that the purchaser would pay an initial deposit of $2 million followed by two instalments of $3.5 million (including total interest of $1 million) payable on 31 May 2005 and 2006. The purchaser was in financial difficulties at the year-end and subsequently went into liquidation on 10 June 2005. No payment is expected from the liquidator. The deposit had been received on 28 February 2005 but the first instalment was not received. The terms of the agreement were such that Jay maintained title to the machinery until the first instalment was paid. The machinery was still physically held by Jay and the machinery had been treated as sold in the financial statements. The amount outstanding of $6 million is included in current assets and no interest has been accrued in the financial statements.

(d) Gee is considered to be a cash-generating unit in its own right. At 31 May 2005, Jay has determined that the recoverable amount of Gee is $64 million and that of Hem is $68 million.

(e) Group policy is to depreciate plant and equipment on the reducing balance basis over ten years. Depreciation is calculated on a time-apportionment basis.

(f) There are no inter-company amounts outstanding at 31 May 2005.

Required:

Prepare the consolidated balance sheet of the Jay Group as at 31 May 2005 in accordance with International Financial Reporting Standards.

(ACCA 3.5int June 2005)

12 On 1 June 2005, Egin, a public limited company, was formed out of the reorganisation of a group of companies with foreign operations. The directors require advice on the disclosure of related party information but are reluctant to disclose information as they feel that such transactions are a normal feature of business and need not be disclosed.

Under the new group structure, Egin owns 80% of Briars, 60% of Doye, and 30% of Eye. Egin exercises significant influence over Eye. The directors of Egin are also directors of Briars and Doye but only one director of Egin sits on the management board of Eye. The management board of Eye comprises five directors. Originally the group comprised five companies but the fifth company, Tang, which was a 70% subsidiary of Egin, was sold on 31 January 2006. There were no transactions between Tang and the Egin Group during the year to 31 May 2006. 30% of the shares of Egin are owned by another company, Atomic, which exerts significant influence over Egin. The remaining 40% of the shares of Doye are owned by Spade.

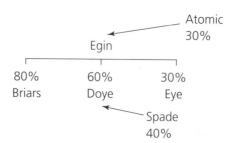

During the current financial year to 31 May 2006, Doye has sold a significant amount of plant and equipment to Spade at the normal selling price for such items. The directors of Egin have proposed that where related party relationships are determined and sales are at normal selling price, any disclosures will state that prices charged to related parties are made on an arm's-length basis.

The directors are unsure how to treat certain transactions relating to their foreign subsidiary, Briars. Egin purchased 80% of the ordinary share capital of Briars on 1 June 2005 for €50 million when its net assets were fair valued at €45 million. At 31 May 2006, it is established that goodwill is impaired by €3 million. Additionally, at the date of acquisition, Egin had made an interest free loan to Briars of $10 million. The loan is to be repaid on 31 May 2007. An equivalent loan would normally carry an interest rate of 6% taking into account Briars' credit rating. The exchange rates were as follows:

	Euros to $
1 June 2005	2
31 May 2006	2.5
Average rate of year	2.3

Financial liabilities of the Group are normally measured at amortised cost.

One of the directors of Briars, who is not on the management board of Egin, owns the whole of the share capital of a company, Blue, that sells goods at market price to Briars. The director is in charge of the production at Briars and also acts as a consultant to the management board of the group.

Required:

(i) Discuss why it is important to disclose related party transactions, explaining the criteria which determine a related party relationship.

(ii) Describe the nature of any related party relationships and transactions which exist:

- within the Egin Group including Tang
- between Spade and the Egin Group
- between Atomic and the Egin Group

commenting on whether transactions should be described as being at 'arm's length'.

(ACCA 3.5int June 2006)

FOREIGN CURRENCY TRANSLATION

29

OBJECTIVES After studying this chapter you should be able to:

- explain the necessity for foreign currency conversion and translation

- describe the IAS regulations in respect of foreign currency transactions for individual entities

- appraise the position where foreign currency investments and borrowings are matched

- critically appraise the IAS regulations in respect of translation of the accounts of foreign branches and subsidiaries, etc.

- translate accounts of foreign entities

- describe the disclosure requirements of IAS regulations in respect of foreign currency translation.

INTRODUCTION

Business is increasingly international. Whenever a business has any dealings abroad, it will be involved in 'foreign' currencies. Since an entity generally keeps its accounting records and prepares its accounting reports in its own 'home' currency, figures expressed in foreign money units need to be re-expressed in 'home' units or whatever the reporting currency is. If foreign currency exchange rates remain absolutely constant, i.e. if the value of one currency in terms of the other does not change, then no difficulties arise. But this is rarely the case and, as we all know, exchange rates can and do fluctuate very considerably over relatively short periods of time.

CURRENCY CONVERSION

Currency conversion is required when a foreign currency transaction is completed within an accounting period. A transaction, foreign or otherwise, can be regarded as comprising two events:

- the purchase or sale of an asset or the incurring of an expense or item of income
- the receipt or payment of monies for these assets, expenses or items of income.

These events need to be recorded in an entity's books as they occur (see Activity 29.1).

CURRENCY TRANSLATION

Activity 29.1 involved a transaction that was completed by the year-end but we need to consider how to deal with foreign transactions that are not completed by the year-end. (See Activity 29.2.)

ACTIVITY 29.1

A UK entity sells goods to a Swiss entity on 1 May 20X2 for SWFr 750 000. Payment is received on 1 August 20X2.

Exchange rate 1 May 20X2 is £1 = SWFr3.5544.
1 August 20X2 is £1 = SWFr3.7081.

The year end for the entity is 30 September 20X2 and the reporting currency is sterling. Record this transaction in the entity's books and name the balance on the accounts receivable account.

Activity feedback
Remembering the transaction comprises two events, we need to record the sale of goods immediately, but we must record the event in £s not SWFrs.

Sales account	
	1.5.X2 acc rec, 211 006

Accounts receivable	
1.5.X2 sales 211 006	

750 000/3.5544 (exchange rate 1.5.X2) = 211 006. When payment is received on 1 August X2 it will be in the form of SWFr750 000 which we must convert to sterling at the exchange rate at the time = 750 000/3.7081 = £202 260.
Event will be recorded as:

	£	£
Dr. Cash	202 260	
Cr. Accounts receivable		202 260

Thus, there will be a balance on the accounts receivable account of £8746, which is obviously a loss on exchange which will need to be reported in the income statement for ordinary activities.

Similarly, if the exchange rate had decreased from May to August a profit on exchange would have occurred which again would be reported as profit on ordinary activities.

ACTIVITY 29.2

Let us assume in Activity 29.1 that the entity's year-end is 30 June 20X2 when the exchange rate is £1 = SWFr3.6573. Record this transaction in the entity's books.

Activity feedback

The initial sale will be recorded as before but at the year-end 30 June 20X2 the accounts receivable account will show a balance of £211 006. This balance is not correct because if the debt was paid at this date we would receive SWFr750 000 = 205 069 which is the value of the debt at 30 June 20X2. Thus we translate the accounts receivable account at the year-end at the exchange rate ruling, which is known as the spot rate, at a given date:

Accounts receivable

1.5.X2 sales	211 006	30.6.X2 Income statement	5 937
		loss on exchange	
		30.6.X2	
		balance c/d	205 069
	211 006		211 006
1.7.X2 balance b/d	205 069	1.8.X2 cash	202 260
		30.6.X3 IS loss on exchange	2 809

The balancing figure of £5937 is the loss on exchange identified as at 30 June X2, which will be debited to the income statement. When the debt is finally paid on 1 August 20X2 a further loss of £2809 is identified for the next year. Notice the total loss of £8746 is now split over the two years.

The currency translation follows the idea of prudence as we are taking account of the loss as soon as we are aware of it. However, what would we have done if on 30 June 20X2 the exchange rate were £1 = SWFr3.4973?

This time at the year-end the debtor would translate as 750 000/3.4973 = £214 451 giving a profit on exchange of £3445 and on 1 August 20X2 when the debt is finally settled a loss of £12 191. The gain of £3445 is an unrealised gain and prudence might suggest that we should not recognise this gain.

Let us see what IAS 21 says on this issue.

IAS 21 REQUIREMENTS FOR INDIVIDUAL ENTITY'S FOREIGN CURRENCY TRANSACTIONS

The Standard was issued in 1983, revised in 1993 and revised again under the improvement project 2004. IAS 21 states in para. 28:

> Exchange differences arising on the settlement of monetary items or on translating monetary items at rates different from those at which they were translated on initial recognition during the period, or in previous financial statements, should be recognised in profit or loss in the period in which they arise, except as described in para. 32.

Further, para. 29 goes on to state:

> When monetary items arise from a foreign currency transaction and there is a change in the exchange rate between the transaction date and the date of settlement, an exchange difference results. When the transaction is settled within the same accounting period as that in which it occurred, all the exchange difference is recognised in that period. However, when the transaction is settled in a subsequent accounting period, the exchange difference recognised in each period up to the period of settlement is determined by the change in exchange rates during each period.

ACTIVITY 29.3

An entity, Axel, purchases an asset for €10 000 from a foreign entity on 1.3.X2 when the exchange rate between the two currencies involved was 1FC = €2. The functional currency of Axel is FCs. At the balance sheet date of Axel, 30.6.X2, the exchange rate is 1FC = €1. Show the entries by Axel to record this transaction initially and those required at the balance sheet date.

Activity feedback

Assets in FC				Accounts payable in FC			
1.3.X2 Purchases	5 000	30.6.X2		30.6.X2		1.3.X2 Purchase	5 000
		Balance c/d	5 000	Balance c/d	10 000	Exchange difference	5 000
	5 000		5 000		10 000		10 000
30.6.X2						1.7.X2 Balance b/d	10 000
Balance b/d	5 000						

Thus, the IAS is telling us to recognise an unrealised gain in the accounts (in the activity this was £3445). This treatment can be justified on the grounds that:

- where exchange gains arise on short-term monetary items their ultimate cash realisation can normally be assessed with reasonable certainty and they are therefore realised in accordance with realisation conventions
- it provides symmetry with losses.

In Activity 29.3 only the monetary item, accounts payable, has been reported using the closing rate at the balance sheet date. Under the requirements of IAS 21 only foreign currency monetary items should be reported using closing rate; non-monetary items which are carried at historical cost denominated in a foreign currency should be reported using the exchange rate at the date of acquisition or, if the fair value is used, the exchange rate prevalent when the fair value was determined.

Reporting currency

The improvement project to IAS 21 removed the notion of 'reporting currency' and replaced it with two further definitions of currency.

Functional currency is the currency of the primary economic environment in which the entity operates.

Presentation currency is the currency in which the financial statements are presented.

When determining its functional currency an entity has to consider the following in accordance with IAS 21, paras 9–12:

The primary economic environment in which an entity operates is normally the one in which it primarily generates and expends cash. An entity considers the following factors in determining its functional currency:

(a) the currency:

   (i) that mainly influences sales prices for goods and services; and

   (ii) of the country whose competitive forces and regulations mainly determine the sales prices of its goods and services;

(b) the currency that mainly influences labour, material and other costs of providing goods or services.

The following factors may also provide evidence of an entity's functional currency:

- the currency in which funds from financing activities are generated
- the currency in which receipts from operating activities are usually retained.

The following additional factors are considered in determining the functional currency of a foreign operation, and whether its functional currency is the same as that of the reporting entity:

- Whether the activities of the foreign operation are carried out as an extension of the reporting entity, rather than being carried out with a significant degree of autonomy. An example of the former is when the foreign operation only sells goods imported from the reporting entity and remits the proceeds to it. An example of the latter is when the operation accumulates cash and other monetary items, incurs expenses, generates income and arranges borrowings, all substantially in its local currency.
- Whether transactions with the reporting entity are a high or low proportion of the foreign operation's activities.
- Whether cash flows from the activities of the foreign operation directly affect the cash flows of the reporting entity and are readily available for remittance to it.
- Whether cash flows from the activities of the foreign operation are sufficient to service existing and normally expected debt obligations without funds being made available by the reporting entity.

When these indicators are mixed and the functional currency is not obvious, management uses its judgement to determine the functional currency that most faithfully represents the economic effects of the underlying transactions, events and conditions.

Once determined the functional currency is not changed unless the factors just outlined change.

We provide below some examples where determination of an entity's functional currency is less than apparent.

Example 29.1

For each of the following determine the functional currency:

1 An entity operating in France owns several buildings in Paris that are rented to foreign companies, mostly US companies. The lease contracts are determined in US dollars and payment can be made in either US dollars or euros.

   We have a mixed situation here and therefore need to consider the factors outlined in IAS 21, paras 9–12:

   - The local circumstances in Paris determine the rental yields thus indicating the euro as functional currency.
   - Lease payments denominated and could be paid in US dollars indicates the dollar as the functional currency.
   - Presumably labour and other expenses are paid in euros indicating the euro as the functional currency.

Overall it is the euro that would appear to most faithfully represent the economic effects of the entity and therefore should be taken as the functional currency.

2 A US entity has a foreign subsidiary located in Greece. The Greek subsidiary imports a product manufactured by its parent, paying in dollars, which it sells throughout Greece with selling prices denominated in euros and determined primarily by local competition. The subsidiary's long-term financing is primarily in the form of dollar loans from its parent and distribution of its profits is under parental control. Proceeds of the subsidiary are remitted to the parent on a regular basis.

Again we have a mixed situation and need to consider the factors outlined in IAS 21, paras 9–12:

- The currency mainly influencing sales prices is the euro.
- The currency mainly influencing labour and other expenses is again presumably the euro except that purchases of inventory are made in US dollars.

ACTIVITY 29.4

The balance sheet of Zhou Ltd at 31.12.X4 is as follows:

	FCs	FCs
Share capital		300
Retained profits		100
		400
Equipment at cost	350	
less Depreciation	50	300
Inventory	80	
Net monetary current assets	60	140
Long-term loans		(40)
		400

The presentation currency for Zhou Ltd. is Crowns (CRs) and as at:

	FCs to CRs
1 January X4	5
Average for the year to 31 December X4	4.5
Average for closing inventory acquisition	4.6
31 December X4	4.2

Income statement for the year ended 31.12.X4 is as follows:

	FCs
Sales	600
less Cost of sales	400
Gross profit	200
less Depreciation	(50)
Less other expenses	(50)
	100

Translate the financial statements of Zhou Ltd into the presentation currency from the functional currency and show clearly where any exchange difference is recognised.

Activity feedback

Balance sheet as at 31.12.X4

	Rate	CRs	CRs
Share capital	5	60	
Retained profits		21.4	
Exchange difference		13.8	95.2
Equipment at cost	4.2	83.3	
Depreciation	4.2	11.9	71.4
Inventory	4.2	19	
Net monetary current assets	4.2	14.3	
Long-term loans	4.2	(9.5)	23.8
			95.2

Income statement for the year ended 31.12.X4:

Sales	4.5		133.3
less Cost of sales	4.5		88.9
Gross profit			44.4
Depreciation	4.2	11.9	
Other expenses		11.1	23
			21.4

The exchange difference is the amount required to balance the statements.

- The currency in which funds from financing activities are generated is the dollar and the subsidiary has little autonomy, merely acting as an agent in Greece for the parent.

On balance the functional currency is the dollar.

An entity entering into a foreign currency transaction records that transaction initially by applying to the foreign currency amount the spot exchange rate between the functional currency and the foreign currency at the date of the transaction. This is what we did in Activity 29.3.

As far as preparation of financial statements is concerned an entity can present them in any currency. This means that where the functional and presentation currency differ then a further translation of results and financial position into the presentational currency is required. This commonly occurs where individual entities within a group who all have different functional currencies have to present in the group currency.

The translation from functional to presentation currency occurs as follows:

1 assets and liabilities for each balance sheet presented shall be translated at the closing rate at the date of that balance sheet

2 income and expenses for each income statement shall be translated at exchange rates at the date of the transactions

3 all resulting exchange differences shall be recognised as a separate component of equity.

Look at Activity 29.4 on the previous page.

Loans

IAS 21 defines monetary items as 'units of currency held and assets and liabilities to be received or paid in fixed or determinable number of units of currency' (para. 7). Thus a loan will be translated as any other monetary item at closing rate and the exchange gain or loss credited or charged to income. We might question the rationale for taking the unrealised exchange gain on the loan at the balance sheet date to the income statement here but it at least provides consistent symmetrical treatment with the loss which is equally unrealised.

Hedge accounting or investments matched by borrowings

An entity that has made a foreign entity investment is exposed to an exchange risk on that investment. However, it is possible for the investing entity to protect itself by raising loans in a foreign country denominated in the foreign currency and using the money from these borrowings to make the investment. From the point of view of the home (investing) entity it has:

- an asset, exposed to an exchange risk
- a liability also exposed to an exchange risk.

Since the asset and liability, in principal equal in amount, are in effect part of one overall transaction and since the exchange risks are equal and opposite, the effects of exchange rate movements on these items should simply be cancelled out.

Normally, however, a foreign currency investment, a long-term non-monetary item, would not be translated in the accounts at the year-end but the loan, a long-term monetary item, would be translated. IAS 21 allows us to classify as equity exchange differences arising on a foreign currency liability where that liability is used as a 'hedge'. Once the investment is disposed of then the exchange difference on the loan will be recognised as income or expense.

Interestingly, IAS 21 does not deal with hedge accounting for foreign currency items in much detail and we have to refer to IAS 39 for further guidance. The criteria in IAS 39 used to identify a hedge are as follows:

- At the inception of the hedge there is a formal document to support classification as a hedge.
- The hedge is expected to be highly effective.
- A forecasted transaction which is the subject of the hedge must be highly probable.
- The effectiveness of the hedge can be reliably measured.
- The hedge was assessed on an ongoing basis and determined actually to have been highly effective throughout the financial reporting period.

ACTIVITY 29.5

An entity whose year-end is 31 March, and which prepares its accounts in £s sterling, takes out two loans on 1 August, one for 5 000 000 X FCs and one for 200 000 Z FCs when the exchange rates were £1 = 180 X FCs = X FCs10. The Z FCs loan is used to make an equity investment of $30 000; £1 = $1.60. At the same time another equity investment is the purchase of 100 000 Australian dollars (A$). £1 = A$1.9. How would this be shown in the entity's books at the year-end when £1 = 186 X FCs = Z FCs 9.7 = $1.5 = A$1.95 given the reporting currency is £?

Activity feedback

Initially, when the loans and investments are taken up they will need to be recorded in the books in £s as follows:

Loan X FCs	
	1/8 cash 27 778
	(5 000 000/180)

Investment $	
1/8 cash 18 750	
(30 000/1.6)	

Loan Z FCs	
	1/8 cash 20 000
	(200 000/10)

Investment A$	
1/8 cash 52 632	
(100 000/1.9)	

Long-term monetary items, i.e. X FCs loan and Z FCs loan will be translated at year-end exchange rates, but can the investments be translated at year-end? The answer is generally no. In this case, however, it is possible that the dollar investment is hedged with the Z FC loan therefore the loss on this loan avoids the income statement and is taken directly to equity.

Loan X FCs	
31/3 gain IS 896	1/8 cash 27 778
31/3 bal c/d 26 882	

Z FCs	
31/3bal.c/d 20 619	1/8 cash 20 000
	31/3 loss equity reserves 619

Note that in Activity 29.5 we assume there is no need for the hedged loan and investment to be in the same currency. It is perfectly clear that where investments and loans are in the same currency the loss on one will offset the gain on the other due to the change in currency rate. However, the logic of hedging using different currencies is rather unclear, as you cannot be certain the risk will be covered. It is interesting to note, in Activity 29.5, that if the Z FC loan and dollar investment had not been treated as hedged then the income statement would have borne a further loss of £619!

Summary of individual entity transactions

1 Settled transactions: gain or loss is obviously realised and reflected in cash flows.

2 Unsettled transactions: short-term monetary items translate at year-end exchange rate and gain or loss, although unrealised, is taken to income statement, as it is reasonably certain.

3 Long-term monetary items treated the same as short term.

4 If a liability forms a hedge to a net investment then the exchange difference on the liability is classified as equity.

TRANSLATION METHODS FOR FINANCIAL STATEMENTS OF FOREIGN OPERATIONS

When translating any particular item we can take two basic possible views:

1 We can use the exchange rate ruling when the item was created (historic rate).

2 We can use the exchange rate ruling when the item is being reported (current or closing rate).

Since we can apply this choice to each item in the financial statements one at a time, it is clear that many different combinations are possible. Four that have been suggested are now outlined.

Single rate (closing rate)

This is based on the idea that the holding entity has a net investment in the foreign operation and that what is at risk from currency fluctuations is this net financial investment. All assets, liabilities, revenues and expenses will be translated at the closing (balance sheet date) rate. Exchange differences will arise if the closing rate differs from the previous year's closing rate or from the date when the transaction occurred.

Mixed rate (current/non-current)

Here, current assets and liabilities would be translated at the closing rate, whereas fixed assets and non-current liabilities would be translated at the rate ruling when the item was established (i.e. current items are translated at current rates and fixed items are translated at fixed rates).

Mixed rate (monetary/non-monetary)

This proposal would translate monetary assets and liabilities at the closing rate and all non-monetary assets and liabilities at the rate ruling when the item was established. There is an analogy here with the arguments for CPP accounting. Monetary items are automatically expressed in current monetary units, so use the current rate for them and non-monetary items are expressed in out-of-date monetary units, so use the out-of-date rate for them.

Mixed rate (temporal)

This is based on the idea that the foreign operations are simply a part of the group that is the reporting entity. Some of the individual assets and liabilities of the group just 'happen' to be abroad. The valuation basis used to value the assets and liabilities determines the appropriate exchange rate. Those assets recorded on a HC basis would be translated at the historic rate – the rate ruling when the item was established. Assets recorded on a current value basis would be translated at the current (closing) rate. Revenues and expenses should theoretically be translated at the rate ruling on the date when the amount shown in the accounts was established, i.e. assuming an even spread of trading at the average rate for the year.

It is important to avoid the assumption that the temporal method means using historic exchange rates. The words temporal and historic are sometimes, quite wrongly, used interchangeably in this context. 'Temporal' means literally 'at the time', i.e. consistent with the underlying valuation basis. So the temporal method does mean using historic exchange rates when applied to HC accounts. But the temporal method means using current exchange rates when applied to current value accounts. This would broadly reduce the temporal method to the single rate method.

There has been controversy over the appropriate method to use. The two favoured possibilities are the closing rate method and the temporal method but both the UK and the US have had changes of heart over the years as to which method should be used when.

IAS 21 RULES FOR TRANSLATION OF FINANCIAL STATEMENTS OF FOREIGN OPERATIONS

IAS 21 requires each entity to determine its functional currency and to then translate its foreign currency items into the functional currency using the temporal method. Exchange differences arising are recognised in the profit or loss of the period. Where an entity has to translate from its functional currency to a presentation currency, for example where consolidated financial statements are required for a group containing individual entities using functional currencies different to the presentation currency, then essentially the closing rate method is used.

However, the closing rate method requires that income and expenses are translated at the dates of transactions and this is usually approximated by an average rate for the period and exchange gains and losses are classified as equity until the disposal of the net investment. There is an exception to this and that is when the foreign entity operates in a hyperinflationary economy when IAS 29 applies.

Tables 29.1 and 29.2 provide a useful summary of both methods.

TABLE 29.1	Financial statements of a foreign operation translated into presentation currency
Item	**Translation rate**
All assets and liabilities whether monetary or non-monetary	Closing rate
Income and expense items	Rate at date of transaction
Exchange difference	Equity

TABLE 29.2	Financial statements of a foreign operation translated into functional currency
Item	**Translation rate**
Cost and depreciation of property, plant and equipment and intangible assets	Rate at date of acquisition or fair valuation date
Inventories	Rate when cost incurred
Monetary items	Closing rate
Income and expense items	Rate at date of transaction or average rate for period if rates do not fluctuate significantly
Exchange difference	Income statement

Activity 29.6 shows the differences between the two methods.

Try Activity 29.7 to test your understanding of foreign currency translation and the requirements of IAS 21.

Some other issues

Disposal of a foreign entity is dealt with in accordance with para. 48 of IAS 21:

> On the disposal of a foreign operation, the cumulative amount of the exchange differences deferred in the separate component of equity relating to that foreign operation should be recognised in profit or loss when the gain or loss on disposal is recognised.

Presumably now we can assume the gain or loss is realised and therefore treated as other realised gains or losses.

IAS 21 does allow a change in an entity's functional currency. However, this can only happen where there is a change in the underlying transaction events and conditions. This could occur when there is a change in the currency that mainly influences the sale prices of goods and services. A good example of this is when European countries adopt the euro. Paragraph 37 of IAS 21 tells us to account for the change in the functional currency prospectively as follows:

> An entity translates all items into the new functional currency using the exchange rate at the date of the change. The resulting translated amounts for non-monetary items are treated as their historical cost. Exchange differences arising from the translation of a foreign operation previously classified in equity in accordance with paragraphs 32 and 39(c) are not recognised in profit or loss until the disposal of the operation.

ACTIVITY 29.6

Home established a 100% ownership of Away on 1 January year 8 by subscribing to €25 000 of shares in cash when the exchange rate was 12 'tickets' to the €. Away raised a long-term loan of 100 000 tickets locally on 1 January year 8 and immediately purchased equipment costing 350 000 tickets, which was expected to last ten years with no residual value. It was to be depreciated under the straight line method. The accounts of Away in the foreign currency for year 8 follow, during which the relevant exchange rates were:

	Tickets to €
1 January	12
Average for year	11
Average for period in which closing inventory acquired	10.5
31 December	10

Income statement for year 8

	Tickets
Sales	450 000
less Cost of sales	(360 000)

Gross profit	90 000
less Depreciation	(35 000)
Other expenses	(15 000)
Net profit	40 000

Balance sheet as at 31 December year 8

Share capital	300 000
Retained profits	40 000
	340 000
Equipment at cost	350 000
less Depreciation	35 000
	315 000
Inventory	105 000
Net monetary current assets	20 000
less Long-term loans	(100 000)
	340 000

Translate the accounts for the foreign operation using both the closing rate and temporal method and identify what to do with the exchange differences.

Activity feedback

Income statement for year 8	Rate	Closing	Temporal	Rate
Sales	11	40 909	40 909	11
less Cost of sales	11	32 727	32 727	11
Gross profit		8 182	8 182	
less Depreciation	10	(3 500)	(2 917)	12
Other expenses	11	(1 364)	(1 364)	11
Net profit		3 318	3 901	

Balance sheet as at 31 December year 8				
Share capital		25 000	25 000	
Retained profits		3 318	3 901	
		28 318	28 901	
Equipment at cost	10	35 000	29 167	12
less Depreciation	10	3 500	2 917	12
		31 500	26 250	
Inventory	10	10 500	10 000	10.5
Net monetary current assets	10	2 000	2 000	10
less Long-term loans	10	(10 000)	(10 000)	10
		34 000	28 250	
Exchange difference		(5 682)	651	
		28 318	28 901	

ACTIVITY 29.6 (Continued)

TABLE 29.3 Retranslation at closing rate

Item	Closing rate	Opening rate	Difference
Opening fixed assets	350 000/10	350 000/12	£5 834 credit
Opening net current assets	50 000/10	50 000/12	£ 833 credit
Opening long-term loans	100 000/10	100 000/12	£1 667 debit
Net profit	40 000/10 = 4 000	40 000/average = 3 318	£ 682 credit

The share capital figure in the closing rate method is translated at the original rate to highlight the exchange differences.

The exchange difference, a loss, of €651 under the temporal method should be charged to the income statement for the current year. Had it been a gain it would have been credited to the income statement in accordance with IAS 21. You might question whether this is prudent but it is treating the exchange differences of the foreign entity as if they were the exchange differences of the reporting entity.

Under the closing rate method, the issue is more complex. Differences have arisen in respect of each type of balance sheet item because the opening balances (representing the net investment in the overseas subsidiary by the holding company) have been retranslated back into sterling at the closing rate. The total gain of €5682 can be broken down as in Table 29.3.

IAS 21 requires that this gain is taken to equity. You could argue that the gain of €833 on the short-term mon-

etary items be taken to income statement and only the long-term items to equity. The allocation of these exchange differences to either equity or income certainly has an effect on the information provided to users as can be seen from the example and the final balance sheets.

	Closing rate – foreign entity	Temporal method – integral
Share capital	25 000	25 000
Equity reserves	5 682	
	30 682	
Retained profits	3 318	3 250
Net assets	34 000	28 250

Note the difference in the net assets, once translated, of the foreign entity.

Disclosure requirements

We refer you to paras 51–57 of the Standard for these, but the following from the Illustrative Corporate Consolidated Financial Statements 2004 [Footsy & Co. Group] published by Pricewaterhouse Coopers illustrates the disclosure required.

2.4 Foreign currency translation

(a) *Functional and presentation currency*
Items included in the financial statements of each of the Group's entities are measured using the currency of the primary economic environment in which the entity operates ('the functional currency'). The consolidated financial statements are presented in euros, which is the Company's functional and presentation currency.

(b) *Transactions and balances*
Foreign currency transactions are translated into the functional currency using the exchange rates prevailing at the dates of the transactions. Foreign

exchange gains and losses resulting from the settlement of such transactions and from the translation at year-end exchange rates of monetary assets and liabilities denominated in foreign currencies are recognised in the income statement, except when deferred in equity as qualifying cash flow hedges and qualifying net investment hedges.

Translation differences on non-monetary items, such as equities held at fair value through profit or loss, are reported as part of the fair value gain or loss. Translation differences on non-monetary items, such as equities classified as available-for-sale financial assets, are included in the fair value reserve in equity.

ACTIVITY 29.7

The final accounts for the year to 31 March year 5 of Otters, an overseas wholly owned subsidiary of Seals of London, follow.

The relevant exchange rates of the two currencies were:

Date	Tails to €s
1 January year 1	16.00 when shares issued
1 April year 1	16.20 when property bought
1 September year 3	18.00 when loans issued
31 March year 4	19.80
Average for January – March year 4	19.70 when opening inventory bought
31 March year 5	20.10
Average for January – March year 5	20.05 when closing inventory bought
Average for year to 31 March year 5	20.00

Retained profits from previous years were €10 240 under temporal and €9950 under closing rate. Paid dividends were 150 000 tails, €7394 as received in London.

Income statement for year to 31 March year 5

Sales		10 000
less Cost of sales		
Opening inventory	1 800	
Purchases	7 700	
	9 500	
less Closing inventory	2 000	7 500
Gross profit		2 500
less Wages and salaries	600	

Sundry expenses	380	
Property depreciation	100	
Equipment depreciation	100	
Loan interest	120	1 300
Net profit		1 200
Tax		600
		600
Retained profits previous years		200
		800

Balance sheet as at 31 March year 5

Ordinary shares		3 000
Retained profits		650
		3 650
8% loans		1 500
Current liabilities		
Accounts payable	2 000	
Tax	600	2 600
		7 750
Property	2 500	
Depreciation	500	2 000
Plant and equipment	500	
Depreciation	250	250
Current assets		
Inventory	2 000	
Accounts receivable	2 000	
Cash	1 500	5 500
		7 750

Translate the accounts of Otters using both the closing rate and temporal rate. Identify the exchange gain or loss and its accounting treatment according to IAS 21.

ACTIVITY 29.7   (Continued)

Activity feedback

Income statement for year to 31 March year 5:

		Temporal method			Closing rate	
		€	€		€	€
Sales	20.		500 000	20		500 000
less Cost of sales						
Opening inventory	19.7	91 371		19.7	91 371	
Purchases	20	385 000		20	385 000	
		476 371			476 371	
Closing inventory	20.05	99 751	376 620	20.05	99 751	376 620
Gross profit			123 380			123 380
Wages and salaries	20	30 000		20	30 000	
Sundry expenses	20	19 000		20	19 000	
Property depreciation	16.2	6 173		20	4 975	
Equipment depreciation	18	5 556		20	4 975	
Loan interest	20	6 000	66 729	20	6 000	64 950
Net profit			56 651			58 430
Tax	20		30 000	20		30 000
			26 651			28 430
Profits previous years	Given		10 240	Given		9 950
			36 891			38 380
Dividends	Actual		7 394	Actual		7 394
			29 497			30 986
Balance sheet as at 31 March year 5						
Shares	16		187 500	16		187 500
Exchange difference	Balancing figure					150 605
					(36 895)	
Retained profits	Above	29 497		Above		30 986
Exchange difference	Balancing figure	(9 751)	19 746			
			207 246			
8% loan	20.1		74 627	20.1		74 627
Current liabilities						
Accounts payable	20.1	99 502		20.1	99 502	
Tax	20.1	29 851	129 353	20.1	29 851	129 353
			411 226			385 571
Property	16.2	154 321		20.1	124 378	
Depreciation	16.2	30 864	123 457	20.1	24 876	99 502
Equipment	18	27 778		20.1	24 876	
Depreciation	18	13 889	13 889	20.1	12 438	12 438
Current assets						
Inventory	20.05	99 751		20.1	99 502	
Accounts receivable	20.1	99 502		20.1	99 502	
Cash	20.1	74 627	273 880	20.1	74 627	273 631
			411 226			385 571

Under the temporal method the loss of €9751 on exchange is charged to profits for the year and will need to be shown within the income statement as an operating expense, i.e. profits for the year will only be €16 900.

Under the closing method the exchange loss of €36 895 is taken to equity not profit.

The figures for incorporation with the reporting entity are noticeably different under each method.

(c) *Group companies*

The results and financial position of all the group entities (none of which has the currency of a hyperinflationary economy) that have a functional currency different from the presentation currency are translated into the presentation currency as follows:

(i) assets and liabilities for each balance sheet presented are translated at the closing rate at the date of that balance sheet;

(ii) income and expenses for each income statement are translated at average exchange rates (unless this average is not a reasonable approximation of the cumulative effect of the rates prevailing on the transaction dates, in which case income and expenses are translated at the dates of the transactions); and

(iii) all resulting exchange differences are recognised as a separate component of equity.

On consolidation, exchange differences arising from the translation of the net investment in foreign entities, and of borrowings and other currency instruments designated as hedges of such investments, are taken to shareholders' equity. When a foreign operation is sold, such exchange differences are recognised in the income statement as part of the gain or loss on sale.

Goodwill and fair value adjustments arising on the acquisition of a foreign entity are treated as assets and liabilities of the foreign entity and translated at the closing rate.

27. Net foreign exchange gains/(losses)

The exchange differences (charged)/credited to the income statement are included as follows:

	2004	2003
Sales	333	(150)
Cost of goods sold	(125)	50
Selling and marketing costs	(250)	200
Administration expenses	(235)	100
Finance costs – net (Note 25)	2 594	(1 995)
	2 317	(1 795)

FINANCIAL REPORTING IN HYPERINFLATIONARY ECONOMIES

At several points throughout this chapter we noted differences to the requirements for IAS 21 for those entities reporting in a currency of a hyperinflationary economy. The financial statements of such a foreign entity have to be dealt with in accordance with IAS 29 before the requirements of IAS 21 are applied. IAS 29 requires (in para. 8) that:

The financial statements of an entity whose functional currency is the currency of a hyperinflationary economy, whether they are based on a historical cost approach or a current cost approach, should be stated in terms of the measuring unit current at the balance sheet date. The corresponding figures for the previous period required by IAS 1, *Presentation of Financial Statements*, and any information in respect of earlier periods should also be stated in terms of the measuring unit current at the balance sheet date.

Paragraph 9 goes on to state: 'The gain or loss on the net monetary position should be included in profit or loss and separately disclosed'.

FOREIGN SUBSIDIARY CONSOLIDATION

We finish here with a series of activities to demonstrate consolidation of a foreign subsidiary. This should help you when attempting exercises 7, 8 and 9.

ACTIVITY 29.8

A UK entity Bei has a wholly-owned US subsidiary Jing which was acquired for US$1m on 31 December 20X1. The fair value of the net assets at the date of acquisition was US$800 000 giving rise to goodwill on acquisition of $200 000.

Exchange rates were as follows:

31 December 20X1	£1 = US$ 2.0
Average rate during year	£1 = US$ 1.5
31 December 20X2	£1 = US$ 1.65

During the year Jing paid a dividend of $28 000 when the exchange rate was £1 = US$ 1.75. The summarised financial statements for Jing were as follows:

Jing income statement for the year ended 31 December 20X2

	$000
Operating profit	270
Interest paid	(30)
Profit before tax	240
Tax	(60)
Profit after tax	180

Jing balance sheet as at 31 December

	20X2	20X1
	$000	$000
Non-current assets at cost	510	450
Depreciation	(196)	(90)
	314	360
Current assets		
Inventory	348	252
Trade receivables	420	290
Cash	480	420
	1 248	962

	20X2	20X1
	$000	$000
Current liabilities		
Trade payables	(250)	(226)
Tax	(60)	(36)
	(310)	(262)
Net current assets	938	700
Loans	(300)	(260)
Net assets	952	800
Share capital	400	400
Retained profits	552	400
	952	800

Translate the financial statements of Jing prior to consolidation with Bei the holding entity.

Activity feedback

Jing's financial statements need to be translated into the presentation currency before consolidation thus we need to use the closing rate method. Therefore income statement items will be translated at the average rate of 1.65 and all assets and liabilities at the closing rate of 1.5 for 20X2, 2.0 for 20X1.

Jing income statement for the year ended 31 December 20X2

	$000		£000
Operating profit	270	1.65	163.7
Interest paid	(30)	1.65	(18.2)
Profit before tax	240		145.5
Tax	(60)	1.65	(36.4)
Profit after tax	180	1.5	109.1

(continued)

ACTIVITY 29.8 (Continued)

Jing balance sheet as at 31 December

	20X2 $000	1.5 £000	20X1 $000	2.0 £000
Non-current assets at cost	510	340	450	225
Depreciation	(196)	(130.7)	(90)	(45)
	314	209.3	360	180
Current assets				
Inventory	348	232	252	126
Trade receivables	420	280	290	145
Cash	480	320	420	210
	1248	832	962	481
Current liabilities				
Trade payables	(250)	(166.7)	(226)	(113)
Tax	(60)	(40)	(36)	(18)
	(310)	(206.7)	(262)	(131)
Net current assets	938	625.3	700	350
Loans	(300)	(200)	(260)	(913)
Net assets	952	634.6	800	400
Share capital	400	100 @ 2.0 = 200	400	200
Retained profits	552	434.6	400	200
	952	634.6	800	400

We now need to analyse the retained profit figure of £434 600 to identify the translation adjustment.

	$000	Translation rate	£000
Pre acquisition profit b/f	400	2.0	200
Profits for the year	180	See above	109.1
Dividends paid	(28)	1.75	(16)
	552		293.1
Exchange difference	–		141.5
	552		434.6

ACTIVITY 29.9

Analyse the exchange difference of £141 500 identified in Activity 29.8.

Activity feedback
We need to do this analysis to identify that part that needs to be shown as a separate component of equity.

On retranslating the net assets of Jing excluding goodwill at acquisition we have:

	$000	Exchange rate	£000
Acquired net assets at opening rate	800	2.0	400
Acquired net assets at closing rate	800	1.5	533.3
Exchange gain on net assets			133.3
Exchange gain from translating retained profits from average to closing rate, i.e. 180 from 1.65 to 1.5			10.9
Exchange loss from translating dividend from actual to closing rate (28) @ 1.5 – (16)			(2.7)
			141.5

ACTIVITY 29.9   *(Continued)*

	$000	Exchange rate	£000
Exchange difference on goodwill assuming no impairment – 200 000 from 2.0 to 1.5			33.3
Total exchange difference included in consolidated balance sheet as separate component of equity			174.8

ACTIVITY 29.10

If we further assume that Bei's functional currency is pound sterling and noting that it received a dividend from Jing you should, given the summarised balance sheet of Bei be able to complete the consolidation.

Summarised balance sheet of Bei 31 December 20X2

	20X2	20X1
Investment in subsidiary		
(1m @ 2.0 date of acquisition)	500	500
Cash	416	400
	916	900
Share capital	900	900
Retained profits (dividend received		
28 @ 1.75 date of translation)	16	–
	916	900

Note that the balance sheet of Bei uses the temporal method to translate the dividend and investment in subsidiary as we are translating these to the functional currency.

Activity feedback

Consolidated income statement 31 December 20X2

Operating profit of Jing	163.7
Operating profit of Bei	16
	179.7
Elimination of inter-entity dividend	(16)
	163.7
Interest paid	(18.2)
	145.5
Tax	(36.4)
	109.1

Consolidated balance sheet as at 31 December 20X2

Goodwill	133.3
Non-current assets nbv	209.3
	342.6
Current assets	
Inventory	232
Trade receivables	280
Cash (416+320)	736
	1 248
Current liabilities	
Trade payables	(166.7)
Tax	(40)
	206.7
Net current assets	1 041.3
Loan	(200)
	1 183.9
Share capital	900
Retained profits	109.1
Cumulative translation adjustment	174.8
	1 183.9

GAAP comparisons

IAS v UK Foreign currency is dealt with under FRS 23 in the UK. This is convergent with IAS 21.

IAS v US Foreign currency is dealt with in SFAS 52, which is generally similar to IAS 21.

SUMMARY

A fascinating topic but not an easy one. It is difficult to get to grips with the logic of applying one set of rules to translation to functional currency and another to presentation currency. Some of the logic used might also be questionable and the information that is eventually provided for users might be less than understandable.

Remember:

- For individual entity transactions non-monetary items are translated at originating exchange rate but monetary items at balance sheet rate if not settled. Thus unrealised gains and losses due to foreign currency fluctuations will be taken to the income statement generally as part of ordinary activities.

- Foreign entities recording to functional currency use the temporal method.

- Foreign entities translating to presentation currency use the closing rate for balance sheet and average rate (generally) for income statement. This usually occurs when there is a need to prepare consolidated financial statements.

- Where exchange differences result from severe devaluations and there is no practical means to hedge, these are carried as part of the cost of the asset.

- Foreign operations in hyperinflationary economies have to be stated in the measuring unit current at the balance sheet date before translation.

- IFRIC 16, *Hedges of a Net Investment in a Foreign Operation* was issued in July 2008 and should be referenced for further guidance on hedging.

EXERCISES

Suggested answers to exercises marked ✓ are to be found on the Student side of the companion website.

Suggested answers to the remaining exercises are to be found on the Instructor side of the companion website.

1 Explain the differences in treatment and the effect of translating financial statements using the temporal and closing rate method.

2 Identify the circumstances under which IAS 21 permits the use of the closing rate method and the temporal method for translation of financial statements.

✓ **3** Should exchange differences appear in the income statement of an entity or be charged direct to reserves? State the reasons for your answer.

4   What is the difference between foreign currency conversion and foreign currency translation?

✓ **5**   Critically appraise the concepts on which the closing rate and temporal methods are based and discuss the factors that will be taken into account by a group choosing between the two methods.

6   What is 'hedge accounting'? Identify the requirements of IAS 21 in accounting for hedges.

7   The income statements for Home and its wholly-owned subsidiary Foreign for the year ended 31 July 2006 are shown below:

	Home	Foreign
	$000	Crowns 000
Revenue	3 000	650
Cost of sales	(2 400)	(550)
Gross profit	600	100
Distribution costs	(32)	(41)
Administrative expenses	(168)	(87)
Finance costs	(15)	(10)
Profit (Loss) before tax	385	(38)
Income tax	(102)	10
Profit (Loss) for the period	283	(28)

NOTES

1   The presentation currency of the group is the $ and Foreign's functional currency is the Crown.

2   Home acquired 100% of the ordinary share capital of Foreign on 1 August 2004 for 204 000 Crowns. Foreign's share capital at that date comprised 1000 ordinary shares of 1 Crown each, and its reserves were 180 000 Crowns. In view of its subsidiary's losses, Home's directors conducted an impairment review of the goodwill at 31 July 2006. They concluded that the goodwill had lost 20% of its value during the year (before taking exchange differences into account). The impairment should be reflected in the consolidated financial statements for the year ended 31 July 2006.

3   On 1 June 2006, Home purchased an item of plant for 32 000 Florins. At the year end, the payable amount had not yet been settled. No exchange gain or loss in respect of this item is reflected in Home's income statement above.

4   Exchange rates are as follows:

On 1 August 2004:	1.7 Crowns = $1
On 31 July 2006:	2.2 Crowns = $1
Average rate for year ended 31 July 2006:	2.4 Crowns = $1
On 1 June 2006:	1.5 Florins = $1
On 31 July 2006:	1.6 Florins = $1

Required:

Prepare the consolidated income statement for the Home group for the year ended 31 July 2006. (Work to the nearest $100)

8   Memo, a public limited company, owns 75% of the ordinary share capital of Random, a public limited company which is situated in a foreign country. Memo acquired Random on 1 May 2003 for 120 million crowns (CR) when the retained profits of Random were 80 million crowns. Random has not revalued its assets or issued any share capital since its acquisition by Memo. The following financial statements relate to Memo and Random:

Balance sheets at 30 April 2004

	Memo $m	Random CRm
Tangible non-current assets	297	146
Investment in Random	48	–
Loan to Random	5	–
Current assets	355	102
	705	248
Capital and reserves		
Ordinary shares of $1/1CR	60	32
Share premium account	50	20
Accumulated profit	360	95
	470	147
Non current liabilities	30	41
Current liabilities	205	60
	705	248

Income statements for year ended 30 April 2004

	Memo $m	Random CRm
Revenue	200	142
Cost of sales	(120)	(96)
Gross profit	80	46
Distribution and administrative expenses	(30)	(20)
Operating profit	50	26
Interest receivable	4	–
Interest payable	–	(2)
Profit before taxation	54	24
Income tax expense	(20)	(9)
Profit after taxation	34	15

The following information is relevant to the preparation of the consolidated financial statements of Memo:

(a) The directors wish to treat goodwill in accordance with recent proposals as a foreign currency asset. Goodwill has been subjected to an impairment review as at 30 April 2004 and is deemed to be impaired by $2 million.

(b) During the financial year Random has purchased raw materials from Memo and denominated the purchase in crowns in its financial records. The details of the transaction are set out below:

	Date of transaction	Purchase price $m	Profit percentage on selling price
Raw materials	1 February 2004	6	20%

At the year-end, half of the raw materials purchased were still in the inventory of Random. The inter-company transactions have not been eliminated from the financial statements and the goods were recorded by Random at the exchange rate ruling on 1 February 2004. A payment of $6 million was made to Memo when the exchange rate was 2.2 crowns to $1. Any exchange gain or loss arising on the transaction is still held in the current liabilities of Random.

(c) Memo had made an interest free loan to Random of $5 million on 1 May 2003. The loan was repaid on 30 May 2004. Random had included the loan in non-current liabilities and had recorded it at the exchange rate at 1 May 2003.

(d) The fair value of the net assets of Random at the date of acquisition is to be assumed to be the same as the carrying value.

(e) Random operates with a significant degree of autonomy in its business operations.

(f) The following exchange rates are relevant to the financial statements:

Crown to $

30 April/1 May 2003	2.5
1 November 2003	2.6
1 February 2004	2
30 April 2004	2.1
Average rate for year to 30 April 2004	2

(g) Memo has paid a dividend of $8 million during the financial year and this is not included in the income statement.

Required:
Prepare a consolidated income statement for the year ended 30 April 2004 and a consolidated balance sheet at that date in accordance with International Financial Reporting Standards.
    (Candidates should round their calculations to the nearest $100 000.)
                                                                        (ACCA June 2004)

9 Small was incorporated in 1985 and prior to its acquisition by Big had built up its own customer base and local supplier network. This was not disturbed when Small became a subsidiary of Big as the directors of Big were anxious that the local expertise of the management of Small should be utilised as much as possible. Therefore all the day-to-day operational decisions regarding Small continued to be made by the existing management, with the directors of Big exercising 'arm's-length' strategic control.

The balance sheets of Big and Small at 31 March 2003 are given below. The balance sheet of Small is prepared in florins, the functional currency for Small.

	Big $000	$000	Small FL'000	FL'000
Non-current assets:				
Property, plant and equipment	60 000		80 000	
Investments	9 500			
		69 500		80 000
Current assets:				
Inventories	30 000		40 000	
Trade receivables	25 000		32 000	
Cash	3 000		4 000	
		58 000		76 000
		127 500		156 000
Issued capital and reserves:				
Called up share capital (50 cents/½ florin shares)		30 000		40 000
Revaluation reserve		15 000		–
Accumulated profits		34 500		44 000
		79 500		84 000
Non-current liabilities:				
Interest-bearing borrowings	15 000		30 000	
Deferred tax	5 000		9 000	
		20 000		39 000
Current liabilities:				
Trade payables	12 000		15 000	
Tax	16 000		18 000	
		28 000		33 000
		127 500		156 000

Notes to the balance sheets

Note 1 – Investment by Big in Small

On 1 April 1997, Big purchased 60 million shares in Small for 57 million florins. The accumulated profits of Small showed a balance of 20 million florins at that date. The accounting policies of Small are the same as those of Big except that Big revalues its land, whereas Small carries its land at historical cost. Small's land had been purchased on 1 April 1994. On 1 April 1997, the fair value of the land of Small was 6 million florins higher than its carrying value in the individual financial statements of that entity. By 31 March 2003, the difference between fair value and carrying value had risen to 11 million florins. Apart from this accounting policy difference, no other fair value adjustments were necessary when initially consolidating Small as a subsidiary.

Note 2 – Intra-group trading

On 6 March 2003, Big sold goods to Small at an invoiced price of $6 000 000, making a profit of 25% on cost. Small recorded these goods in inventory and payables using an exchange rate of 5 florins to $1 (there were minimal fluctuations between the two currencies in the month of March 2003). The goods remained in the inventory of Small at 31 March 2003 but on 29 March 2003, Small sent Big a cheque for 30 million florins to clear its payable. Big received and recorded this cash on 3 April 2003.

Note 3 – Exchange rates

Date	Exchange rate (florins to $1)
1 April 1994	7
1 April 1997	6
31 March 2002	5.5
31 March 2003	5
Weighted average for the year to 31 March 2003	5.2
Weighted average for the dates of acquisition of closing inventory	5.1

Required:

Translate the balance sheet of Small at 31 March 2003 into $s and prepare the consolidated balance sheet of the Big group at 31 March 2003.

(CIMA May 2003)

10 East is an entity incorporated in Asia. East has a subsidiary, West, that is located in Africa and prepares its financial statements under local accounting standards. West prepares its financial statements in African Francs (AFr). Financial information relating to the two entities for the financial year ended 30 September 2004 is given below:

Balance sheets at 30 September 2004	East $m	East $m	West AFrm	West AFrm
Assets				
Non-current assets:				
Property, plant and equipment [Note 1]	100		120	
Intangible assets [Note 2]	–		20	
Investments [Note 3]	27		–	
		127		140
Current assets:				
Inventories [Note 4]	40		50	
Receivables	45		60	
Cash and bank balances	15		–	
		100		110
		227		250

Balance sheets at 30 September 2004

	East $m	East $m	West AFrm	West AFrm
Equity and liabilities				
Capital and reserves:				
Called up share capital [$1/AFr1 shares]	75		60	
Accumulated profits	52		53	
		127		113
Non-current liabilities:				
Interest bearing borrowings	50		60	
Deferred tax	15		12	
		65		72
Current liabilities:				
Trade and other payables	35		45	
Short-term borrowings	–		20	
		35		65
		227		250

Income statements for the year ended 30 September 2004

	East $m	West AFrm
Revenue	200	240
Cost of sales	(120)	(145)
Gross profit	80	95
Other operating expenses	(35)	(40)
Profit from operations	45	55
Intra-group investment income	4.5	–
Finance cost	(7.5)	(10)
Profit before tax	42	45
Income tax expense	(10)	(15)
Net profit for the period after tax	32	30
Balance at 1 October 2003	111	98
Net profit for the period	32	30
Dividends paid	(16)	(15)
Balance at 30 September 2004	127	113

Notes to the financial statements

Note 1 When East acquired West (see note 3 below) the fair value of the plant and equipment of West was AFr20 million higher than its carrying value in West's balance sheet. These assets were being depreciated over their estimated useful economic lives and, at the date of acquisition, the directors estimated that the future useful lives of these assets was four years. This depreciation is recognised as part of cost of sales.

Note 2 The intangible assets of West comprise internally developed brands that have no ascertainable market value. At the date of acquisition of West by East (see note 3 below) the carrying value of such brands was AFr12 million. The brands are not amortised and no change occurred in their carrying value during the year ended 30 September 2004.

Note 3 On 1 October 2001, when the accumulated profits of West showed a credit balance of AFr25 million, East purchased 45 million shares in West for AFr1.80 each. East amortises purchased goodwill over ten years, presenting the amortisation under other operating expenses. East has not provided West with any loan finance.

Note 4 On 1 September 2004, East sold a supply of components to West for $12 million. These components had cost East $10 million to manufacture. All of these components were included in the inventory of West at 30 September 2004. West had paid for half of the consignment before the year-end and the balance of the liability was included in its payables. Apart from this transaction, and the payment of a dividend by West on 30 June 2004, there were on other intra-group transactions.

Note 5 Exchange rates on relevant dates were:

Date	Exchange rate AFr to $1
1 October 2001	3.00
30 September 2003	2.70
30 June 2004	2.50
1 September 2004	2.45
30 September 2004	2.40

The weighted average exchange rate for the year ended 30 September 2004 was AFr2.5 = $1.

Note 6 In preparing the consolidated financial statements, the directors of East treat fair value adjustments and purchased goodwill as part of the net investment in West and so both are subject to exchange fluctuations. The closing rate [or net investment] method is appropriate for translating the financial statements of West for consolidation purposes.

Required:

(a) Translate the balance sheet of West at 30 September 2004 into $s and prepare the consolidated balance sheet of East at 30 September 2004.

(b) Translate the income statement of West for the year ended 30 September 2004 into $s and prepare the consolidated income statement of East for the year ended 30 September 2004.

(CIMA paper November 2004)

11 Little was incorporated over 20 years ago, operating as an independent entity for 15 years until 1998 when it was taken over by Large. Large's directors decided that the local expertise of Little's management should be utilised as far as possible, and since the takeover they have allowed the subsidiary to operate independently, maintaining its existing supplier and customer bases. Large exercises 'arm's-length' strategic control, but takes no part in day-to-day operational decisions.

The balance sheets of Large and Little at 31 March 2004 are given below. The balance sheet of Little is prepared in francos (*F*), its reporting currency.

	Large $000	$000	Litte F000	F000
Non-current assets:				
Property, plant and equipment	63 000		80 000	
Investments	12 000		–	
		75 000		80 000
Current assets:				
Inventories	25 000		30 000	
Trade receivables	20 000		28 000	
Cash	6 000		5 000	
		51 000		63 000
		126 000		143 000
Issued capital and reserves:				
Called up share capital				
(50 cents/1 Franco shares)		30 000		40 000
Revaluation reserve		–		6 000
Accumulated profits		35 000		34 000
		65 000		80 000
Non-current liabilties:				
Interest-bearing borrowings	20 000		25 000	
Deferred tax	6 000		10 000	
		26 000		35 000
Current liabilties:				
Trade payables	25 000		20 000	
Tax	7 000		8 000	
Bank overdraft	3 000		–	
		35 000		28 000
		126 000		143 000

NOTES TO THE BALANCE SHEETS

Note 1 – Investment by Large in Litte

On 1 April 19W8. Large purchased 36 000 shares in Little for 72 million francos. The accumulated profis of Little at that date were 26 million francos. Large's accounting policy in respect of goodwill on acquisition is to amortise it on a straight line basis over five years.

Note 2 – Intra-group trading

Little sells goods to Large, charging a mark-up of one-third on production cost. At 31 March 20X4, Large held $1 million (at cost to Large) of goods purchased from Little in its inventories. The goods were purchased during March 20X4 and were recorded by Large using an exchange rate of $1 = 5 francos. (There were minimal fluctuations between the two currencies during March 20X3). At 31 March 20X3, Large's inventories included no goods purchased from Litte. On 29 March 20X4, Large sent Little a cheque for $1 million to clear the intra-group payable. Little received and recorded this cash on 3 April 20X4.

Note 3 – Accounting policies

The accounting policies of the two companies are the same, except that the directors of Little have decided to adopt a policy of revaluation of property, whereas Large includes all property in its balance sheet at depreciated historical cost. Until 1 April 20X3, Little operated from rented warehouse premises. On that date, the entity purchased a leasehold building for 25 million francos, taking out a long-term loan to finance the purchase. The building's estimated useful life at 1 April 20X3 was 25 years, with an estimated residual value of nil, and the directors decided to adopt a policy of straight line depreciation. The building was professionally revalued at 30 million francos on 31 March 20X4, and the directors have included the revalued amount in the balance sheet.[1]

Note 4 – Exchange rates

Date	Exchange rate (francos to $1)
1 April 19W8	6·0
31 March 20X3	5·5
31 March 20X4	5·0
Weighted average for the year to 31 March 20X4	5·2
Weighted average for the dates of acquisition of closing inventory	5·1

[1] Depreciation during the year ended 31.3.X4 was calculated on the historic cost. No other property was owned by Little during the year.

Required:

(a) Explain (with reference to relevant accounting standards to support your argument) how the financial statements (balance sheet and income statement) of Little should be translated into $s for the consolidation of Large and Little.

(b) Translate the balance sheet of Little at 31 March 20X4 into $s and prepare the consolidated balance sheet of the Large group at 31 March 20X4.

Note: Ignore any deferred tax implications of the property revaluation and the intra-group trading.

PART FOUR
FINANCIAL ANALYSIS

In Part One we focused on what financial reporting is all about – what it is trying to achieve and how the accountant sets about achieving it. Parts Two and Three presented the rules that accountants have created for themselves to govern financial reporting. In those three parts, a preparer's approach to financial reporting is taken as we describe the mechanisms and rules through which financial information is provided to users. In Part Four, a user's approach is followed. In this part we analyse how different stakeholders of a company can use the information provided in the annual accounts to gain some insight as to the reporting entity's stability, performance, future prospects and/or whatever else may interest them.

INTERPRETATION OF FINANCIAL STATEMENTS

30

OBJECTIVES After studying this chapter you should be able to:

- explain how industry analysis can be useful in the context of financial analysis

- explain why knowledge of the corporate strategy is important for financial analysis

- describe the different incentives for annual accounts' management

- identify the practices which are used for annual accounts' management purposes

- explain the purpose of entity analysis

- describe what is meant by quality of disclosure

- describe what is meant by accounting quality.

INTRODUCTION

Financial statements provide valuable information for different stakeholders. In Chapters 1 and 11 we identified the users of accounting information and their differing needs. The following activity provides a useful piece of revision.

ACTIVITY 30.1

Identify the users of accounting information and their needs/objectives.

Activity feedback

- Investors/owners – is the money invested in the business making a suitable return for them or could it earn more if invested elsewhere? Is the business a safe investment, that is, is it likely to become insolvent/bankrupt? Should the investors invest more money in the business?

- Suppliers – is the business able to pay for the goods bought on credit? Will the business continue to be a recipient of the goods the supplier produces?

- Customers – is the business able to supply the goods the customer requires and when it requires them? Will the business continue in operation so that guarantees on goods purchased will be met?

- Lenders – is there adequate security for the loan made? Does the business make a sufficient profit and have enough cash available to make the necessary payments to the lender of interest and capital?

- Employee – does the business make sufficient profit and have enough cash available to make the necessary payments to the employees? Will the business continue in operation at its current level so that the employee has secure employment?

- Government – for example to calculate taxation due or to aid decision-making in respect of the economy as a whole of a country.

- Public – the majority of their needs is in respect of employment, pollution and health and safety which is not particularly, as yet, provided by financial statements.

A prime source of information for all these economic decision makers are the financial statements published by the company.

Since the financial statements serve as a means of communication with the external stakeholders of a firm, they may sometimes be 'managed' to convey a certain message to the outside world. As well as the financial statements, the whole annual report together with interim statements and other releases of financial information and non-financial information, are subject to this phenomenon of 'manipulation'. Therefore, it is extremely important for users of financial accounting information to be able to 'undo' this manipulation and to uncover the underlying economic performance of the firm. Economic decision makers must therefore be aware of the incentives a company may have to influence the annual accounts, and of the available discretion management enjoys to pursue these incentives and the means they have available for this purpose.

The knowledge about 'annual accounts management incentives and practices' is as important as a sound knowledge about the techniques of financial analysis in order to understand and judge properly the information provided through the annual accounts. In Part Four we discuss both elements in depth. The 'annual accounts management incentives and practices' will be discussed in this chapter. The techniques of financial analysis (trend analysis, common size financial statements, ratio analysis and cash flow analysis) are presented and illustrated in Chapter 31.

Financial statements are a source of information about a company since they present a picture of the economic performance of a firm. This economic performance, however, is determined to a large extent by the adopted business strategy of a firm and by the economic and industrial environment in which a firm is operating. As a result the business strategy of a firm and the industry characteristics will have an impact on the accounting data represented in the financial statements. Therefore, it is worthwhile gaining a clear insight into the industry and business characteristics of a company before starting with the analysis of its financial statements. Studying the economic and industrial environment of a company together with its strategy is often called 'industry analysis' in textbooks on financial and corporate reporting and analysis.

INDUSTRY ANALYSIS

In order to determine whether a company is, in fact, liquid or whether it is making a reasonable profit or is worthwhile to invest in, we need to compare the performance of the company with a benchmark. Besides gaining insight into how a firm's strategy and its business environment have an impact on the data in the annual accounts, industry analysis also provides benchmarking data to financial analysts and other users of accounting information. Further, boards of directors judge the performance of the top management of the company by comparing the company's performance with the competitors in the same industry. Through industry analysis we can obtain benchmarks against which the current performance, the financial status and the investment potential of a particular company can be compared. However, we need to take great care in carrying out this benchmarking so that we do not invalidate the results. In setting benchmarks against which we can compare a company, we must remain aware of the limitations of this comparison. This item will be further elaborated in the next chapter.

Activity 30.2 below repeats information from Chapter 11, but it is included here in a slightly different format for pedagogical reasons.

Each of the four benchmarks identified is commonly used in assessing business status, performance and potential, but interpretation of accounts is highly subjective and requires skilled judgement, bearing in mind the limitations of these benchmarks.

In the next two sections a brief overview of the elements to be considered in the context of industry analysis will be presented.

Analysis of the business environment

As different elements of the business and the economic environment of a company have an impact on the revenue and costs levels of the firm, we may state that the

ACTIVITY 30.2

What other benchmarks/indicators could you think of besides benchmarks taken from industry analysis? Consider also their limitations.

Activity feedback

- *Past period achievements*. Uses – to identify whether current activity is better or worse than previous periods. Limitations – external factors may have influenced activity levels, e.g. public awareness of environmental issues may have necessitated a change in manufacturing process leading to increased costs.

- *Budgets*. Uses – has current activity matched planned activity? Limitations – the budget may not be a valid standard of performance, e.g. underlying assumptions may have been unrealistic or set at too high a level.

Within the scope of industry analysis, data from other businesses in the same industry or industry averages could be used for benchmarking purposes. What could be their limitations?

Activity feedback

● *Other businesses*. Uses – is our business performing as well? Limitations – businesses may not be truly comparable with regard to size and type, e.g. grocery sole trader compared to supermarket; manufacturer compared to retailer. Further external factors may affect one business, e.g. a lengthy strike. Accounting standards and accounting policies on which accounting information is prepared may be different, e.g. inventory valuations, depreciation, historic cost or revalued amount, treatment of research and development, treatment of goodwill.

● *Industry averages*. Industry averages have uses and limitations very similar to those of other businesses. Additionally, an average is simply a figure which takes account of the best but also of the worst.

environment determines to a certain extent the profit potential of a company. An important element with regard to industry profitability is the level of competition in an industry. This level of competition is influenced by the type of competition, the barriers to entry, the production capacity available in the industry, the existing relationships, agreements and alliances.

The degree of competition in an industry determines to a large extent the price which can be charged for the products or services to the customer. The competition can be perfect competition, monopoly or any form in between. Firms in a monopoly position with no substitutes for their products or services can charge higher prices than firms in a situation of perfect competition with a high number of substitutes and high price elasticity of demand. The danger of substitute products can be avoided if firms are able to differentiate their products or services. This possibility will be determined by the existing switching costs.

The level of price competition in an industry is also a function of the cost structure which is related to the technology used and the existence of economies of scale. If the ratio fixed to variable costs is high, firms have a tendency to engage in price wars in order to fully utilise the production capacity they have invested in. Many economic textbooks mention the airline industry as a typical example of an industry where such a policy is often applied. However, if we analyse more closely the value chain of an airline company then this observation (= high fixed costs) relates only to the transport activities in the value chain of the airline. Other activities in the value chain (such as reservations and sales, catering, handling) have a higher proportion of variable costs in their total cost structure. Therefore, price wars intended to fill up the empty seats in the airplanes will increase costs in the other activity areas of the value chain of an airline, where costs are much more variable. The outcome of such a policy of filling up seats through price reductions is not always beneficial, as we will see later.

Another element which characterises the competitive environment of a firm is the presence of high or low barriers to entry. In industries with low barriers to entry the pricing of existing firms within that industry is more constrained and so is the potential for abnormal profits. Barriers to entry could be created through the technology used, the access to channels of distribution, the supplier relationships and the existence of excess capacity.

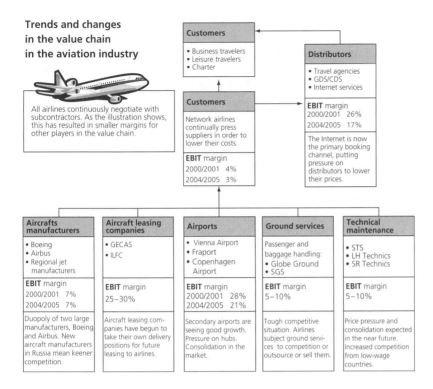

Trends and changes in the value chain in the aviation industry

All airlines continuously negotiate with subcontractors. As the illustration shows, this has resulted in smaller margins for other players in the value chain.

Customers
- Business travelers
- Leisure travelers
- Charter

Distributors
- Travel agencies
- GDS/CDS
- Internet services

EBIT margin
2000/2001 26%
2004/2005 17%

The Internet is now the primary booking channel, putting pressure on distributors to lower their prices.

Customers

Network airlines continually press suppliers in order to lower their costs.

EBIT margin
2000/2001 4%
2004/2005 3%

Aircrafts manufacturers
- Boeing
- Airbus
- Regional jet manufacturers

EBIT margin
2000/2001 7%
2004/2005 7%

Duopoly of two large manufacturers, Boeing and Airbus. New aircraft manufacturers in Russia mean keener competition.

Aircraft leasing companies
- GECAS
- ILFC

EBIT margin
25–30%

Aircraft leasing companies have begun to take their own delivery positions for future leasing to airlines.

Airports
- Vienna Airport
- Fraport
- Copenhagen Airport

EBIT margin
2000/2001 28%
2004/2005 21%

Secondary airports are seeing good growth. Pressure on hubs. Consolidation in the market.

Ground services

Passenger and baggage handling:
- Globe Ground
- SGS

EBIT margin
5–10%

Tough competitive situation. Airlines subject ground services to competition or outsource or sell them.

Technical maintenance
- STS
- LH Technics
- SR Technics

EBIT margin
5–10%

Price pressure and consolidation expected in the near future. Increased competition from low-wage countries.

The financial outcome of a company will be influenced not only by decisions taken with regard to its own competitive position, but these figures will also be influenced by evolutions in the industry value chain in which the company is active. In order to judge the performance or financial position of a firm properly, its value chain should be compared with the value chain of competitors and the industry value chain.

Corporate strategy Some firms operate in only one industry but others are competitive in more industries (see Activity 30.4).

At corporate level the management can choose to be active only in one business or to operate in multiple businesses. Corporate strategy decisions focus on where corporate resources will be invested. Business strategy decisions are concerned with how to compete in defined product markets.

ACTIVITY 30.4

Think of companies such as Unilever, Walt Disney Corporation, McDonald's and BMW. In how many businesses are they competitive?

Activity feedback

Single industry	Multiple businesses
McDonald's (fast food)	Unilever (food, cleansing agents, skincare products)
BMW (car manufacture)	Walt Disney Corporation (movies, TV channel, theme parks, real estate)

Some companies prosper by competing in one industry whereas others operate successfully in different industries.

For financial analysis purposes it is important to know whether a company is a multi-business company, in which case, the consolidated annual accounts reflect the performance of the group as a whole. In the consolidated profit and loss account, costs of different businesses will be presented in an aggregated way. Only through the segmental data included in the notes to the financial statements can the user of these statements get a glimpse of the profitability of the individual businesses. The Scandinavian SAS group, for example, is active in the airline business but is also a well-known player in the hotel sector. This implies that, for example, the item leasing costs in the profit and loss account of the group's financial statements of SAS not only relates to lease expenses for airplanes, but also to the lease costs of assets employed in the hotel business of the group. In the case of inter-firm comparison one must be vigilant as regards whether or not companies are in the same business or in the same portfolio of businesses. The risks involved in these different business segments may evolve around different patterns.

The main aim of undertaking industry analysis before one starts with accounting analysis is to get to know the business as the business context gives meaning to the information presented in the annual accounts. According to the industry or strategy chosen the value of certain ratios will be lower or higher or the volatility of earnings will be different.

ACCOUNTING ANALYSIS

We have already illustrated that the performance of a firm is influenced to a large extent by the adopted business strategy and by the economic and industrial environment in which the firm is operating. As a result, the business strategy of the firm and the industry characteristics will be reflected in the accounting data. An understanding of that process is useful for an analysis of the accounts in a meaningful way. However, there is more to be taken into account before one can start with financial analysis. As annual accounts are used to communicate the underlying business reality to outside investors, managers may use financial reporting strategies to manipulate investors' perceptions or the perception of other stakeholders. Managers may choose accounting and disclosure policies that make it more or less difficult for external users of financial statements to understand the true economic performance of the business.

Besides adopting a business strategy, the management can also adopt what is called an 'accounting strategy'. Management may employ a number of accounting methods, accounting estimates and real decisions such that the published accounting numbers begin to deviate widely from the underlying economic performance. This toolkit of methods, estimates and real decisions is used to influence the accounting numbers according to the accounting strategy defined by top management with or without approval from the board of directors. The purpose of accounting analysis is to gain insight into the 'accounting strategy' of the firm. The 'accounting strategy' of a firm consists of the incentives management has to influence the accounting numbers, the adopted reporting strategy in order to obtain the 'target' or 'preferred' accounting numbers and the methods which have been used to manage these accounting numbers in response to the incentives. Knowledge about the adopted 'accounting strategy' will enable the external user of the annual accounts to detect more easily the underlying economic performance of the firm and make a more reliable judgement about the performance of that firm. The academic literature has devoted most of its attention to the management of earnings numbers. In order to detect earnings management most studies focus on the presence of abnormal or discretionary accruals. Accruals result from the use of accounting estimates like the creation or the use of a provision, write-downs, impairments, etc. In the business world, real operating decisions are also used to manage the accounting numbers. However, real choices employed to influence accounting numbers are more difficult to observe.

Accounting strategy: incentives to manage the annual accounts

The management of a company can have different incentives to manage the financial statements. Academic research into earnings management has shown that earnings management incentives result from the external and internal contracts governing the firm. This stream of research is inspired mainly by the agency paradigm. Among the external contracts governing the firm, we can distinguish between contracts with shareholders, debt holders and the government and other regulatory authorities. The most important internal contract of the firm is that with top management. Academic research provides evidence that incentives to manage accounting numbers are embedded in all contracts. In the sections below we make a pedagogical presentation of these incentives towards earnings management, taking into account the contract from which they originate.

Incentives driven by the contract with shareholders In accounting literature there is ample evidence of different characteristics of accounting numbers, which are viewed favourably by current and potential shareholders. Shareholders will appreciate those accounting numbers and react with high share prices and a lower cost of capital. High share prices are beneficial for the company (e.g. when an initial public offering (IPO) is planned), but also for top management (e.g. where they have stock options). These characteristics of accounting numbers and disclosure are: small loss avoidance (Burghstahler and Dichev, 1997); recurrent and increasing stream of earnings (Barth, Elliot and Finn, 1995; De Angelo, De Angelo and Skinner, 1996); low earnings volatility (Trueman and Titman, 1988; Hand, 1989; Bartov, 1993; Hunt, Moyer and Shevlin, 1995); meeting earnings targets or benchmarks (Degeorge, Patel and Zeckhauser, 1999 and Kasznik, 1999); and reducing information asymmetry through increased voluntary and mandatory disclosure (Healy and Palepu, 1993; Botosan, 1997; Sengupta, 1998; Healy, Hutton and Palepu, 1999; Leuz and Verrechia, 2000).

Low earnings volatility Investors and analysts evaluate an investment in a firm as more risky when the reported results are volatile. This volatility has an impact on the market price of the shares. A higher risk perception means a lower share price. Thus, managers may have an incentive to influence the perception of the capital market with regard to the volatility of the business.

Recurrent and increasing stream of earnings In periods preceding a capital increase (i.e pre-IPO period) the management of the company might be tempted to produce a steady stream of increasing earnings over the years. In this situation earnings are not only smoothed and reported as less volatile but an upward trend of the results is also shown. Some recent studies show that earnings are managed prior to or around IPOs (Friedlan, 1994; Neil, Pourciau and Schaefer, 1995) or seasoned equity offerings (Shivakumar, 1998; Rangan, 1998).

Meeting earnings targets and benchmarks The first earnings target a company must achieve in order to be appreciated by the capital market is to meet the previous year's earnings. In addition, top management usually present targets to the capital markets (e.g. in presentations made to financial analysts) which include an improvement in relation to prior periods. When a company does not meet these targets, the company faces a drop in share price (unless the whole industry is facing the same situation). Therefore, the management of a company will always try to meet the target it has put forward. Further top management must also make sure that they do not perform below the industry average, since the latter is a benchmark used by current and potential shareholders.

Small loss avoidance behaviour It has been noticed that companies tend to avoid small losses and prefer instead to report small profits instead. Earnings management research has provided evidence for this practice which the research calls 'small loss avoidance'. De George, Patel and Zeckhauser (1999) and Burgstahler and Dichev (1997) present evidence that managers of US firms use accounting discretion to avoid reporting small losses. Small losses are more likely to lie within the bounds of insiders' reporting discretion and, consequently, can be avoided through earnings management. This implies, further, that if a loss cannot be avoided by accounting decisions companies have a tendency to go for a one-time big loss, which is known as 'big bath accounting'.

Incentives driven by debt contracts – accounting-based debt covenants Very often the terms of a lending agreement involve debt covenants which are specified as accounting ratios and may not be violated. A violation of these debt covenants might entail an increase of the interest rate applied to a loan or an immediate repayment of that loan or an extra collateral. So managers have an incentive to choose those accounting methods and estimates which reduce the violation of the debt covenant (Sweeney, 1994). Sweeney found further that firms approaching default respond with income increasing accounting changes. Using actual debt covenant violations, Defond and Jiambalvo (1994) found support for earnings management by managers of firms with debt covenant violations.

It is not compulsory under most GAAP systems to disclose information about debt covenants. The following example taken from the annual accounts of Barry-Callebaut (the largest manufacturer worldwide of cocoa and chocolate products) in the year 2002/2003 is the result of a voluntary disclosure decision made by the firm:

> The term and revolving facilities agreement also contains certain financial covenants, including, amongst others, a maximum senior leverage ratio, a minimum interest cover ratio and a minimum solvency ratio, next to a number of potentially restrictive undertakings limiting or preventing specific business transactions.
>
> (Note 13, financial statements 2002/2003, p. 96)

As can be seen below, cash flow figures are included in Euro Disney SCA's information on debt covenants:

Debt Covenants

The Group's debt agreements include covenants between the Group and the lenders, which were significantly modified as a result of the Restructuring. The renegotiated covenants continue to include restrictions on additional indebtedness and capital expenditures, the provision of certain financial information and compliance with the financial covenant based upon the ratios of certain actual and forecasted cash flows (as defined in our bank agreements) to the Group's debt service payment requirements. Compliance with the latter does not begin until fiscal year 2006.

(Euro Disney SCA Annual Report 2005, p. 25)

Contracts with governments and regulatory authorities Tax authorities use accounting data in order to determine the tax base of a company. Accounting methods might be chosen with a tax effect in mind. Especially in continental Europe (e.g. Germany, Belgium, France) there is a strong link between the reported income in the individual accounts of the company and the tax income.

Regulatory agencies may use accounting data to evaluate regulatory policies (e.g. import tariffs, anti-trust actions). Empirical evidence can be found that earnings management is induced by political or regulatory processes (Key, 1997; Guenther, Maydew and Nutter, 1997).

Articles in company laws with regard to dividend payments, companies in distress and bankruptcy conditions often refer to ratios in the individual or group accounts of a company which may or may not be exceeded or violated. This results in an incentive to manage these ratios if there is a risk that ratios may be violated.

In relation to these contracts with top management there is the implicit incentive that top managers want to keep their jobs. Therefore they have an incentive to equal the industry average performance. Research results do indeed indicate that top managers are dismissed when their firms perform below the average industry performance (Pourciau, 1993).

Alongside such implicit incentives, contracts with top management often also include explicit incentives.

Management compensation Top management compensation often consists of three individual components, a base salary, a bonus plan linked to a certain indicator and shares or share options. When the bonus plans of top management are linked to reported profits, there is an incentive to choose those accounting methods and accounting estimates which make the company exceed the profit targets stipulated in their compensation contract. This finding not only holds for top management compensation but also for lower level managers compensated on the basis of accounting numbers. Linking compensation to accounting numbers does not only create incentives for managing those numbers. Jensen and Murphy (1990) claim that paying executives on the basis of accounting profits rather than on changes in shareholder wealth not only generates incentives to manipulate the accounting system but also generates incentives to ignore projects with large net present values in favour of less valuable projects with larger immediate accounting profits.

In his seminal paper in this area Healy (1985) found support for earnings management by managers of firms with bonus plans linked to accounting numbers. Healy shows that ceilings (i.e. the upper earnings found in the bonus scheme) in compensation contracts have a predictable effect on accounting accruals.

Due to this possible negative effect of accounting numbers-based compensation other forms of management compensation emerged. Stock option plans became very popular and 'stock-based performance measures' are often argued to be superior to accounting-based performance measures. However, short-term behaviour of the management might arise when the exercise period of the options is short.

In order to avoid short-termism, bonuses with a long-term perspective can be introduced and combined with a stock option plan that is in alignment with shareholders' interest, in order to stimulate top management behaviour.

In the Annual Report of Adidas 2004, we find a description of a compensation plan in which many mechanisms for compensation are used:

Structure of Executive Board Remuneration

In accordance with its Rules of Procedure, our Supervisory Board has assigned matters relating to the compensation structure of the Executive Board to its General Committee. As this system has proven successful, the General Committee that also deals in detail with the performance of the Executive Board members will continue to discuss and resolve upon the structure of compensation of the Executive Board. The compensation structure is based on the Group's economic and financial position and the outlook of the Group. Criteria for determining the level of Executive Board compensation include the responsibilities and the contribution of the respective Board member, his personal performance as well as the performance of the entire Executive Board. The remuneration of the members of the Executive Board comprises the following components:

- A fixed component which is paid monthly.

- A variable component in the form of a performance bonus, which is paid out following the end of the year and is dependent on individual performance and the Group's results. The variable component also comprises a further bonus under a Long-Term Incentive Plan (LTIP), the amount being linked to the attainment of certain goals during a three-year period. This bonus is dependent on the accumulated earnings improvement (income before taxes) in the period 2003 to 2005 and the earnings increase in 2005 versus the prior year. Provided the targets are achieved, payment will be made following approval of the consolidated financial statements for the year ending December 31, 2005. The allocation to the accrued expenses is shown as variable remuneration.

- Benefits in kind, such as a company car, etc.

- Stock options, which were granted under the Management Share Option Plan (MSOP) adopted by the Annual General Meeting on May 20, 1999 and amended by resolution of the Annual General Meeting on May 8, 2002 and May 13, 2004, as a compensation component with a long-term incentive effect and with risk character.

According to a resolution passed at the Annual General Meeting in 1999, a maximum of approximately 10% of the total issue volume was granted to Executive Board members. The stock options were given out in tranches and are exercisable over five years following a two-year vesting period, provided that at least one of the following performance objectives has been attained:

- During the period between the issue and exercise of the stock options, the stock market price for the adidas-Salomon share has increased by an average annual rate of at least 8% ('absolute performance').

Between the issue and exercise of the stock options, the stock market price for the adidas-Salomon share has grown by an annual average of 1% more favorably than the stock market prices of the major competitors of adidas-Salomon globally and in absolute terms has not fallen ('relative performance').

Compensation from the stock option plan consists of a performance discount which is composed of the absolute and relative performance components.

The variable components are structured in such a way as to represent a clear incentive to achieve the defined goals.

Executive Board Members' Remuneration for 2004 € in thousands

	2004	2003
Cash compensation	**11 137**	7 308
Fixed components	**3 141**	3 108
Variable components:		
Performance bonus	**3 446**	3 450
LTIP[1]	**4 550**	750
Benefits in kind	**239**	159
Share-based compensation (MSOP)	**3 606**	35
Total compensation	**14 982**	7 502

[1]Accrued expenses, which will be paid out upon attainment of certain targets following approval of the consolidated financial statements for the year ending December 31, 2005

(Adidas Annual Report 2004, p. 116)

Adidas communicates, in a transparent way, the individual impact of the different compensation components on total compensation. The higher the influence of the bonus and the stock option plan in the total compensation of managers, the stronger the incentive towards earnings management and towards influencing the accounting numbers of the company in such a way that the capital market reacts with an increase in the share price.

Another possibility is to base compensation on performance measured relative to aggregate performance in the industry. An example of such a plan is the 'performance' programmes that Lufthansa offers to its senior executives (Lufthansa Annual Report 2007, p. 38):

Performance-related remuneration

Incentive programmes as an element of remuneration have a long tradition at Lufthansa; not only for Board members but for all managers and employees.

For managers, there is a remuneration programme with a variable, performance-related remuneration component, which is oriented both towards value creation of the Company, as measured by the CVA, and towards attaining personal targets. Since 1997, Lufthansa has also offered its managers a share programme known as 'LH-Performance' as a general and longer-term component. This programme combines a personal investment by the participants in Lufthansa shares with the granting of appreciation rights. The Executive Board members have also been taking part in 'LH-Performance' since 2002. In 2003 the programme was extended to non-contracted staff. Lufthansa gives a discount on shares purchased as part of this programme. The shares may not be sold before the end of the programme. Since 2007, the appreciation rights have been made up of a performance and an outperformance option. Lufthansa makes a payout on the performance option when the performance of the Lufthansa share reaches a set hurdle based on the cost of equity. The participants receive a payment from the outperformance option if the Lufthansa share has performed better than the shares of the main European competitors over the course of the programme. The amount of the payment depends on the performance or outperformance level, up to a defined cap. This makes the participants shareholders on the one hand, with all related risks and rewards, and on the other, provides them with remuneration for a Company-specific performance.

Results 'LH-Performance'

	Expiry of programme	Actual outperformance in %
LH-Performance 2007	2011	0.4
LH-Performance 2006	2010	11.8
LH-Performance 2005	2009	37.4
LH-Performance 2004	2008	20.5
LH-Performance 2003	2007	−30.3

The combination of a personal investment in shares and performance-related options gives Lufthansa an exemplary scheme, which has been commended for many years as one of the best share programmes of all the 30 DAX companies.

For many years Lufthansa employees have received a profit-share payment in addition to their basic salary. Since 1970, they have had the option of choosing between a cash payment and share-based payments. They can either purchase traditional employee shares or take advantage of the equity model LH-Chance to acquire a larger number of shares with an interest-free loan. In 2007, the LH-Chance programme was run for the tenth time. Around 40 per cent of the German workforce opted to take their profit-share payment in the form of shares.

Despite the expectations that stock option plans would align shareholders' interests with the interest of management, research evidence is now available which shows that stock option plans also induce top management towards earnings management.

Incentives at the time of executive turnover Annual accounts management may be observed when executive changes take place within companies. Executive changes can be forced or voluntary (e.g. retirement). The outgoing CEO or executive team as well as the incoming CEO or executive team can have incentives to influence the accounts. Research on CEO turnover and annual accounts management distinguishes between CEO turnover in troubled firms and CEO turnover in non-troubled firms. Dechow and Sloan (1991) investigated the hypothesis that CEOs, in their final years of office (before retirement), manage discretionary investment expenditures to improve short-term earnings performance (for example, spending less on R&D). LaSalle, Jones and Jain (1993) report evidence that is consistent with the hypothesis that new CEOs exploit their accounting discretion to blame their predecessors for poor performance, establish a lower benchmark for subsequent performance evaluation and relieve future earnings of charges that would otherwise have to be made. Murphy and Zimmerman (1993) also found evidence that incoming CEOs of poorly performing firms took 'baths'.

However, it is important to stress that reduced profits or losses when a new CEO or new management team comes in could also be the result of the 'income borrowing behaviour' of the former CEO. The outgoing CEO could have improved his perform-ance through accounting decisions in the immediate years before the turnover which increases the reported results, or through income-smoothing behaviour above sustain-able levels for several years. So, the outgoing CEO in this case has increased the reported income by using accounting practices which borrow income from the future.

In these circumstances, the new CEO will be faced with less profit or even a loss due to the reversal effect of the practices used by his predecessor (this is discussed later).

The new incoming top management team is often tempted to undertake 'big bath' accounting. In their first year in office, compensation will not be tied greatly to the results of the company. In later years, however, compensation will be tied to the performance of the company. Through this 'big bath' a new CEO is able to front-load costs and secure himself higher profits in the years to follow.

'Big bath' accounting, which is observed not only in terms of executive turnover, will be explained below.

'Big bath accounting' to manage future earnings Setting the objective to maximise the loss is referred to in the literature as big bath accounting. Of course, there are limits to the loss one can present to the stakeholders without influencing their actions. Big bath accounting occurs in two circumstances. First of all, big bath accounting can occur in case of a (one-time) heavy loss that cannot be avoided by income maximising accounting interventions (see small loss avoidance). Faced with such a situation the firm's management may choose to maximise the loss in the current accounting period. In years of economic downturn, this practice is often observed.

Second, big bath accounting can occur when the annual accounts will be cleaned up before or after an acquisition, a merger or other form of business cooperation. Big bath accounting usually implies the frontloading of costs through large asset write downs and increases in provisions (restructuring provisions are extremely popular for this purpose) in order to enhance the future performance of the firm. In the financial year where 'a bath is taken' a substantial loss is reported, however, in the following years, performance will rise partly due to reduced depreciation charges or a decrease of provisions.

Third, big bath accounting occurs at the time of executive handover, especially when the prior CEO was dismissed for poor performance (for a discussion on this see prior section). This practice has received increasing levels of critique over recent years. The reinforcement of the conditions for creating restructuring provisions under IAS 37 is a result of those practices. The extract below refers to the practice of big bath accounting and the methods used to achieve this accounting strategy:

Cookie jar reserves

One of the accounting 'hot spots' that we are considering this morning is accounting for restructuring charges and restructuring reserves. A better title would be accounting for general reserves, contingency reserves, rainy day reserves or cookie jar reserves.

Accounting for so-called restructurings has become an art form. Some companies like the idea so much that they establish restructuring reserves every year. Why not? Analysts seem to like the idea of recognising as a liability today, a budget of expenditures planned for the next year or next several years in down-sizing, right-sizing or improving operations and portraying that amount as a special, below-the-line charge in the current period's income statement. This year's earnings are happily reported in press releases as 'before charges'. CNBC analysts and commentators talk about earnings 'before charges'. The financial press talks about earnings before 'special charges'. (Funny, no one talks about earnings before credits-only charges.) It's as if special charges are not real. Out of sight, out of mind . . .

The occasion of a merger also spawns the wholesale establishment of restructuring or merger reserves. The ingredients of the merger reserves and merger charges look like the makings of a sausage. In the Enforcement Division, I have seen all manner and kind of things that ordinarily would be charged to operating earnings instead being charged 'below the line'. Write-offs of the carrying amounts of bad receivables. Write-offs of cost of obsolete inventory. Write-downs of plant and equipment costs, which, miraculously at the date of the merger, become non-recoverable, whereas those same costs were considered recoverable the day before the merger. Write-offs of previously capitalised costs such as goodwill, which all of a sudden are not recoverable because of a merger. Adjustments to bring warranty liabilities up to snuff. Adjustments to bring claim liabilities in line with management's new view of settling or litigating cases. Adjustments to bring environmental liabilities up to snuff or in line with management's new view of the manner in which the company's obligations to comply with EPA will be satisfied. Recognition of liabilities to pay for future services by investment bankers, accountants and lawyers. Recognition of liabilities for officers' special bonuses. Recognition of liabilities for moving people. For training people. For training people not yet hired. For retraining people. Recognition of liabilities for moving costs and refurbishing costs. Recognition of liabilities for new software that may be acquired or written, for ultimate sale to others. Or some liabilities that go by the title 'other'.

It is no wonder that investors and analysts are complaining about the credibility of the numbers.

(Source: Speech by Walter R. Schuetze, Chief Accountant, Enforcement Division, US Securities and Exchange Commission, 22 April 1999. *http: www.sec.gov/ news/speeches/spcha76.htm*)

Other incentives

Competitive pressures: Data from the annual accounts might be useful for the competition. Especially in a situation where one company is obliged to disclose more proprietary information due to national GAAP requirements, companies have a tendency either to avoid this disclosure or to decrease the quality of disclosure. For example, segmental data will be disclosed on a more aggregated level or high recurring profits might be topped off to avoid entry in the industry by new firms.

Union negotiations: Facing forthcoming union negotiations the management might have an incentive to decrease the net result of the company. Strong company profits might incite the unions to ask for a salary increase. These incentives will be more present in companies, industries or countries with strong labour union power.

ACTIVITY 30.5

Which of the incentives listed above could be classified as 'recurring' and which could be classified as 'non-recurring'?

Activity feedback

Recurring incentives could be: reducing earnings volatility for listed companies, efforts to sustain share prices when stock options are granted. Further, regulatory incentives can be recurring if, for example, a company is located in a country where there is a link between tax income and accounting income. Non-recurring incentives could be present in the situation of an individual public offering, a merger or acquisition or an executive turnover.

If we consider the incentives listed we can see that some of them are recurring and others are non-recurring incentives to manage the accounts (see Activity 30.5).

In current research related to earnings management the notion of implicit contracts is introduced. Contracts can be between the firm and its customers, suppliers, short-term creditors, employees, capital providers and other stakeholders. Bowen, Du Charme and Cheres (1995) and Kasanen, Kinnunen and Niskanen (1996) find evidence that implicit contracts induce earnings management. While explicit contracts seem important incentives for earnings management in companies with widespread ownership, implicit contracts are especially important in creating earnings management incentives in firms with concentrated ownership. Concentrated ownership might create implicit contracts between a firm and its major shareholders which often have a seat on the board of directors. (Kasanen, Kinnunen and Niskanen (1996) reveals implicit contracts on dividends with institutional shareholders.)

Before we start with a case on earnings management and the incentives towards earnings management, we end this section by citing the most used definition of earnings management found in the academic literature. Earnings management is the alteration of a firm's related economic performance by using judgement in financial reporting and in structuring transactions to either mislead some stakeholders or to influence contractual outcomes (Healy and Wahler, 1999).

The story of Sabena and the airline industry Different companies from the airline industry will be used for illustrative purposes throughout Part Four. The published financial statements and annual reports of Austrian Airlines, KLM, British Airways, Lufthansa, Ryanair, easyJet, SAS, the former SAir Group and the late Sabena will be used. In relation to the airline Sabena, data from the last ten years of its existence (1991–2001) will be used throughout both this chapter and for educational purposes. Sabena was the Belgian national flag carrier which was declared bankrupt in 2001. Within the time span covered the analysis will mainly focus on the period 1995–2001 during which Sabena was linked to the SAir Group. The SAir Group was the majority shareholder of the airline Swissair which also ceased to exist at the beginning of 2002. If we need to compare the performance of Sabena and the Swissair/SAir·Group with the other airlines, then we use the financial statements of the years 1999, 2000, 2001. For an analysis of the existing carriers today we use the most recent financial statements available. A short overview of the last ten years of the existence of Sabena is presented in Activity 30.6.

Accounting analysis: Reporting strategy

In the previous section we have discussed the incentives to manage the accounting numbers embedded in the contracts governing the firm. According to the type of incentive a different reporting strategy and as a result a different type of annual accounts management will be used. For example, if a firm is involved in union negotiations the aim will be the decrease of the reported profits in the period before the negotiations. In the literature on reporting strategies a distinction is often made between management of the profit and loss account (also called earnings management) and management of the balance sheet numbers. Further, when earnings management is used to present the published results in a more favourable way than the underlying economic results, we are able to distinguish two major patterns. First of all, the result of one particular year might be influenced in a particular direction (increase or decrease) and, second, earnings management can also take the form of

ACTIVITY 30.6

When reading the following information about Sabena, keep in mind the overview of the literature given above. Which elements from the literature could possibly be related to this company?

Sabena, Belgium's national flag carrier, was founded in 1923. Sabena was a state-owned entity, characterised by a weak financial performance for as long as it existed. Due to the deregulation of the airline industry which would gradually take place in the European Union from the beginning of the 1990s, airlines were investigating all forms of cooperations and alliances with each other. It was already clear at that time that it would be extremely difficult for Sabena to survive on its own. In order to make Sabena an attractive bride for a partnership a major restructuring had taken place in 1991. Subsequently Sabena entered in 1992 into a cooperation with Air France. The French partner acquired 37% of the shares of Sabena. The partnership with Air France came to an end two years later in 1994. Mid-1995 Swissair acquired a large minority holding of 49.5% in the capital of Sabena. Together with the investment in the share capital of Sabena, a loan of 151 million CHF was granted by Swissair to the Belgian government, which remained the majority shareholder with 50.5% of the shares. The loan to the Belgian government entitled Swissair at that time to raise its equity holding in Sabena from 49.5% to 62.25% later on.

The shareholder agreement signed by the two shareholders (SAir and the Belgian government) included, among other things, the following items. The articles of the shareholders' and masters' agreement stipulated that the managing director (CEO) be appointed at the suggestion of both shareholders (Belgian state and SAir). Further, the articles stipulated that the other members of the management committee of Sabena could be appointed or dismissed by the board of directors on the proposal of the managing director.

In February 1996 one of the top executives of the SAir Group became President and CEO of Sabena. From the management team in place at Sabena at the beginning of 1996 only one person remained on the board of the management team at the time of the bankruptcy in 2001. In this short time frame many management positions were occupied by several persons; the position of chief financial officer changed hands three times in those five years.

Sabena was the first airline in which the SAir Group took a substantial minority shareholding. The acquisition of this substantial minority shareholding (49.5%) fitted into the new strategy of Swissair. Their new corporate strategy was presented in their Annual Report 1996 (p. 1):

Swissair has moved from its traditional structure as an airline to become a corporate group that conducts airline-related activities in addition to actual airline operations. The new group structure, named the SAir Group will underscore the diversity of the new corporation.

Together with this new corporate strategy, a new CEO, a former controller from within the company, was appointed in the SAir group. The strategy of the business segment airlines of the SAir Group was to obtain a market share of 20% in Europe (Lüchinger, p. 210). This strategy, called the 'hunter' strategy would be pursued by taking substantial minority shareholdings in EU airlines. Sabena was the first one and later on French (AOM, Air Litoral), German (LTU), Italian (Volare) and Portuguese Airlines (Portugalia, TAP) followed. As Switzerland was not a member of the EU, acquiring a majority shareholding in the EU airlines would result in these airlines becoming non-EU airlines.

The acquisition of minority holdings by SAir in other airlines was beneficial not only for obtaining a market share of 20% but also for the so-called second pillar of the SAir Group, namely the airline-related business segments (e.g. catering, ground handling, technics, logistics, information systems). Illustrations of this practice can be found in several annual reports of the SAir Group. The following evidence is found on p. 18 of the 1996 SAir Group Annual Report:

Atraxis' first year as an independent information technology company was very challenging . . . Several reservations and handling systems were delivered to third-party customers and made operational, including the complete migration of the Sabena booking and handling system.

Further:

On December 16, Swisscargo and Sabena signed an agreement whereby Swisscargo's distribution network would market the entire freight capacity of Sabena's fleet of aircraft as of January 1, 1997. Swisscargo thereby enlarged its freight capacity by almost one quarter and is taking full advantage of the chance to create a cargo hub in Brussels.

(SAir Group 1997 Annual Report, p. 20)

In the notes to the annual accounts of the SAir Group of 1997 we find the following explanation concerning the operating revenues: 'Results for 1997 also include the assumption by Swisscargo of Sabena's

ACTIVITY 30.6   (Continued)

cargo business, which increased the relevant operating revenue item by CHF160 million.' It is interesting to note here that the so-called 'assumption' of the cargo business of Sabena by SAir is, in fact, a non-event in the annual report of Sabena. In the annual reports of Sabena the titles in the narrative part switch from cargo to cargo handling and in the five-year overview of summary airline operating statistics the statistics relating to cargo are replaced by the words 'assumed by SAir'. The growth in the airline-related activities came from acquisitions and from providing services to the Qualiflyer Group, which included all the airlines in which SAir hold substantial shareholdings. (SAir Group Annual Report 2000, p. 4): 'Group companies active in the airline-related businesses generated added revenue by performing maintenance, catering, IT and cargo services for Qualiflyer Group airlines.'

Whereas Sabena had only two shareholders (the Belgian Government 50.5% and the SAir Group 49.5%), the SAir Group was listed with dispersed ownership. Even employees held shares in SAir as we learn from the notes to the annual accounts of the SAir Group (e.g. note 4 of the Annual Report of the SAir Group of 1998, p. 19): 'The SAir Group also issues shares to its personnel. These shares carry dividend and voting rights, but cannot be sold for three years after their issuance.' As in many large listed groups stock options were also granted to staff members.

At the end of 1996 both SAir and Sabena were headed by new CEOs who had committed themselves to growth and profitability. With regard to Sabena evidence of this commitment to profitability can be found in the consecutive annual reports of 1995, 1996 and 1997:

> Our collaboration with Swissair, the strengthening of our balance sheet achieved in 1995 and the commercial growth witnessed over the last three years are all strong building blocks which enable us to achieve our objective of profitability from 1998.
> (Sabena Annual Report, 1995)

> A year of transition for Sabena, 1996 was hallmarked by the creation of a new management team headed by a new CEO. The Horizon '98 plan points the way to a return to profitability in 1998.
> (Sabena Annual Report 1996, p. 5)

> Sabena succeeded in 1997 in reaping the first benefits of the Horizon '98 programme in the drive to balance the books and make the airline profitable again.... [p. 9] The aim of all these measures

(Horizon '98 plan) is to return Sabena to profitability in 1998.
> (Sabena Annual Report 1997, p. 5)

In 1998 Sabena 'showed' the promised profit. Figure 30.1 shows the operating result and the net result of Sabena NV over the period 1991–2000 and the 1998 figures are, indeed, in the black.

Sabena NV represents the holding company of the Sabena Group but at the same time it is also the airline. The revenue of Sabena NV makes up 90% of the revenue of the Sabena Group and the total assets of Sabena NV represent 85% of the total assets of the Sabena Group. For this reason it makes sense to look at the behaviour of the individual accounts of Sabena NV. These individual accounts are prepared according to Belgian GAAP for the whole time frame. The results of 1998 were commented on by the board of directors in the Annual Report as follows:

> The main reason why the year has been such a turning point is because we have managed to re-establish our profitability. The efforts made to cut costs, to increase productivity and to occupy more aircraft seats, have clearly borne fruit . . . In summary we can state that, this year, Sabena has finalised the groundwork done in 1996 and 1997 within the framework of the 'Horizon '98 Plan'. Its task is now to ensure profitable growth based on continued restraint in matters of expenditure.

The fact that in 1997, and especially 1998, the economic climate was very favourable for the airline industry was not mentioned as a possible explanation for the positive figures. In line with the growth strategy of the SAir Group the board of directors of Sabena took the decision in 1997 to renew and expand the fleet in the coming years. To fill this extra seat capacity offered on the market Sabena engaged heavily in price competition. The number of passengers indeed grew as we will see later, but the mix of passengers was very unfavourable. In the main, it was economy class passengers who were attracted, among them many transfer passengers. These transfer passengers create extra variable costs (handling, etc.) and are therefore not very profitable for an airline. The percentage of business class passengers decreased especially from 2000 on, the year when the sale of the tickets for both airlines (Swissair and Sabena) was for the first time carried out for a period of 12 months through the newly created Airline Management Partnership (AMP) between the two airlines.

(continued)

ACTIVITY 30.6 (Continued)

FIGURE 30.1 Ten-year overview of the operating and net result of Sabena NV

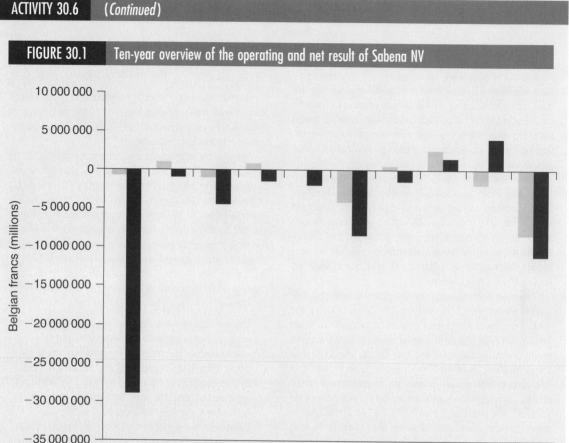

SOURCE: ANNUAL ACCOUNTS OF SABENA NV, 1991–2000

The results of the Sabena Group over the same time frame show a rather similar pattern, except for 1992 and 1999 (group accounts are only available from 1992 on) (see Figure 30.2). In those years the results of the individual accounts of Sabena NV were positively influenced by gains on intra-group sale of assets (for example, in 1999, the creation of a new 100% owned subsidiary Sabena Technics NV which would be responsible for maintenance, repair and overhaul of planes). These intra-group results are, of course, eliminated in the process of consolidation (see Part 3 consolidated or group accounts).

From 1999 on the group accounts of Sabena are prepared with the use of IAS. The group loss of 1999 was explained in the message of the board of directors as follows:

1999 turned into another year of strong growth for the Sabena Group in spite of an ever more demanding competitive climate. It was a year that saw us exceed

the 10-million passenger mark. But the unexpected increase in certain costs, particularly in the price of fuel, lowered operating results. Because of certain extraordinary transactions, amongst which the sale of Equant shares, the net results of the Sabena Group show a slight profit. Nonetheless, the Board has decided to absorb into the 1999 figures part of the restructuring costs linked to the Airline Management Project (AMP).

The message of the board of directors reported further on the start of AMP and what it meant for Swissair and Sabena:

As initially provided in the 1995 agreements, the two airline companies have decided to combine their commercial activities by the formation of a partnership.

ACTIVITY 30.6 (*Continued*)

FIGURE 30.2 Overview of the operating and net result of the Sabena Group

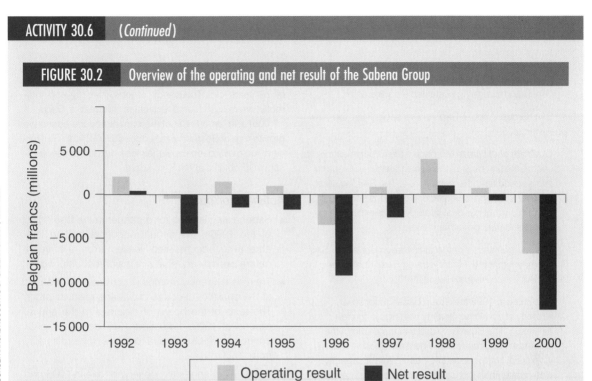

The divisions of the two companies have been restructured and spread over 2 administrative headquarters: Brussels for Marketing, Product and Sales, Zurich for the Management of the network and support functions. Because of the permanency of this new agreement, the Board of Directors asked the 2 main shareholders of Sabena, being the Belgian State and the SAir Group, for an agreement on matters pertaining to the future shareholding structure.

It is obvious from the description in the annual report that the creation of AMP will have an impact on the structure of the Sabena Group and maybe on the SAir Group as well. Employees from the SAir Group and from Sabena were transferred to AMP. Concerning the impact on costs and revenues, the annual report remains vague.

The agreement between the shareholders on the future shareholding structure, talked about in the report of 1999, was reported in the annual report of Sabena of 2000 as follows (Annual Report 2000, p. 3):

Two principal events distinguished the year 2000: the agreement between the shareholders under which the SAir Group would take a majority holding of 85 per cent in Sabena as soon as the bilateral agreements between Switzerland and the 15

Member States of the European Union have been ratified. This ratification is expected to take place by the end of 2001.... The establishment of the AMP as a partnership under British law with affiliates in every country in which Sabena and Swissair operate.

The agreement talked about in the Sabena report of 2000, was signed on 25 January 2001.

The economic climate deteriorated in 2000 (economic crises, high fuel prices and an unfavourable exchange rate with the dollar) and Sabena's financial situation became dramatic. At the level of the SAir Group difficulties also started to emerge mid-2000.

The 'old' CEO left Sabena mid-2000 and the company was headed by a new CEO whom the Swiss had recruited a year earlier from a competitor airline. At the beginning of 2001 two CEO changes shortly after each other were witnessed at the top of the SAir Group as well. Both new CEOs got the task to turn the tide and restore profitability. In both annual reports the reader is informed about how each company will proceed in achieving this target. Sabena Annual Report 2000:

In order to improve the result sharply in the short term, the 'Blue Sky' restructuring programme was

(*continued*)

ACTIVITY 30.6   *(Continued)*

launched.... The Board of Directors will give every priority in 2001 to redressing the performance of the Group and to signing sustainable partnerships.

SAir Group Annual Report, Message from the new Chairman, p. 5:

Our main priority is to reorganise the Group's airline sector, the first pillar of the dual strategy, and restore it to a sound financial condition.... The SAir logistics, SAir services and SAir relations divisions, forming the second pillar of our dual strategy, have either met or surpassed their performance targets.

The reorganisation of the airline segment at the SAir Group meant that the 'hunter' strategy was abandoned in 2001. SAir Group Annual Report 2000, p. 4:

Beginning in 1995 the Group began to follow a strategy of acquiring minority holdings in foreign airlines.... The Board realised that the depth of the resources required to implement the chosen strategy, in terms of time, capital and management capacity, was greater than the Group could provide. The lack of ample financial resources to pursue additional acquisitions and to carry out the required refinancing plans in Germany, Belgium and France forced the abandonment of this strategy. Subsequent to a thorough investigation, the Board decided to shift the strategy of the Group's airline sector in January 2001.

Due to the further deterioration of the economic climate, the events of 11 September 2001, social unrest, an extreme unfavourable cost structure due to prior management decisions and, last but not least, the withdrawal of the SAir Group at the end of September 2001 from Sabena, the Belgian airline had to file for bankruptcy. The oldest carrier in Europe at that time was declared bankrupt on 7 November 2001 and ceased to exist, at the age of 78 years old. Thousands of jobs (directly and indirectly) were lost (some estimates suggest a figure of 17 000) and, as a result of the bankruptcy the economic growth rate of Belgium was reduced by 0.2%. In Switzerland, too many people lost their jobs due to the serious financial problems at the SAir Group.

Activity feedback

- Sabena was looking for a partner in the beginning of the 1990s, the annual accounts had to look attractive. Accumulated losses from the years before were cleaned up in a major restructuring.

- There is evidence of implicit contracts on the part of the board of directors of Sabena towards profit. The texts of the board of directors in the annual reports of 1995, 1996 and 1997 contain implicit contracts which make a promise for profitability from 1998 on.

- Two CEO changes are observed: one in 1996 and the other in 2000. However, there is a difference between the first CEO change and the second. The CEO coming on board in 1996 had the goal of pursuing growth and profitability. The CEO of the new millennium was facing a company in distress.

- Regulatory aspects could also play a role.

Taxes: In Belgium, there is a strong link between reported accounting income in the individual accounts and the income which is used to determine taxable profit.

Regulatory aspects: Although there has been deregulation since the beginning of the 1990s, the airline business is still a highly regulated industry.

income smoothing which is a recurring activity. The purpose of income smoothing is to reduce the variability in reported earnings over time. Although a wide variety of incentives to manage the financial statements exists, the same reporting strategy can often be used for different incentives.

Management of the balance sheet structure is often done to influence the accounting numbers, which are used to evaluate the financial position of the company (see the liquidity ratio and solvency ratios discussed in Chapter 11) in a favourable way. As well as accounting numbers from the balance sheet and profit and loss account cash flow data can also be manipulated. This happens through real decisions.

Since each company is subject to a different set of contracts, the incentives for accounting numbers management and the resulting reporting strategies will also differ among companies. Although general checklists to detect earnings management

ACTIVITY 30.7

Consider some of the different types of incentives presented earlier to manage the annual accounts. What type of accounting strategy would be appropriate for these different types of incentives?

Activity feedback

● *Capital market considerations.*

– *Risk perception.* The accounting strategy of the firm would be to engage in earnings management with the purpose of presenting earnings or results which are less volatile than the underlying economic results that the firm has obtained. In this situation income smoothing would be pursued and this practice would be a 'rerecurring activity'. In periods with 'high' economic income, profits would be topped off and in periods with ' lower' income increasing measures would be used.

– *Prepare for an initial public offering.* In this case the accounting strategy could consist of showing a good performance over the years before the IPO and an improvement of the balance sheet structure. Different types of annual accounts management might be combined into the overall reporting strategy: income smoothing in order to influence the perceived risk of the company, balance sheet management to improve the structure of the balance sheet and increasing the result upwards over a time period before the IPO.

● *Tax incentives.* In countries where there is a link between accounting income and taxable income, the accounting strategy is to decrease the reported profit in order to reduce taxable profit. This type of management will be recurring as long as the company exists.

● *Compensation contracts.* In the case of stock options, an increasing share price is desired. The reporting strategy could consist of income smoothing practices, undertaken to reduce the perceived risk of the company, and further income increasing measures might be used as well. Bonus plans with ceilings might entail one-time earnings management upwards to the ceiling or one-time earnings management below the ceiling.

are available (see Nelson, Elliot and Tarpley, 2003; Penman, 2003), the toolbox used by corporate management will be unique to each company. We will return to this issue at the end of this chapter.

Discussing the concept of reporting strategy, it is also worthwhile mentioning that, although a distinction is made between earnings management and balance sheet management, the impact of the methods used for those purposes are not isolated to the income statement or the balance sheet alone. In reality, earnings management also has an indirect impact on certain balance sheet items. For example, an accounting method change with regard to depreciation (change from declining method to straight line method) will influence not only the depreciation expense on the profit and loss account, but also the reported book value of the assets on the balance sheet. The same indirect effect can be observed when a company decides to manage the balance sheet. If a company wants to improve the debt/equity ratio through switching from owned assets to assets acquired under operational leasing contracts, not only the liability structure of the balance sheet will be altered. As a consequence the character of the costs involved will change as well. A large part of the costs related to the use of the asset will switch from depreciation costs to rental costs. For financial analysis purposes the former are regarded as non-cash costs whereas the latter are considered as cash costs.

To conclude this section on accounting strategy the operating results, the extraordinary results (which relate to gains and losses on sales of assets) and the net result of a company named DAT Airlines NV are presented in Figure 30.3 for the period 1997–2000. DAT was a 100% subsidiary of Sabena NV and these data were taken from the individual accounts of DAT. The data reflect two items which evolve in the

| FIGURE 30.3 | Results of DAT Airlines NV, 1997–2000 |

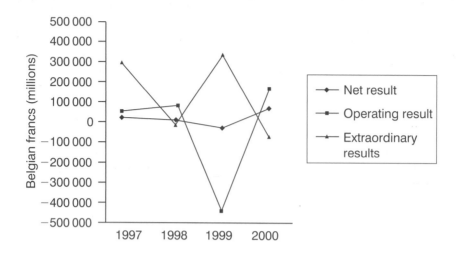

opposite way (operating result and extraordinary result) and the sum of the two reflects a more stable pattern (net result). Can you think of a possible explanation?

Accounting analysis: Methods of accounting numbers management

After the discussion on the incentives for annual accounts management and the applied accounting strategy (earnings management and management of balance sheet elements) we now focus on the methods or practices used to influence these accounting numbers. The practices or methods used for annual accounts management are usually divided in most textbooks and articles into three categories, namely accounting method choices, accounting estimate choices and real decisions (operating decisions, financing decisions or investment decisions). Besides these three main instruments, other mechanisms can be used as well to manage the impression of the reader of the financial statements towards a more favourable impression about the performance of the company. In this respect Francis (2001) lists the following elements: timing of adoption of new Standards; choices about display (number of statements, layout of statement); aggregation decisions; and classification decisions. Accounting method choice and accounting estimate choice are accounting decisions with no direct first order effect on cash flows (Jiambalvo, 1996). These practices are called accrual methods in the literature and the use of them is called accruals management. Academic research in the area of earnings management has constructed variables which are proxies for earnings management, for example total accruals, working capital accruals, discretionary accruals, a measure for income smoothing and small loss avoidance. In many of these articles the underlying assumption in the calculation of these proxies is that cash flow figures are not managed. However, when real earnings management is included, there is a direct impact on the cash flow. Further, a company can pick a single element to manage the accounts but most often a portfolio of elements is used. A portfolio could mean either several individual methods or practices used to achieve a reporting strategy or a combination of an accrual method linked to a real decision.

As we saw in the earlier parts of this volume, preparing financial statements implies complying with the regulation which governs financial reporting (general accepted accounting principles: e.g. US GAAP, IAS/IFRS, UK GAAP, German GAAP). However, since most GAAP are not a rigid set of principles, the management of a company has a certain flexibility with regard to the choice of valuation methods and accounting estimates to use. The level of flexibility will depend on the GAAP being applied. Insight into the accounting flexibility available to a company might enable the external analyst to separate true information from noise or distortion to a certain extent. An explicit consideration of the flexibility allowed by GAAP applied for the presentation of the annual accounts is a necessity for financial analysis.

Accounting standards that are characterised by more flexibility allow managers more easily to report income in those financial periods when managers have incentives to present better results. Empirical research has provided evidence that the so-called 'low-quality' accounting standards provide more flexibility to management for earnings management purposes (see Chapter 2). These standards are found in countries with a code law system and a creditor orientation in financial reporting. However, we also learned in Chapter 2 that 'high-quality' accounting standards on their own are no guarantee for 'high-quality' financial reporting. The institutional environment (= shareholder protection, degree of enforcement of accounting standards and risk of litigation) play a significant role in the quality of financial reporting in a country.

The aim of the IASB (Foundation Constitution, part A, para. 2) is 'to develop in the public interest, a single set of high-quality, understandable and enforceable global accounting standards that require high-quality, transparent and comparable information in financial statements and other financial reporting to help participants in the world's capital markets and other users make economic decisions'. As a result, we observe over recent years that the flexibility in the IAS/IFRS becomes less. In most Standards, the allowable treatment has been removed, leaving only the prior benchmark treatment in place (e.g. with IAS 8 the prospective application of accounting method or policy changes was deleted from the Standard). Since more countries and more regulatory authorities require listed groups to comply with IFRS, it is somewhat easier for users to compare the difference in available accounting flexibility among listed companies. For non-listed companies, and especially SMEs, differences in accounting flexibility are to a large extent influenced by the national GAAP they use.

The following is a brief discussion of a number of methods or practices used for annual accounts management.

Accounting method choice Accounting method choice is present when there are several possible valuation methods for the same item under the GAAP which has to be applied for the preparation of the annual accounts. Some examples are listed now which could be categorised under the heading accounting method choice:

- choice of depreciation method (e.g. declining method, straight line or accelerated method)
- choice of inventory valuation (LIFO, FIFO or weighted average)
- choice whether or not to capitalise certain expenditures (e.g. R&D, software, advertising)
- choice with regard to the valuation base (historical cost versus fair value).

With regard to accounting method choice the possibility of influencing the accounts can be limited by the accounting standard setter. A standard setter can always remove options from the available set of accounting valuation methods. This evolution is observable recently in relation to IAS/IFRS. The IASB has been removing a number of alternative treatments from the Standards. This implies that the level of accounting flexibility with regard to accounting method choice is declining.

Accounting method choices are not the most popular item to be used for annual accounts' management purposes as the visibility of those choices is perceived as rather high. If one applies an accounting method change the impact on the results of the company and the equity should be disclosed in the notes (for further discussion see the section on quality of disclosure). Chapter 8 presented the accounting treatment of accounting method changes and the necessary information disclosure in relation to such a change. The aim of IAS 8 is to enhance comparability in a situation of an accounting method change.

The use of accounting estimates for annual accounts' management purposes is often preferred by management above accounting method changes because they are less visible and less costly than changes in accounting methods.

Accounting estimates For the preparation of the financial statements accounting decisions not only relate to the choice of valuation methods to be applied but also to the accounting estimates to be used for valuation purposes. Below a few items of the financial statements in which accounting estimates play a role are now presented.

Bad debt allowances: Research has revealed that this type of accrual is often used for management purposes (e.g. McNichols and Wilson, 1988). A change in the amount of bad debt allowance is often not visible as this amount is netted off from the receivables. The use of bad debt allowances is one of the oldest methods practised for earnings management purposes. Influencing the amount of bad debt allowance is a typical example of accounts management.

Inventory: Related to inventories there is, first of all, the accounting method choice (FIFO, LIFO, weighted average). Next full costing is often required for inventory valuation purposes for industrial companies. In this case, overhead should be allocated to the production. Many standards on inventory valuation require that the allocation of the overhead be based on the company's normal level of activity. Companies in distress are sometimes tempted to allocate part of the unused capacity to the products instead of charging that amount to the P&L account. As a result, these costs related to the unused capacity will be carried forward through the inventory to 'hopefully' more favourable financial years.

For contracts which are valued with the use of the 'percentage of completion method', judgement can be used in determining the exact percentage of completion as well as the costs still to incur on the contract.

Provisions: Provisions are a very popular balance sheet item for managing earnings. Provisions are used for smoothing purposes as well as for one time increases or decreases of the results. External analysts should always investigate the reasons why provisions are created. Sometimes they have the character of amounts set aside for intentional use later on.

This use of provisions for the increase of reported profit when 'economic profit' is lower is also called rainy day accounting. An example of this rainy day accounting can be found in the annual accounts of Sabena in the time frame 1991 to 1995. A substantial amount of provisions was created in the annual accounts of 1991 before the cooperation with Air France. These provisions were then released until 1996 when a new management team headed by a Swiss CEO had taken over. The gradual release of these provisions reduced the negative reported results over that period.

Provisions can also be used to 'frontload' costs, frontloading meaning bringing future costs to the current period. The purpose is to enhance the profitability in future periods. This frontloading of costs by increasing provisions was encountered in the first years of the cooperation between Sabena and the SAir Group. Evidence of this practice is found in the following annual report:

(Sabena Annual Report 1995, p. 5) The group result for 1995 remained in the red to the tune of BEF 1.620 Million. This includes an exceptional provision of BEF 1.090 million for the renewal of the fleet ... [p. 22]. Following the decision by the Board of Directors to make exceptional provisions of BEF 1.090 million to effect a rapid standardisation of the long haul fleet, consolidated results in 1995 showed a net loss of BEF 1.620 million BEF.

ACTIVITY 30.8

Is this provision created in 1995 in accordance with conceptual frameworks governing financial reporting?

Activity feedback

This provision does not really match with definitions and concepts found in the conceptual frameworks.

More provisions follow in the financial year 1996:

The Board of Directors has decided to set off the exceptional charges in 1996 against major reductions in values and provisions designed to ease the fleet harmonisation and modernisation process. The total amount of money involved in the reduction of values and provisions for the fleet (A310–B747) is BEF 1531 million.

(Annual Report 1996, p. 9)

The evolution of the provisions over the period 1991–2000 in the annual accounts of Sabena is presented in Figure 30.4.

FIGURE 30.4   Evolution of provisions of Sabena NV

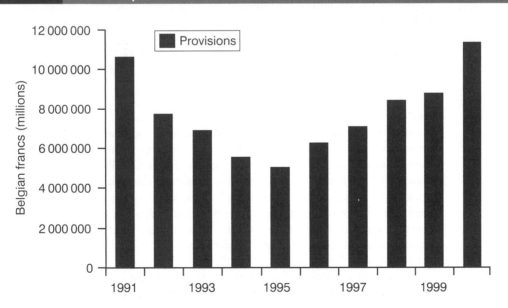

High-quality Standards are characterised by their stringent rules for the creation and the use of provisions. A provision for the renewal of the fleet, would under strict compliance with IAS/IFRS not have been possible. So these practices are more easy to apply for managers when they use low-quality accounting standards. However if managers are operating in countries with weak shareholder protection and low risk of litigation it might be tempting to use this type of earnings management even when high-quality accounting standards are used for the preparation of the financial statements. Due to the low risk of litigation the costs of non-compliance with accounting standards are low. The latter is referred to in the literature as GAAP–application quality.

Impairment of assets: Through impairment of assets costs in the current period are increased. The remaining book value is lower and, as a result, future depreciation costs will be lower. Sabena recorded, beside the creation of provisions for fleet renewal, impairment of assets on the aircraft present in their fleet as we saw in the extract of the annual report of 1996 (p. 9), cited earlier. Large impairments of assets also occurred in 1997:

> The board of directors decided actively to pursue the recovery plan to redress the accounts of Sabena and its subsidiaries in order to provide them with the maximum resources for the future. Within Sabena, the pursuit of this recovery plan was mainly reflected in the value reductions made to aircraft, above all in the case of the 2 Boeing 747s.
>
> (Annual Report 1997 p. 9)

These aircraft were later the subject of sale and leaseback transactions. The surplus realised at the moment of the sale of the aircraft was spread over the leasing period of those planes in 1998 and in 1999. As a result the impact of the leasing costs of those planes on the profit and loss account was softened in those years. Here we observe a combination of an accrual accounting decision (recording of impairments) followed by a real transaction (sale and leaseback of a plane).

Under low-quality accounting standards there is usually less guidance on how to determine the amount of the impairment. Very often these standards of lower quality only stipulate that in case of a major reduction in value an impairment should be recorded. In this book we illustrated how under IAS 36 the amount of the impairment should be determined. We recall from Chapter 12 in Part Two that managers have fewer degrees of freedom for the determination of the impairment under standards of higher quality.

Real transactions Companies are constantly engaged in operating, financing and investment transactions. These real transactions, however, can also be used for annual account's management purposes. Common examples are the deferral of transactions to future periods, such as purchases and R&D. In some cases, the choice of a particular transaction (e.g. financing through a finance lease or operating lease) is not neutral with regard to the impact on the annual accounts. As a result the choice of operating, investment and financing decisions might be influenced or even determined by accounting valuation or presentation issues. Sometimes, real transactions are only undertaken with the purpose of annual accounts management.

A common example is the sale of assets with a gain on disposal. This has an immediate favourable effect on the result of that year (except for certain sale and leaseback transactions; see Chapter 14). The possibility of creating profit through a sale of assets depends to a large extent on the valuation principles which are applied in the company or are required by the GAAP to which the company complies. In a historical cost environment the possibilities for these one-time big gains are much larger than in an environment dominated by fair value valuation.

The impact of these one-time gains could even be enhanced by combining the real transactions (sale of asset) with a large write-down or impairment the year before the sale. This practice was applied by Sabena. The airplanes on which large impairments had been recorded were sold. A number of those planes were leased back for a short time period. The profits realised on those planes were deducted from the rental costs for the years 1998 and 1999; as a result the operating costs for the airline were lower in 1998 and 1999.

Gains or losses realised on the sale of assets always have an influence on the individual accounts of the entity that undertakes the transaction. However, if the sale is realised within a group, these intra-group sales with gains or losses have no influence on the group accounts. In circumstances in which individual accounts are used for regulatory, tax or legal purposes, one must be vigilant for these intra-group profits. The profit reported in 1999 in the individual accounts of Sabena NV was mainly created through the transfer of assets from Sabena NV to a newly created subsidiary Sabena Technics NV. It had no effect on the result in the group accounts.

It is clear that not all changes in accounting estimates, accounting method changes and real transactions are induced by earnings management motives or balance sheet management motives. It is important for an analyst to consider all possible explanations for these changes or transactions when they occur. This will be illustrated by the following example.

In the individual accounts of Sabena NV a change in allowances for bad debts is noticed in the year 2000 – a year in which the company is already seriously in distress. The evolution of allowances for bad debts is presented in Table 30.1. In 2000 there is a decrease in the allowances for bad debt, whereas in prior years there was an increase related to the change in allowances for bad debt (see Activity 30.9).

At the end of the discussion on annual accounts' management practices it is important to highlight that most methods of annual accounts management have what is called a *reversal effect*. Reversal means that income increasing accounting interventions in the current period lead to a decrease in income in future periods and vice versa. In fact, many of the methods applied involve only inter-temporal shifts in accounting income. In the literature accounting method choices are often labelled as having a reversal effect (declining depreciation will have lower profits in the beginning than the straight line method, but after a certain moment in the life span of the asset the situation reverses), whereas a real transaction is often labelled as having a one-time effect. However, all three practices (accounting method changes, accounting estimates and real transactions) might entail reversing effects. If one sells, for example, a fuel hedge contract to have an increase in profits in the year the contract is sold, the company will probably suffer from higher fuel prices in the period thereafter. So the sale of the contract is not limited to a one-time effect.

An element that might differ between the different methods for annual accounts management is the timing of the reversal effect (see Activity 30.10 on p. 783).

Bowen, DuCharme and Chores (1995) found that management in general chooses accounting interventions with a long-term positive effect on accounting income.

ACTIVITY 30.9

If you relate the change in bad debt allowance to the elements of the annual accounts (balance sheet total, turnover, equity) of Sabena do you think the amount is material (balance sheet total 61 billion BEF, revenue see Table 30.1, equity at 31.12.2000, 220 392 (000) BEF)?

Activity feedback

At first sight the amount does not seem to be material, at least not in relation to the balance sheet total of 61 billion BEF or to the total revenue of 94 billion BEF. However if we relate the amount to the equity of the company we get a different picture. The equity in 2000 declined to 220 392 (000) BEF. The difference between an increase of bad debt allowances of +/ 40 million BEF (year 1999) and a decrease of 57 million BEF (year 2000) amounts to 90 million BEF. This 90 million BEF compared with 220 million BEF is not that immaterial. However, economic explanations for this change in allowances for bad debts should always be considered. It could be that the sepa-

ration of Sabena Technics from Sabena NV in 1999 was the explaining factor. Maybe customers of Sabena Technics have another payment profile. In order to investigate for this possibility the data of Technics are added in 1999 and 2000 to the Sabena NV data.

Another explanation could be the creation of the Airline Management Partnership. Does the AMP play a role in the treatment of uncollectable receivables? Note that in the annual report of Sabena, AMP is announced as a major restructuring for a number of activities under which come 'marketing, product and sales'. A further explanation could be that Sabena is pursuing a stricter collection policy due to her own liquidity problems. In an effort to improve cash flow, the management of firms in serious distress usually take action to accelerate the collection of receivables. This leads to a lower balance in receivables and a decrease in allowances for bad debt. These are questions which cannot be answered by an external analyst on the basis of published information. Only insiders know the answer.

| TABLE 30.1 | Evolution of turnover and bad debt allowances in the financial statements of Sabena NV and Sabena Technics NV |

In (000 BEF)	Turnover		Changes in bad debt allowances	
	Sabena	Sabena + Technics	Sabena	Sabena + Technics
1997	65 384 958	65 384 958	38 266	38 266
1998	80 363 967	80 363 967	90 515	90 515
1999	76 975 634	89 544 618	47 634	138 294
2000	94 747 785	106 598 381	(57 069)	(204 309)

Source: Financial statements of Sabena NV and Sabena Technics NV.

However, if the compensation scheme of the management had short-term perspectives, practices with shorter reversal periods were used.

The story of Sabena In Figure 30.1 we presented the net results of Sabena NV over the years 1991–2000 and in Figure 30.2 the results of the Sabena Group over the years 1992–2000. In this section we link together all the information we have collected so far on Sabena and re-analyse the evolution of the reported results. The aim of this illustration is to analyse the accounting and reporting strategy and to get an idea of the underlying economic result.

ACTIVITY 30.10

Think of some methods to be used for annual accounts management purposes with a short reversal time and methods with a longer reversal time.

Activity feedback

A change in accounting methods or estimates in the area of the working capital of a firm might have a short reversal period, e.g. a switch from one inventory valuation method to another, a change in the estimates of bad debt allowances.

Working capital accruals reverse in the short term as these elements are short-term assets and liabilities. This implies that if the results fall short the year after, additional earnings influence practices must be used if one does not want the result to drop. The reversal period in relation to non-working capital items is longer. For example the gain realised on sale and leaseback transactions is spread out over the life span of the leased asset.

In 1991 big bath accounting was practised in order to enhance the future of Sabena. Figure 30.1 clearly illustrates this. In 1992 the cooperation with Air France started. The figure presents the operating result and the net result of the individual accounts of Sabena NV over the period 1992–2000. Figure 30.2 presents the consolidated results of the Sabena Group over the same period. In Figure 30.5 the important company events are mentioned.

In the first time frame, namely the cooperation with Air France, the results fluctuate almost within a more narrow band-width. The results were kept within that bandwidth partly due to the release of provisions over those years (see Figure 30.4) In 1992 the individual accounts were positively influenced due to the sale of the charter activities to another entity, namely Sabena Leasing NV, which is also part of the Sabena group. This intra-group sale was only beneficial for the individual accounts of Sabena, in the group accounts this intra-group profit was eliminated.

At the start of the second time frame, namely the cooperation with the SAir Group, especially in 1996, the financial year where the new CEO comes in, the results drop sharply. The subsequent messages of the board of directors even provide information on the goal they were pursuing and on the methods they were using to obtain the goal. The accounting strategy was making it possible for Sabena to show profit from 1998 on. The subsequent messages of the board of directors could be regarded as implicit contracts for profitability from 1998 on. For example (Annual Report 1997, p. 30):

> In 1997 the Sabena Group's exceptional result was influenced, as it had been in 1996, by the implementation of the balance sheet recovery plan with the intention that certain factors should no longer have an adverse effect on the profit and loss account in the coming years.

The two time frames can also be distinguished if we represent the exceptional costs and exceptional revenues in a graphical way (Figure 30.6). During the cooperation with Air France it is a rather stable pattern. From 1996 to 1999 we observe a gradual increase of exceptional revenue. In 2000 a new CEO comes in.

If we return to the second time frame in Figure 30.5 we might state that the frontloading of costs, a favourable economic climate and gains on disposal of assets resulted in the 'promised' profit in 1998 in the individual accounts as well as in the consolidated accounts. The gain in the number of planes (mainly Boeings) acquired under a sale and leaseback agreement also favourably influenced the result of 1999,

FIGURE 30.5 Net and operating result of Sabena NV, 1992–2000

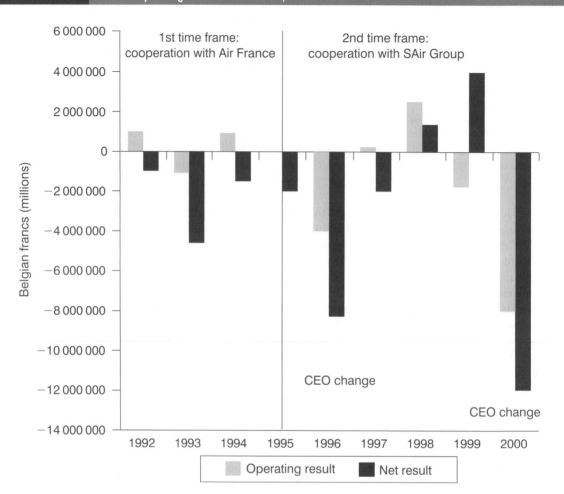

SOURCE: ANNUAL ACCOUNTS OF SABENA NV, 1992–2000

as part of the gain was carried forward. In 1999 the group results were negative again (see Figure 30.2); the individual accounts, however, showed a good profit figure of 4 billion BEF through intra-group sales as explained earlier. The 'reported' results of Sabena looked fair in 1998, although whether the underlying economic performance had also improved could not yet be judged. This would only become clear after a few years, since Sabena had practised to some extent what is called big bath accounting in the years before 1998. Many stakeholders involved considered this reported profit as a major breakthrough. In many textbooks, however, warnings with regard to big bath accounting can be found. For example, Penman (2001, p. 601):

> This intertemporal shifting of income means that earnings quality is not only doubtful in the year of the manipulation but also in subsequent years when borrowing or saving of income 'comes home to roost'.

It is important to note here that the board of directors of Sabena had made in their messages the necessary disclosures, so that external parties who had taken the time

FIGURE 30.6   Evaluation of exceptional results within Sabena NV, 1992–2000

to look at the annual reports of prior years, knew they had to judge the results of 1998 with the necessary caution.

Due to the elements mentioned in the introduction to this chapter on Sabena – unfavourable economic climate, rising costs due to prior management decisions, extensive and expensive fleet renewal and to a lesser extent rather expensive outsourcing of activities (evidence of the latter can be found in interviews given by the management of Sabena to the press and by declarations of the members of the management before the parliamentary investigation committee in Belgium), high fuel prices, unfavourable exchange rate with the dollar – but also due to the reversal effect of certain of the accounting methods used, the results of 2000 collapsed.

The purpose of this section on practices of annual accounts' management was to highlight the importance of gaining understanding into the accounting flexibility which is available to the management of a company. For financial analysis purposes it is not only important to understand the accounting flexibility which was available, but it is also necessary to know which valuation rules and estimates are used in the presentation of those annual accounts. In order to get an idea about the valuation methods used and accounting estimates applied the quality and the level of disclosure in the financial statements is an important determinant of the visibility of accounting interventions. Unfortunately, the level of disclosure differs among companies.

Quality of disclosure

When management provides the necessary disclosures in the notes to the balance sheet, profit and loss account and cash flow statement and in the management discussion report, it facilitates the analysis of the business reality of the company by external parties. Financial statements are meant to inform the stakeholders of the firm about the result, the cash flow and the financial position of the firm. In principle, the published figures should represent the underlying economic situation of the firm. However, due to the flexibility that exists in the accounting standards to be applied and the incentives top executives face towards earnings management a situation might be created in which the published figures in the financial statements do not translate the underlying economic condition of the firm. Although companies must provide a minimum level of disclosure as required by the GAAP they are complying with, the management team can always make more voluntary disclosures. Disclosure quality refers to the compliance of a company to all the disclosures required by the GAAP and to the informativeness of the voluntary disclosures which are presented in the annual report. So disclosure quality and the level of disclosure can also be extended to the narrative part of the annual report. This will be discussed further in Chapter 31. Empirical and analytical accounting research has paid attention to disclosure practices. Most empirical research studies provide evidence that an increase in disclosure leads to lower costs of capital due to the reduction in information asymmetry (e.g. Leuz and Verrechia, 2003). The analytical research, however, indicates that there is an optimal level of disclosure for a company.

Disclosure quality is an important benchmark when inter-firm comparisons are made and it relates to several aspects. Some examples of disclosure quality will now be illustrated.

Description of accounting methods and accounting estimates So far we have learned that the choice of accounting valuation methods and accounting estimates can influence the reported profit and the balance sheet structure. Adequate disclosure in the notes on the methods and the estimates used might enable external analysts to get an idea of the impact of the choice and to reconcile earnings of different firms when executing a comparative financial analysis of companies. Further, a company can also explain why a particular choice has been made. If we compare the different airlines we notice that the level of explanation with regard to, for example, how frequent flyer obligations are accounted for differs. Frequent flyer programmes could create obligations for an airline. However, the obligation is dependent on several terms of the contract between the airline and the customer. On top of that several ways exist to account for these obligations: the incremental cost approach whereby the costs are charged to P&L when passengers make use of the bonus miles or the revenue minus approach whereby part of the revenue of the ticket sale is deferred to the moment the passenger makes use of the bonus miles (a provision is then created).

In the notes containing the description of the accounting policies of Sabena we find the following brief disclosure (Annual Report 2000, p. 50, n. 5.7):

> Appropriate provisions are also made for liabilities arising from mileages accrued via the Qualiflyer frequent flyer programme. These provisions are equal to the costs to be incurred as such credits are redeemed.

In the accounts of British Airways, the programmes themselves are described together with the way they are accounted for:

Revenue recognition – Mileage programmes
The Group operates two principal loyalty programmes. The airline frequent flyer programme operates through the airline's 'Executive Club' and allows frequent

travellers to accumulate 'BA Miles' mileage credits which entitle them to a choice of various awards, primarily free travel. The estimated direct incremental cost of providing free redemption service, including British Airways' flights, in exchange for redemption of miles earned by members of the Group's 'Executive Club' is accrued as members of the scheme accumulated mileage. These costs are charged to selling costs.

In addition, 'BA Miles' are sold to commercial partners to use in promotional activity. The fair value of the miles sold is deferred and recognised as revenue on redemption of the miles by the participants to whom the miles are issued. The incremental cost of providing free redemption services is recognised when the miles are redeemed.

The Group also operates the AIRMILES scheme, operated by the Company's wholly-owned subsidiary Airmiles Travel Promotions Limited. The scheme allows companies to purchase miles for use in their own promotional activities. Miles can be redeemed for a range of benefits, including flights on British Airways and other carriers. The fair value of the miles sold is deferred and recognised as revenue on redemption of the miles by the participants to whom the miles are issued. The incremental cost of providing free redemption services is recognised when the miles are redeemed.

(British Airways Annual Report 2005/2006, p. 61)

Explanation of significant changes in accounting methods and accounting estimates
Accounting method changes hinder external users of the financial statements in comparing the results and the balance sheet structures over the years. Adequate disclosure of the new accounting method applied and the impact on comparability could facilitate the analysis.

When Ryanair changed its accounting policies for the provision for maintenance of aircraft and for depreciation of aircraft (Annual Report 1999, p. 29, n. 1: prior year adjustment) extensive explanation was provided regarding the impact of this change on the profit and loss account, the tangible assets, the provisions and the equity of the company.

For airlines complying with IAS the issuance of SIC 23 (*Property, Plant and Equipment – Major Inspection or Overhaul Costs*) implied changes with regard to the treatment of major inspection or overhaul costs. The level of disclosure with regard to this change, however, differed among the airlines.

Level of information disclosure Another example which relates to quality of disclosure is the level of compliance with disclosures required by GAAP and the extra-voluntary disclosure provided on that item. With regard to related parties a separate disclosure has to be made under several GAAP, e.g. IAS/IFRS (see Chapter 29). If we compare the item 'related party disclosures' between the annual accounts of Lufthansa and those of the SAir Group and Sabena we observe differences, even though both airlines prepare their annual accounts using IAS/IFRS.

SAir limits the explicit note on related parties to note 29 'Transactions with board members and key shareholders'. Board members and key shareholders are indeed third parties, however; we know that the airlines in which SAir holds a substantial minority shareholding qualify as related parties due to the way they are accounted for in the books of SAir, namely by using the equity method. Information on those third parties is distributed over several different items in the notes of the financial statements of the SAir Group (SAir Annual Report 2000, p. 33). For example n. 12, p. 21 on the accounts receivable includes elements which classify in fact as related party disclosures:

> Trade accounts receivable: of which CHF 66 million due from associated undertakings, other accounts receivable: of which CHF 12 million due from associated undertakings, current loans: of which CHF 13 million due from associated undertakings.

Related party information is also found in the notes on lease payments (see Chapter 31). Sabena on the other hand included the following disclosure with regard to related parties:

> No transactions were effected with Board members, affiliated companies or key shareholders in the course of the year. There are no receivables or liabilities outstanding between the Sabena Group and its Board members or key shareholders.
>
> (Annual Report 2000, note 28 'Transactions with Board members and key shareholders', p 67)

Given the information available on the relation between SAir and Sabena, it is doubtful that this disclosure is even true.

In the annual accounts of Lufthansa, however (Annual Report 2005, n. 46) the information on related party disclosures is bundled into one note, and the information disclosed is much more extensive. Together with the kind of relationship, a list is presented with the amount of services rendered to the related party and the amount of services utilised:

46) Related party transactions

The business segments of the Lufthansa Group render numerous services to non-consolidated affiliated companies within the scope of their ordinary activities. In turn, the respective investments render services to the Lufthansa Group within the scope of their business purpose. These extensive supply and service relationships are managed on the basis of market prices.

In addition, the Group and certain non-consolidated subsidiaries have concluded numerous settlement agreements regulating the partly mutual utilisation of services. Administrative services rendered are in this case charged as cost allocations.

The cash management of the Lufthansa Group is centralised, and in this respect the Lufthansa Group assumes a 'banking function' also in respect of non-consolidated group companies. The non-consolidated group companies included in the Group's cash management invest their available cash in the Group or borrow funds from the Group and effect their derivative hedging transactions there. All of the transactions are managed under market conditions.

Because of the geographical proximity, a large number of sub-rental contracts have been concluded between the Lufthansa Group and certain related parties; in these cases, the Lufthansa Group usually re-debits the rental costs and incidental expenses incurred to the respective companies on a pro rata basis.

The volume of material services rendered to or provided by related parties may be gathered from the following table:

	Volume of services rendered		Volume of services utilised	
	2005	*2004*	*2005*	*2005*
	€m	*€m*	*€m*	*€m*
Subsidiaries				
Albatros Versicherungsdienste GmbH	4	14	72	106
Cargo Future Communications (CFC) GmbH	0*	1	6	6
Delvag Lufftahrtversicherungs-AG	7	19	6	7
Global Tele Sales (PTY) Ltd., Südafrika	0*	0*	5	4
Global Tele Sales Ltd. Ireland	1	1	7	6
Global Telesales of Canada, Inc.	0*	1	6	5
LRS Lufthansa Revenue Services GmbH	15	19	63	65
Lufthansa Engineering and Operational Services GmbH	4	5	24	21
Lufthansa Global Tele Sales GmbH	1	1	8	7
Lufthansa Service-Center Kassel GmbH	1	–	8	–
Lufthansa Systems FlightNav AG, Schweiz	1	1	6	1
Lufthansa Systems Hungaria Kft	1	1	12	8
Lufthansa Systems Network Services GmbH	0*	0*	21	18
Lufthansa Technical Training GmbH	8	9	24	24
Lufthansa Technik Budapest Repülogép Nagyjavító Kit	1	2	23	18
Lufthansa Technik Logistik of America LLC	2	2	11	10
Lufthansa Technik Malta Limited	0*	1	5	6
Lufthansa Technik Tulsa Corporation	3	2	7	5
Lufthansa Technik Turbine Shannon Limited	2	3	11	11
Lufthansa WorldShop GmbH	2	1	42	32
LZ-Catering GmbH	9	10	15	11
Miles & More International GmbH	55	40	1	1
Joint Ventures				
AFC Aviation Fuel Company mbH	2	2	320	212
Alitalia Maintenance Systems S.p.A.	31	27	31	34
Lufthansa Bombardier Aviation Services GmbH	12	7	0*	0*
Star Alliance Services GmbH	5	0*	0*	6
Thomas Cook AG (plus Condor Flugdienst GmbH)	240	185	7	45
Associated Companies				
AviationPower GmbH	0*	–	7	–
British Midland plc	0*	11	21	34
HEICO Aerospace Holdings Corp.	–	–	13	13
Terminal 2 Betriebsgesellschaft mbH & Co oHG	3	3	109	96

*Rounded below € 1m.

There are no individual shareholders of Lufthansa AG with a significant influence on the Group. As regards relationships with Executive and Supervisory Board members, cf. note 47.

(Lufthansa Annual Report, pp. 121–122)

ENTITY ANALYSIS

In the earlier section on methods of annual accounts' management we saw that results of the individual accounts can be influenced through intra-group sales. If there is a relationship of control these results are eliminated in the group accounts in the consolidation process (see Part Three of this textbook). This means, however, that it is important to look into the different relationships one company might have with other companies. There are different kinds of relationship between an investor company and the company it has invested in. These different kinds of relationship need different accounting treatments. The following treatments are laid down in all GAAP: control (the investee is consolidated), significant influence (equity method) and no influence (valuation at cost).

When there is a control relationship, there is always the possibility of transferring profits from one company to the other by means of transfer prices for goods and services transferred between group members. These intra-group profits are eliminated when all companies over which a holding company has control are fully consolidated.

In case of a significant influence in a company, but without control, the undertaking is accounted for by the equity method. In situations where there is control but the undertaking is accounted for by the equity method, the accounts of both parties involved do not present a true picture of the underlying relationship and position of the group.

The 'real' nature of the relationship should be considered and compared with the accounting treatment applied in the annual accounts. Sometimes it might be that the accounting treatment does not comply with the underlying relationship. As an external analyst it is extremely useful to know why there is this difference and what the impact on the published accounts is. Especially under rules-based GAAP, companies can set up separate entities using legal constructions in such a way that the legal form of the relationship does not comply with the definition of control embedded in the GAAP used by the controlling company. In these circumstances, a change in the accounting standards might turn an associated company into a subsidiary for reporting purposes. We will elaborate this item further at the end of this section.

Through the following activity we will illustrate the impact on the annual accounts of the investor according to the accounting method applied: full consolidation or equity method. This activity illustrates further the reporting procedures presented in Part Three.

We notice that if the transactions with associated entities are accounted for in a correct manner the impact on the net result of the investor company is the same as under full consolidation. The only difference concerning the profit and loss account relates to the lines where the result is eliminated (see Activities 30.11 and 30.12). The operating result under the equity method is always 10 000, in the case of consolidation the loss or profit made by B on the sale is reflected in the operating result. Although the net result is the same amount under both the equity method and full consolidation, the amounts representing the operating revenue and the operating result are different. This might have an impact on ratios calculated where sales or operating results are included in the nominator or denominator. (See Chapter 31 for more information on ratio analysis.) The main difference with regard to full consolidation or equity relates mainly to the balance sheet. The amount of debt is much higher in the case of full consideration.

A further element with regard to entity analysis is the question whether all entities with which a company has a link have been included in the consolidated accounts and are properly accounted for (consolidated, equity method or valued at cost according to the relation). In this context the creation of special purpose entities is important.

ACTIVITY 30.11

Company A owns 45% of the shares of company B; company A bought the shares on 1.1.X. Company A sells goods or services to company B. Company B sells the goods or services further to their clients. The beginning balance sheets of the individual accounts of company A and B follow. Assume that company A sells a product to company B, at year-end 31.12.X company B has sold all products to third parties. The cost of the products for company A amounts to €40 000. Company A sells the products to company B for €50 000. In the first situation company B is able to realise a turnover of €56 000 with the sale of the products to its customers. In the second situation company B realises only a turnover of €42 000. This sale of products is the only activity for company A and B in the year X.

	Balance sheet A company 1.1.X	Balance sheet company B 1.1.X
Financial assets	45 000	
Other assets	755 000	400 000
Total assets	800 000	400 000
Equity	300 000	100 000
Liabilities	500 000	300 000
Total equity + liabilities	800 000	400 000

Consider, for both situations, the impact on the profit and loss account for company B. Take further into account the regulation on accounting for associated entities and consider the impact on the profit and loss account of company A, the investor, if the shareholding in B is accounted for under the equity method. When solving this activity bear in mind what you learned about the equity method and accounting for associated companies in prior chapters of this book.

Activity feedback

Situation 1: Company B is able to sell the products for €56 000

	Individual accounts, company A	Individual accounts, company B	Group accounts, company A
Balance sheet			
Financial assets	45 000		47 700
Other assets	765 000	406 000	765 000
Total assets	810 000	406 000	812 700
Equity	310 000	106 000	312 700
Liabilities	500 000	300 000	500 000
Equity + liabilities	810 000	406 000	812 700
Profit and loss account			
Operating revenue	50 000	56 000	50 000
Operating costs	40 000	50 000	40 000
Operating results	10 000	6 000	10 000
Results from associated undertakings			2 700
Net result	10 000	6 000	12 700

Situation 2: Company B sells the products for €42 000

	Individual accounts, company A	Individual accounts, company B	Group accounts, company A
Balance sheet			
Financial assets	45 000		41 400
Other assets	765 000	392 000	765 000
Total assets	810 000	392 000	806 400
Equity	310 000	92 000	306 400
Liabilities	500 000	300 000	500 000
Equity − liabilities	810 000	392 000	806 400
Profit and loss account			
Operating revenue	50 000	42 000	50 000
Operating costs	40 000	50 000	40 000
Operating results	10 000	(8 000)	10 000
Results from associated undertakings			(3 600)
Net result	10 000	(8 000)	6 400

In the last decades of the 20th century SPEs were created for various reasons, in the beginning especially for lease purposes and later on, for other reasons (e.g. increasing revenue). The entity analysis performed should take into account whether or not all special purpose entities set up by a company are included or left out from the consolidation process. However, there can be differences in the GAAP which is applied. It is said that the SPEs which Enron had created and which they could

ACTIVITY 30.12

Assume that there are underlying contracts between the management of company *A* and the shareholders of company *B* in which agreements are made that company *A* has the power to control the operating and financing activities of company *B*. Remember what you learned about consolidation in Part Three. Consider also the definition of control in IFRS 3 and the accounting method prescribed in IAS 27. How should company *A* now account for company *B* and what would be the difference with the situation presented under Activity 30.11?

Activity feedback

Company *A* would now have to consolidate company *B*. The consolidated accounts of the group *AB* would present the following picture.

	B sold the products for €56 000	B sold the products for €42 000
Group balance sheet		
Total assets	1 171 000	1 157 000
Equity (capital – reserves)	300 000	300 000
Results of the year	12 700	6 400
Minority interests	58 300	50 600
Liabilities	800 000	800 000
Total equity and liabilities	1 171 000	1 157 000

	B sold the products for €56 000	B sold the products for €42 000
Group profit and loss account		
Operating revenue	56 000	42 000
Operating costs	40 000	40 000
Net result	16 000	2 000
Share of minority interests	(3 300)	4 400
Net result for the group	12 700	6 400

exclude from consolidation under US GAAP would have been consolidated if Enron would have applied IAS/IFRS.

In the wake of the accounting scandals, the FASB looked into these issues. In January 2003, the FASB issued FASB Interpretation no. 46, *Consolidation of Variable Interest Entities – VIE (FIN 46)* and amended it in October 2003. Variable interest entities are entities that lack sufficient equity to finance their activities without additional financial support from other parties or whose equity holders lack adequate decision-making ability based on the criteria set forth in that Interpretation.

Economic criteria such as 'lack of sufficient equity to finance the activities' or 'lack of decision-making ability' now dominate the decision whether or not to consolidate an entity in the group accounts. Due to this change in the standards on variable interest entities, the Walt Disney Company now has to include its two theme parks, Euro Disney in France and Hong Kong Disneyland, in its group accounts with the use of the full consolidation method. Up until 2003 both theme parks were included in the group accounts of the Walt Disney Company with the use of the equity method. With regard to the investment Euro Disney, the economic situation of Euro Disney and its relationship with the Walt Disney Company are now presented in Activity 30.13.

ACTIVITY 30.13

When you read the following information, consider the characteristics of a variable interest entity. Which elements embedded in FIN 46 do you recognise in the relation between the Walt Disney Company and Euro Disney?

The Walt Disney Company holds 39% of the capital of Euro Disney SCA, but Euro Disney SCA is managed by Euro Disney SA, which is an indirect 99% owned subsidiary of the Walt Disney Company. Further in connection with a financial restructuring of Euro Disney in 1994, Euro Disney Associe's SNC, a wholly owned affiliate of the Walt Disney Company, entered into a lease arrangement with a financing company with a non-cancellable term of 12 years related to substantially all of the Disneyland Park assets and then entered into a 12-year sub-lease agreement with Euro Disney on substantially the same terms. At the conclusion of the sub-lease term, Euro Disney will have the option of assuming Disney SNC's rights and obligations under the lease for a payment of $90 million over the ensuing 15 months. If Euro Disney does not exercise its option, Disney SNC may purchase the assets, continue to lease the assets or elect to terminate the lease. In the event the lease is terminated, Disney SNC would be obligated to make a termination payment to the lessor equal to 75% of the lessor's then outstanding debt related to the Disneyland Park assets, which payment would be approximately $1.3 billion. Disney SNC would then have the right to sell or lease the assets on behalf of the lessor to satisfy the remaining debt, with any excess proceeds payable to Disney SNC. Euro Disney's financial difficulties, notwithstanding, the company believes it is unlikely that Disney SNC would be required to pay the 75% lease termination payment as the company currently expects that in order for Euro Disney to continue its business it will either exercise its assumption option in 2006 or that the assumption of the lease by Euro Disney will otherwise be provided for in the resolution to Euro Disney's financial situation.

Activity feedback

We distinguish the 'lack of management power'. Euro Disney is, in fact, managed by a subsidiary of the Walt Disney Company. Further we notice that due to the weak financial situation of Euro Disney from the start, a subsidiary of the Walt Disney Company bears the financial risks in relation to the lease agreements Euro Disney has with the lessor of the assets. Euro Disney SNC is obliged to fulfil the commitments towards the lessor if Euro Disney SCA is not able to pay the lessor.

Although the economic situation and the legal situation of the relationship between the Walt Disney Company and Euro Disney did not change from 2003 to 2004, the accounting method the Walt Disney Company will use to account for its investment in Paris will be different. This change in method is a result of a change in accounting standards. In its annual report the Walt Disney Company informs its readers (see the extract from the annual report, which follows (note 2 of the annual accounts of TWDC, 2003)). The impact of a change in accounting standards is illustrated with the use of the economic situation of the Walt Disney Company and Euro Disney. The financial figures of Euro Disney will also be used further in this chapter.

	As Reported	Euro Disney	Hong Kong Disneyland	Adjustments	As Adjusted
Results of Operations					
Revenues	$ 27 061	$ 1 077	$ 5	$ (10)	$ 28 133
Cost and expenses	(24 330)	(1 032)	(7)	9	(25 360)
Amortisation of intangibles assets	(18)	–	–	–	(18)
Gain on sale of business	16	–	–	–	16
Net interest expense	(793)	(101)	–	–	(894)
Equity in the income of investees	334	–	–	24	358
Restructuring and impairment charges	(16)	–	–	–	(16)
Income before income taxes, minority interest and the cumulative effect of accounting change	2 254	(56)	(2)	23	2 219

	As Reported	Euro Disney	Hong Kong Disneyland	Adjustments	As Adjusted
Income taxes	(789)	–	–	13	(776)
Minority interests	(127)	–	–	22	(105)
Cumulative effect of accounting change	(71)	–	–	–	(71)
Net income/(loss)	$ 1 267	$ (56)	$ (2)	$ 58	$ 1 267
Balance Sheet:					
Cash and cash equivalents	$ 1 583	$ 103	$ 76	$ –	$ 1 762
Other current assets	6 731	191	9	(9)	6 922
Total current assets	8 314	294	85	(9)	8 684
Investments	1 849	–	–	(623)	1 226
Fixed assets	12 678	2 951	524	–	16 153
Intangible assets	2 786	–	–	–	2 786
Goodwill	16 966	–	–	–	16 966
Other assets	7 395	128	9	–	7 532
Total assets	$ 49 988	$ 3 373	$ 618	$ (632)	$ 53 347
Current portion of borrowings[1]	$ 2 457	$ 2 528	$ –	$ (388)	4 597
Other current liabilities	6 212	487	61	(85)	6 675
Total current liabilities	8 669	3 015	61	(473)	11 272
Borrowings	10 643	–	237	–	10 880
Deferred income taxes	2 712	–	–	–	2 712
Other long-term liabilities	3 745	289	–	(71)	3 963
Minority interests	428	–	–	301	729
Shareholders' equity	23 791	69	320	(389)	23 791
Total liabilities and shareholders' equity	$ 49 988	$ 3 373	$618	$(632)	$ 53 347

[1] All of Euro Disney's borrowings are classified as current as they are subject to acceleration if a long-term solution to Euro Disney's financing needs is not achieved by March 31, 2004.

Impact of FIN 46 on Equity Investments

As discussed in Note 2, the implementation of FIN 46 will likely require the Walt Disney Company to consolidate both Euro Disney and Hong Kong Disneyland for financial reporting purposes in the first quarter of fiscal 2004. The above tables present consolidated results of operations and financial position for the Walt Disney Company as of and for the year ended September 30 2003 as if Euro Disney and Hong Kong Disneyland had been consolidated based on our current analysis and understanding of FIN 46.

Now take a look of Activity 30.14.

ACCOUNTING ANALYSIS: THE AVAILABLE ACCOUNTING DISCRETION

As already mentioned, we know that accounting analysis involves an evaluation of the accounting flexibility available to the management of the company. Accounting flexibility is first influenced by the type of GAAP a company applies. This aspect will be elaborated further below in the section 'Impact of accounting standards used on annual accounts'. In order, however, to make a judgement

ACTIVITY 30.14

Lufthansa has acquired 49% of the shares of the Swiss company Air Trust AG in late 2005. Air Trust AG owns 100% of the shares of the airline SWISS, the combination of the bankrupt airline Swissair with Crossair. The other shareholder of the company, Air Trust AG, is the Swiss Almea Foundation which holds 51% of the shares. A direct takeover of SWISS in 2005–2006 is not possible because the traffic rights of SWISS might lose their value then. (See Lufthansa Annual Report 2005, p. 55):

> The traffic rights of SWISS are based on bilateral agreements with the target countries and are tied to Switzerland as the home location. In the wake of a direct takeover of Swiss by Lufthansa these traffic rights would lose their value. That is why the full integration of SWISS will occur only after talks have been held with the target countries in which the traffic rights are to be secured. This process is progressing well. It is unlikely, however, that the negotiations will be concluded before the end of 2006.
>
> On 3 May 2005, Lufthansa acquired eleven per cent of the shares in AirTrust AG at a price of TCHF 11. The purpose of this company is to purchase and hold shares of Swiss International Air Lines AG. Following approval by the EU commission and the US antitrust enforcement agency, the share in AirTrust AG was increased by 38 percent at a price of TCHF 38 to in total 49 per cent on 27 July 2005. The remaining 51 percent will be acquired as soon as negotiations with regard to securing air traffic rights have been concluded and the respective arrangements provided. AirTrust AG is treated as a special purpose entity under SIC 12 fully consolidated in the consolidated financial statements. Since the purchase price was equal to the acquired equity share, the transaction has not resulted in any goodwill.

Balance sheet of Air Trust AG immediately before and after the acquisition date:

	1.7.2005 TCHF
Assets	
Liquid funds	100
Equity and liabilities	
Equity	100

> After 27 July 2005, AirTrust AG successively acquired shares from Swiss International Air Lines AG, which purchase was financed by loans from Deutsche Lufthansa AG. As at 31 December 2005, AirTrust AG held 99.4 per cent of the SWISS shares. However, it does not exercise any controlling influence because it has no representative in the administrative board of Swiss International Air Lines AG and no other means of control. The majority of the members of the administrative board is provided by Almea Shiftung, with two of the five seats being currently assigned to Deutsche Lufthansa AG. Swiss International Airlines AG is, therefore, accounted for at equity in the consolidated financial statements. The profit contribution of AirTrust AG including this investment in Swiss International Airlines AG accounted for under the equity method amounted to in total €292m in financial year 2005. The result includes income of €291m from the excess balance of the assets and liabilities of Swiss International Air Lines AG acquired through Air Trust AG and measured at fair value over the acquisition cost of such shares. Even with complete inclusion in the group of consolidated companies as from the beginning of financial year 2005, the profit contribution would be unchanged.
>
> (Lufthansa Annual Report 2006, pp. 82–83)

The comment about the profit contribution not being influenced by the choice between the equity method and full consolidation is correct. However, what would change if Lufthansa would fully consolidate SWISS into its accounts?

Activity feedback

The external debt of SWISS would increase the debt figure of the Lufthansa Group. Further, minority interests (51% in this case) would have to be recognised. Intrafirm transactions would have to be eliminated. This might change the amounts of revenues and expenses, but would not affect the net result of the group (see also the example of the Walt Disney Company).

Lufthansa acquired the remaining 51% of the shares of SWISS in 2007 and SWISS is now fully consolidated in the annual accounts of Lufthansa from 2007 onwards.

about the latitude of action, top management has to influence the accounts in the direction which is favourable to them; more elements play a role than just the flexibility of the GAAP applied. Research results indicate that certain company characteristics, characteristics of the board of directors, auditors' characteristics and the institutional environment influence all the accounting discretion available to top management. We will enumerate below the most important findings of these research streams in order to facilitate a judgement about the available accounting discretion.

Company characteristics

Research results provide evidence that the degree of ownership concentration affects the nature of contracting and demonstrate that accounting informativeness declines as ownership concentration increases (Donelly and Lynch, 2002; Fan and Wong, 2002). Further, due to improved visibility, and more dispersed ownership and listing requirements, the quality of earnings of listed companies is found to be higher than in non-listed companies, especially in those countries where securities regulators have sufficient qualified staff and the legal power to enforce full compliance with the domestic accounting standards or the accounting standards accepted for listing. The amount of accounting flexibility will be less.

Audit quality

The quality of the auditors has a direct impact on the available accounting discretion of the management. Research results so far have provided evidence that the presence of the big four auditors seems to constrain earnings management.

Board Characteristics

Governance research has focused extensively on the question whether or not certain board characteristics are indicators of weaker board monitoring. Research results do indicate that board monitoring becomes weaker when the chairman of the board is also the CEO of the company, when the majority of board members are internal company members or directors with family or economic ties to the company, when there are interlocking directorships, and where no audit committee exists.

It is important to note in relation to the research results on company characteristics, audit quality and board characteristics mentioned above that they represent the behaviour of the 'average' firm. They may give an indication in an individual case, but they have no absolute power of prediction in a particular case. We will concentrate now on the impact of the quality of the accounting standards and the quality of the application of the accounting standards on the available accounting flexibility to top management.

IMPACT OF ACCOUNTING STANDARDS USED ON ANNUAL ACCOUNTS

As already mentioned, we know that accounting analysis involves an evaluation of the accounting flexibility available to the management of a company. This accounting flexibility is, to a large extent, determined by the type of GAAP which is applied. Some GAAP systems allow more valuation choices for one item than others or simply require other valuation or presentation methods. According to the GAAP applied the same transactions or operations can be accounted for in a different way.

A clear illustration of the impact which GAAP can have on the annual accounts, is found in the annual accounts of Euro Disney SCA. We will follow this example in the years 2003–2005 as it not only illustrates differences between the different GAAP system at one point in time, but it also illustrates the convergence of the GAAP systems taking place. The structure of Euro Disney SCA is presented in n. 1 of the consolidated financial statements 2003:

> Euro Disney SCA (the 'Company') and its wholly-owned subsidiaries (collectively, the 'Group') commenced operations with the official opening of Disneyland Park on April 12, 1992. The Group operates the Disneyland Resort Paris, which includes two theme parks, Walt Disney Studios Park and the Disneyland Park (the 'Theme Park'), seven themed hotels, two convention centres, the Disney Village entertainment centre and a golf course in Marne-la-Valleé, France. In addition, the Group manages the real estate development and expansion of the related infrastructure of the property. The company, a publicly held French company, is owned 39% by indirect, wholly-owned subsidiaries of the Walt Disney Company ('TWDC') and managed by Euro Disney SA (the Company's Gérant), an indirect, 99%-owned subsidiary of TWDC. The General Partner is EDL Participations SA, also an indirect, wholly-owned subsidiary of TWDC.

The balance sheet structure and the cost structure of the company differ significantly according to the GAAP applied over the period 1992–2003. Euro Disney SCA presented during that period its financial statements according to French GAAP and according to US GAAP. The biggest difference relates to the treatment of the lease agreements in the accounts of Euro Disney SCA (nn. 1–2 of the consolidated financial statements 2001):

> The Group owns Walt Disney Studios Park, the Disneyland Hotel, the Davy Crockett Ranch, the golf course, the underlying land thereof and the land on which the five other hotels and the Disney Village entertainment centre are located and leases substantially all the remaining operating assets.

This implies that all attractions in the theme park, the hotels (New York, Newport Bay Club, Sequoia Lodge, Cheyenne and Santa Fe) and the Disney Village entertainment centre are operated under lease agreements which qualify under French GAAP as operational leases (note 2, consolidated financial statements 2003).

The balance sheet and profit and loss account of Euro Disney SCA under French GAAP are as follows:

Profit and loss account of Euro Disney SCA (in € million)	*Year ended September 30*			
	2003	*2002*	*2001*	*2000*
Revenues	1 053.1	1 076.0	1 005.2	959.2
Cost and expenses	(920.7)	(900.3)	(820.0)	(783.4)
Income before lease and financial charges 132.4		175.7	185.2	175.8
– lease rental expense	(193.8)	(188.8)	(185.8)	(151.1)
– financial income	49.0	59.1	89.8	74.8
– financial expense	(55.5)	(41.1)	(51.5)	(62.0)
Income before exceptional items	(67.9)	4.9	37.7	37.5
– exceptional income/(loss) net	11.9	(38.0)	(7.2)	1.2
Net income	(56.0)	(33.1)	30.5	38.7

Balance sheet Euro Disney SCA
(€ in millions)

	Year ended September 30			
	2003	*2002*	*2001*	*2000*
Current assets	210.7	232.4	784.5	645.9
Deferred charges	55.1	86.7	88.1	63.3
Fixed assets	2 317.8	2 389.5	2 233.5	2 084.6
Total assets	2 583.6	2 708.6	3 106.1	2 793.8
Current liabilities	271.2	359.5	425.8	379.6
Deferred revenues	87.6	94.7	77.3	75.3
Provisions	120.1	35.5	31.1	21.8
Borrowings	867.5	821.3	1 141.2	916.8
Shareholders' equity	1 084.4	1 244.8	1 277.9	1 247.5
Quasi-equity	152.8	152.8	152.8	152.8
Total liabilities and equity	2 583.6	2 708.6	3 106.1	2 793.8

In the annual accounts a reconciliation to US GAAP was included. The largest impact stemmed from a different treatment of the lease contracts:

> The Group leases substantially all of its operating assets under various agreements. Under French GAAP, the Group has not capitalised these leases and is accounting for them as operating leases. Under US GAAP, the underlying assets and liabilities and related depreciation and interest expense are reflected in the Group's financial statements.

Besides the reconciliation of the leasing agreements, there were also other elements which also had an impact on the accounts but the amount was minor compared to the lease impact (see annual accounts):

	Year ended September 30			
(€ in millions)	*2003*	*2002*	*2001*	*2000*
Net result, as reported under French GAAP	(56.0)	(33.1)	30.5	38.7
Lease and interest adjustments	7.2	(35.7)	(78.4)	(106.0)
Other	(5.6)	1.5	(2.7)	1.1
Net loss under US GAAP	(54.4)	(67.3)	(50.6)	(66.2)
Comprehensive income items:				
Interest rate hedges	2.1	0.7	(8.1)	–
Comprehensive loss under US GAAP	(52.3)	(66.6)	(58.7)	(66.2)

This reconciliation to US GAAP brings the result of Euro Disney SCA in the red in the years 2000 and 2001. After the reconciliation of shareholders' equity to US GAAP a much smaller amount of equity was left.

Reconciliation of shareholders' equity
(€ in millions)

	Year ended September 30			
	2003	*2002*	*2001*	*2000*
Shareholders' equity, as reported under French GAAP	1 084.3	1 244.8	1 277.9	1 247.5
Cumulative lease and interest adjustments	(1 279.8)	(1 278.0)	(1 251.3)	(1 172.9)
Effect of revaluing the ORAs and sale/leaseback transactions	178.1	178.1	178.1	178.1
Other	77.8	(23.3)	(25.0)	(14.6)
Shareholders' equity under US GAAP	60.4	112.6	179.7	238.1

As well as a change from one set of GAAP to another set of GAAP, new standards within the same set of GAAP could also result in major differences with regard to balance sheet and profit and loss accounts.

This happened for Euro Disney in 2004:

Effective from the beginning of fiscal year 2004 (October 1, 2003), the Group adopted new accounting rules mandated by Article 133 of the Financial Security Law (Loi de Securite Financiere) with respect to the consolidation of financing companies that are not legally controlled by the Group. Under these new rules, the Financing Companies, from which the Company leases a substantial portion of its operating assets, have been included in the Group's consolidated accounts. In the past, lease payments to the Financing Companies were recorded as incurred, along contractual commitments for lease rentals, and the related debt obligations of the Financing Companies. As a result of the new consolidation rules, these operating assets are now consolidated resulting in increased fixed assets and borrowings. The Group's receivables from the Financing Companies have been eliminated in consolidation and shareholders' equity has been reduced. The reduction in the consolidated shareholder's equity primarily reflects past depreciation charges related to the operating assets owned by the Financing Companies, which were greater than the lease payments expensed for classification and amount of costs reported in the income statement, resulting in increased operating expenses and depreciation and reduced lease rental expense.

(Euro Disney SCA Financial Report 2005, n. 2, p. 16)

The result of this change in French GAAP was that the difference between the French GAAP figures and the US GAAP figures became smaller. The operational leases were now treated under the new French GAAP as financial leases. We will present below only the most important figures of Euro Disney SCA according to French GAAP and US GAAP in 2004 and 2005.

In € millions	2004	2005
Revenues	1 048.2	1 076.0
Results in French GAAP	(145.2)	(94.9)
Results according to US GAAP	(130)	(100)
Total assets – French GAAP	2 876.6	2 894.1
Total assets – US GAAP	2 906.6	2 917.4
Equity–French GAAP	(59.9)	295.7
Equity – US SAAP	(48.7)	366.8

This is in fact an illustration of convergence between different GAAP systems. The accounts prepared according to French GAAP no longer provide accounting numbers, which are totally different from the US GAAP figures. As all listed companies are now moving to compliance with IAS, the differences between the GAAP applied will no longer influence international comparisons. However in many countries the majority of businesses consist of small and medium-sized companies. So the issue of comparability of different national GAAP still applies to that category of companies.

Changes within GAAP systems will, however, always need our attention since they remain an obstacle to comparability over time or even between companies when different companies choose different adoption dates in relation to a new revised accounting standard.

British Airways experienced this some time ago. When it had to make substantial changes to its accounts following the introduction of several new financial reporting standards (FRS) by the Accounting Standards Board in the UK at the beginning of the 1990s. FRS 5 particularly had an enormous impact. The following illustration relates to this:

British Airways plc

This company, because of FRS 5, *Reporting the Substance of Transactions* is having to make very significant changes to its published financial statements. For example, as of 1994 twenty-four aircraft previously accounted for under extendable operating lease arrangements, and therefore off the balance sheet, will need to be included as assets on the balance sheet with the corresponding liabilities also included. British Airways also, in order to avoid problems of protection policies by foreign governments, has set up 49%-owned operating companies, i.e. TAT European airlines and Deutsche BA. Under FRS 2 these were classified as associate undertakings and dealt with accordingly in the group accounts. However, under FRS 5 they will need to be classified as quasi-subsidiaries and therefore treated in the accounts as if they were subsidiary undertakings. There are obviously a whole variety of detailed effects on the numbers in the published financial statements resulting from FRS 5. Noteworthy, for example, is an increase in the value of fixed assets and related borrowings by some £1100 million!

It is interesting to refer here to Chapter 2 of this book where reference was made to academic research, which revealed that accounting quality and the degree of compliance with accounting standards was influenced by the institutional environment (see the references to the research results of Leuz, Nanda and Wysocki (2003) and Hope (2003)). The latter implies that it is not sufficient just to check whether or not a company is using high-quality accounting standards to be able to evaluate the accounting flexibility available to management. Since these research results indicate that the application quality might differ among countries, one needs also to consider the institutional environment before one gets a complete picture of the available accounting quality and sources of discretion.

High-quality GAAP are recognised as leaving less room for the kind of accounting flexibility which allows management to report the results in the period they wish them to appear in the profit and loss account.

In their Annual Report, the corporate management of Adidas explained in their own words what the change from a low-quality GAAP to higher-quality GAAP meant for them when they complied for the first time with IFRS:

3 Framework for Accounting Policies in accordance with IFRS and Explanation of Major Differences compared with German Accounting Policies

The major differences between the accounting policies and consolidation methods according to IFRS and German law as set out in § 292a section 2 No. 4b of the German Commercial Code (HGB) are outlined below.

a) Framework for Accounting Policies in Accordance with IFRS

The accounting policies of entities in accordance with IFRS are based on the objective of providing investors with decision-relevant information.

Based on the assumption that decision-relevant information should be provided to investors, it follows that accounting policies should be aimed at showing an entity's operating results, rather than determining the amount of distributable profits, whilst bearing in mind the need for protection of creditors.

As a rule, accounting policies in accordance with IFRS have a lower level of prudence than German accounting policies, which leads to the following major differences:

● Minimisation of possibilities for establishing and releasing hidden reserves.

● The consistency requirement (recognition, valuation, classification, consolidation) is to be strictly followed; changes in accounting policies are only permitted if it can be proven that the change leads to an improvement in the fair presentation of the financial statements.

● Economic substance has precedence over legal form. The principle of substance over form has a stronger influence in accounting policies in accordance with IFRS than in German GAAP.

(Adidas Annual Report 2004, p. 138)

SUMMARY

The purpose of financial statements is to give external parties a picture of the performance of a company and its financial position. At the same time, however, financial statements are viewed by the management of a company as a means of communication to the outside world. Sometimes, a tension may arise to publish a result somewhat different from the underlying economic result. In this case, the company will adopt a certain accounting strategy. The aim of this chapter was to describe and analyse the different building blocks of such an accounting strategy (incentives towards management of accounting numbers and methods used to manipulate accounting numbers) and the discretion available to pursue such an accounting strategy. Trying to detect the accounting strategy of a firm and clarify the published result free from the disturbing elements of the accounting strategy is called accounting analysis. The purpose of accounting analysis is to get an idea of the underlying economic result and only this result is useful or value relevant for decision-making purposes.

It is important to remember however that each toolkit for manipulation (accounting methods, accounting estimates and real decisions) is unique to the needs and the environment of each individual company.

EXERCISES

Suggested answers to exercises marked ✓ are to be found on the Student side of the companion website.

Suggested answers to the remaining exercises are to be found on the Instructor side of the companion website.

1 Identify as many examples as possible where the choice of accounting policy could significantly affect the analysis and interpretation of published financial statements.

2 The summarised balance sheets of three businesses in the same industry are shown below for 200X.

	A	B	C
	£000	£000	£000
Intangibles	100	–	10
Tangible fixed assets	886	582	580
Current assets	920	580	950
Current liabilities	(470)	(252)	(486)
	1 436	910	1 054
Long-term liabilities	(100)	(20)	(50)
	1 336	890	1 004
Share capital	200	40	300
Revaluation reserve	80		
Retained profits	1 056	850	704
	1 336	890	1 004

The operating profit and sales for the three companies for the years in question were:

Operating profit	282	194	148
Sales	2 100	1 500	1 750

The companies had different treatments for the intangibles. Company A is amortising this at £10 000 per annum and company C at £2000 per annum. Company B has written off goodwill of £40 000 to retained profits in the year. Included in the depreciation expense of company A is an extra £4000 over and above the historical cost depreciation caused by an earlier revaluation of its premises.

Appraise the financial performance and stability of each of these three companies within the limits of the information given.

3   If you consider companies such as McDonald's, Kentucky Fried Chicken, Burger King, etc., what are the value drivers in their industries? What are the critical factors in their industrial environment? Comment on these. Subsequently, contrast your findings with an analysis of the value drivers of companies like Boeing and Airbus. What do you observe? How will these different industry characteristics and value drivers have an impact on the financial statements of these companies? You might look up their annual reports on their websites for inspiration.

4   Identify as many examples as possible where the choice of accounting methods, accounting estimates or even real transactions could significantly affect the analysis and interpretation of the financial statements. Comment on how these choices affect the financial statements.

5   Consider again the examples you have listed in answering question 3. Relate these findings to the national GAAP of your own country. Does the national GAAP in your country allow accounting flexibility on many of the items listed?

6   Compare the accounting flexibility of the national GAAP in your own country with the flexibility in IAS/IFRS. Which of the two systems allows less flexibility to the preparer of the financial statements?

7 Would the information provided through financial statements improve if you could eliminate accounting flexibility from the standards?

8 You, as an accountant, are asked by your financial director, to choose suitable companies to compare your own company with. Explain, in a report to her, what would influence your choice and how you would adjust for differing accounting policies, if any.

TECHNIQUES OF FINANCIAL ANALYSIS

31

OBJECTIVES After studying this chapter you should be able to:

- identify potential red flags that obstruct comparability of financial accounting data

- perform the following types of analysis and appraise the results:

  - trend analysis
  - common size analysis
  - ratio analysis
  - segmental analysis
  - cash flow analysis.

INTRODUCTION

The purpose of financial analysis is to evaluate the performance of a firm given the strategy of the firm, the economic and industrial environment in which the company is competitive and the accounting strategy applied. Several techniques of financial analysis exist. The most well-known technique is the technique of ratio analysis, in which items of the balance sheet and profit and loss account are related to each other. This technique has been introduced to you in Chapter 11. In order to review the elements discussed in Chapter 11, we start with the activity below

ACTIVITY 31.1

Using the annual accounts of Euro Disney 2003 which ratios would you calculate?

Activity feedback

Any reader of this text who has some introduction to this topic will come up with ratios such as:

- current assets/current liabilities to judge the ability of a company to repay its debt in the short term
- debt/equity to evaluate the financial risk of a company in the long term
- results/equity to decide whether or not the investments are used in a profitable way.

ACTIVITY 31.2

Can you judge the financial situation of Euro Disney SCA properly based only on the ratios of one particular year? Why or why not?

Activity feedback

Judging the performance of a firm based on the results of a particular year or even two years is not that meaningful. First of all, one has no external benchmark to compare the performance of the firm with, for example, a competitor in the same industry. Second, information from one or two years is too short a time frame to build an internal benchmark on.

Think of the example of Sabena in Chapter 30. Had you been given only the annual accounts of 1998 or even 1998 and 1999, would you have been able to make a proper judgement on the economic and financial situation of Sabena? The answer is simply, No! The profits of 1998 and the figures of 1999 tell a different story if the data from 1995, and more especially 1996 and 1997, are added.

In order to evaluate the performance of a firm in a meaningful way a comparison is needed with firms in the industry, with the past performance of the firm or with an absolute benchmark. In ratio analysis, however, no absolute benchmarks exist, except maybe that profitability should be above the weighted average cost of capital. But even that absolute benchmark in some industries is not always fulfilled.

From the illustrations in the activities thus far it becomes clear that the performance of a firm should be judged in a relevant time frame and against some industry benchmarks. The analysis of the performance of the firm over time is called horizontal analysis or trend analysis. The comparison with the performance of other companies or a whole industry is done by vertical analysis or common size analysis. Before trend analysis and vertical analysis can be undertaken, it is necessary to check that there are no elements present which would disturb the comparison over time and between companies. The elements of industry analysis and accounting analysis (both discussed in Chapter 30) should be kept in mind here.

In the following section we illustrate these pitfalls related to comparability.

ACTIVITY 31.3

Which elements can you think of that would disturb the comparison of firm performance over time or between companies?

Activity feedback

- Changes in the structure of the company through a merger, acquisition or creation of new subsidiaries

- differences in valuation methods or accounting estimates applied
- differences in presentation
- different time spans.

ELEMENTS OF NON-COMPARABILITY IN FINANCIAL STATEMENTS

Activity 31.3 listed some red flags that should be checked before one starts with analysing the performance and the financial position of a company. A number of red flags will now be illustrated with real life examples taken from the airline industry.

Changes with regard to the time span of the financial year

Companies might decide to change the time span of a particular year for several reasons. We can observe this practice if a company suffers from a huge loss (e.g. trading losses on financial contracts), the company may decide to extend the financial year from 12 months to 15 months by changing the reporting date. As a result, this huge loss is then compensated by profits of 15 months instead of 12.

Companies can also create very short financial years in which huge losses or restructurings are accounted for. An example can be found in the annual accounts of the 1991 financial year of Sabena. For the purpose of big bath accounting, the financial year 1991 of Sabena was split into two financial years. The first financial year covered three months (1.1.1991–31.3.1991). The second financial year of 1991 covered the other nine months (1.4.1991–31.12.1991). The bath was located in the first annual report of 1991, the second annual report of 1991 showed a profit.

Financial year	1.1.1991–31.3.1991 in 000 BEF	1.4.1991–31.12.1991 in 000 BEF
Operating profit/(loss)	(2 808 673)	2 161 465
Net profit/(loss)	(30 230 650)	1 132 000

When the ten-year overview of the results of Sabena (1991–2000) were presented (Figure 30.1) the results of the two annual reports of the year 1991 were added up. In this way we obtained a result for a period of 12 months which does not disturb the ten-year comparability over those ten years. In the annual reports of Sabena, however, the data of 1991 were never included in an overview of comparative data over a time frame. The following argument was always put forward: The data of 1991 are not comparative with the other data due to restructuring of Sabena World Airlines in 1991. The comparative figures in the annual accounts of 1992 were those of the second annual report of 1991.

As mentioned earlier, for comparative purposes in this text Sabena's two financial years of 1991 have been combined to gain results for a 12-month period. This is done in the figures presented in this book and also in the data used for trend analysis and common size analysis later on in this chapter.

Different balance sheet dates

Companies use different closing dates for their financial statements. Even within the same industry differences can be observed. For example, in the airline business the following dates are used as balance sheet dates by the different airlines:

31 March: British Airways, Air France–KLM, Ryanair
31 September: easyJet
31 December: Lufthansa, Sabena and SAS.

If we compare the annual accounts of the two low-cost carriers for the financial year with closing dates in 2001, we have to take into account that easyJet closed its financial statements after the 11 September terrorist attacks on the WTC in New York and Pentagon in Washington by terrorists; and Ryanair and Birtish Airways had done so before that event.

Changes in company structure

Over the years companies merge, acquire other companies or parts of other companies or restructure activities into different separate legal business entities. If a company is involved in mergers or acquisitions observed growth is often not organic but rather through acquisition. This should be considered in a different way.

Often companies disclose in the notes to the accounts the main drivers of the growth. For example, the SAir Group, to which the airline Swissair belonged, grew mainly through acquisitions in the last years of the 20th century. In note 1 of the annual report of SAir (financial year 2000) information is provided on the causes of the growth in revenue:

> The increase of 24.8% in operating revenue from 1999 to 2000 can be split up in 48% growth through acquisition, 14% positive impact of currency movements and 38% resulting from organic growth.
>
> (Annual accounts 2000, p. 14, n.1)

These changes in company structures are especially hindering for trend analysis. Some company restructurings can create an impression of decline, although in reality part of the activities has been moved to a separate entity. The accounts of the airline Sabena NV seem to suggest a decline in total operating revenue from 1998 to 1999 (see Table 31.1).

In reality, however, the activities of maintenance and repair were, in 1999, separated into Sabena Technics NV. In order to make a proper comparison over three years we need a constant entity structure. If we add up the data of Sabena Technics NV with those of Sabena NV and correct for intra-group transactions then (data taken from the segmental information in the group accounts) we get a picture which shows growth. In Table 31.2 we present the evolution of the total operating revenue and some operating cost items of Sabena NV, whereby the necessary corrections are made to obtain a constant entity.

Although we have now managed to keep the entity of analysis constant, the influence of the changes in book value of the assets is not eliminated. With the transfer of

TABLE 31.1	Operating revenue and some operating cost items of Sabena NV (%)		
	1998	*1999*	*2000*
Operating revenue	100	97.51	110.88
Materials and consumables	100	92.04	139.11
Services and goods delivered	100	111.68	139.02
Personnel cost	100	91.24	88.38
Depreciation fixed assets	100	50.58	46.16

Source: Sabena NV Annual Reports, 1998, 1999 and 2000.

TABLE 31.2	Operating revenue and some operating cost items of Sabena NV totalled with operating revenue and operating cost items of Sabena Technics NV (%)		
	1998	*1999*	*2000*
Operating revenue	100	105.17	118.77
Materials and consumables	100	112.41	158.11
Services and goods delivered	100	112.61	139.98
Personnel cost	100	109.18	107.42
Depreciation fixed assets	100	74.96	93.44

Source: Sabena NV Annual Reports 1998, 1999 and 2000 and Sabena Technics NV Annual Reports 1999 and 2000.

assets from Sabena NV to Sabena Technics NV, the book value of those assets was increased as well. As a result the depreciation costs rise.

As Sabena Technics was a 100% subsidiary of Sabena NV the accounts of the Sabena Group were not influenced by this restructuring. The increase in book value of the assets now remaining with Sabena Technics has no influence on the group accounts, because this increase is eliminated in the consolidation process.

Although group accounts are not affected by this kind of restructuring whereby the new entity is fully consolidated in the group accounts, we must always keep in mind that individual accounts are still used for different purposes, for example, tax. It also happens that group management decides to undertake an IPO in relation to individual legal entities belonging to the group. For example, the Deutsche Post Group offered a part of the shares of its subsidiary the Deutsche Post Bank to the capital market in 2004. The individual accounts are then used as a piece of information in the business valuation process of that particular business unit. If restructurings take the form of bringing activities into joint ventures or other forms of cooperation which are no longer fully consolidated, then there is also an impact on the consolidated accounts. When operations are discontinued due to a restructuring of activities, shareholders need information on the share of these discontinued activities in the results, the financial position and the cash flow of the group. IFRS 5 stipulates that in case of discontinued activities the impact should be disclosed to the reader of the accounts. The main objective is to ensure comparability for the reader of the annual accounts. Sometimes companies are very active in acquiring businesses and divesting from them. In the notes to the annual accounts of Danone 2007, we notice some activities that impact on the structure of the group. Danone is a company active in fresh diary products, waters, baby food and medical nutrition.

Acquisitions

In 2007, the main acquisitions were the following:

- acquisition, for an amount of € 12 189 million, of a 98.85% interest in Royal Numico N.V. ('Numico'): the company and its subsidiaries have been fully consolidated since October 31, 2007;

- acquisition of all the shares of the Calpis Ajinomoto Danone joint-venture, renamed Danone Japan (Fresh Dairy Products). This company, which was previously accounted for under the equity method, has been fully consolidated since the first half of 2007;

- acquisition of an 80% interest in a joint-venture with Caglar (Waters – Turkey). The company, named Danone Hayat Antalya, is fully consolidated;

- acquisition of a 70% interest in a joint-venture with Vialat (Fresh Dairy Products – Chile). The company, named Danone Chile, is fully consolidated;

- acquisition of a 51% interest in a joint-venture with Alqueria (Fresh Dairy Products – Colombia). The company, named Danone Colombia, is fully consolidated;

- acquisition of an additional interest in Danone Industria (Fresh Dairy Products – Russia), increasing the Group's interest ownership from 70% to 85%.

In 2006, the main acquisitions related to additional investments in Danone Asia Pte Ltd. (holding company), Danone Djurdjura Algeria (Fresh Dairy Products) and Danone Romania (Fresh Dairy Products), bringing the Group's shareholding in these companies to 100%, as well as the acquisition of a 100% shareholding in Rodich (Fresh Dairy Products – Ukraine), a 22.18% interest in Hui Yuan Juice Holdings Co (Waters – China) and a 49% interest in Aqua d'Or (Waters – Denmark).

Disposals

The principal disposals in 2007 included:

- the Biscuits and Cereal Products businesses: the sale of these business activities, which occurred in November 2007, generated a net capital gain of approximately € 3105 million. As the Group has discontinued its activities, this gain is reflected under the line item 'Net income from discontinued operations' (see Note 3);

- the disposal of this company, finalised in July 2007, generated a net capital loss of € 8 million, reflected under the line item 'Net income (loss) of equity-accounted affiliates' (see Note 6).

In 2006, the main disposals related to the Sauces business activities in Asia, and the Group's equity interest in Griffins (Biscuits – New Zealand), in Danone Waters of Canada (HOD – Canada) and in Bakoma (Fresh Dairy Products – Poland).

Companies that merge or are involved in acquisition have increasing absolute numbers for revenue, EBIT (earnings before interest and taxes), results and total assets. These firms often like to stress this increase in absolute amounts of revenue, EBIT and results, without putting in the spotlight the fact that the increase derives mainly from acquisition. Impression management is often observed in these circumstances; fortunately we also observe companies that disclose the origin of the increase in these absolute figures in a transparent way. For example, Nestlé uses a construct called RIG, which is equal to 'real internal growth'. In this figure the impact of acquisitions, mergers or spin-offs are eliminated, together with the impact of inflation and price changes.

ACCOUNTING METHOD CHANGES AND ACCOUNTING ESTIMATE CHANGES

All GAAP have the consistency principle in their standards: companies are supposed to apply the same accounting policies from one period to the next. The purpose of this consistency principle is enhancing comparability between financial statements over time. However, in practice, changes are observed and the user of the financial statements should take them into account. As these elements have been discussed extensively in Chapter 30 in the context of annual accounts management we will not elaborate on them further here.

A change in GAAP applied

Companies not only change accounting methods or estimates over the years, they sometimes switch from one set of accounting regulation or standards to another set of standards. This is a one-time change that might have a serious impact on the results and on the balance sheet of the company. The impact of a different set of GAAP on the financial statements of a company was illustrated at the end of Chapter 30 with the difference between the net result and the equity of Euro Disney SCA presented both according to French and US GAAP. Since listed companies worldwide (except for American companies on US stock exchanges) comply with IFRS, this issue of non-comparability mainly applies to comparisons of annual accounts of non-listed companies.

In the time period of the Sabena case study, several major airlines have switched from their national GAAP to IAS/IFRS. The financial year of the change differed between them, the first financial years in which IAS group accounts were published for the different airlines were: Lufthansa in 1997, SAS in 1997, the SAir Group in 1996, Austrian Airlines in 2000 and Sabena in 1999. British Airways, Ryanair and Air France–KLM changed to IAS from 2005 onwards as a result of the EU regulation which made compliance with IAS standards compulsory for listed companies. This hinders not only the comparability of company data over a longer time span, but it also makes inter-firm comparisons less obvious in those periods. The switch to IAS/IFRS is usually done for the group accounts only.

When new standards are issued by standard setters and companies have some flexibility to choose the period of first-time adoption of the new standard, comparability will be threatened.

Differences in presentation

With regard to differences in presentation we observe two main issues. First of all, the contents of 'similar' items used in the annual accounts can be different. Second, different companies use different ways of presentation, classification, aggregation and layout. Standardised formats for balance sheet and profit and loss accounts facilitate comparison. In practice, however, companies use different formats and layouts. Several GAAP require a minimum layout with which companies have to comply. IAS prescribes only a minimum layout for the profit and loss account, which allows substantial room for company-specific choices with regard to the layout of the profit and loss account. The same observation holds for the balance sheet or the statement of financial position.

It is clear from Activity 31.4 that in order to compare the operating income of the three airlines reconciliations need to be made.

ACTIVITY 31.4

Look at the consolidated income statements of British Airways, Air France-KLM and Lufthansa. Can you compare the operating profit of the three airlines as such? Is the information published on operating costs easily comparable? Which items can easily be compared?

British Airways group consolidated income statement for the year ended 31 March, 2008

£ million	Note	2008	Group 2007
Traffic revenue			
Passenger		**7 541**	7 263
Cargo		**616**	598
		8 157	7 861
Other revenue		**596**	631
Revenue	3	**8 753**	8 492
Employee costs	7	**2 166**	2 277
Depreciation, amortisation and impairment	4	**692**	714
Aircraft operating lease costs		**68**	81
Fuel and oil costs		**2 055**	1 931
Engineering and other aircraft costs		**451**	414
Landing fees and en route charges		**528**	517
Handling charges, catering and other operating costs		**977**	930
Selling costs		**359**	436
Currency differences		**6**	18
Accommodation, ground equipment and IT costs		**576**	618
Total expenditure on operations before non-recurring items		**7 878**	7 936
Operating profit before non-recurring items		**875**	556
Credit arising on changes to pension scheme	35	**–**	396
Provision for settlement of competition investigations	29	**–**	(350)
Operating profit	4	**875**	602
Fuel derivative gains/(losses)		**12**	(12)
Finance costs	8	**(175)**	(168)
Finance income	8	**111**	129
Net financing income/(expense) relating to pensions	8	**34**	(19)
Retranslation (charges)/credits on currency borrowings	8	**(11)**	13
Profit on sale of property, plant and equipment and investments	9	**14**	47
Share of post-tax profits in associates accounted for using the equity method	19	**26**	5
(Charges)/income relating to financial assets	10	**(3)**	14
Profit before tax		**883**	611
Tax	11	**(187)**	(173)
Profit after tax from continuing operations		**696**	438
Loss from discontinued operations (after tax)	5	**(2)**	(134)
Profit after tax		**694**	304
Attributable to:			
Equity holders of the parent		**680**	290
Minority interest		**14**	14
		694	304
Earnings/(loss) per share			
Continuing operations:			
Basic	12	**59.2p**	37.2p
Diluted	12	**58.8p**	36.8p

ACTIVITY 31.4   (Continued)

£ million	Note	2008	Group 2007
Discontinued operations:			
Basic	12	**(0.2)p**	*(11.7)p*
Diluted	12	**(0.2)p**	*(11.7)p*
Total:			
Basic	12	**59.0p**	*25.5p*
Diluted	12	**58.6p**	*25.2p*

Air France–KLM Group consolidated income statement

In € millions	Notes	2008	2007	2006
Period from April 1 to March 31				
Sales	5	**24 114**	**23 073**	**21 448**
Other revenues		4	4	4
Revenues		**24 118**	**23 077**	**21 452**
External expenses	6	(13 814)	(13 100)	(12 127)
Salaries and related costs	7	(7 018)	(6 689)	(6 357)
Taxes other than income taxes		(250)	(263)	(228)
Amortisation and depreciation	8	(1 606)	(1 782)	(1 656)
Other income and expenses	9	(8)	5	(76)
Income from current operations		**1 405**	**1 240**	**936**
Sales of aircraft equipment	10	9	13	2
Negative goodwill	4	40		5
Other non-current income and expenses	10	(182)	(20)	512
Income from operating activities		**1 272**	**1 233**	**1 455**
Cost of financial debt		(387)	(407)	(392)
Income from cash and cash equivalents		288	267	168
Net cost of financial debt	11	**(99)**	**(140)**	**(224)**
Other financial income and expenses	11	(24)	25	(31)
Income before tax		**1 149**	**1 118**	**1 200**
Income taxes	12	(358)	(248)	(256)
Net income of consolidated companies		**791**	**870**	**944**
Share of profits (losses) of associates	20	(24)	17	(23)
Net income from continuing operations		**767**	**887**	**921**
Net income from discontinued operations	13	–	–	–
Net income for the period		**767**	**887**	**921**
– Group		**748**	**891**	**913**
– Minority interests		19	(4)	8
Earnings per share – Group (in euros)	14.1			
– basic		2.63	3.35	3.47
– diluted		2.47	3.05	3.25
Earnings per share from continuing operations (in euros)	14.2			
– basic		2.69	3.33	3.50
– diluted		2.53	3.03	3.28

The accompanying notes are an integral part of these consolidated financial statements.

(continued)

ACTIVITY 31.4   *(Continued)*

Lufthansa consolidated income statement for the financial year 2007

in €m	Notes	2007	2006
Traffic revenue	3)	17 568	15 354
Other revenue	4)	4 852	4 495
Total revenue		**22 420**	**19 849**
Changes in inventories and work performed by the enterprise and capitalised	5)	119	152
Other operating income	6)	1 571	1 399
Cost of materials and services	7)	−11 553	−10 302
Staff costs	8)	−5 498	−5 029
Depreciation, amortisation and impairment	9)	−1 204	−1 051
Other operating expenses	10)	−4 269	−3 940
Profit from operating activities		**+ 1 586**	**+ 1 078**
Result of equity investments accounted for using the equity method	11)	+ 223	+ 216
Result from other equity investments	11)	+ 131	**+ 89**
Interest income	12)	177	207
Interest expense	12)	−371	−461
Other financial items	13)	−133	**−84**
Financial result		**+ 27**	**−33**
Profit before income taxes		**+ 1 613**	**+ 1 045**
Income taxes	14)	−356	−230
Profit from continuing operations		**+ 1 257**	**+ 815**
Profit from the discontinued Leisure Travel segment	15)	**+ 503**	**+ 82**
Profit after income taxes		**+ 1 760**	**+ 897**
Minority interests		−105	−94
Net profit attributable to shareholders of Lufthansa AG		**+ 1 655**	**+ 803**
Basic earnings per share in €	16)	+ 3.61	+ 1.75
Diluted earnings per share in €	16)	+ 3.60	+ 1.75

Activity feedback

At first glance we get the impression that the operating profit or income from operations or profit from operations (notice that we have three different labels) is comparable straight away. However if we analyse the income statement in more detail we notice that the profit on sale of property, plant and equipment and investments (see income statement British Airways) is reported below the operating profit. The other two airlines include this item in the operating results. Air France-KLM includes a part under the income from operating activities under the caption 'sales of aircraft equipment' and 'other non-current income and expenses'. Lufthansa includes these items under other operating income and other operating expenses. So in order to compare the results of the three airlines reconciliations need to be made.

With regard to the different items represented under the operating costs we notice that British Airways presents the operational costs by function on the profit and loss account and the two other airlines use an approach that classifies costs by nature in the first place. Analysing further the notes on operational costs of British Airways and those on the operational costs of Lufthansa we notice that the only cost components which are directly comparable on the basis of the published information are the fuel costs, the staff and personnel costs, the depreciation and amortisation cost and the lease and rental costs.

Further we observe that British Airways makes a distinction between recurring and non-recurring items on the face of the income statement. This information is interesting if one wants to estimate the future performance of a company. Financial analysts always distinguish recurring items from non-recurring items. Only recurring revenue and recurring costs are useful to make projections about the future.

ILLUSTRATION

Many airlines use headings such as operating profit (British Airways, Ryanair), operating income (KLM, SAS) or result from operating activities (Austrian Airlines, Lufthansa). These items sound similar and one is tempted to calculate an operating margin (operating result/operating revenue) in order to compare the operating profitability of the different airlines. To illustrate the impact of differences in presentation on the comparability of accounting numbers, we reconcile the different published operating margins of the airlines in the Sabena case.

If we investigate the contents of the profit and loss accounts and the notes on the operating revenues and operating costs of the different airlines, for example, for the financial years 1999 and 2000 we notice certain differences. An element to be reckoned with are the different balance sheet dates (see earlier discussion). Further the differences relate mainly to the treatment of gains and losses on disposal of assets and on whether or not the income from associated companies is included in the operating income.

- Ryanair, British Airways, easyJet and KLM exclude results on the sale of fixed assets and financial assets from the operating revenues, operating costs and operating result. Income from

associated entities is also not included in the operating result. British Airways has two separate lines in its profit and loss account: operating profit and operating profit including associates.

- SAS includes items as share of income in affiliated entities, income from the sale of shares in affiliated companies, income from the sale of aircraft as separate items contributing to the operating income. For a comparison with BA, KLM, Ryanair and easyJet these elements need to be excluded.

- Austrian Airlines includes under other operating revenue, income from disposal of non-current assets excluding financial assets. For comparison, these items should be excluded.

- Lufthansa includes under other operating revenue income from disposal of fixed assets; the operating expenses include losses from the disposal of fixed assets.

In Table 31.3 the operating margin of each airline before and after correction for comparability is presented using the financial statements of 1999–2000, which relate to the period of the Sabena case study. For some airlines we notice a not insignificant difference.

TABLE 31.3	Operating margin of different European airlines before and after some corrections to improve comparability (%)			
Operating margin	Before correction		After correction for comparability	
	31.12.1999 or 31.3.2000	31.12.2000 or 31.3.2001	31.12.1999 or 31.3.2000	31.12.2000 or 31.3.2001
UK GAAP				
Ryanair	22.71	23.39	22.71	23.39
easyJet (31.9)	10.87	11.74	10.87	11.74
BA	0.94	4.10	0.94	4.10
Dutch GAAP				
KLM	1.51	3.98	1.51	3.98
IAS/IFRS				
Lufthansa	7.12	8.78	5.32	6.53
SAS	3.99	6.42	1.51	3.22
Austrian Airlines	1.23	4.22	0.59	−0.69

Source: Annual accounts of Ryanair, easyJet, British Airways, KLM, Lufthansa, SAS and Austrian Airlines.

Table 31.3 only illustrates how comparability can be obstructed by including different elements under the same heading. Corrections of this type can only be executed if one is analysing a small number of companies, however, in large-scale analyses (e.g. for large industry analyses or for academic research) these corrections are often not made. These differences have not vanished with the compulsory introduction of IAS. These differences also influenced the accounting numbers in databases like Worldscope, Amadeus, Osiris, Datastream, etc, which are extensively used for academic research purposes.

TREND ANALYSIS OR HORIZONTAL ANALYSIS

That benchmarks are necessary to make a sound judgement about the performance of a company has already been illustrated in this chapter. With the use of trend analysis we compare the performance of the firm to its own history. In annual reports we often find change statistics comparing the figures of two consecutive years. However, some caution is needed when using this published information (see Activity 31.5).

With trend analysis or horizontal analysis we analyse how financial statement items have changed over time. According to the literature a five-year time frame is necessary; longer periods, for example, ten years are also possible, although the number of elements which disturb comparison only increases over such a long period. For the purpose of trend analysis a base year is chosen and all the financial statement items are then expressed as an index relative to the base year. Therefore, the choice of the base year is relatively important, as the performance over the years to follow is benchmarked to this base year.

ACTIVITY 31.5

Table 31.4 presents percentages of change between 1999 and 2000 published in the Sabena Annual Report 2000, p. 9. Is a reported increase always positive?

Activity feedback

If negative amounts are involved, care should be taken with the presented statistics. The change in net result and the change in treasury position is not favourable at all.

TABLE 31.4   Sabena Group consolidated: key figures, 2000/1999

	1999 (million EUR)	2000 (million EUR)	% 2000/1999
Turnover	2 228	2 436	9.3
Operating result	15	(163)	−1 208.7
Net result	(14)	(325)	2 226.1
Operating cash flow	138	(51)	−137.1
Cash flow net result	124	(108)	−187.1
Changes in treasury position	(80)	(225)	182.1
Balance sheet total	2 471	2 358	−4.6
Equity	223	(97)	−143.3
Ratio long-term debt/equity	5.0	10.9	118.0

Source: Sabena Annual report 2000, p. 9.

If trend analysis is applied on the items of the profit and loss account the focus lies on the evolution of the revenue or turnover and the costs related to it. Whether or not the relation between the evolution of the sales and the costs should be linear, depends on the industry characteristics. From the section on industry analysis we know that for the airline industry only catering and handling costs are somewhat variable and are a function of the number of passengers transported. The other costs related to the air transport are a function of the output capacity of the airline which is measured as available seat kilometre or available ton kilometre. We illustrate trend analysis on the basis of the evolution of the operating revenue and operating costs of British Airways and Ryanair in Tables 31.5 and 31.6. The year 2004 was chosen as the starting year for the trend analysis. This was the first financial year for which IFRS data became available for both airlines.

If we analyse the data and focus on the growth rate of turnover, we notice much higher growth rates for Ryanair. The addition of new destinations, especially in eastern Europe, contributed to a certain extent to this growth. If we focus on the trend in the operational costs in comparison to the revenue trend, we notice that BA managers were able to keep the growth path of the operational costs more in line with the growth of the revenues. A cost element which is responsible to a large extent for the growth in operating costs are the fuel and oil costs.

Although fuel costs are a function of distance flown and the number of takeoffs, the steep increase in fuel costs does not necessarily mean that more flights were offered. The fuel cost component is also a function of the kerosene price and fluctuations in the dollar currency. From 2000 the kerosene price started to rise again and airlines were facing higher fuel costs for the same flights offered. The impact could be postponed for a period if the airline had been able to hedge against these fuel price increases. The costs of Ryanair related to output capacity (e.g. depreciation, amortisation and aircraft leasing) increased more in comparison to the turnover than did the same cost item for BA. This is due to the fact that Ryanair added a number of new airplanes to its fleet. This decreased the average fleet life of Ryanair.

TABLE 31.5	Horizontal analysis, Ryanair, 2004–2008				
	Horizontal analysis (%)				
	2004	2005	2006	2007	2008
Operating revenue	100.00	124.42	157.56	208.23	252.63
Operating expenses	100.00	122.38	160.10	214.49	264.51
Fuel and oil costs	100.00	151.59	264.28	396.21	452.21
Staff costs	100.00	114.05	138.66	183.28	230.82
Depreciation	100.00	97.35	122.70	141.53	173.54
Aircraft rentals	100.00	290.02	410.50	504.14	629.67
Maintenance, materials and repairs	100.00	87.37	86.17	96.84	130.61
Marketing and distribution costs	100.00	121.57	86.19	147.42	106.36
Route charges	100.00	123.04	149.25	180.68	235.13
Airport and handling charges	100.00	121.17	146.92	185.85	269.20
Other	100.00	124.35	102.03	134.38	156.30
Operating profit – continuing operations	100.00	131.12	149.25	187.73	213.73
Profit before tax	100.00	129.52	148.32	197.41	192.11

TABLE 31.6	Horizontal analysis, British Airways, 2004–2008				
	Horizontal analysis (%)				
	2004	*2005*	*2006*	*2007*	*2008*
Turnover	100.00	103.35	112.63	112.33	115.78
Operating expenses	100.00	101.65	109.15	110.92	110.10
Fuel and oil costs	100.00	122.34	177.01	209.44	222.89
Staff	100.00	104.27	107.61	104.45	99.36
Depreciation, amortisation and impairment	100.00	101.18	105.60	105.15	101.91
Aircraft leasing	100.00	78.52	82.96	60	50.37
Engineering and other aircraft costs	100.00	98.24	92.56	81.02	88.26
Landing fees and route charges	100.00	101.28	101.82	94.17	96.17
Handling, catering and other operating costs	100.00	99.57	102.25	99.57	104.60
Selling costs	100.00	88.09	81.05	78.70	64.80
Accommodation, ground equipment costs and currency differences	100.00	87.26	82.05	92.04	84.23
Operating profit – before non-recurring items	100.00	133.33	174.07	137.28	216.05
Profit before tax	100.00	180.43	269.57	265.65	383.91

In both companies the growth path of the operating profit is similar. Ryanair achieves this growth path through more revenue increases, whereas BA managed to achieve a slower increase in operational costs in comparison to the increase in revenues. Common size analysis in the next section will show that although both airlines face a positive trend in income, the percentage of income realised on revenue differs for both airlines.

As an external user of financial statements one must always keep in mind that competitors also watch evolutions of costs and breakdown of those costs (common size analysis). Anecdotal evidence exists that smoothing around certain levels for certain cost items is practised in several industries. Consumers also keep an eye on the annual accounts. For example, which airline in the world would publish a profit and loss account showing decreasing costs with regard to maintenance if the fleet capacity remains constant or increases?

COMMON SIZE ANALYSIS

The benchmark to compare the performance of a firm within trend analysis was its own past performance. In common size analysis the benchmarking element is the performance of other firms, usually taken from the same industry. For the purpose of external benchmarking the size effect needs to be eliminated and this is done by expressing the items of the profit and loss account as percentage of sales and the items of the balance sheet in percentages of total assets.

The Table 31.7 common size analysis indicates that for one monetary unit of revenue, British Airways generates one tenth of profit, whereas Ryanair realises 20% of operating profit on this one monetary unit.

Through common size balance sheets we are able to compare, on the one hand, the financing structure of different companies and, on the other, where they have

TABLE 31.7	Common size analysis of the operational profit of British Airways and Ryanair

	British Airways	Ryanair
Turnover	100.00	100.00
Operating expenses	90.00	80.21
Fuel and oil costs	23.48	29.16
Staff	24.75	10.51
Depreciation, amortisation and impairment	7.91	6.48
Aircraft leasing	0.78	2.68
Other	33.10	31.37
Operating profit	10.00	19.79

invested these resources. Balance sheet data provide information on the financing and the investment policy of a company. The items on the balance sheets of Lufthansa, British Airways, Air France–KLM and Ryanair will now be reformulated or regrouped so that the headings include similar items which are comparable.

For the year 2007 (British Airways, Air France-KLM and Ryanair balance sheet date 31.3.2008) the common size balance sheets reveal the structure set out in Table 31.8.

TABLE 31.8	Common size analysis of group balance sheet

	Common size analysis of group balance sheet (%)			
	British Airways	Ryanair	Air France-KLM	Lufthansa
	31 March, 2008	31 March, 2008	31 March, 2008	31 Dec., 2007
Total non-current assets	71.70	62.27	66.93	63.06
Intangible assets	1.99	0.74	2.78	4.70
Tangible assets	65.30	56.61	47.16	48.11
Financial assets	3.65	4.92	9.68	10.25
Pension assets	0.76	–	7.32	–
Total current assets	28.30	37.73	33.07	36.94
Inventory	1.01	0.03	1.65	2.29
Liquid assets	16.76	23.25	14.28	9.31
Other current assets	10.54	14.45	17.14	25.33
Total assets	100.00	100.00	100.00	100.00
Total equity	29.07	39.54	34.58	30.91
Total non-current liabilities	41.77	35.85	35.47	32.03
Provisions and pension liabilities	15.23	0.68	4.69	12.59
Other non-current liabilities	26.54	35.17	30.78	19.44
Total current liabilities	29.16	24.61	29.95	37.06
Total equity and liabilities	100.00	100.00	100.00	100.00

Source: Annual reports of British Airways 2007/2008, Air France/KLM 2007/2008, Lufthansa, 2007 and Ryanair 2007/2008.

Studying the way in which those companies are financed we notice that British Airways and Lufthansa are more financed through external debt than Ryanair and Air France-KLM. In the case of Lufthansa, the debt is made up of a large proportion of provisions. These provisions relate to a large extent to pension benefits which are financed through internal funding. In Chapter 21 we mentioned that there are significant differences in the organisation and the funding of these benefits. Internal funding is a common practice in German companies and this is an illustration of it.

In the annual accounts of Lufthansa we notice however that Lufthansa is planning to switch in the future to external pension funding. This will definitely improve the debt/equity ratio and make the debt structure of the company more comparable with other companies, who practise external funding as well.

> Company pension schemes and transitional pension arrangements for Germany are financed mainly by pension provisions. Obligations are measured annually using the projected unit credit method. In the 2004 financial year work began on building up plan assets to fund future pension payments and transfer them to the Lufthansa Pension Trust. The aim is to outsource the pension obligations in full within 10 to 15 years. In 2007, a further EUR 1 565m was transferred, taking the total transferred to the pension trust to EUR 3 200m.
>
> Staff abroad are also entitled to retirement benefits and in some cases to medical care based mainly on length of service and salary earned. As a rule, benefits are financed by means of external funds.
>
> In the course of acquiring Swiss International Air Lines on 1 July 2007, pension obligations, mainly statutory obligations, were also taken on. The retirement benefits are funded via pension funds known as collective foundations. The SWISS schemes have surplus plan assets which cannot be used to reduce current contributions or be reimbursed, and are therefore subject to an asset ceiling under the provisions of IAS 19.
>
> In measuring pension provisions and determining pension costs the 10 per cent corridor rule is applied. Actuarial profits or losses are disregarded if they do not exceed 10 per cent of the pension commitment or 10 per cent of the fair value of existing plan assets. The amount that exceeds the corridor is divided over the expected average remaining years of service of active staff through profit or loss and recognised in the balance sheet.

For Air France-KLM a net pension asset on the Dutch pension plans represents about 7% of the total assets of the group. Ryanair's equity represents 40% of the financial resources, in 2005 the equity represented even 50% of Ryanair's financial sources. This substantial amount of equity is not only a result from the profit generated by the company, but it results also from the appeal the company has made to the capital market in the past year and the years before. On the asset side of the balance sheet we notice that fixed assets make up a large proportion of the assets of the airlines. However if we compare categories of assets we need to take into account that, for example, Lufthansa is active in many more segments of the air transport industry than Ryanair, who is solely concentrating on passenger transport. We will elaborate this issue later on in this chapter. Ryanair has a substantial part of current assets invested in liquid assets and securities. Again we have to mention that this common size analysis is carried out on the group accounts of those companies. Whether the groups have similar structures will be discussed later in this chapter.

Common size analysis carried out on the profit and loss accounts is only meaningful if the individual items of the profit and loss account can be compared. Based on the available data in the Sabena case study, we have undertaken a common size analysis of a number of items of the profit and loss account of all airlines included in the case. This common size analysis will be used to illustrate further a number of elements which are of importance in comparing performances of different companies. From a number of airlines in Europe we have taken those cost items which are comparable and used them in a common size profit and loss account with regard to operating revenue, some operating costs and operating result. Since the following illustrations and those further on in this chapter benefit from the presence of the data of the SAir group and Sabena, we present the figures for the year 2000. Further the corrections for comparability with regard to the inclusion of gains and losses on disposal of assets have been taken into account (see Table 31.3) We still have to remember that British Airways and Ryanair use UK GAAP, KLM uses Dutch GAAP and all the others use IAS/IFRS (see Table 31.9).

TABLE 31.9	Common size analysis of operating revenue and operating cost components (%)							
	BA	Lufthansa	SAS	AA	KLM	Ryanair	SAir	Sabena
Operating revenue	100	100	100	100	100	100	100	100
Operating costs	95.90	93.47	96.78	100.69	96.02	76.61	96.28	105.75
Fuel	11.88	9.13	8.33	11.38	14.91	13.02	6.35	10.74
Staff	25.61	22.08	31.40	18.76	24.07	12.56	27.77	22.17
Depreciation	7.71	6.23	4.61	12.88	6.16	12.14	6.11	4.75
Lease cost	2.38	0.38	3.99	1.66	4.89	1.49	5.47	13.89
Other	48.32	55.66	8.45	56.01	45.99	37.40	50.59	54.19
Operating result	4.10	6.53	3.22	−0.69	3.98	23.39	3.72	−5.75

Source: Austrian Airlines Annual Report 2000, British Airways Annual Report 2000/2001, KLM Annual Report 2000/2001, Lufthansa Annual Report 2000, Ryanair Annual Report 2000/2001, Sabena Annual Report 2000, SAir Annual Report 2000, and SAS Annual Report 2000.

ACTIVITY 31.6

What kinds of difference do you notice? Can you think of an explanation, taking into account all the elements which have been discussed already concerning airlines?

Activity feedback

Ryanair has substantially lower staff costs than the other companies. Further, the lease costs differ among the airlines. However, the lease costs which refer to operating lease contracts should always be considered in combination with depreciation and amortisation costs. Airlines which own a large percentage of their fleet or operate their fleet under financial lease agreements have higher depreciation costs than airlines leasing most of their aircraft under operating lease contracts. The quality of disclosure with regard to the

item owned aircraft, aircraft under financial lease or aircraft under operating lease differs among the airlines. Some comparative data are presented with regard to this item. Some airlines disclose in the narrative part of the annual accounts the breakdown of their fleet according to the way it is financed. A few examples are listed in Table 31.10.

We learn from this comparative analysis that Lufthansa is the only carrier which still owns a large part of its fleet. Whether or not a plane is accounted for as a financial lease or an operating lease depends not only on the contract, but also on the GAAP applied. To illustrate the impact we present an historic overview of the composition of the fleet and the way it is accounted for in Table 31.11. The data included in Table 31.11 will be used again later in this chapter.

ACTIVITY 31.6   (Continued)

TABLE 31.10   Information on fleet capacity of British Airways, KLM, Lufthansa and Sabena

	Aircraft owned	Financial leading	On balance sheet	Operational leasing	Total
Lufthansa	273 (82%)	49 (15%)	322 (97%)	9 (3%)	331 (100%)
KLM	87 (41%)	78 (37%)	165 (77%)	48 (23%)	213 (100%)
Sabena	8 (9%)	32 (37%)	40 (46%)	47 (54%)	87 (100%)
British Airways			226 (67%)	112 (33%)	338 (100%)

Source: British Airways Annual Report, KLM Annual Report 2000/2001, Lufthansa Annual Report 2000 and Sabena Annual Report 2000.

TABLE 31.11   Aircraft operated by the Sabena Group

Year	Aircraft owned		Aircraft under financial leasing		Aircraft under operational leasing		Total
1993	33	49.25%	15	22.39%	19	28.36%	67
1994	27	38.57%	19	27.14%	24	34.29%	70
1995	26	33.77%	19	24.68%	32	41.56%	77
1996	38	48.72%	8	10.26%	32	41.03%	78
1997	35	50.00%	4	5.71%	31	44.29%	70
1998	10	13.51%	3	4.05%	61	82.43%	74
1999	8	9.76%	31	37.80%	43	52.44%	82
2000	8	9.20%	32	36.78%	47	54.02%	87

Source: Sabena Annual Reports 1993–2000

The fuel cost expressed as a percentage of operating revenue differs drastically among these companies. We know already that distance flown, number of take-offs and kerosene price has an influence, but that alone does not explain the differences which appear in Table 31.9.

ACTIVITY 31.7

Can you think of another explanation for the observed differences in the cost structures of the airlines?

Activity feedback

When we compare British Airways and Ryanair at 31.3.2001 these companies are almost 100% airlines, with very few other activities at that time. The group accounts of SAS, however, do not only present revenues and costs from the airline business – the costs and the revenues stemming from their hotel business are included as well. Further Lufthansa and SAir have, besides their airlines, other airline-related businesses such as catering, ground handling, IT, etc. This explains the lower percentage of fuel costs in relation to operating revenue, whereas British Airways and Ryanair were not active in these airline-related businesses at that time.

Corporate strategic decisions determine the different business lines in which a company is active. The consolidated group accounts represent the overall performance of the different industries or businesses in which a company competes. Segmental information provides an overview of the different businesses and the proportion of each business unit in the total revenue and the results before interest and taxes (EBIT). A discussion on segmental reporting under IAS can be found in Chapter 24. In the next section we illustrate how the use of segmental data could shed extra light on the analysis of the group's profit and loss account and balance sheet included in the group accounts.

SEGMENTAL ANALYSIS

Segmental reporting informs the user of the group accounts on the breakdown of the total revenue over the different business segments. For an evaluation of the breakdown of the operational costs in the common size analysis (see Tables 31.7 and 31.8) in a more meaningful way, the segmental data included in the accounts also need to be considered. A comparative analysis between airline activities (passengers and freight and mail) versus airline-related activities reveals that SAS, Lufthansa but especially the SAir Group have diversified activities (Table 31.12).

The data of the SAir Group do not come as a surprise, as their corporate strategy since 1996 is their so-called two pillar strategy. Growth in the so-called second pillar is among acquisitions and organic growth also obtained by integrating the airline-related activities of the airlines in which they acquire a substantial minority shareholding into the SAir Group. If we analyse the annual report of Sabena of 1994, we observe that before the cooperation with SAir (Sabena Annual Report 1994, p. 6) passenger traffic made up 75.1% of total revenue, cargo and other airline-related activities amounted to 25% of the total revenue. These proportions had been changing up to 2000. So we learn from the Sabena Annual Report 2000, p. 24, that in 2000 the catering activities were further integrated and outsourced to Gate Gourmet, the catering company from the SAir Group.

The analysis of the segmental disclosure of a company can shed light on the corporate strategy of the group and on the importance of the different business or geographical segments of the group. In Table 31.13 the horizontal analysis of the different business segments of the SAir Group are presented (the analysis is based not on total revenue, which includes inter-segment revenue, but on external revenue).

Focusing on the business segment airlines of the SAir Group we learn from their annual report that for the years 1998, 1999 and 2000 the revenue and earnings before interest and taxes (EBIT) of the leasing activities of their company, Flightlease, are combined with the revenue and EBIT of the airlines Swissair, Crossair and Balair into one business segment airline.

Segmental reporting data may also be subject to manipulation. When a company plans for an IPO on a particular segment there is an incentive to present increasing non-volatile results for that segment. On the other hand if a company considers segmental data as proprietary data, which it does not want to disclose to the competition, then an incentive for manipulation will arise as well.

TABLE 31.12	Breakdown of total group revenue over different business segments (%)

	Passenger traffic	Freight and mail	Other (technics, ground handling, catering etc.)
Ryanair	88		12
British Airways	84	6	10
SAS	70	5	25
Lufthansa	61	14	25
KLM	65	17	18
Austrian Airlines	75	6	19
SAir Group	41	10	49
Sabena	85	Assumed by SAir in 1997	15

Source: Financial statements of 2000, Austrian Airlines, 2000, British Airways and KLM, 2000/2001, Lufthansa, 2000, Ryanair, 2000/2001, Sabena, SAir, and SAS, 2000.

TABLE 31.13	Horizontal analysis of different business segments of the SAir Group (%)

	1997	1998	1999	2000
External revenue	100	107.02	123.17	153.74
SAirlines	100	106.54	116.37	130.40
SAir Services	100	120.37	147.00	243.86
SAir Logistics	100	105.18	110.61	141.77
SAir Relations	100	104.61	131.79	170.58
SAir Group	100	2700	2400	8200

Source: SAir Group Annual Report of the 1997, 1998, 1999, 2000.

ACTIVITY 31.8

The combination of leasing and airline activities into one business segment, 'Airlines', in the financial years 1999 and 2000 (Table 13.13): what do you think of this approach?

Activity feedback

Earlier in the chapter we mentioned that depreciation and rental and lease costs should always be considered together in order to determine the impact of the airplane capacity costs on the results. According to the financing policy chosen (financial leasing, operational leasing or owned and financed through equity or loans) the depreciation and rental costs will be higher or lower. In 1998 Swissair sold and leased back a large part of its fleet. The leasing company, Flightlease, was involved in these transactions. In order to make EBIT and other data of the SAirlines (Swissair, Crossair and Balair) comparable with other airlines, the leasing activities were added to the business segment airlines. That was the explanation given by financial analysts.

This argument would have been acceptable had Flightlease been responsible only for the leasing activities of Swissair, Crossair and Balair, the airlines in which the SAir Group was the majority shareholder. However, Flightlease also leases planes to associated entities such as Sabena and its subsidiary, Sobelair, LTU and several other airlines. Taking that information into account the argument is less acceptable. In the notes to the annual accounts of SAir we find with regard to leased assets the following information (SAIR annual accounts, 2000, n. 26, p. 30) 'Future lease income from aircraft lease agreements amounts to CHF 1.6 billion and will stem largely from associated undertakings.'

ILLUSTRATION

The case of Sabena (1991–2000)

Before we turn to the next technique of financial analysis, ratio analysis, we apply trend analysis and common size analysis on the operating revenue and operating cost data of Sabena NV over the last ten years (1991–2000) of its existence. We use the individual accounts of Sabena NV because they have been prepared according to Belgian GAAP for the whole time frame of the analysis, whereas the group accounts were published in Belgian GAAP up to 1998 and from 1999 according to IAS. As already mentioned Sabena NV represents the airline and accounts for 90% of the revenue of the Sabena Group. In the data presented, comparability is enhanced by adding the cost and revenue data of Sabena Technics (the subsidiary created in 1999) to the data of Sabena NV after correction for inter-segment revenue. Many elements resulting from the accounting strategy of Sabena (see subsequent reports of the board of directors, discussed in Chapter 30) were reported as exceptional costs and exceptional revenue, so the operating revenue and operating costs reported relate to the operating activities. The evolution of some airline operating statistics is also presented.

ACTIVITY 31.9

Taking into account the information given about Sabena in Chapter 30, the discussion on trend analysis, common size analysis and segmental analysis, what evolutions do you observe in Table 31.14 and 31.15? What explanations can you give? What extra information would you like to have in addition in order to make a better judgement?

Activity feedback

Most meaningful is to focus the analysis on those operating cost components which are less influenced by accrual accounting decisions. Operating cost items such as changes in values in current assets and provisions will therefore be left out of this analysis.

Taking into account all the data presented so far on Sabena in Chapters 30 and 31 we know that there have been at least three 'events' which had an impact on the structure of Sabena NV in that period, namely the 'assumption' of cargo by the SAir Group, the creation of Sabena Technics NV and the creation of the Airline Management Partnership. Only with regard to the creation of Sabena Technics can the external user of the annual accounts judge the impact as Sabena Technics is fully consolidated in the group accounts and its individual accounts are

TABLE 31.14   Horizontal analysis of the operating result of Sabena NV + Sabena Technics (%)

Sabena + Technics	1991	1992	1993	1994	1995	1996	1997	1998	1999	2000
Operating revenue	100.00	98.24	100.99	108.86	112.82	115.24	132.98	162.43	170.83	192.92
Mat. cons	100.00	90.96	102.68	105.23	94.94	107.78	71.51	71.84	80.75	113.58
Serv. goods	100.00	99.81	112.49	121.94	133.11	145.49	192.05	247.31	278.48	346.18
Personnel cost	100.00	92.81	86.09	86.08	93.75	100.87	99.73	108.32	118.26	116.35
Dep. fix assets	100.00	117.11	115.97	118.36	118.02	118.17	111.48	112.54	84.36	105.16
Current assets	100.00	33.33	8.89	8.92	3.62	10.66	−36.65	15.65	−7.02	−33.40
Provisions	100.00	88.30	6.88	29.63	−27.62	2.60	−33.90	0.66	57.50	68.22
Other	100.00	88.42	81.07	72.06	55.70	110.21	98.41	132.60	138.52	128.85
Operating cost	100.00	95.33	101.71	106.02	111.45	121.44	130.79	156.08	171.21	205.54
Operating result	100.00	−140.97	160.05	−125.10	−0.42	625.45	−47.75	−359.65	202.21	1231.30
Activity data	1991	1992	1993	1994	1995	1996	1997	1998	1999	2000
Actual production										
# passengers	100.00	104.11	120.96	141.20	165.69	171.41	227.69	289.86	332.46	362.19
# hours	100.00	104.74	118.31	126.41	142.99	164.98	170.88	208.46	239.94	258.51
# km	100.00	104.15	117.54	126.69	143.57	162.00	166.11	209.33	243.61	263.82

Source: Sabena Annual reports 1991–2000.

(continued)

ACTIVITY 31.9   *(Continued)*

TABLE 31.15   Vertical analysis of the operating result of Sabena NV + Sabena Technics NV (%)

Sabena + Technics	1991	1992	1993	1994	1995	1996	1997	1998	1999	2000
Operating revenue	100.00	100.00	100.00	100.00	100.00	100.00	100.00	100.00	100.00	100.00
Mat. cons	23.61	21.86	24.01	22.83	19.87	22.08	12.70	10.44	11.16	13.90
Serv. goods	40.44	41.09	45.05	45.30	47.71	51.06	58.40	61.57	65.93	72.57
Personnel cost	32.66	30.85	27.84	25.82	27.13	28.58	24.49	21.78	22.61	19.69
Dep. fix assets	4.39	5.23	5.04	4.77	4.59	4.50	3.68	3.04	2.17	2.39
Current assets	1.64	0.56	−0.14	0.13	0.05	0.15	−0.45	0.16	−0.07	−0.28
Provisions	−1.86	−1.67	−0.13	−0.51	0.46	−0.04	0.47	−0.01	−0.63	−0.66
Other	0.35	0.32	0.28	0.23	0.17	0.34	0.26	0.29	0.29	0.24
Operating cost	101.23	98.23	101.95	98.59	100.00	106.68	99.56	97.28	101.46	107.85
Operating result	−1.23	1.77	−1.95	1.41	0.00	−6.68	0.44	2.72	− 1.46	−7.85

Source: Sabena and Sabena Technics NV Annual Reports 1991–2000

published. The impact of the 'assumption of the cargo business' by SAir on the operating revenue and the operating costs of Sabena is not clear for an external user of the annual accounts. We only know from the annual report of SAir that their group operating revenue increased positively as a result of the assumption of Sabena's cargo business. The impact of this assumption on the revenues and costs of Sabena is not disclosed. This hinders further the comparability of the airline statistics over time. So more information on the impact of the 'assumption' of the cargo business by SAir would be welcome.

That the creation of the AMP will have an impact on the operating revenues and operating costs of Sabena is clear. Personnel costs, for example, decrease in 2000 as a number of employees of Sabena are transferred to the Airline Management Partnership. The same happens at the level of the SAir Group, employees from SAir are also transferred to the AMP. Evaluating the impact of the AMP on the situation of Sabena is rendered more difficult for the external analysts as the AMP was organised under the legal form of a partnership located in the UK. One of the characteristics of a partnership under the European Directives is that the financial statements do not have to be made public.

Further we learn from the annual report of SAir (see Chapter 30, extract SAir Annual Report 1999, financial statements (p. 19) and financial statements year 2000 (p. 17) that in 1998 and in 1999 shares which could be sold after three years have been given to personnel and share options were also granted to staff members. It would be interesting to know how many of the AMP employees own shares of the SAir Group.

We will now turn to the evolution of the individual operating cost items.

In this ten-year period the two time frames (namely the cooperation with Air France and the cooperation with the SAir Group) clearly step out of the data. Different patterns can be observed from 1991 to 1995 and from 1996 until 2000. In the first time frame, the cooperation with Air France, there is a smooth growth of operating revenue. The different operating cost categories follow more or less at the same pace. The vertical analysis shows that the proportion of each cost component in total revenue remains stable in the first half of the last decade of the 20th century. In the second time frame when the SAir Group took a substantial minority shareholding (49.5%) in Sabena, the growth rate increased. The aim of SAir was to acquire, together with its associated undertakings, a market share of 20% in Europe. Those airline operating statistics, which are comparable over the ten-year time span show an enormous increase in the last years of the 20th century. This was a result of the fleet expansion. From Table 31.10 we learn that there is an enormous increase in the fleet capacity in the year 1999. From Chapter 30 we know that Sabena tried to fill up the increased seat capacity by price reductions. This policy did result in a growing number of passengers carried, but most of the extra passengers were economy class. These passengers increase the rather variable costs such as handling and catering, which represent activities which had to be bought for a large part from the airline-related segments or the second pillar of the SAir Group in the last years of the existence of Sabena. As a result of this policy, the trend pattern of the cost components and the proportion of each cost component in the total revenue lost their stability in the second half of the 1990s.

ACTIVITY 31.9 *(Continued)*

The decrease in the component 'materials and consumables' until 1998 can be explained by the policy of outsourcing, but also by the favourable fuel prices and the favourable exchange rate to the dollar. An unfavourable change in these last two years at the end of the 20th century explains the steep rise in component materials and consumables costs.

Due to the outsourcing of activities the component 'services and other goods' rose, but that is not the sole explanation. The steep rise in this component in the last two years is also due to the enormous fleet expansion of Sabena, financed through operating lease contracts. The impact of this fleet expansion on the costs of 1999 was somewhat softened as the realised gains on the sale of planes were offset with the lease costs. In 2000 this effect disappeared to a large extent and the costs of the fleet expansion now hit the profit and loss account with their full impact. (The impact of this fleet expansion on the finance structure of Sabena is illustrated in the section on ratio analysis.) The personnel cost decreases in 2000; this could be due to the creation of the AMP, but we cannot be completely sure of this as the only information received about AMP is that: 'The partnership constituted a complete merger of the commercial departments of Sabena and Swissair . . . From the economic aspect of achieving savings, AMP realised a reduction in expenditure for the two airlines of around EUR 100 million per annum' (Sabena Annual Report 2000, p. 14).

Depreciation costs remain rather stable over the ten-year period. This is due to the fact that capacity cost for the airplanes switch from depreciation to lease costs over the years (Sabena NV used Belgian GAAP). The increase from 1999 to 2000 can be explained by the increase in book values of the fixed assets transferred from Sabena NV to Sabena Technics NV together with the goodwill created in the course of the creation of this subsidiary. This results in higher depreciation costs.

Further care should be taken in evaluating the trend data of the operating result. As the base year had a negative operating result, years with a positive operating result get a negative sign. Years with a negative operating result have a positive sign.

RATIO ANALYSIS

Financial statements identify a multitude of figures for us, for example, profit before tax, gross profit, total of fixed assets, net current assets. As already mentioned these figures do not mean very much unless we can compare them to something else. In previous sections of this chapter on techniques of financial analysis we have benchmarked the whole balance sheet and profit and loss account of a company against its own historical data (trend analysis) or against the data of other companies (common size profit and loss account and common size balance sheets) in order to be able to evaluate the overall performance. In Chapter 11 we discussed the technique of ratio analysis. This technique enables us to focus on specific questions concerning the financial situation of the company. We repeat the issues analysed in Chapter 11 here again in broader context.

- Can the business meet its financial commitments? Can the business pay its debt? Is it liquid (financial status)?
- How successful is the business? Is it making a reasonable profit? Is it utilising its assets to the fullest? Is it, in fact, profitable and efficient?
- Is the business a suitable investment for shareholders or would returns be greater if they invested elsewhere? Is it a good investment?

Balance sheet items or profit and loss account items related to these questions will be combined in a ratio to provide useful information to the user of the accounts for his/her decision-making.

With ratios we relate certain items of the balance sheet and profit and loss account to each other in order to evaluate the financial status, performance or investment potential of a business.

Before starting with ratio analysis, one must always check the pitfalls which may hinder the comparability of financial statement data. We have discussed these pitfalls to a large extent in the first part of this chapter so we will not repeat them here. Besides data from the airline industry, in this section on ratio analysis we will also use data from the annual accounts of several groups specialised in consumer goods, namely Nestlé, Unilever and Danone. The main objective in including these accounts is to illustrate the different ratios which might be calculated on the basis of these financial statements rather than compare the financial situation of the two multinationals, which have as similarities that they are recognisable worldwide and are active in consumer goods. Nestlé is active in the following business segments: beverages, milk products, nutrition and ice cream, prepared dishes, cooking aids, pet care, chocolate, confectionery and biscuits and pharmaceutical products. Unilever is active in the following segments: savoury and dressings, spread and cooking products, beverages, ice cream and frozen products, foods and home and personal care products. Danone is active in the fresh dairy products, waters, baby food and medical nutrition segments.

In the accompanying tables the data on the balance sheet and profit and loss account of Unilever (Table 31.16), Nestlé (Table 31.17) and Danone (Table 31.18) are presented.

With respect to Unilever we also provide an extract of the notes in order to see information on the breakdown of the operating costs.

We observe that Unilever has already moved towards the improved IAS 1. Unilever presents a consolidated income statement and a consolidated statement of recognised income and expense. This latter statement presents information on the total recognised income and expense which consists of the net profit of the company (a breakdown of this net profit is found in the income statement) and the net income/(expense) recognised directly in equity. In prior years the net income recognised directly in equity was a larger amount compared to the net profit, than in 2007. A fluctuating amount in this income recognised directly in equity are the actuarial gains and losses on pension schemes net of tax.

In Table 31.17, on the consolidated statement of recognised income and expense and changes in equity, the reader finds information on how much income and expenses are recognised directly in equity in the accounts of Nestlé. The amount is about 5% of the profit for the period recognised in the income statement. However this amount is a result from larger negative amounts and a number of smaller positive amounts. Currency translations, pensions and share-based payment are the items with material amounts in the elements which are recognised directly in equity.

In Table 31.18 information on income and expenses directly recognised in equity is to be found in the Danone financial statements in the consolidated statement of changes in shareholders' equity. This is the old IAS 1. The information on income and expenses directly recognised in equity, is more difficult to retrieve from this statement than, for example, in the presentation of Unilever, which is according to the new IAS 1.

Before we start with a discussion of the ratios which are helpful in assessing the following questions:

- How successful is the business?
- Is it making a reasonable profit?
- Is it utilising its assets to the fullest?
- Is it in fact profitable and efficient?

we will pay attention to the characteristics of IAS accounts.

TABLE 31.16 | Financial statements Unilever Group

Consolidated income statement
for the year ended 31 December

	€ million	€ million	€ million
	2007	**2006**	**2005**
Continuing operations			
Turnover 2	**40 187**	39 642	38 401
Operating profit 2	**5 245**	5 408	5 074
After (charging)/crediting:			
Restructuring 3	**(875)**	(704)	(328)
Business disposals, impairments and other 3	**306**	196	(249)
Gain on US healthcare and UK pensions 3	**–**	266	–
Net finance costs 5	**(252)**	(721)	(613)
Finance income	**147**	128	129
Finance costs	**(550)**	(590)	(689)
Preference shares provision	**(7)**	(300)	
Pensions and similar obligations	**158**	41	(53)
Share of net profit/(loss) of joint ventures	**102**	78	47
Share of net profit/(loss) of associates	**50**	36	(25)
Other income from non-current investments 11	**39**	30	33
Profit before taxation	**5 184**	4 831	4 516
Taxation 6	**(1 128)**	(1 146)	(1 181)
Net profit from continuing operations	**4 056**	3 685	3 335
Net profit from discontinued operations 27	**80**	1 330	640
Net profit	**4 136**	5 015	3 975
Attributable to:			
Minority interests	**248**	270	209
Shareholders' equity	**3 888**	4 745	3 766
Combined earnings per share 7			
From continuing operations			
Basic earnings per share	**€1.32**	€1.19	€1.07
Diluted earnings per share	**€1.28**	€1.15	€1.04
From discontinued operations			
Basic earnings per share	**€0.03**	€0.46	€0.22
Diluted earnings per share	**€0.03**	€0.45	€0.21
From total operations			
Basic earnings per share	**€1.35**	€1.65	€1.29
Diluted earnings per share	**€1.31**	€1.60	€1.25

References in the consolidated income statement, consolidated statement of recognised income and expense, consolidated cash flow statement and consolidated balance sheet relate to notes on pages 72 to 121, which form an integral part of the consolidated financial statements.

Accounting policies of the Unilever Group are set out in note 1 on pages 72 to 76.

(continued)

TABLE 31.16   (Continued)

Consolidated statement of recognised income and expense

for the year ended 31 December

	€ million	€ million	€ million
	2007	**2006**	**2005**
Fair value gains/(losses) net of tax:			
On cash flow hedges	**84**	6	14
On available-for-sale financial assets	**2**	15	–
Actuarial gains/(losses) on pension schemes net of tax	**542**	853	(49)
Currency retranslation gains/(losses) net of tax[a]	**(413)**	(335)	513
Net income/(expense) recognised directly in equity	**215**	539	478
Net profit	**4 136**	5 015	3 975
Total recognised income and expense 21	**4 351**	5 554	4 453
Attributable to:			
Minority interests	**237**	242	249
Shareholders' equity	**4 114**	5 312	4 204

(a) Includes fair value gains/(losses) on net investment hedges of €(692) million (2006: €(779) million; 2005: €332 million).

Consolidated balance sheet

as at 31 December

	€ million	€ million
	2007	**2006**
Goodwill 9	**12 244**	12 425
Intangible assets 9	**4 511**	4 781
Property, plant and equipment 10	**6 284**	6 276
Pension asset for funded schemes in surplus 20	**2 008**	1 697
Deferred tax assets 12	**1 003**	1 266
Other non-current assets 11	**1 324**	1 126
Total non-current assets	**27 374**	27 571
Inventories 13	**3 894**	3 796
Trade and other current receivables 14	**4 194**	4 254
Current tax assets	**367**	125
Cash and cash equivalents 15	**1 098**	1 039
Other financial assets 15	**216**	273
Assets held for sale 27	**159**	14
Total current assets	**9 928**	9 501
Financial liabilities 16	**(4 166)**	(4 458)
Trade payables and other current liabilities 18	**(8 017)**	(7 838)
Current tax liabilities	**(395)**	(579)

TABLE 31.16   (Continued)

Consolidated balance sheet
as at 31 December

	€ million	€ million
	2007	**2006**
Provisions 19	**(968)**	(1 009)
Liabilities associated with assets held for sale 27	**(13)**	–
Total current liabilities	**(13 559)**	(13 884)
Net current assets/(liabilities)	**(3 631)**	(4 383)
Total assets less current liabilities	**23 743**	23 188
Financial liabilities due after one year Provisions 19	**5 483**	4 377
Non-current tax liabilities	**233**	272
Pensions and post-retirement healthcare liabilities:		
Funded schemes in deficit 20	**827**	1 379
Unfunded schemes 20	**2 270**	3 398
Provisions 19	**694**	826
Deferred tax liabilities 12	**1 213**	1 003
Other non-current liabilities	**204**	261
Total non-current liabilities	**10 924**	11 516
Called up share capital 21	**484**	484
Share premium account 21	**153**	165
Other reserves 21	**(3 412)**	(2 143)
Retained profit 21	**15 162**	12 724
Shareholders' equity	**12 387**	11 230
Minority interests 21	**432**	442
Total equity	**12 819**	11 672
Total capital employed	**23 743**	23 188

Commitments and contingent liabilities are shown in note 25 on page 112.
These financial statements, together with the Report of the Directors, were approved by the Directors on 10 March 2008.

3 Gross profit and operating costs

	€ million	€ million	€ million
	2007	**2006**	**2005**
Turnover	**40 187**	39 642	38 401
Cost of sales	**(20 558)**	(20 093)	(19 539)
Gross profit	**19 629**	19 549	18 862
Distribution and selling costs	**(9 489)**	(9 486)	(9 078)
Administrative expenses[a]	**(4 895)**	(4 655)	(4 710)
Operating profit	**5 245**	5 408	5 074

(a) Includes amortisation of finite-lived intangible assets and impairment of goodwill and intangible assets.

TABLE 31.16 (Continued)

The following items are disclosed on the face of the income statement as separate disclosure provides additional information to users to help them better understand underlying business performance.

	€ million	€ million	€ million
	2007	2006	2005
Restructuring	(875)	(704)	(328)
Business disposals, impairments and other:			
Gain/(loss) on disposals of group companies	297	179	132
Impairments	–	(14)	(397)
(Provision for)/release of Brazilian sales tax	9	31	16
Gains on US healthcare and UK pensions	–	266	–

Restructuring costs are incurred as Unilever continues to simplify the organisation, reorganise operations and support functions and redevelop the portfolio. They primarily relate to redundancy and retirement costs. The significant costs incurred in 2007 are in respect of new multi-country organisations announced and several factory closures. Business disposals generate both costs and revenues which are not reflective of underlying performance. Impairment charges are primarily recognised for goodwill other than where included in restructuring or as part of business disposals. In 2005 an impairment charge of €363 million was recognised in respect of *Slim Fast*.

The gains on US healthcare arose from the introduction of an annual cap on the benefits which each participant can claim. The gain in the UK resulted from reducing deferred pensions where they are taken early.

Other items within operating costs include:

	€ million	€ million	€ million
	2007	2006	2005
Staff costs	(5 537)	(5 355)	(5 745)
Raw and packaging materials and goods purchased for resale	(15 588)	(15 655)	(15 106)
Amortisation of finite-lived intangible assets and software	(140)	(157)	(99)
Depreciation of property, plant and equipment	(804)	(787)	(770)
Advertising and promotions	(5 289)	(5 203)	(4 918)
Exchange gains/(losses):	(15)	(25)	19
On underlying transactions	(10)	(10)	(6)
On covering forward contracts	(5)	(15)	25
Lease rentals:	(477)	(451)	(421)
Minimum operating lease payments	(488)	(455)	(423)
Contingent operating lease payments	–	(3)	(3)
Less: Sub-lease income relating to operating lease agreements	11	7	5

Total expenditure on research and development in 2007, including costs incurred under some of the headings reported above, was €868 million (2006: €906 million; 2005: €932 million).

TABLE 31.17 Nestlé consolidated financial statements for the year ended 31 December 2007

Consolidated income statement

In millions of CHF

	Notes	2007		2006
Sales	1	**107 552**		**98 458**
Cost of goods sold		(45 037)		(40 713)
Distribution expenses		(9 104)		(8 244)
Marketing and administration expenses		(36 512)		(34 465)
Research and development costs		(1 875)		(1 734)
EBIT Earnings Before Interest, Taxes, restructuring and impairments	1	**15 024**		**13 302**
Net other income/(expenses)	2	(590)		(516)
Profit before interest and taxes		**14 434**		**12 786**
Net financing cost	3			
Financial income		576	537	
Financial expense		(1 492)	(1 218)	
		(916)		(681)
Profit before taxes and associates		**13 518**		**12 105**
Taxes	5	(3 416)		(3 293)
Share of results of associates	6	1 280		963
Profit from continuing operations		**11 382**		**9 775**
Net profit/(loss) on discontinued operations	25	–		74
Profit for the period		**11 382**		**9 849**
of which attributable to minority interests		733		652
of which attributable to shareholders of the parent (Net profit)		10 649		9 197
As percentages of sales				
EBIT Earnings Before Interest, Taxes, restructuring and impairments		14.0%		13.5%
Profit for the period attributable to shareholders of the parent (Net profit)		9.9%		9.3%
Earnings per share from continuing operations (in CHF)				
Basic earnings per share	7	27.81		23.71
Fully diluted earnings per share	7	27.61		23.56

(continued)

TABLE 31.17 (Continued)

Consolidated balance sheet

In millions of CHF

	Notes	2007		2006	
Assets					
Current assets					
Liquid assets					
Cash and cash equivalents	18	6 594		5 278	
Short term investments		2 902		6 197	
			9 496		11 475
Trade and other receivables	8/18		15 421		14 577
Assets held for sale	25		22		74
Inventories	10		9 272		8 029
Derivative assets			754		556
Prepayments and accrued income	9/18		805		594
Total current assets			**35 770**		**35 305**
Non-current assets					
Property, plant and equipment	11				
Gross value		49 474		47 077	
Accumulated depreciation and impairment		(27 409)		(26 847)	
			22 065		20 230
Investments in associates	6		8 936		8 430
Deferred tax assets	16		2 224		2 433
Financial assets	18		4 213		2 778
Employee benefits assets	14		811		343
Goodwill	12		33 423		28 513
Intangible assets	13		7 217		3 773
Total non-current assets			**78 889**		**66 500**
Total assets			**114 659**		**101 805**
Liabilities and equity					
Current liabilities					
Trade and other payables	18		14 179		12 572
Liabilities directly associated with assets held for sale	25		7		–
Financial liabilities	18		24 541		15 494

TABLE 31.17 (*Continued*)

In millions of CHF	Notes	2007	2006
Tax liabilities		856	884
Derivative liabilities	9/18	477	470
Accruals and deferred income		3 266	3 059
Total current liabilities		**43 326**	**32 479**
Non-current liabilities			
Financial liabilities	18	6 129	6 952
Employee benefits liabilities	14	5 165	5 415
Deferred tax liabilities	16	1 398	706
Other payables		1 091	366
Provisions	17	3 316	3 039
Total non-current liabilities		**17 099**	**16 478**
Total liabilities		**60 425**	**48 957**
Equity			
Share capital [a]	20	393	401
Share premium and reserves			
Share premium [a]		5 883	5 926
Reserve for treasury shares [a]		7 839	4 550
Translation reserves		(6 302)	(5 205)
Retained earnings [a]		52 285	49 963
Treasury shares [a]	21	59 705	55 234
		(8 013)	(4 644)
Total equity attributable to shareholders of the parent		**52 085**	**50 991**
Minority interests		2 149	1 857
Total equity		**54 234**	**52 848**
Total liabilities and equity		**114 659**	**101 805**

(a) At the Annual General Meeting on 19 April 2007, the shareholders approved the cancellation of 7 663 200 shares.

(*continued*)

TABLE 31.17 (Continued)

Consolidated statement of recognised income and expense and changes in equity

Statement of recognised income and expense for the year ended 31 December 2007

In millions of CHF

	Share capital	Share premium	Reserve for treasury shares	Translation reserve	Retained earnings	Less: Treasury shares	Total equity attributable to shareholders of the parent	Minority interests	Total equity
Profit for the period recognised in the income statement					10 649		10 649	733	11 382
Currency retranslations				(1 097)			(1 097)	(98)	(1 195)
Fair value adjustments on available-for-sale financial instruments									
– Unrealised results					(15)		(15)		(15)
– Recognition of realised results in the income statement					(18)		(18)		(18)
Fair value adjustments on cash flow hedges									
– Recognised in hedging reserve					94		94		94
– Removed from hedging reserve					(168)		(168)		(168)
Actuarial gains/(losses) on defined benefit schemes					600		600	(3)	597
Changes in equity of associates					(631)		(631)		(631)
Equity-settled share-based transactions cost					222		222	24	246
Taxes on equity items					(213)		(213)	—	(213)
Income and expense recognised directly in equity				(1 097)	(129)		(1 226)	(77)	(1 303)
Total recognised income and expense for the year ended 31 December 2007				(1 097)	10 520		9 423	956	10 079

TABLE 31.18 Danone Group: Consolidated financial statements

Consolidated income statement

(In € millions)	Notes	Year ended December 31	
		2006	**2007**
Net sales		**12 068**	**12 776**
Cost of goods sold		(6 163)	(6 380)
Selling expenses		(3 170)	(3 498)
General and administrative expenses		(878)	(943)
Research and development expenses		(103)	(121)
Other (expense) income	20	(157)	(138)
Trading operating income		**1 597**	**1 696**
Other operating (expense) income	21	(37)	(150)
Operating income		**1 560**	**1 546**
Interest income		*178*	*132*
Interest expense		*(179)*	*(307)*
Cost of net debt	22	*(1)*	*(175)*
Other financial (expense) income	22	*(29)*	*(2)*
Income before tax		**1 530**	**1 369**
Income tax	23	(287)	(410)
Income from consolidated companies		**1 243**	**959**
Net income (loss) of equity-accounted affiliates	6	(49)	87
Net income from continuing operations		**1 194**	**1 046**
Net income from discontinued operations	3	366	3 292
Net income		**1 560**	**4 338**
– Attributable to the Group		**1 353**	**4 180**
– Attributable to minority interests		**207**	**158**

Per Share Information (see note 13)

(In euros, except for number of shares)	2006	2007
Number of shares used in calculating:		
– earnings per share	485 468 188	476 355 811
– diluted earnings per share	489 377 826	479 863 143
Earnings per share attributable to the Group		

(continued)

TABLE 31.18 (Continued)

Per Share Information (see note 13)

(In euros, except for number of shares)

	2006	2007
– underlying	2.46	2.49
– total	2.79	8.77
Diluted earnings per share attributable to the Group		
– underlying	2.44	2.47
– total	2.76	8.71

Consolidated balance sheets

As of December 31

(In € millions)	Notes	2006	2007
ASSETS			
Brand names		962	3 961
Other intangible assets, net		175	401
Goodwill, net		4 145	12 869
Intangible assets, net	4	5 282	17 231
Property, plant and equipment, net	5	3 020	3 035
Investments accounted for under the equity method	6	1 093	1 263
Investments in non-consolidated companies	7	827	772
Long-term loans	8	22	67
Other long-term assets	9	115	205
Deferred taxes	23	343	609
Non-current assets		**10 702**	**23 182**
Inventories	10	628	861
Trade accounts and notes receivable	11	1 594	1 548
Other accounts receivable and prepaid expenses	11	601	763
Short-term loans		34	30
Marketable securities	12	2 564	493
Cash and cash equivalents		655	548
Assets held for sale	3	78	151
Current assets		**6 154**	**4 394**
Total Assets		**16 856**	**27 576**

TABLE 31.18 (*Continued*)

Liabilities and Shareholders' Equity	Note		
Capital stock		130	128
Additional paid-in capital		203	255
Retained earnings		6 460	9 594
Cumulative translation adjustments		34	(190)
Treasury stock		(1 414)	(1 270)
Net income recognised directly in equity		410	501
Shareholders' equity attributable to the Group		**5 823**	**9 018**
Minority interests		246	82
Shareholders' equity		**6 069**	**9 100**
Non-current financial liabilities	25	5 705	9 855
Pension liabilities	16	147	190
Deferred taxes	23	296	1 157
Other non-current liabilities	17	391	461
Shareholders' equity and non-current liabilities		**6 539**	**11 663**
Trade accounts and notes payable	18	1 861	2 306
Accrued expenses and other current liabilities	18	1 971	2 047
Current financial liabilities	25	416	2 447
Liabilities held for sale	3	–	13
Current liabilities		**4 248**	**6 813**
Total Liabilities and Shareholders' Equity		**16 856**	**27 576**

TABLE 31.18 (Continued)

Consolidated Statement of Changes in Shareholders' Equity

(Number of shares *) (In € millions)

	Issued	Excluding treasury stock	Capital stock	Additional paid-in capital	Retained earnings	Cumulative translation adjustments	Treasury stock	Net income recognised directly in equity	Share- holders' equity – Group	Minority interests	Share- holders' equity
As of January 1, 2006	528 470,380	489 038,722	132	244	5 728	258	(1 149)	67	5 280	341	5 621
Translation adjustments						(224)			(224)	(33)	(257)
Unrealised gain (loss) on available-for-sale securities					3			340	343		343
Cash flow hedges								2	2		2
Stock options					14			1	15		15
Net income recognised directly in equity					17	(224)		343	136	(33)	103
Net income for 2006					1 353				1 353	207	1 560
Total recognised income and expenses for 2006					1 370	(224)		343	1 489	174	1 663
Capital stock issues	1 259 112	1 259 112	0	45					45	7	52
Capital stock reduction	(8 000 000)	(8 000 000)	(2)	(86)	(225)				(313)		(313)
Changes in treasury stock		(1 478 684)			3		(265)		(262)		(262)
Dividends paid					(416)				(416)	(194)	(610)
Changes in the scope of consolidation										(80)	(80)
Put options granted to minority shareholders										(2)	(2)
As of December 31, 2006	521 729 492	480 819 150	130	203	6 460	34	(1 414)	410	5 823	246	6 069
Translation adjustments						(224)			(224)	(20)	(244)
Unrealised gain (loss) on available-for-sale securities								89	89		89

TABLE 31.18 (Continued)

Consolidated Statement of Changes in Shareholders' Equity

(In € millions)

	(Number of shares *) Issued	Excluding treasury stock	Capital stock	Additional paid-in capital	Retained earnings	Cumulative translation adjustments	Treasury stock	Net income recognised directly in equity	Share-holders' equity – Group	Minority interests	Share-holders' equity
Cash flow hedges								2	2		2
Stock options					16				16		16
Net income recognised directly in equity					16	(224)		91	(117)	(20)	(137)
Net income for 2007					4 180				4 180	158	4 338
Total recognised income and expenses for 2007					4 196	(224)		91	4 063	138	4 201
Capital stock issues	1 121 968	1 121 968	1	52					53	13	66
Capital stock reduction	(10 000 000)	(6 485 217)	(3)		(580)				(583)		(583)
Change in treasury stock					(2)		144		142		142
Dividends paid					(480)				(480)	(143)	(623)
Changes in the scope of consolidation										(184)	(184)
Put options granted to minority shareholders										12	12
As of December 31, 2007	**512 851 460**	**475 455 901**	**128**	**255**	**9 594**	**(190)**	**(1 270)**	**501**	**9 018**	**82**	**9 100**

*After taking into account the two-for-one share split that occurred on June 1, 2007.
As of December 31, 2007, the number of treasury shares held by GROUPE DANONE and its subsidiaries amounted to 37 395 559 (40 910 342 as of December 31, 2006 and 39 431 658 as of December 31, 2005).

RATIO ANALYSIS AND THE IAS ACCOUNTS

The IASB foresees a minimum content for the balance sheet and the profit and loss account. Since the revision of IAS 1, the profit and loss account is one element of the statement of comprehensive income. The balance sheet is renamed in IAS 1 and is now called the statement of financial position. Application of the revised IAS 1 is for annual periods beginning after 1 January 2009. Therefore we use for the discussion the balance sheet and profit and loss accounts published by companies in compliance with the 'old' IAS 1.

In some countries domestic GAAP prescribes extensive detailed layouts of the balance sheet and profit and loss account. The IASB did not opt for such an approach. When you look at the profit and loss account of Nestlé and compare it with the layout and the contents of the profit and loss account of Unilever, you will understand the consequence of the IASB's choice. Remember the activity with the income statements of Lufthansa, British Airways and Air France-KLM, which illustrated the issue of comparability. With the approach of the IASB the preparer of the annual accounts has more freedom with regard to presentation. In these circumstances classification and presentation decisions may be used to create a certain impression. The user, however, is left with the task of reorganising the information presented in order to try to achieve some comparability, before even ratio analysis or any other financial technique can be applied.

The issue of comparability relates not only to items on the face of the balance sheet or profit and loss account, which are presented under different headings, but also to items which are presented by one company in the notes where the other companies opt for a disclosure on the face of the balance sheet.

In some countries the national GAAP prescribe the use of a specified layout with a specified number of items which must appear on the balance sheet and the profit and loss account. If an item is not present or does not apply to the company, the preparer must insert a zero or the words not available. In relation to the IAS solution companies can disclose a certain item under another line item and hide the information from the public by not presenting that specific single line item on the face of the balance sheet or the profit and loss account.

For example, when Sabena switched in 1999 from Belgian GAAP to IAS for its group accounts, a deferred tax asset of €24 million was created. This information could be found in the notes to the accounts:

> The principles of valuation, consolidation and classification have been changed; as from 1998 the IAS are applied. The first time application of IAS gives rise to the following impact on equity:

	in mio of EUR
Equity 1998 before IAS-application	213
IAS adjustments:	
• application of IAS 17–leases	(23)
• application IAS 19 – end of career indemnities	(27)
• valuation of the current investments at market value	25
• deferred tax asset on loss carry forward	24
Equity 1998 after IAS – application	212

(Sabena Annual Report, 1999, p. 10)

This was the only information provided to explain the first time application of IAS. If we know that other companies usually publish several pages as explanation, this is in fact an indication of a low quality of disclosure by Sabena.

Although IAS mentions explicitly that deferred tax assets must be disclosed as single line items, the deferred tax asset was included in other assets on the balance sheet. The deferred tax asset was not visible as a single line item. Since this deferred tax asset is about 10% of the company's equity, this item is not immaterial. For the user of the annual accounts it is impossible to know whether all single line items which must be disclosed are actually disclosed.

Under the IAS a number of items in the equity account must be recognised immediately. In relation to other items (e.g. actuarial gains and losses and past service costs in relation to pension plans) companies have a choice. Comparing performance ratios between companies, we need to consider items which have been recorded immediately in equity. If, for example, we compare Vodafone with British Airways, we need to consider the difference in the treatment of actuarial gains and losses. Vodafone opted for immediate recognition in the statement of recognised income and expenses, whereas British Airways opted for the corridor approach (see Chapter 21).

IASB mixed valuation model

In the early years the IASC opted for the historical cost model. In recent years the fair value approach gained more ground, especially in the later IASs and the new IFRS. Adaptations were also made to early IASs in order to allow for revaluations of asset items. As a result companies often have the choice between the historical cost model or the fair value model. A user of the accounts must be aware of the difference. Ideally, a company would provide the two values (historical cost and fair value) so that users of the accounts could carry out a reconciliation of the asset values in order to improve comparability. For example, if we analyse the balance sheet of Unilever, we notice the presence of biological assets (see Activity 31.10).

If we consult the notes of the annual accounts of Unilever we notice that Unilever applies the fair value method:

> The fair value of tea bushes older than 10 years is based on the market price of the estimated recoverable tea leaf volumes, net of harvest costs. The fair value of palm trees older than 8 years is based on the market price of the estimated recoverable palm oil volumes, net of harvest costs. The fair value of immature tea bushes and oil palm trees is based on the present value of the net cash flows expected to be generated by the plants at maturity.
>
> (Unilever Annual Report 2005, p. 102, n. 12.)

ACTIVITY 31.10

After consulting IAS 41, *Agricultural Products* on the website accompanying this book, figure out which valuation model the IASB prefers for biological assets and agricultural products.

Activity feedback

IAS 41 prefers the fair value model for agricultural products and biological assets.

If we analyse the balance sheet of LVMH (Louis Vuitton Moët Hennesy – a company active in the wine and spirits segment, the jewellery and watches segment, and fashion and leather goods) we do not observe biological assets, although IAS 1 requires them to be mentioned as a single line item on the face of the balance sheet. The notes of the accounts however inform us that the group has biological assets, but that they are valued according to the historical cost model and that they are included in the single line item 'property, plant and equipment':

> Vines, for champagnes, cognacs and other wines produced by the Group, are considered as biological assets as defined in IAS 41 *Agriculture*. As their valuation at market value differs little from that recognised at historical cost, no revaluation is undertaken for these assets.
>
> LVMH Annual Report 2005, p. 76, n. 1.10.

Besides the three points highlighted above, the 'classical' differences in accounting methods and accounting estimates used should always be taken into account.

Performance of the firm

Ratios which try to give a picture of a firm's profitability combine the result of a firm with the investments made for the generation of that result. The two most common ratios are return on equity (ROE) and return on assets (ROA).

$$\text{Return on equity (ROE)} = \text{Profit/Equity}$$

The profit figure used in this ratio can be before or after tax. In case of group accounts one has to make sure that if the minority interests are not added up to the equity of the group, the share in the profit of the company of the minority interests should be excluded from the profit in the numerator as well. Besides ROE another widely used profitability ratio is ROA:

$$\text{Return on assets (ROA)} = (\text{Profit before tax} + \text{Interest})/\text{Total assets}$$

Instead of using the total assets in the denominator, net total assets can be used. The net assets are equal to the equity of the company and the long term debts. This ratio is also often called return on capital employed (ROCE) or return of net total assets:

$$\text{Return on capital employed (ROCE)} = (\text{Profit before tax} + \text{Long-term interest})$$
$$/(\text{Equity} + \text{Long-term debt})$$

A remark which applies to the calculation of all performance ratios, ROA, ROE and ROCE or RNA is the question with regard to the choice of the investment base to which one should compare the result: investment base of the beginning of the year or an average equity base. In practice, very often the equity base at the end of the year is taken. If one has data available only for one year, then in that case there is not much of a choice.

In order to determine whether the obtained profitability is sufficient or excellent, one needs a benchmark. Suitable benchmarks for these ratios, besides the already known time series data and competitor or industry data, could be the proceeds of an investment in risk-free loans. The latter could answer the question: would the owners be better off selling the business and placing the proceeds in a bank deposit account?

ACTIVITY 31.11

Calculate the ROA and the ROE of Nestlé, Unilever and Danone. Evaluate what the difference between the outcome of the ratios will be according to the different investment bases used (investment base at the begin-ning of the year (= t − 1) and investment base at the end of the year (= t)). Compare also the difference of an ROE, whereby minority interests are included with an ROE with minority interests (= MI) are not included.

Activity feedback

	Nestlé		Unilever		Danone	
ROA_{t-1}	$\frac{13518}{101805}$	13.28%	$\frac{5184}{37072}$	13.98%	$\frac{1369}{16856}$	8.12%
ROA_t	$\frac{13518}{114659}$	11.79%	$\frac{5184}{37302}$	13.90%	$\frac{1369}{27576}$	
ROE_{t-1}	$\frac{10649}{50991}$	20.88%	$\frac{3888}{11230}$	34.62%	$\frac{4180}{5823}$	71.78%
$ROE_{t\ Without\ MI}$	$\frac{10649}{52085}$	20.45%	$\frac{3888}{12387}$	31.39%	$\frac{4180}{9018}$	46.35%
$ROE_{t\ With\ MI}$	$\frac{11382}{54234}$	20.99%	$\frac{4136}{12819}$	32.26%	$\frac{4338}{9100}$	47.67%

If we compare the profitability ratios of the three companies, we notice that Danone's financing structure was responsible for a positive gearing which turned the lower position on ROA into a leading position on ROE. When a company is making profit then ROA and ROE are always lower if the investment base at the end of the year is taken.

The return on total assets can be calculated at corporate level, the information is available through segmental disclosure, and the profitability of the reportable segments can be calculated as well. To retrieve information on operating decisions and investment decisions, the profitability ratio ROA can be broken down further by relating results to sales and sales to the investment base:

$$\text{Return on assets} = \frac{\text{Profit}}{\text{Total sales}} \times \frac{\text{Total sales}}{\text{Assets}}$$

The first ratio (profit/total sales) is called the profit margin ratio which expresses the result in a currency generated by each currency unit of sales. This ratio focuses on profitability and is a result of the operating decisions taken in the company. The second ratio (total sales/assets) focuses on efficiency and provides information on investment decisions and how efficiently these investments are used.

An analysis of the different cost components in relation to the sales figures could reveal interesting differences between companies. If costs are classified in the profit and loss account according to their function, then the following ratios could be calculated:

- cost of sales/sales
- marketing and sales costs/sales
- distribution cost/sales
- administrative cost/sales.

ACTIVITY 31.12

Which 'profit' is the most meaningful to be combined with sales in the ratio (profit/total sales)? Look at the profit and loss account of Unilever, Nestlé and Danone.

Activity feedback

There is the choice between the operating result and the net result of the company. The operating result is related directly to the sales, whereas the net result is also influenced by financing activities. So the most obvious choice is the operating result. If the net result is used, then the combination with the asset turnover (total sales/assets) results in the ROA figure again.

ACTIVITY 31.13

Calculate the ratios for Nestlé, Unilever and Danone.

Activity feedback

	Nestlé		Unilever		Danone	
Profit margin	$\dfrac{14\,434}{107\,552}$	13.42%	$\dfrac{5\,245}{40\,187}$	13.05%	$\dfrac{1\,546}{12\,776}$	12.10%
Asset turnover	$\dfrac{107\,552}{114\,659}$	0.94	$\dfrac{40\,187}{37\,302}$	1.08	$\dfrac{12\,776}{27\,576}$	0.46

The profit margins are more clustered than the asset turnover ratio. This implies that with regard to operating issues management arrives at similar returns on sales, but with regard to efficient use of the assets invested, we do observe a difference. The asset turnover of Danone is smaller, this explains why in the end Danone ends up with a lower ROA.

In the section on industry analysis in Chapter 30 we discussed factors influencing the pricing policy of a company and those influencing the cost levels. Sales price levels and cost levels together determine the profit margin.

ACTIVITY 31.14

Try to calculate the ratios for cost of sales/sales, marketing and sales cost/sales, distribution cost/sales and administrative cost/sales for the three groups. What do you observe?

Activity feedback

The layouts of the profit and loss accounts are different and for Unilever the information is not on the face of the profit and loss account, but is to be found in the notes. For comparative purposes we have added up distribution costs, marketing costs and selling and administrative costs. All three companies make a different subdivision so that the individual components cannot be compared:

	Nestlé	Unilever	Danone
Cost of goods sold/sales	41 87%	51 16%	49 94%
Marketing, sales, distribution and administrative costs\sales	42.41%	48.95%	34.76%

The figures confirm what is generally known: these companies spent fortunes on marketing and sales, especially Nestlé and Unilever. Nestlé's cost of goods sold in relation to sales is lowest.

The information obtained from these ratios which relate the different cost components to the sales figure can also be obtained from a common size analysis of the profit and loss account. For example, the common size analysis of the operating cost items revealed similar information.

The next group of ratios to be examined concentrates on the investment decisions and how effectively these assets in which the firm has invested are used. The performance of a firm is influenced not only by the profit margin obtained on its products or services but also by the effectiveness of its operations. The turnover of assets can be regarded as an efficiency ratio, however, it is one of a very general nature. Long-term as well as short-term assets are included in the overall ratio total sales/total assets. With regard to efficiency, the short-term elements are the centre of attention, although in some industries the efficient use of the long term assets is much more crucial.

The following ratios focus on the turnover of short-term assets.

Turnover of inventory The turnover of inventory is calculated as the 'cost of goods sold/inventory'. The average inventory level is used as denominator. The turnover of the inventory could also be expressed in days, the ratio then becomes ((average inventory/cost of goods sold) 365). (See Activity 31.15.)

Using the same ratio structure the turnover of trade receivables and trade payables can be calculated, and the average collection or payment period. The following ratios provide that information (and see Activity 31.16):

- sales/trade receivables
- (trade receivables/sales) × 365
- purchases/trade payables
- (trade payables/purchases) × 365.

Not only efficiency influences the outcome of these ratios. They could be influenced by industry characteristics. Average collection periods are often determined by industry practice. Also country influences can play a role.

The ratios concerning the trade payables can only be calculated if information on the purchases is provided in the annual accounts.

ACTIVITY 31.15

Calculate the inventory turnover and the number of inventory days for the three companies.

Activity feedback

	Nestlé Group		Unilever Group		Groupe Danone	
Inventory turnover	$\dfrac{45\,037}{8\,650.50}$	5.21	$\dfrac{20\,558}{3\,845}$	5.35	$\dfrac{6\,380}{744.5}$	8.57
Number of inventory days		70 days		68 days		43 days

Although the total asset turnover of Danone was lower, we find a different result when we focus on the inventory turnover. However one must be cautious since a higher turnover rate could be due either to more efficient inventory management or to the perishable nature of the products.

ACTIVITY 31.16

Calculate the trade receivable turnover and the collection period for Nestlé, Unilever and Danone.

	Nestlé		Unilever		Danone	
Trade receivables turnover	$\dfrac{107\,552}{14\,999}$	7.17	$\dfrac{40\,187}{4\,224}$	9.51	$\dfrac{12\,776}{1\,571}$	8.13
Collection period		51 days		38 days		45 days

Activity feedback

Nestlé uses in its presentation for financial analysts the concept 'cash conversion cycle' which consists of the collection period plus the number of days in inventory minus the days of credit granted by suppliers. In order to calculate the last item, it uses cost of goods sold in the denominator, whereas more correctly it should use the amount purchased. The figure they present in this presentation is lower than the figure we arrive at. We notice that Unilever is able to collect its receivables about ten days earlier than Nestlé.

As well as the value obtained for the ratios presented differing between industries, the usefulness of the ratios will also differ according to the industry.

Industry-specific ratios The ratio cost of goods sold/sales is more meaningful for companies active in consumer and industrial goods than for companies in a service industry such as insurance companies and banks. Some industries have their own specific ratios (like banks, insurance companies, airlines) which characterise the key drivers of performance in that specific industry. For the airline industry such ratios are, for example, unit revenue or yield which represent the average amount of traffic revenue per RPK/RPM or RTK/ RTM. In this ratio revenue passenger kilometres/miles (RPK/M) is defined as the number of paying passengers multiplied by the distance they are flown in kilometres/miles. Revenue tonne kilometres/miles (RTK/M) is defined as the number of tonnes of paid traffic (passengers, freight and mail) multiplied by the distance this traffic is flown in kilometres or miles.

These operating statistics or industry-specific key ratios are disclosed by companies on a voluntary basis. Industry practice is usually the driving force for this type of disclosure. This implies that the level of disclosure of these industry-specific ratios differs significantly between companies. The issue of quality of disclosure, which was discussed in Chapter 30, is relevant in this context. Further it is essential to keep in mind that these operating statistics or ratios are presented in the non-audited part of the annual report. A proper comparison between companies based on these voluntary disclosed industry ratios is therefore not always possible and should be executed with great caution as it concerns non-audited data.

Financial status

In order to judge the financial situation of a firm the external stakeholders want answers to questions such as: Can the business meet its financial commitments? Can the business pay its debt? Is it liquid? External stakeholders need information on the financial status of a company. It is essential for a business to be able to pay its debts as and when they fall due, otherwise its chances of remaining in operation become

ACTIVITY 31.17

Calculate both current and acid test ratios for Nestlé, Unilever and Danone.

Activity feedback

	Nestlé		Unilever		Danone	
Current ratio	$\dfrac{35\,770}{43\,326}$	0.83	$\dfrac{9\,928}{13\,559}$	0.73	$\dfrac{4\,394}{6\,813}$	0.64
Acid test ratio	$\dfrac{26\,498}{43\,326}$	0.61	$\dfrac{6\,034}{13\,559}$	0.45	$\dfrac{3\,533}{6\,813}$	0.52

remote. For that purpose there is a need to analyse the assets available to the company to meet its liabilities. This can be done in the short, medium and long term.

Short-term financial status or the liquidity of a firm If we analyse the assets available in order to meet the short-term liabilities of the firm, we focus on the structure of the working capital of a company, namely the relation between current assets and current liabilities. The acid test ratio or quick ratio and the current ratio can be used for this purpose (see Activity 31.17).

$$\text{Current ratio} = \text{Current assets/Current liabilities}$$

$$\text{Acid test ratio} = (\text{Current assets} - \text{Inventory})/\text{Current liabilities}$$

If one calculates the current liabilities on the basis of IAS financial statements, one always needs to check whether long-term borrowings due within 12 months have not been mentioned under the amount of long-term liabilities. For the calculation of the above ratios we have taken the amounts of current liabilities mentioned on the face of the balance sheet. If a company fully complies with IAS 1 and it includes this amount of long-term borrowing due within 12 months under the long-term debt, then this implies that there is already a refinance agreement for those amounts (IAS 1) and as such those amounts are not 'economically speaking' due within 12 months.

Current assets are supposed to be converted into cash in the current operating cycle of the company. The higher the ratio the more resources a company has available to repay the short-term debts. In the acid test or quick ratio the inventory is excluded from the current assets as it is the least convertible item of the group. It is often observed that companies in distress keep production levels constant although their sales drop. If these companies use a full cost approach for inventory valuation purposes then they are able to capitalise a part of their overhead in a growing inventory amount. The IAS/IFRS only allow the full cost approach for inventory valuation purposes (see Chapter 16). This improves the comparability among the data published by firms complying with IAS/IFRS.

Long-term financial status The financial status of a company also refers to the ability of a company to meet its debt in the long run. A key element in this respect is the capital structure of the firm. Companies have two main sources of funds, namely debt and equity. Each has different well-known characteristics (e.g. fixed versus variable rewards, fixed repayment schedules versus repayment when the company liquidates). The financial risk or financial strength of a company is measured by ratios which relate debt to equity. The most commonly used ratio worldwide in this respect is the debt/equity ratio. A high debt/equity ratio implies higher financial risk, since a higher

ACTIVITY 31.18

Calculate debt/equity ratios for the three companies.

Activity feedback

	Nestlé		Unilver		Danone	
Debt/equity	$\dfrac{60\,425}{54\,234}$	1.11	$\dfrac{24\,483}{12\,819}$	1.91	$\dfrac{18\,476}{9\,100}$	2.03
Debt/equity + debt	$\dfrac{60\,425}{114\,659}$	0.53	$\dfrac{24\,483}{37\,302}$	0.66	$\dfrac{18\,476}{27\,576}$	0.67
Long-term debt/equity	$\dfrac{17\,099}{54\,234}$	0.32	$\dfrac{10\,924}{12\,819}$	0.85	$\dfrac{11\,663}{9\,100}$	1.28
Equity/debt + equity		0.47		0.34		0.33

Danone and to a certain extent Unilever are heavily financed through external debt, whereas Nestlé is financed to a large extent by equity. Half of the debt of Unilever is short-term debt. Through this high leverage

Danone and Unilever is able to increase its ROE substantially if ROA is above the cost of debt. However this high leverage also implies that they face a higher financial risk than Nestlé.

ratio points at higher interest charges and a wider exposure to possible interest changes. Further, debt needs to be repaid often at a fixed date irrespective of whether or not the company has sufficient funds available.

Several alterations can be made to the numerator and the denominator of this ratio in relation to the focus of the analysis: e.g. Debt/(Equity + Debt), Long-term Debt/Equity (see Activity 31.18).

Further, the debt/equity ratio could be influenced by national or institutional differences (see Chapter 2). In countries with a shareholder orientation the debt/equity ratio will be lower than in countries with a credit orientation. Information on the financial risk of a company can be provided by the ratios but also by a common size analysis of the balance sheet structure (see the section on common size analysis in this chapter) or by trend analysis with ratios as input data. Ratio analysis and common size analysis are complementary techniques of analysis rather than substitutes.

Up to now in this section on ratio analysis we have used ratios taken from other companies as benchmarks. Another possibility is to benchmark a ratio against its own historical performance within the same firm. In this type of analysis, trend analysis is combined with ratio analysis. The red flags of comparability should also be taken into account when interpreting the data. As an illustration of a trend analysis performed on ratios we will analyse the evolution of the debt/equity ratio of the Sabena Group over the years 1992–2000. The trend analysis of the debt/equity ratio clearly reveals an increasing financial risk over the years towards the final stage of bankruptcy. Before we start with the analysis of the data the pitfalls of comparability need to be checked. If we check for comparability over time, we notice the following elements. With regard to the Sabena Group as a whole no major structural changes have taken place over the time frame considered except for the year 2000 when the Airline Management Partnership was created. Further, we have noticed some structural changes within the group (e.g. 1992 the sale of the charter company Sobelair from Sabena NV to Sabena Leasing, 1999 the creation of a new subsidiary Sabena Technics NV). These within-group structural changes have no influence on the overall group structure. A second element which needs to be taken into account in the

TABLE 31.19	Evolution of the debt situation of the Sabena Group, 1992–2000								
	1992	*1993*	*1994*	*1995*	*1996*	*1997*	*1998*	*1999*	*2000*
Debt/equity IAS switch in 1999	5.87	7.28	6.10	3.14	5.42	6.23	6.31	9.68	−26.92
Debt/equity IAS switch in 1998							8.49	9.68	−26.92
'Extended' debt/Equity (*)				3.99	6.7	9.28	9.17	13.21	−42.73

*Balance sheet debt + off balance sheet debt relating to operating lease contracts
Source: Group accounts of Sabena, 1992–2000.

period of analysis (1992–2000) is the change of the applied GAAP. Up to 1998 the annual group accounts complied with Belgian GAAP. From 1999 on the group accounts were published using IAS/IFRS. The group accounts of 1999 include comparative data on 1998 which were also prepared with the use of IAS/IFRS.

In Table 31.19 the evolution of the debt/equity ratio of the Sabena group is presented. For the year 1998 the debt/equity ratio is calculated twice, once with data originating from the Belgian GAAP group accounts (D/E = 6.31) published in 1998 and then with the comparative data included in the IAS group accounts data (D/E = 8.49) of 1999.

We notice that when in 1998 Belgian GAAP data are used the debt/equity ratio is lower. The higher ratios under IAS are due to the fact that a number of lease contracts which could be accounted for as operating lease contracts under Belgian GAAP qualified under IAS/IFRS as finance lease contracts. Since from 1995 on we could find in the notes to the annual accounts information on future operating lease payments, we have added up these future operating lease payments with the debt included on the face of the balance sheet. Using this amount (balance sheet debt + off-balance sheet debt relating to operating lease contracts) in the numerator, we have calculated a ratio which we have labelled the 'extended' debt/equity ratio.

The 'Belgian' debt/equity ratio fluctuates around six until 1998. The improvement of the ratio in 1995 was due to a capital increase, the positive effect of which did not last very long. Due to the accounting strategy followed by the board of directors, which was communicated in the annual report of 1996, equity decreased substantially. The debt/equity ratio shows an increase in financial risk only from 1999 (or 1998 with IAS accounts) on. The 'extended' debt/equity ratio revealed the deterioration of the financial situation of the Sabena Group much sooner.

The evolution of the 'extended' debt/equity ratio shows clearly that from the start of the cooperation with the SAir Group in 1995 the financial risk increased each year. In 1997 the situation has become critical; in 2000 both ratios (debt/equity and 'extended' debt/equity) point to a dramatic situation. The extreme deterioration of the debt/equity ratio in 2000 is caused by two elements. First of all the huge losses of 2000 turns the equity into the red. The second cause of the steeply rising ratios is the increasing lease commitments due to the fleet expansion.

The debt/equity ratio is often used in debt covenants. In Chapter 30 we discussed how a threat of a possible violation of the debt covenants could lead to annual accounts management. A ratio which tries to circumvent the effect of these practices

ACTIVITY 31.19

Calculate the interest cover ratio for the three companies.   *Activity feedback*

	Nestlé Group		Unilever Group		Groupe Danone	
Interest cover ratio	$\dfrac{15\,010}{1\,492}$	10.06	$\dfrac{5\,734}{550}$	10.43	$\dfrac{1\,676}{307}$	5.46

Nestlé and Unilever have a higher safety margin than Danone. This ratio is no surprise if we remember the high gearing of Danone.

of annual accounts management is the interest cover ratio. This ratio (see Activity 31.19) indicates the safety margin between profit and interest charges:

Interest cover ratio = Profit before interest and taxation/Net interest costs

The financial risk of a company is directly linked to the capital structure of a company. A company with a high proportion of debt financing is highly leveraged. High financial leverage implies high risk. To get an idea about the leverage of the firm the debt/equity ratio is often used. Financial leverage influences the financial risk of a company and further it has an impact on the relation between ROE and ROA.

Whether or not ROE is bigger than ROA depends on two elements. First of all the leverage of the company and second the difference between ROA and the interest cost of the firm. The latter is often called the spread. If the obtained ROA is higher than the interest cost, a company can increase the level of ROE compared to ROA by switching from equity financing to debt financing. If, however, ROA is lower than the interest cost of the firm, the relation works in the opposite way. ROE will be lower than ROA and the difference will increase with higher leverage.

Investment perspective

Potential investors in a company use different sets of information in order to decide whether or not to buy shares of a certain company. The question on their mind is whether the company is a worthwhile investment. When investors possess shares in a company they continuously assess their investment. The decision to be taken is a 'hold' or 'sell' decision.

Although for these 'buy' or 'sell' decisions the ratios on the profitability, efficiency and financial status of a company provide useful information, specific ratios are developed with regard to this investment decision. These ratios focus on those elements which are specifically relevant for shareholders, namely the return obtained on their investment. This return can take the form of dividends and/or capital appreciation.

In Chapter 11 we presented a number of different ratios which could be used by investors to evaluate the profit potential of their investment. These ratios concentrated on the dividend performance of these companies (net dividend and dividend cover ratio), on the earnings potential of the investment (earnings per share) and on the evolution of the share price of those companies (price earnings ratio). The earnings per share ratio and the price earnings ratio have been discussed in Chapter 24.

These investment ratios are usually included and discussed in reports of financial analysts or reports of industry analysts. Investors and potential investors use the information contained in those reports to make buy, hold or sell decisions.

In order to illustrate these investor ratios, we present the EPS and ROE of the four airlines which we have studied in 2005 and compare these with the price/earnings ratio (PE ratio taken from Davy European Transport and Leisure Report 2006; see Ryanair website).

	BEPS	DEPS	PE	ROE
Air France/KLM	3.47 Ec	3.25 Ec	11.6	11%
British Airways	40.4p	39.8p	10	24%
Lufthansa	0.99 Ec	0.95 Ec	23	10.4%
Ryanair	40.00 Ec	39.74 Ec	20	15.3%

Air France–KLM, British Airways, Lufthansa, and Ryanair annual accounts.

What do these figures mean?

At the time the report was made, the market wanted to pay 20 times the EPS of Ryanair and Lufthansa, whereas investors wanted to pay only ten times the EPS of Air France–KLM and British Airways. Further we observe that there is not exactly a link between ROE and PE. This is because in the PE ratio much more information is included than in ROE, which is a historical measure. The appraisal by the investors of opportunities for the company and the way in which the top management of the company can react to threats and opportunities in the market all influence the share price and, as a result, the PE ratio. On the other hand the 10 PE value of British Airways and Air France–KLM could also mean that these companies were undervalued at the time of the report.

Companies try to influence the share price not only by providing those accounting numbers to the market which the market appreciates (see Chapter 30), but also by providing information to the market outside the financial statements. This information is non-audited and therefore can be more subject to impression management. Conference calls and financial analysts' presentations have become a 'classical' means of communicating with the investor community, as well as putting information on the website of the company. Very often the company management translates the accounting numbers into new numbers which suit their message better. They create their own ratios, such as 'like for like sales,' 'profit before one time expenditures, before goodwill and impairment', and many others. All the ratios presented by companies in their financial analysts' presentations and as key figures in the annual reports must be regarded with caution. Very often these are figures taken from the annual accounts but corrected for negative elements; those corrections are never presented as corrections but as improvements of the figures of the annual accounts. In the following sections we are going to analyse a number of new measures created for shareholders in order to measure the value of the company.

Shareholder value and total shareholder return These ratios could be labelled as the more 'traditional' ones to use for assessing the attractiveness of an investment in certain shares. In the 1980s the concept of shareholder value emerged. Total shareholder return represents the change in capital value of a company over a one-year period, plus dividends, expressed as a plus or minus percentage of the opening value.

The concept of 'total shareholder return' is used by Unilever, as described in the following extract from the company's 2004 Annual Report:

Total Shareholder Return

Total Shareholder Return (TSR) is a concept used to compare the performance of different companies' stocks and shares over time. It combines share price appreciation and dividends paid to show the total return to the shareholder. The absolute level of the TSR will vary with stock markets, but the relative position reflects the market perception of overall performance relative to a reference group.

Unilever calculates TSR over a three-year rolling period. This period is sensitive enough to reflect changes but long enough to smooth out short-term volatility. The return is expressed in US dollars, based on the equivalent US dollar share price for NV and PLC. US dollars were chosen to facilitate comparison with companies in Unilever's chosen reference group. The choice of currency affects the absolute TSR but not the relative ranking.

Unilever's TSR target is to be in the top third of a reference group of 21 international consumer goods companies on a three-year rolling basis. At the end of 2003 we were positioned 6th, and at the end of 2004 the ranking was 13th. In 2004, the following companies formed the peer group of comparative companies:

Altria Group	Kao
Avon	Lion
Beiersdorf	L'Oréal
Cadbury Schweppes	Nestlé
Clorox	Orkla
Coca-Cola	Pepsico
Colgate	Procter & Gamble
Danone	Reckitt Benckiser
Gillette	Sara Lee
Heinz	Shiseido

Unilever's position relative to the TSR reference group

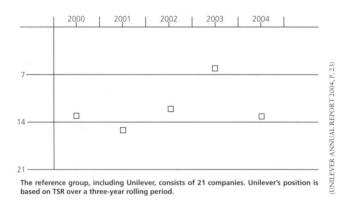

The reference group, including Unilever, consists of 21 companies. Unilever's position is based on TSR over a three-year rolling period.

(UNILEVER ANNUAL REPORT 2004, P. 23)

The founding father of the concept of shareholder value was Rappaport (1998) and the idea behind the concept was that the future stream of forecast earnings would be a much better starting point to evaluate the future economic potential of a firm. Future cash flows are often used as a proxy for future earnings. Various metrics were developed in the wake of this shareholder value approach. Within the set of 'new' ratios two groups can be distinguished, namely one group of metrics which is developed around the economic value added concept and, second, a group of ratios which focuses on the future cash flows of a firm.

Some of these new metrics have really been developed recently, while others have already been around for years under another name. Those that have been around for years have been relabelled after minor modifications to the existing metric. The most well known is the EVA® concept which builds on the residual income concept and has been trademarked by Stern Stewart & Co:

> The foundations for these new performance measures are residual income and internal rate of return concepts developed in the 1950s and 1960s. Stern Stewart & Co's trademarked 'economic value added' however is the firm's proprietary adaptation of residual income.
>
> (Ittner and Larcker, 2001)

In essence, economic value added is created when the net operating profit after tax is higher than the company's cost of capital (including debt and equity). Stern Stewart suggest several corrections to the different items of the concept in order to undo accounting distortions resulting from accrual accounting.

As EVA® is a single-period measure and in order to be useful for financial analysis it should be judged against prior year data. Further, EVA® is a monetary measure which is less useful for inter-firm comparison. These shortcomings for external analysis are not surprising since EVA® was developed in the first place as a management tool for driving the value creation within the firm. A firm can increase its economic value added through the following actions:

- increasing the net operating profit after tax by operational measures which could increase revenues, decrease costs or both of them

- reducing the cost of capital by changing the financing structure of the company

- improving the utilisation of the capital employed.

The second group of 'new' ratios represents multi-period metrics which are built on cash flow information. The most well-known metric is the cash flow return on investment (CFROI). This concept is developed by the Boston Consulting Group and represents an economic measure of a company's performance that reflects the average underlying IRR on all existing investment projects. The CFROI can be defined as annual gross cash flow relative to the invested capital of the business unit.

Based on a simplified CFROI rate the Boston Consulting Group developed a residual income measure, which is called cash value added (CVA). CVA is the spread between CFROI and the real cost of capital, multiplied with the investment in fixed assets plus working capital.

These new metrics not only serve as a communication tool to the outside world, but they are also used internally for management and strategic purposes. SAS for example now focuses its communication on CFROI. In their annual accounts of 2007, the SAS group has put forward a CFROI target of 25% to reach in 2011 (SAS group, Annual Report and Sustainability Report 2007, page 10).

We learn from the annual report of Lufthansa, financial year 2007 (pp. 36–38) that CVA is their central financial performance indicator. An illustration of Lufthansa's interpretation of value-based management is reproduced here.

Value-based management

An established concept Since late 1999, Deutsche Lufthansa AG has been run according to the principles of value-based management, with the objective of a sustainable increase in Company value. The aim of this approach, applied to all planning, steering and monitoring processes, is a purposeful, long-term and steady increase in the value of the Company in the investors' and lenders' interests. Achievement of this target is measured continuously and is included in internal and external reporting. As the concept is anchored in the performance-related pay scheme, managers are encouraged to act as entrepreneurs according to the corporate goals.

The central financial performance indicator at Lufthansa is the cash value added (CVA). The CVA is based on the return on investment expected by the investors and lenders. It provides information on the value being created in a given period. In contrast to other concepts of residual profit (e.g. EVA©) the advantage of the CVA approach is that, by using, for instance, the historical cost of assets, performance measurement is not affected by changes of the capital base due to depreciation and amortisation. With the system of value-based Group management, Lufthansa ensures that the requirements of investors and lenders are embedded in all management processes.

In the past years, the CVA was constantly increased.

Calculating CVA Cash value added is an absolute residual amount providing information on the value created in a financial year. It is calculated by comparing the cash flow generated in a year (EBITDA^{plus} as explained below) with the cost of capital employed expressed as a required minimum cash flow. The CVA is the difference between the two figures. Value is generated when the actual cash flow is higher than the minimum cash flow. The following graph shows the value drivers of this top-level indicator:

Calculation of cash value added

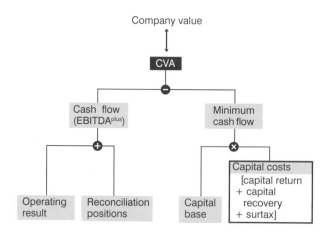

The minimum cash flow is calculated from the required return on capital employed, the capital recovery rate and the tax paid.

The capital base is made up of non-current and currents assets, less non-interest bearing liabilities. In this approach the capital base is determined at historical cost, so that the calculation of value created and its evolution over time are independent of the depreciation or amortisation method applied.

The return on capital is calculated using the weighted average cost of capital (WACC), which considers both debt and equity. The factors covered are presented in the following table.

Calculation return on capital 2007

in%	
Risk-free interest rate	4.4
Market risk premium	5.7
Beta factor	1.1x
Share of equity	50.0
Share of debt	50.0
Cost of equity	**10.7**
Cost of debt	**4.7**

In 2006, the WACC was calculated as 7.9 per cent, based on the parameters shown and a target capital structure of 50 per cent quoted equity to 50 per cent balance sheet debt. This figure was reconfirmed in 2007, due to the difference in some parameters of this return on capital being insignificant.

Cost of capital (WACC)

for the Group and the business segments

in %	2007	2006	2005	2004	2003
Group	7.9	7.9	8.6	8.6	8.6
Passenger Transportation	7.9	7.9	8.6	8.6	8.6
Logistics	8.2	8.2	8.9	8.9	8.9
MRO	7.6	7.6	8.3	8.3	8.3
IT Services	7.6	7.6	8.3	8.3	8.9
Catering	7.9	7.9	8.6	8.6	7.7

In addition to the return on capital, the capital recovery has to be considered in the calculation of the minimum cash flow, which is expressed by the economic depreciation of an asset. It is measured by the capital recovery rate. If this is applied to the capital base, the result is the percentage of the historical cost of assets which needs to be earned annually over its useful life in order to recover the historical cost, after accounting for interest. Finally, the expected tax payment is added – in simplified form, by applying a surcharge of currently 1.2 per cent of the capital base.

The generated cash flow is represented by the EBITDA[plus] figure: this is derived from the operating result, whereby essentially non-cash items are adjusted. These are mainly depreciation and amortisation and net changes to pension provisions. Other items are the pre-tax results of equity investments which are not fully consolidated and book gains on the disposal of assets. EBITDA[plus] therefore includes all cash-relevant items which are influenced by management decisions.

Reconciliation EBITDA[plus]

in €m	2007	2006
Operating result	1 378	845
Depreciation/amortisation	1 160	1 051
Result from tangible asset disposal	13	3
Income from reversal of provisions	163	129
Impairment losses	−44	–
Change in pension provisions before interests	190	178
Cash flow from operating activities EBITDA[plus]	**2 860**	**2 206**
Pro rata results of non-consolidated subsidiaries	406	256

Reconciliation EBITDA*plus*

in €m	2007	2006
Interest income	186	269
Result from financial asset disposal	481	**70**
Financial cash flow EBITDA	**1 073**	**595**
Cash flow EBITDAplus	**3 933**	**2 801**

In order to obtain the CVA the minimum cash flow is deducted from the EBITDA^plus. In 2007, the CVA for the Group was almost tripled. It stands at EUR 1 546m (+180 per cent).

Value creation (CVA) of the Lufthansa Group and the individual business segments

in €m	2007	2006	2005	2004
Group	1 546	552	386	151
Passenger Transportation	768	317	−53	64
Logistics	59	37	39	−26
MRO	205	85	121	86
IT Services	−16	32	36	40
Catering	21	−50	−71	−274
Service and Financial Companies	7	−88	239	403

Value-based management using operating indicators at all levels of management In order to influence positively the value creation and thereby the CVA, the Lufthansa Group developed a system of key performance indicators. It contains the major levers which can be influenced by management decisions. Changes in these value drivers have a direct effect on the operating result, the capital base and thus on the CVA.

Limitations of ratio analysis

The limitations of ratio analysis also apply to analysis of financial statements in general. We have already discussed items such as changes in environment, absence of comparable data, different accounting policies, which may limit the usefulness of the information resulting from ratio analysis, horizontal analysis or common size analysis. In this section we point out a few more limitations.

Non-monetary factors Non-monetary factors are not reflected in financial statements. Thus, such factors as the quality of the product or service are not reflected, neither is whether labour relations are good or bad. In the section on disclosure of non-financial data we will see how companies are trying to overcome this lack of information. More and more non-financial indicators of performance are introduced in the annual reports.

Historic cost accounting The historical nature of accounts must always be borne in mind as our interpretation of the business is based on this historical information, but this may not be the best guide as to the future performance, financial status and investment potential. However, with recent evolutions in IAS/IFRS and US GAAP the impact of historical cost accounting might diminish in the coming years.

Short-term fluctuations Ratio analysis does not identify short-term fluctuations within one year in assets and liabilities as our appraisal is based on a balance sheet which provides values of assets and liabilities as at a point in time. By using these year-end figures we may, for example, present a better view of liquidity than has been the case throughout the year.

ACTIVITY 31.20

The following sales figures are available for David plc:

X0	X1
£000	£000
700	800

The price of goods sold has been subject to an increase of 10% at the beginning of X1. What is the magnitude of the increase in the volume of trade?

Activity feedback

Sales have increased by £100 000 from X0 to X1 but £70 000 of this is due to the price increase, inflation in the price of goods sold. Volume of sales has only increased by £30 000, that is 4% not 14%.

Changes in the value of money We all know how inflation can affect the value of the euro, pound, dollar, yen in our pocket and this is no different for a business. In fact, inflation and price changes could render the whole of our ratio analysis invalid. Short-term fluctuations are better reflected in interim reports.

Multivariate analysis

The ratio analysis we have considered so far is of a univariate type. This is where one ratio is considered at a time and then all ratios, once calculated, are assessed together and the analyst makes a considered judgement on the state of the entity. By way of contrast, multivariate analysis combines some of the ratios together in a specified manner by applying weightings to each of the ratios. The result is an index number that is compared to previous years, other companies and industrial averages. Multivariate analysis has been widely used in predicting corporate failure. In 1968 Professor Altman combined five ratios to produce what he named a Z score:

$$Z = 0.012X1 + 0.014X2 + 0.033X3 + 0.006X4 + 0.999X5$$

$X1$ = Working capital/Total assets

$X2$ = Retained earnings/Total assets

$X3$ = Earnings before interest and tax/Total assets

$X4$ = Market capitalisation/Book value of debt

$X5$ = Sales/Total assets

In his seminal article companies with Z scores above 2.99 had not failed whereas those companies with a Z score below 1.81 had. His research was undertaken in the manufacturing sector of the United States. In the context of this type of multivariate analysis it is important to remember that results of such multivariate analyses in relation to the economic health of a company must be used with extreme caution. The results of these multivariate analyses are only valid for companies located in the same region, active in the same industry and existing more or less in the same time period. The reason for this limited application is that national environments influence reporting practices (see Chapter 2), that the economic climate constantly changes and that the value of the ratios is influenced by industry characteristics.

Another internationally well-known model is that of Taffler, who carried out similar work in the UK, but have not published the details of this as it is used as a working model and they need to retain the commercial interest. What we do know about the model are the ratios included:

$$Z = c_0 + c_1X1 + c_2X2 + c_3X3 + c_4X4$$

$X1$ = Profit before tax/Current assets

$X2$ = Current assets/Current liabilities

$X3$ = Current liabilities/Total assets

$X4$ = Length of time which the company can continue to finance
its operations using its own assets with no revenue inflow.

The usefulness of these models is, unfortunately, still often limited to the region from which the company data were taken for the estimation procedure. Our view is that the use of several ratios with additional information (such as trend, common size, industry and accounting analysis) and a good deal of common sense should enable you to make a reasonable assessment of a company's financial status, performance, potential and position in the market. The multivariate models used the individual ratios as input without making a proper assessment on the quality of the data and typical characteristics of the data.

DISCLOSURE OF NON-FINANCIAL DATA

The current company performance as well as the long-term company performance is influenced by several factors which are called in the literature drivers of performance or drivers of value creation. These drivers relate to elements such as customer satisfaction, internal organisation of the business processes, the quality and service of the products, the innovation capability of the firm. In the last two decades of the 20th century these drivers of performance started to play a much more prominent role in the management control systems of companies. Internal performance evaluation systems within companies are now built around financial as well as non-financial performance indicators. Many of these indicators are chosen because they are the drivers of future value creation. The most well-known scorecard in which financial indicators are combined with non-financial indicators is the balanced scorecard, a normative concept developed by Kaplan and Norton (1992).

Since elements such as customer satisfaction, innovative capabilities, organisational efficiency, etc. are key drivers of performance in the long run, information on these value drivers or performance drivers is also interesting for external users of annual accounts. These indicators might help external users to forecast future performance.

Over recent years we observe that companies which have this information on non-financial indicators available in their internal management information systems also include them in their annual reports. This information on non-financial key drivers for success is always included in the narrative or descriptive part of the annual report and is therefore non-audited.

Since these non-financial data became integrated in a number of annual reports, the academic community started to research the information content of this non-financial information. The focus of the research relates to the information contents of non-financial data and to the predictive value of the data or what is called the value relevance of the data (e.g. Amir and Lev, 1996; Ittner and Larcker, 2001). Research results so far show that non-financial data are complementary to financial data and the value relevance of financial accounting data continues. Further (using customer satisfaction data) Ittner and Larcker obtained evidence that non-financial data have predictive value, however the relation is non-linear

In Chapter 12 the communication of additional information to the balance sheet, the income statement, the changes in equity and the notes to the accounts were discussed. Most popular these days are additional statements on the environmental policy of the company, product information, market growth and social policies. Very often this information is bundled in a sustainability report. These additional reports contain interesting information to relate to the annual report. However one must keep in mind that this information is non-audited. In order to provide some guidance on this extra information the IASB has paid attention to the disclosure of management information to the annual accounts.

CASH FLOW STATEMENT

The cash flow statement, its preparation and its contents have been discussed in Chapter 23. Cash flow information helps the external user to get an idea whether or not a company is able to generate net positive cash flows. To be able to sort out the different origins of cash, the cash flows are divided in three groups in the cash flow statement, namely cash flow from operating activities, cash flow from investment activities and cash flow from financing activities.

Studying cash flow data, users of this statement want to know, in the first place, if a company can generate cash from its operations. In the second place, the analyst will try to find out whether this internally generated cash is sufficient to finance the investments of the company or whether the firm needs to rely on external borrowing or an equity increase. The relations between the three components of the cash flow will differ according to the financial situation of the company. The cash flow patterns in a fast growing company will differ from those of a company in distress. For example, if we analyse the cash flow statement of the fast growing low-cost airline Ryanair we notice that the growth is financed through a combination of internally generated operating cash flow, external borrowing and an increase in equity. The stock market is an important provider of capital for Ryanair.

Companies in distress often show different patterns, their cash flow generated from operating activities is often negative. This negative cash flow can be compensated through a disposal of assets and borrowing extra funds from creditors or a capital increase. However, cash flow patterns are not always that predictable. If we analyse the cash flow statement of Sabena the year before bankruptcy we still find a positive operating cash flow; however, the remainder of the picture is not that positive (see Table 31.20).

Looking into the details of the operating cash flow of Sabena we notice that the loss in 2000 is almost offset by non-cash expenses which were recorded in the profit and loss account. The operating cash flow turns positive in the end through a rather substantial decrease in working capital, especially if we compare the movement in working capital with the previous year (1999). Further, the company keeps investing, however external funds from creditors are not used to finance these investments. The cash flow from financing activities has turned negative and represents substantial cash outflows. Finally, looking at the bottom line of the cash flow, we notice that the company suffers from a substantial decrease in liquid assets in the year 2000.

Although one might have the impression that the comparability issue is less important with cash flow data, one still has to be alert for differences. For example, dividends, taxation and interests can be presented differently among companies. Further, one has to be sure that the bottom line represents an increase or decrease in

TABLE 31.20	Consolidated cash flow statement of the Sabena Group, 1999 and 2000	
	1999 in million euros	**2000 in million euros**
Net result for the year	(10)	(323)
Minority interests	(3)	(2)
Depreciation of intangible, tangible fixed and financial assets	127	128
Profits/losses realised sustained on assets sales	(30)	(14)
Taxation	1	2
Other corrections and value adjustments	115	204
Cash flow operations before changes in working capital	**200**	**(5)**
Changes in working capital excluding disposable funds	123	330
Interest paid	(56)	(34)
Taxes paid	(1)	(11)
Interest received	14	19
Dividends received		
Decrease in liabilities	(82)	(129)
Total	(124)	(155)
Net cash inflow operating activities (A)	**199**	**170**
Investments in tangible fixed and financial assets	(315)	(143)
Proceeds from sales of tangible fixed assets	169	40
Net cash inflow from investment activities (B)	**(146)**	**(102)**
Net cash inflow from financing activities (C)	**(99)**	**(202)**
Net decrease/increase in disposable funds (A + B + C)	**(46)**	**(134)**
Cash and cash equivalents at beginning of year	324	278
Decrease/increase in disposable funds	(46)	(134)
Adjustments for foreign currency translations on opening	(1)	
Cash and cash equivalents at year-end	**278**	**143**

Source: Sabena Group accounts 2000.

cash and cash equivalents available in the company. Sometimes the bottom line is working capital movements.

From Chapter 30 we know that information provided through the balance sheet and profit and loss account might be biased or distorted through annual accounts management (accounting method choices, changes in accounting estimates or real transactions). It is believed that in situations where large accruals are recorded cash flow information gives a more reliable picture of the performance of the firm than the result reported in the profit and loss account. However, the usefulness of cash flow information in general and in relation to undoing the effect of accrual accounting varies from firm to firm (empirical evidence can be found in Dechow, 1994). Cash flow figures can be influenced by real decisions. Further, clarification and presentation decisions can be made in order to provide the impressions of a healthy operating cash flow.

So in order to make a proper assessment about the economic situation and performance of a company data from the balance sheet, profit and loss account, the notes and the cash flow statement should always be combined. This is often called the cash flow check.

TABLE 31.21	Cash flow and result information of SAir, 1999–2000	
CHF million	**1999**	**2000**
Net result	273	(2 885)
Cash flow from operations	1 423	1 191

If we analyse the profit and loss account of the SAir Group for the year 2000 in combination with the cash flow statement of the same group we notice indeed that cash flows are less influenced by accruals.

According to the report of the new incoming CEO, the financial difficulties at the SAir group necessitated the following measures:

> The realignment of our Group's overall business thrust requires corrective action in balance sheet terms, with the charging of extensive depreciation and provisions to the 2000 results. This will enable the Swissair Group to focus on its new corporate objectives free of the financial burdens of the past.
>
> (SAir Group Annual Report 2000, p. 5)

The financial year 2000 ended for the SAir Group with a loss of 2885 million CHF whereas the year 1999 ended with a profit of 273 million CHF. Looking at the cash flow statements of 1999 and 2000 we notice in both years positive cash flows from operating activities and an increase in cash and cash equivalents at the bottom line of the cash flow statement (see Table 31.21).

With the discussion of the analysis of the cash flow statement the most important techniques of financial analysis have been discussed.

SUMMARY

External parties use financial statement data to obtain information on several aspects of a company, e.g. is the company liquid, can the company repay its debt, is the company performing well? Several techniques exist to extract information from the financial statements in order to answer those questions. One purpose of this chapter was to explain and illustrate these techniques (trend analysis, common size analysis, ratio analysis, segmental analysis and cash flow analysis). A common characteristic of all these techniques is that benchmarks (internal and external) with which to compare the company data are needed in order to have information value for decision purposes. A necessary condition for benchmarking is the comparability of data. As a result, the second purpose of this chapter was to point out and illustrate several pitfalls which might hinder the comparability of financial accounting data. If accounting analysis is combined with several techniques of financial analysis, external parties should be able to judge the performance and the financial position of a company in a proper perspective.

EXERCISES

Suggested answers to exercises marked ✓ *are to be found on the Student side of the companion website.*

Suggested answers to the remaining exercises are to be found on the Instructor side of the companion website.

1 You are the management accountant of Expand, a company incorporated in Dollarland. The company is seeking to grow by acquisition and has identified two potential investment opportunities. One of these, Hone, is also a company incorporated in Dollarland. The other, Over, is a company incorporated in Francland.

You have been presented with financial information relating to both companies. The financial information is extracted from their published financial statements. In both cases, the financial statements conform to domestic accounting standards. The financial statements of Hone were drawn up in $s while those of Over were drawn up in Francs. The information relating to Over has been expressed in $s by taking the figures in Francs and dividing by 1.55 – the $/Franc exchange rate at 31 December 2000. The financial information is given below.

Income statements

	Hone		Over	
	31 March	*31 March*	*31 December*	*31 December*
Year ended	*2001*	*2000*	*2000*	*1999*
	$ million	*$ million*	*$ million*	*$ million*
Revenue	600	550	620	560
Cost of sales	(300)	(250)	(320)	(260)
Gross profit	300	300	300	300
Other operating expenses	(120)	(105)	(90)	(85)
Profit from operations	180	195	210	215
Finance cost	(20)	(18)	(22)	(20)
Profit before tax	160	177	188	195
Income tax expense	(50)	(55)	(78)	(90)
Net profit for the period	110	122	110	105

Statements of changes in equity

	Hone		Over	
	31 March	*31 March*	*31 December*	*31 December*
Year ended	*2001*	*2000*	*2000*	*1999*
	$ million	*$ million*	*$ million*	*$ million*
Balance brought forward	470	418	265	240
Net profit for the period	110	122	110	105
Dividends	(70)	(70)	(80)	(80)
Balance carried forward	510	470	295	265

Balance sheets

	Hone		Over	
	31 March	31 March	31 December	31 December
	2001	2000	2000	1999
	$ million	$ million	$ million	$ million
Non-current assets	600	570	455	440
Inventories	60	50	55	50
Trade receivables	80	75	90	80
Cash	10	20	15	15
	750	715	615	585
Issued share capital	150	150	110	110
Reserves	360	320	185	155
	510	470	295	265
Interest-bearing borrowings	150	150	240	240
Current liabilities	90	95	80	80
	750	715	615	585

Expand is more concerned with the profitability of potential investment opportunities than with liquidity. You have been asked to review the financial statements of Hone and Over with this concern in mind.

Required:

(a) Prepare a short report to the directors of Expand that, based on the financial information provided, assesses the relative profitability of Hone and Over.

(b) Discuss the validity of using this financial information as a basis to compare the profitability of the two companies.

(CIMA May 2001)

✓ **2** It has been suggested that cash is king and that readers of a company's accounts should pay more attention to information concerning its cash flows and balances than to its profits and other assets. It is argued that cash is more difficult to manipulate than profit and that cash flows are more important.

Required:

(a) Explain whether you agree with the suggestion that cash flows and balances are more difficult to manipulate than profit and non-cash assets.

(b) Explain why it might be dangerous to concentrate on cash to the exclusion of profit when analysing a set of financial statements.

(CIMA – adapted)

3 Look up the financial statements of two companies competing in the same industry in your country. Calculate their return on equity (ROE). First, try to explain the difference observed with the use of ratio analysis. Subsequently, add trend analysis, common size analysis, segmental analysis and cash flow analysis to it. What extra information do these supplemental analyses give you? If you were to carry out an industry analysis, would this give you extra information on top of it?

4 Look up the PE ratios of several airlines; what do you observe? How does the market value the prospects of each of these companies? Do the underlying financial statements confirm the market appreciation? Or do you observe conflicts?

5 Question 4 can be repeated for listed companies in several industries. Do you observe industry differences?

6 In which industries would you expect inventory turnover to be lower, in which industries would you expect this ratio to be higher? Comment on this (discuss this in relation to asset turnover also).

7 In which industries would you expect profit margins to be lower, in which industries would you expect this ratio to be higher?

8 Heavy Goods plc carries on business as a manufacturer of tractors. In 2004 the company was looking for acquisitions and carrying out investigations into a number of possible targets. One of these was a competitor, Modern Tractors plc. The company's acquisition strategy was to acquire companies that were vulnerable to a takeover and in which there was an opportunity to improve asset management and profitability.

The chief accountant of Heavy Goods plc has instructed his assistant to calculate ratios from the financial statements of Modern Tractors plc for the past three years and to prepare a report based on these ratios and the industry average ratios that have been provided by the trade association. The ratios prepared by the assistant accountant and the industry averages for 2004 are set out as follows.

Required:
You are required to write a full appraisal and report.

		2002	2003	2004	Industry average 2004
Sales growth	%	30.00	40.00	9.52	8.25
Sales/total assets		1.83	2.05	1.60	2.43
Sales/net fixed assets		2.94	3.59	2.74	16.85
Sales/working capital		−21.43	−140.00	38.33	10.81
Sales/debtors		37.50	70.00	92.00	16.00
Gross profit/sales	%	18.67	22.62	19.57	23.92
Profit before tax/sales	%	8.00	17.62	11.74	4.06
Profit before interest/interest		6.45	26.57	14.50	4.95
Profit after tax/total assets	%	9.76	27.80	13.24	8.97
Profit after tax/equity	%	57.14	75.00	39.58	28.90
Net fixed assets/total assets	%	62.20	57.07	58.54	19.12
Net fixed assets/equity		3.64	1.54	1.75	0.58
Equity/total assets	%	18.29	37.07	33.45	32.96
Total liabilities/total assets	%	81.71	62.93	66.55	69.00
Total liabilities/equity		4.47	1.70	1.99	2.40
Long-term debt/total assets	%	36.59	18.54	29.27	19.00
Current liabilities/total assets	%	45.12	44.39	37.28	50.00

		Industry average			2004
		2002	2003	2004	
Current assets/current liabilities		0.84	0.97	1.11	1.63
(Current assets – stock)/ current liabilities		0.43	0.54	0.72	0.58
Stock/total assets	%	17.07	18.54	14.63	41.90
Cost of sales/stock		8.71	8.55	8.81	4.29
Cost of sales/creditors		6.10	6.25	6.17	12.87
Debtors/total assets	%	4.88	2.93	1.70	18.40
Cash/total assets	%	15.85	21.46	25.08	9.60

Note

Total assets = (fixed assets at net book value + current assets) and net fixed assets = fixed assets at net book value.

(ACCA – adapted)

9   Seville plc is a rapidly expanding trading and manufacturing company. It is currently seeking to extend its product range in new markets. To achieve this growth it needs to raise €800 000. The directors are considering two sources of funds:

(i)   A rights issue at €2.00 per share. The shares are trading at €2.50 (2000 €2.20) per share.

(ii) A bank loan at an interest rate of 15% and repayable by instalments after two years. The bank would want to secure the loan with a charge over the company's property. The following are extracts from the draft financial statements.

Seville plc
Draft P&L account extract year ended 31.12.01

	2000 €000	2001 €000
Turnover	1 967	1 991
Operating profit	636	698
Interest payable	(45)	(55)
Profit before taxation	591	643
Taxation	(150)	(140)
Profit after taxation	441	503
Extraordinary item	(90)	–
Profit for the year	361	453
Fixed assets		
tangible	1 132	1 504
intangible	247	298
Draft balance sheet	1 379	1 802
Current assets		
stocks	684	679
debtors	471	511
cash in hand and at bank	80	117

	2000 €000	2001 €000
Creditors: due within one year		
trade	(336)	(308)
taxation	(140)	(190)
dividends	(80)	(80)
Creditors: due after more than one year		
10% debentures, repayable 2004	(450)	(450)
finance lease	–	(100)
	1 608	1 981
Capital and reserves		
ordinary share capital €1 shares	800	800
revaluation reserve	144	144
profit and loss	664	1 037
	1 608	1 981

Operating profit

Operating profit has been arrived at after charging or crediting the following:

	2000 €000	2001 €000
Depreciation	110	150
Gain on disposal of property (as part of a sale and leaseback transaction)	–	95

Extraordinary item The extraordinary loss consists of reorganisation costs in a branch where a reduction in activity involved various measures including redundancies. Attributable tax credit is €38 000.

Deferred taxation Deferred taxation has not been provided because it is not considered probable that a liability will crystallise. If deferred taxation had been provided in full then a liability for the year of €7000 would have arisen (2000 €8000).

Contingent liability There is a contingent liability of €85 000 (2000 €80 000) in respect of bills of exchange discounted with bankers.

Further investigation has revealed that stock includes items subject to reservation of title of €40 000 and obsolete or slow moving items of €28 000 (2000 €28 000).

An age analysis of debtors has revealed that debts overdue by more than one year amount to €40 000 (2000) €40 000.

The auditors are yet to report and there is some discussion as to the classification of the gain on disposal and the reorganisation costs.

The directors forecast that the new funds will generate an operating profit of €300 000, and that the 2001 operating profit will be repeated. If new shares are issued the dividend will increase to €150 000.

Required:

Prepare a full report on progress, strengths and weaknesses, supported by ratio analysis.

(ACCA – adapted)

10 Recycle plc is a listed company which recycles toxic chemical waste products. The waste products are sent to Recycle plc from all around the world. You are an accountant (not employed by Recycle plc) who is accustomed to providing advice concerning the performance of companies, based on the data which are available from their published financial statements. Extracts from the financial statements of Recycle plc for the two years ended 30 September 2007 are as follows:

Profit and loss accounts – year ended 30 September:

	2007 €m	2006 €m
Turnover	3 000	2 800
Cost of sales	(1 600)	(1 300)
Gross profit	1 400	1 500
Other operating expenses	(800)	(600)
Operating profit	600	900
Interest payable	(200)	(100)
Profit before taxation	400	800
Taxation	(150)	(250)
Profit after taxation	250	550
Proposed dividend	(200)	(200)
Retained profit	50	350
Retained profit b/fwd	900	550
Retained profit c/fwd	950	900

Balance sheets at 30 September

	2007 €m	2007 €m	2006 €m	2006 €m
Tangible fixed assets		4 100		3 800
Current assets:				
Stocks	500		350	
Debtors	1 000		800	
Cash in hand	50		50	
	1 550		1 200	
Current liabilities:				
Trade creditors	600		600	
Taxation payable	150		250	
Proposed dividend	200		200	
Bank overdraft	750		50	
	1 700		1 100	
Net current (liabilities)/assets		(150)		100
Long-term loans (repayable 2009)		(1 000)		(1 000)
		2 950		2 900
Capital and reserves:				
Called-up share capital (€1 shares)		2 000		2 000
Profit and loss account		950		900
		2 950		2 900

You ascertain that depreciation of tangible fixed assets for the year ended 30 September 2007 was €1200 million. Disposals of fixed assets during the year ended 30 September 2007 were negligible. You are approached by two individuals.

A is a private investigator who is considering purchasing shares in Recycle plc. *A* considers that Recycle plc has performed well in 2007 compared with 2006 because turnover has risen and the dividend to shareholders has been maintained.

B is resident in the area immediately surrounding the premises of Recycle plc and is interested in the contribution made by Recycle plc to the general well-being of the community. *B* is also concerned about the potential environmental effect of the recycling of chemical waste. *B* is uncertain how the published financial statements of Recycle plc might be of assistance in addressing social and environmental matters.

Required:
Write a full report addressed to *A*, supported by appropriate ratios.

(CIMA – adapted)

11 H plc manufactures vehicle parts. The company sells its products to a number of independent distributors who resell the goods to garages and other retail outlets in their areas. H plc has a policy of having only one distributor in any given geographical area. Distributors are selected mainly on the basis of financial viability. H plc is keen to avoid the disruption of sales and loss of credibility associated with the collapse of a distributor. The company is currently trying to choose between two companies which have applied to be its sole distributor in Geetown, a new sales area.

The applicants have supplied the following information:

	Applicant X			Applicant Y		
	1993	*1994*	*1995*	*1993*	*1994*	*1995*
Sales (£ 000)	1280	1600	2000	1805	1900	2000
Gross profit %	22	20	18	23	22	24
Return on capital employed %	8	12	16	14	15	16
Current ratio	1.7:1	1.9:1	2.1:1	1.7:1	1.65:1	1.7:1
Quick ratio	1.4:1	1.1:1	0.9:1	0.9:1	0.9:1	0.9:1
Gearing %	15	21	28	29	30	27

Requirements:

(a) Explain why trends in accounting ratios could provide a more useful insight than the latest figures taken on their own.

(b) Using the information provided above, explain which of the companies appears to be the safer choice for the role of distributor.

(CIMA – adapted)

12 Arizona plc has carried on business for a number of years as a retailer of a wide variety of 'do it yourself' goods. The company operates from a number of stores around the United Kingdom.

In recent years, the company has found it necessary to provide credit facilities to its customers in order to achieve growth in turnover. As a result of this decision, the liability to the company's bankers has increased substantially.

The statutory accounts of the company for the year ended 31 March 1998 have recently been published, and extracts are provided below, together with comparative figures for the previous two years.

Profit and loss accounts for the years ended 31 March

	1996	1997	1998
	£m	£m	£m
Turnover	1850	2200	2500
Cost of sales	(1250)	(1500)	(1750)
Gross profit	600	700	750
Other operating costs	(550)	(640)	(700)
Operating profit	50	60	50
Interest from credit sales	45	60	90
Interest payable	(25)	(60)	(110)
Profit before taxation	70	60	30
Taxation	(23)	(20)	(10)
Profit after taxation	47	40	20
Dividends	(30)	(30)	(20)
Retained profit	17	10	–

Balance sheets at 31 March

	1996	1997	1998
	£m	£m	£m
Tangible fixed assets	278	290	322
Stocks	400	540	620
Debtors	492	550	633
Cash	12	12	15
Trade creditors	(270)	(270)	(280)
Taxation	(20)	(20)	(8)
Proposed dividends	(30)	(30)	(20)
Bank overdraft	(320)	(520)	(610)
Debentures	(200)	(200)	(320)
	342	352	352
Share capital	90	90	90
Reserves	252	262	262
	342	352	352

Other information:

- Depreciation charged for the three years was as follows:

Year-ended 31 March	1996	1997	1998
	£m	£m	£m
	55	60	70

- The debentures are secured by a floating charge over the assets of Arizona plc. Their repayment is due on 31 March 2008.

- The bank overdraft is unsecured. The bank has set a limit of £630 million on the overdraft.
- Over the past three years, the level of credit sales has been:

Year-ended 31 March	1996	1997	1998
	£m	£m	£m
	213	263	375

Given the steady increase in the bank overdraft which has taken place in recent years, the company has recently written to its bankers to request an increase in the limit. The request was received by the bank on 15 May 1998, two weeks after the 1998 statutory accounts were published.

You are an accountant employed by the bankers of Arizona plc. The bank is concerned at the steep escalation in the level of the company's overdraft and your regional manager has asked for a report on the financial performance of Arizona plc for the last three years.

Required:

Write a report to your regional manager which analyses the financial performance of Arizona plc for the period covered by the financial statements.

Your report may take any form you wish, but should specifically address the particular concern of the bank regarding the rapidly increasing overdraft. Therefore, your report should identify aspects of poor performance which could have contributed to the increase in the overdraft.

(CIMA)

13 You are an investment analyst. A client of yours, Mr A, owns 3.5% of the share capital of Price. Price is a listed company and prepares financial statements in accordance with International Accounting Standards. The company supplies machinery to agricultural businesses. The year-end of Price is 31 July and the financial statements for the year ended 31 July 2001 were approved by the directors on 30 September 2001. Following approval, copies of the financial statements were sent to all shareholders in readiness for the annual general meeting which is due to be held on 30 November 2001. Extracts from these financial statements are given below:

Income statements – year ended 31 July	2001	2000
	$000	$000
Revenue	54 000	51 000
Cost of sales	(42 000)	(40 000)
Gross profit	12 000	11 000
Other operating expenses	(6 300)	(6 000)
Profit from operations	5 700	5 000
Finance cost	(1 600)	(1 000)
Profit before tax	4 100	4 000
Income tax expense	(1 200)	(1 200)
Net profit for the period	2 900	2 800

Balance sheets – at 31 July	2001		2000	
	$000	$000	$000	$000
Non-current assets:				
Property plant and equipment		44 200		32 000
Current assets:				
Inventories	8 700		7 500	
Receivables	13 000		12 000	
Cash and cash equivalents	200		1 500	
		21 900		21 000
		66 100		53 000
Capital and reserves:				
Issued share capital		20 000		20 000
Reserves		20 300		14 000
		40 300		34 000
Non-current liabilities		15 400		10 000
Current liabilities:				
Trade payables	8 000		7 800	
Tax	1 200		1 200	
Bank overdraft	1 200		Nil	
		10 400		9 000
		66 100		53 000

Statement of changes in equity

	$000
Balance at 31 July 2000	34 000
Surplus on revaluation of properties	5 000
Net profit for the period	2 900
Dividends	(1 600)
Balance at 31 July 2001	40 300

Extracts from notes to the financial statements
Finance cost – year ended 31 July

	2001	2000
	$000	$000
On 10% interest-bearing borrowings	1 000	1 000
On zero-rate bonds	400	Nil
On bank overdraft	200	Nil
	1 600	1 000

Non-current liabilities at 31 July

	2001	2000
	$000	$000
10% borrowings repayable 31 July 2006	10 000	10 000
Zero-rate bonds	5 400	Nil
	15 400	10 000

The zero-rate bonds were issued for proceeds of $5 million on 1 August 2000. The lenders are not entitled to interest during their period of issue. The bonds are repayable on 31 July 2004 for a total of $6 802 450. The bonds are quoted on a recognised stock exchange. However, the company intends to hold the bonds until they mature and then repay them.

Revaluation of properties: This is the first time the company has revalued any of its properties.

Depreciation of non-current assets: Depreciation of non-current assets for the year totalled $4 million (2000 – $3 million).

Your client always attends the annual general meeting of the company and likes to put questions to the directors regarding the financial statements. However, he is not a financial specialist and does not wish to look foolish by asking inappropriate questions. Mr A intends to ask the following three questions and seeks your advice based on the information provided. The points he wishes to make are as follows:

Point 1: Why, when the company has made almost the same profit as last year and has borrowed more money through a bond issue, has the company got a bank overdraft of $1.2 million at the end of the year when there was a positive balance of $1.5 million in the bank at the end of the previous year? This looks wrong to me.

Point 2: The company has a revaluation surplus of $5 million included in the statement of changes in equity. I have never understood this statement. Surely surpluses are shown in the income statement. Perhaps our accountants are unaware of the correct accounting treatment?

Point 3: I don't understand the treatment of the zero-rate bonds. The notes tell me that these were issued for $5 million and no interest was paid to the investors. The accounts show a finance cost of $400 000 and a balance owing of $5.4 million. Is this an error? On the other hand, perhaps the $5.4 million is the fair value of the bonds? I feel sure an International Accounting Standard has been issued that requires companies to value their borrowings at fair value.

Required:
Prepare a reply to Mr A that evaluates the issues he has raised in the three points and provides appropriate advice. You should support your advice with references to International Accounting Standards.

(CIMA November 2001)

14 You are the Management Accountant of Drax. The entity prepares financial statements to 31 March each year. Earnings per share is regarded as a key performance indicator and the executive directors receive a bonus if the earnings per share exceeds a given target figure. Good corporate governance is ensured by the appointment of a number of non-executive directors, who rigorously scrutinise the financial statements each year to ensure that the earnings per share figure has been correctly computed.

Drax has recently appointed a new non-executive director who seeks your advice regarding the financial statements for the year ended 31 March 2003. Extracts from these financial statements (excluding the comparative figures) are given below. The financial statements comply with relevant Accounting Standards in all material respects.

STATEMENTS OF FINANCIAL PERFORMANCE:
Income statement – year ended 31 March 2003

	Continuing operations $ million	Discontinuing operations $ million	Total $ million
Revenue	1 000	100	1 100
Cost of sales	(520)	(70)	(590)
Gross profit	480	30	510
Other operating expenses	(200)	(40)	(240)
Profit from operations	280	(10)	270
Loss on disposal of discontinuing operations (*Note 1*)	–	(30)	(30)
Profit before finance costs	280	(40)	240
Finance costs			(55)
Profit before tax			185
Income tax expense			(55)
Profit after tax			130
Minority interests			(45)
Group profit for the period			85

Earnings per equity share 59.13 cents

Statement of changes in equity – year ended 31 March 2003

	$ million	$ million
Balance at 1 April 2002		270
Profit for the financial year		85
Unrealised surplus on the revaluation of properties		22
Currency translation differences on foreign currency net investments	12	
Less exchange losses on related foreign currency loans	(9)	
		3
Dividends (all equity)		(50)
Issue of share capital (*Note 2*)		60
Balance at 31 March 2003		390

NOTES TO THE FINANCIAL STATEMENTS:

Note 1

During the year Drax disposed of a subsidiary. The loss on disposal shown in the income statement consists of two elements:

Disposal proceeds less related net assets less related goodwill	$45 million **loss**
Gain on curtailment of retirement benefits relating to disposal	$15 million **profit**.

Note 2

At the start of the period, Drax had 120 million $1 equity shares in issue. Drax had no non-equity shares. On 1 July 2002, Drax made a rights issue to existing shareholders of one share for every four held at $2 per share. The market value of each share immediately before the rights issue was $2.50.

Note 3 – Defined benefit pension plan

	At 31 March 2003 $ million	At 31 March 2002 $ million
Present value of funded obligations	5 000	4 500
Fair value of plan assets	(2 600)	(2 700)
Unrecognised actuarial losses	(380)	(350)
Net liability in balance sheet	2 020	1 450

The new non-executive director has sent you a list of questions to which he requires answers:

(a) Please show how the earnings per share figure has been computed.

(b) I am a non-executive director for another entity operating in the same industry as Drax with roughly the same revenue and with very similar unit costs of raw materials. The nominal value of the shares of this other entity is $1 yet its earnings per share is quite different from that of Drax. How can this be?

(c) I am very suspicious about some of the figures in the statement of changes in equity and in the pension plan liability. It would seem to me that exchange losses on loans and actuarial losses relating to the pension plan should be in the income statement. Are the executive directors trying to maximise the earnings per share for their own ends?

(d) I don't understand how the 'gain on curtailment of retirement benefits' is a gain that goes to the income statement. Shouldn't it be treated in the same way as the actuarial losses that seem to be included in the balance sheet figure for the pension plan liability?

Required:
Prepare a reply to the questions the non-executive director has raised. You should refer to the provisions of relevant Accounting Standards where appropriate. Assume that the non-executive director has a reasonable general knowledge of business but that he is not familiar with the detail of Accounting Standards.

(CIMA May 2003)

15 You are the accountant of Acquirer. Your entity has the strategy of growth by acquisition and your directors have identified an entity, Target, which they wish to investigate with a view to launching a takeover bid. Your directors consider that the directors of Target will contest any bid and will not be very cooperative in providing background information on the entity. Therefore, relevant financial information is likely to be restricted to the publicly available financial statements.

Your directors have asked you to compute key financial ratios from the latest financial statements of Target [for the year ended 30 November 2002] and compare the ratios with those for other entities in a similar sector. Accordingly, you have selected ten broadly similar entities and have presented the directors with the following calculations:

Ratio	Basis of calculation	Ratio for Target	Spread of ratios for comparative entities		
			Highest	Average	Lowest
Gross profit margin	$\dfrac{\text{Gross profit}}{\text{Revenue}}$	42%	44%	38%	33%
Operating profit margin	$\dfrac{\text{Profit from operations}}{\text{Revenue}}$	29%	37%	30%	26%
Return on total capital	$\dfrac{\text{Profit from operations}}{\text{Total capital}}$	73%	92.5%	69%	52%
Interest cover	$\dfrac{\text{Profit from operations}}{\text{Finance cost}}$	1.8 times	3.2 times	2.5 times	1.6 times
Gearing	$\dfrac{\text{Debt capital}}{\text{Total capital}}$	52%	56%	40%	28%
Dividend cover	$\dfrac{\text{Profit after tax}}{\text{Dividend}}$	5.2 times	5 times	4 times	3 times
Turnover of inventory	$\dfrac{\text{Cost of sales}}{\text{Closing inventory}}$	4.4 times	4.5 times	4 times	3.2 times
Receivables days	$\dfrac{\text{Trade receivables}}{\text{1 day's sales revenue}}$	51 days	81 days	62 days	49 days

Required:

(a) Using the ratios provided, write a report that compares the financial performance and position of Target to the other entities in the survey. Where an issue arises that reflects particularly favourably or unfavourably on Target, you should assess its relevance to a potential acquirer.

(b) Identify any reservations you have regarding the extent to which the ratios provided can contribute to an acquisition decision by the directors of Acquirer. You should highlight the extent to which the financial statements themselves might help you to overcome the reservations you have identified.

(CIMA November 2003)

16 BHG is a successful listed entity that designs and markets specialist business software. BHG's directors have decided to adopt a policy of expansion into overseas territories through the acquisition of similar software businesses possessing established shares of their domestic markets. BHG's aim is to obtain control, or at the minimum, significant influence (represented by at least 40% of issued share capital) of investee entities. Target investee entities are likely to be listed entities in their own countries, but the acquisition of unlisted entities is not ruled out.

You are a senior accountant in BHG, and you have been asked by the Chief Financial Officer (CFO) to establish a set of key accounting ratios for use in:

1 the initial appraisal of potential acquisitions;

2 ongoing appraisal following acquisitions.

The ratios will be used as part of a suite of quantitative and non-quantitative measurements to compare businesses with each other. The CFO has suggested that it would be appropriate to identify no more than five–seven key financial ratios.

One of your assistants has suggested a list of five key accounting ratios as suitable for both initial and ongoing appraisal and comparison. She has provided reasons to support the case for their inclusion as key ratios.

1   Earnings per share: 'one of the most important investor ratios, widely used by all classes of investor to assess business performance'.

2   Dividend yield: 'this ratio provides a very useful measurement that allows comparison with yields from other equity and non-equity investments'.

3   Gearing: 'this is of critical importance in determining the level of risk of an equity investment'.

4   Gross profit margin: 'allows investors to assess business performance, and is of particular use over several accounting periods within the same organisation. It is also very useful for comparing performances between businesses'.

5   Asset turnover ratios: 'allow the investor to compare the intensity of asset usage between businesses, and over time'.

Required:

(a) Discuss the extent to which each of the five suggested accounting ratios is likely to be useful to BHG for both initial and ongoing appraisal and comparison, and the extent to which your assistant's assessments of the value of the ratios are justified.

(b) Explain the problems and limitations of accounting ratio analysis in making inter-firm and international comparisons.

(CIMA May 2008)

17   ST, UV and WX are listed entities operating in the same business sector. At 31 October 2006, their PE ratios were reported as follows:

ST 16.2
UV 12.7
WX 8.4

Which ONE of the following statements about these PE ratios is correct?
The PE ratios suggest that

(a) ST is regarded by the market as the riskiest of the three entities.

(b) ST has the highest earnings per share of the three entities.

(c) UV represents the safest investment because its PE lies approximately mid-way between the other two.

(d) WX's share price may be relatively lower than that of ST and UV because of an adverse effect such as a profit warning.

(CIMA May 2006)

REFERENCES

International accounting

Chapter 2

Alexander, D. and Nobes, C. (2004) *Financial accounting: an international introduction*, 2nd edn, Pearson Education, Harlow.

Ali, A. and Hwang, L-S. (2000) 'Country-specific factors related to financial reporting and the value relevance of accounting data', *Journal of Accounting Research*, 38(1), Spring.

American Accounting Association (1977) *The Accounting Review*, Supplement to volume 52.

Ball, R., Kothari, S.P. and Robin, A. (2000) 'The effect of international institutional factors on properties of accounting earnings', *Journal of Accounting and Economics*, 29, 1–51.

Ball, R. and Shivakumar, L. (2002) 'Earning quality in UK private firms', Working paper, London Business School, 53.

Basu, S. (1997) 'The conservatism principle and the asymmetric timeliness of earnings', *Journal of Accounting and Economics*, 24, 3–37.

Burghstahler, D.C., Hail, L. and Leuz, C. (2006) 'The importance of reporting incentives: earnings management in European private and public firms', *The Accounting Review* (Forthcoming).

Choi, F. and Mueller, G. (1992) *International Accounting*, Prentice Hall, Englewood Cliffs.

da Costa, R.C., Bourgeois, J.C. and Lawson, W.M. (1978) 'A classification of international financial accounting practices', *The International Journal of Accounting (education and research)*, Spring, 73–85.

Frank, W.G. (1979) An empirical analysis of international accounting principles, *Journal of Accounting Research*, Autumn, 593–605.

Gonzalo, J.A. and Gallizo, J.L. (1992) *Spain*, Routledge, London.

Gray, S. (1988) 'Towards a theory of cultural influence on the development of accounting systems internationally', *Abacus*, March.

Guenther, D. and Young, D. (2000) 'The association between financial accounting measures and real economic activity: A multinational study', *Journal of Accounting and Economics*, 29, 53–72.

Hatfield, H.R. (1966) 'Some variations in accounting practices in England, France, Germany and the US', *Journal of Accounting Research*, Autumn.

Hofstede, G. (1984) *Culture's consequences: international differences in work-related values*. Sage, Beverly Hills, CA.

Hope, O.-K. (2003a) 'Disclosure practices, enforcement of accounting standards, and analysts' forecast accuracy: an international study', *Journal of Accounting Research*, 41(2), 235–272.

Hope, O.-K. (2003b) 'Firm-level disclosures and the relative roles of culture and legal origin', *Journal of International Management and Accounting*, 41(3), 218–248.

La Porta, R., Lopez-de-Silanes, F., Schleifer, A. and Vishny, R. (1997) 'Legal determinants of external finance', *Journal of Finance*, 52, 1131–50.

La Porta, R., Lopez-de-Silanes, F., Schleifer, A. and Vishny, R. (1998) 'Law and finance', *Journal of Political Economy*, 106, 1113–55.

Leuz, C., Nanda, D. and Wysocki, P. (2003) 'Earnings management and investor protection: An international comparison', *Journal of Financial Economics*, 69(3), 505–28.

Leuz, C. and Verrechia, R.E. (2000) 'The economic consequences of increased disclosure', *Journal of Accounting Research*, 38, supplement, 91–124.

Maijoor, S. and Vanstraelen, A. (2006) 'Earnings management: The effects of national audit environment, audit quality and international capital markets', *Accounting and Business Research*, 36(1), 33–52.

Mey, A. (1996) 'Theodore Limperg and his theory of values and costs', *Abacus*, 2(1), September 3–23.

Mueller, G.G. (1967) *International Accounting*, Macmillan, New York.

Nair, R.D. and Frank, W.G. (1980) 'The impact of disclosure and measurement on international accounting classificating', *The Accounting Review*, July, 426–50.

Nobes, C.W. (1980) 'International classification of accounting systems', unpublished paper.

Nobes, C.W. and Parker, R. (2003) *Comparative International Accounting*, 7th edn, Prentice Hall, London.

Ordelheide, D. and KPMG (eds) (2001) *Transnational Accounting*, 2nd edn, Palgrave, London.

Penman, S.H. and Zhang, X-J. (2002) 'Accounting conservatism, the quality of earnings, and stock returns', *The Accounting Review*, 77(2), April, 237–64.

Pope, P. and Walker, M. (1999) 'International differences in the timeliness, conservatism and classification of earnings', *Journal of Accounting Research*, 37, supplement, 53–87.

Schipper, K. (2000) 'Accounting research and the potential use of international accounting', *British Accounting Review*, 32, 243–56.

Schmalenbach, E. (1927) 'Der Kontenrahmen', *Zeitschrift für betriebswirtschaftliche Forschung*, 21, 385–402.

Seidler, L.J. (1967) 'International accounting – the ultimate theory course', The *Accounting Review*, October, 775–81.

Chapter 3

Jorissen, A., Lybaert, N. and K. Van de Poel (2006) 'Lobbying towards a global standard-setter – do national characteristics matter? An analysis of comment letter written to the IAS' in Gregoriou, Greg N. (ed.) *International Accounting: standards, regulation and financial reporting*, Oxford, Elsevier, 1–40.

Schipper, K. (2005) International Accounting Standards in Europe: Implications for International Convergence, *European Accounting Review*, 14(1), 101–126.

Sutton, T.G. (1984) 'Lobbying of Accounting Standards-Setting Bodies in the UK and the USA: a downsian analysis', *Accounting Organisations and Society*, 9(1), 81–95.

Watts, R.L. and Zimmerman, J.L. (1978) 'Towards a Positive Theory of the Determination of Accounting Standards'. *The Accounting Review*, 53(1), 112–134.

Chapter 4

Edwards, E.O. and Bell, P.W. (1961) *The Theory and Measurement of Business Income*, University of California Press, Berkeley, CA.

Fisher, I. (1930) *The Theory of Interest*. Macmillan, New York. (Reprinted as 'Income and capital', in Parker and Harcourt, 1969.)

Hicks, J. (1946) *Value and Capital*, Clarendon Press, Oxford. (Reprinted as 'Income' in Parker and Harcourt, 1969.)

Parker, R.H. and Harcourt, G.C. (1969) *Readings in the Concept and Measurement of Income*, Cambridge University Press, Cambridge.

Chapter 7

Bonbright, J.C. (1937) *The Valuation of Property*, McGraw-Hill, New York.

Mey, A. (1966) 'Theodore Limperg and his theory of values and costs', *Abacus*, 2(1), September, 3–23.

Sandilands Report (1975) *Inflation Accounting Committee*, MND 6225, HMSO, London.

Schmalenbach, E. (1959) *Dynamic Accounting*, Gee & Co., London.

Sweeney, H.W. (1936) *Stabilised Accounting*, Harper & Bros, New York.

Chapter 8

Belkaoui, A. (2000) *Accounting Theory*, 4th edn, Thomson Learning, London.

Devine, C.T. (1960) 'Research methodology and accounting theory formation', *The Accounting Review*, July.

Edwards, E.O. and Bell, P.W. (1961) *The Theory and Measurement of Business Income*, University of California Press, Berkeley, CA.

Hendriksen, E.S. (1977) *Accounting Theory*, 3rd edn, Irwin, Homewood, IL.

Jensen, M.C. (1976) *Reflections on the state of accounting research and the regulation of accounting*, Stanford lectures in Accounting, Stanford University.

Lehman, G. (2001) *Accounting Forum*, Editorial 25, March.

Littleton, A.C. (1953) *Structure of Accounting Theory*. Monograph no. 5. American Accounting Association.

McDonald, D.L. (1972) *Comparative Accounting Theory*, Addison-Wesley, Reading, MA.

Paton, W.A. (1922) *Accounting Theory*, The Ronald Press, New York.

Scott, D.R. (1941) 'The basis for accounting principles', *Accounting Review*, December.

Sorter, G.H. (1969) 'An events approach to basic accounting theory', *The Accounting Review*, January.

Yu, S.C. (1976) *The Structure of Accounting Theory*, The University Press of Florida, Gainesville.

Chapter 10

Adams, R. (1994) 'Ready for a greening' *Accountancy Age*, 5 May.

Adams, R. (1997) *Linking environmental and financial performance: a survey of best practice techniques*, International standards of accounting and reporting.

Bayer Ag Annual Report 2001.

Beiersdorf Annual Report 2000.

Corporate report 1975, UK Accounting Standards Committee.

Corporate social responsibility, a government update 2004 DTI, UK gov.

FRC Combined code on corporate governance 2008 (Turnbull), FRC.

Gray, R.H., Owen, D. and Adams, C. (1996) *Accounting and accountability: changes and challenges in corporate social and environmental reporting*, Prentice Hall, London.

Greenbury committee report 1995.

Hampel committee report 1998.

Hicks, J.R. (1946) *Value and capital*, 2nd edn, Oxford University Press, Oxford.

IFAC code of ethics for professional accountants 2005, IFAC.

Kaplan, R.S. and Norton, D. (1996) *The balances scorecard: translating strategy into action*, Harvard Business School Press, Boston.

Moore, D. (1997) *Position paper on accounting for environmental costs and liabilities*, Canadian Institute of Chartered Accountants.

OECD Code of ethics for professional accountants 2004, OECD.

OECD Principles of corporate governance, 2004 OECD.

Report of the committee on financial aspects of corporate governance, the Cadbury code 1992.

Chapter 21

Black, F. and Scholes, M. (1973) 'The pricing of options and corporate liabilities', *Journal of Political Economy*, 81, 637–59.

Lane, Clark and Peacock, 'Accounting for Pensions Survey', 2005.

Chapter 24

Fields, T., Lys, T. and Vincent L. (2001) 'Empirical research on accounting choice', *Journal of Accounting and Economics*, 31, 255–307.

Chapter 30

Banker, R. and Johnston, H. (1993) 'An empirical study of cost drivers in the U.S. airline industry', *The Accounting Review*, 68(3), July, 576–601.

Barth, M., Elliot, J. and Finn, M. (1995) 'Market rewards associated with increasing earnings patterns', Working paper, Cornell University.

Bartov, E. (1993) 'The timing of asset sales and earnings manipulation', *The Accounting Review*, 68, 840–855.

Botosan, C.A. (1997) 'Disclosure level and the cost of equity capital', *The Accounting Review*, 72, 323–349.

Bowen, R., DuCharme, L. and Chores, D. (1995) 'Stakeholders implicit claims and accounting method choice', *Journal of Accounting and Economics*, 255–96.

Burgstahler, D. and Dichev, I. (1997) 'Earnings management to avoid earnings decreases and losses', *Journal of Accounting and Economics*, 99–126.

DeAngelo, H., DeAngelo, L. and Skinner, D. (1996) 'Reversal of fortune: Dividend signaling and the disappearance of sustained earnings growth', *Journal of Financial Economics*, 40, 341–371.

DeFond, M.L. and Jiambalvo, J. (1994) 'Debt covenant violation and manipulation of accruals', *Journal of Accounting and Economics*, 17, 145–76.

DeGeorge, F., Patel, J. and Zeckhauser, R. (1999) 'Earnings management to exceed thresholds', *Journal of Business*, 72, 1–33.

Dechow, P. and Sloan, R. (1991) 'Executive incentives and the horizon problem: an empirical investigation' *Journal of Accounting and Economics*, 14, 51–89.

Donnelly, R. and Lynch C. (2002) 'The ownership structure of UK firms and the informativeness of accounting earnings', *Accounting and Business Research*, 32(4), 245–257.

Fan, J.P.H. and Wong, T.J. (2002) 'Corporate ownership structure and the informativeness of accounting earnings in East Asia', *Journal of Accounting and Economics*, 33, 401–425.

Francis, J. (2001) 'Discussion of empirical research on accounting choice', *Journal of Accounting and Economics*, 31, 309–19.

Friedlan, J.M. (1994) 'Accounting choices of issuers of initial public offerings', *Contemporary Accounting Research*, 11, 1–31.

Guenther, D., Maydew, E. and Nutter, S. (1997) 'Financial reporting, tax costs and book-tax conformity', *Journal of Accounting and Economics*, 23, 225–48.

Hand, J.R. (1989) 'Did firms undertake debt-equity swaps for an accounting paper profit or true financial gain?', *The Accounting Review*, 64, 423–462.

Healy, P.M. (1985) 'The effect of bonus schemes on accounting decisions', *Journal of Accounting and Economics*, 7, 85–107.

Healy, P., Hutton, A. and Palepu, K. (1999) 'Stock Performance and Intermediation Changes Surrounding Sustained Increases in Disclosure', *Contemporary Accounting Research*, 485–520.

Healy, P. and Palepu K. (1993) 'The Effect of Firms' Financial Disclosure Strategies on Stock Prices', *Accounting Horizons*, 7, 1–11.

Healy, P. and Wahlen, J. (1999) 'A review of the earnings management literature and its implications for standard settings', *Accounting Horizons*, 13, 365–383.

Hope, O. (2003) 'Disclosure practices, enforcement of Accounting Standards and analyst's forecast accuracy: an international study', *Journal of Accounting Research*, 41(2), 235–272.

Horngren, C., Bhimani, A., Datar, S. and Foster, G. (2002) *Management and Cost Accounting*, 2nd edn, Financial Times – Prentice Hall, London.

Hunt, A., Moyer, S. and Shevlin, T. (1995) 'Earnings volatility, earnings management, and equity value', Working paper, University of Washington.

Jensen, M. and Murphy, K. (1990) 'Performance pay and top management', *Journal of Political Economy*, 98, 2, 225–64.

Jiambalvo, J. (1996) 'Causes and consequences of earnings manipulation: an analysis of firms subject to enforcement actions by the SEC', *Contemporary Accounting Research*, 13, 37–47.

Kasanen, E., Kinnunen, J. and Niskanen, J. (1996) 'Dividend based earnings management: empirical evidence from Finland', *Journal of Accounting and Economics*, 283–312.

Kasznik, R. (1999) 'On the association between voluntary disclosure and earnings management', *Journal of Accounting Research*, 37, 57–81.

Key, K.G. (1997) 'Political cost incentives for earning management in the cable television industry', *Journal of Accounting and Economics*, 309–37.

LaSalle, R.E., Jones, S.K. and Jain, R. (1993) 'The association between executive succession and discretionary accounting changes: earning management or different perspectives?' *Journal of Business Finance and Accounting*, 653–71.

Leuz, C. and Verrecchia, R.E. (2003) 'The Economic Consequences of Increased Disclosure', *Journal of Accounting Research*, 38, supplement 2000, 91–124.

Leuz, C., Nanda, D. and Wysocki, P. (2003) 'Earning's management and inventor protection: an international comparison', *Journal of Financial Economics*, 69, 505–527.

McNichols, M. and Wilson, G.P. (1988) 'Evidence of earnings management from the provision for bad debts', *Journal of Accounting Research*, 1–31.

Murphy, K.J. and Zimmerman, J.L. (1993) 'Financial performance surrounding CEO turnover', *Journal of Accounting and Economics*, 273–316.

Nelson, M., Elliott, J. and Tarpley, R. (2003) 'How are earnings managed? Examples from auditors' *Accounting Horizons*, 17 (suppl), 17–35.

Neil, J.D., Pourciau, S.G. and Schaefer, T.F. (1995) 'Accounting method choice and IPO valuation', *Accounting Horizons*, 9, 68–80.

Penman, S. (2001) *Financial Statement Analysis and Security Valuation*, McGraw-Hill/Irwin, Boston, MA.

Penman, S. (2003) *Financial Statement Analysis and Security Valuation*, 2nd edn, McGraw Hill, New York, 740.

Porter, M. (1985) *Competitive Advantage: Creating and Sustaining Superior Performance*, The Free Press, New York.

Pourciau, S. (1993) 'Earnings management and nonroutine executive changes', *Journal of Accounting and Economics*, 16, 317–336.

Rangan, S. (1998) 'Earnings management and the performance of seasoned equity offerings', *Journal of Financial Economics*, 50, 101–22.

Sengupta, P. (1998) 'Corporate disclosure quality and the cost of debt', *The Accounting Review*, 73, 459–474.

Shank, J. and Govindarajan, V. (1992) 'Strategic cost management and the value chain', *Journal of Cost Management*, winter, 5–21.

Shivakumar, L. (1998) 'Market reaction to seasoned equity offering announcements and earnings management', working paper, London Business School.

Sweeney, A.P. (1994) 'Debt-covenant violations and managers' accounting responses', *Journal of Accounting and Economics*, 17, 281–308.

Trueman, B. and Titman, S. (1988) 'An explanation for accounting income smoothing', *Journal of Accounting Research*, 26, 127–139.

Chapter 31

Altman, E. (1968) 'Financial ratios, discriminant analysis and the prediction of corporate bankruptcy', *Journal of Finance*, 23(4), 589–609.

Amir, E. and Lev, B. (1996) 'Value-relevance of non-financial information: the wireless communications industry', *Journal of Accounting and Economics*, 22, 3–30.

Dechow, P. (1994) 'Accounting earnings and cash flows as measures of firm performance: The role of accounting accruals', *Journal of Accounting and Economics*, 138–56.

Decraene, S., Denruyter, P. and Sciot, G. (2002) *De crash van SABENA*, Uitgeverij Van Halewyck, Leuven.

De Zitter, A. (2002) *Het avontuur van SABENA: groei en val van een* luchtvaartmaatschappij, Lannoo, Tielt.

Ittner, C. and Larcker, D.F. (2001) 'Assessing empirical based research in managerial accounting: a value based management perspective', *Journal of Accounting and Economics*, 349–411.

INDEX